MEN'S LIVES

SEVENTH EDITION

MEN'S LIVES

Michael S. Kimmel
State University of New York, Stony Brook

Michael A. Messner
University of Southern California

PEARSON

Boston   New York   San Francisco
Mexico City   Montreal   Toronto   London   Madrid   Munich   Paris
Hong Kong   Singapore   Tokyo   Cape Town   Sydney

Senior Series Editor: Jeff Lasser
Editoral Assistant: Erikka Adams
Senior Marketing Manager: Kelly May
Senior Production Administrator: Donna Simons
Cover Administrator: Joel Gendron
Composition Buyer: Linda Cox
Manufacturing Buyer: JoAnne Sweeney
Editorial-Production Service: Publishers' Design and Production Services, Inc.
Electronic Composition: Publishers' Design and Production Services, Inc.
Cover Designer: Jenny Hart

For related titles and support materials, visit our online catalog at www.ablongman.com

Between the time website information is gathered and then published, it is not unusual for some sites to have closed. Also, the transcription of URLs can result in typographical errors. The publisher would appreciate notification where these errors occur so that they may be corrected in subsequent editions.

Library of Congress Cataloging-in-Publication Data

Men's lives / [compiled by] Michael S. Kimmel, Michael A. Messner. —7th ed.
    p. cm.
  Includes bibliographical references.
  ISBN 0-205-48545-6
  1. Men—United States—Attitudes. 2. Masculinity—United States.
 3. Men—United States—Sexual behavior. I. Kimmel, Michael S.
 II. Messner, Michael A.
 HQ1090.3.M465 2007
 305.31—dc22   2006041597

Printed in the United States of America

10 9 8 7 6 5 4 3 2 1   RRD-VA   10 09 08 07 06

To our fathers

Edwin H. Kimmel (1926–)

Russell John Messner, Jr., 1920–1977

and how they helped to shape our lives.

CONTENTS

PREFACE

Over the past twenty years, we have been teaching courses on the male experience, or "men's lives." Our courses have reflected both our own education and recent research by feminist scholars and profeminist men in U.S. society. (By profeminist men, we mean active supporters of women's efforts against male violence and claims for equal opportunity, political participation, sexual autonomy, family reform, and equal education.) Gender, scholars have demonstrated, is a central feature of social life—one of the chief organizing principles around which our lives revolve. Gender shapes our identities and the institutions in which we find ourselves. In the university, women's studies programs and courses about women in traditional disciplines have explored the meaning of gender in women's lives. But what does it mean to be a man in contemporary U.S. society?

This anthology is organized around specific themes that define masculinity and the issues men confront over the course of their lives. In addition, a social-constructionist perspective has been included that examines how men actively construct masculinity within a social and historical context. Related to this construction and integrated in our examination are the variations that exist among men in relation to class, race, and sexuality.

We begin Part One with issues and questions that unravel the "masculine mystique" and reveal various dimensions of men's position in society and their relationships with women and with other men. Parts Two through Ten examine the different issues that emerge for men at different times of their lives and the ways in which their lives change over time. We touch on central moments related to boyhood, adolescence, sports, occupations, marriage, and fatherhood, and we explore men's emotional and sexual relationships with women and with other men. In this edition, we've added a new section on Violence and Masculinities. We have done so because violence remains the single behavior, attitude, or trait for which there are overwhelming, significant, and seemingly intractable gender differences. It affects so many other arenas of our lives that we have decided that we need to highlight this important feature of men's lives. The final part, "Men, Movements, and the Future," explores some of the ways in which men are changing and some possible directions in which they might continue to change.

Although a major component of the traditional, normative definition of masculinity is independence, we are pleased to acknowledge those colleagues and friends whose criticism and support have been a constant help throughout our work on this project. Karen Hanson and Jeff Lasser, our editors at Allyn and Bacon, inherited this project and have embraced it as their own, facilitating our work at every turn. Chris Cardone and Bruce Nichols, our original editors, were supportive from the start and helped get the project going. Many other scholars who work on issues of masculinity, such as Bob Blauner, Robert Brannon, Harry Brod, Rocco Capraro, Bob Connell, James Harrison, Jeff Hearn, Joe Pleck, Tony Rotundo, Don Sabo, and Peter Stein, have contributed to a supportive intellectual community in which to work.

Colleagues at the State University of New York at Stony Brook and the University of Southern California have been supportive of this project. We are especially grateful to Diane Barthel-Bouchier, John Gagnon, Barry Glassner, Norman Goodman, Carol Jacklin, and Barrie Thorne. A fellowship from the Lilly Foundation supported Kimmel's work on pedagogical issues of teaching about men and masculinity.

This book is the product of the profeminist men's movement as well—a loose network of men who support a feminist critique of traditional masculinity and women's struggles to enlarge the scope of their personal autonomy and public power. These men are engaged in a variety of efforts to transform masculinity in ways that allow men to live fuller, richer, and healthier lives. The editors of *Changing Men* (with whom we worked as Book Review Editor and Sports Editor), the late Mike Biernbaum and Rick Cote, labored for more than a decade to provide a forum for anti-sexist men. We acknowledge their efforts with gratitude and respect.

Our families, friends, and colleagues have provided a rare atmosphere that combines intellectual challenge and emotional support. We thank the reviewers of this edition: Cheryl Bartholomew, George Mason University; Evan Cooper, Ithaca College; Jackie Eller, Middle Tennessee State University; Kevin D. Henson, Loyola University; Caitlin Killian, Drew University; Ami Lynch, The George Washington University; Todd Migliaccio, California State University, Sacramento; and Amanda Udis-Kessler, Colorado College. We want especially to acknowledge our fathers and mothers for providing such important models—not of being women or men, but of being adults capable of career competence, emotional warmth, and nurturance (these are not masculine or feminine traits).

Finally, we thank Amy Aronson and Pierette Hondagneu-Sotelo, who have chosen to share our lives, and our sons, who didn't have much of a choice about it. Together they fill our lives with so much joy.

M.S.K.
M.A.M.

INTRODUCTION

This is a book about men. But unlike other books about men, which line countless library shelves, this is a book about men *as men*. It is a book in which men's experiences are not taken for granted as we explore the "real" and significant accomplishments of men, but a book in which those experiences are treated as significant and important in themselves.

Men as "Gendered Beings"

But what does it mean to examine men "as men"? Most courses in a college curriculum are about men, aren't they? But these courses routinely deal with men only in their public roles, so we come to know and understand men as scientists, politicians, military figures, writers, and philosophers. Rarely, if ever, are men understood through the prism of gender.

But listen to some male voices from some of these "ungendered" courses. Take, for example, composer Charles Ives, debunking "sissy" types of music; he said he used traditional tough guy themes and concerns in his drive to build new sounds and structures out of the popular musical idiom (cf. Wilkinson 1986: 103). Or architect Louis Sullivan, describing his ambition to create "masculine forms": strong, solid, commanding respect. Or novelist Ernest Hemingway, retaliating against literary enemies by portraying them as impotent or homosexual.

Consider also political figures, such as Cardinal Richelieu, the seventeenth-century French First Minister to Louis XIII, who insisted that it was "necessary to have masculine virtue and do everything by reason" (cited in Elliott 1984: 20). Closer to home, recall President Lyndon Baines Johnson's dismissal of a political adversary: "Oh him. He has to squat to piss!" Or President Johnson's boast that during the Tet offensive in the Vietnam War, he "didn't just screw Ho Chi Minh. I cut his pecker off!"

Democrats have no monopoly on unexamined gender coloring their political rhetoric. Indeed, recent political campaigns have revolved, in part, around gender issues, as each candidate attempted to demonstrate that he was not a "wimp" but was a "real man." (Of course, female politicians face the double task of convincing the electorate that they are not the "weak-willed wimps" that their gender implies in the public mind while at the same time demonstrating that they are "real women.")

These are just a few examples of what we might call gendered speech, language that uses gender terms to make its case. And these are just a few of the thousands of examples one could find in every academic discipline of how men's lives are organized around gender issues and how gender remains one of the organizing principles of social life. We come to know ourselves and our world through the prism of gender—only we act as if we didn't know it.

Fortunately, in recent years, the pioneering work of feminist scholars, both in traditional disciplines and in women's studies, and of feminist women in the political arena has made us aware of the centrality of gender in our lives. In the social sciences, gender has now taken its place alongside class and race as one of the three central mechanisms by which power and resources are distributed in our society and the three central themes out of which we fashion the meanings of our lives.

We certainly understand how this works for women. Through women's studies courses and also in courses about women in traditional disciplines, students have explored the complexity of women's lives, the hidden history of exemplary women, and the daily experiences of women in the routines of their lives. For women, we know how gender works as one of the formative elements out of which social life is organized.

The Invisibility of Gender: A Sociological Explanation

Too often, though, we treat men as if they had no gender, as if only their public personae were of interest to us as students and scholars, as if their interior experience of gender was of no significance. This became evident when one of us was in a graduate seminar on feminist theory several years ago. A discussion between a white woman and a black woman revolved around the question of whether their similarities as women were greater than their racial differences as black and white. The white woman asserted that the fact that they were both women bonded them, in spite of their racial differences. The black woman disagreed.

"When you wake up in the morning and look in the mirror, what do you see?" she asked.

"I see a woman," replied the white woman.

"That's precisely the issue," replied the black woman. "I see a black woman. For me, race is visible every day, because it is how I am not privileged in this culture. Race is invisible to you, which is why our alliance will always seem somewhat false to me."

Witnessing this exchange, Michael Kimmel was startled. When he looked in the mirror in the morning, he saw, as he put it, "a human being: universally generalizable. The generic person." What had been concealed—that he possessed both race and gender—had become strikingly visible. As a white man, he was able not to think about the ways in which gender and race had affected his experiences.

There is a sociological explanation for this blind spot in our thinking: the mechanisms that afford us privilege are very often invisible to us. What makes us marginal (unempowered, oppressed) are the mechanisms that we understand, because those are the ones that are most painful in daily life. Thus, white people rarely think of themselves as "raced" people, and rarely think of race as a central element in their experience. But people of color are marginalized by race, and so the centrality of race both is painfully obvious and needs study urgently. Similarly, middle-class people do not acknowledge the importance of social class as an organizing principle of social life, largely because for them class is an invisible force that makes everyone look pretty much the same. Working-class people, on the other hand, are often painfully aware of the centrality of class in their lives. (Interestingly, upper-class people are often more aware of class dynamics than are middle-class people. In part, this may be the result of the emphasis on status within the upper class, as lineage, breeding, and family honor take center stage. In part, it may also be the result of a peculiar marginalization of the upper class in our society, as in the overwhelming number of television shows and movies that are ostensibly about just plain [i.e., middle-class] folks.)

In this same way, men often think of themselves as genderless, as if gender did not matter in the daily experiences of our lives. Certainly, we can see the biological sex of individuals, but we rarely understand the ways in which *gender*—that complex of social meanings that is attached to biological sex—is enacted in our daily lives. For example, we treat male scientists as if their being men had nothing to do with the organization of their experiments, the logic of scientific inquiry, or the questions posed by science itself. We treat male political figures as if masculinity were not even remotely in their consciousness as they do battle in the political arena.

This book takes a position directly opposed to such genderlessness for men. We believe that men are also "gendered" and that this gendering process, the transformation of biological males into socially interacting men, is a central experience for men. That we are unaware of it only helps to perpetuate the inequalities based on gender in our society.

In this book, we will examine the various ways in which men are gendered. We have gathered together some of the most interesting, engaging, and convincing materials from the past decade that have been written about men. We believe that *Men's Lives* will allow readers to explore the meanings of masculinity in contemporary U.S. culture in a new way.

Earlier Efforts to Study Men

Certainly, researchers have been examining masculinity for a long time. Historically, there have been three general models that have governed social scientific research on men and masculinity. *Biological models* have focused on the ways in which innate biological differences between males and females program different social behaviors. *Anthropological models* have examined masculinity cross-culturally, stressing the variations in the behaviors and attributes associated with being a man. And, until recently, *sociological models* have stressed how socialization of boys and girls includes accommodation to a "sex role" specific to one's biological sex. Although each of these perspectives helps us to understand the meaning of masculinity and femininity, each is also limited in its ability to explain fully how gender operates in any culture.

Relying on differences in reproductive biology, some scholars have argued that the physiological organization of males and females makes inevitable the differences we observe in psychological temperament and social behaviors. One perspective holds that differences in endocrine functioning are the cause of gender difference, that testosterone predisposes males toward aggression, competition, and violence, whereas estrogen predisposes females toward passivity, tenderness, and exaggerated emotionality. Others insist that these observed behavioral differences derive from the differences between the size or number of sperm and eggs. Since a male can produce 100 million sperm with each ejaculation, whereas a female can produce fewer than 20 eggs capable of producing healthy offspring over the course of her life, these authors suggest that men's "investment" in their offspring is significantly less than women's investment. Other authors arrive at the same conclusion by suggesting that the different size of egg and sperm, and the fact that the egg is the source of the food supply, impels temperamental differences. Reproductive "success" to males means the insemination of as many females as possible; to females, reproductive success means carefully

choosing one male to mate with and insisting that he remain present to care for and support their offspring. Still other authors argue that male and female behavior is governed by different halves of the brain; males are ruled by the left hemisphere, which controls rationality and abstract thought, whereas females are governed by the right hemisphere, which controls emotional affect and creativity. (For examples of these works, see Trivers 1972; Goldberg 1975; Wilson 1976; and Goldberg, 1986.)

Observed normative temperamental differences between women and men that are assumed to be of biological origin are easily translated into political prescriptions. In this ideological sleight of hand, what is *normative* (i.e., what is prescribed) is translated into what is *normal*, and the mechanisms of this transformation are the assumed biological imperative. George Gilder, for example, assembles the putative biological differences between women and men into a call for a return to traditional gender roles. Gilder believes that male sexuality is, by nature, wild and lusty, "insistent" and "incessant," careening out of control and threatening anarchic disorder, unless it can be controlled and constrained. This is the task of women. When women refuse to apply the brakes to male sexuality—by asserting their own or by choosing to pursue a life outside the domestic sphere—they abandon their "natural" function for illusory social gains. Sex education, abortion, and birth control are all condemned as facilitating women's escape from biological necessity. Similarly, he argues against women's employment, since the "unemployed man can contribute little to the community and will often disrupt it, but the woman may even do more good without a job than with one" (Gilder 1986: 86).

The biological argument has been challenged by many scholars on several grounds. The implied causation between two observed sets of differences (biological differences and different behaviors) is misleading, since there is no logical reason to assume that one caused the other, or that the line of causation moves only from the biological to the social. The selection of biological evidence is partial, and generalizations from "lower" animal species to human beings are always suspect. One sociologist asks, if these differences are "natural," why must their enforcement be coercive, and why must males and females be forced to assume the rules that they are naturally supposed to play (see Epstein 1986: 8)? And one primatologist argues that the evidence adduced to support the current status quo might also lead to precisely the opposite conclusions, that biological differences would impel female promiscuity and male fragility (see Hrdy 1981). Biological differences between males and females would appear to set some parameters for differences in social behavior, but would not dictate the temperaments of men and women in any one culture. These psychological and social differences would appear to be the result far more of the ways in which cultures interpret, shape, and modify these biological inheritances. We may be born males or females, but we become men and women in a cultural context.

Anthropologists have entered the debate at this point, but with different positions. For example, some anthropologists have suggested that the universality of gender differences comes from specific cultural adaptations to the environment, whereas others describe the cultural variations of gender roles, seeking to demonstrate the fluidity of gender and the primacy of cultural organization. Lionel Tiger and Robin Fox argue that the sexual division of labor is universal because of the different nature of bonding for males and females. "Nature," they argue, "intended mother and child to be together" because she is the source of emotional security and food; thus, cultures have prescribed various behaviors for women that emphasize nurturance and emotional connection (Tiger and Fox 1984: 304). The bond between men is forged through the necessity of "competitive cooperation" in hunting; men must cooperate with members of their own tribe in the hunt and yet compete for scarce resources with men in other tribes. Such bonds predispose men toward the organization of the modern corporation or governmental bureaucracy.

Such anthropological arguments omit as much as they include, and many scholars have pointed out problems with the model. Why didn't intelligence become sex linked, as this model (and the biological model) would imply? Such positions also reveal a marked conservatism: The differences between women and men are the differences that nature or cultural evolution intended and are therefore not to be tampered with.

Perhaps the best-known challenge to this anthropological argument is the work of Margaret Mead. Mead insisted that the variations among cultures in their prescriptions of gender roles required the conclusion that culture was the more decisive cause of these differences. In her classic study, *Sex and Temperament in Three Primitive Societies* (1935), Mead observed such wide variability among gender role prescriptions—and such marked differences from our own—that any universality implied by biological or anthropological models had to be rejected. And although the empirical accuracy of Mead's work has been challenged in its specific arguments, the general theoretical arguments remain convincing.

Psychological theories have also contributed to the discussion of gender roles, as psychologists have specified the developmental sequences for both males and females. Earlier theorists observed psychological distancing from the mother as the precondition for independence and autonomy or suggested a sequence that placed the capacity for abstract reason as the developmental stage beyond relational reasoning. Because it is normative for males to exhibit independence and the capacity for abstract reason, it was argued that males are more successful at negotiating these psychological passages and implied that women somehow lagged behind men on the ladder of developmental success. (Such arguments may be found in the work of Freud, Erikson, and Kohlberg.)

But these models, too, have been challenged, most recently by sociologist Nancy Chodorow (1978), who argued that women's ability to connect contains a more fundamentally human trait than the male's need to distance, and by psychologist Carol Gilligan (1982), who claimed that women's predisposition toward relational reasoning may contain a more humane strategy of thought than recourse to abstract principles. Regardless of our assessment of these arguments, Chodorow and Gilligan rightly point out that the highly ideological assumptions that make masculinity the normative standard against which the psychological development of *both* males and females was measured would inevitably make femininity problematic and less fully developed. Moreover, Chodorow explicitly insists that these "essential" differences between women and men are socially constructed and therefore subject to change.

Finally, sociologists have attempted to synthesize these three perspectives into a systematic explanation of "sex roles." These are the collection of attitudes, attributes, and behaviors that is seen as appropriate for males and appropriate for females. Thus, masculinity is associated with technical mastery, aggression, competitiveness, and cognitive abstraction, whereas femininity is associated with emotional nurturance, connectedness, and passivity. Sex role theory informed a wide variety of prescriptive literature (self-help books) that instructed parents on what to do if they wanted their child to grow up as a healthy boy or girl.

The strongest challenge to all these perspectives, as we have seen, has come from feminist scholars, who have specified the ways in which the assumptions about maturity, development, and health all made masculinity the norm against which both genders were measured. In all the social sciences, these feminist scholars have stripped these early studies of their academic facades to reveal the unexamined ideological assumptions contained within them. By the early 1970s, women's studies programs began to articulate a new paradigm for the study of gender, one that assumed nothing about men or women beforehand and that made no assumptions about which gender was more highly

developed. And by the mid-1970s, the first group of texts about men appeared that had been inspired by these pioneering efforts by feminist scholars.

Thinking about Men: The First Generation

In the mid-1970s, the first group of works on men and masculinity appeared that was directly influenced by these feminist critiques of the traditional explanations for gender differences. Some books underscored the costs to men of traditional gender role prescriptions, exploring how some aspects of men's lives and experiences are constrained and underdeveloped by the relentless pressure to exhibit other behaviors associated with masculinity. Books such as Marc Feigen-Fasteau's *The Male Machine* (1974) and Warren Farrell's *The Liberated Man* (1975) discussed the costs to men's health—both physical and psychological—and to the quality of relationships with women, other men, and their children of the traditional male sex role.

Several anthologies explored the meanings of masculinity in the United States by adopting a feminist-inspired prism through which to view men and masculinity. For example, Deborah David and Robert Brannon's *The Forty-Nine Percent Majority* (1976) and Joseph Pleck and Jack Sawyer's *Men and Masculinity* (1974) presented panoramic views of men's lives from within a framework that accepted the feminist critique of traditional gender arrangements. Elizabeth Pleck and Joseph Pleck's *The American Man* (1980) suggested a historical evolution of contemporary themes. These works explored both the costs and the privileges of being a man in modern U.S. society.

Perhaps the single most important book to criticize the normative organization of the male sex role was Joseph Pleck's *The Myth of Masculinity* (1981). Pleck carefully deconstructed the constituent elements of the male sex role and reviewed the empirical literature for each component part.

After demonstrating that the empirical literature did not support these normative features, Pleck argued that the male sex role model was incapable of describing men's experiences. In its place, he posited a male "sex role strain" model that specified the contemporary sex role as problematic, historically specific, and also an unattainable ideal.

Building on Pleck's work, a critique of the sex role model began to emerge. Sex roles had been cast as the static containers of behaviors and attitudes, and biological males and females were required to fit themselves into these containers, regardless of how ill-fitting these clusters of behaviors and attitudes felt. Such a model was ahistorical and suggested a false cultural universalism, and was therefore ill equipped to help us understand the ways in which sex roles change, and the ways in which individuals modify those roles through the enactments of gender expectations. Most telling, however, was the way in which the sex role model ignored the ways in which definitions of masculinity and femininity were based on, and reproduced, relationships of power. Not only do men as a group exert power over women as a group, but the definitions of masculinity and femininity reproduce those power relations. Power dynamics are an essential element in both the definition and the enactments of gender.

This first generation of research on masculinity was extremely valuable, particularly since it challenged the unexamined ideology that made masculinity the gender norm against which both men and women were measured. The old models of sex roles had reproduced the domination of men over women by insisting on the dominance of masculine traits over feminine traits. These new studies argued against both the definitions of either sex and the social institutions in which those differences were embedded. Shapers of the new model looked at "gender relations" and understood how the definition of either masculinity or femininity was relational, that is, how the definition of one gender depended, in part, on the understanding of the definition of the other.

In the early 1980s, the research on women again surged ahead of the research on men and masculinity. This time, however, the focus was not on the ways in which sex roles reproduce the power relations in society, but rather on the ways in which femininity is experienced differently by women in various social groups. Gradually, the notion of a single femininity—which was based on the white middle-class Victorian notion of female passivity, langorous beauty, and emotional responsiveness—was replaced by an examination of the ways in which women differ in their gender role expectations by race, class, age, sexual orientation, ethnicity, region, and nationality.

The research on men and masculinity is now entering a new stage, in which the variations among men are seen as central to the understanding of men's lives. The unexamined assumption in earlier studies had been that one version of masculinity—white, middle-aged, middle-class, heterosexual—was the sex role into which all men were struggling to fit in our society. Thus, working-class men, men of color, gay men, and younger and older men were all observed as departing in significant ways from the traditional definitions of masculinity. Therefore, it was easy to see these men as enacting "problematic" or "deviant" versions of masculinity. Such theoretical assertions, however, reproduce precisely the power relationships that keep these men in subordinate positions in our society. Not only does middle-class, middle-aged, heterosexual white masculinity become the standard against which all men are measured, but this definition, itself, is used against those who do not fit as a way to keep them down. The normative definition of masculinity is not the "right" one, but it is the one that is dominant.

The challenge to the hegemonic definition of masculinity came from men whose masculinity was cast as deviant: men of color, gay men, and ethnic men. We understand now that we cannot speak of "masculinity" as a singular term, but must examine *masculinities*: the ways in which different men construct different versions of masculinity. Such a perspective can be seen in several recent works, such as Harry Brod's *The Making of*

Masculinities (1987), Michael Kimmel's *Changing Men: New Directions in Research on Men and Masculinity* (1987), and Tim Carrigan, Bob Connell, and John Lee's "Toward a New Sociology of Masculinity" (1985). Bob Connell's *Gender and Power* (1987) and Jeff Hearn's *The Gender of Oppression* (1987) represent the most sophisticated theoretical statements of this perspective. Connell argues that the oppression of women is a chief mechanism that links the various masculinities, and that the marginalization of certain masculinities is an important component of the reproduction of male power over women. This critique of the hegemonic definition of masculinity as a perspective on men's lives is one of the organizing principles of our book, which is the first college-level text in this second generation of work on men and masculinities.

Now that we have reviewed some of the traditional explanations for gender relations and have situated this book within the research on gender in general, and men in particular, let us briefly outline exactly the theoretical perspective we have employed in the book.

The Social Construction of Masculinities

Men are not born, growing from infants through boyhood to manhood, to follow a predetermined biological imperative encoded in their physical organization. To be a man is to participate in social life as a man, as a gendered being. Men are not born; they are made. And men make themselves, actively constructing their masculinities within a social and historical context.

This book is about how men are made and how men make themselves in contemporary U.S. society. It is about what masculinity means, about how masculinity is organized, and about the social institutions that sustain and elaborate it. It is a book in which we will trace what it means to be a man over the course of men's lives.

Men's Lives revolves around three important themes that are part of a social scientific perspective. First, we have adopted a *social constructionist* perspective. By this, we mean that the important fact of men's lives is not that they are biological males, but that they become men. Our sex may be male, but our identity as men is developed through a complex process of interaction with the culture in which we both learn the gender scripts appropriate to our culture and attempt to modify those scripts to make them more palatable. The second axis around which the book is organized follows from our social constructionist perspective. As we have argued, the experience of masculinity is not uniform and universally generalizable to all men in our society. Masculinity differs dramatically in our society, and we have organized the book to illustrate the *variations* among men in the construction of masculinity. Third, we have adopted a *life course* perspective, to chart the construction of these various masculinities in men's lives and to examine pivotal developmental moments or institutional locations during a man's life in which the meanings of masculinity are articulated. Social constructionism, variations among men, and the life course perspective define the organization of this book and the criteria we have used to select the articles included.

The Social Constructionist Model

The social constructionist perspective argues that the meaning of masculinity is neither transhistorical nor culturally universal, but rather varies from culture to culture and within any one culture over time. Thus, males become men in the United States in the early twenty-first century in a way that is very different from men in Southeast Asia, or Kenya, or Sri Lanka.

Men's lives also vary within any one culture over time. The experience of masculinity in the contemporary United States is very different from that experience 150 years ago. Who would argue that what it meant to be a "real man" in seventeenth-century France (at least among the upper classes)—high-heeled patent leather shoes, red velvet jackets covering frilly white lace shirts, lots of rouge and white powder makeup, and a taste for the elegant refinement of ornate furniture—bears much resemblance to the meaning of masculinity among a similar class of French men today?

A perspective that emphasizes the social construction of gender is, therefore, both *historical* and *comparative*. It allows us to explore the ways in which the meanings of gender vary from culture to culture, and how they change within any one culture over historical time.

Variations among Men

Masculinity also varies *within* any one society according to the various types of cultural groups that compose it. Subcultures are organized around other poles, which are the primary way in which people organize themselves and by which resources are distributed. And men's experiences differ from one another according to what social scientists have identified as the chief structural mechanisms along which power and resources are distributed. We cannot speak of masculinity in the United States as if it were a single, easily identifiable commodity. To do so is to risk positing one version of masculinity as normative and making all other masculinities problematic.

In the contemporary United States, masculinity is constructed differently by class culture, by race and ethnicity, and by age. And each of these axes of masculinity modifies the others. Black masculinity differs from white masculinity, yet each of them is also further modified by class and age. A 30-year-old middle-class black man will have some things in common with a 30-year-old middle-class white man that he might not share with a 60-year-old working-class black man, although he will share with him elements of masculinity that are different from those of the white man of his class and age. The resulting matrix of *masculinities* is complicated by cross-cutting elements; without understanding this, we risk collapsing all masculinities into one hegemonic version.

The challenge to a singular definition of masculinity as the normative definition is the second axis around which the readings in this book revolve.

The Life Course Perspective

The meaning of masculinity is not constant over the course of any man's life but will change as he grows and matures. The issues confronting a man about proving himself and feeling successful and the social institutions in which he will attempt to enact his definitions of masculinity will change throughout his life. Therefore, we have adopted a *life course perspective* to discuss the ways in which different issues will emerge for men at different times of their lives and the ways in which men's lives, themselves, change over time. The life course perspective that we have employed will examine men's lives at various pivotal moments in their development from young boys to adults. As in a slide show, these points will freeze the action for a short while, to afford us the opportunity to examine in more detail the ways in which different men in our culture experience masculinity at any one time.

The book's organization reflects these three concerns. Part One sets the context through which we shall examine men's lives. Parts Two through Ten follow those lives through their full course, examining central moments experienced by men in the United States today. Specifically, Parts Two and Three touch on boyhood and adolescence, discussing some of the institutions organized to embody and reproduce masculinities in the United States, such as fraternities, the Boy Scouts, and sports groups. Part Four, "Men and Work," explores the ways in which masculinities are constructed in relation to men's occupations. Part Five, "Men and Health: Body and Mind," deals with heart attacks, stress, AIDS, and other health problems among men. Part Six, "Men in Relationships," describes men's emotional and sexual relationships. We deal with heterosexuality and homosexuality, mindful of the ways in which variations are based on specific lines (class, race, ethnicity). Part Seven, "Male Sexualities," studies the normative elements of heterosexuality and probes the controversial political implications of pornography as a source of both straight and gay men's sexual information. Part Eight,

"Men in Families," concentrates on masculinities within the family and the role of men as husbands, fathers, and senior citizens. Part Nine, "Masculinities in the Media," explores the different ways the media present modes of masculinity. Part Ten, "Violence and Masculinities," looks at violence as the most obdurate, intractable behavioral gender difference. Part Eleven, "Men, Movements, and the Future," examines some of the ways in which men are changing and points to some directions in which men might continue to change.

Our perspective, stressing the social construction of masculinities over the life course, will, we believe, allow a more comprehensive understanding of men's lives in the United States today.

References

Brod, Harry, ed. *The Making of Masculinities.* Boston: Unwin, Hyman, 1987.

Carrigan, Tim, Bob Connell, and John Lee. "Toward a New Sociology of Masculinity" in *Theory and Society,* 1985, *5*(14).

Chodorow, Nancy. *The Reproduction of Mothering.* Berkeley: University of California Press, 1978.

Connell, R. W. *Gender and Power.* Stanford, CA: Stanford University Press, 1987.

David, Deborah, and Robert Brannon, eds. *The Forty-Nine Percent Majority.* Reading, MA: Addison-Wesley, 1976.

Elliott, J. H. *Richelieu and Olivares.* New York: Cambridge University Press, 1984.

Epstein, Cynthia Fuchs. "Inevitability of Prejudice" in *Society,* Sept./Oct., 1986.

Farrell, Warren. *The Liberated Man.* New York: Random House, 1975.

Feigen-Fasteau, Marc. *The Male Machine.* New York: McGraw-Hill, 1974.

Gilligan, Carol. *In a Different Voice.* Cambridge, MA: Harvard University Press, 1982.

Gilder, George. *Men and Marriage.* Gretna, LA: Pelican Publishers, 1986.

Goldberg, Steven. *The Inevitability of Patriarchy.* New York: William Morrow & Co., 1975.

———— "Reaffirming the Obvious" in *Society,* Sept./Oct., 1986.

Hearn, Jeff. *The Gender of Oppression.* New York: St. Martin's Press, 1987.

Hrdy, Sandra Blaffer. *The Woman That Never Evolved.* Cambridge, MA: Harvard University Press, 1981.

Kimmel, Michael S., ed. *Changing Men: New Directions in Research on Men and Masculinity.* Newbury Park, CA: Sage Publications, 1987.

Mead, Margaret. *Sex and Temperament in Three Primitive Societies.* New York: McGraw-Hill, 1935.

Pleck, Elizabeth, and Joseph Pleck, eds. *The American Man.* Englewood Cliffs, NJ: Prentice-Hall, 1980.

Pleck, Joseph. *The Myth of Masculinity.* Cambridge, MA: M.I.T. Press, 1981.

———— and Jack Sawyer, eds. *Men and Masculinity.* Englewood Cliffs, NJ: Prentice-Hall, 1974.

Tiger, Lionel, and Robin Fox. *The Imperial Animal.* New York: Holt, Rinehart & Winston, 1984.

Trivers, Robert. "Parental Investment and Sexual Selection" in *Sexual Selection and the Descent of Man* (B. Campbell, ed.). Chicago: Aldine Publishers, 1972.

Wilkinson, Rupert. *American Tough: The Tough Guy Tradition and American Character.* New York: Harper & Row, 1986.

Wilson, E. O. *Sociobiology: The New Synthesis.* Cambridge, MA: Harvard University Press, 1976.

PART ONE

Perspectives on Masculinities

A quick glance at any magazine rack or television talk show is enough to make you aware that these days, men are confused. What does it mean to be a "real man"? How are men supposed to behave? What are men supposed to feel? How are men to express their feelings? Who are we supposed to be like: Eminem or Boyz II Men? Jimmy Kimmel or Carson Kressley? Derek Jeter or Kobe Bryant? Rhett Butler or Ashley Wilkes?

We are bombarded daily with images and handy rules to help us negotiate our way through a world in which all the rules seem to have suddenly vanished or changed. Some tell us to reassert traditional masculinity against all contemporary challenges. But a strength that is built only on the weakness of others hardly feels like strength at all. Others tell us that men are in power, the oppressor. But if men are in power as a group, why do individual men often feel so powerless? Can men change?

These questions will return throughout this book. These articles in Part One begin to unravel the "masculine mystique" and suggest various dimensions of men's position in society, their power, their powerlessness, and their confusion.

But we cannot speak of "masculinity" as some universal category that is experienced in the same ways by each man. "All men are alike" runs a popular saying. But are they really? Are gay men's experiences with work, relationships, love, and politics similar to those of heterosexual men? Do black and Chicano men face the same problems and conflicts in their daily lives that white men face? Do middle-class men have the same political interests as blue-collar men? The answers to these questions, as the articles in this part suggest, are not simple.

Although earlier studies of men and masculinity focused on the apparently universal norms of masculinity, recent work has attempted to demonstrate how different the worlds of various men are. Men are divided along the same lines that divide any other group: race, class, sexual orientation, ethnicity, age, and geographic region. Men's lives vary in crucial ways, and understanding these variations will take us a long way toward understanding men's experiences.

Earlier studies that suggested a single universal norm of masculinity reproduced some of the problems they were trying to solve. To be sure, *all* benefit from the inequality between women and men; for example, think of how rape jokes or male-exclusive sports culture provide contexts for the bonding of men across class, race, and ethnic lines while denying full participation to women. But the single, seemingly universal masculinity obscured ways in which some men hold and maintain power over other men in our society, hiding the fact that

men do not all share equally in the fruits of gender inequality.

Here is how sociologist Erving Goffman put it in his important book *Stigma* (New York: Doubleday, 1963, p. 128):

> In an important sense there is only one complete unblushing male in America: a young, married, white, urban, northern, heterosexual Protestant father of college education, fully employed, of good complexion, weight, and height, and a recent record in sports. Every American male tends to look out upon the world from this perspective, this constituting one sense in which one can speak of a common value system in America. Any male who fails to qualify in any one of these ways is likely to view himself—during moments at least—as unworthy, incomplete, and inferior.

As Goffman suggests, middle-class, white, heterosexual masculinity is used as the marker against which other masculinities are measured, and by which standard they may be found wanting. What is *normative* (prescribed) becomes translated into what is *normal*. In this way, heterosexual men maintain their status by the oppression of gay men; middle-aged men can maintain their dominance over older and younger men; upper-class men can exploit working-class men; and white men can enjoy privileges at the expense of men of color.

The articles in this section explore the variety of masculinities. James Messerschmidt discusses what sorts of experiences, behaviors, and traits are associated with being "real men" for a number of different men. Yen Le Espiritu, José Torres, and Shaun Harper focus on the different ways in which different groups of men (Asian, American, Latino, and African American) experience masculinities. Michelle Fine and her colleagues examine the same questions for white working-class men in a world that seems to be passing them by. Taken together, these articles suggest that an understanding of class, ethnic, and racial minorities requires an understanding of how political, social, and economic factors shape and constrain the possibilities and personal lifestyle choices for different groups of men. Calls for "changing masculinities," these articles suggest, must involve an emphasis on *institutional transformation*. Steven Schacht's reflective self-examiniation enumerates the various ways in which he is privileged, just by being a man.

Michael Kimmel's article explores the gendered dimensions of terrorism, particularly examining the similarities between the perpetrators of America's two most horrific acts of terrorism: the bombing of the Murrah Federal Building in Oklahoma City in 1995 and the attack on the World Trade Center and the Pentagon on September 11, 2001.

James Messerschmidt

Varieties of "Real Men"

It was a theoretical breakthrough in social theory when the family came to be recognized generally as both gendered and political. Feminist work has now begun to reveal theoretically what we have known for some time in practice—that other social milieux, such as the street and workplace, are not only political but also gendered (Cockburn 1983; Connell 1987; Acker 1990). I extend this theoretical insight through an analysis of how the social structures of labor, power, and sexuality constrain and enable social action within three specific social settings: the street, the workplace, and the family. I focus on how some men, within particular social situations, can make use of certain crimes to construct various public and private adult masculinities.

Research reveals that men construct masculinities in accord with their position in social structures and, therefore, their access to power and resources. Because men situationally accomplish masculinity in response to their socially structured circumstances, various forms of crime can serve as suitable resources for doing masculinity within the specific social contexts of the street, the workplace, and the family. Consequently, I emphasize the significant differences among men and how men utilize different types of crimes to situationally construct distinct forms of masculinities. We begin with the street and an examination of pimping.

From *Masculinities and Crime: Critique and Reconceptualization of Theory,* pp. 119–153. Rowman and Littlefield Publishers, 1993. Reprinted by permission.

The Street

Middle-class, working-class, and lower-working-class young men exhibit unique types of public masculinities that are situationally accomplished by drawing on different forms of youth crime. Moreover, class and race structure the age-specific form of resources employed to construct the cultural ideals of hegemonic masculinity. Such public arenas as the school and street are lush with gendered meanings and signals that evoke various styles of masculinity and femininity. Another type of public masculinity found in the social setting of the street is that of the adult pimp. This particularized form of masculinity is examined here within the context of "deviant street networks."

The Pimp and His Network

Eleanor Miller's (1986, 35–43) respected work *Street Women* reports that in Milwaukee, Wisconsin, African American men in their mid to late twenties and early thirties dominate what she calls "deviant street networks." Deviant street networks are groups of men and women assembled to conduct such illegal profit-making ventures as prostitution, check and credit-card fraud, drug trafficking, burglary, and robbery. Although both men and women engage in various aspects of these "hustling activities," gender relations are unequal, reflecting the social structures of labor, power, and normative heterosexuality. Miller (p. 37) found that a major source of continuous income in these networks "derives from the hustling activity of women who turn their earnings over to the men in exchange for affection, an allowance, the status of their company, and some measure of protection." Commonly referred to as "pimps," the men act as agents and/or companions of these women, substantially profiting from their labor. Miller found that to work as street hustlers, it is essential that women have a "male" sponsor and protector. However, this "essential" has not always existed in the history of prostitution.

Throughout the 1800s, U.S. prostitution was condemned but not classified as a criminal offense, and was conducted primarily under the direction of a "madam" in brothels located in specific red-light districts (Rosen 1982, 27–30). In an attempt to halt prostitution, state legislatures enacted laws in the early 1900s in order to close down these red-light districts and, contemporaneously, women-controlled brothels. Predictably, rather than halting prostitution, new forms of prostitution emerged from this attempt at legislating morality. As Rosen (p. 32) shows in *The Lost Sisterhood,* the closing of the brothels simply increased streetwalking for women; because prostitutes could no longer receive "johns" "in the semiprotected environment of the brothel or district, . . . they had to search for business in public places—hotels, restaurants, cabarets, or on the street." This search for customers in public places exposed prostitutes to violent clients and police harassment. Consequently, these women turned to men for help in warding off dangers, providing legal assistance, and offering some emotional support. Eventually, the overall prostitution business came to be dominated by individual pimp entrepreneurs or masculine-dominated syndicated crime.

In today's deviant street network, the pimp usually controls two to three women (labeled "wives-in-law") on the street (Miller 1986, 37–38). The women turn over their earnings to the pimp and he decides how it will be spent. The disciplinarian of the network, the pimp also "decides upon and metes out the punishment" (Romenesko and Miller 1989, 120). Indeed, as Romenesko and Miller (p. 117) show in their interviews with street hustlers, the pimp demands unquestioned respect:

Showing respect for "men" means total obedience and complete dedication to them. Mary reports that in the company of "men" she had to "talk mainly to the women—try not to look at the men if possible at all—try not to have conversations with them." Rita, when asked about the rules of the street, said, "Just basic, obey. Do what he wants to do. Don't disrespect him. . . . I could not disrespect him in any verbal or physical way. I never attempted to hit him back. Never." And, in the same vein, Tina said that when her "man" had others over to socialize, the women of the family were relegated to the role of servant. "We couldn't speak to them when we wasn't spoken to, and we could not foul up on orders. And you cannot disrespect them."

This authority and control exercised by pimps over women is also clearly exemplified in biographies of pimp life (Malcolm X, 1965; Slim, 1967). Christina Milner and Richard Milner (1972, 52–53) reported a similar form of gendered power in their study of African American pimps in San Francisco:

First and foremost, the pimp must be in complete control of his women; this control is made conspicuous to others by a series of little rituals which express symbolically his woman's attitude. When in the company of others she must take special pains to treat him with absolute deference and respect. She must light his cigarettes, respond to his every whim immediately, and never, never, contradict him. In fact, a ho [prostitute] is strictly not supposed to speak in the company of pimps unless spoken to.

Gender is a situated accomplishment in which we produce forms of behavior seen by others in the same immediate situation as masculine or feminine. Within the confines and social setting of the street, economically marginal men and women create street networks for economic survival, yet simultaneously "do gender" in the process of surviving. In this manner, deviant street networks become the condition that produces material survival as well as the social setting that reaffirms one's gender. The result is a gendered, deviant street network in which men and women do masculinity and femininity, albeit in a distinct manner.

In short, the division of street network labor is concerned both with rationally assigning specific tasks to network members and with the symbolic affirmation and assertion of specific forms of masculinity and femininity (discussed further below). Consequently, pimps simultaneously do pimping and masculinity. As marginalized men, street pimps choose pimping in preference to unemployment and routine labor for "the man." Lacking other avenues and opportunities for accomplishing gender, the pimp lifestyle is a survival strategy that is exciting and rewarding for them as men. The deviant street network provides the context within which to construct one's "essential nature" as a man and to survive as a human being.

The Cool Pose of the Badass

African American street pimps engage in specific practices (constrained by class and race) intended to construct a specific "cool pose" as an important aspect of their specific type of masculinity (Majors 1986; Majors and Billson 1992). In the absence of resources that signify other types of masculinity, sex category is held more accountable and physical presence, personal style, and expressiveness take on an increased importance (Messner 1989, 82). Consequently, as Richard Majors (1986, 5) argues, many "black males have learned to make great use of 'poses' and 'postures' that connote control, toughness and detachment," adopting a specific carriage that exemplifies an expressive and distinct assertion of masculinity.

The often flamboyant, loud, and ostentatious style of African American pimps signifies aspects of this cool pose. The exaggerated display of luxury (for example, in the form of flashy clothing) is also a specific aspect of the cool pose distinctively associated with African American pimps. Majors and Billson (1992, 81–84) argue that the "sharp" and "clean" look of pimps is intended to upstage other men in the highly competitive arena of the street where they earn street applause for

their style, providing an "antidote to invisibility." Pimps literally prance above their immediate position in the class and race divisions of labor and power, thereby constructing a specific masculine street upper-crust demeanor.

Notwithstanding, this cool presence complements an intermittent and brutal comportment to construct masculinity and, in the process, show that the pimp means business. In other words, the African American pimp must always be prepared to employ violence both for utilitarian reasons and for constructing and maintaining a formidable, portentious profile (Katz 1988, 97). The following account by Milner and Milner (1972, 232) illustrates this unpredictable use of violence:

> One ho known as Birthday Cake said she worked for a pimp for four years, gave him a new Cadillac every year, and one night came home from work with her money "funny" and got the beating of her life. She walked in and handed over the money; he counted it and said, "That's all right, honey," drew her a bath, laid her down afterwards on the bed, went to the closet and got a tire iron and beat her senseless with it. She showed us the long scars which required hundreds of stitches and demonstrated her permanent slight limp.

This "badass" form of masculinity (Katz 1988, 80–113) is also publicly displayed for, and supported by, other pimps. Milner and Milner (1972, 56) discuss how a pimp took one of "his" prostitutes (who was also a dancer) into the dancer's dressing room and "began to shout at her and slap her around" loud enough for everyone in the bar to hear. "The six pimps sitting at the back of the bar near the dressing room began to clap and whistle loudly," seemingly for the current dancer, "but in reality to cover the noise of the beating from the ears of the straight customers" (p. 56). Emerging from the dressing room and joining the others, the pimp exclaimed, "Well, I took care of that bitch." Then they all began to "joke around." In contrast, when the prostitute emerged, not "one of them (pimps) felt it proper to comfort her in any way" (p. 56). Such violence, neither out-of-control nor ungovernable, is situationally determined and regulated. Thus, pimp violence becomes a means of disciplining the prostitute and of constructing a badass public masculinity.

The combined cool pose and badass identity of African American pimps clearly represent a specialized means with which to transcend class and race domination. Yet, it also demonstrates the socially constrained nature of social action, and how African American pimps rework the ideals of hegemonic masculinity as a vehicle for achieving that transcendence. Pimping, then, is a resource for surmounting oppressive class and race conditions and for reasserting the social dominance of men. Moreover, like other men, pimps associate masculinity with work, with authority and control, and with explicit heterosexuality.

Within deviant street networks, the prostitute/pimp relationship represents a reworking of these hegemonic masculine ideals under specifically structured social possibilities/constraints. Through their authority and control within deviant street networks, pimps create a class- and race-specific type of masculine meaning and configuration, resulting in a remodeling of heterosexual monogamy in which the pimp provides love, money, and an accompanying sense of security for his "wives-in-law" (Romenesko and Miller 1989, 123).

Normative heterosexuality is the major focus of activities: wives-in-law are expected to be sexually seductive to men, receptive to the sexual "drives" and special "needs" of men (including the pimp), and to work for men who "protect" them and negotiate the "rough spots."[1] Pimping, as a resource for demonstrating that one is a "real man," distinguishes pimps from prostitutes in a specific way. Within the social context of the deviant street network, this pimp type of masculinity is sustained by means of collective and gendered practices that subordinate women, manage the expression of violence against women, and exploit women's labor and sexuality. Indeed, the individual style of the pimp is somewhat meaningless outside the group (Connell 1991, 157); it

is the deviant street network that provides meaning and currency for this type of masculinity.[2] Pimping, in short, is a practice that facilitates a particular gender strategy.

In spite of the above, in attempting to transcend oppressive social structures, African American pimps ultimately reproduce them. Their masculine style is at once repugnant to "conventionality"—their source of wealth anathema to traditional morality (Katz 1988, 97)—yet simultaneously reactionary and reproductive of the gendered social order. In other words, African American pimps respond in a gender-specific manner to race and class oppression, which in turn locks them into the very structured constraints they attempt to overcome. Thus, pimping becomes a form of social action that ultimately results in the reproduction of the gender divisions of labor and power as well as normative heterosexuality.

The following section examines two distinct types of masculinity constructed in the workplace.

The Workplace

The gender divisions of labor and power and normative heterosexuality structure gender relations in the workplace. The workplace not only produces goods and provides services but is the site of gendered control and authority. Because women historically have been excluded from paid work or segregated within it, today the gender division in the workplace is both horizontally and vertically segregated (Game and Pringle 1984; Walby 1986; Reskin and Roos 1987).[3] The result is that women are concentrated overwhelmingly at the lower levels of the occupational hierarchy in terms of wages and salary, status, and authority. Indeed, a recent study of nearly four hundred firms revealed that the vast majority of women were either completely or nearly completely segregated by gender (Bielby and Baron 1986). Consequently, gender relations throughout much of the paid-labor market—like gender relations in schools, youth groups, and deviant street networks—embody relations of power: the domination of men and the subordination of women. Moreover, the creation of "male" and "female" jobs helps to maintain and reproduce this power relationship. Accordingly, gender differences are maintained through gender segregation, and occupational segregation is born of practices ultimately based on conceptions of what constitutes the "essential" natures of men and women.

In addition, the concepts "worker" and "a job" are themselves gendered. As Joan Acker (1990) recently demonstrated, these concepts embody the gender divisions of labor and power. Historically, the idea of a job and who works it has assumed a specific gendered organization or public and private life: a man's life centers on full-time work at a job outside the household; a woman's life focuses on taking care of all his other needs. Consequently, as the abstract worker is masculinized (p. 152):

> it is the man's body, his sexuality, minimal responsibility in procreation, and conventional control of emotions that pervades work and organizational processes. Women's bodies—female sexuality, their ability to procreate and their pregnancy, breast feeding, childcare, menstruation, and mythic "emotionality"—are suspect, stigmatized, and used as grounds for control and exclusion.

Because organization and sexuality occur simultaneously, the workplace is sexualized and normative heterosexuality actually conditions work activities (Hearn and Parkin 1987). As Rosemary Pringle (1989, 162) recently reported, heterosexuality in the workplace is actively perpetuated in a range of practices and interactions exemplified in "dress and self-presentation, in jokes and gossip, looks and flirtations, secret affairs and dalliances, in fantasy and in the range of coercive behaviors that we now call sexual harassment."

Within the social situation of gendered segregation, power, and normative heterosexuality, men and women in the paid-labor market actively construct specific types of masculinity and femininity, depending upon their position in the work-

place. In other words, social action is patterned in the workplace in terms of a distinction between masculine and feminine. Regarding men specifically, a power hierarchy exists in the workplace among men and, not surprisingly, different forms of masculinity correspond to particular positions in this hierarchy.

Let us now look at two differing forms of masculinity in the workplace: (1) workers and their relation to a specific type of sexual harassment and (2) corporate executives and their involvement in a variant form of sexual harassment. In each case, I demonstrate how specific crimes are a resource for constructing particularized representations of private masculinity—those that are occluded from the vision, company, or intervention of outsiders.

Workers and Sexual Harassment

Studies highlight the persistence and dominance of normative heterosexuality on the shop floor— such practices as exhibiting men's sexuality as biologically driven and perpetually incontinent, whereas women are the objects of a sexuality that precipitates men's "natural urges" (Willis 1979; Cockburn 1983; Hearn 1985; Gray 1987). This macho sexual prowess, mediated through bravado and sexist joking, is constructed and encouraged on the shop floor (Collinson and Collinson 1989, 95–98). Moreover, failure to participate in this specific interaction raises serious questions about one's masculinity. In this way, situationally specific notions of heterosexuality are reproduced through the construction of shop-floor masculinity and center on men's insistence on exercising power over women.

Under such conditions, when women enter the shop floor as coworkers, a threatening situation (for the men, that is) results. In this situation, some shop-floor men are likely to engage in forms of interaction quite different from their interaction with women outside the workplace. Not surprising, sexual harassment is more prevalent in this type of social setting. For example, one study of a manufacturing firm (in which the vast majority of manual laborers were men) found (DiTomaso 1989, 81):

> the men in the plant acted differently than they would if they interacted with these women in any other context. Their behavior, in other words, was very much related to the work context itself. It appeared to provide a license for offensive behavior and an occasion for attempting to take advantage of many of the women in the plant.

In DiTomaso's study, the younger women on the shop floor were perceived by the men as the most threatening because they were competing directly for the same kinds of jobs as were the men. Consequently, these women were more likely than other women to be subjected to demeaning forms of social interaction: the men's behavior was more likely to exceed simple flirtation and to involve specific forms of sexual harassment. The following are comments from several women in the plant (pp. 80–81):

> "The men are different here than on the street. It's like they have been locked up for years."

> "It's like a field day."

> "A majority of the men here go out of their way to make you feel uneasy about being inside the plant and being a female; nice guys are a minority."

Research reveals that sexual harassment occurs at all levels in the workplace—from shop floor to management. However, sexual harassment by men on the shop floor generally is twice as serious and persistent, and is different from sexual harassment by managers (Hearn 1985, 121). In the shop-floor setting (where men are the majority), sexual harassment is "a powerful form of economic protection and exclusion from men's territory. Women workers are perceived as a threat to solidarity between men" (pp. 121–122). Studies of shop-floor sexual harassment suggest that 36 to 53 percent of women workers report some type of sexual harassment (Gruber and Bjorn 1982); furthermore, a recent study of workplace sexual assault suggests that manual workers

(as opposed to other men in the firm) committed the overwhelming majority of both attempted and completed assaults within the entire firm (Schneider 1991, 539).

Notwithstanding, the most common types of sexual harassment on the shop floor involve such demeaning acts as sexual slurs, pinches or grabs, and public displays of derogatory images of women (Carothers and Crull 1984, 222; Schneider 1991, 539). Perceptively, women shop-floor coworkers are more likely than women coworkers in other occupational settings to describe this sexual harassment as designed to label them as "outsiders." The "invasion" of women on the shop floor poses a threat to men's monopoly over these jobs, and one way to discourage women from attempting to compete in this domain is to remind them, through remarks and behavior, of their "female fragility" (Carothers and Crull 1984, 224). In this way, then, shop-floor men attempt to secure the "maleness" of the job by emphasizing the "femaleness" of women coworkers (DiTomaso 1989, 88).

Although most shop-floor workers clearly do not engage in sexual harassment, the unique social setting of the shop floor increases the likelihood that this particular type of sexual harassment will occur. Indeed, this specific shop-floor sexual harassment must be seen as a practice communicating anger against women for invading a "male" bastion and for threatening the economic and social status of men (Carothers and Crull 1984, 224). In addition, however, the shop floor is an ideal arena for differentiating between masculinity and femininity—performing manual labor demonstrates to others that such workers are "real men." The presence of women on the shop floor dilutes this gender distinction: if women can do what "real men" do, the value of the practice for accomplishing masculinity is effectively challenged. Because "doing gender" means creating differences between men and women, by maintaining and emphasizing the "femaleness" of women coworkers, shop-floor men are attempting to distinguish clearly between women and men manual laborers, thus preserving the peculiar masculinity of the shop floor. This type of sexual harassment serves as an effective (albeit primitive) resource for solidifying, strengthening, and validating a specific type of heterosexual shop-floor masculinity, while simultaneously excluding, disparaging, and ridiculing women (Segal 1990, 211).[4]

Moving from shop floor to boardroom, we will next consider how a different type of sexual harassment provides certain white corporate executives with resources for constructing a specific form of private masculinity.

White Corporate Executives and Sexual Harassment

Sexual harassment is a resource available to corporate executives for constructing a specific type of masculinity. Because of their subordinate position in the corporation, women "are vulnerable to the whim and fancy of male employers or organizational superiors, who are in a position to reward or punish their female subordinate economically" (Box 1983, 152). In other words, corporate-executive men are in a unique position to sexually exploit, if they desire, women subordinates. Executive exploitation of sexuality is often a means of reinforcing men's power at the same time as making profits. For example, secretaries frequently are treated as conspicuous "possessions"; therefore, by hiring the "best looking" instead of the most competent secretary, managers exploit secretarial sexuality to "excite the envy of colleagues, disarm the opposition and obtain favors from other departments" (Hearn 1985, 118). Thus, as Jeff Hearn (p. 118) points out, exploitation of secretarial sexuality is not only a matter of directly objectifying women but also of using their sexuality for the eyes of other men. Economic and gender relations are produced simultaneously through the same ongoing sexual practices.

In addition to this direct exploitation of secretarial sexuality, corporate executives sometimes engage in specific types of sexual harassment. While shop-floor men who engage in sexual harassment are more likely to undertake practices that create a sexually demeaning work environ-

ment characterized by slurs, pictures, pinches, and grabs, white corporate-executive men are more likely to threaten women workers and lower-level managers who refuse to comply with demands for sexual favors with the loss of their jobs (Carothers and Crull 1984, 222). One secretary described this type of sexual harassment from a corporate executive as follows (cited in Carothers and Crull 1984, 222):

> He always complimented me on what I wore. I thought he was just being nice. It got to the place that every time he buzzed for me to come into his office for dictation, my stomach turned. He had a way of looking at me as if he were undressing me. This time as his eyes searched up and down my body and landed on my breast, he said, "Why should your boyfriend have all the fun. You could have fun with me *and* it could pay off for you. *Good* jobs are really scarce these days."

The harassment of women in subordinate positions by an executive man more likely involves hints and requests for dates or sexual favors, which, when rejected, are likely followed by work retaliation (p. 224). Essentially, this particular type of sexual harassment involves economic threats by white, corporate-executive men such that if a woman employee or would-be employee refuses to submit, she will, on the one hand, not be hired, retained, or promoted or, on the other hand, will be fired, demoted, or transferred to a less-pleasant work assignment. Assuming that the woman employee or potential employee does not desire a sexual relationship with the executive, such threats are extremely coercive. Given the economic position of many of these women, termination, demotion, or not being hired is economically devastating. When women depend on men for their economic well-being, some men take advantage of their economic vulnerability and engage in this particular practice of sexual harassment.

Although the imbalance of corporate gender power can be exercised coercively, sexual harassment is by no means automatic. Women often enter into genuine and humane relationships with men in the workplace, notwithstanding the fact that these men may be in supervisory positions vis-à-vis the women.[5] Nevertheless, the general power imbalance within the corporation often creates conditions such that men in supervisory positions may exercise economic coercion to gain sexual access without genuine overt consent. Indeed, the corporate structural position of white executive men ensures that such exploitation will more likely be manipulative than violent.

One recent study of workplace assaults found that shop-floor workers utilized physical force more often than other forms of coercion because they lack the institutionalized economic means with which to force compliance. Corporate executives are much more likely to use economic coercion than physical force as a means with which to obtain sexual access to women subordinates (Schneider 1991). Two women who experienced this type of sexual assault stated in part (cited in MacKinnon 1979, 32):

> "If I wasn't going to sleep with him, I wasn't going to get my promotion."

> "I was fired because I refused to give at the office."

When women refuse to "give at the office," some corporate executives retaliate by exercising their power over women's careers. In one case, an executive, "following rejection of his elaborate sexual advances, barraged the woman with unwarranted reprimands about her job performance, refused routine supervision or task direction, which made it impossible for her to do her job, and then fired her for poor work performance" (MacKinnon 1979, 35).

The social construction of masculinity/ femininity in the executive/secretary relationship shows clearly how this specific type of sexual harassment comes about. A secretary is often expected to nurture the executive by stroking his ego, making his coffee, cleaning the office, and ensuring he is presentable (Sokoloff 1980, 220). Secretaries are often symbolically hired as "office wives." In one case, an executive had his secretary do all his grocery shopping and even go to his home and take his washing off the line! (Pringle 1989, 169–170)

Rosabeth Moss Kanter (1977, 88) noted some time ago that a "tone of emotional intensity" pervades the relationship between secretary and executive. The secretary comes to "feel for" the executive, "to care deeply about what happens to him and to do his feeling for him." In fact, according to Kanter (p. 88), secretaries are rewarded for their willingness "to take care of bosses' personal needs." In other words, women subordinates construct a specific type of femininity by performing an extensive nurturing service for the executive.[6] Women do in the workplace what they traditionally have done in the home. It should come as no surprise that some executives come to expect such nurturance from women subordinates, just as they do from their wives, and that some take this nurturance further to include sexual nurturing. The result is that some women are coerced to exchange sexual services for material survival. As Carothers and Crull (1984, 223) observe in their important study of sexual harassment:

> The male boss can use his power over women within the organizational structure to impose sexual attentions on a woman, just as he can coerce her into getting his coffee. They both know that if she does not go along, she is the one who will lose in terms of job benefits.

Corporate-executive harassment and sexual coercion are practices that simultaneously construct a specific form of masculinity. This type of sexual harassment arrogantly celebrates hegemonic masculinity, its presumed heterosexual urgency, and the "normality of pursuing women aggressively." In an attempt to "score" with "his" secretary, the corporate-executive sexual harasser strengthens gender hierarchy, thereby "affirming in men a shared sense of themselves as the dominant, assertive and active sex" (Segal 1990, 244). The corporate executive enjoys an immediate sensation of power derived from this practice, power that strengthens his masculine self-esteem.

In this way, in addition to normative heterosexuality, white, corporate-executive sexual harassers attempt to reproduce their gender power.

Through the practice of corporate sexual harassment, executives exhibit, as MacKinnon (1979, 162) argues, "that they can go this far any time they wish and get away with it." White, corporate-executive sexual harassment, constructed differently than by shop-floor men, provides a resource for constructing this specific type of heterosexual masculinity that centers on the "driven" nature of "male" sexuality and "male" power.

Although clearly most corporate executives do not engage in sexual harassment, the social setting of the executive/secretary relationship increases the probability that this specific form of sexual harassment will occur. Corporate executives engage in sexual harassment to reinforce their power by sexualizing women subordinates, creating "essential" differences between women and men by constructing this particular type of masculinity.

The Family

In addition to the street and the workplace, the divisions of labor and power frame social interactions and practices in the contemporary nuclear family where, for example, women remain responsible primarily for unpaid housework and child care while men remain responsible primarily for paid labor. Indeed, the gender division of household labor defines not only who does most of the unpaid household labor but also the kind of household labor assigned to men and women. Moreover, the sociological evidence indicates clearly that in Western industrialized societies gender asymmetry in the performance of household labor continues to exist (Hartmann 1981; Berk 1985; Messerschmidt 1986, 74; Andersen 1988, 141–145; Hochschild 1989, 1992) and women share less in the consumption of household goods (from food to leisure time) than do men (Walby 1986, 221).

It is true that barely 10 percent of all U.S. heterosexual households consist of a husband and wife with two children living at home, where the husband is the sole breadwinner (Messerschmidt 1986, 74). Further, as fertility is delayed or de-

clines, and with more and more women working during pregnancy and child-rearing years, active motherhood is shrinking as a component of most women's lives (Petchesky 1984, 246). Nevertheless, evidence indicates that women continue to perform most of the household labor, even as these demographic changes occur and women's participation in the paid-labor market increases dramatically. Indeed, Arlie Hochschild (1992, 512) concluded in her study of fifty-two heterosexual couples over an eight-year period that just as "there is a wage gap between men and women in the work place, there is a 'leisure gap' between them in the home. Most women work one shift at the office or factory and a 'second shift' at home."

This gender division of labor embodies the husband's power to define the household setting in his terms. While conscious efforts are being made in many households to dismantle familial power relations (Connell 1987, 124), especially in the middle class (Ehrenreich 1983), for most couples the capacity of each spouse to determine the course of their shared life is unequal: men alone make the "very important" decisions in the household; women alone make few "important" decisions (Komter 1989). In many dual-career families, men's power is deemed authentic and an acceptable part of social relations. This legitimized power in the family provides men with considerably greater authority (Bernard 1982; Komter 1989; Pahl 1992). Concomitantly, the marital sexual relationship, as with other aspects of marriage, likely embodies power, unless consciously dismantled, and "in most cases it is the husband who holds the initiative in defining sexual practice" (Connell 1987, 123).

The concept of patriarchy has lost its strength and usefulness as a theoretical starting point for comprehending gender inequality in Western industrialized societies. Nevertheless, the concept is helpful to describe a certain type of masculinity that persists today: some men are simply *patriarchs* in the traditional sense. Patriarchs fashion configurations of behavior and pursue a gender strategy within the family setting that control women's labor and/or sexuality. Moreover, these men will most likely use violence against women in the family. In the final section of this chapter, the discussion focuses on two forms of violence against women in the family—wife beating and wife rape—and analyzes how these crimes serve as a resource for the construction of specific types of patriarchal masculinities.

Wife Beating and Battering Rape

Victimization surveys indicate that in the home, wives are assaulted much more often by their husbands than husbands are by their wives (less than 5 percent of domestic violence involves attacks on husbands by their wives) and women are much more likely than men to suffer injury from these assaults (Dobash, Dobash, Wilson, and Daly 1992).[7] Wife beating also develops within a setting of prolonged and persistent intimidation, domination, and control over women (Dobash and Dobash 1984; Pagelow 1984; Dobash et al. 1992). Accordingly, wife beating is the "chronic battering of a person of inferior power who for that reason cannot effectively resist" (Gordon 1988, 251).

Violence by men in the household derives from the domestic authority of men and is intimately linked to the traditional patriarchal expectation (1) that men are the credible figures within monogamous relationships and (2) that men possess the inherent right to control those relationships. As Susan Schechter (1982, 222) argues, "a man beats to remind a woman that the relationship will proceed in the way he wants or that ultimately he holds the power."

Katz's (1988, 18–31) discussion of "righteous slaughter"—killing among family members, friends, and acquaintances—by men aids in understanding how this focus on household authority and control results in wife beating as a resource for masculine construction. Katz argues that for the typical killer, murder achieves *Good* by obliterating *Bad*. Moreover, the killer has no capacity to "ignore a fundamental challenge" to his self-worth and identity. From the killer's perspective, the victim teases, dares, defies, or pursues the killer. Accordingly, the killer sees himself as simply "defending his rights." In other words, the killer's identity and self-worth have been taken away—by an insult, losing an argument, an act of infidelity—and such events attack an "eternal human value" that calls for a "last stand in defense of his basic worth." The "eternally humiliating situation" is transformed into a blinding rage and the compulsion to wipe away the stigmatizing stain through the act of murder. And the rage is not random and chaotic but, rather, "coherent, disciplined action, cunning in its moral structure" (p. 30). The killer "does not kill until and unless he can fashion violence to convey the situational meaning of defending his rights" (p. 31).

Investigations of wife beating indicate further the application of the notion "defending his rights." Violence is regarded by the husband as achieving *Good* by pulverizing *Bad;* such men engage in a coherent and disciplined rage to defend what they consider to be their rights. According to interviews with wife beaters, their wife is perceived as not "performing well," not accomplishing what her "essential nature" enjoins and stipulates. Women are beaten for not cooking "up to standards," for not being obeisant and deferential, and for not completing or performing housework sufficiently—for not being a "good wife" (Ptacek 1988, 147). According to the offender, the "privileges of male entitlement have been unjustly denied" because the wife is not submissive and, therefore, not conforming to his standards of "essential femininity" (p. 148). Irene Frieze's (1983, 553) interviews with wife beaters found that they believe "it is their right as men to batter wives who disobey them."

Dobash and Dobash (1984, 274) similarly found that most wife beating is precipitated by verbal confrontations centering on possessiveness and jealousy on the part of the husband and a husband's demand concerning domestic labor and services. During an argument over such issues, "the men were most likely to become physically violent at the point when the woman could be perceived to be questioning his authority or challenging the legitimacy of his behavior or at points when she asserted herself in some way" (p. 274).

In other words, wife beating arises not solely from gendered subordination but also from women actively contesting that subordination (Gordon 1988, 286). In such situations, the wife beater is punishing "his wife" for her failure to fulfill adequately her "essential" obligations in the gender division of labor and power and for her challenge to his dominance. The wife beater perceives that he has an inherent patriarchal right to punish "his woman" for her alleged wrongdoing.

Wife beaters are piously sure of their righteousness, and thus fashion their violence to communicate the situational meaning of defending their patriarchal rights. Indeed, the more traditional the gender division of labor (regardless of class and race position) the greater the likelihood of wife beating (Edleson, Eisikovits, and Guttman, 1986; Messerschmidt 1986; Smith 1990a). In such traditional patriarchal households, both husband and wife tend to perceive the lopsided gender division of labor and power as "fair" (Berk 1985). Linda Gordon's (1988, 260–261) historical study of family violence found that in households where wife beating is prevalent:

> Women as well as men professed allegiance to male-supremacist understandings of what relations between the sexes should be like. These shared assumptions, however, by no means prevented conflict. Women's assumptions of male dominance did not mean that they quit trying to improve their situations.

The wife beater attempts to resolve in *his* way what he regards as a conflict over this "fair" arrangement, even when the wife is not actively or consciously contesting that "fair" household organization.[8] Accordingly, as West and Zimmerman (1987, 144) argue, "It is not simply that household labor is designated as 'women's work,' but that a woman to engage in it and a man not to engage in it is to draw on and exhibit the 'essential nature' of each." By engaging in practices that maintain gender divisions of labor and power, husbands and wives do not simply produce household goods and services, but also produce gender. Indeed, husbands and wives develop gendered ra-

tionalizations and justifications for this asymmetrical household labor. What follows are selected but representative examples (Komter 1989, 209):

> *By wives:*
> "He has no feeling for it."
> "He is not born to it."
> "It does not fit his character."
>
> *By husbands:*
> "She has more talent for it."
> "It is a woman's natural duty."

When this asymmetry is questioned (whether consciously or not), the wife beater assumes that his "essential rights" are being denied—an injustice has occurred, a violation of the "natural" order of things. The "essential nature" of wife beaters is that they control familial decision making and thus dominate the family division of labor and power. When wives "question" this decision making, through words or actions, they threaten their husband's control of the gender division of labor and power. In other words, the husband interprets such behavior as a threat to his "essential nature"—control and domination of the household. Because spousal domestic labor is a symbolic affirmation of a patriarch's masculinity and his wife's femininity, such men are extremely vulnerable to disappointment when that labor is not performed as they expect (Gordon 1988, 268).

According to the wife beater, it is his duty to determine, for example, what constitutes a satisfactory meal, how children are cared for, when and how often sexual relations occur, and the nature of leisure activities (Ferraro 1988, 134). Women are beaten for some of the most insignificant conduct imaginable: for example, preparing a casserole instead of a meat dish for dinner, wearing their hair in a ponytail, or remarking that they do not like the pattern on the wallpaper. Kathleen Ferraro (p. 135) discusses a case in which even the issue of wearing a particular piece of clothing was perceived by the husband as a threat to his control:

> On her birthday, she received a blouse from her mother that she put on to wear to a meeting she

was attending without Steven. He told her she could not wear the blouse, and after insisting that she would, Steven beat her. It was not only her insistence on wearing the blouse that evening that triggered Steven's abuse. It was the history of his symbolic control, through determining her appearance that was questioned by wearing the new blouse.

Wife beaters (regardless of class and race position) presume they have the patriarchal right—because it is part of their "essential nature"—to dominate and control their wives, and wife beating serves both to ensure continued compliance with their commands and as a resource for constructing a "damaged" patriarchal masculinity. Thus, wife beating increases (or is intended to do so) their control over women and, therefore, over housework, child care, and sexual activity.

Yet wife beating is related not only to the husband's control over familial decision making, but also develops from another form of control, possessiveness. For some wife beaters, spousal demonstration of loyalty is a focal concern and is closely monitored. For instance, time spent with friends may be interpreted by a wife beater simply as disloyalty. Indeed, sexual jealousy of friends is a common theme in the literature on wife beating (Dobash and Dobash 1979, 1984; Frieze 1983; Ferraro 1988), and indicates the importance of the social structure of normative heterosexuality to understanding wife beating. The wife's uncommitted wrong is the potential to be unfaithful, which to her husband is not only a serious challenge to his patriarchal ideology, but his very real fear that his wife will choose another man and, thereby, judge him less "manly" than his "competitor." Thus, because time spent with friends endangers his ongoing interest in heterosexual performance, wife beating reassures him that his wife is his to possess sexually.

Moreover, not only potential sexual competitors can threaten a patriarchal husband, but relatives may also pose threats to a wife's loyalty. Pregnancy, for example, is closely associated with wife beating, and reflects the husband's resentment of the fetal intruder (Ferraro 1988). Walker

(1979, 83–84) offers an example of a husband and wife who planned to spend the day together, but the wife broke off the plans, choosing instead to baby-sit her three-year-old granddaughter. Her husband (Ed) seems to have interpreted this choice as disloyal behavior and a challenge to his ultimate control.

> Ed became enraged. He began to scream and yell that I didn't love him, that I only loved my children and grandchildren. I protested and said, "Maybe you would like to come with me," thinking that if he came, he might feel more a part of the family. He just became further enraged. I couldn't understand it. . . . He began to scream and yell and pound me with his fists. He threw me against the wall and shouted that he would never let me leave, that I had to stay with him and could not go. I became hysterical and told him that I would do as I saw fit. . . . Ed then became even further enraged and began beating me even harder.

Thus, under conditions where labor services are "lacking" and possessiveness is "challenged," a wife beater's masculinity is threatened. In such a scenario, predictably, the wife beater attempts to reestablish control by reconstructing his patriarchal masculinity through the practice of wife beating.

Approximately 30 to 40 percent of battered women are also victims of wife rape (Walker 1979; Russell 1982; Frieze 1983). These "battering rapes," as Finkelhor and Yllö (1985) describe them, do not result from marital conflicts over sex; rather, the rape is an extension of other violence perpetrated on the victim. The wife beating/rape represents punishment and degradation for challenging his authority and, thus, the traditional division of labor and power. In fact, although wife beating and battering rapes extend across all classes and races (for the reasons discussed above), they occur most frequently in working-class and lower-working-class households wherein the traditional patriarchal gender division of labor and power—husband decision maker and wife caretaker—is strongest (Walker 1977–78; Straus, Gelles, and Steinmetz 1980; Finkelhor and Yllö

1985; Messerschmidt 1986, 144; Smith 1990b). Research consistently shows that class conditions are associated with wife beating: for example, low-income (Straus et al. 1980; DeKeseredy and Hinch 1991) and working-class wives are approximately twice as likely as middle-class wives to experience wife beating (Stets and Straus 1989; Smith 1990a). Moreover, among couples in which the husband is unemployed or employed part-time, the level of husband-to-wife violence is three times as high as the level among couples in which the husband is fully employed (Straus et al. 1980; DeKeseredy and Hinch 1991).

Finally, Michael Smith's (1990b, 49) study of risk factors in wife beating found that "the lower the income, the higher the probability of abuse." This same study went on to report that the chances of a low-income woman being severely battered during marriage exceed those of a middle-class woman by a factor of ten. Smith's (1990a, 267) data reveals that "men with relatively low incomes, less educated men, and men in low-status jobs were significantly more likely than their more privileged counterparts to subscribe to an ideology of familial patriarchy. These men were also more likely to have beaten their wives."

Although at work he is individually powerless, at home the working-class battering rapist is a patriarch endowed with individual authority. His ability to earn money (if available) "authorizes" his patriarchal power as husband/father. But his masculine identity depends on the demarcation of public and private responsibility; consequently, any challenge to the status quo in the home is taken personally as a confrontation (Tolson 1977, 70). In seeking to sustain this specific type of patriarchal masculinity, working-class men develop an intense emotional dependency on the family/household (Donaldson 1987), demanding nurturance, services, and comfort on their terms when at home. As Lynne Segal (1990, 28) points out, "the sole site of authority" for such men is in the home. And when their power and authority are threatened or perceived to be threatened at home, working-class men are more likely than other men to employ battering rapes to accomplish

gender and reestablish their control. As Harris and Bologh (1985, 246) point out in their examination of "blue collar battering," "If he can establish an aura of aggression and violence, then he may be able to pass as a 'real man,' for surely it is admirable to use violence in the service of one's honor."

Battering in this sense is a resource for affirming "maleness." Because of their structural position in the class division of labor, working-class men—in particular, lower-working-class men—lack traditional resources for constructing their masculinity and, as a result, are more likely than are middle-class men to forge a particular type of masculinity that centers on ultimate control of the domestic setting through the use of violence. Moreover, unemployment and low occupational status undermine the patriarchal breadwinner/good provider masculinity: he cannot provide for his wife and children. Such men are more likely than are economically advantaged husbands to engage in wife beating and battering rapes to reestablish their masculinity. As Kathleen Ferraro (1988, 127) puts it, "for men who lack any control in the civil realm, dominance within the private realm of the home becomes their sole avenue for establishing a sense of self in control of others."[9]

In sum, most working- and lower-working-class husbands do not abuse their wives, nor is this particular type of abuse limited to this class of men. Nevertheless, the peculiar social conditions prevalent in working- and lower-working-class families increase the incidence of this type of abuse. For these men, power is exercised in the home in ways that hegemonic masculinity approves: men are allowed to be aggressive and sexual. Lacking dominance over others at work or the ability to act out a breadwinner (or even economic contributor) masculinity, sex category is particularly important, and working- and lower-working-class men are more likely to express their masculinity as patriarchs, attempting to control the labor and sexuality of "their women." Consequently, when patriarchal relations are "challenged," their taken-for-granted "essential nature" is undermined and, accordingly, doing masculinity requires extra effort. Wife beating/rape is a specific practice designed with an eye to one's accountability as a "real man" and, therefore, serves as a suitable resource for simultaneously accomplishing gender and affirming patriarchal masculinity.

Force-Only Rape

However, wife rape is not limited to the victims of wife beating. Indeed, in Finkelhor and Yllö's (1985) study, 40 percent of their sample were "force-only rapes"—situations in which husbands use only the force necessary to coerce their wives into submission. The perpetrators and victims of force-only rapes were significantly more educated than those of battering rapes, more often middle-class, and almost half held business- or professional-level jobs.[10] Moreover, the perpetrators and victims of force-only rapes were much less likely to have been in a relationship based on the traditional gender divisions of labor and power. Sex was usually the issue in force-only rapes, and the offenders were "acting on some specifically sexual complaint," such as how often to have sex or what were acceptable sexual activities (p. 46).

In some sectors of the "progressive" middle class, there have been serious attempts to become truly equal marriage partners, where the wife has a career and where the husband participates equally in child care and housework. However, the greater the income differential between husbands and wives, the less involved some husbands are in parenting and housework, and there exists greater equality in dual-career families than in dual-income families (Segal 1990, 38). Consequently, as Barbara Ehrenreich (1989, 218–220; see also 1983, 1984) argues, a new heterosexual masculinity on the part of certain progressive, middle-class men has emerged, consisting of choosing a mate who can "pull her own weight" economically and who is truly committed to sharing household labor equally.

Notwithstanding, this progressive "dual-career" relationship is not supplemented, in many cases, by a progressive sexual relationship. As Andrew Tolson (1977, 121) argued as early as 1977, for many progressive, middle-class men, sexual passion is "still acted out in familial terms of masculine 'conquest'—to which women could only 'respond.'" Although many progressive, middle-class men seriously seek "free women" who live for themselves and their careers (Ehrenreich 1984), in bed they continue to demand submission and the affirmation of masculinity through heterosexual performance (Tolson 1977, 121). That is, many progressive, middle-class men continue to adhere to the hegemonic masculine ideology that "entitles" them to sex with their wives whenever they want it. For example, Finkelhor and Yllö (1985, 62–70) discuss the case of Ross, a middle-class businessman who somewhat represents this progressive middle class, yet who frequently raped his wife. Ross describes below how one such rape occurred during an argument over sex that his wife was winning (p. 66):

> She was standing there in her nightie. The whole thing got me somewhat sexually stimulated, and I guess subconsciously I felt she was getting the better of me. It dawned on me to just throw her down and have at her . . . which I did. I must have reached out and grabbed at her breast. She slapped my hand away. So I said, "Lay down. You're going to get it." She replied, "Oh, no, you don't," so I grabbed her by the arms and she put up resistance for literally fifteen seconds and then just resigned herself to it. There were no blows or anything like that. It was weird. I felt very animalistic, and I felt very powerful. I had the best erection I'd had in years. It was very stimulating. . . . I walked around with a smile on my face for three days.

Ross believed his wife not only controlled the sexuality in their lives, but that she had "completely and totally emasculated" him (p. 68). The rape was both a way to overcome that loss of power in his life and a means to construct a specific type of patriarchal masculinity centering on heterosexual performance and the domination and control of women's sexuality.

Another businessman, Jack, stated to Finkelhor and Yllö (p. 72), "When she would not give it freely, I would take it." He felt that his wife did not have the right to deny sex, he had the right to sex when he pleased, and it was her duty to satisfy his sexual needs. Similarly, in Irene Frieze's (1983, 544, 553) study of wife rape, the vast majority of wife rapists engaged in this form of violence in order to prove their "manhood," believing "that their wives were obligated to service them sexually in whatever ways they desired."

Thus, in force-only rapes, the assaults are practices of masculine control based on expectations that sex is a right. Both battering and force-only rapists consciously choose such violent action to facilitate a patriarchal gender strategy and to protect what they view as their "essential" privileges. The resulting masculine construction is not only an exhibition of their "essential nature," but also illustrates the seductive quality of violence for displaying that "essential nature." For these men, masculine authority is quite simply expressed through the violent control of women.

Nevertheless, such personal choices become enigmatic when detached from social structures. In battering rapes, because the traditional division of labor and power is prevalent and the struggle is over authority and control of that division, these men construct a patriarchal form of masculinity that punishes and degrades the wife for deviating from her "essential" duties. In force-only rapes, however, the gender division of labor is not the issue: this is the classic, middle-class, dual-career family in which both partners participate in decision making and household tasks, and in which the husband accepts, in a general way, his wife's autonomous right to develop her own interests. However, the force-only rapist feels specifically wronged, cheated, and deprived in the sexual realm. Some progressive, middle-class men simply adhere to the hegemonic masculine ideology that entitles them to sex whenever they want it. Sex is considered a marriage right by which gender is accomplished through effective performance in the sexual realm. Like sexual harassment, a similar type of crime, wife rape can be a resource for accomplishing masculinity differently. And as the social setting within the nuclear family changes, so does the conceptualization of what is normative masculine behavior. Different social settings generate different masculinities, even when the particular resource (crime) is similar.

In sum, the structure of the gender division of labor and power and normative heterosexuality impinges on the construction of masculinity. These structural features both preclude and permit certain forms of crime as resources that men may use to pursue a gender strategy and construct their masculinity. Although both battering and force-only rapists try to control their wives, they do so in qualitatively different ways. The social relations extant within their respective gender divisions of labor and power are different, and different options exist for maintaining their control. The choices made by each type of rapist, and the resources available to carry out those choices, develop in response to the specific social circumstances in which they live. For these reasons, then, these men employ different forms of violence to construct different types of private masculinities.

This chapter has attempted to demonstrate that men produce specific configurations of behavior that can be seen by others within the same immediate social setting as "essentially male." These different masculinities emerge from practices that utilize different resources, and class and race relations structure the resources available to construct specific masculinities. Pimps, workers, executives, and patriarchs generate situationally accomplished, unique masculinities by drawing on different types of crime indigenous to their distinct positions within the structural divisions of labor and power. Because men experience their everyday world from a uniquely individualistic position in society, they construct the cultural ideals of hegemonic masculinity in different ways.

Social structures are framed through social action and, in turn, provide resources for constructing masculinity. As one such resource, specific types of crime ultimately are based on these social structures. Thus, social structures both enable and constrain social action and, therefore, masculinities and crime.

Notes

1. Prostitutes, or "wives-in-law," are constructing a femininity that both confirms and violates stereotypical "female" behavior. In addition to the conventional aspects of femininity just mentioned, prostitute femininity also ridicules conventional morality by advocating sex outside marriage, sex for pleasure, anonymous sex, and sex that is not limited to reproduction and the domesticated couple. This construction of a specific type of femininity clearly challenges, in certain respects, stereotypical femininity. Nevertheless, the vast majority of prostitutes do not consider themselves feminists: they know very little about the feminist movement, do not share its assumptions, and believe men and women are "naturally" suited for different types of work (Miller 1986, 160).

2. The masculinity constructed by African American pimps is fittingly comparable to the masculinity associated with men (usually from working-class backgrounds) who are members of white motorcycle gangs. The men in such groups act extremely racist and similarly exploit the sexuality and labor of "biker women." However, biker men do not display a "cool pose" with an accompanying show of luxury in the form of flashy clothing and exotic hairstyles. On the contrary, a biker usually has long unkempt hair, a "rough" beard, and his "colors" consist of black motorcycle boots, soiled jeans, and a simple sleeveless denim jacket with attached insignia (see Willis 1978; Hopper and Moore 1990).

3. Horizontal segregation allocates men and women to different types of jobs; vertical segregation concentrates men and women in different occupations at different steps in an occupational hierarchy.

4. Nevertheless, it should be pointed out that increasing numbers of men are attempting to counter sexism on the shop floor and, therefore, reconstruct shop-floor masculinity. For an excellent example, see Gray 1987.

5. Indeed, office romances seem to be flourishing because women more routinely work beside men in professional and occupational jobs (Ehrenreich 1989, 219).

6. This particular form of femininity has been explored by Pringle (1988).

7. Despite devastating criticisms of the Conflict Tactics Scale as a methodological tool (Dobash, Dobash, Wilson, and Daly 1992), some researchers (remarkably) continue to use it to guide their work, concluding that women are about as violent as men in the home (Straus and Gelles 1990) or even, in some cases, that more men are victimized in the home than are women (McNeely and Mann 1990).

8. Unfortunately, there is scant research on wife beating in racial-minority households. Nevertheless, what evidence there is on African American households suggests that when violence does occur, both husband and wife are likely to accept the traditional patriarchal division of labor and power as natural and that complete responsibility for the battering, when questioned, "lies with white society" (Richie 1985, 42; see also Asbury 1987). Consequently, I am forced to concentrate solely on class and wife beating.

9. This is not to deny that many middle-class men engage in wife beating for the reasons discussed earlier in this section. What I suggest, following Segal (1990, 255) and others, is that it is clearly less common in middle-class households because such men have access to other resources, possibly more effective resources, through which they exert control over women without employing violence.

10. Because Finkelhor and Yllö (1985, 9) found no significantly higher rate of marital rape among African Americans than among whites, I do not distinguish by race.

References

Andersen, Margaret. (1988). *Thinking About Women.* New York: Macmillan.

Berk, Sarah Fenstermaker. (1985). *The Gender Factory: The Apportionment of Work in American Households.* New York: Plenum Press.

Bernard, Jessie. (1992). "The Good-Provider Role: Its Rise and Fall." In *Men's Lives,* ed. Michael S. Kimmel and Michael A. Messner, 203–21. New York: Macmillan.

Bielby, William, and James N. Baron. (1986). "A Woman's Place Is with Other Women: Sex Segregation within Organizations." In *Sex Segregation in the Workplace: Trends, Explanations, Remedies,* ed. Barbara Reskin, 27–55. Washington, DC: National Academy Press.

Box, Steven. (1983). *Power, Crime and Mystification.* New York: Tavistock.

Carothers, Suzanne C., and Peggy Crull. (1984). "Contrasting Sexual Harassment in Female- and Male-Dominated Occupations." In *My Troubles Are Going to Have Trouble with Me,* ed. Karen Brodkin Sacks and Dorothy Remy, 219–28. New Brunswick, NJ: Rutgers University Press.

Cockburn, Cynthia. (1983). *Brothers: Male Dominance and Technological Change.* London: Pluto Press.

Collinson, David L., and Margaret Collinson. (1989). "Sexuality in the Workplace: The Domination of Men's Sexuality." In *The Sexuality of Organization,* ed. Jeff Hearn, Deborah L. Sheppard, Peta Tancred-Sheriff, and Gibson Burrell, 91–109. Newbury Park, CA: Sage.

Connell, R. W. (1991). "Live Fast and Die Young: The Construction of Masculinity among Young Working-Class Men on the Margin of the Labour Market." *Australian and New Zealand Journal of Sociology* 27 (2): 141–71.

Connell, R. W. (1987). *Gender and Power.* Stanford, CA: Stanford University Press.

DeKeseredy, Walter, and Ronald Hinch. (1991). *Woman Abuse: Sociological Perspectives.* Lewiston, NY: Thompson Educational Pub., Inc.

D'Emilio, John, and Estelle B. Freedman. (1988). *Intimate Matters: A History of Sexuality in America.* New York: Harper and Row.

DiTomaso, Nancy. (1989). "Sexuality in the Workplace: Discrimination and Harassment." In *The Sexuality of Organization,* eds. Jeff Hearn, Deborah L. Sheppard, Peta Tancred-Sheriff, and Gibson Burrell, 71–90. Newbury Park, CA: Sage.

Dobash, R. Emerson, and Russell P. Dobash. (1984). "The Nature and Antecedents of Violent Events." *British Journal of Criminology* 24 (3): 269–88.

Dobash, R. Emerson, and Russell P. Dobash. (1979). *Violence Against Wives.* New York: Free Press.

Dobash, Russell P., R. Emerson Dobash, Margo Wilson, and Martin Daly. (1992). "The Myth of Sexual Symmetry in Marital Violence." *Social Problems* 39 (1): 71–91.

Donaldson, Mike. (1987). "Labouring Men: Love, Sex and Strife." *Australian and New Zealand Journal of Sociology* 23 (2): 165–84.

Edleson, Jeffrey L., Zvi Eisikovits, and Edna Guttman. (1986). "Men Who Batter Women: A Critical Review of the Evidence." *Journal of Family Issues* 6 (2): 229–47.

Ehrenreich, Barbara. (1983). *The Hearts of Men.* New York: Doubleday.

Ferraro, Kathleen J. (1988). "An Existential Approach to Battering." In *Family Abuse and its Consequences,* ed. Gerald T. Hotaling, David Finkelhor, John T. Kirkpatrick, and Murray Straus, 126–38. Newbury Park, CA: Sage.

Finkelhor, David, and Kristi Yllö. (1985). *License to Rape: Sexual Abuse of Wives.* New York: Holt, Rinehart and Winston.

Frieze, Irene H. (1983). "Investigating the Causes and Consequences of Marital Rape." *Signs* 8 (3): 532–53.

Game, Ann, and Rosemary Pringle. (1984). *Gender at Work.* Boston: Allen and Unwin.

Gordon, Linda. (1988). *Heroes of Their Own Lives.* New York: Viking.

Gray, Stan. (1987). "Sharing the Shop Floor." In *Beyond Patriarchy,* ed. Michael Kaufman, 216–34. New York: Oxford University Press.

Gruber, James, and Lars Bjorn. (1982). "Blue Collar Blues: The Sexual Harassment of Women Autoworkers." *Work and Occupations* 9 (3): 271–98.

Harris, Richard N., and Roslyn Wallach Bologh. (1985). "The Dark Side of Love: Blue and White Collar Wife Abuse." *Victimology* 10 (1–4): 242–52.

Hartmann, Heidi. (1981). "The Unhappy Marriage of Marxism and Feminism: Towards a More Progressive Union." In *Women and Revolution,* ed. Lydia Sargent, 1–41. Boston: South End Press.

Hearn, Jeff. (1985). "Men's Sexuality at Work." In *The Sexuality of Men,* ed. Andy Metcalf and Martin Humphries, 110–28. London: Pluto Press.

Hochschild, Arlie. (1989). *The Second Shift.* New York: Viking.

Hochschild, Arlie. (1992). "The Second Shift: Employed Women Are Putting in Another Day of Work at Home." In *Men's Lives,* ed. Michael S. Kimmel and Michael A. Messner, 511–15. New York: Macmillan.

Kanter, Rosabeth Moss. (1977). *Men and Women of the Corporation.* New York: Basic Books.

Katz, Jack. (1988). *Seductions of Crime: Moral and Sensual Attractions in Doing Evil.* New York: Basic Books.

Komter, Aafke. (1989). "Hidden Power in Marriage." *Gender and Society* 3 (2): 187–216.

MacKinnon, Catherine A. (1979). *Sexual Harassment of Working Women.* New Haven, CT: Yale University Press.

Majors, Richard. (1986). "Cool Pose: The Proud Signature of Black Survival." *Changing Men* 17: 5–6.

Majors, Richard, and Janet Mancini Billson. (1992). *Cool Pose: The Dilemma's of Black Manhood in America.* New York: Macmillan.

Messerschmidt, James W. (1986). *Capitalism, Patriarchy and Crime: Toward a Socialist Feminist Criminology.* Totowa, NJ: Rowman and Littlefield.

Miller, Eleanor. (1986). *Street Woman.* Philadelphia: Temple University Press.

Milner, Christina, and Richard Milner. (1972). *Black Players: The Secret World of Black Pimps.* Boston: Little, Brown.

Pagelow, Mildred D. (1984). *Family Violence.* New York: Praeger.

Pahl, Jan. (1992). "Money and Power in Marriage." In *Gender, Power and Sexuality,* ed. Pamela Abbott and Claire Wallace, 41–57. London: Macmillan.

Petchesky, Rosalind. (1984). *Abortion and Woman's Choice.* New York: Longman.

Pringle, Rosemary. (1989). "Bureaucracy, Rationality and Sexuality: The Case of Secretaries." In *The Sexuality of Organization,* ed. Jeff Hearn, Deborah L. Sheppard, Peta Tancred-Sheriff, and Gibson Burell, 158–77. Newbury Park, CA: Sage.

Ptacek, James. (1988). "Why Do Men Batter Their Wives?" In *Feminist Perspectives on Wife Abuse,* ed. Kersti Yllö and Michele Bogard, 133–57. Newbury Park, CA: Sage.

Reskin, Barbara, and Patricia Roos. (1987). "Status Hierarchies and Sex Segregation." In *Ingredients for Women's Employment Policy,* ed. Christine Bose and Glenna Spitze, 3–21. Albany: State University of New York Press.

Romenesko, Kim, and Eleanor M. Miller. (1989). "The Second Step in Double Jeopardy: Appropriating the Labor of Female Street Hustlers." *Crime and Delinquency* 35 (1): 109–35.

Rosen, Ruth. (1982). *The Lost Sisterhood: Prostitution in America: 1900–1918.* Baltimore: Johns Hopkins University Press.

Russell, Diana E. H. (1982). *Rape in Marriage.* New York: Macmillan.

Schechter, Susan. (1982). *Women and Male Violence.* Boston: South End Press.

Schneider, Beth E. (1991). "Put Up and Shut Up: Workplace Sexual Assaults." *Gender and Society* 5 (4): 533–48.

Segal, Lynne. (1990a). *Slow Motion: Changing Masculinities, Changing Men.* New Brunswick, NJ: Rutgers University Press.

Smith, Michael D. (1990b). "Patriarchal Ideology and Wife Beating: A Test of a Feminist Hypothesis." *Violence and Victims* 5 (4): 257–73.

Smith, Michael D. (1990a). "Sociodemographic Risk Factors in Wife Abuse: Results from a Survey of Toronto Women." *Canadian Journal of Sociology* 15 (1): 39–58.

Sokoloff, Natalie J. (1980). *Between Money and Love.* New York: Praeger.

Stets, Jan E., and Murray A. Straus. (1989). "The Marriage License as a Hitting License: A Comparison of Assaults in Dating, Cohabitating and Married Couples." In *Violence in Dating Relationships,* ed. Maureen A. Pirog-Good and Jan E. Stets, 38–52. New York: Praeger.

Straus, Murray A., and Richard J. Gelles. (1990). "How Violent Are American Families? Estimates from the National Family Violence Survey and Other Studies." In *Physical Violence in American Families,* ed. Murray A. Straus and Richard J. Gelles, 95–112. New Brunswick, NJ: Transaction.

Straus, Murray A., Richard J. Gelles, and Susan Steinmetz. (1980). *Behind Closed Doors.* New York: Doubleday.

Tolson, Andrew. (1977). *The Limits of Masculinity.* New York: Harper and Row.

Walby, Sylvia. (1986). *Patriarchy at Work: Patriarchal and Capitalist Relations in Employment.* Minneapolis: University of Minnesota Press.

Walker, Lenore E. (1979). *The Battered Woman.* New York: Harper and Row.

Walker, Lenore E. (1977–78). "Battered Women and Learned Helplessness." *Victimology* 2 (4): 525–34.

West, Candace, and Don H. Zimmerman. (1987). "Doing Gender." *Gender and Society* 1 (2): 125–51.

Willis, Paul E. (1979). "Shop Floor Culture, Masculinity and the Wage Form." In *Working Class Culture,* ed. John Clarke, Chas Critcher, and Richard Johnson, 185–98. London: Hutchinson.

Yen Le Espiritu

All Men Are *Not* Created Equal: Asian Men in U.S. History

Today, virtually every major metropolitan market across the United States has at least one Asian American female newscaster. In contrast, there is a nearly total absence of Asian American men in anchor positions (Hamamoto, 1994, p. 245; Fong-Torres, 1995). This gender imbalance in television news broadcasting exemplifies the racialization of Asian American manhood: Historically, they have been depicted as either asexual or hypersexual; today, they are constructed to be less successful, assimilated, attractive, and desirable than their female counterparts (Espiritu, 1996, pp. 95–98). The exclusion of Asian men from Eurocentric notions of the masculine reminds us that not all men benefit—or benefit equally—from a patriarchal system designed to maintain the unequal relationship that exists between men and women. The feminist mandate for gender solidarity tends to ignore power differentials among men, among women, and between white women and men of color. This exclusive focus on gender bars traditional feminists from recognizing the oppression of men of color: the fact that there are men, and not only women, who have been "feminized" and the fact that some white middle-class women hold cultural power and class power over certain men of color (Cheung, 1990, pp. 245–246; Wiegman, 1991, p. 311). Presenting race and gender as relationally constructed, King-Kok Cheung (1990) exhorted white scholars to acknowledge that, like female voices, "the voices of many men of color have been historically silenced or dismissed" (p. 246). Along the same line, black feminists have referred to "racial patriarchy"—a

Reprinted by permission of the author.

concept that calls attention to the white/patriarch master in U.S. history and his dominance over the black male as well as the black female (Gaines, 1990, p. 202).

Throughout their history in the United States, Asian American men, as immigrants and citizens of color, have faced a variety of economic, political, and ideological racism that have assaulted their manhood. During the pre–World War II period, racialized and gendered immigration policies and labor conditions emasculated Asian men, forcing them into womanless communities and into "feminized" jobs that had gone unfilled due to the absence of women. During World War II, the internment of Japanese Americans stripped *Issei* (first generation) men of their role as the family breadwinner, transferred some of their power and status to the U.S.-born children, and decreased male dominance over women. In the contemporary period, the patriarchal authority of Asian immigrant men, particularly those of the working class, has also been challenged due to the social and economic losses that they suffered in their transition to life in the United States. As detailed below, these three historically specific cases establish that the material existences of Asian American men have historically contradicted the Eurocentric, middle-class constructions of manhood.

Asian Men in Domestic Service

Feminist scholars have argued accurately that domestic service involves a three-way relationship between privileged white men, privileged white women, and poor women of color (Romero,

1992). But women have not been the only domestic workers. During the pre–World War II period, racialized and gendered immigration policies and labor conditions forced Asian men into "feminized" jobs such as domestic service, laundry work, and food preparation.[1] Due to their non-citizen status, the closed labor market, and the shortage of women, Asian immigrant men, first Chinese and later Japanese, substituted to some extent for female labor in the American West. David Katzman (1978) noted the peculiarities of the domestic labor situation in the West in this period: "In 1880, California and Washington were the only states in which a majority of domestic servants were men" (p. 55).

At the turn of the twentieth century, lacking other job alternatives, many Chinese men entered into domestic service in private homes, hotels, and rooming houses (Daniels, 1988, p. 74). Whites rarely objected to Chinese in domestic service. In fact, through the 1900s, the Chinese houseboy was the symbol of upper-class status in San Francisco (Glenn, 1986, p. 106). As late as 1920, close to 50 percent of the Chinese in the United States were still occupied as domestic servants (Light, 1972, p. 7). Large numbers of Chinese also became laundrymen, not because laundering was a traditional male occupation in China, but because there were very few women of any ethnic origin—and thus few washerwomen—in gold-rush California (Chan, 1991, pp. 33–34). Chinese laundrymen thus provided commercial services that replaced women's unpaid labor in the home. White consumers were prepared to patronize a Chinese laundryman because as such he "occupied a status which was in accordance with the social definition of the place in the economic hierarchy suitable for a member of an 'inferior race'" (cited in Siu, 1987, p. 21). In her autobiographical fiction *China Men*, Maxine Hong Kingston presents her father and his partners as engaged in their laundry business for long periods each day—a business considered so low and debased that, in their songs, they associate it with the washing of menstrual blood (Goellnicht, 1992, p. 198). The existence of the Chinese houseboy and launderer—and their

forced "bachelor" status—further bolstered the stereotype of the feminized and asexual or homosexual Asian man. Their feminization, in turn, confirmed their assignment to the state's labor force which performed "women's work."

Japanese men followed Chinese men into domestic service. By the end of the first decade of the twentieth century, the U.S. Immigration Commission estimated that 12,000 to 15,000 Japanese in the western United States earned a living in domestic service (Chan, 1991, pp. 39–40). Many Japanese men considered housework beneath them because in Japan only lower-class women worked as domestic servants (Ichioka, 1988, p. 24). Studies of Issei occupational histories indicate that a domestic job was the first occupation for many of the new arrivals; but unlike Chinese domestic workers, most Issei eventually moved on to agricultural or city trades (Glenn, 1986, p. 108). Filipino and Korean boys and men likewise relied on domestic service for their livelihood (Chan, 1991, p. 40). In his autobiography *East Goes West*, Korean immigrant writer Younghill Kang (1937) related that he worked as a domestic servant for a white family who treated him "like a cat or a dog" (p. 66).

Filipinos, as stewards in the U.S. Navy, also performed domestic duties for white U.S. naval officers. During the ninety-four years of U.S. military presence in the Philippines, U.S. bases served as recruiting stations for the U.S. armed forces, particularly the navy. Soon after the United States acquired the Philippines from Spain in 1898, its navy began actively recruiting Filipinos—but only as stewards and mess attendants. Barred from admissions to other ratings, Filipino enlistees performed the work of domestics, preparing and serving the officers' meals, and caring for the officers' galley, wardroom, and living spaces. Ashore, their duties ranged from ordinary housework to food services at the U.S. Naval Academy hall. Unofficially, Filipino stewards also have been ordered to perform menial chores such as walking the officers' dogs and acting as personal servants for the officers' wives (Espiritu, 1995, p. 16).

As domestic servants, Asian men became subordinates of not only privileged white men but also privileged white women. The following testimony from a Japanese house servant captures this unequal relationship:

> Immediately the ma'am demanded me to scrub the floor. I took one hour to finish. Then I had to wash windows. That was very difficult job for me. Three windows for another hour! . . . The ma'am taught me how to cook. . . . I was sitting on the kitchen chair and thinking what a change of life it was. The ma'am came into the kitchen and was so furious! It was such a hard work for me to wash up all dishes, pans, glasses, etc., after dinner. When I went into the dining room to put all silvers on sideboard, I saw the reflection of myself on the looking glass. In a white coat and apron! I could not control my feelings. The tears so freely flowed out from my eyes, and I buried my face with my both arms (quoted in Ichioka, 1988, pp. 25–26).

The experiences of Asian male domestic service workers demonstrate that not all men benefit equally from patriarchy. Depending on their race and class, men experience gender differently. While male domination of women may tie all men together, men share unequally in the fruits of this domination. For Asian American male domestic workers, economic and social discriminations locked them into an unequal relationship with not only privileged white men but also privileged white women (Kim, 1990, p. 74).

The racist and classist devaluation of Asian men had gender implications. The available evidence indicates that immigrant men reasserted their lost patriarchal power in racist America by denigrating a weaker group: Asian women. In *China Men*, Kingston's immigrant father, having been forced into "feminine" subject positions, lapses into silence, breaking the silence only to utter curses against women (Goellnicht, 1992, pp. 200–201). Kingston (1980) traces her father's abuse of Chinese women back to his feeling of emasculation in America: "We knew that it was to feed us you had to endure demons and physical labor" (p. 13). On the other hand, some men

brought home the domestic skills they learned on the jobs. Anamaria Labao Cabato relates that her Filipino-born father, who spent twenty-eight years in the navy as a steward, is "one of the best cooks around" (Espiritu, 1995, p. 143). Leo Sicat, a retired U.S. Navy man, similarly reports that "we learned how to cook in the Navy, and we brought it home. The Filipino women are very fortunate because the husband does the cooking. In our household, I do the cooking, and my wife does the washing" (Espiritu, 1995, p. 108). Along the same line, in some instances, the domestic skills which men were forced to learn in their wives' absence were put to use when husbands and wives reunited in the United States. The history of Asian male domestic workers suggests that the denigration of women is only one response to the stripping of male privilege. The other is to institute a revised domestic division of labor and gender relations in the families.

Changing Gender Relations: The Wartime Internment of Japanese Americans

Immediately after the bombing of Pearl Harbor, the incarceration of Japanese Americans began. On the night of 7 December 1941, working on the principle of guilt by association, the Federal Bureau of Investigation (FBI) began taking into custody persons of Japanese ancestry who had connections to the Japanese government. On 19 February 1942, President Franklin Delano Roosevelt signed Executive Order 9066, arbitrarily suspending civil rights of U.S. citizens by authorizing the "evacuation" of 120,000 persons of Japanese ancestry into concentration camps, of whom approximately 50 percent were women and 60 percent were U.S.-born citizens (Matsumoto, 1989, p. 116).

The camp environment—with its lack of privacy, regimented routines, and new power hierarchy—inflicted serious and lasting wounds on Japanese American family life. In the crammed twenty-by-twenty-five-foot "apartment" units, tensions were high as men, women, and children struggled to recreate family life under very trying conditions. The internment also transformed the balance of power in families: husbands lost some of their power over wives, as did parents over children. Until the internment, the Issei man had been the undisputed authority over his wife and children: he was both the breadwinner and the decision maker for the entire family. Now "he had no rights, no home, no control over his own life" (Houston and Houston, 1973, p. 62). Most important, the internment reverted the economic roles—and thus the status and authority—of family members. With their means of livelihood cut off indefinitely, Issei men lost their role as breadwinners. Despondent over the loss of almost everything they had worked so hard to acquire, many Issei men felt useless and frustrated, particularly as their wives and children became less dependent on them. Daisuke Kitagawa (1967) reports that in the Tule Lake relocation center, "the [Issei] men looked as if they had suddenly aged ten years. They lost the capacity to plan for their own futures, let alone those of their sons and daughters" (p. 91).

Issei men responded to this emasculation in various ways. By the end of three years' internment, formerly enterprising, energetic Issei men had become immobilized with feelings of despair, hopelessness, and insecurity. Charles Kikuchi remembers his father—who "used to be a perfect terror and dictator"—spending all day lying on his cot: "He probably realizes that he no longer controls the family group and rarely exerts himself so that there is little family conflict as far as he is concerned" (Modell, 1973, p. 62). But others, like Jeanne Wakatsuki Houston's father, reasserted their patriarchal power by abusing their wives and children. Stripped of his roles as the protector and provider for his family, Houston's father "kept pursuing oblivion through drink, he kept abusing Mama, and there seemed to be no way out of it for anyone. You couldn't even run" (Houston and Houston, 1973, p. 61). The experiences of the Issei men underscore the intersections of racism and sexism—the fact that men of color

live in a society that creates sex-based norms and expectations (i.e., man as breadwinner) which racism operates simultaneously to deny (Crenshaw, 1989, p. 155).

Camp life also widened the distance and deepened the conflict between the Issei and their U.S.-born children. At the root of these tensions were growing cultural rifts between the generations as well as a decline in the power and authority of the Issei fathers. The cultural rifts reflected not only a general process of acculturation, but were accelerated by the degradation of everything Japanese and the simultaneous promotion of Americanization in the camps (Chan, 1991, p. 128; see also Okihiro, 1991, pp. 229–232). The younger *Nisei* also spent much more time away from their parents' supervision. As a consequence, Issei parents gradually lost their ability to discipline their children, whom they seldom saw during the day. Much to the chagrin of the conservative parents, young men and women began to spend more time with each other unchaperoned—at the sports events, the dances, and other school functions. Freed from some of the parental constraints, the Nisei women socialized more with their peers and also expected to choose their own husbands and to marry for "love"—a departure from the old customs of arranged marriage (Matsumoto, 1989, p. 117). Once this occurred, the prominent role that the father plays in marriage arrangements—and by extension in their children's lives—declined (Okihiro, 1991, p. 231).

Privileging U.S. citizenship and U.S. education, War Relocation Authority (WRA) policies regarding camp life further reverted the power hierarchy between the Japan-born Issei and their U.S.-born children. In the camps, only Nisei were eligible to vote and to hold office in the Community Council; Issei were excluded because of their alien status. Daisuke Kitagawa (1967) records the impact of this policy on parental authority: "In the eyes of young children, their parents were definitely inferior to their grown-up brothers and sisters, who as U.S. citizens could elect and be elected members of the Community

Council. For all these reasons many youngsters lost confidence in, and respect for, their parents" (p. 88). Similarly, the WRA salary scales were based on English-speaking ability and on citizenship status. As a result, the Nisei youths and young adults could earn relatively higher wages than their fathers. This shift in earning abilities eroded the economic basis for parental authority (Matsumoto, 1989, p. 116).

At war's end in August 1945, Japanese Americans had lost much of the economic ground that they had gained in more than a generation. The majority of Issei women and men no longer had their farms, businesses, and financial savings; those who still owned property found their homes dilapidated and vandalized and their personal belongings stolen or destroyed (Broom and Riemer, 1949). The internment also ended Japanese American concentration in agriculture and small businesses. In their absence, other groups had taken over these ethnic niches. This loss further eroded the economic basis of parental authority since Issei men no longer had businesses to hand down to their Nisei sons (Broom and Riemer, 1949, p. 31). Historian Roger Daniels (1988) declared that by the end of World War II, "the generational struggle was over: the day of the Issei had passed" (286). Issei men, now in their sixties, no longer had the vigor to start over from scratch. Forced to find employment quickly after the war, many Issei couples who had owned small businesses before the war returned to the forms of manual labor in which they began a generation ago. Most men found work as janitors, gardeners, kitchen helpers, and handymen; their wives toiled as domestic servants, garment workers, and cannery workers (Yanagisako, 1987, p. 92).

Contemporary Asian America: The Disadvantaged

Relative to earlier historical periods, the economic pattern of contemporary Asian America is considerably more varied, a result of both the postwar restructured economy and the 1965 Immigration Act.[2] The dual goals of the 1965 Immigration Act—to facilitate family reunification and to admit educated workers needed by the U.S. economy—have produced two distinct chains of emigration from Asia: one comprising the relatives of working-class Asians who had immigrated to the United States prior to 1965; the other of highly trained immigrants who entered during the late 1960s and early 1970s (Liu, Ong, and Rosenstein, 1991). Given their dissimilar backgrounds, Asian Americans "can be found throughout the income spectrum of this nation" (Ong, 1994, p. 4). In other words, today's Asian American men both join whites in the well-paid, educated, white collar sector of the workforce *and* join Latino immigrants in lower-paying secondary sector jobs (Ong and Hee, 1994). This economic diversity contradicts the model minority stereotype—the common belief that most Asian American men are college educated and in high-paying professional or technical jobs.

The contemporary Asian American community includes a sizable population with limited education, skills, and English-speaking ability. In 1990, 18 percent of Asian men and 26 percent of Asian women in the United States, age 25 and over, had less than a high school degree. Also, of the 4.1 million Asians 5 years and over, 56 percent did not speak English "very well" and 35 percent were linguistically isolated (U.S. Bureau of the Census, 1993, Table 2). The median income for those with limited English was $20,000 for males and $15,600 for females; for those with less than a high school degree, the figures were $18,000 and $15,000, respectively. Asian American men and women with both limited English-speaking ability and low levels of education fared the worst. For a large portion of this disadvantaged population, even working full-time, full-year brought in less than $10,000 in earnings (Ong and Hee, 1994, p. 45).

The disadvantaged population is largely a product of immigration: Nine tenths are immigrants (Ong and Hee, 1994). The majority enter as relatives of the pre-1956 working-class Asian immigrants. Because immigrants tend to have socioeconomic backgrounds similar to those of their sponsors, most family reunification immigrants represent a continuation of the unskilled and semiskilled Asian labor that emigrated before 1956 (Liu, Ong, and Rosenstein, 1991). Southeast Asian refugees, particularly the second-wave refugees who arrived after 1978, represent another largely disadvantaged group. This is partly so because refugees are less likely to have acquired readily transferable skills and are more likely to have made investments (in training and education) specific to the country of origin (Chiswick, 1979; Montero, 1980). For example, there are significant numbers of Southeast Asian military men with skills for which there is no longer a market in the United States. In 1990, the overall economic status of the Southeast Asian population was characterized by unstable, minimum-wage employment, welfare dependency, and participation in the informal economy (Gold and Kibria, 1993). These economic facts underscore the danger of lumping all Asian Americans together because many Asian men do not share in the relatively favorable socioeconomic outcomes attributed to the "average" Asian American.

Lacking the skills and education to catapult them into the primary sector of the economy, disadvantaged Asian American men and women work in the secondary labor market—the labor-intensive, low-capital service, and small manufacturing sectors. In this labor market, disadvantaged men generally have fewer employment options than women. This is due in part to the decline of male-occupied manufacturing jobs and the concurrent growth of female-intensive industries in the United States, particularly in service, microelectronics, and apparel manufacturing. The garment industry, microelectronics, and canning industries are top employers of immigrant women (Mazumdar, 1989, p. 19; Takaki, 1989, p. 427; Villones, 1989, p. 176; Hossfeld, 1994, pp. 71–72). In a study of Silicon Valley (California's famed high-tech industrial region), Karen Hossfeld (1994) reported that the employers interviewed preferred to hire immigrant women over immigrant men for entry-level, operative jobs (p. 74).

The employers' "gender logic" was informed by the patriarchal and racist beliefs that women can afford to work for less, do not mind dead-end jobs, and are more suited physiologically to certain kinds of detailed and routine work. As Linda Lim (1983) observes, it is the "*comparative disadvantage* of women in the wage-labor market that gives them a comparative advantage vis-à-vis men in the occupations and industries where they are concentrated—so-called female ghettoes of employment" (p. 78). A white male production manager and hiring supervisor in a California Silicon Valley assembly shop discusses his formula for hiring:

> Just three things I look for in hiring [entry-level, high-tech manufacturing operatives]: small, foreign, and female. You find those three things and you're pretty much automatically guaranteed the right kind of work force. These little foreign gals are grateful to be hired—very, very grateful—no matter what (Hossfeld, 1994, p. 65).

Refugee women have also been found to be more in demand than men in secretarial, clerical, and interpreter jobs in social service work. In a study of Cambodian refugees in Stockton, California, Shiori Ui (1991) found that social service agency executives preferred to hire Cambodian women over men when both had the same qualifications. One executive explained his preference, "It seems that some ethnic populations relate better to women than men. . . . Another thing is that the pay is so bad" (cited in Ui, 1991, p. 169). As a result, in the Cambodian communities in Stockton, it is often women—and not men—who have greater economic opportunities and who are the primary breadwinners in their families (Ui, 1991, p. 171).

Due to the significant decline in the economic contributions of Asian immigrant men, women's earnings comprise an equal or greater share of the family income. Because the wage each earns is low, only by pooling incomes can a husband and wife earn enough to support a family (Glenn, 1983, p. 42). These shifts in resources have challenged the patriarchal authority of Asian men. Men's loss of status and power—not only in the public but also in the domestic arena—places severe pressure on their sense of well-being. Responding to this pressure, some men accepted the new division of labor in the family (Ui, 1991, pp. 170–173); but many others resorted to spousal abuse and divorce (Luu, 1989, p. 68). A Korean immigrant man describes his frustrations over changing gender roles and expectations:

> In Korea [my wife] used to have breakfast ready for me. . . . She didn't do it any more because she said she was too busy getting ready to go to work. If I complained she talked back at me, telling me to fix my own breakfast. . . . I was very frustrated about her, started fighting and hit her (Yim, 1978, quoted in Mazumdar, 1989, p. 18).

Loss of status and power has similarly led to depression and anxieties in Hmong males. In particular, the women's ability—and the men's inability—to earn money for households "has undermined severely male omnipotence" (Irby and Pon, 1988, p. 112). Male unhappiness and helplessness can be detected in the following joke told at a family picnic, "When we get on the plane to go back to Laos, the first thing we will do is beat up the women!" The joke—which generated laughter by both men and women—drew upon a combination of "the men's unemployability, the sudden economic value placed on women's work, and men's fear of losing power in their families" (Donnelly, 1994, pp. 74–75). As such, it highlights the interconnections of race, class, and gender—the fact that in a racist and classist society, working-class men of color have limited access to economic opportunities and thus limited claim to patriarchal authority.

Conclusion

A central task in feminist scholarship is to expose and dismantle the stereotypes that traditionally have provided ideological justifications for women's subordination. But to conceptualize oppression only in terms of male dominance and female subordination is to obscure the centrality of classism, racism, and other forms of inequality in U.S. society (Stacey and Thorne, 1985, p. 311). The multiplicities of Asian men's lives indicate that ideologies of manhood and womanhood have as much to do with class and race as they have to do with sex. The intersections of race, gender, and class mean that there are also hierarchies among women and among men and that some women hold power over certain groups of men. The task for feminist scholars, then, is to develop paradigms that articulate the complicity among these categories of oppression, that strengthen the alliance between gender and ethnic studies, and that reach out not only to women, but also to men, of color.

Notes

1. One of the most noticeable characteristics of pre–World War II Asian America was a pronounced shortage of women. During this period, U.S. immigration policies barred the entry of most Asian women. America's capitalist economy also wanted Asian male workers but not their families. In most instances, families were seen as a threat to the efficiency and exploitability of the workforce and were actively prohibited.

2. The 1965 Immigration Act ended Asian exclusion and equalized immigration rights for all nationalities. No longer constrained by exclusion laws, Asian immigrants began arriving in much larger numbers than ever before. In the 1980s, Asia was the largest source of U.S. legal immigrants, accounting for 40 percent to 47 percent of the total influx (Min, 1995, p. 12).

References

Broom, Leonard and Ruth Riemer. 1949. *Removal and Return: The Socio-Economic Effects of the War on Japanese Americans*. Berkeley: University of California Press.

Chan, Sucheng. 1991. *Asian Americans: An Interpretive History*. Boston: Twayne.

Cheung, King-Kok. 1990. "The Woman Warrior Versus the Chinaman Pacific: Must a Chinese American Critic Choose Between Feminism and Heroism?" In *Conflicts in Feminism*, edited by

Marianne Hirsch and Evelyn Fox Keller (pp. 234–251). New York and London: Routledge.

Chiswick, Barry. 1979. "The Economic Progress of Immigrants: Some Apparently Universal Patterns." In *Contemporary Economic Problems* edited by W. Fellner (pp. 357–399). Washington, DC: American Enterprise Institute.

Crenshaw, Kimberlee. 1989. "Demarginalizing the Intersection of Race and Sex: A Black Feminist Critique of Antidiscrimination Doctrine, Feminist Theory and Antiracist Politics." In *University of Chicago Legal Forum: Feminism in the Law: Theory, Practice, and Criticism* (pp. 139–167). Chicago: University of Chicago Press.

Daniels, Roger. 1988. *Asian America: Chinese and Japanese in the United States Since 1850*. Seattle: University of Washington Press.

Donnelly, Nancy D. 1994. *Changing Lives of Refugee Hmong Women*. Seattle: University of Washington Press.

Espiritu, Yen Le. 1995. *Filipino American Lives*. Philadelphia: Temple University Press.

Espiritu, Yen Le. 1996. *Asian American Women and Men: Labor, Laws, and Love*. Thousand Oaks, CA: Sage.

Fong-Torres, Ben. 1995. "Why Are There No Male Asian Anchormen on TV?" In *Men's Lives*, 3rd ed., edited by Michael S. Kimmel and Michael A. Messner (pp. 208–211). Boston: Allyn and Bacon.

Gaines, Jane. 1990. "White Privilege and Looking Relations: Race and Gender in Feminist Film Theory." In *Issues in Feminist Film Criticism*, edited by Patricia Erens (pp. 197–214). Bloomington: Indiana University Press.

Glenn, Evelyn Nakano. 1983. "Split Household, Small Producer and Dual Wage Earner: An Analysis of Chinese-American Family Strategies." *Journal of Marriage and the Family*, February: 35–46.

Glenn, Evelyn Nakano. 1986. *Issei, Nisei, War Bride: Three Generations of Japanese American Women at Domestic Service*. Philadelphia: Temple University Press.

Goellnicht, Donald C. 1992. "Tang Ao in America: Male Subject Positions in *China Men*." In *Reading the Literatures of Asian America*, edited by Shirley Geok-lin-Lim and Amy Ling (pp. 191–212). Philadelphia: Temple University Press.

Gold, Steve and Nazli Kibria. 1993. "Vietnamese Refugees and Blocked Mobility." *Asian and Pacific Migration Review* 2:27–56.

Hamamoto, Darrell. 1994. *Monitored Peril: Asian Americans and the Politics of Representation*. Minneapolis: University of Minnesota Press.

Hossfeld, Karen J. 1994. "Hiring Immigrant Women: Silicon Valley's 'Simple Formula.' " In *Women of Color in U.S. Society*, edited by Maxine Baca Zinn and Bonnie Thornton Dill (pp. 65–93). Philadelphia: Temple University Press.

Houston, Jeanne Wakatsuki and James D. Houston. 1973. *Farewell to Manzanar*. San Francisco: Houghton Mifflin.

Ichioka, Yuji. 1988. *The Issei: The World of the First Generation Japanese Immigrants, 1885–1924*. New York: The Free Press.

Irby, Charles and Ernest M. Pon. 1988. "Confronting New Mountains: Mental Health Problems Among Male Hmong and Mien Refugees. *Amerasia Journal* 14: 109–118.

Kang, Younghill. 1937. *East Goes West*. New York: C. Scribner's Sons.

Katzman, David. 1978. "Domestic Service: Women's Work." In *Women Working: Theories and Facts in Perspective*, edited by Ann Stromberg and Shirley Harkess (pp. 377–391). Palo Alto: Mayfield.

Kim, Elaine. 1990. " 'Such Opposite Creatures': Men and Women in Asian American Literature." *Michigan Quarterly Review*, 68–93.

Kingston, Maxine Hong. 1980. *China Men*. New York: Knopf.

Kitagawa, Daisuke. 1967. *Issei and Nisei: The Internment Years*. New York: Seabury Press.

Kitano, Harry H. L. 1991. "The Effects of the Evacuation on the Japanese Americans." In *Japanese Americans: From Relocation to Redress*, edited by Roger Daniels, Sandra C. Taylor, and Harry Kitano (pp. 151–162). Seattle: University of Washington Press.

Light, Ivan. 1972. *Ethnic Enterprise in America: Business and Welfare Among Chinese, Japanese, and Blacks*. Berkeley and Los Angeles: University of California Press.

Lim, Linda Y. C. 1983. "Capitalism, Imperialism, and Patriarchy: The Dilemma of Third-World Women Workers in Multinational Factories." In *Women, Men, and the International Division of Labor*, edited by June Nash and Maria Patricia Fernandez-Kelly (pp. 70–91). Albany: State University of New York.

Liu, John, Paul Ong, and Carolyn Rosenstein. 1991. "Dual Chain Migration: Post-1965 Filipino Immigration to the United States." *International Migration Review* 25 (3): 487–513.

Luu, Van. 1989. "The Hardships of Escape for Vietnamese Women." In *Making Waves: An Anthology of Writings by and About Asian American Women*, edited by Asian Women United of California (pp. 60–72). Boston: Beacon Press.

Matsumoto, Valerie. 1989. "Nisei Women and Resettlement During World War II." In *Making Waves: An Anthology of Writings by and about Asian American Women*, edited by Asian Women United of California (pp. 115–126). Boston: Beacon Press.

Mazumdar, Sucheta. 1989. "General Introduction: A Woman-Centered Perspective on Asian American History." In *Making Waves: An Anthology by and about Asian American Women*, edited by Asian Women United of California (pp. 1–22). Boston: Beacon Press.

Min, Pyong Gap. 1995. "Korean Americans." In *Asian Americans: Contemporary Trends and Issues*, edited by Pyong Gap Min (pp. 199–231). Thousand Oaks, CA: Sage.

Modell, John, ed. 1973. *The Kikuchi Diary: Chronicle from an American Concentration Camp*. Urbana: University of Illinois Press.

Montero, Darrell. 1980. *Vietnamese Americans: Patterns of Settlement and Socioeconomic Adaptation in the United States*. Boulder, CO: Westview.

Okihiro, Gary Y. 1991. *Cane Fires: The Anti-Japanese Movement in Hawaii, 1865–1945*. Philadelphia: Temple University Press.

Ong, Paul. 1994. "Asian Pacific Americans and Public Policy." In *The State of Asian Pacific America: Economic Diversity, Issues, & Policies*, edited by Paul Ong (pp. 1–9). Los Angeles: LEAP Asian Pacific American Public Policy Institute and UCLA Asian American Studies Center.

Ong, Paul and Suzanne Hee. 1994. "Economic Diversity." In *The State of Asian Pacific America: Economic Diversity, Issues, & Policies*, edited by Paul

Ong (pp. 31–56). Los Angeles: LEAP Asian Pacific American Public Policy Institute and UCLA Asian American Studies Center.

Romero, Mary. 1992. *Maid in the U.S.A.* New York: Routledge.

Siu, Paul. 1987. *The Chinese Laundryman: A Study in Social Isolation*. New York: New York University Press.

Stacey, Judith and Barrie Thorne. 1985. "The Missing Feminist Revolution in Sociology." *Social Problems* 32: 301–316.

Takaki, Ronald. 1989. *Strangers from a Different Shore: A History of Asian Americans*. Boston: Little, Brown.

Ui, Shiori. 1991. " 'Unlikely Heroes': The Evolution of Female Leadership in a Cambodian Ethnic Enclave." In *Ethnography Unbound: Power and Resistance in the Modern Metropolis*, edited by Michael Burawoy et al. (pp. 161–177). Berkeley: University of California Press.

U.S. Bureau of the Census. 1993. *We the American Asians*. Washington, DC: U.S. Government Printing Office.

Villones, Rebecca. 1989. "Women in the Silicon Valley." In *Making Waves: An Anthology of Writings by and About Asian American Women*, edited by Asian Women United of California (pp. 172–176). Boston: Beacon Press.

Wiegman, Robyn. 1991. "Black Bodies/American Commodities: Gender, Race, and the Bourgeois Ideal in Contemporary Film." In *Unspeakable Images: Ethnicity and the American Cinema*, edited by Lester Friedman (pp. 308–328). Urbana and Chicago: University of Illinois Press.

Yanagisako, Sylvia Junko. 1987. "Mixed Metaphors: Native and Anthropological Models of Gender and Kinship Domains." In *Gender and Kinship: Essays Toward a Unified Analysis*, edited by Jane Fishburne Collier and Sylvia Junko Yanagisako (pp. 86–118). Palo Alto, CA: Stanford University Press.

José B. Torres

Masculinity and Gender Roles among Puerto Rican Men: Machismo on the U.S. Mainland

My father was a gentle man. His mestizo face lovingly carved by joys, sorrows, and warm sunny rays. His greenish, greyish eyes always squinting like lips with half smiles. I remember watching him sitting in the backyard, his mind, spirit, and body in quiet harmony. He was a man of sayings: "It all comes out in the mirror" and "Words are like oil." My favorite has become my definition for coalitions: "juntos pero no revuel-tos" (together but not scrambled).

When he talked to us, my brother, my mother, and me, he spoke about truth, in-tegrity, and love. He did sit at the head of the table, and demanded our deference. He loved and treated my mother as a partner, a lover, a mother, and a wife. You see, my father was a macho . . . and I loved him. Machismo in my cultural dictionary is hom-bria, *manhood. A macho is not the oiled, tan, muscular guy with a woman hanging from his left shoulder in a shaving cream commercial. He is not the woman hater or the wife beater. He is not the enemy in the battle of the sexes, or the tough man with a distorted view of his manhood. He is who he is and not who he is made to be. So machismo—it's okay with me.*

—Gladys Benavides
(Unpublished writing)

As a result of changing socioeconomic and labor market conditions in the United States, conflict has developed for Puerto Rican men in their marital relationships and in certain gender-role characteristics. Much of the conflict stems from their desire to retain traditional ideals of masculinity that may no longer be attainable. Today's urban environment is characterized by rapidly changing sociopolitical conditions, gender-role ambiguities, and contradictory cultural expectations and values. A central source of conflict can be found in the cultural form of masculinity known as machismo that is observed among Puerto Ricans on the U.S. mainland. Machismo may be defined as the complex interaction of social, cultural, and behavioral components forming male gender-role identity in the sociopolitical context of the Latino society (De La Cancela, 1986; Deyoung & Zigler, 1994).

Traditionally, researchers have focused on such negative connotations of machismo as male dominance, aggression, patriarchy, authoritarianism, and oppressive behavior toward women and children. They have often failed, however, to recognize that machismo can have positive expression, such as emphasis on self-respect and on responsibility for protecting and providing for the family. They have also failed to consider the sociopolitical realities for Puerto Rican men, and the "ideal" of masculinity and gender roles held by Puerto Rican women. Studies of these factors

From *American Journal of Orthopsychiatry*, 68(1), January 1998, pp. 16–26.

might result in less emphasis on the sexual and aggressive aspects of machismo, and more on such traits as patience, sensitivity, artistic appreciation, and open verbal communication that exist within Puerto Rican culture.

Although machismo is popularly viewed as the major factor in Latino men's masculine identity, research on the topic, particularly with Puerto Rican men, is limited compared to research with socioeconomically advantaged white Americans of European ancestry (Levant & Pollack, 1995). Kimmel and Messner (1992) have argued that "the meaning of masculinity varies from culture to culture" (p. 9), and that, consequently, masculinity is reflected in many different forms. This oversight in the literature has left Puerto Rican men, and Latinos in general, burdened with stereotyped characteristics that have negative implications for their emotional, social, and physical well-being. Among these implications are anxiety, confusion, depression, hostility, isolation, loneliness, panic, tension, sexual dysfunction, and a sense of emasculation (De La Cancela, 1988).

Puerto Rican men are often told that their culture, attitudes, and behavior are irredeemably sexist (De La Cancela, 1986; Ramirez, 1993). In truth, this perspective is secondary to the fact that the dominant culture does not permit them to explore adaptive options. They are not, for example, given access to economic opportunities equal to those of the women in their culture; the result is a reversal of traditional gender roles in which Puerto Rican women become the primary source of income and achieve greater levels of economic self-sufficiency than the men. It is hardly surprising that, challenged at the very core of their traditional masculinity, many Puerto Rican men feel vulnerable and off balance, expressing dissatisfaction, discontent, and confusion, while struggling for emotional survival.

In this context, it is a matter of concern whether Puerto Rican men will be able to tolerate, accept, or survive the new active role of Puerto Rican women. To do so, they must relinquish some kinds of traditional behavior in order to explore the potential benefits of a more egalitarian relationship with their partners. A dilemma for the Puerto Rican community on the U.S. mainland is the tendency of educated Puerto Rican women to marry white Americans of European background (Anglos), possibly to bypass the threat presented to some Puerto Rican men by the women's changing roles (Comas-Díaz, 1989). Others are choosing to leave unhealthy or unsatisfying relationships with Puerto Rican men through separation or divorce; still others are remaining single female heads of households.

To help Puerto Rican men and their families deal effectively with this changing environment, a more thorough understanding of how machismo operates within traditional family systems is necessary. The intent of this article is to identify common conceptions and misconceptions about machismo, describe the adaptive role machismo has traditionally played within the Puerto Rican family system, and discuss ways of enhancing the ability of Puerto Rican men to adapt more effectively to shifts in gender and role identities among Puerto Rican women.

Machismo: Characteristics and Misconceptions

Historically, the male gender-socialization process and popular perspective on masculinity for Anglos in the United States has emphasized such traits as assertiveness; obsession with achievement and success; individualism; status; aggression, toughness, and winning; restricted emotionality and affectionate behavior; concerns about power, control, and competition; and homophobia (Levant, 1992; Levant & Pollack, 1995; O'Neil, 1982). The Puerto Rican male gender-socialization process and view of masculinity has historically emphasized bravery, strength, male dominance, honor, virility, aggression, and autonomy.

Although the mental health literature depicts machismo as one of the major forces in the ethos of Latino males (Gonzalez, 1982; Mirandé, 1988; Ramírez, 1993), it has defined it in inconsistent, contradictory, superficial, and negatively stereotypic ways that are as ambiguous and misunderstood as any other aspect of the Latino culture. Among the stereotyped characteristics are physical aggression, sexual promiscuity, insecurity, alcohol abuse, spousal violence (i.e., emotional and physical abuse of women and children), and other oppressions of women (Ramírez, 1993; Valdéz, Barón, & Ponce, 1987). Other such characterizations have focused on irresponsible behavior, immaturity, feelings of inferiority, latent homosexuality, narcissistic personality, ambivalence toward women, and sexual anxiety (Aramoni, 1972; Ramírez, 1993; Ruiz, 1981). While these traits might be important dimensions of the machismo construct, they reflect only a narrow perspective on gender-role identity of Puerto Rican men.

In contrast, De La Cancela (1991) and Mayo (1993) have suggested that machismo is characterized by other important and positive, though less culturally profiled, elements. These include: forcefulness of personality, strength of will, daring, self-assertiveness, and self-confidence, in conjunction with softer and more emotional aspects such as affection, caring, tenderness, love, respect for self and others, and protectiveness toward women, children, and less fortunate members of society; provision for and protection of the family, strength in adverse situations, uncompromising positions on matters of great personal importance, pride, respect, dignity, and honor. De La Cancela (1986) further included stoicism; varying levels of intimacy among men, leading to attachments in certain contexts and disengagement in others; attempts to avoid shame and gain *respeto* (respect) and *dignidad* (dignity) for self and family; the displacement of stress related to economic and social factors onto the interpersonal and familial sphere; and patterns of assertiveness and dominance like those caricatured in the literature.

Among Puerto Ricans, the concept of *respeto* governs all positive reciprocal interpersonal relations (Diaz-Royo, 1976); it particularly dictates appropriate deferential behavior toward others—

especially older people, parents, and relatives—on the basis of age, socioeconomic position, and authority. Often associated with *respeto, dignidad* refers to a strong belief in the worth and value of each individual as a human being, whatever his or her social standing. This aspect of machismo primarily refers to how Latino males carry out their functions within the family, the community, and the culture at large.

Regardless of the origin or construction of machismo and the variants of macho or *machista* (exaggerated manliness), Latino men's adherence to and tolerance of its negative attitudinal and behavioral characteristics not only make life difficult, emotionally and physically, for their female partners and families, but are also dangerous. Alcoholism, infidelity, domestic and other forms of violence, minimal involvement with child rearing, and abandonment of partners and families are only a few of the dysfunctional and destructive consequences for family life when machismo is exercised as an exaggerated masculinity.

In general, Latino men have been socialized to perceive themselves as dominant of women, with rights and privileges that can be asserted legitimately by force. Puerto Rican men are not given *respeto* and *dignidad* in the traditional way on the U.S. mainland, where male *machismo* and female *marianismo* are deprecated (Ghali, 1977).

Marianismo, based on the cult of the Virgin Mary, serves as the counterpoint to machismo; it stipulates that women are morally and spiritually superior to men and, therefore, better able to endure suffering (Stevens, 1973). Women are, however, expected to accept male authority (Ramos-McKay, Comas-Díaz, & Rivera, 1988; Stevens, 1973). Implicit in their socialization process is the expectation of self-sacrifice in favor of their children and husbands, repression or sublimation of sexual drives and consideration of sex as an obligation to their husband, chastity until marriage, and conformity to husbands' *macho* (male) behavior (Comas-Díaz, 1988). Gil and Vazquez (1996) stressed that, like *machismo, marianismo* has a positive and lighter side, including loyalty, compassion, and generosity, and that accessing and harnessing these qualities can fuel women's empowerment and provide healthy support to those around them (p. 6).

Adjustment to changing gender roles in the Puerto Rican family demands sensitivity to changing *marianismo* and *machismo* constructs, and to the people most affected by different levels of acculturation. Adaptive acculturation may be expected to influence the emergence of *la nueva marianisma* (the new Latina), manifested as a competent, assertive, self-assured, and empowered Latina (Gil & Vazquez, 1996, p. 15).

In their effort to integrate the demands of their Latino heritage into the accepted male gender role on the mainland, Puerto Rican men may persist in maintaining a sense of autonomy and independence and a show of manliness. How these are expressed is influenced by such factors as level of education, generational shifts, acculturation patterns, ethnic identity, responsibility to the extended family, and socioeconomic status. Redefinition and reconstruction of the Puerto Rican male gender-role identity demands attention both to the male role and to the interface of machismo with other individuals and systems within the mainland culture. It must also identify valid and constructive aspects of the traditional Puerto Rican male code and target obsolete and dysfunctional aspects for change (Levant & Pollack, 1995).

In view of the historically fragmented aspects of machismo, ongoing investigations would best be served by viewing Puerto Rican male gender role and machismo as a dynamic set of both positive and negative traits; by identifying the prevalence of and distinctions between positive and negative forms (Mirandé, 1988); and by recognizing that its behavioral manifestations occur on a continuum from negative to positive.

Male-to-Male Behavior

While macho behavior has often been discussed in terms of male-female relationships, machismo has rarely been considered in relationships among males. Early studies focusing on male relationships (Landy, 1959) noted that Puerto Rican males constantly try to form relationships *de confianza* (of confidence, trust, intimacy) with other males, while at the same time fearing the possibility of being exploited by them. As Landy (1959) stated:

> The more he seeks a close relationship with other males, the less the young man is apt to find it. When relationships are established, they are brittle and easily fragmented. Thus, the male's poignant desires find little permanent gratification, and repeated short-lived relationships lead to distrust of others. At the same time however, he longs for nothing so much as to be able to trust the relationship of other men. And so he looks continually for trust, or confianza relationships. But he looks within a lonely crowd in which confianza relationships are rare because while the demand is great, supply is short. (p. 246)

De La Cancela (1991) and Mayo (1993) have suggested that similar patterns of behavior still persist, although more flexible and adaptive roles are developing with the advent of greater education and acculturation.

In the past, relationships among Puerto Rican men, and between men and women, have been structurally and culturally defined according to specific values, such as *afecto* (affection), *personalismo* (the need to relate to people and not to institutions), *respeto, dignidad,* and *confianza.* Any man, whatever his situation in life, is thought to be worthy of *respeto.* In modern Puerto Rico, men still treat each other with more formality than one finds on the U.S. mainland. Any *falta de respeto* (lack of respect) toward a man violates his dignity and contributes to a stressful situation. Other behavioral patterns observed among Puerto Rican males are a) a tendency to be more open than men in general in expressing emotion, particularly extremes of joy and anger; and b) casual, routine, and unembarrassed expression of affection toward other males by handshaking, an embrace on meeting, and frequent touching during conversation (Padilla & Ruiz, 1973).

Given the paucity of serious analytic and qualifying data on machismo in the literature, the preceding observations must be viewed with caution and as an attempt to open up the multidimensional aspects of the construct. Whether machismo is perceived as a negative behavioral pattern or as a cultural norm with both negative and positive attributes, it must be understood, when used for descriptive purposes, as reflecting a complex interaction of cultural, sociopolitical, economic, psychological, and behavioral components of personality (De La Cancela, 1986).

Machismo in a Changing Environment

With the exception of Mexican Americans, Puerto Ricans are the largest Latino group on the U.S. mainland. Although they share with other Latino groups a language and cultural traits and values reflecting their Spanish heritage (e.g., religion, *familism*), there are demographic, historical, political, and socioeconomic indicators that distinguish Puerto Ricans and contribute significantly to their oppressed socioeconomic condition (De La Cancela, 1986).

Consistent with previous demographic and socioeconomic data profiles, recent census reports on Puerto Ricans reflect both positive and negative socioeconomic indicators of well-being. During the past decade, they have achieved some socioeconomic progress (e.g., increased average household income). However, they continue to lag far behind other Latino groups on several socioeconomic dimensions, and behind the majority population on virtually all of them. According to the U.S. Bureau of the Census (1994), while the employed portion of the Latino male labor force ranged from 63% to 83% as of March 1994, that of Puerto Rican men was 66%. Like other Latino males, Puerto Rican men were more likely to be employed as operators, fabricators, and nonskilled laborers, and in service occupations. During the period 1982–1994, Latino unemployment rates were consistently higher than those of non-Latinos. While the March 1994 unemployment rate among all Latinos was nearly twice that of non-Latino whites (11.1% and 5.7%, respectively), the rate among Latinos ranged from 6.8% for Cubans to 14.2% for Puerto Ricans. Of the Latino male unemployment figures, Puerto Rican men represented the highest rate at 15.9% (Institute for Puerto Rican Policy, 1995).

The mainland's societal criteria for "manhood" intensify for Puerto Rican men the psychological stress and role strains stemming from immigration, acculturation, racism, and poverty. The inability to find employment and be good providers for their families adds to this stress, causing many of these men to experience guilt, feelings of inadequacy, and a form of psychological emasculation stemming from fear of not being able to live up to the male role (Doyle, 1983).

The symptomatic behavioral reactions of many Puerto Rican men to such personal crises tend to be aggressive rather than depressive, and aimed at protecting personal vulnerability. Drinking, gambling, fighting, and promiscuity are common reported manifestations of attempts to maintain *hombria* (manhood). Baca-Zinn (1982) observed:

> Perhaps manhood takes on greater importance for those who do not have access to socially valued roles. Being male is one sure way to acquire status when other roles are systematically denied by the workings of society. (p. 39)

Such reactions can also be seen as attempts to salvage their pride in terms of *dignidad* and *respeto.* They have also been found to create panic, confusion, marital discord, and breakdown of family ties (De La Cancela, 1991). A different self-concept and better self-esteem may be experienced by Puerto Rican men who have better access to resources and the ability to regulate their behavior in conformity with the prescribed male and female norms of the majority culture (Bem, 1985).

Clinical Recommendations

The preceding discussion on gender roles and the construct of machismo among mainland Puerto

Rican men holds several implications for the development and delivery of mental health services to this population.

Ethnic or Cultural Biases

It is necessary that practitioners working with Puerto Rican men commit themselves to a process of self-exploration designed to overcome personal biases, prejudices, and racism, and to develop their own integrative ethnic identity. This self-exploration should disclose any preconceptions they may have regarding Puerto Rican men, their communication and relationship patterns with both sexes, and their particular cultural values and norms. Practitioners must also become aware of the impact of culture, history, socioeconomic and political conditions, religion, and racism on these men and their families. They must then reach an understanding of their own level of comfort with personal flexibility and appropriate self-disclosure when this is therapeutically necessary.

Mental health practitioners must exercise caution in using traditional Anglo models of psychological counseling (e.g., psychodynamic theory) with Puerto Rican clients, who are likely to resist such treatment approaches, since they reflect several assumptions that are inconsistent with Puerto Rican values, particularly among those who are bicultural or of low acculturation levels. Among these is the view that it is appropriate and beneficial to discuss personally sensitive issues, and the belief that achieving an intellectual understanding of a problem is likely to reveal a course of action that can rectify it. Puerto Rican men, in particular, are usually reluctant to participate in an activity that involves revelation of personal information, sharing of deep feelings, and submission to a situation in which they perceive themselves as helpless and weak.

Cultural Importance of Family

For non-Puerto Rican practitioners, knowledge of the role played by Puerto Rican men in the family is of utmost importance. Appreciation of male and female gender roles and the impact of machismo and marianismo at all levels of Puerto Rican family life requires familiarity with specific cultural values, including *dignidad, respeto, personalismo,* and *familismo* or *familism.* Counseling with Puerto Rican men also requires constant and acute sensitivity to the difficulties encountered by them as they strive to achieve success within the dominant sociocultural context. In a society where success is often associated with economic wealth, reconciling cultural, masculine, and gender-role identities with economic and social obstacles is critical for Puerto Rican and other men of color (Lazur & Majors, 1995).

Much of the literature has reported the significance of *la familia* (the family) as a primary source of emotional and economic support among Latino families. This is particularly true in the Puerto Rican community, where the extended family system is its "heart and soul" (Canino & Canino, 1980). Bearing this in mind, practitioners should display understanding and appreciation of the cultural dictates, roles, structure, values, and complex relationships that comprise the interactive, mutually supportive, and strong family orientation in the Puerto Rican community. It is within this family and community that Puerto Rican men draw on their culture of machismo to define their male gender role in the face of the demands of the dominant culture.

Adapting the Concept of Machismo

To understand better the multidimensional and dynamic components of Puerto Rican men's individual identity and thus maximize their openness to counseling, practitioners must be prepared to expand their own clinical conceptualization of male gender role and machismo beyond an exclusive intrapsychic or sociocultural view (De La Cancela, 1991). This requires enough flexibility to reach out from an individualistic to a collective or systemic perception of intervention so as to permit an integration of individual treatment with family dynamics that is consistent with Puerto Rican culture.

Culturally sensitive assessment and treatment planning can be attained through an ecosystemic orientation that takes into account the elements of cultural, linguistic, educational, economic, gender, political, and environmental context. Diagnostic assessment must include not only presenting concerns and personal history, but an exploration of the individual's level of acculturation, period of migration, education, adherence to traditional cultural role expectations, and experiences with racism. Also important are the client's understanding of his own symptomatology, evaluation of motivation, capacity for change, and available opportunities in his community.

Overall, the therapeutic intervention must encourage empowerment of the individual through his acknowledgment of responsibility for his role of *respeto* within his family and community. The socioeconomic and political forces obstructing fulfillment of this role must also be considered. Confrontation of the client's resistance must itself be respectful, and attentive to his wounded self-esteem.

With practitioners' help, Puerto Rican men may learn not to respond to changes in Puerto Rican women by entrenching themselves in or attempting to regain their former male prerogatives. Instead, they may learn to redefine the concept of masculinity so as to encompass greater egalitarianism, achieving a better balance between individuality, gender, and culture, whatever their present level of machismo. Only through such a process can these men survive, flourish, and ultimately attain a healthy personal self apart from a world predicated on men's power over women (Rodriguez, 1996).

Change often involves loss, and the integration of loss requires mourning. Therefore, it is of the utmost importance that any therapeutic intervention with Puerto Rican men be designed to help them to bear, and gain perspective on, their sense of loss as they let go their traditional forms of masculinity and patriarchal privilege, a loss none the smaller for being politically unacceptable or personally dysfunctional (Pollack & Levant, 1995). The reconstruction of masculinity in more functional form could produce many benefits for Puerto Rican men, as well as women (Brooks & Silverstein, 1995). Clinical help in working through the mourning process and moving on to a richer, more empowered level of gender-role identity may be necessary, depending on the form or level of machismo involved, which in turn reflects stages of acculturation and development.

Contradictory Aspects of Machismo

Therapeutic work with Puerto Rican male clients requires attention to the contradictory aspects of machismo and to any tendency by the practitioner to minimize the client's personal responsibilities. According to De La Cancela (1991), this task is notable for the attention needed to:

> The danger of displacing employment-related conflicts onto his mate; the utilization of the family, sex and substance abuse as a refuge from the world; the distinction between protection of the family and paternalism; how social institutions like welfare and schools encourage displacing the Puerto Rican man; and the oppression of women. (p. 200).

Of course, not all Puerto Rican men adhere to the traditional negative perspectives of machismo. In fact, some Puerto Ricans, men and women, reject the negative construct of machismo outright.

Behavioral Manifestations of Machismo

The approach to clinical interventions with Puerto Rican men must, then, be both micro- and macrosystemic, taking into consideration the behavioral manifestations of male gender role and machismo as they fall on a continuum from negative to positive (Martinez, 1994), or the degree to which maladaptive behavior is rendered functional by modification to the cultural context. Ability to reframe culturally maladaptive behavior without diminishing either the client's self-esteem on the one hand, or the behavior's potential for destructive consequences on the other may further increase the possibility of engaging Puerto Rican men in counseling.

Practitioners will also find De La Cancela's (1991) dialectical perspective on machismo useful: he sees it as both progressive and reactionary, and as intimately related to the socioeconomic and historical forces maintaining the colonization of Puerto Ricans; he suggests that "the Puerto Rican male role is neither a Latino malady that must be eliminated nor a healthy cultural value that must be reinforced" (p. 198).

Use by clinicians of such key cultural dimensions as dignity, integrity, honor, and pride will also be conducive to establishing trust in the therapeutic relationship.

Practitioners who view macho behavior only in terms of physical aggression, sexual promiscuity, dominance over women, and excessive use of alcohol, and who pathologize these kinds of behavior without understanding their other cultural aspects, will significantly limit opportunities for engaging Puerto Rican men and their families in a counseling relationship. Development of culturally competent clinical skills should take into consideration the positive elements of machismo, the Puerto Rican male gender role, and other cultural values such as *respeto* and *dignidad.*

Psychological Empowerment

Emphasis on empowering Puerto Rican male clients—by increasing their sense of personal control over their lives, helping them feel good about themselves, and supporting their assumption of personal responsibility for change—should also further continuation of their engagement in counseling (Goldstein, 1995). Reframing the client's concerns about treatment, addressing his strong sense of obligation and responsibility for himself and his family, and appealing to his sense of honor may also be in keeping with his own gender-role expectations. Attention to the individual as a whole—psychological, social, and physical health—also implies openness by practitioners to collaborative work with medical and other health-care-related professionals (Casas, Wagenheim, Banchero, & Mendoza-Romero, 1994).

Facilitative Approaches

The positive qualities of the male gender role (e.g., respect, loyalty, fairness, responsibility, and family centrality) can be used as bridges instead of barriers in the process of therapeutic engagement. In addition to promoting and nurturing personal change, such a focus can help the client reach a level of empowerment from which he can more effectively advocate for himself and contribute to collective efforts for change in the community and larger society.

Other potentially facilitative approaches include psychoeducational groups; same-gender consciousness-raising groups; group-oriented work focused on discovering a different understanding of masculinity; and a combination of individual, marital, and family therapy approaches.

Practitioners must be vigilant about the contradictory and inconsistent behavioral patterns presented among Puerto Rican men. While some are readily making satisfactory adaptations to the dominant culture and socioeconomic situation, others remain oblivious and resistant to the need to reevaluate certain dysfunctional characteristics (e.g., aggression and emotional inhibition) that can provoke negative psychological or physical consequences for themselves and others. Instead of dwelling on these negative aspects, or on clients' limitations or deficits, practitioners should consider exploring their strengths, competence, resilience, and resourcefulness. Validation and strengthening of ethnic identity may need to be fostered as part of their quest for a healthy personal adjustment. Also, hope for good results from behavioral changes should be encouraged.

Overall, competent practice requires cultural awareness and sensitivity, as well as excellent diagnostic and treatment skills that can accurately distinguish culturally related conflicts and issues from problems of psychopathology and daily life. In general, treatment should be active, structured, time-limited, and goal-oriented; it may also require a degree of self-disclosure on the part of practitioners; regardless of which culturally sensitive intervention approach is used, the practitioner's authentic presentation of self will remain his or her most valuable therapeutic tool.

Systemic Change

Mental health practitioners must recognize and acknowledge that not all Puerto Rican men, and certainly not all females, subscribe to the machismo perspective, and may be actively seeking a profound revision of the man-woman relationship. They must, however, bear in mind that many individuals of both genders are more affected by machismo than they themselves realize, often through the social system at large. Change and transformation are necessary not only in individuals, but also in social, political, and legal institutions that affect work, marriage, and family life and are the architects of the dominant cultural society. Attitudes, values, and expected behavior within these structures must change if there is to be large-scale, collective, and systematic modification that will have an impact on culturally defined gender roles.

Role of Puerto Rican Women

The liberation of Puerto Rican women could also have a liberalizing effect on the traditional confining attitudes and behavior of Puerto Rican men. Some men may resist the gender-role reversals associated with the pressures of economic survival, or other changes perceived as challenging their role as providers and protectors of the family. Others, however, may welcome the opportunity to reduce the stress of maintaining sole responsibility for their traditional family role as provider.

The changing position of Puerto Rican women has been reported as detrimental to some Puerto Rican men (Comas-Diaz, 1989; Torres-Matrullo, 1976), but it may also contribute to men's personal growth. By modifying the attitudes and behavior associated with machismo, women may help to liberate men from the oppressive and constricting aspects of their traditionally defined roles. This could lead to men's better self-integration and balance, and have beneficial effects on gender and family interactions (e.g.,

increased communication, cohesiveness, and stable relationships).

For these changes to occur, Puerto Rican women, like their sisters world-wide, must pursue efforts to establish cultural and social norms that allow a wider range of human expression and endeavor. As the sociocultural role of Puerto Rican women changes and thereby broadens their personal choices (i.e., greater independence without loss of interdependence, responsibility, and maturity), the role of Puerto Rican men need not be diminished but may be expanded, empowered, and enriched.

Social Services

To improve their economic status and thus let them fulfill their expected role as a family provider, Puerto Rican men need adequate opportunities for education and training. Assumption of a proper status as equal partner or titular family head would benefit personal relationships, families, and community.

Social and psychological services for Puerto Ricans on the U.S. mainland need to be tailored to meet their characteristics and needs. Policy makers and program developers share the responsibility to address Puerto Ricans more adequately as a unique ethnic group. Acknowledgment and respect for the cultural elements that distinguish Puerto Ricans from other ethnic populations may enable development of more comprehensive programs for improved social and mental health services for this population.

Implications for Research

Because of the lack of literature about the distinct cultural values and behavior of different Latino subgroups in the U.S., the ways in which men from these groups form their gender-role identity are misunderstood and unappreciated. This very lack of information, however, suggests some interesting avenues for further research. How do men from different ethnic groups in the U.S. view traditional norms of masculinity? Are there variations of machismo between Puerto Ricans and other Latino groups on the mainland? Are there significant differences in how machismo is perceived by mainland and island Puerto Ricans? Are there differences in how men and women view machismo across and within each of the Latino groups? What, specifically, are the functional versus dysfunctional attitudinal and behavioral manifestations of the construct of machismo in the Latino culture and within each individual Latino group?

Rigorous research to answer these questions could help diffuse some of the unrealistic stereotypes that exist for Latino men on the U.S. mainland, as well as differentiate variations of machismo among Latino subgroups. Investigations of Puerto Rican patterns of adaptation and acculturation to their new environments on the mainland should, by focusing on culture-specific behavior, reveal different levels of help-seeking and the different engagement skills needed by practitioners to be consistent with the culture. Such research would help practitioners increase their understanding of how male gender role and the construct of machismo operate within a Latino multicultural society and how they can more effectively provide mental health services to Puerto Rican men and their families.

Conclusion

The preceding discussion on masculinity and gender roles among Puerto Rican men is a response to the persistent negative stereotyping of Latino men by what is popularly referred to as machismo, and the paucity of available literature addressing the needs of this large Latino group in the United States. A contributing factor to the lack of understanding of Puerto Ricans, their distressing socioeconomic problems, and their lack of visibility has been the tendency to lump them together with other Latino groups.

The discussion has noted the prevalent use, misuse, and abuse of the highly volatile concept of machismo in its association with Latino men. Too often given a narrow interpretation by Anglos and some Latinos as self-aggrandizement

and exaggerated masculinity, machismo and male gender role have been presented here as distinct aspects of Puerto Rican men's lives. Specifically, machismo has been considered as a significant component of the broader Latino male gender role construct that needs to be understood in its historical, sociopolitical, and cultural context.

Although numerous behavioral traits associated with machismo have certainly been evidenced among the diverse Latino groups, the discussion has noted the critical need for further serious dialogue and in-depth study of machismo. Other, less prominent, elements of the broader male gender role norm have been presented that contrast with the machismo aspect.

Finally, this analysis should encourage clinical practitioners to facilitate Puerto Rican men's gender-role transitions by exploring their restricted traditional masculine identity and helping adapt it to healthier roles in their personal and social lives.

References

Aramoni, A. (1972). Machismo. *Psychology Today, 5,* 69–72.

Baca-Zinn, M. (1982). Chicano men and masculinity. *Journal of Ethnic Studies, 10,* 20–44.

Bem, S.L. (1985). Gender schema theory: a cognitive account of sex typing. *Psychological Review, 88,* 354–364.

Brooks, G.R. & Silverstein, L.B. (1995). In R.F. Levant & W.S. Pollack (Eds.), *A new psychology of men* (pp. 280–333). New York: Basic Books.

Canino, I., & Canino, G. (1980). Impact of stress on the Puerto Rican family: Treatment considerations. *American Journal of Orthopsychiatry, 50,* 535–541.

Casas, J.M., Wagenheim, B.R., Banchero, R., & Mendoza-Romero, J. (1994). Hispanic masculinity: Myth or psychological schema meriting clinical considerations. *Hispanic Journal of Behavioral Sciences, 16,* 315–331.

Comas-Diaz, L. (1989). Culturally relevant issues and treatment implications for Hispanics. In D.R. Koslow, & E. Salet (Eds.), *Crossing cultures in mental health* (pp. 31–48). Washington, D.C.: Society for International Educational Education Training and Research.

De La Cancela, V. (1986). A critical analysis of Puerto Rican machismo: Implications for clinical practice. *Psychotherapy, 23,* 291–296.

De La Cancela, V. (1988). Labor pains: Puerto Rican males in transition. *Centro de Estudios Puertorriqueños Bulletin, 2,* 40–55.

De La Cancela, V. (1991). Working affirmatively with Puerto Rican men: Professional and personal reflections. In M. Bograd (Ed.), *Feminist approaches for men in family therapy* (pp. 195–211). New York: Hawthorn Press.

Deyoung, Y., & Zigler, E.F. (1994). Machismo in two cultures: Relation to punitive child-rearing practices. *American Journal of Orthopsychiatry, 64,* 386–395.

Diaz-Royo, A. (1976). *Dignidad y respeto. Dos temas centrales en la cultura puertorriqueña tradicional* [Dignity and respect: Two central themes in the traditional Puerto Rican culture]. Unpublished manuscript, Department of Psychology, University of Puerto Rico, Rio Piedras, Puerto Rico.

Doyle, J.A. (1983). *The male experience.* Dubuque, IA: William C. Brown.

Ghali, S.B. (1977). Cultural sensitivity and the Puerto Rican Client. *Social Casework, 58,* 459–468.

Gil, R.M., & Vazquez, C.A. (1996). *The Maria paradox: How Latina women can merge old world traditions with new world self-esteem.* New York: Putnam.

Goldstein, E.G. (1995). *Ego psychology and social work practice* (2nd ed.). New York: Free Press.

Gonzalez, A. (1982). Sex roles of the traditional Mexican American family: A comparison of Chicano and Anglo students' attitudes. *Journal of Cross-Cultural Psychology, 13,* 330–339.

Institute for Puerto Rican Policy. (1995, August). *IPR datanote on the Puerto Rican community.* New York: Author.

Kimmel, M.S., & Messner, M.A. (Eds.). (1992). *Men's lives.* New York: Macmillian.

Landy, D. (1959). *Tropical childhood: Cultural transmission and learning in a rural Puerto Rican village.* Chapel Hill: University Press of North Carolina.

Lazur, R.F. & Majors, R. (1995). Men of color: Ethnocultural variations of male gender role strain. In R.F. Levant & W.S. Pollack (Eds.), *A new psychology on men.* New York: Basic Books.

Levant, R.F. (1992). Toward the reconstruction of masculinity. *Journal of Family Psychology, 5,* 379–402.

Levant, R.F., & Pollack, W.S. (1995). *A new psychology on men.* New York: Basic Books.

Martinez, K.J. (1994). Cultural sensitivity in family therapy gone awry. *Hispanic Journal of Behavioral Sciences, 16,* 75–89.

Mayo, Y. (1993). *The utilization of mental health services, acculturation, and machismo among Puerto Rican men.* Unpublished doctoral dissertation, School of Social Work, Adelphi University, Garden City, NY.

Mirandé, A. (1988). Qué gacho es ser macho: It's a drag to be a macho man. *Aztlan, 17,* 63–69.

O'Neil, J.M. (1982). Gender-role conflict and strain in men's lives. In K. Solomon & N. Levy (Eds.), *Men in transition: Theory and therapy* (pp. 5–44). New York: Plenum.

Padilla, A.M., & Ruiz, R.A. (1973). *Latino mental health. A review of literature.* Washington, DC: Government Printing Office.

Ramirez, R.L. (1993). *Dime capitán: Reflexiones sobre la masculinidad* [Tell me: Reflections on masculinity]. Rio Piedras, PR: Ediciones Huracán.

Ramos-MacKay, J.M., Comas-Diáz, L., & Rivera, L.A. (1988). Puerto Ricans. In L. Comas-Diáz & E.E.E. Griffith (Eds.), *Clinical guidelines in cross-cultural mental health* (pp. 204–232). New York: Wiley.

Rodriguez, L.J. (1996). On macho. In R. González (Ed.), *Muy macho: Latino men confront their manhood* (pp. 187–201). New York: Anchor Books.

Ruiz, R.A. (1981). Cultural and historical perspective in counseling Hispanics. In D.W. Sue (Ed.), *Counseling the culturally different: Theory and practice* (pp. 186–216). New York: Wiley.

Stevens, E. (1972). Machismo and marianismo. *Transaction-Society, 10,* 57–63.

Torres-Matrullo, C. (1976). Acculturation and psychopathology among Puerto Rican women in mainland United States. *American Journal of Orthopsychiatry, 46,* 710–719.

U.S. Bureau of the Census. (1994). *Hispanics-Latinos: Diverse people in a multicultural society. A Special Report. Population characteristics, Current Population Reports, 1995.* Washington, DC: National Association of Hispanic Publications.

Valdes, L., Baron, A., & Ponce, F. (1987). Counseling Hispanic men. In M. Scher, M. Stevens, G. Good, & Eichennfield (Eds.), *Handbook of counseling & psychotherapy with men* (pp. 203–217). Newbury Park, CA: Sage.

Shaun R. Harper

The Measure of a Man: Conceptualizations of Masculinity among High-Achieving African American Male College Students

Previous inquiry confirms that a healthy, conflict-free masculine identity leads to a strong self-concept and positive outcomes in a wide array of areas, including academics (Gilbert and Gilbert 1998; Price 2000). Despite this, little attention has been given to exploring identity development and conceptualizations of masculinity among male students on college and university campuses. Research regarding within-group variations among 18–24 year-old African American male collegians is virtually nonexistent, and the intersection between race and gender among this population remains particularly understudied. The proverbial saying, "Boys will be boys," has not been adequately disaggregated by race and ethnicity within various age groups in much of the mainstream literature on masculinity. Theoretical perspectives on masculine identity development in schools have been largely based on data collected from White male students, thus offering limited applicability to men of color. Consequently, structured efforts to assist African American male students in developing strong masculine identities that lead to academic, social, and long-term post-undergraduate success have not been implemented at most postsecondary educational institutions. Given that two-thirds of all African American men who start college never graduate (Mortenson 2001), it is essential to explore the nexus between identity development, definitions of self, and outcomes, including academic achievement and retention.

Reprinted by permission of the author.

African American college students have received considerable attention in the social-science literature over the past 30 years (Sedlacek 1987). However, few studies focus exclusively on African American men, and even fewer examine the needs and experiences of high-achieving African American male undergraduates (Bonner 2001; Fries-Britt 1997, 1998). As a result, current scholarship contains limited insight into the gender politics and peer interactions of African American male college students. To help address the paucity of research on this population, this article explores definitions of masculinity among African American male college students, and perceptions of those definitions by high-achievers within this group.

Literature Review

Previous research on masculinity and its role in identity development has almost exclusively been based on data collected from young boys, adolescents, and male adults who were not enrolled in college during the time at which the studies were conducted. Therefore, the majority of the literature reviewed in this section is not specific to traditional-aged college students.

Social Context and Masculine Identity Formation

Many foundational studies on masculinity suggest that identity development among boys is primarily characterized by autonomy, achievement concerns, competence, mastery, supremacy, and competitiveness (Gilligan 1993). This body of literature provides many of the generally accepted theories regarding masculine identity development, and consistently confirms that same-sex peers are largely influential in the development of masculine identities among young boys, which help shape long-lasting definitions of what it means to be a man (Blos 1962, 1979; Chodorow 1978; LaVoire 1976; Stoller 1964; Wainrib 1992). Connell (1993) suggests that men of all ages and ethnicities are often forced to negotiate their masculinities with other males—meaning that their manhood must be approved and validated by their peers. Morrison and Eardley's (1985) assertions fully capture and describe what most of the published literature reports about the impact of peers on identity development in young boys:

> Boys grow up to be wary of each other. We are taught to compete with one another at school, and to struggle to prove ourselves outside it, on the street, the playground and the sports field. Later we fight for status over sexual prowess, or money, or physical strength or technical know-how . . . the pressure is on to act tough. We fear humiliation or exclusion, or ultimately the violence of other boys if we fail to conform (19).

These claims are supported by Gilligan (1993) and Head (1999), who also suggest that men are more competitive, less apt to collaborate with one another, and far more rule- and authority-bound than women. Accordingly, male peer group interactions typically result in some sort of contest to see who can outpace, outrun, and overpower the others.

For boys at almost all levels of schooling, peer promotion of sports and athleticism play an influential role in the shaping of their masculine identities (Morrison & Eardley 1985). Quite often, interests beyond football and active outdoor play for young boys are seen as abnormal and unacceptable by peers (Harris 1995). Alternative expressions of manliness, such as doing well in school or participating in non-sports related school activities, must be approved by other male peer group members. Gilbert and Gilbert (1998: 63)

contend that rule-based sports both afford boys the opportunity to rehearse their masculinities and also factor into what it means to be deemed "cool" by peers: "Unfortunately, this image of the cool sociable sportsman is constantly set against the picture of the boy whose interests might be to read a book, a practice most often associated with girls." They posit that sports are chief among the masculine endeavors that conflict with a commitment to school achievement.

Through the adolescence and young adulthood periods, being good at sports becomes more important than simple participation. Usually, the "coolest guys" on campus are those who are standouts on the athletic field or court (Askew & Ross 1988; Gilbert & Gilbert 1998). By contrast, rarely, if ever, is the class president or smartest student in the class considered the most "manly" by his peers—unless of course he also participates in sports. Furthermore, those who can overpower opponents in athletic competition are also usually more sought after for romantic relationships by young women than male students who demonstrate leadership in other areas on campus and make good grades. Kunjufu (1988) asserts that African American boys must make a choice between school achievement and peer acceptance. The title of his book, *To Be Popular or Smart: The Black Peer Group,* captures the essence of this struggle. To this end, young men generally prefer to identify themselves as standout athletes instead of academic achievers or campus leaders.

This fascination with sports, accumulating points, beating out opponents, and demonstrating masculinity and superiority through competitive exercises has an enduring effect on the male identity, which extends into the college years. For example, the accumulation of points to surpass others in childhood games usually turns into a motivation to accumulate wealth, power, and monetary status during adulthood (Wainrib 1992). Likewise, most boys who strive for autonomy and superiority during the childhood years develop identities characterized by a desire to compete with and outperform others through the mastery of non-collaborative tasks. The peer influences discussed herein are largely shaped by perceivably rigid societal standards regarding male-appropriate behaviors (Askew & Ross 1988; Gilbert & Gilbert 1998; Harris 1995; Head 1999; Martino & Meyenn 2001).

Westwood (1990: 58) argues that society has provided "the insistence of 'the male role' against which all men must be measured." Society has historically suggested that boys should play sports, suppress outward displays of emotion, and compete rigorously against each other. Parents have also been influenced by these societal indices of masculinity, as many communicate messages of power, toughness, and competitiveness to their young sons. No father wants his son to grow up being a "pussy," "sissy," "punk," or "softy"—terms commonly associated with boys and men who fail to live up to the traditional standards of masculinity in America. Masculine identity is largely impacted by societal messages that say men should be the breadwinners for and protectors of their families; should be legends in college and professional sports; and should be leaders and executives in the organizations by which they are employed.

Expressions of Masculinity among African American Males

Harris (1995) argues that the traditional pathway to masculine identity development is limited in its applicability to African American men, and offers the following:

> Pressures to meet European American standards of manhood as provider, protector, and disciplinarian are representative of such a dilemma for African American men . . . Inequities in earning potential and employment and limited access to educational opportunities prevent the expression of these behaviors . . . To compensate for feelings of powerlessness, guilt, and shame that result from the inability to enact traditional masculine roles, some African American male youth have redefined masculinity to emphasize sexual promiscuity,

toughness, thrill seeking, and the use of violence in interpersonal interactions (279–280).

Harris suggests that traditionally White masculine ideals are often unattainable for African American men due to the material constraints of race, and that expectations for African American men to assume these seemingly unachievable masculine roles exacerbate identity conflicts. In turn, these perceptions and experiences force them to find alternative ways to prove their manliness. Instead of the mainstream definitions of masculinity—accumulation of wealth, status, and power—Oliver (1988, 1989) asserts that masculinity for African American men is often characterized by two primary orientations: "tough guy" and "player of women."

Tough guys are those who are good at fighting, are not afraid to defend themselves, and incite fear in others. Although most boys attempt to exude toughness and are generally "naughty by nature," displays of hyperactivity and roughness among African American males of all ages are perceived as dangerous and disproportionately lead to a harsher set of penalties in schools and society (Ferguson 2000). In a national study of more than 25 million public school students, Gregory (1997) found that African American males were more likely to be punished at school, suspended, or expelled than any other racial/ethnic group. In fact, they were 16 times more likely than their White female counterparts to experience disciplinary actions or school expulsion. Davis and Jordan (1994) found a nexus between school discipline, suspensions, grade retention, and academic failure. Despite these negative outcomes, African American males often set the standards for popularity, hip-hop culture, and athleticism at school (Davis 2003). Those who are perceived as tough, rough, and athletically talented enjoy peer admiration and respect, but usually garner negative reactions from teachers and school administrators.

The "player of women" concept is usually more prevalent in the teenage and young adulthood years, and is often linked to the "tough guy" orientation. Having multiple girlfriends and sexual partners typifies the "player." Those who are unsuccessful at these aims are generally made fun of, have their heterosexuality questioned, or are considered less masculine than their peers. Again, this characteristic also applies to men of different races and ethnicities, but it is extremely common among African Americans. Media and commercial images overwhelmingly depict, popularize, and celebrate certain types of African American men—namely pimps, rappers, and athletes, who are surrounded by attractive women (usually more than one at a time) and appear to be financially prosperous. In turn, young African American boys are socialized to believe that these behaviors are in fact indicative of Black masculinity and success. Those who are glorified usually share a certain communication and self-presentation style and approach to interacting with women. Majors and Billson (1992) introduced the term "cool pose," which is displayed by many African American men of all ages. Trendy and baggy clothing (usually urban wear), an overall relaxed look and informal presence, and a "pimp-style" strut are characteristic of this pose.

The African American male middle school students in Davis' (2001) study had developed a strict masculine code of conduct in their school that was characterized by various elements of the aforementioned "player of women" and "cool pose" concepts. He offers the following analysis:

> Boys who do not adhere to the prescribed rigid masculine orthodoxy are victimized . . . Black boys who dare to verbalize alternative views on masculinity and any aspect of the code in effect violate the masculine code. These actions conflict with the notions of what is appropriately male, and thus he is usually expelled from the confines and benefits of boy networks at the school (177–178).

These findings are consistent with Connell's (1993: 193) assertion that masculinity "must be seen as an active process of construction, occurring in a field of power relations that is often tense and contradictory, and often involving negotiation of alternative ways of being masculine." Connell calls for more inquiry that examines the masculine identities of African American men who assume roles other than the cool posing tough guys, players of women, and athletes.

As previously mentioned, insight into within-group masculine negotiations among African American men in college is scarce, as most research has been conducted either with young African American boys or with White male students. How do those who choose to excel in postsecondary education resolve the conflicts noted above? How do African American men on college and university campuses define masculinity? Do high-achieving African American male undergraduates ignore societal and peer messages regarding what is masculine, or are their identities in conflict? The paucity of research regarding masculine variability among this population makes the investigation of these questions especially interesting and important. The present study seeks to fill this void. Exploring and understanding the ways in which masculine identities are conceptualized and negotiated among African American male undergraduates could offer practical implications that lead to more positive academic and psychosocial outcomes.

Methodology

This article is based on a larger qualitative data set regarding the experiences of high-achieving African American undergraduate men. The phenomenological study sought to understand what it is like to be a high-achieving African American male college student at a large, predominantly White university, and included questions regarding the ways in which the participants deemed themselves different from other African American male undergraduates on their campuses. The phenomenology tradition in qualitative research focuses on understanding and describing the "lived experiences" of the participants involved in the study (Moustakas 1994). This type of qualitative study usually provides full, detailed descriptions of the phenomenon under study (Denzin & Lincoln 2000; Miles & Huberman 1994). The aim of the present study was to capture, in the students' words, what they had experienced and observed within their same-race male peer groups at their respective institutions.

Sites

This study was conducted at six large, public research universities in the Midwest—Indiana University, Michigan State University, Purdue University, The Ohio State University, the University of Illinois, and the University of Michigan. These six institutions are similar in terms of size, age, reputation, and selectivity; they are also in close geographic proximity to each other and are affiliated with the same athletic conference. On average, 6.3 percent of the students at the institutions were African American during the time at which the data were collected, with African American undergraduate enrollments ranging from 3.1 percent to 8.8 percent. Approximately 34 percent of the African American students at these universities were male.

Sample

Key administrators on the six campuses (i.e. deans, vice presidents, and directors of campus programs) were asked to identify African American male students who had made the most of their college experience. This was defined as earning cumulative grade point averages above 3.0; establishing lengthy records of leadership and involvement in multiple campus organizations; earning the admiration of their peers (as determined by peer elections to campus leadership positions); developing quality relationships with faculty and high-ranking campus administrators; participating in enriching educational experiences (e.g. study abroad programs, internships, and summer research programs); and earning numerous collegiate awards and honors. Using these criteria, 32 high-achieving African American undergraduate men were identified and selected for participation in this study.

The sample included four sophomores, 12 juniors, and 16 seniors, representing a wide variety of academic majors. The mean GPA for the sample was 3.32. All of the participants were between the ages of 18–22 years old and single with no dependents. Twelve participants grew up in single-parent homes and the remaining 20 were from homes with two parents. Collectively, they had been awarded more than $489,000 in merit-based scholarship awards. The participants expressed high educational and career aspirations, with 72 percent indicating the intent to someday earn a doctoral degree (including the J.D.). The remaining 28 percent planned to pursue master's degrees, usually in business. None of the high-achievers were student athletes. All but two identified themselves as heterosexual—one was openly gay and the other was privately bisexual.

Data Collection Procedures

Each of the 32 African American men was asked to participate in a 2–3 hour face-to-face interview, and at least two follow-up interviews via telephone. I visited each campus at least once to conduct the first-round individual interviews; four campuses were visited twice. A semi-structured interview technique was used in the face-to-face interview sessions, which enabled me to gather information without making the dialogue exchange inflexible and restrictive (Holstein & Gubrium 1995). Although specific questions and interview protocol were used in this study, the discussions often became conversational, thus allowing the participants to reflect upon the experiences, perceptions, and observations they deemed most important. Transcripts from all sessions were sent to each participant for confirmation within eight weeks following his interviews.

Data Analysis

Several techniques prescribed by Moustakas (1994) were used to analyze the data collected from interviews with the 32 participants. I first bracketed out my thoughts and assumptions as I read each line of the participants' transcripts. The margins of the transcripts were marked with reflective comments regarding my own presumptions and experiences. After bracketing, the transcripts were sorted and key phases were linearly arranged under tentative headings in NVivo®. This process resulted in the identification of 36 invariant constituents, which were sub-themes that did not vary more than 84.7 percent of the time (Moustakas, 1994). The invariant constituents were helpful for understanding the participants' experiences, and were later clustered into thematic categories. I identified seven thematic categories that captured the essence of the participants' shared experiences.

Findings

Participants on the six campuses consistently noted that their African American male peers used a limited number of variables to describe masculinity—dating and pursuing romantic (oftentimes sexual) relationships with women; any type of athletic activity (organized sports, individual exercise and bodybuilding, etc.); competition, namely through sports and video games; and the accumulation and showing off of material possessions. Some participants added fraternity membership to the list based on the observation that fraternity members seemed to attract and date more women. The participants were convinced that activities in which they were engaged—such as, holding multiple leadership positions; achieving top academic honors in the classroom; and maintaining a high-profile status on campus—would not have made it into the African American undergraduate male portfolio of masculinity. One University of Illinois student commented:

> Playing basketball in the rec. center, lifting weights, shooting hoops, partying, and showing off . . . they think those are masculine activities. I can be blunt, right? How many girls they can screw and who they've slept with. Those are the activities that most brothas' on this campus would use to define masculinity. You'll find them talking about these things in a boastful way all the time. I don't believe that holding a leadership position in student government has quite found its way onto the list of masculinity.

Participants from the other five campuses consistently reported similar ways of thinking among their fellow African American male peers.

Lenny, a senior at Purdue, was dumbfounded when asked if other African American male students would perceive leadership and out-of-class involvement as masculine. Instead of speculating, he posed the following question in return: "He's slept with 30 girls or he's the Vice President in an organization on campus . . . which would you think the majority of 18–21 year-old Black males would consider more masculine?" The participants believed their peers were seeking validation from other African American males, and had something to prove by attempting to date and have sex with as many women as possible. Reportedly, competition to see who could sleep with the most female students on campus was commonplace—extra points were awarded for interracial sexual encounters. Males who successfully conquered the most women were considered "the big men on campus."

Because of their active pursuit of dating opportunities and attention from the opposite sex, many of their male peers spent a significant amount of time in the gym working out and enhancing their physiques. Michael, a student at Michigan State, believed women somehow occupied most African American male students' time on campus. "Women probably take a good 80 percent of that time because when they aren't actually spending time with women, they're working out to look good for the ladies." One Indiana University student noted that one of his closest male friends spent more time lifting weights and playing basketball in the campus fitness center than the combined hours he spent attending class and doing homework. "Sure, his body is on point, but his grades and resume are not," the participant added.

Second to women, competition influenced many of their peers' perceptions of masculinity. Specifically, defeating opponents at video games and on the basketball court were two key ways in which "real men" could flaunt their manhood.

Marshawn, another Indiana University student, observed that competition among African American males, while quite prevalent on campus, was not "cutthroat." That is, his peers derived tremendous satisfaction from outpacing each other in intramural and recreational sports and outscoring each other on video games. Thus, they did not seek to bring about harm, injury, or widespread insult to other African American males. Instead, Marshawn noticed that competition on his campus had more to do with building masculine reputations and earning respect. An Ohio State student remembered an excerpt from a speech given by a visiting lecturer who was directly addressing the African American males in the audience:

> He was like, when you're on the basketball court and you're about to take someone to the hole, you're talking trash and grabbing your [genitals] like, 'bring it on'! Now, why is it when brothas' are in the classroom, they act like 'little punks?' You can be hard out there, but then you get in here and you're a 'little punk'!

The participants also thought other African American male students on their campuses defined masculinity and achievement through the accumulation and exhibition of material possessions. Anyone who appeared to have a pocket full of money earned the respect of other African American males on campus. Nice cars with flashy rims were at the top of the list. One student shared the following story:

> I've sat down with different brothas' and asked them why they were here. This one African American guy told me something that really shocked me. He said he was here in college so he could get a good enough job to buy a Ford Excursion [sports utility vehicle]. This really shocked me. His idea of achievement was to have this truck with some rims on it. That was his sole reason for attending college.

In addition to cars, the participants' African American male peers also relied on expensive clothing and shoes to show they were excelling and doing

well, the participants claimed. Those who sported the "flyest gear" were often dubbed coolest among the African American students on campus. The participants considered their peers to be quite materialistic and disproportionately focused on showing off to impress women and other male students.

By contrast, the participants in this study offered different definitions of masculinity. Though they too enjoyed playing recreational sports and pursuing romantic relationships (time permitting), the high-achievers did not consider those activities paradigmatic examples of masculinity. Instead, their shared definition overwhelmingly included "taking care of business." For example, many participants talked about the importance of working hard to secure their futures, and handling the business that would protect them from dropping out or failing out of school. Failing to do well and having to return home to their mothers did not strike them as being very masculine, especially for men who called themselves adults.

They also strongly believed that leadership and community advancement had been historically associated with men. Bryant, a senior at the University of Michigan commented: "Real men assume responsibility and take the lead on making improvements; they don't leave problems for others to solve. College is the place where you learn to be a leader." The participants also acknowledged that most of the historical icons and celebrated figures in the African American community were male leaders. "Look at Dr. Martin Luther King, Malcolm X, Jesse Jackson, Louis Farrakhan . . . they're masculine; they weren't athletes, but they were out in the streets fighting for the rights of Black folks. To me, that's masculine."

Reportedly, the participants' African American male peers (though uninvolved themselves) supported, appreciated, and applauded the participants' display of leadership on the six campuses. In fact, both their African American male and female peers elected them to serve in a variety of important leadership capacities in minority and mainstream student organizations. Keely, a junior at the University of Illinois, commented,

"They don't really know what the organization does, but because they feel this camaraderie with another African American student who's running for a particular leadership position, they're going to vote for that student because he or she is Black." The participants felt a special sense of support from other African American males on campus and believed their peers would not have elected them to major leadership positions if they deemed such activities inappropriately "un-masculine." "When I ran for student body president, brothas' turned out in record numbers to cast their ballots in my favor; they wouldn't have done that if they didn't at least respect me as an African American male peer who could be their leader," a Purdue student added.

The participants believed their previous track records for contributing to the advancement of the minority and African American student communities on campus helped them win favor with their fellow African American male peers. Though they were involved in an array of clubs and student organizations on their campuses, the high-achievers primarily held leadership positions in African American and minority student organizations. Their involvement enabled them to programmatically address issues and communicate the concerns of the African American community to university administrators. The participants often likened their roles to leading a family. In essence, their fellow African American peers comprised a "family" that these student leaders were providing for and protecting from social isolation, racism, and discrimination on their predominantly White campuses.

Regarding masculinity, the participants strongly believed that being a man had a lot to do with preparing to take care of a family. They often asked what good would a man who wasted his time in college and consequently ended up in dead-end jobs for the rest of his life be to his family and community. Or how useful was a man who did not stand up for his family and attempt to make their lives better. Robert's remarks provided an excellent synopsis of the high-achievers' shared opinion:

First of all, a real man honors God. Secondly, a real man takes care of his family and the people he is directly or indirectly responsible for . . . to me, anything outside of that is not very masculine. If you're not a person who's honoring God, you're not a man. If you're not doing things right now to take care of the family you're going to have in the future because you're so bent on self-gratification, you're not a man. Real men know that most decisions they make today will affect the family they're going to have in the future.

The participants believed they would be better off in the long-term by striving to become like older African American male leaders from their communities, instead of validating their manhood through their fellow African American college peers who would presumably achieve limited success later in life.

Although their definitions of masculinity were relatively unconventional and the activities in which they were most engaged were not part of the traditional African American male portfolio of manliness, the participants indicated that their masculinities were never questioned or challenged by their African American male peers or anyone else. This even held true for the gay and bisexual men in the sample. They had never been the victims of ridicule because they chose to spend their out-of-class time differently. The high-achievers received an incredible amount of support and praise from other African American male students on their campuses, including the uninvolved. "Though the things that I'm involved in wouldn't be in their criteria for being a man, they wouldn't look at me and say, 'Cullen isn't masculine.'"

The high-achievers had a different perspective on the perceived nexus between masculinity, materialism, and achievement. For instance, one participant from the University of Michigan noted:

Being "the man" isn't about the money, the clothes, and the cars that you have right now. You're "the man" when you're at a company and you're in a position to hire other African Americans; when you're in a position to give dollars back to the Black community; when you have time to go be a mentor to young African American boys in your city, that's masculine . . . to me, being an executive someday who's able to reach back and help other African Americans is the measure of a man.

Discussion

The 32 high-achieving African American men's conceptualizations of masculinity, in comparison to their fellow African American male peers, offer several intriguing contrasts to previous inquiries on this topic. The participants were comfortable with themselves and had apparently developed conflict-free masculine identities, despite their unconventional views and the ways in which their out-of-class time was spent. Morrison and Eardley (1985) contend that boys who fail to live up to traditional standards of masculinity usually experience ridicule and sometimes become victims of violent acts committed by their male peers. The experiences of these 32 high-achievers contradicted that claim. Instead they felt extremely supported by other African American male students on their campuses, and were not ridiculed or deemed heterosexually-suspect because of the decisions they made regarding the allocation of their out-of-class time. This held true for the openly gay student in the sample. He believed his African American male peers fully supported and treated him with an enormous amount of respect. The sexual orientation of the one bisexual participant remained private and undisclosed among his African American male peers, and he too experienced no ridicule from other men on his campus. Reportedly, this was largely due in part to their previous track records of service, leadership, and contributions to the African American communities at their universities.

These reports of peer approval coincide with Connell's (1993) claim that masculinities must be negotiated within male peer groups. It appears that committing one's time to the advancement of the African American community and assuming responsibility for bringing about changes that

would improve the quality of life for minority students were the primary ways by which the high-achievers were able to negotiate with their uninvolved male peers who would ultimately benefit from the improved campus conditions.

Unlike Kunjufu's (1988) characterization, the participants did not have to choose between being popular or smart—they were accepted as both. That they were elected to multiple campus leadership positions suggests the participants were popular and highly-regarded by their peers. Gilligan (1993) and Head (1999) found that most men were competitive and generally disinterested in collaboration. In the present study, competitiveness manifested itself vis-à-vis the participants' reports of vying for multiple leadership positions on campus. However, collaboration is a necessary attribute of a successful undergraduate student leader. In fact, this was one of the key skills the participants deemed important for future success.

The high-achievers devoted a sizeable portion of their out-of-class time to purposeful activities—participating in clubs and organizations, leading various student groups on campus, studying and preparing for class, interacting with university administrators, and so on. In contrast, most of their African American male peers spent their time in residence hall rooms doing nothing, pursuing romantic (oftentimes sexual) relationships with women, exercising in the campus recreation facility, and playing video games and intramural sports. This finding is consistent with previous reports of traditionally African American masculine activities (Askew & Ross 1988; Head 1999; Martino & Meyenn 2001).

It does appear, however, that the high-achievers held certain beliefs and aspired to roles that are consistent with traditional, mainstream White definitions of masculinity (i.e. provider, family man, and executive). At the same time, their motives were strikingly different. They were involved in leadership roles for selfless reasons and believed their work as student leaders was central to the advancement of the African American community on their campuses. Even in discussing their aspirations of becoming top executives and leaders in their future professions, the participants consistently emphasized the importance of being in a position to help, hire, and provide opportunities to other African Americans. There was no mention of solely personal gain or competing for the sake of simply being on top. This social commitment is inconsistent with the self-serving, ultra-competitive depiction of White men who subscribe to traditional definitions of masculinity. Moreover, the high-achievers' views of masculinity were clearly alternative and inconsistent with those of fellow African American male peers.

Oliver (1988, 1989) found that many African American men take on the "tough guy" or "players of women" identities to compensate for their inability to meet traditional White standards of masculinity. While there was no mention of "tough guys" or violent peers, many African American men on the six campuses reportedly devoted tremendous time and energy to romantic and sexual conquests with female students (oftentimes multiple women simultaneously). Although 30 participants identified themselves as heterosexual and admittedly engaged in romantic and sexual endeavors with women, they did not deem the high priority and disproportionate emphasis that their peers placed on opposite-sex relationships healthy or productive. Moreover, instead of relying on indicators such as money, cars, and the exhibition of material possessions to define masculinity, the participants' conceptualizations included campus involvement, community improvement, and the indemnity of long-term career success beyond the undergraduate years.

Implications and Recommendations

According to data from Mortenson (2001), 67.6 percent of all African American men who started college in 1996 withdrew before completing their bachelor's degrees in 2000, compared to 56 percent of African American women and 58.1 percent of White male undergraduates. Mortenson's findings also indicate that African American men

had the lowest retention rates among both sexes and all racial/ethnic groups in higher education in 2000. While the causes of student attrition are extensive and complex (Tinto 1993), identity conflict—confusion about who one is, challenges with fitting into a community within the college environment, and unresolved psychosocial insecurities—is largely responsible for a significant number of student departures from the college campus (Evans, Forney, & Guido-DiBrito 1998). In fact, Gilbert and Gilbert (1998) and Price (2000) suggest that a healthy, conflict-free masculine identity positively affects a variety of student outcomes, including academic achievement. If colleges and universities are to improve retention and graduation rates for African American male undergraduates, faculty and administrators must implement effective programs that will assist these students in resolving identity conflicts and developing masculinities with which they are comfortable.

Highly-involved African American male student leaders, such as the participants in the present study, should be used as a resource in efforts to broaden or redefine within-group conceptualizations of masculinities. Programs and structured dialogues in which students candidly share their perspectives on manhood may broaden the scope of masculine attitudes and behaviors that are deemed acceptable by and garner respect from peers.

Organizations specifically designed for African American male students are also important, as they typically attract many men who would otherwise remain completely uninvolved. Programs that focus on masculine identity issues and diversified conceptualizations of what it means to be a man would naturally complement the mission of this type of student organization. These initiatives must be student-led with some faculty and administrative guidance, as undergraduates are more likely to listen to peers who challenge them to see issues in a different light. Given that fraternity membership was occasionally deemed highly masculine among men on the six campuses, it would be advantageous for advisors and administrators to encourage the African American fraternities to sponsor semi-structured programs that focus on explorations of masculinity.

It is also important to connect African American male undergraduates to African American mentors who can expose them to alternative definitions of what it means to be a man. These mentors could include male faculty, staff, administrators, and graduate students, as well as alumni who serve in important positions in their professions and are actively involved in their communities. These mentors could share their personal success stories, encourage mentees to spend their out-of-class time more meaningfully, deconstruct longstanding myths about masculinity and help undergraduates understand how the choices they make today will affect future success and employability. These mentoring relationships are especially critical for African American male students who come from single-parent homes or communities where they were not exposed to African American male professionals and leaders.

Campus counseling centers should also consider approaches that focus on masculinity for African American men. Private, individualized sessions and small group therapy may help these students unpack their identity issues and come to terms with their alternative conceptualizations of masculinity. Given the sexual promiscuity that the study participants described among their peers, campus health centers should expand their safe-sex campaigns to include information about masculinity. Programs and materials that emphasize to male students (African American and otherwise) that being a man is not all about sex would likely inspire some students to rethink their priorities. A "men's only" session at new student orientation would be an appropriate venue for spreading this message. African American male student leaders could also participate in these orientation sessions and suggest to newcomers that they balance their romantic and sexual pursuits with out-of-class activities that will yield meaning-

ful post-college outcomes. Gender-specific orientation sessions would also give advanced male student leaders the opportunity to share with new students their definitions of what it means to be a man and provide recommendations for how to survive in college despite peer pressure to live up to traditional standards of masculinity. These sessions would also confirm that it is possible to maintain intact masculine reputations without participating in sports, showing off material possessions, and constantly pursuing women.

Similar to women's centers that exist on hundreds of college and university campuses across the country, administrators should also consider devoting financial and staff resources to the establishment of men's centers. These centers could provide activities, resources, and support for male students. In addition to regularly sponsoring structured dialogues regarding identity and definitions of masculinity, the centers could also offer information and programs on rape prevention, aggression, health and wellness, sexuality, and male/female relationships, and facilitate opportunities for the cultivation of friendships and male bonding. If resources are not available to start this type of center, perhaps multicultural affairs offices could expand their scope to include programming on gender, particularly men's issues. These and other initiatives designed to address identity issues and definitions of masculinity among undergraduate men in general and African American male students specifically, would help students feel better about their definitions of self. The resolution of identity issues is necessary for retention and success in college, and is especially critical for African American male undergraduates.

Limitations

The most glaring limitation of this study is the reliance on self-reported data of peer perceptions. Interviews were only conducted with the 32 high-achieving African American undergraduate men, not their peers. Although the participants believed their African American male peers held certain views regarding masculinity or disproportionately devoted their out-of-class time to traditionally masculine activities, their peers may have reported something different. Also, the participants believed their peers perceived them to be masculine and never questioned their heterosexuality; no data were collected to confirm these speculations.

References

Askew, S., and Ross, C. 1988. *Boys don't cry: Boys and sexism in education.* Philadelphia, PA: Open University Press.

Blos, P. 1962. *On adolescence.* New York: Free Press.
———.1979. *The adolescence passage.* New York: International Universities Press.

Bonner II, F.A. 2001. *Gifted African American male college students: A phenomenological study.* Storrs, CT: The National Research Center on the Gifted and Talented.

Chodorow, N. 1978. *The reproduction of mothering.* Berkeley, CA: University of California Press.

Connell, R.W. 1993. "Disruptions: Improper masculinities." In *Beyond silenced voices.* Edited by L. Weis and M. Fine, 191–208. Albany, NY: State University of New York Press.

Davis, J.E. 2001. "Black boys at school: Negotiating masculinities and race." In *Educating our Black children: New directions and radical approaches.* Edited by R. Majors, 169–182. New York: RoutledgeFalmer.

———.2003. Early schooling and academic achievement of African American males. *Urban Education, 38*(5): 515–533.

Davis, J.E., and Jordan, W.J. 1994. The effects of school context, structure, and experience on African American males in middle and high school. *Journal of Negro Education, 63:* 570–587.

Denzin, N., and Lincoln, Y. 2000. Introduction: The discipline and practice of qualitative research. In *Handbook of qualitative research 2nd ed.,* Edited by N. Denzin & Y. Lincoln, 1–28. Thousand Oaks, CA: Sage.

Evans, N.J., Forney, D.S., and Guido-DiBrito, F. 1998. *Student development in college: Theory, research, and practice.* San Francisco: Jossey-Bass.

Fries-Britt, S. 1997. Identifying and supporting gifted African American men. In *Helping African American men succeed in college. New Directions for Student Services, No. 80.* Edited by M.J. Cuyjet, 65–78. San Francisco: Jossey-Bass.

———.1998. Moving beyond Black achiever isolation: Experiences of gifted Black collegians. *Journal of Higher Education, 69*(5): 556–576.

Ferguson, A.A. 2000. *Bad boys: Public schools in the making of black male masculinity.* Ann Arbor: The University of Michigan Press.

Gilbert, R., and Gilbert, P. 1998. *Masculinity goes to school.* New York: Routledge.

Gilligan, C. 1993. *In a different voice: Psychological theory and women's development.* Cambridge, MA: Harvard University Press.

Gregory, J.F. 1997. Three strikes and they're out: African American boys and American schools' responses to misbehavior. *International Journal of Adolescence and Youth, 7*(1), 25–34.

Harris, S.M. 1995. Psychosocial development and Black male masculinity: Implications for counseling economically disadvantaged African American male adolescents. *Journal of Counseling and Development,* 73, 279–287.

Head, J. 1999. *Understanding the boys: Issues of behaviour and achievement.* London: Falmer Press.

Holstein, J.A., and Gubrium, J.F. 1995. *The active interview. Qualitative research method series, No. 37.* Thousand Oaks, CA: Sage.

Kunjufu, J. 1988. *To be popular or smart: The Black peer group.* Chicago: African American Images.

LaVoire, J. 1986. Ego identity formation in middle adolescence. *Journal of Youth and Adolescence, 5:* 371–385.

Majors, R., and Billson, J.M. 1992. *Cool pose: The dilemmas of Black manhood in America.* New York: Lexington Press.

Martino, W., and Meyenn, B., eds. 2001. *What about the boys? Issues of masculinity in schools.* Philadelphia, PA: Open University Press.

Miles, M.B., and Huberman, A.M. 1994. *Qualitative data analysis: An expanded sourcebook, 2nd ed.* Thousand Oaks, CA: Sage.

Morrison, P., and Eardley, T. 1985. *About men.* Philadelphia, PA: Open University Press.

Mortenson Research Seminar on Public Policy Analysis of Opportunity for Postsecondary Education. 2001, July. College participation by gender age 18 to 24, 1967 to 2000. *Postsecondary Education Opportunity,* 109: 1–16.

Moustakas, C. 1994. *Phenomenological research methods.* Thousand Oaks, CA: Sage.

Oliver, W. 1988. Black males and social problems: Prevention through Afrocentric socialization. *Journal of Black Studies,* 24: 379–390.

———.1989. Sexual conquest and patterns of Black-on-Black violence: A structural-cultural perspective. *Violence and Victims,* 4: 257–273.

Price, J.N. 2000. *Against the odds: The meaning of school and relationships in the lives of six young African-American men.* Stamford, CT: Ablex.

Sedlacek, W.E. 1987. Black students on White campuses: 20 years of research. *Journal of College Student Personnel,* 28: 484–495.

Stoller, R.J. 1964. A contribution to the study of gender identity. *International Journal of Psychoanalysis,* 45: 220–226.

Tinto, V. 1993. *Leaving college: Rethinking the causes and cures of student attrition,* 2nd ed. Chicago: University of Chicago Press.

Wainrib, B.R. 1992. *Gender issues across the lifecycle.* New York, Springer.

Westwood, S. 1990. Racism, Black masculinity and the politics of space. In *Men, masculinities and social theory.* Edited by J. Hearn and D. Morgan, 55–71. Cambridge, MA: Unwin Hyman.

Michelle Fine
Lois Weis
Judi Addelston
Julia Marusza Hall

(In) Secure Times:
Constructing White Working-Class
Masculinities in the Late 20th Century

In the late 1980s and early 1990s, the poor and working-class white boys and men whom we interviewed have narrated "personal identities" as if they were wholly independent of corroding economic and social relations. Drenched in a kind of postindustrial, late twentieth-century individualism, the discourse of "identity work" appears to be draped in Teflon. The more profoundly that economic and social conditions invade their personal well-being, the more the damage and disruption is denied. Hegemony works in funny ways, especially for white working-class men who wish to think they have a continued edge on "Others"—people of color and white women.

Amid the pain and anger evident in the United States in the 1990s, we hear a desperate desire to target, to pin the tail of blame on these "Others" who have presumably taken away economic and social guarantees once secure in a nostalgic yesteryear. Our work in this article follows this pain and anger, as it is narrated by two groups of poor and working-class white boys in the Northeast, in high school and at their public sector jobs. Through pooled analyses of two independent qualitative studies, we look at the interiors and

From *Gender & Society* 11(1) © 1998 by Michelle Fine et al. pp. 52–68. Reprinted by permission of Sage Publications, Inc.

fragilities of white working-class male culture, focusing on the ways in which both whiteness and maleness are constructed through the setting up of "Others." Specifically, the two populations in this study include white working-class boys in high school and poor and working-class white men in their communities and workplaces—including a group of firefighters—between the ages of 24 and 35. These two groups were purposefully selected to demonstrate how white working-class men construct identities at different stages of adulthood. Although some of the men in this study are poor, the analytic focus remains on the identity formation of white working-class men, as the poor men come from working-class backgrounds and, as their articulations indicate, they routinely fluctuate between poor and working-class status.

Through these narratives we cut three analytic slices, trying to hear how personal and collective identities are formed today by poor and working-class white men. The first slice alerts us to their wholesale *refusal to see themselves inside history,* drowning in economic and social relations, corroding the ever-fragile "privilege" of white working-class men. The second slice takes us to the *search for scapegoats* and the ways in which these men scour their "local worlds" for those who have robbed them of their presumed privilege—finding answers in historically likely suspects,

Blacks and white women. The third slice, taken up in the conclusion, distressingly reveals the erosion of union culture in the lives of these boys and men and the *refusal to organize along lines of class or economic location,* with women and men across racial/ethnic groups, in a powerful voice of protest or resistance. These themes document the power of prevailing ideologies of individualism and meritocracy—as narrated by men who have, indeed, lost their edge but refuse to look up and fetishistically only look "down" to discover who stole their edge. These are men who belong to a tradition of men who think they "did it right," worked hard and deserve a wife, a house, a union job, a safe community, and public schools. These are men who confront the troubled pastiche of the 1990s, their "unsettled times," and lash out at pathetically available "Others." By so doing, they aspire toward the beliefs, policies, and practices of a white elite for whom their troubles are as trivial as those of people of color. Yet, these boys and men hold on, desperate and vigilant, to identities of white race and male gender as though these could gain them credit in increasingly class-segregated worlds.

The poor and working-class white boys and men in this [study] belong to a continuum of white working-class men who, up until recently in U.S. history, have been relatively privileged. These men, however, do not articulate a sense of themselves inside that history. In current economic and social relations that felt sense of privilege is tenuous at best. Since the 1970s, the U.S. steel industry has been in rapid decline as have other areas of manufacturing and production, followed by the downward spiral of businesses that sprang up and around larger industry (Bluestone and Harrison 1982). In the span of a few decades, foreign investment, corporate flight, downsizing, and automation have suddenly left members of the working class without a steady family wage, which, compounded with the dissipation of labor unions, has left many white working-class men feeling emasculated and angry (Weis 1990; Weis, Proweller, and Centrie 1996). It seems that overnight, the ability to work hard and provide

disappeared. White working-class men, of course, are not more racist or sexist than middle-class and upper-class white men. In this analysis, however, we offer data that demonstrate how white working-class male anger takes on virulent forms as it is displaced in a climate of reaction against global economic change.

As they search for someone who has stolen their presumed privilege, we begin to understand ways in which white poor and working-class men in the 1980s and 1990s manage to maintain a sense of self in the midst of rising feminism, affirmative action, and gay/lesbian rights. We are given further insight into ways in which they sustain a belief in a system that has, at least for working- and middle-class white men, begun to crumble, "e-racing" their once relatively secure advantage over white women and women and men of color (Newman 1993). As scholars of the dominant culture begin to recognize that "white is a color" (Roman 1993; Wong 1994), our work makes visible the borders, strategies, and fragilities of white working-class male culture, in insecure times, at a moment in history when many feel that this identity is under siege.

Many, of course, have theorized broadly about the production of white working-class masculinity. Willis (1977), for example, focuses on how white working-class "lads" in the industrial English Midlands reject school and script their futures on the same shopfloor on which their fathers and older brothers labor. Because of the often tense and contradictory power dynamics inherent in any single cultural context, Connell (1995) draws attention to the multiplicity of masculinities among men. In the absence of concrete labor jobs in which poor and working-class white men partially construct a sense of manhood, Connell also explores how the realm of compulsory heterosexuality becomes a formidable context for the production of white working-class male subjectivities. Various strands within the literature on masculine identity formation consider the construction of the "Other." For instance, researchers who explore all-male spaces in schools for white working-class and middle-class boys indicate that they often become potent breeding grounds for negative attitudes toward white women and gay men, whether in college fraternities (Sanday 1990), high school and college sports teams (Messner and Sabo 1994), or on an all-male college campus (Addelston and Stirratt, forthcoming). The look at the formation of white working-class masculinity in this study draws on this significant literature, while bringing to the forefront of analysis the current effects that the deindustrializing economy has on the meaning-making processes among poor and working-class white boys and men, particularly as it translates to the construction of a racial "Other."

On Whiteness

In the United States, the hierarchies of race, gender, and class are embodied in the contemporary "struggle" of working-class white men. As their stories reveal, these boys and men are trying to sustain a *place* within this hierarchy and secure the very *hierarchies* that assure their place. Among the varied demographic categories that spill out of this race/gender hierarchy, white men are the only ones who have a vested interest in maintaining both their position and their hierarchy—even, ironically, working-class boys and men who enjoy little of the privilege accrued to their gender/race status.

Scholars of colonial thought have highlighted the ways in which notions about non-Western "Others" are produced simultaneously with the production of discourse about the Western white "self," and these works become relevant to our analyses of race/gender domination. Analysts of West European expansion document the cultural disruptions that took place alongside economic appropriation, as well as the importance of the production of knowledge about groups of people that rendered colonization successful. As Frankenberg states,

> The notion of "epistemic violence" captures the idea that associated with West European colonial expansion is the production of modes of knowing that enabled and rationalized colo-

nial domination from the standpoint of the West, and produced ways of conceiving other societies and cultures whose legacies endure into the present (1993, 16).

Central, then, to the colonial discourse is the idea of the colonized "Other" being wholly and hierarchically different from the "white self." In inventing discursively the colonial "Other," whites were parasitically producing an apparently stable Western white self out of a previously nonexistent self. Thus the Western (white) self and the colonial "Other" both were products of discursive construction. The work of Chakravorty Spivak (1985), which explores how Europe positioned itself as sovereign in defining racial "Others" for the purposes of administration and expanding markets, is useful on this point.

One continuing effect of colonial discourse is the production of an unnamed, unmarked white/Western self against which all others can be named and judged. It is the unmarked self that must be deconstructed, named, and marked (Frankenberg 1993). This article takes up this challenge. As we will argue here, white working-class male identity is parasitically coproduced as these men name and mark others, largely African Americans and white women. Their identity would not exist in its present form (and perhaps not at all) if these simultaneous productions were not taking place. At a moment of economic crisis in which white working-class men are being squeezed, the disparaging constructions of others proliferate.

Racism and the Construction of the "Other"

The first study we focus on involves an ethnographic investigation conducted by Lois Weis in the mid-1980s. This is an exploration of white working-class high school students in a deindustrializing urban area called "Freeway." Data were collected in the classrooms, study halls, during extracurricular activities, and through in-depth interviews with over 60 juniors, most of their teachers, the vice-principal, social workers, guidance counselors, and others over the course of an academic year. Data collection centered on the junior class since this is the year when some students begin to plan for further schooling, and in the state where Freeway is located, college entrance exams are administered.

While there are several facets to the production of the boys' identity, we focus on the ways in which young white boys coproduce African American male identities and their own identities. For the most part, these young white boys narrate a sense of self grounded in the sphere of sexuality, in which they script themselves as the protectors of white women whom they feel are in danger of what they regard as a deviant African American male sexuality. Not only are these young working-class boys unable to see themselves as belonging to a tradition of privilege in their being white and male, their felt loss of that historic status in a restructuring economy leaves them searching in their school, their neighborhood, and surrounding communities for those responsible. Perhaps due, in part, to student peer culture contextualized within the lived culture of the school in which these interviews took place, this examination of white male working-class youths of high school age reveals meaning-making processes that are strikingly uniform, at least in relation to the construction of a racial "Other."

Freeway is a divided city and a small number of Arabs and Hispanics live among African Americans largely on one side of the "tracks," and whites on the other, although there are whites living in one section of Freeway just adjacent to the steel mill, which is in the area populated by people of color. Virtually no people of color live in the white area, unlike many large cities in the United States, where there are pockets of considerable mix. Most African Americans came up from the South during and after World War II, drawn by the lure of jobs in the steel industry. Having been relegated to the dirtiest and lowest paid jobs, most are now living in large public housing projects, never having been able to amass the necessary capital to live elsewhere. Although we have no evidence to this effect, we also assume

that even had they been able to accumulate capital, mortgages would have been turned down if African Americans had wished to move into the white area. Also, there are no doubt informal agreements among those who rent, not to rent to African Americans in the white areas, further contributing to the segregated nature of the town. Today, most of project residents receive welfare and have done so for a number of years.

Among these white adolescent men, people of color are used consistently as a foil against which acceptable moral, and particularly sexual, standards are established. The goodness of white is always contrasted with the badness of Black— Blacks are involved with drugs, Blacks are unacceptable sexually, Black men attempt to "invade" white sexual space by talking with white women, Black women are simply filthy. The binary translates in ways that complement white boys. As described by Jim, there is a virtual denial of anything at all good being identified with Blackness and of anything bad identified with whiteness:[1]

> The minorities are really bad into drugs. You're talking everything. Anything you want, you get from them. A prime example, the _____ ward of Freeway; about 20 years ago, the _____ ward was predominately white, my grandfather used to live there. Then Italians, Polish, the Irish people, everything was fine. The houses were maintained; there was a good standard of living. . . . The Blacks brought drugs. I'm not saying white people didn't have drugs; they had drugs, but to a certain extent. But drugs were like a social thing. But now you go down to the _____ ward; it's amazing; it's a ghetto. Some of the houses are okay. They try to keep them up. Most of the homes are really, really terrible. They throw garbage on the front lawn; it's sickening. You talk to people from [surrounding suburbs]. Anywhere you talk to people, they tend to think the majority of our school is Black. They think you hang with Black people, listen to Black music. . . . A few of them [Black] are starting to go into the _____ ward now [the white side], so they're moving around. My parents will be around there when that happens, but I'd like to be out of there.

Much expressed racism centers on white men's entitled access to white women, thus serving the dual purpose of fixing Blacks and white women on a ladder of social relations. Clint expresses these sentiments as he relays that the fighting between Blacks and whites in the community is a result of white men protecting white women:

> [The Blacks] live on the other side of town. . . . A lot of it [fights] starts with Blacks messing with white girls. That's how a lot of them start. Even if they [white guys] don't know the white girl, they don't like to see [it] . . . I don't like it. If I catch them [Blacks] near my sister, they'll get it. I don't like to see it like that. Most of them [my friends] see it that way [the same way he does] . . . I don't know many white kids that date Black girls.

This felt need to protect white girls also translates as a code of behavior for white male students inside school. Within school walls, white working-class male anger toward African American men is magnified. As Bill bitterly accounts, white male students are not seen as doing the right thing:

> Like my brother, he's in ninth grade. He's in trouble all the time. Last year he got jumped in school . . . about his girlfriend. He don't like Blacks. They come up to her and go, "Nice ass," and all that shit. My brother don't like that when they call her "nice ass" and stuff like that. He got suspended for saying "fucking nigger"; but it's all right for a Black guy to go up to whites and say stuff like that ["nice ass"]. . . . Sometimes the principals aren't doing their job. Like when my brother told [the assistant principal] that something is going to happen, Mr. _____ just said, "Leave it alone, just turn your head." . . . Like they [administrators] don't know when fights start in this school. Like there's this one guy's kid sister, a nigger [correction]—a Black guy—grabbed her ass. He hit him a couple of times. Did the principal know about it? No!

These young white men construct white women as if they were in need of their protection. The young men fight for these young women. Their complaints are communicated through a language of property rights. Black boys intruding onto *white property*. It is the fact that *Black* men are invading *white* women, the property of *white* men, that is at issue here. The discursive construction of Black men as oversexualized enables white men to elaborate their own "appropriate" heterosexuality. At a time of heightened concern with homosexuality, by virtue of their age, the collective nature of their lives, the fear of being labeled homosexual, and the violence that often accompanies such labeling in high school, these boys assert virulently and publicly their concern with Black men, while expressing their own heterosexuality and their ability to "take care of their women."

There is a grotesqueness about this particular set of interactions, a grotesqueness that enables white men to write themselves as pure, straight, and superior, while authoring Black men as dirty, oversexualized, and almost animal-like. The white female can be put on a pedestal, in need of protection. The Black female disparaged; the Black male avenged. The elevation of white womanhood, in fact, has been irreducibly linked to the debasement of both Black women and men (Davis 1990). By this Davis asserts that in the historic positioning of Black females as unfeminine and Black males as predators, the notion of what is feminine has become an idealized version of white womanhood. It is most interesting that not one white female in this study ever discussed young Black men as a "problem." This is not to say that white women were not racist, but this discursive rendering of Black men was quite noticeably the terrain of white men.

The word *nigger* flows freely from the lips of white men and they treat Black women far worse than they say Black men treat white women. During a conversation at the lunch table, for example, Mike says that Yolanda [a Black female] should go to "Niggeria" [Nigeria]. In another conversation about Martin Luther King Day, Dave says, "I have a wet dream—about little white boys and little Black girls." On another occasion, when two African American women walk into the cafeteria, Pete comments that "Black people . . . they're yecch. They smell funny and they [got] hair under their arms." The white boys at this table follow up their sentiment by making noises to denote disgust.

Young white men spend a great deal of time expressing and exhibiting disgust for people of color. This is done at the same time they elaborate an uninvited protectionist stance toward white women. If white women are seen as the property of white men, it is all the more acceptable for them to say and do anything they like. This set of discursive renditions legitimates their own "cultural wanderings" since they are, without question, "on the top." For the moment, this symbolic dominance substitutes for the real material dominance won during the days of heavy industry. Most important, for present purposes, is the coproduction of the "white self," white women, and the African American male "Other."

Young Adults: White Poor and Working-Class Men in an Economic Stranglehold

The second set of narratives stems from an ongoing study of poor and working-class young adults who grew up in the Reagan–Bush years, conducted by Michelle Fine, Lois Weis, and a group of graduate students, including Judi Addelston. In broad strokes we are investigating constructions of gender, race, ethnic, and class identities; participation in social and community-based movements for change; participation in self-help groups; participation in religious institutions; experiences within and outside the family; and experiences within and outside the new economy. We have adopted a quasi-life history approach in which a series of in-depth interviews are conducted with young people—poor and working-class—of varying racial backgrounds. Data were gathered in Buffalo, New York, and Jersey City, New Jersey. Seventy-five to 80 adults were interviewed in each city. While the larger aspects of the project are as stated above, in this [study] we focus on the bordered constructions of whiteness

as articulated by young white men—a combined sample of poor and working-class men, some of whom are firefighters.[2]

As with the Freeway boys, we hear from these somewhat older men a set of identities that are carved explicitly out of territory bordered by African Americans and white women. Similar to the Freeway study, these groups are targeted by young white adult men as they search their communities, work sites, and even the local social service office for those who are responsible for stealing their presumed privilege. While most of these men narrate hostile comparisons with "Others," some offer sympathetic, but still bordered, views. Like cartographers working with different tools on the same geopolitical space, all these men—from western New York and northern New Jersey—sculpt their identities as if they were discernibly framed by, and contrasted through, race, gender, and sexuality.

As with the teens, the critique by young adult white men declares the boundaries of acceptable behavior at themselves. The white male critique is, by and large, a critique of the actions/behaviors taken by African Americans, particularly men. This circles around three interrelated points: "not working," welfare abuse or "cheats," and affirmative action.

Because many, if not most, of the white men interviewed have themselves been out of work and/or received welfare benefits and food stamps, their critique serves to denigrate African Americans. It also draws the limits of what constitutes "deserving" circumstances for not working, receiving welfare, and relying on government-sponsored programs at themselves.

By young adulthood, the target site for this white male critique shifts from sexuality to work but remains grounded *against* men of color. When asked about the tensions in their neighborhood, Larry observes,

> Probably not so much [tension] between them [Blacks and Hispanics]. But like for us. I mean, it gets me angry sometimes. I don't say I'm better than anybody else. But I work for the things that I have, and they [Blacks and Hispanics]

figure just because you're ahead, or you know more and you do more, [that it's] because you're white. And that's not really it. We're all equal, and I feel that what I've done, I've worked for myself to get to where I'm at. If they would just really try instead of just kind of hanging out on the street corners. That's something that really aggravates me, to see while I'm rushing to get to work, and everybody is just kind of milling around doing nothing.

In Larry's view, he is a hardworking man, trying to live honestly, while African Americans and Hispanics do nothing all day long. Larry talks about the anger he feels for those who are Black and Hispanic and in so doing sets up a binary opposition between whites and "Others," with whites as morally superior. From this flows an overt racial critique of affirmative action programs, as well as a more racially coded critique of welfare abusers and cheats.

We take up the issue of affirmative action first. Many of these white men focus on what they consider to be unfair hiring practices, which they see as favoring people of color and white women. Pete, for example, has a great deal to say about his experience at work and the Civil Rights movement more generally, and then how such movements have hurt him as a white man:

> For the most part, it hasn't been bad. It's just that right now with these minority quotas, I think more or less, the white male has become the new minority. And that's not to point a finger at the Blacks, Hispanics, or the women. It's just that with all these quotas, instead of hiring the best for the job, you have to hire according to your quota system, which is still wrong . . . Civil rights, as far as I'm concerned, is being way out of proportion . . . granted, um, the Afro-Americans were slaves over 200 years ago. They were given their freedom. We as a country, I guess you could say, has tried to, well, I can't say all of us, but most of us, have tried to, like, make things a little more equal. Try to smooth over some of the rough spots. You have some of these militants who are now claiming that after all these years, we still owe them. I think the owing time is over for every-

body. Because if we go into that, then the Poles are still owed [he is Polish]. The Germans are still owed. Jesus, the Jews are definitely still owed. I mean, you're, you're getting cremated, everybody wants to owe somebody. I think it's time to wipe the slate clean . . . it's all that, um, you have to hire a quota of minorities. And they don't take the best qualified, they take the quota number first . . . . So that kind of puts you behind the eight ball before you even start. . . . Well, I'm a minority according to some people now, because they consider the white male now a minority.

Larry focuses on what he interprets as a negative effect of the Civil Rights movement—government-sponsored civil service tests. For Larry, these exams favor white women and "minorities" and exclude qualified white men from employment:

> I mean, in theory, a whole lot of it [Civil Rights movement] is good. I feel that is worthwhile, and there has to be some, not some, there has to be equality between people. And just because of . . . I feel that the federal government sometimes makes these laws or thinks that there's laws that are bad, but they themselves break them. I mean, I look at it as where—this is something that has always irked me—taking civil service exams. I feel that, I mean, I should be given a job based on my abilities and my knowledge, my background, my schooling, everything as a whole, rather than sometimes a Black man has to have a job just because he's Black. And really you're saying, you're not basing it on being Black or whether you're a male or female, but that's exactly what they're doing . . . I really, I completely disagree with quotas. I don't feel it's, they're fair. I mean, me as a white male, I'm really being pushed, turned into a minority. I mean, it doesn't matter. We have to have so many Blacks working in the police department or in the fire department, or women. And even though, well, say, I'm not just saying this because I'm a white male, but white males, you know, will be pushed, you know, pushed away from the jobs or not given the jobs even though they might qualify more so for them, and have more of the capabilities

to do the job. And they just won't get it because they're white males.

According to Tom, "color" is not an issue—there are lazy people all over and he even has friends who are Black. Tom, however, accuses African Americans and white women of unfairly playing up minority status to get jobs. From politicians to other lazy minorities, in Tom's view, Blacks in particular have a lock hold on all the good jobs:

> I have nothing against Blacks. Whether you're Black, white, you know, yellow, whatever color, whatever race. But I don't like the Black movement where, I have Black friends. I talk to them and they agree. You know, they consider themselves, you know. There's white trash and there's white, and there's Black trash, and there's Blacks. And the same in any, you know, any race. But as soon as they don't get a job, they right away call, you know, they yell discrimination. That's where I think some of our, you know, politicians come in too. You have your [council members in Buffalo], and I think they do that. But I think maybe if you went out there, and educated yourself. And you know, there's a lot of educated Blacks, and you don't hear them yelling discrimination because they've got good jobs. Because they got the know-how behind them. But the ones that are really lazy, don't want it, they, they start yelling discrimination so they can just get the job and they're not even qualified for it. And then they might take it away from, whether it's a, you know, a woman or a guy.

The white male critique of affirmative action is that it is not "fair." It privileges Blacks, Hispanics, and at times white women, above white men. According to these men, white men are today being set up as the "new minority," which contradicts their notions of equal opportunity. Nowhere in these narratives is there any recognition that white men as a group have historically been privileged, irrespective of individual merit. These assertions about affirmative action offer white men a way of "Othering" African Americans, in particular. This theme is further elaborated in discussions of welfare abusers and

cheats. Like talk of sexuality among the younger men, as exemplified by Pete, the primary function of discussions about welfare abusers is to draw the boundaries of acceptable welfare at their own feet:

> [The Welfare system] is a joke. . . . They treat you like absolute garbage. They ask you everything except your sexual preference to be quite honest with you. They ask how many people are in the house. What time do you do this? What time do you do that? Where do you live? Do you pay your gas? Do you pay your electric? Um, how come you couldn't move into a cheaper apartment? Regardless of how much you're paying to begin with. If you ask them for a menial item, I mean . . . like your stove and refrigerator. They give me a real hard time. . . . There's definitely some people who abuse the system, I can see that. But then there are people who, when you need it, you know, it's like they have something to fall on to. And they're [the case workers] basically shoving everybody into one category. They're all users. But these [case workers] are the same people that if the country closes them off, they won't have a job and they're going to be there next too.

Ron, a white working-class man who has been in and out of instances of stable employment, makes observations on welfare and social services that are based on his own varied experiences. Ron says that he has never applied for welfare and takes pride in this fact, and he compares himself with those who abuse the system—who he believes are mostly Black. Later, Ron reveals that he has used social services:

> You know, we [spouse] look at welfare as being something, um, less than admirable . . . I think for the most part, I think most people get out of life what they put into it. You know, because some people have more obstacles than others, there's no doubt about it. But I think a lot of people just expect things to come to them, and when it doesn't, you know, they've got the government to fall back on. . . . You know I think it [falling back on the government] is more common for Black people. I mean social services, in general, I think, is certainly necessary,

and Kelly and I have taken advantage of them. We've got food stamps several times. Um, one of the things about the home improvement [business he was in], when I first got into that, before I really developed my skills better and, and the first company, like I said, when they were doing some change over. And, just before they left [the city], we were at a point where business was starting to slack off and um, especially in the winter time. So, a lot of times in the winter when my income was quite low, we'd go on food stamps, and I think, I think that's the way it should be used. I mean, it's help there for people. But, you know, as soon as I was able to get off it, I did. And not for any noble reasons, but just, you know, I think I'd rather be able to support myself than have things handed to me.

Since most of the case workers are white, Ron is aligning himself with the hardworking white people who have just fallen on hard times, unlike the abusers, largely Black, who exploit the system. Along these same lines, Pete's criticism of the case workers is that they treat *all* welfare recipients as cheats. Many of the white men who have been out of work, or are now in a precarious economic state, speak with a strong disdain for African American men and, if less so, for white women as well. Others, however, narrate positions relative to white women and people of color within a discourse of concern and connection. This more liberal discourse is typically spoken by working-class men who occupy positions of relative economic security. But even here the borders of their identity nevertheless fall along the same fault lines of race and gender (Roediger 1994).

The white working-class firefighters interviewed in our study narrate somewhat similar views. Joe, for instance, works in a fire department in Jersey City. He, like so many of our informants, insists that he is "not a racist," but he vehemently feels that "Civil Rights has [sic] gone far enough." As we discovered, the fire and police departments in Jersey City have historically garnered a disproportionate share of the city's public sector investment and growth over the last decade, and they

employ a disproportionate share of white men. We began to hear these departments as the last public sector spaces in which white working-class men could at once exercise identities as white, working, and men. Joe offers these words to describe his raced and gendered identity:

> No, I'm not racist. I'm not prejudiced. There are definitely lowlifes in this community where we live in. If you see somebody do something stupid, you call them stupid. You don't call them a stupid Black person because there's no need for those extra words. Just stupid. That's how I feel, I look at things. I'm not racist at all. If there is such a thing, racist towards a person. That's how I see it.

Although Joe makes the disclaimer that he is not racist, ironically, he specifically marks the Black person "who does something stupid." Later, in his interview, we hear greater clarity. Joe is tired of hearing about race and has come to some frightening conclusions about how such issues should be put to rest:

> Civil rights, I think they're going overboard with it. Everything is a race issue now. Everything you see on TV, all of the talk shows. You have these Black Muslims talking, preaching hate against whites, the whites should be dead. And then you got these Nazi fanatics who say Blacks and Jews should be dead. That's fine, let them [Blacks and Jews] go in their own corner of the world.

In characterizing African Americans as "lowlifes" and "stupid," Joe ostensibly creates a subclass used to buttress what he sees as the higher moral character of whites. Sick of the race "issue," Joe also critiques gains won during progressive movements for social change. On the streets of his community and on television, Joe maintains that he is bombarded with examples of irresponsible African Americans and others whom he feels are taking over and, therefore, should be pushed back into "their own corner of the world." Interestingly, Joe revised his otherwise critical look at affirmative action because it *positively* affected him:

I would say, what you call affirmative action, I would say that helped me to get this job. Because if it wasn't for minorities pressing the issue two or three years ago about the test being wrong, I would have scored a 368 on the test [and would have failed].

Joe passed the exam only after it had been modified to be more equitable. For Joe, public sector commitments to equity, including affirmative action and welfare, could be helpful if they help whites. But they are racist if they don't. In talking about his sister, Joe points out how she is being discriminated against because she is white. In Joe's logic, because so many Blacks and Asians are using and abusing the system, whites, unfairly, are the ones who are being cheated. Again, Joe places his sister in a position of superiority in relation to people of color. While his sister is a hard worker, "Others," who do not really need the assistance, are simply bilking the system:

She just had a baby. She works as a waitress. Not too much cash in there because they cut her hours, and she's getting welfare and from what I understand from her, there are people, Black or Asian people, that aren't having as much problems as she is. It seems that the system is trying to deter her from using it. The impression she gets is you're white, you can get a job. If it's true, and I think that's definitely not right. You could be Black, white, gold, or brown, if you need it, you should have it.

Mark is another white firefighter. Echoing much of what Joe has said, Mark portrays the firehouse as a relatively protected and defended space for whiteness. By extension, the firehouse represents the civic goodness of [white] public institutions. In both Joe's and Mark's interviews, there is a self-consciousness about "not sounding racist," yet both consistently link any mention of people of color and the mention of social problems—be it child neglect, violence, or vandalism. Whiteness preserves the collective good, whereas people of color periodically threaten the collective good:

I wouldn't say there is tension in the fire department but people are prejudiced. I guess I am to a certain degree. I don't think I'm that bad. I think there's good Blacks and bad Blacks, there's good whites and bad whites. I don't know what the percentage of minorities are, but Jersey City is linked with other cities and they have to have a certain percentage of minorities. Where I live right now, it's not too bad. I don't really hang out. . . . I have no problems with anybody. Just the vandalism. You just got to watch for that.

Mark doesn't describe how he got to be a firefighter, and he also does not know how Joe successfully landed the job. Although he is secure in his vocation, Joe is somehow certain that "minorities" have gained access unfairly. When asked what he might like to see changed about the job, Mark responds,

Have probably testing be more well-rounded. More straightforward and fair. It seems to be a court fight every time to take a test. Everybody takes the same test. I just don't understand why it's so difficult. I understand you have to have certain minorities in the job and that's only fair, but sometimes I think that's not fair. It's not the fire department, it's the people that fight it . . . I think everybody should take the same test and that's it. The way you score is the way you score.

Frank, on the other hand, embodies the white working-class "success" story. He has completed college and graduate school and speaks from an even greater distance about his community's sentiments about race, safety and crime. Frank complicates talk of race/ethnicity by introducing social class as the social border that cannot easily be crossed. His narrative of growing up unravels as follows:

Well, because, you know, we were white, and these other places were, were much less white, and I think there was kind of that white fear of, minorities, um, particularly Blacks and Hispanics. And you know, I'm not proud of that, but I mean, that's just, that's part of the history of it. But it was also perceiving that things were changing, very radically, very dramatically. And what's happened over the years is that a lot of people who lived there for generations have moved away. But, you know, it was, I think, they just, a fear of, of the changes going on in the 60s and 70s, and seeing, you know, crime increase. . . . And wanting to keep, you know, this neighborhood as intact as possible. . . . I sense that there's a lot of apprehension [among whites]. You know, I think . . . I mean, a lot of it comes out of people talking about, um, their fear, you know, um, getting mugged, or getting their, you know their car stolen.

Seemingly embarrassed by racialized biases embedded in the community in which he was raised, Frank nevertheless shifts responsibly off of whites and onto "minorities" when he discusses solutions to racial problems:

> Indian women have these . . . marks on their foreheads. And um, you know, they're apparently, just racists (referring to white youths who beat on these women). . . . You know, ignorant. Yeah, they're, they're young white, ignorant people who go around beating up Indians, in particular because the Indians tend to be passive. Um, it's something they need to learn to do, which is to be more assertive, I think and to be, um, you know, to stand up for their, their basic human rights.

We hear, from these young white males, a set of identities carved inside, and against, demographic and political territories. The borders of gender, race/ethnicity, and, for Frank, class, mark the borders of self, as well as "Other." While all of our interviewees are fluent in these comparisons, those who sit at the collapsing "bottom" of the economy or in sites of fragile employment rehearse identities splintered with despair, verbal violence, and hostile comparisons of self and "Other." Those more economically secure also speak through these traditional contours of identity but insist that they have detached from the moorings of hostile attitudes and oppositional identities. Even this last group, however, has little social experience from which to invent novel

constructions of self, as white, working-class, male, and positively engaged with others.

From men like Frank we hear the most stretch, the greatest desire to connect across borders. But even these men feel the pull of tradition, community, historic, and contemporary fears. They are simply one job away from the narrations of their more desperate and hostile or perhaps more honest white brothers. With few noticing that the economy has produced perverse relations of scarcity, along lines of race, class, and gender, these white men are the mouths that uphold, as if truth, the rhetoric of the ruling class. Elite white men have exploited these men's fears and provided them with the language of hate and the ideology of the "Other." To this end, many of the working-class men in this sample believe that there are still good jobs available for those who work hard, only "minorities" are blocking any chance for access to such employment. Refusing analyses of collapsing urban economies and related race relations, these young adult white men hold Black and Latino men accountable for their white misery and disappointments.

Conclusion

The U.S. economy is rapidly changing, moving from an industrial to a postindustrial society. Jobs that once served to secure the lives and identities of many working-class people are swiftly becoming a thing of the past. The corrosion of white working-class male felt privilege—as experienced by the boys and men in this analysis—has also been paralleled by the dissipation of labor unions, which are being washed away as quickly as industry. Even though capital has traditionally used fundamental cleavages such as racism and sexism as tools to fracture a working-class consciousness from forming, labor unions have typically played a strong role in U.S. history in creating a space for some workers to organize against capital for change (Roediger 1994). Historical ties to white working-class union activity are fading fast, particularly among young white working-class men, whose fathers, uncles, and older brothers no longer have a union tradition to pass on to the next generation. With the erosion of union culture and no formal space left to develop and refine meaningful critique, some white working-class men, instead, scramble to reassert their assumed place of privilege on a race-gender hierarchy in an economy that has ironically devalued all workers. Unorganized and angry, our data indicate that white working-class boys and men consistently displace their rage toward historically and locally available groups.

We have offered two scenes in which white men in various stages of adulthood, poor and working-class, are constructing identities on the backs of people of color and white women. Clearly this is not only the case for white working-class men, nor is it generalizable to *all* white working-class men, but these men are among the best narrators of virulent oppositional hostility. It is important that the boys and young adult men in both studies in different geographic locations exhibit similar sentiments. These white men are a race/class/gender group that has been dramatically squeezed relative to their prior positions. Meanwhile, the fantasies and stereotypes of "Others" continue to be promoted, and these delicate, oppositional identities constantly require "steroids" of denigration to be maintained. As the Freeway data suggest, white working-class men also virulently construct notions of identity around another historically available "Other"—gays. Many studies, such as that by Messner and Sabo (1994), evidence how homophobia is used as a profound foil around which to forge aggressive forms of heterosexuality. Heteromasculinity, for the working class in the United States, may indeed be endangered.

As these white boys and men comment on their sense of mistreatment, we reflect, ironically, on their stone-faced fragility. The 1980s and 1990s have marked a time when the women they associate with got independent, their jobs got scarce, their unions got weak, and their privileged access to public institutions was compromised by the success of equal rights and affirmative action. Traditional bases of white male material power—

head of the family, productive worker, and exclusive access to "good" public sector and/or unionized jobs—eroded rapidly. Sold out by elites, they are in panic and despair. Their reassertions of status reveal a profound fragility masked by the protection of "their women," their fight for "fairness" in the workplace, and their demand for "diversity" among (but not within) educational institutions. As they narrate a precarious white heteromasculinity, perhaps they speak for a narrow slice of men sitting at the white working-class nexus. More likely, they speak for a gendered and raced group whose privilege has been rattled and whose wrath is boiling over. Their focus, almost fetishistically, is on themselves as victims and "Others" as perpetrators. Research conducted by Janoff-Bulman (1979) documents that an exclusive focus on individual "perpetrators" of injustice [real or imagined] is the *least* likely strategy for transforming inequitable social conditions and the *most* likely strategy for creating poor mental health outcomes. Comforted by Howard Stern and Rush Limbaugh, these men are on a treacherous course for self, "Others," and the possibilities for broad-based social change.

The responsibility of educators, researchers, and citizens committed to democratic practice is not simply to watch passively or interrupt responsively when these boys/men get "out of hand." We must embark on serious social change efforts aimed at both understanding and transforming what we uncover here. Spaces must be located in which men/boys are working together to affirm white masculinity that does not rest on the construction of the viral "Other." Such spaces must be imagined and uncovered, given the attention that they deserve. Schools, churches, and work sites all offer enormous potential for such transformative cultural activity. We need to make it our task to locate spaces in which white men and boys are reimagining what it means to be white and male in the 1990s. Activists and researchers can profitably work with such groups to chronicle new images of white masculinity that are not based on the aggressive "Othering" that we find to be so prevalent.

Notes

1. We must point out that although we focus on only the white boys' construction of Blacks, we do not mean to imply that they authored the race script in its entirety nor that they wrote the meaning of Black for the African American students. We are, for present purposes, simply focusing on the ways in which young white men discursively construct the "Other."

2. We include men of different ages and statuses to represent an array of voices that are white, male, and working-class.

References

Addelston, J., and M. Stirratt. Forthcoming. The last bastion of masculinity: Gender politics and the construction of hegemonic masculinity at the Citadel. In *Masculinities and organizations,* edited by C. Change. Thousand Oaks, CA: Sage.

Bluestone, B., and B. Harrison. 1982. *The deindustrialization of America.* New York: Basic Books.

Connell, R. 1995. *Masculinities.* Berkeley: University of California Press.

Davis, A. 1990. *Women, culture, and politics.* New York: Vintage.

Frankenberg, R. 1993. *The social construction of whiteness: White women, race matters.* Minneapolis: University of Minnesota Press.

Janoff-Bulman, R. 1979. Characterological versus behavioral self-blame: Inquiries into depression and rape. *Journal of Social Psychology* 37:1798–1809.

Messner, M., and D. Sabo. 1994. *Sex, violence, and power in sports: Rethinking masculinity.* Freedom, CA: Crossing.

Newman, K. 1993. *Declining fortunes: The withering of the American dream.* New York: Basic Books.

Roediger, D. 1994. *The wages of whiteness: Race and the making of the American working class.* New York: Verso.

Roman, L. 1993. White is a color!: White defensiveness, postmodernism, and anti-racist pedagogy. In *Race, identity and representation in education.* New York: Routledge.

Sanday, P. R. 1990. *Fraternity gang rape: Sex, brotherhood, and privilege on campus.* New York: New York University Press.

Spivak, C. 1985. The Rani of Sirmur. In *Europe and its others,* edited by F. Barker. Colchester, UK: University of Essex Press.

Weis, L. 1990. *Working class without work: High school students in a de-industrializing economy.* New York: Routledge.

Weis, L., A. Proweller, and C. Centrie. 1996. Re-examining a moment in history: Loss of privilege inside white, working class masculinity in the 1990s. In *Off white,* edited by M. Fine, L. Powell, L. Weis, and M. Wong. New York: Routledge.

Willis, Paul. 1977. *Learning to labor: How working-class kids get working-class jobs.* New York: Columbia University Press.

Wong, L. M. 1994. Di(s)-secting and di(s)-closing whiteness. Two tales from psychology. *Feminism and Psychology* 4:133–153.

Michael S. Kimmel

Gender, Class, and Terrorism

The events of September 11 [2001] have sent scholars and pundits alike scrambling to make sense of those seemingly senseless acts. While most analyses have focused on the political economy of globalization or the perversion of Islamic teachings by Al Qaeda, several commentators have raised gender issues.

Some have reminded us that in our haste to lionize the heroes of the World Trade Center collapse, we ignored the many women firefighters, police officers, and rescue workers who also risked their lives. We've been asked to remember the Taliban's vicious policies toward women; indeed, even Laura Bush seems to be championing women's emancipation.

A few have asked us to consider the other side of the gender coin: men. Some have rehearsed the rather tired old formulae about masculine bloodlust or the drive for domination and conquest, with no reference to the magnificent humanity displayed by so many on September 11. In an article in *Slate,* the Rutgers anthropologist Lionel Tiger trotted out his old male-bonding thesis but offered no understanding of why Al Qaeda might appeal to some men and not others. Only the journalist Barbara Ehrenreich suggests that there may be a link between the misogyny of the Taliban and the masculinity of the terrorists.

As for myself, I've been thinking lately about a letter to the editor of a small, upstate–New York newspaper, written in 1992 by an American GI after his return from service in the Gulf War. He

complained that the legacy of the American middle class had been stolen by an indifferent government. The American dream, he wrote, has all but disappeared; instead, most people are struggling just to buy next week's groceries.

That letter writer was Timothy McVeigh from Lockport, N.Y. Two years later, he blew up the Murrah federal building in Oklahoma City in what is now the second-worst act of terrorism ever committed on American soil.

What's startling to me are the ways that McVeigh's complaints were echoed in some of the fragmentary evidence that we have seen about the terrorists of September 11, and especially in the portrait of Mohammed Atta, the suspected mastermind of the operation and the pilot of the first plane to hit the World Trade Center.

Looking at these two men through the lens of gender may shed some light on both the method and the madness of the tragedies they wrought.

McVeigh was representative of the small legion of white supremacists—from older organizations like the John Birch Society, the Ku Klux Klan, and the American Nazi Party, to newer neo-Nazi, racist-skinhead, white-power groups like Posse Comitatus and the White Aryan Resistance, to radical militias.

These white supremacists are mostly younger (in their early 20s), lower-middle-class men, educated at least through high school and often beyond. They are the sons of skilled workers in industries like textiles and tobacco, the sons of the owners of small farms, shops, and grocery stores. Buffeted by global political and economic forces, the sons have inherited little of their fathers' legacies. The family farms have been lost to foreclosure, the small shops squeezed out by

From *The Chronicle of Higher Education* (Feb. 8, 2002): B11–B12. Copyright © Michael Kimmel. Reprinted by permission of Chronicle of Higher Education and the author.

Wal-Marts and malls. These young men face a spiral of downward mobility and economic uncertainty. They complain that they are squeezed between the omnivorous jaws of global capital concentration and a federal bureaucracy that is at best indifferent to their plight and at worst complicit in their demise.

As one issue of *The Truth at Last,* a white-supremacist magazine, put it:

> Immigrants are flooding into our nation willing to work for the minimum wage (or less). Super-rich corporate executives are flying all over the world in search of cheaper and cheaper labor so that they can lay off their American employees. . . . Many young White families have no future! They are not going to receive any appreciable wage increases due to job competition from immigrants.

What they want, says one member, is to "take back what is rightfully ours."

Their anger often fixes on "others"—women, members of minority groups, immigrants, gay men, and lesbians—in part because those are the people with whom they compete for entry-level, minimum-wage jobs. Above them all, enjoying the view, hovers the international Jewish conspiracy.

What holds together these "paranoid politics"—antigovernment, anti-global capital but pro-small capitalist, racist, sexist, anti-Semitic, homophobic—is a rhetoric of masculinity. These men feel emasculated by big money and big government—they call the government "the Nanny State"—and they claim that "others" have been handed the birthright of native-born white men.

In the eyes of such downwardly mobile white men, most white American males collude in their own emasculation. They've grown soft, feminized, weak. White supremacists' Web sites abound with complaints about the "whimpering collapse of the blond male"; the "legions of sissies and weaklings, of flabby, limp-wristed, non-aggressive, non-physical, indecisive, slack-jawed, fearful males who, while still heterosexual in theory and practice, have not even a vestige of the old macho spirit."

American white supremacists thus offer American men the restoration of their masculinity—a manhood in which individual white men control the fruits of their own labor and are not subject to emasculation by Jewish-owned finance capital or a black- and feminist-controlled welfare state. Theirs is the militarized manhood of the heroic John Rambo, a manhood that celebrates their God-sanctioned right to band together in armed militias if anyone, or any government agency, tries to take it away from them. If the state and the economy emasculate them, and if the masculinity of the "others" is problematic, then only "real" white men can rescue America from a feminized, multicultural, androgynous melting pot.

Sound familiar? For the most part, the terrorists of September 11 come from the same class, and recite the same complaints, as American white supremacists.

Virtually all were under 25, educated, lower middle class or middle class, downwardly mobile. The journalist Nasra Hassan interviewed families of Middle Eastern suicide bombers (as well as some failed bombers themselves) and found that none of them had the standard motivations ascribed to people who commit suicide, such as depression.

Although several of the leaders of Al Qaeda are wealthy—Osama bin Laden is a multimillionaire, and Ayman al-Zawahiri, the 50-year-old doctor thought to be bin Laden's closest adviser, is from a fashionable suburb of Cairo—many of the hijackers were engineering students for whom job opportunities had been dwindling dramatically. (Judging from the minimal information I have found, about one-fourth of the hijackers had studied engineering.) Zacarias Moussaoui, who did not hijack one of the planes but is the first man to be formally charged in the United States for crimes related to September 11, earned a degree at London's South Bank University. Marwan al-Shehhi, the chubby, bespectacled 23-year-old from the United Arab Emirates who flew the second plane into the World Trade Center, was an engineering student, while Ziad Jarrah, the 26-year-old Lebanese who flew the plane that crashed in Pennsylvania, had studied aircraft design.

Politically, these terrorists opposed globalization and the spread of Western values; they opposed what they perceived as corrupt regimes in several Arab states (notably Saudi Arabia and Egypt), which they claimed were merely puppets of American domination. "The resulting anger is naturally directed first against their rulers," writes the historian Bernard Lewis, "and then against those whom they see as keeping those rulers in power for selfish reasons."

Central to their political ideology is the recovery of manhood from the emasculating politics of globalization. The Taliban saw the Soviet invasion and westernization of Afghanistan as humiliations. Bin Laden's October 7 videotape describes the "humiliation and disgrace" that Islam has suffered "for more than 80 years." And over and over, Nasra Hassan writes, she heard the refrain: "The Israelis humiliate us. They occupy our land, and deny our history."

Terrorism is fueled by a fatal brew of antiglobalization politics, convoluted Islamic theology, and virulent misogyny. According to Ehrenreich, while these formerly employed or self-employed males "have lost their traditional status as farmers and breadwinners, women have been entering the market economy and gaining the marginal independence conferred by even a paltry wage." As a result, "the man who can no longer make a living, who has to depend on his wife's earnings, can watch Hollywood sexpots on pirated videos and begin to think the world has been turned upside down."

The Taliban's policies thus had two purposes: to remasculinize men and to refeminize women. Another journalist, Peter Marsden, has observed that those policies "could be seen as a desperate attempt to keep out that other world, and to protect Afghan women from influences that could weaken the society from within." The Taliban prohibited women from appearing in public un-

escorted by men, from revealing any part of their body, and from going to school or holding a job. Men were required to grow their beards, in accordance with religious images of Muhammad, yes; but also, perhaps, because wearing beards has always been associated with men's response to women's increased equality in the public sphere, since beards symbolically reaffirm biological differences between men and women, while gender equality tends to blur those differences.

The Taliban's policies removed women as competitors and also shored up masculinity, since they enabled men to triumph over the humiliations of globalization and their own savage, predatory, and violently sexual urges that might be unleashed in the presence of uncovered women.

All of these issues converged in the life of Mohammed Atta, the terrorist about whom the most has been written and conjectured. Currently, for example, there is much speculation about Atta's sexuality. Was he gay? Was he a repressed homosexual, too ashamed of his sexuality to come out? Such innuendoes are based on no more than a few circumstantial tidbits about his life. He was slim, sweet-faced, neat, meticulous, a snazzy dresser. The youngest child of an ambitious lawyer father and a pampering mother, Atta grew up shy and polite, a mama's boy. "He was so gentle," his father said. "I used to tell him, 'Toughen up, boy!'"

When such revelations are offered, storytellers seem to expect a reaction like "Aha! So that explains it!" (Indeed, in a new biography of Adolf Hitler, *The Hidden Hitler,* Lothar Machtan offers exactly that sort of explanation. He argues that many of Hitler's policies—such as the killing of longtime colleague and avowed homosexual Ernst Rohm, or even the systematic persecution and execution of gay men in concentration camps—were, in fact, prompted by a desire to conceal his own homosexuality.)

But what do such accusations actually explain? Do revelations about Hitler's or Atta's possible gay propensities raise troubling connections between homosexuality and mass murder? If so, then one would also have to conclude that the discovery of Shakespeare's "gay" sonnet explains the Bard's genius at explicating Hamlet's existential anguish, or that Michelangelo's sexuality is the decisive factor in his painting of God's touch in the Sistine Chapel.

Such revelations tell us little about the Holocaust or September 11. They do, however, address the consequences of homophobia—both official and informal—on young men who are exploring their sexual identities. What's relevant is not the possible fact of Hitler's or Atta's gayness, but the shame and fear that surround homosexuality in societies that refuse to acknowledge sexual diversity.

Even more troubling is what such speculation leaves out. What unites Atta, McVeigh, and Hitler is not their repressed sexual orientation but gender—their masculinity, their sense of masculine entitlement, and their thwarted ambitions. They accepted cultural definitions of masculinity, and needed someone to blame when they felt that they failed to measure up. (After all, being called a mama's boy, a sissy, and told to toughen up are demands for gender conformity, not matters of sexual desire.) Gender is the issue, not sexuality.

All three failed at their chosen professions. Hitler was a failed artist—indeed, he failed at just about every job he ever tried except dictator. McVeigh, a business-college dropout, found his calling in the military during the Gulf War, where his exemplary service earned him commendations; but he washed out of Green Beret training—his dream job—after only two days. And Atta was the odd man out in his family. His two sisters both became doctors—one a physician and one a university professor. His father constantly reminded him that he wanted "to hear the word 'doctor' in front of his name. We told him, your sisters are doctors and their husbands are doctors and you are the man of the family."

Atta decided to become an engineer, but his degree meant little in a country where thousands of college graduates were unable to find good jobs. After he failed to find employment in Egypt, he went to Hamburg, Germany, to study architecture. He was "meticulous, disciplined, and highly intelligent, an ordinary student, a quiet, friendly guy who was totally focused on his studies," according to another student in Hamburg.

But his ambitions were constantly undone. His only hope for a good job in Egypt was to be hired by an international firm. He applied and was continually rejected. He found work as a draftsman—highly humiliating for someone with engineering and architectural credentials and an imperious and demanding father—for a German firm involved with razing low-income Cairo neighborhoods to provide more scenic vistas for luxury tourist hotels.

Defeated, humiliated, emasculated, a disappointment to his father and a failed rival to his sisters, Atta retreated into increasingly militant Islamic theology. By the time he assumed the controls of American Airlines Flight 11, he evinced a hysteria about women. In the message he left in his abandoned rental car, he made clear what mattered to him in the end. "I don't want pregnant women or a person who is not clean to come and say good-bye to me," he wrote. "I don't want women to go to my funeral or later to my grave." Of course, Atta's body was instantly incinerated, and no burial would be likely.

The terrors of emasculation experienced by lower-middle-class men all over the world will no doubt continue, as they struggle to make a place for themselves in shrinking economies and inevitably shifting cultures. They may continue to feel a seething resentment against women, whom they perceive as stealing their rightful place at the head of the table, and against the governments that displace them. Globalization feels to them like a game of musical chairs, in which, when the music stops, all the seats are handed to others by nursemaid governments.

The events of September 11, as well as of April 19, 1995 (the Oklahoma City bombing), resulted from an increasingly common combination of factors—the massive male displacement that accompanies globalization, the spread of American consumerism, and the perceived corruption of local political elites—fused with a masculine sense of entitlement. Someone else—some "other"—had to be held responsible for the terrorists' downward mobility and failures, and the failure of their fathers to deliver their promised inheritance. The terrorists didn't just get mad. They got even.

Such themes were not lost on the disparate bands of young, white supremacists. American Aryans admired the terrorists' courage and chastised their own compatriots. "It's a disgrace that in a population of at least 150 million White/Aryan Americans, we provide so few that are willing to do the same [as the terrorists]," bemoaned Rocky Suhayda, the chairman of the American Nazi Party. "A bunch of towel head/sand niggers put our great White Movement to shame."

It is from such gendered shame that mass murderers are made.

Steven P. Schacht

Teaching about Being an Oppressor: Some Personal and Political Considerations

I believe the truth about any subject only comes when all sides of the story are put together, and all their different meanings make a new one. Each writer writes the missing parts of the other writer's story. And the whole truth is what I am after.

—Walker 1983, p. 49

Women's studies programs have been established on the vast majority of college and university campuses in the United States over the past twenty-five years. While the founding and continued existence of these programs has frequently been met with resistance, they have also realized untold successes. Women's studies programs have seriously challenged every academic discipline's conceptualizations of gender, ethnicity, class, and sexuality. These programs have also reinvigorated several fields of studies' ongoing dialogues, many of which had long since grown tired and stale. Correspondingly, it has been one of the fastest growing academic fields. In many ways, women's studies has forever changed the face of academia.

A perhaps somewhat latent but nevertheless important outcome of this transformation has been the impact that women's studies (and feminism in general) has had on people like myself. That is, being a white heterosexual[1] male from an upper middle-class background meant I was born into a social status that afforded me limitless opportunities to obtain immeasurable amounts of male prestige, privilege, power, and concordant wealth. Yet, as I enter my middle-age years (often another privileged male social status in our society) I find myself covertly and overtly rejecting

From *Men and Masculinities* 4(2), pp. 201–208; reprinted by permission of Sage Publications, Inc.

the oppressive roles a male dominated society has cast for me, and replacing them with a feminist center and personal way of being (Schacht and Ewing 1998; Schacht 2000a).

This essay explores my attempts as a white male to meaningfully contribute to the Women's Studies programs on the various campuses I have taught and to the larger feminist movement. Recognizing that I must travel a disparate path than women to realize a feminist worldview (Schacht and Ewing 1997), I similarly acknowledge that as a male (pro)feminist[2] instructor, the potential contribution I can make to women's studies is also quite different than female instructors (Schacht 2000b). The experiential knowledge I bring into my classes is very much situated in.that of an incredibly privileged societal member: I am male, white, heterosexual, and from an upper middle class background (Haraway 1988). While being privileged has significantly decreased the likelihood of me being oppressed—as defined by Young (1988), I honestly can claim no experiences of being oppressed—it has correspondingly increased the likelihood of me being an oppressor. That is, both in action and mere presence, much of my life has been spent being oppressive to others. Accordingly, much of my privilege and status has been purchased at the expense of societal subordinates, as they were the real estate and obvious requisites for me being superior and doing masculinity: it was through the humiliation and degradation of others (sometimes in the form of their bruised and bloodied bodies),[3] the resultant terror and pain in their eyes, and the typical powerlessness and helplessness of their response that I came to experience and fallaciously believe myself to be superior to so many others.

A great deal of what feminists have written about and is taught in women's studies courses, however, is about experiences of being oppressed and the unjust basis of these all too common societal realities. Since I lack any experiences of being oppressed, it would initially appear that I would have little to contribute to women's and other subordinated people's emancipation. Yet I believe that it is exactly through my experiences of being an oppressor that I can contribute to the creation of a more just world. By telling my different story of the how's and why's of being an oppressor, I hope to become a meaningful collaborator in the "whole story being written," ultimately done in hopes that new, non-oppressive stories might be envisioned and acted upon.

On Being Male and Over-Privileged

As I have written elsewhere (Schacht 2000 a & b), I increasingly try to teach my classes using a feminist pedagogy. This has meant that both the materials I use in all my courses and the way I approach the classroom has changed significantly over the past fifteen years that I have been teaching. While I have previously explored in detail how I have personally benefitted from a feminist instructional approach and students' positive responses to my attempts, I have yet to clearly consider what exactly it is that I am personally trying to accomplish as a white heterosexual male professing feminism in my classes.

There are obviously numerous ways I could answer this question. Moreover, I would guess that many of my answers would be quite consistent with what women feminist instructors hope to accomplish in their classes. Ultimately, however, I hope to teach the participants of my courses that the reason that women, people of color, the

poor, and so forth are truly disadvantaged is that certain individuals, such as myself, are truly over-privileged in our society. More specifically, combining the feminist materials I use in my classes that explore the various ways certain people are categorically oppressed and exploited with my experiences as a white male from an upper middle-class background, I attempt to share with the participants of my courses the ways in which much of the privilege that has been conferred upon me has been unearned, how I have benefitted from others' oppression, the often unjust nature of the rewards I have received, and what I am personally trying to do to change this.

Peggy McIntosh (2000) in her classic and frequently reprinted article, "White Privilege and Male Privilege," explores the numerous ways that white people enjoy unearned skin privilege. Since I frequently use this article in my classes, I believe it provides an excellent model of how I attempt to explain the oppressive basis of my being (male, in particular, as this is the primary focus of my essay) to the participants of my classes. Her essay lists numerous (although far from exhaustive) ways that her being white confers unearned privilege to her on a daily basis. As she also notes, the conditions she chooses "attach somewhat more to skin-color privilege than to class, religion, ethnic status, or geographical location" and are ones that as far as she can tell her "African American coworkers, friends, and acquaintances . . . cannot count on most of these conditions" (p. 477).

In her analysis McIntosh makes the important distinction between "positive advantages" and "negative advantages." Positive advantages are things such as adequate housing, nutrition, and health care that all people should be entitled to. As she argues, we should work to extend these types of advantages to all people and to make them the norms of a just society. Since many of these positive advantages, however, are only available to certain people, they remain an unearned and unfair privilege. On the other hand, negative types of advantage are ones that, because of certain people's blind acceptance and/or unwillingness to reject them, further reinforce the hierarchical realities of our society. These are privileges that not only subordinate and oppress people but they also often further reinforce and enhance the status of the dominant party who is exercising them.

Although I explore both types of advantages in my classes, I most strongly emphasize the negative privileges that men have bestowed upon them in our society. The following list is a sampling of status conferring conditions I discuss in my classes that through my own past experiences—as either a witness to or an active participant of—I have learned I can count on during any given day. As such, although academic research can be found in support of all these conditions, since they are based on my experiences, I accordingly prefer to list them as just that, my observations and realizations. In keeping with McIntosh's framework, these are all unearned privileges granted to me that women are largely and, in some cases, entirely denied. Because of the limits of my own partial and situated perspective, this list should obviously be considered far from exhaustive.

1. I can be reasonably sure that most jobs I might apply for I will not only have a better chance of getting them than a comparably qualified woman, but I will be paid more than a woman doing the same job. In addition to having more and better paying employment opportunities available to me than women, should I decide to venture into a traditional female vocation (e.g., nursing or schoolteacher) I can still count on being paid better and promoted more often than my female counterparts.

2. When I go to lease/buy a car or home (or to have work done on them), I can expect to not only be treated in a far more professional manner than a woman (who are often patronized in these business transactions), but in most cases, to ultimately pay less for the product or service.

3. When I read the newspaper or watch the nightly news, I can largely assume that the vast majority of the stories will be about the accomplishments of men. Moreover, throughout the media I can rest assured that most positive portrayals are about men and their importance. Conversely, when women are made visible, it typically will be in a trivializing manner; as models (sex objects) to sell some good or service, or in the form of some self-help/defective-being product all "real" women need (e.g., cosmetics and weight loss products).

4. Should I enjoy watching sports, I am virtually guaranteed that all the important, most skilled participants will also be men who are paid unbelievable sums of money to reinforce my masculine and seemingly superior sense of being. Alternatively, I am almost equally guaranteed that when women are presented at these events it most often will be in the form of them being sidelined cheerleaders for the far more important men on the field. And in the few events that women are exclusively found, they will most typically be presented in a manner that largely denigrates their skills in comparison to men's. Moreover, I am virtually guaranteed that all the sporting teams I might cheer for will have virile names to further reinforce my masculine sense of importance. Sometimes when these same names are applied to their female counterparts, one's left with quite strange results: the women's basketball team at my alma mater is called the Lady Rams.

5. If I am sexually active, even promiscuous, I can largely count on not being seen as a slut, a whore, or a prostitute. To the contrary, most typically I will be held in high regard, perhaps seen as a "stud," with such behavior attesting to my superior sense of being.

6. I can largely count on clothes fashions that ensure my mobility and reinforce my status as an important person whereas women often are expected to wear restrictive clothing de-

signed to objectify their status as a subordinate in our society. Moreover, since women's fashions are largely designed by men, I am virtually assured that the fashions available to me will both stay in style longer and cost less money.

7. I am not expected to spend my discretionary income on makeup, skin lotion, and age defying potions to cover my flaws, nor am I expected to spend money on dieting products (unless severely obese), all so I can be seen as attractive and socially acceptable.

8. If I am married or even cohabiting, I can count on my "wife" doing most of the housework and being responsible for most of the childcare should we have children, regardless of whether she works or not.

9. Should my "wife" unexpectedly become pregnant—or for that matter, any women I might have sex with—I can rest assured that it will be almost entirely be seen as her fault and responsibility to take care of, especially if the pregnancy is not desired on my part.

10. Should I decide to rape a woman in my quest to feel superior, I can rest assured that it is highly unlikely that she will report my misogynist criminal activity to the police. If, however, I should incur the unfortunate charge of rape, unlike any other crime, I can count on my accuser's life and status to simultaneously be on trial to determine if she is worthy of being named my "victim."

11. To demonstrate my superiority, should I feel the need to physically assault my "wife" (or other women that I might purport to love), even to the point I might kill her, I can be reasonably assured that I will largely not be held accountable for my actions. Conversely, should a woman partake in these same actions against me, especially murder, I can count on her being held far more accountable for her actions.

12. Moreover, should abusing my "wife" not be sufficient, I can additionally turn my perversely exercised authority on my children.

Should I get caught, unless it is someone else's child, I know that the most typical punishment will be for my children to be removed from my home, and that my "wife" will also largely be held accountable and blamed for my actions; thus, diffusing some, if not most of my responsibility for what I have done.

13. Should I decide to divorce my spouse, or have this decision forced upon me, if children are involved, I can count on her being the primary caretaker of them (unless I should desire otherwise), and to correspondingly experience an increase in my standard of living often with the full knowledge that hers will significantly drop.

14. Should I not have a woman immediately at my disposal to denigrate and further support my false notions of superiority, I can easily and cheaply go out and purchase or rent pornographic depictions to serve as a surrogate for this purpose. If this does not sufficiently reinforce my feelings of superiority, I can go to a strip club, a peep show, or a mud wrestling/wet T-shirt contest to have live depictions of female subordination (in the flesh), or even better yet, go out and purchase a prostitute for these same purposes.

15. When venturing out in public I can reasonably rest assured that I will not be sexually harassed or sexually assaulted. Conversely, should I come across a woman in these same contexts, I can largely count on a simple terrorist/manly man stare on my part to make her feel uncomfortable in my presence. The same also holds true for most public drinking places. If I am especially brave, I can expose myself to a woman or masturbate in front of her to even further reinforce my masculinity, and forever implant this image into her head, yet largely count on not getting caught or punished.

16. Should I have specialized medical problems, I can rest assured that the majority of research dollars being spent are to find cures for male health problems using largely male

research subjects (an extreme example of this would be Viagra, which was developed for male impotence that has promising yet unproven usage possibilities for female sexual dysfunction).

17. Should I feel the desire to search for positive role models in positions of authority, nearly everywhere I look I can easily find a male to fill this need. If my identification with these specific male role models is not sufficient to bolster my perceived self-importance, I can easily further reinforce this perception by largely seeing most women in subordinate positions throughout our society.

18. When I listen to my radio or watch music videos, I can be assured that most of the performers I will listen to will be male who often explicitly denigrate women in the verses of their songs. Moreover, most of the few female artists who make it on the airways will be conversely singing songs that reinforce male dominance and female subordination.

19. When attending school I can often count on the teacher (he or she) to perceive my inquiries and presence as more important than the females that are in attendance.

20. At the schools I attend I can count on more monies being spent on the activities men traditionally partake in, especially sports (even with the passage of Title IX over 25 years ago), and in general have a wider array of activities available for me to participate in.

21. I can also be pretty confident that my parents will be supportive of a wider array of activities for me to partake in, spend more money on them, and give me more freedom to explore my surroundings.

22. When undertaking conversations with women, I can largely count on my voice being heard more often by both of us, my comments to be more validated, and should I feel the need to interrupt a woman while she is talking (further reinforcing the importance of my voice) I will in all likelihood be generously forgiven for my transgression.

23. Should I ever feel the need to verbally denigrate someone to boost my masculinity and false sense of being, I will have available an endless cache of derogatory terms that refer explicitly to women to accomplish this task. Conversely, the few derogatory terms that refer explicitly to my male gender I can often use in a positive, affirming manner: "Scott, you're such a 'dick head' or 'prick,' buddy."

24. If I so choose, I can count on numerous all male contexts to be available to me for my pleasure and affirmation. And although there are a few exclusive female settings (some auxiliaries to men's groups), I can still count on the ones I might attend to almost always be perceived as more important replete with activities to support this assertion.

25. Finally, should I choose *not to partake* in any of the above conditions, the mere fact that I can make this choice is in itself indicative and quite telling of the privilege upon which it is predicated. Moreover, I can still count on other men partaking in them, which ultimately still maintains my superior status in society. All that is expected of me is to remain silent and I, too, will cash in on my patriarchal dividend.

I am guessing that it is quite easy for the reader to see the unjust nature of each of the above conditions. Although a handful of participants in my classes will sometimes challenge their prevalence and/or applicability to their own experiences, most easily ascertain the unjust nature of these and numerous other privileges. Once each of these unfair negative advantages are presented and discussed, I always reserve a significant amount of class time to discuss what each of us might do to resist their occurrence. For the female participants of my classes this is usually accomplished by exploring the various attitudes women hold—internalized oppression—and corresponding behaviors that women often undertake to support such outcomes. For the male participants this usually involves me exploring ways men might release the firm grip they have on maintaining their existence—quite literally in some cases—and coming up with more just approaches to life.

Release the Penis and Let the Blood Flow to the Brain. Isn't It Amazing the Things One Might Ascertain?

We live in a society where ignorance truly is bliss, especially for those with unearned male privilege and status, which in turn often provides men with an excuse to deny the existence of the very real and harmful sexist hierarchical realities that surround us and the active role men must play in their maintenance. While some men are willing to admit that women are disadvantaged in our society, very few men are willing to acknowledge that they are over-privileged (McIntosh 2000). After all, to actually do so would mean that men would not only have to admit the unearned and unjust basis of their advantage but perhaps even personally change and give up some of their privilege. In the highly competitive world we live in giving up any advantages—earned or unearned—one might have in the game of life would seem foolish at best to the vast majority of men.

And yet, as a partner, a mother, a sister, a daughter or just a friend, most men have significant women in their lives that they deeply care about, love, and sometimes even view as equals. I believe herein lies the true promise of the feminist pedagogy that I bring to my classes. Instead of abstractly talking about male dominance and women's subordination, I attempt to put a face on oppression. I offer my own experiences of doing unearned male privilege, and recognize the harm it inflicted on others, both female and male. Often courageous male students will also offer their experiences of doing male dominance. In all classroom discussions female students freely and frequently offer their experiences of being oppressed by men. Combined with constant reminders by me that the "who's" and "what's" we are talking about are our partners, parents, sib-

lings, children, friends, and each of us, emerges lived images of the oppressor and oppressed. These "faces" of sort demonstrate how all too common oppression is, how harmful it is for so many, and why each of us—women and men—should join together to bring about its end.

By making men aware of the unearned advantages that society confers upon them, coupled with the knowledge of how this is oppressive to the significant women in their lives, many men are left in an ideological bind: how can they personally express concern and respect for the welfare of these women all the while supporting realities that cause women's oppression in larger societal settings? While I realistically have no meaningful way to measure the answer to this question, I have witnessed many men (although admittedly not all) in my classes very much loosen the otherwise firm grip they have on justifying and living the male privilege that society so unjustly confers upon them. A world without unearned male privilege would be a significant step in the pursuit of a non-oppressive, egalitarian future.

Notes

1. While in my classes and personal interactions I increasingly refer to and identify myself as queer and/or simply sexual, since my partner is a woman, and acknowledging that most people still view and treat me as "heterosexual," I am using the term accordingly here and throughout this essay.

2. I use "(pro)feminist" as an inclusive way to recognize both men who identify as profeminist and a perhaps equal number of other men who think of themselves as male feminists.

3. The ethos of the various male groups I belonged to prescribed that one should never be violent towards a woman. Accordingly, although I have severely injured innumerable men, I never have been physically violent towards a women. Nevertheless, when I was younger I often did use economic resources to be controlling and abusive to many women.

References

Haraway, Donna. 1988. "Situated Knowledges: The Science Question in Feminism and the Privilege of a Partial Perspective." *Feminist Studies* 14: 575–591.

McIntosh, Peggy. 2000. "White Privilege and Male Privilege: A Personal Account of Coming to See Correspondences through Work in Women's Studies." Pp. 475–485 in *The Social Construction of Difference and Inequality,* edited by Tracy E. Ore. Mountain View, CA: Mayfield.

Schacht, Steven P. 2000a. "*Paris Is Burning:* How Society's Stratification Systems Makes Drag Queens of Us All." *Race, Gender & Class* 7(1): 147–166.

Schacht, Steven P. 2000b. "The Promise of Men Using a Feminist Pedagogy: The Possibilities and Limits of a Partial and Situated Perspective." Unpublished manuscript.

Schacht, Steven P. and Doris Ewing. 1997. "The Many Paths of Feminism: Can Men Travel Any of Them?" *Journal of Gender Studies* 6(2): 159–176.

Schacht, Steven P. and Doris Ewing. 1998. *Feminism and Men: Reconstructing Gender Relations.* New York: New York University Press.

Walker, Alice. 1983. *In Search of Our Mothers' Garden.* New York: Harcourt-Brace-Jovanovich.

Young, Iris. 1988. "The Five Faces Of Oppression." *Philosophical Forum* 19:270–90.

PART TWO

Boyhood

"**O**ne is not born, but rather becomes, a woman," wrote the French feminist thinker Simone de Beauvoir in her ground-breaking book *The Second Sex* (New York: Vintage, 1958). The same is true for men. And the social processes by which boys become men are complex and important. How does early childhood socialization differ for boys and girls? What specific traits are emphasized for boys that mark their socialization as different? What types of institutional arrangements reinforce those traits? How do the various institutions in which boys find themselves—school, family, and circles of friends—influence their development? What of the special institutions that promote "boys' life" or an adolescent male subculture?

During childhood and adolescence, masculinity becomes a central theme in a boy's life. *New York Times* editor A. M. Rosenthal put the dilemma this way: "So there I was, 13 years old, the smallest boy in my freshman class at DeWitt Clinton High School, smoking a White Owl cigar. I was not only little, but I did not have longies—long trousers—and was still in knickerbockers. Obviously, I had to do something to project my fierce sense of manhood" (*New York Times*, 26 April 1987). That the assertion of manhood is part of a boy's natural development is sug-

gested by Roger Brown, in his textbook *Social Psychology* (New York: Free Press, 1965, p. 161):

> In the United States, a real boy climbs trees, disdains girls, dirties his knees, plays with soldiers, and takes blue for his favorite color. When they go to school, real boys prefer manual training, gym, and arithmetic. In college the boys smoke pipes, drink beer, and major in engineering or physics. The real boy matures into a "man's man" who plays poker, goes hunting, drinks brandy, and dies in the war.

The articles in this section address the question of how boys develop, focusing on the institutions that shape boys' lives. Ellen Jordan and Angela Cowan describe the gender socialization of schooling, both inside and outside the classroom. Ritch Savin-Williams and Ann Ferguson examine issues of boys' development from the perspectives of different groups of boys—those who feel different and those who are made to feel different. Anyone walking down any hallway in middle school or high school in the United States would probably tell you that the most common put down is "That's so gay." Homophobia is one of the founding principles of masculinity, as the articles by C. J. Pascoe and Daniel Farr detail. Asked recently about why he is constantly rapping about "faggots," one of our favorite contemporary gender theorists, Eminem, said:

> The lowest degrading thing you can say to a man when you're battling him is to call him a faggot and try to take away his manhood. Call him a sissy, call him a punk. "Faggot" to me doesn't necessarily mean gay people. "Faggot" to me just means taking away your manhood.

The association between sexual orientation and gender begins early in boys' lives and continues as they grow to be men.

Photo by Mike Messner.

Ellen Jordan

Angela Cowan

Warrior Narratives in the Kindergarten Classroom: Renegotiating the Social Contract?

Since the beginning of second wave feminism, the separation between the public (masculine) world of politics and the economy and the private (feminine) world of the family and personal life has been seen as highly significant in establishing gender difference and inequality (Eisenstein 1984). Twenty years of feminist research and speculation have refined our understanding of this divide and how it has been developed and reproduced. One particularly striking and influential account is that given by Carole Pateman in her book *The Sexual Contract* (1988).

Pateman's broad argument is that in the modern world, the world since the Enlightenment, a "civil society" has been established. In this civil society, patriarchy has been replaced by a fratriarchy, which is equally male and oppressive of women. Men now rule not as fathers but as brothers, able to compete with one another, but presenting a united front against those outside the group. It is the brothers who control the public world of the state, politics, and the economy. Women have been given token access to this world because the discourses of liberty and universalism made this difficult to refuse, but to take part they must conform to the rules established to suit the brothers.

This public world in which the brothers operate together is conceptualized as separate from

From *Gender & Society* 9(6): 727–743. Copyright © 1995 by Sage Publications. Reprinted by permission of Sage Publications, Inc.

the personal and emotional. One is a realm where there is little physicality—everything is done rationally, bureaucratically, according to contracts that the brothers accept as legitimate. Violence in this realm is severely controlled by agents of the state, except that the brothers are sometimes called upon for the supreme sacrifice of dying to preserve freedom. The social contract redefines the brawling and feuding long seen as essential characteristics of masculinity as deviant, even criminal, while the rest of physicality—sexuality, reproduction of the body, daily and intergenerationally—is left in the private sphere. Pateman quotes Robert Unger, "The dichotomy of the public and private life is still another corollary of the separation of understanding and desire. . . . When reasoning, [men] belong to a public world. . . . When desiring, however, men are private beings" (Pateman 1989, 48).

This is now widely accepted as the way men understand and experience their world. On the other hand, almost no attempt has been made to look at how it is that they take these views on board, or why the public/private divide is so much more deeply entrenched in their lived experience than in women's. This article looks at one strand in the complex web of experiences through which this is achieved. A major site where this occurs is the school, one of the institutions particularly characteristic of the civil society that emerged with the Enlightenment (Foucault 1980, 55–57). The school does not deliberately condition boys and not girls into this dichotomy, but it is, we believe, a site where what Giddens (1984, 10–13) has called a cycle of practice introduces little boys to the public/private division.

The article is based on weekly observations in a kindergarten classroom. We examine what happens in the early days of school when the children encounter the expectations of the school with their already established conceptions of gender. The early months of school are a period when a great deal of negotiating between the children's personal agendas and the teacher's expectations has to take place, where a great deal of what Genovese (1972) has described as accommodation and resistance must be involved.

In this article, we focus on a particular contest, which, although never specifically stated, is central to the children's accommodation to school: little boys' determination to explore certain narratives of masculinity with which they are already familiar—guns, fighting, fast cars—and the teacher's attempts to outlaw their importation into the classroom setting. We argue that what occurs is a contest between two definitions of masculinity: what we have chosen to call "warrior narratives" and the discourses of civil society—rationality, responsibility, and decorum—that are the basis of school discipline.

By "warrior narratives," we mean narratives that assume that violence is legitimate and justified when it occurs within a struggle between good and evil. There is a tradition of such narratives, stretching from Hercules and Beowulf to Superman and Dirty Harry, where the male is depicted as the warrior, the knight-errant, the superhero, the good guy (usually called a "goody" by Australian children), often supported by brothers in arms, and always opposed to some evil figure, such as a monster, a giant, a villain, a criminal, or, very simply, in Australian parlance, a "baddy." There is also a connection, it is now often suggested, between these narratives and the activity that has come to epitomize the physical expression of masculinity in the modern era: sport (Duthie 1980, 91–94; Crosset 1990; Messner 1992, 15). It is as sport that the physicality and desire usually lived out in the private sphere are permit-

ted a ritualized public presence. Even though the violence once characteristic of the warrior has, in civil society and as part of the social contract, become the prerogative of the state, it can still be re-enacted symbolically in countless sporting encounters. The mantle of the warrior is inherited by the sportsman.

The school discipline that seeks to outlaw these narratives is, we would suggest, very much a product of modernity. Bowles and Gintis have argued that "the structure of social relations in education not only inures the student to the discipline of the work place, but develops the types of personal demeanor, modes of self-presentation, self-image, and social-class identifications which are the crucial ingredients of job adequacy" (1976, 131). The school is seeking to introduce the children to the behavior appropriate to the civil society of the modern world.

An accommodation does eventually take place, this article argues, through a recognition of the split between the public and the private. Most boys learn to accept that the way to power and respectability is through acceptance of the conventions of civil society. They also learn that warrior narratives are not a part of this world; they can only be experienced symbolically as fantasy or sport. The outcome, we will suggest, is that little boys learn that these narratives must be left behind in the private world of desire when they participate in the public world of reason.

The Study

The school where this study was conducted serves an old-established suburb in a country town in New South Wales, Australia. The children are predominantly Australian born and English speaking, but come from socioeconomic backgrounds ranging from professional to welfare recipient. We carried out this research in a classroom run by a teacher who is widely acknowledged as one of the finest and most successful kindergarten teachers in our region. She is an admired practitioner of free play, process writing, and creativity. There was no gender definition of games in her classroom. Groups composed of both girls and boys had turns at playing in the Doll Corner, in the Construction Area, and on the Car Mat.

The research method used was nonparticipant observation, the classic mode for the sociological study of children in schools (Burgess 1984; Thorne 1986; Goodenough 1987). The group of children described came to school for the first time in February 1993. The observation sessions began within a fortnight of the children entering school and were conducted during "free activity" time, a period lasting for about an hour. At first we observed twice a week, but then settled to a weekly visit, although there were some weeks when it was inconvenient for the teacher to accommodate an observer.

The observation was noninteractive. The observer stationed herself as unobtrusively as possible, usually seated on a kindergarten-sized chair, near one of the play stations. She made pencil notes of events, with particular attention to accurately recording the words spoken by the children, and wrote up detailed narratives from the notes, supplemented by memory, on reaching home. She discouraged attention from the children by rising and leaving the area if she was drawn by them into any interaction.

This project thus employed a methodology that was ethnographic and open-ended. It was nevertheless guided by certain theories, drawn from the work on gender of Jean Anyon, Barrie Thorne, and R. W. Connell, of the nature of social interaction and its part in creating personal identity and in reproducing the structures of a society.

Anyon has adapted the conceptions of accommodation and resistance developed by Genovese (1972) to understanding how women live with gender. Genovese argued that slaves in the American South accommodated to their contradictory situation by using certain of its aspects, for example, exposure to the Christian religion, to validate a sense of self-worth and dignity. Christian beliefs then allowed them to take a critical view of slavery, which in turn legitimated certain forms of resistance (Anyon 1983, 21). Anyon lists

a variety of ways in which women accommodate to and resist prescriptions of appropriate feminine behavior, arguing for a significant level of choice and agency (Anyon 1983, 23–26).

Thorne argues that the processes of social life, the form and nature of the interactions, as well as the choices of the actors, should be the object of analysis. She writes, "In this book I begin not with individuals, although they certainly appear in the account, but with *group life*—with social relations, the organization and meanings of social situations, the collective practices through which children and adults create and recreate gender in their daily interactions" (1993, 4).

These daily interactions, Connell (1987, 139–141) has suggested, mesh to form what Giddens (1984, 10–13) has called "cyclical practices." Daily interactions are neither random nor specific to particular locations. They are repeated and recreated in similar settings throughout a society. Similar needs recur, similar discourses are available, and so similar solutions to problems are adopted; thus, actions performed and discourses adopted to achieve particular ends in particular situations have the unintended consequence of producing uniformities of gendered behavior in individuals.

In looking at the patterns of accommodation and resistance that emerge when the warrior narratives that little boys have adapted from television encounter the discipline of the classroom, we believe we have uncovered one of the cyclical practices of modernity that reveal the social contract to these boys.

Warrior Narratives in the Doll Corner

In the first weeks of the children's school experience, the Doll Corner was the area where the most elaborate acting out of warrior narratives was observed. The Doll Corner in this classroom was a small room with a door with a glass panel opening off the main area. Its furnishings—stove, sink, dolls' cots, and so on—were an attempt at a literal re-creation of a domestic setting, revealing the school's definition of children's play as a preparation for adult life. It was an area where the acting out of "pretend" games was acceptable.

Much of the boys' play in the area was domestic:

> Jimmy and Tyler were jointly ironing a tablecloth. "Look at the sheet is burnt, I've burnt it," declared Tyler, waving the toy iron above his head. "I'm telling Mrs. Sandison," said Jimmy worriedly. "No, I tricked you. It's not really burnt. See," explained Tyler, showing Jimmy the black pattern on the cloth. (February 23, 1993)

> "Where is the baby, the baby boy?" Justin asked, as he helped Harvey and Malcolm settle some restless teddy babies. "Give them some potion." Justin pretended to force feed a teddy, asking "Do you want to drink this potion?" (March 4, 1993)

On the other hand, there were attempts from the beginning by some of the boys and one of the girls to use this area for nondomestic games and, in the case of the boys, for games based on warrior narratives, involving fighting, destruction, goodies, and baddies.

> The play started off quietly, Winston cuddled a teddy bear, then settled it in a bed. Just as Winston tucked in his bear, Mac snatched the teddy out of bed and swung it around his head in circles. "Don't hurt him, give him back," pleaded Winston, trying vainly to retrieve the teddy. The two boys were circling the small table in the center of the room. As he ran, Mac started to karate chop the teddy on the arm, and then threw it on the floor and jumped on it. He then snatched up a plastic knife, "This is a sword. Ted is dead. They all are." He sliced the knife across the teddy's tummy, repeating the action on the bodies of two stuffed dogs. Winston grabbed the two dogs, and with a dog in each hand, staged a dog fight. "They are alive again." (February 10, 1993)

> Three boys were busily stuffing teddies into the cupboard through the sink opening. "They're in jail. They can't escape," said Malcolm. "Let's pour water over them." "Don't do that. It'll hurt them," shouted Winston, rushing into the

Doll Corner. "Go away, Winston. You're not in our group," said Malcolm. (February 12, 1993)

The boys even imported goodies and baddies into a classic ghost scenario initiated by one of the girls:

> "I'm the father," Tyler declared. "I'm the mother," said Alanna. "Let's pretend it's a stormy night and I'm afraid. Let's pretend a ghost has come to steal the dog." Tyler nodded and placed the sheet over his head. Tyler moaned, "ooooOOOOOOOOAHHHH!!!" and moved his outstretched arms toward Alanna. Jamie joined the game and grabbed a sheet from the doll's cradle, "I'm the goody ghost." "So am I," said Tyler. They giggled and wrestled each other to the floor. "No! you're the baddy ghost," said Jamie. Meanwhile, Alanna was making ghostly noises and moving around the boys. "Did you like the game? Let's play it again," she suggested. (February 23, 1993)

In the first two incidents, there was some conflict between the narratives being invoked by Winston and those used by the other boys. For Winston, the stuffed toys were the weak whom he must protect knight-errant style. For the other boys, they could be set up as the baddies whom it was legitimate for the hero to attack. Both were versions of a warrior narrative.

The gender difference in the use of these narratives has been noted by a number of observers (Paley 1984; Clark 1989, 250–252; Thorne 1993, 98–99). Whereas even the most timid, least physically aggressive boys—Winston in this study is typical—are drawn to identifying with the heroes of these narratives, girls show almost no interest in them at this early age. The strong-willed and assertive girls in our study, as in others (Clark 1990, 83–84; Walkerdine 1990, 10–12), sought power by commandeering the role of mother, teacher, or shopkeeper, while even the highly imaginative Alanna, although she enlivened the more mundane fantasies of the other children with ghosts, old widow women, and magical mirrors, seems not to have been attracted by warrior heroes.[1]

Warrior narratives, it would seem, have a powerful attraction for little boys, which they lack for little girls. Why and how this occurs remains unexplored in early childhood research, perhaps because data for such an explanation are not available to those doing research in institutional settings. Those undertaking ethnographic research in preschools find the warrior narratives already in possession in these sites (Paley 1984, 70–73, 116; Davies 1989, 91–92). In this research, gender difference in the appeal of warrior narratives has to be taken as a given—the data gathered are not suitable for constructing theories of origins; thus, the task of determining an explanation would seem to lie within the province of those investigating and theorizing gender differentiation during infancy, and perhaps, specifically, of those working in the tradition of feminist psychoanalysis pioneered by Dinnerstein (1977) and Chodorow (1978). Nevertheless, even though the cause may remain obscure, there can be little argument that in the English-speaking world for at least the last hundred years—think of Tom Sawyer playing Robin Hood and the pirates and Indians in J. M. Barrie's *Peter Pan*—boys have built these narratives into their conceptions of the masculine.

Accommodation through *Bricolage*

The school classroom, even one as committed to freedom and self-actualization as this, makes little provision for the enactment of these narratives. The classroom equipment invites children to play house, farm, and shop, to construct cities and roads, and to journey through them with toy cars, but there is no overt invitation to explore warrior narratives.

In the first few weeks of school, the little boys un-self-consciously set about redressing this omission. The method they used was what is known as *bricolage*—the transformation of objects from one use to another for symbolic purposes (Hebdige 1979, 103). The first site was the Doll Corner. Our records for the early weeks contain a number of examples of boys rejecting the usages ascribed to the various Doll Corner objects by the teacher and by the makers of equipment and as-

signing a different meaning to them. This became evident very early with their use of the toy baby carriages (called "prams" in Australia). For the girls, the baby carriages were just that, but for many of the boys they very quickly became surrogate cars:

> Mac threw a doll into the largest pram in the Doll Corner. He walked the pram out past a group of his friends who were playing "crashes" on the Car Mat. Three of the five boys turned and watched him wheeling the pram toward the classroom door. Mac performed a sharp three-point turn; raced his pram past the Car Mat group, striking one boy on the head with the pram wheel. (February 10, 1993)

> "Brrrrmmmmmm, brrrrrmmmmm," Tyler's revving engine noises grew louder as he rocked the pram back and forth with sharp jerking movements. The engine noise grew quieter as he left the Doll Corner and wheeled the pram around the classroom. He started to run with the pram when the teacher could not observe him. (March 23, 1993)

The boys transformed other objects into masculine appurtenances: knives and tongs became weapons, the dolls' beds became boats, and so on.

> Mac tried to engage Winston in a sword fight using Doll Corner plastic knives. Winston backed away, but Mac persisted. Winston took a knife but continued to back away from Mac. He then put down the knife, and ran away half-screaming (semi-seriously, unsure of the situation) for his teacher. (February 10, 1993)

In the literature on youth subcultures, bricolage is seen as a characteristic of modes of resistance. Hebdige writes:

> It is through the distinctive rituals of consumption, through style, that the subculture at once reveals its "secret" identity and communicates its forbidden meanings. It is predominantly the way commodities are *used* in subculture which mark the subculture off from more orthodox cultural formations. . . . The concept of *bricolage* can be used to explain how subcultural styles are constructed. (1979, 103)

In these early weeks, however, the boys did not appear to be aware that they were doing anything more than establishing an accommodation between their needs and the classroom environment.

This mode of accommodation was rejected by the teacher, however, who practiced a gentle, but steady, discouragement of such bricolage. Even though the objects in this space are not really irons, beds, and cooking pots, she made strong efforts to assert their cultural meaning, instructing the children in the "proper" use of the equipment and attempting to control their behavior by questions like "Would you do that with a tea towel in your house?" "Cats never climb up on the benches in *my* house." It was thus impressed upon the children that warrior narratives were inappropriate in this space.

The children, our observations suggest, accepted her guidance, and we found no importation of warrior narratives into the Doll Corner after the first few weeks. There were a number of elaborate and exciting narratives devised, but they were all to some degree related to the domestic environment. For example, on April 20, Justin and Nigel used one of the baby carriages as a four-wheel drive, packed it with equipment and went off for a camping trip, setting out a picnic with Doll Corner tablecloths, knives, forks, and plates when they arrived. On May 18, Matthew, Malcolm, Nigel, and Jonathan were dogs being fed in the Doll Corner. They then complained of the flies, and Jonathan picked up the toy telephone and said, "Flycatcher! Flycatcher! Come and catch some flies. They are everywhere." On June 1, the following was recorded:

> "We don't want our nappies [diapers] changed," Aaron informed Celia, the mum in the game. "I'm poohing all over your clothes mum," Mac declared, as he grunted and positioned himself over the dress-up box. Celia cast a despairing glance in Mac's direction, and went on dressing a doll. "I am too; poohing all over your clothes mum," said Aaron. "Now mum will have to clean it all up and change my nappy," he informed Mac, giggling. He turned to the dad [Nigel], and said in a baby voice,

> "Goo-goo; give him [Mac] the feather duster." "No! give him the feather duster; he did the longest one all over the clothes," Mac said to Nigel. (June 1, 1993)

Although exciting and imaginative games continued, the bricolage virtually disappeared from the Doll Corner. The intention of the designer of the Doll Corner equipment was increasingly respected. Food for the camping trip was bought from the shop the teacher had set up and consumed using the Doll Corner equipment. The space invaded by flies was a domestic space, and appropriate means, calling in expert help by telephone, were used to deal with the problem. Chairs and tables were chairs and tables, clothes were clothes and could be fouled by appropriate inhabitants of a domestic space, babies. Only the baby carriages continued to have an ambiguous status, to maintain the ability to be transformed into vehicles of other kinds.

The warrior narratives—sword play, baddies in jail, pirates, and so on—did not vanish from the boys' imaginative world, but, as the later observations show, the site gradually moved from the Doll Corner to the Construction Area and the Car Mat. By the third week in March (that is, after about six weeks at school), the observer noticed the boys consistently using the construction toys to develop these narratives. The bricolage was now restricted to the more amorphously defined construction materials.

> Tyler was busy constructing an object out of five pieces of plastic straw (clever sticks). "This is a water pistol. Everyone's gonna get wet," he cried as he moved into the Doll Corner pretending to wet people. The game shifted to guns and bullets between Tyler and two other boys. "I've got a bigger gun," Roger said, showing off his square block object. "Mine's more longer. Ehehehehehehehe, got you," Winston yelled to Roger, brandishing a plastic straw gun. "I'll kill your gun," Mac said, pushing Winston's gun away. "No Mac. You broke it. No," cried Winston. (March 23, 1993)

> Two of the boys picked up swords made out of blue- and red-colored plastic squares they had

displayed on the cupboard. "This is my sword," Jamie explained to Tyler. "My jumper [sweater] holds it in. Whichever color is at the bottom, well that's the color it shoots out. Whoever is bad, we shoot with power out of it." "Come on Tyler," he went on. "Get your sword. Let's go get some baddies." (March 30, 1993)

The toy cars on the Car Mat were also pressed into the service of warrior narratives:

> Justin, Brendan, and Jonathan were busy on the Car Mat. The game involved police cars that were chasing baddies who had drunk "too much beers." Justin explained to Jonathan why his car had the word "DOG" written on the front. "These are different police cars, for catching robbers taking money." (March 4, 1993)
>
> Three boys, Harvey, Maurice, and Marshall, were on the Car Mat. "Here comes the baddies," Harvey shouted, spinning a toy car around the mat. "Crasssshhhhh everywhere." He crashed his car into the other boys' cars and they responded with laughter. "I killed a baddie everyone," said Maurice, crashing his cars into another group of cars. (May 24, 1993)

A new accommodation was being proposed by the boys, a new adaptation of classroom materials to the needs of their warrior narratives.

Classroom Rules and Resistance

Once again the teacher would not accept the accommodation proposed. Warrior narratives provoked what she considered inappropriate public behavior in the miniature civil society of her classroom. Her aim was to create a "free" environment where children could work independently, learn at their own pace, and explore their own interests, but creating such an environment involved its own form of social contract, its own version of the state's appropriation of violence. From the very first day, she began to establish a series of classroom rules that imposed constraints on violent or disruptive activity.

The belief underlying her practice was that firmly established classroom rules make genuine free play possible, rather than restricting the range

of play opportunities. Her emphasis on "proper" use of equipment was intended to stop it being damaged and consequently withdrawn from use. She had rules of "no running" and "no shouting" that allowed children to work and play safely on the floor of the classroom, even though other children were using equipment or toys that demanded movement, and ensured that the noise level was low enough for children to talk at length to one another as part of their games.

One of the outcomes of these rules was the virtual outlawing of a whole series of games that groups of children usually want to initiate when they are playing together, games of speed and body contact, of gross motor self-expression and skill. This prohibition affected both girls and boys and was justified by setting up a version of public and private spaces: The classroom was not the proper place for such activities, they "belong" in the playground.[2] The combined experience of many teachers has shown that it is almost impossible for children to play games involving car crashes and guns without violating these rules; therefore, in this classroom, as in many others (Paley 1984, 71, 116), these games were in effect banned.

These rules were then policed by the children themselves, as the following interchange shows:

> "Eeeeeheeeeeeheeeeh!" Tyler leapt about the room. A couple of girls were saying, "Stop it Tyler" but he persisted. Jane warned, "You're not allowed to have guns." Tyler responded saying, "It's not a gun. It's a water pistol, and that's not a gun." "Not allowed to have water pistol guns," Tony reiterated to Tyler. "Yes, it's a water pistol," shouted Tyler. Jane informed the teacher, who responded stating, "NO GUNS, even if they are water pistols." Tyler made a spear out of Clever Sticks, straight after the banning of gun play. (March 23, 1993)

The boys, however, were not prepared to abandon their warrior narratives. Unlike gross motor activities such as wrestling and football, they were not prepared to see them relegated to the playground, but the limitations on their expression and the teacher disapproval they evoked led the boys to explore them surreptitiously; they found ways of introducing them that did not violate rules about running and shouting.

As time passed, the games became less visible. The warrior narratives were not so much acted out as talked through, using the toy cars and the construction materials as a prompt and a basis:

> Tyler was showing his plastic straw construction to Luke. "This is a Samurai Man and this is his hat. A Samurai Man fights in Japan and they fight with the Ninja. The bad guys who use cannons and guns. My Samurai is captain of the Samurai and he is going to kill the sergeant of the bad guys. He is going to sneak up on him with a knife and kill him." (June 1, 1993)

> Malcolm and Aaron had built boats with Lego blocks and were explaining the various components to Roger. "This ship can go faster," Malcolm explained. "He [a plastic man] is the boss of the ship. Mine is a goody boat. They are not baddies." "Mine's a steam shovel boat. It has wheels," said Aaron. "There it goes in the river and it has to go to a big shed where all the steam shovels are stopping." (June 11, 1993)

It also became apparent that there was something covert about this play. The cars were crashed quietly. The guns were being transformed into water pistols. Swords were concealed under jumpers and only used when the teacher's back was turned. When the constructed objects were displayed to the class, their potential as players in a fighting game was concealed under a more mundane description. For example:

> Prior to the free play, the children were taking turns to explain the Clever Stick and Lego Block constructions they had made the previous afternoon. I listened to Tyler describe his Lego robot to the class: "This is a transformer robot. It can do things and turn into everything." During free play, Tyler played with the same robot explaining its capacities to Winston: "This is a terminator ship. It can kill. It can turn into a robot and the top pops off." (March 23, 1993)

Children even protested to one another that they were not making weapons, "This isn't a gun, it's

a lookout." "This isn't a place for bullets, it's for petrol."

The warrior narratives, it would seem, went underground and became part of a "deviant" masculine subculture with the characteristic "secret" identity and hidden meanings (Hebdige 1979, 103). The boys were no longer seeking accommodation but practicing hidden resistance. The classroom, they were learning, was not a place where it was acceptable to explore their gender identity through fantasy.

This, however, was a message that only the boys were receiving. The girls' gender-specific fantasies (Paley 1984, 106–108; Davies 1989, 118–122) of nurturing and self-display—mothers, nurses, brides, princesses—were accommodated easily within the classroom. They could be played out without contravening the rules of the miniature civil society. Although certain delightful activities—eating, running, hugging, and kissing (Best 1983, 110)—might be excluded from this public sphere, they were not ones by means of which their femininity, and thus their subjectivity, their conception of the self, was defined.

Masculinity, the School Regime, and the Social Contract

We suggest that this conflict between warrior narratives and school rules is likely to form part of the experience of most boys growing up in the industrialized world. The commitment to such narratives was not only nearly 100 percent among the boys we observed, but similar commitment is, as was argued above, common in other sites. On the other hand, the pressure to preserve a decorous classroom is strong in all teachers (with the possible exception of those teaching in "alternative" schools) and has been since the beginnings of compulsory education. Indeed, it is only in classrooms where there is the balance of freedom and constraint we observed that such narratives are likely to surface at all. In more formal situations, they would be defined as deviant and forced underground from the boys' first entry into school.

If this is a widely recurring pattern, the question then arises: Is it of little significance or is it what Giddens (1984, 10–3) would call one of the "cyclical practices" that reproduce the structures of our society? The answer really depends on how little boys "read" the outlawing of their warrior narratives. If they see it as simply one of the broad constraints of school against which they are continually negotiating, then perhaps it has no significance. If, on the other hand, it has in their minds a crucial connection to the definition of gender, to the creation of their own masculine identity, to where they position particular sites and practices on a masculine to feminine continuum, then the ostracism of warrior narratives may mean that they define the school environment as feminine.

There is considerable evidence that some primary school children do in fact make this categorization (Best 1983, 14–15; Brophy 1985, 118; Clark 1990, 36), and we suggest here that the outlawry of the masculine narrative contributes to this. Research by Willis (1977) and Walker (1988) in high schools has revealed a culture of resistance based on definitions of masculinity as *antagonistic* to the demands of the school, which are construed as feminine by the resisters. It might therefore seem plausible to see the underground perpetuation of the warrior narrative as an early expression of this resistance and one that gives some legitimacy to the resisters' claims that the school is feminine.

Is the school regime that outlaws the warrior narratives really feminine? We would argue, rather, that the regime being imposed is based on a male ideal, an outcome of the Enlightenment and compulsory schooling. Michel Foucault has pointed out that the development of this particular regime in schools coincided with the emergence of the prison, the hospital, the army barracks, and the factory (Foucault 1980, 55–57). Although teachers in the first years of school are predominantly female, the regime they impose is perpetuated by male teachers (Brophy 1985, 121), and this preference is endorsed by powerful and influential males in the society at large. The kind of demeanor and self-management that teachers are trying to inculcate in the early school years is the behavior expected in male-dominated public arenas like boardrooms, courtrooms, and union mass meetings.[3]

Connell (1989, 291) and Willis (1977, 76, 84) provide evidence that by adolescence, boys from all classes, particularly if they are ambitious, come to regard acquiescence in the school's demands as compatible with constructing a masculine identity. Connell writes:

> Some working class boys embrace a project of mobility in which they construct a masculinity organized around themes of rationality and responsibility. This is closely connected with the "certification" function of the upper levels of the education system and to a key form of masculinity among professionals. (1989, 291)

Rationality and responsibility are, as Weber argued long ago, the primary characteristics of the modern society theorized by the Enlightenment thinkers as based on a social contract. This prized rationality has been converted in practice into a bureaucratized legal system where "responsible" acceptance by the population of the rules of civil society obviates the need for individuals to use physical violence in gaining their ends or protecting their rights, and where, if such violence is necessary, it is exercised by the state (Weber 1978, 341–354). In civil society, the warrior is obsolete, his activities redefined bureaucratically and performed by the police and the military.

The teacher in whose classroom our observation was conducted demonstrated a strong commitment to rationality and responsibility. For example, she devoted a great deal of time to showing that there was a cause and effect link between the behavior forbidden by her classroom rules and classroom accidents. Each time an accident occurred, she asked the children to determine the cause of the accident, its result, and how it could have been prevented. The implication throughout was that children must take responsibility for the outcomes of their actions.

Mac accidentally struck a boy, who was lying on the floor, in the head with a pram wheel. He was screaming around with a pram, the victim was playing on the Car Mat and lying down to obtain a bird's eye view of a car crash. Mac rushed past the group and struck Justin on the side of the head. Tears and confusion ensued. The teacher's reaction was to see to Justin, then stop all play and gain children's attention, speaking first to Mac and Justin plus Justin's group:

T. How did Justin get hurt?

M. [No answer]

T. Mac, what happened?

M. I was wheeling the pram and Justin was in the way.

T. Were you running?

M. I was wheeling the pram.

The teacher now addresses the whole class:

T. Stop working everyone, eyes to me and listen. Someone has just been hurt because someone didn't remember the classroom rules. What are they, Harvey?

(Harvey was listening intently and she wanted someone who could answer the question at this point.)

H. No running in the classroom.

T. Why?

Other children offer an answer.

Chn. Because someone will get hurt.

T. Yes, and that is what happened. Mac was going too quickly with the pram and Justin was injured. Now how can we stop this happening next time?

Chn. No running in the classroom, only walk. (February 10, 1993)

Malcolm, walking, bumped Winston on the head with a construction toy. The teacher intervened:

T. [To Malcolm and Winston] What happened?

W. Malcolm hit me on the head.

M. But it was an accident. I didn't mean it. I didn't really hurt him.

T. How did it happen?

M. It was an accident.

W. He [Malcolm] hit me.

T. Malcolm, I know you didn't mean to hurt Winston, so how did it happen?

M. I didn't mean it.

T. I know you didn't mean it, Malcolm, but why did Winston get hurt?

Chn. Malcolm was running.

M. No I wasn't.

T. See where everyone was sitting? There is hardly enough room for children to walk. Children working on the floor must remember to leave a walking path so that other children can move safely around the room. Otherwise someone will be hurt, and that's what has happened today. (February 23, 1993)

This public-sphere masculinity of rationality and responsibility, of civil society, of the social contract is not the masculinity that the boys are bringing into the classroom through their warrior narratives. They are using a different, much older version—not the male as responsible citizen, the producer and consumer who keeps the capitalist system going, the breadwinner, and caring father of a family. Their earliest vision of masculinity is the male as warrior, the bonded male who goes out with his mates and meets the dangers of the world, the male who attacks and defeats other males characterized as baddies, the male who turns the natural products of the earth into weapons to carry out these purposes.

We would argue, nevertheless, that those boys who aspire to become one of the brothers who wield power in the public world of civil society ultimately realize that conformity to rationality and responsibility, to the demands of the school, is the price they must pay. They realize that although the girls can expect one day to become the brides and mothers of their pretend games, the boys will never, except perhaps in time of war, be allowed to act out the part of warrior hero in reality.

On the other hand, the school softens the transition for them by endorsing and encouraging the classic modern transformation and domestication of the warrior narrative, sport (Connell 1987, 177; Messner 1992, 10–12). In the school where this observation was conducted, large playground areas are set aside for lunchtime cricket, soccer, and basketball; by the age of seven, most boys are joining in these games. The message is conveyed to them that if they behave like citizens in the classroom, they can become warriors on the sports oval.

Gradually, we would suggest, little boys get the message that resistance is not the only way to live out warrior masculinity. If they accept a public/private division of life, it can be accommodated within the private sphere; thus, it becomes possible for those boys who aspire to respectability, figuring in civil society as one of the brothers, to accept that the school regime and its expectations are masculine and to reject the attempts of the "resisters" to define it (and them) as feminine. They adopt the masculinity of rationality and responsibility as that appropriate to the public sphere, while the earlier, deeply appealing masculinity of the warrior narratives can still be experienced through symbolic reenactment on the sports field.

Conclusion

We are not, of course, suggesting that this is the only way in which the public/private division becomes part of the lived awareness of little boys. We do, however, believe that we have teased out one strand of the manner in which they encounter it. We have suggested that the classroom is a major site where little boys are introduced to the masculinity of rationality and responsibility characteristic of the brothers in civil society; we have been looking at a "cycle of practice" where, in classroom after classroom, generation after generation, the mode of masculinity typified in the warrior narratives is first driven underground and then transferred to the sports field. We are, we would suggest, seeing renegotiated for each generation and in each boy's own life the conception of the "social contract" that is characteristic of the era of modernity, of the Enlightenment, of democracy, and of capitalism. We are watching reenacted the transformation of violence and power as exercised by body over body, to control through surveillance and rules (Foucault 1977, 9; 1984, 66–67), the move from domination by individual superiors to acquiescence in a public sphere of decorum and rationality (Pateman 1988).

Yet, this is a social *contract*, and there is another side to the bargain. Although they learn that they must give up their warrior narratives of masculinity in the public sphere, where rationality and responsibility hold sway, they also learn that in return they may preserve them in the private realm of desire as fantasy, as bricolage, as a symbolic survival that is appropriate to the spaces of leisure and self-indulgence, the playground, the backyard, the television set, the sports field. Although this is too large an issue to be explored in detail here, there may even be a reenactment in the school setting of what Pateman (1988, 99–115) has defined as the sexual contract, the male right to dominate women in return for accepting the constraints of civil society. Is this, perhaps, established for both boys and girls by means of the endemic misogyny—invasion of girls' space (Thorne 1986, 172; 1993, 63–88), overt expressions of aversion and disgust (Goodenough 1987, 422; D'Arcy 1990, 81), disparaging sexual innuendo (Best 1983, 129; Goodenough 1987, 433; Clark 1990, 38–46)—noted by so many observers in the classrooms and playgrounds of modernity? Are girls being contained by the boys' actions within a more restricted, ultimately a private, sphere because, in the boys' eyes, they have not earned access to the public sphere by sharing their ordeal of repression, resistance, and ultimate symbolic accommodation of their gender-defining fantasies?

Author's Note: The research on which this article is based was funded by the Research Management Committee of the University of Newcastle. The observation was conducted at East Maitland Public School, and the authors would like to thank the principal, teachers, and children involved for making our observer so welcome.

Notes

1. Some ethnographic studies describe a "tomboy" who wants to join in the boys' games (Best 1983, 95–97; Davies 1989, 93, 123; Thorne 1993, 127–129), although in our experience, such girls are rare, rarer even than the boys who play by choice with girls. The girls' rejection of the warrior narratives does not appear to be simply the result of the fact that the characters are usually men. Bronwyn Davies, when she read the role-

reversal story *Rita the Rescuer* to preschoolers, found that many boys identified strongly with Rita ("they flex their muscles to show how strong they are and fall to wrestling each other on the floor to display their strength"), whereas for most girls, Rita remained "other" (Davies 1989, 57–58).

2. This would seem to reverse the usual parallel of outdoor/indoor with public/private. This further suggests that the everyday equation of "public" with "visible" may not be appropriate for the specialized use of the term in sociological discussions of the public/private division. Behavior in the street may be more visible than what goes on in a courtroom, but it is nevertheless acceptable for the street behavior to be, to a greater degree, personal, private, and driven by "desire."

3. There are some groups of men who continue to reject these modes of modernity throughout their lives. Andrew Metcalfe, in his study of an Australian mining community, has identified two broad categories of miner, the "respectable," and the "larrikin" (an Australian slang expression carrying implications of nonconformism, irreverence, and impudence). The first are committed to the procedural decorums of union meetings, sporting and hobby clubs, welfare groups, and so on; the others relate more strongly to the less disciplined masculinity of the pub, the brawl, and the racetrack (Metcalfe 1988, 73–125). This distinction is very similar to that noted by Paul Willis in England between the "ear'oles" and the "lads" in a working-class secondary school (Willis 1977). It needs to be noted that this is not a *class* difference and that demographically the groups are identical. What distinguishes them is, as Metcalfe points out, their relative commitment to the respectable modes of accommodation and resistance characteristic of civil society of larrikin modes with a much longer history, perhaps even their acceptance or rejection of the social contract.

References

Anyon, Jean. 1983. Intersections of gender and class: Accommodation and resistance by working-class and affluent females to contradictory sex-role ideologies. In *Gender, class and education*, edited by Stephen Walker and Len Barton. Barcombe, Sussex: Falmer.

Best, Raphaela. 1983. *We've all got scars: What girls and boys learn in elementary school*. Bloomington: Indiana University Press.

Bowles, Samuel, and Herbert Gintis. 1976. *Schooling in capitalist America: Educational reform and the contradictions of economic life*. London: Routledge and Kegan Paul.

Brophy, Jere E. 1985. Interactions of male and female students with male and female teachers. In *Gender influences in classroom interaction*, edited by L. C. Wilkinson and C. B. Marrett. New York: Academic Press.

Burgess, R. G., ed. 1984. *The research process in educational settings: Ten case studies*. Lewes: Falmer.

Chodorow, Nancy. 1978. *The reproduction of mothering: Psychoanalysis and the sociology of gender*. Berkeley: University of California Press.

Clark, Margaret. 1989. Anastasia is a normal developer because she is unique. *Oxford Review of Education* 15:243–255.

———. 1990. *The great divide: Gender in the primary school*. Melbourne: Curriculum Corporation.

Connell, R. W. 1987. *Gender and power: Society, the person and sexual politics*. Sydney: Allen and Unwin.

———. 1989. Cool guys, swots and wimps: The interplay of masculinity and education. *Oxford Review of Education* 15:291–303.

Crosset, Todd. 1990. Masculinity, sexuality, and the development of early modern sport. In *Sport, men and the gender order*, edited by Michael E. Messner and Donald F. Sabo. Champaign, IL: Human Kinetics Books.

D'Arcy, Sue. 1990. Towards a non-sexist primary classroom. In *Dolls and dungarees: Gender issues in the primary school curriculum*, edited by Eva Tutchell. Milton Keynes: Open University Press.

Davies, Bronwyn. 1989. *Frogs and snails and feminist tales: Preschool children and gender*. Sydney: Allen and Unwin.

Dinnerstein, Myra. 1977. *The mermaid and the minotaur: Sexual arrangements and human malaise*. New York: Harper and Row.

Duthie, J. H. 1980. Athletics: The ritual of a technological society? In *Play and culture*, edited by Helen B. Schwartzman. West Point, NY: Leisure.

Eisenstein, Hester. 1984. *Contemporary feminist thought*. London: Unwin Paperbacks.

Foucault, Michel. 1977. *Discipline and punish: The birth of the prison*. Translated by Alan Sheridan. New York: Pantheon.

———. 1980. Body/power. In *power/knowledge: Selected interviews and other writings 1972–1977*, edited by Colin Gordon. Brighton: Harvester

————. 1984. Truth and power. In *The Foucault reader*, edited by P. Rabinow. New York: Pantheon.

Genovese, Eugene E. 1972. *Roll, Jordan, roll: The world the slaves made*. New York: Pantheon.

Giddens, Anthony. 1984. *The constitution of society: Outline of the theory of structuration*. Berkeley: University of California Press.

Goodenough, Ruth Gallagher. 1987. Small group culture and the emergence of sexist behaviour: A comparative study of four children's groups. In *Interpretive ethnography of education*, edited by G. Spindler and L. Spindler. Hillsdale, NJ: Lawrence Erlbaum.

Hebdige, Dick. 1979. *Subculture: The meaning of style*. London: Methuen.

Messner, Michael E. 1992. *Power at play: Sports and the problem of masculinity*. Boston: Beacon.

Metcalfe, Andrew. 1988. *For freedom and dignity: Historical agency and class structure in the coalfields of NSW*. Sydney: Allen and Unwin.

Paley, Vivian Gussin. 1984. *Boys and girls: Superheroes in the doll corner*. Chicago: University of Chicago Press.

Pateman, Carole. 1988. *The sexual contract*. Oxford: Polity.

————. 1989. The fraternal social contract. In *The disorder of women*. Cambridge: Polity.

Thorne, Barrie. 1986. Girls and boys together . . . but mostly apart: Gender arrangements in elementary schools. In *Relationships and development*, edited by W. W. Hartup and Z. Rubin. Hillsdale, NJ: Lawrence Erlbaum.

————. 1993. *Gender play: Girls and boys in school*. New Brunswick, NJ: Rutgers University Press.

Walker, J. C. 1988. *Louts and legends: Male youth culture in an inner-city school*. Sydney: Allen and Unwin.

Walkerdine, Valerie. 1990. *Schoolgirl fictions*. London: Verso.

Weber, Max. 1978. *Selections in translation*. Edited by W. G. Runciman and translated by Eric Matthews. Cambridge: Cambridge University Press.

Willis, Paul. 1977. *Learning to labour: How working class kids get working class jobs*. Farnborough: Saxon House.

Ritch C. Savin-Williams

Memories of Same-Sex Attractions

Recalling their childhood, gay/bisexual youths often report the pervasiveness of distinct, early memories of same-sex attractions. They remember particular feelings or incidents from as young as four or five years of age that, in retrospect, reflect the first manifestations of sexual orientation. These memories often comprise some of the youths' earliest recollections of their lives, present in some rudimentary form for many years before the ability to label sexual feelings and attractions emerges, usually after pubertal onset.[1]

Indeed, over 80 percent of the interviewed youths reported same-sex attractions prior to the physical manifestations of puberty. By the completion of puberty, all youths recalled attractions that they later labeled as "homosexual." Nearly half noted that their feelings for other males were some of their very first memories, present prior to beginning elementary school. Revelation for one youth came through his kindergarten naps: "Dreams of naked men and curious about them. Really wanting to look at them." Another youth was acting on his sexually charged feelings at age four: "I particularly remember an incident with a cousin in the bathroom and we both having hard-ons and feeling a tingling sensation when we rubbed against each other. I wanted to repeat it, and did!"

The origins of these feelings and their meanings are difficult to discern because prepubertal children are seldom asked if they have sexual attractions for other boys or girls. Thus, clinicians, educators, researchers, and other interested pro-

fessionals must rely on retrospective data from adolescents and young adults. Although these later recollections may be distorted by an awareness of current sexual identity, they provide an invaluable source of information.

Gay/bisexual youths often recall a vague but distinct sense of *being different* from other boys. Indeed, characterizing most developmental models of sexual identity is an introductory stage in which an individual has an unequivocal cognitive and/or emotional realization that he or she is "different" from others. An individual may feel alienated from others with very little awareness that homosexuality is the relevant issue.[2] For example, sociologist and sex educator Richard Troiden proposes a coming-out model that begins with an initial sense that one is marginalized in conjunction with perceptions of being different from peers.[3] This undeniable feeling may be the first internal, emotional revelation of sexual orientation, although it is not likely to be perceived initially as sexual but rather as a strongly experienced sense of not fitting in or of not having the same interests as other boys/girls.

The existence of these early feelings implies that youths have both an awareness of a normative standard of how boys are supposed to act, feel, and behave and a belief that they violate this ideal. Troiden describes this conflation of feeling different and gender inappropriate:

> It is not surprising that "prehomosexuals" used gender metaphors, rather than sexual metaphors, to interpret and explain childhood feelings of difference. . . . Children do not appear to define their sexual experimentation in heterosexual or homosexual terms. The socially created categories of homosexual, heterosexual,

and bisexual hold little or no significance for them. (p. 52)

Retrospectively, the gay/bisexual youths interviewed for this book reported three somewhat overlapping sources as a basis for their initial awareness of differentness:

- a pervasive and emotional captivation with other boys that felt passionate, exotic, consuming, and mysterious;
- a strongly felt desire to engage in play activities and to possess traits usually characteristic of girls;
- disinterest or, in more extreme cases, a revulsion in typical boys' activities, especially team sports and rough-and-tumble physical play.[4]

These three sources are not mutually exclusive— many youths recalled instances of all three during their childhood. For example, one youth who felt apart and isolated during his childhood was obsessed with wanting to be around adult men, frequently developed crushes on male teachers, and spent considerable time with neighborhood girls, particularly enjoying their games of hopscotch and jump rope. He was called "sissy" and "girly" by other boys, and he detested team sports and all things athletic, especially locker rooms.

The prevalence of these three is difficult to determine because few researchers have systematically asked boys the relevant questions that probe these issues. It also bears noting that not all gay or bisexual individuals recall this sense of being different during childhood and adolescence and that these feelings and attractions are not solely the domain of sexual-minority youths. Heterosexual boys may also feel different, have same-sex attractions or desires, enjoy feminine activities, and avoid aggressive pursuits.

Youths interviewed for this book easily and at times graphically remembered these same-sex attractions that emanated from their earliest childhood memories. Despite the dramatic significance that these early homoerotic attractions would have, at the time they felt natural, om-

nipresent. Many recalled these attractions to other males by identifying concrete, distinct memories prior to first grade. Without great fanfare, with no clashing of cymbals, and with no abiding shock, later homoerotic attractions were felt to be contiguous with these early feelings.

Captivation with Masculinity

Of the three sources for feeling different, the vast majority of the gay/bisexual youths interviewed for this book attributed to themselves an early sense that in some fundamental way they differed from other boys. This difference was an obsession of always wanting to be near other males. Most boys did not at the time believe that these attractions were sexually motivated; they were just overwhelmed with an all-consuming desire to be with other males. Some became flushed or excited when they made contact, especially physical, with other boys or men; some arranged their lives so as to increase time spent with males, while others avoided males because they were frightened by the male aura. Above all else, their obsession with males was mysterious and pervasive. It was also present from an early age, from first memories.

One youth's childhood was one massive memory of men. He decided that the death of his father ten years earlier was the reason that he would always need guys in his life.

I can remember wanting the men who visited us to hug me when I was real little, maybe three or four. I've always wanted to touch and be touched by guys, and I was a lot. Guys loved to manhandle me. They would throw me up in the air and I'd touch the ceiling and I'd scream and would love it and would do anything to make it happen more and more. It never was enough and I'd tire them out or I'd go to someone else who would toss me. Sometimes I would be teased for the "little points" [erections] in my pants, but no one, including myself, made much of it.

I think I spent my childhood fantasizing about men, not sexually of course, but just being close to them and having them hold me or hug me. I'd feel safe and warm. My dad gave me this and my older brother Mitchell gave me this but all of this was never enough. With the other men I'd feel flushed, almost hot. Maybe those were hot flashes like what women get! Those were good days.

Although he may have been an extreme case, other youths also recalled distinct attractions to men that a decade or more later were still vivid, emotional, and construed as significant. This obsession with males remained at the time nameless for the following three youths:

I was seven at the time and Will, who was working for us doing yard work, was twenty-one and a college student/athlete. One night when my parents went to a hotel for their anniversary dinner and whatever, they asked Will to stay the night to watch over me. He was in a sleeping bag on the floor and I knew he was nude and he was next to my bed and I kept wondering what was in the sleeping bag. I just knew that I wanted to get in with him but I didn't know why or that I could because I didn't want to bother him. I didn't sleep the whole night.

Maybe it was third grade and there was an ad in the paper about an all-male cast for a movie. This confused me but fascinated—intrigued—me so I asked the librarian and she looked all flustered, even mortified, and mumbled that I ought to ask my parents.

It was very clear to me around six years of age. There was a TV beer commercial which featured several soccer players without shirts on. I mentioned to my brother how much I liked this TV show because the guys didn't have shirts on. I remember this but I'm sure I had thoughts before this.

Those who monopolized their attention were occasionally same-age boys, but were more often older teenagers and adults—male teachers, coaches, cousins, or friends of the family. Public male figures were also sources of fantasies—Superman, Scott Baio, Duran Duran, John Ritter, Bobby Ewing, and Hulk Hogan. Others turned pages in magazines and catalogs to find male models in various stages of undress; especially popular were underwear advertisements. The captivation with men had a familiar tone—a drive for male contact or the male image from an early age with little understanding of what it meant—and a common emotional quality—excitement, euphoria, mystery.

These same-sex attractions were not limited to gay boys. Bisexual youths recalled similar early homoerotic captivation with men.

Technically it could be either male or female, no matter. I just was into naked bodies. I had access and took, without him knowing it, dad's *Penthouse* magazines. Such a big fuss, but actually in them and whatever else I could find, turned on by both the girls and the men. The men I recall most vividly. It was the hairless, feminine guys with big penises and made-up faces. I loved make-up on my guys, the eyelashes and the eyes, blue shadow, but mostly it was the look. Tight jeans, lean bodies.

Homoerotic desires were often interpreted as natural and hence characteristic of all boys. Many youths articulated that their desire for the "male touch" was deeply embodied in their natural self. By this they implied that their attractions to boys were not a matter of choice or free will but were of early and perhaps, they speculated, genetic origins. For example, one youth never felt that he had a choice regarding his intense attractions to adult males:

My infatuation with my day camp counselor I didn't choose. Why him and not his girlfriend? I never chose my love objects but I was always attracted to guys. In all of my early dreams and fantasies I always centered on guys whether they were sexual or not. What I wanted to do was to get close to them and I knew that innately, perhaps even by the age of six or seven. I felt it was okay because God said it was okay.

Similarly, many other youths noted that their homoerotic desires were never a matter of choice but "just were." Most believed that they were gay or bisexual in large part because of genetic factors or the "way the cards were dealt—luck of the draw, like something in the neuro-structure or hormonal."

I'd dream of my uncle and wake up all euphoric and sweaty and eroticized. Another dream that I had at six was of my [boy] classmates playing around in their underwear with these big cocks sticking out. It just happened. How could I choose these things to dream about, to check out the cocks in my mom's *Playgirl*, and to cut out pictures of guys from movie magazines? I was very intrigued by all of this and knew somehow it related to me.

Maybe my child sex play taught me how to be gay but then maybe it only reinforced what already was. I know that I've been gay for a long time, probably I was born with it. I assumed when I was young that all people had a pee pee. It doesn't have to be genetic but then it could happen during the first year of life. I think I was born being gay, leaning toward homosexuality, and development just sort of pushed it further.

My brother is gay, my uncle is gay, my father acts like he is gay sometimes, and my mother is hanging out with feminist support groups and really butch-looking women. Did I really have a choice?!

I can't stand the smell of women. Who really cares? I could have gone straight but it would have been torture. I am what I am, from birth.

Some youths simply assumed, based on the egocentric principle that their thoughts and feelings were shared by others, that all boys must feel as they do but were simply not talking about their desires. With age, however, they came to realize that perhaps they were more "into it."

I guess I was pretty touchable—and I still am based on what guys I know or am with tell me. I didn't understand why because I thought all kids liked it. Others have told me that they liked it too but somehow I think I liked it more. I craved and adored it and my day would not be a good one unless I had this contact. Only later did I find out why I liked being touched by guys.

Another youth decided that he would simply "outgrow" his obsession with males. He was not, however, going to let this future keep him from enjoying this wonderful pleasure at the moment.

As a child I knew I was attracted to males. I was caught by my mother looking at nude photographs of men in her magazines and I heard my father say to her that, "He'll grow out of it," and so I thought and hoped I would. But until then I just settled back and enjoyed my keen curiosity to see male bodies.

You see, it did not feel threatening because (a) it felt great, and (b) father said I would grow out of it, and he was always right. So why not enjoy it until it went away?

Other youths, however, recognized that these undeniably homoerotic attractions were not typical of other boys. They knew they were extreme cases but they "could not help it."

Even at eight I could tell that my interest in guys was way beyond normal. Like this time that we were out with my friend Chad's big brother catching fireflies and he took off his shirt and I forgot about the fireflies and just stared at his chest. Chad got really irritated and called out, "Hey homo give me the jar!" I'm sure I blushed.

When we played truth-or-dare I always wanted to be dared to kiss one of the guys. No one ever dared me to do that, probably because they knew that I'd like it. And I would have! I knew it was strange of me and that they didn't want to kiss boys. They all knew that too but I really didn't care.

Eventually, most youths understood that these undeniable attractions were the wrong ones to have. Despite the belief that they had no choice in matters of their attractions, most inevitably came to appreciate that they should hide their attractions. Snide remarks made by peers, prohibitions taught by parents, and the silence imposed by religion and by teachers all contributed to this realization. Thus, although early obsessions with males were experienced as instinctive, most of the gay/bisexual youths acknowledged from an early age that their impulses were somehow "wrong" but not necessarily "bad."

Despite the presence of an older gay brother, one youth was vulnerable to society's negative messages about homosexuality. His concern centered on being "strike two" for his mother.

Well, I knew enough to hide Sean's *Jock* after I looked at it. It was not guilt—it was too much fun!—but fear that I felt. I was afraid if mother found out that she would feel bad that she had two failures and that Sean would kill me for getting into his stockpile.

Very few youths made the connection during their childhood that these attractions that felt so natural and significant placed them in the stigmatized category of "homosexual." Although most had a passing acquaintance with the concept and had seen "homosexuals" displayed in the media, relatively few would have situated themselves in this category at this point in their lives. One youth believed that "it" was something to be outgrown: "I thought maybe that it was just a stage that I was going through. But if it wasn't a stage then it was probably no problem for me to worry about now." Other youths, however, were worried.

> Something was different about me. I knew that. I was afraid of what it meant, and I prayed to God that whatever it was that He would take it away. It was a burden but I liked it, and so I felt guilty about liking it.

It was not until many years later, with the onset of sexual maturations that these attractions would be fully linked with sexuality and perhaps a sexual identity. Homosensuality for these youths was not foreign but natural, a lifelong intrigue with men's bodies. However, as the societal wrongness of their intuitive obsession with masculinity became increasingly apparent, many youths hoped that their attractions were a phase to be outgrown or that their feelings would make sense in some distant future.

The feared repercussions from family members and peers if they were known to have gay traits served as a powerful reason for the boys to feel that their same-sex desires and acts were improper and should not be shared with others. Acting on them was thought to be wrong because if caught, punishment would likely ensue. Balancing desire and fear became a significant dilemma. Eventually, many of the youths recognized that others rarely shared or understood their same-sex desires. This pact of secrecy with themselves was a major theme for many of the youths. It did not, however, always inhibit their sexual behavior; a significant number of the boys acted on their sexual desires during childhood. . . .

Acting Like a Girl

A second source of feeling different, not explicitly linked with same-sex attractions, involved cultural definitions of gender—how a boy should *not* act, think, and feel. Characteristics deemed not appropriate for boys included observable behaviors such as play with girl-typed toys, especially dolls; involvement in female activities and games; cross-dressing; sex-role motor behavior including limp wrists, high-pitched voices, and dramatic gestures; and stated interests such as wishing to be a girl, imagining self as dancer or model, and preferring female friends and being around older women. These boys did not wonder, "Why am I gay?" but "Why do I act like a girl?"[5] For example, one youth recalled his childhood in the following way:

> I knew that a boy wasn't supposed to kiss other boys, although I did. I knew it was wrong, so this must be some indication that I knew. I also knew that I wasn't supposed to cross my legs at the knees, but I wouldn't like quickly uncross my legs whenever that was the case. So this is certainly at a young age that I noticed this. I think I knew that it was sort of a female thing, sort of an odd thing, and I knew that boys weren't supposed to do that.

Many boys who fit the category of gender bending were at once erotically drawn to boys and men (the first source) but were repelled by their behavior, their standard of dress and cleanliness, and their barbarian nature. They felt ambivalent regarding their attractions to males; intrigued by male bodies and the masculinity mystique, these youths saw men as enigmatic and unapproachable.

Psychotherapist Richard Isay characterizes this sense of gender atypicality in some pregay boys: "They saw themselves as more sensitive than other boys; they cried more easily, had their feelings more readily hurt, had more aesthetic interests, enjoyed nature, art, and music, and were drawn to other 'sensitive' boys, girls, and adults" (p. 23).[6] Indeed, research amply demonstrates that gender nonconformity is one of the best childhood predictors of adult homosexuality in men.[7] Findings from prospective studies are fairly straightforward: The proportion of *extremely* feminine boys who eventually profess a same-sex sexual orientation approaches 100 percent. However, the fraction of these gender-nonconforming boys in the total population remains considerably below that of gay men. Thus, while the vast majority of extremely feminine boys eventually adopt a gay or bisexual identity in adulthood, so do an unknown number of boys who are not particularly feminine.

Feeling more similar to girls than to boys, one youth described his experience "as if I was from a different planet than other boys." He was not alone; a substantial proportion of the gay/bisexual youths recalled that this "girl-like syndrome" was the basis of how they differed from their male peers. Of all boys interviewed, over one-third described their self-image as being more similar to that of girls than boys, and nearly all of these boys reported that this sense of themselves permeated areas of their lives.

One consequence of having more culturally defined feminine than masculine interests was that many boys with gender-atypical characteristics felt most comfortable in the company of girls and women or preferred spending time alone. Two youths described their gender nonconformity during their childhood years.

I had mostly friends who were girls and I can remember playing jump rope, dolls, and hopscotch with them, and I can remember being very interested in hairstyling and practicing on dolls. I got into sewing and knitting. I played make-believe, read spy and adventure stories, house with my sisters. I had a purse and dolls that they gave me. We did everything together. I was never close with my brother and we never

did anything together. I was always accepted by girls and few other boys were.

Thinking back I did play with girls in the neighborhood a lot. I loved actually to kiss girls and I was always wanting to kiss girls and I thought this might be a little strange or weird because I liked girls so much at such a young age. I just felt very comfortable with them. I felt more self-conscious around boys because I always wondered what they were thinking about.

The extent to which such behavior could produce a gender-bender who is accepted by girls as one of them is illustrated by a third youth:

I was even invited to slumber parties and I always went. They were so much fun! Just the five of us in our gowns, with lace and bows that my mom had made for my sister and I "borrowed," laughing, sneaking cigarettes, and gossiping about other girls.

Thus, almost without exception boys who displayed early gender-atypical behavior strongly preferred hanging out with girls rather than with boys. Girls were far less likely to reject the "feminine" boys, a reaction that has been confirmed by research studies.[8] If such youths had male friends it was usually one best friend, perhaps a neighbor who also disliked masculine activities.

I have always been gay although I did not know what that meant at the time. But I knew that I always felt queer, out of place in my hometown. . . . Mostly I spent my time alone in the house or with girls at school. We ate lunch together and talked in between classes. I always felt that girls received the short end of the stick. I really did not have many friends because I lived in a rural area. I felt rejected and I feared being rejected.

I have usually had one best male friend, who might change every other year or so but who always was like me in hating sports. Like Tim who was one of my best friends because he lived across the street and was handy, someone so I would not be alone. We spent time together but I am not sure what else we ever did. Otherwise I hung with girls.

Not uncommonly, boys who displayed interest in gender-atypical pursuits fervently expressed strong preferences for solo activities such as reading and make-believe games, or for artistic endeavors.

> But my major activity during childhood was drawing and I was sort of known as "The Artist," even as early as third and fourth grades. Today I can see some very gay themes in my drawings! Whenever anyone in the class wanted anything drawn then they asked me. No matter how much they had ridiculed me I agreed to do it.

A second youth made up plays for the neighborhood, role-played TV characters, and cartooned.

> I took part in dance, ballet, singing, and had good manners. I liked Broadway musicals, Barbra, Bette, Joan, Liz, Judy, and Greta . . . I did drama, lots and lots of drama! Anything pretend. I did lots of skits for the Mickey Mouse Club, play writing, and office decorating.

Unclear from these accounts is whether the decision to spend time alone was one freely chosen by the gay/bisexual youths or was a consequence of exclusion dictated by others. That is, were they loners by choice or by circumstance? Although most evidence supports the banishment hypothesis, time alone may have been desired and pursued for creative reasons; time alone may have enhanced their creative efforts. One youth found that he spent a lot of time "doing nothing, just being alone, playing the violin, planting flowers, and arranging flowers." Another youth loved "building and creating things like castles and bridges and rivers in the backyard. Maybe it was because I was an only child but I was into any kind of art and I also composed on the piano." When asked about his childhood activities, a third youth was merely succinct: "Shopped. Homework. Masturbated. Read."

Most difficult for many gender-atypical gay/bisexual boys was the almost universal harassment they received from their peers. As a consequence

of associating with girls and not boys, spending considerable time alone, and appreciating female activities, they faced almost daily harassment from peers, usually boys but sometimes girls, teachers, parents, and siblings. Perhaps most insufferable to their male peers was the gay/bisexual boys' feminine gross and fine motor behavior. Their hand gestures, standing and sitting posture, leg and hip movement, voice pitch and cadence, and head tilt conveyed to others that these boys were girllike and hence weak and deplorable. The reactions they received from peers went beyond mere teasing, which most youths receive during childhood and adolescence as a mechanism for social bonding, to outright verbal abuse that was harassing and sometimes extremely destructive to a sense of self. The abuse was occasionally physically expressed and always had emotional and self-image consequences.

Below is a list of names that boys with gender-atypical characteristics reported that they were called by age mates. Not all youths recalled or wanted to remember the exact names.

• sissy	• clumsy	• bitchy	• fag
• queer	• little girl	• cry baby	• fem
• gayson	• faggot	• super fem	• queer bait
• fruitcake	• wimpy	• fruit	• gay
• schoolboy	• pansy	• gaylord	• Janus
• fairy	• softy	• girl	• fag boy
• girly	• homo	• cocksucker	• lisp
• wimp	• gay guy	• Avon Lady	• Safety Girl
• Tinkerbell	• flamer	• mommy's boy	

One youth reported that in grammar school he was voted "The Person Most Likely to Own a Gay Bar."

The specific provocation that elicited these names during school, on the bus, and in the neighborhood varied, but several patterns are discernible. The abuse usually occurred because a boy was perceived as a misfit, as acting too much "like a girl." Three youths provided testimonies from their lives:

> Because I was somewhat effeminate in my behavior and because I wore "girly" shoes. Some

said that I was a little girl because I couldn't play baseball. I played the clarinet in school and this was defined as a female instrument so I got some teasing for that. I thought I could control my behavior but it got so bad that my family decided to pull me out of the public school to go to a private Catholic school where the teasing receded.

Because I was weak and a cry baby. I was not in the "in" crowd. Also because of the way I dressed and that I got good grades. I was very thin and got every disease that came around. I had all sorts of allergies and was always using all sorts of drugs. I was told I looked like a girl. I played with Barbies and taught her how to sit up and later how to fly. I just wasn't masculine enough I guess.

People thought that perhaps I might be gay because they thought I was just way too nice and also because I was flamboyant. They really didn't think I was like homosexually gay. It was just a term they used for me because it seemed to fit my personality. People said I'm gay because of my mannerisms, also because I slur my s's and I'm so flamboyant. I think it's the way that I walked, the way I talked, the way I carried myself. I had a soft voice. Lots of boys blew me kisses. My voice is just not masculine. Also I tended to be very giggly and flighty and flaky and silly at times.

One youth believed that "most kids were just looking for a laugh" and that he was the easiest target, because of his femininity, they could find. He was their "amusement for the day."

In no story were girls the only ones who verbally abused a youth for being gender nonconforming. On many occasions, however, boys acted alone. Perhaps the most usual pattern was for boys, or a subset of boys, to be the persistent ridiculers with a few girls chiming in when present.

Some of the jocks really bothered me but mostly it was these three guys every day making my life miserable. Always done by males who really had this pecking order. Real bullies!

This was mostly males—this one guy seemed to have it out for me. But some of the girls who

hung out with him also did it. The girls thought I was bitchy and called me "fag" and "homo."

Although reactions to being victimized by peer ridicule were diverse, the most common responses, illustrated by three youths, were to ignore, withdraw, or cry.

I took it without saying anything back. I'd pretend that I didn't hear them or hide my feelings. I hated it but didn't say anything back. Guess I was benign to it. Just sat there and took it. I did that for protection. I was so much of a misfit that bullies did it to me. I offended them in some way. Just a horrible, wrenching experience.

I became more withdrawn and thus more of an outcast. I'd cower and keep my distance, keeping it inside myself. I did nothing or remained silent or said "leave me alone." Once I fought back and lost, which made me withdraw even more.

I was very, very sensitive and would cry very easily. I had very little emotional control at the time. Cry, yell at them, cry some more. I would tell my mother and cry and she'd try to comfort me or she'd just dismiss it all. I would tell the guys that I had told my mother and they would make more fun of me.

Not all boys reacted so passively to the verbal assault. Several developed innovative, self-enhancing ways to cope with peer harassment. For example, one youth noted an unusual situation:

All my boyfriends, the jock types, always protected me and punished those who teased me. I would just turn away as if I never gave notice because I knew that I would be protected by all the guys, the jocks, that I was having sex with. I never did try to get back at them [the harassers]. Once they realized this then they kept quiet.

Another used his intelligence and experience as strategies for coping with peer harassment.

I think it was because I was so flamboyant and I was not so sports-oriented. If they said it to my face then I would say "get out of my face!" Or I would point out their stupidity. I considered them to be rather stupid, so immature. I'd been around the world and I knew I could say things that would damage them because I was smarter than them and because I had so many female friends. I tried to ignore it because I knew that I was better than them. I sort of got respect for not fighting back or sometimes I would say, "I like girls! What's *your* problem?"

It is difficult to ascertain the true impact on a youth of this constant bombardment of negative peer review. Few of the boys thought it was anything but negative. Most felt that the most significant effect of the verbal harassment was what it did to their personality: They became increasingly withdrawn from social interactions, despondent, and self-absorbed. The aftermath for the four youths below was a decrease in their self-image and self-worth.

I felt very conscious about my voice and somewhat shameful that I wasn't masculine enough. I actually just sort of retreated more and became more introverted. I felt rejected and it hurt my self-esteem. I took the ridicule to heart and I blamed myself.

Because I knew that indeed I had the attractions to guys I knew that they were right and that I was a disgusting human being. I just spent a lot more time alone to avoid the pain. I just sort of blocked it all internally because it hurt so much. I just sort of erased all my memories of my childhood so I can't give you much detail.

A real nightmare! I really felt like I had no friends. It really did lower my self-esteem and it made me focus on sort of my outer appearance and ignore the inner. It devastated me because I felt everything they said was true. I was quiet and kept it inside.

Heightened my sense of being different. Caused me to withdraw and not feel good about myself. Cut off from people and became shy. Became introverted, guilty. I hated that time. Childhood was supposed to be happy times but it was not. Later, I dropped out of school, thought about suicide, and ran away from home.

Although none of the boys felt that the labeling made him gay, many believed that the name-calling contributed to their negative image of homosexuality. Hence, the ridicule became a central factor in who they are. The abuse also kept them in the closet for a considerably longer period of time. These effects are apparent in the two narratives below:

It just sort of reinforced that men are scum. I viewed being a fag as so negative that it hurt my self-image for them to call me that. I didn't like myself, so being gay is bad and what they're saying I knew it to be true because I am bad and being gay is bad and I'm gay. It's made me think of males only as sex objects because I wanted to be hated by men because I didn't like myself. I started back in elementary school to believe it was true.

I had such a hostile view towards homosexuality, so it was hard to come out as a result of this stigma because I had really low self-esteem. It affected me by not having a positive attitude about homosexuality in general. I needed at least a positive or even neutral point of view and that would have made my gay life so much easier. I continue to suppress things.

It was the rare youth for whom anything positive emerged from the verbal ridicule. One youth noted that "teasing sort of helped me to deal with my gay identity at a very early age because everyone was calling my attention to it." He was proud to be effeminate; he reported that the teasing made him stronger and was thus beneficial.

I wore stylish clothes and was my own individual self. My teachers appreciated this but not the slobs. Because of this a lot of them said that I was gay and so I thought I must be, although I did not know what this meant except that it meant I would not be shoveling cow shit!

Unfortunately, few youths could recall such positive aspects to their gender atypicality. More often, the consequences of being true to their nature were that other boys viewed them as undesirable playmates and as "weird." Labeled sissy or effeminate, they were rejected by boys, and, equally important, they had little desire to fraternize with their male peers. Because other boys did not constitute an enjoyable or safe context for play or socializing, the youths often turned to girls for activities and consolation. They preferred to dance rather than shovel shit, to sing rather than yell "hike," and to draw rather than bash heads. Thus, childhood was usually experienced as a traumatizing time by youths who did not conform to cultural sex roles. The fortunate ones sought and found girls for solace and support. Girls became their saviors, offering sources of emotional sustenance as the male world of childhood became increasingly distasteful. It was to these girls that many gay/bisexual males subsequently disclosed their sexual affiliations during middle or late adolescence. . . .

Not Acting Like a Boy

A third source of feeling different among the interviewed youths originated from a disinterest or abhorrence of typical masculine activities, which may or may not have occurred in the presence of a captivation with masculinity (first source) or of high levels of femininity (second source). Thus, a lack of masculinity did not necessarily imply that such youths were fond of female activities or were drawn to or hung out with girls. Many reported never playing house, dressing up as a girl, or having a passing acquaintance with Barbie. In the absence of typical expressions of femininity, boys without masculine interests were usually loners or spent time with one or several best male friends.

Compared with what is known about gender-atypical boys, considerably less is known concerning those who during childhood do not fit cultural images of how a boy should act, think, and feel. Characteristics labeled as unmasculine or as failure to conform to gender expectations include observable behaviors such as avoidance of rough-and-tumble play, typical boys' games, and athletic activities; no imagining of oneself as a sports figure; and no desire to grow up to be like one's father. These boys did not wonder, "Why am I gay?" but "Why don't I act like a boy?"[9]

Childhood activities that constitute "unmasculine" all share the characteristic of being gender

neutral by North American standards, suitable for both boys and girls. Within this gender non-partisanship, active and passive patterns were evident in the interviews. Some boys were as active as masculine-inclined peers but in nonmasculine, nonathletic—at least in a team sports sense—activities.

> My friend and me made roads and gardens. I liked to sort of build cities and bridges outside and in the garden. Played in the woods, hiked in the woods, camped out, and hide and seek. Ted and I were almost inseparable for a couple of years. I also biked, swam a lot, jumped on the trampoline. Biking was my way of dealing with stress. I was into matchbox cars.

> I enjoyed playing office, playing grow-up, walking around the city basically looking at other people. Mind games and chess with my brothers. Creative imaginative play. Discovering and enjoying spending a lot of time on bike trips, going to new places. Getting out of the house and being outside, just wandering off by myself.

More common were boys who spent considerable time alone pursuing passive activities. This passivity should not be equated, however, with having a bad time or having a bad childhood. Many recalled an enjoyable if unconventional life during childhood.

> At school I hung out with myself but on weekends it was primarily guys in the neighborhood and we would like watch TV and videos. They were like my best friends and we were not really into moving sports. We were more into passive activities like music and cards. I've always been in the band. Hanging out at the mall. A couple of us guys would do this.

> Very quiet pursuits, stamps, cooking, which my mother liked. Guess I played verbal games, board games with the family, Risk and Candyland, and crossword puzzles. Did a lot with my family, like family vacations, visiting historical things. I read, played with Lincoln Logs, fantasizing, spending time by myself, drawing, and swinging. I loved the freedom of the swing and I'd do it for hours. Oh yes, I loved croquet!

> I read a lot—like the encyclopedia, the phone book, science fiction, science, mystery, and

gothic novels. I had a comic book collection and Star Wars cards. I spent most of my other time drawing maps. I was really into getting any information anywhere I could, even from the atlas or an almanac. I can remember actually setting out to read the dictionary, although I don't think I got very far. Almost every book in the public library later on.

Most explicitly, unmasculine youths felt particularly ill at ease with archetypal male sports, especially loathing team sports such as baseball, basketball, and football. If they became involved in competitive, aggressive sports it was in response to family or peer pressure. Perhaps forced by a father or coach to participate in sports as a right fielder, a defensive back, or a bench warmer, they deeply resented such coercion and their inevitable failure. Severely repulsed by many typical masculine pursuits, this source of trauma was to be avoided at all costs, even at the price of disappointing parents. Unmasculine youths often shared with the following very gender-atypical youth his rejection of masculine activities and hence of masculinity.

> I did not play basketball or wrestle and I was not a farmer nor a slob nor did I shovel cow shit like my classmates. Girl, they would come in smelling like they looked and you can be sure it was not a number Chanel ever heard of! There was no way that I was going to let this be a part of what I wanted for my life.
>
> Well they [parents] wanted me to try at least one sport but I was always sort of the last chosen. I knew I was effeminate and clumsy and my father ridiculed me for it. So I avoided sports and I did this by going home for lunch and visiting my female friends rather than playing sports with the other guys during recess.

For one youth, the appeal or even logic of sports baffled and befuddled him.

> I really did not care about most sports and I still do not. I liked more intellectual than physical things. I enjoyed more talking philosophy, writing poetry, and drawing than spending time throwing stupid balls away, then running after the stupid balls, trying to find the stupid balls,

and then throwing the stupid balls back to the same person so that he could throw it away again and have somebody run after it, find it, and throw it back to him again. Sounds real intelligent does it not?! Doing these stupid ball tricks made Bill [twin brother] real popular and me really unpopular. Where is the fairness in that?

> I only played sports during recess when I had to. I hated little boy games such as basketball, kickball, football, baseball, or anything that had a ball or a peck order. It was very aggressive and used all of the wrong parts of my anatomy and my personality.

The most aversive aspect of sports was its aggressive, dominant, physical nature. One youth remarked that in sports someone always has to lose—"and it was usually me!" This reflected not only his own personal experience of losing but also an antipathy to his life philosophy of peace, harmony, cooperation. Another youth astutely recognized another reason not to become involved in sports—his true nature might emerge and become figuratively and physically visible.

> I was not on any team sport because I was so self-conscious about being around other males. I was afraid of how I might be looked upon by them and what I might do or say or look at if I was around them a lot. What would I do in the locker room? What would happen to "George," who has a mind of his own? Maybe my feelings might come out and then where would I be?

Other youths reported that they wanted to participate in sports but could not because of physical problems. One noted, "I could never much be a sports person because I had a coordination problem because of my vision that caused me to be physically awkward." Another compensated by reading about sports: "Well, I read the sports pages and sports books! I hated gym because I was overweight. I could not do sports because I felt so evil watching men strip naked in the locker room and I couldn't take it." A third youth was on the swim team before getting pneumonia, forcing him to quit. His restitution was to remain active: "I hung out at the beach (yes, looking at the guys!), played Atari, skateboarded, and played Pogo."

Those who became involved in sports almost preferred individual to team sports. These "jocks" included the two youths below.

> Some track, cross-country, swimming. I never liked the team sports. I had to do soccer in fourth grade because my best friends were into it but I disliked it immensely. Guess I was mid-level in ability and lower than that in interest but it gave me something to do and kept me around guys. I lived in a very sex-segregated rural area. I gave all of these up in junior high, except swimming in the Scout pool.
>
> I was really into sports. Let's see. Gymnastics in fourth to sixth grades; bowling in third; darts in third; ping pong whenever; dodge the ball in second to fourth; volleyball in sixth.

Perhaps because of their paltry athleticism and low levels of masculine interests, these boys were not immune to peer ridicule and teasing. They were not, however, ridiculed nearly to the degree that gender-noncomforming boys were. They were often teased for non-gender-related characteristics or for individualized perceived deficits in physical features ("fatty"), in normative masculine behavior ("wimp"), or in desirable kinds of intelligence ("nerd"). Some were also called names more typical of effeminate youths ("fag") without, they almost universally acknowledged, the connotation of sexuality. One youth defended himself by asserting, "Being called a fag really was not a sexual thing. It was more that it reflected on my low self-esteem and that I was so wimpy."

The most common name callers were same-age, same-sex peers, although occasionally girls also participated. One youth had an unusual experience. Called "nerd" by three girls who were making his life miserable, "several boys seemed to go out of their way to protect me and shield me from this kind of teasing. Of course I was giving them answers on their exams!" Otherwise he simply withdrew. Because ridicule was seemingly random and seldom daily, it was sometimes dif-

ficult for unmasculine youths to understand what provoked the name calling.

One youth reported that he enjoyed his life as a loner and that others seemed more upset than he was that he was spending so much time alone. With his involvement in computers, the complaints lessened, perhaps, he guessed, because others envied his knowledge and saw it as a means to earn a good living. He was subject, however, to the taunts of male peers. Occasionally he was ridiculed by several boys on the school bus and during recess for reasons that were beyond his control.

> At first I didn't understand why they were on my case, but since I didn't fit in in a lot of ways, they had their way. It was just the usual thing. Probably because I wasn't good at sports but I can't remember what I was called. In gym classes primarily by macho males. Nothing I didn't want to remember. I really can't remember too much of it or certainly not the names. It just seemed like I was teased about as much as anyone else was. Not every day, maybe once a month, and I just sort of reacted passively. Never really a major thing or very threatening, just sort of stupid kids' stuff. Just sort of let it go away.
>
> I didn't fit in because I was against the intellectualism of the smart kids and I wasn't a jock. Hence I was not respected. I have no real memories of the exact names but I think they weren't happy ones because I was thin and, oh yes, my ears stuck out so I was called "monkey face."

The name-calling message might be that the boy was too feminine or not masculine enough, but more commonly it was because he was simply different or had undesirable characteristics. Very few felt that being gay was a cause of the verbal abuse. The following youths recounted the reasons they believed they suffered at the hands of their peers.

> I was awkward and wore glasses. I had a speech impediment and a birthmark. I was ostracized, sort of left out because I wasn't conforming and I was very shy. I was sort of known as an only

child and thus a spoiled brat with very little so-cial skills. I was never teased about being gay. For being fat and overweight. Maybe I was teased more than average. It did hurt. I reacted by just crying because I really couldn't ignore it. It was a weight issue and not a sexual identity issue.

Because I was quiet, shy, and geekish. For being physically awkward, being different, bookish. As a kid I was teased for having cow eyes be-cause my eyes were large. For not going to church. Very low-class assholes, mostly males. Then I went to a school for gifted children and it stopped.

I was ridiculed about being a softy and brain box because I was so intellectual or consumed in the books. They said I got good grades because I was kissing teachers' asses. I think I was just different from all of them and the teachers liked me because I liked learning. Perhaps it hap-pened because I went to an all-male Catholic school.

I was shy and I got called Spock a lot because of my eyes which were real dark. They thought I was wearing eye shadow.

The most common response of the youths was to remain silent. One youth felt scared and frightened but "later it just got to be an annoyance. My response was to remain rather stoic." Another hated gym because he was not "graceful" and be-cause of a particular nemesis.

A classic case of one guy on my case which I usually ignored. But one day he threw me to the gym floor but a guy came to my rescue. He was bigger than me so my reaction was basi-cally to brave it, to try to show that it did not af-fect me by just walking away. I would usually not talk back and I would not cry.

A second common response was to simply avoid situations where one might be ridiculed. This was not always an easy task.

Being not good at sports, I tried to avoid all sporting situations if at all possible. I just felt like I was left out of everything. I sort of inter-nalized it but I can't really remember how I re-acted. I dreaded going to the gym. I was afraid

and felt that I was bullied. I was not verbally equipped to deal with this kind of teasing. I re-ally didn't fight back until high school.

A third response, somewhat less prevalent, was to feel extremely hurt and cry, either publicly or in private. One youth grew to hate and fear school. "It was very painful and I was upset by it and I cried. In fact, so much so I didn't want to go to school." Another cried in private.

I was teased for being very heavy and for being slow. I reacted by being very hurt; I couldn't accept it. I cried a lot, not in front of them but in the bathroom or my room. My out was al-ways, "Well, I'm smart."

Finally, several youths reported that they surprised their tormentors by behaving in a very masculine way, fighting back against the name-calling.

I rode the bus. I felt singled out and ridiculed. Initially what I did was simply relax and ignore it but then at one point I actually fought back, physically and verbally attacking sort of the main person who was ridiculing me the most. If I did fight back, which was the case occa-sionally, I would usually win. Because it was a small school, the word got out and after that I had no problems. I gained in popularity and the teasing tapered off to almost nothing.

There were rumors about me being gay. I got teasing when my friend told others that we had slept together. I confronted these people but it didn't help. I ended up going back at others or attacking them. I confronted them, "Why are you so interested in my sexuality?" After awhile they left me alone. I denied being gay but I knew I was. I wasn't ashamed but I wanted the ridiculing to stop. I was very wicked to others.

The immediate effects of the ridicule are difficult to determine. However, based on their reports, consequences appear far less severe than they were for youths who enacted femininity, perhaps because the ridicule was not as frequent and did not focus on a central aspect of their sex-uality. For example, one youth noted that the name-calling had no repercussion on his sexuality because he did not interpret the ridicule as emanating from his unconventional sexuality. He did not feel that the abuse made him gay or caused him to delay self-identifying as gay. He felt, however, that the ridicule contributed to this tendency to withdraw from social settings, causing him to be more introverted and self-effacing.

> It had no real implications for my sexual identification. Everybody in my school was teased; everyone was called faggot, so I really didn't feel like I was singled out. But it made me trust people less. Hurt my self-esteem. I still need to be liked by others and if not, it upsets me. Maybe why I spent so much time alone. People hurt you. On the good side, I developed good sarcastic skills and a dry wit.

Including those who had many feminine characteristics during childhood, as many as three-quarters of the gay/bisexual youths interviewed had few interests or characteristics usually attributed to men in North American culture. Being *neither* particularly masculine *nor* feminine resulted in youths occupying the middle rung of the peer-group status hierarchy. When not alone, they were usually with a best buddy or a small group of male friends with whom they spend considerable time. Although they were seldom as frequently ridiculed by peers as were youths who were gender atypical in their lifestyle, such youths still faced verbal abuse, usually from same-age boys. The personal characteristics that became targets of abuse were notably analogous to those that heterosexual boys also receive teasing about if they are "unconventional": physical features, personality characteristics, and intelligence. Similar to other gay/bisexual youths, however, most recalled early, intense, natural attractions to other boys and men.

Acting Like a Boy

Not all of the gay/bisexual boys felt different from peers, acted in gender-atypical ways, expressed effeminate gestures and postures, or disliked team sports during their childhood. One in ten was masculine in appearance, behavior, and interests—

nearly indistinguishable from their childhood masculine heterosexual peers. Although these relatively rare boys recalled, in retrospect, that they might have had "nonsexual" attractions to males during early childhood, they had few memories of *sexual* attractions to girls, boys, or anything else. Now, however, they believe that their same-sex attractions have always been a natural part of who they are.

Many of these youths reminisced that as children they chased girls, but this was more of a game that they joined with other boys than a statement about their sexuality or their true sexual interests. As adolescents they were simply disinterested in sexual relations with girls, in being emotionally intimate with girls, or in developing romantic relationships with girls. Most never fantasized about girls. The gay youths with masculine characteristics often had difficulty articulating precisely what it was about sexuality that excited them. Many failed to recall any prepubertal sexual or erotic attractions; thus, in some respects, they appeared to be asexual, especially during the years preceding adolescence. One youth reported "a vague sense that although I did not desire intimate relations with girls, I was not sure what I wanted." Unsure of how they "became gay," the youths characterized their life before puberty as "sexless" and as deeply invested in masculine activities, especially sports.

One youth, who would later run track and play high-school baseball and football, remembered his childhood as his "glory years." Girls were not an integral part of his life.

> As a child I used to run a lot, just everywhere I could, and play tag, swimming, kickball, and softball. Loved making forts. Building blocks, Legos, war games. Just like my best buddy, which changed from time to time, well at least every year I would develop a best buddy, and it was always the best looking guy in my class who was my best friend—always an athlete. I hung around totally guys.
>
> Maybe I just did not have time but I was not into sex. I would have to say that I was sexless because I cannot remember any sexual thoughts. I

was not interested in girls even though I had several girlfriends. In general I felt left out of what my teammates said they were going through.

When asked during the interview to elaborate *any* aspect of his childhood sexuality, he drew a blank. He had many stories of athletic exploits but no sexual ones. Years after pubertal onset he discovered his sexuality and expressed wonderment regarding the location of his sexual desires during childhood.

Similar to this youth, others appeared in most respects to be the traditional, heterosexual boy next door. This was especially evident in their play activities and partners. They enjoyed their popularity with other boys, and they often developed a best friendship with another boy, usually a teammate on a sports team. One swimmer noted that the time he spent "with Jared and the other guys on the swim team was the happiest time of my life."

The sports acumen of these youths was equal or superior to many of their heterosexual peers. However, a distinct bias existed in terms of liking and participating in individual rather than team sports. While many played competitive team sports, their participation appeared more obligatory as an important aspect of male culture than a real choice. Their true love was more apparent in individual sports, especially swimming, track, tennis, and wrestling. Similar to other gay/bisexual youths, many disliked the aggressive, competitive nature of team sports.

> For Dad I did baseball—and it wasn't that I was bad, because I made the team and started— but I just couldn't get into it. Like I refused to slide because I was afraid I'd hurt the other guy, and I was just not going to go crashing into fences to catch a ball! I didn't like being challenged at sports because I was afraid I wasn't good enough so I went into individual sports like tennis, track, and swimming. Dad and I reached a compromise with my track, especially when I won the state 1000M.

> As a child I really liked horseplay, tag, and wrestling. I have to admit that I hated the Little League but as a kid I played Little League for

five years, usually at second base. Later tennis, two years of which were on varsity and I lettered. Also track and lifted weights. I was accepted by everyone, but the baseball guys who were so cutthroat; every game was the end of the universe for them!

As a result of their peer status, few of these boys were teased by others. When they were, it was usually within the context of normative male bonding—teasing in good humor. Although relatively few heard references to being gay, they nonetheless dreaded such accusations. One youth feared that his friends would notice his head turning when a good-looking guy passed by.

In contrast to the gay/bisexual youths previously discussed, masculine youths by disposition looked and acted like other boys their age, participated in typical masculine pursuits, and "fooled" peers into believing that they were heterosexual. They claimed no memories of homoerotic or even sexual attractions during childhood, perhaps, one might speculate, because the realization that the true objects of their sexual desires were boys would have caused them considerable grief and confusion. They were often perceived to be social butterflies and they actively engaged in male–male competitive sports, although their preference was individual sports. Their male friendships were critical to maintain; they wanted and needed to be members of the "male crowd." From all appearances they succeeded in creating a facade of heterosexuality, in being accepted as "one of the guys."

Reflections on the Childhood of Gay/Bisexual Youths

From an early age, the vast majority of the gay/bisexual youths believed that they were different from other boys their age and that regardless of the source of this feeling, it was a natural, instinctual, and omnipresent aspect of themselves. The pattern that most characterized the youths' awareness, interpretation, and affective responses to childhood attractions consisted of an overwhelming desire to be in the company of men. They wanted to touch, smell, see, and hear masculinity. This awareness originated from earliest childhood memories; in this sense, they "always felt gay."

Most ultimately recognized, however, that these feelings were not typical of other boys and that it would be wrong or unwise to express them because of family and peer prohibitions. Others simply assumed that all boys felt as they did and could not understand why their friends were not as preoccupied as they were with homoerotic desires. Although these attractions may have felt natural, the youths were told by parents, friends, religious leaders, teachers, and dogma that such desires were evil and sinful. Many knew that their homosensuality was ill-advised, but they did not thus conclude that it made them sick or immoral.

Beyond this common pattern, two other sources of "feeling different" characterized the vast majority of the gay/bisexual youths. Many were dominated by an overwhelming sense that their difference was attributed to their feminine appearance, behavior, and interests. In many respects these characteristics typify the stereotype that many, gay and nongay alike, have of gay males. Youths so feminized felt natural and true to self, despite the fact that their gender noncomformity was frequently and severely punished with ostracism. Most of these youths detested cultural definitions of masculinity and felt at odds with other boys because they did not share their peers' interest in team sports, competition, and aggressive pursuits. Being an outcast in the world of male peers was usually felt to be unfair and unnecessary, but also inevitable. To avoid becoming expatriated, these boys developed friendships with girls, perhaps because of common interests such as attractions to boys and appreciation of the arts, creativity, clothing, and manners. They felt more comfortable and had greater comradery with girls than with boys. Few wanted to change either their genitalia or their behavior; they did not view themselves as women in disguise—they were simply repulsed by the "grossness" of masculinity and attracted to the sensitivities of femininity.

Other youths failed to duplicate standard masculine characteristics without necessarily assuming feminine traits. In this they may well have resembled heterosexual peers who were also neither particularly masculine nor feminine in behavior. They differed, however, in the direction of their sexual attractions. Being disinterested in team sports and other typical aggressive and competitive pursuits caused them to feel unmasculine, but they did not thus necessarily construe themselves as feminine. Relatively few spent time with girls or participated in girl games. Rather, their activities can be characterized as "appropriate" for either girls or boys.

Many of these youths felt that they simply faded into the background when with peers. Most were loners for a considerable period during their childhood; when they socialized with peers they were usually with one or two male friends. Although they were spared the vicious, pervasive verbal abuse that their effeminate counterparts received during childhood, they were not immune from harassment. Boys still ridiculed them for their physical features, lack of ability in athletic pursuits, and unconventional behavior or intelligence.

In contrast to these gay/bisexual youths was a much smaller group of youths who were nearly indistinguishable from masculine heterosexual boys their age. Constituting at least one of every ten youths interviewed, their participation in typical masculine pursuits, especially individual and team sports, blended them into the fabric of male culture. Many were socially active and one might speculate that their male friendships were an enjoyable sublimation of homoerotic attractions that they only later, often during adolescence or young adulthood, recognized. Their failure to recognize any sexual feelings during childhood could be attributed to the direction their sexual attractions might take if they were allowed into consciousness. In this respect, their psychic investment was to conceal this secret from themselves and others.

Unknown is the etiology of these patterns and their long-term effects on other aspects of development, including participation in sexual activities, self-recognition of a sexual identity, disclosure of that identity to others, romantic relationships with other males, and developing a positive sense of self.

Although several of the interviewed youths experienced same-sex attractions as arising abruptly and unexpectedly, for the vast majority these feelings emerged as gradual, inevitable, and not particularly surprising. In this sense, these findings are at odds with the theme of this book—diversity in developmental patterns. Few if any youths believed that they could control the direction of their sexual feelings and no youth believed that he ultimately chose his sexual orientation or sexual attractions. The incorporation of the various masculine and feminine behavioral patterns was felt by youths to be less a matter of choice than an experienced naturalness that was derived from their biological heritage and, less commonly, from early socialization processes beyond their control. On his emerging sexuality, one youth reflected, "It was like being visited by an old friend." This awareness may have emerged early or late, surfaced gradually or arrived instantaneously, felt normal or wrong, motivated sexual activity or abstinence—but it was one aspect of the self that was present without invitation. Future development [. . .] was simply an unfolding of that which was already present, with puberty playing a crucial turning point for many youths in clarifying for them that their homosensuality had a sexual component. From this awareness often loomed first sexual encounters, which occurred during the earliest years of childhood or waited until young adulthood. They too were interpreted by the youths in diverse ways, thus having a differential impact on the eventual incorporation of a gay or bisexual identity.

Notes

1. See early account in A. P. Bell, M. S. Weinberg, and S. K. Hammersmith (1981), *Sexual Preference: Its Development in Men and Women* (Bloomington, IN: Indiana University Press). For data on gay youths see G. Herdt and A. Boxer (1993), *Children of Horizons: How Gay and Lesbian Teens Are Leading a New Way Out*

of the Closet (Boston: Beacon) and R. C. Savin-Williams (1990), *Gay and Lesbian Youth: Expressions of Identity* (New York: Hemisphere).

2. J. Sophie presents a synthesis of coming-out models in her 1985–1986 article, "A Critical Examination of Stage Theories of Lesbian Identity Development," *Journal of Homosexuality, 12,* 39–51.

3. Revised in his 1989 article, R. R. Troiden, "The Formation of Homosexual Identities," *Journal of Homosexuality, 17,* 43–73. Additional empirical evidence is available in references in note 1 and B. S. Newman and P. G. Muzzonigro (1993), "The Effects of Traditional Family Values on the Coming Out Process of Gay Male Adolescents," *Adolescence, 28,* 213–226, and S. K. Tellijohann and J. P. Price (1993), "A Qualitative Examination of Adolescent Homosexuals' Life Experiences: Ramifications for Secondary School Personnel," *Journal of Homosexuality, 26,* 41–56.

4. For a comprehensive review of this literature see J. M. Bailey and K. J. Zucker (1995), "Childhood Sex-Typed Behavior and Sexual Orientation: A Conceptual Analysis and Quantitative Review," *Developmental Psychology, 31,* 43–55.

5. For a review of studies using these measures, see note 4 and J. M. Bailey (1996), "Gender Identity," in R. C. Savin-Williams and K. M. Cohen (Eds.), *The Lives of Lesbians, Gays, and Bisexuals: Children to Adults,* pp. 71–93 (Fort Worth, TX: Harcourt Brace); R. Green (1987), *The "Sissy Boy Syndrome" and the Development of Homosexuality* (New Haven: Yale University Press); G. Phillips and R. Over (1992), "Adult Sexual Orientation in Relation to Memories of Childhood Gender Conforming and Gender Nonconforming Behaviors," *Archives of Sexual Behavior, 21,* 543–558; and B. Zuger (1984), "Early Effeminate Behavior in Boys: Outcome and Significance for Homosexuality," *Journal of Nervous and Mental Disease, 172,* 90–97.

6. From R. A. Isay (1989), *Being Homosexual: Gay Men and Their Development* (New York: Farrar Straus Grove).

7. See sources in notes 1 and 4.

8. Experimental evidence is supplied in K. J. Zucker, D. N. Wilson-Smith, J. A. Kurita, and A. Stern (1995), "Children's Appraisals for Sex-Typed Behavior in their Peers," *Sex Roles, 33,* 703–725.

9. See references in notes 4 and 5.

Ann Ferguson

Making a Name for Yourself: Transgressive Acts and Gender Performance

Though girls as well as boys infringe the rules, the overwhelming majority of violations in every single category, from misbehavior to obscenity, are by males. In a disturbing tautology, transgressive behavior is that which constitutes masculinity. Consequently, African American males in the very act of identification, of signifying masculinity, are likely to be breaking rules.

I use the concept of sex/gender not to denote the existence of a stable, unitary category that reflects the presence of fundamental, natural biological difference, but as a socially constructed category whose form and meaning [vary] culturally and historically. We come to know ourselves and to recognize others as of a different sex through an overdetermined complex process inherent in every sphere of social life at the ideological and discursive level, through social structures and institutional arrangements, as well as through the micropolitics of social interactions.[1] We take sex difference for granted, as a natural form of difference as we look for it, recognize it, celebrate it; this very repetition of the "fact" of difference produces and confirms its existence. Indeed, assuming sex/gender difference and identifying as one or the other gender is a precursor of being culturally recognizable as "human."

While all these modes of constituting gender as difference were palpable in the kids' world, in the following analysis of sex/gender as a

From *Bad Boys: Public Schools in the Making of Black Masculinity,* by Ann Ferguson. Ann Arbor: University of Michigan Press, 2000. © University of Michigan. Reprinted with permission.

heightened and highly charged resource for self-fashioning and making a name for oneself, the phenomenological approach developed by ethnomethodologists and by poststructuralist feminist Judith Butler is the most productive one to build on. Here gender is conceptualized as something we do in a performance that is both individually and socially meaningful. We signal our gender identification through an ongoing performance of normative acts that are ritually specific, drawing on well-worked-over, sociohistorical scripts and easily recognizable scenarios.[2]

Butler's emphasis on the coerced and coercive nature of these performances is especially useful. Her work points out that the enactment of sex difference is neither voluntary nor arbitrary in form but is a compulsory requirement of social life. Gender acts follow sociohistorical scripts that are policed through the exercise of repression and taboo. The consequences of an inadequate or bad performance are significant, ranging from ostracism and stigmatization to imprisonment and death. What I want to emphasize in the discussion that follows are the rewards that attach to this playing out of roles; for males, the enactment of masculinity is also a thoroughly embodied display of physical and social power.

Identification as masculine through gender acts, within this framework, is not simply a matter of imitation or modeling, but is better understood as a highly strategic attachment to a social category that has political effects. This attachment involves narratives of the self and of Other, constructed within and through fantasy and imagination, as well as through repetitious, referential acts.

The performance signals the individual as socially connected, embedded in a collective membership that always references relations of power.

African American boys at Rosa Parks School use three key constitutive strategies of masculinity in the embrace of the masculine "we" as a mode of self-expression. These strategies speak to and about power. The first is that of heterosexual power, always marked as male. Alain's graffiti become the centerpiece of this discussion. The second involves classroom performances that engage and disrupt the normal direction of the flow of power. The third strategy involves practices of "fighting." All three invoke a "process of iterability, a regularized and constrained repetition of norms," in doing gender, constitute masculinity as a natural, essential, corporeal style; and involve imaginary, fantasmatic identifications.[3]

These three strategies often lead to trouble, but by engaging them a boy can also make a name for himself as a real boy, the Good Bad Boy of a national fantasy. All three illustrate and underline the way that normative male practices take on a different, more sinister inflection when carried out by African American boys. Race makes a significant difference both in the form of the performance as well as its meaning for the audience of adult authority figures and children for whom it is played.

Heterosexual Power: Alain's Graffiti

One group of transgressions specifically involves behavior that expresses sexual curiosity and attraction. These offenses are designated as "personal violations" and given more serious punishment. Inscribed in these interactions are social meanings about relations of power between the sexes as well as assumptions about male and female difference at the level of the physical and biological as well as the representational. It is assumed that females are sexually passive, unlikely to be initiators of sexual passes, while males are naturally active sexual actors with strong sexual drives. Another assumption is that the feminine is a contaminated, stigmatizing category in the sex/gender hierarchy.

Typically, personal violations involved physical touching of a heterosexual nature where males were the "perpetrators" and females the "victims." A few examples from the school files remind us of some of the "normal" displays of sexual interest at this age.

- Boy was cited with "chasing a girl down the hall" [punishment: two days in the Jailhouse].
- Boy pulled a female classmate's pants down during recess [punishment: one and a half days in the Jailhouse].
- Boy got in trouble for, "touching girl on private parts. She did not like" [punishment: a day in the Jailhouse].
- Boy was cited for "forcing girl's hand between his legs" [punishment: two and a half days in the Jailhouse].

In one highly revealing case, a male was cast as the "victim" when he was verbally assaulted by another boy who called him a girl. The teacher described the "insult" and her response to it on the referral form in these words:

> During the lesson, Jonas called Ahmed a girl and said he wasn't staying after school for detention because "S" [another boy] had done the same thing. Since that didn't make it ok for anyone to speak this way I am requesting an hour of detention for Jonas. I have no knowledge of "S" saying so in my presence.

This form of insult is not unusual. When boys want to show supreme contempt for another boy they call him a girl or liken his behavior to female behavior. What is more troubling is that adults capitulate in this stigmatization. The female teacher takes for granted that a comment in which a boy is called a girl is a symbolic attack, sufficiently derogatory to merit punishment. All the participants in the classroom exchange witness the uncritical acknowledgment of adult authority to a gender order of female debasement.

Of course, this is not news to them. Boys and girls understand the meaning of being male and being female in the field of power; the binary opposition of male/female is always one that expresses a norm, maleness, and its constitutive outside, femaleness. In a conversation with a group of boys, one of them asserted and then was supported by others that "a boy can be a girl, but a girl can never be a boy." Boys can be teased, controlled, punished by being accused of being "a girl." A boy faces the degradation of "being sissified," being unmanned, transferred to the degraded category of female. Girls can be teased about being a tomboy. But this is not the same. To take on qualities of being male is the access to and performance of power. So females must now fashion themselves in terms of male qualities to partake of that power. Enactments of masculinity signal value, superiority, power.

Let us return to Alain, the 11-year-old boy who while cooling off and writing lines as a punishment in the antechamber of the Punishing Room, writes on the table in front of him: "Write 20 times. I will stop fucking 10 cent teachers and this five cent class. Fuck you. Ho! Ho! Yes Baby." Alain's message can be read in a number of ways. The most obvious way is the one of the school. A child has broken several rules in one fell swoop and must be punished: he has written on school property (punishable); he has used an obscenity (punishable); he has committed an especially defiant and disrespectful act because he is already in the Punishing Room and therefore knows his message is likely to be read (punishable). Alain is sent home both as a signal to him and to the other witnesses as well as to the students and adults who will hear it through the school grapevine that he cannot get away with such flagrant misbehavior.

An alternative reading looks at the content of the message itself and the form that Alain's anger takes at being sent to the Punishing Room. Alain's anger is being vented against his teacher and the school itself, expressing his rejection, his disidentification with school that he devalues as monetarily virtually worthless. His message expresses his anger through an assertion of sexual power—to fuck or not to fuck—one sure way that a male can conjure up the fantasmatic as well as

the physical specter of domination over a female of any age. His assertion of this power mocks the authority of the teacher to give him orders to write lines. His use of "baby" reverses the relations of power, teacher to pupil, adult to child; Alain allies himself through and with power as the school/teacher becomes "female," positioned as a sex object, as powerless, passive, infantilized. He positions himself as powerful through identification with and as the embodiment of male power as he disidentifies with school. At this moment, Alain is not just a child, a young boy, but taking the position of "male" as a strategic resource for enacting power, for being powerful. At the same time, this positioning draws the admiring, titillated attention of his peers.

These moments of sex trouble exemplify some of the aspects of the performance of sex/gender difference that is naturalized through what is deemed punishable as well as punishment practices. Judging from the discipline records, girls do not commit sexual violations. It is as if by their very nature they are incapable. To be female is to be powerless, victimizable, chased down the hallway, an object to be acted upon with force, whose hand can be seized and placed between male legs. To be female is also to be sexually passive, coy, the "chaste" rather than the chaser, in relation to male sexual aggressiveness. In reality, I observed girls who chased boys and who interacted with them physically. Girls, in fact, did "pants" boys, but these acts went unreported by the boys. For them to report and therefore risk appearing to be victimized by a girl publicly would be a humiliating outcome that would only undermine their masculinity. In the production of natural difference, boys' performances work as they confirm that they are active pursuers, highly sexualized actors who must be punished to learn to keep their burgeoning sexuality under control. There is a reward for the behavior even if it may be punished as a violation. In the case of African American boys, sex trouble is treated as egregious conduct.

African American males have historically been constructed as hypersexualized within the national imagination. Compounding this is the process of the adultification of their behavior. Intimations of sexuality on their part, especially when directed toward girls who are bused in—white girls from middle-class families—are dealt with as grave transgressions with serious consequences.

Power Reversals: Class Acts

Performance is a routine part of classroom work. Students are called upon to perform in classes by teachers to show off their prowess or demonstrate their ineptitude or lack of preparation. They are required to read passages aloud, for example, before a highly critical audience of their peers. This display is teacher initiated and reflects the official curricula; they are command performances with well-scripted roles, predictable in the outcome of who has and gets respect, who is in control, who succeeds, who fails.

Another kind of performance is the spontaneous outbreaks initiated by the pupils generally defined under the category of "disruption" by the school. These encompass a variety of actions that punctuate and disrupt the order of the day. During the school year about two-thirds of these violations were initiated by boys and a third by girls. Here are some examples from the discipline files of girls being "disruptive":

- Disruptive in class—laughing, provoking others to join her. Purposely writing wrong answers, being very sassy, demanding everyone's attention.
- Constantly talking; interrupting; crumpling paper after paper; loud.

Some examples of boys' disruption:

- Constant noise, indian whoops, face hiccups, rapping.
- Chanting during quiet time—didn't clean up during art [punishment: detention].
- Joking, shouting out, uncooperative, disruptive during lesson.

From the perspective of kids, what the school characterizes as "disruption" on the referral slips is often a form of performance of the self: comedy, drama, melodrama become moments for self-expression and display. Disruption adds some lively spice to the school day; it injects laughter, drama, excitement, a delicious unpredictability to the classroom routine through spontaneous, improvisational outbursts that add flavor to the bland events.

In spite of its improvisational appearance, most performance is highly ritualized with its own script, timing, and roles. Teachers as well as students engage in the ritual and play their parts. Some kids are regular star performers. Other kids are audience. However, when a substitute is in charge of the class and the risk of being marked as a troublemaker is minimal, even the most timid kids "act up." These rituals circulate important extracurricular knowledge about relations of power.

These dramatic moments are sites for the presentation of a potent masculine presence in the classroom. The Good Bad Boy of our expectations engages power, takes risks, makes the class laugh, and the teacher smile. Performances mark boundaries of "essential difference"—risk taking, brinkmanship. The open and public defiance of the teacher in order to get a laugh, make things happen, take center stage, be admired, is a resource for doing masculinity.

These acts are especially meaningful for those children who have already been marginalized as outside of the community of "good," hardworking students. For the boys already labeled as troublemakers, taking control of the spotlight and turning it on oneself so that one can shine, highlights, for a change, one's strengths and talents. Already caught in the limelight, these kids put on a stirring performance.

Reggie, one of the Troublemakers, prides himself on being witty and sharp, a talented performer. He aspires to two careers: one is becoming a Supreme Court justice, the other an actor. He had recently played the role of Caliban in the school production of *The Tempest* that he described excitedly to me:

I always try to get the main characters in the story 'cause I might turn out to be an actor because I'm really good at acting and I've already did some acting. Shakespeare! See I got a good part. I was Caliban. I had to wear the black suit. Black pants and top. Caliban was a beast! In the little picture that we saw, he looks like the . . . the . . . [searching for image] the beast of Notre Dame. The one that rings the bells like *fing! fing! fing!*

Here is one official school activity where Reggie gets to show off something that he is "good at." He is also proud to point out that this is not just a role in any play, but one in a play by Shakespeare. Here his own reward, which is not just doing something that he is good at, but doing it publicly so that he can receive the attention and respect of adults and peers, coincides with the school's educational agenda of creating an interest in Shakespeare among children.

Reggie also plays for an audience in the classroom, where he gets in trouble for disruption. He describes one of the moments for me embellished with a comic imitation of the teacher's female voice and his own swaggering demeanor as he tells the story:

> The teacher says [he mimics a high-pitched fussy voice], "You not the teacher of this class." And then I say [adopts a sprightly cheeky tone], "Oh, yes I am." Then she say, "No, you're not, and if you got a problem, you can just leave." I say, "Okay" and leave.

This performance, like others I witnessed, are strategies for positioning oneself in the center of the room in a face-off with the teacher, the most powerful person up to that moment. Fundamental to the performance is engagement with power; authority is teased, challenged, even occasionally toppled from its secure heights for brief moments. Children-generated theatrics allow the teasing challenge of adult power that can expose its chinks and weaknesses. The staged moments heighten tension, test limits, vent emotions, perform acts of courage. For Reggie to have capitulated to the teacher's ultimatum would have been to lose what he perceives as the edge in the struggle. In addition, he has won his escape from the classroom.

Horace describes his challenge to the teacher's authority in a summer school math class:

> Just before the end of the period he wrote some of our names on the board and said, "Whoever taught these students when they were young must have been dumb." So I said, "Oh, I didn't remember that was you teaching me in the first grade." Everyone in the room cracked up. I was laughing so hard, I was on the floor. He sent me to the office.

Horace is engaging the teacher in a verbal exchange with a comeback to an insult rather than just passively taking it. In this riposte, Horace not only makes his peers laugh at the teacher, but he also defuses the insult through a quick reversal. The audience in the room, raised on TV sitcom repartee and canned laughter, is hard to impress, so the wisecrack, the rejoinder, must be swift and sharp. Not everyone can get a laugh at the teachers' expense, and to be topped by the teacher would be humiliating, success brings acknowledgment, confirmation, applause from one's peers. For Horace, this is a success story, a moment of gratification in a day that brings few his way.

The tone of the engagement with power and the identity of the actor is highly consequential in terms of whether a performance is overlooked by the teacher or becomes the object of punishment. In a study of a Texas high school, Foley documents similar speech performances.[4] He describes how both teacher and students collaborate to devise classroom rituals and "games" to help pass the time given the context of routinized, alienating classroom work. He observes that upper-middle-class male Anglo students derail boring lessons by manipulating teachers through subtle "making out" games without getting in trouble. In contrast, low-income male Hispanic students, who were more likely to challenge teachers openly in these games, were punished. Foley concluded that one of the important lessons learned by all participants in these ritual games was that the subtle manipulation of authority was a much more effective way of getting your way than openly confronting power.

Style becomes a decisive factor in who gets in trouble. I am reminded of comments made by one of the student specialists at Rosa Parks who explained the high rate of black kids getting in trouble by remarking on their different style of rule breaking: "The white kids are sneaky, black kids are more open."

So why are the black kids "more open" in their confrontations with power? Why not be really "smart" and adopt a style of masculinity that allows them to engage in these rituals that spice the school day and help pass time, but carry less risk of trouble because it is within certain mutually understood limits?

These rituals are not merely a way to pass time, but are also a site for constituting a gendered racial subjectivity. For African American boys, the performance of masculinity invokes cultural conventions of speech performance that draw on a black repertoire. Verbal performance is an important medium for black males to establish a reputation, make a name for yourself, and achieve status.[5] Smitherman points out that black talk in general is

> a functional dynamic that is simultaneously a mechanism for learning about life and the world and a vehicle for achieving group recognition. Even in what appears to be only casual conversation, whoever speaks is highly conscious of the fact that his personality is on exhibit and his status at stake.[6]

Oral performance has a special significance in black culture for the expression of masculinity. Harper points out that verbal performance functions as an identifying marker for masculinity only when it is delivered in the vernacular and that "a too-evident facility in white idiom can quickly identify one as a white-identified uncle Tom who must also be therefore weak, effeminate, and probably a fag."[7] Though the speech performances that I witnessed were not always delivered in the strict vernacular, the nonverbal, bodily component accompanying it was always delivered in a manner that was the flashy, boldly flamboyant popular

style essential to a good performance. The body language and spoken idiom openly engage power in a provocative competitive way. To be indirect, "sly," would not be performing masculinity.

This nonstandard mode of self-representation epitomizes the very form the school seeks to exclude and eradicate. It is a masculine enactment of defiance played in a black key that is bound for punishment. Moreover, the process of adultification translates the encounter from a simple verbal clash with an impertinent child into one interpreted as an intimidating threat.

Though few white girls in the school were referred to the office for disruptive behavior, a significant number of African American girls staged performances, talked back to teachers, challenged authority, and were punished. But there was a difference with the cultural framing of their enactments and those of the boys. The bottom line of Horace's story was that "everyone in the room cracked up." He engaged authority through a self-produced public spectacle with an eye for an audience that is at home with the cultural icon of the Good Bad Boy as well as the "real black man." Boys expect to get attention. Girls vie for attention too, but it is perceived as illegitimate behavior. As the teacher described it in the referral form, the girl is "demanding attention." The prevailing cultural framework denies her the rights for dramatic public display.

Male and female classroom performance is different in another respect. Girls are not rewarded with the same kind of applause or recognition by peers or by teachers. Their performance is sidelined; it is not given center stage. Teachers are more likely to "turn a blind eye" to such a display rather than call attention to it, for girls are seen as individuals who operate in cliques at most and are unlikely to foment insurrection in the room. Neither the moral nor the pragmatic principle prods teachers to take action. The behavior is not taken seriously; it is rated as "sassy" rather than symptomatic of a more dangerous disorder. In some classrooms, in fact, risk taking and "feistiness" on the part of girls is subtly encouraged given the prevailing belief that what they need is to become more visible, more assertive in the classroom. The notion is that signs of self-assertion on their part should be encouraged rather than squelched.

Disruptive acts have a complex, multifaceted set of meanings for the male Troublemakers themselves. Performance as an expression of black masculinity is a production of a powerful subjectivity to be reckoned with, to be applauded; respect and ovation are in a context where none is forthcoming. The boys' anger and frustration as well as fear motivate the challenge to authority. Troublemakers act and speak out as stigmatized outsiders.

Ritual Performances of Masculinity: Fighting

Each year a substantial number of kids at Rosa Parks get into trouble for fighting. It is the most frequent offense for which they are referred to the Punishing Room. Significantly, the vast majority of the offenders are African American males.[8]

The school has an official position on fighting; it is the wrong way to handle any situation, at any time, no matter what. Schools have good reasons for banning fights: kids can get hurt and when fights happen they sully the atmosphere of order, making the school seem like a place of danger, of violence.

The prescribed routine for schoolchildren to handle situations that might turn into a fight is to tell an adult who is then supposed to take care of the problem. This routine ignores the unofficial masculine code that if someone hits you, you should solve the problem yourself rather than showing weakness and calling an adult to intervene. However, it is expected that girls with a problem will seek out an adult for assistance. Girls are assumed to be physically weaker, less aggressive, more vulnerable, more needy of self-protection; they must attach themselves to adult (or male) power to survive. This normative gen-

der distinction, in how to handle both problems of a sexual nature and physical aggression, operates as a "proof" of a physical and dispositional gender nature rather than behavior produced through discourses and practices that constitute sex difference.

Referrals of males to the Punishing Room, therefore, are cases where the unofficial masculine code for problem resolution has prevailed. Telling an adult is anathema to these youth. According to their own codes, the act of "telling" is dangerous for a number of reasons. The most practical of these sets it as a statement to the "whole world" that you are unable to deal with a situation on your own—to take care of yourself—an admission that can have disastrous ramifications when adult authority is absent. This is evident from the stance of a Troublemaker who questions the practical application of the official code by invoking knowledge of the proper male response when one is "attacked" that is shared with the male student specialist charged with enforcing the regulation: "I said, 'Mr. B, if somebody came up and hit you, what would you do?' 'Well,' he says, 'We're not talking about me right now, see.' That's the kind of attitude they have. It's all like on you."

Another reason mentioned by boys for not relying on a teacher to take care of a fight situation is that adults are not seen as having any real power to effectively change the relations among kids:

> If someone keep messing with you, like if someone just keep on and you tell them to leave you alone, then you tell the teacher. The teacher can't do anything about it because, see, she can't hit you or nothing. Only thing she can do is tell them to stop. But then he keep on doing it. You have no choice but to hit 'em. You already told him once to stop.

This belief extends to a distrust of authority figures by these young offenders. The assumption that all the children see authority figures such as teachers, police, and psychologists as acting on their behalf and trust they will act fairly may be true of middle- and upper-class children brought up to expect protection from authority figures in society. This is not the case with many of the children at the school. Their mistrust of authority is rooted in the historical and locally grounded knowledge of power relations that come from living in a largely black and impoverished neighborhood.

Fighting becomes, therefore, a powerful spectacle through which to explore trouble as a site for the construction of manhood. The practice takes place along a continuum that ranges from play—spontaneous outbreaks of pummeling and wrestling in fun, ritualistic play that shows off "cool" moves seen on video games, on TV, or in movies—to serious, angry socking, punching, fistfighting. A description of some of these activities and an analysis of what they mean provides the opportunity for us to delve under the surface of the ritualized, discrete acts that make up a socially recognizable fight even into the psychic, emotional, sensuous aspects of gender performativity. The circular, interactive flow between fantasmatic images, internal psychological processes, and physical acts suggest the dynamics of attachment of masculine identification.

Fighting is one of the social practices that add tension, drama, and spice to the routine of the school day. Pushing, grabbing, shoving, kicking, karate chopping, wrestling, fistfighting engage the body and the mind. Fighting is about play and games, about anger and pain, about hurt feelings, about "messing around." To the spectator, a fight can look like serious combat, yet when the combatants are separated by an adult, they claim, "We were only playing." In fact, a single fight event can move along the continuum from play to serious blows in a matter of seconds. As one of the boys explained, "You get hurt and you lose your temper."

Fighting is typically treated as synonymous with "aggression" or "violence," terms that already encode the moral, definitional frame that obscures the contradictory ways that the practice, in all its manifestations, is used in our society. We, as good citizens, can distance ourselves from aggressive and violent behavior. "Violence" as

discourse constructs "fighting" as pathological, symptomatic of asocial, dangerous tendencies, even though the practice of "fighting" and the discourses that constitute this practice as "normal," are in fact taken for granted as ritualized resources for "doing" masculinity in the contemporary United States.

The word *fighting* encompasses the "normal" as well as the pathological. It allows the range of meanings that the children, specifically the boys whom I interviewed and observed, as well as some of the girls, bring to the practice. One experience that it is open to is the sensuous, highly charged embodied experience before, during, and after fighting; the elating experience of "losing oneself" that I heard described in fight stories.

War Stories

I began thinking about fights soon after I started interviews with the Troublemakers and heard "fight stories." Unlike the impoverished and reluctantly told accounts of the school day, these stories were vivid, elaborate descriptions of bodies, mental states, and turbulent emotional feelings. They were stirring, memorable moments in the tedious school routine.

Horace described a fight with an older boy who had kept picking on him. He told me about the incident as he was explaining how he had broken a finger one day when we were trading "broken bones" stories.

> When I broke this finger right here it really hurted. I hit somebody in the face. It was Charles. I hit him in the face. You know the cafeteria and how you walk down to go to the cafeteria. Right there. That's where it happened. Charles picked me up and put me on the wall, slapped me on the wall, and dropped me. It hurt. It hurt bad. I got mad because he used to be messing with me for a long time so I just swung as hard as I could, closed my eyes, and just *pow*, hit him in the face. But I did like a roundhouse swing instead of doing it straight and it got the index finger of my right hand. So it was right there, started right here, and all

around this part [he is showing me the back of his hand] it hurt. It was swollen. Oooh! It was like this! But Charles, he got hurt too. The next day I came to school I had a cast on my finger and he had a bandage on his ear. It was kinda funny, we just looked at each other and smiled.

The thing that most surprised and intrigued me about Horace's story was that he specifically recalled seeing Charles the next day and that they had looked at each other and smiled. Was this a glance of recognition, of humor, of recollection of something pleasing, of all those things? The memory of the exchanged smile derailed my initial assumption that fighting was purely instrumental. This original formulation said that boys fight because they have to fight in order to protect themselves from getting beaten up on the playground. Fighting from this instrumental perspective is a purely survival practice. Boys do fight to stave off the need to fight in the future, to stop the harassment from other boys on the playground and in the streets. However, this explains only a small group of boys who live in certain environments; it relegates fighting to the realm of the poor, the deviant, the delinquent, the pathological. This position fails to address these physical clashes as the central normative practice in the preparation of bodies, of mental stances, of self-reference for manhood and as the most effective form of conflict resolution in the realm of popular culture and international relations.

I listened closely to the stories to try to make sense of behavior that was so outside of my own experience, yet so familiar a part of the landscape of physical fear and vulnerability that I as a female walked around with every day. I asked school adults about their own memories of school and fighting. I was not surprised to find that few women seemed to recall physical fights at school, though they had many stories of boys who teased them or girlfriends whom they were always "fighting" with. This resonated with my own experience. I was struck, however, by the fact that all of the men whom I talked to had had to position themselves in some way with regard to fighting. I was also struck that several of these men framed

the memory of fighting in their past as a significant learning experience.

Male adults in school recall fighting themselves, but in the context both of school rules and of hindsight argue that they now know better. One of the student specialists admitted that he used to fight a lot. I found it significant that he saw "fighting" as the way he "learned":

> I used to fight a lot. [Pause.] I used to fight a lot and I used to be real stubborn and silent. I wouldn't say anything to anybody. It would cause me a lot of problems, but that's just the way I learned.

The after-school martial arts instructor also admitted to fighting a lot when he was younger:

> There were so many that I had as a kid that it's hard to remember all of them and how they worked out. But yes, I did have a lot of arguments and fights. A lot of times I would lose my temper, which is what kids normally do, they lose their temper, and before they have a chance to work things out they begin punching and kicking each other. Right? Well I did a lot of those things so I know from experience those are not the best thing to do.

As I explored the meaning of fighting I began to wonder how I, as female, had come to be shaped so fighting was not a part of my own corporeal or mental repertoire. A conversation with my brother reminded me of a long forgotten self that could fight, physically, ruthlessly, inflict hurt, cause tears. "We were always fighting," he recalled. "You used to beat me up." Memories of these encounters came back. I am standing with a tuft of my brother's hair in my hand, furious tears in my eyes. Full of hate for him. Kicking, scratching, socking, feeling no pain. Where had this physical power gone? I became "ladylike," repressing my anger, limiting my physical contact to shows of affection, fearful. I wondered about the meaning of being female in a society in which to be female is to be always conscious of men's physical power and to consciously chart one's everyday routines to avoid becoming a victim of this power, but to never learn the bodily and mental pleasure of fighting back.

Bodily Preparations: Pain and Pleasure

Fighting is first and foremost a bodily practice. I think about fighting and physical closeness as I stand observing the playground at recess noticing a group of three boys, bodies entangled, arms and legs flailing. In another area, two boys are standing locked closely in a wrestling embrace. Children seem to gravitate toward physical contact with each other. For boys, a close, enraptured body contact is only legitimate when they are positioned as in a fight. It is shocking that this bodily closeness between boys would be frowned on, discouraged if it were read as affection. Even boys who never get in trouble for "fighting" can be seen engaging each other through the posturing and miming, the grappling of playfight encounters.

This play can lead to "real" fights. The thin line between play and anger is crossed as bodies become vulnerable, hurt, and tempers are lost. One of the white boys in the school who was in trouble for fighting describes the progression this way:

> Well we were messing with each other and when it went too far, he started hitting me and then I hit him back and then it just got into a fight. It was sorta like a game between me, him and Thomas. How I would get on Thomas's back an—he's a big guy—and Stephen would try to hit me and I would wanta hit him back. So when Thomas left it sorta continued and I forgot which one of us wanted to stop—but one of us wanted to stop and the other one wouldn't.

Fighting is about testing and proving your bodily power over another person, both to yourself and to others through the ability to "hurt" someone as well as to experience "hurt."

HORACE: You know Claude. He's a bad boy in the school. When I was in the fifth grade, he was in the fifth grade. I intercepted his pass and he threw the ball at my head and then I said, "You're mad," and I twisted the ball on the floor. I said, "Watch this," and y'know spiraled it on the floor, and he kicked it and it hit my leg, and I said, "Claude, if you hit me one more time with the ball or anything I'm going to hurt you." He said. "What if you do?" I said, "Okay, you expect me not to do anything, right?" He said, "Nope." Then I just *pow, pow, pow,* and I got him on the floor and then I got him on his back. I wanted to hurt him badly but I couldn't.

ANN: Why couldn't you?

HORACE: I didn't want to get in trouble. And if I did really hurt him it wouldn't prove anything anyway. But it did. It proved that I could hurt him and he didn't mess with me anymore.

Pain is an integral part of fighting. Sometimes it is the reason for lashing out in anger. This description by Wendell also captures the loss of self-control experienced at the moment of the fight:

> Sometimes it starts by capping or by somebody slams you down or somebody throws a bullet at you. You know what a bullet is, don't you? [He chuckles delightedly because I think of a bullet from a gun.] The bullet I am talking about is a football! You throw it with all your might and it hits somebody. It just very fast and they call it bullets. You off-guard and they throw it at your head, and bullets they throw with all their might so it hurts. Then that sorta gets you all pissed off. Then what happens is, you kinda like, "Why you threw it?" " 'Cause I wanted to. Like, so?" "So you not going to do that to me." Then: "So you going to do something about it?" Real smart. "Yeah!" And then you tap the person on the shoulder and your mind goes black and then *shweeeee* [a noise and hand signal that demonstrates the evaporation of thought] you go at it. And you don't stop until the teacher comes and stops it.

Fighting is a mechanism for preparing masculinized bodies through the playful exercise of bodily moves and postures and the routinized rehearsal of sequences and chains of stances of readiness, attack, and defense. Here it is crucial to emphasize that while many boys in the school never ever engage in an actual physical fight with another boy or girl during school hours, the majority engage in some form of body enactments of fantasized "fight" scenarios. They have observed boys and men on TV, in the movies, in video games, on the street, in the playground adopting these stances.

These drills simultaneously prepare and cultivate the mental states in which corporeal styles are grounded. So for instance, boys are initiated into the protocol of enduring physical pain and mental anguish—"like a man"—through early and small infusions of the toxic substance itself in play fights. The practice of fighting is the site for a hot-wiring together of physical pain and pleasure, as components of masculinity as play and bodily hurt inevitably coincide.

Consequently, it also engages powerful emotions. Lindsey described the feelings he experienced prior to getting into a fight:

> Sometimes it's play. And sometimes it's real. But that's only sometimes, because they can just suddenly make you angry and then, it's like they take control of your mind. Like they manipulate your mind if you angry. Little by little you just lose it and you get in a temper.

One of the white boys in the school who had gotten in trouble for fighting described his thoughts and feelings preceding a fight and the moment of "just going black" in a loss of self:

> My mind would probably be going through how I would do this. If I would stop it now or if I would follow through with it. But once the fight actually happens I sort of go black and just fight 'em.

Fighting is a practice, like sports, that is so symbolically "masculine" that expressions of emotion or behavior that might call one's manhood into question are allowed without danger of jeopardizing one's manliness. Even crying is a permissible expression of "masculinity" under these circumstances. One of the boys who told me he never cried, corrected himself:

> But if I be mad, I cry. Like if I get into a fight or something like that, I cry because I lose my temper and get so mad. But sometimes, I play football and if I cry that mean I'm ready to tumble—throw the ball to me because I'm going.

Fighting in school is a space in which boys can feel free to do emotional work.[9] In a social practice that is so incontrovertibly coded as masculine, behaviors marked as feminine, such as crying, can be called upon as powerful wellsprings for action.

One of the questions that I asked all the boys about fighting came out of my own ignorance. My query was posed in terms of identity work around the winning and losing of fights. Did you ever win a fight? Did you ever lose a fight? How did you feel when you lost? How did you feel when you won? I found the answers slippery, unexpected, contradictory. I had anticipated that winning would be described in proud and boastful ways, as success stories. But there seemed to be a surprising reluctance to embellish victory. I learned that I was missing the point by posing the question the way I had in terms of winning and losing. Trey enlightened me when he explained that what was at stake was not winning or losing per se but in learning about the self:

> I won a lot of fights. You know you won when they start crying and stuff or when they stop and leave. I lost fights. Then you feel a little okay. At least you lost. I mean like you ain't goin' win every fight. At least you fought back instead of just standing there and letting them hit you.

Another boy expressed the function that fighting played in establishing yourself as being a particular kind of respectable person:

> It's probably like dumb, but if somebody wants to fight me, I mean, I don't care even if I know I can't beat 'em. I won't stop if they don't stop. I mean I'm not scared to fight anybody. I'm not a coward. I don't let anybody punk me around. If you let people punk you around, other peoples want to punk you around.

Proving yourself to others is like a game, a kind of competition:

> Me and Leslie used to fight because we used to be the biggest boys, but now we don't care anymore. We used to get friends and try and fight each other. I fought him at Baldwin school all the time. We stopped about the fifth grade [the previous year]. Just got tired, I guess.

Standing and proving yourself today can be insurance against future harassment in the yard as you make a name for yourself through readiness to fight: "Like if somebody put their hands on you, then you have to, you have to hit them back. Because otherwise you going be beat up on for the rest of your life."

Eddie, who has avoided fights because he does not want to get in trouble, is now seen as a target for anyone to beat up, according to one of his friends, who characterized Eddie's predicament this way: "He can't fight. *He can't fight.* Every girl, every boy in the whole school fixing to beat him up. Badly. They could beat him up badly."

Eddie explains his own perspective on how he has come to actually lose a reputation.

> Yeah, I won a fight in preschool. Like somebody this tall [his gesture indicates a very tall someone] I had to go like this [reaches up to demonstrate] so I could hit him. He was older than me. He was the preschool bully. Till I mess him up.

But Eddie's parents came down hard on him for getting in trouble for fighting in elementary school:

> Yeah, I lost fights. See when I got to Rosa Parks my parents told me not to fight unless I had to—so I lost my face. 'Cause I was so used to telling them to stop, don't fight, don't fight.

In constructing the self through fight stories, it is not admirable to represent oneself as the aggressor or initiator in a fight. All the boys whom I talked to about fighting presented themselves as responding to a physical attack that had to be answered in a decisive way. No one presented himself as a "bully," though I knew that Horace had

that reputation. Yet he told me that "only fights I been in is if they hit me first."

There are, however, times when it is legitimate to be the initiator. When verbal provocation is sufficient. This is when "family" has been insulted. Talking about "your momma" is tantamount to throwing down the gauntlet:

> Mostly I get in fights if somebody talk about my grandfather because he's dead. And I loved my grandfather more than I love anybody and then he died. [Tears are in Jabari's eyes as we talk.] That's why I try to tell people before they get ready to say anything, I'm like, "Don't say anything about my grandfather, 'cause if you say something about him, I'm goin' hit you."

The boys talked about how they learned to fight. How one learns to fight and what one learns about the meaning of fighting—why fight, to fight or not to fight—involved both racial identity and class positioning. Ricky and Duane, two of the Schoolboys, have been enrolled by their parents in martial arts classes. Fighting remains a necessary accoutrement of masculinity that is "schooled," not a "natural" acquisition of doing. As such, it becomes a marker of higher class position. Fighting takes place in an institutionalized arena rather than spontaneously in just any setting. The mind seems to control the body here, rather than vice versa.

Horace, on the other hand, like the majority of boys with whom I talked, explained that he had learned to fight through observation and practice:

> I watched people. Like when I was younger, like I used to look up to people. I still do. I look up to people and they knew how to fight so I just watched them. I just like saw people fight on TV, you know. Boxing and stuff.

Another boy told me that he thought kids learned to fight "probably from theirselves. Like their mom probably say, if somebody hit you, hit them back." This advice about proper behavior is grounded in the socialization practices that are brought into school as ways of responding to confrontations.

Gender Practice and Identification

Fighting acts reproduce notions of essentially different gendered natures and the forms in which this "difference" is grounded. Though class makes some difference in when, how, and under what conditions it takes place, fighting is the hegemonic representation of masculinity. Inscribed in the male body—whether individual males fight or not, abjure fighting or not—is the potential for this unleashing of physical power. By the same token, fighting for girls is considered an aberration, something to be explained.

Girls do get in fights at school. Boys asserted that girls can fight, even that "sometimes they get in fights easier. Because they got more attitude." Indeed, girls do make a name for themselves this way. One of the girls at Rosa Parks was in trouble several times during the school year for fighting. Most of her scrapes were with the boys who liked to tease her because she was very tall for her age. This, however, was not assumed to be reflective of her "femaleness" but of her individuality. Mr. Sobers, for example, when I asked him about her, made a point of this singularity rather than explaining her in terms of race, class, or gender: "Oh, Stephanie is just Stephanie."

Notes

1. Here are a very few examples of the enormous body of work concerned with the production of gender differences in the last two decades. At the ideological and discursive level see Mullings, "Images, Ideology"; Teresa de Lauretis, *Technologies of Gender: Essays on Theory, Film, and Fiction* (Bloomington: Indiana University Press, 1987); and Michele Barrett, *Women's Oppression Today: Problems in Marxist Feminist Analysis* (London: New Left Books, 1980). For processes of social structure and institutional arrangements see R. W. Connell et al., *Making the Difference: Schools, Families, and Social Division* (London: George Allen and Unwin, 1982); Mariarosa Dalla Costa, "Women and the Subversion of the Community," in *The Power of Women and the Subversion of Community,* ed. Mariarosa Dalla Costa and Selma James (Bristol, England: Falling Wall Press, 1973); Catharine A. MacKinnon, *Feminism Unmodified: Discourses on Life and Law* (Cambridge: Harvard University Press, 1987). For micropolitics see Arlie Russell Hochschild, *The Second Shift: Working Parents and the Revolution at Home* (New York: Viking, 1989); Donna Eder, Catherine Colleen Evans, and Stephen Parker, *School Talk: Gender and Adolescent Culture* (New Brunswick, N.J.: Rutgers University Press, 1995); and Candace West and Don H. Zimmerman, "Doing Gender," *Gender & Society* 1, no. 2 (1987).

2. Judith Butler, "Performative Acts and Gender Constitution: An Essay in Phenomenology and Feminist Theory," *Theatre Journal* 40, no. 4 (1988).

3. Judith Butler, *Bodies That Matter: On the Discursive Limits of "Sex"* (New York: Routledge, 1993), 95.

4. Douglas E. Foley, *Learning Capitalist Culture: Deep in the Heart of Tejas* (Philadelphia: University of Pennsylvania, 1990).

5. Geneva Smitherman, *Talkin and Testifyin: Language of Black America* (Detroit: Wayne State University Press, 1977); Lawrence Levine, *Black Culture and Black Consciousness: Afro-American Folk Thought from Slavery to Freedom* (New York: Oxford University Press, 1977); Philip Brian Harper, *Are We Not Men? Masculine Anxiety and the Problem of African-American Identity* (New York: Oxford University Press, 1996); Keith Gilyard, *Voices of the Self: A Study of Language Competence* (Detroit: Wayne State University Press, 1991).

6. Smitherman, *Talkin and Testifyin,* 80.

7. Harper, *Are We Not Men?* 11.

8. One-quarter of the 1,252 referrals to the Punishing Room were for fighting; four-fifths of the incidents involved boys, nine out of ten of whom were African Americans. All except three of the girls who were in fights were black.

9. Arlie Russell Hochschild, *The Managed Heart: Commercialization of Human Feeling* (Berkeley and Los Angeles: University of California Press, 1983). Hochschild explores the feeling rules that guide and govern our own emotional displays as well as how we interpret the emotional expression of others.

ARTICLE 11

C. J. Pascoe

"Dude, You're a Fag": Adolescent Masculinity and the Fag Discourse

"There's a faggot over there! There's a faggot over there! Come look!" yelled Brian, a senior at River High School, to a group of 10-year-old boys. Following Brian, the 10-year-olds dashed down a hallway. At the end of the hallway Brian's friend, Dan, pursed his lips and began sashaying towards the 10-year-olds. He minced towards them, swinging his hips exaggeratedly and wildly waving his arms. To the boys Brian yelled, "Look at the faggot! Watch out! He'll get you!" In response the 10-year-olds raced back down the hallway screaming in terror. (From author's fieldnotes)

The relationship between adolescent masculinity and sexuality is embedded in the specter of the faggot. Faggots represent a penetrated masculinity in which "to be penetrated is to abdicate power" (Bersani, 1987: 212). Penetrated men symbolize a masculinity devoid of power, which, in its contradiction, threatens both psychic and social chaos. It is precisely this specter of penetrated masculinity that functions as a regulatory mechanism of gender for contemporary American adolescent boys.

Feminist scholars of masculinity have documented the centrality of homophobic insults to masculinity (Lehne, 1998; Kimmel, 2001) especially in school settings (Wood, 1984; Smith, 1998; Burn, 2000; Plummer, 2001; Kimmel, 2003). They argue that homophobic teasing often characterizes masculinity in adolescence and early adulthood, and that anti-gay slurs tend to primarily be directed at other gay boys.

This article both expands on and challenges these accounts of relationships between homo-

From *Sexualities*. Copyright © 2005 Sage Publications (London, Thousand Oaks, CA, and New Delhi). Vol. 8(3):329–346.

phobia and masculinity. Homophobia is indeed a central mechanism in the making of contemporary American adolescent masculinity. This article both critiques and builds on this finding by (1) pointing to the limits of an argument that focuses centrally on homophobia, (2) demonstrating that the fag is not only an identity linked to homosexual boys[1] but an identity that can temporarily adhere to heterosexual boys as well and (3) highlighting the racialized nature of the fag as a disciplinary mechanism.

"Homophobia" is too facile a term with which to describe the deployment of "fag" as an epithet. By calling the use of the word "fag" homophobia—and letting the argument stop with that point—previous research obscures the gendered nature of sexualized insults (Plummer, 2001). Invoking homophobia to describe the ways in which boys aggressively tease each other overlooks the powerful relationship between masculinity and this sort of insult. Instead, it seems incidental in this conventional line of argument that girls do not harass each other and are not harassed in this same manner.[2] This framing naturalizes the relationship between masculinity and homophobia, thus obscuring the centrality of such harassment in the formation of a gendered identity for boys in a way that it is not for girls.

"Fag" is not necessarily a static identity attached to a particular (homosexual) boy. Fag talk and fag imitations serve as a discourse with which boys discipline themselves and each other through joking relationships.[3] Any boy can temporarily become a fag in a given social space or interaction. This does not mean that those boys who identify as or are perceived to be homosexual are not subject to intense harassment. But becoming a fag has as much to do with failing at the masculine tasks of competence, heterosexual prowess and strength or in any way revealing weakness or femininity, as it does with a sexual identity. This fluidity of the fag identity is what makes the specter of the fag such a powerful disciplinary mechanism. It is fluid enough that boys police most of their behaviors out of fear of having the fag identity permanently adhere and definitive enough so that boys recognize a fag behavior and strive to avoid it.

The fag discourse is racialized. It is invoked differently by and in relation to white boys' bodies than it is by and in relation to African-American boys' bodies. While certain behaviors put all boys at risk for becoming temporarily a fag, some behaviors can be enacted by African-American boys without putting them at risk of receiving the label. The racialized meanings of the fag discourse suggest that something more than simple homophobia is involved in these sorts of interactions. An analysis of boys' deployments of the specter of the fag should also extend to the ways in which gendered power works through racialized selves. It is not that this gendered homophobia does not exist in African-American communities. Indeed, making fun of "Negro faggotry seems to be a rite of passage among contemporary black male rappers and filmmakers" (Riggs, 1991: 253). However, the fact that "white women and men, gay and straight, have more or less colonized cultural debates about sexual representation" (Julien and Mercer, 1991: 167) obscures varied systems of sex-

ualized meanings among different racialized ethnic groups (Almaguer, 1991; King, 2004).

Theoretical Framing

The sociology of masculinity entails a "critical study of men, their behaviors, practices, values and perspectives" (Whitehead and Barrett, 2001: 14). Recent studies of men emphasize the multiplicity of masculinity (Connell, 1995) detailing the ways in which different configurations of gender practice are promoted, challenged or reinforced in given social situations. This research on how men do masculinities has explored gendered practices in a wide range of social institutions, such as families (Coltrane, 2001) schools (Skelton, 1996; Parker, 1996; Mac an Ghaill, 1996; Francis and Skelton, 2001), workplaces (Cooper, 2000), media (Craig, 1992), and sports (Messner, 1989; Edly and Wetherel, 1997; Curry, 2004). Many of these studies have developed specific typologies of masculinities: gay, Black, Chicano, working class, middle class, Asian, gay Black, gay Chicano, white working class, militarized, transnational business, New Man, negotiated, versatile, healthy, toxic, counter, and cool masculinities, to name a few (Messner, 2004). In this sort of model the fag could be (and often has been) framed as a type of subordinated masculinity attached to homosexual adolescent boys' bodies.

Heeding Timothy Carrigan's admonition that an "analysis of masculinity needs to be related as well to other currents in feminism" (Carrigan et al., 1987: 64), in this article I integrate queer theory's insights about the relationships between gender, sexuality, identities and power with the attention to men found in the literature on masculinities. Like the sociology of gender, queer theory destabilizes the assumed naturalness of the social order (Lemert, 1996). Queer theory is a "conceptualization which sees sexual power as embedded in different levels of social life" and interrogates areas of the social world not usually seen as sexuality (Stein and Plummer, 1994). In this sense queer theory calls for sexuality to be looked at not only as a discrete arena of sexual practices and identities, but also as a constitutive element of social life (Warner, 1993; Epstein, 1996).

While the masculinities' literature rightly highlights very real inequalities between gay and straight men (see for instance Connell, 1995), this emphasis on sexuality as inhered in static identities attached to male bodies, rather than major organizing principles of social life (Sedgwick, 1990), limits scholars' ability to analyze the myriad ways in which sexuality, in part, constitutes gender. This article does not seek to establish that there are homosexual boys and heterosexual boys and the homosexual ones are marginalized. Rather this article explores what happens to theories of gender if we look at a *discourse* of sexualized identities in addition to focusing on seemingly static identity categories inhabited by men. This is not to say that gender is reduced only to sexuality, indeed feminist scholars have demonstrated that gender is embedded in and constitutive of a multitude of social structures—the economy, places of work, families and schools. In the tradition of post-structural feminist theorists of race and gender who look at "border cases" that explode taken-for-granted binaries of race and gender (Smith, 1994), queer theory is another tool which enables an integrated analysis of sexuality, gender and race.

As scholars of gender have demonstrated, gender is accomplished through day-to-day interactions (Fine, 1987; Hochschild, 1989; West and Zimmerman, 1991; Thorne, 1993). In this sense gender is the "activity of managing situated conduct in light of normative conceptions of attitudes and activities appropriate for one's sex category" (West and Zimmerman, 1991: 127). Similarly, queer theorist Judith Butler argues that gender is accomplished interactionally through "a set of repeated acts within a highly rigid regulatory frame that congeal over time to produce the appearance of substance, of a natural sort of being" (Butler, 1999: 43). Specifically she argues that gendered beings are created through processes of citation

and repudiation of a "constitutive outside" (Butler, 1993: 3) in which is contained all that is cast out of a socially recognizable gender category. The "constitutive outside" is inhabited by abject identities, unrecognizably and unacceptably gendered selves. The interactional accomplishment of gender in a Butlerian model consists, in part, of the continual iteration and repudiation of this abject identity. Gender, in this sense, is "constituted through the force of exclusion and abjection, on which produces a constitutive outside to the subject, an abjected outside, which is, after all, 'inside' the subject as its own founding repudiation" (Butler, 1993: 3) This repudiation creates and reaffirms a "threatening specter" (Butler, 1993: 3) of failed, unrecognizable gender, the existence of which must be continually repudiated through interactional processes.

I argue that the "fag" position is an "abject" position and, as such, is a "threatening specter" constituting contemporary American adolescent masculinity. The fag discourse is the interactional process through which boys name and repudiate this abjected identity. Rather than analyzing the fag as an identity for homosexual boys, I examine uses of the discourse that imply that any boy can become a fag, regardless of his actual desire or self-perceived sexual orientation. The threat of the abject position infuses the faggot with regulatory power. This article provides empirical data to illustrate Butler's approach to gender and indicates that it might be a useful addition to the sociological literature on masculinities through highlighting one of the ways in which a masculine gender identity is accomplished through interaction.

Method

Research Site

I conducted fieldwork at a suburban high school in north-central California which I call River High.[4] River High is a working class, suburban 50-year-old high school located in a town called Riverton. With the exception of the median household income and racial diversity (both of which are elevated due to Riverton's location in California), the town mirrors national averages in the percentages of white collar workers, rates of college attendance and marriages, and age composition (according to the 2000 census). It is a politically moderate to conservative, religious community. Most of the students' parents commute to surrounding cities for work.

On average Riverton is a middle-class community. However, students at River are likely to refer to the town as two communities: "Old Riverton" and "New Riverton." A busy highway and railroad tracks bisect the town into these two sections. River High is literally on the "wrong side of the tracks," in Old Riverton. Exiting the freeway, heading north to Old Riverton, one sees a mix of 1950s-era ranch-style homes, some with neatly trimmed lawns and tidy gardens, others with yards strewn with various car parts, lawn chairs and appliances. Old Riverton is visually bounded by smoke-puffing factories. On the other side of the freeway New Riverton is characterized by wide sidewalk-lined streets and new walled-in home developments. Instead of smokestacks, a forested mountain, home to a state park, rises majestically in the background. The teens from these homes attend Hillside High, River's rival.

River High is attended by 2000 students. River High's racial/ethnic breakdown roughly represents California at large: 50 percent white, 9 percent African-American, 28 percent Latino and 6 percent Asian (as compared to California's 46, 6, 32, and 11 percent respectively, according to census data and school records). The students at River High are primarily working class.

Research

I gathered data using the qualitative method of ethnographic research. I spent a year and a half conducting observations, formally interviewing 49 students at River High (36 boys and 13 girls), one male student from Hillside High, and conducting countless informal interviews with students, faculty and administrators. I concentrated on one school because I explore the richness rather

than the breadth of data (for other examples of this method see Willis, 1981; MacLeod, 1987; Eder et al., 1995; Ferguson, 2000).

I recruited students for interviews by conducting presentations in a range of classes and hanging around at lunch, before school, after school and at various events talking to different groups of students about my research, which I presented as "writing a book about guys." The interviews usually took place at school, unless the student had a car, in which case he or she met me at one of the local fast food restaurants where I treated them to a meal. Interviews lasted anywhere from half an hour to two hours.

The initial interviews I conducted helped me to map a gendered and sexualized geography of the school, from which I chose my observation sites. I observed a "neutral" site—a senior government classroom, where sexualized meanings were subdued. I observed three sites that students marked as "fag" sites—two drama classes and the Gay/Straight Alliance. I also observed two normatively "masculine" sites—auto-shop and weightlifting.[5] I took daily field notes focusing on how students, faculty and administrators negotiated, regulated and resisted particular meanings of gender and sexuality. I attended major school rituals such as Winter Ball, school rallies, plays, dances and lunches. I would also occasionally "ride along" with Mr. Johnson (Mr J.), the school's security guard, on his battery-powered golf cart to watch which, how and when students were disciplined. Observational data provided me with more insight to the interactional processes of masculinity than simple interviews yielded. If I had relied only on interview data I would have missed the interactional processes of masculinity which are central to the fag discourse.

Given the importance of appearance in high school, I gave some thought as to how I would present myself, deciding to both blend in and set myself apart from the students. In order to blend in I wore my standard graduate student gear— comfortable, baggy cargo pants, a black t-shirt or sweater and tennis shoes. To set myself apart I carried a messenger bag instead of a back-pack, didn't wear makeup, and spoke slightly differently than the students by using some slang, but refraining from uttering the ubiquitous "hecka" and "hella."

The boys were fascinated by the fact that a 30-something white "girl" (their words) was interested in studying them. While at first many would make sexualized comments asking me about my dating life or saying that they were going to "hit on" me, it seemed eventually they began to forget about me as a potential sexual/romantic partner. Part of this, I think, was related to my knowledge about "guy" things. For instance, I lift weights on a regular basis and as a result the weightlifting coach introduced me as a "weight-lifter from U.C. Berkeley" telling the students they should ask me for weight-lifting advice. Additionally, my taste in movies and television shows often coincided with theirs. I am an avid fan of the movies *Jackass* and *Fight Club*, both of which contain high levels of violence and "bathroom" humor. Finally, I garnered a lot of points among boys because I live off a dangerous street in a nearby city famous for drug deals, gang fights and frequent gun shots.

What Is a Fag?

"Since you were little boys you've been told, 'hey, don't be a little faggot,'" explained Darnell, an African-American football player, as we sat on a bench next to the athletic field. Indeed, both the boys and girls I interviewed told me that "fag" was the worst epithet one guy could direct at another. Jeff, a slight white sophomore, explained to me that boys call each other fag because "gay people aren't really liked over here and stuff." Jeremy, a Latino Junior, told me that this insult literally reduced a boy to nothing, "To call someone gay or fag is like the lowest thing you can call someone. Because that's like saying that you're nothing."

Most guys explained their or others' dislike of fags by claiming that homophobia is just part of what it means to be a guy. For instance Keith, a white soccer-playing senior, explained, "I think

guys are just homophobic." However, it is not just homophobia, it is a *gendered* homophobia. Several students told me that these homophobic insults only applied to boys and not girls. For example, while Jake, a handsome white senior, told me that he didn't like gay people, he quickly added, "Lesbians, okay that's *good*." Similarly Cathy, a popular white cheerleader, told me "Being a lesbian is accepted because guys think 'oh that's cool.'" Darnell, after telling me that boys were told not to be faggots, said of lesbians, "They're [guys are] fine with girls. I think it's the guy part that they're like ewwww!" In this sense it is not strictly homophobia, but a gendered homophobia that constitutes adolescent masculinity in the culture of this school. However, it is clear, according to these comments, that lesbians are "good" because of their place in heterosexual male fantasy not necessarily because of some enlightened approach to same-sex relationships. It does however, indicate that using only the term homophobia to describe boys' repeated use of the word "fag" might be a bit simplistic and misleading.

Additionally, girls at River High rarely deployed the word "fag" and were never called "fags." I recorded girls uttering "fag" only three times during my research. In one instance, Angela, a Latina cheerleader, teased Jeremy, a well-liked white senior involved in student government, for not ditching school with her, "You wouldn't 'cause you're a faggot." However, girls did not use this word as part of their regular lexicon. The sort of gendered homophobia that constitutes adolescent masculinity does not constitute adolescent femininity. Girls were not called dykes or lesbians in any sort of regular or systematic way. Students did tell me that "slut" was the worst thing a girl could be called. However, my field notes indicate that the word "slut" (or its synonym "ho") appears one time for every eight times the word "fag" appears. Even when it does occur, "slut" is rarely deployed as a direct insult against another girl.

Highlighting the difference between the deployment of "gay" and "fag" as insults brings the gendered nature of this homophobia into focus.

For boys and girls at River High "gay" is a fairly common synonym for "stupid." While this word shares the sexual origins of "fag," it does not *consistently* have the skew of gender-loaded meaning. Girls and boys often used "gay" as an adjective referring to inanimate objects and male or female people, whereas they used "fag" as a noun that denotes only un-masculine males. Students used "gay" to describe anything from someone's clothes to a new school rule that the students did not like, as in the following encounter:

> In auto-shop Arnie pulled out a large older version black laptop computer and placed it on his desk. Behind him Nick said "That's a gay laptop! It's five inches thick!"

A laptop can be gay, a movie can be gay or a group of people can be gay. Boys used "gay" and "fag" interchangeably when they refer to other boys, but "fag" does not have the non-gendered attributes that "gay" sometimes invokes.

While its meanings are not the same as "gay," "fag" does have multiple meanings which do not necessarily replace its connotations as a homophobic slur, but rather exist alongside. Some boys took pains to say that "fag" is not about sexuality. Darnell told me "It doesn't even have anything to do with being gay." J.L., a white sophomore at Hillside High (River High's cross-town rival) asserted "Fag, seriously, it has nothing to do with sexual preference at all. You could just be calling somebody an idiot you know?" I asked Ben, a quiet, white sophomore who wore heavy metal t-shirts to auto-shop each day, "What kind of things do guys get called a fag for?" Ben answered "Anything . . . literally, anything. Like you were trying to turn a wrench the wrong way, 'dude, you're a fag.' Even if a piece of meat drops out of your sandwich, 'you fag!'" Each time Ben said "you fag" his voice deepened as if he were imitating a more masculine boy. While Ben might rightly *feel* like a guy could be called a fag for "anything . . . literally, anything," there are actually specific behaviors which, when enacted by most boys, can render him more vulnerable to a fag epithet. In this instance Ben's comment high-lights the use of "fag" as a generic insult for incompetence, which in the world of River High, is central to a masculine identity. A boy could get called a fag for exhibiting any sort of behavior defined as non-masculine (although not necessarily behaviors aligned with femininity) in the world of River High: being stupid, incompetent, dancing, caring too much about clothing, being too emotional or expressing interest (sexual or platonic) in other guys. However, given the extent of its deployment and the laundry list of behaviors that could get a boy in trouble it is no wonder that Ben felt like a boy could be called "fag" for "anything."

One-third (13) of the boys I interviewed told me that, while they may liberally insult each other with the term, they would not actually direct it at a homosexual peer. Jabes, a Filipino senior, told me

> I actually say it [fag] quite a lot, except for when I'm in the company of an actual homosexual person. Then I try not to say it at all. But when I'm just hanging out with my friends I'll be like, "shut up, I don't want you hear you any more, you stupid fag."

Similarly J.L. compared homosexuality to a disability, saying there is "no way" he'd call an actually gay guy a fag because

> There's people who are the retarded people who nobody wants to associate with. I'll be so nice to those guys and I hate it when people make fun of them. It's like, "bro do you realize that they can't help that." And then there's gay people. They were born that way.

According to this group of boys, gay is a legitimate, if marginalized, social identity. If a man is gay, there may be a chance he could be considered masculine by other men (Connell, 1995). David, a handsome white senior dressed smartly in khaki pants and a white button-down shirt said, "Being gay is just a lifestyle. It's someone you choose to sleep with. You can still throw around a football and be gay." In other words there is a possibility, however slight, that a boy can be gay and masculine. To be a fag is, by definition, the opposite of masculine, whether or not the word is deployed with sexualized or non-sexualized meanings. In explaining this to me, Jamaal, an African-American junior, cited the explanation of popular rap artist, Eminem,

> Although I don't like Eminem, he had a good definition of it. It's like taking away your title. In an interview they were like, "you're always capping on gays, but then you sing with Elton John." He was like "I don't mean gay as in gay."

This is what Riki Wilchins calls the "Eminem Exception. Eminem explains that he doesn't call people 'faggot' because of their sexual orientation but because they're weak and unmanly" (Wilchins, 2003). This is precisely the way in which this group of boys at River High uses the term "faggot." While it is not necessarily acceptable to be gay, at least a man who is gay can do other things that render him acceptably masculine. A fag, by the very definition of the word, indicated by students' usages at River High, cannot be masculine. This distinction between "fag" as an unmasculine and problematic identity and "gay" as a possibly masculine, although marginalized, sexual identity is not limited to a teenage lexicon, but is reflected in both psychological discourses (Sedgwick, 1995) and gay and lesbian activism.

Becoming a Fag

"The ubiquity of the word faggot speaks to the reach of its discrediting capacity" (Corbett, 2001: 4). It is almost as if boys cannot help but shout it out on a regular basis—in the hallway, in class, across campus as a greeting, or as a joke. In my fieldwork I was amazed by the way in which the word seemed to pop uncontrollably out of boys' mouths in all kinds of situations. To quote just one of many instances from my fieldnotes:

> Two boys walked out of the P.E. locker room and one yelled "fucking faggot!" at no one in particular.

This spontaneous yelling out of a variation of "fag" seemingly apropos of nothing happened repeatedly among boys throughout the school.

The fag discourse is central to boys' joking relationships. Joking cements relationships between boys (Kehily and Nayak, 1997; Lyman, 1998) and helps to manage anxiety and discomfort (Freud, 1905). Boys invoked the specter of the fag in two ways: through humorous imitation and through lobbing the epithet at one another. Boys at River High imitated the fag by acting out an exaggerated "femininity," and/or by pretending to sexually desire other boys. As indicated by the introductory vignette in which a predatory "fag" threatens the little boys, boys at River High link these performative scenarios with a fag identity. They lobbed the fag epithet at each other in a verbal game of hot potato, each careful to deflect the insult quickly by hurling it toward someone else. These games and imitations make up a fag discourse which highlights the fag not as a static but rather as a fluid identity which boys constantly struggle to avoid.

In imitative performances the fag discourse functions as a constant reiteration of the fag's existence, affirming that the fag is out there; at any moment a boy can become a fag. At the same time these performances demonstrate that the boy who is invoking the fag is *not* a fag. By invoking it so often, boys remind themselves and each other that at any point they can become fags if they are not sufficiently masculine.

> Mr McNally, disturbed by the noise outside of the classroom, turned to the open door saying "We'll shut this unless anyone really wants to watch sweaty boys playing basketball." Emir, a tall skinny boy, lisped "I wanna watch the boys play!" The rest of the class cracked up at his imitation.

Through imitating a fag, boys assure others that they are not a fag by immediately becoming masculine again after the performance. They mock their own performed femininity and/or same-sex desire, assuring themselves and others that such an identity is one deserving of derisive laughter.

The fag identity in this instance is fluid, detached from Emir's body. He can move in and out of this "abject domain" while simultaneously affirming his position as a subject.

Boys also consistently tried to put another in the fag position by lobbing the fag epithet at one another.

> Going through the junk-filled car in the auto-shop parking lot, Jay poked his head out and asked "Where are Craig and Brian?" Neil, responded with "I think they're over there," pointing, then thrusting his hips and pulling his arms back and forth to indicate that Craig and Brian might be having sex. The boys in auto-shop laughed.

This sort of joke temporarily labels both Craig and Brian as faggots. Because the fag discourse is so familiar, the other boys immediately understand that Neil is indicating that Craig and Brian are having sex. However these are not necessarily identities that stick. Nobody actually thinks Craig and Brian are homosexuals. Rather the fag identity is a fluid one, certainly an identity that no boy wants, but one that a boy can escape, usually by engaging in some sort of discursive contest to turn another boy into a fag. However, fag becomes a hot potato that no boy wants to be left holding. In the following example, which occurred soon after the "sex" joke, Brian lobs the fag epithet at someone else, deflecting it from himself:

> Brian initiated a round of a favorite game in auto-shop, the "cock game." Brian quietly, looking at Josh, said, "Josh loves the cock," then slightly louder, "Josh loves the cock." He continued saying this until he was yelling "JOSH LOVES THE COCK!" The rest of the boys laughed hysterically as Josh slinked away saying "I have a bigger dick than all you mother fuckers!"

These two instances show how the fag can be mapped, momentarily, on to one boy's body and how he, in turn, can attach it to another boy, thus deflecting it from himself. In the first instance Neil makes fun of Craig and Brian for simply hanging out together. In the second instance Brian goes from being a fag to making Josh into a fag, through the "cock game." The "fag" is transferable. Boys move in and out of it by discursively creating another as a fag through joking interactions. They, somewhat ironically, can move in and out of the fag position by transforming themselves, temporarily, into a fag, but this has the effect of reaffirming their masculinity when they return to a heterosexual position after imitating the fag.

These examples demonstrate boys invoking the trope of the fag in a discursive struggle in which the boys indicate that they know what a fag is—and that they are not fags. This joking cements bonds between boys as they assure themselves and each other of their masculinity through repeated repudiations of a non-masculine position of the abject.

Racing the Fag

The fag trope is not deployed consistently or identically across social groups at River High. Differences between white boys' and African-American boys' meaning making around clothes and dancing reveal ways in which the fag as the abject position is racialized.

Clean, oversized, carefully put together clothing is central to a hip-hop identity for African-American boys who identify with hip-hop culture.[6] Richard Majors calls this presentation of self a "cool pose" consisting of "unique, expressive and conspicuous styles of demeanor, speech, gesture, clothing, hairstyle, walk, stance and handshake." developed by African-American men as a symbolic response to institutionalized racism (Majors, 2001: 211). Pants are usually several sizes too big, hanging low on a boy's waist, usually revealing a pair of boxers beneath. Shirts and sweaters are similarly oversized, often hanging down to a boy's knees. Tags are frequently left on baseball hats worn slightly askew and perched high on the head. Meticulously clean, unlaced athletic shoes with rolled up socks under the tongue complete a typical hip-hop outfit.

This amount of attention and care given to clothing for white boys not identified with hip-hop culture (that is, most of the white boys at River High) would certainly cast them into an abject, fag position. White boys are not supposed to appear to care about their clothes or appearance, because only fags care about how they look. Ben illustrates this:

> Ben walked in to the auto-shop classroom from the parking lot where he had been working on a particularly oily engine. Grease stains covered his jeans. He looked down at them, made a face and walked toward me with limp wrists, laughing and lisping in a in a high pitch sing-song voice "I got my good panths all dirty!"

Ben draws on indicators of a fag identity, such as limp wrists, as do the boys in the introductory vignette to illustrate that a masculine person certainly would not care about having dirty clothes. In this sense, masculinity, for white boys, becomes the carefully crafted appearance of not caring about appearance, especially in terms of cleanliness.

However, African-American boys involved in hip-hop culture talk frequently about whether or not their clothes, specifically their shoes, are dirty:

> In drama class both Darnell and Marc compared their white Adidas basketball shoes. Darnell mocked Marc because black scuff marks covered his shoes, asking incredulously "Yours are a week old and they're dirty—I've had mine for a month and they're not dirty!" Both laughed.

Monte, River High's star football player, echoed this concern about dirty shoes when looking at the fancy red shoes he had lent to his cousin the week before, and told me he was frustrated because after his cousin used them, the "shoes are hella scuffed up." Clothing, for these boys, does not indicate a fag position, but rather defines membership in a certain cultural and racial group (Perry, 2002).

Dancing is another arena that carries distinctly fag associated meanings for white boys and masculine meanings for African-American boys who participate in hip-hop culture. White boys often associate dancing with "fags." J.L. told me that guys think "'nSync's gay" because they can dance. 'nSync is an all white male singing group known for their dance moves. At dances white boys frequently held their female dates tightly, locking their hips together. The boys never danced with one another, unless engaged in a round of "hot potato." White boys often jokingly danced together in order to embarrass each other by making someone else into a fag:

> Lindy danced behind her date, Chris. Chris's friend, Matt, walked up and nudged Lindy aside, imitating her dance moves behind Chris. As Matt rubbed his hands up and down Chris's back, Chris turned around and jumped back startled to see Matt there instead of Lindy. Matt cracked up as Chris turned red.

However dancing does not carry this sort of sexualized gender meaning for all boys at River High. For African-American boys dancing demonstrates membership in a cultural community (Best, 2000). African-American boys frequently danced together in single sex groups, teaching each other the latest dance moves, showing off a particularly difficult move or making each other laugh with humorous dance moves. Students recognized K.J. as the most talented dancer at the school. K.J. is a sophomore of African-American and Filipino descent who participated in the hip-hop culture of River High. He continually wore the latest hip-hop fashions. K.J. was extremely popular. Girls hollered his name as they walked down the hall and thrust urgently written love notes folded in complicated designs into his hands as he sauntered to class. For the past two years K.J. won first place in the talent show for dancing. When he danced at assemblies the room reverberated with screamed chants of "Go K.J.! Go K.J.! Go K.J.!" Because dancing for African-American boys places them within a tradition of masculinity, they are not at risk of becoming a fag for this particular gendered practice. Nobody called K.J. a fag. In fact in several of my interviews boys of multiple racial/ethnic backgrounds spoke admiringly of K.J.'s dancing abilities.

Implications

These findings confirm previous studies of masculinity and sexuality that position homophobia as central to contemporary definitions of adolescent masculinity. These data extend previous research by unpacking multilayered meanings that boys deploy through their uses of homophobic language and joking rituals. By attending to these meanings I reframe the discussion as one of a fag discourse, rather than simply labeling this sort of behavior as homophobia. The fag is an "abject" position, a position outside of masculinity that actually constitutes masculinity. Thus, masculinity, in part, becomes the daily interactional work of repudiating the "threatening specter" of the fag.

The fag extends beyond a static sexual identity attached to a gay boy. Few boys are permanently identified as fags; most move in and out of fag positions. Looking at "fag" as a discourse rather than a static identity reveals that the term can be invested with different meanings in different social spaces. "Fag" may be used as a weapon with which to temporarily assert one's masculinity by denying it to others. Thus "fag" becomes a symbol around which contests of masculinity take place.

The fag epithet, when hurled at other boys, may or may not have explicit sexual meanings, but it always has gendered meanings. When a boy calls another boy a fag, it means he is not a man, not necessarily that he is a homosexual. The boys in this study know that they are not supposed to call homosexual boys "fags" because that is mean. This, then, has been the limited success of the mainstream gay rights movement. The message absorbed by some of these teenage boys is that "gay men can be masculine, just like you." Instead of challenging gender inequality, this particular discourse of gay rights has reinscribed it. Thus we need to begin to think about how gay men may be in a unique position to challenge gendered as well as sexual norms.

This study indicates that researchers who look at the intersection of sexuality and masculinity need to attend to the ways in which racialized identities may affect how "fag" is deployed and what it means in various social situations. While researchers have addressed the ways in which masculine identities are racialized (Connell, 1995; Ross, 1998; Bucholtz, 1999; Davis, 1999; Price, 1999; Ferguson, 2000; Majors, 2001) they have not paid equal attention to the ways in which "fag" might be a racialized epithet. It is important to look at when, where and with what meaning "the fag" is deployed in order to get at how masculinity is defined, contested, and invested in among adolescent boys.

Research shows that sexualized teasing often leads to deadly results, as evidenced by the spate of school shootings in the 1990s (Kimmel, 2003). Clearly the fag discourse affects not just homosexual teens, but all boys, gay and straight. Further research could investigate these processes in a variety of contexts: varied geographic locations, sexualized groups, classed groups, religious groups and age groups.

Acknowledgments

The author would like to thank Natalie Boero, Leslie Bell, Meg Jay and Barrie Thorne for their comments on this article. This work was supported by the Center for the Study of Sexual Culture at University of California, Berkeley.

Notes

1. While the term "homosexual" is laden with medicalized and normalizing meanings, I use it instead of "gay" because "gay" in the world of River High has multiple meanings apart from sexual practices or identities.

2. Girls do insult one another based on sexualized meanings. But in my own research I found that girls and boys did not harass girls in this manner with the same frequency that boys harassed each other through engaging in joking about the fag.

3. I use discourse in the Foucauldian sense, to describe truth producing practices, not just text or speech (Foucault, 1978).

4. The names of places and respondents have been changed.

5. Auto-shop was a class in which students learned how to build and repair cars. Many of the students in this course were looking into careers as mechanics.

6. While there are several white and Latino boys at River High who identify with hip-hop culture, hip-hop is identified by the majority of students as an African-American cultural style.

References

Almaguer, Tomas (1991) "Chicano Men: A Cartography of Homosexual Identity and Behavior," *Differences* 3: 75–100.

Bersani, Leo (1987) "Is the Rectum a Grave?" *October* 43: 197–222.

Best, Amy (2000) *Prom Night: Youth, Schools and Popular Culture.* New York: Routledge.

Bucholtz, Mary (1999) "'You Da Man': Narrating the Racial Other in the Production of White Masculinity," *Journal of Sociolinguistics* 3/4: 443–60.

Burn, Shawn M. (2000) "Heterosexuals' Use of 'Fag' and 'Queer' to Deride One Another: A Contributor to Heterosexism and Stigma," *Journal of Homosexuality* 40: 1–11.

Butler, Judith (1993) *Bodies That Matter.* Routledge: New York.

Butler, Judith (1999) *Gender Trouble.* New York: Routledge.

Carrigan, Tim, Connell, Bob and Lee, John (1987) "Toward a New Sociology of Masculinity," in Harry Brod (ed.) *The Making of Masculinities: The New Men's Studies,* pp. 188–202. Boston, MA: Allen & Unwin.

Coltrane, Scott (2001) "Selling the Indispensable Father," paper presented at *Pushing the Boundaries Conference: New Conceptualizations of Childhood and Motherhood,* Philadelphia.

Connell, R.W. (1995) *Masculinities.* Berkeley: University of California Press.

Cooper, Marianne (2000) "Being the 'Go-to Guy': Fatherhood, Masculinity and the Organization of Work in Silicon Valley," *Qualitative Sociology* 23: 379–405.

Corbett, Ken (2001) "Faggot = Loser," *Studies in Gender and Sexuality* 2: 3–28.

Craig, Steve (1992) *Men, Masculinity and the Media.* Newbury Park: Sage.

Curry, Timothy J. (2004) "Fraternal Bonding in the Locker Room: A Profeminist Analysis of Talk about Competition and Women," in Michael Messner and Michael Kimmel (eds.) *Men's Lives.* Boston, MA: Pearson.

Davis, James E. (1999) "Forbidden Fruit, Black Males' Constructions of Transgressive Sexualities in Middle School," in William J. Letts IV and James T. Sears (eds.) *Queering Elementary Education: Advancing the Dialogue about Sexualities and Schooling,* pp. 49 ff. Lanham, MD: Rowan & Littlefield.

Eder, Donna, Evans, Catherine and Parker, Stephen (1995) *School Talk: Gender and Adolescent Culture.* New Brunswick, NJ: Rutgers University Press.

Edly, Nigel and Wetherell, Margaret (1997) "Jockeying for Position: The Construction of Masculine Identities," *Discourse and Society* 8: 203–17.

Epstein, Steven (1996) "A Queer Encounter," in Steven Seidman (ed.) *Queer Theory/Sociology,* pp. 188–202. Cambridge, MA: Blackwell.

Ferguson, Ann (2000) *Bad Boys: Public Schools in the Making of Black Masculinity.* Ann Arbor: University of Michigan Press.

Fine, Gary (1987) *With the Boys: Little League Baseball and Preadolescent Culture.* Chicago, IL: University of Chicago Press.

Foucault, Michel (1978) *The History of Sexuality, Volume I.* New York: Vintage Books.

Francis, Becky and Skelton, Christine (2001) "Men Teachers and the Construction of Heterosexual Masculinity in the Classroom," *Sex Education* 1: 9–21.

Freud, Sigmund (1905) *The Basic Writings of Sigmund Freud,* (translated and edited by A.A. Brill). New York: The Modern Library.

Hochschild, Arlie (1989) *The Second Shift.* New York: Avon.

Julien, Isaac and Mercer, Kobena (1991) "True Confessions: A Discourse on Images of Black Male Sexuality," in Essex Hemphill (ed.) *Brother to Brother: New Writings by Black Gay Men,* pp. 167–73. Boston, MA: Alyson Publications.

Kehily, Mary Jane and Nayak, Anoop (1997) "Lads and Laughter: Humour and the Production of Heterosexual Masculinities," *Gender and Education* 9: 69–87.

Kimmel, Michael (2001) "Masculinity as Homophobia: Fear, Shame, and Silence in the Construction of Gender Identity," in Stephen Whitehead and Frank Barrett (eds.) *The Masculinities Reader,* pp. 266–187. Cambridge: Polity.

Kimmel, Michael (2003) "Adolescent Masculinity, Homophobia, and Violence: Random School Shootings, 1982–2001," *American Behavioral Scientist* 46: 1439–58.

King, D. L. (2004) *Double Lives on the Down Low.* New York: Broadway Books.

Lehne, Gregory (1998) "Homophobia among Men: Supporting and Defining the Male Role," in Michael Kimmel and Michael Messner (eds.) *Men's Lives,* pp. 237–49. Boston, MA: Allyn and Bacon.

Lemert, Charles (1996) "Series Editor's Preface," in Steven Seidman (ed.) *Queer Theory/Sociology.* Cambridge, MA: Blackwell.

Lyman, Peter (1998) "The Fraternal Bond as a Joking Relationship: A Case Study of the Role of Sexist Jokes in Male Group Bonding," in Michael Kimmel and Michael Messner (eds.) *Men's Lives,* pp. 171–93. Boston, MA: Allyn and Bacon.

Mac an Ghaill, Martain (1996) "What about the Boys—School, Class and Crisis Masculinity," *Sociological Review* 44: 381–97.

MacLeod, Jay (1987) *Ain't No Makin It: Aspirations and Attainment in a Low Income Neighborhood.* Boulder, CO: Westview Press.

Majors, Richard (2001) "Cool Pose: Black Masculinity and Sports," in Stephen Whitehead and Frank Barrett (eds.) *The Masculinities Reader,* pp. 208–17. Cambridge: Polity.

Messner, Michael (1989) "Sports and the Politics of Inequality," in Michael Kimmel and Michael Messner (eds.) *Men's Lives.* Boston, MA: Allyn and Bacon.

Messner, Michael (2004) "On Patriarchs and Losers: Rethinking Men's Interests," paper presented at Berkeley *Journal of Sociology* Conference, Berkeley.

Parker, Andrew (1996) "The Construction of Masculinity within Boys' Physical Education," *Gender and Education* 8: 141–57.

Perry, Pamela (2002) *Shades of White: White Kids and Racial Identities in High School.* Durham, NC: Duke University Press.

Plummer, David C. (2001) "The Quest for Modern Manhood: Masculine Stereotypes, Peer Culture and the Social Significance of Homophobia," *Journal of Adolescence* 24: 15–23.

Price, Jeremy (1999) "Schooling and Racialized Masculinities: The Diploma, Teachers and Peers in the Lives of Young, African-American Men," *Youth and Society* 31: 224–63.

Riggs, Marlon (1991) "Black Macho Revisited: Reflections of a SNAP! Queen," in Essex Hemphill (ed.) *Brother to Brother: New Writings by Black Gay Men,* pp. 153–260. Boston, MA: Alyson Publications.

Ross, Marlon B. (1998) "In Search of Black Men's Masculinities," *Feminist Studies* 24: 599–626.

Sedgwick, Eve K. (1990) *Epistemology of the Closet.* Berkeley: University of California Press.

Sedgwick, Eve K. (1995) " 'Gosh, Boy George, You Must be Awfully Secure in Your Masculinity!' " in Maurice Berger, Brian Wallis and Simon Watson (eds.) *Constructing Masculinity,* pp. 11–20. New York: Routledge.

Skelton, Christine (1996) "Learning to be Tough: The Fostering of Maleness in One Primary School," *Gender and Education* 8: 185–97.

Smith, George W. (1998) "The Ideology of 'Fag': The School Experience of Gay Students," *The Sociological Quarterly* 39: 309–35.

Smith, Valerie (1994) "Split Affinities: The Case of Interracial Rape," in Anne Herrmann and Abigail Stewart (eds.) *Theorizing Feminism,* pp. 155–70. Boulder, CO: Westview Press.

Stein, Arlene and Plummer, Ken (1994) " 'I Can't Even Think Straight': 'Queer' Theory and the Missing Sexual Revolution in Sociology," *Sociological Theory* 12: 178 ff.

Thorne, Barrie (1993) *Gender Play: Boys and Girls in School.* New Brunswick, NJ: Rutgers University Press.

Warner, Michael (1993) "Introduction," in Michael Warner (ed.) *Fear of a Queer Planet: Queer Politics and Social Theory,* pp. vii–xxxi. Minneapolis: University of Minnesota Press.

West, Candace and Zimmerman, Don (1991) "Doing Gender," in Judith Lorber (ed.) *The Social Construction of Gender,* pp. 102–21. Newbury Park: Sage.

Whitehead, Stephen and Barrett, Frank (2001) "The Sociology of Masculinity," in Stephen Whitehead and Frank Barrett (eds.) *The Masculinities Reader,* pp. 472–6. Cambridge: Polity.

Wilchins, Riki (2003) "Do You Believe in Fairies?" *The Advocate,* 4 February.

Willis, Paul (1981) *Learning to Labor: How Working Class Kids Get Working Class Jobs.* New York: Columbia University Press.

Wood, Julian (1984) "Groping Toward Sexism: Boy's Sex Talk," in Angela McRobbie and Mica Nava (eds.) *Gender and Generation.* London: Macmillan Publishers.

Daniel Farr

Sissy Boy, Progressive Parents

Gender is part of our lives from the very beginning. From early on, children begin to conceptualize and integrate an understanding of gender into their identities and actions (Jordan and Cowan 1995; Rogers 1999; Thorne 1986). Families, the media, and other children continually recreate, develop, and perpetuate regulating behaviors both within and between individuals that work to legitimize and maintain the dichotomous nature of gender. One is either a boy or a girl, a man or a woman. When gender is not evident in this conventional way, there can be disapproval, concern, and even loathing. These responses may torment both girls (tomboys) and boys (sissy boys) who do not conform to dichotomous gender characteristics. Some research suggests that tomboys may be less stigmatized than sissy boys (Martin 1995), but the experience of growing up as a "too masculine" girl does have lifetime implications (Carr 1998).

In adulthood, many of the gendering events that shape one's life have been forgotten or minimized. For most, the act of fitting into one's socially approved gender feels natural—seamless and simple. The social rules about how to behave in the spheres of work, education, and recreation or in the private sphere of the family are so deeply imbedded into our persona we can be unaware of their existence. Not only does one learn how to behave, but how *not* to behave. These rules and norms unwittingly limit us in our daily lives in how and to whom we should speak, how we should dress, perhaps even how we should think if we wish to adhere to our "natural" gender.

From *Couples, Kids, and Family Life,* edited by Jaber Guborium and James Holstein (NY: Oxford UP, 2006). Used by permission of the author.

Our introduction into a gendered world is so deeply ingrained that individuals who do not seem to support the gendered norms of appropriate masculinity and femininity stand out in stark relief. We can be ill-at-ease if we are unable to neatly allocate individuals the appropriate slots of man or woman (see Lucal 1999). Without being able to categorize individuals, we don't know how to interact or interpret the behaviors, situations, and interactions we are encountering.

Looking Back at Childhood

Applying an autoethnographic analysis of my experience growing up as a gender non-conforming boy—yes, a "sissy boy"—offers insight into the social construction of gender and the manner in which gender is incorporated into the various social organizations and structures that guide our lives. As a sissy boy, I seldom interacted with tomboys so I cannot offer insight into their experience, but I will explore facets of my own early experience as an effeminate male to describe the way gender dichotomy affects those who don't readily fit into one gender category or the other.

Critically evaluating and looking back at one's experience offers a rich tapestry of information about the social world. Informed in part by Arlie Hochschild's concept of the "magnified moment" (1994: 4), I explore several of the key moments and events of my life that have reverberated through my memories. These are happenings which, at the time they occur, seem to tell it all, so to speak. In the process, I point to the many threads of gender socialization and related power dynamics at play in our society, which, oddly enough, work themselves out in the smallest ways, such as through toy selection and favored books. Setting out to examine my own social history in terms of magnified moments has been both challenging and insightful. These memories, while sometimes painful or embarrassing, offer a glimpse into the moments when experience can telescope our understanding of our selves and society. Clearly, my perception and interpretation of these moments are not representative of the experience of all sissy boys, but they do offer insight into the experience of growing up as an effeminate boy in a culture, where the two words—"effeminate" and "boy"—are considered anomalous terms of reference.

Looking back to being children, we all can probably recall being called a cruel name or feeling out of place. Fortunately, most of us do find a place or group in which to fit and we learn to cope with those with whom we don't fit. Sometimes we cope by setting ourselves apart from the groups that treat us poorly. Sometimes we cope by demeaning the group that we are apart from. Sometimes we pretend the others are unimportant and don't matter. Sometimes we cope by reaffirming the importance of our own group. Regardless of how we deal with this, we've all experienced these varying social mechanisms at play as we grew up. The scary reality is that we can experience these mechanisms our entire lives if we aren't careful, perhaps without even noticing it.

Looking to childhood, one is likely to recall a quiet boy who never quite fit in. Maybe he was shy. Maybe he was socially awkward with boys but comfortable with girls. Maybe he liked music and art too much. Maybe he was too smart. Maybe he was too fat or too skinny, or not athletic. Perhaps he was a bit too effeminate (girly acting)—who knows what specifically marked him as different, but surely you knew this boy. This boy was probably picked on and teased, perhaps even physically assaulted in some manner, but he was clearly marked as the outsider, the one you knew you didn't want to be—even if he was you. This chapter will examine some of the experiences of one such boy, the trials and tribulations

that he experienced, the pains felt, and the victories that can be won. Examining the various moments that have shaped my early life will allow us to explore the numerous manners in which the notions of gender and sexuality are taught, learned, lived, and challenged.

Growing up I was what many might call a precocious child. I was intelligent, creative, imaginative, and "too" sensitive to fit into the social conception of boyhood. I was the boy who was constantly picked on by my peers for being unmanly, for being a sissy, and later for supposedly being a faggot. I don't know that I can pinpoint when I first realized I was unique and different, but I certainly recognized I was not just unlike other boys, but other children in general, at any early age (at least by first or second grade). The path of my unique childhood is not the same as all other effeminate boys or even other outsider boys in general, but the various experiences I will examine are ones to which we can all relate in one way or another.

Boy versus Girl Toys

As children of the late 20th century, many of us have a collection of toys and other recreational and educational objects. Coming from a middle-class background, I was fortunate to have a respectable assortment of toys and tools at my disposal, to help ward off childhood boredom. Looking back to my childhood, I don't think my parents took too strongly to the idea that there were specific toys for boys and specific toys for girls. I know my sister got dolls and I got teddy bears, but at the time I only saw this as their giving us what we each liked.

Is this a matter of what we instinctively prefer or is it what we are taught to prefer? Had I been more like other "normal" boys of my age group, maybe I would have received more action figures and appropriately masculine toys. For example, *Transformers* were all the rage at the time. I don't recall ever expressing desire for, or interest in, them. My one friend had a large collection of these types of toys, but I never found them especially interesting. The time I spent playing with this friend and his toys was more the result of neighborhood proximity than strong feelings of camaraderies. Fortunately, my parents were able to step away from some, though of course not all, of the categorization of toys by gender. Despite the frequent gender stereotyping of toys by parents (see Campenni 1999), my own parents were more open about the types of toys my siblings and I could play with. I was thus able to enjoy "masculine" toys, such as Legos™ and Construx™, as well as "feminine" toys like looms and cooking kits. My parents were exceptional in this way. As far as I knew, they never stereotyped my interests. They never discouraged what my peers viewed with disdain as sissy boy inclinations. To my progressive parents, I was simply their son—the one who was good at so many things and who loved his family—not the boy child in their lives.

One of the favorite toys I received as a child was a Fisher-Price™ loom. It's used to weave yarn into fabric, to make scarves, for example. I didn't view it as a girly type of gift; I saw it as a cool new crafty toy. I still recall the circumstances of receiving the loom; it was an unexpected gift, unassociated with a holiday or birthday. It was new and exciting. As I look back, I can still vaguely see the box. It seems that there was a boy on the box cover. I have unsuccessfully searched online trying to locate a picture of this box. I believe it was a boy on the cover, but it may have been a girl with a "masculine" haircut. This led me to assume that this was a gender-appropriate gift. It there was a boy on the cover, it must have been okay for me to also play with the loom.

The freedom of toy selection I experienced at home was not something I would experience in school. One winter, in second grade, my class had a holiday party and a gift exchange. On the day of the big party, we each drew numbers for the gifts that were sorted as being either a masculine toy or a feminine toy. I was lucky in that I drew the number for the biggest box! After all the boxes were distributed, the tension grew as we

all opened our gifts at the same time. My initial excitement of receiving the biggest box was squelched when I opened it to find a Nerf™ football. I was disappointed; I had no clue about what to do with it. I had grown up in a household where sports were rarely, if ever, watched on TV. I promptly made a trade for a cool dinosaur kit where you could put the bones together to build a T-rex. I loved building that T-rex and kept it for many years, but the boys of my class branded me a "wuss" because I didn't want the football. One would think that bones and dinosaurs would be adequately masculine, but a football superseded this in the toy-related hierarchy of masculinity in the classroom.

Hobbies and Books

Through much of my childhood I had an interest in artistic endeavors. Despite my parents' lack of concern for gender-appropriate toys and interests, I soon became aware of the gendered division of hobbies and how to regulate and manage the public (school) and private (home) side of this. I had grown up with parents who both enjoyed arts and crafts. From as back as I can remember, my mother had sewn, quilted, crocheted, and cross-stitched. My father also had interest in crafts, particularly working with wood and stained glass. Given the dangers innate to a wood shop, I was primarily exposed to the fiber arts my mother was working with. From an early age, I found her hobbies intriguing and was eager to learn. I was six or seven when my mother showed me how to cross-stitch. Her efforts to teach me didn't work out very well. I had a hard time emulating what she was doing. I ultimately did learn to cross-stitch from a book. I can still remember the first piece I stitched of a little brown bear.

Looking back, I now know that my interest in cross-stitch must have been challenging for my parents. Sewing is culturally regarded in our society as a craft for women. I feel it was quite progressive of my parents to not have told me "cross-stitch is for girls" and push me toward stereotypical masculine pastimes. I even recall my father's positive support for my first little project. My parents never instilled shame or embarrassment in me because of my "feminine" hobbies.

Early in my school years, I found great joy in the world of books. I became a hungry little reader, taking out as many as three books a week from the library—a heavy stack for such a little person. At the pace I worked through the library books, it was inevitable that I would hit upon books that boys "shouldn't" read. I recall one series of books where a doll traveled to different places around the world. I don't recall ever having an interest in dolls as a child, but I enjoyed those books because of the travel aspect and the exposure to different cultures and places.

The other children in my class did take notice. Since boys aren't supposed to read books about dolls, I used to hide them from my classmates. I don't recall if they teased me about this, but I knew, even at that age, that these were books for girls. Further reflection upon these books makes me wonder about my parents' response. I don't remember any. As far as I can recall, my parents never made any negative or derogatory comment about it; they simply supported my interest in reading, even if my books weren't really boy books.

Later, in this same library, I discovered a children's series of biographies where I was exposed to individuals such as Abraham Lincoln, Martin Luther King, Jr., and Thomas Jefferson. These books were most certainly appropriate for a boy. I checked out a new one every week. One week, I got one about a woman, for which I received a great deal of harassment from my male classmates. Over and over, I heard, "Why would you want to read about a girl?" I was embarrassed and dejected. Helen Keller remains the only woman from the series I ever read about. It's odd how a simple act of reading about a woman can put one's masculinity at risk.

A growing interest in arts and crafts, combined with my love of books, led me to borrow various arts books. Initially, I was vaguely familiar with the craft of crocheting, having seen my mother working with the funny hooked needle. I was curious, so this was the topic of the first of these books I borrowed. I took the book home and taught myself how to crochet, making a white washcloth.

I was proud of that little project, so I took it to school for show-and-tell. This led to another magnified moment, in which I learned one of the harshest lessons of my gender socialization. My classmates picked me on endlessly. I was beginning to see that there were certain hobbies and activities that I might be interested in and had talent in doing, but which could never be shared with the kids at school. The teacher was supportive and said what a nice job I had done, but the kids were cruel. I was confused. After all, we all took the same art classes. How was this different? I had no idea that this wasn't stuff I was supposed to be doing. I had two options: give up this hobby entirely or continue it at home and keep it secret from my peers. I chose the latter.

At first blush, the library would seem to be gender-neutral territory, a place of knowledge and entertainment. But this is gendered too. A boy must be careful not to overstep the boundaries that define appropriate masculinity. One is constricted by the gendered information we are taught by peers, teachers, and families. While adults certainly have a profound influence upon youth, it also seems that much of the gender policing of boys is accomplished by their male peers. Girls, who may participate in taunting and harassment in conjunction with other boys, are unlikely to police and taunt boys for feminine behaviors or interests on their own (Zucker et al. 1995). In my experience this was true. Girls were much more willing to accept my interest in art and the books that they may have also read, and they enjoyed discussing them with me. This probably helped lay the groundwork for my ability to establish friendships more readily with girls than with boys.

Moving Along in School

The lesson learned about what constitutes an appropriate book extended beyond the library to schooling. There is an expectation that both girls and boys in our culture will attend schools, but the types of involvement and the interest demonstrated by the differing genders is regulated differently. Subjects and information taught and presented to children help to reinforce conceptions of masculinity and femininity, as well as power, in our culture. Subjects that have the connotation of being of "lesser" importance, such as handwriting, tend to be associated with the feminine. Thus, it may be socially expected that girls will earn higher grades than boys in such subjects. People notice the "girly" writing of a man who writes nicely. The social construction of gender also reaches out from the books of the classroom to suggest that there are subjects, topics, and careers that are for girls and others that are for boys.

By the fourth grade, I was selected to join my school district's Academically Gifted Program (AGP). This became another nail in the coffin of my popularity. It's strange how as children we tease and insult both the over-achievers and the under-achievers. I yearned through those years to merely be "average." Alas, I was not, as I was in a special program where I was permitted to leave my regular school one whole day a week and ride a bus to another school to interact with other "gifted" students in a special class. We had access to various academic and activity-experience opportunities. It was a good experience while I was at AGP, at least initially. This was the first time that I had a chance to mingle with peers who seemed to be at my own intellectual level. I also was no longer the main target of harassment in my class. I was grouped with those who I can only assume were also targets in their own schools. In a funny kind of way, it was rewarding to be grouped up with the other nerds, geeks, sissies, and weirdos, one of the first times I didn't feel alone.

Children can be incredibly cruel and I was an easy target, being in a gifted program, being a bit pudgy, being too effeminate, and wearing glasses. It was in fourth grade when I first tried to go on a diet in hopes of fitting in better with my classmates. I knew to hide this from my peers, because, as with so many other things in my world, being on a diet was something girls did, not boys. So even in my aim to fit in better, I was trying to get there by way of non-masculine approved routes (though as adults we know that both men and women go on diets).

During those years of fourth through sixth grade, I found myself becoming increasingly isolated and distant. I was a sad child in many ways. I spent a lot of time reading and doing artistic projects by myself. I struggled with the emotional limitations of schooling, with my inability to fit in with my peers. I spent many nights hiding under my quilt in bed crying about it. I simply could not understand why my peers held such a negative view of me. I tried to reason the circumstances away as being the result of superior intellect, but this didn't work. I'm sure it was not an easy thing for my parents to see me so sad, so I also tried to keep it hidden from them. (Isn't that what boys are supposed to do?) I sought to reconcile some of the emotional strain of the situation by withdrawing and convincing myself that I was fine alone.

Having relocated to a new town towards the end of sixth grade, I merged into the life of junior high school much like my peers. We were all new to the school, with an equally low status in the grade hierarchy, all seeking to establish our standing in the local scheme of things. I was placed in all the advanced classes that were offered. While this was great in that I was with a group of intellectual peers, I also was separated from the majority of my classmates, who I only met in gym, chorus, and maybe in the cafeteria.

During the seventh grade, all students were required to take a home economics class. For the first time, I was able to flaunt my domestic abilities with a needle and thread as well as in the kitchen. From a young age, I had learned to cook, in part because of personal interest, but also in part because I was a Cub Scout. I no longer had to hide the fact that I could cook and sew from my peers, but I did have to be careful in showing how much I knew and how much I enjoyed these activities. I ended up being at the head of my class for home economics and even started helping other students with some of the sewing and embroidery assignments. It was the first time that the feedback I was receiving from peers was not reinforcing the negative associations of my gender identity in connection with stereotypically feminine activities.

Because the course was required and I was part of a class of high achieving students, I wasn't seen as a boy participating in feminine activities. Instead, I was just a student who was doing well in class. But as soon as the semester in home economics ended and I entered the wood shop class, I had to send my domestic abilities and interests into the gender closet. This produced another magnified moment, this time highlighting how quickly valued abilities in one context can become a source of embarrassment and taunting in another.

Heading into wood shop, many of my peers expected that I would be uncomfortable and fall flat on my face. I surprised them when they learned that I actually knew as much or more about the tools and equipment as they did. All the time I had spent with my father in the garage had paid off. I was a competent woodworker and did just fine in making the semester's big lamp project. One might think that the ability to fulfill both the roles and tasks traditionally classified as feminine and those classified as masculine would have been regarded positively by my peers. Unfortunately, this was not the case, because the dichotomous nature of gender reared its head once again. While both my feminine and masculine skills required similar abilities—precise measurement, the operation of machines (be it a sewing machine and mixer, or a table saw and drill press), envisioning how differing parts or different ingredients work together to create a final product—the incongruity of being a boy who was successful in the feminine tasks was unacceptable. We seem more likely to recognize difference while remaining blind to the similarity that is demonstrated by differently gendered youth (Messner 2000). This is especially true for boys who demonstrate "feminine" skills.

I was never blessed as a child with good hand-eye coordination or balance; I was a "big ol' klutz." Early on, I learned to dread gym class, in part because of a disinterest in athletics and in part because of my peers' responses to my lack of athletic prowess. There were, of course, some things I loved about gym class, such as the little wheelie carts for scooting around, dodge-ball, playing with the big parachute, and square-dancing, which I adored. Another magnified moment unfolded at this time. It was a Wednesday and we had gym in late morning, right after lunch. My second tooth was loose. It had gotten to that cool stage where you could spin the tooth round and round, but it held tight by a single thread. It was climb-the-rope day. To me, the rope was the very worst part of gym classes. I did not have the upper body strength to climb the rope; I even had problems with the interval knots. I was waiting in line, spinning the tooth with all my might, and it finally came out when there was just one person remaining between me and the dreaded rope. I felt tremendous relief in being able to avoid the rope and go to the nurse's office. But I also knew this could have been a gender-defining moment.

In those early years, in addition to scouting, my parents also offered me the opportunity to join various local youth sports teams, like baseball. My one sister and I had both taken swim lessons when we were young and enjoyed that greatly, but the thought of an organized team sport didn't appeal to me. As it was, I was already spending enough time figuring ways to get out of gym class. But my parents never forced these opportunities on me. They surely knew that I was not the most masculine boy, but they never demeaned me for lacking an interest in sports. Actually, in contrast to many of my classmates' parents, my own parents weren't very interested in sports. Organized sports were rarely, if ever, seen on television in my house. One could argue that this could have "caused" me not be interested in sports, but this is unlikely considering that both my siblings participated in various sports in their youth.

When I was about six years old, I had another of those eye-opening experiences (another magnified moment) during which I began to understand some of the "real world" differences between males and females. I had mastered riding my bike with training wheels and was finally ready to move on to riding without them. At the time, I was only allowed to bike back and forth on the sidewalks on either side of my house. Two sisters, Ann and Stella, lived in the house on the left and had a driveway that was perfect for turning around. In the transition to riding without training wheels, one of the hardest parts is learning to turn, continue to stay upright, and keep going where you want to go. At the side of Ann and Stella's driveway was a large bush. During one of my first efforts to turn around, I turned abruptly, crashed into their bush, and simultaneously learned what happens when a hard object—like handle bars—hits a boy in the groin. I was stuck, entangled in both the bush and bike, and in tremendous pain. I cried and was very upset, of course. Who knew that such an occurrence could hurt so badly? As I was a modest child, I was embarrassed by the entire incident. I knocked on Ann and Stella's door to apologize for breaking branches on their bush. They took me very seriously, inspected the bush, and actually thanked me for having broken out the branch that had some rot on it. (At least, that was their story.) I was so relieved. I eventually mastered the act of turning on my bike with not too many scars to my ego or body, but my neighbors' support and understanding stayed with me.

Third grade brought my first regular visits to the playground. Of course, we had gone outside to play in the past, but it had been intermittent, as the big kids in higher grades were "too wild" and might hurt us. While it is common for children to create single-sex play groups (Martin and Fabes 2001), I found I was more comfortable playing with the girls. They were less violent and didn't always talk about the stereotypically masculine toys about which I had little knowledge or interest. I didn't fit in well and was picked on and posited to the lowest boy status. However, with the group of girls, I was able to be one of the leaders and had a lot of social support from them. I learned how to play cat's cradle at lunch, got to

just relax and sit and talk in the sun at play time, and compete on the swings for who could go highest and jump off.

The dread of gym class persisted throughout my junior and high school years. My gym class loathing was reinforced one year when I was placed with students two years my senior because of my academic and choral schedule. That was a very rough year of gym class for me. As one might suspect, my classmates (who seemingly comprised the majority of the football team) were not pleased to have to count me among them. Making matters worse, the gym teacher "inadvertently" mentioned that I was in a class of seniors "because of chorus." Involvement of any male in choir was regarded with disgust by most of the boys of my school.

I had learned to deal with the psychological harm accompanying this masculine departure, but that year I understood that gender violations could also result in physical pain. That fall, one of the games of flag football, which was supposed to be non-contact, resulted in my first cast. This was the first concrete example of my life in which the disapproval of my gender portrayal by my peers, together with the bolstering disapproval of adults (my gym teacher), caused me real harm. I had always wanted to believe that each of my classmates felt different and out-of-place to at least some degree, but from that point on I became increasingly critical and distant from my peers and even wary of the adults of my school. I was disappointed that adults would not present a better example for students, but I now recognize that deeply imbedded categories of masculinity are not only part of youth culture but of adult culture as well.

Athletic interest and involvement have long been held a bastion of masculinity. Being a successful athlete enables men/boys to affirm and define who and what they are, especially in opposition to femininity (Connell 1995; Messner 1992). Having had little athletic interest or skill as a child (and I still don't today), my experience of masculinity was problematized in this regard by my peers as well as the adults of my world. I had become a large-bodied, strongly built youth, with the quintessential football figure. The idea that I was disinterested in the football and wrestling teams seemed utterly foreign to my athletics teachers.

Cub Scouts and Masculinity

While I didn't participate in organized sports in my youth, I did become involved in an organization that is commonly regarded as a cornerstone of masculine childhood socialization, the Cub Scouts. I do not recall if I joined of my own volition or if I had been encouraged to do so by my parents. Looking back, I can see how I might initially have perceived Cub Scouts as the "in thing" to do, but I can also see how my parents, like many other parents, may have been encouraged to involve their sons in activities such as this. My scout troop was small because of the area where I lived. It was just me, Gus (a boy who was even more of an outsider than myself), and Brian (whose dad was our pack leader). Such a small pack was limited in the activities it could undertake. I remember the occasional craft projects and the emergence of my competitive nature as I sought various beads and patches that marked one's ranking and skill as a scout. As the years passed, I obtained quite a few badges, but I did not find the overall experience fulfilling.

While "character development" is the first purpose of scouting, I do not know if I experienced much of this within the Scouts or if, instead, I was encouraged to regard certain behaviors, activities, and characteristics as masculine and thus appropriate, or feminine and thus inappropriate. There were many conflicting messages in this regard. While we primarily participated in "masculine" activities such as woodworking, nature and environmental appreciation, and various competitions such as the building and racing of small wooden cars, we also had an annual cake bake contest. Fathers and sons were to bake cakes without the help of a mother to raise funds for the troop. At the time, I did not understand why my mother wasn't allowed to help with the cake. I felt that since my mother did most of the cooking and baking at home, she would be the appropriate parent for the task. In other scouting tasks, such as seeking patches, my mother was able to help, so why couldn't she here? The annual cake-baking contest was in many respects a magnified moment, an affirmation for me that men and women were in opposition in our society. To be a real man meant to be separate and independent of girls. Any task a woman could do, a man could do better—if he wanted to.

I eventually left the Cub Scouts, just before advancing to Boy Scouts. My parents encouraged continued participation, but I asserted that I was not enjoying the activities, especially given the shortcomings that resulted from my troop's small size. My parents sympathized and allowed me to make the final decision; I always appreciated the choices they allowed me to make.

Cooking and Clothing

While there were conflicting messages conveyed in the cake baking of Cub Scouts, it didn't reduce my interest in cooking. I found I loved mixing and making things in the kitchen. It amazed me that you could put various ingredients together, add heat, and presto! I first learned the miracles of kitchen chemistry through the use of *Bisquick*. I would get up early on the weekend, not only for the cartoons, but to make pancakes for the family. I became quite skilled at it, even though it took many bad pancakes to master the timing. My parents were always encouraging and around the age of 7 or 8, I received my first cookbook. I loved that book and have kept it. The first real thing I ever made from it was potato salad, which was a hit with the family. Despite all the comfort and praise I received from my family for my cooking, and despite my cookbook having pictures of both boys and girls, I somehow knew that this was not something I should mention at school. I was already labeled an outsider; no need to add fodder to my peers' ammunition.

It is odd how, as children, we receive such mixed messages about what establishes various tasks as masculine and feminine. We often see our parents completing similar tasks, at least on occasion. If raised in the home of a single parent, with all the adult tasks needing to be accomplished by that one parent, how is it that certain tasks and skills are then demarcated masculine and feminine? I recall most cooking and kitchen tasks being done by my mother, but I can also vividly recall occasions when my father cooked and worked in the kitchen. We probably all experience childhood in this way, but at the same time we create a cultural understanding of gender through the subtle messages surrounding us, such as that while both men and women cook, kitchen and cooking are gendered feminine.

During my early adolescence, like most of my peers, I became fashion conscious. I aspired to dress in style and to fit in. I was never quite able to pull it off. When I was in junior high, I had a pair of jeans that caused me problems and sparked a new wave of taunting. When I sat, the jeans would bunch up in front, causing the zippered area to visibly bulge. At the time, we were having our first big sex education sections in health class. All the sex talk combined with my bulging jeans led one of my male classmates to ask me loudly whether I was gay because I was allegedly looking in his direction while sexually aroused. I was completely embarrassed and angered, prompting another magnified moment.

Regardless of my response, I was branded. No longer was I just a nerd, geek, and sissy boy, but I was to become the gay boy of the class. The months that followed were horrendous. Despite assertions to the contrary, no one listened. Being regarded as gay was the worst thing anyone could be branded.

Dating, Sex, and College

In time, I became increasingly aware of dating and sex. However, unlike many of my peers, I did not date. There were some girls who I had crushes

on, but given my outsider and stigmatized status, it did not seem likely that I could get a date. The combination of rumors that I was gay, my participation in music, art, and theater, and my academic achievements put me in a tough spot. Socially, I did spend some time with a small group of my classmates, much of it during lunch. It was reassuring to have some bonds with a group of other nerds, sissies, and outsiders of both genders. Few members of this group dated or were sexually active as far as I knew, and we were all disparaged to varying degrees by the "populars."

High school is not an easy journey. It is particularly difficult if you do not adhere to established gender norms. Even though those norms are sometimes unclear, and the ability to cross the borders of gendered behavior is occasionally warranted, there is privilege associated with adhering to normative gender behaviors. In our society, we privilege those who clearly demark their homosexual status by having a romantic partner of the opposite six. This affirms one's gender identity as appropriate. An appropriately masculine male should be emotionally and erotically oriented to appropriately feminine females. Sexuality especially seems to supersede the other gendered markers that we take into account when viewing another person. Had I been more inclined to date or establish a heterosexual relationship in my teen years, perhaps my journey would have been less painful.

College offered me a clean slate on which I hoped to write a new story. After years of being labeled and taunted for not being masculine enough, I found college to be a liberating experience. I had visions of being a new person, a man who would be masculine and free of taunts and labels, someone who would leave behind gender-bending attributes. But I found I could not be anyone other than who I was—a man who enjoyed sewing and quilting, a man who loved to cook, a man who enjoyed art and music, and a man who became immersed in the soap operas the girls would watch at lunch time. College was a world away from the one I had known. Not only was I no longer picked on, teased, or taunted, but I was finally accepted by my floormates, classmates, instructors, and co-workers. With this new freedom, I became more confident and outgoing. Those unique "non-masculine" activities and interests that had confined me as a youth now worked to my benefit, making me special. I reveled in newfound popularity with my peers and found the obstacles that had impeded dating in the past were now all but gone.

Then and Now

As the years have passed, I have often reflected on my past and contrasted my own experience with that of other men with whom I've spoken. I have realized my parents were far more progressive than I had imagined, providing me with a regular refuge at home to be myself. In our culture, the acceptable expressions of masculinity are quite restrictive, but my parents somehow managed to establish an environment that offered flexibility. My parents are not psychiatrists; they had not even acquired college degrees when I was growing up. But they supported my own, as well as my sibling's, choices to live our lives as we chose, to be the individuals we preferred. I believe it is their acceptance and support that made my childhood successful despite the odds.

Today, I am proud to admit that I still partake in many feminine stereotyped activities. I no longer feel shame for the ways that I challenge the stereotypes of gender. Yes, I am clearly a man. I dress in appropriately masculine clothes. I wear my hair in a masculine style. I am "masculine" in many ways. Yet, I suspect my sexual orientation is often in question. Many may wonder—am I gay or am I straight? Were all those taunts and teases of my youth correct? I actually find this to be humorous, something reflecting the need for clear dichotomies. Perhaps some readers did not question my sexuality as they read this chapter, but I suspect that most did, given the "demasculinizing" title of the chapter and the various masculinity-challenging behaviors exhibited throughout my life. I know that I challenge the

conceptions of masculinity in numerous ways, but nearly every man challenges our stereotypical beliefs of masculinity in some manner. In practice, gender for many is an endless range of grays.

Yes, many gay men do express recollections of a childhood in which they experienced masculinity in problematic and stigmatizing manners (Savin-Williams 1998). There also are many gay men who experienced a fairly non-problematic masculine gender identity as they grew up. We see little problem in questioning the experiences of gay men, presuming that somehow their gender inclinations are clear, but we rarely question the gender of heterosexual men whose gender depictions challenge our conceptions of masculinity.

Does it matter? Why do we tie together gender and sexual orientation—are they really the same thing? Don't you, yourself, know individuals whose gendered behavior and depiction do not align with our stereotypical beliefs about homosexuality and heterosexuality? Why do we stigmatize and label the sissy boys of our culture as gay, but are more accepting of tomboys? There are tomboys who grow up to be heterosexual women and there are tomboys who grow up to be homosexual women. The same is true for sissy boys. Is masculinity so much more valuable than femininity? This sissy boy has grown up, and I have been fortunate to find a wonderful person to share my life—a progressive individual like my parents who supports my interests and abilities and loves me for the sissy boy I am.

Summing Up

Based on my own social history, I have examined the experience of growing up as a boy/man who embraces stereotypically feminine activities. Through this autoethnography, some of the complexities of socialization have been examined for those who are different. Looking at the education system, one of the primary socialization environments for youth, we can readily recognize the mechanisms of peer policing and gender regulation, which are further linked with society at large. Individuals who do not adhere to dichotomous definitions of masculinity or femininity are often stigmatized, considered polluted, and suspect. Negative responses often conflate sexuality and gender, whose magnified moments showcase difference.

References

Campenni, C. Estelle. 1999. "Gender Stereotyping of Children's Toys: A Comparison of Parents and Nonparents." *Sex Roles* 40: 121–138.

Carr, C. Lynn. 1998. "Tomboy Resistance and Conformity: Agency in Social Psychological Gender Theory." *Gender & Society* 12: 528–553.

Connell, Robert W. 1995. *Masculinities*. Berkeley, CA: University of California Press.

Hochschild, Arlie Russell. 1994. "The Commercial Spirit of Intimate Life and the Abduction of Feminism: Signs from Women's Advice Books." *Theory, Culture & Society* 11: 1–24.

Jordan, Ellen, and Angela Cowan. 1995. "Warrior Narratives in the Kindergarten Classroom: Renegotiating the Social Contract?" *Gender & Society* 9: 727–743.

Lucal, Betsy. 1999. "What It Means to Be Gendered Me: Life on the Boundaries of a Dichotomous Gender System." *Gender & Society* 13: 781–797.

Martin, Carol Lynn. 1995. "Stereotypes about Children with Traditional and Nontraditional Gender Roles." *Sex Roles* 33: 727–751.

Martin, Carol Lynn, and Richard A. Fabes. 2001. Research cited in Marianne Szegedy-Maszak's, "The Power of Gender." *U.S. News & World Report* 130(22): 52.

Messner, Michael. 1992. *Power at Play: Sports and the Problem of Masculinity*. Boston: Beacon.

Rogers, Mary F. 1999. *Barbie Culture*. Thousand Oaks, CA: Sage.

Savin-Williams, Ritch C. 1998. *. . . And Then I Became Gay: Young Men's Stories*. New York: Routledge.

Thorne, Barrie. 1986. "Girls and Boys Together . . . but Mostly Apart: Gender Arrangements in Elementary Schools." Pp. 167–221 in *Relationships and Development*, edited by W. W. Hartup and Z. Rubin. Hillsdale, NJ: Lawrence Erlbaum.

Zucker, K. J., D. N. Wilson-Smith, J. A. Kurita, and A. Stern. 1995. "Children's Appraisals for Sex-Typed Behavior in their Peers." *Sex Roles* 33: 703–725.

Paul Kivel

The Act-Like-a-Man Box

How are boys trained in the United States? What is the predominant image of masculinity that boys must deal with while growing up?

From a very early age, boys are told to "Act Like a Man." Even though they have all the normal human feelings of love, excitement, sadness, confusion, anger, curiosity, pain, frustration, humiliation, shame, grief, resentment, loneliness, low self-worth, and self-doubt, they are taught to hide the feelings and appear to be tough and in control. They are told to be aggressive, not to back down, not to make mistakes, and to take charge, have lots of sex, make lots of money, and be responsible. Most of all, they are told not to cry.

My colleagues and I have come to call this rigid set of expectations the "Act-Like-a-Man" box because it feels like a box, a 24-hour-a-day, seven-day-a-week box that society tells boys they must fit themselves into. One reason we know it's a box is because every time a boy tries to step out he's pushed back in with names like wimp, sissy, mama's boy, girl, fag, nerd, punk, mark, bitch, and others even more graphic. Behind those names is the threat of violence.

These words are little slaps, everyday reminders designed to keep us in the box. They are also fighting words. If someone calls a boy a "wimp" or a "fag," he is supposed to fight to prove that he is not. Almost every adult man will admit that as a kid, he had to fight at least once to prove he was in the box.

The columns on either side of the box show the expectations our society holds for men. The abuse, pressure, and training boys receive to meet

these expectations and stay in the box produce a lot of feelings, some of which are listed in the middle of the box above. Yet they have to cover over those feelings and try to act like a man because one of the strictures of being a man is not to show your feelings.

Notice that many of the words we get called refer to being gay or feminine. This feeds into two things we're taught to fear: (1) that we are not manly enough and (2) that we might be gay. Homophobia, the fear of gays or of being taken for gay, is an incredibly strong fear we learn as boys and carry with us throughout our lives. Much too often we try to relieve our fears of being gay or effeminate by attacking others.

There is other training that keeps us in the box. Besides getting into fights, we are ostracized and teased, and girls don't seem to like us when we step out of the box. Many adults keep pushing us to be tough, and that process begins early. They seem convinced that if they "coddle" us, we will be weak and vulnerable. Somehow, withdrawal of affection is supposed to toughen us and prepare us for the "real" world. Withdrawal of affection is emotional abuse. And that's bad enough. But it often does not stop there. One out of every six of us is sexually abused as a child. Often, the verbal, physical, and sexual abuse continues throughout our childhood.

There are many cultural variations of this theme, but its prevalence in Western cultures is striking. All boys have different strategies for trying to survive in the box. Some might even sneak out of it at times, but the scars from living within the walls of the box are long-lasting and painful.

If we pay attention we can easily see the box's effects on boys. Just watch a group of them

"Act Like a Man" Box

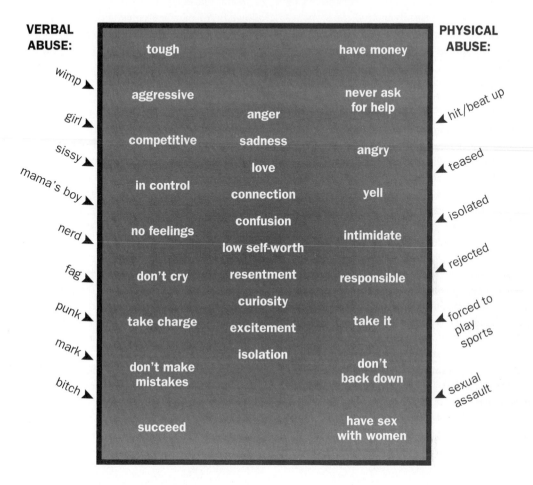

VERBAL ABUSE:

wimp
girl
sissy
mama's boy
nerd
fag
punk
mark
bitch

PHYSICAL ABUSE:

hit/beat up
teased
isolated
rejected
forced to play sports
sexual assault

tough   have money

aggressive   never ask for help

anger

competitive   sadness

angry

love

in control   connection   yell

confusion

no feelings   intimidate

low self-worth

don't cry   resentment   responsible

curiosity

take charge   excitement   take it

isolation

don't make mistakes   don't back down

succeed   have sex with women

together. They are constantly challenging each other, putting each other down, hitting each other, testing to see who is in the box. They are never at ease, always on guard. At an early age they start to hide their feelings, toughen up, and will make a huge emotional effort not to cry. They stop wearing colorful clothing or participating in activities that they think might make them vulnerable to being labeled gay. They walk more stiffly, talk more guardedly, move more aggressively. Behind this bravura they are often confused, scared, angry, and wanting closeness with others. But being in the box precludes closeness and makes intimacy unlikely.

The key to staying in the box is control. Boys are taught to control their bodies, control their feelings, control their relationships—to protect themselves from being vulnerable. Although the box is a metaphor for the pressures all boys must respond to, the possibility that a boy will have control over the conditions of his life varies depending on his race, class, and culture.

Being in control is not the same as being violent. In Western societies hitting people is frowned upon except in particular sports or military settings. It is deemed much more refined to retain control by using verbal, emotional, or psychological means rather than physical force.

Financial manipulation, coercion and intimidation, and sexual pressure are also condoned as long as no one is physically injured.

Clearly, the more money, education, and connections a man has, the easier it is for him to buy or manipulate what he wants. Wealthy and upper- or middle-class white men are generally promoted and celebrated for being in control and getting what they want. Poor or working-class men and men of color are usually punished for these same behaviors, especially, but not only, if they use physical force.

Why are boys trained to be in control? Most boys will end up with one of three roles in society—to be workers, consumers, or enforcers. A small percentage of boys are trained to give orders—to be bosses, managers, or officers. The box trains boys for the roles they will play, whether they will make decisions governing the lives of others or carry out the decisions made by those at the top. The box prepares boys to be police officers, security cops, deans, administrators, soldiers, heads of families, probation officers, prison guards—the roles that men, primarily white men, are being trained to fill. Men of color, along with women and young people, are the people more often being controlled.

Many men are under the illusion that being in the box is like being in an exclusive club. No girls allowed. All men are equal. For working- and middle-class white men and for those men of color who aspire to be accepted by them, the box creates a false feeling of solidarity with men in power and misleads many of them into thinking they have more in common with the corporate executives, political and religious leaders, generals, and bosses than they have with women.

Nobody is born in the Act-Like-a-Man box. It takes years and years of enforcement, name-calling, fights, threats, abuse, and fear to turn us into men who live in this box. By adolescence we believe that there are only two choices—we can be a man or a boy, a winner or a loser, a bully or a wimp, a champ or a chump.

Nobody wants to live in a box. It feels closed in; much of us is left out. It was a revelation to realize how I had been forced into the box. It was a relief to understand how it had been accomplished and to know it didn't have to be that way. Today, it inspires me to see adult men choose to live outside the box. It is a choice each of us can, and must make—to step outside the box and back into our families and communities.

PART THREE

Collegiate Masculinities: Privilege and Peril

The old social science orthodoxy about sex role socialization, from the 1950s until today, held that three institutions—family, church, and school—formed the primary sites of socialization, and the impact of education, family values, and religious training was decisive in shaping people's lives. This view tended to emphasize the centrality of adults in boys' lives. Because adults themselves were constructing the models of socialization, this conclusion seems understandable. But as social scientists began to ask boys and girls about the forces that influenced them, they heard about the increasing importance of peer groups and the media—two arenas where adults had far less reach. In recent years, researchers have begun to explore how homosocial peer groups affect men's lives.

The articles in Part Three focus on masculinities in college, a place where the all-male peer group is especially salient. How does collegiate life organize and reproduce the definitions of masculinity that we learn as young boys? How do specific all-male subcultures develop within these institutions, and what roles do they play? Part Three explores male bonding within collegiate organizations, such as fraternities and athletic teams, and within the traditions of formerly all-male military institutions. In recent years these institutions have been increasingly scrutinized and criticized, and some group members have felt besieged and unfairly picked on. Who is right?

Three of the articles in this section focus specifically on fraternities and the role of fraternity culture in campus life. The articles by Peter Lyman, A. Ayres Boswell and Joan Spade, and Michael Kimmel ask: How is hegemonic masculinity reproduced in fraternity life? Why are fraternity men more likely to be accused of sexual assault? Rocco Capraro provides a fascinating gender analysis of male drinking culture in college, and Kirby Schroeder looks at military schooling. Jason Schultz proposes some new rules of dating etiquette for college men, and Eric Anderson explores different versions of masculinity among male cheerleaders.

Photo courtesy of Barbara Kruger.

Peter Lyman

The Fraternal Bond as a Joking Relationship: A Case Study of the Role of Sexist Jokes in Male Group Bonding

One evening during dinner, 45 fraternity men suddenly broke into the dining room of a nearby campus sorority, surrounded the 30 women residents, and forced them to watch while one pledge gave a speech on Freud's theory of penis envy as another demonstrated various techniques of masturbation with a rubber penis. The women sat silently, staring downward at their plates, and listened for about 10 minutes, until a woman law student who was the graduate resident in charge of the house walked in, surveyed the scene and demanded, "Please leave immediately!" As she later described that moment, "There was a mocking roar from the men, 'It's tradition.' I said, 'That's no reason to do something like this, please leave!' And they left. I was surprised. Then the women in the house started to get angry. And the guy who made the penis-envy speech came back and said to us, 'That was funny to me. If that's not funny to you I don't know what kind of sense of humor you have, but I'm sorry.' "

That night the women sat around the stairwell of their house discussing the event, some angry and others simply wanting to forget the whole thing. They finally decided to ask the university to require that the men return to discuss the event. When university officials threatened to take action, the men agreed to the meeting. I had served as a faculty resident in student housing for two years and had given several talks in the dorm

From *Changing Men*, Michael Kimmel (ed.). Newbury Park, CA: Sage Publications, 1987. Reprinted by permission.

about humor and gender, and was asked by both the men and the women involved to attend the discussion as a facilitator, and was given permission to take notes and interview the participants later, provided I concealed their identities.

The penis-envy ritual had been considered a successful joke in previous years by both "the guys and the girls," but this year it failed, causing great tension between two groups that historically had enjoyed a friendly joking relationship. In the women's view, the joke had not failed because of its subject; they considered sexual jokes to be a normal part of the erotic joking relationship between men and women. They thought it had failed because of its emotional structure, the mixture of sexuality with aggression and the atmosphere of physical intimidation in the room that signified that the women were the object of a joking relationship between the men. A few women argued that the failed joke exposed the latent domination in men's relation to women, but this view was labeled "feminist" because it endangered the possibility of reconstituting the erotic joking relationship with the men. Although many of the men individually regretted the damage to their relationship with women friends in the group, they argued that the special male bond created by sexist humor is a unique form of intimacy that justified the inconvenience caused the women. In reinterpreting these stories as social constructions of gender, I will focus upon the way the joke form and joking relationships reveal the emotional currents underlying gender in this situation.

The Sociology of Jokes

Although we conventionally think of jokes as a meaningless part of the dramaturgy of everyday life, this convention is part of the way that the social function of jokes is concealed and is necessary if jokes are to "work." It is when jokes fail that the social conflicts that the joke was to reconstruct or "negotiate" are uncovered, and the tensions and emotions that underlie the conventional order of everyday social relations are revealed.

Joking is a special kind of social relationship that suspends the rules of everyday life in order to preserve them. Jokes indirectly express the emotions and tensions that may disrupt everyday life by "negotiating" them (Emerson 1969, 1970), reconstituting group solidarity by shared aggression and cathartic laughter. The ordinary consequences of forbidden words are suspended by meta-linguistic gestures (tones of voice, facial expressions, catch phrases) that send the message "this is a joke," and emotions that would ordinarily endanger a social relationship can be spoken safely within the micro-world created by the "the joke form" (Bateson 1972).

Yet jokes are not just stories, they are a theater of domination in everyday life, and the success or failure of a joke marks the boundary within which power and aggression may be used in a relationship. Nearly all jokes have an aggressive content, indeed shared aggression toward an outsider is one of the primary ways by which a group may overcome internal tension and assert its solidarity (Freud 1960, p. 102). Jokes both require and renew social bonds; thus Radcliffe-Brown pointed out that "joking relationships" between mothers-in-law and their sons-in-law provide a release for tension for people structurally bound to each other but at the same time feeling structural conflict with each other (Radcliffe-Brown 1959). Joking relationships in medicine, for example, are a medium for the indirect expression of latent emotions or taboo topics that if directly expressed would challenge the physician's authority or disrupt the need to treat life and death

situations as ordinary work (see Coser 1959; Emerson 1969, 1970).

In each of the studies cited above, the primary focus of the analysis was upon the social function of the joke, not gender, yet in each case the joke either functioned through a joking relationship between men and women, such as in Freud's or Radcliffe-Brown's analysis of mother-in-law jokes, or through the joking relationship among men. For example, Coser describes the role of nurses as a safe target of jokes: as a surrogate for the male doctor in patient jokes challenging medical authority; or as a surrogate for the patient in the jokes with which doctors expressed anxiety. Sexist jokes, therefore, should be analyzed not only in general terms of the function of jokes as a means of defending social order, but in specific terms as the mechanism by which the order of gender domination is sustained in everyday life. From this perspective, jokes reveal the way social organizations are gendered, namely, built around the emotional rules of male bonding. In this case study, gender is not only the primary content of men's jokes, but the emotional structures of the male bond is built upon a joking relationship that "negotiates" the tension men feel about their relationship with each other, and with women.

Male bonding in everyday life frequently takes the form of a group joking relationship by which men create a serial kind of intimacy to "negotiate" the latent tension and aggression they feel toward each other. The humor of male bonding relationships generally is sexual and aggressive, and frequently consists of sexist or racist jokes. As Freud (1960, p. 99) observed, the jokes that individual men direct toward women are generally erotic, tend to clever forms (like the double entendre), and have a seductive purpose. The jokes that men tell about women in the presence of other men are sexual and aggressive rather than erotic and use hostile rather than clever verbal forms; and, this paper will argue, have the creation of male group bonding as their purpose. While Freud analyzed jokes in order to reveal the unconscious, in this article, relationships will be analyzed to uncover the emotional dynamics of male friendships.

The failed penis-envy joke reveals two kinds of joking relationships between college men and women. First, the attempted joke was part of an ongoing joking relationship between "the guys and the girls," as they called each other. The guys used the joking relationship to negotiate the tension they felt between sexual interest in the girls and fear of commitment to them. The guys contrasted their sense of independence and play in male friendships to the sense of dependence they felt in their relationships with women, and used hostile joking to negotiate their fear of the "loss of control" implied by intimacy. Second, the failure of the joke uncovered the use of sexist jokes in creating bonds between men; through their own joking relationships (which they called friendship), the guys negotiated the tension between their need for intimacy with other men and their fear of losing their autonomy as men to the authority of the work world.

The Girls' Story

The women frequently had been the target of fraternity initiation rites in the past, and generally enjoyed this joking relationship with the men, if with a certain ambivalence. "There was a naked Christmas Carol event, they were singing 'We wish you a Merry Christmas,' and 'Bring on the hasty pudding' was the big line they liked to yell out. And we had five or six pledges who had to strip in front of the house and do naked jumping jacks on the lawn, after all the women in the house were lined up on the steps to watch." The women did not think these events were hostile because they had been invited to watch, and the men stood with them watching, suggesting that the pledges, not the women, were the targets of the joke. This made the joke sexual, not sexist, and part of the normal erotic joking relationship between the guys and girls. Still, these jokes were ritual events, not real social relationships; one woman said, "We were just supposed to watch, and the guys were

watching us watch. The men set up the stage and the women are brought along to observe. They were the controlling force, then they jump into the car and take off."

At the meeting with the men, two of the women spoke for the group while 11 others sat silently in the center, surrounded by about 30 men. Each tried to explain to the men why the joke had not been funny. The first began, "I'm a feminist, but I'm not going to blame anyone for anything. I just want to talk about my feelings." When she said, "these guys pile in, I mean these huge guys," the men exploded in loud cathartic laughter, and the women joined in, releasing some of the tension of the meeting. She continued, "Your humor was pretty funny as long as it was sexual, but when it went beyond sexual to sexist, then it became painful. You were saying 'I'm better than you.' When you started using sex as a way of proving your superiority it hurt me and made me angry."

The second woman speaker criticized the imposition of the joke form itself, saying that the men's raid had the tone of a symbolic rape. "I admit we knew you were coming over, and we were whispering about it. But it went too far, and I felt afraid to say anything. Why do men always think about women in terms of violating them, in sexual imagery? You have to understand that the combination of a sexual topic with the physical threat of all of you standing around terrified me. I couldn't move. You have to realize that when men combine sexuality and force it's terrifying to women." This woman alluded to having been sexually assaulted in the past, but spoke in a nonthreatening tone that made the men listen silently.

The women spoke about feeling angry about the invasion of their space, about the coercion of being forced to listen to the speeches, and about being used as the object of a joke. But they reported their anger as a psychological fact, a statement about a past feeling, not an accusation. Many began by saying, "I'm not a feminist, but . . . ," to reassure the men that although they felt angry, they were not challenging traditional gender relations. The women were caught in a double-bind; if they spoke angrily to the men they would violate the taboo against the expression of anger by women (Miller 1976, p. 102). If they said nothing, they would internalize their anger, and traditional feminine culture would encourage them to feel guilty about feeling angry at all (Bernardez 1978; Lerner 1980). In part they resolved the issue by accepting the men's construction of the event as a joke, although a failed joke; accepting the joke form absolved the men of responsibility, and transformed a debate about gender into a debate about good and bad jokes.

To be accepted as a joke, a cue must be sent to establish a "frame" [for] the latent hostility of the joke content in a safe context; the men sent such a cue when they stood next to the women during the naked jumping jacks. If the cue "this is a joke" is ambiguous, or is not accepted, the aggressive content of the joke is revealed and generally is responded to with anger or aggression, endangering the relationship. In part the women were pointing out to the men that the cue "this is a joke" had not been given in this case, and the aggressive content of the joke hurt them. If the cue is given properly and accepted, the everyday rules of social order are suspended and the rule "this is fun" is imposed on the expression of hostility.

Verbal aggression mediated by the joke form generally will be [accepted] without later consequences in the everyday world, and will be judged in terms of the formal intention of jokes, shared play marked by laughter in the interest of social order. By complaining to the university, the women had suspended the rules of joke culture, and attempted to renegotiate them by bringing in an observer; even this turned out to be too aggressive, and the women retreated to traditional gender relationships. The men had formally accepted this shift of rules in order to avoid punishment from the university, however their defense of the joke form was tacitly a defense of traditional gender rules that would define male sexist jokes toward women as erotic, not hostile.

In accepting the construction of the event as "just a joke" the women absolved the men of responsibility for their actions by calling them "little boys." One woman said, "It's not wrong, they're just boys playing a prank. They're little boys, they don't know what they're doing. It was unpleasant, but we shouldn't make a big deal out of it." In appealing to the rules of the joke form the men were willing to sacrifice their relationship to the women to protect the rules. In calling the men "little boys" the women were bending the rules trying to preserve the relationship through a patient nurturing role (see Gilligan 1982, p. 44).

In calling the guys "little boys," the girls had also created a kind of linguistic symmetry between "the boys and the girls." With the exception of the law student, who called the girls "women," the students called the men "guys" and the women "girls." Earlier in the year the law student had started a discussion about this naming practice. The term "women" had sexual connotations that made "the girls" feel vulnerable, and "gals," the parallel to "guys," connoted "older women" to them. While the term "girls" refers to children, it was adopted because it avoided sexual connotations. Thus the women had no term like "the guys," which is a bonding term that refers to a group of friends as equals; the women often used the term "the guys" to refer to themselves in a group. As the men's speeches were to make clear, the term "guys" refers to a bond that is exclusively male, which is founded upon the emotional structure of the joke form, and which justifies it.

The Guys' Story

Aside from the roar of laughter when a woman referred to their intimidating size, the men interrupted the women only once. When a woman began to say that the men obviously intended to intimidate them, the men loudly protested that the women couldn't possibly judge their intentions, that they intended the whole event only as a joke, and the intention of a joke is, by definition, just fun.

At this point the two black men in the fraternity intervened to explain the rules of male joke culture to the women. The black men said that in a sense they understood what the women meant, it is painful being the object of aggressive jokes. In fact, they said, the collective talk of the fraternity at meals and group events was made up of nothing but jokes, including many racist jokes. One said, "I know what you mean. I've had to listen to things in the house that I'd have hit someone for saying if I'd heard them outside." There was again cathartic laughter among the guys, for the male group bond consisted almost entirely of aggressive words that were barely contained by the responsibility absolving rule of the joke form. A woman responded, "Maybe people should be hit for saying those things, maybe that's the right thing to do." But the black speaker was trying to explain the rules of male joke culture to the women, "if you'd just ignored us, it wouldn't have been any fun." To ignore a joke, even though it makes you feel hurt or angry, is to show strength or coolness, the two primary masculine ideals of the group.

Another man tried to explain the failure of the joke in terms of the difference between the degree of "crudeness" appropriate among the guys and between "guys and girls." He said, "As I was listening at the edge of the room, near the door, and when I looked at the guys I was laughing but when I looked at the girls I was embarrassed. I could see both sides at the same time. It was too crude for your sense of propriety. We have a sense of crudeness you don't have. That's a cultural aspect of the difference between girls and guys."

The other men laughed as he mentioned "how crude we are at the house," and one of the black men added, "you wouldn't believe how crude it gets." Many of the men said privately that while they individually found the jokes about women vulgar, the jokes were justified because they were necessary for the formation of the fraternal bond. These men thought the mistake had been to reveal their crudeness to the women, this was "in bad taste."

In its content, the fraternal bond was almost entirely a joking relationship. In part, the joking was a kind of "signifying" or "dozens," a ritual exchange of insults that functioned to create group solidarity. "If there's one theme that goes on, it's the emphasis on being able to take a lot of ridicule, of shit, and not getting upset about it. Most of the interaction we have is verbally abusing each other, making disgusting references to your mother's sexuality, or the women you were seen with, or your sex organ, the size of your sex organ. And you aren't cool unless you can take it without trying to get back." Being cool is an important male value in other settings as well, such as sports or work; the joke form is a kind of male pedagogy in that, in one guy's words, it teaches "how to keep in control of your emotions."

But the guys themselves would not have described their group as a joking relationship or even as a male bond; they called it friendship. One man said he had found perhaps a dozen guys in the house who were special friends, "guys I could cry in front of." Yet in interviews, no one could recall any of the guys actually crying in front of each other. One said, "I think the guys are very close, they would do nearly anything for each other, drive each other places, give each other money. I think when they have problems about school, their car, or something like that, they can talk to each other. I'm not sure they can talk to each other about problems with women though." The image of crying in front of the other guys was a moving symbol of intimacy to the guys, but in fact crying would be an admission of vulnerability, which would violate the ideals of "strength" and "being cool."

Although the fraternal bond was idealized as a unique kind of intimacy upon which genuine friendship was built, the content of the joking relationship was focused upon women, including much "signifying" talk about mothers. The women interpreted the sexist jokes as a sign of vulnerability. "The thing that struck me the most about our meeting together," one said, "was when the men said they were afraid of trusting women, afraid of being seen as jerks." According to her, this had been the women's main reaction to the meeting by the other women, "How do you tell men that they don't have to be afraid, and what do you do with women who abuse that kind of trust?" One of the men on the boundary of the group remarked that the most hostile misogynist jokes came from the men with the fewest intimate relationships with women. "I think down deep all these guys would love to have satisfying relationships with women. I think they're scared of failing, of having to break away from the group they've become comfortable with. I think being in a fraternity, having close friendships with men is a replacement for having close relationships with women. It'd be painful for them because they'd probably fail."

Joking mobilized the commitment of the men to the group by policing the individual men's commitments to women and minimized the possibility of dyadic withdrawal from the group (see Slater 1963). "One of the guys just acquired a girlfriend a few weeks ago. He's someone I don't think has had a woman to be friends with, maybe ever, at least in a long time. Everybody has been ribbing him intensely the last few weeks. It's good natured in tone. Sitting at dinner they've invented a little song they sing to him. People yell questions about his girlfriend, the size of her vagina, does she have big breasts."

Since both the jokes and the descriptions of the parties have strong homoerotic overtones, including the exchange of women as sexual partners, jokes were also targeted at homosexuality, to draw an emotional line between the homosocial male bond and homosexual relationships. Being called "queer," however, did not require a sexual relationship with another man, but only visible signs of vulnerability or nurturing behavior.

Male Bonding as a Joking Relationship

Fraternal bonding is an intimate kind of male group friendship that suspends the ordinary rules and responsibilities of everyday life through joking relationships. To the guys, dyadic friendship with a woman implied "loss of control," namely, responsibility for work and family. In dealing with women, the group separated intimacy from sex, defining the male bond as intimate but not sexual (homosocial), and relationships with women as sexual but not intimate (heterosexual). The intimacy of group friendship was built upon shared spontaneous action, "having fun," rather than the self-disclosure that marks women's friendships (see Rubin 1983, p. 13). One of the men had been inexpressive as he listened to the discussion, but spoke about fun in a voice filled with emotion, "The penis-envy speech was a hilarious idea, great college fun. That's what I joined the fraternity for, a good time. College is a stage in my life to do crazy and humorous things. In 10 years when I'm in the business world I won't be able to carry on like this [again cathartic laughter from the men]. The initiation was intended to be humorous. We didn't think through how sensitive you women were going to be."

This speech gives the fraternal bond a specific place in the life cycle. The joking relationship is a ritual bond that creates a male group bond in the transition between boyhood and manhood, after the separation from the family, where the authority of mothers limits fun, but before becoming subject to the authority of work. One man later commented on the transitional nature of the male bond, "I think a lot of us are really scared of losing total control over our own lives. Having to sacrifice our individuality. I think we're scared of work in the same way we're scared of women." In this sense individuality is associated with what the guys called "strength," both the emotional strength suggested by being cool, and the physical strength suggested by facing the risks of sports and the paramilitary games they liked to play.

The emotional structure of the joking relationship is built upon the guys' latent anger about the discipline that middle-class male roles imposed upon them, both marriage rules and work rules. The general relationship between organization of men's work and men's domination of women was noted by Max Weber (1958, pp.

345–346), who described "the vocational special- ist" as a man mastered by the rules of organization that create an impersonal kind of dependence, and who therefore seeks to create a feeling of in- dependence through the sexual conquest of women. In each of the epochs of Western history, Weber argues, the subordination of men at work has given rise to a male concept of freedom based upon the violation of women. Although Weber tied dependence upon rules to men's need for sexual conquest through seduction, this may also be a clue to the meaning of sexist jokes and jok- ing relationships among men at work. Sexist jokes may not be simply a matter of recreation or a means of negotiating role stress, they may be a reflection of the emotional foundations of orga- nizational life for men. In everyday work life, sexist jokes may function as a ritual suspension of the rules of responsibility for men, a with- drawal into a microworld in which their anger about dependence upon work and women may be safely expressed.

In analyzing the contradictions and vulnera- bilities the guys felt about relationships with women and the responsibilities of work, I will focus upon three dimensions of the joking rela- tionship: (1) the emotional content of the jokes; (2) the erotics of rule breaking created by the rules of the joke form; and (3) the image of strength and "being cool" they pitted against the depen- dence represented by both women and work.

The Emotional Dynamic of Sexist Jokes

When confronted by the women, the men de- fended the joke by asserting the formal rule that the purpose of jokes is play, then by justifying the jokes as necessary in order to create a special male bond. The defense that jokes are play defines ag- gressive behavior as play. This defense was far more persuasive to the men than to the women, since many forms of male bonding play are rule- governed aggression, as in sports and games. The second defense, asserting the relation between sex- ist jokes and male bonds, points out the social function of sexist jokes among the guys, to control the threat that individual men might form intimate

emotional bonds with women and withdraw from the group. Each defense poses a puzzle about the emotional dynamics of male group friendship, for in each case male group friendship seems more like a defense against vulnerability than a positive ideal.

In each defense, intimacy is split from sexu- ality in order to eroticize the male bond, thereby creating an instrumental sexuality directed at women. The separation of intimacy from sexual- ity transforms women into "sexual objects," which both justifies aggression at women by sus- pending their relationships to the men and deval- ues sexuality itself, creating a disgust at women as the sexual "object" unworthy of intimate at- tention. What is the origin of this conjunction between the devaluation of sexuality and the ap- propriation of intimacy for the male bond?

Chodorow (1978, p. 182) argues that the sense of masculine identity is constructed by an early repression of the son's erotic bond with his mother; with this repression the son's capacity for intimacy and commitment is devalued as fem- inine behavior. Henceforth men feel ambivalent about intimate relationships with women, seeking to replicate the fusion of intimacy and sexuality that they had experienced in their primal rela- tionships to their mothers, but at the same time fearing engulfment by women in heterosexual re- lationships, like the engulfment of their infant selves by their mothers (Chodorow 1976). Cer- tainly the content of the group's joke suggests this repression of the attachment to the mother, as well as hostility to her authority in the family. One man reported, "There're an awful lot of jokes about people's mothers. If any topic of conversa- tion dominates the conversation it's 'heard your mother was with Ray [one of the guys] last night.' The guys will say incredibly vulgar things about their mothers, or they'll talk about the anatomy of a guy's girlfriends, or women they'd like to sleep with." While the guys' signifying mother jokes suggest the repression Chodorow describes, the men realized that their view of women made it unlikely that marriage would be a positive expe- rience. One said, "I think a lot of us expect to marry someone pretty enough that other men will think we got a good catch, someone who is at least marginally interesting to chat with, but not someone we'd view as a friend. But at the same time, a woman who will make sufficient demands that we won't be able to have any friends. So we'll be stuck for the rest of our lives without friends."

While the emotional dynamic of men's "heterosexual knots" may well begin in this primordial separation of infant sons from mothers, its structure is replicated in the guys' ambivalence about their fathers, and their anger about the dependence upon rules in the work world. Yet the guys themselves described the fraternal bond as a way of creating "strength" and overcoming dependence, which suggests a positive ideal of male identity. In order to explore the guys' sense of the value of the male bond, their conception of strength and its consequences for the way they related to each other and to women has to be taken seriously.

Strength

Ultimately the guys justified the penis-envy joke because it created a special kind of male intimacy, but while the male group is able to appropriate its members' needs for intimacy and commitment, it is not clear that it is able to satisfy those needs, because strength has been defined as the opposite of intimacy. "Strength" is a value that represents solidarity rather than intimacy, the solidarity of a shared risk in rule-governed aggressive competition; its value is suggested by the cathartic laughter when the first woman speaker said, "These guys poured in, these huge guys."

The eros detached from sexuality is attached to rules, not to male friends; the male bond consists of an erotic toward rules, and yet the penis-envy joke expresses most of all the guys' ambivalence about rules. Like "the lads," the male gangs who roam the English countryside, "getting in trouble" by enforcing social mores in unsocial ways (Peters 1972), "the guys" break the rules in rule-governed ways. The joke form itself suggests this ambivalence about rules and

acts as a kind of pedagogy about the relationship between rules and aggression in male work culture. The joke form expresses emotions and tensions that might endanger the order of the organization, but that must be spoken lest they damage social order. Jokes can create group solidarity only if they allow dangerous things to be said; allow a physical catharsis of tension through laughter; or create the solidarity of an "in group" through shared aggression against an "out group." In each case there is an erotic in joke forms: an erotic of shared aggression, of shared sexual feeling, or an erotic of rule breaking itself.

It has been suggested that male groups experience a high level of excitement and sexual arousal in public acts of rule breaking (Thorne & Luria 1986). The penis-envy speech is precisely such an act, a breaking of conventional moral rules in the interest of group arousal. In each of the versions of the joking relationship in this group there is such an erotic quality: in the sexual content of the jokes, in the need for women to witness dirty talk or naked pledges, in the eros of aggression of the raid and jokes themselves. The penis-envy speech, a required event for all members of the group, is such a collective violation of the rules, and so is the content of their talk, a collective dirty talking that violates moral rules. The cathartic laughter that greeted the words, "You wouldn't believe what we say at the house," testifies to the emotional charge invested in dirty talk.

Because the intimacy of the guys' bond is built around an erotic of rule breaking, it has the serial structure of shared risk rather than the social structure of shared intimacy. In writing about the shared experience of suffering and danger of men at war, J. Glenn Gray (1959, pp. 89–90) distinguishes two kinds of male bonding, comradeship and friendship. Comradeship is based upon an erotic of shared danger, but is based upon the loss of an individual sense of self to a group identity, while friendship is based upon an individual's intellectual and emotional affinity to another individual. In the eros of friendship one's sense of self is heightened; in the eros of comradeship a sense of self is replaced by a sense of group membership. In this sense the guys were seeking comradeship, not friendship, hence the group constructed its bond through an erotic of shared activities with an element of risk, shared danger, or rule breaking: in sports, in paramilitary games, in wild parties, in joking relations. The guys called the performance of these activities "strength," being willing to take risks as a group and remaining cool.

Thus the behavior that the women defined as aggressive was seen by the men as a contest of strength governed by the rules of the joke form, to which the proper response would have been to remain "cool." To the guys, the masculine virtue of "strength" has a positive side, to discover oneself and to discover a sense of the other person through a contest of strength that is governed by rules. To the guys, "strength" is not the same as power or aggression because it is governed by rules, not anger; it is anger that is "uncool."

"Being Cool"

It is striking that the breaking of rules was not spontaneous, but controlled by the rules of the joke form: that aggressive talk replaces action; that talk is framed by a social form that requires the consent of others; that talk should not be taken seriously. This was the lesson that the black men tried to teach the women in the group session: In the male world, aggression is not defined as violent if it is rule governed rather than anger governed. The fraternal bond was built upon this emotional structure, for the life of the group centered upon the mobilization of aggressive energies in rule-governed activities (in sports, games, jokes, parties). In each arena aggression was highly valued (strength) only when it was rule governed (cool). Getting angry was called "losing control" and the guys thought they were most likely to lose control when they experienced themselves as personally dependent, as in relationships with women and at work.

Rule-governed aggression is a conduct that is very useful to organizations, in that it mobilizes aggressive energies but binds them to order by rules (see Benjamin 1980, p. 154). The male sense of order is procedural rather than substantive because the male bond is formal (rule governed), rather than personal (based upon intimacy and commitment). Male groups in this sense are shame cultures, not guilt cultures, because the male bond is a group identity that subordinates the individual to the rules, and because social control is imposed through collective judgments about self-control, such as "strength" and "cool." The sense of order within such male groups is based upon the belief that all members are equally dependent upon the rules and that no personal dependence is created within the group. This is not true of the family or of relations with women, both of which are intimate, and, from the guys' point of view, are "out of control" because they are governed by emotion.

The guys face contradictory demands from work culture about the use of aggressive behavior. Aggressive conduct is highly valued in a competitive society when it serves the interests of the organization, but men also face a strong taboo against the expression of anger at work when it is not rule governed. "Competition" imposes certain rules upon aggressive group processes: Aggression must be calculated, not angry; it must be consistent with the power hierarchy of the organization, serving authority and not challenging it; if expressed, it must be indirect, as in jokes; it must serve the needs of group solidarity, not of individual autonomy. Masculine culture separates anger from aggression when it combines the value "strength" with the value "being cool." While masculine cultures often define the expression of anger as "violent" or "loss of control," anger, properly defined, is speech, not action; angry speech is the way we can defend our sense of integrity and assert our sense of justice. Thus it is anger that challenges the authority of the rules, not aggressive behavior in itself, because anger defends the self, not the organization.

The guys' joking relationship taught them a pedagogy for the controlled use of aggression in the work world, to be able to compete aggressively without feeling angry. The guys recognized the relationship between their male bond and the work world by claiming that "high officials of the university know about the way we act and they understand what we are doing." While this might be taken as evidence that the guys were internalizing their fathers' norms and thus inheriting the mantle of patriarchy, the guys described their fathers as slaves to work and women, not as patriarchs. The guys also asserted themselves against the authority of their fathers by acting out against the authority of rules in the performance of "strength."

The guys clearly benefited from the male authority that gave them the power to impose the penis-envy joke upon the women with essentially no consequences. Men are allowed to direct anger and aggression toward women because social norms governing the expression of anger or humor generally replicate the power order of the group. It is striking, however, that the guys would not accept the notion that men have more power than women do; to them it is not men who rule, but rules that govern men. These men had so internalized the governing of male emotions by rules that their anger itself could emerge only indirectly through rule-governed forms, such as jokes and joking relationships. In these forms their anger could serve only order, not their sense of self or justice.

References

Bateson, G. (1972). A theory of play and fantasy. In *Steps toward an ecology of mind* (pp. 177–193). New York: Ballantine.

Benjamin, J. (1978). Authority and the family revisited, or, A world without fathers. *New German Critique, 4*(3), 13, 35–57.

Benjamin, J. (1980). The bonds of love: Rational violence and erotic domination. *Feminist Studies, 6*(1), 144–174.

Berndardez, T. (1978). Women and anger. *Journal of the American Medical Women's Association, 33*(5), 215–219.

Bly, R. (1982). What men really want: An interview with Keith Thompson. *New Age,* pp. 30–37, 50–51.

Chodorow, N. (1976). Oedipal asymmetries, heterosexual knots. *Social Problems, 23,* 454–468.

Chodorow, N. (1978). *The reproduction of mothering.* Berkeley: University of California Press.

Coser, R. (1959). Some social functions of laughter: A study of humor in a hospital setting. *Human Relations, 12,* 171–182.

Emerson, J. (1969). Negotiating the serious import of humor. *Sociometry, 32,* 169–181.

Emerson, J. (1970). Behavior in private places. In H. P. Dreitzel (Ed.), *Recent sociology: Vol. 2. Patterns in communicative behavior.* New York: Macmillan.

Freud, S. (1960). *Jokes and their relation to the unconscious.* New York: Norton.

Gilligan, C. (1982). *In a different voice.* Cambridge, MA: Harvard University Press.

Gray, G. J. (1959). *The warriors: Reflections on men in battle.* New York: Harper & Row.

Lerner, H. E. (1980). Internal prohibitions against female anger. *American Journal of Psychoanalysis, 40,* 137–148.

Miller, J. B. (1976). *Toward a new psychology of women.* Boston: Beacon.

Peters, E. L. (1972). Aspects of the control of moral ambiguities. In M. Gluckman (Ed.), *The allocation of responsibility* (pp. 109–162). Manchester: Manchester University Press.

Radcliffe-Brown, A. (1959). *Structure and function in primitive society.* Glencoe, IL: Free Press.

Rubin, L. (1983). *Intimate strangers.* New York: Harper & Row.

Slater, P. (1963). On social regression. *American Sociological Review, 28,* 339–364.

Thorne, B., & Luria, Z. (1986). Sexuality and gender in children's daily worlds. *Social Problems, 33*(3), 176–190.

Weber, M. (1958). Religions of the world and their directions. In H. Gerth & C. W. Mills (Eds.), *From Max Weber.* New York: Oxford University Press.

A. Ayres Boswell
Joan Z. Spade

Fraternities and Collegiate Rape Culture: Why Are Some Fraternities More Dangerous Places for Women?

Date rape and acquaintance rape on college campuses are topics of concern to both researchers and college administrators. Some estimate that 60 to 80 percent of rapes are date or acquaintance rape (Koss, Dinero, Seibel, and Cox 1988). Further, 1 out of 4 college women say they were raped or experienced an attempted rape, and 1 out of 12 college men say they forced a woman to have sexual intercourse against her will (Koss, Gidycz, and Wisniewski 1985).

Although considerable attention focuses on the incidence of rape, we know relatively little about the context or the *rape culture* surrounding date and acquaintance rape. Rape culture is a set of values and beliefs that provides an environment conducive to rape (Herman 1984; Buchwald, Fletcher, & Roth 1993). The term applies to a generic culture surrounding and promoting rape, not the specific settings in which rape is likely to occur. We believe that the specific settings also are important in defining relationships between men and women.

Some have argued that fraternities are places where rape is likely to occur on college campuses (Martin and Hummer 1989; Sanday 1990; O'Sullivan 1993) and that the students most likely to accept rape myths and be more sexually aggressive

are more likely to live in fraternities and sororities, consume higher doses of alcohol and drugs, and place a higher value on social life at college (Gwartney-Gibbs and Stockard 1989; Kalof and Cargill 1991). Others suggest that sexual aggression is learned in settings such as fraternities and is not part of predispositions or preexisting attitudes (Boeringer, Shehan, and Akers 1991). To prevent further incidences of rape on college campuses, we need to understand what it is about fraternities in particular and college life in general that may contribute to the maintenance of a rape culture on college campuses.

Our approach is to identify the social contexts that link fraternities to campus rape and promote a rape culture. Instead of assuming that all fraternities provide an environment conducive to rape, we compare the interactions of men and women at fraternities identified on campus as being especially *dangerous* places for women, where the likelihood of rape is high, to those seen as *safer* places, where the perceived probability of rape occurring is lower. Prior to collecting data for our study, we found that most women students identified some fraternities as having more sexually aggressive members and a higher probability of rape. These women also considered other fraternities as relatively safe houses, where a women could go and get drunk if she wanted to and feel secure that the fraternity men would not take advantage of her. We compared parties at houses identified as high-risk and low-risk houses as well as at two local bars

From *Gender & Society* 10(2): 133–147. Copyright © 1996 A. Ayres Boswell and Joan Z. Spade. Reprinted by permission of Sage Publications, Inc.

frequented by college students. Our analysis provides an opportunity to examine situations and contexts that hinder or facilitate positive social relations between undergraduate men and women.

The abusive attitudes toward women that some fraternities perpetuate exist within a general culture where rape is intertwined in traditional gender scripts. Men are viewed as initiators of sex and women as either passive partners or active resisters, preventing men from touching their bodies (LaPlante, McCormick, and Brannigan 1980). Rape culture is based on the assumptions that men are aggressive and dominant whereas women are passive and acquiescent (Herman 1984; Buchwald, Fletcher, & Roth 1993). What occurs on college campuses is an extension of the portrayal of domination and aggression of men over women that exemplifies the double standard of sexual behavior in U.S. society (Barthel 1988; Kimmel 1993).

Sexually active men are positively reinforced by being referred to as "studs," whereas women who are sexually active or report enjoying sex are derogatorily labeled as "sluts" (Herman 1984; O'Sullivan 1993). These gender scripts are embodied in rape myths and stereotypes such as "She really wanted it; she just said no because she didn't want me to think she was a bad girl" (Malamuth 1986; Jenkins and Dambrot 1987; Muehlenhard and Linton 1987; Peterson and Franzese 1987; Lisak and Roth 1988; Burke, Stets, and Pirog-Good 1989). Because men's sexuality is seen as more natural, acceptable, and uncontrollable than women's sexuality, many men and women excuse acquaintance rape by affirming that men cannot control their natural urges (Miller and Marshall 1987).

Whereas some researchers explain these attitudes toward sexuality and rape using an individual or a psychological interpretation, we argue that rape has a social basis, one in which both men and women create and recreate masculine and feminine identities and relations. Based on the assumption that rape is part of the social construction of gender, we examine how men and women "do gender" on a college campus (West and Zimmerman 1987). We focus on fraternities because they have been identified as settings that encourage rape (Sanday 1990). By comparing fraternities that are viewed by women as places where there is a high risk of rape to those where women believe there is a low risk of rape as well as two local commercial bars, we seek to identify characteristics that make some social settings more likely places for the occurrence of rape.

Method

We observed social interactions between men and women at a private coeducational school in which a high percentage (49.4 percent) of students affiliate with Greek organizations. The university has an undergraduate population of approximately 4,500 students, just more than one third of whom are women; the students are primarily from upper-middle-class families. The school, which admitted only men until 1971, is highly competitive academically.

We used a variety of data collection approaches: observations of interactions between men and women at fraternity parties and bars, formal interviews, and informal conversations. The first author, a former undergraduate at this school and a graduate student at the time of the study, collected the data. She knew about the social life at the school and had established rapport and trust between herself and undergraduate students as a teaching assistant in a human sexuality course.

The process of identifying high- and low-risk fraternity houses followed Hunter's (1953) reputational approach. In our study, 40 women students identified fraternities that they considered to be high risk, or to have more sexually aggressive members and higher incidence of rape, as well as fraternities that they considered to be safe houses. The women represented all four years of undergraduate college and different living groups (sororities, residence halls, and off-campus housing). Observations focused on the four fraternities named most often by these women as high-risk houses and the four identified as low-risk houses.

Throughout the spring semester, the first author observed at two fraternity parties each weekend at two different houses (fraternities could have parties only on weekends at this campus). She also observed students' interactions in two popular university bars on weeknights to provide a comparison of students' behavior in non-Greek settings. The first local bar at which she observed was popular with seniors and older students; the second bar was popular with first-, second-, and third-year undergraduates because the management did not strictly enforce drinking age laws in this bar.

The observer focused on the social context as well as interaction among participants at each setting. In terms of social context, she observed the following: ratio of men to women, physical setting such as the party decor and theme, use and control of alcohol and level of intoxication, and explicit and implicit norms. She noted interactions between men and women (i.e., physical contact, conversational style, use of jokes) and the relations among men (i.e., their treatment of pledges and other men at fraternity parties). Other than the observer, no one knew the identity of the high- or low-risk fraternities. Although this may have introduced bias into the data collection, students on this campus who read this article before it was submitted for publication commented on how accurately the social scene is described.

In addition, 50 individuals were interviewed including men from the selected fraternities, women who attended those parties, men not affiliated with fraternities, and self-identified rape victims known to the first author. The first author approached men and women by telephone or on campus and asked them to participate in interviews. The interviews included open-ended questions about gender relations on campus, attitudes about date rape, and their own experiences on campus.

To assess whether self-selection was a factor in determining the classification of the fraternity, we compared high-risk houses to low-risk houses on several characteristics. In terms of status on campus, the high- and low-risk houses we studied attracted about the same number of pledges; however, many of the high-risk houses had more members. There was no difference in grade point averages for the two types of houses. In fact, the highest and lowest grade point averages were found in the high-risk category. Although both high- and low-risk fraternities participated in sports, brothers in the low-risk houses tended to play intramural sports whereas brothers in the high-risk houses were more likely to be varsity athletes. The high-risk houses may be more aggressive, as they had a slightly larger number of disciplinary incidents and their reports were more severe, often with physical harm to others and damage to property. Further, in year-end reports, there was more property damage in the high-risk houses. Last, more of the low-risk houses participated in a campus rape-prevention program. In summary, both high- and low-risk fraternities seem to be equally attractive to freshmen men on this campus, and differences between the eight fraternities we studied were not great; however, the high-risk houses had a slightly larger number of reports of aggression and physical destruction in the houses and the low-risk houses were more likely to participate in a rape prevention program.

Results

The Settings

Fraternity Parties We observed several differences in the quality of the interaction of men and women at parties at high-risk fraternities compared to those at low-risk houses. A typical party at a low-risk house included an equal number of women and men. The social atmosphere was friendly, with considerable interaction between women and men. Men and women danced in groups and in couples, with many of the couples kissing and displaying affection toward each other. Brothers explained that, because many of the men in these houses had girlfriends, it was normal to see couples kissing on the dance floor. Coed groups engaged in conversations at many of these houses, with women and men engaging in friendly exchanges, giving the impression that they knew each other well. Almost no cursing and yelling was observed at parties in low-risk houses; when pushing occurred, the participants apologized. Respect for women extended to the women's bathrooms, which were clean and well supplied.

At high-risk houses, parties typically had skewed gender ratios, sometimes involving more men and other times involving more women. Gender segregation also was evident at these parties, with the men on one side of a room or in the bar drinking while women gathered in another area. Men treated women differently in the high-risk houses. The women's bathrooms in the high-risk houses were filthy, including clogged toilets and vomit in the sinks. When a brother was told of the mess in the bathroom at a high-risk house, he replied, "Good, maybe some of these beer wenches will leave so there will be more beer for us."

Men attending parties at high-risk houses treated women less respectfully, engaging in jokes, conversations, and behaviors that degraded women. Men made a display of assessing women's bodies and rated them with thumbs up or thumbs down for the other men in the sight of the women. One man attending a party at a high-risk fraternity said to another, "Did you know that this week is Women's Awareness Week? I guess that means we get to abuse them more this week." Men behaved more crudely at parties at high-risk houses. At one party, a brother dropped his pants, including his underwear, while dancing in front of several women. Another brother slid across the dance floor completely naked.

The atmosphere at parties in high-risk fraternities was less friendly overall. With the exception of greetings, men and women rarely smiled or laughed and spoke to each other less often than was the case at parties in low-risk houses. The few one-on-one conversations between women and men appeared to be strictly flirtatious (lots of eye contact, touching, and very close talking). It was rare to see a group of men and women together talking. Men were openly hostile, which

made the high-risk parties seem almost threatening at times. For example, there was a lot of touching, pushing, profanity, and name calling, some done by women.

Students at parties at the high-risk houses seemed self-conscious and aware of the presence of members of the opposite sex, an awareness that was sexually charged. Dancing early in the evening was usually between women. Close to midnight, the sex ratio began to balance out with the arrival of more men or more women. Couples began to dance together but in a sexual way (close dancing with lots of pelvic thrusts). Men tried to pick up women using lines such as "Want to see my fish tank?" and "Let's go upstairs so that we can talk; I can't hear what you're saying in here."

Although many of the same people who attended high-risk parties also attended low-risk parties, their behavior changed as they moved from setting to setting. Group norms differed across contexts as well. At a party that was held jointly at a low-risk house with a high-risk fraternity, the ambience was that of a party at a high-risk fraternity with heavier drinking, less dancing, and fewer conversations between women and men. The men from both high- and low-risk fraternities were very aggressive; a fight broke out, and there was pushing and shoving on the dance floor and in general.

As others have found, fraternity brothers at high-risk houses on this campus told about routinely discussing their sexual exploits at breakfast the morning after parties and sometimes at house meetings (cf. Martin and Hummer 1989; Sanday 1990; O'Sullivan 1993). During these sessions, the brothers we interviewed said that men bragged about what they did the night before with stories of sexual conquests often told by the same men, usually sophomores. The women involved in these exploits were women they did not know or knew but did not respect, or *faceless victims*. Men usually treated girlfriends with respect and did not talk about them in these storytelling sessions. Men from low-risk houses, however, did not describe similar sessions in their houses.

The Bar Scene   The bar atmosphere and social context differed from those of fraternity parties. The music was not as loud, and both bars had places to sit and have conversations. At all fraternity parties, it was difficult to maintain conversations with loud music playing and no place to sit. The volume of music at parties at high-risk fraternities was even louder than it was at low-risk houses, making it virtually impossible to have conversations. In general, students in the local bars behaved in the same way that students did at parties in low-risk houses with conversations typical, most occurring between men and women.

The first bar, frequented by older students, had live entertainment every night of the week. Some nights were more crowded than others, and the atmosphere was friendly, relaxed, and conducive to conversation. People laughed and smiled and behaved politely toward each other. The ratio of men to women was fairly equal, with students congregating in mostly coed groups. Conversation flowed freely and people listened to each other.

Although the women and men at the first bar also were at parties at low- and high-risk fraternities, their behavior at the bar included none of the blatant sexual or intoxicated behaviors observed at some of these parties. As the evenings wore on, the number of one-on-one conversations between men and women increased and conversations shifted from small talk to topics such as war and AIDS. Conversations did not revolve around picking up another person, and most people left the bar with same-sex friends or in coed groups.

The second bar was less popular with older students. Younger students, often under the legal drinking age, went there to drink, sometimes after leaving campus parties. This bar was much smaller and usually not as crowded as the first bar. The atmosphere was more mellow and relaxed than it was at the fraternity parties. People went there to hang out and talk to each other.

On a couple of occasions, however, the atmosphere at the second bar became similar to that of a party at a high-risk fraternity. As the number of people in the bar increased, they removed chairs and tables, leaving no place to sit and talk. The music also was turned up louder, drowning out conversation. With no place to dance or sit, most people stood around but could not maintain conversations because of the noise and crowds. Interactions between women and men consisted mostly of flirting. Alcohol consumption also was greater than it was on the less crowded nights, and the number of visibly drunk people increased. The more people drank, the more conversation and socializing broke down. The only differences between this setting and that of a party at a high-risk house were that brothers no longer controlled the territory and bedrooms were not available upstairs.

Gender Relations

Relations between women and men are shaped by the contexts in which they meet and interact. As is the case on other college campuses, *hooking up* has replaced dating on this campus, and fraternities are places where many students hook up. Hooking up is a loosely applied term on college campuses that had different meanings for men and women on this campus.

Most men defined hooking up similarly. One man said it was something that happens

> when you are really drunk and meet up with a woman you sort of know, or possibly don't know at all and don't care about. You go home with her with the intention of getting as much sexual, physical pleasure as she'll give you, which can range anywhere from kissing to intercourse, without any strings attached.

The exception to this rule is when men hook up with women they admire. Men said they are less likely to press for sexual activity with someone they know and like because they want the relationship to continue and be based on respect.

Women's version of hooking up differed. Women said they hook up only with men they cared about and described hooking up as kissing and petting but not sexual intercourse. Many women said that hooking up was disappointing because they wanted longer-term relationships. First-year women students realized quickly that hook-ups were usually one-night stands with no strings attached, but many continued to hook up because they had few opportunities to develop relationships with men on campus. One first-year woman said that "70 percent of hook-ups never talk again and try to avoid one another; 26 percent may actually hear from them or talk to them again, and 4 percent may actually go on a date, which can lead to a relationship." Another first-year woman said, "It was fun in the beginning. You get a lot of attention and kiss a lot of boys and think this is what college is about, but it gets tiresome fast."

Whereas first-year women get tired of the hook-up scene early on, many men do not become bored with it until their junior or senior year. As one upperclassman said, "The whole game of hooking up became really meaningless and tiresome for me during my second semester of my sophomore year, but most of my friends didn't get bored with it until the following year."

In contrast to hooking up, students also described monogamous relationships with steady partners. Some type of commitment was expected, but most people did not anticipate marriage. The term *seeing each other* was applied when people were sexually involved but free to date other people. This type of relationship involved less commitment than did one of boyfriend/girlfriend but was not considered to be a hook-up.

The general consensus of women and men interviewed on this campus was that the Greek system, called "the hill," set the scene for gender relations. The predominance of Greek membership and subsequent living arrangements segregated men and women. During the week, little interaction occurred between women and men after their first year in college because students in fraternities or sororities live and dine in separate quarters. In addition, many non-Greek upper-class students move off campus into apartments. Therefore, students see each other in classes or in the library, but there is no place where students can just hang out together.

Both men and women said that fraternities dominate campus social life, a situation that everyone felt limited opportunities for meaningful interactions. One senior Greek man said:

> This environment is horrible and so unhealthy for good male and female relationships and interactions to occur. It is so segregated and male dominated. . . . It is our party, with our rules and our beer. We are allowing these women and other men to come to our party. Men can feel superior in their domain.

Comments from a senior woman reinforced his views: "Men are dominant; they are the kings of the campus. It is their environment that they allow us to enter; therefore, we have to abide by their rules." A junior woman described fraternity parties as:

> good for meeting acquaintances but almost impossible to really get to know anyone. The environment is so superficial, probably because there are so many social cliques due to the Greek system. Also, the music is too loud and the people are too drunk to attempt to have a real conversation, anyway.

Some students claim that fraternities even control the dating relationships of their members. One senior woman said, "Guys dictate how dating occurs on this campus, whether it's cool, who it's with, how much time can be spent with the girlfriend and with the brothers." Couples either left campus for an evening or hung out separately with their own same-gender friends at fraternity parties, finally getting together with each other at about 2 A.M. Couples rarely went together to fraternity parties. Some men felt that a girlfriend was just a replacement for a hook-up. According to one junior man, "Basically a girlfriend is someone you go to at 2 A.M. after you've hung out with the guys. She is the sexual outlet that the guys can't provide you with."

Some fraternity brothers pressure each other to limit their time with and commitment to their

U - V G

5. 00

Clean —
Inscription on
Facing Page

er-
de-
and
for
ing.
arks
and
said
ends;
n said
ew he
on this
in my
ave too

commit-
ment to girlfriends, ... ue of all
fraternities or of all men on campus. Couples attended low-risk fraternity parties together, and men in the low-risk houses went out on dates more often. A man in one low-risk house said that about 70 percent of the members of his house were involved in relationships with women, including the pledges (who were sophomores).

Treatment of Women

Not all men held negative attitudes toward women that are typical of a rape culture, and not all social contexts promoted the negative treatment of women. When men were asked whether they treated the women on campus with respect, the most common response was "On an individual basis, yes, but when you have a group of men together, no." Men said that, when together in groups with other men, they sensed a pressure to be disrespectful toward women. A first-year man's perception of the treatment of women was that "they are treated with more respect to their faces, but behind closed doors, with a group of men present, respect for women is not an issue." One senior man stated, "In general, college-aged men don't treat women their age with respect because 90 percent of them think of women as merely a means to sex." Women reinforced this perception. A first-year women stated, "Men here are more

interested in hooking up and drinking beer than they are in getting to know women as real people." Another woman said, "Men here use and abuse women."

Characteristic of rape culture, a double standard of sexual behavior for men versus women was prevalent on this campus. As one Greek senior man stated, "Women who sleep around are sluts and get bad reputations; men who do are champions and get a pat on the back from their brothers." Women also supported a double standard for sexual behavior by criticizing sexually active women. A first-year woman spoke out against women who are sexually active: "I think some girls here make it difficult for the men to respect women as a whole."

One concrete example of demeaning sexually active women on this campus is the "walk of shame." Fraternity brothers come out on the porches of their houses the night after parties and heckle women walking by. It is assumed that these women spent the night at fraternity houses and that the men they were with did not care enough about them to drive them home. Although sororities now reside in former fraternity houses, this practice continues and sometimes the victims of hecklings are sorority women on their way to study in the library.

A junior man in a high-risk fraternity described another ritual of disrespect toward women called "chatter." When an unknown woman sleeps over at the house, the brothers yell degrading remarks out the window at her as she leaves the next morning such as "Fuck that bitch" and "Who is that slut?" He said that sometimes brothers harass the brothers whose girlfriends stay over instead of heckling those women.

Fraternity men most often mistreated women they did not know personally. Men and women alike reported incidents in which brothers observed other brothers having sex with unknown women or women they knew only casually. A sophomore woman's experience exemplifies this anonymous state: "I don't mind if 10 guys were watching or it was videotaped. That's expected on this campus. It's the fact that he didn't apologize or even offer to drive me home that really upset me." Descriptions of sexual encounters involved the satisfaction of men by nameless women. A brother in a high-risk fraternity described a similar occurrence:

> A brother of mine was hooking up upstairs with an unattractive woman who had been pursuing him all night. He told some brothers to go outside the window and watch. Well, one thing led to another and they were almost completely naked when the woman noticed the brothers outside. She was then unwilling to go any further, so the brother went outside and yelled at the other brothers and then closed the shades. I don't know if he scored or not, because the woman was pretty upset. But he did win the award for hooking up with the ugliest chick that weekend.

Attitudes toward Rape

The sexually charged environment of college campuses raises many questions about cultures that facilitate the rape of women. How women and men define their sexual behavior is important legally as well as interpersonally. We asked students how they defined rape and had them compare it to the following legal definition: the perpetration of an act of sexual intercourse with a female against her will and consent, whether her will is overcome by force or fear resulting from the threat of force, or by drugs or intoxicants; or when, because of mental deficiency, she is incapable of exercising rational judgment. (Brownmiller 1975, 368)

When presented with this legal definition, most women interviewed recognized it as well as the complexities involved in applying it. A first-year woman said, "If a girl is drunk and the guy knows it and the girl says, 'Yes, I want to have sex,' and they do, that is still rape because the girl can't make a conscious, rational decision under the influence of alcohol." Some women disagreed. Another first-year woman stated, "I don't think it is fair that the guy gets blamed when both people involved are drunk."

The typical definition men gave for rape was "when a guy jumps out of the bushes and forces himself sexually onto a girl." When asked what date rape was, the most common answer was "when one person has sex with another person who did not consent." Many men said, however, that "date rape is when a woman wakes up the next morning and regrets having sex." Some men said that date rape was too gray an area to define. "Consent is a fine line," said a Greek senior man student. For the most part, the men we spoke with argued that rape did not occur on this campus. One Greek sophomore man said, "I think it is ridiculous that someone here would rape someone." A first-year man stated, "I have a problem with the word rape. It sounds so criminal, and we are not criminals; we are sane people."

Whether aware of the legal definitions of rape, most men resisted the idea that a woman who is intoxicated is unable to consent to sex. A Greek junior man said, "Men should not be responsible for women's drunkenness." One first-year man said, "If that is the legal definition of rape, then it happens all the time on this campus." A senior man said, "I don't care whether alcohol is involved or not; that is not rape. Rapists are people that have something seriously wrong with them." A first-year man even claimed that when women get drunk, they invite sex. He said, "Girls get so drunk here and then come to us. What are we supposed to do? We are only human."

Discussion and Conclusion

These findings describe the physical and normative aspects of one college campus as they relate to attitudes about and relations between men and women. Our findings suggest that an explanation emphasizing rape culture also must focus on those characteristics of the social setting that play a role in defining heterosexual relationships on college campuses (Kalof and Cargill 1991). The degradation of women as portrayed in rape culture was not found in all fraternities on this campus. Both group norms and individual behavior changed as students went from one place to another. Although individual men are the ones who rape, we found that some settings are more likely places for rape than are others. Our findings suggest that rape cannot be seen only as an isolated act and blamed on individual behavior and proclivities, whether it be alcohol consumption or attitudes. We also must consider characteristics of the settings that promote the behaviors that reinforce a rape culture.

Relations between women and men at parties in low-risk fraternities varied considerably from those in high-risk houses. Peer pressure and situational norms influenced women as well as men. Although many men in high- and low-risk houses shared similar views and attitudes about the Greek system, women on this campus, and date rape, their behaviors at fraternity parties were quite different.

Women who are at highest risk of rape are women whom fraternity brothers did not know. These women are faceless victims, nameless acquaintances—not friends. Men said their responsibility to such persons and the level of guilt they feel later if the hook-ups end in sexual intercourse are much lower if they hook up with women they do not know. In high-risk houses, brothers treated women as subordinates and kept them at a distance. Men in high-risk houses actively discouraged ongoing heterosexual relationships, routinely degraded women, and participated more fully in the hook-up scene; thus, the probability that women would become faceless victims was higher in these houses. The flirtatious nature of the parties indicated that women go to these parties looking for available men, but finding boyfriends or relationships was difficult at parties in high-risk houses. However, in the low-risk houses, where more men had long-term relationships, the women were not strangers and were less likely to become faceless victims.

The social scene on this campus, and on most others, offers women and men few other options to socialize. Although there may be no such thing as a completely safe fraternity party for women, parties at low-risk houses and commercial bars encouraged men and women to get to know each

other better and decreased the probability that women would become faceless victims. Although both men and women found the social scene on this campus demeaning, neither demanded different settings for socializing, and attendance at fraternity parties is a common form of entertainment.

These findings suggest that a more conducive environment for conversation can promote more positive interactions between men and women. Simple changes would provide the opportunity for men and women to interact in meaningful ways such as adding places to sit and lowering the volume of music at fraternity parties or having parties in neutral locations, where men are not in control. The typical party room in fraternity houses includes a place to dance but not to sit and talk. The music often is loud, making it difficult, if not impossible, to carry on conversations; however, there were more conversations at the low-risk parties, where there also was more respect shown toward women. Although the number of brothers who had steady girlfriends in the low-risk houses as compared to those in the high-risk houses may explain the differences, we found that commercial bars also provided a context for interaction between men and women. At the bars, students sat and talked and conversations between men and women flowed freely, resulting in deep discussions and fewer hook-ups.

Alcohol consumption was a major focus of social events here and intensified attitudes and orientations of a rape culture. Although pressure to drink was evident at all fraternity parties and at both bars, drinking dominated high-risk fraternity parties, at which nonalcoholic beverages usually were not available and people chugged beers and became visibly drunk. A rape culture is strengthened by rules that permit alcohol only at fraternity parties. Under this system, men control the parties and dominate the men as well as the women who attend. As college administrators crack down on fraternities and alcohol on campus, however, the same behaviors and norms may transfer to other places such as parties in apartments or private homes where administrators have much less control. At commercial bars, interaction and socialization with others were as important as drinking, with the exception of the nights when the bar frequented by under-class students became crowded. Although one solution is to offer nonalcoholic social activities, such events receive little support on this campus. Either these alternative events lacked the prestige of the fraternity parties or the alcohol was seen as necessary to unwind, or both.

In many ways, the fraternities on this campus determined the settings in which men and women interacted. As others before us have found, pressures for conformity to the norms and values exist at both high-risk and low-risk houses (Martin and Hummer 1989; Sanday 1990; Kalof and Cargill 1991). The desire to be accepted is not unique to this campus or the Greek system (Horowitz 1988; Moffat 1989; Holland and Eisenhart 1990). The degree of conformity required by Greeks may be greater than that required in most social groups, with considerable pressure to adopt and maintain the image of their houses. The fraternity system intensifies the "groupthink syndrome" (Janis 1972) by solidifying the identity of the in-group and creating an us/them atmosphere. Within the fraternity culture, brothers are highly regarded and women are viewed as outsiders. For men in high-risk fraternities, women threatened their brotherhood; therefore, brothers discouraged relationships and harassed those who treated women as equals or with respect. The pressure to be one of the guys and hang out with the guys strengthens a rape culture on college campus by demeaning women and encouraging the segregation of men and women.

Students on this campus were aware of the contexts in which they operated and the choices available to them. They recognized that, in their interactions, they created differences between men and women that are not natural, essential, or biological (West and Zimmerman 1987). Not all men and women accepted the demeaning treatment of women, but they continued to participate in behaviors that supported aspects of a rape culture. Many women participated in the hook-up scene even after they had been humiliated and hurt

because they had few other means of initiating contact with men on campus. Men and women alike played out this scene, recognizing its injustices in many cases but being unable to change the course of their behaviors.

Although this research provides some clues to gender relations on college campuses, it raises many questions. Why do men and women participate in activities that support a rape culture when they see its injustices? What would happen if alcohol were not controlled by groups of men who admit that they disrespect women when they get together? What can be done to give men and women on college campuses more opportunities to interact responsibly and get to know each other better? These questions should be studied on other campuses with a focus on the social settings in which the incidence of rape and the attitudes that support a rape culture exist. Fraternities are social contexts that may or may not foster a rape culture.

Our findings indicate that a rape culture exists in some fraternities, especially those we identified as high-risk houses. College administrators are responding to this situation by providing counseling and educational programs that increase awareness of date rape including campaigns such as "No means no." These strategies are important in changing attitudes, values, and behaviors; however, changing individuals is not enough. The structure of campus life and the impact of that structure on gender relations on campus are highly determinative. To eliminate campus rape culture, student leaders and administrators must examine the situations in which women and men meet and restructure these settings to provide opportunities for respectful interaction. Change may not require abolishing fraternities; rather, it may require promoting settings that facilitate positive gender relations.

Author's Note: An earlier version of this article was presented at the annual meeting of the American Sociological Association, August 1993. Special thanks go to Barbara Frankel, Karen Hicks, and Jennifer Vochko for their input into the process and final version and to Judith Gerson, Sue Curry Jansen, Judith Lasker, Patricia Yancey

Martin, and Ronnie Steinberg for their careful readings of the draft of this article and for many helpful comments.

References

Barthel, D. 1988. *Putting on appearances: Gender and advertising*. Philadelphia: Temple University Press.

Boeringer, S. B., C. L. Shehan, and R. L. Akers, 1991. Social contexts and social learning in sexual coercion and aggression: Assessing the contribution of fraternity membership. *Family Relations* 40:58–64.

Brownmiller, S. 1975. *Against our will: Men, women and rape*. New York: Simon & Schuster.

Buchwald, E., P. R. Fletcher, and M. Roth, eds. 1993. *Transforming a rape culture*. Minneapolis, MN: Milkweed Editions.

Burke, P., J. E. Stets, and M. A. Pirog-Good. 1989. Gender identity, self-esteem, physical abuse and sexual abuse in dating relationships. In *Violence in dating relationships: Emerging social issues*, edited by M. A. Pirog-Good and J. E. Stets. New York: Praeger.

Gwartney-Gibbs, P., and J. Stockard. 1989. Courtship aggression and mixed-sex peer groups. In *Violence in dating relationships: Emerging social issues*, edited by M. A. Pirog-Good and J. E. Stets. New York: Praeger.

Herman, D. 1984. The rape culture. In *Women: A feminist perspective*, edited by J. Freeman. Mountain View, CA: Mayfield.

Holland, D. C., and M. A. Eisenhart. 1990. *Educated in romance: Women, achievement, and college culture*. Chicago: University of Chicago Press.

Horowitz, H. L. 1988. *Campus life: Undergraduate cultures from the end of the 18th century to the present*. Chicago: University of Chicago Press.

Hunter, F. 1953. *Community power structure*. Chapel Hill: University of North Carolina Press.

Jenkins, M. J., and F. H. Dambrot. 1987. The attribution of date rape: Observer's attitudes and sexual experiences and the dating situation. *Journal of Applied Social Psychology* 17:875–895.

Janis, I. L. 1972. *Victims of groupthink*. Boston: Houghton Mifflin.

Kalof, L., and T. Cargill. 1991. Fraternity and sorority membership and gender dominance attitudes. *Sex Roles* 25:417–423.

Kimmel, M. S. 1993. Clarence, William, Iron Mike, Tailhook, Senator Packwood, Spur Posse, Magic . . . and us. In *Transforming a rape culture*, edited by E. Buchwald, P. R. Fletcher, and M. Roth. Minneapolis, MN: Milkweed Editions.

Koss, M. P., T. E. Dinero, C. A. Seibel, and S. L. Cox. 1988. Stranger and acquaintance rape: Are there differences in the victim's experience? *Psychology of Women Quarterly* 12:1–24.

Koss, M. P., C. A. Gidycz, and N. Wisniewski. 1985. The scope of rape: Incidence and prevalence of sexual aggression and victimization in a national sample of higher education students. *Journal of Consulting and Clinical Psychology* 55:162–170.

LaPlante, M. N., N. McCormick, and G. G. Brannigan. 1980. Living the sexual script: College students' views of influence in sexual encounters. *Journal of Sex Research* 16:338–355.

Lisak, D., and S. Roth. 1988. Motivational factors in nonincarcerated sexually aggressive men. *Journal of Personality and Social Psychology* 55:795–802.

Malamuth, N. 1986. Predictors of naturalistic sexual aggression. *Journal of Personality and Social Psychology* 50:953–962.

Martin, P. Y., and R. Hummer. 1989. Fraternities and rape on campus. *Gender & Society* 3:457–473.

Miller, B., and J. C. Marshall. 1987. Coercive sex on the university campus. *Journal of College Student Personnel* 28:38–47.

Moffat, M. 1989. *Coming of age in New Jersey: College life in American culture*. New Brunswick, NJ: Rutgers University Press.

Muehlenhard, C. L., and M. A. Linton. 1987. Date rape and sexual aggression in dating situations: Incidence and risk factors. *Journal of Counseling Psychology* 34:186–196.

O'Sullivan, C. 1993. Fraternities and the rape culture. In *Transforming a rape culture*, edited by E. Buchwald, P. R. Fletcher, and M. Roth. Minneapolis, MN: Milkweed Editions.

Peterson, S. A., and B. Franzese. 1987. Correlates of college men's sexual abuse of women. *Journal of College Student Personnel* 28:223–228.

Sanday, P. R. 1990. *Fraternity gang rape: Sex, brotherhood, and privilege on campus*. New York: New York University Press.

West, C., and D. Zimmerman. 1987. Doing gender. *Gender & Society* 1:125–151.

Michael S. Kimmel

Ritualized Homosexuality in a Nacirema Subculture

Students of anthropology have long been aware of the esoteric customs of the Nacirema, a culture situated in the northern hemisphere in the territory between the Canadian Cree, the Yaqui and Tarahumare of Mexico, and the Carib and the Arawak of the Antilles (see Miner, 1956). According to Horace Miner, the Michigan anthropologist who first discovered them, the Nacirema exhibit a strange and almost perverse preoccupation with the body and its ritual purification, spending enormous amounts of time, and exchanging significant amounts of currencies to purify what they believe is an essentially disgusting and fetid physical form.

We have recently become aware of an even more esoteric subculture among the Nacirema, one more curiously preoccupied with body ritual, and especially with ritualized homosexuality. This subculture, known as the Tarfs, is the subject of this essay.

I.

Ritual homosexual behavior is certainly not unknown to cultural anthropologists. In perhaps the most famous example, Gilbert Herdt (1981) described the sexual rituals of the Sambia, a mountain people who live in Papua New Guinea. The Sambia practice ritualized homosexuality as a way to initiate young boys into full adult manhood. Young boys ritually daily fellate the older boys and men so that they (the younger boys) can re-

Forthcoming in *Sexualities* 9(1) 2006, pp. 117–127. Reprinted with permission of the author.

ceive the vital life fluid (semen) from the older men and thus become men. "A boy must be initiated and [orally] inseminated, otherwise the girl betrothed to him will outgrow him and run away to another man," was the way one Sambia elder put it. "If a boy doesn't eat semen, he remains small and weak."

When they reach puberty, these boys are then fellated by a new crop of younger boys. Throughout this initiation, the boys scrupulously avoid girls, and have no knowledge of heterosexuality until they are married. Neither the boys nor the older men think of themselves as engaging in homosexual behavior. In fact, when Herdt suggested that this behavior made them homosexual, or at least bisexual, they grew angry and diffident. This had nothing whatever to do with homosexuality, they assured Herdt. The older men are married to women, and the younger men fully expect to be. There is no adult homosexuality among the Sambia. But these young boys must become, as Herdt puts it, "reluctant warriors." How else are the boys to receive the vital life force that will enable them to be real men and warriors? (Herdt, 1981:1, 165, 82).

A nearby culture, the Keraki, engage in a related practice. There, the boys are sodomized by older men, because the Keraki believe that without the older men's semen, the boys will not grow to be men. This ritual practice occurs until the boys hit puberty and secondary sex characteristics appear—facial hair, dropped voice—at which point the ritual has accomplished its task. When an anthropologist asked Keraki men if they had been sodomized, many responded by saying

"Why, yes! Otherwise how should I have grown?" Other ritualized homosexual practices have been reported from other cultures (Williams, 1936: 159; see also Schiefflin, 1976; Carrier, 1977; Kelly, 1977).

Interestingly, such ritual practices, as among the Sambia and Keraki, are more evident in cultures in which sex segregation is high and women's status is low. This conforms to other ethnographic evidence that suggests that elaborate rituals of male bonding have the effect of excluding women from ritual life and thus correlate with women's lower status (Davenport, 1977; see also Herdt, ed. 1984: 66).

Herdt's book was greeted with significant academic acclaim and equally significant shock and disbelief among undergraduate students. When this writer has asked students what they think they would do if they were brought up among the Sambia, the male students invariably declare that they would be the first Sambian youth to refuse to ingest the life force. They may end up sterile outcasts, but better that than to be gay.

II.

Among the Nacirema, there is ample evidence of homosexual activity, especially among males, that is neither experienced nor understood to be homosexual in nature. A researcher named Prok, who studied sexual behavior among Nacirema males, found that fully two in five had had at least one homosexual experience to orgasm. In the largest villages, for example, there is often a group of young males, many of whom are married and virtually all of whom consider themselves to be heterosexual, who have sex with other men for money. The "reltsuh" (pronounced *relt-suh*), as he is known, will typically only perform certain acts (anal penetration) or will only allow certain acts (permitting themselves to be fellated, but they will not reciprocate). By remaining the "insertor" in homosexual acts, these males maintain a heterosexual identity, and identify as "men." Men are insertors, whether with women or with men, so as

long as they remain insertors, they believe their masculinity is not compromised.

A casual observer may believe that if two males are engaging in sex, it is, by definition, "gay sex." However, these particular Nacirema males do not see it that way. They believe that the meaning of sexual acts does not inhere in the gender identity of the actor, but rather either in the sexual orientation of the actor or in the acts themselves. Thus, they believe, if two heterosexual males engage in sex, it may be heterosexual sex; conjointly, if one of the males performs as heterosexual males perform—that is, remains the penetrator and scrupulously avoids being penetrated—he is still a male, i.e., heterosexual.[1]

However, these relatively exotic denizens of the Nacirema demimonde are only the tip of the ritualized homosexual iceberg. It turns out that there is a large subculture of Nacirema males who engage in ritualized homosexual activities quite openly. They are the "Tarf" subculture.

The Tarf subculture has developed in villages where the youth of the culture gather for education and entertainment. The youth of the culture who gather in these villages are called "dentstuds" (pronounced *dent-stoods*). While most of the village's youth are dentstuds, not all are Tarfs. Tarfs are a special group of dentstuds.

Dentstuds congregate within these villages in an enclosed area called the "supmac" (prounced *sup-mack*). Supmacs encompass many buildings for ceremonial inductions, Nacirema instruction, and often also have a special type of building called an "mrod" (pronounced *em-rod*). Mrods are long houses where the members of the village, dentstuds, live and socialize. They eat in special dining huts and are often expected to eat inferior food.

Tarfs, however, most often live apart in ceremonial men's huts that abut or are adjacent to the supmac. These men's huts are ritually forbidden to women; indeed, Tarfs celebrate sex segregation as a necessary ingredient in their main activity: exclusionary bonding. It is the defining feature of the Tarf subculture that they develop hyperextended kinship networks, appropriating kinship terms like "brother" to denote the specialness of their relationship. However, as we shall see, this further complicates the ritualized homosexuality among the Tarf subculture, lending also an element of incest to its mix.

Tarf huts are residential huts, in which the Tarfs live, eat and socialize. Tarfs are apparently exempt from most of the formal educational activities that occupy the time of the majority of dentstuds in the village, for they spend virtually no time in formal training, and most would have a hard time finding the "yrarbil" (pronounced *y-ar-bill*), which is where the sacred texts of the village are housed. Ceremonial activities occupy most of the Tarfs' time.

Some of these ceremonies include bacchanalian festivals, at which there is a significant amount of ingestion of alcoholic libations and copious feigned heterosexual contact. Their substance abuse rivals that of the Yanomamo and Jibaro. During their festivals, Tarfs frequently become intoxicated and then attempt to perform heterosexual activities. They call these attempts at heterosexual coupling "pukooh" (pronounced *pook-oo*). Obviously, heterosexual activity is so distasteful to the Tarfs that they need to be sufficiently drunk in order to accomplish it.

When a Tarf is successful in a pukooh, he immediately tells the other Tarfs, and they then credit him with successful heterosexual accomplishment. Tallies may be kept of these pukoohs, and the names and physical descriptions of the heterosexual women with whom the Tarfs have "pukooh-ed" are written down in a sacred book, to be consulted only by other members of the Tarf subculture.

However, it is clear that the purpose of the pukooh is not the sexual satisfaction that might accompany sexual relations among typical heterosexuals in Nacirema culture, or, indeed, among non-Tarfs in the same supmac. It is clear that the main purpose of these feigned heterosexual events is to win the praise of the other Tarfs. Even in Tarf heterosexual behavior, there is a strong undercurrent of homosocial validation.

Tarfs live for the validation of other Tarfs. They are willing to undergo extreme punishment and degradation in order to do so. Tarfs begin their career not as full-fledged Tarfs, but they must undergo an arduous initiation period, during which time they are probationary Tarfs. When a Tarf is in this probationary stage, he is called a "Jelp."

Like many cultures, Tarfs have developed elaborate rituals of initiation (see, for example, Gilmore, 1990). These initiation rituals demand that the young novice prove his worth to enter the society as a full-fledged member, often after undergoing some severe test or hardship. For example, in some East African cultures, the 12-year-old boys live alone and isolated for four years. When they return, they are circumcised without anesthesia by a stone knife. They must not flinch. Mende boys, a West African culture, are scarified by a "monster" (an elder in disguise). Pueblo Indian (Hopi, Zuni) kachinas whip the boys with yucca whips until they bleed (kachinas are animal-human hybrids, also elders in disguise). Others use nasal incision to stimulate bleeding. But as several of these examples illustrate, these rituals are supervised and conducted by elders who prepare the initiation ritual, preside over the events and confer *their* validation of masculinity on the successful initiates.

Tarf subcultural norms are slightly different. For one thing, the "elders" who supervise the ritual initiations are elders only in a symbolic sense; they are usually no more than two or three years older than the Jelps. Tarf initiation rituals are, in fact, organized to take place away from any and all adult supervision by the elders who administer the life of the supmac. In this way, the administrators can maintain a façade of "plausible deniability" in case any legal challenges are made to the homosexual excesses of the Tarf rituals. Administrators routinely feign surprise and shock when the structure and content of Tarf rituals are disclosed.

For this reason, Tarf rituals are shrouded in the deepest of secrecy. Tarfs and also the Jelps swear oaths to maintain the strictest of secrecy about their activities, perhaps because there is some shame about their overtly homosexual content. (Nacirema society is among the least permissive of the advanced cultures we have studied when it comes to homosexual behavior.)

It is during his apprenticeship as a Jelp that the true homosexual nature of Tarf life is revealed. To prove himself worthy to be a Tarf, he must engage in a variety of homosexual practices with the other Jelps. Although, as we have noted, these are often veiled in secrecy, we have been able to describe several of them here. These are by no means universal among all Tarfs, nor does every Tarf hut require these. However, they are well known among most Tarfs, either in practice or as a reference point for other, more inventive, local variations.

Bagging Tea

In Nacirema culture, the small pouch employed to concoct morning libations, drunk hot, is believed to resemble the male scrotum. In the "Bagging Tea" ritual, the Tarf removes his trousers and loin cloth, and squats over a sleeping Jelp. The Jelp is then awakened to find a dangling scrotum directly over his face. While this is intended to be humiliating to the Jelp, it is not clear whether he then is expected to engage with the other man's scrotum orally.

The Walk of the Elephants

In this ritual, all the Jelps are stripped naked and stand in a straight line, one behind the other. Each Jelp reaches through the legs of the Jelp standing in from of him and grabs that man's penis. The entire effect resembles a line of elephants walking in a single line, in which each holds the other's tail in his trunk. By performing the Walk of the Elephants, the Jelps learn the homosexual behavior that is expected of them by other Tarfs. Apparently, it is not typical for Tarfs to walk around their secret men's hut in this way during non-ritual periods or secular time. Only during ritual events are they permitted to do so.

Anal Egg Transport

In this collective ritual, each Jelp is asked to place a peeled hard boiled egg in his rectum, and then all proceed to walk a certain distance, either inside the ceremonial men's hut or in a secluded place. While this ritual clearly signifies anal intercourse, it is unclear whether Tarfs themselves insert the eggs into the Jelp's rectum or whether the Jelp is required to do this himself.

Block Party

In this ritual, Tarfs and Jelps stand on a balcony or ledge of a building. The Tarfs measure a rope, with a cinderblock tied to one end, so that it reaches almost, but not quite, to the ground. Then the Tarfs tie the other end of the rope to the Jelp's penis. They tell him that only if his penis is large enough will the cinderblock reach the ground; otherwise, the weight of the block falling will likely rip the Jelp's penis off. While the manifest function, according to Tarfs, of this ritual is to test how much trust the Jelp has for his future brothers, it also reveals Tarf and Jelp anxiety about penis size. Since Tarf culture revolves so centrally around ritualized homosexuality, anxiety about penis size—whether they measure up—is heightened for the Jelps.

Ookie Cookie

As if in imitation of the Sambia, this ritual is one of the most overtly homosexual of the entire Tarf subculture. Tarfs masturbate together (although they are prohibited from masturbating each other) and ejaculate on a cookie. Jelps are then required to eat the cookie. In this homosexual form of communion, bonds of solidarity are forged, and the Jelps can ingest the Tarf life force from their elders. Among all dentstuds within a particular supmac, Tarfs are the most closely allied with their Sambia cousins.

Gnag Gnab

This is a particularly odious variation of the *ookie cookie*, in which the shared semen is located in the genitals of a drugged female, who is often unconscious or at least incapable of consenting to heterosexual sex. The unconscious or unconsenting woman is then said to "have sex" with several Tarfs or Jelps. This homosexual activity is a most cleverly disguised homosexual ritual, since it involves many different male Tarfs seemingly having heterosexual sex with the same woman. However, as Sanday and others have observed, participants in Gnag Gnabs often say that the best part was feeling the semen of the other Tarfs inside the unconscious woman. While this ritual is technically illegal, the absence of any supmac administrators, and the veneer of "plausible deniability" that such activities are taking place, ensure that the illegal activities often go unpunished.

Of course, like Herdt's Sambia, the Tarfs vigorously deny the obvious homosexual elements in their rituals. Indeed, when it is pointed out to them by the naïve researcher, several threatened physical harm to the researcher for suggesting it. This reaction leads us to the obvious psychoanalytic conclusion: *The vigorousness of the denial is directly related to the obviousness of the behavior being denied.*

There is one other ritual that we must consider: *norp*. Norp consists of images and pictures, and also movies, of naked people engaged in sexual relations. Originally, we suspect that these films were created for physicians and other health professionals because they use extreme close-ups of the genitals to reveal the various methods people use to engage in sexual intercourse. The actors in the movies possess enormous penises, so as to enable the viewer to observe all facets of erection, coitus, and ejaculation. Concerns for birth control are evident, as well, because the male in the norp movie ejaculates outside the female, to ensure that she will not conceive. (We can only briefly comment here that such a method of birth control is obviously ineffective, judging from the high rates of unwanted pregnancies among the Nacirema. However, it should be noted that other cultures whose territories abut that of the Nacirema are far more adept at providing adequate contraception and therefore have lower rates of unwanted pregnancy.) These clinical depictions of sex are interesting to the anthropologist because we can only conclude from watching them that the Nacirema do not like sex very much at all.

Yet norp is everywhere in Nacirema society. It is especially prevalent in educational villages, where it may appear on the information boxes that all the dentstuds use to record information. And it is omnipresent in the Tarf subculture. We understand from our informants that they enjoy norp because it facilitates masturbation. Its function is to arouse the viewer sexually, and he then proceeds to masturbate. (Virtually all Nacirema males of this age cohort, regardless of Tarf status, engage in masturbation, although few actually discuss it publicly.) Only a small fraction of the Nacirema—and an even smaller percentage of Tarfs—employs norp in their heterosexual unions; its use is mostly a solitary experience.

Naïve readers may assume that since the depictions of sexual congress contained in norp are images of heterosexual couples, then the viewing experience would hardly qualify as ritualized homosexuality. However, in our field research, we noticed that within the Tarf subculture, even the most evidently heterosexual experiences can be transformed into ritualized homosexuality. Indeed, it may be that the Tarf subculture feels a bit ashamed about its evident rampant homosexuality, and so the Tarfs attempt to conceal it under a veil of surface heterosexuality. If norp is manifestly heterosexual, its latent function may be to provide an outlet for ritualized homosexuality.

Tarfs tend to view norp collectively. They will gather together, drink alcoholic libations, and sit very close to one another on the sofa. As they watch the norp together, they will, of course, begin to become sexually aroused, but there are strict prohibitions against acknowledgement of that arousal, let alone permission to masturbate in the presence of the other Tarfs. Thus, Tarfs are frustrated in the gratification of their arousal, and we can only conclude that this frustration is intentional: they want to have their heterosexual impulses (heterosexual fantasies tend to accompany their masturbation) frustrated in order to facilitate their ritualized homosexual arousal.

However, Tarfs also feel so guilty about their homosexual arousal that their frustration becomes aggression, as would be predicted by social psychologists. Again, however, this aggression is often directed not at the other males but at the images of the women depicted in norp. The Tarfs will yell at the image of the woman, hoping that the male actor will hurt her, hit her, or "nail her." (We assume that this bears some relationship to Nacirema spiritual beliefs.) In this way, the Tarfs reaffirm their secret homosexual identities, as they repudiate their interest in women so that they can remain together.

IV. Toofball and Ritualized Homosexuality among the Tarf Subculture

Many of the most overtly homosexual rituals occur following ceremonial sporting events known as Toofball. In this athletic contest, the contestants dress in gladiatorial costumes that exaggerate masculine musculature in the shoulders and thighs while ensuring that any observer can view the entire buttocks without obstruction. Armored helmets conceal their faces. This is no doubt to enable them to engage in overtly homoerotic behavior anonymously, as adult homosexuals among the Nacirema often do.

The object of this athletic contest, as Berkeley folklorist Alan Dundes has eloquently pointed out, is itself ritually homosexual (Dundes, 1985). "The object of the game, simply stated, is to get into the opponent's endzone while preventing the opponent from getting into one's own endzone," Dundes writes (1985:121). This helps to explain the "bottom patting" that is often observed among players. "A good offensive or defensive play deserves a pat on the rear end. The recipient has held up his end and has thereby helped protect

the collective 'end' of the entire team. One pats one's teammates' ends, but one seeks to violate the endzone of one's opponents!" (Ibid.).

In one particularly homoerotic display, the largest of the Toofball players make themselves vulnerable to anal penetration by their teammates, facing their opponents. The largest and heaviest men bend over into an untenable stooped position, leaning forward so far (to expose their buttocks to their teammates) that they need to rest their heavy frame on one hand as well. This three-point stance is simultaneously more impervious to one's opponents and exceptionally vulnerable to one's trusted teammates.

When arrayed for competition, the most handsome of these warriors is required to place his hands on the buttocks of the largest and least mobile of the other combatants. (Only he may do so; all others are enjoined from this display.) He recites a ceremonial incantation as he moves his hands rhythmically. The larger man does not move, nor does he indicate sexual gratification from this simulation of masturbation. At a specified point, he passes the oblong projectile through his legs, and the handsome warrior either gives it away to another combatant or throws it in the air. Regardless, as soon as the initial homosexual rubbing is over and the "toofball" is passed, all the combatants in both colored costumes fall on top of each other, grabbing each other's bodies, until they lie together in a big undulating pile. Adults, wearing costumes like zebras, run to the pile and blow a whistle to ensure that all the combatants are stimulated fairly. (The zebra-men are dressed this way to make sure that the experience is as natural as the jungle that their costumes signify.)

Observing such a spectacle of public homosexuality is obviously arousing for the many spectators. Many wear strange costumes themselves to the spectacle, perhaps to indicate their fanatic allegiance to the combatants from one side or the other. After the large piles are dispersed, strangers often hug each other and show other forms of affection such as holding hands for a fraction of a second or slapping a neighbor's hand or buttocks.

Many drink ceremonial libations from bottles in paper bags.

Tarfs are regular spectators; indeed, they are the most consistent attendees at these Toofball spectacles. Perhaps it is their heightened state of sexual arousal that leads to the Tarfs' ritualized homosexual behavior; their rituals often take place in the evenings following these Toofball events.

V.

That Tarfs routinely engage in such ritualized homosexuality need not concern citizens of open and tolerant societies. Indeed, the only concerns we raise here about ritualized homosexuality in Tarf culture are about the layers of homophobic denial that so often accompany it and the ways in which women become a vehicle by which the ritualized homosexuality is simultaneously enacted and denied.

Attitude surveys have consistently found high levels of homophobia among the Tarf subculture—which is ironic when one considers that the Tarfs spend virtually all their time together in their men's hut engaging in ritualized homosexual activity. Since the Tarf males so evidently want to be with each other, and want to have sex with each other, we can only hope that they become active campaigners for more tolerant attitudes and laws regarding homosexuality. Surely that is in their interests as Tarfs.

Second, we must register concern for the ways in which Tarf denial of the obvious homoeroticism in their rituals leads to certain compensatory efforts to demonstrate heterosexuality. Male heterosexual predatory sexual behavior has been consistently remarked upon by observers of Nacirema life, especially in its supmacs. While it is no doubt the case that an overall decline in cultural homophobia among the Nacirema in general might reduce such behavior, we also hope that the acknowledgment of the manifest homosexual content of Tarf rituals will enable Tarfs, particularly, to relax their obsession with proving what they are unable to prove.

Further, the specific forms of ritualized homosexuality knows as gnag gnabs must be vigorously prosecuted as crimes against the women whose sole function is to provide a vessel by which the ritualized homosexuality can take place. This requires the active intervention of administrators and other elders in the supmac.

Surely, now that the ritualized homosexuality of the Tarf subculture has been described, future researchers will be able to better understand the activities of this strange and esoteric tribe.

Authors Note: While I intend this essay to be provocative, it should also be clear that in no way do I assume that all members of the Tarf subculture engage in these practices. For research on the subculture, I am grateful to Lauren Joseph and Tyson Smith for their insights and explanations. Denny Gilmore helped to situate the Tarf subculture in a wider cross-cultural literature. Three anonymous reviewers helped me to sharpen the analysis and restrain potential excesses.

Notes

1. While these particuilar "reltsuhs" may believe the meaning of acts do not inhere in the gender of the actors, their view is not widely shared. Generally, Nacirema believe in the "one drop rule," in which one sexual experience with a member of the same sex brands the person indelibly as gay.

References

Carrier, J. 1977. "'Sex Role Preference' as a Explanatory Variable in Homosexual Behavior" in *Archives of Sexual Behavior*, 6(1), 53–65.

Davenport, W. 1977. "Sex in Cross-Cultural Perspective" in *Human Sexuality in Four Perspectives*, (F. Beach and M. Diamond, eds.). Baltimore: The Johns Hopkins University Press.

Dundes, A. 1985. "The American Game of 'Smear the Queer' and the Homosexual Component of Male Competitive Sport and Warfare." *Journal of Psychoanalytic Anthropology*, 8, 115–129.

Gilmore, D. 1990. *Manhood in the Making*. New Haven: Yale University Press.

Herdt, G. 1981. *Guardians of the Flutes*, Chicago: University of Chicago Press.

————, ed. 1984. *Ritualized Homosexuality in Melanesia*. Berkeley: University of California Press.

Kelly, R. 1977. *Etero Social Structure*. Ann Arbor: University of Michigan Press.

Miner, H. 1956. "Body Ritual among the Nacirema." *American Anthropologist,* 58(3), 503–507.

Schiefflin, E. L. 1976. *The Sorrow of the Lonely and the Burning of the Dancers*. New York: St. Martin's Press.

Williams, F. 1936. *Papuans of the Trans-Fly*. Oxford: Oxford University Press.

Rocco L. Capraro

Why College Men Drink: Alcohol, Adventure, and the Paradox of Masculinity

And you drink this burning liquor like your life
Your life which you drink like an eau-de-vie.

Apollinaire[1]

Though terror speaks to life and death and distress makes of the world a vale of tears, yet
shame strikes deepest into the heart of man.

Tomkins[2]

Given the magnitude of the negative consequences of some college men's drinking—for themselves and for those around them—on campuses across the nation,[3] college health professionals and alcohol prevention educators might well wonder: "Why *do* college men drink?" Because most college men drink in unproblematic ways and only to be sociable,[4] those men who drink in a way that is likely to be harmful to themselves or others are actually the central focus of this article—that is, those men "for whom drinking has become a central activity in their way of life."[5(p100)]

Writing from a men's health studies perspective, I articulate what is necessarily only a tentative answer to the question of men's problem drinking by offering a model for conceptualizing the complex connections between college men and alcohol. Men's health studies, a subfield of men's studies, describes and analyzes men's experience

of health, injury, morbidity, and mortality in the context of masculinity.[6,7] I also suggest an answer to the companion question that immediately presents itself to us: "What can we do about it?"

Part one of this article discusses the connections between alcohol, men, and masculinity generally; part two, the cultural and developmental aspects of men in a college setting; and part three, conceptual and programmatic responses to the men's problem drinking.

In general, I conclude that when college men drink, they are simply *being* men in college: that is the best context for understanding why they drink. I further conclude, in what is perhaps my central insight in this article, that college men's drinking appears to be profoundly paradoxical in a way that seems to replicate a larger paradox of masculinity itself: that men's alcohol use is related to both men's power and men's powerlessness. Stated most succinctly, my interpretation of a variety of evidence suggests that many college men may be drinking not only to enact male privilege but also to help them negotiate the emotional hazards of being a man in the contemporary American college.

From *Journal of American College Health* 48: 307–315. Copyright © 2000. Reprinted with permission of the Helen Dwight Reid Foundation. Published by Heldref Publication, Washington, DC.

Alcohol and Masculinity

Drinking as a Male Domain

If we want to understand why college men drink, then we might embed drinking and college in masculinity and ask in what ways each might be seen as a specific male experience.[6] When we look for connections between drinking, men, and masculinity, we observe that the most prominent feature on the social landscape of drinking is that drinking is a "male domain."[3(p6)] By *male domain,* I suggest that drinking is male dominated, male identified, and male centered.[8]

Men outnumber women in virtually every category of drinking behavior used in research for comparison—prevalence, consumption, frequency of drinking and intoxication, incidence of heavy and problem drinking, alcohol abuse and dependence, and alcoholism.[4,9–12] Although most college men and women say they drink to be sociable, men are more likely than women to say they drink for escapism or to get drunk.[4(p125)]

These findings hold true for the categories of age, ethnicity, geographic region, religion, education, income, and marital status.[9] Although there has been some speculation that changing gender roles may be narrowing the gap between women and men vis-á-vis alcohol, discussed by scholars as the *convergence hypothesis,* research tends to reject that proposition.[3]

In a classic and often-cited article, Lemle and Miskind[9] asked, "Why should it be that males drink and abuse alcohol in such magnitude and in such marked contrast to females?" Citing empirical research that placed men mostly in the company of other men in the life course of their drinking, they suggested that drinking was a symbol of masculinity and speculated that men may drink to be manly.[9(p215)] They found little or no empirical evidence to support many of the theoretical possibilities they discussed, particularly for any theories concerned with men's abusive drinking, yet they remained intrigued with the idea that men were affirming their manliness by drinking.

More recently, McCreary et al.[10] ask what *specific* aspects of the male gender role correlate with alcohol involvement. In addition to the personality traits of instrumentality and expressiveness, they explore the traits of traditional male-role attitudes and masculine gender-role stress. For their research, traditional male-role attitudes represent a "series of beliefs and assumptions that men should be in high-status positions in society, act in physically and emotionally toughened ways, and avoid anything stereotypically feminine." *Masculine gender-role stress* is a term used to "describe the stress resulting from a man's belief that he is unable to meet society's demands of what is expected from men or the male role or from having to respond to a situation in a feminine-typed manner."[10(pp111–112).]

McCreary et al.[10] identify traditional male-role attitudes as the *one* aspect of the male gender role they studied that predicts alcohol *use* among men. Alcohol use itself correlates with alcohol problems. However, masculine gender-role stress, while statistically unrelated to alcohol *use,* does predict alcohol *problems* for men (p. 121). In short, this study suggests that, from the point of view of masculinity or culture of manhood as a factor among many others, men *qua* men might arrive at alcohol problems by two routes: one route starts at traditional male-role attitudes, passes through alcohol use, and ends in alcohol problems; another route starts at masculine gender-role stress and ends directly in alcohol problems.

Variations on a Theme: Conflict and Strain, Shame and Fear, Depression, and the Paradox of Masculinity

The Paradox of Masculinity Traditional male-role attitudes and masculine gender-role stress are actually not very far apart; in some aspects, they are correlated.[10,13] Their correlation reveals the contradictory nature of masculinity.[14] Reflecting upon the contradictory nature of the male role, researchers in the field of men's studies have articulated the paradox of masculinity, or the paradox of men's power, as follows: *men are powerful and powerless.*[15–18]

What is the resolution of the apparent contradiction that constitutes the paradox? How can men be both powerful and powerless? Men's studies observe two aspects of men's lives. First, in objective social analysis, *men as a group have power over women as a group:* but, in their subjective experience of the world, *men as individuals do not feel powerful.* In fact, they feel powerless. As at first articulated, and then later resolved by men's studies, the concept of a paradox of men's power offers an important insight into men's lives, one that seems to capture and to explain many of the contradictory claims made by and about men.

Ironically, it is men themselves who make the "rules of manhood" by which men as individuals are "disempowered."[17(p138)] Kaufman[16] aptly concludes that men's power is actually the cause of men's pain: "men's social power is the source of individual power and privilege . . . it is also the source of the individual experience of pain and alienation."[16(pp142–143)]

The paradoxical nature of masculinity is further illuminated in other men's studies research on at least three critical psychosocial aspects of masculinity: gender-role conflict and strain, shame and fear, and depression. Interestingly, those same aspects of masculinity are themselves important possible connections between men and alcohol. Consequently, the concept of the paradox of men's power draws us to an important conceptual understanding of some men's connections to alcohol.

Conflict and Strain   O'Neil[19] provides a useful series of interlocking definitions that locate gender-role conflict and strain in relation to the gender role itself. Gender roles are "behaviors, expectations, and values defined by society as masculine or feminine," or "as appropriate behavior for men and women." Gender-role conflict is "a psychological state in which gender roles have negative consequences on the individual or others" through the restriction, devaluation, or vi-olation of oneself or others. Gender-role strain is "physical or psychological tension experienced as an outcome of gender-role conflict." At the bottom of gender-role strain is a "discrepancy between the real self and the gender role" (pp. 24, 25). Strain can follow from both conformity and nonconformity to the male role.

In his writings on strain, Pleck[14,20] provides additional insight into the relation between the masculine gender role and conflict or strain. Pleck maintains that the masculine gender role itself is "dysfunctional,"[14(p147)] fraught with contradictions and negative consequences. Even when men live up to the role, they suffer well-documented adverse consequences. But, very often, men do not live up to the role. In fact, conflict and strain are inherent in the role, and they are actually the best rubrics under which to understand most men's identity and experience.

In Pleck's[14] role-strain paradigm, social approval and situational adaptation replace innate psychological need as the social and psychological mechanisms by which men achieve manhood. Violating gender roles (norms and stereotypes) results in social condemnation, a negative consequence experienced as sex-role strain and anxiety, a negative psychological consequence (pp. 145, 146). At least one study has connected role conflict and alcohol use. Blazina and Watkins[21] found that masculine gender-role conflict, in particular the factor cluster of "success, power, and competition," were significantly related to college men's reported use of alcohol.

Shame and Fear   Krugman,[22] reflecting on Pleck's foundational work on gender-role strain, characterizes male-role strain, with its grounding in feelings of inadequacy and inferiority, as a shame-based experience. "Role strain generates shame affect as males fail to live up to the cultural and peer group standards they have internalized."[22(p95)] The essence of shame for Krugman is "painful self-awareness" or "a judgment against the self" (p. 99). He advises that shame is active in both male gender-role strain and normal male socialization.

Recent research suggests that normative male socialization employs shame to shape boys' and men's behaviors and attitudes.[22,23] In common and nonpathological forms, shame becomes integrated into the self and transformed into a cue that tells us when to modify our behaviors and feelings in response to shame's messages about their appropriateness. But although shame may be the powerful leverage to enforce boys' and men's conformity to the male role, men are less likely than women to transform shame because they find shame to be *repugnant* to their masculinity. Consequently, for Krugman,[22] boys and men internalize male gender roles to avoid shame; but they also learn that dependency needs, for example, are shameful, especially under the gaze of their peer group.

Shame is related to fear.[2] Shame can magnify fear by linking similar episodes of fear into what Tomkins refers to as a family of episodes, creating a behavioral template in which fear can be anticipated and become more pervasive. In adversarial cultures, and I would include our own society generally in that category, fear and shame are conjoined, resulting in the mutually reinforcing "fear of shame" and "shame of fear."[2(p538)]

Kimmel[17] places fear and shame at the very center of the social construction of men's identity. For him, men "fear that other men will unmask us, emasculate us, reveal to us and the world that we do not measure up, that we are not real men. Fear makes us ashamed" (p. 131). To avoid shame, Kimmel writes, men distance themselves from the feminine and all associations with it, including mothers, the world of feelings, nurturing, intimacy, and vulnerability.

Without the transformation of shame, men learn to manage shame in other ways. Alcohol is one of the significant ways men manage shame: drinking is a "maladaptive male solution to the pressure of undischarged shame."[22(p120)] Speaking metaphorically, Krugman observes that alcohol "dissolves acute shame" (p. 94). Referring to Lansky's study of shame in families, Krugman reports that alcohol, as a disinhibitor, is used by some men "to handle vulnerable and exposed states that generate shameful feelings." Krugman, citing M. Horowitz, advises that alcohol "softens ego criticism" and "facilitates interpersonal connections and self-disclosures" (p. 120). Drinking may also reduce fear.[2] It seems to me that shame may also be the mechanism that leads men directly to alcohol, which is used to instill conformity to the dictates of traditional masculinity that encourage men to drink.

Depression   In addition to anxiety and shame, male gender-role strain and conflict make themselves known in the lives of men in depression. Depression is significantly related to all four aspects of gender-role conflict: (a) success, power, and competition; (b) restrictive emotionality; (c) restrictive affectionate behavior between men; and (d) conflicts between work and family relations.[13,24] Traditional masculinity insidiously puts men at risk for depression and also masks the depression, should it actually develop.[25,26]

Whereas Kaufman[16] uses a discourse of power to explain men's unacknowledged emotions, Lynch and Kilmartin[25] offer an alternative approach to the pitfalls of masculinity drawn from the point of view of social relations. Men's socialization encourages them to disconnect, or dissociate, from their feelings. An emotionally restrictive masculinity permits men to show their feelings only "in disguised form," and so they become "mostly unrecognized, unexpressed, and misunderstood by self and others" (p. 45). Men, instead, express their feelings in indirect ways, often through behavior that is destructive to themselves or others. Dissociation from feelings and destructive behavior are the two major characteristics of what Lynch and Kilmartin refer to as "masculine depression."[25(pp9,10)]

Heavy drinking, or binge drinking, is one of the ways some depressed men may act out, or manifest, their depression.[4] Lynch and Kilmartin[25] cite research indicating that depression is a strong risk factor for substance abuse problems. Krugman[22] notes a study showing strong correlations between alcohol abuse and major depression, especially among men. Although they do not cite empirical evidence for it, Blazina and Watkins[21] speculate that traditional men may "self-medicate their pain and depression with alcohol" (p. 461). Although research findings suggest only a possible correlation between alcohol use or abuse and depression, perhaps alcohol use or abuse may actually precede depression. Alcohol and depression are certainly connected in the lives of some men.

Alcohol and the Paradox of Men's Power

Men in our society are supposed to be powerful.[27] According to the empirical findings of McClelland et al.,[28] when men are not powerful, they may often compensate for their lack of power or seek an "alternative to obtaining social power" with alcohol. Stated most dramatically by McClelland, drinking is "part of a cluster of actions which is a principal manifestation of the need for power" (p. 119). For this research, feeling powerful means "feeling that one is vigorous and can [have] an impact on others" (p. 84). But men's power motivation can be personalized (i.e., for "the greater glory or influence of the individual") or socialized for "the good of others" (p. 137).

According to McClelland,[28] a few drinks will stimulate socialized power thoughts for most men, and that is one of the reasons they like to drink. Higher levels of drinking tend to decrease inhibitions and stimulate personalized power thoughts. Heavy drinking in men is uniquely associated with personalized power, McClelland says. Heavy drinking makes men feel strong and assertive and, I would argue, the way they are supposed to feel.

Drinking may be related to men's power in a more profound and paradoxical way. In the aggregate, the connection between some men and heavy or problem drinking appears to be of two sorts: (a) that which follows from simple, apparently uncomplicated, conformity to traditional masculinity—drinking simply because men are supposed to drink; and (b) that which is informed by complex, perceived inadequacy as men, either from men's own point of view, or from that of society. If they do not feel inadequate, then at least

they experience a kind of doubt, or a sense of falling short of the cultural ideal of manhood—drinking because of gender-role conflicts.

This distinction may be, after all, only a conceptual, or theoretical, distinction; in practice, the two sorts of connection co-occur. I wonder if traditional masculinity does not contain within it, socially constructed over time in the course of men's history, the use of alcohol to accommodate gender-role conflict. Given the way traditional masculinity has been constructed, is not gender-role conflict of the sort described by Pleck[14] and O'Neil[19] and documented in the lives of the men studied by Tomkins,[2] Krugman,[21] Lynch and Kilmartin,[25] Real,[26] and Kimmel[17] inherent in most men's lives? Have not men as historical agents, therefore, made provision for taking care of their own? If so, traditional masculine drinking would encompass conflicted drinking; certainly, in the culture of manhood, it does.

If heavy and problem drinking is associated with conformity, overconformity, or conflicted or strained resistance to the imperatives of traditional masculinity, why should this be the case? It would appear that drinking is a kind of fatally flawed defense mechanism, or compensatory behavior. It protects men's objective power as a group, even as it reveals men's subjective powerlessness as individuals and results in a diminution of men's power, particularly through the loss of control of emotions, health, and a variety of other negative consequences.

If this is the case, then drinking would have much in common with other documented psychological defense mechanisms that correlate with male gender-role conflict. And gender-role conflict, following from either conformity or nonconformity, might itself be seen as a defense mechanism that "protects a man's sense of well-being."[29(p253)] Like men's silence,[30] men's drinking turns out to be in the interest of men's power, even as it disempowers individual men. And alcohol, in my view, is the paradoxical drug that is a part of the larger whole, a trope, of a paradoxical masculinity.

As I ponder this material, then, it seems to me that a significant part of men's drinking, like male gender-role stress and strain, men's shame, and masculine depression themselves, is a reflection of both men's power and men's powerlessness about men's privilege and men's pain. Heavy and problem drinking join other aspects of masculinity as they, too, come to be seen as manifestations of the paradox of masculinity. Drinking thus falls into a line of masculine icons, including body building, sexual assault, and pornography, that reveal the paradoxical nature of masculinity itself.[31–34] As I review those icons, it strikes me that at those times men *appear* most powerful socially, they *feel* most powerless personally.

College and Masculinity

College Drinking

What happens when we look at *college* men? College students, mostly men, are among the heavy drinkers in Rorabaugh's[35] history of drinking in early American society. Contemporary college men drink more than they did in high school and more heavily than their noncollege counterparts, and the gap is widening.[3,36–38] Men have been the primary public purveyors of alcohol to the college campus. All of the differences in drinking behavior for men and women generally hold true for college men and women.[3,4]

Given today's college students' preference for alcohol, one could not really imagine most colleges void of alcohol.[39] However, given the great variety of colleges and universities, the diversity of today's student populations, and the sweeping nature of the concerns I express in this article, most of what follows must necessarily speak primarily to an ideal type, represented for me by the relatively small, residential liberal arts college, occupied by a mostly traditionally aged student population.[40] In the following pages, I shall discuss critical aspects of college that seem to define college men's experience and help explain much of the presence of alcohol on college campuses: adventure, adult development, and permissiveness.

College as Adventure

Green[41] conceptualizes adventure as a domain of transgression. For Green, adventure takes shape around the themes of "eros" and "potestas"—love and power. Following Bataille, Green asks us to think about civil society "as based on the purposes and values of work, which means the denial of all activities hostile to work, such as both the ecstasies of eroticism and those of violence." Adventure lies in the conceptual space where heroes, "men acting with power," break free of ordinary restraints and "sample the repressed pleasures of sex and violence."[42(p17)]

Although Green[41] makes no reference to drinking in his essays on adventure, we can easily recognize that the terrain of adventure is the same terrain as that of alcohol: "a boy's first drink, first prolonged drinking experience, and first intoxication tend to occur with other boys away from home."[9(p214)] Sports and the military are contexts for both adventure and drinking. Drinking games "are an important factor in the socialization of new students into heavy use," particularly for men.[42(p105)] Drinking, in general, can be an adventure, insofar as it takes men through a "breach" of the social contract and into the realms of violence, sex, and other adventure motifs.

In what way might college be conceptualized as an adventure? College is not literally, or predominantly, a scene of eros and potestas. It is, however, a time and place of an imaginative assertion of manhood outside of civil society, away from home and family, where a kind of heroism is possible. By analogy, we can observe that student life in 19th-century American colleges developed outside of the civil society represented by the faculty and administration in what I would regard as the realm of adventure. Horowitz[43] argues that what we think of as student life was actually "born in revolt" (p. 23) against the faculty and administration. It is a "world made by the undergraduates," she says (p. 3).

Levine and Cureton[39] find that colleges today are occupied by a transitional generation that reflects the changing demographics of contemporary American society. Horowitz's history, however, employs a simple tripartite typology of college students that is still largely applicable as a model for understanding students on many campuses in more recent times. That typology deeply resonates with my own many years of experience in student affairs: (a) college men—affluent men in revolt against the faculty and administration who created campus life as "the culture of the college man" (p. 32); (b) outsiders—hardworking men who identify with the faculty (p. 14); and (c) rebels—creative, modernist, and expressive men who conform neither to campus life nor to the faculty (p. 15). Horowitz[43] observes that these three student types were distinctly *male* when they first made their appearance, but their female counterparts eventually found their place alongside the men.

Nuwer[44] argues that there are historical links between traditional male undergraduate life and danger, a key adventure motif. Social interactions initiating students into various campus communities have continuously subjected college men to high risk. Acceptance by their peers is granted in exchange for successfully undertaking the risk involved. A variety of college rituals and traditions often mix danger and alcohol.[44] Alcohol, itself, is associated with risk in men's lives.[9] Seen this way, college and campus life become an adventurescape, where young men (college men) imagine their manhood in a developmental moment that is socially dominated by alcohol.

Green[41] identifies a number of arenas or institutions of adventure: manhood before marriage, hunting, battle, travel, sports, and politics, to name a few. Although there may be feminine variants, Green links adventure to masculinity because society gives men the freedom to "apply forces to the world to assert power and identity." Adventure is an act of assertion by which men "imagine themselves" in "a breach of the social contract" (p. 19).

College as a Male Developmental Moment

Beyond seeing the sociology of college and student life organized as adventure, we must also consider the role of individual developmental psychology in the college environment. Paradoxically, just at the moment the great adventure begins, college men feel the most vulnerable. Rotundo[45] observes that in the 19th century, "male youth culture" made its appearance in men's development as the vehicle for the transition from boyhood to manhood. Boys' principal developmental task was disengagement from home, which created conflict between the imperatives of wordly ambition young men's psychological needs for attachment. Young men of Rotundo's period gathered in business districts and colleges. Wherever they gathered, a "special culture" developed to support them in a time of need (pp. 56–62).

Lyman[46] carries us forward from Rotundo's[45] historical analysis to the present. In his essay on male bonding in fraternities, he locates college as a developmental time and place between the authority of home and family (in the high school years), and that of work and family (after graduation). He identifies college men's anger, their "latent anger about the discipline that middle-class male roles impose upon them, both marriage rules and work rules" (p. 157). Their great fear is loss of control and powerlessness. Lyman concludes that joking relationships (banter, sexual humor, etc.) among men allow a needed connection without being self-disclosive or emotionally intimate, that is, with little vulnerability. Recent research on first-year college men has characterized their transition to college as often involving separation anxiety and loss, followed by grieving. Among the significant responses that may manifest some college men's grief, we find self-destructive behaviors, including alcohol use.[47]

Shame theory advises that to avoid shame, boys need to distance themselves from their mothers because of the "considerable discomfort with dependency needs at the level of the peer group."[22(p107)] College men in groups, such as Lyman's fraternity men, perceive homosexuality and intimate emotional relationships with women to be a threat to their homosocial world. Thus, men are encouraged to treat women as sexual objects, which confirms their heterosexuality, but prevents true intimacy with women.

Alcohol plays a role in men's emotional management under these conditions. Drinking remains a "socially acceptable way for men to satisfy their dependency needs while they maintain a social image of independence,"[48(p187)] even as it masks those needs. For example, recent research on drinking games suggests they are actually an environmental context for drinking where a variety of students' social and psychological needs come into play.[49] When men (and women) give reasons for playing drinking games, they are likely to be "tapping into more general motives for drinking" (p. 286). Alcohol may be an effective way to cope in the short term, but it is ultimately "self-destructive."[48(p191)]

For Nuwer,[44] as was true for Horowitz,[43] fraternities are the quintessential emblems of traditional college life. They provide a "feeling of belonging" for students who "crave relationships and acceptance" in their college years (p. 38). They are also the riskiest environments for heavy and problem drinking.[4] Nationally, just over 80 percent of fraternity residents binge drink, whereas just over 40 percent of all college students binge.[50] Drinking in fraternities is perhaps best understood as an extreme on a continuum of college men's drinking, dramatizing what may be going on to a lesser extent in traditional student life among a range of men. From the point of view of men's needs assessments, we have much to learn from the psychology of brotherhood.

Permissiveness—Real and Imagined

Alcohol is "one of the oldest traditions in the American college," and alcohol-related problems have also been a benchmark of campus life. Until very recently, though, college administrations have been permissive about alcohol, voicing "official condemnation tempered by tacit toleration."[51(pp81–83)] Myers[52] provides a model for "institutional (organizational) denial" of the presence (or extent) of alcohol abuse that could easily apply to college campuses nationally (p. 43). In 1995, Wechsler[11] was explicit about the widespread denial about alcohol on college campuses.

With the increase in the drinking age from 18 to 21 years and increased awareness of the dangers of alcohol abuse, colleges now "typically have policies which promote responsible drinking" and attempt the "management of student drinking and its consequences."[51(pp84–88)] My own informal observations are that liability case law, awareness of the negative impact of alcohol on the achievement of educational mission, and enrollment management concerns for retention have also encouraged colleges to be more vigilant about the role of alcohol in campus cultures.

But among students, permissiveness persists, both in drinking behavior and in attitudes toward drinking. Permissiveness itself is, in part, the result of students' own misperceptions of campus norms for alcohol behavior and attitudes.[53,54] With reference to the consumption of alcohol and the acceptability of intoxication, students generally perceive themselves to be in a permissive environment. In reality, the environment is not as permissive as they think. Misperceiving the norm leads students who are inclined to drink to consume more alcohol than they otherwise would drink were they to perceive the norm correctly.[55] This social norms research indicates that correcting the misperception through public information campaigns can reduce both problem drinking and binge drinking on college campuses.[56,57]

How well do social norms approaches work with college men who are heavy drinkers? How are masculinity, permissive attitudes about drinking, and misperceptions of the norm related? How accurately do college men perceive their campus norms? For social norms theory and research, the heaviest drinking results from the interaction of the most permissive personal attitudes toward alcohol and the greatest misperception of the norm as more permissive than it actually is. Men as a group are the heaviest drinkers on campus. We might conclude that the heaviest drinking men have the most permissive attitudes about drinking and that they misperceive the norm at the greatest rates. But, theoretically, they should also be most susceptible to the benefits of social norms approaches.

However, in one study, the heaviest drinking college men proved to be the least susceptible to social norms interventions. From 1995 to 1998 Western Washington University implemented a campus-wide social norms approach. Although most students on the campus changed their patterns of drinking in positive ways, the "students reporting they had seven or more drinks on peak occasions [the most consumed at one time in the past month] remained virtually unchanged [at about 35 percent]." The most recalcitrant students at Western Washington were underage men: "nearly two thirds of the underage men still reported having seven or more drinks on a peak occasion. Only one third of the underage women reporting the same"[56(p3)] level of consumption.

In view of the significance of personal attitudes toward alcohol,[55] permissive personal attitudes about alcohol in the group of recalcitrant underage men might have been so robust that they simply overwhelmed any other perceptions of the environment. Prentice and Miller[58] found that men and women in their study did respond differently to corrections of misperceptions. Perhaps, in the case of at least some college men, personal attitudes about drinking and misperception of the campus norm are so inextricably linked that research and prevention work that addresses the one (personal attitudes) must necessarily be done in conjunction with the same kind of work on the other (misperception of the norm).

Perkins once characterized "the perceived male stereotype of heavy use as a misperception to which males do not need to conform."[3(p6)] Some college men's misperceptions of their campus alcohol norms may be "contained" in their personal attitudes about drinking. Baer found that differences in the perception of campus drinking norms among students in different housing situations on one campus "*already existed prior to college enrollment*"[42(p98)] [emphasis mine]. Certainly, if "the impact of public behavior and conversation" on campus can generate misperceptions of the norm,[54(p17)] a lifetime of powerful messages about the connection between alcohol and manhood would produce great distortions of its own.

Social norms theory, research, and strategies would be enhanced by a closer look at gender in the creation of drinking attitudes and behaviors, in possible differences in the misperception of norms, and in the social mechanisms that lie behind the actual norms. Social norms research surveys should include measures of traditional masculine role strain and should look for correlations between attitudes and perceptions of the norm and actual drinking behavior.

In addition, surveys should replace the generic "college student" with "male student" or "female student" when asking college students about how much students are drinking and asking about their attitudes toward drinking. So, for example, we should ask, "How many drinks does a *male* [or *female*] student typically have at a party on this campus?" instead of "do *students* typically have" or "Is it acceptable for men [or women] to drink with occasional intoxication as long as it does not interfere with other responsibilities?"[54(p15)]

The results would have implications for norms-based prevention programs. It would make sense if, in fact, masculinity were found to predispose men to misperceive the norm because assumptions and attitudes about drinking and how drinking relates to manhood are built into masculinity. It would also make sense that the actual and perceived social norms be gender specific.

What Is to Be Done?

Concrete Responses

Men, alcohol, and college are connected by the paradoxical nature of men's power. What can we do about college men's frequent, heavy, and problem drinking? Following from the model that has been developed in this essay, nothing short of radical reconstruction of masculinity and a reimagining of the college experience are likely to bring about significant change in college men's drinking. The same paradox that characterizes college men's drinking also provides a pedagogy for change. This is because, while the paradox acknowledges men's pain and powerlessness, it also discourages men from seeing themselves simply as victims, and it insists that men take responsibility for their actions.

Colleges, in collaboration with high schools and community agencies, should integrate gender awareness into alcohol education, prevention, and risk-reduction programs. For men, I recommend a comprehensive educational program that addresses four central themes in men's lives: friendship, health, life/work/family, and sexual ethics (see also, Good and Mintz[24(p20)]).

As in the case of effective rape prevention education workshops for men, the pedagogy should be workshops that are all male, small group, interactive, and peer facilitated. Such programs have been shown to change some men's attitudes and values that are associated with the perpetration of rape.[59] It may be that the rape prevention workshops are changing attitudes because they correct men's misperceived norm of other men's attitudes about women, or vice versa.[60]

Attitudes and values associated with problem drinking could be similarly changed. Developing what Lynch and Kilmartin[25] refer to as "healthy masculinity" that connects men in healthy relationships with other men, family, and intimate partners would be a succinct statement of the goal of such programming (pp. 46, 47).

The transition to college is a critical juncture in the consumption of alcohol.[4] Programming should therefore begin early in the first year and continue well beyond orientation week. Broad-based, fully integrated, social norms educational programs, interventions, and public information initiatives should be implemented.[55] I would add that such programs should be gender-informed along the lines I have suggested in this article. College men should understand how the paradox-

ical masculinity I have discussed may orient them to alcohol use and abuse.

College students should be strongly encouraged to get involved in clubs and organizations on campus, to run for office, and to be involved in sports as ways of meeting power orientation needs in socially responsible ways.[23] Those activities themselves must have alcohol education components; otherwise, involvement could have the ironic consequence of promoting heavier drinking.[3] Associations between men and beer in campus media should be discouraged.[61,62] Given their powerful influence over men's drinking in the first year,[43] the hazards of drinking games should be especially discussed in educational programming.

In general, college as adventure is a theme that should be discouraged. A "boys will be boys" permissiveness should be rejected. Recognizing and affirming that alcohol does harm, colleges must assert themselves as "moral communities" and move from permissive to restrictive stances on alcohol by first articulating what the harm is, then establishing policies to prevent college community members from harming themselves or others.[51(pp135,150–159)] Wechsler and associates[63] recommend a comprehensive approach to alcohol use on college campuses, including scrutiny of alcohol marketing, more alcohol-free events and activities, and more restrictive policies that control the flow of alcohol on campus. Their recommendation would benefit from more deeply gendered approaches to the problem because the problem, itself, is deeply gendered.

In addition to promoting social norms approaches, preventive education, and risk-reduction education, college administrators should require that frequent violators of alcohol policy seek treatment or seek their education elsewhere. Although critics of treatment may say it addresses the symptoms and not the real problem, which is the campus culture itself, colleges must offer treatment as part of a comprehensive program for renewed campus life. Treatment should seamlessly integrate men's health studies approaches.[66,67] Unfortunately, some college men will be untouched and untouchable by education or treatment, and they must lose the privilege of attending their chosen college and be asked to leave.

Conceptual Responses

Speaking most globally about solving the problem of college men's drinking and solving the problem of the connections between alcohol and masculinity, I would paraphrase what I have previously written about the problem of rape: Our understanding of the specific act of drinking should be embedded in our understanding of masculinity. Drinking is not an isolated behavior; it is a behavior linked to larger systems of attitudes, values, and modalities of conduct in men's lives that constitute masculinity and men's social position relative to women. In this model, alcohol prevention work with men begins with them *as* men, and with men's questioning of prevailing assumptions about masculinity and what it means to be a man. I am extremely skeptical of any alcohol prevention work that proposes solutions to the problem of drinking that leave masculinity, as we know it, largely intact.[68(p22)]

The educational challenge, which is really the psychological and political resistance to this solution, lies in the fact that alcohol benefits men as a group, even as it injures men as individuals. Men are likely to resist this global approach because we fear losing the benefits of masculinity conferred upon the group. The path to a reconstructed masculinity or alternatives to the dominant masculinity that includes more variety of men's identities and experiences may look something like Helms's[69] stage-development model for a positive racial-cultural identity for minority groups. It will not be easy getting there.

In the meantime, in our work with college men who drink, we must look to the bottom of their glasses and find the *men* inside. For when college men drink, they are simply being men at college, or what they perceive men at college to be. By this I mean that the most useful way to interpret their behavior is not so much in its *content,* but in its *context*—first, the imperatives of manhood, then the psychosocial particulars of college life, both of

which put men at risk for drinking. Basically, at the bottom of heavy and problematic drinking among college men are the paradoxical nature of masculinity and the corresponding paradoxical nature of alcohol in men's lives. Once we know college men *as* men, we will know more about why they drink and what we can do about it.

Acknowledgment

This article is dedicated to Alan D. Berkowitz, longtime friend and colleague. I would also like to thank others for their extremely helpful and supportive readings of its various drafts: John Lynch, H. Wesley Perkins, Jan E. Regan, David A. Diana, and David DeVries.

References

1. Apollinaire G. Zone. In: *Selected Writings of Guillaume Apollinaire* (trans. Roger Shattuck). New York: New Directions, 1971.

2. Tomkins S. *Affect, Imagery, Consciousness.* Vol 3, 1962–1992. New York: Springer, 1991.

3. Perkins H. W. Gender patterns in consequences of collegiate alcohol abuse: A 10-year study of trends in an undergraduate population. *J Stud Alcohol.* 1992, September: 458–462.

4. Berkowitz A. D., Perkins H. W. Recent research on gender differences in collegiate alcohol use. *J Am Coll Health.* 1987, 36:123–129.

5. Fingarette H. *Heavy Drinking: The Myth of Alcoholism as a Disease.* Berkeley, CA: University of California Press, 1989.

6. Brod H. The case for men's studies. In: Brod H., ed. *The Making of Masculinities: The New Men's Studies.* Boston: Allen Unwin, 1987.

7. Sabo D., Gordon D. F. Rethinking men's health and illness. In: Sabo D., Gordon D. F. eds. *Men's Health and Illness: Gender, Power, and the Body.* Thousand Oaks, CA: Sage, 1995.

8. Johnson A. G. *The Gender Knot: Unraveling Our Patriarchal Legacy.* Philadelphia: Temple University Press, 1997.

9. Lemle R., Mishkind M. E. Alcohol and masculinity. *Journal of Substance Abuse Treatment.* 1989, 6:213–222.

10. McCreary D. R., Newcomb M. D., Sadave S. The male role, alcohol use, and alcohol problems. *Journal of Counseling Psychology*. 1999, 46(1): 109–124.

11. Wechsler H., Deutsch C., Dowdell G. Too many colleges are still in denial about alcohol abuse. (1995) http://www.hsph.harvard.edu/cas/test/articles/chronicle2.shtm/.

12. Courtenay W. H. Behavioral factors associated with disease, injury, and death among men: Evidence and implications for prevention. *The Journal of Men's Studies*. In press.

13. Sharpe M. J. Heppner P. P. Gender role, gender-role conflict, and psychological well-being in men. *Journal of Counseling Psychology*. 1991, 39(3):323–330.

14. Pleck J. H. *The Myth of Masculinity*. Cambridge, MA: The MIT Press, 1981.

15. Pleck J. Men's power with women, other men, and society: A men's movement analysis. In: Kimmel M. S., Messner M. A. eds. *Men's Lives*. New York: Macmillan, 1989.

16. Kaufman M. Men, feminism, and men's contradictory experiences of power. In: Brod H., Kaufman M., eds. *Theorizing Masculinities*. Newbury Park, CA: Sage, 1994.

17. Kimmel M. S. Masculinity as homophobia: Fear, shame, and silence in the construction of gender identity. In: Brod H., Kaufman M., eds. *Theorizing Masculinities*. Newbury Park, CA: Sage, 1994.

18. Capraro R. L. Review of *Theorizing Masculinities*. Brod H., Kaufman M., eds. Sage; 1994. *Journal of Men's Studies*. 1995, 4(2):169–172.

19. O'Neil J. Assessing men's gender role conflict. In: Moore D., Leafgren F., eds. *Problem Solving Strategies and Interventions for Men in Conflict*. Alexandria, VA: American Association for Counseling and Development, 1990.

20. Pleck J. The gender role strain paradigm: An update. In: Levant R. L., Pollack W. S., eds. *A New Psychology of Men*. New York: Basic, 1995.

21. Blazina C., Watkins C. E. Masculine gender role conflict: Effects on college men's psychological well-being, chemical substance usage, and attitudes toward help-seeking. *Journal of Counseling Psychology*. 1995, 43(4):461–465.

22. Krugman S. Male development and the transformation of shame. In: Levant R. F., Pollack W. S., eds. *A New Psychology of Men*. New York: Basic, 1995.

23. Pollack W. *Real Boys*. New York: Henry Holt, 1999.

24. Good G. E., Mintz L. Gender role conflict and depression in college men: Evidence for compounded risk. *Journal of Counseling and Development*. 1990, 69 (September/October):17–21.

25. Lynch J., Kilmartin C. *The Pain Behind the Mask: Overcoming Masculine Depression*. New York: Haworth, 1999.

26. Real T. *I Don't Want to Talk About It*. New York: Simon & Schuster, 1997.

27. David D. S., Brannon R., eds. *The Forty-Nine Percent Majority: The Male Sex Role*. New York: Random House, 1976.

28. McClelland D. C., David W. N., Kalin R., Wanner E. *The Drinking Man*. New York: The Free Press, 1972.

29. Mahalik J. R., Cournoyer R. J., DeFran W., Cherry M., Napolitano J. M. Men's gender role conflict in relation to their use of psychological defenses. *Journal of Counseling Psychology*. 1998, 45(3):247–255.

30. Sattel J. W. Men, inexpressiveness, and power. In: Thorne K. H. *Language, Gender and Society*. Newbury House, 1983.

31. Fussell W. S. *Muscle: Confessions of an Unlikely Body-builder*. New York: Avon Books, 1991.

32. Berkowitz A. D., Burkhart B. R., Bourg S. E. *Research on College Research and Prevention Education in Higher Education*. San Francisco: Jossey-Bass, 1994.

33. Brod H. Pornography and the alienation of male sexuality. In: Hearn J., Morgan D., eds. *Men, Masculinities and Social Theory*. London: Unwin Hyman, 1990.

34. Kimmel M. S. *Men Confront Pornography*. New York: Crown, 1990.

35. Rorabaugh W. J. *The Alcoholic Republic: An American Tradition*. New York: Oxford University Press, 1981.

36. Maddox G. L., ed. *The Domesticated Drug: Drinking Among Collegians*. New Haven: College and University Press, 1970.

37. Bacon S. D., Strauss R. *Drinking in College*. New Haven: Yale University Press, 1953.

38. Johnston L., Bachman J. G., O'Malley P. M. *Monitoring the Future*. Health and Human Services Dept., US Public Health Service, National Institutes of Health, National Institute of Drug Abuse, 1996.

39. Levine A., Cureton J. S. *When Hope and Fear Collide: A Portrait of Today's College Student.* San Francisco: Jossey-Bass, 1998.

40. *Daedalus.* Distinctively American: The residential liberal arts colleges. Winter 1999.

41. Green M. *The Adventurous Male: Chapters in the History of the White Male Mind.* University Park, PA: The Pennsylvania State University Press, 1993.

42. Adams C. E., Nagoshi C. T. Changes over one semester in drinking game playing and alcohol use and problems in a college sample. *Subst Abuse.* 1999, 20(2):97–106.

43. Horowitz H. L. *Campus Life: Undergraduate Cultures from the End of the Eighteenth Century to the Present.* Chicago: University of Chicago Press, 1987.

44. Nuwer H. *Wrongs of Passage: Fraternities, Sororities, Hazing, and Binge Drinking.* Bloomington, IN: Indiana University Press, 1999.

45. Rotundo E. A. *American Manhood: Transformations in Masculinity from the Revolution to the Modern Era.* New York: HarperCollins, 1993.

46. Lyman P. The fraternal bond as a joking relationship. In: Kimmel M. S., ed. *Changing Men: New Directions in Research on Men and Masculinity.* Newbury Park, CA: Sage, 1987.

47. Gold J., Neururer J., Miller M. Disenfranchised grief among first-semester male university students: Implications for systemic and individual interventions. *Journal of the First Year Experience.* 2000, 12(1):7–27.

48. Burda P. C., Tushup R. J., Hackman P. S. Masculinity and social support in alcoholic men. *Journal of Men's Studies.* 1992, 1(2):187–193.

49. Johnson T. J., Hamilton S., Sheets V. L. College students' self-reported reasons for playing drinking games. *Addict Behav.* 1999, 24(2):279–286.

50. Wechsler H., Dowdall G. W., Maener G., Gledhill-Hoyt J., Lee H. Changes in binge drinking and related problems among American college students between 1993 and 1997. *J Am Coll Health.* 1998, 47:57–68.

51. Hoekema D. A. *Campus Rules and Moral Community: In Place of In Loco Parentis.* Lanham, MD: Rowman & Littlefield, 1994.

52. Myers P. L. Sources and configurations of institutional denial. *Employee Assistance Quarterly.* 1990, 5(3):43–53.

53. Berkowitz, A. D. From reactive to proactive prevention: Promoting an ecology of health on campus. In: Rivers P. C., Shore E. R., eds. *Substance Abuse on Campus: A Handbook for College and University Personnel.* Westport, CT: Greenwood Press, 1997.

54. Perkins H. W. Confronting misperceptions of peer drug use norms among college students: An alternative approach for alcohol and other drug education programs. In: *The Higher Education Leaders/Peer Network Peer Prevention Resource Manual.* US Dept. of Education, FIPSE Drug Prevention Program, 1991.

55. Perkins H. W., Wechsler H. Variation in perceived college drinking norms and its impact on alcohol abuse: A nationwide study. *Journal of Drug Issues.* 1996, 26(4):961–974.

56. Fabiano P. M., McKinney G. R., Hyun Y.-R., Mertz H. K., Rhoads K. Lifestyles, 1998: Patterns of alcohol and drug consumption and consequences among Western Washington University students—An extended executive study. *Focus: A Research Summary.* 1999, 4(3):1–8.

57. Haines M. *A Social Norms Approach to Preventing Binge Drinking at Colleges and Universities.* Newton, MA: The Higher Education Center for Alcohol and Other Drug Prevention, 1998.

58. Prentice D. A., Miller D. T. Pluralistic ignorance and alcohol use on campus: Some consequences of misperceiving the social norms. *J Pers Soc Psychol.* 1993, 65:243–256.

59. Berkowitz A. D. A model acquaintance rape prevention program for men. In: Berkowitz A. D., ed. *Men and Rape: Theory, Research, and Prevention Education in Higher Education.* San Francisco: Jossey-Bass, 1994.

60. Berkowitz A. D. Applications of social norms theory to other health and social justice issues. Paper presented at: Annual Social Norms Conference. July 28–30, 1999, Big Sky, Mont.

61. Postman N., Nystrom C., Strate L., Weingartner C. *Myths, Men, and Beer: An Analysis of Beer Commercials on Broadcast Television, 1987.* Washington, DC: AAA Foundation for Traffic Safety, undated.

62. Courtenay W. H. Engendering health: A social constructionist examination of men's health beliefs and behaviors. *Psychology of Men and Masculinity.* In press.

63. Wechsler H., Kelley K., Weitzman E. R., San Giovanni J. P., Seebring M. What colleges are doing about student binge drinking: A survey of college administrators. (March 2000)

http://www.hsph.Harvard.edu/cas/test/alcohol/surveyrpt.shtm/.

64. Scher M., Steven M., Good G., Eichenfield G. A. *Handbook of Counseling and Psychotherapy with Men.* Newbury Park, CA: Sage, 1987.

65. Moore D., Leafgren F., eds. *Problem Solving Strategies and Intervention for Men in Conflict.* Alexandria, VA: American Association for Counseling and Development, 1990.

66. Levant R. F., Pollack, W. S., eds. *A New Psychology of Men.* New York: Basic, 1995.

67. Mahalik M. R. Incorporating a gender role strain perspective in assessing and treating men's cog-

nitive distortions. *Professional Psychology: Research and Practice.* 1999, 30(4):333–340.

68. Capraro R. L. Disconnected lives: Men, masculinity, and rape prevention. In: Berkowitz A. D., ed. *Men and Rape: Theory, Research, and Prevention Programs in Higher Education.* San Francisco: Jossey-Bass, 1994.

69. Helms J. An Update of Helms' *White and People of Color Racial Identity Models.* In: Ponterretto J., et al., eds. *Handbook of Multicultural Counseling.* Newbury Park, CA: Sage, 1995.

Kirby D. Schroeder

Hard Corps: How to End Sexual Assault at Military Academies

In April, I returned to the rainy Vermont campus of Norwich University, the nation's oldest private military college and birthplace of the R.O.T.C. program, which I'd attended as a cadet nearly three years before. The annual Junior Ring Ceremony was scheduled to take place in two short days, and three years' worth of anticipation was about to be released in a barrage of blank 75mm Pack Howitzer shells, the presentation of a treasure trove of enormous glittering rings, a six-hour dance in Plumely Armory, and by some long-awaited off-campus comradery. The members of the freshman "Rook" platoon with whom I'd shared the first few months of my cadet experience—the two dozen men and women of Golf Company, Second Platoon, Class of 2004—had rented a condo for the weekend in the ski-resort town of Rutland about an hour's drive south of campus—along with several other Norwich platoons. On Saturday night, proudly sporting their new rings and after dancing at the ball, most of the platoon gathered there.

At some point in the night, one of the men from my platoon wandered over to another platoon's condo to hang out. While there, Cadet "Garcia" had been opening various doors, drunkenly searching for a bathroom, when he came across a young woman he didn't recognize, passed out on a bed in the dark, alone. He lay down next to her and started to touch her sexually. As it happened, she was not deeply unconscious—only snoozing—and she woke up to discover that the

man accosting her was an intoxicated stranger and not her cadet husband. She called out for her husband who immediately phoned the police, and within an hour the local authorities had arrived to arrest Garcia on a sexual assault charge.

At Norwich, as at any military college, rumors travel faster than a 30 caliber round. Two of my Rook buddies decided to host a "Rookie Meeting" in their room the following night, and called everyone from our platoon on campus to attend. No one missed the meeting who could have been there. About 15 of us assembled in the two-person room, closed the door, and began to talk. It was a sobering conversation; if Garcia's attitudes and behavior towards women had been unique within the platoon, we could simply have condemned him and moved on. But they were not: I had heard cadets tell stories in the past about sex with passed-out or intoxicated women, stories which were meant to be humorous. The men in these incidents may have understood that such behavior was morally suspect, but they certainly wouldn't have called it rape. Faced with Garcia's arrest for an otherwise seemingly trivial act, we started to confront our own complicity. One of the men present had the courage to put it this way: "The fact is, there are probably four of you here that I would trust to be in a room alone with my sister. And I hate that—I *hate* that about us." I could see some of the men glancing around the room as he said this, forming their own short mental tallies of those in whom they would dare place such a trust. We may have all been "buddies," but we also knew that not all our buddies shared the same set of values when it came to sexual decision-making and the understanding of what constitutes a sexual assault.

It would have been too awkward for any of us to have shared the names on our lists with each other, but I like to think my buddies' lists would have included my name. I was a full-time graduate student in the department of sociology at the University of Chicago when, with the support of the Norwich administration and the notification of its Corps of Cadets, I had enrolled as a 30-year-old freshman recruit in the fall of 2000. I was to have the same experiences there as all other cadets while gathering material for my dissertation on gender, institutions, and emotion management. The Housing Office found me a compatible 17-year-old roommate with whom I would share living space in the barracks. I participated in the Navy R.O.T.C. program and attended undergraduate classes, and on the night of Dec. 11, 2000, I was recognized as a Norwich cadet along with the rest of the Class of 2004 in a ceremony which was genuinely one of the proudest moments of my adult life. As a doctoral student, I was nicknamed "Doc," and I became a part of the corps' social fabric. But like many cadets I also grew deeply ambivalent about Norwich: I loved the corps, but behavior like Garcia's was one of the things I hated also. It was a malignancy within male-cadet identity.

The general public has only recently been made aware of the degree of the sexual-assault problem within military academies, a problem which administrators have been confronting since the academies decided to enroll women in 1976. This past spring, a female cadet at the Air Force Academy in Colorado Springs told authorities she had been assaulted outside the campus gymnasium. The case was well publicized, and other victims began to come forward; the Air Force Academy is now confronting claims by 61 current and former cadets that they were sexually assaulted while they were enrolled at the school over the past 20 years. The male cadets in these scenarios engaged in sexual blackmail, systematically abused the cadet power structure, and used alcohol to make their victims pass out before taking

advantage of them. Air Force officials at the Academy who reviewed these claims ultimately decided that only a slim minority warranted any action under the Uniform Code of Military Justice, and many of the cases that passed this test resulted in only administrative forms of punishment for the attackers. The charges triggered an investigation by the Department of Defense's Inspector General whose report, issued last month, revealed a gruesome litany of rapes at the academy. Over the last 20 years, the IG found, 12 percent of all female cadets enrolled there had been raped. Worse, the IG's report noted that the Academy's administration had ignored the problems; for the first 20 years of gender integration the Air Force Academy did not even maintain records of reported assaults.

The Air Force Academy scandals have received an extensive public airing, and Sens. Wayne Allard (R-Colo.) and Patty Murray (D-Wash.) have successfully pressed for some reforms, from character development training to improved night-time monitoring of cadet behavior; negligent commanders have already been replaced. These are necessary and positive steps, but by themselves they may still prove inadequate because they miss a crucial point: The real root of the pervasive sexual assault problems of military academies lies not with the administration or with the programs it implements, but within the minds of the cadets themselves.

The military academies have integrated women into their cadet corps, but they have yet to produce a corresponding change in the essential nature of the corps—its values, its ideals, and its behavior. As I saw at Norwich, cadet culture is defined by an amplified masculinity whose more noble values—service to one's country, performance of duty under pressure, and the emphasis of team success over personal achievement—are sometimes offset by chronic patterns of rule-breaking, gratuitous physical abuse, and drinking to the point of self-oblivion. Serious change in the military academies will only be possible when administrators confront that aspect of cadet culture itself which promotes anachronistic ideas of gender-relations and undermines administrative efforts to reform them.

Made to Be Broken

The freshman year at any military college is designed to be a test of physical, mental, and emotional limits. The Class of 2004 began its freshman year at Norwich by standing in a tense and silent formation on the campus Upper Parade Ground dressed in the mandatory "Rookie storm" uniform: black shoes, tan slacks, white dress t-shirt, black neck tie, and maroon baseball cap embroidered with the word "ROOK" in large gold letters. Soon, AC/DC's "Hell's Bells" began to toll slowly and ominously through the campus loudspeakers. As the 12th toll sounded, the Norwich artillery unit fired a jarring cannon blast that signaled the arrival of a swarm of upperclassmen instructors called "cadre." They poured out of the barracks and began the process of adversative training which would make life in my platoon extremely difficult. The nine men and one woman assigned to train Golf Company became both our deeply respected leaders and our ruthlessly hostile enemies. They put us to bed by kicking our garbage cans into our rooms, and woke us up by pounding on our doors with clenched fists.

The Corps of Cadets at Norwich consists of about 1,000 individuals, approximately 15 percent of them female and virtually all between the ages of 17 and 23. It is overwhelmingly white, though 20 percent of my own platoon was native Spanish speaking. Alcohol consumption was par for the course, though a few members of my own platoon were avowed non-drinkers. The men and women who make up the corps live on the Norwich campus in barracks rooms next to each other, attend academic classes together, and conduct all military training together. Signs on the doors of the latrines warning of a "Class-One Offense" signal the only place where the corps mandates gender segregation, but adherence to even this regulation is sometimes lax. Norwich was the nation's first military school to admit women to its Corps of Cadets, and in '97 became the first to have a female cadet as its Regimental Commander. If there is a vanguard in gender relations among military schools, Norwich is it.

Which is not to say that things at Norwich are gender-neutral or that its women do not feel the strains of tokenism. Male cadets still teach each other by example that it is okay to approach an unconscious, possibly drunk woman and attempt to have sex with her. In this sense, Garcia had been following a script he had come to believe was acceptable. But Garcia was just clumsy enough to pick a married woman and the wife of another cadet as his target. I am certain he thought he had not done anything unusual or wrong until the moment the police arrived and placed him in custody, and I can imagine him deeply confused as they escorted him away for committing a sexual assault.

That April, my platoon still had four of its original six women (one woman left at the end of her first week as a recruit, saying that she believed Rookdom would interfere with her ability to perform academically; another left at the end of the first semester citing a number of issues including a damaged ankle). As the details of the assault in Rutland became clear, I wondered what these women might say given the opportunity to address their wayward Rook Brothers. But during the Rookie Meeting, all four of the women carefully kept quiet, and only while thinking about this weeks afterwards did I feel I accurately understood why: military school is not a place that welcomes feminist critiques of inappropriate male behavior. Further, women, by virtue of their gender, are always at risk of becoming labeled as disruptive and confrontational and—even worse—"feminist" if they indicate that they disapprove of the things the men around them do. Instead, they learn to shake their heads in silence because the social costs of speaking up are simply too large: becoming ostracized at military school is a social death sentence for men and women alike. When the *men* start speaking up—when they as a class finally start saying those things which the women cannot—then the climate for change becomes hospitable.

Of course, assaults like those at Norwich and the Air Force Academy are not unique to military schools. Date rape is endemic to colleges of every size and academic purpose, and it frequently goes hand in hand with alcohol: Young men and women get together and drink, inhibitions and good judgment succumb to desire, and seemingly innocent gestures of attraction become grounds for stained reputations and expulsions. What is different in the military school setting, however, is the extent to which such a script is emphasized and validated: Masculinity is often defined in part by sexual performance, and military schools offer young men the opportunity for masculine certification like few other institutions. They officially test military bearing, the limits of strength and speed, the ability to perform under enormous pressure, and skill at concealing emotions (both negative and positive). This package also includes an unofficial emphasis on other, less-savory aspects of masculinity, including demonstrations of heterosexual conquest.

The administration at Norwich fights a steady battle against the behavior of many of its cadets. Despite the severe consequences for possession, the campus floats on a contraband bed of alcohol. Cadets regularly put themselves, their undergraduate careers, and their commissions as officers on the line by indulging in it. For the first "Violation of the Alcohol Policy" (abbreviated "V.A.P." and called "a vap") Norwich cadets are subject to several weeks of close military confinement, loss of all cadet rank, and more than two dozen tours: each tour is one hour of monotonous pacing on the Campus Upper Parade Ground while wearing a class-A uniform and bearing a nine-pound M-14 rifle at right-shoulder arms. If caught twice, a cadet faces dismissal from the school and loss of federal commission. Every year, some cadets take these chances and lose: During my freshman experience, two of the campus' five notorious Command Sergeants Major (the campus' highest ranking juniors and the bulldogs of the corps) were humiliatingly demoted after one such incident, and they were neither the first nor the last cadets demoted that year. The awkward-

ness of their demotion did more to foster a sense of bitterness between the corps and the administration, however, than it did to affect the consumption of alcohol.

As with alcohol, so with sex: At the end of my first week of freshman training, my cadre explicitly told my platoon that sex between platoon members was a strictly forbidden act, as was sex between freshmen and upperclassmen—within a month, both rules had been broken. The intention of those involved was to circumvent the seemingly frivolous rule, and since cadet life is replete with such rules, cadets quickly become resourceful at circumventing them.

Norwich University maintains on its staff a Title IX coordinator whose full-time job is to monitor and advise the school on its gender environment. However, unlike many members of the administration, the woman who held this position during my tenure as a cadet had never served in the military, did not wear a uniform, was not involved in any of the physical aspects of cadet training, and was manifestly unfamiliar with cadet values and culture. In a setting where symbols of authority have enormous importance, she appeared in the minds of the cadets to lack them all: They were required to listen to her lectures on equal opportunity and gender equality, but did so with low-voiced, mocking incredulity and complete dismissal. Contrast her to another campus figure of that year, the man who headed the Norwich Navy/Marine Corps R.O.T.C. department. This colonel's impeccable uniform, combat service in the Marines, truly superhuman physicality in spite of his near-retirement age, and awe-inspiring presence made him a campus figure of mythical proportions known to the entire corps—he was deeply respected, honored, even feared, and when he spoke cadets would listen with rapt attention. He was the antithesis of the Title IX coordinator.

Eyes Wide Shut

There are two ways the academies can facilitate changes in cadet culture: They can seek to change the kind of people they choose to admit, and they can try to modify the socialization experience of those who enter. Obviously, arriving at a one-to-one ratio of men to women would have dramatic effects, but the fact is only a small number of women are interested in military education—even at Norwich, with its tradition of progressive attitudes towards women and the 1995 implementation of an innovative recruitment campaign targeted at potential female candidates. Preventative education programs and sexual-assault awareness training can have some impact, but only if handled sensitively and carried out by respected senior officials.

Useful examples from other American institutions that have endured a similarly rough transition away from all-male environments are sparse, in large part because there are few other settings like military universities which are so defined by a set of masculine values. Police and fire departments, however, may represent the closest approximations: Their experiences in the 1970s and 1980s, while not promising certain success, suggest why at least some of these institutions have been able to change their cultures while others have not.

One famous example comes from the Los Angeles County Sheriff's Department. Despite a 1993 court order to change unprofessional working conditions in the department, four years later the LASD was still found to have done little or nothing to correct them. One of the plaintiff's attorneys in the case even suggested that the order's only effect was to generate increased tension and resentment between male and female officers. Another called the court order an "abysmal failure." Subsequent incidents where female deputies had become the subject of rude jokes and ridicule and had found sex toys and pornographic Polaroids in their patrol cars were clear indications that the underlying masculine culture had not changed. Fire departments around the country have faced similar hurdles, but a study done by the RAND Corporation in 1993 found that the smooth integration of female firefighters depended in large part upon the vocal and public leadership

of the department's Chief Officers, and sexual harassment appeared to be more frequent in those departments that had not seen forceful advocacy from their leadership.

While these strategies offer some guidance, however, the solution for military colleges is unlikely to be as intuitive. Certainly the most senior administrators must emphatically and repeatedly tell their cadets that sexual assaults will not be tolerated, and must consistently impose appropriate punishments on offenders, but simply making these penalties more severe may have small effect on the actual problems, though the fair and even evaluation of individual claims of assault would be a start—something which was not practiced in the past by the now-replaced leadership at the Air Force Academy.

Officers and Gentlemen

The search for the solution to the problem begins with an understanding of the dual university-leadership structures of adult administrators and the upperclassmen who often wield vast but subtle influence. An important part of the creed of military schools holds that the interaction between more senior and more junior cadets is what models and prepares them for commissioned life in the military, but this relationship also allows cadets to resist administrative efforts to alter the nature of the corps. When the administration tells students that drinking is not permitted, the cadets hear from upperclassmen that there is a long tradition of delicately circumventing this particular rule; when the administration tells students that sexual assault is unacceptable, they hear from juniors and seniors that having sex with passed-out girls is actually okay. In both of these cases the cadets often adopt, through a simple logic, older peers rather than administrators as the acceptable model for their own understanding of what it means to be a cadet.

Exclusive administrative use of new carrot-and-stick strategies to change such behaviors from the top down is likely to lead to a dead end. Educational seminars and training sessions designed to initiate changes in behavior from the bottom up will hit resistance from a cadet culture which has its own deeply held masculine values and an established and efficient system for transmitting them. The objective needs to be to turn cadets into gentlemen—gentlemen who do not engage in blind inebriation as a form of entertainment and who do not consider women to be objects of male sexual convenience. But while cadets may often ignore those regulations which conflict with the extant masculine value system, they also regularly adopt formally prescribed yet functionally useless behaviors of cadet life with enthusiasm. One of these prescriptions is actually a ritualistic *pro*-scription involving some red bricks.

Set flush into the ground directly in front of the entrance to the 1993 Kreitzberg Library on the Norwich campus is a small collection of red bricks arranged in a square. During Rook Week, the cadre of each freshman platoon bring their charges to these bricks and explain that they are all that is left of the Old South Barracks. The cadre also explain that no cadet entering or leaving the library ever deliberately steps on these bricks, and if one watches cadets leave or enter the library at any hour of the day or night, in a group or alone, Norwich cadets always step around the bricks. There are no consequences for failing to do so, no regulation protecting the bricks, and a cadet whose foot slips is unlikely to be chastised by his peers. All that protects the bricks is the fact that Norwich cadets are not supposed to step on them—and the behavior is self-reinforcing because it has

become part of the definition of what it means to be a cadet at Norwich.

Respect for bricks is not the same as respect for women or respect for sexual boundaries, but the behavior suggests a crucial transferability. If the definition of a cadet can be remade to actually include such values rather than merely to render them lip service, then the incidence of sexual assault in military schools can only go down.

On the Monday after the Junior Ring Ball, I packed my bags and got ready to leave Norwich. While my two Rook buddies were in class, I combed the room for stray clothing and misplaced toiletries. As I did this, I suddenly realized that the decor of the room had experienced a small but critical change—a change that forced me to smile amidst all the weekend's sadness and drama. And as I left the room, I felt a renewed sense of hope, an unanticipated confirmation that the Norwich Corps of Cadets is still worth loving in spite of its many problems, that regardless all of the machismo, the men of my platoon—many of whom will become U.S. officers within the next year—are fully capable of introspection and change with respect to how they view women. And all I could think as I walked to my car was, *He figured it out! He actually figured it out!* Sometime earlier in the day, in my absence and with no encouragement from me, one of my buddies had taken down the picture of the woman in uniform and lingerie which had been taped to his wall locker, and had replaced it with a picture of his swim team.

Jason Schultz

The Antirape Rules

"This will probably offend you," she said, looking down for a moment, "but I need to ask you something." She clenched her hands together in a small ball as she leaned back against the headboard of my bed and took a deep breath. "I need to know why it doesn't bother you." Her eyes reopened and looked to me for answers. My lips pursed and separated.

I thought back to other conversations I'd had like this one. Six years back. You'd think that after half a decade of educating, counseling, and supporting survivors that you've heard everything—every story, every question, every nightmare. But this was a new one. "Well," I said, "it doesn't bother me because I didn't do it. And because letting it bother me would make us both victims of his attack. It doesn't mean I don't hate him. It means I know the difference between hating him and hating you because of what he did to you."

She stared back at me. "You probably don't believe that," I continued. "But it's the truth and it's the same answer I'm going to give you every time you ask. It may not help you feel any better, and that's fine because I'm not saying it to make you feel better. You're going to have to figure out how to believe me. It's my job to understand how you feel and yours to believe that I care."

Ever since I became a rape educator in 1990, I've been acutely aware of the impact of violence against women in my life. On an external level, I now worry much more about my female friends and family. I always try to offer them a ride or walk home. I always wait for them to get inside safely before driving away. I give way to women on the street at night. I make sure other men know I'm watching when they make their moves.

On a more personal level, I've felt the pain of being mistrusted for no good reason, the frustration when past hurts affect present attempts at intimacy, the disbelief when cycles of violence repeat themselves. I've felt the emotional impact of rape in my relationships, my friendships, even my family.

The Cascade Effect

The first time is always the worst. That cold, hard realization of the effect of rape. The first woman ever to tell me she was raped was a good friend of mine in college. We were both in our first semester at Duke University, giddy with excitement over the future and full of arrogance about our newfound college independence. "No more curfews!" we would shout, fantasizing about all the rules we would break and trouble we would cause.

Eight weeks into the semester, there was a knock at my door. I opened it and in she collapsed, sobbing. She crawled over to my futon and curled up in a shell. "What's wrong?" I asked. "He raped me tonight" was all she could murmur.

In the following months I learned what rape does to friendship. The anger, the sadness, the hurt—it all came flooding out. I tried every method of support I could think of—the strong shoulder to cry on, the overprotective brother, the vindictive vigilante. Nothing changed how she felt. "How can I trust you?" she would blurt out in private. "You could be just like him."

"You could be just like him." Those words echo in my ears every time I talk to men about rape and every time I hear them talk about it. "But I'm not a rapist!" they'll say—all the words that I once said myself. They're right, of course. They're always right. But that's the horror of rape. It doesn't change anything. It doesn't make a difference to a survivor that you're not a rapist. They simply don't care.

I joined the Duke Acquaintance Rape Education Program. I felt stronger, more in control. I learned what caused rape: patriarchy, socialization, cycles of violence. I also felt in control of my own emotions. I knew that when survivors talked to me that it wasn't my fault—I hadn't caused their pain. I was helping them. I was part of the solution, not part of the problem.

But they just kept on coming. A friend . . . a classmate . . . a fellow editor at the student newspaper. Someone I met at a party. Someone I hooked up with after a basketball game. My senior-year girlfriend. Her roommate. The numbers started to build and so did the horrors. Child sexual abuse, STDs, gang rape. I started to keep count. The Number kept growing. All the time I kept thinking and saying to myself, "It's okay. You're helping them. You're making a difference."

And I was. I received countless thank-yous from people I helped and from others as well—faculty in the women's studies department, campus administrators who had their hands tied by the legal department. But no matter how hard I tried to help, no matter how much I listened, The Number kept growing. Sisters, old friends from high school, the cab driver on my way home for Thanksgiving. How? I would wonder. How can we live in a world where every woman I meet has been tortured in this way?

In some ways it was a perverse high. I was the savior. I was the good guy. I heard their stories and believed them. If only more men could be like me, I would think to myself, there wouldn't be all this hurt and madness.

December of my senior year, I lost it. I called up a close friend of mine—someone with whom I had shared much of my adolescent and adult life, someone with whom I could break the rules. "I need to ask you a question," I prefaced. "It's going to sound weird and might possibly embarrass you, but I need to know if you've ever been raped." I went on for a minute explaining what was happening to me, how all the violence in the lives of the people around me was overwhelming my sense of hope.

"Jason," she interrupted. "I have *never* been raped. By anyone. Anytime in my life." My stomach relaxed and the air slowly left my chest in relief. "Thank you," I said. "Thank you so much."

I have no idea how one learns to live with being raped. I can't even imagine what it means to carry that around with you. But I know what it means to live with and care for people who have been raped. I know the frantic phone calls, the frustration of starting over, the joy of witnessing recovery. I know that it's hard to be a man and care for women who've been raped. I know how not to blame myself and not to blame them.

As part of the national antirape movement, I've spent the last eight years talking about sexual violence, mostly on college campuses and mostly to men. Looking back on that now, I realize that we don't need to simply educate men on how not to rape. The reality is that most of us don't rape women. But we do need to educate all men on how to live with, love, care for, and communicate with survivors. We need to share the rules we've learned.

The Antirape Rules

When I first heard of *The Rules,* I laughed. *The Rules: Time-Tested Secrets for Capturing the Heart of Mr. Right* was a surprising best-seller self-help book that gave women traditional and prefeminist guidelines for snagging men. Encouraging mind games, *The Rules* include such tidbits as "Let him take the lead," and "Don't call him." What a ridiculous idea, I thought. How could anyone imagine finding the key to a successful relationship in this semblance of pop-cult grocery-store-line pocket trash? I figured the hype about the book was simply the logical outcome of media conspiracy, lack of education, and yet another market built on women's insecurities. Yet as many of us do, I forced myself to read *The Rules,* just to be sure.

I pretty much found what I suspected. Manipulative psychobabble and social conditioning. There were, of course, a few feminist intonations about the "modern girl" and the need to be independent in one's life. But these were couched in the frantic language of the man-crazy woman and the "horror" of being unmarried.

So why was this book selling? I wandered about, asking various female friends. They gave me three reasons: (1) Despite all our good wishes about bicycles and fish, many women *are* frustrated with their attempts to find the right guy; (2) despite the stereotypes, every woman I talked to knew at least one man whom they thought would respond to *The Rules;* and (3) even if you completely disagree with *The Rules,* you still want to read it as a gut check—just to make sure you're still not doing anything wrong.

So while the content of *The Rules* disturbed me, the brilliance of the approach to writing it intrigued me. Then it clicked. Rules . . . that's what men need—not on how to find the right woman (well, maybe, but that's more like a book instead of an essay), but for handling the issue of rape— a topic that makes men about as neurotic as women are made about marriage.

Where to Start

That being said, starting to learn about rape is almost always weird for men. There are so many subtle moments and brief insights that we all need to learn. But every journey starts with a single

step, or four in this case. Below are several experiences and "rules" that have helped me support survivors of sexual assault in my own life. I offer them up in the hope that we all will start to think about what "rules" truly help us care for, and about, each other.

Rule #1: Believe the Hype

As much of a cliché as it sounds, you probably know someone who has been raped. They may have told you by now or not, but sooner or later they will. When they do, they will most likely disclose information to you in doses. Maybe just the fact that it happened. Maybe the story leading up to it. They may even disguise it as bad sex or a drunken blur. Whatever they do when they tell you, there's one rule to follow: Don't reject them.

Rape centers on control. After someone is assaulted, it often takes great effort to regain control of her or his life. One of the quickest ways to do this is to control who knows about the rape and what they know about it. That is why it is often difficult to get survivors to talk to the police or a doctor or even answer their phone. There are many other reasons why survivors don't tell anyone, such as fear of retaliation, desire to put it behind them and move on, and so on. But the need to control who knows about the rape is often a primary concern. (Hence the need for rape crisis centers to maintain confidentiality.)

When a survivor tells you about her rape, she is beginning to trust again. She is reaching out to you with one of the few parts of her life that she does feel control over. When she does this, she generally wants two things: (1) to have you believe her, and (2) to have you accept her. Often a survivor's worst fear is that telling someone about the rape will trigger another attack or betrayal, this time a verbal or emotional one.

Marilyn Van Derbur Atler, an incest survivor and former Miss America, once talked at Duke about disclosing her survivor status on an airplane. She was sitting next to a businessman, reading a magazine, when he struck up a conversation with her. At one point in the conversation, he mentioned his occupation. He then proceeded to ask her what she did. "I talk about how I survived child sexual abuse," she replied. As you can imagine, the man was struck silent by her comment.

After taking a moment to compose himself, though, he asked a question I suspect most men think about when a survivor discloses to them: "How should one respond to that?" he asked her.

Ms. Van Derbur Atler calmly looked back at him and said, "You say 'I'm very sorry that happened to you.' And you mean it."

Rule #2: Don't Expect Her to Change, or Try to Change Her

The knock on the door had to be Catherine. I opened it and it was. "Surprise!" she yelled, and marched into the room with not one man in tow, but two—one on each arm. "This is Kevin; and this is Dave! Aren't they cute?" she breathed into my face, fresh and full of keg beer. My heart sank.

"Yeah, I suppose they are. Don't you think you're . . . um . . . a little out of it to be hooking up with two guys?" I asked, regretting each word as I spoke.

"Fuck you," she retorted. "I'm a big girl. I'm in control. I'll do whatever I want." She turned around, pushed the two men out the door, and slammed it behind her.

The next afternoon she came to apologize. We both knew she was having a tough time dating again after the rape, especially on campus. She admitted that last night she had been scared of being alone with her dates and said that she came by my room with the hope that I would intervene. I told her that I can't intervene—that part of being supportive is following her lead and letting her run her own life again, not simply transferring control to me.

I asked her why she chose Kevin and Dave. "They don't particularly seem your type," I said, still trying to tread cautiously. Catherine had always gone for more introverted guys as long as I had known her. She started to list a number of

excuses: She was turning over a new leaf. They liked her, so why not? She didn't care who she hooked up with anymore.

Finally, she told the truth. "I knew what they wanted," she said. "I knew they wanted sex, so I knew there wouldn't be any surprises. No rape. No force. No betrayal. I knew that if I took the initiative with them that I would be in control and never out of it. I wouldn't have to be afraid that it would happen again." She leaned against the wall, picking off pieces of paint with her fingernails. "I just can't take that risk anymore."

I sat at my desk. I had no idea what to say. "You'll figure it out," I responded.

Watching survivors make dumb decisions and take horrible risks is probably the most frustrating part of being there for them. When Catherine left with the two men, it took every ounce of self-control not to run after her and make sure she wasn't going to be attacked again. But the number-one rule with survivors is to let them forge their own recovery. Catherine also later admitted that she had been testing me in some ways by bringing the men home—to see if I would trust her. I've learned time and time again to be honest with survivors about how I feel—to express disappointment, concern, anger, fear—but ultimately to leave the decisions up to them. Right or wrong, they will need you as a friend the next day more than a savior the night before.

Rule #3: Ask for It

"I've been thinking about kissing you all night," I said.

"Really?" she asked whimsically, testing the waters a bit more.

"And then touching you. All over."

The wind whistled past our ears as we headed back to the hotel. A sudden silence arose between us. "I hope that's okay," I added.

"Sure," she said. "I just . . . well—no one's ever said that to me so far in advance before." She blushed a little. "Usually we're already drunk and naked and at least somewhere near the bed."

I laughed. "Well, I figured it'd be better to make my intentions clear before we got in the elevator. That way you could decide what floor to get off on . . . so to speak." We laughed again, and I felt the tension ease a bit. I opened the outside door for her and we scurried into the lobby.

"So it's really my choice?"

"Yeah," I replied.

She reached out with one hand for the elevator button, then reached with the other for my arm. She smiled as we waited for the doors to open.

Much has been said about supposed politically correct sex: that asking for consent is unsexy, that talking ruins the mood. And for the most part, I agree—if that's all you do. In the midst of confronting violence, it's easy to forget about the fact that being sexy is important to both men and women, to survivors and nonsurvivors alike. Being too clinical, too cautious, or even too earnest often clashes with our fantasies about what turns us on. And no matter how many rape awareness workshops we attend or late-night dorm conversations we have, antiseptic sexual conversations will rarely hit the right spot.

Being sexy means knowing what you really want. If you truly know what you want with the other person, you'll know how to tell them you want it. And you'll also know when they want it too. Spend some time thinking about it. Fantasize about what you think will make you both happy, then take a deep breath and tell her. Style, nuance, attitude, and mystery are all still important elements of seduction. Don't lose them. Just use them in the way they were meant to be used: to elicit true desire and temptation.

Rule #4: Sometimes the Tough Thing Is the Right Thing

I stayed up very late last night, trying to clean the kitchen. It's something I do when I'm nervous—cleaning. It had been a pretty rough day, with the trip to the hospital and all. I wondered what Laura was doing right now. I thought about the hug she

had given me right before they took her to her room. "Don't disappear on me," she said, as if I were the one leaving the rest of the world behind. "Remember, I know where you live," she added as the duty nurse searched her suitcase. I nodded, turned, and walked down the hallway, hands in my pockets, eyes on the red carpet beneath my feet.

The counter was a mess. I emptied the wine bottle from the night before and dumped the ashtray. We'd decided that they probably wouldn't allow her to drink or smoke once she was inside, so we took advantage of her last night to binge a little. At one point I caught her staring at me from her seat near the windowsill, bright blue eyes flickering as she exhaled away form my face. "It really means a lot to me," she said softly, turning back toward the light. "I really don't know who else I can trust."

That was exactly twenty-four hours ago. Now she was tucked away inside the psych ward on the other side of town and I was home, loading dishes into the dishwasher. I felt a tremendous sense of relief, mixed with sadness from the separation. I thought about calling the hallway phone number she had left me. I let the thought pass. I took her last cigarette from off the counter and grabbed a match.

Helping survivors recover can hurt. Many of the men I've talked to over the years have told me about "secondary syndrome"—a condition whereby people who are close to a victim of violence begin to experience similar symptoms of post-traumatic stress disorder—almost like emotional osmosis. Lack of sleep, difficulty concentrating, and depression are a few of the common experiences.

But beyond secondary syndrome is an even greater issue for men who support survivors—our own general health and happiness. No matter how giving you are, no matter how gentle you want to be, there are limits to what any one person can offer to another. Anger, depression, and burnout can creep up on us, and before we know it, we're of little use to them or to ourselves.

The bottom line is always to know your limits and make sure you have support for yourself. Find friends to talk to about the situation. Call a help line whenever you feel like it. Take time away from the crisis. Checking Laura into the psychiatric hospital was a difficult decision for both her and me, but we agreed that she needed more help than I could ever give her. Recognizing that limit not only saved her life, but saved our friendship as well. In the end, we realized we wanted both to survive.

Eric Anderson

Orthodox and Inclusive Masculinity: Competing Masculinities among Heterosexual Men in a Feminized Terrain

This research uses 68 in-depth interviews of collegiate male cheerleaders and ethnographic field-work from four selected cheerleading teams to examine the construction of masculinity among heterosexual men in a feminized terrain. Previous studies maintain that a hegemonic process of masculine dominance and submission (Connell 1987, 1995) influences most heterosexual men in feminized arenas to bolster their masculinity through the approximation of orthodox masculine requisites, including the expression of homophobic and antifeminine-acting attitudes (Davis 1990; Majors 1990; Messner 1992; Sargent 2001; Williams 1989, 1993, 1995). This research, however, shows that men in collegiate cheerleading today exhibit two contrasting and competing forms of normative masculinity, each supported by organizational and institutional culture and each with near equal membership.

The first category of masculine performance is labeled as *orthodox*. The men categorized into this group are shown to perform masculinity in a manner consistent with previous studies of men in feminized terrain: they attempt to approximate the hegemonic form of masculinity, largely by devaluing women and gay men (Adams 1993; Davis 1990; Hanson 1995; Sargent 2001; Williams 1993, 1995). The performance of masculinity among men in this group is influenced by a number of factors, including the institutional culture of one of the two major cheerleading governing bodies, the "Orthodox Cheerleading Association."

From *Sociological Perspectives*, 48(3) pp. 337–355, 2006. Used by permission of the author.

The second category of masculine performance is labeled as *inclusive*. The men in this group view orthodox masculinity as undesirable and do not aspire to many of its tenets. Particularly important to the study of men in feminized terrain, this research shows that inclusive masculinity is based less on homophobia and antifemininity than on orthodox masculinity. Men in this group willingly embrace the feminized underpinnings of their sport and largely value their gay teammates. Notably, the construction of inclusive masculinity is influenced by the institutional culture of the other major governing cheerleading body, the "Inclusive Cheerleading Association."

Whereas previous studies of heterosexual men in feminized terrain found that men near-unanimously attempt to align themselves with orthodox masculinity, this research finds that heterosexual men in collegiate cheerleading are nearly evenly split between these two normative forms of masculine expression. The emergence of a more inclusive form of masculinity is attributed to many factors, including the structure of the sport; the reduction of cultural, institutional, and organizational homophobia; and the resocialization of men into a gender-integrated sport.

Background

David and Brannon (1976: 12) have categorized four basic tenets that "seem to comprise the core requirements" of American masculinity. These include (1) No sissy stuff; (2) Be a big wheel; (3)

Be a sturdy oak; and (4) Give 'em hell. While all four rules are important in understanding the construction and stratification of masculine power and privilege, it is the *no sissy stuff* principle about which this research is mostly concerned. This is because there is a durable sociological understanding that contemporary masculinity is largely based in opposition to femininity (Bourdieu 2001; Chodorow 1978; Connell 1987; David and Brannon 1976; Dellinger 2004; Frye 1983; Gilmore 1990; Kimmel 1996, 2004; Lorber 1994; Lucal 1999; West and Zimmerman 1987). Kimmel (2004: 97) says, "While different groups of men may disagree about other traits and their significance in gender definitions, the antifemininity component of masculinity is perhaps the single dominant and universal characteristic."

The marginalization of men in feminine fields had been shown effective in deterring heterosexual men from engaging in these settings (Adams 1993; Davis 1990; Sargent 2001; Williams 1993, 1995), perhaps because men who enter these fields find their sexuality publicly scrutinized (Martin and Collinson 1999). Accordingly, it has also been shown that North American masculinity is based in a disassociation from homosexuality (Chauncey 1995; Gorer 1964; Halperin 1989; Kimmel 1994; Lancaster 1988; Plummer 2001; Pollack 1998), something particularly true to athletic settings (Adams 1993; Anderson 2005; Pronger 1990). When one adds homophobia to David and Brannon's (1976) tenets, it produces an orthodox form of masculinity. Orthodox masculinity is reflected in, and reproduced through, an institutionalized, gender-segregated, and highly competitive sporting culture in North America (Anderson 2005; Burstyn 1999).

Previous investigations into the social construction of masculinities have shown a relationship between the dominant form of masculine expression and subordinate forms (Anderson 2002; Connell 1987, 1995; Gramsci 1971; Messner 1992). Connell (1995: 77) has described hegemonic masculinity as a social process in which one form of institutionalized masculinity is "culturally exalted" above all others. Key to understanding the operation of hegemony in relationship to masculinity, Connell (1987, 1995) maintains that most men exhibiting a subordinate form of masculinity actually desire to obtain the hegemonic form. Essentially, the process of hegemony influences the oppressed to maintain the rightfulness or naturalization of their oppression. Indeed, it is this aspiration that makes the process hegemonic (Gramsci 1971). Thus, if hegemony applies to masculinity, one would expect most who transgress masculine-defined boundaries to preserve, if not inflate, their position by adopting as many tenets of orthodox masculinity as possible. These identity management techniques might include (1) being homophobic, (2) devaluing femininity, (3) increasing masculine bravado, and (4) claiming masculine space within the larger feminized arena.

Examinations of feminized terrain have consistently shown men to approximate orthodox masculinity and to justify their transgression as consistent with hegemonic expectations of masculinity (Adams 1993; Anderson 2002; Davis 1990; Klein 1993; Majors 1990; Williams 1993, 1995). For example, men who occupy feminized space are quick in defending their transgressions as being consistent within normative boundaries of orthodox masculinity, maintaining that they have not transgressed masculine acceptability but rather that the space has been inappropriately gendered. Or, if men do acknowledge the feminine underpinnings of their field, they attempt to select a particular role within that space and define it as masculine (Davis 1990; McGuffey and Rich 1999; Sargent 2001; Williams 1993, 1995). Accordingly, heterosexual male cheerleaders have been shown to emphasize that certain tasks within cheerleading (such as lifting women above their heads) are masculine, believing that women lack the strength to perform this task as well as men. Conversely, they designate other tasks (such as erotic dancing) to be exclusively feminine (Davis 1990; Hanson 1995).

While the types of identity management techniques men in feminized terrain exhibit are considered to be a reflection of the social process of hegemonic masculinity (Connell 1987, 1995), it is important to clarify that hegemonic masculinity is not an archetype. "It is, rather, the masculinity that occupies the hegemonic position in a given pattern of gender relations, a position always contestable" (Connell 1995: 76). And while Connell does describe the contemporary form of hegemonic masculinity as including the tenets of homophobia and antifemininity, he does not assign a categorical label to this group. This makes it easy to erroneously conflate the process of hegemonic masculinity with an archetype of masculinity. I therefore refrain from using "hegemonic masculinity" as a categorical label; instead, it is used to describe a social process of subordination and stratification. In this research, the difference between an archetype and a social process of dominance is understood by delineating the traditionally hegemonic category of masculinity as *orthodox masculinity*. Thus, I recognize traditionally marginalized masculinities (such as gay, nonathletic, or feminine-acting men) as occupying the lower rungs of the hierarchy based in defiance to orthodox masculinity (Anderson 2005; Messner 1992, 1997).

Methods

This research uses in-depth interviews and participant observations to examine how heterosexual men in collegiate cheerleading construct masculinity through micro and macro processes (Dellinger 2004). Because cheerleading is commonly understood to be a feminized terrain, this research also examines the relationship between hegemonic processes of masculine dominance and individual agency (Dilorio 1989; Glaser and Strauss 1967) in the social construction of gendered identities. Considering that previous investigations of masculine construction in cheerleading were conducted over a decade ago, this research might also capture the effect of decreasing homophobia in recent years.

The informants are 68 self-identified heterosexual men who used to play high school football

but became collegiate cheerleaders because they were unable to make their university football teams. While a self-selection process cannot be ruled out (i.e., it is possible that men most affected by the masculinization process of football do not become cheerleaders), most of the informants reported that upon entering cheerleading, they held orthodox notions of masculinity, including sexist view and overt homophobia. The men, between 18 and 23 years of age, represent diverse regions and city sizes from throughout the United States, but the informants represent about 80% white, middle-class men, so generalizations can be made only for this group.

Orientation into the culture of collegiate cheerleading began with informal discussions with friends who were collegiate male cheerleaders and through the analysis of cheerleading web pages. Next, 12 collegiate male cheerleaders were contacted for interviews by using the member profile search on America Online, which provides a search engine for accessing the stated interests of AOL's 33 million subscribers. After conversations with these cheerleaders through instant messaging, they were asked for in-depth, taped telephone interviews. From these initial informants, snowball and theoretical sampling techniques (Corbin and Strauss 1990) were used to obtain an additional 12 interviews. The 44 informant interviews were obtained randomly at cheerleading competitions by asking potential informants if they were willing to participate in academic research. In total, 68 interviews with self-identified heterosexual male cheerleaders were transcribed and coded.

The interviews began by asking informants to discuss their life history in sport and the process by which they came into cheerleading. They were then asked about their views on homosexuality and feminine expression among men, as well as their perceptions of women's athleticism and leadership qualities. They were also asked to discuss how they maintained a heterosexual identity in cheerleading and how their identity, or identity management techniques, might vary from when they were in football. In addition to those coded and transcribed interviews, 12 informal group interviews (60 to 120 minutes) were conducted on co-ed cheerleading teams throughout the United States, some of which included women, coaches, and gay men. Men in these groups were asked about their relationships with women and gay men and about the gendered underpinnings of cheerleading.

In addition to these interviews, 300 hours of participant observation were conducted on four selected co-ed teams. These teams were solicited in advance of a major competition, and each agreed to be observed and interviewed over three- to four-day competitions, but observations also took place at practices in their home states and while socializing away from the athletic arena. Field notes (with either a micro recorder or pocket-sized memo pad) were recorded outside of their direct presence. The teams' willingness to be observed was made in part by my experience as a coach. During the analysis of this research, I maintained relationships with several heterosexual male cheerleaders (from both cheerleading institutions) and used them as key informants for understanding the complexities of cheerleading rules, maneuvers, and cultural practices.

Categorizing informants as belonging to one form of masculinity or the other was based largely on an informant's perceptions of how men and women should act and what tasks men should or should not perform within the sport of cheerleading. Categorization was also influenced by the informant's views on homosexuality and feminine-acting men. For example, athletes who expressed dislike of gay men or held antifeminine or misogynistic attitudes were grouped as orthodox cheerleaders, while those expressing support for gay men and femininity among men were classified as inclusive. Men who stigmatized the performance of certain roles within co-ed cheerleading as strictly feminine (such as erotic dancing or being thrown into the air) were classified as orthodox, and men who comfortably performed these feminine-coded roles were grouped as inclusive.

It is important to understand that there are two major competing associations that control the world of cheerleading. This research, however,

analyzes these associations only as far as they relate to collegiate cheerleading. This is not an analysis of high school or professional cheerleading. Each cheerleading association is a profit-oriented corporation that markets cheerleading instruction, merchandise, and training camps. At the collegiate level, each of these two associations maintains near equal university membership and each organizes a series of competitions leading to a national meet that draws hundreds of college teams. To protect their identities, the names of these associations have been changed to the Inclusive Cheerleading Association and the Orthodox Cheerleading Association. Since these two cheerleading associations maintain different institutionalized perspectives on gender (in collegiate cheerleading), data collection was evenly split between them.

It is also important to understand that the given names of the two cheerleading associations are intentionally conflated with the categorized forms of masculine expression found in this study. This is primarily for simplicity but also because, as one might expect, the informants of each association largely reflect the institutional creed of their governing body. Men who belonged to the Orthodox Cheerleading Association largely displayed and valued the tenets of orthodox masculinity, while the men in the Inclusive Cheerleading Association largely displayed and valued the tenets of inclusive masculinity. During the coding of the research, however, men were classified as belonging to one group of men or the other, independent of their organizational (university) or cheerleading association affiliation.

Results

Cheerleading has long evolved from the days of simply cheering for the victory of other athletic teams. Cheerleading squads today compete against each other in complex athletic performances where contestants dance, cheer, stunt, and tumble to rhythmically synchronized, high-energy music. Higher, faster, and more complicated are the hallmarks of winning squads, and these qualities demand cheerleaders (of both sexes) to be fearless acrobats who perform dangerously complicated maneuvers.

Research on cheerleading, however, shows that despite the evolution of cheerleading from the sidelines to the main stage, the sport has largely maintained its cultural ascription of femininity (Adams and Bettis 2003). Hanson (1995) says, "The overriding contemporary perception that cheerleader equals girl is reinforced by popular culture which defines it strictly in feminized terms" (p. 116). Adams and Bettis (2003) have even shown that young women who play other (masculinized) sports often participate in cheerleading as a way to counter stereotypes of their masculinization, reporting that cheerleading offered young women "a space to revel in what they called being a 'girlie girl' " (p. 84).

Men who cheer in college, however, have been shown to view themselves as being far from "girlie men." Previous studies of these men have found that they maintain themselves to be "real men": daring, heterosexual, and strong enough to hold a woman (or two) above their heads while still agile enough to perform gymnastic feats (Davis 1990; Hanson 1995). Despite the fact that the entire field is culturally feminized, many cheerleaders, of both sexes, maintain that certain tasks within the sport are actually highly masculinized activities, even if women perform the exact tasks in the all-women's division of cheerleading.

Gendering certain tasks as masculine has been credited with paving the way for more men to join cheerleading (Hanson 1995). Still, because not enough men cheer in high school, most collegiate teams competing in the co-ed division must recruit men who have no experience in cheerleading. They often look to football players, believing them well suited for the complexities of competitive cheerleading because they are strong, used to rigorous training, and value self-sacrifice in the pursuit of victory. But because football players have been socialized into a highly sexist and homophobic arena (Messner 1992; Pronger 1990) and because cheerleading is culturally defined as

a feminine activity (Adams and Bettis 2003; Davis 1990; Hanson 1995), convincing men to *give up* football is not effective. After all, football players occupy a space described to accrue social power, prestige, and privilege (Anderson 2005; Bissinger 1990; Connell 1987, 1995; Messner 1992, 1997; Miracle and Rees 1994; Pronger 1990). Football, however, is also a highly competitive sport, and there are a large number of former high school football players who do not make their university teams during tryouts. It is these men who become the recruitment targets for cheerleading squads.

Threatened by a disengagement from their previous athletic identity (Messner 1987) and desiring an association with the highly masculinized ethos attributed to men in team sports, former football players report a desire to join other competitive athletic teams. However, they are generally not trained in the rigors of other team sports (such as baseball or basketball), which also maintain a competitive selection process. Thus, cheerleading becomes a common avenue for "getting back into the game."

While having lunch with a group of male cheerleaders, I asked, "How many of you would rather be on the football team?" All six resoundingly answered, "I would." After indicating a fondness for the cultural power that came to him as a football player, Richie said, "Yeah, I wish I could have made the football team; I really miss football." He added, "But I wasn't going to make any other team, so cheerleading was a way of getting back into the game. Well, as close as I could anyhow." This was the *leitmotif* among men who were recruited to cheerleading after playing football. To these men, cheerleading became an acceptable last effort to return to sport. For them, being in a feminized athletic arena was judged to be better than being outside of it altogether.

Performing Orthodox Masculinity

During the first day of cheerleading, Randy (a college senior) instructed the younger men:

> It is really important for you guys to give these women a lot of respect. . . . You are going to be putting your hands in certain places, and

catching them when they fall, so be sure to be respectful. . . . Remember that we do things better; we pick up on things faster than women do, so don't rub that in by telling them, "We are better than you." Be respectful of the fact that guys are better. Just as important, when you are out in the field you have to portray a masculine image. When you are on the field, you must be the king of masculinity. We don't care what your sexual orientation is; that is none of our business. What you are at home is none of our business. But when you are here you have to be masculine. And if anyone gives you shit, and says you are gay or whatever, remind them that while they are out there playing with guys, you are out here with all these beautiful women.

Randy's talk illustrates the institutional and cultural attitudes of masculinity, homophobia, and sexism among men categorized as belonging to the orthodox group. This speech, in some variation, is traditional for veteran male cheerleaders to give to new men in the Orthodox Cheerleading Association. It is something they call "guy talk," and it best exemplifies orthodox masculinity because it maintains that men should strictly avoid activities culturally determined to be feminine, and portrays women as less intelligent and less athletic than men. The form of masculinity promoted in Randy's speech also subjugates homosexuality and sends a message to gay men that in order to be accepted they must downplay their sexuality and act in accordance with dominant notions of orthodox masculinity (Anderson 2002; Connell 1987, 1995; David and Brannon 1976; Messner 1992). Thus, similar to previous investigations of men in feminized terrain and synonymous with the findings of marginalized men in masculinized terrain, this study found that the orthodox group of men in collegiate cheerleading attempted to mitigate and justify their transgression into feminized terrain (Anderson 2002; Davis 1990; Majors 1990; Messner 1992; Williams 1989, 1993, 1995).

Those who valued orthodox masculinity often relied upon the same identity management techniques discussed in previous investigations of collegiate cheerleading (Davis 1990; Hanson 1995). Namely, they maintained that their role within the sport was consistent with orthodox expectations of masculinity and that the feminized nature of their terrain was falsely attributed. Daren said, "I know that people don't think that this is a masculine sport, but I challenge them to throw a girl up in the air and then catch her as she falls. Besides, the original cheerleaders *were* men." Daren, like many men in cheerleading, postulates that not only is cheerleading a sport in which men and women are polarized into masculine and feminine roles, but that it is also a sport that requires men to be "really" masculine. "Yeah, most of the guys are *really* masculine, . . . We aren't a bunch of fairies out here dancing in skirts."

There was variance about attitudes toward women among those classified as belonging to the orthodox group. While some held misogynistic attitudes, viewing women as purely sex objects, most maintained that they respected women as athletes but usually relegated them as inferior to men in their athleticism. Patrick agreed:

I was asked to be on the team because the women needed me to help them do their routines better. They just can't throw girls as high as guys can. I'm not saying that they can't throw girls, but I am saying that the best cheerleading comes from the co-ed squads, and that's because we give them a better show. We can do what women can't.

In addition to the maintenance of sexist attitudes, many of the men categorized as belonging to the orthodox group also expressed varying degrees of homophobia. While this was sometimes found in overt expressions, it was most often expressed covertly. Perhaps much of this group's homophobic and/or heterosexist sentiment was used to challenge cultural assumptions that male cheerleaders are gay. Indeed, it is common for heterosexual men to confront (or displace) accusations of homosexuality with homophobia (Anderson 2002; Martin and Collinson 1999; McGuffey and Rich 1999; Messner 1992; Plummer 1999, 2001; Smith 1998), and these men certainly found themselves inundated with homosexual suspicion. In fact, the suspicion of homosexuality may be even more prominent among male cheerleaders today than among male cheerleaders of yesteryear.

Loftus (2001) used General Social Survey data to show that homosexuality was not as visible two decades ago as it is today, and Ibson (2002) has shown that the mere awareness that homosexuality exists is enough to alter men's behaviors. Furthermore, Pronger (1990) suggests that homosexuality in the 1980s was largely thought incompatible with athletic men, but recently, it has been shown that athleticism no longer provides the same veneer of heterosexuality (Anderson 2005). Finally, the reduction of cultural homophobia in recent years may also have encouraged a larger percentage of male cheerleaders to come out of the closet, and this might place the heterosexuality of other male cheerleaders under suspicion through a guilt-by-association process (Anderson 2000, 2005). Therefore, heterosexual men who cheered a decade or more ago may not have had to prove their heterosexuality in the same manner that heterosexual cheerleaders do today.

However, the reduction of cultural homophobia and the increased presence of openly gay men seems to have made the expression of homophobia somewhat outmoded, even among many members of the orthodox group. The expression of homophobia is therefore largely accomplished through covert mechanisms of heterosexism. One such manner comes in the form of *defensive heterosexuality*.

Defensive heterosexuality is characterized by the expressive signaling of heterosexuality through a variety of repeated mechanisms. For example, the most common narrative that heterosexual male cheerleaders used to explain their transgression into feminized space was a well-crafted and collectively constructed story about men lusting for their female teammates. Patrick told me, "Yeah, there are all these hot chicks in cheerleading. That is why I came out for the team." Another said, "Who wouldn't want to be out here with all these beautiful women?" The story was common:

so compelled to be around hot women, heterosexual male cheerleaders were sexually drawn to the feminized arena of cheerleading.

These heterosexist and objectifying remarks even dominated the Orthodox Cheerleading Association's website. In one discussion forum, the question was asked, "How do I get more guys to cheer in high school?" Fifteen of nineteen responses included the "Tell-them-about-the-girls" pitch. It was also common for men classified in the orthodox group to make heterosexualized and/or objectifying comments about women, often talking about whom they slept with or whom they would like to. One night, five heterosexual male cheerleaders sat in a hotel room when one said, "Let's order a prostitute." The men then talked about this for the better part of an hour. It was doubtful this would happen, however, for they had had the same conversation the previous night.

For the orthodox men in this study, masculinity is constructed within well-established feminist findings (Chodorow 1978; David and Brannon 1976; Frye 1983; Kimmel 1994; Lorber 1994; Lucal 1999; Plummer 1999, 2001; Pronger 1990; Smith 1998), namely, that in order to be a "real man," one must not be "like a woman" and one must "not be gay." Most of the men in the orthodox group stressed their athleticism and their masculinity, and they attempted to distance themselves from acting feminine or being perceived as gay. They justified their transgression into feminized terrain by challenging the feminine attributes of the arena and by claiming that their particular tasks (e.g., holding women above their heads) were inappropriately labeled as feminine.

Unlike previous studies of masculine construction in cheerleading, however, only about half of the men in collegiate cheerleading were categorized as subscribing to the orthodox form of masculinity. The other half were shown to perform masculinity in a surprising, fascinating, and theoretically important manner.

Performing Inclusive Masculinity

With their competition finished, dinner eaten, and the movie over, a group of seven men (five straight and two gay) walked back to their hotel. Howie said, "Time for some drinking games. I've invited over the guys from Lincoln." When asked if he was worried that the cheerleaders from the other team might think him gay, since he was sharing not only a room with a gay man, but also a bed, he responded, "No. Why would I?"

After an hour of drinking games, one of the heterosexual men said, "Hey, guys, do you want to see if Coach will drive us to a club?" Howie responded, "You guys know of any around here?" His best friend Steve answered, "There is Gold Diggers, the Slush House, and then of course there is the Phoenix; it's a gay club." Howie interrupted, "Let's go there," and the others agreed. When asked why they would rather go to a gay club than a straight one, Howie answered, "The vibe is better, the music is better, and there are still good-looking women, so why wouldn't we want to go there?" When asked, "Aren't you worried about being thought gay?," the five heterosexual men shook their heads no, "Why would we?" They rounded up more teammates, piled into two vans, and headed for the club. Once there, heterosexual men danced with both women *and* gay men; two heterosexual men even freaked each other (a term used by these men to describe two people dancing with their groins together).

While there was not a universal position on homosexuality among men in the inclusive group (just as there was not in the orthodox group), these men had few inhibitions about homosexuality. Their variance in attitudes ran from tolerant to celebratory. Typical comments included "I don't care what people think of me" and "Why is it necessary to have a label?" One male cheerleader even said, "I used to go to gay clubs all the time, and then I actually got a job at a gay club. I got hit on all the time. It was flattering." Still another said, "Why should I care? Why should people care if I'm straight?"

These attitudes are particularly unusual given that these men had previously played high school football. "I used to hate gays," one inclusive cheerleader told me. "But now I don't care. I've gotten over it." His teammate added, "Yeah, most of my teammates used to just hate gays; I mean, what football player doesn't?" Perhaps most telling, another cheerleader said, "To be honest with you, I used to be homophobic. I used to be one of the guys calling the cheerleaders on my high school team fags." He continued, "Now, I'm on the other side. I mean, I'm not gay, but others sometimes think I am because I cheer, and if that's what they want to think, I don't bother to try to tell them different."

Data suggests that this shift in attitude from homophobic to gay-friendly might be made possible for several reasons. First, gay male cheerleaders seem to have strong support from female and older male teammates. For example, Dan said, "Oh yeah, you learn not to be homophobic real quick. I mean, you can't be. The women and coaches in cheer would never stand for that." Another said, "I made some homophobic comment when I first joined, and one of the guys pulled me to the side and schooled me on it." Second, heterosexual men generally befriended at least one gay male teammate. Jeffrey, a fourth-year cheerleader, said:

> I grew up in a town of 2,000. I never met a gay person. In my town, you were just taught to hate them, even though we didn't know who it was we were supposed to hate. So I did . . . until I met Jaime [who was the only openly gay member on his team]. I mean, I used to call guys fags all the time, but I'd never call him that. He was a real cool guy, and now I think that gay people are just really cool people.

Third, institutional support has helped in shaping a new understanding of homosexuality. While overt homophobia was generally replaced with heterosexism in the Orthodox Cheerleading Association, homosexuality and femininity among men was institutionally supported in the Inclusive Cheerleading Association. This has led many gay men who cheered in high school to self-select into colleges that compete for the Inclusive Cheerleading Association. Thus, there are more openly gay athletes in this association, and this makes it easier for closeted men to come out.

The men classified as belonging to the inclusive group are not only less concerned with mitigating homosexual suspicion through homophobia and heterosexism, but also less concerned with associating with femininity. That is to say, men who ascribed to inclusive masculinity are far less concerned with the expression of femininity among other men. In fact, discussions of what behaviors were considered feminine or masculine often suggest a great deal of thought and critical thinking as to the nature of gender performance in the sport. Men in this group were willing, often eager, to participate in role-reversal activities that were stigmatized by men in the orthodox group. Some men in the inclusive group agreed that certain behaviors were understood to be feminine but displayed irreverence for such essentialist thinking. Other men questioned the usefulness of categorizing things as gendered. Men from one inclusive squad even wore sleeveless shirts that zipped up the back (something associated with women's uniforms in this sport). In this respect, the gendered perspectives of many men in this group might best be understood from a queer theory perspective (Jargose 1996; Kosofsky 1993; Seidman 1996).

For example, Jeff, a heterosexual cheerleader, practiced with another male teammate for nearly half an hour, trying to put a female into the air with perfect form. But after growing bored he said, "My turn." The athletes switched positions, and Jeff stood atop the hands of a male and a female. According to those with an orthodox understanding of masculinity, this position is one of the most feminine things a man can do in cheerleading. Jeff, however, was unconcerned. He willingly embraced the coded femininity of such tasks. In this respect, men in this group were shown to be less concerned with performing consistently with some of the tenets of traditional masculinity, as well as challenging the bifurcation of gender.

When men in this group were asked about their masculine identities, many indicated that they considered themselves to be "metrosexual," a recent pop-culture term they understand to describe a gay-friendly heterosexual male who presents himself with the style-conscious behaviors otherwise attributed to gay men (Cashmore and Parker 2003; Flocker 2004; Hyman 2004). Thus, in a similar manner to how "guy talk" was a useful defining construct for men in the orthodox group, the term "metrosexual" was useful for men in the inclusive group.

It is also important to note that in the collegiate cheerleading arena, it would be inappropriate to describe the men categorized as belonging to the inclusive group as maintaining a subordinate form of masculinity. That label does not work for these men because (like hegemonic masculinity) subordination describes a social process, not an archetype. Specifically, Connell (1987, 1995) describes subordinate masculinity in relation to a dominant (and hegemonic) form of masculinity. But because these men construct a hierarchy that esteems inclusivity and stigmatizes orthodox masculinity, it would be hard to say that they are subordinate. Furthermore, Connell describes subordinate masculinity as existing *only* in relationship to a dominant *institutionalized* form of masculinity, and in the Inclusive Cheerleading Association, it is inclusive masculinity that is institutionalized, not orthodox masculinity. This highlights that the process of gender construction in collegiate cheerleading is a product of individuals, organizations and institutions.

Structure and Agency in Constructing Masculinity

Individuals are not simply free to construct any version of identity that they desire; identity construction is influenced and constrained by a number of micro and macro processes (Acker 1990; Connell 1987; Messner 1997; Walkerdine 1993; West and Zimmerman 1987). In order to understand how cultural scripts and organizational rules institutionalize gender in collegiate cheerleading, I rely upon Acker's (1990) theory of gendered institutions—the same theory used in other investigations of men in feminized terrain (Davis 1990; Williams 1993, 1995).

Acker views organizational hierarchies, job descriptions, and informal workplace practices as containing deeply gendered assumptions that eventually become naturalized. In this manner, gender is institutionalized by employing hegemonic processes that reify gender myths and stigmatize those who do not follow institutional norms. Within the same institution, however, there can be variances in gender expression, suggesting that organizational culture and individual agency also maintain influence in the process of gender construction (Dellinger 2004).

The Orthodox Cheerleading Association institutionalizes masculinity along the lines of other masculinized team sports. It values a bifurcation of gender and views homosexuality as a threat to this polarization. In the maintenance of orthodox masculinity, this cheerleading association uses covert and overt techniques to police masculine behaviors. For example, cultural norms stigmatize men (or entire teams) that perform in ways contrary to orthodox masculine perspectives. Men who dance complicated or erotic choreography (similar to women) find that their showmanship lowers their team's score. Because of this, men move in a rigid fashion, leaving the hip-swinging and body-eroticizing choreography exclusively to women.

In the Inclusive Cheerleading Association, however, men are expected to dance as competently and erotically as women. Men often take center stage, thrusting their pelvises and caressing their bodies to the thunderous approval of the audience, while their female teammates wait on the side. In the Inclusive Cheerleading Association, men even throw other men into the air, the strictest taboo in the Orthodox Cheerleading Association. While this does not happen with regular frequency (largely because it is more difficult to throw and catch a 180-pound man than a 100-pound woman), one squad concluded their national championships routine in the Inclusive Cheerleading Association by having a man fly over a two-person high pyramid and land into the arms of four other men. This finale brought cheers of deafening approval that carried on longer than customary. In this respect, the Inclusive Cheerleading Association's competitions are widely rec-

ognized as being more dynamic and daring than those of the Orthodox Cheerleading Association, whose members, in turn, feel that they uphold the traditional form of cheerleading.

The institutional variance of gender roles between these two associations is fiercely contested and politically charged. The Orthodox Cheerleading Association even bans (for three years) any collegiate team that participates in an Inclusive Cheerleading Association event. In this manner, the Orthodox Cheerleading Association relies on traditional tools of marginalization, stigmatization, and institutional punishment for associating with femininity. The Inclusive Cheerleading Association makes no such demands of its participants.

The two leading cheerleading associations also maintain near-opposite perspectives on homosexuality. Highlighting the institutional perspective on homosexuality in the Orthodox Cheerleading Association, men who are out or who act in less than masculinized ways are equated with being unprofessional. Accordingly, it was harder to find openly gay cheerleaders in the Orthodox Cheerleading Association. Similar to the "don't ask, don't tell" policy found among openly gay athletes in highly masculinized team sports (Anderson 2005), their status was often privately recognized but not publicly discussed. Conversely, in many cases, gay members of the Inclusive Cheerleading Association talked more freely about their sexuality.

But just because a cheerleading association sanctions a particular version of masculinity does not imply that all of the cheerleaders who belong to that governing body agree with this perspective. Some individuals, and in some cases entire teams, publicly protested their association's gender paradigm.

The best example of organizational contestation in reformulating representations of institutionalized masculinity comes from participant observations of the Troubadours. Unlike the rigid masculinity observed in most teams of the Orthodox Cheerleading Association, the Troubadours' coaches made a decision to challenge the tough guy image that their governing body esteems. One of the coaches told me, "Oh, I say to hell with all that macho stuff. We are just here to have fun, and if others don't like us for who we are, to hell with them." One of his athletes agreed, "Everyone here is like 'that's just stupid, acting so macho and stuff.'" His comments were supported by participant observations, which showed a great deal of physical intimacy (hugging and holding) between men on the Troubadours team. In a restaurant after competition, one heterosexual man even kissed another on the cheek, in an endearing expression of his friendship.

The Troubadours have also taken a political stand against the conservative nature of the Orthodox Cheerleading Association. The coach reflected, "I remember one year, well, I knew we would be dinged points for it, but I had this male flyer (one who is thrown into the air) that was just amazing. So I took a chance. I figured why not? I put a guy into the air." When asked, "Isn't that like the most feminine thing you can do in cheer?" He answered, "Of course, and we were dinged points for it too. But I didn't care."

The gender rebellion the Troubadours exhibited in the Orthodox Cheerleading Association made them highly ostracized by other Orthodox Cheerleading Association teams. One coach raised his eyebrow even at the mention of the Troubadours, saying, "Oh, you don't want to talk to them; they are not what cheerleading is all about," despite the fact that the Troubadours held five consecutive national championship titles in their division. Furthermore, the Orthodox Cheerleading Association has recently responded to the Troubadours' embracing of femininity and homosexuality by removing points for the dance portion of cheerleading routines. One coach told me that this was a direct response to the fact that *some* judges had ceased to demerit the Troubadours for dancing in other than masculinized ways, suggesting that the institutional creed of this organization is contested by individuals as well as organizations.

Likewise, not all teams that belonged to the Inclusive Cheerleading Association reflected an inclusive form of masculinity. Several teams competed in the style of the Orthodox Cheerleading Association, even interrupting their high-energy and dynamic performances to yell cheers like "Go! Fight! Win!" to the crowd (something considered taboo in this association). Upon finishing an orthodox-style performance at the Inclusive Cheerleading Association's National Championship meet, one team even handed out Bibles to other teams. When asked why, one of the male cheerleaders said, "So others can see God's word." When asked, "See God's word on what?," he answered, "Well, like on homosexuality."

Discussion

Previous investigations of masculine construction among men in feminized terrain have shown that hegemonic processes serve to stigmatize the expression of masculinity in ways that do not meet orthodox perspectives (Davis 1990; Williams 1995). This is attributable to the hegemonic understandings of masculine construction, which requires cultural and institutional punishment for those that fail to meet the mandates of the dominant form, in whichever form it currently exists. The hegemonic privileging of one form of masculine expression and the subordination of all others is made particularly salient among men in feminized terrain because these arenas have been shown to be more permissive of marginalized men than masculinized arenas (Connell 1995). Thus, a greater variance of masculinities is exhibited among men in feminized terrain than among men in highly masculinized fields (Anderson 2005).

The presence of feminized, gay, or otherwise marginalized men in feminized terrain has not, however, been shown to influence a significant number of men to challenge the dominant form of masculinity. In fact, just the opposite has been shown to occur. Previous investigations of heterosexual men in feminized occupational and/or recreational terrain find that orthodox masculinity retains its hegemonic position. Men in these terrains have been shown to distance themselves from subordinate status by aligning themselves with orthodox masculinity (Adams 1993; Anderson 2002, 2005: Davis 1990; Hanson 1995; Sargent 2001; Williams 1993, 1995). Thus, men in feminized spaces have been shown to preserve and/or inflate their masculine identities by being homophobic, devaluing femininity, and claiming their space to be erroneously labeled as feminized.

In this study, male cheerleaders who subscribed to orthodox understandings of masculinity also relied on these identity management techniques. Men in this group were shown to inflate their masculine worth, distance themselves from acting feminine, and use "guy talk" to socialize new cheerleaders into their gendered perspective. Men in this group also reproduced heterosexism by classifying gay male cheerleaders who discussed their sexuality as "unprofessional" and sexism by stressing that they are athletically superior to women. In other words, most men within the orthodox category devalued and distanced themselves from homosexuality and femininity.

Additionally, this research found that, similar to the fashion in which men must prove and reprove their masculinity (Kimmel 2004), male cheerleaders who desire a public image of heterosexuality had to prove and reprove their heterosexuality. Most heterosexual men in the orthodox group signaled their heterosexuality through a variety of overt and covert methods. One method of doing this was found in the display of defensive heterosexuality, which included overt sexualization of women and, for those who did not desire to be thought overtly homophobic, prefacing many statements with "I'm not gay, but. . . ."

Conversely, those who ascribed to inclusive masculinity were shown to behave in effeminate ways without experiencing social stigma. This group largely chose not to value whether people perceived them as gay or straight, masculine or feminine. In this respect, they were less (or not at all) defensive about their heterosexuality, and they regularly stated support for homosexuality. Because of their culturally positive association with homosexuality, homophobia ceased to be a tool of masculine marginalization. Conversely,

homophobic expression was stigmatized among men in this group. In fact, the inclusive form of masculinity proposed by this group was the near-antithesis of orthodox masculinity. Many self-identified heterosexual men in this (equally large) group found the label "metrosexual" useful for self-identification of their modified masculine perspective.

Men in the inclusive group also participated in tasks traditionally defined as feminine and supported women who performed tasks traditionally defined as masculine. This included allowing themselves to be tossed into the air (flying), standing atop the shoulders of others, wearing clothing defined as feminine, and dancing in the same erotic fashion as their female teammates. This understanding questions the utility of binary thinking. Thus, about half the men in the world of collegiate cheerleading contested the masculine/feminine binary that previous studies have shown to be intensely policed.

To be clear, the existence of marginalized men in feminized terrain is not new. What is significant with these findings, however, is that about half of the heterosexual men in collegiate cheerleading were found to align themselves politically away from the orthodox form of masculinity. They responded differently to their transgression than previous investigations of men in feminized terrain. In fact, they resisted many of the tenets of orthodox masculinity and constructed a normative form of masculinity based on inclusiveness. What is also new is that their inclusive prescription of masculinity was institutionally supported by one of the two dominating cheerleading associations, as there was found to be a variance in the institutionalization of masculinity between the two dominating cheerleading associations that govern the sport.

The Orthodox Cheerleading Association was shown to codify orthodox masculine behaviors by penalizing those who perform in ways it deems feminine, while the Inclusive Cheerleading Association rewarded behaviors that break the traditional mode. Foucault (1984) suggests that power must be understood as a multiplicity of factors emanating from individuals, organizations, and institutions. In this manner, men are not merely subject to institutional modeling on masculinity; they are simultaneously active in shaping institutional perspectives through their complacency or protest. Foucault's analysis of power seems fitting in describing gender construction in these cheerleading associations because, despite attempts toward universal solidarity, both associations experienced internal dissension from both individuals and organizations (teams).

I suggest that the emergence of inclusive masculinity as a group with an institutionalized power and membership equal to orthodox masculinity is the product of a number of influences. First, the increasing structural demands for originality and innovation in cheerleading routines have compelled the Inclusive Cheerleading Association to replace the "go, fight, win" mantra of yesteryear's cheerleading (Hanson 1995) with a choreographic philosophy of "higher, faster, and more complicated." But this is not the sole or even the primary impetus for the creation of an inclusive form of masculinity. If this were the case, one might expect to see men dance in feminized ways and then, when away from competition, return to orthodox prescriptions of masculinity. This did not occur. Observations confirm that men who exhibited inclusive masculinity during competition also expressed it while socializing away from competition. These men also self-reported a reconstructed understanding of homophobia and sexism in other social spaces (family, school, work), although these self-reports were not confirmed with observations.

Second, the research design provides evidence of a strong institutional influence on the construction of gender within collegiate cheerleading. While virtually all informants mentioned that as football players they displayed orthodox notions of masculinity, those who happened to attend a university with membership in the Inclusive Cheerleading Association substantially reformulated their masculine perspectives compared to men who happened to attend a university belonging to the Orthodox Cheerleading Associa-

tion. Men who ended up at universities belonging to the Inclusive Cheerleading Association also exhibited a greater openness to homosexuality and feminine-acting men than men from teams belonging to the Orthodox Cheerleading Association.

Because orthodox masculinity is largely predicated on homophobia, I also suggest the emergence of inclusive masculinity to be a product of the rapidly decreasing levels of cultural homophobia in American society (Laumann et al. 2004; Loftus 2001; Persell, Green, and Gurevich 2001; Widmer, Treas, and Newcomb 2002). It is reasonable to suspect that if masculinity is based largely on homophobia, then as homophobia declines, there might also be a change in the manner masculinity is constructed and valued (Carillo 2003; Gutmann 2003). Accordingly, even men in the orthodox group reported that they maintained *less* homophobia than they had as football players.

Finally, the emergence of inclusive masculinity in this feminized arena might also be influenced by the athletes' introduction to the narratives and experiences of women and gay men as teammates. Men in cheerleading, from both associations, reported that their relationships with women and gay men had helped them reconstruct their views on homosexuality and femininity among men, a finding that has implications for the sex-segregated manner in which competitive, institutionalized team sports are currently structured in North American society.

References

Acker, Joan. 1990. "Hierarchies, Jobs, Bodies: A Theory of Gendered Organizations." *Gender & Society*, 4 (June): 139–158.

Adams, Marie Louise. 1993. "To Be an Ordinary Hero: Male Figure Skaters and the Ideology of Gender." In *Men and Masculinities,* edited by T. Haddad. Toronto: Canadian School Press.

Adams, Natalie & Bettis, Pamela. 2003. "Commanding the Room in Short Skirts: Cheering as the Embodiment of Ideal Girlhood." *Gender & Society*, 17(1): 73–91.

Anderson, Eric. 2000. *Trailblazing: The True Story of America's First Openly Gay Track Coach*. Hollywood: Alyson Publications.

Anderson, Eric. 2002. "Openly Gay Athletes: Contesting Hegemonic Masculinity in a Homophobic Environment." *Gender & Society*, 16(6): 860–877.

Anderson, Eric. 2005. *In the Game: Gay Athletes and the Cult of Masculinity*. New York: State University of New York Press.

Berger, Peter & Luckmann, Thomas (1966). *The Social Construction of Reality*, Garden City, NY: Doubleday.

Bissinger, H. G. 1990. *Friday Night Lights: A Town, a Team, and a Dream*. Reading, MA: Addison-Wesley.

Bourdieu, Pierre. 2001. *Masculine Domination*, translated by Richard Nice. Palo Alto, CA: Stanford University Press.

Burstyn, Varda. 1999. *The Rites of Men: Manhood, Politics, and the Culture of Sport*. Toronto: University of Toronto Press.

Carillo, Hector. 2003. "Helping Lift Machismo." In *Changing Men and Masculinities in Latin America,* edited by Matthew Guttman. Durham NC: Duke University Press.

Cashmore, Ellis & Parker, Andrew. 2003. "One David Beckham: Celebrity, Masculinity, and the Soccerati." *Sociology of Sport Journal* 20 (3): 214–231.

Chauncey, George. 1985. "Christian Brotherhood or Sexual Perversion?: Homosexual Identities and the Construction of Sexual Boundaries in the World War One Era." *Journal of Social History,* 19(1985): 189–211. Reprinted in eight collections.

Chodorow, Nancy. 1978. *The Reproduction of Mothering*. Berkeley: University of California Press.

Connell, Robert. 1987. *Gender and Power*. Palo Alto, CA: Stanford University Press.

Connell, Robert. 1995. *Masculinities*. Berkeley: University of California Press.

Corbin, Juliet & Anselm Strauss. 1990. "Grounded Theory Research: Procedures, Canon, and Evaluative Criteria." *Qualitative Sociology*, 13(1): 3–21.

David, Deborah & Robert Brannon. 1976. *The Forty Nine Percent Majority: The Male Sex Role*. Reading MA: Addison Wesley.

Davis, Laurel. 1990. "Male Cheerleaders and the Naturalization of Gender." *Sport, Men and the Gender Order*, edited by M. Messner & D. Sabo (pp. 153–61). Champaign, IL: Human Kinetics.

Dellinger, Kirsten. 2004. "Masculinities in 'Safe' and 'Embattled' Organizations: Accounting for Pornographic and Feminist Magazines." *Gender & Society,* 18(5): 545–566.

Dilorio, Judith 1989. "Feminism, Gender, and the Ethnographic Study of Sport." *Arena Review,* 13(1), 49–59.

Flocker, Michael. 2004. *The Metrosexual Guide to Style: A Handbook for the Modern Man*. New York: DaCapo Press.

Foucault, Michel. 1984. *The History of Sexuality, Volume 1: An Introduction*, translated by Robert Hurley. New York: Vintage Press.

Frye, Marilyn. 1983. *The Politics of Reality: Essays in Feminist Theory*. Berkeley, CA: Crossing Press.

Garfinkle, Harold. 1967. *Studies in Ethnomethodology*. Englewood Cliffs, NJ: Prentice-Hall.

Gilmore, David. 1990. *Manhood in the Making: Cultural Concepts of Masculinity*. New Haven, CT: Yale University Press.

Glaser, Barney & Anselm Strauss. 1967. *The Discovery of Grounded Theory: Strategies for Qualitative Research*. New York: Aldine De Gruyter.

Gorer, Geoffrey. 1964. *The American People: A Study in National Character*. New York: Norton.

Gramsci, Antonio. 1971. *Selections from Prison Notebooks*. London: New Left Books.

Gutmann, Matthew. 2003. *Changing Men and Masculinities in Latin America*. Durham, NC: Duke University Press.

Halperin, David. 1989. *One Hundred Years of Homosexuality: And Other Essays on Greek Love*. New York: Routledge.

Hanson, Mary Ellen. 1995. *Go! Fight! Win! Cheerleading in American Culture*. Bowling Green, OH: Bowling Green State University Popular Press.

Holstein, James & Miller, Gale (eds.). 1993. *Reconsidering Social Constructionism: Debates in Social Problems Theory*. Hawthorne, NY: Aldine de Gruyter.

Hyman, Peter. 2004. *The Reluctant Metrosexual: Dispatches from an Almost Hip Life*. New York: Villard.

Ibson, John. 2002. *A Century of Male Relationships in Everyday American Photography*. Washington DC: Smithsonian Books.

Jargose, Annamarie. 1996. *Queer Theory: An Introduction*. New York: New York University Press.

Klein, Alan. 1993. *Little Big Men: Bodybuilding Subculture and Gender Construction*. New York: State University of New York Press.

Kimmel, Michael. 1994. "Homophobia as Masculinity: Fear, Shame and Silence in the Construction of Gender Identity." *Theorizing Masculinities,* edited by Harry Brod & Michael Kaufman. pp. 119–141. Thousand Oaks, CA: Sage.

Kimmel, Michael. 1996. *Manhood in America: A Cultural History.* New York: The Free Press.

Kimmel, Michael. 2004. *The Gendered Society: Sociological Perspective on Sex and Gender.* London: Oxford University Press.

Kosofsky, Sedgwick. 1993. *Tendencies.* Durham, NC: Duke University Press.

Lancaster, Roger. 1988. "Subject Honor and Object Shame: The Construction of Male Homosexuality and Stigma in Nicaragua." *Ethnomethodology,* 27(2): 111–125.

Laumann, Edward; Ellingson, Stephen; Mahay, Jenna; Paik, Anthony & Youm, Yoosik. 2004. *The Sexual Organization of the City.* Chicago: University of Chicago Press.

Lorber, Judith. 1994. *Paradoxes of Gender.* New Haven, CT: Yale University Press.

Loftus, Jeni. 2001. "America's Liberalization in Attitudes Toward Homosexuality, 1973 to 1998." *American Sociological Review,* 66(5): 762–782.

Lucal, Betsy. 1999. "What It Means to Be Gendered Me: Life on the Boundaries of a Dichotomous Gender System." *Gender & Society,* 13: 781–797.

Majors, Richard. 1990. "Cool Pose: Black Masculinity and Sport." In *Sport, Men and the Gender Order,* edited by M. Messner & D Sabo. Champaign, IL: Human Kinetics.

Martin, Patricia Yancey & Collinson, David. 1999. "Gender and Sexuality in Organizations." *Revisioning Gender,* edited by Myra Marx Ferree, Judith Lorber, & Beth B. Hess. Thousand Oaks, CA: Sage.

McGuffey, Shawn & Lindsey Rich. 1999. "Playing in the Gender Transgression Zone: Race, Class, and Hegemonic Masculinity in Middle Childhood." *Gender & Society,* 13(5): 608–610.

Messner, Michael. 1987. "The Meaning of Success: The Athletic Experience and the Development of Identity." In *The Making of Masculinities: The New Men's Studies,* edited by Harry Brod, pp. 193–209. Melbourne, Australia: Allen & Unwin.

Messner, Michael. 1992. *Power at Play: Sports and the Problem of Masculinity.* Boston: Beacon Press.

Messner, Michael. 1997. *Politics of Masculinities: Men in Movements.* Thousand Oaks, CA: Sage.

Miracle, Andrew & Rees, Roger. 1994. *Lessons of the Locker Room: The Myth of School Sports.* New York: Prometheus Books.

Persell, Caroline, Green, Adam & Gurevich, Liena. 2001. "Civil Society, Economic Distress, and Social Tolerance." *Sociological Forum,* 16: 203–230.

Plummer, David. 1999. *One of the Boys: Masculinity, Homophobia and Modern Manhood.* New York: Harrington Park Press.

Plummer, David. 2001. "Policing Manhood: New Theories about the Social Significance of Homophobia." In *Sexual Positions,* edited by Carl Wood (pp. 60–75). Melbourne, Australia: Hill of Content.

Pollack, William. 1998. *Real Boys: Rescuing Our Sons from the Myth of Boyhood.* New York: Henry Holt and Company.

Pronger, Brian. 1990. *The Arena of Masculinity: Sports, Homosexuality, and the Meaning of Sex.* New York: St. Martin's Press.

Robidoux, Michael. 2001. *Men at Play: A Working Understanding of Professional Hockey.* Quebec: McGill-Queen's University Press.

Sargent, Paul. 2001. *Real Men or Real Teachers: Contradictions in the Lives of Men Elementary School Teachers.* Harriman, TN: Men's Studies Press.

Seidman, Steven. 1996. *Queer Theory Sociology.* Oxford, UK: Blackwell Publishers.

Smith, George. 1998. "The Ideology of Fag: The School Experience of Gay Students." *Sociological Quarterly* (39)2: 309–335.

Walkerdine, Valerie. 1993. "Girlhood through the Looking Glass." In *Girls, Girlhood and Girls' Studies in Transition,* edited by Mario de Ras & Mieke Lunenberg. Amsterdam: Het Spinhuis.

West, Candice & Don Zimmerman. 1987. "Doing Gender." *Gender & Society,* 1(2): 125–151.

Widmer, Eric D., Treas, Judith & Newcomb, Robert. 1998. "Attitudes toward Nonmarital Sex in 24 Countries." *Journal of Sex Research,* 35(4): 349–357.

Williams, Christine L. 1989. *Gender Differences at Work.* Berkeley: University of California Press.

Williams, Christine L. (ed.). 1993. *Doing "Women's Work:" Men in Nontraditional Occupations.* Newbury Park, CA: Sage.

Williams, Christine L. 1995. *Still a Man's World: Men Who Do "Women's Work."* Berkeley: University of California Press.

PART FOUR

Men and Work

In what ways is work tied to male identity? Do men gain a sense of fulfillment from their work, or do they view it as necessary drudgery? How might the organization of workplaces play on, reinforce, or sometimes threaten the types of masculinity that males have already learned as youngsters? How does the experience of work (or of not having work) differ for men of different social classes, ethnicities, and sexual preference groups? And how do recent structural changes in society affect the masculinity–work relationship? The articles in this section address these issues and more.

The rise of urban industrial capitalism saw the creation of separate "public" and "domestic" spheres of social life. As women were increasingly relegated to working in the home, men were increasingly absent from the home, and the male "breadwinner role" was born. The sexual division of labor, this gendered split between home and workplace, has led to a variety of problems and conflicts for women and for men. Women's continued movement into the paid labor force, higher levels of unemployment, and the rise of a more service-oriented economy have led to dramatic shifts in the quality and the quantity of men's experiences in their work.

Articles by Jennifer Pierce and Marianne Cooper explore how men "do" gender in the workplace; those by Christine Williams and Kevin Henson and Jackie Krasas Rogers explore how men who do women's work also "do" gender by ensuring that their masculinity is validated. The work world has also become an arena of the battle between the sexes, as the continuing debates over sexual harassment make clear. The article by Beth Quinn examines sexual harassment in that most commonplace behavior: girl watching.

Jennifer Pierce

Rambo Litigators: Emotional Labor in a Male-Dominated Occupation

Litigation is war. The lawyer is a gladiator and the object is to wipe out the other side.
—Cleveland lawyer quoted in *The New York Times*

A recent spate of articles in *The New York Times* and a number of legal dailies characterized some of America's more flamboyant and aggressive trial lawyers as "Rambo litigators."[1] This hypermasculine, aggressive image is certainly not a new one. In popular culture and everyday life, jokes and stories abound that characterize lawyers as overly aggressive, manipulative, unreliable, and unethical individuals.[2] What jokes, as well as the popular press, fail to consider is that such behavior is not simply the result of individual failings but is actually required and reinforced by the legal profession itself.

Legal scholar Carrie Menkel-Meadow (1985) suggests that the adversarial model with its emphasis on "zealous advocacy" and "winning" encourages a "macho ethic" in the courtroom (pp. 51–54). Lawyers and teachers of trial lawyers argue that the success of litigators depends on their ability to manipulate people's emotions (Brazil 1978; Turow 1987). Trial lawyers must persuade judges and juries, as well as intimidate witnesses and opposing counsel in the courtroom, in deposition, and in negotiations. The National Institute of Trial Advocacy, for example, devotes a three-week training seminar to teaching lawyers

From *Masculinities in Organizations,* Cheng (ed.), pp. 1–27. Sage Publications, 1993. © Sage Publications. Reprinted by permission.

to hone such emotional skills, thereby improving their success in the courtroom (Rice 1989). This chapter makes this aspect of lawyering explicit by examining the emotional dimension of legal work in a particular specialty of law—litigation. Sociological studies of the legal profession have yet to seriously examine the emotional dimension of lawyering.[3] Although a few studies make reference to the emotional dimension of work, it is not the central focus of their research.[4] For example, Nelson (1988) reduces lawyering to three roles— "finders, minders and grinders," meaning "lawyers who seem to bring in substantial clients . . . lawyers who take care of the clients who are already here and there are the grinders who do the work" (senior partner quoted in Nelson 1988, p. 69). Nelson's reduction of these roles to their instrumental and intellectual dimensions neglects the extent to which instrumental tasks may also contain emotional elements.

The sparse attention other sociological studies have given to this dimension of lawyering is contradicted by my 15 months of field research (from 1988 to 1989) at two large law firms in San Francisco—six months at a private firm (Lyman, Lyman, and Portia) and nine months in the legal department of a large corporation (Bonhomie Corporation).[5] Litigators make use of their emotions to persuade juries, judges, and witnesses in the courtroom and in depositions, in communications with opposing counsel, and with clients. However, in contrast to the popular image, intimidation and aggression constitute only one component of the emotional labor required by this profession. Lawyers also make use of strategic friendliness, that is, the use of charm or flattery to manipulate others. Despite the apparent differences in these two types of emotional labor, both use the manipulation of others for a specific end—winning a case. Although other jobs require the use of manipulation to achieve specific ends, such labor may serve different purposes and be embedded in a different set of relationships. Flight attendants, for example, are friendly and reassuring to passengers so as to alleviate their anxiety about flying (Hochschild 1983). However, flight attendants' friendliness takes the form of deference: Their relationship to passengers is supportive and subordinate. By contrast, in litigation, the goal of strategic friendliness is to *win over* or dominate another. As professionals who have a monopoly over specialized knowledge, attorneys hold a superordinate position with respect to clients, witnesses, and jurors and a competitive one with other lawyers. If trial lawyers want to win their cases, they must be able to successfully manipulate and ultimately dominate others for their professional ends.

By doing whatever it takes within the letter of the law to win a case, lawyers effectively fulfill the goal of zealous advocacy: persuading a third party that the client's interests should prevail. In this way, intimidation and strategic friendliness serve to reproduce and maintain the adversarial model. At the same time, by exercising dominance and control over others, trial lawyers also reproduce gender relations. The majority of litigators who *do dominance* are men (88 percent of litigators are male) and those who defer are either female secretaries and paralegals,[6] other women, or men who become feminized in the process of losing. In addition to creating and maintaining a gendered hierarchy, the form such emotional labor takes is gendered. It is a masculinized form of emotional labor, not only because men do it but because dominance is associated with masculinity

in our culture. West and Zimmerman (1987) argue, for example, that displays of dominance are ways for men to "do gender."[7] Similarly, psychoanalytic feminists equate masculinity with men's need to dominate women (Chodorow 1978; Benjamin 1988). In the case of trial lawyers, the requirements of the profession deem it appropriate to dominate women as well as other men. Such *conquests* or achievements at once serve the goals of effective advocacy and become the means for the trial lawyer to demonstrate a class-specific form of masculinity.

Gamesmanship and the Adversarial Model

Popular wisdom and lawyer folklore portray lawyering as a game, and the ability to play as gamesmanship (Spence 1988). As one of the trial attorneys I interviewed said,

> The logic of gamesmanship is very interesting to me. I like how you make someone appear to be a liar. You know, you take them down the merry path and before they know it, they've said something pretty stupid. The challenge is getting them to say it without violating the letter of the law.

Lawyering is based on gamesmanship—legal strategy, skill, and expertise. But trial lawyers are much more than chess players. Their strategies are not simply cerebral, rational, and calculating moves but highly emotional, dramatic, flamboyant, and shocking presentations that invoke sympathy, distrust, or outrage. In my redefinition of the term, *gamesmanship* involves the utilization of legal strategy through a presentation of an emotional self designed specifically to influence the feelings and judgment of a particular legal audience—the judge, the jury, the witness, or opposing counsel. Furthermore, in my definition, the choices litigators make about selecting a particular strategy are not simply individual, they are institutionally constrained by the structure of the legal profession, formal and informal professional norms such as the American Bar Association's

(1982) *Model Code of Professional Responsibility* and training in trial advocacy through programs sponsored by the National Institute of Trial Advocacy.

The rules governing gamesmanship derive from the adversarial model that underlies the basic structure of our legal system. This model is a method of adjudication that involves two advocates (e.g., the attorneys) presenting their case to an impartial third party (i.e., the judge and the jury) who listens to evidence and argument and declares one party the winner (Menkel-Meadow 1985; Luban 1988). As Menkel-Meadow (1985) observes, the basic assumptions that underlie this set of arrangements are "advocacy, persuasion, hierarchy, competition and binary results (win or lose)." She writes, "The conduct of litigation is relatively similar . . . to a sporting event—there are rules, a referee, an object to the game, and a winner is declared after play is over" (p. 51).

Within this system, the attorney's main objective is to persuade the impartial third party that his client's interests should prevail (American Bar Association 1982, p. 34). However, clients do not always have airtight, defensible cases. How, then, does the *zealous advocate* protect his clients interests and achieve the desired result? When persuasion by appeal to reason breaks down, an appeal to emotions becomes tantamount (Cheatham 1955, pp. 282–283). As legal scholar John Buchan (1939) writes, "The root of the talent is simply the *power to persuade*" [italics added] (pp. 211–213). By appealing to emotions, the lawyer becomes a "con man."[8] He acts "as if" he has a defensible case, he puffs himself up, he bolsters his case. Thus, the successful advocate must not only be smart, but as famous turn-of-the-century trial lawyer Francis Wellman (1903/1986, p. 13) observes, he must also be a "good actor." In his book, *The Art of Cross-Examination*, first published in 1903 and reprinted to the present, Wellman describes how carefully the litigator must present himself to the judge and jury:

> The most cautious cross-examiner will often elicit a damaging answer. Now is the time for the greatest self-control. If you show by your face how the answer hurt, you may lose by that

one point alone. How often one sees a cross-examiner fairly staggered by such an answer. He pauses, blushes . . . [but seldom regains] control of the witness. With the really experienced trial lawyer, such answers, instead of appearing to surprise or disconcert him, will seem to come as a matter of course, and will fall perfectly flat. He will proceed with the next question as if nothing happened, or else perhaps give the witness an incredulous smile, as if to say, "Who do you suppose would believe that for a minute?" (pp. 13–14).

More recently, teacher and lawyer David Berg (1987) advises lawyers to think of themselves as actors, and the jury, an audience. He writes,

> Decorum can make a difference, too. . . . *Stride* to the podium and *exude confidence*, even if there is a chance that the high school dropout on the stand is going to make you look like an idiot. *Take command* of the courtroom. Once you begin, do not grope for questions, shuffle through papers, or take breaks to confer with co-counsel. Let the jury know that you are prepared, that you do not need anyone's advice, and that *you care* about the case . . . because if *you don't care, the jurors won't care.* (1987, p. 28, italics added)

Wellman (1903/1986) and Berg (1987) make a similar point: Trials are the enactment of a drama in the courtroom, and attorneys are the leading actors. Appearance and demeanor are of utmost importance. The lawyer's manner, his tone of voice, his facial expressions are all means to persuade the jury that his client is right. Outrageous behavior is acceptable, as long as it remains within the letter of the law. Not only are trial lawyers expected to act but with a specific purpose in mind: to favorably influence feelings of the jurors. As Berg points out, "if you don't show you care, the jurors won't care."

This emphasis on acting is also evident in the courses taught by the National Institute for Trial Advocacy (NITA) where neophyte litigators learn the basics in presenting a case for trial. NITA's emphasis is on "learning by doing" (Kilpatrick, quoted in Rice 1989). Attorneys do not simply read about cases but practice presenting them in a simulated courtroom with a judge, a jury, and witnesses. In this case, doing means acting. As one of the teacher–lawyers said on the first day of class, "Being a good trial lawyer means being a good actor. . . . Trial attorneys love to perform." Acting, in sociological terms, translates into emotional labor, that is, inducing or suppressing feelings in order to produce an outward countenance that influences the emotions of others. Teacher–lawyers discuss style, delivery, presentation of self, attitude, and professionalism. Participants, in turn, compare notes about the best way to "handle" judges, jurors, witnesses, clients, and opposing counsel. The efforts of these two groups constitute the teaching and observance of "feeling rules" or professional norms that govern appropriate lawyerlike conduct in the courtroom.

The three-week course I attended[9] took students through various phases of a hypothetical trial—jury selection, opening and closing statements, and direct and cross-examination. Each stage of the trial has a slightly different purpose. For example, the objective of jury selection is to uncover the biases and prejudices of the jurors and to develop rapport with them. On the other hand, an opening statement sets the theme for the case, whereas a direct examination lays the foundation of evidence for the case. Cross-examination is intended to undermine the credibility of the witness, whereas closing represents the final argument. Despite the differing goals that each of these phases has, the means to achieve them is similar in each case, that is, the attempt to persuade a legal audience favorably to one's client through a particular emotional presentation of self.

In their sessions on direct and cross-examination, students were given primarily stylistic, as opposed to substantive, responses on their presentations. They were given finer legal points on the technicalities of their objections—the strength or weakness of their arguments. But in the content analysis of my field notes, I found that 50 percent to 80 percent of comments were directed toward the attorney's particular style. These comments fell into five categories: (a) personal appearance, (b) presentation of self (nice, aggressive, or sincere manner), (c) tone and level of voice, (d) eye contact, and (e) rapport with others in the courtroom.

For example, in one of the sessions, Tom, a young student–lawyer in the class, did a direct examination of a witness to a liquor store robbery. He solemnly questioned the witness about his work, his special training in enforcing liquor laws, and how he determined whether someone was intoxicated. At one point when the witness provided a detail that Tom had not expected, rather than expressing surprise, Tom appeared nonchalant and continued with his line of questions. At the end of his direct, the teacher–lawyer provided the following feedback:

> Good background development of a witness. Your voice level was appropriate but try modulating it a bit more for emphasis. You also use too many thank you's to the judge. You should ingratiate yourself with the judge but not overly so. You also made a good recovery when the witness said something unexpected.

When Patricia, a young woman attorney, proceeded nervously through the same direct examination, opposing counsel objected repeatedly to some of her questions, which flustered her. The teacher–lawyer told her,

> You talk too fast. And you didn't make enough eye contact with the judge. Plus, you got bogged down in the objections and harassment from opposing counsel. You're recovery was too slow. You've got to be more forceful.

In both these examples, as in most of the sessions that I observed, the focus of the comments was not on the questions asked but on *how* the questions were asked. Tom was told to modulate his voice; Patricia was told not to talk so fast. In addition, the teacher–lawyer directed their attention to rapport with others in the courtroom. Tom was encouraged not to be overly ingratiating with the judge, whereas Patricia was told to pay more attention to the judge. Moreover, the teacher commended Tom for his "recovery," that is, regaining self-composure and control of the witness. He criticized Patricia, on the other hand, for not recovering well from an aggressive objection made by opposing counsel.[10]

In my fieldwork at NITA and in the two law offices, I found two main types of emotional labor: intimidation and strategic friendliness. Intimidation entails the use of anger and aggression, whereas strategic friendliness uses politeness, friendliness, or playing dumb. Both forms are related to gamesmanship. Each involves an emotional presentation of self that is intended to favorably influence the feelings of a particular legal audience toward one's client. Many jobs appear to require strategic friendliness and intimidation. Domestic workers, for example, sometimes "play dumb" so as not to alienate their white female employers (Rollins 1985). For domestic workers, however, this strategy is a means for someone in a subordinate position to survive a degrading job. By contrast, for litigators, strategic friendliness, like intimidation, is a means for an individual with professional status to control and dominate others in an effort to win one's case. Although both the litigator and the domestic worker may play dumb, in each job, the behavior serves different goals that are indicative of their divergent positions in relationship to others.

Intimidation and strategic friendliness not only serve the goals of the adversarial model, but they exemplify a masculine style of emotional labor. They become construed as masculine for several reasons. First, emotional labor in the male-dominated professional strata of the gendered law firm is interpreted as masculine, simply because men do it. Ruth Milkman (1987), for example, suggests that "idioms of sex-typing can be applied to whatever women and men happen to be doing" (p. 50). Male trial attorneys participate in shaping this idiom by describing their battles in the courtroom and with opposing counsel as "macho," "something men get into," and "a male thing." In addition, by treating women lawyers as outsiders

and excluding them from professional networks, they further define their job as exclusively male.

In addition, the underlying purpose of gamesmanship itself, that is, the control and domination of others through manipulation, reflects a particular cultural conception of masculinity. Connell (1987), for example, describes a hegemonic form of masculinity that emphasizes the domination of a certain class of men—middle- to upper-middle class—over other men and over women. Connell's cultural conception of masculinity dovetails neatly with feminist psychoanalytic accounts that interpret domination as a means of asserting one's masculinity (Chodorow 1978; Benjamin 1988). The lawyers I studied also employed a ritual of degradation and humiliation against other men and women who were witnesses or opposing counsel. The remainder of this chapter describes the two main components of emotional labor—intimidation and strategic friendliness—the purpose of each, and shows how these forms become construed as masculine. These forms of emotional labor are explored in practices, such as cross-examination, depositions, jury selection, and in opening and closing statements.

Intimidation

The first and most common form of emotional labor associated with lawyers is intimidation. In popular culture, the tough, hard-hitting, and aggressive trial lawyer is portrayed in television shows, such as *L.A. Law* and *Perry Mason* and in movies, such as *The Firm*, *A Few Good Men*, and *Presumed Innocent*. The news media's focus on famous trial attorneys such as Arthur Liman, the prosecutor of Oliver North in the Iran-Contra trial, also reinforces this image. Law professor Wayne Brazil (1978) refers to this style of lawyering as the *professional combatant*. Others have used terms such as *Rambo litigator*, *legal terrorists*, and *barbarians of the bar* (Margolick 1988; Miner 1988; Sayler 1988). Trial attorneys themselves call litigators from large law firms "hired guns" (Spangler 1986). The central figure that appears again and again in these images is not only intimidating but strongly masculine. In the old West, hired guns were sharpshooters, men who were hired to kill other men. The strong, silent movie character Rambo is emblematic of a highly stylized, super masculinity. Finally, most of the actors who play tough, hard-hitting lawyers in the television shows and movies mentioned above are men. Thus, intimidation is not simply a form of emotional labor associated with trial lawyers, it is a masculinized form of labor.

Intimidation is tied to cultural conceptions of masculinity in yet another way. In a review of the literature on occupations, Connell (1987) observes that the cult of masculinity in working-class jobs centers on physical prowess and sexual contempt for men in managerial or office positions (p. 180). Like the men on the shop floor in Michael Burawoy's (1979) study who brag about how much they can lift or produce, lawyers in this study boast about "destroying witnesses," "playing hardball," "taking no prisoners," and about the size and amount of their "win." In a middle-class job such as the legal profession, however, intimidation depends not on physical ability but on mental quickness and a highly developed set of social skills. Thus, masculinizing practices, such as aggression and humiliation, take on an emotional and intellectual tone specific to middle-class occupations and professions.

This stance is tied to the adversarial model's conception of the "zealous advocate" (American Bar Association 1982). The underlying purpose of this strategy is to intimidate, scare, or emotionally bully the witness of opposing counsel into submission. A destructive cross-examination is the best example.[11] Trial attorneys are taught to intimidate the witness in cross-examination, "to control the witness by never asking a question to which he does not already know the answer and to regard the impeachment of the witness as a highly confrontational act" (Menkel-Meadow 1985, p. 54). Wellman (1903/1986) describes cross-examination in this way:

It requires the greatest ingenuity; a habit of logical thought; clearness of perception; infinite patience and self-control; the power to read men's minds intuitively, to judge of their characters by their faces, to appreciate their motives; ability to act with force and precision; a masterful knowledge of the subject matter itself; an extreme caution; and, above all *the instinct to discover the weak point in the witness under examination* . . . It is a *mental duel* between counsel and witness. (p. 8, italics added)

Berg (1987) echoes Wellman's words when he begins his lecture on cross-examination by saying, "The common denominator for effective cross-examination is not genius, however. It's a combination of preparation and an instinct for the jugular" (p. 27). Again, cross-examination involves not only acting mean but creating a specific impression on the witness.

In the sections on cross-examination at NITA, teachers trained lawyers how to *act mean*. The demonstration by the teachers on cross-examination best exemplified this point. Two male instructors reenacted an aggressive cross-examination in a burglary case. The prosecutor relentlessly hammered away, until the witness couldn't remember any specific details about what the burglar looked like. At its conclusion, the audience clapped vigorously. Three male students who had been asked to comment on the section responded unanimously and enthusiastically that the prosecutor's approach has been excellent. One student commentator said, "He kept complete control of the witness." Another remarked, "He blasted the witness's testimony." And the third added, "He destroyed the witness's credibility." The fact that a destructive cross-examination served as the demonstration for the entire class underlines the desirability of aggressive behavior as a model for appropriate lawyerlike conduct in this situation. Furthermore, the students' praise for the attorney's tactics collectively reinforce the norm for such behavior.

Teachers emphasized the importance of using aggression on an individual level as well. Before a presentation on cross-examination, Tom, one of the students, stood in the hallway with one of the instructors trying to "psyche himself up to get mad." He repeated over and over to himself, "I hate it when witnesses lie to me, it makes me so mad!" The teacher coached him to concentrate on that thought, until Tom could actually evoke the feeling of anger. He said to me later in an interview, "I really felt mad at the witness when I walked into the courtroom." In the actual cross-examination, each time the witness made an inconsistent statement, Tom became more and more angry: "First, you told us you could see the burglar, now you say your vision was obstructed! So, which is it, Mr. Jones?" The more irate he became, the more intimidated and confused the witness became, until he completely backed down and said, "I don't know," in response to every question. The teacher characterized Tom's performance as "the best in the class," because it was the "the most forceful" and "the most intimidating." Students remarked that he deserved to "win the case."

NITA's teachers also used mistakes to train students in the rigors of cross-examination. For example, when Laura cross-examined the same witness in the liquor store case, a teacher commented on her performance:

> Too many words. You're asking the witness for information. Don't do that in cross-examination. You tell them what the information is. You want to be destructive in cross-examination. When the other side objects to an answer, *you were too nice. Don't be so nice!* [italics added]. Next time, ask to talk to the judge, tell him, "This is crucial to my case." You also asked for information when you didn't know the answer. Bad news. You lost control of the witness.

By being nice and losing control of the witness, Laura violated two norms underlying the classic confrontational cross-examination. A destructive cross-examination is meant to impeach the witness's credibility, thereby demonstrating to the jury the weakness in opposing counsel's case.

In situations that call for such an aggressive cross-examination, being nice implies that the lawyer likes the witness and agrees with his or her testimony. By not being aggressive, Laura created the wrong impression for the jury. Second, Laura lost control of the witness. Rather than guiding the witness through the cross with leading questions[12] that were damaging to opposing counsel's case, she allowed the witness to make his own points. As we will see in the next section of the chapter, being nice can also be used as a strategy for controlling a witness; however, such a strategy is not effective in a destructive cross-examination.

Laura's violation of these norms also serves to highlight the implicitly masculine practices used in cross-examination. The repeated phrase, "keeping complete control of the witness," clearly signals the importance of dominating other women and men. Furthermore, the language used to describe obtaining submission—"blasting the witness," "destroying his credibility," or pushing him to "back down"—is quite violent. In addition, the successful control of the witness often takes on the character of a sexual conquest. One brutal phrase used repeatedly in this way is "raping the witness." Within this discursive field, men who "control," "destroy," or "rape" the witness are seen as "manly," whereas those who lose control are feminized as "sissies" and "wimps" or, in Laura's case, as "too nice."

The combative aspect of emotional labor carries over from the courtroom to other lawyering tasks, such as depositions. Attorneys not only "shred" witnesses in the courtroom but in depositions as well. When I worked at this private firm, Daniel, one of the partners, employed what he called his "cat and mouse game" with one of the key witnesses, Jim, in a deposition that I attended. During the deposition, Daniel aggressively cross-examined Jim. "When did you do this?" "You were lying, weren't you?" Jim lost his temper in response to Daniel's hostile form of interrogation—"You hassle me, man! You make me mad!" Daniel smiled and said, "I'm only trying to get to the truth of the situation." Then, he became aggressive again and said, "You lied to the IRS about how much profit you made, didn't you, Jim!" Jim lost his temper again and started calling Daniel a liar. A heated interchange between Daniel and opposing counsel followed, in which opposing counsel objected to Daniel's "badgering the witness." The attorneys decided to take a brief recess.

When the deposition resumed, Daniel began by accusing John, the other attorney, of withholding crucial documents to the case, while pointing his index finger at him. Opposing counsel stood up and started yelling in a high-pitched voice, "Don't you ever point your finger at me! Don't you ever do that to me! This deposition is over . . . I'm leaving." With that he stood up and began to cram papers into his briefcase in preparation to leave. Daniel immediately backed down, apologized, and said, "Sit down, John, I promise I won't point my finger again." He went on to smooth the situation over and proceeded to tell John in a very calm and controlled voice what his objections were. John made some protesting noises, but he didn't leave. The deposition continued.

In this instance, the deposition, rather than the courtroom, became the *stage* and Daniel took the leading role. His cross-examination was confrontational and his behavior with the witness and opposing counsel was meant to intimidate. After the deposition, Daniel boasted to me and several associates about how mad he had made the witness and how he had "destroyed his credibility." He then proceeded to reenact the final confrontation by imitating John standing up and yelling at him in a falsetto voice. In the discussion that followed, Daniel and his associates gave the effects of his behavior on the "audience" utmost consideration. Hadn't Daniel done a good job forcing the witness to lose control? Hadn't he controlled the situation well? Didn't he make opposing counsel look like a "simpering fool"?

The reenactment and ensuing discussion reveal several underlying purposes of the deposition.

First, it suggests that the deposition was not only a fact-finding mission for the attorney but a show designed to influence a particular audience—the witness. Daniel effectively flustered and intimidated the witness. Second, Daniel's imitation of John with a falsetto voice, "as if" he were a woman, serves as a sort of "degradation ceremony" (Garfinkel 1956). By reenacting the drama, he ridicules the man on the other side before an audience of peers, further denigrating him by inviting collective criticism and laughter from colleagues. Third, the discussion of the strategy builds up and elevates Daniel's status as an attorney for his aggressive, yet rational control of the witness and the situation. Thus, the discussion creates a space for collectively reinforcing Daniel's intimidation strategy.

In addition to highlighting the use of intimidation in depositions, this example also illustrates the way aggression as legal strategy or rule-governed aggression (Lyman 1987; Benjamin 1988) and masculinity become conflated, whereas aggression, which is not rule governed, is ridiculed as feminine. John shows his anger, but it is deemed inappropriate, because he loses control of the situation. Such a display of hostility does not serve the interests of the legal profession, because it does not achieve the desired result—a win for the case. As a result, Daniel and his associate regard John's behavior—his lack of control, his seeming hysteria and high voice, with contempt. This contempt takes on a specific sexual character. Just as the working class "lads" in Paul Willis's (1977) book, *Learning to Labor*, denigrate the "earholes" or sissies for their feminine attributes, Daniel and his colleagues ridicule John for his femalelike behavior. Aggression as legal strategy or maleness is celebrated; contempt is reserved for aggression (or behavior) that is not rule governed and behavior that is also associated with the opposite sex.

Attorneys also used the confrontational approach in depositions at Bonhomie Corporation. In a deposition I sat in on, Mack, a litigator, used an aggressive cross-examination of the key witness.

Q: What were the names of the people that have migrated from one of the violators, as you call it, to Bonhomie Corporation?

A: I don't remember as of now.

Q: Do you have their names written down?

A: No.

Q: Well, if you don't remember their names and they're not written down, how can you follow their migration from one company to another?

A: You can consider it in the process of discovery that I will make some inquiring phone calls.

Q: Did you call anyone to follow their migration?

A: Well, I was unsuccessful as of yet to reach other people.

Q: Who have you attempted to call?

A: I can't tell you at this time. I have a list of processes in my mind to follow.

Q: Do you recall who you called and were not able to reach?

A: No.

Q: What's the list of processes in your mind to follow?

A: It's hard to describe.

Q: In other words, you don't have a list?

A: [quietly] Not really.

Q: Mr. Jensen, instead of wasting everyone's time and money, answer the question yes or no!

Opposing Counsel: Don't badger the witness.

Q: Answer the question, Mr. Jensen, yes or no!

Opposing Counsel: I said, don't badger the witness.

Q: Mr. Jensen, you are still required to answer the question!

A: [quietly] No.

In this case, Mack persisted in badgering the witness, who provided incoherent and vague an-

swers. In response to the question, "Well, if you don't remember their names and they're not written down, how can you follow their migration from one company to another?" the witness gave the vague reply: "You can consider it in the process of discovery that I will make some inquiring phone calls." As the witness became more evasive, the attorney became more confrontational, "Answer the question, Mr. Jensen, yes or no!" By using this approach, the lawyer succeeded in making the witness appear even more uncooperative than he actually was and eventually pushed him to admit that he didn't have a list.

Later, in the same deposition, the attorney's confrontational tactics extended to opposing counsel.

Q: Let's change the subject. Mr. Jensen, can you tell me what representations were made to you about the reliability of the Bonhomie Corporation's spider system?

A: Nancy, the saleslady, said they use it widely in the United States, and could not be but very reliable. And, as we allege, fraudulent, and as somebody referred to it, was the, they wanted to give us the embrace of death to provide us more dependency, and then to go on and control our operation totally [sic].

Q: Who said that?

A: My attorney.

Q: When was that?

Opposing Counsel: Well, I . . .

Mack: I think he's already waived it. All I want to know is when it was supposedly said.

A: Well . . .

Opposing Counsel: I do use some great metaphors.

Mack: Yes, I know, I have read your complaint.

Opposing Counsel: Sorry?

Mack: I have read your complaint. That will be all for today, Mr. Jensen.

Here, the attorney did not stop with badgering the witness. When the witness made the statement about the "embrace of death," Mack was quick to find out who said it. And when opposing counsel bragged about his "great metaphors," Mack parried back with a sarcastic retort, "Yes, I know, I have read your complaint." Having had the final word, he abruptly ended the deposition. Like the other deposition, this one was not only an arena for intimidating the witness but for ridiculing the attorney on the other side. In this way, intimidation was used to control the witness and sarcasm to dominate opposing counsel. In doing so, Mack had achieved the desired result—the witness's submission to his line of questioning and a victory over the other side. Furthermore, in his replay of the deposition to his colleagues, he characterized his victory as a "macho blast against the other side," thereby underscoring the masculine character of his intimidation tactics.

Strategic Friendliness

> Mr. Choate's appeal to the jury began long before final argument. . . . His manner to the jury was that of a *friend* [italics added], a friend solicitous to help them through their tedious investigation; never an expert combatant, intent on victory, and looking upon them as only instruments for its attainment. (Wellman 1903/1986, pp. 16–17)

The lesson implicit in Wellman's anecdote about famous 19th-century lawyer Rufus Choate's trial tactics is that friendliness is another important strategy the litigator must learn and use to be successful in the courtroom. Like the use of aggression, the strategic use of friendliness is another feature of gamesmanship and, hence, another component of emotional labor. As Richard, one of the attorney–teachers at NITA stated, "Lawyers have to be able to vary their styles, they have to be able to have multiple speeds, personalities and style." In his view, intimidation did not always work and he proposed an alternative strategy, what he called "the toe-in-the-sand, aw shucks routine." Rather than adopting an intimidating stance vis-à-vis the witness, he advocated "play-

ing dumb and innocent." "Say to the witness, 'Gee, I don't know what you mean. Can you explain it again?' until you catch the witness in a mistake or an inconsistent statement." Other litigators, such as Leonard Ring (1987), call this the "low-key approach." As an illustration of this style, Ring describes how opposing counsel delicately handled the cross-examination of a child witness:

> The lawyer for the defendant . . . stood to cross-examine. Did he attack the details of her story to show inconsistencies? Did he set her up for impeachment by attempting to reveal mistakes, uncertainties and confusion? I sat there praying that he would. But no, he did none of the things a competent defense lawyer is supposed to do. He was old enough to be the girl's grandfather . . . the image came through. He asked her very softly and politely: "Honey, could you tell us again what you saw?" She told it exactly as she had on my direct. I felt relieved. He still wasn't satisfied. "Honey, would you mind telling us again what you saw?" She did again exactly as she had before. He still wasn't satisfied. "Would you do it once more?" She did. She repeated, again, the same story—the same way, in the same words. By that time I got the message. The child had been rehearsed by her mother the same way she had been taught "Mary Had a Little Lamb." I won the case, but it was a very small verdict. (pp. 35–36)

Ring concludes that a low-key approach is necessary in some situations and advises against adhering rigidly to the prototypical combative style.

Similarly, Scott Turow (1987), lawyer and novelist, advises trying a variety of approaches when cross-examining the star witness. He cautions against adopting a "guerrilla warfare mentality" in cross-examination and suggests that the attorney may want to create another impression with the jury:

> Behaving courteously can keep you from getting hurt and, in the process, smooth the path for a win. [In one case I worked on] the cross examination was conducted with a politesse appropriate to a drawing room. I smiled to show

that I was not mean-spirited. The chief executive officer smiled to show that he was not beaten. The commissioners smiled to show their gratitude that everybody was being so nice. And my client won big. (pp. 40–42)

Being nice, polite, welcoming, playing dumb, or behaving courteously are all ways that a trial lawyer can manipulate the witness to create a particular impression for the jury. I term this form of gamesmanship *strategic friendliness*. Rather than bully or scare the witness into submission, this tactic employs the opposite—friendliness, politeness, and tact. Despite this seeming difference, it shares with the former an emphasis on the emotional manipulation of another person for a strategic end—winning one's case. For instance, the attorney in Ring's account is gentle and considerate of the child witness for two strategic reasons. First, by making the child feel comfortable, he brings to light the fact that her testimony has been rehearsed. Second, by playing the polite, gentle grandfatherly role, he has created a favorable impression of himself with the jury. Thus, he simultaneously demonstrates to the jury that the witness has been rehearsed and that he, as opposing counsel, is a nice guy. In this way, he improves his chances for winning. And, in fact, he did. Although he didn't win the case, the verdict for the other side was "small."

Although strategic friendliness may appear to be a softer approach than intimidation, it carries with it a strongly instrumental element. Consider the reasoning behind this particular approach. Ring's attorney is nice to the child witness not because he's altruistically concerned for her welfare. He utilizes gentility as a strategy to achieve the desired result—a big win in the courtroom. It is simply a means to an end. Although this approach may be less aggressive than intimidation, it is no less manipulative. Like the goal of intimidation, the central goal of this component of gamesmanship is to dominate and control others for a specific end. This end is best summed up by litigator Mark Dombroff (1989) who writes, "So long as you don't violate the law, including the rules of procedure and evidence or do violence to the

canons of ethics, winning is the only thing that matters" (p. 13).

This emphasis on winning is tied to hegemonic conceptions of masculinity and competition. Sociologist Mike Messner (1989) argues that achievement in sporting competitions, such as football, baseball, and basketball, serve as a measure of men's self-worth and their masculinity. This can also be carried over into the workplace. For example, in her research on men in sales, Leidner (1993) finds that defining the jobs as competition becomes a means for construing the work as masculine.

For litigators, comparing the number of wins in the courtroom and the dollar amount of damages or settlement awards allows them to interpret their work as manly. At Bonhomie Corporation and at Lyman, Lyman, and Portia, the first question lawyers often asked others after a trial or settlement conference was "Who won the case?" or "How big were the damages?" Note that both Ring and Turow also conclude their pieces with descriptions of their win—"I won the case, but the verdict was small" and "I won big." Trial attorneys who did not "win big" were described as "having no balls," "geeks," or "wimps." The fact that losing is associated with being less than a man suggests that the constant focus on competition and winning is an arena for proving one's masculinity.

One important area that calls for strategic friendliness and focuses on winning is jury selection or *voir dire*. The main purpose of *voir dire* is to obtain personal information about prospective jurors to determine whether they will be fair, "favorably disposed to you, your client, and your case, and will ultimately return a favorable verdict" (Mauet 1980, p. 31). Once an attorney has made that assessment, biased jurors can be eliminated through challenges for cause and peremptory challenges. In an article on jury selection, attorney Peter Perlman (1988) maintains that the best way to uncover the prejudices of the jury "is to conduct *voir dire* in an atmosphere that makes prospective jurors comfortable about disclosing their true feelings" (p. 5). He provides a checklist of strategies for lawyers to use that enable jurors to feel more comfortable. Some of these include the following:

- Given the initial intimidation that jurors feel, try to make them feel as comfortable as possible; approach them in a *natural, unpretentious, and clear manner.*
- Because jurors don't relate to "litigants" or "litigation," humanize the client and the dispute.
- *Demonstrate the sincere* desire to learn of the jurors's feelings. (pp. 5–9, italics added)

Perlman's account reveals that the underlying goal of jury selection is to encourage the jury to open up so that the lawyer can eliminate the jurors he doesn't want and develop a positive rapport with the ones who appear favorable to his case. This goal is supported not only by other writings on jury selection (Cartwright 1977; Blinder 1978; Mauet 1980; Ring 1983) but also through the training offered by NITA. As a teacher–judge said after the class demonstration on jury selection, "Sell your personality to the jury. Try to get liked by the jury. You're not working for a fair jury but one favorable to your side."

At NITA, teachers emphasized this point on the individual level. In their sessions on *voir dire*, students had to select a jury for a case that involved an employee who fell down the steps at work and severely injured herself. (Jurors in the class were other students, in addition to myself.) Mike, one of the students, proceeded with his presentation. He explained that he was representing the wife's employer. He then went on to tell the jury a little bit about himself. "I grew up in a small town in Indiana." Then, he began to ask each of the jurors where they were from, whether they knew the witness or the experts, whether they played sports, had back problems, suffered any physical injuries, and ever had physical therapy. The instructor gave him the following comments:

> The personal comments about yourself seem forced. Good folksy approach, but you went overboard with it. You threw stuff out and let the jury nibble and you got a lot of information. But the main problem is that you didn't find out how people *feel* about the case or about their relatives and friends.

Another set of comments:

> Nice folksy approach but a bit overdone. Listen to what jurors say, don't draw conclusions. Don't get so close to them, it makes them feel uncomfortable. Use body language to give people a good feeling about you. Good personality, but don't cross certain lines. Never ask someone about their ancestry. It's too loaded a question to ask. Good sense of humor, but don't call one of your prospective jurors a "money man." And don't tell the jury jokes! You don't *win them over* [italics added] that way.

The sporting element to *voir dire* becomes "winning over the jury." This theme also became evident in discussions student lawyers had before and after jury selection. They discussed at length how best "to handle the jurors," "how to get personal information out of them," "how to please them," "how to make them like you," and "how to seduce them to your side." The element of sexual seduction is no more apparent than in the often used phrase, "getting in bed with the jury." The direct reference to sexual seduction and conquest suggests, as it did with the intimidation strategy used in cross-examination, that "winning over the jury" is also a way to prove one's masculinity. Moreover, the desired result in both strategic friendliness and intimidation is similar: obtaining the juror's submission and winning.

Strategic friendliness is used not only in jury selection but in the cross-examination of sympathetic witnesses. In one of NITA's hypothetical cases, a husband's spouse dies of an illness related to her employment. He sues his deceased wife's former employer for her medical bills, her lost wages, and "lost companionship." One of the damaging facts in the case that could hurt his claim for lost companionship was the fact that he had a girlfriend long before his wife died. In typical combative adversarial style, some of the student lawyers tried to bring this fact out in cross-examination to discredit his relationship with his wife. The teacher–judge told one lawyer who presented such an aggressive cross-examination,

> It's too risky to go after him. Don't be so confrontational. And don't ask the judge to reprimand him for not answering the question. This witness is too sensitive. Go easy on him.

The same teacher gave the following comment to another student who had "come on too strong":

> Too stern. Hasn't this guy been through enough already! Handle him with kid gloves. And don't cut him off. It generates sympathy for him from the jury when you do that. It's difficult to control a sympathetic witness. It's best to use another witness's testimony to impeach him.

And to yet another student:

> Slow down! This is a dramatic witness. Don't lead so much. He's a sympathetic witness—the widower—let him do the talking. Otherwise you look like an insensitive jerk to the jury.

In the cross-examination of a sympathetic witness, teachers advised students not to be aggressive but to adopt a gentler approach. Their concern, however, is not for the witness's feelings but how their treatment of the witness appears to the jury. The jury already thinks the witness is sympathetic, because he is a widower. As a result, the lawyers were advised not to do anything that would make the witness appear more sympathetic and them less so. The one student who did well on this presentation demonstrated great concern for the witness. She gently asked him about his job, his marriage, his wife's job, and her illness. Continuing with this gentle approach, she softly asked him whether anyone had been able to provide him comfort during this difficult time. By doing so, she was able to elicit the testimony about the girlfriend in a sensitive manner. By extracting the testimony about the girlfriend, she decreased the jury's level of sympathy for the bereaved widower. How much companionship did he lose, if he was having an affair? At the same time, because she did so in a gentle manner, she

increased the jury's regard for her. She presented herself as a nice person. Her approach is similar to Laura's in using "niceness" as a strategy. However, in Laura's case, being nice was not appropriate to a destructive cross-examination. In the case of cross-examining a sympathetic witness, such an approach is necessary.

Opening statements also provide an opportunity for using the nonconfrontational approach. NITA provided a hypothetical case called *BMI v. Minicom*, involving a large corporation that sues a small business for its failure to pay a contract. Minicom signed a contract for a $20,000 order of computer parts from BMI. BMI shipped the computer parts through UPS to Minicom, but they never arrived. According to the law in the case, the buyer bears the loss, typically through insurance, when the equipment is lost in mail. Mark gave an opening statement that portrayed Minicom as a small business started by ambitious, hard-working college friends "on their way to the big league in business." He played up the difficulties that small businesses face in trying to compete with giant corporations. And at a dramatic moment in the opening, he asked the jury to "imagine a world where cruel giants didn't squeeze out small companies like Minicom." The teacher provided the following comments:

> Good use of evocative imagery. BMI as cruel giant. Minicom squeezing in between the cracks. Great highlighting of the injustice of the situation.

The lawyer for Minicom attempted to gain sympathy from the jury by playing up the underdog role of his client—the small company that gets squeezed between the cracks of the cruel, dominating giant.

In his attempt to counter this image, Robert, the lawyer for BMI, used a courteous opening statement. He attempted to present himself as a nice guy. He took off his jacket, loosened his tie, smiled at the jury, and said, in a friendly conversational tone, "This case is about a broken contract. BMI fulfilled their side of the contract. Mr. Blakey, my client, worked round the clock to get the shipment ready for Minicom. He made phone call after phone call to inventory to make sure the parts got out on time. He checked and rechecked the package before he sent it to Minicom." He paused for dramatic emphasis and, looking sincere and concerned, said, "It's too bad UPS lost the shipment, but that's not BMI's fault. And now, BMI is out $20,000." He received the following comments from the teacher:

> Great use of gestures and eye contact. Good use of voice. You made the case sound simple but important. You humanized yourself and the people at BMI. Good building of sequence.

Here, the attorney for BMI tried to play down his client's impersonal, corporate image by presenting himself as a nice guy. Before he began his opening statement, he took off his jacket and loosened his tie to suggest a more casual and ostensibly less corporate image. He smiled at the jury to let them know that he was friendly—not the cruel giant depicted by opposing counsel. He used a friendly conversational tone to begin his opening statement. And he even admitted that it was not fair that the other side didn't get their computer parts. As the teacher's comments suggest, this strategy was most effective for this particular kind of case.

This approach can also be used in closing statements. In a hypothetical case, during which an insurance company alleged that the claimant set fire to his own business, the lawyer for the store owner tried to defuse the insurance company's strategy with a highly dramatic closing statement:

> Visualize Elmwood Street in 1952. The day Tony Rubino came home from the Navy. His father took him outside to show him a new sign he had made for the family business. It read "Rubino & Son." Standing under the sign "Rubino & Son" with his father was the happiest day of his life. [Pause] The insurance company wants you to believe, ladies and gentlemen of the jury, that Tony set fire to this family jewel. "I'll carry on," he told his father, and he did. ... [With tears in her eyes, the lawyer concludes] You don't set fire to your father's dream.

The teacher's comments for Janine's closing statement were effusive:

> Great! Well thought out, sounded natural. Good use of details and organization. I especially liked "I don't know what it's like to have a son, but I know what it's like to have a father." And you had tears in your eyes! Gave me the closing-argument goose bumps. Pitched emotion felt real, not phony.

Janine's use of sentimental and nostalgic imagery, the son returning home from the Navy, the beginning of a father and son business, the business as the "family jewel" is reminiscent of a Norman Rockwell painting. It also serves to counter the insurance company's allegation that Tony Rubino set fire to his own store. With the portrait the lawyer paints and the concluding line, "You don't set fire to your father's dream," she rallies the jury's sympathy for Tony Rubino and their antipathy for the insurance company's malicious claim against them. Moreover, her emotional presentation of the story is so effective that the instructor thought it "sounded natural" and "felt real, not phony." The great irony here is that this is not a real case—it is a hypothetical case with hypothetical characters. There is no Tony Rubino, no family store, and no fire. Yet Janine's "deep acting" was so convincing that the teacher believed it was true—it gave him "the closing-argument goose bumps."

Strategic friendliness carries over from the courtroom to depositions. Before deposing a particularly sensitive or sympathetic witness, Joe, one of the attorneys in the private firm, asked me whether "there is anything personal to start the interview with—a sort of warm up question to start things off on a personal note?" I had previously interviewed the woman over the phone, so I knew something about her background. I told him that she was a young mother who had recently had a very difficult delivery of her first child. I added that she was worried about the baby's health, because he had been born prematurely. At the beginning of the deposition later that afternoon, Joe said in a concerned voice that he understood the witness had recently had a baby and was concerned about its health. She appeared slightly embarrassed by the question, but with a slow smile and lots of encouragement from him, she began to tell him all about the baby and its health problems. By the time Joe began the formal part of the deposition, the witness had warmed up and gave her complete cooperation. Later, the attorney bragged to me and one of the associates that he had the witness "eating out of his hand."

After recording these events in my field notes, I wrote the following impressions:

> On the surface, it looks like social etiquette to ask the witness these questions, because it puts her at ease. It lets her know he takes her seriously. But the "personal touch" is completely artificial. He doesn't give a shit about the witness as a person. Or, I should say, only insofar as she's *useful* to him.

Thus, something as innocuous as a personal remark becomes another way to create the desired impression with a witness and thereby manipulate him or her. Perhaps what is most ironic about strategic friendliness is that it requires a peculiar combination of sensitivity to other people and, at the same time, ruthlessness. The lawyer wants to appear kind and understanding, but that is merely a cover for the ulterior motive—winning. Although the outward presentation of self for this form of emotional labor differs from intimidation, the underlying goal is the same: the emotional manipulation of the witness for a favorable result.

Conclusion

In this chapter, I have redefined gamesmanship as the utilization of legal strategy through a presentation of emotional self designed specifically to influence the feelings and judgments of a particular legal audience, such as the judge, the jury, opposing counsel, or the witness. Gamesmanship as emotional labor constitutes two main components—intimidation and strategic friendliness. Despite their apparent differences, both

share an emphasis on the manipulation of others toward a strategic end, that is, winning a case. Whereas, the object of intimidation is to "wipe out the other side," playing dumb and being polite represent strategically friendly methods for controlling legal audiences and bringing about the desired "win." Furthermore, I have shown that the attempt to dominate and control judges, juries, and opposing counsel not only serves the goals of the adversarial model but also becomes a means for trial lawyers to assert a hegemonic form of masculinity. Lawyers who gain the other side's submission characterize their efforts as a "macho blast," "a male thing," or "something men get into," whereas those who do not are regarded as "sissies" and "wimps." Thus, it is through their very efforts to be successful litigators that emotional labor in this male-dominated profession is masculinized.

This chapter also suggests many questions for future research on the role of masculinity and emotions in organizations. Masculinity is often a taken-for-granted feature of organizational life. Yet the masculinization of occupations and professions has profound consequences for workers located within them. Not only do male litigators find themselves compelled to act in ways they may find morally reprehensible, but women working in these jobs[13] are increasingly marginalized—facing sex discrimination and sexual harassment (Rhode 1988; Rosenberg, Perlstadt, & Phillips 1993). At the same time, because of its informal and seemingly invisible nature, emotional labor too is often unexamined and unquestioned (Fineman 1993). Given that organizations often intrude on emotional life means that the line between the individual and the job becomes a murky one. The litigator who refuses to play Rambo may not only be unsuccessful, he may find himself without a job. Thus, many questions still require our attention. Is emotional labor gendered in other jobs? Under what conditions? When does emotional labor take on racialized or classed dimensions? When is it exploitative and when is it not? And finally, what role, if any, should emotions play in the workplace?

Notes

1. For examples, see Goldberg (1987), Margolick (1988), Miner (1988), and Sayler (1988).

2. For example, see the *National Law Journal*'s (1986) article, "What America Really Thinks About Lawyers."

3. Classic studies on the legal profession have typically focused on the tension between professionalism and bureaucracy. For examples, see Carlin (1962), Smigel (1969), Spangler (1986), and Nelson (1988).

4. For example, in their classic book, *Lawyers and Their Work*, Johnstone and Hopson (1967) describe 19 tasks associated with the lawyering role. In only two of these 19 tasks do Johnstone and Hopson allude to the emotional dimension of lawyering—"emotional support to client" and "acting as a scapegoat" (pp. 119–120).

5. In addition to my field research, I also conducted 60 interviews with lawyers, paralegals, and secretaries, as well as eight interviews with personnel directors from some of San Francisco's largest law firms. Field work and interviews were also conducted at the National Institute of Trial Advocacy where I spent three weeks with litigators during a special training course on trial preparation. These methodological decisions are fully discussed in the introductory chapter to my book, *Gender Trials* (Pierce 1995). Please note, names of organizations and individuals have been changed throughout to protect confidentiality.

6. See Chapter 4, "Mothering Paralegals: Emotional Labor in a Feminized Occupation," in *Gender Trials* (Pierce 1995).

7. West and Zimmerman (1987) conceptualize gender as "a routine accomplishment embedded in everyday interaction" (p. 1).

8. Blumberg (1967) describes lawyers as practicing a "confidence game." In his account, it is the client who is the "mark" and the attorney and other people in the court who collude in "taking him out." In my usage, litigators "con" not only their clients but juries, judges, and opposing counsel as well.

9. Special thanks to Laurence Rose, Lou Natali, and the National Institute of Trial Advocacy for allowing me to attend and observe NITA's special three-week training seminar on trial advocacy. All interpretations of NITA and its practices are my own and are *not* intended to reflect the goals or objectives of that organization.

10. Women were much more likely to be criticized for being "too nice." The significance of women being singled out for these kinds of "mistakes" is examined in Chapter 5, "Women and Men as Litigators," in *Gender Trials* (Pierce 1995).

11. Mauet describes two approaches to cross-examination. In the first, the purpose is to elicit favorable testimony by getting the witness to agree with the facts that support one's case. On the other hand, a destructive cross-examination "involves asking questions which will discredit the witness or his testimony" (1980, p. 240).

12. The proper form of leading questions is allowed in cross-examination but *not* in direct examination. Mauet (1980) defines a leading question as "one which suggests the answer" and provides examples, such as "Mr. Doe, on December 13, 1977, you owned a car, didn't you?" (p. 247). In his view, control comes by asking "precisely phrased leading questions that never give the witness an opening to hurt you" (p. 243).

13. Women trial lawyers negotiate the masculinized norms of the legal profession in a variety of ways. See Chapter 5, "Women and Men as Litigators," in *Gender Trials* (Pierce 1995).

References

American Bar Association (1982). *Model code of professional responsibility and code of judicial conduct*. Chicago: National Center for Professional Responsibility and ABA.

Benjamin, J. (1988). *The bonds of love: Psychoanalysis, feminism and the problem of domination*. New York: Pantheon.

Berg, D. (1987). Cross-examination. *Litigation: Journal of the Section of Litigation, American Bar Association, 14*(1), 25–30.

Blinder, M. (1978). Picking juries. *Trial Diplomacy, 1*(1), 8–13.

Blumberg, A. (1967). The practice of law as confidence game: Organizational co-optation of a profession. *Law and Society Review, 1*(2), 15–39.

Brazil, W. (1978). The attorney as victim: Toward more candor about the psychological price tag of litigation practice. *Journal of the Legal Profession, 3*, 107–117.

Buchan, J. (1939). The judicial temperament. In J. Buchan, *Homilies and recreations* (3rd ed.). London: Hodder & Stoughton.

Burawoy, M. (1979). *Manufacturing consent*. Chicago: University of Chicago Press.

Carlin, J. (1962). *Lawyers on their own*. New Brunswick, NJ: Rutgers University Press.

Cartwright, R. (1977, June). Jury selection. *Trial, 28*, 13.

Cheatham, E. (1955). *Cases and materials on the legal profession* (2nd ed.). Brooklyn, NY: Foundation.

Chodorow, N. (1978). *The reproduction of mothering: Psychoanalysis and the sociology of gender*. Berkeley & Los Angeles: University of California Press.

Connell, R. W. (1987). *Gender and power: Society, the person and sexual politics*. Palo Alto, CA: Stanford University Press.

Dombroff, M. (1989, September 25). Winning is everything! *National Law Journal*, p. 13, col. 1.

Fineman, S. (Ed.). (1993). *Emotions in organizations*. Newbury Park, CA: Sage.

Garfinkel, H. (1956). Conditions of successful degradation ceremonies. *American Journal of Sociology, 61*(11), 420–424.

Goldberg, D. (1987, July 1). Playing hardball. *American Bar Association Journal*, p. 48.

Hochschild, A. (1983). *The managed heart: Commercialization of human feeling*. Berkeley & Los Angeles: University of California Press.

Johnstone, Q., & Hopson, D., Jr. (1967). *Lawyers and their work*. Indianapolis, IN: Bobbs-Merrill.

Leidner, R. (1993). *Fast food, fast talk: Service work and the routinization of everyday life*. Berkeley: University of California Press.

Luban, D. (1988). *Lawyers and justice: An ethical study*. Princeton, NJ: Princeton University Press.

Lyman, P. (1987). The fraternal bond as a joking relationship: A case study of sexist jokes in male group bonding. In M. Kimmel (Ed.), *Changing men: New directions in research on men and masculinity* (pp. 148–163). Newbury Park, CA: Sage.

Margolick, D. (1988, August 5). At the bar: Rambos invade the courtroom. *New York Times*, p. B5.

Mauet, T. (1980). *Fundamentals of trial techniques*. Boston: Little, Brown.

Menkel-Meadow, C. (1985, Fall). Portia in a different voice: Speculations on a women's lawyering process. *Berkeley Women's Law Review*, pp. 39–63.

Messner, M. (1989). Masculinities and athletic careers. *Gender & Society, 3*(1), 71–88.

Milkman, R. (1987). *Gender at work*. Bloomington: University of Indiana Press.

Miner, R. (1988, December 19). Lawyers owe one another. *National Law Journal*, pp. 13–14.

Nelson, R. (1988). *Partners with power*. Berkeley & Los Angeles: University of California Press.

Perlman, P. (1988). Jury selection. *The Docket: Newsletter of the National Institute for Trial Advocacy, 12*(2), 1.

Pierce, J. L. (1995). *Gender trials: Emotional lives in contemporary law firms*. Berkeley & Los Angeles: University of California Press.

Rhode, D. (1988). Perspectives on professional women. *Stanford Law Review, 40*, 1163–1207.

Rice, S. (1989, May 24). Two organizations provide training, in-house or out. *San Francisco Banner*, p. 6.

Ring, L. (1983, July). *Voir dire:* Some thoughtful notes on the selection process. *Trial, 19*, 72–75.

Ring, L. (1987). Cross-examining the sympathetic witness. *Litigation: Journal of the Section of Litigation, American Bar Association, 14*(1), 35–39.

Rollins, J. (1985). *Between women: Domestics and their employers*. Philadelphia: Temple University Press.

Rosenberg, J., Perlstadt, H., & Phillips, W. (1993). Now that we are here: Discrimination, disparagement and harassment at work and the experience of women lawyers. *Gender & Society, 7*(3), 415–433.

Sayler, R. (1988, March 1). Rambo litigation: Why hardball tactics don't work. *American Bar Association Journal*, p. 79.

Smigel, E. (1969). *The Wall Street lawyer: Professional or organizational man?* (2nd ed.). New York: Free Press.

Spangler, E. (1986). *Lawyers for hire: Salaried professionals at work*. New Haven: Yale University Press.

Spence, G. (1988). *With justice for none*. New York: Times Books.

Turow, S. (1987). Crossing the star. *Litigation: Journal of the Section of Litigation, American Bar Association, 14*(1), 40–42.

Wellman, F. (1986). *The art of cross-examination: With the cross-examinations of important witnesses in some celebrated cases* (4th ed.). New York: Collier. (Original work published 1903.)

West, C., & Zimmerman, D. (1987). Doing gender. *Gender & Society, 1*(2), 125–151.

What America really thinks about lawyers. (1986, October). *National Law Journal*, p. 1.

Willis, P. (1977). *Learning to labor*. Farnborough, UK: Saxon House.

Christine L. Williams

The Glass Escalator: Hidden Advantages for Men in the "Female" Professions

The sex segregation of the U.S. labor force is one of the most perplexing and tenacious problems in our society. Even though the proportion of men and women in the labor force is approaching parity (particularly for younger cohorts of workers) (U.S. Department of Labor 1991:18), men and women are still generally confined to predominantly single-sex occupations. Forty percent of men or women would have to change major occupational categories to achieve equal representation of men and women in all jobs (Reskin and Roos 1990:6), but even this figure underestimates the true degree of sex segregation. It is extremely rare to find specific jobs where equal numbers of men and women are engaged in the same activities in the same industries (Bielby and Baron 1984).

Most studies of sex segregation in the work force have focused on women's experiences in male-dominated occupations. Both researchers and advocates for social change have focused on the barriers faced by women who try to integrate predominantly male fields. Few have looked at the "flip-side" of occupational sex segregation: the exclusion of men from predominantly female occupations (exceptions include Schreiber 1979; Zimmer 1988; Williams 1989). But the fact is that men are less likely to enter female sex-typed occupations than women are to enter male-dominated jobs (Jacobs 1989). Reskin and Roos, for exam-

ple, were able to identify 33 occupations in which female representation increased by more than nine percentage points between 1970 and 1980, but only three occupations in which the proportion of men increased as radically (1990:20–21).

In this paper, I examine men's underrepresentation in four predominantly female occupations—nursing, librarianship, elementary school teaching, and social work. Throughout the twentieth century, these occupations have been identified with "women's work"—even though prior to the Civil War, men were more likely to be employed in these areas. These four occupations, often called the female "semi-professions" (Hodson and Sullivan 1990), today range from 5.5 percent male (in nursing) to 32 percent male (in social work). (See Table 22.1.) These percentages have not changed substantially in decades. In fact, as Table 22.1 indicates, two of these professions—librarianship and social work—have experienced declines in the proportions of men since 1975. Nursing is the only one of the four experiencing noticeable changes in sex composition, with the proportion of men increasing 80 percent between 1975 and 1990. Even so, men continue to be a tiny minority of all nurses.

Although there are many possible reasons for the continuing preponderance of women in these fields, the focus of this paper is discrimination. Researchers examining the integration of women into "male fields" have identified discrimination as a major barrier to women (Reskin and Hartmann 1986; Reskin 1988; Jacobs 1989). This discrimination has taken the form of laws or in-

■ **TABLE 22.1**
Percent Male in Selected Occupations,
Selected Years

Profession	1990	1980	1975
Nurses	5.5	3.5	3.0
Elementary teachers	14.8	16.3	14.6
Librarians	16.7	14.8	18.9
Social workers	31.8	35.0	39.2

Source: U.S. Department of Labor. Bureau of Labor Statistics. *Employment and Earnings* 38:1 (January 1991), Table 22 (Employed civilians by detailed occupation), 185; 28:1 (January 1981), Table 23 (Employed persons by detailed occupation), 180; 22:7 (January 1976), Table 2 (Employed persons by detailed occupation), 11.

stitutionalized rules prohibiting the hiring or promotion of women into certain job specialties. Discrimination can also be "informal," as when women encounter sexual harassment, sabotage, or other forms of hostility from their male co-workers resulting in a poisoned work environment (Reskin and Hartmann 1986). Women in nontraditional occupations also report feeling stigmatized by clients when their work puts them in contact with the public. In particular, women in engineering and blue-collar occupations encounter gender-based stereotypes about their competence which undermine their work performance (Martin 1980; Epstein 1988). Each of these forms of discrimination—legal, informal, and cultural—contributes to women's underrepresentation in predominantly male occupations.

The assumption in much of this literature is that any member of a token group in a work setting will probably experience similar discriminatory treatment. Kanter (1977), who is best known for articulating this perspective in her theory of tokenism, argues that when any group represents less than 15 percent of an organization, its members will be subject to predictable forms of discrimination. Likewise, Jacobs argues that "in some ways, men in female-dominated occupations experience the same difficulties that women

in male-dominated occupations face" (1989:167), and Reskin contends that any dominant group in an occupation will use their power to maintain a privileged position (1988:62).

However, the few studies that have considered men's experience in gender-atypical occupations suggest that men may not face discrimination or prejudice when they integrate predominantly female occupations. Zimmer (1988) and Martin (1988) both contend that the effects of sexism can outweigh the effects of tokenism when men enter nontraditional occupations. This study is the first to systematically explore this question using data from four occupations. I examine the barriers to men's entry into these professions; the support men receive from their supervisors, colleagues, and clients; and the reactions they encounter from the public (those outside their professions).

Methods

I conducted in-depth interviews with 76 men and 23 women in four occupations from 1985–1991. Interviews were conducted in four metropolitan areas: San Francisco/Oakland, California; Austin, Texas; Boston, Massachusetts; and Phoenix, Arizona. These four areas were selected because they show considerable variation in the proportions of men in the four professions. For example, Austin has one of the highest percentages of men in nursing (7.7 percent), whereas Phoenix's percentage is one of the lowest (2.7 percent) (U.S. Bureau of the Census 1980). The sample was generated using "snowballing" techniques. Women were included in the sample to gauge their feelings and responses to men who enter "their" professions.

Like the people employed in these professions generally, those in my sample were predominantly white (90 percent).[1] Their ages ranged from 20 to 66 and the average age was 38. The interview questionnaire consisted of several open-ended questions on four broad topics: motivation to enter the profession; experiences in training;

career progression; and general views about men's status and prospects within these occupations. I conducted all the interviews, which generally lasted between one and two hours. Interviews took place in restaurants, my home or office, or the respondent's home or office. Interviews were tape-recorded and transcribed for the analysis.

Data analysis followed the coding techniques described by Strauss (1987). Each transcript was read several times and analyzed into emergent conceptual categories. Likewise, Strauss's principle of theoretical sampling was used. Individual respondents were purposively selected to capture the array of men's experiences in these occupations. Thus, I interviewed practitioners in every specialty, oversampling those employed in the *most* gender atypical areas (e.g., male kindergarten teachers). I also selected respondents from throughout their occupational hierarchies—from students to administrators to retirees. Although the data do not permit within-group comparisons, I am reasonably certain that the sample does capture a wide range of experiences common to men in these female-dominated professions. However, like all findings based on qualitative data, it is uncertain whether the findings generalize to the larger population of men in nontraditional occupations.

In this paper, I review individuals' responses to questions about discrimination in hiring practices, on-the-job rapport with supervisors and coworkers, and prejudice from clients and others outside their profession.

Discrimination in Hiring

Contrary to the experience of many women in the male-dominated professions, many of the men and women I spoke to indicated that there is a *preference* for hiring men in these four occupations. A Texas librarian at a junior high school said that his school district "would hire a male over a female."

I: Why do you think that is?

R: Because there are so few, and the . . . ones that they do have, the library directors

seem to really . . . think they're doing great jobs. I don't know, maybe they just feel they're being progressive or something, [but] I have had a real sense that they really appreciate having a male, particularly at the junior high. . . . As I said, when seven of us lost our jobs from the high schools and were redistributed, there were only four positions at the junior high, and I got one of them. Three of the librarians, some who had been here longer than I had with the school district, were put down in elementary school as librarians. And I definitely think that being male made a difference in my being moved to the junior high rather than an elementary school.

Many of the men perceived their token status as males in predominantly female occupations as an *advantage* in hiring and promotions. I asked an Arizona teacher whether his specialty (elementary special education) was an unusual area for men compared to other areas within education. He said,

> Much more so. I am extremely marketable in special education. That's not why I got into the field. But I am extremely marketable because I am a man.

In several cases, the more female-dominated the specialty, the greater the apparent preference for men. For example, when asked if he encountered any problem getting a job in pediatrics, a Massachusetts nurse said,

> No, no, none. . . . I've heard this from managers and supervisory-type people with men in pediatrics: "It's nice to have a man because it's such a female-dominated profession."

However, there were some exceptions to this preference for men in the most female-dominated specialties. In some cases, formal policies actually barred men from certain jobs. This was the case in some rural Texas school districts, which refused to hire men in the youngest grades (K–3). Some nurses also reported being excluded from positions in obstetrics and gynecology wards, a policy encountered more frequently in private Catholic hospitals.

But often the pressures keeping men out of certain specialties were more subtle than this. Some men described being "tracked" into practice areas within their professions which were considered more legitimate for men. For example, one Texas man described how he was pushed into administration and planning in social work, even though "I'm not interested in writing policy; I'm much more interested in research and clinical stuff." A nurse who is interested in pursuing graduate study in family and child health in Boston said he was dissuaded from entering the program specialty in favor of a concentration in "adult nursing." A kindergarten teacher described the difficulty of finding a job in his specialty after graduation: "I was recruited immediately to start getting into a track to become an administrator. And it was men who recruited me. It was men that ran the system at that time, especially in Los Angeles."

This tracking may bar men from the most female-identified specialties within these professions. But men are effectively being "kicked upstairs" in the process. Those specialties considered more legitimate practice areas for men also tend to be the most prestigious, better paying ones. A distinguished kindergarten teacher, who had been voted city-wide "Teacher of the Year," told me that even though people were pleased to see him in the classroom, "there's been some encouragement to think about administration, and there's been some encouragement to think about teaching at the university level or something like that, or supervisory-type position." That is, despite his aptitude and interest in staying in the classroom, he felt pushed in the direction of administration.

The effect of this "tracking" is the opposite of that experienced by women in male-dominated occupations. Researchers have reported that many women encounter a "glass ceiling" in their efforts to scale organizational and professional hierarchies. That is, they are constrained by invisible barriers to promotion in their careers, caused mainly by sexist attitudes of men in the highest positions (Freeman 1990).[2] In contrast to the "glass ceiling," many of the men I interviewed seem to encounter a "glass escalator." Often, despite their intentions, they face invisible pressures to move up in their professions. As if on a moving escalator, they must work to stay in place.

A public librarian specializing in children's collections (a heavily female-dominated concentration) described an encounter with this "escalator" in his very first job out of library school. In his first six-months' evaluation, his supervisors commended him for his good work in storytelling and related activities, but they criticized him for "not shooting high enough."

> Seriously. That's literally what they were telling me. They assumed that because I was a male—and they told me this—and that I was being hired right out of graduate school, that somehow I wasn't doing the kind of management-oriented work that they thought I should be doing. And as a result, really they had a lot of bad marks, as it were, against me on my evaluation. And I said I couldn't believe this!

Throughout his ten-year career, he has had to struggle to remain in children's collections.

The glass escalator does not operate at all levels. In particular, men in academia reported some gender-based discrimination in the highest positions due to their universities' commitment to affirmative action. Two nursing professors reported that they felt their own chances of promotion to deanships were nil because their universities viewed the position of nursing dean as a guaranteed female appointment in an otherwise heavily male-dominated administration. One California social work professor reported his university canceled its search for a dean because no minority male or female candidates had been placed on their short list. It was rumored that other schools on campus were permitted to go forward with their searches—even though they also failed to put forward names of minority candidates—because the higher administration perceived it to be "easier" to fulfill affirmative action goals in the social work school. The interviews provide greater evidence of the "glass escalator" at work in the lower levels of these professions.

Of course, men's motivations also play a role in their advancement to higher professional positions. I do not mean to suggest that the men I talked to all resented the informal tracking they experienced. For many men, leaving the most female-identified areas of their professions helped them resolve internal conflicts involving their masculinity. One man left his job as a school social worker to work in a methadone drug treatment program not because he was encouraged to leave by his colleagues, but because "I think there was some macho shit there, to tell you the truth, because I remember feeling a little uncomfortable there . . . ; it didn't feel right to me." Another social worker, employed in the mental health services department of a large urban area in California, reflected on his move into administration:

> The more I think about it, through our discussion, I'm sure that's a large part of why I wound up in administration. It's okay for a man to do the administration. In fact, I don't know if I fully answered a question that you asked a little while ago about how did being male contribute to my advancing in the field. I was saying it wasn't because I got any special favoritism as a man, but . . . I think . . . because I'm a man, I felt a need to get into this kind of position. I may have worked harder toward it, may have competed harder for it, than most women would do, even women who think about doing administrative work.

Elsewhere I have speculated on the origins of men's tendency to define masculinity through single-sex work environments (Williams 1989). Clearly, personal ambition does play a role in accounting for men's movement into more "male-defined" arenas within these professions. But these occupations also structure opportunities for males independent of their individual desires or motives.

The interviews suggest that men's underrepresentation in these professions cannot be attributed to discrimination in hiring or promotions. Many of the men indicated that they received preferential treatment because they were men.

Although men mentioned gender discrimination in the hiring process, for the most part they were channelled into the more "masculine" specialties within these professions, which ironically meant being "tracked" into better paying and more prestigious specialties.

Supervisors and Colleagues: The Working Environment

Researchers claim that subtle forms of workplace discrimination push women out of male-dominated occupations (Reskin and Hartmann 1986; Jacobs 1989). In particular, women report feeling excluded from informal leadership and decision-making networks, and they sense hostility from their male co-workers, which makes them feel uncomfortable and unwanted (Carothers and Crull 1984). Respondents in this study were asked about their relationships with supervisors and female colleagues to ascertain whether men also experienced "poisoned" work environments when entering gender atypical occupations.

A major difference in the experience of men and women in nontraditional occupations is that men in these situations are far more likely to be supervised by a member of their own sex. In each of the four professions I studied, men are overrepresented in administrative and managerial capacities, or, as in the case of nursing, their positions in the organizational hierarchy are governed by men (Grimm and Sterm 1974; Phenix 1987; Schmuck 1987; York, Henley, and Gamble 1987; Williams 1989). Thus, unlike women who enter "male fields," the men in these professions often work under the direct supervision of other men.

Many of the men interviewed reported that they had good rapport with their male supervisors. Even in professional school, some men reported extremely close relationships with their male professors. For example, a Texas librarian described an unusually intimate association with two male professors in graduate school:

> I can remember a lot of times in the classroom there would be discussions about a particular

topic or issue, and the conversation would spill over into their office hours, after the class was over. And even though there were . . . a couple of the other women that had been in on the discussion, they weren't there. And I don't know if that was preferential or not . . . it certainly carried over into personal life as well. Not just at the school and that sort of thing. I mean, we would get together for dinner . . .

These professors explicitly encouraged him because he was male:

I: Did they ever offer you explicit words of encouragement about being in the profession by virtue of the fact that you were male? . . .

R: Definitely. On several occasions. Yeah. Both of these guys, for sure, including the Dean who was male also. And it's an interesting point that you bring up because it was, oftentimes, kind of in a sign, you know. It wasn't in the classroom, and it wasn't in front of the group, or if we were in the student lounge or something like that. It was . . . if it was just myself or maybe another one of the guys, you know, and just talking in the office. It's like . . . you know, kind of an opening-up and saying, "You know, you are really lucky that you're in the profession because you'll really go to the top real quick, and you'll be able to make real definite improvements and changes. And you'll have a real influence," and all this sort of thing. I mean, really, I can remember several times.

Other men reported similar closeness with their professors. A Texas psychotherapist recalled his relationships with his male professors in social work school:

I made it a point to make a golfing buddy with one of the guys that was in administration. He and I played golf a lot. He was the guy who kind of ran the research training, the research part of the master's program. Then there was a sociologist who ran the other part of the research program. He and I developed a good friendship.

This close mentoring by male professors contrasts with the reported experience of women in nontraditional occupations. Others have noted a lack of solidarity among women in nontraditional occupations. Writing about military academies, for example, Yoder describes the failure of token women to mentor succeeding generations of female cadets. She argues that women attempt to play down their gender difference from men because it is the source of scorn and derision.

Because women felt unaccepted by their male colleagues, one of the last things they wanted to do was to emphasize their gender. Some women thought that, if they kept company with other women, this would highlight their gender and would further isolate them from male cadets. These women desperately wanted to be accepted as cadets, not as *women* cadets. Therefore, they did everything from not wearing skirts as an option with their uniforms to avoiding being a part of a group of women. (Yoder 1989:532)

Men in nontraditional occupations face a different scenario—their gender is construed as a *positive* difference. Therefore, they have an incentive to bond together and emphasize their distinctiveness from the female majority.

Close, personal ties with male supervisors were also described by men once they were established in their professional careers. It was not uncommon in education, for example, for the male principal to informally socialize with the male staff, as a Texas special education teacher describes:

Occasionally I've had a principal who would regard me as "the other man on the campus" and "it's us against them," you know? I mean, nothing really that extreme, except that some male principals feel like there's nobody there to talk to except the other man. So I've been in that position.

These personal ties can have important consequences for men's careers. For example, one California nurse, whose performance was judged marginal by his nursing supervisors, was transferred to the emergency room staff (a prestigious promotion) due to his personal friendship with the physician in charge. A Massachusetts teacher acknowledged that his principal's personal interest in him landed him his current job.

> **I:** You had mentioned that your principal had sort of spotted you at your previous job and had wanted to bring you here [to this school]. Do you think that has anything to do with the fact that you're a man, aside from your skills as a teacher?
>
> **R:** Yes, I would say in that particular case, that was part of it. . . . We have certain things in common, certain interests that really lined up.
>
> **I:** Vis-à-vis teaching?
>
> **R:** Well, more extraneous things—running specifically, and music. And we just seemed to get along real well right off the bat. It is just kind of a guy thing; we just liked each other . . .

Interviewees did not report many instances of male supervisors discriminating against them, or refusing to accept them because they were male. Indeed, these men were much more likely to report that their male bosses discriminated against the *females* in their professions. When asked if he thought physicians treated male and female nurses differently, a Texas nurse said:

> I think yeah, some of them do. I think the women seem like they have a lot more trouble with the physicians treating them in a derogatory manner. Or, if not derogatory, then in a very paternalistic way than the men [are treated]. Usually if a physician is mad at a male nurse, he just kind of yells at him. Kind of like an employee. And if they're mad at a female nurse, rather than treat them on an equal basis, in terms of just letting their anger out at them as an employee, they're more paternalistic or there's some sexual harassment component to it.

A Texas teacher perceived a similar situation where he worked:

> I've never felt unjustly treated by a principal because I'm a male. The principals that I've seen that I felt are doing things that are kind of arbitrary or not well thought out are doing it to everybody. In fact, they're probably doing it to the females worse than they are to me.

Openly gay men may encounter less favorable treatment at the hands of their supervisors. For example, a nurse in Texas stated that one of the physicians he worked with preferred to staff the operating room with male nurses exclusively—as long as they weren't gay. Stigma associated with homosexuality leads some men to enhance, or even exaggerate their "masculine" qualities, and may be another factor pushing men into more "acceptable" specialties for men.

Not all men who work in these occupations are supervised by men. Many of the men interviewed who had female bosses also reported high levels of acceptance—although levels of intimacy with women seemed lower than with other men. In some cases, however, men reported feeling shut-out from decision making when the higher administration was constituted entirely by women. I asked an Arizona librarian whether men in the library profession were discriminated against in hiring because of their sex:

> Professionally speaking, people go to considerable lengths to keep that kind of thing out of their [hiring] deliberations. Personally, is another matter. It's pretty common around here to talk about the "old girl network." This is one of the few libraries that I've had any intimate knowledge of which is actually controlled by women. . . . Most of the department heads and upper level administrators are women. And there's an "old girl network" that works just like the "old boy network," except that the important conferences take place in the women's room rather than on the golf course. But the political mechanism is the same, the exclusion of the other sex from decision making is the same. The reasons are the same. It's somewhat discouraging . . .

Although I did not interview many supervisors, I did include 23 women in my sample to ascertain their perspectives about the presence of men in their professions. All of the women I interviewed claimed to be supportive of their male colleagues, but some conveyed ambivalence. For example, a social work professor said she would like to see more men enter the social work profession, particularly in the clinical specialty (where they are underrepresented). Indeed, she favored affirmative action hiring guidelines for men in the profession. Yet, she resented the fact that her department hired "another white male" during a recent search. I questioned her about this ambivalence:

> **I:** I find it very interesting that, on the one hand, you sort of perceive this preference and perhaps even sexism with regard to how men are evaluated and how they achieve higher positions within the profession, yet, on the other hand, you would be encouraging of more men to enter the field. Is that contradictory to you, or . . . ?
>
> **R:** Yeah, it's contradictory.

It appears that women are generally eager to see men enter "their" occupations. Indeed, several men noted that their female colleagues had facilitated their careers in various ways (including mentorship in college). However, at the same time, women often resent the apparent ease with which men advance within these professions, sensing that men at the higher levels receive preferential treatment which closes off advancement opportunities for women.

But this ambivalence does not seem to translate into the "poisoned" work environment described by many women who work in male-dominated occupations. Among the male interviewees, there were no accounts of sexual harassment. However, women do treat their male colleagues differently on occasion. It is not uncommon in nursing, for example, for men to be called upon to help catheterize male patients, or to lift especially heavy patients. Some librarians also said that women asked them to lift and move heavy boxes of books because they were men. Teachers sometimes confront differential treatment as well, as described by this Texas teacher:

> As a man, you're teaching with all women, and that can be hard sometimes. Just because of the stereotypes, you know. I'm real into computers . . . and all the time people are calling me to fix their computer. Or if somebody gets a flat tire, they come and get me. I mean, there are just a lot of stereotypes. Not that I mind doing any of those things, but it's . . . you know, it just kind of bugs me that it is a stereotype, "A man should do that." Or if their kids have a lot of discipline problems, that kiddo's in your room. Or if there are kids that don't have a father in their home, that kid's in your room. Hell, nowadays that'd be half the school in my room (laughs). But you know, all the time I hear from the principal or from other teachers, "Well, this child really needs a man . . . a male role model" (laughs). So there are a lot of stereotypes that . . . men kind of get stuck with.

This special treatment bothered some respondents. Getting assigned all the "discipline problems" can make for difficult working conditions, for example. But many men claimed this differential treatment did not cause distress. In fact, several said they liked being appreciated for the special traits and abilities (such as strength) they could contribute to their professions.

Furthermore, women's special treatment sometimes enhanced—rather than poisoned—the men's work environments. One Texas librarian said he felt "more comfortable working with women than men" because "I think it has something to do with control. Maybe it's that women will let me take control more than men will." Several men reported that their female colleagues often cast them into leadership roles. Although not all savored this distinction, it did enhance their authority and control in the workplace. In subtle (and not-too-subtle) ways, then, differential treatment contributes to the "glass escalator" men experience in nontraditional professions.

Even outside work, most of the men interviewed said they felt fully accepted by their female colleagues. They were usually included in informal socializing occasions with the women—

even though this frequently meant attending baby showers or Tupperware parties. Many said that they declined offers to attend these events because they were not interested in "women's things," although several others claimed to attend everything: The minority men I interviewed seemed to feel the least comfortable in these informal contexts. One social worker in Arizona was asked about socializing with his female colleagues:

> **I:** So in general, for example, if all the employees were going to get together to have a party, or celebrate a bridal shower or whatever, would you be invited along with the rest of the group?
>
> **R:** They would invite me, I would say, somewhat reluctantly. Being a black male, working with all white females, it did cause some outside problems. So I didn't go to a lot of functions with them . . .
>
> **I:** You felt that there was some tension there on the level of your acceptance . . . ?
>
> **R:** Yeah. It was OK working, but on the outside, personally, there was some tension there. It never came out, that they said, "Because of who you are we can't invite you" (laughs), and I wouldn't have done anything anyway. I would have probably respected them more for saying what was on their minds. But I never felt completely in with the group.

Some single men also said they felt uncomfortable socializing with married female colleagues because it gave the "wrong impression." But in general, the men said that they felt very comfortable around their colleagues and described their workplaces as very congenial for men. It appears unlikely, therefore, that men's underrepresentation in these professions is due to hostility towards men on the part of supervisors or women workers.

Discrimination from "Outsiders"

The most compelling evidence of discrimination against men in these professions is related to their dealings with the public. Men often encounter negative stereotypes when they come into contact with clients or "outsiders"—people they meet outside of work. For instance, it is popularly assumed that male nurses are gay. Librarians encounter images of themselves as "wimpy" and asexual. Male social workers describe being typecast as "feminine" and "passive." Elementary school teachers are often confronted by suspicions that they are pedophiles. One kindergarten teacher described an experience that occurred early in his career which was related to him years afterwards by his principal:

> He indicated to me that parents had come to him and indicated to him that they had a problem with the fact that I was a male. . . . I recall almost exactly what he said. There were three specific concerns that the parents had: One parent said, "How can he love my child; he's a man." The second thing that I recall, he said the parent said, "He has a beard." And the third thing was, "Aren't you concerned about homosexuality?"

Such suspicions often cause men in all four professions to alter their work behavior to guard against sexual abuse charges, particularly in those specialties requiring intimate contact with women and children.

Men are very distressed by these negative stereotypes, which tend to undermine their self-esteem and to cause them to second-guess their motivations for entering these fields. A California teacher said,

> If I tell men that I don't know, that I'm meeting for the first time, that that's what I do, . . . sometimes there's a look on their faces that, you know, "Oh, couldn't get a real job?"

When asked if his wife, who is also an elementary school teacher, encounters the same kind of prejudice, he said,

> No, it's accepted because she's a woman. . . . I think people would see that as a . . . step up, you know. "Oh, you're not a housewife, you've got a career. That's great . . . that you're out there working. And you have a daughter, but you're still out there working. You decided not

to stay home, and you went out there and got a job." Whereas for me, it's more like I'm supposed to be out working anyway, even though I'd rather be home with [my daughter].

Unlike women who enter traditionally male professions, men's movement into these jobs is perceived by the "outside world" as a step down in status. This particular form of discrimination may be most significant in explaining why men are underrepresented in these professions. Men who otherwise might show interest in and aptitudes for such careers are probably discouraged from pursuing them because of the negative popular stereotypes associated with the men who work in them. This is a crucial difference from the experience of women in nontraditional professions: "My daughter, the physician," resonates far more favorably in most people's ears than "My son, the nurse."

Many of the men in my sample identified the stigma of working in a female-identified occupation as the major barrier to more men entering their professions. However, for the most part, they claimed that these negative stereotypes were not a factor in their own decisions to join these occupations. Most respondents didn't consider entering these fields until well into adulthood, after working in some related occupation. Several social workers and librarians even claimed they were not aware that men were a minority in their chosen professions. Either they had no well-defined image or stereotype, or their contacts and mentors were predominantly men. For example, prior to entering library school, many librarians held part-time jobs in university libraries, where there are proportionally more men than in the profession generally. Nurses and elementary school teachers were more aware that mostly women worked in these jobs, and this was often a matter of some concern to them. However, their choices were ultimately legitimized by mentors, or by encouraging friends or family members who implicitly reassured them that entering these occupations would not typecast them as feminine. In some cases, men were told by recruiters there were special advancement opportunities for men in these fields, and they entered them expecting rapid promotion to administrative positions.

I: Did it ever concern you when you were making the decision to enter nursing school, the fact that it is a female-dominated profession?

R: Not really. I never saw myself working on the floor. I saw myself pretty much going into administration, just getting the background and then getting a job someplace as a supervisor and then working, getting up into administration.

Because of the unique circumstances of their recruitment, many of the respondents did not view their occupational choices as inconsistent with a male gender role, and they generally avoided the negative stereotypes directed against men in these fields.

Indeed, many of the men I interviewed claimed that they did not encounter negative professional stereotypes until they had worked in these fields for several years. Popular prejudices can be damaging to self-esteem and probably push some men out of these professions altogether. Yet, ironically, they sometimes contribute to the "glass escalator" effect I have been describing. Men seem to encounter the most vituperative criticism from the public when they are in the most female-identified specialties. Public concerns sometimes result in their being shunted into more "legitimate" positions for men. A librarian formerly in charge of a branch library's children's collection, who now works in the reference department of the city's main library, describes his experience:

R: Some of the people [who frequented the branch library] complained that they didn't want to have a man doing the storytelling scenario. And I got transferred here to the central library in an equivalent job . . . I thought that I did a good job. And I had been told by my supervisor that I was doing a good job.

I: Have you ever considered filing some sort of lawsuit to get that other job back?

R: Well, actually, the job I've gotten now . . . well, it's a reference librarian; it's what I wanted in the first place. I've got a whole lot more authority here. I'm also in charge of the circulation desk. And I've recently been promoted because of my new stature, so . . . no, I'm not considering trying to get that other job back.

The negative stereotypes about men who do "women's work" can push men out of specific jobs. However, to the extent that they channel men into more "legitimate" practice areas, their effects can actually be positive. Instead of being a source of discrimination, these prejudices can add to the "glass escalator effect" by pressuring men to move *out* of the most female-identified areas, and *up* to those regarded as more legitimate and prestigious for men.

Conclusion: Discrimination Against Men

Both men and women who work in nontraditional occupations encounter discrimination, but the forms and consequences of this discrimination are very different. The interviews suggest that unlike "nontraditional" women workers, most of the discrimination and prejudice facing men in the "female professions" emanates from outside those professions. The men and women interviewed for the most part believed that men are given fair—if not preferential—treatment in hiring and promotion decisions, are accepted by supervisors and colleagues, and are well-integrated into the workplace subculture. Indeed, subtle mechanisms seem to enhance men's position in these professions—a phenomenon I refer to as the "glass escalator effect."

The data lend strong support for Zimmer's (1988) critique of "gender neutral theory" (such as Kanter's [1977] theory of tokenism) in the study of occupational segregation. Zimmer argues that women's occupational inequality is more a consequence of sexist beliefs and practices embedded in the labor force than the effect of numerical un-derrepresentation per se. This study suggests that token status itself does not diminish men's occupational success. Men take their gender privilege with them when they enter predominantly female occupations: this translates into an advantage in spite of their numerical rarity.

This study indicates that the experience of tokenism is very different for men and women. Future research should examine how the experience of tokenism varies for members of different races and classes as well. For example, it is likely that informal workplace mechanisms similar to the ones identified here promote the careers of token whites in predominantly black occupations. The crucial factor is the social status of the token's group—not their numerical rarity—that determines whether the token encounters a "glass ceiling" or a "glass escalator."

However, this study also found that many men encounter negative stereotypes from persons not directly involved in their professions. Men who enter these professions are often considered "failures" or sexual deviants. These stereotypes may be a major impediment to men who otherwise might consider careers in these occupations. Indeed, they are likely to be important factors whenever a member of a relatively high status group crosses over into a lower status occupation. However, to the extent that these stereotypes contribute to the "glass escalator effect" by channeling men into more "legitimate" (and higher paying) occupations, they are not discriminatory.

Women entering traditionally "male" professions also face negative stereotypes suggesting they are not "real women" (Epstein 1981; Lorber 1984; Spencer and Podmore 1987). However, these stereotypes do not seem to deter women to the same degree that they deter men from pursuing nontraditional professions. There is ample historical evidence that women flock to male-identified occupations once opportunities are available (Cohn 1985; Epstein 1988). Not so with men. Examples of occupations changing from predominantly female to predominantly male are very rare in our history. The few existing cases—such as medicine—suggest that redefinition of the occupations as appropriately "masculine" is necessary before men will consider joining them (Ehrenreich and English 1978).

Because different mechanisms maintain segregation in male- and female-dominated occupations, different approaches are needed to promote their integration. Policies intended to alter the sex composition of male-dominated occupations—such as affirmative action—make little sense when applied to the "female professions." For men, the major barriers to integration have little to do with their treatment once they decide to enter these fields. Rather, we need to address the social and cultural sanctions applied to men who do "women's work" which keep men from even considering these occupations.

One area where these cultural barriers are clearly evident is in the media's representation of men's occupations. Women working in traditionally male professions have achieved an unprecedented acceptance on popular television shows. Women are portrayed as doctors ("St. Elsewhere"), lawyers ("The Cosby Show," "L.A. Law"), architects ("Family Ties"), and police officers ("Cagney and Lacey"). But where are the male nurses, teachers, and secretaries? Television rarely portrays men in nontraditional work roles, and when it does, that anomaly is made the central focus—and joke—of the program. A comedy series (1991–1992) about a male elementary school teacher ("Drexell's Class") stars a lead character who *hates children!* Yet even this negative portrayal is exceptional. When a prime-time hospital drama series ("St. Elsewhere") depicted a male orderly striving for upward mobility, the show's writers made him a "physician's assistant," not a nurse or nurse practitioner—the much more likely "real life" possibilities.

Presenting positive images of men in nontraditional careers can produce limited effects. A few social workers, for example, were first inspired to pursue their careers by George C. Scott, who played a social worker in the television drama series, "Eastside/Westside." But as a policy strategy to break down occupational segregation, changing media images of men is no panacea.

The stereotypes that differentiate masculinity and femininity, and degrade that which is defined as feminine, are deeply entrenched in culture, social structure, and personality (Williams 1989). Nothing short of a revolution in cultural definitions of masculinity will effect the broad scale social transformation needed to achieve the complete occupational integration of men and women.

Of course, there are additional factors besides societal prejudice contributing to men's underrepresentation in female-dominated professions. Most notably, those men I interviewed mentioned as a deterrent the fact that these professions are all underpaid relative to comparable "male" occupations, and several suggested that instituting a "comparable worth" policy might attract more men. However, I am not convinced that improved salaries will substantially alter the sex composition of these professions unless the cultural stigma faced by men in these occupations diminishes. Occupational sex segregation is remarkably resilient, even in the face of devastating economic hardship. During the Great Depression of the 1930s, for example, "women's jobs" failed to attract sizable numbers of men (Blum 1991:154). In her study of American Telephone and Telegraph (AT&T) workers, Epstein (1989) found that some men would rather suffer unemployment than accept relatively high paying "women's jobs" because of the damage to their identities this would cause. She quotes one unemployed man who refused to apply for a female-identified telephone operator job:

> I think if they offered me $1000 a week tax free, I wouldn't take that job. When I . . . see those guys sitting in there [in the telephone operating room], I wonder what's wrong with them. Are they pansies or what? (Epstein 1989: 577)

This is not to say that raising salaries would not affect the sex composition of these jobs. Rather, I am suggesting that wages are not the only—or perhaps even the major—impediment to men's entry into these jobs. Further research is needed to explore the ideological significance of the "woman's wage" for maintaining occupational stratification.[3]

At any rate, integrating men and women in the labor force requires more than dismantling barriers to women in male-dominated fields. Sex segregation is a two-way street. We must also confront and dismantle the barriers men face in predominantly female occupations. Men's experiences in these nontraditional occupations reveal just how culturally embedded the barriers are, and how far we have to travel before men and women attain true occupational and economic equality.

Author's Note: This research was funded in part by a faculty grant from the University of Texas at Austin. I also acknowledge the support of the sociology departments of the University of California, Berkeley; Harvard University; and Arizona State University. I would like to thank Judy Auerbach, Martin Button, Robert Nye, Teresa Sullivan, Debra Umberson, Mary Waters, and the reviewers at *Social Problems* for their comments on earlier versions of this paper.

Notes

1. According to the U.S. Census, black men and women comprise 7 percent of all nurses and librarians, 11 percent of all elementary school teachers, and 19 percent of all social workers (calculated from U.S. Census 1980: Table 278, 1–197). The proportion of blacks in social work may be exaggerated by these statistics. The occupational definition of "social worker" used by the Census Bureau includes welfare workers and pardon and parole officers, who are not considered "professional" social workers by the National Association of Social Workers. A study of degreed professionals found that 89 percent of practitioners were white (Hardcastle 1987).

2. In April 1991, the Labor Department created a "Glass Ceiling Commission" to "conduct a thorough study of the underrepresentation of women and minorities in executive, management, and senior decision-making positions in business" (U.S. House of Representatives 1991:20).

3. Alice Kessler-Harris argues that the lower pay of traditionally female occupations is symbolic of a patriarchal order that assumes female dependence on a male breadwinner. She writes that pay equity is fundamentally threatening to the "male worker's sense of self, pride, and masculinity" because it upsets his individual standing in the hierarchical ordering of the sexes (1990:125). Thus, men's reluctance to enter these occupations may have less to do with the actual dollar amount recorded in their paychecks, and more to do with the damage that earning "a woman's wage" would wreak on their self-esteem in a society that privileges men. This conclusion is supported by the interview data.

References

Bielby, William T., and James N. Baron
1984 "A woman's place is with other women: Sex segregation within organizations." In *Sex Segregation in the Workplace: Trends, Explanations, Remedies*, ed. Barbara Reskin, 27–55. Washington, D.C.: National Academy Press.

Blum, Linda M.
1991 *Between Feminism and Labor: The Significance of the Comparable Worth Movement*. Berkeley and Los Angeles: University of California Press.

Carothers, Suzanne C., and Peggy Crull
1984 "Contrasting sexual harassment in female-dominated and male-dominated occupations." In *My Troubles Are Going to Have Trouble with Me: Everyday Trials and Triumphs of Women Workers*, ed. Karen B. Sacks and Dorothy Remy, 220–227. New Brunswick, N.J.: Rutgers University Press.

Cohn, Samuel
1985 *The Process of Occupational Sex-Typing*. Philadelphia: Temple University Press.

Ehrenreich, Barbara, and Deirdre English
1978 *For Her Own Good: 100 Years of Expert Advice to Women*. Garden City, N.Y.: Anchor Press.

Epstein, Cynthia Fuchs
1981 *Women in Law*. New York: Basic Books.
1988 *Deceptive Distinctions: Sex, Gender and the Social Order*. New Haven: Yale University Press.
1989 "Workplace boundaries: Conceptions and creations." *Social Research* 56: 571–590.

Freeman, Sue J. M.
1990 *Managing Lives: Corporate Women and Social Change*. Amherst, Mass.: University of Massachusetts Press.

Grimm, James W., and Robert N. Stern
1974 "Sex roles and internal labor market structures: The female semi-professions." *Social Problems* 21: 690–705.

Hardcastle, D. A.
1987 "The social work labor force." Austin, Tex.: School of Social Work, University of Texas.

Hodson, Randy, and Teresa Sullivan

1990 *The Social Organization of Work*. Belmont, Calif.: Wadsworth Publishing Co.

Jacobs, Jerry

1989 *Revolving Doors: Sex Segregation and Women's Careers*. Stanford, Calif.: Stanford University Press.

Kanter, Rosabeth Moss

1977 *Men and Women of the Corporation*. New York: Basic Books.

Kessler-Harris, Alice

1990 *A Woman's Wage: Historical Meanings and Social Consequences*. Lexington, Ky.: Kentucky University Press.

Lorber, Judith

1984 *Women Physicians: Careers, Status, and Power*. New York: Tavistock.

Martin, Susan E.

1980 *Breaking and Entering: Police Women on Patrol*. Berkeley, Calif.: University of California Press.

1988 "Think like a man, work like a dog, and act like a lady: Occupational dilemmas of policewomen." In *The Worth of Women's Work: A Qualitative Synthesis*, ed. Anne Statham, Eleanor M. Miller, and Hans O. Mauksch, 205–223. Albany, N.Y.: State University of New York Press.

Phenix, Katharine

1987 "The status of women librarians." *Frontiers* 9: 36–40.

Reskin, Barbara

1988 "Bringing the men back in: Sex differentiation and the devaluation of women's work." *Gender & Society* 2: 58–81.

Reskin, Barbara, and Heidi Hartmann

1986 *Women's Work, Men's Work: Sex Segregation on the Job*. Washington, D.C.: National Academy Press.

Reskin, Barbara, and Patricia Roos

1990 *Job Queues, Gender Queues: Explaining Women's Inroads into Male Occupations*. Philadelphia: Temple University Press.

Schmuck, Patricia A.

1987 "Women school employees in the United States." In *Women Educators: Employees of Schools in Western Countries*, ed. Patricia A. Schmuck, 75–97. Albany, N.Y.: State University of New York Press.

Schreiber, Carol

1979 *Men and Women in Transitional Occupations*. Cambridge, Mass.: MIT Press.

Spencer, Anne, and David Podmore

1987 *In a Man's World: Essays on Women in Male-Dominated Professions*. London: Tavistock.

Strauss, Anselm L.

1987 *Qualitative Analysis for Social Scientists*. Cambridge, England: Cambridge University Press.

U.S. Bureau of the Census

1980 *Detailed Population Characteristics*, Vol. 1, Ch. D. Washington, D.C.: Government Printing Office.

U.S. Congress. House

1991 *Civil Rights and Women's Equity in Employment Act of 1991*. Report. (Report 102-40, Part I.) Washington, D.C.: Government Printing Office.

U.S. Department of Labor. Bureau of Labor Statistics

1991 *Employment and Earnings*. January. Washington, D.C.: Government Printing Office.

Williams, Christine L.

1989 *Gender Differences at Work: Women and Men in Nontraditional Occupations*. Berkeley, Calif.: University of California Press.

Yoder, Janice D.

1989 "Women at West Point: Lessons for token women in male-dominated occupations." In *Women: A Feminist Perspective*, ed. Jo Freeman, 523–537. Mountain View, Calif.: Mayfield Publishing Company.

York, Reginald O., H. Carl Henley, and Dorothy N. Gamble

1987 "Sexual discrimination in social work: Is it salary or advancement?" *Social Work* 32: 336–340.

Zimmer, Lynn

1988 "Tokenism and women in the workplace." *Social Problems* 35: 64–77.

Kevin D. Henson
Jackie Krasas Rogers

"Why Marcia You've Changed!": Male Clerical Temporary Workers Doing Masculinity in a Feminized Occupation

To say that organizations are gendered has many meanings, from gender segregation at work to the part organizations play in the cultural reproduction of gender inequality (Acker 1990; Britton 2000). We know that "advantage and disadvantage, exploitation and control, action and emotion, meaning and identity are patterned through and in terms of a distinction between male and female, masculine and feminine" (Acker 1990, 146). Interaction and identity are but two means through which gender is constituted and reproduced in the workplace. Men and women "do gender" (West and Fenstermaker 1995; West and Zimmerman 1987) at work in organizations that are themselves gendered, and organizational imperatives shape interaction that "naturalizes" and essentializes cultural constructions of masculinity and femininity for men and women. This study provides a look at men doing gender in the highly feminized context of temporary clerical employment.

Doing gender "appropriately" in the workplace has consequences, including material ones, for both women and men. A significant portion of the existing sociological literature explores how women are required to do gender at work, including emotional labor, which often reinforces vulnerability and inequality (Hochschild 1983;

From *Gender & Society* 15(2): 218–238. Copyright © 2001 Sociologists for Women in Society.

Leidner 1993; Pierce 1995; Williams 1989, 1995; Rogers and Henson 1997). Yet, men are also required to do gender on the job, and although less well documented, men do perform emotional labor, albeit subject to a different set of constraints, expectations, and outcomes than women's emotional labor (Pierce 1995; Cheng 1996). Indeed, emotional work is implicated in the microprocesses of doing gender that reinforce, uphold, and even naturalize male dominance and hegemonic masculinity (Collinson and Hearn 1996).[1]

In contrast with Kanter's (1977) position that any token, male or female, is subject to a distinct set of negative experiences, a recent avenue of inquiry has demonstrated how some men "benefit" from their token status in "women's work"— riding the "glass escalator" to more prestigious, better-paid positions within women's professions (Pierce 1995; Williams 1995; Maume 1999). Although men who cross over into women's work are often seen as less manly, this disadvantage has paled in comparison to the material benefits available to (white) male tokens, who self-segregate (or are pushed) into higher pay and higher status specialties or administrative positions in female-dominated professions (see Williams 1989, 1995).

What happens, however, when men find themselves in a female-dominated occupation with limited opportunities to ride the glass escalator? Temporary clerical work is such an occupation. As externalized employment that institutionalizes limited access to internal labor markets, there is no glass escalator to ride in temporary clerical work. Temporary clerical work does not provide the opportunities for men (or women) to elevate their status through additional credentialing, specialization, or promotions. Indeed, upward mobility into permanent employment—hailed as a major benefit by the temporary industry—is extremely elusive (Smith 1998; Rogers 2000).[2] Therefore, male tokens in female-dominated temporary clerical work present an interesting case concerning the gendered nature of work. How does men's gender privilege operate in the absence of opportunities for upward mobility? Does men's presence in a dead-end, female-dominated occupation disrupt the gender order and challenge hegemonic masculinity?

In this article, we argue that although men's presence in temporary clerical work has the potential to challenge the "naturalness" of the gendered organization of work, in everyday practice it is assumed to say more about the essential nature of the individual men. Male clerical temporaries, as with other men who cross over into women's work, fall increasingly short of the ideals of hegemonic masculinity on at least two fronts. First, they face gender assessment through their lack of a "real" job (i.e., a full-time career in "men's work"). Second, their location in a feminized occupation that requires the performance of emphasized femininity, including deference and caretaking behaviors, calls into question their presumed heterosexuality. The resulting gender strategies (Hochschild 1989) these men adopt reveal how male clerical temporary workers "do masculinity" to reassert the feminine identification of the job while rejecting its application to them. In particular, we argue that men in clerical temporary work do masculinity through renaming and reframing the work, distancing themselves from the work with a cover story, and resisting the demands to perform deference. Paradoxically, rather than disrupting the gender order, the gender strategies adopted help reproduce and naturalize the gendered organization of work and reinvigorate hegemonic masculinity and its domination over women and subaltern men.

The Gendered Character of Temporary Clerical Employment

While temporary employment has increased dramatically in the past 15 years in response to employers' demands (Golden and Appelbaum 1992), researchers have only recently begun to systematically document the effects of this trend for workers and workplace relations. The rapid expansion of temporary employment is profoundly changing the experience, meaning, and conditions of work for temporaries who, like other contingent workers, fall through the cracks of existing workplace protections and provision of benefits (Parker 1994; Henson 1996; Rogers and Henson 1997; Rogers 2000).

The clerical sector of temporary employment, like the permanent clerical sector, is predominantly composed of women (Bureau of Labor Statistics 1995). Historically, this association of temporary work with women's work was reflected in the common inclusion of the infantilizing term *girl* in the names of the earliest temporary agencies (e.g., Kelly Girl). While temporary agencies have formally modernized their names (i.e., Kelly Girl became Kelly Services), the continued popular usage of the outdated names accurately reflects the gendered composition of the temporary clerical workforce. Indeed, a survey by the National Association of Temporary Services (1992) estimated that 80 percent of member agency temporaries were women. A recent government survey concluded that "workers employed by temporary help agencies in February 1997 were more likely than other workers to be young, female, Black or Hispanic" (Cohany 1998, 13).

Contemporary clerical temporary employment, like permanent clerical work, is so completely identified as women's work that until recently, it was considered inappropriate employment for a man, even by the temporary industry. Until the 1960s, in fact, it was common policy within the industry not to accept male applicants for clerical temporary work (Moore 1963, 35). Men, it was asserted, should be seeking a permanent, full-time career-type job—a "real job"—that would allow them to work hard, be financially successful, and take on the idealized (male) bread-winner role (Connell 1987, 1995; Cheng 1996).

Recently, however, men have come to constitute a greater proportion of temporary agency workers, although they are still more likely to be working as industrial than clerical temporaries (see Parker 1994). In fact, the continued numerical predominance of women in both the permanent and temporary clerical workforce often leads to the assumption that clerical temporary workers are women. Indeed, the job of clerical temporary worker is gendered—more specifically feminized—as women's work. Consequently, temporary work, clerical work, and especially temporary clerical work are perceived as women's work.

Given temporaries' low status and vulnerability to work deprivation, the expectations of temporary agencies and clients become de facto job requirements that shape temporary workers' interactions in such a way that one's gender and sexuality are prominently featured as aspects of the work (see Rogers and Henson 1997). For example, the demands of temporary agencies and client companies for particular (gendered or sexy) physical presentations, and the embedded expectations for deference and caretaking behaviors, highlight the gendered (feminized) and sexualized nature of temporary clerical work (Henson 1996; Rogers and Henson 1997). Indeed, the common association of temporary work with promiscuity, or "occupational sleeping around," highlights the ways in which clerical work and temporary work intersect to create a highly feminized job (see Rogers 2000 for a discussion of the gendering of temporary versus clerical work). In other words, temporary clerical work is a gendered (as well as raced, classed, aged, and heterosexualized) occupation that requires workers to do gender (and race, class, and so forth) in certain forms, recreating them and making them appear natural (see West and Zimmerman 1987; Acker 1990, West and Fenstermaker 1995). The type of gender one must "do" in clerical temporary work is primar-

ily white, middle-class, heterosexual femininity. Consequently, while certain exceptions are made, it is nearly impossible to do this brand of femininity appropriately if you are a man or a woman of color. After describing our research methodology, we examine the gendered (feminized) context of clerical temporary employment, the institutionalized challenges to masculinity such employment poses for token men, and the gender strategies token men adopt to buttress their sense of masculinity. Finally, we discuss how these gender strategies reproduce rather than challenge the gender order.

Method

This research is based on in-depth interviews and extensive participant observation from two broader studies on temporary clerical work we conducted in Chicago in 1990–1991 (Henson 1996) and Los Angeles in 1993–1994 (Rogers 2000). During the participant observation component of our studies, each of us worked as a clerical temporary worker for more than one year on a variety of assignments in many different types of organizations. We entered our temporary employment with many common characteristics such as relatively high educational attainment, whiteness, and youthfulness (Kevin was 26; Jackie was 28), yet our different respective genders affected our temporary work experiences in many dissimilar and revealing ways.

In addition to our participant–observation work, each of us conducted open-ended, semi-structured interviews with temporaries and agency personnel, yielding 68 interviews in all (35 in Chicago and 33 in Los Angeles). Our interview participants included 10 temporary agency personnel and one client company representative, but the majority (57) were temporary clerical workers. We located participants of this highly fluid and difficult-to-access workforce through a variety of methods—personal contacts made on assignment, responses to fliers placed at temporary agency offices, and personal referrals. We pursued a grounded theory approach in our research, including an emphasis on theoretical sampling (Glaser and Strauss 1965, 1967). Consequently, we sought out participants who maximized the range of temporary work experiences we studied rather than pursuing a strictly representative sample of the temporary workforce. In the end, our sample of temporary clerical workers included a relatively diverse group of participants, including 20 men and 37 women ranging in age from 20 to 60 (see Table 23.1).[3] Indeed, our sample approximates the age and race distribution of the general temporary workforce. However, our sample differs in at least one important way from the general clerical temporary workforce. We deliberately oversampled for men in this female-dominated occupation. Collectively, our interview participants had worked through more than 40 temporary agencies with individual tenure in temporary employment ranging from a few months to more than 10 years.

We followed flexible open-ended interview schedules, addressing themes that we had identified as salient during our participant–observation work and pursued new themes as they emerged. We both interviewed women and men in our respective locales, and although evidence of participants' negotiation of the "gendered context of the [interview] interaction" emerged (e.g., men talked

directly about feeling "less manly" to Jackie but talked more abstractly about feeling like "failures" to Kevin), there was a remarkable overlap and consistency in the substance of participants' responses (see Williams and Heikes 1993). We tape-recorded, transcribed, and analyzed all of the interviews. Although at first we pursued an open coding process focusing on general concepts such as stigmatization and coping strategies, eventually our analysis revealed consistent gendered patterns in our data. All names indicated in the body of the article are pseudonyms.

What's He Doing Here?

Male temporary clerical workers initially disrupt the gendered landscape of an organization since both the permanent and temporary clerical workforces are female dominated. This is reflected in the consistency with which token male clerical temporaries were met with surprise on the job. Indeed, the reaction to token men highlights the almost complete feminization of the work and the associated expectation that temporary workers will be women. The male temporaries we interviewed, for example, universally commented on their experiences as token men in women's work:

> There are areas where I felt that I did not fit in properly because I was a man on a temp assignment. (Michael Glenn, 26-year-old Asian American man)

> People are looking at me like, "What are you doing here?" Like they're thinking, "Gee, what's the deal? Shouldn't you be, I don't know, doing something else?" I mean it's like it's sort of fine if you're just out of school. They kind of expect well, you're doing this until you get a regular job. (Harold Koenig, 29-year-old white man)

Similarly, Henson was conscious on more than one of his assignments of steady streams of chuckling female workers conspicuously moving past his workstation, (apparently) to see the male receptionist. While there might be socially acceptable reasons for a young man's location in

■ **TABLE 23.1**
Race/Ethnicity and Gender of Temporary
Clerical Workers

Race/Ethnicity	Men	Women
White	13	28
African American	3	7
Asian	1	2
Latino/Latina	1	0
Other	2	0
Total	20	37

temporary work (e.g., "just out of school" or "until you get a regular job"), for men, it is generally employment requiring an explanation.[4]

In fact, the disruption of the taken-for-granted naturalness of workplace gender segregation by the presence of male temporaries was often a source of humor for permanent workers. For example, Henson repeatedly encountered variants of a joke that played on themes of gender and mistaken identity. Permanent workers, especially men, upon seeing him for the first time at a (female) permanent worker's desk, would declare with mock seriousness, "Why (Marcia, Faye, Lucy) you've changed!" The humor of this joke, apparently, derived from the mismatch between the expected gender of the worker and Henson's gender. Another widespread joke, playing on similar themes, was to knowingly misattribute ownership of a permanent female employee's personal (and feminine) belongings to a male temporary through a mock compliment such as, "Nice pumps." Jackie, however, experienced neither the need to explain her employment nor the jokes.

The feminized nature of the work was further highlighted when others failed to recognize a male temporary as the secretary, mistaking him for someone with higher organizational status. Jon Carter, for example, described the confusion callers experienced when they heard his masculine voice at the receptionist's desk: "I get a lot of people, you know, that are confused as to who I am because it's a male voice" (23-year-old gay white man). Henson also experienced being mistaken for a permanent (higher status) new hire. One coworker, realizing his error after warmly welcoming Kevin and introducing himself, quickly pulled back his extended hand and retreated in embarrassment.

Finally, the feminized nature of temporary work was revealed by the extent to which "male" continues to be the verbally marked category. Note, for example, Linda Schmidt's verbal marking of both "male secretaries" and "male temps":

> Roger Piderat. He was a male secretary. He was very good. And then we had a male temp come in. And he was English. He was a nice guy. And he did reception for a while. And he worked at Anne's desk for a while. But he was a very pleasant person too. So we've had male secretaries before. (Linda Schmidt, 38-year-old white woman)

As with women in nontraditional occupations (e.g., female doctors or female lawyers), men in nontraditional (secretarial and clerical) work are the marked category.

The expectation, indeed assumption, that (requested) temporary workers will be women sometimes is expressed as an overt preference for women—or aversion to men—in these positions. Although temporary agencies are legally required to operate under equal opportunity employer legislation (i.e., to hire workers without regard to race, sex, or age), temporaries are nevertheless often placed for non-skill-specific characteristics including their race, gender, age, and physical attractiveness (Henson 1996; Rogers and Henson 1997; Rogers 2000). Cindy Beitz, a temporary counselor, described how client companies sometimes explicitly, and quite illegally, requested female temporaries:

> You can call them and say, "We have a young gentleman who will be coming in there tomorrow for you." And sometimes they will say . . . they'll come out and say, "Well, I don't want him. I told you I wanted a woman." (Cindy Beitz, 33-year-old white woman)

Without prompting, approximately half of the agency representatives mentioned similar illegal requests. Similarly, temporary workers like Irene Pedersen, who were privy to client company–agency interactions, reported overhearing illegal requests:

> I worked on a temp assignment somewhere in the Personnel Department at this company, and the client wanted a temp receptionist. And he would come in and beat on the personnel manager, he didn't want a man. He didn't want anybody who was Black, he didn't want anybody who was this. (Irene Pedersen, 25-year-old white woman)

Temporary workers were often aware, or at least suspected, that personal characteristics such as gender determined their access to jobs. Arnold Finch, for example, hypothesized that he had lost a job because of his gender:

> I was working a temp job and I left there. I did really good work. They wouldn't call me back. The only reason why, I was a male. They only wanted females to work that job. . . . It's just that I guess companies that . . . when somebody comes in the door, they want a pretty, happy, smiling female face behind the counter. (Arnold Finch, 23-year-old white man)

In addition, Henson lost at least one clerical assignment admittedly on the basis of his gender: "The client isn't sure if they want a male temporary or not. Whoever placed the order is going to check and see if it's okay" (Henson's field notes, 1990). Although Kevin had cross-trained in preparation at the agency's office on a specific word processing program (without pay), the assignment was withdrawn. Neither Rogers nor any of the women we interviewed experienced a negative gender screening similar to Henson's—they were the right gender.[5]

Not only is clerical temporary work feminized, it is also heterosexualized, especially for women. Clients, for example, often included demands for particular feminized (even sexy) physical presentations when placing an order for temporary help:

> When we get a position like that in where they say, "She should wear this outfit" or "She should look like this." Whatever. We'll still recommend . . . we can still call men in too, but . . . (Cindy Beitz, 33-year-old white woman)

> They'll ask for blond and blue eyes and stuff like that. Always for the front office. We tell them that we'll send the best qualified. If we send a qualified person and they send 'em back because they're not blond, we obviously wouldn't be able to fill that order. They'll go to another agency that will. (Regina Mason, 44-year-old Latina agency manager)

Indeed, female temporary secretaries, like women serving higher status men in other traditional women's work (MacKinnon 1979; Hall 1993), were often expected to make an offering of their gender, including their sexual attractiveness, as part of the job. Since the agencies' interests are in pleasing clients, even some of the more egregious requests for female temporary workers as sex objects (e.g., for a young, blond woman with great legs) are often honored (Henson 1996; Rogers and Henson 1997; Rogers 2000). Because temporary agencies depend on client companies for revenue, they are under considerable pressure to comply with these client requests. Agencies that assiduously follow the law risk losing their clients.

However, it would be inaccurate to describe the preference for women in temporary secretarial work as simply the desire to employ women as sexual objects. The employers' preference for women is partially explained by employers' essentialized understandings of gender as it relates to workers' capabilities. In other words, client companies and agencies often use a "gender logic" when matching workers with assignments (Hossfeld 1990). Women, in this logic, are often assumed to be innately superior at work calling for certain emotional and relational skills (Hochschild 1983; Leidner 1993; Pierce 1995). In fact, temporary secretaries, as part of the job, are expected to perform emotional labor—to be deferential and nurturing toward managers, coworkers, clients, and agency personnel (Henson 1996; Rogers and Henson 1997). As Pierce (1995, 89) has argued about another feminized occupation (paralegals), "The feminization of this occupation . . . is created not only by employer preference for women, but by the fact that the occupation itself—formally or not—calls for women to cater to men's emotional needs."

Challenges to Masculinity

Men who cross over to work in highly feminized occupations face institutionalized challenges to their sense of masculinity, that is, the extent to which they measure up to the dictates of hegemonic masculinity (Pringle 1993; Pierce 1995; Williams 1989, 1995). Male clerical temporary workers, for example, face gender assessment—highlighting their failure to live up to the ideals of hegemonic masculinity—on at least two fronts. First, they are working temporary rather than permanent, higher paying, full-time jobs ("He should have a real job"), which limits their ability to assume the male breadwinner role. Second, they are doing clerical work (i.e., women's work), including demands for deference and caretaking, which challenges their presumed heterosexuality ("He could be gay"). Yet, unlike the situation of male nurses or elementary schoolteachers (Williams 1989, 1995), clerical temporary work is not a semiprofession with institutionalized room for upward mobility via the glass escalator.

He Should Have a Real Job

Male temporary clerical workers' individual failings, when faced with gender assessment, included questions about their drive, motivation, and competence for male career success (i.e., "Why doesn't he have a real job?"). Indeed, permanent work providing a sufficient financial base to assume the male breadwinner role is a core component of hegemonic masculine identity (Connell 1987, 1995; Kimmel 1994; Cheng 1996). Consequently, men who have jobs that do not allow them to assume the breadwinner role—such as those in part-time or temporary work—are perceived as "less manly" (Epstein et al. 1999; Rogers 2000).

Indeed, the assumption that men, but not women, should hold or desire permanent employment was widely shared by temporary workers, temporary agency staff, and client company supervisors. For example, Dorothy Brooke, a temporary worker, expressed the idea that temporary work was acceptable for women but that men should be striving to get real jobs. In other words, temporary jobs are unsatisfactory jobs that no real man (i.e., white, heterosexual, and middle-class) would or should accept:

> I was surprised by how many older men were working as temporaries. I guess I expected to just see women. But I asked one of these guys if he was looking for full-time work. And he said

he was just hoping that one of his temp jobs was going to turn into a full-time job. I thought you've got to have more spunk than that to get a job. (Henson's field notes, 1991)

Likewise, Regina Mason, a temporary agency manager, struggling to explain the anomalous presence of men in temporary work, tapped into gendered industry rhetoric portraying the work as good for women—a "flexible, secondary wage earning job"—but inadequate for men, except on a truly temporary basis (Henson 1996):

> I think that's the trend that men have never thought of working temporary. I mean that's a new thing to men to go work temp. It's the old attitude that men are breadwinners you know so they gotta have stability, permanency, a real job. But we still have a few men working. I think a lot of housewives don't want anything permanent. So they prefer to come in and just do temping so that they can take off when they want to. (Regina Mason, 44-year-old Latina agency manager)

Ironically, while men in temporary employment are curiosities to be pitied, the low-pay, impermanence, and dead-end nature of these jobs is seen as natural or unproblematic for women. Consequently, an agency manager can bemoan the difficulties she has telling men, but not women, "they'd only be getting maybe $8 an hour and not necessarily steady work" (Rogers's field notes, 1994).

The irregularity, uncertainty, and poor remuneration of clerical temporary work challenged male temporaries' abilities to live up to the breadwinner, and self-sufficiency, ideals contained in hegemonic masculinity. Without prompting, most men in the study detailed the challenges temping presented to their sense of masculinity. Kirk Stevens, for example, felt guilty and ashamed about his inability to take on the idealized (male) breadwinner role. An inadequate supply of assignments left Kirk financially dependent on his girlfriend:

> So far, this summer, Natalie, my girlfriend, has been supporting us both. I really can't stand it.

She leaves at eight thirty and gets home at five thirty or six and she's totally exhausted. She can't stay up past eleven at night. And I feel really guilty 'cause she wouldn't have to be working quite so crazy if I were getting any money in at all. But it's difficult for both of us. (Kirk Stevens, 27-year-old white man)

While financial dependence is seen as an unproblematic aspect of low-wage temporary employment for women (i.e., the income is assumed to be secondary), this same dependence among men often challenges male temporary workers' sense of masculinity. In other words, not only is the male temporary worker unable to provide for others but he also finds himself in the painful position of dependence.

The lack of respect accorded to men who fail to live up to the career orientation ideals embodied in hegemonic masculinity was not lost on male temporary workers. Albert Baxter, for example, described his belief that male temporary workers received less respect than female temporaries:

I think men get a little less respect if they're temping. There's that expectation that they should be like career oriented and like moving up in the world and being a businessman and moving himself forward in business. Where women can do that but it's not an expectation. And so I think that, I think that's where that Kelly Girl image, that temporaries are women is. I have noticed that there is a certain amount, looking down upon. I think that's true of temps in general. They're somewhat looked down upon. I think the men maybe more. (Albert Baxter, 31-year-old white man)

Accordingly, male temporary workers sometimes experienced feelings of inferiority and inadequacy when recognized (and judged) as temporary secretaries by others. Denny Lincoln, for example, articulated feelings of inferiority when others assessed him on the basis of his low-wage, low-status temporary employment:

Why are all these people taking $6.50 and $7.00 an hour jobs? Why? Why can't they go out and get a real job? And I think that's what

goes through people's minds. Like you have a college degree! What the hell's going on here? There must be something wrong with this guy. He can't hold a job, he's working for 7 bucks an hour stuffing envelopes. (Denny Lincoln, 39-year-old white man)

Similarly, Bob Johnson described the embarrassment he felt when recognized on a temporary assignment by old college classmates:

Where I work there's a lot of people who I graduated [from college] with on staff. And when they see me, you know, they go, "What are you doing? Why are you working as a secretary?" And you have to explain yourself. Well, I'm trying to find the ideal job. Maybe it's all in my mind because I feel sort of inferior to that because they're kind of established. I feel really inadequate. (Bob Johnson, 23-year-old gay white man)

Bob's reaction reveals his embarrassment about both the impermanence of his employment ("they're kind of established") and its feminization ("Why are you working as a secretary?").

He Could Be Gay

Male temporary workers' failing, when faced with gender assessment, does not stop with questioning their drive, motivation, and competence for male career success. Their location in a female-dominated occupation that requires and produces emphasized femininity, including deferential and nurturing behaviors, also calls into question their presumed heterosexuality, a core component of hegemonic masculinity. When men do deference and caretaking, they are popularly defined as feminine—like women—and therefore gay. As Donaldson (1993, 648) has noted, any type of powerlessness quickly becomes conflated with the popular stereotype of homosexuality. Male clerical temporaries, as with male secretaries (Pringle 1993), nurses (Williams 1989), elementary schoolteachers (Williams 1995), and paralegals (Pierce 1995), are regularly stereotyped as gay. Patsy Goodrich, for example, accepted the construction of male temporary clerical workers, but not male temporary industrial workers, as gay:

> But, yeah, I think most of the people [in temporary work] that I know have either been gay men or women. Or lesbian women. I don't really know. I can't think of a straight man that I know that's done it. Except for my brother. But he did the kind where it's like the industrial side. (Patsy Goodrich, 27-year-old white lesbian woman)

Similarly, in searching for an explanation for the presence of some men in temporary clerical work, Connie Young described the male temporary workers in her office as unmasculine or effeminate in appearance:

> We've had male temporaries come in to answer the phones and do whatever typing jobs. And, for some reason, all the male temps we've gotten didn't have any masculine features. They're very longhaired, ponytailed, very artsy look. And the men in business suits would look at them and kind of not take them seriously actually. You know like, "Oh, he has an earring." (Connie Young, 25-year-old Asian American woman)

In addition, male temporary workers are feminized as they enter and interact in an organizational environment that requires the performance of emphasized femininity, including deference. Male temporaries' discomfort with the demands for deference, although more limited than the deferential demands made of female temporaries, revealed both the gendered nature of the work and its implicit threat to their sense of masculinity:

> It's a manly thing to be in charge. And men should want to be, supposedly in charge and delegating things. If you're a man and you're being delegated to, it somehow makes you less manly. You know what I'm saying? Whereas it seems to be okay for the person delegating to women. And the women, maybe they're just projecting that to get by. It seems that they're more okay with that than men are. I guess I'm saying that it makes me feel less of the manly kind of qualities, like I'm in charge, you know. And men should be like takin' meetings and barking or-

ders instead of just being subservient. (Harold Koenig, 29-year-old heterosexual white man)

Several male temporary workers remarked that they were surprised by the deferential demands of temporary work—as men with male privilege, they had rarely experienced the requirement to enact deference.

Similarly, Kirk Stevens was outraged when he was asked to perform the subservient work of cleaning bathrooms:

> I got a phone call saying there was this company that needed me to go out and change the light bulbs And I met the guy and he gives me, you know, the obligatory tour. . . . And then he gives me a bucket and a mop, some rubber gloves, and he says, "Now what I'd really like you to do, just to start off, is clean, if you could, the bathrooms need cleaning. Could you clean this bathroom?" And it didn't even . . . I just . . . I just can't believe that I didn't just say. "Go to hell. I'm not going to clean your goddamn bathrooms." (Kirk Stevens, 27-year-old heterosexual white man)

While someone has to clean bathrooms (often work relegated to poor women of color), Kirk Stevens believed he was not the type of person (e.g., white, educated, and male) who should be asked to do so. The negative reactions to deferential demands were strongest (but not exclusive) among white, heterosexual, college-educated men who would fall closest to the cultural ideal of hegemonic masculinity (see Connell 1987, 1995).

Male temporary workers, heterosexual and gay, were aware of the construction of the male temporary as gay. A noted exception, Michael Glenn, positively rather than negatively framed and accepted an essentialized construction of temporary workers as gay:

> But temps usually are women or homosexual men. Um, it's not to say that some heterosexual men don't make good temps, but I think it's harder to find. And then you get into the whole psychology of heterosexual men I suppose. *Men are from Mars* and all of that. But heterosexual men are not as great at being people-people. . . . you have to be flexible. And there's

more of a rigidity to a heterosexual male. And then again in the gradations, I would say there's more rigidity for a homosexual male than for a woman. And I'm not even gonna try to place homosexual women. (Michael Glenn, 26-year-old Asian American gay man)

Note how Michael's assertion that gay men excel over heterosexual men at the emotional and relational demands of the job (being flexible and being "people-people") leads him to the conclusion that gay men are more suited to temporary clerical work. Ironically, while gay men come closer than straight men to naturally making good temps in his account, they still do not measure up to (real, i.e., heterosexual) women, leaving the natural gender order intact.

Gender Strategies/ Hegemonic Bargains

The male temporaries we interviewed, faced with gender assessment, adopted three primary gender strategies—renaming and reframing the work, distancing themselves from the work with a cover story, as well as the more risky strategy of resisting demands for deference—to do masculinity in a feminized occupation. Ironically, rather than disrupting the gender order, each of these strategies "enables men to maintain a sense of themselves as different from and better than women—thus contributing to the gender system that divides men from women in a way that privileges men" (Williams 1995, 123). Indeed, each of these gender strategies represents what Chen (1999, 600), modifying Kandiyoti's (1988) "patriarchal bargain" concept, has described as a "hegemonic bargain"—a situation in which a man's "gender strategy involves trading on (or benefiting from) the advantages conferred by his race, gender, sexuality, class, accent, and/or generational status to achieve "unblushing" manhood."

Doing Masculinity—Renaming and Reframing

One of the primary gender strategies male temporaries use to maintain their sense of masculinity is

to distance themselves from the feminized aspects of the occupation by renaming or reframing the work. Male temporary secretaries, similar to men in other feminized occupations (Pierce 1995; Pringle 1993; Williams 1989, 1995), described their work in terms perceived to be more masculine, or at the very least, gender-neutral (e.g., word processor, administrative assistant, proofreader, bookkeeper). Steve Woodhead, a 35-year-old white gay man, for example, characterized his temporary work assignment as *bookkeeping*. Steven did not mention the temporary nature of his job, framing it more as an independent contracting arrangement. Indeed, male temporaries displayed an almost pathological avoidance of the term *secretarial*. In contrast, most of the female temporaries we interviewed described their work without hesitation as secretarial.

Occasionally, agency personnel and clients also participated in this project of renaming the work in more masculine terms. For example, on one of Henson's temporary assignments, the supervisor wondered aloud how to refer to the position in a more masculine or gender-neutral way: "Word processor? What should we call you? We're not going to call you secretary" (Henson's field notes, 1990). Whether this renaming was simply a courtesy to individual male temporary workers or a way of reconciling clients' discomfort in seeing men crossing over into women's work is unclear.[6]

In addition, some male temporary workers attempted to reframe the work as masculine by focusing on the technical competencies required on their temporary assignments. Indeed, to be technically competent is to be masculine (Cockburn 1985; Messerschmidt 1996; Wright 1996). Bob Johnson, for example, described his work in terms of the computer environment of software he was required to use on his (secretarial) work assignments:

That was mostly work with IBM. You know, cause IBM is incredibly popular. So I used my WordPerfect a lot. And then when they didn't have any WordPerfect, they sent me out on proofreading assignments. To proofread these books that no one would ever, ever read. Basically, it's been a lot of word processing. (Bob Johnson, 23-year-old gay white man)

This focus on the technological aspects (computer) of the work, however, is not just a refusal to name the work. As Cynthia Cockburn (1985, 12) has noted, "Femininity is incompatible with technological competence; to feel technically competent is to feel manly." Therefore, focusing on the technological aspects of the work is part of a gender strategy that bolsters one's sense of power at the same time it reinforces segregation between men's and women's work.

Another reframing technique male temporaries use to maintain their masculinitiy is to borrow the prestige of the employing organization (Pierce 1995; Williams 1995) when describing their work to outsiders, especially other men. A male paralegal in Pierce's (1995) study of gender in law firms described how he used the name of the law firm rather than his job title to impress outsiders. Similarly, Bob Johnson described the unit he was assigned to at a consulting firm in elaborate detail rather than his specific work tasks when asked about his temporary job:

> I work for six managers . . . in the change management services division. Companies hire them to do consulting work and they sort of do a lot of work with organizations that are going through organizational change. Implementing new systems. Both in the workforce and in terms of like information technology. Sort of reeducating them and reorganizing them around different responsibilities and different organizational hierarchies. And the other division I work for is integration services. And they're really technical experts. In terms of different [computer] hardware and software configuration systems. (Bob Johnson, 23-year-old gay white man)

Only in follow-up questions did he detail his more mundane day-to-day secretarial tasks: "I do support work. It's a lot of typing up correspondence between clients and interoffice correspondence. A lot of filing. A lot of typing. Answering phones a lot. Most of the time."

Doing Masculinity—Telling the Cover Story

Male temporaries, almost universally, invoked the "cover story" as a gender strategy to buttress their challenged sense of masculinity. The cover story, told to both self and others, invokes an alternative identity and defines one as truly temporary or occupationally transient (Henson 1996). Male clerical temporaries, through telling the cover story both on and off the job, provide an explanation for their apparent lack of drive or competence in obtaining a real (male) job. Steve Woodhead, for example, described how he strategically used his cover story on new assignments: "Oh, I always told them I was an actor. Immediately. Immediately. And they were, like, 'Great! This is wonderful.' So maybe that's what cut the ice, you know. They knew I wasn't just waiting to get a *real job*. 'Why doesn't this guy have a *real job* yet?'" (35-year-old gay white man). Likewise, Harold Koenig said, "I always wanna tell people that I'm just doing this because I'm a writer and I'm really here because of that. But they really don't want to know that. It's like to save your ego" (29-year-old white man). The cover story, then, explains why a man in clerical temporary employment does not have a real job and asserts a more valuable (masculine) social identity.

While permanent workers might also define themselves as occupationally transient (Williams 1989; Garson 1994; Pierce 1995), the organization of temporary work provided workers with the ready-made temporary label. For example, Pierce (1995, 170) noted that male paralegals frequently asserted their occupational transience despite their permanent, full-time status ("I'm planning to go to law school after working as a legal assistant for a few years"). The organization of their work as permanent, however, required that these workers simultaneously demonstrate commitment and noncommitment to their work.

The organization of temporary work, however, presupposes that male temporary workers are uncommitted and facilitates the assumption that there is an underlying reason to be revealed.

Note, for example, Henson's failed use of his cover story, in response to direct questioning, in this field note excerpt:

> Someone asked me if I just temped all the time or what I did. And I said, "Well no. I'm a graduate student in Sociology at Northwestern." She asked what I was studying and I said, "Clerical temporary work." Which she thought was really funny. I saw her in the elevator today and she asked, "How's your little study going?" Like, "Sure. That's just your little story." And it is. Because I'm [also] doing it for money. So it is just my little story. But I felt really belittled because she just wasn't taking me seriously. (Henson's field notes, 1991)

Coworkers commonly elicited cover stories from men, but seldom from women. While some women did offer cover stories, their use appeared to be motivated by class rather than gender anxieties (i.e., "What am I doing here with a college degree?").[7] In fact, since women's presence in clerical temporary employment is naturalized, coworkers rarely pressed them for explanations of any sort. On the few occasions when this happened, the question was precipitated by the temporary worker's efforts or exceptional work performance. During her fieldwork, for example, Rogers's presence in temporary clerical work was questioned only once when she was found to possess unusually detailed knowledge about insurance benefits.

Doing Masculinity—Refusing to Do Deference

Finally, men in clerical temporary work often adopted the risky gender strategy of resisting demands for deference in an effort to do masculinity. Deference, however, is part of being a "good" temporary worker for both male and female temporaries (Rogers 1995; Henson 1996; Rogers and Henson 1997). Temporaries must enact subservience and deference, for example, to continue getting assignments. While other researchers (Hochschild 1983; Pierce 1995; Williams 1995) have argued that men in women's work are not required to do deference (or at least in the same

way), we believe that there are occupations in which men are required to do deference, including clerical temporary work. While the demands for deference may be different for women and men (and different within genders along dimensions of race, age, and sexual orientation), men were still expected to provide deferential services as clerical temporary workers.

While none of the men reported ever being asked to get coffee, a request many women reported with great irritation, they were still expected to provide deferential services—smiling, waiting, taking orders, and tolerating the bad moods of their supervisors. In other words, women were asked to provide more of the nurturing and caretaking components of deference than men, especially when working for older and more established men. Helen, for example, reported receiving (and resisting) a particularly egregious request for caretaking behavior on one of her assignments:

> They had this glass candy jar this big. And like, "You're supposed to keep that filled with chocolate." Like, "Where do I get the chocolate from?" "Well, you know, just pick something up. Something cheap." Yeah. Like I'm supposed to go and buy a bag of Hershey's Kisses so that the executives can add to their waistlines. I'm like no. And it's been empty ever since I've been there. [Laughs]. (Helen Weinberg, 24-year-old white woman)

Helen, unlike many of the women we interviewed, resisted the most demeaning caretaking requests through a passive "forgetfulness" strategy. Although both female and male temporaries are generally passive in their resistance (Rogers 2000), the significance of deference in temporary employment for masculinity is heightened when we realize that most opportunities for resistance are passive ones.

The refusal to do deference, as doing masculinity, may be so important that male temporary workers risk losing the job rather than feel demeaned. Contrast Helen's forgetfulness strategy above with Bob's overt refusal to do deferential tasks, notably for a female superior:

At my long-term assignment, this one permanent secretary was out sick. I had my own desk and I had things that had to be done. And this woman comes up to me and she hands me a stack of photocopying to do. And I said, "Excuse me." And she said, "Well this is for you to do." And I said, "Well, thank you, but I have my own work to do. This work has to be done by 5." And she goes, "Well, you are just a temp and blah, blah, blah, blah, blah." I said, "Wait a minute. I am a temporary worker, but I do have a desk and assigned work that has to be done." And she threw this little fit. And throughout the day she was really terse and really just a real bitch to me. . . . She was just awful. You know that whole mentality of "just a temp, just a temp." (Bob Johnson, 23-year-old gay white man)

Similarly, Pierce (1995, 92) reports a story of a male paralegal who did not successfully do deference and appropriately "manage his own anger" with an ill-behaved male attorney. He confronted the attorney on his abusive behavior, was removed from the case, and eventually pushed to a peripheral position within the firm.

Similarly, Henson discovered the risks in resisting demands for deference when he failed to adopt a submissive demeanor and was removed from an assignment. Near the end of his first week on a (scheduled) long-term assignment at a small medical college, Henson arrived to find a typed message from Shirley, his work-site supervisor, on his chair. The note clearly asserted the hierarchy of power and demanded deference and submission—especially since Shirley worked only a few feet from Henson's desk and could have easily communicated her request verbally:

"Kevin. RE: Lunch today (12/5). My plans are to be out of the office from about 11:45 AM to 1:00 PM. (If you get hungry early, I suggest you have a snack before I leave at 11:45 AM). Thanks. Shirl."

This annoys me: patronizing and hostile—at least that's the way I take it. So, I very casually and fully aware of the politics, walk to Shirley's door with the note in hand and say, "Oh, about

lunch. . . . That's great! That works out fine with my plans too. No problem." I'm upbeat and polite, but I'm framing it as giving permission or at least as an interaction between equals. (Henson's field notes, 1990)

At the end of the day, Henson said good night to Shirley and left with every intention of returning in the morning. That evening, however, he received a call from his agency counselor: "Hi Kevin. This is Wendy. I don't know how to tell you this, but the college called us today and they said they just didn't think things were working out. They don't want you to come back tomorrow." While Henson had completed the formal work adequately, he had consciously resisted adopting the appropriate submissive demeanor. By refusing to perform deference and doing masculinity instead, he had lost the assignment.

Demands for deference seemed to be the breaking point for the male temporaries in this study. They were no longer able to reframe their way out of their feminized position. Male privilege no longer protected these men from the requirements of the job, including the performance of feminine styles of emotional labor and deference. While men do perform emotional labor and even deference on the job (Hochschild 1983; Pierce 1995), they typically do so in ways that are compatible with hegemonic notions of masculinity. In contrast, male temporaries were required to enact feminine modes of deference. Thus, men's refusals to do deference in temporary clerical work come to serve as proof that men are not suited for temporary clerical work.

Conclusion

Male clerical temporaries, as with other men who cross over into women's work, fail to conform to the dictates of hegemonic masculinity on at least two fronts. First, they are working temporary rather than permanent, higher paying, full-time jobs (i.e., a real job), which limits their ability to assume the male breadwinner role. Second, they are doing clerical work (i.e., women's work), including demands for deference and caretaking, which challenges their presumed heterosexuality.

At first glance, men's presence in a female-dominated job such as temporary clerical work might appear to disrupt the gendered landscape of the workplace. Unlike men in women's semi-professions, however, these men cannot exercise their male privilege by riding the glass escalator to higher paying, more prestigious work. Work that is female dominated and very low status does not provide the credential system and internal labor market necessary for the operation of the glass escalator. Here, occupational specificity makes all the difference in understanding men's interactions in female-dominated work. The experience of male temporary clerical workers neither conforms wholly to Kanter's (1977) theory of tokenism nor to Williams's (1992) glass escalator theory. Rather, these men experience a gendered set of token-related problems that center on maintaining the ideals of hegemonic masculinity.

With little organizational opportunity for upward mobility, men do gender in such a way that they reassert the feminine identification of the job while rejecting its application to them. Through renaming and reframing their individual duties, men distance themselves from the most feminized aspects of the job. Through telling their cover story, men construct their presence in temporary work as truly transient while naturalizing women's numerical dominance in the job. While men's refusal to do female-typed deference places them at risk of job loss individually, the meanings attributed to those actions once again reproduce the gender order as men are confirmed as unsuited for temporary clerical work. Through their gender strategies, male temporary clerical workers strike a hegemonic bargain, retracing the lines of occupational segregation and reinvigorating hegemonic masculinity and its domination over women and subaltern men.

Author's Note: An earlier version of this article was presented at the 1999 meeting of the American Sociological Association in Chicago, Illinois. We would like to thank Marjorie L. DeVault, Ronnie J. Steinberg, Judith Wittner, Anne Figert, Christine Bose, and the reviewers of Gender & Society for their comments on earlier drafts of this article.

Notes

1. Connell (1987, 1995) argues that hegemonic masculinity is not a static and homogeneous trait or role but is the ascendant (dominant) definition of masculinity at any one time to which other men are measured and, almost invariably, found wanting. Although the specific dictates of hegemonic masculinity vary over time, it is "chiefly, though not exclusively, associated with men located in the uppermost reaches of a society's ascriptive hierarchies" (Chen 1999, 587). The power of hegemonic masculinity lies not so much in the extent to which men actually conform to its (impossible) expectations but rather in the practice of masculinity and the patriarchal dividend they collect (Connell 1987, 1995).

2. Nevertheless, men may have different rates of exit from temporary work into permanent employment gained from sources other than temporary agencies.

3. Although we did not systematically collect data on the sexual orientation of respondents, two women and 10 men in our sample self-identified as lesbian and gay. While we make no claims regarding generalizability on this front, we have marked sexual orientation of the interviewee where it is directly relevant as indicated by the respondents.

4. We would specify white men here, if our sample permitted, since race is theoretically an important part of the construction of the socially acceptable male temporary clerical worker.

5. Women did report negative screenings on the basis of race, age, and perceived attractiveness.

6. We documented no systematic pay differences for jobs that were renamed in more masculine terms. In fact, pay increases were seldom reported and difficult to negotiate (Rogers 2000).

7. Class anxiety is apparent in the men's comments as well. While class is an important component of hegemonic masculinity, it is difficult to unravel gender and class at this intersection.

References

Acker, Joan. 1990. Hierarchies, jobs, bodies: A theory of gendered organizations. *Gender & Society* 4:139–158.

Britton, Dana M. 2000. The epistemology of the gendered organization. *Gender & Society* 14:418–434.

Bureau of Labor Statistics. 1995. *Handbook of labor statistics.* Washington, DC: Government Printing Office.

Chen, Anthony S. 1999. Lives at the center of the periphery, lives at the periphery of the center: Chinese American masculinities and bargaining with hegemony. *Gender & Society* 13:584–607.

Cheng, Cliff. 1996. *Masculinities in organizations.* Thousand Oaks, CA: Sage.

Cockburn, Cynthia. 1985. *Machinery of dominance: Women, men, and technical know-how.* Boston: Northeastern University Press.

Cohany, Sharon R. 1998. Workers in alternative employment arrangements: A second look. *Monthly Labor Review* 121:3–21.

Collinson, David L., and Jeff Hearn. 1996. *Men as managers, managers as men: Critical perspectives on men, masculinities and managements.* Thousand Oaks, CA: Sage.

Connell, R. W. 1987. *Gender and power.* Palo Alto, CA: Stanford University Press.

———. 1995. *Masculinities.* Berkeley: University of California Press.

Donaldson, Mike. 1993. What is hegemonic masculinity? *Theory and Society* 22:643–657.

Epstein, C. F., C. Seron, B. Oglensky, and R. Saute. 1999. *The part-time paradox: Time norms, professional life, family and gender.* New York: Routledge.

Garson, Barbara. 1994. *All the livelong day: The meaning and demeaning of routine work.* Rev. 2d ed. New York: Penguin.

Glaser, Barney G., and Anselm L. Strauss. 1965. *Awareness of dying.* Chicago: Aldine.

———. 1967. *The discovery of grounded theory: Strategies for qualitative research.* Chicago: Aldine.

Golden, Lonnie, and Eileen Appelbaum. 1992. What was driving the 1982–88 boom in temporary employment: Preferences of workers or decisions and power of employers? *Journal of Economics and Society* 51:473–494.

Hall, Elaine, J. 1993. Smiling, deferring, and flirting: Doing gender by giving "good service." *Work & Occupations* 20:452–471.

Henson, Kevin, D. 1996. *Just a temp.* Philadelphia: Temple University Press.

Hochschild, Arlie R. 1983. *The managed heart: Commercialization of human feeling.* Berkeley: University of California Press.

———. 1989. *The second shift.* New York: Avon.

Hossfeld, Karen. 1990. Their logic against them: Contradictions in sex, race, and class in Silicon Valley. In *Women workers and global restructuring,* edited by K. Ward, Ithaca, NY: ILR Press.

Kandiyoti, Deniz. 1988. Bargaining with patriarchy. *Gender & Society* 2:274–290.

Kanter, Rosabeth M. 1977. *Men and women of the corporation.* New York: Basic Books.

Kimmel, Michael S. 1994. Masculinity as homophobia: Fear, shame, and silence in the construction of gender identity. In *Theorizing masculinities,* edited by Harry Brod and Michael Kaufman. Thousand Oaks, CA: Sage.

Leidner, Robin. 1993. *Fast food, fast talk: Service work and the routinization of everyday life.* Berkeley: University of California Press.

MacKinnon, Catharine A. 1979. *Sexual harassment of working women: A case of sex discrimination.* New Haven and London: Yale University Press.

Maume, David J. Jr. 1999. Glass ceilings and glass escalators: Occupational segregation and race and sex differences in managerial promotions. *Work & Occupations* 26:483–509.

Messerschmidt, James W. 1996. Managing to kill: Masculinities and the space shuttle Challenger explosion. In *Masculinities in organizations,* edited by C. Cheng. Thousand Oaks, CA: Sage.

Moore, Mack. A. 1963. The role of temporary help-services in the clerical labor market. Ph.D. diss., University of Wisconsin–Madison.

National Association of Temporary Services. 1992. *Report on the temporary help services industry.* Alexandria, VA: DRI/McGraw-Hill.

Parker, Robert E. 1994. *Flesh peddlers and warm bodies: The temporary help industry and its workers.* New Brunswick, NJ: Rutgers University Press.

Pierce, Jennifer. 1995. *Gender trials: Emotional lives in contemporary law firms.* Berkeley: University of California Press.

Pringle, Rosemary. 1993. Male secretaries. In *Doing "women's work": Men in nontraditional occupations,* edited by C. L. Williams. Newbury Park, CA: Sage.

Rogers, Jackie K. 1995. Just a temp: Experience and structure of alienation in temporary clerical employment. *Work and Occupations* 22:137–166.

———. 2000. *Temps: The many faces of the changing workplace.* Ithaca, NY: Cornell University Press.

Rogers, Jackie K., and Kevin D. Henson. 1997. "Hey, why don't you wear a shorter skirt?" Structural vulnerability and the organization of sexual harassment in temporary clerical employment. *Gender & Society* 11:215–237.

Smith, Vicki. 1998. The fractured world of the temporary worker: Power, participation, and fragmentation in the contemporary workplace. *Social Problems* 45:411–430.

West, Candace, and Sarah Fenstermaker. 1995. Doing difference. *Gender & Society* 1:8–37.

West, Candace, and Don H. Zimmerman. 1987. Doing gender. *Gender & Society* 1:125–151.

Williams, Christine L. 1989. *Gender differences at work: Women and men in nontraditional occupations.* Berkeley: University of California Press.

———. 1992. The glass escalator: Hidden advantages for men in the "female" professions. *Social Problems* 39:253–267.

———. 1995. *Still a man's world: Men who do women's work.* Berkeley: University of California Press.

Williams, Christine L., and Joel E. Heikes, 1993. The importance of researcher's gender in the in-depth interview: Evidence from two case studies of male nurses. *Gender & Society* 7:280–291.

Wright, Rosemary. 1996. The occupational masculinity of computing. In *Masculinities in organizations,* edited by C. Cheng. Thousand Oaks, CA: Sage.

Beth A. Quinn

Sexual Harassment and Masculinity: The Power and Meaning of "Girl Watching"

Confronted with complaints about sexual harassment or accounts in the media, some men claim that women are too sensitive or that they too often misinterpret men's intentions (Buckwald 1993; Bernstein 1994). In contrast, some women note with frustration that men just "don't get it" and lament the seeming inadequacy of sexual harassment policies (Conley 1991; Guccione 1992). Indeed, this ambiguity in defining acts of sexual harassment might be, as Cleveland and Kerst (1993) suggested, the most robust finding in sexual harassment research.

Using in-depth interviews with 43 employed men and women, this article examines a particular social practice—"girl watching"—as a means to understanding one way that these gender differences are produced. This analysis does not address the size or prevalence of these differences, nor does it present a direct comparison of men and women; this information is essential but well covered in the literature.[1] Instead, I follow Cleveland and Kerst's (1993) and Wood's (1998) suggestion that the question may best be unraveled by exploring how the "subject(ivities) of perpetrators, victims, and resistors of sexual harassment" are "discursively produced, reproduced, and altered" (Wood 1998, 28).

This article focuses on the subjectivities of the perpetrators of a disputable form of sexual harassment, "girl watching." The term refers to the act of men's sexually evaluating women, often in the company of other men. It may take the form

of a verbal or gestural message of "check it out," boasts of sexual prowess, or explicit comments about a woman's body or imagined sexual acts. The target may be an individual woman or group of women or simply a photograph or other representation. The woman may be a stranger, coworker, supervisor, employee, or client. For the present analysis, girl watching within the workplace is [the focus].

The analysis is grounded in the work of masculinity scholars such as Connell (1987, 1995) in that it attempts to explain the subject positions of the interviewed men—not the abstract and genderless subjects of patriarchy but the gendered and privileged subjects embedded in this system. Since I am attempting to delineate the gendered worldviews of the interviewed men, I employ the term "girl watching," a phrase that reflects their language ("they watch girls").

I have chosen to center the analysis on girl watching within the workplace for two reasons. First, it appears to be fairly prevalent. For example, a survey of federal civil employees (U.S. Merit Systems Protection Board 1988) found that in the previous 24 months, 28 percent of the women surveyed had experienced "unwanted sexual looks or gestures," and 35 percent had experienced "unwanted sexual teasing, jokes, remarks, or questions." Second, girl watching is still often normalized and trivialized as only play, or "boys will be boys." A man watching girls—even in his workplace—is frequently accepted as a natural and commonplace activity, especially if he is in the presence of other men.[2] Indeed, it may be required (Hearn 1985). Thus, girl watching sits on the blurry edge between fun and harm, joking and harassment. An understanding of the process of

From *Gender & Society* 16(3): 386–402. Copyright © 2002 Sociologists for Women in Society.

identifying behavior as sexual harassment, or of rejecting this label, may be built on this ambiguity.

Girl watching has various forms and functions, depending on the context and the men involved. For example, it may be used by men as a directed act of power against a particular woman or women. In this, girl watching—at least in the workplace—is most clearly identified as harassing by both men and women. I am most interested, however, in the form where it is characterized as only play. This type is more obliquely motivated and, as I will argue, functions as a game men play to build shared masculine identities and social relations.

Multiple and contradictory subject positions are also evidenced in girl watching, most notably that between the gazing man and the woman he watches. Drawing on Michael Schwalbe's (1992) analysis of empathy and the formation of masculine identities, I argue that girl watching is premised on the obfuscation of this multiplicity through the objectification of the woman watched and a suppression of empathy for her. In conclusion, the ways these elements operate to produce gender differences in interpreting sexual harassment and the implications for developing effective policies are discussed.

Previous Research

The question of how behavior is or is not labeled as sexual harassment has been studied primarily through experimental vignettes and surveys.[3] In both methods, participants evaluate either hypothetical scenarios or lists of behaviors, considering whether, for example, the behavior constitutes sexual harassment, which party is most at fault, and what consequences the act might engender. Researchers manipulate factors such as the level of "welcomeness" the target exhibits, and the relationship of the actors (supervisor–employee, coworker–coworker).

Both methods consistently show that women are willing to define more acts as sexual harassment (Gutek, Morasch, and Cohen 1983; Padgitt and Padgitt 1986; Powell 1986; York 1989; but see

Stockdale and Vaux 1993) and are more likely to see situations as coercive (Garcia, Milano, and Quijano 1989). When asked who is more to blame in a particular scenario, men are more likely to blame, and less likely to empathize with, the victim (Jensen and Gutek 1982; Kenig and Ryan 1986). In terms of actual behaviors like girl watching, the U.S. Merit Systems Protection Board (1988) survey found that 81 percent of the women surveyed considered "uninvited sexually suggestive looks or gestures" from a supervisor to be sexual harassment. While the majority of men (68 percent) also defined it as such, significantly more men were willing to dismiss such behavior. Similarly, while 40 percent of the men would not consider the same behavior from a coworker to be harassing, more than three-quarters of the women would.

The most common explanation offered for these differences is gender role socialization. This conclusion is supported by the consistent finding that the more men and women adhere to traditional gender roles, the more likely they are to deny the harm in sexual harassment and to consider the behavior acceptable or at least normal (Pryor 1987; Malovich and Stake 1990; Popovich et al. 1992; Gutek and Koss 1993; Murrell and Dietz-Uhler 1993; Tagri and Hayes 1997). Men who hold predatory ideas about sexuality, who are more likely to believe rape myths, and who are more likely to self-report that they would rape under certain circumstances are less likely to see behaviors as harassing (Pryor 1987; Reilly et al. 1992; Murrell and Dietz-Uhler 1993).

These findings do not, however, adequately address the between-group differences. The more one is socialized into traditional notions of sex roles, the more likely it is for both men and women to view the behaviors as acceptable or at least unchangeable. The processes by which gender roles operate to produce these differences remain underexamined.

Some theorists argue that men are more likely to discount the harassing aspects of their behavior because of a culturally conditional tendency to misperceive women's intentions. For example, Stockdale (1993, 96) argued that "patriarchal norms create a sexually aggressive belief system in some people more than others, and this belief system can lead to the propensity to misperceive." Gender differences in interpreting sexual harassment, then, may be the outcome of the acceptance of normative ideas about women's inscrutability and indirectness and men's role as sexual aggressors. Men see harmless flirtation or sexual interest rather than harassment because they misperceive women's intent and responses.

Stockdale's (1993) theory is promising but limited. First, while it may apply to actions such as repeatedly asking for dates and quid pro quo harassment,[4] it does not effectively explain motivations for more indirect actions, such as displaying pornography and girl watching. Second, it does not explain why some men are more likely to operate from these discourses of sexual aggression contributing to a propensity to misperceive.

Theoretical explanations that take into account the complexity and diversity of sexual harassing behaviors and their potentially multifaceted social etiologies are needed. An account of the processes by which these behaviors are produced and the active construction of their social meanings is necessary to unravel both between- and within-gender variations in behavior and interpretation. A fruitful framework from which to begin is an examination of masculine identities and the role of sexually harassing behaviors as a means to their production.

Method

I conducted 43 semistructured interviews with currently employed men and women between June 1994 and March 1995. Demographic characteristics of the participants are reported in Table 24.1. The interviews ranged in length from one to three hours. With one exception, interviews were audiotaped and transcribed in full.

Participants were contacted in two primary ways. Twenty-five participants were recruited

from "Acme Electronics," a Southern California electronic design and manufacturing company. An additional 18 individuals were recruited from an evening class at a community college and a university summer school class, both in Southern California. These participants referred three more individuals. In addition to the interviews, I conducted participant observation for approximately one month while on site at Acme. This involved observations of the public and common spaces of the company.

At Acme, a human resources administrator drew four independent samples (salaried and hourly women and men) from the company's approximately 300 employees. Letters of invitation were sent to 40 individuals, and from this group, 13 women and 12 men agreed to be interviewed.[5]

The strength of organizationally grounded sampling is that it allows us to provide context for individual accounts. However, in smaller organizations and where participants occupy unique positions, this method can compromise participant anonymity when published versions of the research are accessed by participants. Since this is the case with Acme, and since organizational context is not particularly salient for this analysis, the identity of the participant's organization is sometimes intentionally obscured.

The strength of the second method of recruitment is that it provides access to individuals employed in diverse organizations (from self-employment to multinational corporations) and in a range of occupations (e.g., nanny, house painter, accounting manager). Not surprisingly, drawing from college courses resulted in a group with similar educational backgrounds; all participants from this sample had some college, with 22 percent holding college degrees. Student samples and snowball sampling are not particularly robust in terms of generalizability. They are, nonetheless, regularly employed in qualitative studies (Connell 1995; Chen 1999) when the goal is theory development—as is the case here—rather than theory testing.

The interviews began with general questions about friendships and work relationships and

■ **TABLE 24.1**
Participant Demographic Measures

Variable	Men		Women		Total	
	n	**%**	**n**	**%**	**n**	**%**
Student participants and referrals	6	33	12	67	18	42
Racial/ethnic minority	2	33	2	17	4	22
Mean age	27.2		35		32.5	
Married	3	50	3	25	6	33
Nontraditional job	1	17	4	33	5	28
Supervisor	0	0	6	50	6	33
Some college	6	100	12	100	18	100
Acme participants	12	48	13	52	25	58
Racial/ethnic minority	2	17	3	23	5	20
Mean age	42.3		34.6		38.6	
Married	9	75	7	54	16	64
Nontraditional job	0	0	4	31	4	16
Supervisor	3	25	2	15	5	20
Some college	9	75	9	69	18	72
All participants	18	42	25	58	43	100
Racial/ethnic minority	4	22	5	20	9	21
Mean age	37.8		34.9		36.2	
Married	12	67	10	40	22	51
Nontraditional job	1	6	8	32	9	21
Supervisor	3	17	8	32	11	26
Some college	15	82	21	84	36	84

progressed to specific questions about gender relations, sexual harassment, and the policies that seek to address it.[6] Since the main aim of the project was to explore how workplace events are framed as sexual harassment (and as legally bounded or not), the term "sexual harassment" was not introduced by the interviewer until late in the interview.

While the question of the relationship between masculinity and sexual harassment was central, I did not come to the research looking expressly for girl watching. Rather, it surfaced as a theme across several men's interviews in the context of a gender reversal question:

It's the end of an average day. You get ready for bed and fall to sleep. In what seems only a moment, the alarm goes off. As you awake, you find your body to be oddly out of sorts. . . . To your surprise, you find that you have been transformed into the "opposite sex." Even stranger, no one in your life seems to remember that you were ever any different.

Participants were asked to consider what it would be like to conduct their everyday work life in this transformed state. I was particularly interested in their estimation of the impact it would have on their interactions with coworkers and supervisors. Imagining themselves as the opposite sex, participants were forced to make explicit the operation of gender in their workplace, something they did not do in their initial discussions of a typical workday.

Interestingly, no man discussed girl watching in initial accounts of his workplace. I suspect that they did not consider it to be relevant to a discussion of their average *work* day, even though it became apparent that it was an integral daily activity for some groups of men. It emerged only when men were forced to consider themselves as explicitly gendered workers through the hypothetical question, something they were able initially to elide.[7]

Taking guidance from Glaser and Strauss's (1967) grounded theory and the methodological insights of Dorothy Smith (1990), transcripts were analyzed iteratively and inductively, with the goal of identifying the ideological tropes the speaker used to understand his or her identities, behaviors, and relationships. Theoretical concepts drawn from previous work on the etiology of sexual harassment (Bowman 1993; Cleveland and Kerst 1993), the construction of masculine identities (Connell 1995, 1987), and sociolegal theories of disputing and legal consciousness (Bumiller 1988; Conley and O'Barr 1998) guided the analysis.

Several related themes emerged and are discussed in the subsequent analysis. First, girl watching appears to function as a form of gendered play among men. This play is productive of masculine identities and premised on a studied lack of empathy with the feminine other. Second, men understand the targeted woman to be an object rather than a player in the game, and she is most often not the intended audience. This obfuscation of a woman's subjectivity, and men's refusal to consider the effects of their behavior, means men are likely to be confused when a woman complains. Thus, the production of masculinity though girl watching, and its compulsory disempathy, may be one factor in gender differences in the labeling of harassment.

Findings: Girl Watching as "Hommo-Sexuality"

[They] had a button on the computer that you pushed if there was a girl who came to the front counter. . . . It was a code and it said "BAFC"—

Babe at Front Counter. . . . If the guy in the back looked up and saw a cute girl come in the station, he would hit this button for the other dispatcher to [come] see the cute girl.

—Paula, police officer

In its most serious form, girl watching operates as a targeted tactic of power. The men seem to want everyone—the targeted woman as well as coworkers, clients, and superiors—to know they are looking. The gaze demonstrates their right, as men, to sexually evaluate women. Through the gaze, the targeted woman is reduced to a sexual object, contradicting her other identities, such as that of competent worker or leader. This employment of the discourse of asymmetrical heterosexuality (i.e., the double standard) may trump a woman's formal organizational power, claims to professionalism, and organizational discourses of rationality (Collinson and Collinson 1989; Yount 1991; Gardner 1995).[8] As research on rape has demonstrated (Estrich 1987), calling attention to a woman's gendered sexuality can function to exclude recognition of her competence, rationality, trustworthiness, and even humanity. In contrast, the overt recognition of a man's (hetero)sexuality is normally compatible with other aspects of his identity; indeed, it is often required (Hearn 1985; Connell 1995). Thus, the power of sexuality is asymmetrical, in part, because being seen as sexual has different consequences for women and men.

But when they ogle, gawk, whistle and point, are men always so directly motivated to disempower their women colleagues? Is the target of the gaze also the intended audience? Consider, for example, this account told by Ed, a white, 29-year-old instrument technician.

When a group of guys goes to a bar or a nightclub and they try to be manly. . . . A few of us always found [it] funny [when] a woman would walk by and a guy would be like, "I can have her." [pause] "Yeah, OK, we want to see it!" [laugh]

In his account—a fairly common one in men's discussions—the passing woman is simply a visual cue for their play. It seems clear that it is a game played by men for men; the woman's participation and awareness of her role seem fairly unimportant.

As Thorne (1993) reminded us, we should not be too quick to dismiss games as "only play." In her study of gender relations in elementary schools, Thorne found play to be a powerful form of gendered social action. One of its "clusters of meaning" most relevant here is that of "dramatic performance." In this, play functions as both a source of fun and a mechanism by which gendered identities, group boundaries, and power relations are (re)produced.

The metaphor of play was strong in Karl's comments. Karl, a white man in his early thirties who worked in a technical support role in the Acme engineering department, hoped to earn a degree in engineering. His frustration with his slow progress—which he attributed to the burdens of marriage and fatherhood—was evident throughout the interview. Karl saw himself as an undeserved outsider in his department and he seemed to delight in telling on the engineers.

Girl watching came up as Karl considered the gender reversal question. Like many of the men I interviewed, his first reaction was to muse about premenstrual syndrome and clothes. When I inquired about the potential social effects of the transformation (by asking him, Would it "be easier dealing with the engineers or would it be harder?") he haltingly introduced the engineers' "game."

> **Karl:** Some of the engineers here are very [pause] they're not very, how shall we say? [pause] What's the way I want to put this? They're not very, uh [pause] what's the word? Um. It escapes me.
>
> **Researcher:** Give me a hint?
>
> **Karl:** They watch women but they're not very careful about getting caught.
>
> **Researcher:** Oh! Like they ogle?
>
> **Karl:** Ogle or gaze or [pause] stare even, or [pause] generate a commotion of an unusual nature.

His initial discomfort in discussing the issue (with me, I presume) is evident in his excruciatingly formal and hesitant language. The aspect of play, however, came through clearly when I pushed him to describe what generating a commotion looked like: " 'Oh! There goes so-and-so. Come and take a look! She's wearing this great outfit today!' Just like a schoolboy. They'll rush out of their offices and [cranes his neck] and check things out." That this is as a form of play was evident in Karl's boisterous tone and in his reference to schoolboys. This is not a case of an aggressive sexual appraising of a woman coworker but a commotion created for the benefit of other men.

At Acme, several spatial factors facilitated this form of girl watching. First, the engineering department is designed as an open-plan office with partitions at shoulder height, offering a maze-like geography that encourages group play. As Karl explained, the partitions offer both the opportunity for sight and cover from being seen. Although its significance escaped me at the time, I was directly introduced to the spatial aspects of the engineers' game of girl watching during my first day on site at Acme. That day, John, the current human resources director, gave me a tour of the facilities, walking me through the departments and offering informal introductions. As we entered the design engineering section, a rhythm of heads emerged from its landscape of partitions, and movement started in our direction. I was definitely aware of being on display as several men gave me obvious once-overs.

Second, Acme's building features a grand stairway that connects the second floor—where the engineering department is located—with the lobby. The stairway is enclosed by glass walls, offering a bird's eye view to the main lobby and the movements of visitors and the receptionists (all women). Robert, a senior design engineer, specifically noted the importance of the glass walls in his discussion of the engineers' girl watching.

> There's glass walls around the upstairs right here by the lobby. So when there's an attractive young female . . . someone will see the girl in the area and they will go back and inform all

the men in the area. "Go check it out." [laugh] So we'll walk over to the glass window, you know, and we'll see who's down there.

One day near the end of my stay at Acme, I was reminded of his story as I ventured into the first-floor reception area. Looking up, I saw Robert and another man standing at the top of the stairs watching and commenting on the women gathered around the receptionist's desk. When he saw me, Robert gave me a sheepish grin and disappeared from sight.

Producing Masculinity

I suggest that girl watching in this form functions simultaneously as a form of play and as a potentially powerful site of gendered social action. Its social significance lies in its power to form identities and relationships based on these common practices for, as Cockburn (1983, 123) has noted, "patriarchy is as much about relations between man and man as it is about relations between men and women." Girl watching works similarly to the sexual joking that Johnson (1988) suggested is a common way for heterosexual men to establish intimacy among themselves.

   In particular, girl watching works as a dramatic performance played to other men, a means by which a certain type of masculinity is produced and heterosexual desire displayed. It is a means by which men assert a masculine identity to other men, in an ironic "hommo-sexual" practice of heterosexuality (Butler 1990).[9] As Connell (1995) and others (West and Zimmerman 1987; Butler 1990) have aptly noted, masculinity is not a static identity but rather one that must constantly be reclaimed. The content of any performance—and there are multiple forms—is influenced by a hegemonic notion of masculinity. When asked what "being a man" entailed, many of the men and women I interviewed triangulated toward notions of strength (if not in muscle, then in character and job performance), dominance, and a marked sexuality, overflowing and uncontrollable to some degree and natural to the male "species." Heterosexuality is required, for just as the label "girl"

questions a man's claim to masculine power, so does the label "fag" (Hopkins 1992; Pronger 1992). I asked Karl, for example, if he would consider his sons "good men" if they were gay. His response was laced with ambivalence; he noted only that the question was "a tough one."

   The practice of girl watching is just that—a practice—one rehearsed and performed in everyday settings. This aspect of rehearsal was evident in my interview with Mike, a self-employed house painter who used to work construction. In locating himself as a born-again Christian, Mike recounted the girl watching of his fellow construction workers with contempt. Mike was particularly disturbed by a man who brought his young son to the job site one day. The boy was explicitly taught to catcall, a practice that included identifying the proper targets: women and effeminate men.

   Girl watching, however, can be somewhat tenuous as a masculine practice. In their acknowledgment (to other men) of their supposed desire lies the possibility that in being too interested in women the players will be seen as mere schoolboys giggling in the playground. Taken too far, the practice undermines rather than supports a masculine performance. In Karl's discussion of girl watching, for example, he continually came back to the problem of men not being careful about getting caught. He referred to a particular group of men who, though "their wives are [pause] very attractive—very much so," still "gawk like schoolboys." Likewise, Stephan explained that men who are obvious, who "undress [women] with their eyes" probably do so "because they don't get enough women in their lives. Supposedly." A man must be interested in women, but not too interested; they must show their (hetero) sexual interest, but not overly so, for this would be to admit that women have power over them.

The Role of Objectification and (Dis)Empathy

As a performance of heterosexuality among men, the targeted woman is primarily an object onto which men's homosocial sexuality is projected. The presence of a woman in any form—embodied, pictorial, or as an image conjured from words—is required, but her subjectivity and active participation is not. To be sure, given the ways the discourse of asymmetrical sexuality works, men's actions may result in similarly negative effects on the targeted woman as that of a more direct form of sexualization. The crucial difference is that the men's understanding of their actions differs. This difference is one key to understanding the ambiguity around interpreting harassing behavior.

When asked about the engineers' practice of neck craning, Robert grinned, saying nothing at first. After some initial discussion, I started to ask him if he thought women were aware of their game ("Do you think that the women who are walking by . . . ?"). He interrupted, misreading my question. What resulted was a telling description of the core of the game:

> It depends. No. I don't know if they enjoy it. When I do it, if I do it, I'm not saying that I do. [big laugh] . . . If they do enjoy it, they don't say it. If they don't enjoy it—wait a minute, that didn't come out right. I don't know if they enjoy it or not [pause]; that's not the purpose of us popping our heads out.

Robert did not want to admit that women might not enjoy it ("that didn't come out right") but acknowledged that their feelings were irrelevant. Only subjects, not objects, take pleasure or are annoyed. If a women did complain, Robert thought "the guys wouldn't know what to say." In her analysis of street harassment, Gardner (1995, 187) found a similar absence, in that "men's interpretations seldom mentioned a woman's reaction, either guessed at or observed."

The centrality of objectification was also apparent in comments made by José, a Hispanic man in his late 40s who worked in manufacturing. For José, the issue came up when he considered the topic of compliments. He initially claimed that women enjoy compliments more than men do. In reconsidering, he remembered girl watching and the importance of intent.

> There is [pause] a point where [pause] a woman can be admired by [pause] a pair of eyes, but we're talking about "that look." Where, you know, you're admiring her because she's dressed nice, she's got a nice figure, she's got nice legs. But then you also have the other side. You have an animal who just seems to undress you with his eyes and he's just [pause], there's those kind of people out there too.

What is most interesting about this statement is that in making the distinction between merely admiring and an animal look that ravages, José switched subject position. He spoke in the second person when describing both form of looking, but his consistency in grammar belies a switch in subjectivity: you (as a man) admire, and you (as a woman) are undressed with his eyes. When considering an appropriate, complimentary gaze, José described it from a man's point of view; the subject who experiences the inappropriate, violating look, however, is a woman. Thus, as in Robert's account, José acknowledged that there are potentially different meanings in the act for men and women. In particular, to be admired in a certain way is potentially demeaning for a woman through its objectification.

The switch in subject position was also evident in Karl's remarks. Karl mentioned girl watching while imagining himself as a woman in the gender reversal question. As he took the subject position of the woman watched rather than the man watching, his understanding of the act as a harmless game was destabilized. Rather than taking pleasure in being the object of such attention, Karl would take pains to avoid it.

> So with these guys [if I were a woman], I would probably have to be very concerned about my attire in the lab. Because in a lot of cases, I'm working at a bench and I'm hunched over, in which case your shirt, for example, would open at the neckline, and I would just have to be concerned about that.

Thus, because the engineers girl watch, Karl feels that he would have to regulate his appearance if he were a woman, keeping the men from using him in their game of girl watching. When he considered the act from the point of view of a man, girl watching was simply a harmless antic and an act of appreciation. When he was forced to consider the subject position of a woman, however, girl watching was something to be avoided or at least carefully managed.

When asked to envision himself as a woman in his workplace, like many of the individuals I interviewed, Karl believed that he did not "know how to be a woman." Nonetheless, he produced an account that mirrored the stories of some of the women I interviewed. He knew the experience of girl watching could be quite different—in fact, threatening and potentially disempowering—for the woman who is its object. As such, the game was something to be avoided. In imagining themselves as women, the men remembered the practice of girl watching. None, however, were able to comfortably describe the game of girl watching from the perspective of a woman and maintain its (masculine) meaning as play.

In attempting to take up the subject position of a woman, these men are necessarily drawing on knowledge they already hold. If men simply "don't get it"—truly failing to see the harm in girl watching or other more serious acts of sexual harassment—then they should not be able to see this harm when envisioning themselves as women. What the interviews reveal is that many men—most of whom failed to see the harm of many acts that would constitute the hostile work environment form of sexual harassment—did in fact understand the harm of these acts when forced to consider the position of the targeted woman.

I suggest that the gender reversal scenario produced, in some men at least, a moment of empathy. Empathy, Schwalbe (1992) argued, requires two things. First, one must have some knowledge of the other's situation and feelings. Second, one must be motivated to take the position of the other. What the present research suggests is that gender differences in interpreting sexual harassment stem not so much from men's not getting it (a failure of the first element) but

from a studied, often compulsory, lack of motivation to identify with women's experiences.

In his analysis of masculinity and empathy, Schwalbe (1992) argued that the requirements of masculinity necessitate a "narrowing of the moral self." Men learn that to effectively perform masculinity and to protect a masculine identity, they must, in many instances, ignore a woman's pain and obscure her viewpoint. Men fail to exhibit empathy with women because masculinity precludes them from taking the position of the feminine other, and men's moral stance vis-à-vis women is attenuated by this lack of empathy.

As a case study, Schwalbe (1992) considered the Thomas–Hill hearings, concluding that the examining senators maintained a masculinist stance that precluded them from giving serious consideration to Professor Hill's claims. A consequence of this masculine moral narrowing is that "charges of sexual harassment . . . are often seen as exaggerated or as fabricated out of misunderstanding or spite" (Schwalbe 1992, 46). Thus, gender differences in interpreting sexually harassing behaviors may stem more from acts of ignoring than states of ignorance.

The Problem with Getting Caught

But are women really the untroubled objects that girl watching—viewed through the eyes of men—suggests? Obviously not; the game may be premised on a denial of a woman's subjectivity, but an actual erasure is beyond men's power! It is in this multiplicity of subjectivities, as Butler (1990, ix) noted, where "trouble" lurks, provoked by "the unanticipated agency of a female 'object' who inexplicably returns the glance, reverses the gaze, and contests the place and authority of the masculine position." To face a returned gaze is to get caught, an act that has the power to undermine the logic of girl watching as simply a game among men. Karl, for example, noted that when caught, men are often flustered, a reaction suggesting that the boundaries of usual play have been disturbed.[10]

When a woman looks back, when she asks, "What are you looking at?" she speaks as a subject, and her status as mere object is disturbed. When the game is played as a form of hommo-sexuality, the confronted man may be baffled by her response. When she catches them looking, when she complains, the targeted woman speaks as a subject. The men, however, understand her primarily as an object, and objects do not object.

The radical potential of sexual harassment law is that it centers women's subjectivity, an aspect prompting Catharine MacKinnon's (1979) unusual hope for the law's potential as a remedy. For men engaged in girl watching, however, this subjectivity may be inconceivable. From their viewpoint, acts such as girl watching are simply games played with objects: women's bodies. Similar to Schwalbe's (1992) insight into the senators' reaction to Professor Hill, the harm of sexual harassment may seem more the result of a woman's complaint (and law's "illegitimate" encroachment into the everyday work world) than men's acts of objectification. For example, in reflecting on the impact of sexual harassment policies in the workplace, José lamented that "back in the '70s, [it was] all peace and love then. Now as things turn around, men can't get away with as much as what they used to." Just whose peace and love are we talking about?

Reactions to Anti–Sexual Harassment Training Programs

The role that objectification and disempathy play in men's girl watching has important implications for sexual harassment training. Consider the following account of a sexual harassment training session given in Cindy's workplace. Cindy, an Italian American woman in her early 20s, worked as a recruiter for a small telemarketing company in Southern California.

> [The trainer] just really laid down the ground rules, um, she had some scenarios. Saying, "OK, would you consider this sexual harassment?" "Would you . . ." this, this, this? "What level?" Da-da-da. So, um, they just gave us some real numbers as to lawsuits and cases. Just that "you guys better be careful" type of a thing.

From Cindy's description, this training is fairly typical in that it focuses on teaching participants definitions of sexual harassment and the legal ramifications of accusations. The trainer used the common strategy of presenting videos of potentially harassing situations and asking the participants how they would judge them. Cindy's description of the men's responses to these videos reveals the limitation of this approach.

> We were watching [the TV] and it was [like] a studio audience. And [men] were getting up in the studio audience making comments like "Oh well, look at her! I wouldn't want to do that to her either!" "Well, you're darn straight, look at her!"

Interestingly, the men successfully used the training session videos as an opportunity for girl watching through their public sexual evaluations of the women depicted. In this, the intent of the training session was doubly subverted. The men interpreted scenarios that Cindy found plainly harassing into mere instances of girl watching and sexual (dis)interest. The antiharassment video was ironically transformed into a forum for girl watching, effecting male bonding and the assertion of masculine identities to the exclusion of women coworkers. Also, by judging the complaining women to be inferior as women, the men sent the message that women who complain are those who fail at femininity.

Cindy conceded that relations between men and women in her workplace were considerably strained after the training ("That day, you definitely saw the men bond, you definitely saw the women bond, and there was a definite separation"). The effect of the training session, rather than curtailing the rampant sexual harassment in Cindy's workplace, operated as a site of masculine performance, evoking manly camaraderie and reestablishing gender boundaries.

To be effective, sexual harassment training programs must be grounded in a complex understanding of the ways acts such as girl watching operate in the workplace and the seeming necessity of a culled empathy to some forms of masculinity. Sexually harassing behaviors are produced from more than a lack of knowledge, simple sexist attitudes, or misplaced sexual desire. Some forms of sexually harassing behaviors—such as girl watching—are mechanisms through which gendered boundaries are patrolled and evoked and by which deeply held identities are established. This complexity requires complex interventions and leads to difficult questions about the possible efficacy of any workplace training program mandated in part by legal requirements.

Conclusions

In this analysis, I have sought to unravel the social logic of girl watching and its relationship to the question of gender differences in the interpretation of sexual harassment. In the form analyzed here, girl watching functions simultaneously as only play and as a potent site where power is played. Through the objectification on which it is premised and in the nonempathetic masculinity it supports, this form of girl watching simultaneously produces both the harassment and the barriers to men's acknowledgment of its potential harm.

The implications these findings have for anti–sexual harassment training are profound. If we understand harassment to be the result of a simple lack of knowledge (of ignorance), then straightforward informational sexual harassment training may be effective. The present analysis suggests, however, that the etiology of some harassment lies elsewhere. While they might have quarreled with it, most of the men I interviewed had fairly good abstract understandings of the behaviors their companies' sexual harassment policies prohibited. At the same time, in relating stories of social relations in their workplaces, most failed to identify specific behaviors as sexual harassment when they matched the abstract definition. As I have argued, the source of this contradiction lies not so much in ignorance but in acts of ignoring. Traditional sexual harassment

training programs address the former rather than the latter. As such, their effectiveness against sexually harassing behaviors born out of social practices of masculinity like girl watching is questionable.

Ultimately, the project of challenging sexual harassment will be frustrated and our understanding distorted unless we interrogate hegemonic, patriarchal forms of masculinity and the practices by which they are (re)produced. We must continue to research the processes by which sexual harassment is produced and the gendered identities and subjectivities on which it poaches (Wood 1998). My study provides a first step toward a more process-oriented understanding of sexual harassment, the ways the social meanings of harassment are constructed, and ultimately, the potential success of antiharassment training programs.

Author's Note: I would like to thank the members of my faculty writing group—Lisa Aldred, Susan Kollin, and Colleen Mack-Canty—who prove again and again that cross-disciplinary feminist dialogue is not only possible but a powerful reality, even in the wilds of Montana. In addition, thanks to Lisa Jones for her thoughtful reading at a crucial time and to the anonymous reviewers who offered both productive critiques and encouragement.

Notes

1. See Welsh (1999) for a review of this literature.

2. For example, Maria, an administrative assistant I interviewed, simultaneously echoed and critiqued this understanding when she complained about her boss's girl watching in her presence: "If he wants to do that in front of other men . . . you know, that's what men do."

3. Recently, more researchers have turned to qualitative studies as a means to understand the process of labeling behavior as harassment. Of note are Collinson and Collinson (1996), Giuffre and Williams (1994), Quinn (2000), and Rogers and Henson (1997).

4. Quid pro quo ("this for that") sexual harassment occurs when a person with organizational power attempts to coerce an individual into sexual behavior by threatening adverse job actions.

5. This sample was not fully representative of the company's employees; male managers (mostly white) and minority manufacturing employees were under-represented. Thus, the data presented here best represent the attitudes and workplace tactics of white men working in white-collar, technical positions and white and minority men in blue-collar jobs.

6. Acme employees were interviewed at work in an office off the main lobby. Students and referred participants were interviewed at sites convenient to them (e.g., an office, the library).

7. Not all the interviewed men discussed girl watching. When asked directly, they tended to grin knowingly, refusing to elaborate. This silence in the face of direct questioning—by a female researcher—is also perhaps an instance of getting caught.

8. I prefer the term "asymmetrical heterosexuality" over "double standard" because it directly references the dominance of heterosexuality and more accurately reflects the interconnected but different forms of acceptable sexuality for men and women. As Estrich (1987) argued, it is not simply that we hold men and women to different standards of sexuality but that these standards are (re)productive of women's disempowerment.

9. "Hommo" is a play on the French word for man, *homme*.

10. Men are not always concerned with getting caught, as the behavior of catcalling construction workers amply illustrates; that a woman hears is part of the thrill (Gardner 1995). The difference between the workplace and the street is the level of anonymity the men have vis-à-vis the woman and the complexity of social rules and the diversity of power sources an individual has at his or her disposal.

References

Bernstein, R. 1994. Guilty if charged. *New York Review of Books,* 13 January.

Bowman, C. G. 1993. Street harassment and the informal ghettoization of women. *Harvard Law Review* 106:517–580.

Buckwald, A. 1993. Compliment a woman, go to court. *Los Angeles Times,* 28 October.

Bumiller, K. 1988. *The civil rights society: The social construction of victims.* Baltimore: Johns Hopkins University Press.

Butler, J. 1990. *Gender trouble: Feminism and the subversion of identity.* New York: Routledge.

Chen, A. S. 1999. Lives at the center of the periphery, lives at the periphery of the center: Chinese American masculinities and bargaining with hegemony. *Gender & Society* 13:584–607.

Cleveland, J. N., and M. E. Kerst. 1993. Sexual harassment and perceptions of power: An under-articulated relationship. *Journal of Vocational Behavior* 42 (1): 49–67.

Cockburn, C. 1983. *Brothers: Male dominance and technological change.* London: Pluto Press.

Collinson, D. L., and M. Collinson. 1989. Sexuality in the workplace: The domination of men's sexuality. In *The sexuality of organizations,* edited by J. Hearn and D. L. Sheppard. Newbury Park, CA: Sage.

———. 1996. "It's only Dick": The sexual harassment of women managers in insurance sales. *Work, Employment & Society* 10 (1): 29–56.

Conley, F. K. 1991. Why I'm leaving Stanford: I wanted my dignity back. *Los Angeles Times,* 9 June.

Conley, J., and W. O'Barr. 1998. *Just words.* Chicago: University of Chicago Press.

Connell, R. W. 1987. *Gender and power.* Palo Alto, CA: Stanford University Press.

———. 1995. *Masculinities.* Berkeley: University of California Press.

Estrich, S. 1987. *Real rape.* Cambridge, MA: Harvard University Press.

Garcia, L., L. Milano, and A. Quijano. 1989. Perceptions of coercive sexual behavior by males and females. *Sex Roles* 21 (9/10): 569–577.

Gardner, C. B. 1995. *Passing by: Gender and public harassment.* Berkeley: University of California Press.

Giuffre, P., and C. Williams. 1994. Boundary lines: Labeling sexual harassment in restaurants. *Gender & Society* 8:378–401.

Glaser, B., and A. L. Strauss. 1967. *The discovery of grounded theory: Strategies for qualitative research.* Chicago: Aldine.

Guccione, J. 1992. Women judges still fighting harassment. *Daily Journal,* 13 October, 1.

Gutek, B. A., and M. P. Koss. 1993. Changed women and changed organizations: Consequences of and coping with sexual harassment. *Journal of Vocational Behavior* 42 (1): 28–48.

Gutek, B. A., B. Morasch, and A. G. Cohen. 1983. Interpreting social–sexual behavior in a work setting. *Journal of Vocational Behavior* 22 (1): 30–48.

Hearn, J. 1985. Men's sexuality at work. In *The sexuality of men,* edited by A. Metcalf and M. Humphries. London: Pluto Press.

Hopkins, P. 1992. Gender treachery: Homophobia, masculinity, and threatened identities. In *Rethinking masculinity: Philosophical explorations in light of feminism,* edited by L. May and R. Strikwerda. Lanham, MD: Littlefield, Adams.

Jensen, I. W., and B. A. Gutek. 1982. Attributions and assignment of responsibility in sexual harassment. *Journal of Social Issues* 38 (4): 121–136.

Johnson, M. 1988. *Strong mothers, weak wives.* Berkeley: University of California Press.

Kenig, S., and J. Ryan. 1986. Sex differences in levels of tolerance and attribution of blame for sexual harassment on a university campus. *Sex Roles* 15 (9/10): 535–549.

MacKinnon, C. A. 1979. *The sexual harassment of working women.* New Haven: Yale University Press.

Malovich, N. J., and J. E. Stake. 1990. Sexual harassment on campus: Individual differences in attitudes and beliefs. *Psychology of Women Quarterly* 14 (1): 63–81.

Murrell, A. J., and B. L. Dietz-Uhler. 1993. Gender identity and adversarial sexual beliefs as predictors of attitudes toward sexual harassment. *Psychology of Women Quarterly* 17 (2): 169–175.

Padgitt, S. C., and J. S. Padgitt. 1986. Cognitive structure of sexual harassment: Implications for university policy. *Journal of College Students Personnel* 27:34–39.

Popovich, P. M., D. N. Gehlauf, J. A. Jolton, J. M. Somers, and R. M. Godinho. 1992. Perceptions of sexual harassment as a function of sex of rater and incident form and consequent. *Sex Roles* 27 (11/12): 609–625.

Powell, G. N. 1986. Effects of sex-role identity and sex on definitions of sexual harassment. *Sex Roles* 14:9–19.

Pronger, B. 1992. Gay jocks: A phenomenology of gay men in athletics. In *Rethinking masculinity: Philosophical explorations in light of feminism,* edited by L. May and R. Strikwerda. Lanham, MD: Littlefield Adams.

Pryor, J. B. 1987. Sexual harassment proclivities in men. *Sex Roles* 17 (5/6): 269–290.

Quinn, B. A. 2000. The paradox of complaining: Law, humor, and harassment in the everyday work world. *Law and Social Inquiry* 25 (4): 1151–1183.

Reilly, M. E., B. Lott, D. Caldwell, and L. DeLuca. 1992. Tolerance for sexual harassment related to self-reported sexual victimization. *Gender & Society* 6:122–138.

Rogers, J. K., and K. D. Henson, 1997. "Hey, why don't you wear a shorter skirt?" Structural vulnerability and the organization of sexual harassment in temporary clerical employment. *Gender & Society* 11:215–238.

Schwalbe, M. 1992. Male supremacy and the narrowing of the moral self. *Berkeley Journal of Sociology* 37:29–54.

Smith, D. 1990. *The conceptual practices of power: A feminist sociology of knowledge.* Boston: Northeastern University Press.

Stockdale, M. S. 1993. The role of sexual misperceptions of women's friendliness in an emerging theory of sexual harassment. *Journal of Vocational Behavior* 42 (1): 84–101.

Stockdale, M. S., and A. Vaux. 1993. What sexual harassment experiences lead respondents to acknowledge being sexually harassed? A secondary analysis of a university survey. *Journal of Vocational Behavior* 43 (2): 221–234.

Tagri, S., and S. M. Hayes. 1997. Theories of sexual harassment. In *Sexual harassment: Theory, research and treatment,* edited by W. O'Donohue. New York: Allyn and Bacon.

Thorne, B. 1993. *Gender play: Girls and boys in school.* Buckingham, UK: Open University Press.

U.S. Merit Systems Protection Board, 1988. *Sexual harassment in the federal government: An update.* Washington, DC: Government Printing Office.

Welsh, S. 1999. Gender and sexual harassment. *Annual Review of Sociology* 1999:169–190.

West, C., and D. H. Zimmerman, 1987. Doing gender. *Gender & Society* 1:125–151.

Wood, J. T. 1998. Saying makes it so: The discursive construction of sexual harassment. In *Conceptualizing sexual harassment as discursive practice,* edited by S. G. Bingham. Westport, CT: Praeger.

York, K. M. 1989. Defining sexual harassment in workplaces: A policy-capturing approach. *Academy of Management Journal* 32:830–850.

Yount, K. R. 1991. Ladies, flirts, tomboys: Strategies for managing sexual harassment in an underground coal mine. *Journal of Contemporary Ethnography* 19:396–422.

PART FIVE

Men and Health

Why did the gap between male and female life expectancy increase from two years in 1900 to nearly eight years today? Why do men suffer heart attacks and ulcers at such a consistently higher rate than women do? Why are auto insurance rates so much higher for young males than for females of the same age? Are mentally and emotionally "healthy" males those who conform more closely to the dominant cultural prescriptions for masculinity, or those who resist those dominant ideals?

The articles in this section examine the "embodiment" of masculinity, the ways in which men's mental health and physical health expresses and reproduces the definitions of masculinity we have ingested in our society. Don Sabo offers a compassionate account of how men will invariably confront traditional stereotypes as they look for more nurturing roles. Gloria Steinem pokes holes in the traditional definitions of masculinity, especially the putative biological basis for gender expression.

Alongside these dominant cultural conceptions of masculinity, there have always been masculinities that have been marginalized and subordinated. These can often provide models for resistance to the dominant model, as the article by Thomas Gerschick and Adam Miller suggests.

Image courtesy of www.adbusters.org.

Don Sabo

Masculinities and Men's Health: Moving toward Post-Superman Era Prevention

My grandfather used to smile and say, "Find out where you're going to die and stay the hell away from there." Grandpa had never studied epidemiology (the study of variations in health and illness in society), but he understood that certain behaviors, attitudes, and cultural practices can put individuals at risk for accidents, illness, or death. This chapter presents an overview of men's health that proceeds from the basic assumption that aspects of traditional masculinity can be dangerous to men's health (Harrison, Chin, & Ficarrotto 1992; Sabo & Gordon 1995). First, I identify some gender differences in relation to morbidity (sickness) and mortality (death). Next, I examine how the risk for illness varies from one male group to another. I then discuss an array of men's health issues and a preventive strategy for enhancing men's health.

Gender Differences in Health and Illness

When British sociologist Ashley Montagu put forth the thesis in 1953 that women were biologically superior to men, he shook up the prevailing chauvinistic beliefs that men were stronger, smarter, and better than women. His argument was partly based on epidemiological data that show males are more vulnerable to mortality than females from before birth and throughout the life span.

Mortality

From the time of conception, men are more likely to succumb to prenatal and neonatal death than females. Men's chances of dying during the prenatal stage of development are about 12% greater than those of females and, during the neonatal (newborn) stage, 130% greater than those of females. A number of neonatal disorders are common to males but not females, such as bacterial infections, respiratory illness, digestive diseases, and some circulatory disorders of the aorta and pulmonary artery. Table 25.1 compares male and female infant mortality rates across historical time. Though the infant mortality rate decreases over time, the persistence of the higher rates for males than females suggests that biological factors may be operating. Data also show that males have higher mortality rates than females in every age category, from "under one year" through "over 85" (National Center for Health Statistics 1992). In fact, men are more likely to die in 9 out of the 10 leading causes of death in the United States. (See Table 25.2.)

Females have greater life expectancy than males in the United States, Canada, and postindustrial societies (Waldron 1986; Verbrugge and Wingard 1987). This fact suggests a female biological advantage, but a closer analysis of changing trends in the gap between women's and men's life expectancy indicates that social and cultural factors related to lifestyle, gender identity, and behavior are operating as well. Life expectancy among American females is about 78.3 years but 71.3 years for males (National Center for Health

■ **TABLE 25.1**
Infant Mortality Rate

Year	Both Sexes	Males	Females
1940	47.0	52.5	41.3
1950	29.2	32.8	25.5
1960	26.0	29.3	22.6
1970	20.0	22.4	17.5
1980	12.6	13.9	11.2
1989	9.8	10.8	8.8

Note: Rates are for infant (under 1 year) deaths per 1,000 live births for all races.

Source: Adapted from *Monthly Vital Statistics Report*, Vol. 40, No. 8, Supplement 2, January 7, 1992, p. 41.

Statistics 1990). As Waldron's (1995) analysis of shifting mortality patterns between the sexes during the 20th century shows, however, women's relative advantage in life expectancy over men was rather small at the beginning of the 20th century. During the mid-20th century, female mortality declined more rapidly than male mortality, thereby increasing the gender gap in life expectancy. Whereas women benefited from decreased maternal mortality, the midcentury trend toward a lowering of men's life expectancy was slowed by increasing mortality from coronary heart disease and lung cancer that were, in turn, mainly due to higher rates of cigarette smoking among males.

The most recent trends show that differences between women's and men's mortality decreased during the 1980s; that is, female life expectancy was 7.9 years greater than that of males in 1979 and 6.9 years in 1989 (National Center for Health Statistics 1992). Waldron explains that some changes in behavioral patterns between the sexes, such as increased smoking among women, have narrowed the gap between men's formerly higher mortality rates from lung cancer, chronic obstructive pulmonary disease, and ischemic heart disease. In summary, it appears that both biological and sociocultural factors are involved with shaping patterns of men's and women's mortality. In fact, Waldron (1976) suggests that gender-related behaviors rather than strictly biogenic factors account for about three-quarters of the variation in men's early mortality.

Morbidity

Whereas females generally outlive males, females report higher morbidity rates, even after controlling for maternity. National health surveys show

■ **TABLE 25.2**
Death Rates by Sex and 10 Leading Causes: 1989

Cause of Death	Age-Adjusted Death Rate per 100,000 Population			
	Total	**Male**	**Female**	**Sex Differential**
Diseases of the heart	155.9	210.2	112.3	1.87
Malignant neoplasms	133.0	163.4	111.7	1.45
Accidents and adverse effects	33.8	49.5	18.9	2.62
Cerebrovascular disease	28.0	30.4	26.2	1.16
Chronic liver disease, cirrhosis	8.9	12.8	5.5	2.33
Diabetes	11.5	2.0	11.0	1.09
Suicide	11.3	18.6	4.5	4.13
Homicide and legal intervention	9.4	14.7	4.1	3.59

Source: Adapted from the *U.S. Bureau of the Census: Statistical Abstracts of the United States:* 1992 (112th ed., p. 84), Washington, DC.

that females experience acute illnesses such as respiratory conditions, infective and parasitic conditions, and digestive system disorders at higher rates than males do; however, males sustain more injuries (Givens 1979; Cypress 1981; Dawson & Adams 1987). Men's higher injury rates are partly owed to gender differences in socialization and lifestyle, such as learning to prove manhood through recklessness, involvement in contact sports, and working in risky blue-collar occupations.

Females are generally more likely than males to experience chronic conditions such as anemia, chronic enteritis and colitis, migraine headaches, arthritis, diabetes, and thyroid disease. However, males are more prone to develop chronic illnesses such as coronary heart disease, emphysema, and gout. Although chronic conditions do not ordinarily cause death, they often limit activity or cause disability.

After noting gender differences in morbidity, Cockerham (1995) asks whether women really do experience more illness than men—or could it be that women are more sensitive to bodily sensations than men, or that men are not as prone as women to report symptoms and seek medical care? He concludes, "The best evidence indicates that the overall differences in morbidity are real" and, further, that they are due to a mixture of biological, psychological, and social influences (p. 42).

Masculinities and Men's Health

There is no such thing as masculinity; there are only masculinities (Sabo & Gordon 1995). A limitation of early gender theory was its treatment of "all men" as a single, large category in relation to "all women" (Connell 1987). The fact is, however, that all men are not alike, nor do all male groups share the same stakes in the gender order. At any given historical moment, there are competing masculinities—some dominant, some marginalized, and some stigmatized—each with its respective structural, psychosocial, and cultural moorings. There are substantial differences between the health options of homeless men, working-class men, lower-class men, gay men, men with AIDS, prison inmates, men of color, and their comparatively advantaged middle- and upper-class, white, professional male counterparts. Similarly, a wide range of individual differences exists between the ways that men and women act out "femininity" and "masculinity" in their everyday lives. A health profile of several male groups is discussed below.

Adolescent Males

Pleck, Sonenstein, and Ku (1992) applied critical feminist perspectives to their research on problem behaviors and health among adolescent males. A national sampling of adolescent, never-married males aged 15–19 were interviewed in 1980 and 1988. Hypothesis tests were geared to assessing whether "masculine ideology" (which measured the presence of traditional male role attitudes) put boys at risk for an array of problem behaviors. The researchers found a significant, independent association with seven of ten problem behaviors. Specifically, traditionally masculine attitudes were associated with being suspended from school, drinking and use of street drugs, frequency of being picked up by the police, being sexually active, the number of heterosexual partners in the last year, and tricking or forcing someone to have sex. These kinds of behaviors, which are in part expressions of the pursuit of traditional masculinity, elevate boys' risk for sexually transmitted diseases, HIV transmission, and early death by accident or homicide. At the same time, however, these same behaviors can also encourage victimization of women through men's violence, sexual assault, unwanted teenage pregnancy, and sexually transmitted diseases.

Adolescence is a phase of accelerated physiological development, and good nutrition during this period is important to future health. Obesity puts adults at risk for a variety of diseases such as coronary heart disease, diabetes mellitus, joint disease, and certain cancers. Obese adolescents are also apt to become obese adults, thus elevating long-term risk for illness. National Health and

Nutrition Examination Surveys show that obesity among adolescents increased by 6 percent during 1976–1980 and 1988–1991. During 1988–1991, 22 percent of females of 12–18 years were overweight, and 20 percent of males in this age group were as well (*Morbidity and Mortality Weekly Report* 1994a).

Males form a majority of the estimated 1.3 million teenagers who run away from home each year in the United States. For both boys and girls, living on the streets raises the risk of poor nutrition, homicide, alcoholism, drug abuse, and AIDS. Young adults in their 20s comprise about 20 percent of new AIDS cases and, when you calculate the lengthy latency period, it is evident that they are being infected in their teenage years. Runaways are also more likely to be victims of crime and sexual exploitation (Hull 1994).

Clearly, adolescent males face a spectrum of potential health problems—some that threaten their present well-being, and others that could take their toll in the future.

Men of Color

Patterns of health and illness among men of color can be partly understood against the historical and social context of economic inequality. Generally, because African Americans, Hispanics, and Native Americans are disproportionately poor, they are more apt to work in low-paying and dangerous occupations, reside in polluted environments, be exposed to toxic substances, experience the threat and reality of crime, and worry about meeting basic needs. Cultural barriers can also complicate their access to available health care. Poverty is correlated with lower educational attainment, which, in turn, mitigates against adoption of preventive health behaviors.

The neglect of public health in the United States is particularly pronounced in relation to African Americans (Polych & Sabo 1996). For example, in Harlem, where 96 percent of the inhabitants are African American and 41 percent live below the poverty line, the survival curve beyond the age of 40 for men is lower than that of men living in Bangladesh (McCord & Freeman

1990). Even though African American men have higher rates of alcoholism, infectious diseases, and drug-related conditions, for example, they are less apt to receive health care, and when they do, they are more apt to receive inferior care (Bullard 1992; Staples 1995). Statistics like the following led Gibbs (1988) to describe young African American males as an "endangered species":

- The number of young African American male homicide victims in 1977 (5,734) was higher than the number killed in the Vietnam War during 1963–1972 (5,640) (Gibbs 1988:258).
- Homicide is the leading cause of death among young African American males. The probability of a black male dying from homicide is about the same as that of a white male dying from an accident (Reed 1991).
- More than 36% of urban African American males are drug and alcohol abusers (Staples 1995).
- In 1993 the rate of contracting AIDS for African American males aged 13 and older was almost 5 times higher than the rate for white males (*Morbidity and Mortality Weekly Report* 1994b).

The health profile of Native Americans and Native Canadians is also poor. For example, alcohol is the number-one killer of Native Americans between the ages of 14 and 44 (May 1986), and 42 percent of Native American male adolescents are problem drinkers, compared to 34 percent of same-age white males (Lamarine 1988). Native Americans (10–18 years of age) comprise 34 percent of in-patient admissions to adolescent detoxification programs (Moore 1988). Compared to the "all race" population, Native American youth exhibit more serious problems in the areas of depression, suicide, anxiety, substance use, and general health status (Blum et al. 1992). The rates of morbidity, mortality from injury, and contracting AIDS are also higher (Metler, Conway, & Stehr-Green 1991; Sugarman et al. 1993).

Like those of many other racial and ethnic groups, the health problems facing American and Canadian natives correlate with the effects of poverty and social marginalization, such as dropping out of school, a sense of hopelessness, the experience of prejudice, poor nutrition, and lack of regular health care. Those who care about men's health, therefore, need to be attuned to the potential interplay between gender, race/ethnicity, cultural differences, and economic conditions when working with racial and ethnic minorities.

Gay and Bisexual Men

Gay and bisexual men are estimated to constitute 5 percent to 10 percent of the male population. In the past, gay men have been viewed as evil, sinful, sick, emotionally immature, and socially undesirable. Many health professionals and the wider public have harbored mixed feelings and homophobic attitudes toward gay and bisexual men. Gay men's identity, their lifestyles, and the social responses to homosexuality can impact the health of gay and bisexual men. Stigmatization and marginalization, for example, may lead to emotional confusion and suicide among gay male adolescents. For gay and bisexual men who are "in the closet," anxiety and stress can tax emotional and physical health. When seeking medical services, gay and bisexual men must often cope with the homophobia of health care workers or deal with the threat of losing health care insurance if their sexual orientation is made known.

Whether they are straight or gay, men tend to have more sexual contacts than women do, which heightens men's risk for contracting sexually transmitted diseases (STDs). Men's sexual attitudes and behaviors are closely tied to the way masculinity has been socially constructed. For example, real men are taught to suppress their emotions, which can lead to a separation of sex from feeling. Traditionally, men are also encouraged to be daring, which can lead to risky sexual decisions. In addition, contrary to common myths about gay male effeminacy, masculinity also plays a powerful role in shaping gay and bi-

sexual men's identity and behavior. To the extent that traditional masculinity informs sexual activity of men, masculinity can be a barrier to safer sexual behavior among men. This insight leads Kimmel and Levine (1989) to assert that "to educate men about safe sex, then, means to confront the issues of masculinity" (p. 352). In addition to practicing abstinence and safer sex as preventive strategies, therefore, they argue that traditional beliefs about masculinity be challenged as a form of risk reduction.

Men who have sex with men remain the largest risk group for HIV transmission. For gay and bisexual men who are infected by the HIV virus, the personal burden of living with an AIDS diagnosis is made heavier by the stigma associated with homosexuality. The cultural meanings associated with AIDS can also filter into gender and sexual identities. Tewksbury's (1995) interviews with 45 HIV positive gay men showed how masculinity, sexuality, stigmatization, and interpersonal commitment mesh in decision making related to risky sexual behavior. Most of the men practiced celibacy in order to prevent others from contracting the disease; others practiced safe sex, and a few went on having unprotected sex.

Prison Inmates

There are 1.3 million men imprisoned in American jails and prisons (Nadelmann & Wenner 1994). The United States has the highest rate of incarceration of any nation in the world, 426 prisoners for every 100,000 people (American College of Physicians 1992), followed by South Africa and the former Soviet Union (Mauer 1992). Racial and ethnic minorities are overrepresented among those behind bars. Black and Hispanic males, for example, comprise 85 percent of prisoners in the New York State prison system (Green 1991).

The prison system acts as a pocket of risk, within which men already at high risk of having a preexisting AIDS infection are exposed to conditions that further heighten the risk of contracting HIV (Toepell 1992) or other infections such as tuberculosis (Bellin, Fletcher, & Safyer 1993) or hepatitis. The corrections system is part of an institutional chain that facilitates transmission of HIV and other infections in certain North American populations, particularly among poor, inner-city, minority males. Prisoners are burdened not only by social disadvantage but also by high rates of physical illness, mental disorder, and substance abuse that jeopardize their health (Editor, *Lancet* 1991).

AIDS prevalence is markedly higher among state and federal inmates than in the general U.S. population, with a known aggregate rate in 1992 of 202 per 100,000 population (Brewer & Derrickson 1992) compared to a total population prevalence of 14.65 in 100,000 (American College of Physicians 1992). The cumulative total of American prisoners with AIDS in 1989 was estimated to be 5,411, a 72 percent increase over the previous year (Belbot & del Carmen 1991). The total number of AIDS cases reported in U.S. corrections as of 1993 was 11,565 (a minimum estimate of the true cumulative incidence among U.S. inmates) (Hammett; cited in Expert Committee on AIDS and Prisons 1994). In New York State, at least 10,000 of the state's 55,000 prisoners are believed to be infected (Prisoners with AIDS/HIV Support Action Network 1992). In Canadian federal penitentiaries, it is believed that 1 in 20 inmates is HIV infected (Hankins; cited in Expert Committee on AIDS and Prison 1994).

The HIV virus is primarily transmitted between adults by unprotected penetrative sex or by needle sharing, without bleaching, with an infected partner. Sexual contacts between prisoners occur mainly through consensual unions and secondarily through sexual assault and rape (Vaid; cited in Expert Committee on AIDS and Prisons 1994). The amount of IV drug use behind prison walls is unknown, although it is known to be prevalent and the scarcity of needles often leads to sharing of needles and sharps (Prisoners with AIDS/HIV Support Action Network 1992).

The failure to provide comprehensive health education and treatment interventions in prisons not only puts more inmates at risk for HIV infection, but also threatens the public at large. Prisons are not hermetically sealed enclaves set apart from the community, but an integral part of society (Editor, *Lancet* 1991). Prisoners regularly move in and out of the prison system. In 1989, prisons in the United States admitted 467,227 persons and discharged 386,228 (American College of Physicians 1992). The average age of inmates admitted to prison in 1989 was 29.6, with 75 percent between 18 and 34 years; 94.3 percent were male. These former inmates return to their communities after having served an average of 18 months inside (Dubler & Sidel 1989). Within three years, 62.5 percent will be rearrested and jailed. Recidivism is highest among poor black and Hispanic men. The extent to which the drug-related social practices and sexual activities of released or paroled inmates who are HIV positive are putting others at risk upon return to their communities is unresearched and unknown.

Male Athletes

Injury is everywhere in sport. It is evident in the lives and bodies of athletes who regularly experience bruises, torn ligaments, broken bones, aches, lacerations, muscle tears, and so forth. For example, about 300,000 football-related injuries per year require treatment in hospital emergency rooms (Miedzian 1991). Critics of violent contact sports claim that athletes are paying too high a physical price for their participation. George D. Lundberg (1994), editor of the *Journal of the American Medical Association,* has called for a ban on boxing in the Olympics and in the U.S. military. His editorial entreaty, though based on clinical evidence for neurological harm from boxing, is also couched in a wider critique of the exploitative economics of the sport.

Injuries are basically unavoidable in sports, but, in traditional men's sports, there has been a tendency to glorify pain and injury, to inflict injury on others, and to sacrifice one's body in order to "win at all costs." The "no pain, no gain" philosophy, which is rooted in traditional cultural equations between masculinity and sports, can jeopardize the health of athletes who conform to its ethos (Sabo 1994).

The connections between sport, masculinity, and health are evidence in Klein's (1993) study of how bodybuilders use anabolic steroids, overtrain, and engage in extreme dietary practices. He spent years as an ethnographic researcher in the muscled world of the bodybuilding subculture, where masculinity is equated to maximum muscularity and men's striving for bigness and physical strength hides emotional insecurity and low self-esteem.

A nationwide survey of American male high school seniors found that 6.6 percent used or had used anabolic steroids. About two-thirds of this group were athletes (Buckley et al. 1988). Anabolic steroid use has been linked to health risks such as liver disease, kidney problems, atrophy of the testicles, elevated risk of injury, and premature skeletal maturation.

Klein lays bare a tragic irony in American culture—the powerful male athlete, a symbol of strength and health, has often sacrificed his health in pursuit of ideal masculinity (Messner & Sabo 1994).

Men's Health Issues

Advocates of men's health have identified a variety of issues that impact directly on men's lives. Some of these issues may concern you or men you care about.

Testicular Cancer

The epidemiological data on testicular cancer are sobering. Though relatively rare in the general population, it is the fourth most common cause of death among males of 15–35 years accounting for 14 percent of all cancer deaths for this age group. It is the most common form of cancer affecting males of 20–34 years. The incidence of testicular cancer is increasing, and about 6,100 new U.S. cases were diagnosed in 1991 (American Cancer Society 1991). If detected early, the cure rate is high, whereas delayed diagnosis is life threatening. Regular testicular self-examination (TSE), therefore, is a potentially effective means for ensuring early detection and successful treat-

ment. Regrettably, however, most physicians do not teach TSE techniques (Rudolf & Quinn 1988).

Denial may influence men's perceptions of testicular cancer and TSE (Blesch 1986). Studies show that most males are not aware of testicular cancer, and even among those who are aware, many are reluctant to examine their testicles as a preventive measure. Even when symptoms are recognized, men sometimes postpone seeking treatment. Moreover, men who are taught TSE are often initially receptive, but their practice of TSE decreases over time. Men's resistance to TSE has been linked to awkwardness about touching themselves, associating touching genitals with homosexuality or masturbation, or the idea that TSE is not a manly behavior. And finally, men's individual reluctance to discuss testicular cancer partly derives from the widespread cultural silence that envelops it. The penis is a cultural symbol of male power, authority, and sexual domination. Its symbolic efficacy in traditional, male-dominated gender relations, therefore, would be eroded or neutralized by the realities of testicular cancer.

Diseases of the Prostate

Middle-aged and elderly men are likely to develop medical problems with the prostate gland. Some men may experience benign prostatic hyperplasia, an enlargement of the prostate gland that is associated with symptoms such as dribbling after urination, frequent urination, or incontinence. Others may develop infections (prostatitis) or malignant prostatic hyperplasia (prostate cancer). Prostate cancer is the third leading cause of death from cancer in men, accounting for 15.7 deaths per 100,000 population in 1989. Prostate cancer is now more common than lung cancer (Martin 1990). One in 10 men will develop this cancer by age 85, with African American males showing a higher prevalence rate than whites (Greco & Blank 1993).

Treatments for prostate problems depend on the specific diagnosis and may range from medication to radiation and surgery. As is the case with testicular cancer, survival from prostate cancer is enhanced by early detection. Raising men's awareness about the health risks associated with the prostate gland, therefore, may prevent unnecessary morbidity and mortality. Unfortunately, the more invasive surgical treatments for prostate cancer can produce incontinence and impotence, and there has been no systematic research on men's psychosocial reactions and adjustment to sexual dysfunction associated with treatments for prostate cancer.

Alcohol Abuse

Although social and medical problems stemming from alcohol abuse involve both sexes, males comprise the largest segment of alcohol abusers. Some researchers have begun exploring the connections between the influence of the traditional male role on alcohol abuse. Isenhart and Silversmith (1994) show how, in a variety of occupational contexts, expectations surrounding masculinity encourage heavy drinking while working or socializing during after-work or off-duty hours. Some predominantly male occupational groups, such as longshoremen (Hitz 1973), salesmen (Cosper 1979), and members of the military (Pursch 1976), are known to engage in high rates of alcohol consumption. Mass media play a role in sensationalizing links between booze and male bravado. Postman, Nystrom, Strate, and Weingartner (1987) studied the thematic content of 40 beer commercials and identified a variety of stereotypical portrayals of the male role that were used to promote beer drinking: reward for a job well done; manly activities that feature strength, risk, and daring; male friendship and esprit de corps; romantic success with women. The researchers estimate that, between the ages of 2 and 18, children view about 100,000 beer commercials.

Findings from a Harvard School of Public Health (1994) survey of 17,600 students at 140 colleges found that 44 percent engaged in "binge drinking," defined as drinking five drinks in rapid succession for males and four drinks for females. Males were more apt to report binge drinking during the past two weeks than females; 50 percent and 39 percent respectively. Sixty percent of the males who binge three or more times in the past two weeks reported driving after drinking, compared to 49 percent of their female counterparts, thus increasing the risk for accident, injury, and death. Compared to non–binge drinkers, binge drinkers were seven times more likely to engage in unprotected sex, thus elevating the risk for unwanted pregnancy and sexually transmitted disease. Alcohol-related automobile accidents are the top cause of death among 16- to 24-year-olds, especially among males (Henderson & Anderson 1989). For all males, the age-adjusted death rate from automobile accidents in 1991 was 26.2 per 100,000 for African American males and 24.2 per 100,000 for white males, 2.5 and 3.0 times higher than for white and African American females, respectively (*Morbidity and Mortality Weekly Report* 1994d). The number of automobile fatalities among male adolescents that results from a mixture of alcohol abuse and masculine daring is unknown.

Men and AIDS

Human immunodeficiency virus (HIV) infection became a leading cause of death among males in the 1980s. Among men aged 25–44 in 1990, HIV infection was the second leading cause of death, compared to the sixth leading cause of death among same-age women (*Morbidity and Mortality Weekly Report* 1993a). Among reported cases of acquired immunodeficiency syndrome (AIDS) for adolescent and adult men in 1992, 60 percent were men who had sex with other men, 21 percent were intravenous drug users, 4 percent were exposed through heterosexual sexual contact, 6 percent were men who had sex with men and injected drugs, and 1 percent were transfusion recipients. Among the cases of AIDS among adolescent and adult women in 1992, 45 percent were intravenous drug users, 39 percent were infected through heterosexual sexual contact, and 4 percent were transfusion recipients (*Morbidity and Mortality Weekly Report* 1993a).

Because most AIDS cases have been among men who have sex with other men, perceptions of the epidemic and its victims have been tinctured by sexual attitudes. In North American cultures, the stigma associated with AIDS is fused with the stigma linked to homosexuality. Feelings about men with AIDS can be mixed and complicated by homophobia.

Thoughts and feelings about men with AIDS are also influenced by attitudes toward race, ethnicity, drug abuse, and social marginality. Centers for Disease Control data show, for example, that men of color aged 13 and older constituted 51 percent (45,039) of the 89,165 AIDS cases reported in 1993. Women of color made up 71 percent of the cases reported among females aged 13 and older (*Morbidity and Mortality Weekly Report* 1994b). The high rate of AIDS among racial and ethnic minorities has kindled racial prejudices in some minds, and AIDS is sometimes seen as a "minority disease." Although African American or Hispanic males may be at greater risk of contracting HIV/AIDS, just as yellow fingers do not cause lung disease, it is not race or ethnicity that confers risk, but the behaviors they engage in and the social circumstances of their lives.

Perceptions of HIV/AIDS can also be influenced by attitudes toward poverty and poor people. HIV infection is linked to economic problems that include community disintegration, unemployment, homelessness, eroding urban tax bases, mental illness, substance abuse, and criminalization (Wallace 1991). For example, males comprise the majority of homeless persons. Poverty and homelessness overlap with drug addiction, which, in turn, is linked to HIV infection. Of persons hospitalized with HIV in New York City, 9–18 percent have been found to be homeless (Torres et al. 1990). Of homeless men tested for HIV at a New York City shelter, 62 percent of those who took the test were seropositive (Ron & Rogers 1989). Among runaway or homeless youth in New York City, 7 percent tested positive, and this rate rose to 15 percent among the 19- and 20-year-olds. Of homeless men in Baltimore, 85 percent admitted to substance use problems (Weinreb & Bassuk 1990).

Suicide

The suicide rates for both African American and white males increased between 1970 and 1989, whereas female rates decreased. Indeed, males are more likely than females to commit suicide from middle childhood until old age (Stillion 1985, 1995). Compared to females, males typically deploy more violent means of attempting suicide (e.g., guns or hanging rather than pills) and are more likely to complete the act. Men's selection of more violent methods to kill themselves is consistent with traditionally masculine behavior (Stillion et al.).

Canetto (1995) interviewed male survivors of suicide attempts in order to better understand sex differences in suicidal behavior. Although she recognizes that men's psychosocial reactions and adjustments to nonfatal suicide vary by race/ethnicity, socioeconomic status, and age, she also finds that gender identity is an important factor in men's experiences. Suicide data show that men attempt suicide less often than women but are more likely to die than women. Canetto indicates that men's comparative "success" rate points toward a tragic irony in that, consistent with gender stereotypes, men's failure even at suicide undercuts the cultural mandate that men are supposed to succeed at everything. A lack of embroilment in traditionally masculine expectations, she suggests, may actually increase the likelihood of surviving a suicide attempt for some men.

Elderly males in North America commit suicide significantly more often than elderly females. Whereas white women's lethal suicide rate peaks at age 50, white men age 60 and older have the highest rate of lethal suicide, even surpassing the rate for young males (Manton, Blazer, & Woodbury 1987). Canetto (1992) argues that elderly men's higher suicide mortality is chiefly owed to gender differences in coping. She writes:

> older women may have more flexible and diverse ways of coping than older men. Compared to older men, older women may be more willing and capable of adopting different coping

strategies—"passive" or "active," "connected" or "independent"—depending on the situation (p. 92).

She attributes men's limited coping abilities to gender socialization and development.

Erectile Disorders

Men often joke about their penises or tease one another about penis size and erectile potency ("not getting it up"). In contrast, they rarely discuss their concerns about impotence in a serious way. Men's silences in this regard are regrettable in that many men, both young and old, experience recurrent or periodic difficulties getting or maintaining an erection. Estimates of the number of American men with erectile disorders range from 10 million to 30 million (Krane, Goldstein, & Saenz de Tejada 1989; National Institutes of Health 1993). The Massachusetts Male Aging Study of the general population of noninstitutionalized, healthy American men between ages 40 and 70 years found that 52 percent reported minimal, moderate, or complete impotence (Feldman et al. 1994). The prevalence of erectile disorders increased with age, and 9.6 percent of the men were afflicted by complete impotence.

During the 1960s and 1970s, erectile disorders were largely thought to stem from psychological problems such as depression, financial worries, or work-related stress. Masculine stereotypes about male sexual prowess, phallic power, or being in charge of lovemaking were also said to put too much pressure to perform on some males (Zilbergeld 1993). In contrast, physiological explanations of erectile disorders and medical treatments have been increasingly emphasized since the 1980s. Today diagnosis and treatment of erectile disorders should combine psychological and medical assessment (Ackerman & Carey 1995).

Men's Violence

Men's violence is a major public health problem. The traditional masculine stereotype calls on males to be aggressive and tough. Anger is a by-product of aggression and toughness and, ultimately, part of the inner terrain of traditional masculinity (Sabo 1993). Images of angry young men are compelling vehicles used by some males to separate themselves from women and to measure their status in respect to other males. Men's anger and violence derive, in part, from sex inequality. Men use the threat or application of violence to maintain their political and economic advantage over women and lower-status men. Male socialization reflects and reinforces these larger patterns of domination.

Homicide is the second leading cause of death among 15- to 19-year-old males. Males aged 15–34 years made up almost half (49 percent, or 13,122) of homicide victims in the United States in 1991. The homicide rate for this age group increased by 50 percent from 1985 to 1991 (*Morbidity and Morality Weekly Report* 1994c).

Women are especially victimized by men's anger and violence in the form of rape, date rape, wife beating, assault, sexual harassment on the job, and verbal harassment (Thorne-Finch 1992). That the reality and potential of men's violence impact women's mental and physical health can be surely assumed. However, men's violence also exacts a toll on men themselves in the forms of fighting, gang clashes, hazing, gay-bashing, intentional infliction of injury, homicide, suicide, and organized warfare.

Summary

It is ironic that two of the best-known actors who portrayed Superman have met with disaster. George Reeves, who starred in the original black-and-white television show, committed suicide, and Christopher Reeve, who portrayed the "man of steel" in recent film versions, was paralyzed by an accident during a high-risk equestrian event. Perhaps one lesson to be learned here is that, behind the cultural facade of mythic masculinity, men are vulnerable. Indeed, as we have seen in this chapter, some of the cultural messages sewn into the cloak of masculinity can put men at risk for illness and early death. A sensible preventive health strategy for the 1990s calls upon men to critically evaluate the Superman legacy, that is, to challenge the negative aspects of traditional masculinity that endanger their health, while hanging on to the positive aspects of masculinity and men's lifestyles that heighten men's physical vitality.

The promotion of men's health also requires a sharper recognition that the sources of men's risks for many diseases do not strictly reside in men's psyches, gender identities, or the roles that they enact in daily life. Men's roles, routines, and relations with others are fixed in the historical and structural relations that constitute the larger gender order. As we have seen, not all men or male groups share the same access to social resources, educational attainment, and opportunity that, in turn, can influence their health options. Yes, men need to pursue personal change in order to enhance their health, but without changing the political, economic, and ideological structures of the gender order, the subjective gains and insights forged within individuals can easily erode and fade away. If men are going to pursue self-healing, therefore, they need to create an overall preventive strategy that at once seeks to change potentially harmful aspects of traditional masculinity and meets the health needs of lower-status men.

References

Ackerman, M. D., & Carey, P. C. (1995). "Psychology's Role in Assessment of Erectile Dysfunction: Historical Procedure, Current Knowledge, and Methods." *Journal of Counseling & Clinical Psychology, 63*(6), 862–876.

American Cancer Society (1991). Cancer facts and figures—1991. Atlanta, GA: American Cancer Society.

American College of Physicians. (1992). The crisis in correctional health care: The impact of the national drug control strategy on correctional health services. *Annals of Internal Medicine, 117*(1), 71–77.

Belbot, B. A., & del Carmen, R. B. (1991). AIDS in prison: Legal issues. *Crime and Delinquency, 31*(1), 135–153.

Bellin, E. Y., Fletcher, D. D., & Safyer, S. M. (1993). Association of tuberculosis infection with increased time in or admission to the New York City jail system. *Journal of the American Medical Association, 269*(17), 2228–2231.

Blesch, K. (1986). Health beliefs about testicular cancer and self-examination among professional men. *Oncology Nursing Forum, 13*(1), 29–33.

Blum, R., Harman, B., Harris, L., Bergeissen, L., & Restrick, M. (1992). American Indian–Alaska native youth health. *Journal of American Medical Association, 267*(12), 1637–1644.

Brewer, T. F., & Derrickson, J. (1992). AIDS in prison: A review of epidemiology and preventive policy. *AIDS, 6*(7), 623–628.

Buckley, W. E., Yesalis, C. E., Friedl, K. E., Anderson, W. A., Streit, A. L., & Wright, J. E. (1988). Estimated prevalence of anabolic steroid use among male high school seniors. *Journal of the American Medical Association, 260*(23), 3441–3446.

Bullard, R. D. (1992). Urban infrastructure: Social, environmental, and health risks to African-Americans. In B. J. Tidwell (Ed.), *The State of Black America* (pp. 183–196). New York: National Urban League.

Canetto, S. S. (1992). Gender and suicide in the elderly. *Suicide and Life-Threatening Behavior, 22*(1), 80–97.

Canetto, S. S. (1995). Men who survive a suicidal act: Successful coping or failed masculinity? In D. Sabo & D. Gordon (Eds.), *Men's health and illness* (pp. 292–304). Newbury Park, CA: Sage.

Cockerham, W. C. (1995). *Medical sociology.* Englewood Cliffs, NJ: Prentice-Hall.

Connell, R. W. (1987). *Gender and power.* Stanford: Stanford University Press.

Cosper, R. (1979). Drinking as conformity: A critique of sociological literature on occupational differences in drinking. *Journal of Studies on Alcoholism, 40,* 868–891.

Cypress, B. (1981). Patients' reasons for visiting physicians: National ambulatory medical care survey, U.S. 1977–78. DHHS Publication No. (PHS) 82-1717, Series 13, No. 56. Hyattsville, MD: National Center for Health Statistics, December, 1981a.

Dawson, D. A., & Adams, P. F. (1987). Current estimates from the national health interview survey: U.S. 1986. Vital Health Statistics Series, Series

10, No. 164. DHHS Publication No. (PHS) 87-1592, Public Health Service. Washington, D.C: U.S. Government Printing Office.

Dubler, N. N., & Sidel, V. W. (1989). On research on HIV infection and AIDS in correctional institutions. *The Milbank Quarterly, 67*(1–2), 81–94.

Editor, (1991, March 16). Health care for prisoners: Implications of "Kalk's refusal." *Lancet, 337,* 647–648.

Expert Committee on AIDS and Prison. (1994). *HIV/AIDS in prisons: Summary report and recommendations to the Expert Committee on AIDS and Prisons* (Ministry of Supply and Services Canada Catalogue No. JS82-68/2-1994). Ottawa, Ontario, Canada: Correctional Service of Canada.

Feldman, H. A., Goldstein, I., Hatzichristou, D. G., Krane, R. J., & McKinlay, J. B. (1994). Impotence and its medical and psychosocial correlates: Results of the Massachusetts Male Aging Study. *Journal of Urology, 151,* 54–61.

Gibbs, J. T. (Ed.) (1988). *Young, black, and male in America: An endangered species.* Dover, MA: Auburn House.

Givens, J. (1979). Current estimates from the health interview survey: U.S. 1978. DHHS Publication No. (PHS) 80-1551, Series 10, No. 130. Hyattsville, MD: Office of Health Research Statistics, November 1979.

Greco, K. E. & Blank, B. (1993). Prostate-specific antigen: The new early detection test for prostate cancer. *Nurse Practitioner, 18*(5), 30–38.

Green, A. P. (1991). Blacks unheard. *Update* (Winter), New York State Coalition for Criminal Justice, 6–7.

Harrison, J., Chin, J., & Ficarrotto, T. (1992). Warning: Masculinity may be dangerous to your health. In M. S. Kimmel & M. A. Messner (Eds.), *Men's lives* (pp. 271–285). New York: Macmillan.

Harvard School of Public Health. Study reported by Wechler, H., Davenport, A., Dowdall, G., Moeykens, B., & Castillo, S. (1994). Health and behavioral consequences of binge drinking in college: A national survey of students at 140 campuses. *Journal of the American Medical Association, 272*(21), 1672–1677.

Henderson, D. C., & Anderson, S. C. (1989). Adolescents and chemical dependency. *Social Work in Health Care, 14*(1), 87–105.

Hitz, D. (1973). Drunken sailors and others: Drinking problems in specific occupations. *Quarterly Journal of Studies on Alcohol, 34,* 496–505.

Hull, J. D. (1994, November 21). Running scared. *Time, 144*(2), 93–99.

Isenhart, C. E., & Silversmith, D. J. (1994). The influence of the traditional male role on alcohol abuse and the therapeutic process. *Journal of Men's Studies, 3*(2), 127–135.

Kimmel, M. S., and Levine, M. P. (1989). Men and AIDS. In M. S. Kimmel & M. A. Messner (Eds.), *Men's lives* (pp. 344–354) New York: Macmillan.

Klein, A. (1993). *Little big men: Bodybuilding subculture and gender construction.* Albany, NY: SUNY Press.

Krane, R. J., Goldstein, I., & Saentz de Tejjada, I. (1989). Impotence. *New England Journal of Medicine, 321,* 1648–1659.

Lamarine, R. (1988). Alcohol abuse among Native Americans. *Journal of Community Health, 13*(3), 143–153.

Lundberg, G. D. (1994, June 8). Let's stop boxing in the Olympics and the United States military. *Journal of the American Medical Association, 271*(22), 1990.

Manton, K. G., Blazer, D. G., & Woodbury, M. A. (1987). Suicide in middle age and later life: Sex and race specific life table and cohort analyses. *Journal of Gerontology, 42,* 219–227.

Martin, J. (1990). Male cancer awareness: Impact of an employee education program. *Oncology Nursing Forum, 17*(1), 59–64.

Mauer, M. (1992). Men in American prisons: Trends, causes, and issues. *Men's Studies Review, 9*(1), 10–12. A special issue on men in prison, edited by Don Sabo and Willie London.

May, P. (1986). Alcohol and drug misuse prevention programs for American Indians: Needs and opportunities. *Journal of Studies of Alcohol, 47*(3), 187–195.

McCord, C., & Freeman, H. P. (1990). Excess mortality in Harlem. *New England Journal of Medicine, 322*(22), 1606–1607.

Messner, M. A., and Sabo, D. (1994). *Sex, violence, and power in sports: Rethinking masculinity.* Freedom, CA: Crossing Press.

Metler, R., Conway, G., & Stehr-Green, J. (1991). AIDS surveillance among American Indians and Alaskan natives. *American Journal of Public Health, 81*(11), 1469–1471.

Miedzian, M. (1991). *Boys will be boys: Breaking the link between masculinity and violence.* New York: Doubleday.

Montagu, A. (1953). *The natural superiority of women.* New York: Macmillan.

Moore, D. (1988). Reducing alcohol and other drug use among Native American youth. *Alcohol and Drug Abuse and Mental Health, 15*(6), 2–3.

Morbidity and Mortality Weekly Report. (1993a). Update: Mortality attributable to HIV infection/AIDS among persons aged 25–44 years—United States, 1990–91. *42*(25), 481–486.

Morbidity and Mortality Weekly Report. (1993b). Summary of notifiable diseases United States, 1992. *41*(55).

Morbidity and Mortality Weekly Report. (1994a). Prevalence of overweight among adolescents—United States, 1988–91. *43*(44), 818–819.

Morbidity and Mortality Weekly Report. (1994b). AIDS among racial/ethnic minorities—United States, 1993. *43*(35), 644–651.

Morbidity and Mortality Weekly Report. (1994c). Homicides among 15–19-year-old males—United States. *43*(40), 725–728.

Morbidity and Mortality Weekly Report. (1994d). Deaths resulting from firearm- and motor-vehicle-related injuries—United States, 1968–1991. *43*(3), 37–42.

Nadelmann, P., & Wenner, L. (1994, May 5). Toward a sane national drug policy [Editorial]. *Rolling Stone,* 24–26.

National Center for Health Statistics. (1990). *Health, United States, 1989.* Hyattsville, MD: Public Health Service.

National Center for Health Statistics. (1992). Advance report of final mortality statistics, 1989. *Monthly Vital Statistics Report, 40* (Suppl. 2) (DHHS Publication No. [PHS] 92-1120).

National Institutes of Health. (1993). Consensus development panel on impotence. *Journal of the American Medical Association, 270,* 83–90.

Pleck, J., Sonenstein, F. L., & Ku, L. C. (1992). In R. Ketterlinus, & M. E. Lamb (Eds.), *Adolescent problem behaviors.* Hillsdale, NJ: Lawrence Erlbaum Associates.

Polych, C., & Sabo, D. (1996). Gender politics, pain, and illness: The AIDS epidemic in North American prisons. In D. Sabo & D. Gordon (Eds.), *Men's health and illness.* Newbury Park, CA: Sage, pp. 139–157.

Postman, N., Nystrom, C., Strate, L., & Weingartner, C. (1987). *Myths, men and beer: An analysis of beer commercials on broadcast television, 1987.* Falls Church, VA: Foundation for Traffic Safety.

Prisoners with AIDS/HIV Support Action Network. (1992). *HIV/AIDS in prison systems: A comprehensive strategy* (Brief to the Minister of Correctional Services and the Minister of Health). Toronto: Prisoners with AIDS/HIV Support Action Network.

Pursch, J. A. (1976). From quonset hut to naval hospital: The story of an alcoholism rehabilitation service. *Journal of Studies on Alcohol, 37,* 1655–1666.

Reed, W. L. (1991). Trends in homicide among African Americans. *Trotter Institute Review, 5,* 11–16.

Ron, A., & Rogers, D. E. (1989). AIDS in New York City: The role of intravenous drug users. *Bulletin of the New York Academy of Medicine, 65*(7), 787–800.

Rudolf, V., & Quinn, K. (1988). The practice of TSE among college men: Effectiveness of an educational program. *Oncology Nursing Forum, 15*(1), 45–48.

Sabo, D. (1993). Understanding men. In Kimball, G. (Ed.) *Everything You Need to Know to Succeed after College.* Chico, CA: Equality Press, pp. 71–93.

Sabo, D. (1994). The body politics of sports injury: Culture, power, and the pain principle. A paper presented at the annual meeting of the National Athletic Trainers Association, Dallas, TX, June 6, 1994.

Sabo, D., & Gordon, D. (1995). *Men's health and illness: Gender, power, and the body.* Newbury Park, CA: Sage.

Staples, R. (1995). Health and illness among African-American Males. In D. Sabo and D. Gordon (Eds.), *Men's health and illness.* Newbury Park, CA: Sage, pp. 121–138.

Stillion, J. (1985). *Death and the sexes: An examination of differential longevity, attitudes, behaviors, and coping skills.* New York: Hemisphere.

———. (1995). Premature death among males: Rethinking links between masculinity and health. In D. Sabo & D. Gordon (Eds.), *Men's health and illness.* Newbury Park, CA: Sage, pp. 46–67.

Stillion, J., White, H., McDowell, E. E., & Edwards, P. (1989). Ageism and sexism in suicide attitudes. *Death Studies, 13,* 247–261.

Sugarman, J., Soderberg, R., Gordon, J., & Rivera, F. (1993). Racial misclassification of American

Indians: Its effects on injury rates in Oregon, 1989–1990. *American Journal of Public Health, 83*(5), 681–684.

Tewksbury, (1995). Sexual adaptation among gay men with HIV. In D. Sabo & D. Gordon (Eds.), *Men's Health and Illness* (pp. 222–245). Newbury Park, CA: Sage.

Thorne-Finch, R. (1992). *Ending the silence: The origins and treatment of male violence against women.* Toronto: University of Toronto Press.

Toepell, A. R. (1992). *Prisoners and AIDS: AIDS education needs assessment.* Toronto: John Howard Society of Metropolitan Toronto.

Torres, R. A., Mani, S., Altholz, J., & Brickner, P. W. (1990). HIV infection among homeless men in a New York City shelter. *Archives of Internal Medicine, 150,* 2030–2036.

Verbrugge, L. M., & Wingard, D. L. (1987). Sex differentials in health and mortality. *Women's Health, 12,* 103–145.

Waldron, I. (1976). Why do women live longer than men? *Journal of Human Stress, 2,* 1–13.

———. (1986). What do we know about sex differences in mortality? *Population Bulletin of the U.N., No. 18-1985, 59–76.*

———. (1995). Contributions of changing gender differences in behavior and social roles to changing gender differences in mortality. In D. Sabo & D. Gordon (Eds.), *Men's health and illness,* Newbury Park, CA: Sage, pp. 22–45.

Wallace, R. (1991). Traveling waves of HIV infection on a low dimensional "sociogeographic" network. *Social Science Medicine, 32*(7), 847–852.

Weinreb, L. F., & Bassuk, E. L. (1990). Substance abuse: A growing problem among homeless families. *Family and Community Health, 13*(1), 55–64.

Zilbergeld, B. (1993). *The new male sexuality.* New York: Bantam.

Gloria Steinem

If Men Could Menstruate

A white minority of the world has spent centuries conning us into thinking that a white skin makes people superior—even though the only thing it really does is make them more subject to ultraviolet rays and to wrinkles. Male human beings have built whole cultures around the idea that penis-envy is "natural" to women—though having such an unprotected organ might be said to make men vulnerable, and the power to give birth makes womb-envy at least as logical.

In short, the characteristics of the powerful, whatever they may be, are thought to be better than the characteristics of the powerless—and logic has nothing to do with it.

What would happen, for instance, if suddenly, magically, men could menstruate and women could not?

The answer is clear—menstruation would become an enviable, boastworthy, masculine event:

Men would brag about how long and how much.

Boys would mark the onset of menses, that longed-for proof of manhood, with religious rituals and stag parties.

Congress would fund a National Institute of Dysmenorrhea to help stamp out monthly discomforts.

Sanitary supplies would be federally funded and free. (Of course, some men would still pay for the prestige of commercial brands such as John Wayne Tampons, Muhammad Ali's Rope-a-dope Pads, Joe Namath Jock Shields— "For Those Light Bachelor Days," and Robert "Baretta" Blake Maxi-Pads.)

From *Outrageous Acts and Everyday Rebellions* by Gloria Steinem, Holt, Rinehart and Winston. Copyright © 1983 by Gloria Steinem.

Military men, right-wing politicians, and religious fundamentalists would cite menstruation ("*men*-struation") as proof that only men could serve in the Army ("you have to give blood to take blood"), occupy political office ("can women be aggressive without that steadfast cycle governed by the planet Mars?"), be priests and ministers ("how could a woman give her blood for our sins?"), or rabbis ("without the monthly loss of impurities, women remain unclean").

Male radicals, left-wing politicians, and mystics, however, would insist that women are equal, just different; and that any woman could enter their ranks if only she were willing to self-inflict a major wound every month ("you *must* give blood for the revolution"), recognize the preeminence of menstrual issues, or subordinate her selfness to all men in their Cycle of Enlightenment.

Street guys would brag ("I'm a three-pad man") or answer praise from a buddy ("Man, you lookin' *good!*") by giving fives and saying, "Yeah, man, I'm on the rag!"

TV shows would treat the subject at length. ("Happy Days": Richie and Potsie try to convince Fonzie that he is still "The Fonz," though he has missed two periods in a row.) So would newspapers. (SHARK SCARE THREATENS MENSTRUATING MEN. JUDGE CITES MONTHLY STRESS IN PARDONING RAPIST.) And movies. (Newman and Redford in "Blood Brothers"!)

Men would convince women that intercourse was *more* pleasurable at "that time of the month." Lesbians would be said to fear blood and therefore life itself—though probably only because they needed a good menstruating man.

Of course, male intellectuals would offer the most moral and logical arguments. How could a woman master any discipline that demanded a sense of time, space, mathematics, or measurement, for instance, without that in-built gift for measuring the cycles of the moon and planets—and thus for measuring anything at all? In the rarefied fields of philosophy and religion, could women compensate for missing the rhythm of the universe? Or for their lack of symbolic death-and-resurrection every month?

Liberal males in every field would try to be kind: the fact that "these people" have no gift for measuring life or connecting to the universe, the liberals would explain, should be punishment enough.

And how would women be trained to react? One can imagine traditional women agreeing to all these arguments with a staunch and smiling masochism. ("The ERA would force house-wives to wound themselves every month": Phyllis Schlafly. "Your husband's blood is as sacred as that of Jesus—and so sexy, too!": Marabel Morgan.) Reformers and Queen Bees would try to imitate men, and *pretend* to have a monthly cycle. All feminists would explain endlessly that men, too, needed to be liberated from the false idea of Martian aggressiveness, just as women needed to escape the bonds of menses-envy. Radical feminists would add that the oppression of the nonmenstrual was the pattern for all other oppressions. ("Vampires were our first freedom fighters!") Cultural feminists would develop a bloodless imagery in art and literature. Socialist feminists would insist that only under capitalism would men be able to monopolize menstrual blood. . . .

In fact, if men could menstruate, the power justifications could probably go on forever.

If we let them.

Thomas J. Gerschick
Adam Stephen Miller

Coming to Terms: Masculinity and Physical Disability

Men with physical disabilities are marginalized and stigmatized in American society. The image and reality of men with disabilities undermine cultural beliefs about men's bodies and physicality. The body is a central foundation of how men define themselves and how they are defined by others. Bodies are vehicles for determining value, which in turn translates into status and prestige. Men's bodies allow them to demonstrate the socially valuable characteristics of toughness, competitiveness, and ability (Messner 1992). Thus, one's body and relationship to it provide a way to apprehend the world and one's place in it. The bodies of men with disabilities serve as a continual reminder that they are at odds with the expectations of the dominant culture. As anthropologist Robert Murphy (1990: 94) writes of his own experiences with disability:

> Paralytic disability constitutes emasculation of a more direct and total nature. For the male, the weakening and atrophy of the body threaten all the cultural values of masculinity: strength, activeness, speed, virility, stamina, and fortitude.

This article seeks to sharpen our understanding of the creation, maintenance, and re-creation of gender identities by men who, by birth, accident, or illness, find themselves dealing with a physical disability. We examine two sets of social dynamics that converge and clash in the lives of men with physical disabilities. On the one side,

From *Masculinities* 2(1): pp. 34–55. Copyright © 1994. Reprinted by permission by *Masculinities*.

these men must deal with the presence and pressures of hegemonic masculinity, which demands strength. On the other side, societal members perceive people with disabilities to be weak.

For the present study, we conducted in-depth interviews with ten men with physical disabilities in order to gain insights into the psychosocial aspects of men's ability to come to terms with their physical and social condition. We wanted to know how men with physical disabilities respond to the demands of hegemonic masculinity and their marginalization. For instance, if men with disabilities need others to legitimize their gender identity during encounters, what happens when others deny them the opportunity? How do they reconcile the conflicting expectations associated with masculinity and disability? How do they define masculinity for themselves, and what are the sources of these definitions? To what degree do their responses contest and/or perpetuate the current gender order? That is, what are the political implications of different gender identities and practices? In addressing these questions, we contribute to the growing body of literature on marginalized and alternative gender identities.

We will first discuss the general relationship between physical disability and hegemonic masculinity. Second, we will summarize the methods used in this study. Next, we will present and discuss our central findings. Finally, we discuss how the gender identities and life practices of men with disabilities contribute to the politics of the gender order.

Hegemonic Masculinity and Physical Disability

Recently, the literature has shifted toward understanding gender as an interactive process. Thus, it is presumed to be not only an aspect of what one *is*, but more fundamentally it is something that one *does* in interaction with others (West and Zimmerman 1987). Whereas previously, gender was thought to be strictly an individual phenomenon, this new understanding directs our attention to the interpersonal and institutional levels as well. The lives of men with disabilities provide an instructive arena in which to study the interactional nature of gender and its effect on individual gender identities.

In *The Body Silent*, Murphy (1990) observes that men with physical disabilities experience "embattled identities" because of the conflicting expectations placed on them as men and as people with disabilities. On the one side, contemporary masculinity privileges men who are strong, courageous, aggressive, independent, and self-reliant (Connell 1987). On the other side, people with disabilities are perceived to be, and treated as, weak, pitiful, passive, and dependent (Murphy 1990). Thus, for men with physical disabilities, masculine gender identity and practice are created and maintained at the crossroads of the demands of contemporary masculinity and the stigmatization associated with disability. As such, for men with physical disabilities, being recognized as masculine by others is especially difficult, if not impossible, to accomplish. Yet not being recognized as masculine is untenable because, in our culture, everyone is expected to display an appropriate gender identity (West and Zimmerman 1987).

Methods

This research was based on in-depth interviews with ten men. Despite the acknowledged problem of identity management in interviews, we used this method because we were most interested in the subjective perceptions and experiences of our informants. To mitigate this dynamic, we relied on probing questions and reinterviews. Informants were located through a snowball sample, utilizing friends and connections within the community of people with disabilities. All of our informants were given pseudonyms, and we further protected their identity by deleting nonessential personal details. The age range of respondents varied from sixteen to seventy-two. Eight of our respondents were white, and two were African American. Geographically, they came from both coasts and the Midwest. All were "mobility impaired," and most were para- or quadriplegics. Given the small sample size and the modicum of diversity within it, this work must necessarily be understood as exploratory.

We interviewed men with physical disabilities for three primary reasons. First, given the diversity of disabilities and our modest resources, we had to bind the sample. Second, mobility impairments tend to be more apparent than other disabilities, such as blindness or hearing loss, and people respond to these men using visual clues. Third, although the literature in this area is scant, much of it focuses on men with physical disabilities.

Due to issues of shared identities, Adam did all the interviews. Interviews were semi-structured and tape-recorded. Initial interviews averaged approximately an hour in length. Additionally, we contacted all of our informants at least once with clarifying questions and, in some cases, to test ideas that we had. These follow-ups lasted approximately thirty minutes. Each informant received a copy of his interview transcript to ensure that we had captured his perspective accurately. We also shared draft copies of this chapter with them and incorporated their insights into the current version.

There were two primary reasons for the thorough follow-up. First, from a methodological standpoint, it was important for us to capture the experience of our informants as fully as possible. Second, we felt that we had an obligation to allow them to control, to a large extent, the representation of their experience.

Interviews were analyzed using an analytic induction approach (Emerson 1988; Katz 1988; Denzin 1989). In determining major and minor patterns of masculine practice, we used the responses to a series of questions including, What is the most important aspect of masculinity to you? What would you say makes you feel most manly or masculine? Do you think your conception of masculinity is different from that of able-bodied men as a result of your disability? If so, how and why? If not, why not? Additionally, we presented our informants with a list of characteristics associated with prevailing masculinity based on the work of R. W. Connell (1987, 1990a, 1990b, 1991) and asked them to rate their importance to their conception of self. Both positive and negative responses to this portion of our questionnaire guided our insight into how each man viewed his masculinity. To further support our discussion, we turned to the limited academic literature in this area. Much more helpful were the wide range of biographical and autobiographical accounts of men who have physical disabilities (see, for instance, Zola 1982; Callahan 1989; Hahn 1989; Murphy 1990; and Kriegel 1991).

Finally, in analyzing the data we were sensitive to making judgments about our informants when grouping them into categories. People with disabilities are shoehorned into categories too much as it is. We sought to discover what was common among their responses and to highlight what we perceived to be the essence of their views. In doing so, we endeavored to provide a conceptual framework for understanding the responses of men with physical disabilities while trying to be sensitive to their personal struggles.

Disability, Masculinity, and Coming to Terms

While no two men constructed their sense of masculinity in exactly the same way, there appeared to be three dominant frameworks our informants used to cope with their situations. These patterns can be conceived of in relation to the standards inherent in dominant masculinity. We call them

the three Rs: *reformulation*, which entailed men's redefinition of hegemonic characteristics on their own terms; *reliance*, reflected by sensitive or hypersensitive adoptions of particular predominant attributes; and *rejection*, characterized by the renunciation of these standards and either the creation of one's own principles and practices or the denial of masculinity's importance in one's life. However, one should note that none of our interviewees *entirely* followed any one of these frameworks in defining his sense of self. Rather, for heuristic reasons, it is best to speak of the major and minor ways each man used these three patterns. For example, some of our informants relied on dominant standards in their view of sexuality and occupation but also reformulated the prevailing ideal of independence.

Therefore, we discuss the *primary* way in which these men with disabilities related to hegemonic masculinity's standards, while recognizing that their coping mechanisms reflected a more complex combination of strategies. In doing so, we avoid "labeling" men and assigning them to arbitrary categories.

Reformulation

Some of our informants responded to idealized masculinity by reformulating it, shaping it along the lines of their own abilities, perceptions, and strengths, and defining their manhood along these new lines. These men tended not to contest these standards overtly, but—either consciously or unconsciously—they recognized in their own condition an inability to meet these ideals as they were culturally conceived.

An example of this came from Damon, a seventy-two-year-old quadriplegic who survived a spinal-cord injury in an automobile accident ten years ago. Damon said he always desired, and had, control of his life. While Damon required round-the-clock personal care assistants (PCAs), he asserted that he was still a very independent person:

> I direct all of my activities around my home where people have to help me to maintain my

apartment, my transportation, which I own, and direction in where I go. I direct people how to get there, and I tell them what my needs will be when I am going and coming, and when to get where I am going.

Damon said that his sense of control was more than mere illusion; it was a reality others knew of as well. This reputation seemed important to him:

People know from Jump Street that I have my own thing, and I direct my own thing. And if they can't comply with my desire, they won't be around. . . . I don't see any reason why people with me can't take instructions and get my life on just as I was having it before, only thing I'm not doing it myself. I direct somebody else to do it. So, therefore, I don't miss out on very much.

Hegemonic masculinity's definition of independence privileges self-reliance and autonomy. Damon required substantial assistance: indeed, some might term him "dependent." However, Damon's reformulation of the independence ideal, accomplished in part through a cognitive shift, allowed him to think otherwise.

Harold, a forty-six-year-old polio survivor, described a belief and practice akin to Damon's. Also a quadriplegic, Harold similarly required PCAs to help him handle daily necessities: Harold termed his reliance on and control of PCAs "acting through others":

When I say independence can be achieved by acting through other people, I actually mean getting through life, liberty, and the pursuit of happiness while utilizing high-quality and dependable attendant-care services.

As with Damon, Harold achieved his perceived sense of independence by controlling others. Harold stressed that he did not count on family or friends to do favors for him, but *employed* his PCAs in a "business relationship" he controlled. Alternatives to family and friends are used whenever possible because most people with disabilities do not want to burden or be dependent on their families any more than necessary (Murphy 1990).

Social class plays an important role here. Damon and Harold had the economic means to afford round-the-clock assistance. While none of our informants experienced economic hardship, many people with disabilities depend on the welfare system for their care, and the amount and quality of assistance they receive make it much more difficult to conceive of themselves as independent.

A third man who reformulated predominant demands was Brent, a forty-five-year-old administrator. He told us that his paraplegic status, one that he had lived with since he was five years old, had often cast him as an "outsider" to society. This status was particularly painful in his late adolescence, a time when the "sexual revolution" was sweeping America's youth:

A very important measure of somebody's personhood—manhood—was their sexual ability. . . . What bothers me more than anything else is the stereotypes, and even more so, in terms of sexual desirability. Because I had a disability, I was less desirable than able-bodied people. And that I found very frustrating.

His experiences led him to recast the hegemonic notion that man's relations with a partner should be predominantly physical. As a result, he stressed the importance of emotional relations and trust. This appeared to be key to Brent's definition of his manhood:

For me, that is my measure of who I am as an individual and who I am as a man—my ability to be able to be honest with my wife. Be able to be close with her, to be able to ask for help, provide help. To have a commitment, to follow through, and to do all those things that I think are important.

As Connell (1990a) notes, this requires a capacity to not only be expressive, but also to have feelings worth expressing. This clearly demonstrates a different form of masculine practice.

The final case of reformulation came from Robert, a thirty-year-old survivor of a motorcycle accident. Able-bodied for much of his life, Robert's accident occurred when he was twenty-four, leaving him paraplegic. Through five years of intensive physical therapy, he regained 95 percent of his original function, though certain effects linger to this day.

Before his accident, Robert had internalized many of the standards of dominant masculinity exemplified by frequenting bars, leading an active sex life, and riding a motorcycle. But, if our research and the body of autobiographical works from men with physical disabilities has shown anything, it is that coming to terms with a disability eventually changes a man. It appeared to have transformed Robert. He remarked that, despite being generally "recovered," he had maintained his disability-influenced value system:

> I judge people on more of a personal and character level than I do on any physical, or I guess I did; but, you know, important things are guys that have integrity, guys that are honest about what they are doing, that have some direction in their life and know . . . peace of mind and what they stand for.

One of the areas that Robert said took the longest to recover was his sexuality—specifically, his confidence in his sexual ability. While Robert said sexual relations were still important to him, like Brent he reformulated his previous, largely hegemonic notion of male sexuality into a more emotionally and physically egalitarian model:

> I've found a whole different side to having sex with a partner and looking at satisfying the partner rather than satisfying myself; and that has taken the focus off of satisfying myself, being the big manly stud, and concentrating more on my partner. And that has become just as satisfying.

However, reformulation did not yield complete severance from prevailing masculinity's standards as they were culturally conceived. For instance, despite his reformulative inclinations, Robert's self-described "macho" attitude continued in some realms during his recovery. He, and all others we interviewed, represented the complexity of gender identities and practices; no man's masculinity fell neatly into any one of the three patterns.

For instance, although told by most doctors that his physical condition was probably permanent, Robert's resolve was unyielding. "I put my blinders on to all negative insight into it and just totally focused on getting better," he said. "And I think that was, you know, a major factor on why I'm where I'm at today." This typified the second pattern we identified—reliance on hegemonic masculinity's standards. It was ironic, then, that Robert's tenacity, his never-ending work ethic, and his focused drive to succeed were largely responsible for his almost-complete recovery. While Robert reformulated much of his earlier sense of masculinity, he still relied on this drive.

Perhaps the area in which men who reformulate most closely paralleled dominant masculinity was the emphasis they placed on their occupation. Our sample was atypical in that most of our informants were professionally employed on a full-time basis and could, therefore, draw on class-based resources, whereas unemployment among people with disabilities is very high. Just as societal members privilege men who are accomplished in their occupation, Harold said he finds both "purpose," and success, in his career:

> No one is going to go through life without some kind of purpose. Everyone decides. I wanted to be a writer. So I became a writer and an observer, a trained observer.

Brent said that he drew much of his sense of self, his sense of self-esteem, and his sense of manhood from his occupational accomplishments. Initially, Brent denied the importance of the prevailing ideal that a man's occupational worth was derived from his breadwinner status:

> It is not so important to be the breadwinner as it is to be competent in the world. You know, to have a career, to have my name on the door. That is what is most important. It is that recognition that is very important to me.

However, he later admitted that being the breadwinner still was important to him, although he denied a link between his desires and the "stereotypical" conception of breadwinner status. He maintained that "it's still important to me, because I've always been able to make money." Independence, both economic and physical, were important to all of our informants.

Rejection of hegemonic ideals also occurred among men who primarily depended on a reformulative framework. Harold's view of relationships with a partner dismissed the sexually powerful ideal: "The fact of the matter is that I'm not all that upset by the fact that I'm disabled and I'm a male. I mean, I know what I can do." We will have more to say about the rejection of dominant conceptions of sexuality later.

In brief summary, the subset of our informants whose primary coping pattern involved reformulation of dominant standards recognized their inability to meet these ideals as they are culturally conceived. Confident in their own abilities and values, and drawing from previous experience, they confronted standards of masculinity on their own terms. In doing so, they distanced themselves from masculine ideals.

Reliance

However, not all of the men with physical disabilities we interviewed depended on a reformulative approach. We found that many of our informants *were* concerned with others' views of their masculinity and with meeting the demands of hegemonic masculinity. They primarily used the second pattern, reliance, which involves the internalization of many more of the ideals of predominant masculinity, including physical strength, athleticism, independence, and sexual prowess. Just as some men depended on reformulation for much of their masculine definition, others, despite their inability to meet many of these ideals, relied on them heavily. As such, these men did not seem to be as comfortable with their sense of manhood; indeed, their inability to meet society's standards bothered them very much.

This subset of our informants found themselves in a double bind that left them conflicted. They embraced dominant conceptions of masculinity as a way to gain acceptance from themselves and from others. Yet, they were continuously reminded in their interactions with others that they were "incomplete." As a result, the identity behind the facade suffered; there were, then, major costs associated with this strategy.

The tension between societal expectations and the reality of men with physical disabilities was most clearly demonstrated by Jerry, a sixteen-year-old who had juvenile rheumatoid arthritis. While Jerry was physically able to walk for limited distances, this required great effort on his part; consequently, he usually used a wheelchair. He was concerned with the appearance of his awkward walking. "I feel like I look a little, I don't know, more strange when I walk," he said.

The significance of appearance and external perception of manliness is symptomatic of the difficulty men with physical disabilities have in developing an identity and masculinity free of others' perceptions and expectations. Jerry said:

> I think [others' conception of what defines a man] is very important, because if they don't think of you as one, it is hard to think of yourself as one; or, it doesn't really matter if you think of yourself as one if no one else does.

Jerry said that, particularly among his peers, he was not perceived as attractive as the able-bodied teenagers; thus, he had difficulty in male–female relations beyond landing an occasional date. "[The girls believe] I might be a 'really nice person,' but not like a guy per se," he said. "I think to some extent that you're sort of genderless to them." This clearly represents the emasculation and depersonalization inherent in social definitions of disability.

However, Jerry said that he faced a more persistent threat to his autonomy—his independence and his sense of control—from others being "uncomfortable" around him and persisting in offering him assistance he often did not need. This made him "angry," though he usually did not refuse the help out of politeness. Thus, with members of his social group, he participated in a "bargain": they would socialize with him as long as he remained in a dependent position where they could "help" him.

This forced, situational passivity led Jerry to emphasize his autonomy in other areas. For instance, Jerry avoided asking for help in nearly all situations. This was directly tied to reinforcing his embattled manhood by displaying outward strength and independence:

> If I ever have to ask someone for help, it really makes me like feel like less of a man. I don't like asking for help at all. You know, like even if I could use some, I'll usually not ask just because I can't, I just hate asking. . . . [A man is] fairly self-sufficient in that you can sort of handle just about any situation, in that you can help other people, and that you don't need a lot of help.

Jerry internalized the prevailing masculine ideal that a man should be independent; he relied on that ideal for his definition of manhood. His inability to meet this ideal—partly through his physical condition, and partly from how others treated him—threatened his identity and his sense of manhood, which had to be reinforced even at the expense of self-alienation.

One should not label Jerry a "relier" simply because of these struggles. Being only sixteen years of age—and the youngest participant in our study—Jerry was still developing his sense of masculinity; and, as with many teenagers both able-bodied and disabled, he was trying to fit into his peer group. Furthermore, Jerry will continue to mature and develop his self-image and sense of masculinity. A follow-up interview in five years might show a degree of resolution to his struggles.

Such a resolution could be seen in Michael, a thirty-three-year-old manager we interviewed, who also internalized many of the standards of hegemonic masculinity. A paraplegic from an auto accident in 1977, Michael struggled for many years after his accident to come to terms with his condition.

His struggles had several sources, all tied into his view of masculinity's importance. The first was that, before his accident, he accepted much of the dominant conception of masculinity. A high-school student, farm hand, and football and track star at the time, Michael said that independence, relations with the women he dated, and physical strength were central to his conception of self.

After his accident, Michael's doctors told him there was a 50–50 chance that he would regain the ability to walk, and he clung to the hope. "I guess I didn't understand it, and had hope that I would walk again," he said. However, he was "depressed" about his situation, "but not so much about my disability, I guess. Because that wasn't real yet."

But coming home three months after his accident didn't alleviate the depression. Instead, it heightened his anxiety and added a new component—vulnerability. In a span of three months, Michael had, in essence, his sense of masculinity and his security in himself completely stripped away. He was in an unfamiliar situation; and far from feeling strong, independent, and powerful, he felt vulnerable and afraid: "No one," he remarked, "can be prepared for a permanent disability."

His reliance on dominant masculinity, then, started with his predisability past and continued during his recovery as a coping mechanism to deal with his fears. The hegemonic standard Michael strove most to achieve was that of independence. It was central to his sense of masculinity before and at the time of our interview. Indeed, it was so important that it frustrated him greatly when he needed assistance. Much like Jerry, he refused to ask for it:

> I feel that I should be able to do everything for myself and I don't like it. . . . I don't mind asking for things that I absolutely can't do, like hanging pictures, or moving furniture, or having my oil changed in my car; but there are things that I'm capable of doing in my chair, like jumping up one step. That I feel like I should be able to do, and I find it frustrating when I can't do that sometimes. . . . I don't like asking for [help I don't think I need]. It kind of makes me mad.

When asked if needing assistance was "unmanly," Michael replied, "There's probably some of that in there." For both Michael and Jerry, the independence ideal often led to risk-taking behavior in order to prove to themselves that they were more than their social definition.

Yet, much like Robert, Michael had reformulated his view of sexuality. He said that his physical sexuality made him "feel the most masculine"—apparently another reliant response with a stereotypical emphasis on sexual performance. However, it was more complicated. Michael said that he no longer concentrated on pleasing himself, as he did when able-bodied, but that he now had a more partner-oriented view of sexuality. "I think that my compensation for my feeling of vulnerability is I've overcompensated by trying to please my partner and leave little room to allow my partner to please me. . . . Some of my greatest pleasure is exhausting my partner while having sex." Ironically, while he focused more on his partner's pleasure than ever before, he did so at his own expense; a sense of balancing the needs of both partners was missing.

Thus, sex served multiple purposes for Michael—it gave him and his partner pleasure; it reassured him in his fears and his feelings of vulnerability; and it reconfirmed his masculinity. His sexuality, then, reflected both reliance and reformulation.

While independence and sexuality were both extremely important to Scott, a thirty-four-year-old rehabilitation engineer, he emphasized a third area for his sense of manhood—athletics. Scott served in the Peace Corps during his twenties, working in Central America. He described his life-style as "rigorous" and "into the whole sports thing," and used a mountain bike as his primary means of transportation and recreation. He was also an avid hockey player in his youth and spent his summers in softball leagues.

Scott acquired a polio-like virus when he was twenty-five years old that left him permanently paraplegic, a situation that he did not initially accept. In an aggressive attempt to regain his physical ability, and similar to Robert, Scott obsessively attacked his rehabilitation

> . . . thinking, that's always what I've done with all the sports. If I wasn't good enough, I worked a little harder and I got better. So, I kept thinking my walking isn't very good now. If I push it, it will get better.

But Scott's athletic drive led not to miraculous recovery, but overexertion. When ordered by his doctors to scale back his efforts, he realized he could not recover strictly through tenacity. At the time of our interview, he was ambivalent about his limitations. He clearly did not feel like a failure: "I think that if I wouldn't have made the effort, I always would have wondered, could I have made a difference?" Following the athlete's code of conduct, "always give 110 percent," Scott attacked his recovery. But when his efforts were not enough—when he did not "emerge victorious"—he accepted it as an athlete would. Yet, his limitations also frustrated him at times, and in different areas.

For example, though his physical capacity was not what it was, Scott maintained a need for athletic competition. He played wheelchair basketball and was the only wheelchair-participant in a city softball league. However, he did not return to hockey, the sport he loved as a youngster; in fact, he refused to even try the sled-based equivalent.

Here was Scott's frustration. His spirit of athleticism was still alive, but he lamented the fact that he could not compete exactly as before:

> [I miss] the things that I had. I played hockey; that was my primary sport for so many years. Pretty much, I did all the sports. But, like, I never played basketball; never liked basketball before. Which is why I think I can play now. See, it would be like the equivalent to wheelchair hockey. Some friends of mine have talked to me about it, [but] I'm not really interested in that. Because it wouldn't be real hockey. And it would make me feel worse, rather than better.

In this respect, Scott had not completely come to terms with his limitations. He still wanted to be a "real" athlete, competing in the same sports, in the same ways, with the same rules, with others who shared his desire for competition. Wheelchair hockey, which he derogatorily referred to as "gimp hockey," represented the antithesis of this for him.

Scott's other responses added to this emphasis. What he most disliked about having a disability was "that I can't do the things that I want to be able to do," meaning he could not ride his bike or motorcycle, he could not play "real" hockey, and he was unable to live a freewheeling, spontaneous lifestyle. Rather, he had to plan ahead of time where he went and how he got there. The frustration caused by having to plan nearly every move was apparent in almost all of our interviews.

However, on the subject of independence, Scott said "I think I'm mostly independent," but complained that there were some situations where he could not meet his expectations and had to depend on his wife. Usually this was not a "major issue," but "there's still times when, yeah, I feel bad about it; or, you know it's the days where she doesn't feel like it, but she kind of has to. That's what bothers me the most, I guess." Thus, he reflected the general desire among men with disabilities not to be a burden of any kind on family members.

Much of the time, Scott accepted being "mostly independent." His reliance on the ideals of athleticism and independence played a significant part in his conception of masculinity and self. However, Scott learned, though to a limited degree, to let go of some of his previous ideals and to accept a different, reformulated notion of independence and competition. Yet, he could not entirely do so. His emphasis on athletics and independence was still strong, and there were many times when athletics and acceptance conflicted.

However, one should stop short of a blanket assessment of men with disabilities who rely on hegemonic masculinity standards. "Always" is a dangerous word, and stating that "men who rely on hegemonic standards are *always* troubled" is a dangerous assumption. An apparent exceptional case among men who follow a reliant pattern

came from Aaron, a forty-one-year-old paraplegic. Rather than experiencing inner turmoil and conflict, Aaron was one of the most upbeat individuals we interviewed. Aaron said that, before his 1976 accident, he was "on top of the world," with a successful business, a commitment to athletics that included basketball shoot-arounds with NBA prospects, and a wedding engagement. Indeed, from the time of his youth, Aaron relied on such hegemonic standards as sexuality, independence, athleticism, and occupational accomplishment.

For example, when asked what masculinity meant to him before his accident, Aaron said that it originally meant sexual conquest. As a teen, he viewed frequent sexual activity as a "rite of passage" into manhood.

Aaron said he had also enjoyed occupational success, and that this success was central to his definition of self, including being masculine. Working a variety of jobs ranging from assembly-line worker to white-collar professional, Aaron said, "I had been very fortunate to have good jobs, which were an important part of who I was and how I defined myself."

According to Aaron, much of his independence ideal came from his father. When his parents divorced, Aaron's father explained to him that, though he was only five, he would have to be "the man of the house." Aaron took this lesson to heart, and strived to fulfill this role both in terms of independence and providing for the family. "My image of manhood was that of a provider," he said, "one who was able to make a contribution to the financial stability of the family in addition to dealing with the problems and concerns that would come up."

His accident, a gunshot wound injuring his spinal cord, left him completely dependent. Predictably, Aaron could not immediately cope with this. "My whole self-image itself was real integrally tied up with the things I used to do," he said. "I found my desire for simple pleasures to be the greatest part of the pain I had to bear."

His pain increased when he left the hospital. His fiancee had left him, and within two years he lost "everything that was important to me"—his house, his business, his savings, most of his friends, and even, for a while, his hope.

However, much as with Robert, Aaron's resiliency eventually turned his life around. Just as he hit bottom, he began telling himself that "if you hold on long enough, if you don't quit, you'll get through it." Additionally, he attacked his therapy with the vengeance he had always devoted to athletics. "I'd never been confronted with a situation in my entire life before that I was not able to overcome by the efforts of my own merit," he said. "I took the same attitude toward this."

Further, he reasserted his sexuality. Though he then wore a colostomy bag, he resumed frequent sexual intercourse, taking the attitude that "this is who I was, and a woman was either going to have to accept me as I was, or she's got to leave me f——— alone."

However, he realized after those five years that his hard work would not be rewarded nor would he be miraculously healed. Figuring that "there's a whole lot of life that I need to live, and this wasn't the most efficient way to live it," he bought a new sport wheelchair, found a job, and became involved in wheelchair athletics. In this sense, a complex combination of all three patterns emerged in Aaron as reliance was mixed with reformulation and rejection.

Furthermore, his soul-searching led him to develop a sense of purpose in his life, and a reason for going on:

> [During my recovery] I felt that I was left here to enrich the lives of as many people as I could before I left this earth, and it gave me a new purpose, a new vision, a new mission, new dreams.

Tenacity, the quest for independence, athletics, and sexual activity carried Aaron through his recovery. Many of these ideals, which had their source in his father's teachings, remained with him as he continued to be active in athletics (everything from basketball to softball to scuba diving), to assert his sexuality, and to aim for complete autonomy. To Aaron, independence, both physical and financial, was more than just a personal

ideal; it was one that should be shared by all people with disabilities. As such, he aspired to be a role model for others:

> The work that I am involved in is to help people gain control over their lives, and I think it's vitally important that I walk my talk. If . . . we hold ourselves out to be an organization that helps people gain control over their lives, I think it's vitally important for me as the CEO of that organization to live my life in a way that embodies everything that we say we're about.

Clearly, Aaron was not the same man he was before his disability. He said that his maturity and his experience with disability "made me stronger," and that manhood no longer simply meant independence and sexual conquest. Manhood also meant

> . . . being responsible for one's actions; being considerate of another's feelings; being sensitive to individuals who are more vulnerable than yourself, to what their needs would be; standing up on behalf and fighting for those who cannot speak out for themselves, fight for themselves. It means being willing to take a position and be committed to a position, even when it's inconvenient or costly to take that point of view, and you do it only because of the principle involved.

This dovetailed significantly with his occupation, which was of great importance to him. But as alluded to above, Aaron's emphasis on occupation cannot be seen as mere reliance on the hegemonic conception of occupational achievement. It was more a reformulation of that ideal from self-achievement to facilitating the empowerment of others.

Nevertheless, Aaron's struggle to gain his current status, like the struggle of others who rely on hegemonic masculinity's standards, was immense. Constructing hegemonic masculinity from a subordinated position is almost always a Sisyphean task. One's ability to do so is undermined continuously by physical, social, and cultural weakness. "Understandably, in an effort to cope with this stress (balancing the demands for

strength and the societal perception of weakness),"
writes political scientist Harlan Hahn, "many disabled men have tended to identify personally and
politically with the supposed strength of prevalent concepts of masculinity rather than with their
disability" (1989: 3). To relinquish masculinity
under these circumstances is to court gender annihilation, which is untenable to some men.
Consequently, relying on hegemonic masculinity
becomes more understandable (Connell 1990a:
471).

Rejection

Despite the difficulties it presents, hegemony, including that related to gender, is never complete
(Janeway 1980, Scott 1985). For some of our informants, resistance took the form of creating alternative masculine identities and subcultures that
provided them with a supportive environment.
These men were reflected in the final pattern: rejection. Informants who followed this pattern did
not so much share a common ideology or set of
practices; rather, they believed that the dominant
conception of masculinity was wrong, either in
its individual emphases or as a practice. One of
these men developed new standards of masculinity in place of the ones he had rejected. Another
seemingly chose to deny masculinity's importance, although he was neither effeminate nor
androgynous. Instead, they both emphasized their
status as "persons," under the motto of "people
first." This philosophy reflected a key tenet of the
Disability Rights Movement.

Alex, a twenty-three-year-old, first-year law
student, survived an accident that left him an incomplete quadriplegic when he was fourteen. Before that time, he felt he was an outsider at his
private school because he eschewed the superficial, athletically oriented, and materialistic atmosphere. Further, he said the timing of the
accident, when many of his peers were defining
their social roles, added to this outsider perspective, in that it made him unable to participate in
the highly social, role-forming process. "I didn't
learn about the traditional roles of sexuality, and
whatever the rules are for such behavior in our

society, until later," he said. "Because of my
physical characteristics, I had to learn a different
set of rules."

Alex described himself as a "nonconformist."
This simple moniker seemed central to his conception of selfhood and masculinity. Alex, unlike
men who primarily reformulate these tenets, rejected the attitudinal and behavioral prescriptions
of hegemonic masculinity. He maintained that
his standards were his own—not society's—and
he scoffed at commonly held views of masculinity.

For example, Alex blamed the media for
the idea that men must be strong and attractive,
stating "The traditional conception is that everyone has to be Arnold Schwartzenegger . . .
[which] probably lead[s] to some violence, unhappiness, and things like that if they [men] don't
meet the standards."

As for the importance of virility and sexual
prowess, Alex said, "There is a part of me that, you
know, has been conditioned and acculturated
and knows those [dominant] values"; but he sar-
castically laughed at the notion of a man's sexual
prowess being reflected in "making her pass out,"
and summed up his feelings on the subject by
adding, "You have to be willing to do things in a
nontraditional way."

Alex's most profound rejection of a dominant ideal involved the importance of fathering,
in its strictest sense of the man as impregnator:

> There's no reason why we (his fiancee and
> himself) couldn't use artificial insemination or
> adoption. Parenting doesn't necessarily involve
> being the male sire. It involves being a good
> parent. . . . Parenting doesn't mean that it's your
> physical child. It involves responsibility and an
> emotional role as well. I don't think the link
> between parenthood is the primary link with
> sexuality. Maybe in terms of evolutionary pur-
> poses, but not in terms of a relationship.

Thus, Alex rejected the procreation imperative encouraged in hegemonic masculinity. However, while Alex took pride at overtly rejecting
prevailing masculinity as superficial and silly,
even he relied on it at times. Alex said he needed
to support himself financially and would not ever

want to be an emotional or economic "burden" in a relationship. On one level, this is a common concern for most people, disabled or not. But on another level, Alex admitted that it tied in to his sense of masculinity:

> If I was in a relationship and I wasn't working, and my spouse was, what could be the possible reasons for my not working? I could have just been fired. I could be laid off. Who knows what happened? I guess . . . that's definitely an element of masculinity, and I guess I am just as influenced by that as, oh, as I guess as other people, or as within my definition of masculinity. What do you know? I have been caught.

A different form of rejection was reflected in Leo, a fifty-eight-year-old polio survivor. Leo, who had striven for occupational achievement since his youth, seemed to value many hegemonic traits: independence, money-making ability, and recognition by peers. But he steadfastly denied masculinity's role in shaping his outlook.

Leo said the most important trait to him was his mental capacity and intelligence, since that allowed him to achieve his occupational goals. Yet he claimed this was not related to the prevailing standard. Rather, it tied into his ambitions from before his disability and his willingness to do most anything to achieve his goals.

Before we label him "a rejector," however, note that Leo was a believer in adaptive technology and personal assistance, and he did not see a contradiction between using personal-care assistants and being independent. This seemed to be a reformulation, just as with Damon and Harold, but when we asked Leo about this relation to masculinity, he flatly denied any connection.

Leo explained his renunciation of masculinity by saying "It doesn't mean a great deal . . . it's not how I think [of things]." He said that many of the qualities on our list of hegemonic characteristics were important to him on an individual level but did not matter to his sense of manhood. Leo maintained that there were "external" and "internal" reasons for this.

The external factors Leo identified were the Women's and Disability Rights Movements. Both provided support and alternatives that allow a person with a disability the freedom to be a person, and not (to use Leo's words) a "strange bird." Indeed, Leo echoed the call of the Disability Rights Movement when he described himself as a "person first." In this way, his humanity took precedence and his gender and his disability became less significant.

Also, Leo identified his background as a contributing factor to his outlook. Since childhood, he held a group of friends that valued intellectual achievement over physical performance. In his youth, Leo said he was a member of a group "on the college route." He remained in academia.

Internally, his view of masculinity came from maturity. He had dealt with masculinity and related issues for almost sixty years and reached a point at which he was comfortable with his gender. According to him, his gender conceptions ranged across all three patterns. This was particularly evident in his sexuality. When younger, he relied on a culturally valued, genital sexuality and was concerned with his potency. He wanted to "be on top," despite the physical difficulties this presented him. At the time of our interview, he had a reformulated sexuality. The Women's Movement allowed him to remain sexually active without worrying about "being on top." He even rejected the idea (but not necessarily the physical condition) of potency, noting that it was "even a funny word—potent—that's power."

Further, his age allowed Leo to let go of many of the expectations he had for himself when younger. For instance, he used to overcompensate with great physical activity to prove his manhood and to be "a good daddy." But, he said, he gradually learned that such overcompensation was not necessary.

The practice of "letting go," as Leo and many of our other informants had done, was much like that described by essayist Leonard Kriegel (1991) who, in a series of autobiographical essays, discussed the metaphor of "falling into life" as a way of coping with a disability and masculinity. Kriegel described a common reaction to coping with disability; that is, attempting to "overcome" the results of polio, in his case, by building his upper-body strength through endless hours of exercise. In the end, he experienced premature arthritis in his shoulders and arms. The metaphor of giving up or letting go of behavioral expectations and gender practices as a way to gain greater strength and control over one's life was prevalent among the men who primarily rejected dominant masculinity. As Hahn notes, this requires a cognitive shift and a change in reference group as well as a source of social support:

> I think, ironically, that men with disabilities can acquire strength by acknowledging weakness. Instead of attempting to construct a fragile and ultimately phony identity only as males, they might have more to gain, and little to lose, both individually and collectively, by forging a self-concept about the concept of disability. Certainly this approach requires the exposure of a vulnerability that has been a primary reason for the elaborate defense mechanisms that disabled men have commonly employed to protect themselves (1989: 3).

Thus, men with disabilities who rejected or renounced masculinity did so as a process of deviance disavowal. They realized that it was societal conceptions of masculinity, rather than themselves, that were problematic. In doing so, they were able to create alternative gender practices.

Summary and Conclusion

The experiences of men with physical disabilities are important, because they illuminate both the insidious power and limitations of contemporary masculinity. These men have insider knowledge of what the subordinated know about both the gender and social order (Janeway 1980). Additionally, the gender practices of some of these

men exemplify alternative visions of masculinity that are obscured but available to men in our culture. Finally, they allow us to elucidate a process of paramount importance: How men with physical disabilities find happiness, fulfillment, and a sense of self-worth in a culture that has, in essence, denied them the right to their own identity, including their own masculinity.

Based on our interviews, then, we believe that men with physical disabilities depend on at least three patterns in their adjustment to the double bind associated with the demands of hegemonic masculinity and the stigmatization of being disabled. While each of our informants used one pattern more than the others, none of them depended entirely on any one of the three.

To judge the patterns and practices associated with any form of masculinity, it is necessary to explore the implications for both the personal life of the individual and the effect on the reproduction of the societal gender order (Connell 1990a). Different patterns will challenge, comply, or actively support gendered arrangements.

The reliance pattern is reflected by an emphasis on control, independence, strength, and concern for appearances. Men who rely on dominant conceptions of masculinity are much more likely to internalize their feelings of inadequacy and seek to compensate or overcompensate for them. Because the problem is perceived to be located within oneself rather than within the social structure, this model does not challenge, but rather perpetuates, the current gender order.

A certain distancing from dominant ideals occurs in the reformulation pattern. But reformulation tends to be an independent project, and class-based resources play an important role. As such, it doesn't present a formidable challenge to the gender order. Connell (1990a: 474) argues that this response may even modernize patriarchy.

The rejection model, the least well represented in this article, offers the most hope for change. Linked closely to a sociopolitical approach that defines disability as a product of interactions between individuals and their environment, disability (and masculinity) is understood as socially constructed.

Members of the Disability Rights Movement, as a result, seek to reconstruct masculinity through a three-prong strategy. First, they focus on changing the frame of reference regarding who defines disability and masculinity, thereby changing the social-construction dynamics of both. Second, they endeavor to help people with disabilities be more self-referent when defining their identities. To do that, a third component must be implemented: support structures, such as alternative subcultures, must exist. If the Disability Rights Movement is successful in elevating this struggle to the level of collective practice, it will challenge the legitimacy of the institutional arrangements of the current gender order.

In closing, there is much fruitful work to be done in the area of masculinity and disability. For instance, we should expect men with disabilities to respond differently to the demands associated with disability and masculinity due to sexual orientation, social class, age of onset of one's disability, race, and ethnicity. However, *how* and *why* gender identity varies for men with disabilities merits further study. We hope that this work serves as an impetus for others to take up these issues.

Author's Note: We would like to thank our informants for sharing their time, experiences, and insights. Additionally, we would like to thank the following people for their comments on earlier drafts of this work: Sandra Cole, Harlan Hahn, Michael Kimmel, Michael Messner, Don Sabo, and Margaret Weigers. We, of course, remain responsible for its content. Finally, we are indebted to Kimberly Browne and Erika Gottfried for background research and interview transcriptions. This research was supported by a grant from the Undergraduate Research Opportunity Program at the University of Michigan.

References

Callahan, John. 1989. *Don't Worry, He Won't Get Far on Foot*. New York: Vintage Books.

Connell, R. W. 1991. "Live Fast and Die Young: The Construction of Masculinity among Young Working-Class Men on the Margin of the Labor Market." *The Australian and New Zealand Journal of Sociology*, Volume 27, Number 2, August, pp. 141–171.

———. 1990a. "A Whole New World: Remaking Masculinity in the Context of the Environmental Movement." *Gender & Society*, Volume 4, Number 4, December, pp. 452–478.

———. 1990b. "An Iron Man: The Body and Some Contradictions of Hegemonic Masculinity," In *Sport, Men, and the Gender Order*, Michael Messner and Donald Sabo, eds. Champaign, IL: Human Kinetics Publishers, Inc., pp. 83–96.

———. 1987. *Gender and Power: Society, the Person, and Sexual Politics*. Palo Alto, CA: Stanford University Press.

Denzin, Norman. 1989. *The Research Act: A Theoretical Introduction to Sociological Methods*. Englewood Cliffs, NJ: Prentice-Hall.

Emerson, Robert. 1988. "Introduction." In *Contemporary Field Research: A Collection of Readings*, Robert Emerson, ed. Prospect Heights, IL: Waveland Press, pp. 93–107.

Hahn, Harlan. 1989. "Masculinity and Disability." *Disability Studies Quarterly*, Volume 9, Number 3, pp. 1–3.

Janeway, Elizabeth. 1980. *Powers of the Weak*. New York: Alfred A. Knopf.

Katz, Jack. 1988. "A Theory of Qualitative Methodology: The Social System of Analytic Fieldwork." In *Contemporary Field Research: A Collection of Readings*, Robert Emerson, ed. Prospect Heights, IL: Waveland Press, pp. 127–148.

Kriegel, Leonard. 1991. *Falling into Life*. San Francisco: North Point Press.

Messner, Michael A. 1992. *Power at Play: Sports and the Problem of Masculinity*. Boston: Beacon Press.

Murphy, Robert F. 1990. *The Body Silent*. New York: W. W. Norton.

Scott, James C. 1985. *Weapons of the Weak: Everyday Forms of Peasant Resistance*. New Haven: Yale University Press.

West, Candace, and Don H. Zimmerman. 1987. "Doing Gender." *Gender & Society*, Volume 1, Number 2, June, pp. 125–151.

Zola, Irving Kenneth. 1982. *Missing Pieces: A Chronicle of Living with a Disability*. Philadelphia: Temple University Press.

PART SIX

Men in Relationships

Why do many men have problems establishing and maintaining intimate relationships with women? What different forms do male–female relational problems take within different socioeconomic groups? How do men's problems with intimacy and emotional expressivity relate to power inequities between the sexes? Are rape and domestic violence best conceptualized as isolated deviant acts by "sick" individuals, or are they the illogical consequences of male socialization? This complex web of male–female relationships, intimacy, and power is the topic of this section.

And what is the nature of men's relationships with other men? Do men have close friendships with men, or do they simply "bond" around shared activities and interests? How do competition, homophobia, and violence enter into men's relationships with each other? For example, a student recently commented that when he goes to the movies with another male friend, they always leave a seat between them, where they put their coats, because they don't want anyone to think they are there "together."

But what are the costs of this emotional and physical distance? And what are the costs of maintaining emotionally impoverished relationships with other men? How is this emotional distance connected to men's intimate relationships with women? Is it related to Billy Crystal's line in *When Harry Met Sally* that women and men can never be friends because "the sex thing always gets in the way"?

Lillian Rubin begins this section with a psychoanalytic interpretation of male–female relational problems. Early development differences, rooted in the social organization of the nuclear family (especially the fact that it is women who care for infants) have set up the fundamental emotional and sexual differences between women and men that create problems for heterosexual couples. Articles by Karen Walker and Peter Nardi suggest the different ways in which men—both straight and gay—develop and sustain their friendships with each other.

The problems in male–female relationships—that such relationships can be distorted by insecurity, anger, the need for control, the need to assert and demonstrate manliness—can take an ugly turn, as described by Tim Beneke and Terry Kupers in their powerful essays, which invite men to think about rape. Kevin Powell's essay, however, gives us room for hope that the next generation of men may struggle with these issues in new and different ways and develop very different ideas about male–female relationships.

"We've been wandering in the desert for forty years. But he's a man—would he ever ask directions?"

Lillian B. Rubin

The Approach–Avoidance Dance: Men, Women, and Intimacy

For one human being to love another, that is perhaps the most difficult of all our tasks, the ultimate, the last test and proof, the work for which all other work is but preparation.

—Rainer Maria Rilke

Intimacy. We hunger for it, but we also fear it. We come close to a loved one, then we back off. A teacher I had once described this as the "go away a little closer" message. I call it the approach–avoidance dance.

The conventional wisdom says that women want intimacy, men resist it. And I have plenty of material that would *seem* to support that view. Whether in my research interviews, in my clinical hours, or in the ordinary course of my life, I hear the same story told repeatedly. "He doesn't talk to me," says a woman. "I don't know what she wants me to talk about," says a man. "I want to know what he's feeling," she tells me. "I'm not feeling anything," he insists. "Who can feel nothing?" she cries. "I can," he shouts. As the heat rises, so does the wall between them. Defensive and angry, they retreat—stalemated by their inability to understand each other.

Women complain to each other all the time about not being able to talk to their men about the things that matter most to them—about what they themselves are thinking and feeling, about what goes on in the hearts and minds of the men they're relating to. And men, less able to expose themselves and their conflicts—those within themselves or those with the women in their lives—either turn silent or take cover by holding women up to derision. It's one of the norms of male camaraderie to poke fun at women, to complain laughingly about the mystery of their minds, wonderingly about their ways. Even Freud did it when, in exasperation, he asked mockingly, "What do women want? Dear God, what do they want?"

But it's not a joke—not for the women, not for the men who like to pretend it is.

The whole goddamn business of what you're calling intimacy bugs the hell out of me. I never know what you women mean when you talk about it. Karen complains that I don't talk to her, but it's not talk she wants, it's some other damn thing, only I don't know what the hell it is. Feelings, she keeps asking for. So what am I supposed to do if I don't have any to give her or to talk about just because she decides it's time to talk about feelings? Tell me, will you: maybe we can get some peace around here.

The expression of such conflicts would seem to validate the common understandings that suggest that women want and need intimacy more than men do—that the issue belongs to women alone; that, if left to themselves, men would not suffer it. But things are not always what they seem.

From *Intimate Strangers* by Lillian B. Rubin, New York: HarperCollins. Copyright © 1983. Reprinted with permission of the Rhoda Weyr Agency.

And I wonder: "If men would renounce intimacy, what is their stake in relationships with women?"

Some would say that men need women to tend to their daily needs—to prepare their meals, clean their houses, wash their clothes, rear their children—so that they can be free to attend to life's larger problems. And, given the traditional structure of roles in the family, it has certainly worked that way most of the time. But, if that were all men seek, why is it that, even when they're not relating to women, so much of their lives is spent in search of a relationship with another, so much agony experienced when it's not available?

These are difficult issues to talk about—even to think about—because the subject of intimacy isn't just complicated, it's slippery as well. Ask yourself: What is intimacy? What words come to mind, what thoughts?

It's an idea that excites our imagination, a word that seems larger than life to most of us. It lures us, beckoning us with a power we're unable to resist. And, just because it's so seductive, it frightens us as well—seeming sometimes to be some mysterious force from outside ourselves that, if we let it, could sweep us away.

But what is it we fear?

Asked what intimacy is, most of us—men and women—struggle to say something sensible, something that we can connect with the real experience of our lives. "Intimacy is knowing there's someone who cares about the children as much as you do." "Intimacy is a history of shared experience. It's sitting there having a cup of coffee together and watching the eleven o'clock news." "It's knowing you care about the same things." "It's knowing she'll always understand." "It's him sitting in the hospital for hours at a time when I was sick." "It's knowing he cares when I'm hurting." "It's standing by me when I was out of work." "It's seeing each other at our worst." "It's sitting across the breakfast table." "It's talking when you're in the bathroom." "It's knowing we'll begin and end each day together."

These seem the obvious things—the things we expect when we commit our lives to one another in a marriage, when we decide to have chil-

dren together. And they're not to be dismissed as inconsequential. They make up the daily experience of our lives together, setting the tone for a relationship in important and powerful ways. It's sharing such commonplace, everyday events that determines the temper and the texture of life, that keeps us living together even when other aspects of the relationship seem less than perfect. Knowing someone is there, is constant, and can be counted on in just the ways these thoughts express provides the background of emotional security and stability we look for when we enter a marriage. Certainly a marriage and the people in it will be tested and judged quite differently in an unusual situation or in a crisis. But how often does life present us with circumstances and events that are so out of the range of ordinary experience?

These ways in which a relationship feels intimate on a daily basis are only one part of what we mean by intimacy, however—the part that's most obvious, the part that doesn't awaken our fears. At a lecture where I spoke of these issues recently, one man commented also, "Intimacy is putting aside the masks we wear in the rest of our lives." A murmur of assent ran through the audience of a hundred or so. Intuitively we say, "yes." Yet this is the very issue that also complicates our intimate relationships.

On the one hand, it's reassuring to be able to put away the public persona—to believe we can be loved for who we *really* are, that we can show our shadow side without fear, that our vulnerabilities will not be counted against us. "The most important thing is to feel I'm accepted just the way I am," people will say.

But there's another side. For, when we show ourselves thus without the masks, we also become anxious and fearful. "Is it possible that someone could love the *real* me?" we're likely to ask. Not the most promising question for the further development of intimacy, since it suggests that, whatever else another might do or feel, it's we who have trouble loving ourselves. Unfortunately, such misgivings are not usually experienced consciously. We're aware only that our discomfort has risen, that we feel a need to get away. For the person who has seen the "real me" is also the one who reflects back to us an image that's usually not wholly to our liking. We get angry at that, first at ourselves for not living up to our own expectations, then at the other, who becomes for us the mirror of our self-doubts—a displacement of hostility that serves intimacy poorly.

There's yet another level—one that's further below the surface of consciousness, therefore, one that's much more difficult for us to grasp, let alone to talk about. I'm referring to the differences in the ways in which women and men deal with their inner emotional lives—differences that create barriers between us that can be high indeed. It's here that we see how those early childhood experiences of separation and individuation—the psychological tasks that were required of us in order to separate from mother, to distinguish ourselves as autonomous persons, to internalize a firm sense of gender identity—take their toll on our intimate relationships.

Stop a woman in mid-sentence with the question, "What are you feeling right now?" and you might have to wait a bit while she reruns the mental tape to capture the moment just passed. But, more than likely, she'll be able to do it successfully. More than likely, she'll think for a while and come up with an answer.

The same is not true of a man. For him, a similar question usually will bring a sense of wonderment that one would even ask it, followed quickly by an uncomprehending and puzzled response. "What do you mean?" he'll ask. "I was just talking," he'll say.

I've seen it most clearly in the clinical setting where the task is to get to the feeling level—or, as one of my male patients said when he came into therapy, to "hook up the head and the gut." Repeatedly when therapy begins, I find myself having to teach a man how to monitor his internal states—how to attend to his thoughts and feelings, how to bring them into consciousness. In the early stages of our work, it's a common experience to say to a man, "How does that feel?" and to see a blank look come over his face. Over and over, I find myself listening as a man speaks with

calm reason about a situation which I know must be fraught with pain. "How do you feel about that?" I'll ask. "I've just been telling you," he's likely to reply. "No," I'll say, "you've told me what happened, not how you *feel* about it." Frustrated, he might well respond, "You sound just like my wife."

It would be easy to write off such dialogues as the problems of men in therapy, of those who happen to be having some particular emotional difficulties. But it's not so, as any woman who has lived with a man will attest. Time and again women complain: "I can't get him to verbalize his feelings." "He talks, but it's always intellectualizing." "He's so closed off from what he's feeling, I don't know how he lives that way." "If there's one thing that will eventually ruin this marriage, it's the fact that he can't talk about what's going on inside him." "I have to work like hell to get anything out of him that resembles a feeling that's something besides anger. That I get plenty of—me and the kids, we all get his anger. Anything else is damn hard to come by with him." One woman talked eloquently about her husband's anguish over his inability to get problems in his work life resolved. When I asked how she knew about his pain, she answered:

> I pull for it, I pull hard, and sometimes I can get something from him. But it'll be late at night in the dark—you know, when we're in bed and I can't look at him while he's talking and he doesn't have to look at me. Otherwise, he's just defensive and puts on what I call his bear act, where he makes his warning, go-away faces, and he can't be reached or penetrated at all.

To a woman, the world men live in seems a lonely one—a world in which their fears of exposing their sadness and pain, their anxiety about allowing their vulnerability to show, even to a woman they love, is so deeply rooted inside them that, most often, they can only allow it to happen "late at night in the dark."

Yet, if we listen to what men say, we will hear their insistence that they *do* speak of what's inside them, *do* share their thoughts and feelings with the women they love. "I tell her, but she's never satisfied," they complain. "No matter how much I say, it's never enough," they grumble.

From both sides, the complaints have merit. The problem lies not in what men don't say, however, but in what's not there—in what, quite simply, happens so far out of consciousness that it's not within their reach. For men have integrated all too well the lessons of their childhood—the experiences that taught them to repress and deny their inner thoughts, wishes, needs, and fears; indeed, not even to notice them. It's real, therefore, that the kind of inner thoughts and feelings that are readily accessible to a woman generally are unavailable to a man. When he says, "I don't know what I'm feeling," he isn't necessarily being intransigent and withholding. More than likely, he speaks the truth.

Partly that's a result of the ways in which boys are trained to camouflage their feelings under cover of an exterior of calm, strength, and rationality. Fears are not manly. Fantasies are not rational. Emotions, above all, are not for the strong, the sane, the adult. Women suffer them, not men—women, who are more like children with what seems like their never-ending preoccupation with their emotional life. But the training takes so well because of their early childhood experience when, as very young boys, they had to shift their identification from mother to father and sever themselves from their earliest emotional connection. Put the two together and it does seem like suffering to men to have to experience that emotional side of themselves, to have to give it voice.

This is the single most dispiriting dilemma of relations between women and men. He complains, "She's so emotional, there's no point in talking to her." She protests, "It's him you can't talk to, he's always so darned rational." He says, "Even when I tell her nothing's the matter, she won't quit." She says, "How can I believe him when I can see with my own eyes that something's wrong?" He says, "Okay, so something's wrong! What good will it do to tell her?" She cries, "What are we married for? What do you need me for, just to wash your socks?"

These differences in the psychology of women and men are born of a complex interaction between society and the individual. At the broadest social level is the rending of thought and feeling that is such a fundamental part of Western thought. Thought, defined as the ultimate good, has been assigned to men; feeling, considered at best a problem, has fallen to women.

So firmly fixed have these ideas been that, until recently, few thought to question them. For they were built into the structure of psychological thought as if they spoke to an eternal, natural, and scientific truth. Thus, even such a great and innovative thinker as Carl Jung wrote, "The woman is increasingly aware that love alone can give her her full stature, just as the man begins to discern that spirit alone can endow his life with its highest meaning. Fundamentally, therefore, both seek a psychic relation one to the other, because love needs the spirit, and the spirit love, for their fulfillment."[1]

For a woman, "love"; for a man, "spirit"—each expected to complete the other by bringing to the relationship the missing half. In German, the word that is translated here as spirit is *Geist*. But *The New Cassell's German Dictionary* shows that another primary meaning of *Geist* is "mind, intellect, intelligence, wit, imagination, sense of reason." And, given the context of these words, it seems reasonable that *Geist* for Jung referred to a man's highest essence—his mind. There's no ambiguity about a woman's calling, however. It's love.

Intuitively, women try to heal the split that these definitions of male and female have foisted upon us.

> I can't stand that he's so damned unemotional and expects me to be the same. He lives in his head all the time, and he acts like anything that's emotional isn't worth dealing with.

Cognitively, even women often share the belief that the rational side, which seems to come so naturally to men, is the more mature, the more desirable.

> I know I'm too emotional, and it causes problems between us. He can't stand it when I get emotional like that. It turns him right off.

Her husband agrees that she's "too emotional" and complains:

> Sometimes she's like a child who's out to test her parents. I have to be careful when she's like that not to let her rile me up because otherwise all hell would break loose. You just can't reason with her when she gets like that.

It's the rational-man–hysterical-woman script, played out again and again by two people whose emotional repertoire is so limited that they have few real options. As the interaction between them continues, she reaches for the strongest tools she has, the mode she's most comfortable and familiar with: She becomes progressively more emotional and expressive. He falls back on his best weapons: He becomes more rational, more determinedly reasonable. She cries for him to attend to her feelings, whatever they may be. He tells her coolly, with a kind of clenched-teeth reasonableness, that it's silly for her to feel that way, that she's just being emotional. And of course she is. But that dismissive word "just" is the last straw. She gets so upset that she does, in fact, seem hysterical. He gets so bewildered by the whole interaction that his only recourse is to build the wall of reason even higher. All of which makes things measurably worse for both of them.

> The more I try to be cool and calm her the worse it gets. I swear, I can't figure her out. I'll keep trying to tell her not to get so excited, but there's nothing I can do. Anything I say just makes it worse. So then I try to keep quiet, but . . . wow, the explosion is like crazy, just nuts.

And by then it *is* a wild exchange that any outsider would agree was "just nuts." But it's not just her response that's off, it's his as well—their conflict resting in the fact that we equate the emotional with the nonrational.

This notion, shared by both women and men, is a product of the fact that they were born and reared in this culture. But there's also a difference between them in their capacity to apprehend the *logic* of emotions—a difference born in their early childhood experiences in the family, when boys had to repress so much of their emotional side and girls could permit theirs to flower. . . . It should be understood: Commitment itself is not a problem for a man; he's good at that. He can spend a lifetime living in the same family, working at the same job—even one he hates. And he's not without an inner emotional life. But when a relationship requires the sustained verbal expression of that inner life and the full range of feelings that accompany it, then it becomes burdensome for him. He can act out anger and frustration inside the family, it's true. But ask him to express his sadness, his fear, his dependency—all those feelings that would expose his vulnerability to himself or to another—and he's likely to close down as if under some compulsion to protect himself.

All requests for such intimacy are difficult for a man, but they become especially complex and troublesome in relations with women. It's another of those paradoxes. For, to the degree that it's possible for him to be emotionally open with anyone, it is with a woman—a tribute to the power of the childhood experience with mother. Yet it's that same early experience and his need to repress it that raises his ambivalence and generates his resistance.

He moves close, wanting to share some part of himself with her, trying to do so, perhaps even yearning to experience again the bliss of the infant's connection with a woman. She responds, woman style—wanting to touch him just a little more deeply, to know what he's thinking, feeling, fearing, wanting. And the fear closes in—the fear of finding himself again in the grip of a powerful woman, of allowing her admittance only to be betrayed and abandoned once again, of being overwhelmed by denied desires.

So he withdraws.

It's not in consciousness that all this goes on. He knows, of course, that he's distinctly uncomfortable when pressed by a woman for more intimacy in the relationship, but he doesn't know why. And, very often, his behavior doesn't please him any more than it pleases her. But he can't seem to help it.

Notes

1. Carl Gustav Jung, *Contributions to Analytical Psychology* (New York: Harcourt, Brace & Co., 1928), p. 185.

Karen Walker

"I'm Not Friends the Way She's Friends": Ideological and Behavioral Constructions of Masculinity in Men's Friendships

Contemporary ideologies about men's friendships suggest that men's capacity for intimacy is sharply restricted. In this view, men have trouble expressing their feelings with friends. Whether due to the development of the masculine psyche or cultural prescriptions, men are viewed as highly competitive with friends. Because of their competition, they are unlikely to talk about intimate matters such as feelings and relationships. The literature on gender differences in friendship suggests that the ideologies reflect actual behavior. Researchers have found that men limit verbal self-disclosure with friends, especially when compared to women (Caldwell & Peplau 1982; Rubin 1985; Sherrod 1987; Aukett, Ritchie, & Mill 1988; Swain 1989; Reid & Fine 1992). Men share activities with friends (Rubin 1985; Swain 1987). On the other hand, there are also suggestions that the degree of self-disclosure among men may be underestimated (Hacker 1981; Wright 1982; Rawlins 1992), particularly among men from particular groups (Franklin 1992). My research on friendship shows that men and women share the stereotypes about gender differences in friendship, but in specific friendships, men discuss their relationships and report relying on men friends for emotional support and intimacy (Walker 1994). In addition, many activities of friendship—seeing friends for dinner, sharing ritual events, and visiting—are things both men and

From *Masculinities* 2(2): 38–55. Copyright © 1994 by Men's Studies Association. Reprinted with permission.

women do. Barry Wellman (1992) argues that there has been a widespread "domestication" of male friendship, with men seeing friends in their home in much the same way women do.

In much of the literature on gender differences in friendship, ideology has been mistaken for behavior. In part, researchers seem to have made this mistake because they have asked general, instead of specific, questions about friendship.[1] As a result, they have elicited good representations of what respondents *believe* their behavior is—beliefs that are shaped by the respondents' own ideologies. What they have sometimes failed to elicit is information about specific friendships in which variations from the ideologies may be substantial. Because researchers report what respondents tell them, it is easy to understand why researchers make this mistake. What becomes more difficult to understand is how the confusion between the ideology of friendship and friendship behavior comes to be constructed in everyday life. Why do men maintain their belief that men are less open than women in the face of considerable evidence that they do discuss their feelings with their friends? This is even more crucial because the stereotype of intimate friendship that men believe characterizes women's friendship is currently highly valued. Feminist scholars and writers have successfully revalued women's intimate relationships to the detriment of earlier ideals that privileged male bonding. While not all respondents in this study positively evaluated the stereotype of women's openness with friends, many did, as evidenced by one professional man who said:

> I mean, we [men] talk about sports and politics sometimes, any kind of safe [topic], if you will. Not that any [every] kind of interaction needs to be intimate or this and that, but it's much different when you talk to women. Women catch on. I remember once seeing Robert Bly, and he said something that is really so in my experience, that women get to the heart of things and that they get there so quickly that it makes you, uh, it can put men into a rage because women are able to articulate these kinds of things that men can't.

Given the belief that being intimate and "getting to the heart of things" is good, and given the evidence that men are more intimate in practice than the ideology suggests, *why don't men challenge the ideology*?

There seem to be several answers to this question. First, when men do not conform to the masculine ideals about how they should act with their friends, they are occasionally censured. In the practice of masculine friendship, the positive evaluation of feminine intimacy disappears. Because of their friends' reactions, men come to see their behavior as anomalous and bad, and they do not reevaluate the extent to which the ideology of masculine friendship accurately reflects behavior.

Second, social class influences men's capacities for conforming to gender ideologies. Professional men are somewhat more likely than working-class men to conform to gendered norms with respect to intimate behavior (Franklin 1992; Walker 1994). Also, professional men's social class makes them—with other middle-class men—the primary groups on which cultural stereotypes are based. Literature written specifically about men's friendships often relies on research of middle-class men, particularly college-aged men (Caldwell and Peplau 1982; Rubin 1985; Swain 1989; Rawlins 1992; Reid and Fine 1992). Very recently, some researchers have noted that men who are other than middle-class or white may have different types of friendships from the ideology (Franklin 1992; Hansen 1992), but the knowledge of the existence of other forms of masculine friendship among working-class African American and white men has not influenced the ideology of friendship.

Third, there *are* gender differences in behavior, and these differences reinforce stereotypes about gendered forms of friendship, even if the differences differ substantively from the substance of the ideology. For instance, male respondents in this study used the telephone somewhat differently from the ways women used it. Through their use of the telephone men constructed their masculinity, and in so doing they reinforced their notions that men are not open. As I will show, men claimed they called their friends for explicitly instrumental reasons—to make plans, get specific information, and so on—but not to find out how friends were, which they connected to women's telephone use. These practices generally supported the idea that women were better at maintaining friendships and talking to friends about feelings even though men's telephone conversations often included talk about personal matters. But a desire to talk to friends about personal matters was rarely the motive for phone calls.

In this article I examine the ways gender ideology about friendships is maintained through four behaviors and men's interpretations of those behaviors: telephone use, jokes, the use of public space, and how men talk about women. It is only when we understand how men behaviorally construct gender within friendship that we can begin to understand how men use these behavioral constructions to support ideological constructions of masculine friendship practices.

Method of Study

This paper relies on research from a study of men's and women's same-gender and cross-gender friendships. I interviewed 9 working-class and 10 professional men (as well 18 working-class and 15 middle-class women). Within each class I individually interviewed some men who were friends with other respondents in the study. Interviewing friends allowed me to gather information on group interaction that would have been unavailable had I interviewed isolated individuals. In addition, I was able to explore issues that were most salient to groups of friends. Finally, by interviewing friends I could examine the extent to which friends agree on what their interactions were like. This was particularly important when there was a discrepancy between behavior and ideology: Some men did not report on behavior that contradicted the masculine ideology of friendship either because they were unwilling to disclose that their behavior did not match the cultural ideal or because such behavior was somewhat meaningless to them, and they forgot it.

Respondents ranged in age from 27 to 48. Class location was determined by both lifestyle and individuals' work. Thus, working-class respondents tended to have high school educations or less, although one self-employed carpenter had a four-year degree in accounting. Working-class men were in construction and some service occupations. Most working-class men lived in densely populated urban neighborhoods in row houses or twins in Philadelphia. Professional respondents had graduate degrees, and they worked as academics, administrators, lawyers, and therapists. Professionals lived in the suburbs of Philadelphia or in urban apartments.

Interviews were semistructured, and respondents answered both global questions about their friendship patterns as well as questions about activities and topics of conversations in which they engaged with each friend they named. The use of in-depth interviews that included both global and specific questions allowed me to gather data indicating the frequent discrepancies between cultural ideologies of masculine friendships and actual behaviors. In addition, in-depth interviews allowed me to compare working-class and professional respondents' experiences.

Recently, Christine Williams and Joel Heikes (1993) have observed that male nurses shaped responses to interview questions in ways that took into account the gender of the interviewer. In this study, my status as a woman interviewer appeared

to have both positive and negative implications for data collection. On the one hand, being a woman made it more likely that men admitted behavior that contradicted gender ideology. Sociologists studying gender and friendship have consistently argued that men do not engage in self-disclosure with other men (Caldwell & Peplau 1982; Reid & Fine 1992). Other research shows that men are likely to be more self-disclosing with women than with men (Rubin 1985; O'Meara 1989). While my research shows that men engaged in self-disclosure more frequently with friends than the literature suggests, they did so with men they considered close friends. Frequently close friends were people they knew for a long time or people with whom they spent much time. Wright (1982) notes that long-time men friends engage in self-disclosure. I suspected that certain kinds of disclosures that men made during the interviews might have been more difficult to make to an unknown man instead of to me, an unknown woman.

On the other hand, respondents suggested that they more heavily edited their responses to questions about how they discussed women with their men friends than they did other questions. They frequently sprinkled their responses with comments recognizing my gender, "You don't have a gun in there, do you? (laugh)" or "I don't mean to be sexist here." I suspected that responses were much more benign than they would have been if I were a man. Thus, when I discuss men's talk about women below I believe that my data underestimate the extent to which men's talk about women constructs gender tensions.

Behavioral Construction of Masculinity

In recent years sociologists of gender have come to emphasize the active construction of gender. Gender is seen as an ongoing activity fundamental to all aspects of social life rather than a static category in which we place men or women (Connell 1987; West & Zimmerman 1987; Leidner 1991). One advantage of a social constructionist perspective is that it allows researchers to explore both the ideological as well as the behavioral construction of gender. Gender is constructed *ideologically* when men and women believe that certain qualities, such as intimacy, characterize one gender rather than another. The way men and women interpret life and its meaning for them is deeply influenced by their ideological beliefs. Gender is constructed *behaviorally* in the activities men and women do and the way they do them.

Sometimes ideology and behavior match— such as when men talk about gender differences in telephone use and report behavior that differs from women's behavior. Sometimes ideology and behavior do not match. When there is a mismatch, the interesting problem of how ideology is sustained when behavior contradicts it emerges. I argue that, in the specific case of friendship, specific behaviors supported men's gendered ideologies. Men discounted or ignored altogether evidence that discredited a distinctly masculine model of friendship. This occurred because gender is a category culturally defined by multiple qualities. When men included themselves in the masculine gender category based on some behavior, they tended unreflectively to accept as given the cultural boundaries of the entire category *even if other of their behaviors contradicted those boundaries.*

Among respondents there were several ways masculinity was constructed in the activities of friendship. First, where men met, particularly working-class men, became a mark of masculinity. Second, the way men used the telephone distinguished masculine from feminine behavior. Third, men used jokes in particular ways to establish masculinity and also to manage tensions between actual behavior and gender ideologies. Finally, men friends talked about women in ways that emphasized the differences and tensions between men and women.

There are class differences in the behaviors that form particular patterns of masculinity. Differential financial constraints, the social expectations of particular kinds of work, and lifestyle differences played roles in shaping particular forms of masculinity. The use of jokes was some-

what more elaborated among working-class men than among professional men, but reports of jokes and joking behavior emerged in both groups. Professional men talked about wives and the strains of work and family differently from working-class men; as I will discuss, this resulted from different work experiences.

Besides class differences, which I will address throughout the article, there were individual differences. All men did not engage in all the behaviors that I argue contribute to the construction of masculinity. One professional man said that while he talked "about what specific women are like," he did not talk about women in general and men who talked about what women are generally like "would not be my friends." Other men did not report the use of jokes and joking behavior in their friendships. Sociology frequently avoids discussion about individuals who do not participate in the behaviors that the sociologist argues shows the existence of meaningful social patterns. Unfortunately, doing so often reifies behavioral differences. This is a particular problem in the discussion of gender because there is currently (and happily for the existence of a lively, informed debate) a very close link between the results of social research on gender and broad social and political debates about men's and women's differences.

I wish, therefore, to give the reader a general indication of the individual variability in the gendered behaviors in which men engaged. In all the behaviors discussed below at least half, and frequently more, of the men participated in the behaviors whereas few women did. There were, however, individual exceptions to these behaviors, and those exceptions point to a flexibility in gendered behavior that, while not as expansive as many would wish, is broader than we frequently recognize. Current social theory about gender emphasizes the agentic nature of the construction of gender. It is a practice in which men and women have a considerable range of actions from which to choose. At given historical points, certain actions may be dictated more than others, and therefore individual men and women may frequently act in ways that conform to current ideology. But even when cultural ideology demands close adherence to particular practices, the practical nature of gender means that some individuals will not conform. Further, the multiplicity of practices that create gender enables individuals to maintain their positions within gender categories without much difficulty.

Men's Use of Public Space

The use of public space for informal and apparently unplanned socializing is much more common among men than among women, and it marks the gender boundaries between men and women. The frequent use of public space by working-class men for informal socializing emerges in ethnographies of men's groups (Liebow 1967; Kornblum 1974; Anderson 1976; Whyte 1981). Working-class men in this study met in public spaces such as local bars and playgrounds. There they talked about work and family, and they made informal connections with other men. Sometimes they picked up side work, sometimes they hung out. At the time of our interview, one working-class man said that he spent some of his time at a local bar selling advertisements in a book to raise money for a large retirement dinner for a long-time coach of a community football team. He also spent time there drinking and talking to friends.

Working-class men also met in semipublic spaces such as gyms or clubs. While membership in these spaces was frequently restricted, the spaces themselves functioned in similar ways to public spaces. Men met regularly and informally in public and semipublic spaces one or more times a week. Unlike women who made definite plans to meet friends occasionally in bars, the men assumed because of past practice that on particular nights of the week they would meet friends.

Wellman (1992) suggests that the use of public space for male socializing is diminishing, and men's friendships are becoming domesticated as their friendships move into the home and hence more like women's. This phenomenon of domestication was evident among professional respondents, most of whom reported socializing infrequently in public spaces. But it was not evident among the working-class respondents in this study. All but one of the working-class respondents had been brought up in the same communities in which they lived when I interviewed them. Among these men there were long-time, continuous patterns of public socializing. While Wellman's point is important, the domestication of male friendship seems to be influenced by circumstances in men's lives and is probably occurring unevenly. Further, barring significant structural changes in working-class men's formal and informal work lives, the domestication of male friendships is unlikely to be complete.

Men's Telephone Use

Discussions of men's telephone use as a construction of gender make the most sense when contrasted with women's telephone use. Many men noted that their wives used the telephone very differently from them. A few, primarily working-class men, stated that they disliked talking on the telephone, and they used it only for instrumental reasons (e.g., to make appointments or get specific information). Other men, both professional and working class, said their wives called friends just to see how they were doing and then talked for a long time, whereas men did not do so. Thus men ideologically constructed gender through their understandings of telephone practices. In addition, both men and women constructed gender behaviorally through using the telephone in different ways.

Telephone use differed slightly by class and work experiences, but even accounting for the effects of class and work, there were substantial gender differences. Men frequently reported that the purpose of their most recent telephone calls with friends was instrumental: lawyers discussed cases, men discussed upcoming social plans, and some working-class men made plans to do side work together. Because of this instrumental motive for telephone calls to friends, many professional men reported that their frequent telephone contact was from their offices during working hours. Men rarely reported that they called friends just to say "hi" and find out how they were. One professional man, Mike,[2] reported differences between his wife and himself in being friends:

> I'm not friends the way she's friends. *How are you friends differently?* I don't work on them. I don't pick the phone up and call people and say, "How are you?"

While Mike reported that, in fact, he did call one friend to find out how he was doing at least once a year, most telephone contact was initiated when friends made plans to visit from out of town or he had business matters to discuss with friends. One result of this behavior was tremendous attrition in his friendship network over time. Mike was a gregarious man who reported many past and current friends, but he tended to lose touch with past friends once business reasons for keeping in touch with them diminished, even those who continued to live in Philadelphia. He only reported talking to two friends six or more times a year on the telephone. One of those friends was a man with whom he had professional ties, and they called one another when they did business. The other friend, Gene, was one of the few men who called friends for social conversations. The fairly frequent calls between Gene and Mike may have been initiated by Gene.

Gil, a working-class man, usually spoke to friends on the phone to arrange meetings. Although he kept in touch with two friends largely through telephone use (he worked two jobs during the week and one of his friends worked on weekends—theirs was a telephone friendship), he said:

> I don't talk to them a long time because I'm not a phone person. I'd rather see them in person because I don't like holding the phone and talking because you really can't think of things to say too often on the phone, but when you're in person you can think of more things, cause I like prefer sitting and talking to a person face-to-face . . . I'll talk to people 10, 15 minutes sometimes, but I prefer not to if I can. But some

you just can't get off the phone, no matter what you do. And you're like, "Uh, great, well, I'll talk to you a little bit later." And they go into another story. You know [my friend] Cindy will do that, Cindy is great for that. Now Joanne [my wife] can talk on the phone for two to three hours . . . And then the person she's with is not too far away so she could just walk over and talk, you know.

Peter, a young working-class man, reported that he "avoided the phone as much as possible." He did not call friends to chat, and he only used the telephone for social chats with one friend, a woman:

> I'm not a phone person, but yeah, I do [talk to a specific friend] because she talks on the phone, she likes the phone so . . . She'll talk and I'll yes and no (laughs).

Peter did not do side jobs with other men, thus his reasons for using the telephone were sharply limited. Peter and Gil both reported that their telephone preferences were different from those of women they knew. Their general comment "I'm not a phone person" was a representation of their identity, and it was substantiated by their behavior that differs from women's behavior. Typically, working-class men spoke on the telephone once or twice a week to those with whom they did side jobs. One man who ran a bookmaking business with a friend reported that they spoke several times a day about business. Men spoke much less frequently than that to friends for other reasons.

Although most men reported calling friends for instrumental reasons, many men reported that their telephone conversations were not limited to the reason for the call. During telephone calls men discussed their families or their work after they finished with their business. During telephone calls made to discuss social plans several men discussed infertility problems with their wives. Another complained to a friend about his marital problems during a phone call initiated to plan side work. One man called a friend to make plans for a birthday dinner for the caller's wife. During the conversation he told his friend how many feelings the interview I had with him had stirred up (the friend had referred me to him). These conversations, then, had several functions for men's friendships. The telephone was primarily considered a tool for business or to make social plans, but it was also used as means of communicating important personal information. Most men, however, deemphasized the telephone's function in the communication of personal information.

About one fourth of the men reported that they did call friends simply to find out how they were. Most of the time these men reported calling out-of-town friends with whom they lacked other regular means of contact, and most of the time their calls were infrequent—one to three times a year. In one exception, a professional man regularly called friends to see how they were (and sometimes became irritated and upset when the friends did not reciprocate by initiating some percentage of the telephone calls). He talked with one local friend once a week for no other reason than to keep in touch, but this pattern was unique. The friend he called had limited mobility, and the men rarely saw one another. The telephone was a primary vehicle for their friendship. In this instance, the two men's calls differed little from some women's calls.

There was tremendous variation in telephone use among men, but the variation does not erase the differences across genders. While only one quarter of the men in this study reported that they ever called friends to visit over the telephone and three quarters called for instrumental reasons, over four-fifths of the women reported that they called friends to visit. Also, men's reported frequency of telephoning friends was consistently lower than women's. Whereas two-thirds of all women reported that they spoke with at least one friend three or more times a week, less than one quarter of the men did so.

The finding that men use the telephone less than women and that women use it for social visiting has been noted by others (Rakow 1991; Fischer 1992). Fischer (1992) argues:

research shows that, discounting their fewer opportunities for social contact, women are more socially adept and intimate than men, for whatever reasons—psychological constitution, social structure, childhood experiences or cultural norms. The telephone therefore fits the typical female style of personal interaction more closely than it does the typical male style (p. 235).

Fischer's comments may hold a clue about how ideologies of gender are maintained despite the evidence of intimate behaviors among men. Men and women both see the telephone as something women use more than men, and they see it as a way women are intimate. Men's telephone practices provided evidence to respondents that men are incapable of intimacy whereas women are very intimate with friends. Although women used the telephone more often for intimate conversation than men, men used opportunities at work and in public hangouts to talk intimately (one respondent reported that when they got together in the bar "we're worse than a bunch of girls when it comes to that [talking about their spouses]!"). Although telephone patterns are a poor measure of intimacy in friendship, men used them as such. Several men commented on hearing their wives call friends and talk about personal information. Doing so substantiated their impressions of women's friendships. Also, because the men focused on the reasons for their calls rather than on the contents of telephone calls, telephone use acted to provide confirmation that stereotypes about friendship are true.

Men's Jokes

Men's use of jokes is another way in which men construct their masculinity. In his ethnography, *America's Working Man*, David Halle (1984) points to several functions jokes serve among men: they reaffirm values of friendship and generosity, they ritually affirm heterosexuality among men whose social circumstances create a level of physical and emotional intimacy culturally regarded as unmasculine, and they mediate disputes. These functions were evident in the way working-class men talked about jokes and humor in their friendships. They were less evident among the professional men, for reasons suggested by Halle.

Men friends, particularly working-class men, used harsh teasing as a form of social control to reinforce certain behaviors. One working-class man said that he and his friends were the worst "ball breakers" in the world. If a man did not show up at the bar or at some social event then my respondent said they heard about it from all their friends. Among these men the friendship group was highly valued, but also, like many contemporary friendships, somewhat fragile. Work and family responsibilities that kept men away from the friendship group might put a friend at risk of being teased.

Other men said that the failure to reciprocate favors, such as help with household projects, might be a basis for teasing friends. This was a particularly important way of defusing tension as well as reaffirming values of friendship for working-class men. They frequently depended on friends to help them attain higher standards of living: friends provided craft services whose prices are high in the formal market and thus many working-class people's material lives were somewhat improved through the help of friends. Failure to reciprocate had implications not only for friendship but also for family income. Jokes about a friend's failure to reciprocate became a public statement about his failure to conform to recognized norms, and they were a way for someone to handle his anger at his friend.

Another way jokes constructed masculinity was to highlight an activity that was outside the purview of men's activities that they nonetheless did. For instance, Greg and Chris were friends from law school who saw each other seven or eight times a year. One of those times was a yearly shopping trip to buy Christmas presents. Men generally claimed they did not shop—those who did usually said they went to hardware stores when they were doing a project with a friend. The shopping trip Greg and Chris went on was a traditional joke between them both. It began in law school when Greg asked Chris to go with him to

buy a negligee for Greg's girlfriend. When they got to the store Chris ran away and Greg was left feeling terribly embarrassed. Ever since, they went shopping once a year, but both men downplayed the shopping aspect of the trips and highlighted the socializing. They said they did not accomplish very much on their trips. They also said they used the time to buy gag gifts for people instead of serious gifts. Turning the shopping spree into a joke subverted the meaning of shopping as something women do, and the trip became a ritual reaffirmation of masculinity.

Jokes were sometimes used as pseudoinstrumental reasons to call friends on the phone when men lacked instrumental reasons; they thus maintained the masculinity of men's telephone practices. Men called each other and told one another jokes and then moved into more personal topics. Gene, for instance, befriended Al's lover, Ken, before Al died of AIDS. During Al's illness Gene was an important source of support for both men, and he continued to keep in touch with Ken after Al's death. They talked regularly on the telephone, but most of the conversations initiated by Ken began with jokes. After Ken and Gene had exchanged jokes the two men moved on to other topics, including their feelings for Al.

Finally, men used jokes to exaggerate gender differences and denigrate women. Gene considered himself sympathetic to women's issues. He said that he and his friends

> will tell in a joking way, tell jokes that are hostile towards feminism or hostile towards women. It's like there's two levels of it. One is, we think the joke is funny in and of itself or we think the joke is funny because it's so outrageously different from what's politically correct. You know, so we kind of laugh about it, and then we'll laugh that we even had the gall to tell it.

Not all men mentioned the importance of humor to friendship, the existence of jokes among friends, or the tendency to tease friends, but about half the respondents indicated that jokes and teasing were part of their friendship. Also, jokes and joking behavior were not limited solely to men. A few women also told jokes and engaged in joking behavior with their friends, but men emphasized the behavior as part of their friendships, whereas women did not. Also, women reported using jokes in a much more restricted way than men. For men, jokes are an elaborated code with multiple meanings and functions.

Men Talk About Women

Finally, men constructed masculinity through their behavior with men friends through their talk about what women are like. While not every man reported that he engaged in discussions about women with his friends, most men did. Comments about women emphasized men's and women's differences. Men, for instance, discussed how their wives had higher housekeeping standards than they, their wives' greater control over child rearing, and their greater propensity to spend money impulsively; they also discussed women's needs for relationships. These comments helped men interpret their relationships with their wives and served to reassure men that their experiences were not unusual.

> We would talk about like how long it would take them to get dressed . . . my wife took exceptionally long to get dressed, four or five hours in the bathroom. Um, but I mean, I don't think I talk a whole lot about women, when I did I guess I generalized and that kind of stuff, like how a wife expects a husband to kind of do everything for her. (Working-class man)

> What we talked about was the differences, differences we have with our wives in terms of raising kids. . . . And how sometimes we feel, rightly or wrongly, we both agreed that we didn't have quite as much control over the situation or say in the situation as we might have liked . . . That's something that a lot of my friends who have younger kids, I've had that discussion with. I've talked to them about it in terms of something that I think mothers, in particular, have a different input into their child's lives than do fathers. (Professional man)

Through these sorts of discussions with men friends—some brief and jocular, some more sus-

tained and serious—men defined who women are, and who they were, in contrast, as men. These discussions with friends frequently reinforced stereotypes about women and men.

Women were spendthrifts:

> One individual may call me up and say, "Geez, my wife just went out and bought these rugs. I need that like a hole in the head. You know, this is great, I have these oriental rugs now, you know, I'm only going to spill coffee on it." (Professional man)

Women attempted to control men's free time:

> [We might talk about] how much we're getting yelled at or in trouble or whatever, you know what I mean, for not doin' stuff around the house, or workin' over somebody else's house too much or staying out at the bars too late. (Working-class man)

Women were manipulative:

> Sometimes they seem, they don't know what they want, or what they want is something different than what they tell you they want. You know, tough to figure out, [we say] that they can be manipulative . . . Conniving. (Professional man)

Men evaluated women's behaviors and desires through such talk. They reported that such talk was a way of getting feedback on their marital experiences. Talking with friends frequently relieved the tensions men felt in their cross-gender relationships, and it did so without requiring men to change their behaviors vis-à-vis women. Men rarely reported that they accommodated themselves to their wives because their friends suggested that they should: in an unusual case, one working-class man said his friend told him that women needed to be told, "I love you," all the time, and he thought his friend had been helpful in mitigating some strains in his marriage through their talk.

More frequently, men's jokes and comments about women—about their demands for more housekeeping help, their ways with money, and their desires to have men home more often—

served to delegitimize women's demands. Men talked about women as unreasonable; as one man above said, "everybody needs time away." This tendency to delegitimize wives' demands was more apparent among working-class men than among the professional men. Professionals reported that their jobs, not unreasonable wives, prevented them from greater involvement in child care, and they sometimes talked with friends about this as an inevitable part of professional life. The effect, however, was similar because talk among both professional and working-class men friends supported the status quo. Instead of becoming a problem to be solved, professional men and their friends determined that professional life unfortunately, but inevitably, caused men to limit their family involvement. (One man who consistently seemed to play with the boundaries of masculinity had tried to solve the problem through scheduling his work flexibly along the lines that a friend had suggested. He reported that he still did not have enough time for his family.)

These four behaviors: using public spaces for friendship socializing, men's telephone practices, joking, and talking about women in particular ways are some ways that men construct masculinity in their friendships. There are many others. Discussions of sports, for instance, are one obvious other way men construct their masculinity, and such discussions were common among respondents. Like women's telephone use and ease with intimacy, men's talk about sports has become part of our cultural ideology about gendered friendships. Not all respondents, however, participated in such talk, and of those who did, some did not enjoy such talk but engaged in it because it was expected.

Cultural Ideology of Men and Friendship

When I began this article I asked not only how men construct masculinity through their behaviors but also why there was a discrepancy between the cultural ideology of men's friendship's, which maintains that men do not share intimate thoughts

and feelings with one another, and reports of specific behaviors that show that they do. It is in part by recognizing that the construction of gender is an ongoing activity that incorporates many disparate behaviors that this question becomes answerable. While one behavior in an interaction may violate the norms of gender ideology, other behaviors are simultaneously conforming to other ideologies of masculinity. When men reflect back on their behavior they emphasize those aspects of their behavior that give truth to their self-images as men. The other behavior may be reported, but, in this study, it did not discredit men's gender ideologies.

Second, as I noted earlier, masculinity is frequently reified, and behavior that does not conform does not affect the overall picture of masculinity. Men belong in the gender category to which they were assigned at birth, and their past in that category reassures them that they belong there. Occasionally respondents recognized that men do things that contradict gender ideology. One man told me about a friend of his who "does thoughtful things for other men." When I asked what he did, and he said:

> Uh, remembers their birthdays. Will buy them gifts. Uh, and does it in a way that's real, I think, really, uh, I don't know, it's not uh, it's not uh, feminine in the sense of, feminine, maybe in the pejorative sense . . . I mean, I remember that John, uh, John's nurturing I saw, not that I was a recipient of it so much although I was in his company a lot and got to see him. Uh, I thought, boy, this guy's a, this guy's a real man, this guy. This guy's all right, you know.

Though my respondent identified his friend's behavior as different, almost feminine, he made sure to tell me that the man is a "real man." This seemed problematic for him, his language became particularly awkward, full of partial sentences. But in the end, the fact that his friend was a man and that my respondent liked and respected him enabled him to conclude, "this guy's a real man."

At other times, recognition that behavior contradicts gender ideology elicits censure instead of acceptance. When men censure one another for such behavior, they reinforce the idea that such behavior is anomalous and should not be expressed. For instance, Gene, who consciously worked at intimacy with his friends, told me about sitting and drinking with a friend of his one night when Gene was depressed. His friend asked him how things were going and Gene told him he was depressed because he was feeling financial pressures. Gene felt "house poor" and upset with himself for buying a house that would cause him to feel such pressures when he had determined that he would not do such a thing. His friend's response was, "Oh, that's the last time I ask you how you're feeling." On an earlier occasion Gene called his gay friend in California on the telephone crying because he had just broken off with a woman he had been dating. His friend comforted him at the time, but later he said, "I didn't know you had it in you [to express yourself like that]." Gene believed that men had greater difficulties with self-disclosure than women, and these events acted as support for his beliefs instead of counterexamples. In both cases friends had let him know his self-disclosing behavior was either intolerable or unusual. His gay friend seemed to admire Gene's ability to call him up in tears by giving him a back-handed compliment, but this was a man who had rejected many norms of heterosexuality, and who saw Gene as participating in hegemonic masculinity (Connell 1987) and teased him for it. Gene's interpretation of these events coincided with his friends: he was behaving in ways men normally did not.

In another case, Anna, a woman respondent, told me about her husband Tom's experience with his best friend. Anna had been diagnosed with a serious chronic illness that had profound consequences for her lifestyle, and Tom was depressed about it. One night he went out with two friends, Jim, Tom's best friend, and another man who was unhappy about his recent divorce. According to Anna, Jim commented that he wished he did not know either Tom or the other man at the time because they were both so depressed. From this, Anna said she and Tom concluded that men did not express their feelings and were not as intimate with one another as women were.

These sorts of events reinforce men's notions that men are emotionally distant. Self-disclosure and attempts to express one's feelings are seen as anomalous, even if desirable—desirable because the contemporary evaluation on friendship as defined primarily by feminists is that women have better friendships than men. Women, by the way, also reported occasions when their friends were unsympathetic to their expressions of distress. The conclusions women and men drew about their unsympathetic friendship differed, however. Women concluded that particular friends lacked sympathy. Unlike men, they did not think their expressive behavior was inappropriate or unusual.

Conclusion

I have conceptualized gender as an ongoing social creation rather than a role individuals learn or a personality type they develop that causes differences in behavior. Individuals construct gender on an ideological and a behavioral level. On a behavioral level, many social acts contribute to the overall construction of masculinity. Men do not talk on the phone unless they have something specific they wish to find out or arrange. Men friends joke around together. Men hang out in bars. Men also talk about women and their wives in ways that distinguish women from men and define gender tensions and men's solutions to them. Some of these behaviors have become part of the cultural ideology of men's friendships. Respondents, for instance, talked generally about differences between men's and women's telephone use. Some also said that women stayed home with their friends whereas men went out. But the relationship between behavior and ideology is not so direct and simple that behaviors in which most men participate become part of the cultural ideology. To the extent that talking about women, for instance, is perceived as sharing personal information, then talking about women is something men do not recognize as characteristic of their friendships.

Because so many actions construct masculinity and gender is a practice over which individuals have some control, the failure to conform to the cultural ideology of masculine friendship does not necessarily threaten either the cultural ideology or the individual's position in the masculine gender category. This becomes particularly important in understanding why the many men who share personal information with friends continue to believe that men are inexpressive and find intimacy difficult. I have found that the exchange of intimate information is something most respondents, men and women, engaged in, but most people also did it with selected friends. Furthermore, talking about personal matters or sharing feelings frequently constituted a small portion of all friendship interactions. Thus, for men whose identities included a notion that they, as men, were not open with friends, the times when they were open were insignificant. There were many other activities of friendship that men preferred to emphasize.

It is useful to expand the debate over gender differences in friendship to include behaviors other than intimacy that has dominated the recent literature on gender and friendship (Miller 1983; Rubin 1985; Sherrod 1987; Swain 1987; Allan 1989; Rawlins 1992). The narrowness of the debate has limited our understandings of why men's friendships have been meaningful and important to them. Working-class men's reliance on friends for services and material support becomes invisible. The importance of joking behavior as a communicative style and its functions in maintaining stable relationships for both working-class and professional men disappear. Finally, the narrow debate over intimacy obscures some implications of how men talk to one another about women for gender relations and inequality.

A version of this article was presented at the 1993 annual meetings of the American Sociological Association in Miami. The author gratefully acknowledges the comments of Robin Leidner and Vicki Smith.

Notes

1. Some researchers have made this mistake as part of a more general positive evaluation of women. Some of this literature is explicitly feminist and draws on literature which emphasizes and dichotomizes gender differences.

2. All names of the respondents have been changed.

References

Allan, G. (1989). *Friendship: Developing a sociological perspective*. Boulder, CO: Westview.

Anderson, E. (1976). *A place on the corner*. Chicago: University of Chicago Press.

Aukett, R., Ritchie, J., & Mill, K. (1988). Gender differences in friendship patterns. *Sex Roles, 19,* 57–66.

Caldwell, M. A., & Peplau, L. A. (1982). Sex differences in same-sex friendships. *Sex Roles, 8,* 721–732.

Connell, R. W. (1987). *Gender and power*. Palo Alto, CA: Stanford University Press.

Fischer, C. (1992). *America calling: A social history of the telephone to 1940*. Berkeley: University of California Press.

Franklin, C. W. II (1992). Friendship among Black men. In P. Nardi (Ed.), *Men's friendships* (pp. 201–214). Newbury Park, CA: Sage.

Hacker, H. M. (1981). Blabbermouths and clams: Sex differences in self-disclosure in same-sex and cross-sex friendship dyads. *Psychology of Women Quarterly, 5,* 385–401.

Halle, D. (1984). *America's working man: Work, home, and politics among blue-collar property owners*. Chicago: University of Chicago Press.

Hansen, K. V. (1992). Our eyes behold each other: masculinity and intimate friendship in antebellum New England. In P. Nardi (Ed.), *Men's friendships* (pp. 35–58). Newbury Park, CA: Sage.

Kornblum, W. (1974). *Blue collar community*. Chicago: University of Chicago Press.

Leidner, R. (1991). Serving hamburgers and selling insurance: Gender, work, and identity in interactive service jobs. *Gender & Society, 5,* 154–177.

Liebow, E. (1967). *Tally's corner: A study of Negro street-corner men*. Boston: Little, Brown.

Miller, M. (1983). *Men and friendship*. Boston: Houghton Mifflin.

O'Meara, J. D. (1989). Cross-sex friendship: Four basic challenges of an ignored relationship. *Sex Roles, 21,* 525–543.

Rakow, L. F. (1991). *Gender on the line: Women, the telephone, and community life.* Urbana, IL: University of Illinois Press.

Rawlins, W. (1992). *Friendship matters: Communication, dialectics, and the life course.* New York: Aldine de Gruyter.

Reid, H. M., & Fine, G. A. (1992). Self-disclosure in men's friendships. In P. Nardi (Ed.), *Men's friendships* (pp. 132–152). Newbury Park, CA: Sage.

Rubin, L. (1985). *Just friends: The role of friendship in our lives.* New York: Harper & Row.

Sherrod, D. (1987). The bonds of men: Problems and possibilities in close male relationships. In H. Brod (Ed.), *The making of masculinities* (pp. 213–239). Boston: Allen and Unwin.

Swain, S. (1989). Covert intimacy: Closeness in men's friendships. In B. Risman & P. Schwartz (Eds.), *Gender and intimate relationships* (pp. 71–86). Belmont, CA: Wadsworth.

Walker, K. (1994). Men, women and friendship: what they say; what they do. *Gender & Society, 8,* 246–265.

Wellman, B. (1992). Men in networks: Private communities, domestic friendships. In P. Nardi (Ed.), *Men's friendships* (pp. 74–114). Newbury Park, CA: Sage.

West, C., & Zimmerman, D. (1987). Doing gender. *Gender & Society, 1,* 125–151.

Whyte, W. F. (1981). *Street corner society: The social structure of an Italian slum* (3rd ed.). Chicago: The University of Chicago Press.

Williams, C. L., & Heikes, E. J. (1993). The importance of researcher's gender in the in-depth interview: Evidence from two case studies of male nurses. *Gender & Society, 7,* 280–291.

Wright, P. (1982). Men's friendships, women's friendships and the alleged inferiority of the latter. *Sex Roles, 8,* 1–20.

Peter M. Nardi

The Politics of Gay Men's Friendships

Towards the end of Wendy Wasserstein's Pulitzer Prize–winning play, *The Heidi Chronicles*, a gay character, Peter Patrone, explains to Heidi why he has been so upset over all the funerals he has attended recently: "A person has so many close friends. And in our lives, our friends are our families" (Wasserstein 1990: 238). In his collection of stories, *Buddies*, Ethan Mordden (1986: 175) observes: "What unites us, all of us, surely, is brotherhood, a sense that our friendships are historic, designed to hold Stonewall together.... It is friendship that sustained us, supported our survival." These statements succinctly summarize an important dimension about gay men's friendships: Not only are friends a form of family for gay men and lesbians, but gay friendships are also a powerful political force.

Mordden's notion of "friends is survival" has a political dimension that becomes all the more salient in contemporary society where the political, legal, religious, economic, and health concerns of gay people are routinely threatened by the social order. In part, gay friendship can be seen as a political statement, since at the core of the concept of friendship is the idea of "being oneself" in a cultural context that may not approve of that self. For many people, the need to belong with others in dissent and out of the mainstream is central to the maintenance of self and identity (Rubin 1985). The friendships formed by a shared marginal identity, thus, take on powerful political dimensions as they organize around a stigmatized status to confront the dominant culture in solidarity. Jerome (1984: 698) believes that friendships have such economic and political implications,

Reprinted by permission of the author.

since friendship is best defined as "the cement which binds together people with interests to conserve."

Suttles (1970: 116) argues that:

> The very basic assumption friends must make about one another is that each is going beyond a mere presentation of self in compliance with "social dictates." Inevitably, this makes friendship a somewhat deviant relationship because the surest test of personal disclosure is a violation of the rules of public propriety.

Friendship, according to Suttles (1970), has its own internal order, albeit maintained by the cultural images and situational elements that structure the definitions of friendship. In friendship, people can depart from the routine and display a portion of the self not affected by social control. That is, friendships allow people to go beyond the basic structures of their cultural institutions into an involuntary and uncontrollable exposure of self—to deviate from public propriety (Suttles 1970).

Little (1989) similarly argues that friendship is an escape from the rules and pieties of social life. It's about identity: who one is rather than one's roles and statuses. And the idealism of friendship "lies in its detachment from these [roles and statuses], its creative and spiritual transcendence, its fundamental skepticism as a platform from which to survey the givens of society and culture" (Little 1989: 145). For gay men, these descriptions illustrate the political meaning friendship can have in their lives and their society.

The political dimension of friendship is summed up best by Little (1989: 154–155):

[T]he larger formations of social life—kinship, the law, the economy—must be different where there is, in addition to solidarity and dutiful role-performance, a willingness and capacity for friendship's surprising one-to-one relations, and this difference may be enough to transform social and political life. . . . Perhaps, finally, it is true that progress in democracy depends on a new generation that will increasingly locate itself in identity-shaping, social, yet personally liberating, friendships.

The traditional, nuclear family has been the dominant model for political relations and has structured much of the legal and social norms of our culture. People have often been judged by their family ties and history. But as the family becomes transformed into other arrangements, so do the political and social institutions of society. For example, the emerging concept of "domestic partnerships" has affected a variety of organizations, including insurance companies, city governments, private industry, and religious institutions (Task Force on Family Diversity final report 1988).

For many gay people, the "friends as family" model is a political statement, going beyond the practicality of developing a surrogate family in times of needed social support. It is also a way of refocusing the economic and political agenda to include nontraditional family structures composed of both romantic and nonromantic nonkin relationships.

In part, this has happened by framing the discussions in terms of gender roles. The women's movement and the emerging men's movement have highlighted the negative political implications of defining gender roles according to traditional cultural norms or limiting them to biological realities. The gay movement, in turn, has often been one source for redefining traditional gender roles and sexuality. So, for example, when gay men exhibit more disclosing and emotional interactions with other men, it demonstrates the limitations of male gender roles typically enacted among many heterosexual male friends. By call-ing attention to the impact of homophobia on heterosexual men's lives, gay men's friendships illustrate the potentiality for expressive intimacy among all men.

Thus, the assumptions that biology and/or socialization have inevitably constrained men from having the kinds of relationships and intimacies women often typically have can be called into question. This questioning of the dominant construction of gender roles is in itself a sociopolitical act with major implications on the legal, religious, and economic order.

White (1983:16) also sees how gay people's lives can lead to new modes of behavior in the society at large:

> In the case of gays, our childlessness, our minimal responsibilities, the fact that our unions are not consecrated, even our very retreat into gay ghettos for protection and freedom: all of these objective conditions have fostered a style in which we may be exploring, even in spite of our conscious intentions, things as they will someday be for the heterosexual majority. In that world (as in the gay world already), love will be built on esteem rather than passion or convention, sex will be more playful or fantastic or artistic than marital—and friendship will be elevated into the supreme consolation for this continuing tragedy, human existence.

If, as White and others have argued, gay culture in the post-Stonewall, sexual liberation years of the 1970s was characterized by a continuous fluidity between what constituted a friend, a sexual partner, and a lover, then we need to acknowledge the AIDS decade of the 1980s as a source for restructuring of gay culture and the reorganization of sexuality and friendship. If indeed gay people (and men in particular) have focused attention on developing monogamous sexual partnerships, what then becomes the role of sexuality in the initiation and development of casual or close friendships? Clearly, gay culture is not a static phenomenon, unaffected by the larger social order. Certainly, as the moral order in the AIDS years encourages the re-establishment of more traditional relationships, the implications for the ways sexuality and friendships are organized similarly change.

Friends become more important as primary sources of social and emotional support when illness strikes; friendship becomes institutionally organized as "brunch buddies" dating services or "AIDS buddies" assistance groups; and self-help groups emerge centering on how to make and keep new friends without having "compulsive sex." While AIDS may have transformed some of the meanings and role of friendships in gay men's lives from the politicalization of sexuality and friendship during the post-Stonewall 1970s, the newer meanings of gay friendships, in turn, may be having some effect on the culture's definitions of friendships.

Interestingly, the mythical images of friendships were historically more male-dominated: bravery, loyalty, duty, and heroism (see Sapadin 1988). This explained why women were typically assumed incapable of having true friendships. But today, the images of true friendship are often expressed in terms of women's traits: intimacy, trust, caring, and nurturing, thereby excluding the more traditional men from true friendship. However, gay men appear to be at the forefront of establishing the possibility of men overcoming their male socialization stereotypes and restructuring their friendships in terms of the more contemporary (i.e., "female") attributes of emotional intimacy.

To do this at a wider cultural level involves major sociopolitical shifts in how men's roles are structured and organized. Friendships between men in terms of intimacy and emotional support inevitably introduce questions about homosexuality. As Rubin (1985: 103) found in her interviews with men: "The association of friendship with homosexuality is so common among men." For women, there is a much longer history of close connections with other women, so that the separation of the emotional from the erotic is more easily made.

Lehne (1989) has argued that homophobia has limited the discussion of loving male relationships and has led to the denial by men of the real importance of their friendships with other men. In addition, "the open expression of emotion and affection by men is limited by homophobia. . . . The expression of more tender emotions among men is thought to be characteristic only of homosexuals" (Lehne 1989: 426). So men are raised in a culture with a mixed message: strive for healthy, emotionally intimate friendships, but if you appear too intimate with another man you might be negatively labelled homosexual.

This certainly wasn't always the case. As a good illustration of the social construction of masculinity, friendship, and sexuality, one need only look to the changing definitions and concepts surrounding same-sex friendship during the nineteenth century (see Smith-Rosenberg 1975; Rotundo 1989). Romantic friendships could be erotic but not sexual, since sex was linked to reproduction. Because reproduction was not possible between two women or two men, the close relationship was not interpreted as being a sexual one:

> Until the 1880s, most romantic friendships were thought to be devoid of sexual content. Thus a woman or man could write of affectionate desire for a loved one of the same gender without causing an eyebrow to be raised (D'Emilio and Freedman 1988: 121).

However, as same-sex relationships became medicalized and stigmatized in the late nineteenth century, "the labels 'congenital inversion' and 'perversion' were applied not only to male sexual acts, but to sexual or romantic unions between women, as well as those between men" (D'Emilio and Freedman, 1988: 122). Thus, the twentieth century is an anomaly in its promotion of female equality, the encouragement of male–female friendships, and its suspicion of intense emotional friendships between men (Richards 1987). Yet, in ancient Greece and the medieval days of chivalry, comradeship, virtue, patriotism, and heroism were all associated with close male friendship. Manly love, as it was often called, was a central part of the definition of manliness (Richards 1987).

It is through the contemporary gay, women's, and men's movements that these twentieth century constructions of gender are being questioned. And at the core is the association of close male friendships with negative images of homosexuality. Thus, how gay men structure their emotional lives and friendships can affect the social and emotional lives of all men and women. This is the political power and potential of gay friendships.

References

D'Emilio, John, and Freedman, Estelle. (1988). *Intimate Matters: A History of Sexuality in America.* New York: Harper & Row.

Jerome, Dorothy. (1984). Good company: The sociological implications of friendship. *Sociological Review*, 32(4), 696–718.

Lehne, Gregory K. (1989 [1980]). Homophobia among men: Supporting and defining the male role. In M. Kimmel and M. Messner (Eds.), *Men's Lives* (pp. 416–429). New York: Macmillan.

Little, Graham. (1989). Freud, friendship, and politics. In R. Porter and S. Tomaselli (Eds.), *The Dialectics of Friendship* (pp. 143–158). London: Routledge.

Mordden, Ethan. (1986). *Buddies.* New York: St. Martin's Press.

Richards, Jeffrey. (1987). "Passing the love of women": Manly love and Victorian society. In J. A. Mangan and J. Walvin (Eds.), *Manliness and Morality: Middle-Class Masculinity in Britain and America (1800–1940)* (pp. 92–122). Manchester, England: Manchester University Press.

Rotundo, Anthony. (1989). Romantic friendships: Male intimacy and middle-class youth in the northern United States, 1800–1900. *Journal of Social History*, 23(1), 1–25.

Rubin, Lillian. (1985). *Just Friends: The Role of Friendship in Our Lives.* New York: Harper & Row.

Sapadin, Linda. (1988). Friendship and gender: Perspectives of professional men and women. *Journal of Social and Personal Relationships*, 5(4), 387–403.

Smith-Rosenberg, Carroll. (1975). The female world of love and ritual: Relations between women in nineteenth-century America. *Signs*, 1(1): 1–29.

Suttles, Gerald. (1970). Friendship as a social institution. In G. McCall, M. McCall, N. Denzin, G. Suttles, and S. Kurth, *Social Relationships* (pp. 95–135). Chicago: Aldine.

Task Force on Family Diversity. (1988). *Strengthening Families: A Model for Community Action.* City of Los Angeles.

Wasserstein, Wendy. (1990). *The Heidi Chronicles.* San Diego: Harcourt, Brace, Jovanovich.

White, Edmund. (1983). Paradise found: Gay men have discovered that there is friendship after sex. *Mother Jones*, June, 10–16.

Tim Beneke

Men on Rape

Rape may be America's fastest growing violent crime; no one can be certain because it is not clear whether more rapes are being committed or reported. It *is* clear that violence against women is widespread and fundamentally alters the meaning of life for women; that sexual violence is encouraged in a variety of ways in American culture; and that women are often blamed for rape.

Consider some statistics:

- In a random sample of 930 women, sociologist Diana Russell found that 44 percent had survived either rape or attempted rape. Rape was defined as sexual intercourse physically forced upon the woman, or coerced by threat of bodily harm, or forced upon the woman when she was helpless (asleep, for example). The survey included rape and attempted rape in marriage in its calculations. (Personal communication)
- In a September 1980 survey conducted by *Cosmopolitan* magazine to which over 106,000 women anonymously responded, 24 percent had been raped at least once. Of these, 51 percent had been raped by friends, 37 percent by strangers, 18 percent by relatives, and 3 percent by husbands. 10 percent of the women in the survey had been victims of incest. 75 percent of the women had been "bullied into making love." Writer Linda Wolfe, who reported on the survey, wrote in reference to such bullying: "Though such harassment stops short of rape, readers reported that it was nearly as distressing."

- An estimated 2–3 percent of all men who rape outside of marriage go to prison for their crimes.[1]
- The F.B.I. estimates that if current trends continue, one woman in four will be sexually assaulted in her lifetime.[2]
- An estimated 1.8 million women are battered by their spouses each year.[3] In extensive interviews with 430 battered women, clinical psychologist Lenore Walker, author of *The Battered Woman*, found that 59.9 percent had also been raped (defined as above) by their spouses. Given the difficulties many women had in admitting they had been raped, Walker estimates the figure may well be as high as 80 or 85 percent (personal communication). If 59.9 percent of the 1.8 million women battered each year are also raped, then a million women may be raped in marriage each year. And a significant number are raped in marriage without being battered.
- Between one in two and one in ten of all rapes are reported to the police.[4]
- Between 300,000 and 500,000 women are raped each year outside of marriage.[5]

What is often missed when people contemplate statistics on rape is the effect of the *threat* of sexual violence on women. I have asked women repeatedly, "How would your life be different if rape were suddenly to end?" (Men may learn a lot by asking this question of women to whom they are close.) The threat of rape is an assault upon the meaning of the world; it alters the feel of the human condition. Surely any attempt to comprehend the lives of women that fails to take issues of violence against women into account is misguided.

Through talking to women, I learned: *The threat of rape alters the meaning and feel of the night.* Observe how your body feels, how the night feels, when you're in fear. The constriction in your chest, the vigilance in your eyes, the rubber in your legs. What do the stars look like? How does the moon present itself? What is the difference between walking late at night in the dangerous part of a city and walking late at night in the country, or safe suburbs? When I try to imagine what the threat of rape must do to the night, I think of the stalked, adrenalated feeling I get walking late at night in parts of certain American cities. Only, I remind myself, it is a fear different from any I have known, a fear of being raped.

It is night half the time. If the threat of rape alters the meaning of the night, it must alter the meaning and pace of the day, one's relation to the passing and organization of time itself. For some women, the threat of rape at night turns their cars into armored tanks, their solitude into isolation. And what must the space inside a car or an apartment feel like if the space outside is menacing?

I was running late one night with a close woman friend through a path in the woods on the outskirts of a small university town. We had run several miles and were feeling a warm, energized serenity.

"How would you feel if you were alone?" I asked.

"Terrified!" she said instantly.

"Terrified that there might be a man out there?" I asked, pointing to the surrounding moonlit forest, which had suddenly been transformed into a source of terror.

"Yes."

Another woman said, "I know what I can't do and I've completely internalized what I can't do. I've built a viable life that basically involves never leaving my apartment at night unless I'm directly going some place to meet somebody. It's unconsciously built into what it occurs to women to do." When one is raised without freedom, one may not recognize its absence.

The threat of rape alters the meaning and feel of nature. Everyone has felt the psychic nurturance of nature. Many women are being deprived of that nurturance, especially in wooded areas near cities. They are deprived either because they cannot experience nature in solitude because of threat, or because, when they do choose solitude in nature, they must cope with a certain subtle but nettlesome fear.

Women need more money because of rape and the threat of rape makes it harder for women to earn money. It's simple: if you don't feel safe walking at night, or riding public transportation, you need a car. And it is less practicable to live in cheaper, less secure, and thus more dangerous neighborhoods if the ordinary threat of violence that men experience, being mugged, say, is compounded by the threat of rape. By limiting mobility at night, the threat of rape limits where and when one is able to work, thus making it more difficult to earn money. An obvious bind: women need more money because of rape, and have fewer job opportunities because of it.

The threat of rape makes women more dependent on men (or other women). One woman said: "If there were no rape I wouldn't have to play games with men for their protection." The threat of rape falsifies, mystifies, and confuses relations between men and women. If there were no rape, women would simply not need men as much, wouldn't need them to go places with at night, to feel safe in their homes, for protection in nature.

The threat of rape makes solitude less possible for women. Solitude, drawing strength from being alone, is difficult if being alone means being afraid. To be afraid is to be in need, to experience a lack; the threat of rape creates a lack. Solitude requires relaxation; if you're afraid, you can't relax.

The threat of rape inhibits a woman's expressiveness. "If there were no rape," said one woman, "I could dress the way I wanted and walk the way I wanted and not feel self-conscious about the responses of men. I could be friendly to people. I wouldn't have to wish I was ugly. I wouldn't have to make myself small when I got on the bus. I wouldn't have to respond to verbal abuse from men by remaining silent. I could respond in kind."

If a woman's basic expressiveness is inhibited, her sexuality, creativity, and delight in life must surely be diminished.

The threat of rape inhibits the freedom of the eye. I know a married couple who live in Manhattan. They are both artists, both acutely sensitive and responsive to the visual world. When they walk separately in the city, he has more freedom to look than she does. She must control her eye movements lest they inadvertently meet the glare of some importunate man. What, who, and how she sees are restricted by the threat of rape.

The following exercise is recommended for men.

> Walk down a city street. Pay a lot of attention to your clothing; make sure your pants are zipped, shirt tucked in, buttons done. Look straight ahead. Every time a man walks past you, avert your eyes and make your face expressionless. Most women learn to go through this act each time we leave our houses. It's a way to avoid at least some of the encounters we've all had with strange men who decided we looked available.[6]

To relate aesthetically to the visual world involves a certain playfulness, spirit of spontaneous exploration. The tense vigilance that accompanies fear inhibits that spontaneity. The world is no longer yours to look at when you're afraid.

I am aware that all culture is, in part, restriction, that there are places in America where hardly anyone is safe (though men are safer than women virtually everywhere), that there are many ways to enjoy life, that some women may not be so restricted, that there exist havens, whether psychic, geographical, economic, or class. But they are *havens*, and as such, defined by threat.

Above all, I trust my experience: no woman could have lived the life I've lived the last few years. If suddenly I were restricted by the threat of rape, I would feel a deep, inexorable depression. And it's not just rape; it's harassment, battery, Peeping Toms, anonymous phone calls, exhibitionism, intrusive stares, fondlings—all contributing to an atmosphere of intimidation in women's lives. And I have only scratched the surface; it would take many carefully crafted short stories to begin to express what I have only hinted at in the last few pages. I have not even touched upon what it might mean for a woman to be sexually assaulted. Only women can speak to that. Nor have I suggested how the threat of rape affects marriage.

Rape and the threat of rape pervade the lives of women, as reflected in some popular images of our culture.

"She Asked for It"— Blaming the Victim[7]

Many things may be happening when a man blames a woman for rape.

First, in all cases where a woman is said to have asked for it, her appearance and behavior are taken as a form of speech. "Actions speak louder than words" is a widely held belief; the woman's actions—her appearance may be taken as action—are given greater emphasis than her words; an interpretation alien to the woman's intentions is given to her actions. A logical extension of "she asked for it" is the idea that she wanted what happened to happen; if she wanted it to happen, she *deserved* for it to happen. Therefore, the man is not to be blamed. "She asked for it" can mean either that she was consenting to have sex and was not really raped, or that she was in fact raped but somehow she really deserved it. "If you ask for it, you deserve it," is a widely held notion. If I ask you to beat me up and you beat me up, I still don't deserve to be beaten up. So even if the notion that women asked to be raped had some basis in reality, which it doesn't, on its own terms it makes no sense.

Second, a mentality exists that says: a woman who assumes freedoms normally restricted to a man (like going out alone at night) and is raped is doing the same thing as a woman who goes out in the rain without an umbrella and catches a cold. Both are considered responsible for what happens to them. That men will rape is taken to be a legitimized given, part of nature, like rain or snow. The view reflects a massive abdication of responsibility for rape on the part of men. It is so much easier to think of rape as natural than to acknowledge one's part in it. So long as rape is regarded as natural, women will be blamed for rape.

A third point. The view that it is natural for men to rape is closely connected to the view of women as commodities. If a woman's body is regarded as a valued commodity by men, then of course, if you leave a valued commodity where it can be taken, it's just human nature for men to take it. If you left your stereo out on the sidewalk, you'd be asking for it to get stolen. Someone will just take it. (And how often men speak of rape as "going out and *taking* it.") If a woman walks the streets at night, she's leaving a valued commodity, her body, where it can be taken. So long as women are regarded as commodities, they will be blamed for rape.

Which brings us to a fourth point. "She asked for it" is inseparable from a more general "psychology of the dupe." If I use bad judgment and fail to read the small print in a contract and later get taken advantage of, "screwed" (or "fucked over"), then I deserve what I get; bad judgment makes me liable. Analogously, if a woman trusts a man and goes to his apartment, or accepts a ride hitchhiking, or goes out on a date and is raped, she's a dupe and deserves what she gets. "He didn't *really* rape her" goes the mentality—"he merely took advantage of her." And in America it's okay for people to take advantage of each other, even expected and praised. In fact, you're considered dumb and foolish if you don't take advantage of other people's bad judgment. And so, again, by treating them as dupes, rape will be blamed on women.

Fifth, if a woman who is raped is judged attractive by men, and particularly if she dresses to look attractive, then the mentality exists that she attacked him with her weapon so, of course, he counter-attacked with his. The preview to a popular movies states: "She was the victim of her own *provocative beauty*." Provocation: "There is a line which, if crossed, will *set me off* and I will lose

control and no longer be responsible for my behavior. If you punch me in the nose then, of course, I will not be responsible for what happens: you will have provoked a fight. If you dress, talk, move, or act a certain way, you will have provoked me to rape. If your appearance *stuns* me, *strikes* me, *ravishes* me, *knocks me out*, etc., then I will not be held responsible for what happens; you will have asked for it." The notion that sexual feeling makes one helpless is part of a cultural abdication of responsibility for sexuality. So long as a woman's appearance is viewed as a weapon and sexual feeling is believed to make one helpless, women will be blamed for rape.

Sixth, I have suggested that men sometimes become obsessed with images of women, that images become a substitute for sexual feeling, that sexual feeling becomes externalized and out of control and is given an undifferentiated identity in the appearance of women's bodies. It is a process of projection in which one blurs one's own desire with her imagined, projected desire. If a woman's attractiveness is taken to signify one's own lust and a woman's lust, then when an "attractive" woman is raped, some men may think she wanted sex. Since they perceive their own lust in part projected onto the woman, they disbelieve women who've been raped. So long as men project their own sexual desires onto women, they will blame women for rape.

And seventh, what are we to make of the contention that women in dating situations say "no" initially to sexual overtures from men as a kind of pose, only to give in later, thus revealing their true intentions? And that men are thus confused and incredulous when women are raped because in their sexual experience women can't be believed? I doubt that this has much to do with men's perceptions of rape. I don't know to what extent women actually "say no and mean yes"; certainly it is a common theme in male folklore. I have spoken to a couple of women who went through periods when they wanted to be sexual but were afraid to be, and often rebuffed initial sexual advances only to give in later. One point is clear: the ambivalence women may feel about having sex is closely tied to the inability of men to fully accept them as sexual beings. Women have been traditionally punished for being openly and freely sexual; men are praised for it. And if many men think of sex as achievement of possession of a valued commodity, or aggressive degradation, then women have every reason to feel and act ambivalent.

These themes are illustrated in an interview I conducted with a 23-year-old man who grew up in Pittsburgh and works as a file clerk in the financial district of San Francisco. Here's what he said:

"Where I work it's probably no different from any other major city in the U.S. The women dress up in high heels, and they wear a lot of makeup, and they just look really *hot* and really sexy, and how can somebody who has a healthy sex drive not feel lust for them when you see them? I feel lust for them, but I don't think I could find it in me to overpower someone and rape them. But I definitely get the feeling that I'd like to rape a girl. I don't know if the actual act of rape would be satisfying, but the *feeling* is satisfying.

"These women look so good, and they kiss ass of the men in the three-piece suits who are *big* in the corporation, and most of them relate to me like 'Who are *you*? Who are *you* to even *look* at?' They're snobby and they condescend to me, and I resent it. It would take me a lot longer to get to first base than it would somebody with a three-piece suit who had money. And to me a lot of the men they go out with are superficial assholes who have no real feelings or substance, and are just trying to get ahead and make a lot of money. Another thing that makes me resent these women is thinking, 'How could she want to hang out with somebody like that? What does that make her?'

"I'm a file clerk, which makes me feel like a nebbish, a nerd, like I'm not making it, I'm a failure. But I don't really believe I'm a failure because I know it's just a phase, and I'm just doing it for the money, just to make it through this phase. I catch myself feeling like a failure, but I realize that's ridiculous."

What Exactly Do You Go Through When You See These Sexy, Unavailable Women?

"Let's say I see a woman and she looks really pretty and really clean and sexy, and she's giving off very feminine, sexy vibes. I think, 'Wow, I would love to make love to her,' but I know she's not really interested. It's a tease. A lot of times a woman knows that she's looking really good and she'll use that and flaunt it, and it makes me feel like she's laughing at me and I feel *degraded*.

"I also feel dehumanized, because when I'm being teased I just turn off, I cease to be human. Because if I go with my human emotions I'm going to want to put my arms around her and kiss her, and to do that would be unacceptable. I don't like the feeling that I'm supposed to stand there and take it, and not be able to hug her or kiss her; so I just turn off my emotions. It's a feeling of humiliation, because the woman has forced me to turn off my feelings and react in a way that I really don't want to.

"If I were actually desperate enough to rape somebody, it would be from wanting the person, but it would be a very spiteful thing, just being able to say, 'I have power over you and I can do anything I want with you,' because really I feel that *they* have power over *me* just by their presence. Just the fact that they can come up to me and just melt me and make me feel like a dummy makes me want revenge. They have power over me so I want power over them. . . .

"Society says that you have to have a lot of sex with a lot of different women to be a real man. Well, what happens if you don't? Then what are you? Are you half a man? Are you still a boy? It's ridiculous. You see a whiskey ad with a guy and two women on his arm. The implication is that real men don't have any trouble getting women."

How Does It Make You Feel Toward Women to See All These Sexy Women in Media and Advertising Using Their Looks to Try to Get You to Buy Something?

"It makes me hate them. As a man you're taught that men are more powerful than women, and that men always have the upper hand, and that it's a man's society; but then you see all these women and it makes you think, 'Jesus Christ, if we have all the power how come all the beautiful women are telling us what to buy?' And to be honest, it just makes me hate beautiful women because they're using their power over me. I realize they're being used themselves, and they're doing it for money. In *Playboy* you see all these beautiful women who look so sexy and they'll be giving you all these looks like they want to have sex so bad; but then in reality you know that except for a few nymphomaniacs, they're doing it for the money; so I hate them for being used and for using their bodies in that way.

"In this society, if you ever sit down and realize how manipulated you really are it makes you pissed off—it makes you want to take control. And you've been manipulated by women, and they're a very easy target because they're out walking along the streets, so you can just grab one and say, 'Listen, you're going to do what I want you to do,' and it's an act of revenge against the way you've been manipulated.

"I know a girl who was walking down the street by her house, when this guy jumped her and beat her up and raped her, and she was black and blue and had to go to the hospital. That's beyond me. I can't understand how somebody could do that. If I were going to rape a girl, I wouldn't hurt her. I might *restrain* her, but I wouldn't *hurt* her. . . .

"The whole dating game between men and women also makes me feel degraded. I hate being put in the position of having to initiate a relationship. I've been taught that if you're not aggressive with a woman, then you've blown it. She's not going to jump on *you*, so *you've* got to jump on *her*. I've heard all kinds of stories where the woman says, 'No! No! No!' and they end up making great love. I get confused as hell if a woman pushes me away. Does it mean she's trying to be a nice girl and wants to put up a good appearance, or does it mean she doesn't want anything to do with you? You don't know. Probably a lot of men think that women don't feel like real women unless a man tries to force himself on her, unless she brings out the 'real man,' so to speak, and probably too much of it goes on. It goes on in my head that you're complimenting a woman by actually staring at her or by trying to get into her pants. Lately, I'm realizing that when I stare at women lustfully, they often feel more threatened than flattered."

Notes

1. Such estimates recur in the rape literature. See *Sexual Assault* by Nancy Gager and Cathleen Schurr, Grosset & Dunlap, 1976, or *The Price of Coercive Sexuality* by Clark and Lewis, The Women's Press, 1977.

2. *Uniform Crime Reports*, 1980.

3. See *Behind Closed Doors* by Murray J. Strauss and Richard Gelles, Doubleday, 1979.

4. See Gager and Schurr (above) or virtually any book on the subject.

5. Again, see Gager and Schurr, or Carol V. Horos, *Rape*, Banbury Books, 1981.

6. From "Willamette Bridge" in *Body Politics* by Nancy Henley, Prentice-Hall, 1977, p. 144.

7. I would like to thank George Lakoff for this insight.

Terry A. Kupers

Rape and the Prison Code

The prisoner is in "the hole" of a high-security unit in a state prison. He is a slight, gay man in his early twenties who does not display any of the posturing and bravado that is characteristic of so many prisoners. Convicted of drug dealing, he was consigned to a high-security prison because he carried a gun. But in prison, without a gun, his physical size and inexperience in hand-to-hand combat make him an easy mark. He explains to me that, since the time he arrived at the prison, he has been brutalized and raped repeatedly. His overt homosexuality seems to pose a threat to tough prisoners, and they regularly single him out for abuse. And he was told that, if he snitched to a guard, he would be killed. He tried talking to a seemingly friendly correctional officer about his plight, but the officer only insisted that he reveal the name of the prisoner who had raped him. He seemed more interested in busting a guilty tough than in helping his man figure out a way to be safe "inside."

This prison does not have a protective custody unit, a "safer" cell block where potential victims might be placed for their own protection—a place for child molesters, policemen who are serving time, snitches, and others who would not survive on the main line. After suffering rape after rape and multiple injuries from beatings, this man determined that the best way to stay alive while serving his time was to be locked up in the hole. So he hit a guard and, as predicted, he was placed in solitary confinement. He cries as he tells me in private how lonely he feels and how seriously he is contemplating suicide.

The rate of occurrence of rape behind bars is unknown, because many cases go unreported. The Federal Bureau of Prisons estimates that between 9 and 20 percent of prisoners become victims of sexual assault (Polych, 1992), and Daniel Lockwood (1980) reports that 28 percent of prisoners in two New York prisons report that, while in custody they have been the victims of sexual assault. But these figures do not include the huge number of men who "consent" to having sex with a tougher con or consent to having sex with many other prisoners only because they are very afraid that, if they do not, they will be repeatedly beaten or perhaps even killed. In my view, this kind of coerced sex also constitutes rape.

The prevalence of AIDS in prison is also very high, and it is rising (Polych, 1992). Considering how much crime is drug related, this is not surprising. But this problem greatly magnifies the damage done by rape and multiplies the terror connected with sexual assault.

The New Prisoner's Dread

Hans Toch interviewed prisoners who had suffered emotional crises as they entered the prison world and discovered that, in many cases, concern about the violence of prison initiation rites was a major precipitant of their psychological stress. According to one man, "When you're a new fish you're nothing. So you've got pressure coming from all sides. When you first come in, anyway, their first intention when they look at you is that they're going to make this man my pussy, my girl and shit. . . . They aggravate you. They say, 'We're going to test this motherfucker.' " This prisoner assumes, with good reason, that the prisoners aggravate him specifically to lure him to the back of the cell block where they can beat him and sodomize him. "So you come along back from the cell and shit, and you lock in [each prisoner is permitted to remain in his cell and lock the door during certain periods when prisoners are being let out to the day room or the yard] and see these guys, big guys, running down" (1992:82–83).

The Problem with Snitching

For the victim of rape, reporting the assault to security staff is not a simple matter. Even if the victim asks to lock up—to be transferred to a protective custody unit—the perpetrator may retaliate by killing, or by arranging for another prisoner to kill, the snitch. In addition, Toch (1992) describes prisoners' need to appear as "manly men." They must not display any sign of weakness lest other prisoners attack them. According to the code, snitching is the worst offense, but being a punk (the victim of rape or the voluntary passive partner of "butt fucking") or displaying weakness of any kind is not much better—and all are punishable by repeated beatings, rapes, or even death. Moreover, it is not at all clear to the violated male prisoner that the staff will maintain confidentiality, much less protect him if he snitches.

I have spoken to many prisoners who report that, when they have told correctional officers that they were raped, the officers have insisted that they reveal the name of the assailant. The situation is even sadder for the victim who suffers from a serious mental illness and does not really understand the code or the possible ramifications of snitching. These prisoners are especially vulnerable to victimization and rape. And when an officer demands that they give the name of the rapist, they are very likely to comply without realizing that they are violating the code and putting themselves in grave danger. I have talked to several mentally disturbed prisoners who were raped, went to a guard to ask what they should do, and

ended up answering the guard's questions about who committed the rape. Once the word gets out that they have snitched, there is no way for the authorities to protect them.

Systemic Factors

Conditions of confinement are very important factors. A recent lawsuit illustrates how overcrowding and relative understaffing can lead to rape. I was asked to give an opinion about a young man who was raped by two gang members in a protective custody unit of a county jail. He was suing the county for not providing adequate protection. I examined the man and reviewed his file, including school reports and past psychiatric records. There seemed to be a pattern of vulnerability. For example, he had on occasion been the victim of mean pranks by classmates who first "suckered" him into engaging in behaviors at school that would lead to punishment and then laughed at him for being stupid enough to give in to their goading only to get caught. This hapless young man was clearly a potential victim. And after examining him, I concluded that he was suffering from severe post-traumatic stress disorder secondary to rape while he was in jail.

How was it possible, in a protective custody unit, for two gang members who had spent many years in prison to rape a vulnerable man who had never been to prison and never committed a violent crime? The victim, who had given the police the names of his accomplices at the time of his arrest, had asked to be placed in the unit because he feared he would be killed if other prisoners found out he had snitched. The two men who raped him, who were bigger and stronger than he was, had been returned from state prison to this jail only because they had to go to court to stand trial for gang-related violence inside prison. But they had been "outed" by their gangs (perhaps they were perceived as snitches). In other words, because they were in trouble with their gangs and therefore in grave danger anywhere in the correctional system, they had been placed in the protective custody unit.

At the time of the rape, a single officer was responsible for observing a day room, a dining area, and two floors of cells with open doors. It was not possible, at any given time, for that officer to observe the entire unit. In fact, the victim told me that the rape took place over a forty-five-minute time span, in a second floor cell, while the officer was in the day room, where she was unable to see inside the cells on the second floor.

The victim should not have been housed with the men who raped him. But in an overcrowded system, it is unlikely that prisoners of different security levels who are identified as being in need of protective custody will be further segregated—staff members are so far behind classifying the new prisoners that the assignment to protective custody is considered classification enough. And this is just one of the many ways that overcrowding can lead to heightened violence and mental decompensation in correctional settings.

The Code

Rape is not an isolated event in prison. It is part of a larger phenomenon: the hierarchical ranking of prisoners by their fighting ability and manliness. Jack Henry Abbott, who has spent most of his teen years and adult life behind bars, describes the process: "This is the way it is done. If you are a man, you must either kill or turn the tables on anyone who propositions you with threats of force. It is the custom among young prisoners. In so doing, it becomes known to all that you are a man, regardless of your youth. I had been trained from a youth spent in gladiator school (juvenile detention hall) for this. It was inevitable then that a youth in an adult penitentiary at some point will have to attack and kill, or else he most certainly will become a punk—even though it may not be well known he is a punk. If he cannot protect himself, someone else will" (1982:94).

The code, with some changes over time, permeates prison culture. Thus, Irwin and Austin point out that, in the first half of the twentieth century, the prisoners essentially operated prisons

in the United States. They cooked, served meals, landscaped, performed building maintenance, and worked in prison industries. "Collectively, prisoners developed their own self-contained society, with a pronounced stratification system, a strong convict value system, unique patterns of speech and bodily gestures, and an array of social roles. . . . Importantly, their participation in this world with its own powerful value system, the convict code, gave them a sense of pride and dignity. It was them against what they perceived as a cruel prison system and corrupt society. . . . However, society was more accepting of the ex-convict than it is now and apparently most did not return to prison" (1994:66).

The situation is very different today. The "war on drugs" that rages in the inner cities: society's "law and order" sensibility; harsher sentences, including state and federal "three strikes legislation"; huge racial disparities in arrests and sentencing; the waning of prison rehabilitation programs; massive overcrowding of jails and prisons; racial and gang tensions in prison; and high recidivism rates have combined to change the code significantly. For instance, the prisoners no longer operate the prison, and there is less solidarity among prisoners of different races and ages. Still, some parts of the prison code remain the same.

One commandment continues to stand out: "Thou shalt not snitch!" Snitching can be a capital offense in prison. "And you had better not show any signs of weakness, or else others will pounce on you and rape or kill you!" The rules go on and on. For example, if a weapon is found in a double cell, each of the cellies is interrogated separately and encouraged—better, coerced—to snitch on the other in order to receive a pardon for having the weapon in the cell. In other words, the security officers manipulate the code to put teeth in their interrogations. They know that a prisoner who snitches and beats the rap will be attacked by other prisoners. Staff members use the code to maintain order in the prison.

Prison is an extreme environment. The men have to act tough, lift weights, and be willing to fight to settle grudges. Any sign of weakness leads to being labeled a victim, and weaklings are subject to beatings and sodomy. Of course, in this milieu, prisoners do not talk to each other about their pains, their vulnerabilities, or their neediness—to do so with the wrong man could lead to betrayal and death. Consequently, a lot of men choose to spend their time in their cells. Touring a high-security prison in the middle of the day, one is struck by the large number of prisoners lying in their bunks with the lights out—just trying to "do the time and stay alive."

This aspect of the code is not ironclad. I cite here some of the worst-case scenarios. In fact, in my tours through prisons and my interviews with prisoners, I have been impressed by a certain warmth and friendship in spite of the danger. For example, it is not rare for a prisoner to report that he was only able to survive in prison because another prisoner offered him the support and help he needed.

Politically conscious prisoners and activists in the growing prison movement on the outside are trying to build on the camaraderie and feelings of solidarity among prisoners. The goal is to help all prisoners understand that animosity toward other prisoners is misguided and that they must stand together against their real oppressors. The male dominance hierarchy, interracial animosities, and intergang battles are the obstacles that must be overcome in this organizing and consciousness-raising project.

There is even consensual sex in prison. Many men find partners, have sex as a sexual outlet in an all-male world, and do not consider themselves gay before or after release. Sex between mutually consenting prisoners can be quiet and unproblematic. There is even affection—sometimes great affection—but this kind of innovation in male intimacy does not attract the kind of media attention that rape receives. In contrast, prison rape is not about affection at all. It is about domination. A prisoner is either a "real man" who subdues and rapes an adversary, or he is a "punk."

There are four obvious structural elements of the prison code:

1. There is a hierarchy of domination wherein the toughest and the most dominant men rule those who are less dominant. Of course, the hierarchy does not begin or end with the prisoners. The security officers wield power over the prisoners; the warden dominates the security officers; and at the other end of the hierarchy, more than a few prisoners have been known to rape women or beat them and their children. Every prisoner knows his place in the hierarchy and maintains his place by proving himself when challenged.

2. There is a sharp line between those at the top of the hierarchy, the dominants, and those at the bottom of the heap, the weaklings and punks. The rape victims I have described are at the bottom.

3. The bottom is defined in terms of the feminine. Whether a man is known as a loser, a weakling, a snitch, a faggot, or a punk, he is accused of being less than a man—in other words, a woman. Jean Genet describes a man he knew at Mettray reform school: "Bulkaen, on the other hand, was a little man whom Mettray had turned into a girl for the use of the big shots, and all his gestures were the sign of nostalgia for his plundered, destroyed virility" (1966:144). When one man beats up another and sodomizes him, the message is clear: "I, the dominant man, have the right and the power to use you, the loser, sexually, as if you were a woman and my slave."

4. There is a narrowing of personal possibilities, as if the only way to survive is to conform to the rigid hypermasculine posturings of the prison culture. Sanyika Shakur, also known as Monster Kody Scott, a leader of the Crips of South Central Los Angeles, tells the story of a vicious fight between cell mates that occurred at the beginning of his first prison term. Fat Rat began punching B.T. B.T. tried pleading with Fat Rat to stop; after all, they were both Crips from South Central. Fat Rat would not listen, and the more B.T. pleaded, the more Fat Rat gloried in his dominance—calling B.T. "bitch"

and "pussy" and proceeding to humiliate him. According to Shakur, "Fat Rat, like me, was uncut street, straight out of the bush. The only language Fat Rat knew or respected or could be persuaded by was violence. Everything else was for the weak. Action and more action—anything else paled in comparison" (1993:295).

Notice that, in these four elements, the structure of masculine domination in prison mirrors the outside world. This is why films such as *An Innocent Man* and *The Shawshank Redemption* strike such resonant chords in many free men's minds. In both films a successful, middle-class man is framed for a crime he did not commit, sent to prison, and forced to fight in order to avoid rape. In *An Innocent Man,* Tom Selleck avoids rape by killing another prisoner. Middle-class male viewers shudder as Tim Robbins is repeatedly raped in *The Shawshank Redemption.* Of course, on the outside, especially among middle- and upper-class men, dominance is not based solely on physical prowess or gang affiliation. It depends more on one's level of affluence or status in the corporate world, in academia, or in the professions. And the literal threat of "butt fucking" is not as omnipresent as it is in prison; rape is more of a symbol. (Of course, for women the threat is literal.) Thus, men on the outside keep their cards close to their chests in order to avoid "being shafted" and try to avoid giving other men the impression that they might be womanly or gay. A man needs a friend who will "watch his back." And on the outside, there are women to play the role of underdog, so men can rape and oppress women instead of raping each other. But there is also, just as in prison, the ever-present hierarchy, the sharp line between winners and losers, the perpetual fear of being betrayed or defeated and falling to the bottom of the heap (this is one reason that so many men become workaholics), the castigation of those at the bottom as womanly or queer, and the narrowing and constricting of men's possibilities in the interest of maintaining the image of a "real man."

In prison, the penalty for falling to the bottom of the heap is literal. The trick for someone who is not a tough guy is to find a "third alternative," neither "pitcher" nor "catcher," neither king of the mountain nor bottom of the heap. For example, some frail intellectuals make themselves invaluable to other prisoners by becoming knowledgeable about law and learning their way around the law library. They become immune to gladiatorial battles because they have a commodity to sell—law is an invaluable resource in a correctional setting, where many prisoners are very involved in attempts to win habeas corpus motions and appeals of their convictions—so the prison toughs leave them alone.

There are other ways to create a third alternative. I met a slim, blond, effeminate man in a maximum-security prison in the Midwest. He was wearing a flowing red gown that reached to the floor, and he had a shawl draped across his chest in a way that did not allow assessment of the size of his breasts. He wore makeup and sported a very seductive female pose. He explained that, because he had been beaten and raped several times upon arrival at the prison, he decided to become the "woman" of one prison tough. He performed sexual favors for this one man, so that all other prisoners would leave him alone for fear of retaliation by his "sugar daddy." There was coercion involved, so his sex acts were not exactly performed by mutual consent. But at least there were no more beatings and rapes. Still, the exceptions to the "top dog"/"punk" dichotomy merely serve to prove the general rule of domination.

Isolation

Shakur writes, "Fat Rat had a reputation for being a 'booty bandit,' and thrived on weak men with tight asses" (1993:293). The booty bandit, the rapist on the prowl for potential victims, preys on isolated prisoners. This is one reason that prisoners are so intent on joining a gang or a group that eats together and lifts weights together. The loner is a potential victim, especially if he cannot defend himself. Men who lack social skills, for instance mentally disordered and timid prisoners, are easily victimized. And after they are raped, they keep it secret. The tendency on the part of these prisoners to isolate themselves thus works against their recovery from the violation and the resulting posttraumatic stress disorder.

Shame plays a big part not only in victims' refusal to report rapes but also in maintaining their isolation. When a boy is shamed, for instance by an alcoholic father or critical mother, he goes to his room. He does not seek the support of other members of the family. In the school yard, the boy who loses a fight or "chickens out" does not seek the support of his friends to heal his wounds; he keeps to himself, and the wounds fester. Shame leads to isolation, and in isolation there is little hope of transcending shame. In prison, it can be dangerous to speak frankly to others about one's pains—again, the code. After being defeated in a fight, especially if a man is raped, he keeps to himself; perhaps he remains in his cell all day in the dark. But this is precisely the kind of response that deepens depression or leads to chronic post-traumatic stress disorder (Pelka, 1993).

It is not only the individual's shame that makes life in prison unbearable. There is also the prisoners' contempt for a weakling. If a man tries to take his own life and fails, and there are visible scars on his wrist or neck, he is labeled a weakling and is likely to be victimized and possibly raped. Many prisoners suffering from mental disorders are raped.

The code in prison is based on intimidation. Positive outlets for the need to feel powerful are scarce. The demeaned of the land are willing to demean those who are even lower in the hierarchy than they are. And even some of the most demeaned of the prisoners, when eventually they leave prison, find themselves acting abusively toward others.

References

Abbott, Jack Henry. 1982. *In the Belly of the Beast: Letters from Prison.* New York: Vintage.

Genet, Jean. 1966. *Miracle of the Rose.* New York: Grove Press.

Irwin, John, and James Austin. 1994. *It's about Time: America's Imprisonment Binge.* Belmont, Calif.: Wadsworth.

Lockwood, Daniel. 1980. *Prison Sexual Violence.* New York: Elsevier Horth Holland.

Pelka, Fred. 1993. "Raped: A Male Survivor Breaks His Silence." *Changing Men* 25 (Winter/Spring): 41–44.

Polych, C. 1992. "Punishment within Punishment: The AIDS Epidemic in North American Prisons." *Men's Studies Review* 9 (1): 13–17. Quoting T. Hammet, *Update: AIDS in Correctional Facilities* (Washington, D.C.: National Institute of Justice, 1989).

Shakur, Sanyika. 1993. *Monster: The Autobiography of an L.A. Gang Member.* New York: Atlantic Monthly Press.

Toch, Hans. 1992. *Mosaic of Despair: Human Breakdowns in Prison.* Washington, D.C.: American Psychological Association.

Kevin Powell

Confessions of a Recovering Misogynist

I am a sexist male.

I take no great pride in saying this. I am merely stating a fact. It is not that I was born this way; rather, I was born into this male-dominated society, and, consequently, from the very moment I began forming thoughts, they formed in a decidedly male-centered way. My "education" at home with my mother, at school, on my neighborhood playgrounds, and at church all placed males at the center of the universe. My digestion of 1970s American popular culture in the form of television, film, ads, and music only added to my training, so that by as early as age nine or ten I saw females, including my mother, as nothing more than the servants of males. Indeed, like the Fonz on that TV sitcom *Happy Days,* I thought I could snap my fingers and girls would come running.

My mother, working poor and a product of the conservative and patriarchal South, simply raised me as most women are taught to raise boys: The world was mine, there were no chores to speak of, and my aggressions were considered somewhat normal, something that we boys carry out as a rite of passage. Those "rites" included me routinely squeezing girls' butts on the playground. And at school boys were encouraged to do "boy" things: work and build with our hands, fight each other, and participate in the most daring activities during our gym time. Meanwhile, the girls were relegated to home economics, drawing cute pictures, and singing in the school choir. Now that I think about it, school was the place that spearheaded the omission of women from my worldview. Save Betsy Ross (whom I remember chiefly for sewing a flag) and a stoic Rosa Parks (she was unfurled every year as an example of Black achievement), I recall virtually no women making appearances is my American history classes.

The church my mother and I attended, like most Black churches, was peopled mainly by Black women, most of them single parents, who dragged their children along for the ride. Not once did I see a preacher who was anything other than an articulate, emotionally charged, well-coiffed, impeccably suited Black man running this church and, truly, these women. And behind the pulpit of this Black man, where he convinced us we were doomed to hell if we did not get right with God, was the image of our savior, a male, always White, named Jesus Christ.

Not surprisingly the "savior" I wanted in my life was my father. Ten years her senior, my father met my mother, my father wooed my mother, my father impregnated my mother, and then my father—as per *his* socialization—moved on to the next mating call. Responsibility was about as real to him as a three-dollar bill. When I was eight, my father flatly told my mother, via a pay phone, that he felt she had lied, that I was not his child, and that he would never give her money for me again. The one remotely tangible image of maleness in my life was gone for good. Both my mother and I were devastated, albeit for different reasons. I longed for my father's affections. And my mother longed to be married. Silently I began to blame my mother for my father's disappearance. Reacting to my increasingly bad behavior, my mother turned resentful and her beatings became more frequent, more charged. I grew to hate her and all females, for I felt it was women who made men act as we do.

At the same time, my mother, a fiercely independent and outspoken woman despite having only a grade-school education and being poor, planted within me the seeds of self-criticism, of shame for wrongful behavior—and, ultimately, of feminism. Clear that she alone would have to shape me, my mother spoke pointedly about my father for many years after that call, demanding that I not grow up to "be like him." And I noted the number of times my mother rejected low-life male suitors, particularly the ones who wanted to live with us free of charge. I can see now that my mother is a feminist, although she is not readily familiar with the term. Like many women before and since, she fell hard for my father, and only through enduring immense pain did she realize the power she had within herself.

I once hated women, and I take no pride in this confession.

I entered Rutgers University in the mid-1980s, and my mama's-boy demeanor advanced to that of pimp. I learned quickly that most males in college are some variety of pimp. Today I lecture regularly, from campus to campus, all over the country, and I see that not much has changed. For college is simply a place where we men, irrespective of race or class, can—and do—act out the sexist attitudes entrenched since boyhood. Rape, infidelity, girlfriend beat-downs, and emotional abuse are common, and pimpdom reigns supreme. There is the athlete pimp, the frat boy pimp, the independent pimp, and the college professor pimp. Buoyed by the antiapartheid movement and the presidential bids of Jesse Jackson, my social consciousness blossomed along racial lines, and behold—the student leader pimp was born.

Blessed with a gift for gab, a poet's sensibility, and an acute memory for historical facts, I baited women with my self-righteousness by quoting Malcolm X, Frantz Fanon, Machiavelli, and any other figure I was sure they had not studied. It was a polite form of sexism, for I was always cer-

tain to say "my sister" when I addressed women at Rutgers. But my politeness did not lend me tolerance for women's issues, nor did my affiliation with a variety of Black nationalist organizations, especially the Nation of Islam. Indeed, whenever women in our African Student Congress would question the behavior and attitudes of men, I would scream, "We don't have time for them damn lesbian issues!" My scream was violent, mean-spirited, made with the intention to wound. I don't think it is any coincidence that during my four years in college I did not have one relationship with a woman that lasted more than three or four months. For every friend or girlfriend who would dare question my deeds, there were literally hundreds of others who acquiesced to the ways of us men, making it easy for me to ignore the legitimate cries of feminists. Besides, I had taken on demanding role of pimp, of conqueror, of campus revolutionary—there was little time or room for real intimacy, and even less time for self-reflection.

Confessions are difficult because they force me to visit ghettos in the mind I thought I had long escaped.

I was kicked out of college at the end of my fourth year because I drew a knife on a female student. We were both members of the African Student Congress, and she was one of the many "subversive" female leaders I had sought to purge from the organization. She *had* left but for some reason was in our office a few days after we had brought Louis Farrakhan to speak at Rutgers. Made tense by her presence, I ignored her and turned to a male student, asking him, as she stood there, to ask her to jet. As she was leaving, she turned and charged toward me. My instincts, nurtured by my inner-city upbringing and several months of receiving anonymous threats as the Farrakhan talk neared, caused me to reach into my pocket and pull out a knife I had been carrying.

My intent was to scare her into submission. The male student panicked and knocked the knife from my hand, believing I was going to stab this woman. I would like to believe that that was not the case. It did not matter. This woman pressed charges on and off campus, and my college career, the one I'd taken on for myself, my under-educated mother, and my illiterate grandparents, came to a screeching halt.

It is not easy for me to admit I have a problem.

Before I could be readmitted to school I had to see a therapist. I went, grudgingly, and agonized over my violent childhood, my hatred of my mother, my many problems with women, and the nauseating torment of poverty and instability. But then it was done. I did not bother to try to return to college, and I found myself again using women for money, for sex, for entertainment. When I moved to New York City in August 1990, my predator mentality was still in full effect. I met a woman, persuaded her to allow me to live with her, and then mentally abused her for nearly a year, cutting her off from some of her friends, shredding her peace of mind and her spirit. Eventually I pushed her into the bathroom door when she blew up my spot, challenging me and my manhood.

I do not want to recount the details of the incident here. What I will say is that I, like most Black men I know, have spent much of my life living in fear: fear of White racism, fear of the circumstances that gave birth to me, fear of walking out my door wondering what humiliation will be mine today. Fear of Black women—of their mouths, of their bodies, of their attitudes, of their hurts, of their fear of us Black men. I felt fragile, as fragile as a bird with clipped wings that day when my ex-girlfriend stepped up her game and spoke back to me. Nothing in my world, nothing in my self-definition prepared me for dealing with a woman as an equal. My world said women were inferior, that they must at all costs be put in their place, and my instant reaction was to do that. When it was over, I found myself dripping with sweat, staring at her back as she ran barefoot out of the apartment.

Guilt consumed me after the incident. The women I knew through my circle of poet and writer friends begged me to talk through what I had done, to get counseling, to read the books of bell hooks. Pearl Cleage's tiny tome, *Mad at Miles,* the poetry of Audre Lorde, the many meditations of Gloria Steinem. I resisted at first, but eventually I began to listen and read, feeling electric shocks running through my body when I realized that these women, in describing abusive, oppressive men, were talking about me. Me, who thought I was progressive, Me, who claimed to be a leader. Me, who still felt women were on the planet to take care of men.

During this time I did restart therapy sessions. I also spent a good deal of time talking with young feminist women—some friends, some not. Some were soothing and understanding, some berated me and all men. I also spent a great deal of time alone, replaying my life in my mind: my relationship with my mother, how my mother had responded to my father's actions, how I had responded to my mother's response to my father. I thought of my education, of the absence of women in it. How I'd managed to attend a major university affiliated with one of the oldest women's colleges in America, Douglas College, and visited that campus only in pursuit of sex. I thought of the older men I had encountered in my life—the ministers, the high school track coach, the street hustlers, the local businessmen, the college professors, the political and community leaders—and realized that many of the ways I learned to relate to women came from listening to and observing those men. Yeah, I grew up after women's studies classes had appeared in most of the colleges in America, but that doesn't mean feminism actually reached the people it really needed to reach: average, everyday American males.

The incident, and the remorse that followed, brought about something akin to a spiritual epiphany. I struggled mightily to rethink the context that had created my mother. And my aunts. And my grandmother. And all the women I had been intimate with, either physically or emotionally or both. I struggled to understand terms like *patriarchy, misogyny, gender oppression.* A year after the incident I penned a short essay for *Essence* magazine called, simply, "The Sexist in Me," because I wanted to be honest in the most public forum possible, and because I wanted to reach some men, some young Black men, who needed to hear from another male that sexism is as oppressive as racism. And at times worse.

I am no hero. I am no saint. I remain a sexist male.

But one who is now conscious of it and who has been waging in internal war for several years. Some days I am incredibly progressive; other days I regress. It is very lonesome to swim against the stream of American male-centeredness, of Black male bravado and nut grabbing. It is how I was molded, it is what I know, and in rejecting it I often feel mad naked and isolated. For example, when I publicly opposed the blatantly sexist and patriarchal rhetoric and atmosphere of the Million Man March, I was attacked by Black men, some questioning my sanity, some accusing me of being a dupe for the White man, and some wondering if I was just "'trying' to get some pussy from Black women."

Likewise, I am a hip-hop head. Since adolescence I have been involved in this culture, this lifestyle, as a dancer, a graffiti writer, an activist, a concert organizer, and most prominently a hip-hop journalist. Indeed, as a reporter at *Vibe* magazine, I found myself interviewing rap icons like Dr. Dre, Snoop Dogg, and the late Tupac Shakur. And although I did ask Snoop and Tupac some pointed questions about *their* sexism, I still feel I dropped the ball. We Black men often feel so powerless, so sure the world—politically, economically, spiritually, and psychologically—is aligned against us. The last thing any of us wants if for another man to question how we treat women. Aren't we, Black men, the endangered species anyhow? This is how many of us think.

While I do not think hip-hop is any more sexist or misogynist than other forms of American culture, I do think it is the most explicit form of misogyny around today. It is also a form of sexism that gets more than its share of attention, because hip-hop—now a billion-dollar industry—is the sound track for young America, regardless of race or class. What folks don't understand is that hip-hop was created on the heels of the Civil Rights era by impoverished Blacks and Latinos, who literally made something out of nothing. But in making that something out of nothing, many of us men of color have held tightly to White patriarchal notions of manhood—that is, the way to be a man is to have power. Within hip-hop culture, in our lyrics, in our videos, and on our tours, that power translates into material possessions, provocative and often foul language, flashes of violence, and blatant objectification of and disrespect for women. Patriarchy, as manifested in hip-hop, is where we can have our version of power within this very oppressive society. Who would want to consider giving that up?

Well, I have, to a large extent, and these days I am a hip-hopper in exile. I dress, talk, and walk like a hip-hopper, yet I cannot listen to rap radio or digest music videos without commenting on the pervasive sexism. Moreover, I try to drop seeds, as we say, about sexism, whenever and wherever I can, be it at a community forum or on a college campus. Some men, young and old alike, simply cannot deal with it and walk out. Or there is the nervous shifting in seats, the uneasy comments during the question-and-answer sessions, generally in the form of "Why you gotta pick on the men, man?" I constantly "pick on the men" and myself because I truly wonder how many men actually listen to the concerns of women. Just as I feel it is Whites who need to be more vociferous about racism in their communities, I feel it is men who need to speak long and loud about sexism among ourselves.

I am recovering misogynist.

I do not say this with pride. Like a recovering alcoholic or a crack fiend who has righted her on his ways, I am merely cognizant of the fact that I have had some serious problems in my life with and in regard to women. I am also aware of the fact that I can lapse at any time. My relationship with my mother is better than it has ever been, though there are days when speaking with her turns me back into the little boy cowering beneath the belt and tongue of a woman deeply wounded by my father, by poverty, by her childhood, by the sexism that has dominated her life. My relationships since the incident with my ex-girlfriend have been better, no doubt, but not the bomb.

But I am at least proud of the fact I have not reverted back to violence against women—and don't ever plan to, which is why I regularly go to therapy, why I listen to and absorb the stories of women, and why I talk about sexism with any men, young and old, who are down to rethink the definitions we've accepted so uncritically. Few of us men actually believe there is a problem, or we are quick to point fingers at women, instead of acknowledging that healing is a necessary and ongoing process, that women *and* men need to be a part of this process, and that we all must be willing to engage in this dialogue and work if sexism is to ever disappear.

So I fly solo, and have done so for some time. For sure, today I count among my friends, peers, and mentors older feminist women like bell hooks and Johnnetta B. Cole, and young feminists like Nikki Stewart, a girls' rights advocate in Washington, D.C., and Aishah Simmons, who is currently putting together a documentary on rape within the Black community. I do not always agree with these women, but I also know that if I do not struggle, hard and constantly, backsliding is likely. This is made worse by the fact that out-side of a handful of male friends, there are no young men I know whom I can speak with regarding sexism as easily as I do with women.

The fact is, there was a blueprint handed to us in childhood telling us this is the way a man should behave, and we unwittingly followed the script verbatim. There was no blueprint handed to us about how to begin to wind ourselves out of sexism as an adult, but maybe there should have been. Every day I struggle within myself not to use the language of gender oppression, to see the sexism inherent in every aspect of America, to challenge all injustices, not just those that are convenient for me. I am ashamed of my ridiculously sexist life, of raising my hand to my girlfriend, and of two other ugly and hateful moments in college, one where I hit a female student in the head with a stapler during the course of an argument, and the other where I got into a punch-throwing exchange with a female student I had sexed then discarded like an old pair of shoes. I am also ashamed of all the lies and manipulations, the verbal abuse and reckless disregard for the views and lives of women. But with that shame has come a consciousness and, as the activists said during the Civil Rights Movement, this consciousness, this knowing, is a river of no return. I have finally learned how to swim. I have finally learned how to push forward. I may become tired, I may lose my breath, I may hit a rock from time to time and become cynical, but I am not going to drown this time around.

PART SEVEN

Male Sexualities

How do many men learn to desire women? What are men thinking about when they are sexual with women? Are gay men more sexually promiscuous than straight men? Are gay men more obsessed with demonstrating their masculinity than straight men, or are they likely to be more "effeminate"? Recent research indicates that there are no simple answers to these questions. It is increasingly clear, however, that men's sexuality, whether homosexual, bisexual, or heterosexual, is perceived as an experience of their gender.

Since there is no anticipatory socialization for homosexuality and bisexuality, future straight and gay men receive the same socialization as boys.

As a result, sexuality as a gender enactment is often a similar internal experience for all men. Early socialization teaches us—through masturbation, locker-room conversations, sex-ed classes and conversations with parents, and the tidbits that boys will pick up from various media—that sex is private, pleasurable, guilt provoking, exciting, and phallocentric, and that orgasm is the goal toward which sexual experience is oriented.

The articles in this section explore how male sexualities express the issues of masculinity. Michael Messner describes how he "became" 100 percent straight, and M. Rochlin's questionnaire humorously challenges us to question the normative elements of heterosexuality. Julia O'Connell Davidson and Jacqueline Sanchez Taylor examine the recent phenomenon of sex tourism and raise important questions about masculinity on the one hand and global sex trafficking, globalization, and consumer culture on the other. Verta Taylor and Leila Rupp, explore the social and sexual dynamics of drag queens, and Meika Loe examines the use of technologies and drugs to "fix" male sexuality.

Image courtesy of THINK AGAIN 2006, www.agitart.org

Michael A. Messner

Becoming 100 Percent Straight

In 1995, as part of my job as the President of the North American Society for the Sociology of Sport, I needed to prepare an hour-long presidential address for the annual meeting of some 200 people. This presented a challenge to me: how might I say something to my colleagues that was interesting, at least somewhat original, and, above all, not boring. Students may think that their professors are especially dull in the classroom but, believe me, we are usually much worse at professional meetings. For some reason, many of us who are able to speak to our classroom students in a relaxed manner, using relatively jargon-free language, seem to become robots, dryly reading our papers—packed with impressively unclear jargon—to our yawning colleagues.

Since I desperately wanted to avoid putting 200 sport studies scholars to sleep, I decided to deliver a talk which I entitled "Studying up on sex." The title, which certainly did get my colleagues' attention, was intended as a play on words, a double entendre. "Studying up" has one generally recognizable colloquial meaning, but in sociology it has another. It refers to studying "up" in the power structure. Sociologists have perhaps most often studied "down"—studying the poor, the blue- or pink-collar workers, the "nuts, sluts and perverts," the incarcerated. The idea of "studying up" rarely occurs to sociologists unless and until we live in a time when those who are "down" have organized movements that challenge the institutional privileges of elites. For example, in the wake of labor movements, some

sociologists like C. Wright Mills studied up on corporate elites. Recently, in the wake of racial and ethnic civil rights movements, some scholars like Ruth Frankenberg have begun to study the social meanings of "whiteness." Much of my research, inspired by feminism, has involved a studying up on the social construction of masculinity in sport. Studying up, in these cases, has raised some fascinating new and important questions about the workings of power in society.

However, I realized that when it comes to understanding the social and interpersonal dynamics of sexual orientation in sport we have barely begun to scratch the surface of a very complex issue. Although sport studies have benefited from the work of scholars such as Helen Lenskyj (1986, 1997), Brian Pronger (1990), and others who have delineated the experiences of lesbians and gay men in sports, there has been very little extension of their insights into a consideration of the social construction of heterosexuality in sport. In sport, just as in the larger society, we seem obsessed with asking "how do people become gay?" Imbedded in this question is the assumption that people who identify as heterosexual, or "straight," require no explanation, since they are simply acting out the "natural" or "normal" sexual orientation. We seem to be saying that the "sexual deviants" require explanation, while the experience of heterosexuals, because we are considered normal, seems to require no critical examination or discussion. But I knew that a closer look at the development of sexual orientation or sexual identity reveals an extremely complex process. I decided to challenge myself and my colleagues by arguing that although we have begun to "study up" on corporate elites in sport, on whiteness, on

361

masculinity, it is now time to extend that by studying up on heterosexuality.

But in the absence of systematic research on this topic, where could I start? How could I explore, raise questions about, and begin to illuminate the social construction of heterosexuality for my colleagues? Fortunately, for the previous two years I had been working with a group of five men (three of whom identified as heterosexual, two as gay) mutually to explore our own biographies in terms of the earlier bodily experiences that helped to shape our gender and sexual identities. We modeled our project after that of a German group of feminist women, led by Frigga Haug, who created a research method which they call "memory work." In short, the women would mutually choose a body part, such as "hair," and each would then write a short story based on a particularly salient childhood memory that related to their hair (for example, being forced by parents to cut one's hair, deciding to straighten one's curly hair in order to look more like other girls, etc.). Then the group would read all of the stories and discuss them one by one in the hope of gaining a more general understanding of, and raising new questions about, the social construction of "femininity." What resulted from this project was a fascinating book called *Female Sexualization* (Haug 1987), which my men's group used as the inspiration for our project.

As a research method, memory work is anything but conventional. Many sociologists would argue that this is not really a "research method" at all. The information that emerges from the project cannot be used very confidently as a generalizable "truth," and in this sort of project the researcher is simultaneously part of what is being studied. How, my more scientifically oriented colleagues might ask, is the researcher to maintain his or her objectivity? My answer is that in this kind of project objectivity is not the point. In fact, the strength of this sort of research is the depth of understanding that might be gained through a systematic group analysis of one's experience, one's subjective orientation to social processes. A clear understanding of the subjective

aspect of social life—one's bodily feelings, emotions, and reactions to others—is an invaluable window that allows us to see and ask new sociological questions about group interaction and social structure. In short, group memory work can provide an important, productive, and fascinating insight on social reality, though not a complete (or completely reliable) picture.

As I pondered the lack of existing research on the social construction of heterosexuality in sport, I decided to draw on one of my own stories from my memory work in the men's group. Some of my most salient memories of embodiment are sports memories. I grew up as the son of a high school coach, and I eventually played point guard on my dad's team. In what follows, I juxtapose my story with that of a gay former Olympic athlete, Tom Waddell, whom I had interviewed several years earlier for a book on the lives of male athletes (Messner and Sabo 1994).

Many years ago I read some psychological studies that argued that even for self-identified heterosexuals it is a natural part of their development to have gone through "bisexual" or even "homosexual" stages of life. When I read this, it seemed theoretically reasonable, but did not ring true in my experience. I have always been, I told myself, 100 percent heterosexual! The group process of analyzing my own autobiographical stories challenged the concept I had developed of myself, and also shed light on the way in which the institutional context of sport provided a context for the development of my definition of myself as "100 percent straight." Here is one of the stories:

> When I was in the 9th grade, I played on a "D" basketball team, set up especially for the smallest of high school boys. Indeed, though I was pudgy with baby fat, I was a short 5'2", still prepubescent with no facial hair and a high voice that I artificially tried to lower. The first day of practice, I was immediately attracted to a boy I'll call Timmy, because he looked like the boy who played in the *Lassie* TV show. Timmy was short, with a high voice, like me. And like me, he had no facial hair yet. Unlike me, he was very skinny. I liked Timmy right away, and soon we

were together a lot. I noticed things about him that I didn't notice about other boys: he said some words a certain way, and it gave me pleasure to try to talk like him. I remember liking the way the light hit his boyish, nearly hairless body. I thought about him when we weren't together. He was in the school band, and at the football games, I'd squint to see where he was in the mass of uniforms. In short, though I wasn't conscious of it at the time, I was infatuated with Timmy—I had a crush on him. Later that basketball season, I decided—for no reason that I could really articulate then—that I hated Timmy. I aggressively rejected him, began to make fun of him around other boys. He was, we all agreed, a geek. He was a faggot.

Three years later, Timmy and I were both on the varsity basketball team, but had hardly spoken a word to each other since we were freshman. Both of us now had lower voices, had grown to around six feet tall, and we both shaved, at least a bit. But Timmy was a skinny, somewhat stigmatized reserve on the team, while I was the team captain and starting point guard. But I wasn't so happy or secure about this. I'd always dreamed of dominating games, of being the hero. Halfway through my senior season, however, it became clear that I was not a star, and I figured I knew why. I was not aggressive enough.

I had always liked the beauty of the fast break, the perfectly executed pick and roll play between two players, and especially the long twenty-foot shot that touched nothing but the bottom of the net. But I hated and feared the sometimes brutal contact under the basket. In fact, I stayed away from the rough fights for rebounds and was mostly a perimeter player, relying on my long shots or my passes to more aggressive teammates under the basket. But now it became apparent to me that time was running out in my quest for greatness: I needed to change my game, and fast. I decided one day before practice that I was gonna get aggressive. While practicing one of our standard plays, I passed the ball to a teammate, and then ran to the spot at which I was to set a pick on a defender. I knew that one could sometimes get away with setting a face-up screen on a player, and then as he makes contact

with you, roll your back to him and plant your elbow hard in his stomach. The beauty of this move is that your own body "roll" makes the elbow look like an accident. So I decided to try this move. I approached the defensive player, Timmy, rolled, and planted my elbow deeply into his solar plexus. Air exploded audibly from Timmy's mouth, and he crumbled to the floor momentarily.

Play went on as though nothing has happened, but I felt bad about it. Rather than making me feel better, it made me feel guilty and weak. I had to admit to myself why I'd chosen Timmy as the target against whom to test out my new aggression. He was the skinniest and weakest player on the team.

At the time, I hardly thought about these incidents, other than to try to brush them off as incidents that made me feel extremely uncomfortable. Years later, I can now interrogate this as a sexual story, and as a gender story unfolding within the context of the heterosexualized and masculinized institution of sport. Examining my story in light of research conducted by Alfred Kinsey a half-century ago, I can recognize in myself what Kinsey saw as a very common fluidity and changeability of sexual desire over the life course. Put simply, Kinsey found that large numbers of adult, "heterosexual" men had previously, as adolescents and young adults, experienced sexual desire for males. A surprisingly large number of these men had experienced sexual contact to the point of orgasm with other males during adolescence or early adulthood. Similarly, my story invited me to consider what is commonly called the "Freudian theory of bisexuality." Sigmund Freud shocked the post-Victorian world by suggesting that all people go through a stage, early in life, when they are attracted to people of the same sex.[1] Adult experiences, Freud argued, eventually led most people to shift their sexual desire to what he called an appropriate "love object"—a person of the opposite sex. I also considered my experience in light of what lesbian feminist author Adrienne Rich called the institution of compulsory heterosexuality. Perhaps the extremely high levels of homophobia that are often endemic in boys' and men's organized sports led me to deny and repress my own homoerotic desire through a direct and overt rejection of Timmy, through homophobic banter with male peers, and the resultant stigmatization of the feminized Timmy. Eventually I considered my experience in the light of what radical theorist Herbert Marcuse called the sublimation of homoerotic desire into an aggressive, violent act as serving to construct a clear line of demarcation between self and other. Sublimation, according to Marcuse, involved the driving underground, into the unconscious, of sexual desires that might appear dangerous due to their socially stigmatized status. But sublimation involves more than simple repression into the unconscious. It involves a transformation of sexual desire into something else—often into aggressive and violent acting out toward others. These acts clarify the boundaries between oneself and others and therefore lessen any anxieties that might be attached to the repressed homoerotic desire.

Importantly, in our analysis of my story, the memory group went beyond simply discussing the events in psychological terms. The story did perhaps suggest some deep psychological processes at work, but it also revealed the importance of social context—in this case, the context of the athletic team. In short, my rejection of Timmy and the joining with teammates to stigmatize him in ninth grade stands as an example of what sociologist R. W. Connell calls a moment of engagement with hegemonic masculinity, where I actively took up the male group's task of constructing heterosexual/masculine identities in the context of sport. The elbow in Timmy's gut three years later can be seen as a punctuation mark that occurred precisely because of my fears that I might be failing in this goal.

It is helpful, I think, to compare my story with gay and lesbian "coming out" stories in sport. Though we have a few lesbian and bisexual coming out stories among women athletes, there are very few from gay males. Tom Waddell, who as a closeted gay man finished sixth in the decathlon in the 1968 Olympics, later came out and started the Gay Games, an athletic and cultural festival that draws tens of thousands of people every four years. When I interviewed Tom Waddell over a decade ago about his sexual identity and athletic career, he made it quite clear that for many years sports was his closet:

> When I was a kid, I was tall for my age, and was very thin and very strong. And I was usually faster than most other people. But I discovered rather early that I liked gymnastics and I liked dance. I was very interested in being a ballet dancer . . . [but] something became obvious to me right away—that male ballet dancers were effeminate, that they were what most people would call faggots. And I thought I just couldn't handle that . . . I was totally closeted and very concerned about being male. This was the fifties, a terrible time to live, and everything was stacked against me. Anyway, I realized that I had to do something to protect my image of myself as a male—because at that time homosexuals were thought of primarily as men who wanted to be women. And so I threw myself into athletics—I played football, gymnastics, track and field . . . I was a jock—that's how I was viewed, and I was comfortable with that.

Tom Waddell was fully conscious of entering sports and constructing a masculine/heterosexual athletic identity precisely because he feared being revealed as gay. It was clear to him, in the context of the 1950s, that being known as gay would undercut his claims to the status of manhood. Thus, though he described the athletic closet as "hot and stifling," he remained there until several years after his athletic retirement. He even knowingly played along with locker room discussions about sex and women as part of his "cover."

> I wanted to be viewed as male, otherwise I would be a dancer today. I wanted the male, macho image of an athlete. So I was protected by a very hard shell. I was clearly aware of what I was doing . . . I often felt compelled to go along with a lot of locker room garbage because I wanted that image—and I know a lot of others who did too.

Like my story, Waddell's points to the importance of the athletic institution as a context in which peers mutually construct and reconstruct narrow definitions of masculinity. Heterosexuality is considered to be a rock-solid foundation of this concept of masculinity. But unlike my story, Waddell's may invoke a dramaturgical analysis.[2] He seemed to be consciously "acting" to control and regulate others' perceptions of him by constructing a public "front stage" persona that differed radically from what he believed to be his "true" inner self. My story, in contrast, suggests a deeper, less consciously strategic repression of my homoerotic attraction. Most likely, I was aware on some level of the dangers of such feelings, and was escaping the risks, disgrace, and rejection that would likely result from being different. For Waddell, the decision to construct his identity largely within sport was to step into a fiercely heterosexual/masculine closet that would hide what he saw as his "true" identity. In contrast, I was not so much stepping into a "closet" that would hide my identity; rather, I was stepping out into an entire world of heterosexual privilege. My story also suggests how a threat to the promised privileges of hegemonic masculinity—my failure as an athlete—might trigger a momentary sexual panic that can lay bare the constructedness, indeed, the instability of the heterosexual/masculine identity.

In either case, Waddell's or mine, we can see how, as young male athletes, heterosexual masculinity was not something we "were," but something we were doing. It is significant, I think, that although each of us was "doing heterosexuality," neither of us was actually "having sex" with women (though one of us desperately wanted to). This underscores a point made by some recent theorists that heterosexuality should not be thought of simply as sexual acts between women and men. Rather, heterosexuality is a constructed identity, a performance, and an institution that is not necessarily linked to sexual acts. Though for one of us it was more conscious than for the other, we were both "doing heterosexuality" as an ongoing practice through which we sought to do two things:

- avoid stigma, embarrassment, ostracism, or perhaps worse if we were even suspected of being gay;
- link ourselves into systems of power, status, and privilege that appear to be the birthright of "real men" (i.e., males who are able to compete successfully with other males in sport, work, and sexual relations with women).

In other words, each of us actively scripted our own sexual and gender performances, but these scripts were constructed within the constraints of a socially organized (institutionalized) system of power and pleasure.

Questions for Future Research

As I prepared to tell this sexual story publicly to my colleagues at the sport studies conference, I felt extremely nervous. Part of the nervousness was due to the fact that I knew some of them would object to my claim that telling personal stories can be a source of sociological insights. But a larger part of the reason for my nervousness was due to the fact that I was revealing something very personal about my sexuality in such a public way. Most of us are not accustomed to doing this, especially in the context of a professional conference. But I had learned long ago, especially from feminist women scholars, and from gay and lesbian scholars, that biography is linked to history. Part of "normal" academic discourse has been to hide "the personal" (including the fact that the researchers are themselves people with values, feelings, and yes, biases) behind a carefully constructed facade of "objectivity." Rather than trying to hide or be ashamed of one's subjective experience of the world, I was challenging myself to draw on my experience of the world as a resource. Not that I should trust my experience as the final word on "reality." White, heterosexual males like me have made the mistake for centuries of calling their own experience "objectivity," and then punishing anyone who does not share their worldview by casting them as "deviant." Instead, I hope to use my experience as an example of how those of us who are in dominant sexual/racial/gender/class categories can get a new perspective on the "constructedness" of our identities by juxtaposing our subjective experiences against the recently emerging worldviews of gay men and lesbians, women, and people of color.

Finally, I want to stress that in juxtaposition neither my own nor Tom Waddell's story sheds much light on the question of why some individuals "become gay" while others "become" heterosexual or bisexual. Instead, I should like to suggest that this is a dead-end question, and that there are far more important and interesting questions to be asked:

- How has heterosexuality, as an institution and as an enforced group practice, constrained and limited all of us—gay, straight, and bi?
- How has the institution of sport been an especially salient institution for the social construction of heterosexual masculinity?
- Why is it that when men play sports they are almost always automatically granted masculine status, and thus assumed to be heterosexual, while when women play sports, questions are raised about their "femininity" and sexual orientation?

These kinds of questions aim us toward an analysis of the working of power within institutions—including the ways that these workings of power shape and constrain our identities and relationships—and point us toward imagining alternative social arrangements that are less constraining for everyone.

Notes

1. The fluidity and changeability of sexual desire over the life course is now more obvious in evidence from prison and military populations, and single-sex boarding schools. The theory of bisexuality is evident, for example, in childhood crushes on same-sex primary schoolteachers.

2. Dramaturgical analysis, associated with Erving Goffman, uses the theater and performance to develop an analogy with everyday life.

References

Haug, Frigga (1987) *Female Sexualization: A Collective Work of Memory*, London: Verso.

Lenskyj, Helen (1986) *Out of Bounds: Women, Sport and Sexuality*, Toronto: Women's Press.

———. (1997) "No fear? Lesbians in sport and physical education," *Women in Sport and Physical Activity Journal* 6(2): 7–22.

Messner, Michael A. (1992) *Power at Play: Sports and the Problem of Masculinity*, Boston: Beacon Press.

———. (1994) "Gay athletes and the Gay Games: An interview with Tom Waddell," in M. A. Messner and D. F. Sabo (eds), *Sex, Violence and Power in Sports: Rethinking Masculinity*, Freedom, CA: The Crossing Press, pp. 113–119.

Pronger, Brian (1990) *The Arena of Masculinity: Sports, Homosexuality, and the Meaning of Sex*, New York: St. Martin's Press.

M. Rochlin

The Heterosexual Questionnaire

1. What do you think caused your heterosexuality?

2. When and how did you decide you were a heterosexual?

3. Is it possible that your heterosexuality is just a phase you may grow out of?

4. Is it possible that your heterosexuality stems from a neurotic fear of others of the same sex?

5. If you have never slept with a person of the same sex, is it possible that all you need is a good gay lover?

6. Do your parents know that you are straight? Do your friends and/or roommate(s) know? How did they react?

7. Why do you insist on flaunting your heterosexuality? Can't you just be who you are and keep it quiet?

8. Why do heterosexuals place so much emphasis on sex?

9. Why do heterosexuals feel compelled to seduce others into their lifestyle?

10. A disproportionate majority of child molesters are heterosexual. Do you consider it safe to expose children to heterosexual teachers?

11. Just what do men and women *do* in bed together? How can they truly know how to please each other, being so anatomically different?

12. With all the societal support marriage receives, the divorce rate is spiraling. Why are there so few stable relationships among heterosexuals?

13. Statistics show that lesbians have the lowest incidence of sexually transmitted diseases. Is it really safe for a woman to maintain a heterosexual lifestyle and run the risk of disease and pregnancy?

14. How can you become a whole person if you limit yourself to compulsive, exclusive heterosexuality?

15. Considering the menace of overpopulation, how could the human race survive if everyone were heterosexual?

16. Could you trust a heterosexual therapist to be objective? Don't you feel s/he might be inclined to influence you in the direction of her/his own leanings?

17. There seem to be very few happy heterosexuals. Techniques have been developed that might enable you to change if you really want to. Have you considered trying aversion therapy?

18. Would you want your child to be heterosexual, knowing the problems that s/he would face?

Julia O'Connell Davidson

Jacqueline Sanchez Taylor

Fantasy Islands:
Exploring the Demand for Sex Tourism

In a useful review of prostitution cross-culturally and historically, Laurie Shrage observes that "one thing that stands out but stands unexplained is that a large percentage of sex customers seek (or sought) sex workers whose racial, national, or class identities are (or were) different from their own" (Shrage 1994: 142). She goes on to suggest that the demand for African, Asian, and Latin American prostitutes by white Western men may "be explained in part by culturally produced racial fantasies regarding the sexuality of these women" and that these fantasies may be related to "socially formed perceptions regarding the sexual and moral purity of white women" (ibid: 48–50). Kempadoo also draws attention to the "over-representation of women of different nationalities and ethnicities, and the hierarchies of race and color within the [international sex] trade" and observes, "That sex industries today depend upon the eroticization of the ethnic and cultural Others suggest we are witnessing a contemporary form of exoticism which sustains postcolonial and post-cold war relations of power and dominance" (Kempadoo 1995: 75–76).

This chapter represents an attempt to build on such insights. Drawing on our research with both male and female Western heterosexual sex tourists in the Caribbean,[1] it argues that their sexual taste for "Others" reflects not so much a wish

From *Sun, Sex and Gold: Tourism and Sex Work in the Caribbean,* K. Kempadoo, ed. Lanham, MD: Rowan and Littlefield, 1999. © Rowan & Littlefield, reprinted by permission.

to engage in any specific sexual practice as a desire for an extraordinarily high degree of control over the management of self and others as sexual, racialized, and engendered beings. This desire, and the Western sex tourist's power to satiate it, can only be explained through reference to power relations and popular discourses that are simultaneously gendered, racialized, and economic.

White Western Men's Sex Tourism

Empirical research on sex tourism to Southeast Asia has fairly consistently produced a portrait of Western male heterosexual sex tourists as men whose desire for the Other is the flip side of dissatisfaction with white Western women, including white Western prostitute women. Lee, for example, explores the demand for sex tourism as a quest for racially fantasized male power, arguing that this is at least in part a backlash against the women's movement in the West: "With an increasingly active global feminist movement, male-controlled sexuality (or female passivity) appears to be an increasingly scarce resource. The travel advertisements are quite explicit about what is for sale: docility and submission" (Lee 1991: 90; see also Jeffreys 1997). Western sex tourists' fantasies of "docile" and "willing" Asian women are accompanied, as Kruhse-Mount Burton (1995: 196) notes, by "a desexualization of white women . . . who are deemed to be spoiled, grasping and, above all, unwilling or inferior sexual partners." These characteristics are also attributed to white prostitute women. The sex tourists interviewed by Seabrook (1997: 3) compared Thai prostitutes "very favorably with the more mechanistic and functional behavior of most Western sex workers." Kruhse-Mount Burton states that where many impose their own boundaries on the degree of physical intimacy implied by the prostitution contract (for example refusing to kiss clients on the mouth or to engage in unprotected penetrative and/or oral sex) and are also in a position to turn down clients' requests to spend the night or a few days with them is likewise experienced as a threat to, or denial of, traditional male identity.

Though we recognize that sex tourism provides Western men with opportunities "to reaffirm, if only temporarily, the idealized version of masculine identity and mode of being," and that in this sense sex tourism provides men with opportunities to manage and control both themselves and others as engendered beings, we want to argue that there is more to the demand for sex tourism than this (ibid: 202). In the remainder of this chapter we therefore interrogate sex tourists' attitudes toward prostitute use, sexuality, gender, and "race" more closely, and further complicate matters by considering white Western women's and black Western men and women's sex tourism to the Caribbean.

Western Sexuality and Prostitute Use

Hartsock observes that there is "a surprising degree of consensus that hostility and domination, as opposed to intimacy and physical pleasure" are central to the social and historical construction of sexuality in the West (Hartsock 1985: 157). Writers in the psychoanalytic tradition suggest that the kind of hostility that is threaded through Western sexual expression reflects an infantile rage and wish for revenge against the separateness of those upon whom we depend. It is, as Stoller puts it, "a state in which one wishes to harm an object," and the harm wished upon objects of sexual desire expresses a craving to strip them of their autonomy, control, and separateness—that is, to dehumanize them, since a dehumanized sexual object does not

have the power to reject, humiliate, or control (Stoller 1986: 4).

The "love object" can be divested of autonomy and objectified in any number of ways, but clearly the prostitute woman, who is in most cultures imagined and socially constructed as an "unnatural" sexual and social Other (a status which is often enshrined in law), provides a conveniently ready dehumanized sexual object for the client. The commercial nature of the prostitute–client exchange further promises to strip all mutuality and dependency from sexual relations. Because all obligations are discharged through the simple act of payment, there can be no real intimacy and so no terrifying specter of rejection or engulfment by another human being. In theory, then, prostitute use offers a very neat vehicle for the expression of sexual hostility and the attainment of control over self and others as sexual beings. Yet for many prostitute users, there is a fly in the ointment:

> Prostitute women may be socially constructed as Others and *fantasized* as nothing more than objectified sexuality, but in reality, of course, they are human beings. It is only if the prostitute is imagined as stripped of everything bar her sexuality that she can be *completely* controlled by the client's money/powers. But if she were dehumanized to this extent, she would cease to exist as a person. . . . Most clients appear to pursue a contradiction, namely to control as an object that which cannot be objectified. (O'Connell Davidson 1998: 161)

This contradiction is at the root of the complaints clients sometimes voice about Western prostitutes (Graaf et al. 1992: Plumridge and Chetwynd 1997). It is not always enough to buy access to touch and sexually use objectified body parts. Many clients want the prostitute to be a "lover" who makes no claims, a "whore" who has sex for pleasure not money, in short, a person (subject) who can be treated as an object. This reflects, perhaps, deeper inconsistencies in the discourses which surround prostitution and sexuality. The prostitute woman is viewed as acting in a way wholly inconsistent with her gender identity. Her perceived sexual agency degenders her (a woman who takes an impersonal, active, and instrumental approach to sex is not a "real" woman) and dishonors her (she trades in something which is constitutive of her personhood and cannot honorably be sold). The prostitute-using man, by contrast, behaves "in a fashion consistent with the attributes associated with his gender (he is active and sexually predatory, impersonal, and instrumental), and his sexual transgression is thus a minor infraction, since it does not compromise his gender identity" (O'Connell Davidson 1998: 127). A paradox thus emerges:

> The more that men's prostitute use is justified and socially sanctioned through reference to the fiction of biologically determined gender roles and sexuality, the greater the contradiction implicit in prostitution. In order to satisfy their "natural" urges, men must make use of "unnatural" women. (ibid: 128)

All of this helps to explain the fact that, even though their sexual interests may be powerfully shaped by a cultural emphasis on hostility and domination, prostitute use holds absolutely no appeal for many Western men.[2] Fantasies of unbridled sexual access to willingly objectified women are not necessarily fantasies of access to prostitute women. Meanwhile, those who do use prostitutes in the West imagine and manage their own prostitute use in a variety of different ways (see O'Connell Davidson 1998). At one extreme are men who are actually quite satisfied with brief and anonymous sexual use of women and teenagers who they imagine as utterly debased and objectified "dirty whores." (For them, the idea of using a prostitute is erotic in and of itself.) At the other extreme are those who regularly visit the same prostitute woman and construct a fiction of romance or friendship around their use of her, a fiction which helps them to imagine themselves as seen, chosen, and desired, even as they pay for sex as a commodity. Between these two poles are men who indulge in a range of (often very inventive) practices and fantasies designed to create the illusion of balance between sexual hostility and sexual mutuality that they personally find sexually

exciting. How does this relate to the demand for sex tourism?

Let us begin by noting that not all Western male sex tourists subjectively perceive their own sexual practices abroad as a form of prostitute use. This reflects the fact that even within any one country affected by sex tourism, prostitution is not a homogeneous phenomenon in terms of its social organization. In some countries sex tourism has involved the maintenance and development of existing large-scale, highly commoditized sex industries serving foreign military personnel (Truong 1990; Sturdevant and Stoltzfus 1992; Hall 1994). But it has also emerged in locations where no such sex industry existed, for instance, in Gambia, Cuba, and Brazil (Morris-Jarra 1996; Perio and Thierry 1996; Sanchez Taylor 1997). Moreover, even in countries like Thailand and the Philippines, where tourist-related prostitution has been grafted onto an existing, formally organized brothel sector serving military demand, tourist development has *also* been associated with the emergence of an informal prostitution sector (in which prostitutes solicit in hotels, discos, bars, beaches, parks, or streets, often entering into fairly protracted and diffuse transactions with clients).

This in itself gives prostitution in sex tourist resorts a rather different character to that of prostitution in red-light districts in affluent, Western countries. The sense of difference is enhanced by the fact that, in many places, informally arranged prostitution spills over into apparently noncommercial encounters within which tourists who do not self-identify as prostitute users can draw local/migrant persons who do not self-identify as prostitutes into profoundly unequal and exploitative sexual relationships. It also means that sex tourism presents a diverse array of opportunities for sexual gratification, not all of which involve straightforward cash for sex exchanges in brothels or go-go clubs or on the streets, and so provides the sex tourist with a veritable "pic 'n' mix" of ways in which to manage himself as a sexual and engendered being. He can indulge in overt forms of sexual hostility (such as selecting a numbered brothel prostitute from those on display in a bar or brothel for "short time" or buying a cheap, speedy sexual service from one of many street prostitutes), or he can indulge in fantasies of mutuality, picking up a woman/teenager in an ordinary tourist disco, wining and dining and generally simulating romance with her for a day or two and completely denying the commercial basis of the sexual interaction. Or, and many sex tourists do exactly this, he can combine both approaches.

Now it could be argued that, given the fact that Western men are socialized into a view of male sexuality as a powerful, biologically based need for sexual "outlets," the existence of multiple, cheap, and varied sexual opportunities is, in itself, enough to attract large numbers of men to a given holiday resort. However, it is important to recognize the numerous other forms of highly sexualized tourism that could satisfy a wish to indulge in various sexual fantasies and also a desire for control over the self as a sexual and engendered being. Sex tourists could, for example, choose to take part in organized holidays designed to facilitate sexual and romantic encounters between tourists (such as Club 18–30 and other singles holidays), or they could choose to take all-inclusive holidays to resorts such as Hedonism or destinations renowned for promiscuous tourist–tourist sex, such as Ibiza or Cap d'Azur. These latter offer just as many opportunities for anonymous and impersonal sex in a party atmosphere as well as for intense but ultimately brief and noncommitted sexual romances. What they do not offer is the control that comes from paying for sex or the opportunity to indulge in racialized sexual fantasies, which helps to explain why sex tourists reject them in favor of sexual experience in what they term "Third World" countries. This brings us to questions about the relationship between the construction of "Otherness" and sex tourism.

"Otherness" and Western Men's Sex Tourism

For obvious reasons, sex tourists spend their time in resorts and *barrios* where tourist-related prostitution is widespread. Thus they constantly encounter what appear to them as hedonistic scenes—local "girls" and young men dancing "sensuously," draping themselves over and being fondled by Western tourists, drinking and joking with each other, and so on. Instead of seeing the relationship between these scenes and their own presence in the resort, sex tourists tend to interpret all this as empirical vindication of Western assumptions of "non-Western peoples living in idyllic pleasure, splendid innocence or Paradise-like conditions—as purely sensual, natural, simple and uncorrupted beings" (Kempadoo 1995: 76). Western sex tourists (and this is true of black as well as white informants) say that sex is more "natural" in Third World countries, that prostitution is not really prostitution but a "way of life," that "They" are "at it" all of the time.

This explains how men who are not and would not dream of becoming prostitute users back home can happily practice sex tourism (the "girls" are not really like prostitutes and so they themselves are not really like clients, the prostitution contract is not like the Western prostitution contract and so does not really count as prostitution). It also explains the paranoid obsession with being cheated exhibited by some sex tourists, who comment on their belief that women in certain sex tourist resorts or particular brothels or bars are "getting too commercial" and advise each other how to avoid being "duped" and "exploited" by a "real professional," where to find "brand new girls," and so on (see O'Connell Davidson 1995; Bishop and Robinson 1998).

It also points to the complex interrelations between discourses of gender, "race," and sexuality. To begin with, the supposed naturalness of prostitution in the Third World actually reassures the Western male sex tourist of his racial or cultural superiority. Thus we find that sex tourists continue a traditional Western discourse of travel which rests on the imagined opposition between the "civilized" West and the "barbarous" Other (Grewal 1996: 136; Kempadoo 1996: 76; see also Brace and O'Connell Davidson 1996). In "civilized" countries only "bad" women become

prostitutes (they refuse the constraints civilization places upon "good" women in favor of earning "easy money"), but in the Third World (a
corrupt and lawless place where people exist in a
state of nature), "nice girls" may be driven to prostitution in order to survive ("they have to do it because they've all got kids" or "they're doing it for
their families"). In the West, "nice girls" are protected and supported by their menfolk, but in the
Third World, "uncivilized" Other men allow (or
even demand that) their womenfolk enter prostitution. In interviews, Western male sex tourists
contrast their own generosity, humanity, and
chivalry against the "failings" of local men, who
are imagined as feckless, faithless, wife-beaters,
and pimps. Even as prostitute users, Other men
are fantasized as inferior moral beings who cheat
and mistreat the "girls."

In this we see that sex tourism is not only
about sustaining a male identity. For white men it
is also about sustaining a *white* identity. Thus, sex
tourism can also be understood as a collective behavior oriented toward the restoration of a gener-
alized belief about what it is to be white: to be truly
white is to be served, revered, and envied by Others. For the black American male sex tourists we
have interviewed, sex tourism appears to affirm a
sense of Western-ness and so of inclusion in a
privileged world. Take, for example, the following
three statements from a 45-year-old black American sex tourist. He is a New York bus driver and
ex-vice cop, a paid-up member of an American-
owned sex tourist club, Travel & the Single Male,
and he has used prostitutes in Thailand, Brazil,
Costa Rica, and the Dominican Republic:

> There's two sides to the countries that I go to.
> There's the tourist side and then there's the real
> people, and I make a habit of going to the real
> people, I see how the real people live, and when
> I see something like that . . . I tend to look at the
> little bit I've got at home and I appreciate it. . . .
>
> I've always been proud to be an American. . . .
> I always tip in US dollars when I arrive. I always
> keep dollars and pesos, because people tend to
> think differently about pesos and dollars. . . .

> They always say at hotels they don't want you
> to bring the girls in; believe me, that's crap, be-
> cause you know what I do? Reach in my pocket
> and I go anywhere I want.

Meanwhile, sexualized racisms help the sex
tourist to attain a sense of control over himself and
Others as engendered and racialized sexual beings. Here it is important to recognize the subtle
(or not so subtle) variations of racism employed
by white Western men. The sex tourists we have
interviewed in the Caribbean are not a homogeneous group in terms of their "race" politics, and
this reflects differences of national identity, age,
socioeconomic background, and racialized identity. One clearly identifiable subgroup is comprised of white North American men aged forty
and above, who, though perhaps not actually affiliated with the Klan, espouse a white supremacist worldview and consider black people their
biological, social, and cultural inferiors. They use
the word "nigger" and consider any challenge to
their "right" to use this term as "political correctness." As one sex tourist complained, in the
States. "You can't use the N word, nigger. Always
when I was raised up, the only thing was the F
word, you can't use the F word. Now you can't
say cunt, you can't say nigger."

For men like this, black women are imagined
as the embodiment of all that is low and debased,
they are "inherently degraded, and thus the appropriate partners for degrading sex" (Shrage
1994: 158). As unambiguous whores by virtue of
their racialized identity, they may be briefly and
anonymously used, but they are not sought out for
longer term or quasi-romantic commercial sexual
relationships. Thus, the sex tourist quoted above
told us that when he and his cronies (all regular sex
tourists to the Dominican Republic) see another
American sex tourist "hanging round" with a local
girl or woman who has the phenotypical characteristics they associate with African-ness, they call
out to him, "How many bananas did it take to get
her down out of the tree?" and generally deride
him for transgressing a racialized sexual boundary
which should not, in their view, be openly crossed.

The Dominican females that men like this want sexual access to are light skinned and straight haired (this is also true in Cuba and in the Latin American countries where we have undertaken fieldwork). They are not classified as "niggers" by these white racists, but instead as "LBFMs" or "Little Brown Fucking Machines," a catch-all category encompassing any female Other not deemed to be either white or "African." The militaristic and imperialist associations of this term (coined by American GIs stationed in Southeast Asia) simultaneously make it all the more offensive and hostile and all the more appealing to this type of sex tourist, many of whom have served in the armed forces (a disturbing number of whom have also been or currently are police officers in the United States) and the rest of whom are "wanna-be vets"—men who never made it to Vietnam to live out their racialized–sexualized fantasies of masculine glory.

Shrage and Kruhse-Mount Burton's comments on the relationship between fantasies of hypersexual Others and myths about white women's sexual purity are also relevant to understanding this kind of sex tourist's worldview. An extract from an article posted on an Internet site written by and for sex tourists entitled "Why No White Women?" is revealing:

Q: Is it because white women demand more (in terms of performance) from their men during Sex? and white men cannot deliver?

A: In my case, it's just that my dick is not long enough to reach up on the pedestal they like to stand on.

If whiteness is imagined as dominance, and woman is imagined as subordination, then "white woman" becomes something of a contradiction. As Young notes, "For white men, white women are both self and other: they have a floating status. They can reinforce a sense of self through common racial identity or threaten and disturb that sense through their sexual Otherness" (Young 1996: 52). White supremacists have to place white women on a pedestal (iconize them

as racially, morally, and sexually pure), since whiteness and civilization are synonymous and "civilization" is constructed as the rejection of base animalism. But keeping them on their pedestal requires men to constantly deny what they imagine to be their own needs and nature and thus white women become the object of profound resentment.

Not all Western male sex tourists to the Caribbean buy into this kind of overt, denigrating racism. In fact, many of them are far more strongly influenced by what might be termed "exoticizing" racisms. Younger white Europeans and North Americans, for example, have been exposed to such racisms through the Western film, music, and fashion industries, which retain the old-school racist emphasis on blackness as physicality but repackage and commoditize this "animalism" so that black men and women become the ultimate icons of sporting prowess, "untamed" rebelliousness, "raw" musical talent, sexual power, and so on (see hooks 1992, 1994; Young 1996). As a consequence, many young (and some not so young) white Westerners view blackness as a marker of something both "cool" and "hot."

In their own countries, however, their encounters with real live black people are not only few and far between, but also generally something of a disappointment to them. As one British sex tourist to Cuba told us, black people in Britain are "very standoffish. . . . They stick to their own, and it's a shame, because it makes divisions." What a delight it is for men like this to holiday in the Caribbean, then, where poverty combined with the exigencies of tourist development ensure that they are constantly faced by smiling, welcoming black folk. The small black boy who wants to shine their shoes; the old black woman who cleans their hotel room; the cool, young, dreadlocked black man on the beach who is working as a promoter for some restaurant or bar; the fit, young black woman soliciting in the tourist disco—all want to "befriend" the white tourist. Finally, interviews with black American male sex tourists suggest that they too sexualize and exoticize the women they sexually exploit in the Third World ("Latin women are hot," "Latin girls love sex").

Both the sexualized racism that underpins the category LBFM and the exoticizing sexualized racism espoused by other sex tourists help to construct the Other prostitute as the embodiment of a contradiction, that is, as a "whore" who does it for pleasure as much as for money, an object with a subjectivity completely attuned to their own, in short, the embodiment of a masturbatory fantasy. Time and again Western sex tourists have assured us that the local girls really are "hot for it," that Third World prostitutes enjoy their work and that their highest ambition is to be the object of a Western man's desire. Their belief that Third World prostitutes are genuinely economically desperate rather than making a free choice to prostitute for "easy money" is clearly inconsistent with their belief that Third World prostitutes are actually acting on the basis of mutual sexual desire, but it is a contradiction that appears to resolve (at least temporarily) an anxiety they have about the relationship between sex, gender, sexuality, and "race."

The vast majority of the sex tourists we have interviewed believe that gender attributes, including sexual behavior, are determined by biological sex. They say that it is natural for women to be passive and sexually receptive as well as to be homemakers, child rearers, dependent upon and subservient toward men, which is why white Western women (prostitute and nonprostitute alike) often appear to them as unsexed. Thus the sex tourist quoted at the beginning of this chapter could only explain women's presence on traditional male terrain by imagining them as sexually "unnatural" ("Most of these girls are dykes anyways"). White women's relative economic, social, and political power as well as their very whiteness makes it hard for Western male sex tourists to eroticize them as nothing more than sexual beings. Racism/ethnocentrism can collapse such tensions. If black or Latin women are naturally physical, wild, hot, and sexually powerful, there need be no anxiety about enjoying them as pure sex. Equally, racism settles the anxieties some men

have about the almost "manly" sexual power and agency attributed to white prostitutes. A Little Brown Fucking Machine is not unsexed by prostituting, she is "just doing what comes naturally." Since the Other woman is a "natural" prostitute, her prostitution does not make her any the less a "natural woman." All these points are also relevant to understanding the phenomenon of female sex tourism.

"Otherness" and Female Sex Tourism

Western women's sexual behavior abroad (both historically and contemporaneously) is often viewed in a rather different light compared to that of their male counterparts, and it is without doubt true that Western women who travel to Third World destinations in search of sex differ from many of the Western male sex tourists discussed above in terms of their attitudes toward prostitution and sexuality. Few of them are prostitute users back home, and few of them would choose to visit brothels while abroad or to pay street prostitutes for a quick "hand job" or any other sexual service (although it should be noted that some women do behave in these ways). But one of the authors' (Sanchez Taylor) ongoing interview and survey research with female sex tourists in Jamaica and the Dominican Republic suggests that there are also similarities between the sexual behavior of Western women and men in sex tourist resorts.

The Caribbean has long been a destination that offers tourist women opportunities for sexual experience, and large numbers of women from the United States, Canada, Britain, and Germany as well as smaller numbers of women from other European countries and from Japan (i.e., the same countries that send male sex tourists) engage in sexual relationships with local men while on holiday there (Karch and Dann 1981; Chevannes 1993; Pruitt and LaFont 1995). Preliminary analysis of data from Sanchez Taylor's survey of a sample of 104 single Western female tourists in Negril, Sosúa, and Boca Chica shows that almost 40 percent had entered into some form of sexual relationship with a local man.[3] The survey data further suggest that these were not chance encounters but rather that the sexually active female tourists visit the islands in order to pursue one or more sexual relationships. Only 9 percent of sexually active women were on their first trip; the rest had made numerous trips to the islands, and over 20 percent of female sex tourists reported having had two or more different local sexual partners in the course of a two- to three-week stay. Furthermore female sex tourists, as much as male sex tourists, view their sexual experiences as integral to their holiday—"When in Jamaica you have to experience everything that's on offer," one black American woman explained, while a white woman working as a tour representative for a U.S. package operator said: "I tell my single women: come down here to love them, fuck them, and leave them, and you'll have a great time here. Don't look to get married. Don't call them."

Like male sex tourists, these women differ in terms of their age, nationality, social class, and racialized identity, including among their ranks young "spice girl" teenagers and students as well as grandmothers in their sixties, working-class as well as middle-class professionals, or self-employed women. They also differ in terms of the type of sexual encounters they pursue and the way in which they interpret these encounters. Some are eager to find a man as soon as they get off the plane and enter into multiple, brief, and instrumental relationships; others want to be romanced and sweet-talked by one or perhaps two men during their holiday. Around 40 percent described their relationships with local men as "purely physical" and 40 percent described them as "holiday romances." Twenty percent said that they had found "true love." Almost all the sexually active women surveyed stated that they had "helped their partner(s) out financially" by buying them meals, drinks, gifts, or by giving cash, and yet none of them perceived these relationships as commercial sexual transactions. Asked whether they had ever been approached by a gigolo/prostitute during their stay in Jamaica, 90 percent

of them replied in the negative. The data collected in the Dominican Republic revealed similar patterns of denial.

The informal nature of the sexual transactions in these resorts blurs the boundaries of what constitutes prostitution for Western women just as it does for Western men, allowing them to believe that the meals, cash, and gifts they provide for their sexual partners do not represent a form of payment for services rendered but rather an expression of their own munificence. It is only when women repeatedly enter into a series of extremely brief sexual encounters that they begin to acknowledge that, as one put it, "It's all about money." Even this does not lead them to view themselves as prostitute users, however, and again it is notions of difference and Otherness that play a key role in protecting the sex tourist from the knowledge that they are paying for the sexual attentions they receive. As Others, local men are viewed as beings possessed of a powerful and indiscriminate sexuality that they cannot control, and this explains their eagerness for sex with tourist women, regardless of their age, size, or physical appearance. Again, the Other is not *selling* sex, just "doing what comes naturally."

As yet, the number of black female sex tourists in Sanchez Taylor's survey and interview sample is too small to base any generalizations upon,[4] but so far their attitudes are remarkably consistent with those voiced by the central character in Terry Macmillan's 1996 novel *How Stella Got Her Groove Back,* in which a black American woman finds "love and romance" with a Jamaican boy almost half her age and with certainly less than half her economic means.[5] Stella views her own behavior in a quite different light from that of white male sex tourists—she disparages an older white male tourist as "a dirty old man who probably has to pay for all the pussy he gets" (Macmillan 1996: 83). It is also interesting to note the ways in which Macmillan "Otherizes" local men: the Jamaican boy smells "primitive"; he is "exotic and goes with the island"; he is "Mr. Expresso in shorts" (ibid: 142, 154). Like white female sex tourists interviewed in the course of research, Macmillan further explains the young Jamaican man's disinterest in Jamaican women and so his sexual interest in an older American woman by Otherizing local women through the use of derogatory stereotypes. Thus, Jamaican women are assumed to be rapacious, materialistic, and sexually instrumental—they only want a man who owns a big car and house and money—and so Jamaican men long for women who do not demand these things (i.e., American women who already possess them).

Like their male counterparts, Western female sex tourists employ fantasies of Otherness not just to legitimate obtaining sexual access to the kind of young, fit, handsome bodies that would otherwise be denied to them and to obtain affirmation of their own sexual desirability (because the fact is that some female sex tourists are themselves young and fit looking and would be easily able to secure sexual access to equally appealing male bodies at home), but also to obtain a sense of power and control over themselves and others as engendered, sexual beings and to affirm their own privilege as Westerners. Thus they continually stress their belief that people in the Caribbean "are different from Westerners." Sexual life is one of the primary arenas in which this supposed difference is manifest. More than half of the female sex tourists surveyed in Jamaica stated that Jamaicans are more relaxed about teenage sex, casual sex, and prostitution than Westerners. In response to open-ended questions, they observed that "Jamaican men are more up front about sex," that "Jamaicans are uninhibited about sex," that "Jamaicans are naturally promiscuous," and that "sex is more natural to Jamaicans." In interviews, female sex tourists also reproduced the notion of an opposition between the "civilized" West and the "primitive" Third World. One Scots grandmother in her early forties described the Dominican Republic as follows: "It's just like Britain before its industrial phase, it's just behind Britain, just exactly the same. Kids used to get beat up to go up chimneys, here they get beaten up to go polish shoes. There's no difference."

Western female sex tourists' racisms, like those of male sex tourists, are also many-layered and nuanced by differences in terms of nationality, age, and racialized identity. There are older white American female sex tourists whose beliefs about "race" and attitudes toward interracial sex are based upon an ideology that is overtly white supremacist. The black male represents for them the essence of an animalistic sexuality that both fascinates and repels. While in their own country they would not want to openly enter a sexual relationship with a black man, in a holiday resort like Negril they can transgress the racialized and gendered codes that normally govern their sexual behavior, while maintaining their honor and reputation back home. As one Jamaican gigolo commented:

> While they are here they feel free. Free to do what they never do at home. No one looking at them. Get a Black guy who are unavailable at home. No one judge them. Get the man to make they feel good then they go home clean and pure.

This observation, and all the sexual hostility it implies, is born out by the following extract from an interview with a 45-year-old white American woman from Chicago, a regular sex tourist to Negril:

> [Jamaican men] are all liars and cheats. . . . [American women come up Negril because] they get what they don't get back home. A girl who no one looks twice at back home, she gets hit on all the time here, all these guys are paying her attention, telling her she's beautiful, and they really want her. . . . They're obsessed with their dicks. That's all they think of, just pussy and money and nothing else. . . . In Chicago, this could never happen. It's like a secret, like a fantasy and then you go home.

When asked whether she would ever take a black boyfriend home and introduce him to her friends and family, she was emphatic that she would not—"No, no, never. It's not like that. This is something else, you know, it's time out. Like a fantasy." This is more than simply a fantasy about having multiple anonymous sexual encounters without getting caught and disgraced. It is also a highly racialized fantasy about power and vengeance. Women like the sex tourist quoted above are looking for black men with good bodies, firm and muscle-clad sex machines that they can control, and this element of control should not be overlooked. It is also important to female sex tourists who reject white supremacist ideologies, and there are many of these, including white liberals and young white women who value Blackness as a "cool" commodity in the same way that many young white men do, and black American and black British female sex tourists.

These latter groups do not wish to indulge in the overtly hostile racialized sexual fantasy described by the woman quoted above, but they do want to live out other fantasies, whether they be "educating and helping the noble savage," or being the focus of "cool" black men's adoring gaze, or being the central character of a Terry Macmillan novel.[6] No matter what specific fantasy they pursue, female sex tourists use their economic power to initiate and terminate sexual relations with local men at whim, and within those relationships, they use their economic and racialized power to control these men in ways in which they could never command a Western man. These are unaccustomed powers, and even the female sex tourists who buy into exoticizing rather than hostile and denigrating racisms appear to enjoy them as such.

For white women, these powers are very clearly linked to their own whiteness as well as to their status and economic power as tourist women. Thus they contrast their own experience against that of local women (remarking on the fact that they are respected and protected and not treated like local women) *and* against their experience back home (commenting on how safe they feel in the Caribbean walking alone at night and entering bars and discos by themselves, observing that local men are far more attentive and chivalrous than Western men). Take, for example, the comments of "Judy," a white American expatri-

ate in the Dominican Republic, a woman in her late fifties and rather overweight:

> When you go to a disco, [white] men eye up a woman for her body, whatever. Dominicans don't care because they love women, they love women. It's not that they're indifferent or anything. They are very romantic, they will never be rude with you, while a white man will say something rude to you, while Dominican men are not like that at all. A white man will say to me, like, "slut" to me and I have been with a lot of Dominican men and they would never say anything like that to you. They are more respectful. Light cigarettes, open doors, they are more gentlemen. Where white men don't do that. So if you have been a neglected woman in civilization, when you come down here, of course, when you come down here they are going to wipe you off your feet.

The Dominican Republic presents women like Judy with a stage upon which to simultaneously affirm their femininity through their ability to command men and exact revenge on white men by engaging sexually with the competition, i.e., the black male. For the first time she is in a position to call the shots. Where back home white female sex tourists' racialized privilege is often obscured by their lack of gender power and economic disadvantage in relation to white men, in sex tourist resorts it is recognized as a source of personal power and power over others. Meanwhile, their beliefs about gender and sexuality prevent them from seeing themselves as sexually exploitative. Popular discourses about gender present women as naturally sexually passive and receptive, and men as naturally indiscriminate and sexually voracious. According to this essentialist model of gender and sexuality, women can never sexually exploit men in the same way that men exploit women because penetrative heterosexual intercourse requires the woman to submit to the male—she is "used" by him. No matter how great the asymmetry between female tourist and local male in terms of their age or economic, social, and racialized power, it is still assumed that the male derives benefits from sex above and beyond the purely pecuniary and so is not being exploited in the same way that a prostitute woman is exploited by a male client. This is especially the case when the man so used is socially constructed as a racialized, ethnic, or cultural Other and assumed to have an uncontrollable desire to have sex with as many women as he possibly can.

Conclusion

The demand for sex tourism is inextricably linked to discourses that naturalize and celebrate inequalities structured along lines of class, gender, and race/Otherness; in other words, discourses that reflect and help to reproduce a profoundly hierarchical model of human sociality. Although sex tourists are a heterogeneous group in terms of their background characteristics and specific sexual interests, they share a common willingness to embrace this hierarchical model and a common pleasure in the fact that their Third World tourism allows them either to affirm their dominant position within a hierarchy of gendered, racialized, and economic power or to adjust their own position upward in that hierarchy. In the Third World, neocolonial relations of power equip Western sex tourists with an extremely high level of control over themselves and others as sexual beings and, as a result, with the power to realize the fantasy of their choosing. They can experience sexual intimacy without risking rejection; they can evade the social meanings that attach to their own age and body type; they can transgress social rules governing sexual life without consequence for their own social standing; they can reduce other human beings to nothing more than the living embodiments of masturbatory fantasies.

In short, sex tourists can experience in real life a world very similar to that offered in fantasy to pornography users: "Sexuality and sexual activity are portrayed in pornography as profoundly distanced from the activities of daily life. The action in pornography takes place in what Griffin has termed 'pornotopia,' a world outside real time and space" (Harstock 1985: 175). To sex tourists,

the resorts they visit are fantasy islands, variously peopled by Little Brown Fucking Machines, "cool" black women who love to party, "primitive smelling" black studs who only think of "pussy and money," respectful Latin gentlemen who love women. All the sex tourist has to do to attain access to this fantasy world is to reach into his or her pocket, for it is there that the sex tourist, like other individuals in capitalist societies, carries "his social power as also his connection with society" (Marx 1973: 94). That the Western sex tourist's pocket can contain sufficient power to transform others into Others, mere players on a pornographic stage, is a testament to the enormity of the imbalance of economic, social, and political power between rich and poor nations. That so many Westerners *wish* to use their power in this way is a measure of the bleakness of the prevailing model of human nature and the human sociality that their societies offer them.

Notes

1. In 1995 we were commissioned by ECPAT (End Child Prostitution in Asian Tourism) to undertake research on the identity, attitudes, and motivations of clients of child prostitutes. This involved ethnographic fieldwork in tourist areas in South Africa, India, Costa Rica, Venezuela, Cuba, and the Dominican Republic. We are currently working on an Economic and Social Research Council-funded project (Award no. R 000 23 7625), which builds on this research through a focus on prostitution and the informal tourist economy in Jamaica and the Dominican Republic. Taking these projects together, we have interviewed some 250 sex tourists and sexpatriates and over 150 people involved in tourist-related prostitution (women, children, and men working as prostitutes, pimps, procurers, brothel keepers, etc.).

2. The fact that not all men are prostitute users is something that is often forgotten in radical feminist analyses of prostitution which, as Hart has noted, encourage us to view "either all men as prostitutes' clients or prostitutes' clients as somehow standing for/being symbolic of men in general" (Hart 1994: 53).

3. Because the survey aims to support exploration and theory development in a previously underre-

searched field, purposive (nonprobability) sampling methods were employed (Arber 1993: 72). Sanchez Taylor obtained a sample by approaching all single female tourists in selected locations (a particular stretch of beach, or a given bar or restaurant) and asking them to complete questionnaires.

4. Four out of eighteen single black British and American female tourists surveyed had entered into sexual relationships with local men. Sanchez Taylor also interviewed four more black female sex tourists.

5. In Negril, gigolos often refer to black American female sex tourists as "Stellas," after this fictional character.

6. Macmillan hints at the transgressive elements of a black Western female sex tourist's excitement— Stella's desire for the "primitive"-smelling younger man makes her feel "kind of slutty," but she likes the feeling.

References

Arber, Sarah. "Designing Samples." *Researching Social Life*, ed. Nigel Gilbert, 68–92. London: Sage, 1993.

Bishop, Ryan and Lillian S. Robinson. *Night Market: Sexual Cultures and the Thai Economic Miracle.* New York: Routledge, 1998.

Brace, Laura and Julia O'Connell Davidson. "Desperate Debtors and Counterfeit Love: The Hobbesian World of the Sex Tourist." *Contemporary Politics* 2.3 (1996): 55–78.

Chevannes, Barry. "Sexual Behaviour of Jamaicans: A Literature Review." *Social and Economic Studies* 42.1 (1993).

Graaf, Ron de, Ine Vanwesenbeck, Gertjan van Zessen, Straver Visser, and Jan Visser. "Prostitution and the Spread of HIV." *Safe Sex in Prostitution in The Netherlands*, 2-24, Amsterdam: Mr A. de Graaf Institute, 1992.

Grewal, Inderpal. *Home and Harem: Nation, Gender, Empire and the Cultures of Travel*. London, Leicester University Press 1996.

Hall, C. Michael. "Gender and Economic Interests in Tourism Prostitution: The Nature, Development and Implications of Sex Tourism in South-East Asia." *Tourism: A Gender Perspective*, ed. Vivien Kinnaird and D. Hall. London: Routledge, 1994.

Hart, Angie, "Missing Masculinity? Prostitutes' Clients in Alicante, Spain." *Dislocating Masculin-*

ity: Comparative Ethnographics, ed. Andrea Cornwall and Nancy Lindisfarne, 48–65. London: Routledge, 1994.

Harstock, Nancy. *Money, Sex, and Power.* Boston: Northeastern University Press, 1985.

hooks, bell. *Black Looks: Race and Representation*. London: Turnaround; Boston: South End Press, 1992.

——. *Outlaw Culture: Resisting Representations.* London; Routledge, 1994.

Jeffreys, Sheila. *The Idea of Prostitution.* Melbourne: Spinifex, 1997.

Karch, Cecilia A. and G. H. S. Dann, "Close Encounters of the Third Kind." *Human Relations* 34 (1981): 249–68.

Kempadoo, Kamala. "Prostitution, Marginality, and Empowerment: Caribbean Women in the Sex Trade." *Beyond Law* 5.14 (1994): 69–84.

——. "Regulating Prostitution in the Dutch Caribbean." Paper presented at the 20th annual conference of the Caribbean Studies Association, Caraçao, Netherlands Antrilles, May 1995.

——. "Dominicanas en Curaçao: Miros y Realidades." *Genero y Sociedad* 4.1 (May–August 1996): 102–30.

Kruhse-Mount Burton, Suzy. "Sex Tourism and Traditional Australian Male Identity." *International Tourism: Identity and Change*, ed. Marie-Françoise Lanfant, John Allcock, and Edward Bruner, 192–204. London: Sage, 1995.

Lee, Wendy. "Prostitution and Tourism in South-East Asia." *Working Women: International Perspectives on Labour and Gender Ideology*, ed. N. Redclift and M. Thea Sinclair, 79–103. London: Routledge, 1991.

Macmillan, Terry. *How Stella Got Her Groove Back.* New York: Penguin, 1996.

Marx, Karl. *Grundisse.* Harmondsworth, England: Penguin, 1973.

Morris-Jarra, Monica. "No Such Thing as a Cheap Holiday." *Tourism in Focus 26* (Autumn 1996): 6–7.

O'Connell Davidson, Julia. *Prostitution, Power and Freedom.* Cambridge: Polity Press, 1998.

Perio, Gaelle and Dominique Thierry. *Tourisme Sexuel au Bresil et en Colombie.* Rapport D'Enquete, TOURGOING, 1996.

Plumridge, Elizabeth and Jane Chetwynd. "Discourses of Emotionality in Commercial Sex." *Feminism & Psychology* 7.2 (1997): 165–81.

Pruitt, Deborah and Suzanne LaFont. "For Love and Money: Romance Tourism in Jamaica." *Annals of Tourism Research* 22.2 (1995): 422–40.

Sanchez Taylor, Jacqueline. "Marking the Margins: Research in the Informal Economy in Cuba and the Dominican Republic." Discussion Paper No. 597/1, Department of Sociology, University of Leicester, 1997.

Seabrook, Jeremy. *Travels in the Skin Trade: Tourism and the Sex Industry*. London: Pluto Press, 1997.

Shrage, Laurie, *Moral Dilemmas of Feminism*. London: Routledge, 1994.

Steller, Robert, *Perversion: The Erotic Form of Hatred*, London: Karnac, 1986.

Sturdevant, Saundra and Brenda Stolzfus. *Let the Good Times Roll: Prostitution and the U.S. Military in Asia*. New York: The New Press, 1992.

Truong, Than Dam. *Sex, Money and Morality: The Political Economy of Prostitution and Tourism in South East Asia*. London: Zed Books, 1990.

Young, Lola. *Fear of the Dark: "Race," Gender and Sexuality in the Cinema*. London: Routledge, 1996.

Verta Taylor
Leila J. Rupp

Chicks with Dicks, Men in Dresses: What It Means to Be a Drag Queen

One night at the drag show at the 801 Cabaret in Key West, Florida, Sushi reminds the audience, as if it were necessary, "Remember we are drag queens! We do have dicks and two balls!" Another night they call themselves "chicks with dicks, sluts with nuts." At the same time, R.V. Beaumont tells us in an interview, "I'm an actor in a dress," and Margo says, "I'm just a man in a dress." R.V. typically announces at the start of the show: "We may look like women, but we are all homosexual men." These different self-presentations suggest how complicated the question of what it means to be a drag queen can be. In this paper we examine the gender and sexual identities of a troupe of drag queens from Key West, Florida, known as the "801 Girls."[1]

To clarify what we mean by "drag queens," it is important to point out that not all men who dress as women are drag queens. Other categories include transvestites or cross-dressers, generally straight men who wear women's clothing for erotic reasons; preoperative male-to-female transsexuals; and transgendered people who display and embrace a gender identity at odds with their biological sex (Fleisher 1996; Brubach and O'Brien 1999; Meyerowitz 2002; Schacht 2002a). Drag queens, in contrast, are gay men who dress and perform as women but do not want to be women or have women's bodies (although some drag performers are "tittie queens" who acquire breasts through either hormones or implants). Within the category of drag queen, there are further distinctions based on performance style. Es-

From *Journal of Homosexuality*, 46(3/4), 2004 pp. 113–133.

ther Newton, in her classic study *Mother Camp*, distinguished between "stage impersonators," talented performers who sang in their own voices, and "street impersonators," more marginal drag queens who lip-synched their numbers (Newton 1972). Steven Schacht identifies four styles of drag as performance (Schacht 2002a). For our purposes, the most important distinction is one the 801 Girls make between "female impersonators," who generally do celebrity impersonation and keep the illusion of being women, in contrast to drag queens, who regularly break it in order to accentuate the inherently performative nature of gender and sexual meanings. Drag queens create their own—often multiple—personae and, in the case of the 801 Girls, adopt an "in-your-face" style.

One of the burning questions about drag queens—among both scholars and audiences—is whether they are more gender-conservatives than gender-revolutionaries, recognizing that there are elements of both in operation. Some scholars view drag as primarily reinforcing dominant assumptions about the dichotomous nature of gender presentation and sexual desire because drag queens appropriate gender displays associated with traditional femininity and institutionalized heterosexuality (Dolan 1985; Tewksbury 1993, 1994; Gagné and Tewksbury 1996; Schacht 1998, 2000, 2002a, 2002b). Others treat drag in the context of the gay community as more a transgressive action that destabilizes gender and sexual categories by making visible the social basis of femininity and masculinity, heterosexuality and homosexuality, and presenting hybrid and minority genders and sexualities (Butler 1990, 1993;

381

Garber 1992; Lorber 1994, 1999; Halberstam 1998; Muñoz 1999). Despite the fact that many observers see both processes at work in complex ways, the question remains: what, ultimately, is the impact of drag? Whereas the overwhelming majority of writings by queer theorists have explored this question by examining the gender and sexual representations conveyed in drag performances (Butler 1990; 1993; Garber 1992), we address this debate by analyzing the way gender and sexuality shape the personal and collective identities of drag queens.

Our analysis relies upon a social constructionist perspective that treats gender and sexuality as historically variable categories of difference overlaid onto external markers, behaviors, bodies, desires, and practices that typically function to reinforce major structures of inequality (Plummer 1981; Connell 1987; West and Zimmerman 1987; Greenberg 1988; Lorber 1994; Nardi and Schneider 1998; Murray 2000). Most research on gender and sexuality focuses on the processes that create and maintain a binary and hierarchical gender system composed of two genders, male and female, and a heteronormative sexual system consisting of two sexual identities, heterosexual and homosexual (Gagnon and Simon 1973; Goffman 1979; Kessler and McKenna 1978; West and Zimmerman 1987; Plummer 1981; West and Fenstermaker 1995; Butler 1990, 1993; Howard and Hollander 1997; Schwartz and Rutter 1998; Ferree, Lorber, and Hess 1999). Recent writings by gender scholars, influenced by the thinking of queer theorists, have called attention to a wide range of "performative" gender transgressions such as drag, cross-dressing, female masculinity, and other boundary-disruptive tactics used by feminist, queer, transgender, and other social movements (Taylor and Whittier 1992; Gamson 1997; Foster 1999; Lorber 1999). In such protests, the body of the performer highlights the social basis of gender and sexuality and becomes a weapon to contest dominant heterosexual gender codes.

We draw on this approach in our empirical study of the 801 Girls, but we use the extended case method (Burawoy 1991) to add to and revise

queer theory by focusing on the personal identities of the performers. Queer theorists, most notably Judith Butler (1990,1993), postulate the performative nature of gender, siding with sociologists who argue that social identities are always produced within prevailing normative and structural contexts (Stryker 1987; West and Zimmerman 1987; Howard and Hollander 1997). Queer theory, however, has a tendency to adopt what sociologists think of as a strong structuralist bias that ignores the subjectivity and identities of actors as well as the role that individuals play in producing as well as resisting and altering systems of gender and sexual inequality. We draw upon queer theory's view of gender as a performative act. But we expand our understanding of drag as it is actually practiced by examining drag queens' self-conceptions with respect to gender and sexuality and by showing how these are shaped by and, in turn, shape their collective identities as drag performers.

Our study draws from life histories of a troupe of drag queens, observation of their performances, and focus groups with audience members. We begin by exploring the processes through which the 801 Girls became drag queens, pointing to the central role of effeminacy, same-sex desire, and the use of masquerade to engage in gender crossing. We then analyze the personal identities and public performances of the drag queens to show how transgenderism and theatrical performance are used as blatant and deliberate acts to create a collective drag queen identity that establishes new and more fluid gender and sexual meanings. We see drag queens as neither feminine nor masculine but rather presenting their own complex genders (Schacht 2002b).

Setting and Data

The data for this study come from field research conducted from 1998–2001 in a popular drag cabaret in Key West, Florida. Key West is an internationally known gay tourist destination and something of a mecca for drag queens. The 801 Cabaret sits on upper Duval Street, the center of

Key West's dynamic gay life. The 801 Girls are full-time drag queens who, joined by occasional guests, perform different lip-synched shows nightly in the cabaret to anywhere from fifty people on an off-night to several thousand people during festivals, holidays, and other celebrations. The audience is mixed, consisting of men and women, gays and heterosexuals, tourists and locals.

Our research is based on multiple sources of data which we analyzed using qualitative methods. We conducted, tape-recorded, and transcribed semi-structured life histories of twelve performers. We coded the interviews thematically and analyzed them inductively to determine which features of theirs and others' self-concepts the drag queens accentuated. We rely heavily on these interviews in describing drag queen identity, since perhaps the best source of data on identity work is narrative (Baumeister and Newman 1994). In addition, we attended weekly drag queen meetings and observed the performers in their dressing room. All of the drag queens, who ranged in age from twenty-five to sixty-two, identified as gay men. We also observed, tape-recorded, and transcribed fifty performances, including the dialogue, music, and audience interactions. We supplemented these with photographs and field notes. In addition, we conducted twelve focus groups with forty audience members who attended the performances, and we held informal conversations and short interviews with fifty-five additional spectators. Finally, to assess the role of the 801 performers in the larger gay and lesbian community, we examined over a three-year period all stories that contained references to the performers at 801 in the weekly gay newspaper, *Celebrate!* and in the mainstream Key West media. (Fuller description of these drag queens, the political aspects of their performances, and audience reactions to the shows is available in Rupp and Taylor 2003.)

The 801 Girls

We see the 801 Girls as somewhat unusual, since they perform in a gay tourist destination, but we are also convinced that the commonalities and differences among these drag performers, who come from different racial, ethnic, regional, and national backgrounds, can tell us something about what it means to be a drag queen more generally. They certainly see themselves as part of what they proclaim as "Queen Nation."

Sushi, whose mother is Japanese and late father a GI who met and married her in Japan, has a beautiful tall slender body, with thin but muscled arms and a dancer's legs. She is the house queen. Sushi never really looks totally like a man, even when he is dressed as Gary.

Milla is also beautiful as both a man and woman. Dean's mother is Italian and his father a military man from Florida. Dean has short wavy black hair, beautiful eyes, and kissable full lips. With her olive skin and dark eyes, and her fondness for Eryka Badu and similar numbers, Milla is often taken onstage for African American.

Kylie, Sushi's best friend from high school, is much shorter than Sushi and Milla. Kevin is a very handsome preppy man with straight blondish hair that falls over his eyes. The other drag queens are convinced that Kylie could go in drag to one of the straight bars at the other end of Duval Street and easily pass herself off as a woman, although most of the women in our focus groups were unconvinced.

R.V., who grew up in a small town in Ohio and used to split the year between Key West and Provincetown, is short and stocky. The other girls call her "fat girl" on stage. He has a red head's complexion with short curly bleached-blond hair. He wears tee shirts that say "I'm not an alcoholic, I'm a drunk" or "Betty Ford Clinic Alumnae."

Margo is a sixty-two-year-old New Yorker with a deep voice. David is painfully thin and not in good health, having suffered a recurrence of bladder cancer and a heart attack during the latest surgery, for which he had to be airlifted out of Key West as Hurricane Georges hit. He is a local celebrity both as Margo, "the oldest living drag queen in captivity," and as David, a columnist for the local gay newspaper.

Scabola Feces, from Providence, Rhode Island, has no intention of looking beautiful, although as Matthew he is a handsome man. He is very thin, has large expressive eyes, a raspy smoker's voice, and a big evil-sounding laugh. He puts together outlandish costumes and elaborate headdresses that he superglues onto his shaved head.

Inga, the "Swedish bombshell," is really from Sweden, and she is big, tall, blond, soft, and adorable, with beautiful dimples. Out of drag as Roger, he favors long baggy shorts and tee shirts, wearing his hair in a thin ponytail. Inga is curvaceous and icy, prone to giving audience members the finger.

When Inga moved to a club down the street, Gugi, who was an occasional performer, took over Inga's show. Gugi is Puerto Rican, from Chicago, and as Rov he's stunning, with black curly hair, beautiful dark eyes, and an unbelievably sweet face. He is shy, while Gugi is aggressive and outgoing.

This was the roster of the 801 Girls at the time we conducted our research. We talked to all of them about how they became drag queens to ascertain common themes in their life histories.

Becoming a Drag Queen

In telling stories about growing up, the drag queens recounted three ways in which gender and sexual identity influenced how they came to do drag: *gender trangression, masquerade,* and *same-sex sexuality.* As other ethnographic studies of gender crossing have found (Kulick 1998), beginning even before their early teens the drag queens interviewed for our study began to engage in *gender transgression* through dressing in feminine or androgynous clothing, experimenting with make-up, and playing with what would conventionally be seen as "girls' toys." Several of the 801 Girls tell stories about dressing in their mothers' clothes when they were boys. Milla says, "Growing up, Mom and Dad would leave the house for a second and I just had that hour to get in her drawer and put on her panty hose and put her shoes on." Scabola interjects, "Oh, girl, I used to do the same

thing!" Gugi, too, admits to liking to dress in his mother's clothes, although he did not do it as regularly as Milla and Scabby. Milla connects his desire to wear women's clothing to wanting to distance himself from his father, who was abusive. Gugi is not sure why he liked to dress up. "I guess I felt comfortable. That's what I wanted to be."

Effeminacy of some kind or other plays a part in all of the girls' stories. Milla told us, "I don't want to say that I was a sissy, but . . . I always played with Barbies, I wanted to make everybody pretty." Scabby always wanted to take the female roles in play, and Margo, who grew up in the 1940s, remembers tossing away the baseball glove his father gave him. R.V., like Milla, played with Barbie dolls, and he loved to bake in his sister's Easy Bake Oven as well. He says his mother "knew when I was a kid what I was going to be."

Drag also developed out of the use of flamboyant dressing as a *masquerade* or disguise that allowed the drag queens to flaunt femininity and embrace gender fluidity by performing a separate identity which they could put on and take off. Kylie and Sushi, growing up in Oregon in the 1980s, both began by imitating Boy George. After Sushi's father died suddenly of a heart attack when Sushi was fourteen, "Kylie came into my life and we just went crazy." They began ratting their hair, wearing eyeliner, and doing crazy things. They dressed up to "have fun" and "be this other person." By his senior year, Sushi was a "flaming queen," wearing full makeup and platform shoes. Kylie says that at first it was not really drag, it was offbeat, but "suddenly I remember one time I was making a dress. And it just dawned on me, 'this is a dress, this is like completely all the way into dressing like a woman.'" Scabby, too, began as a "club kid," wearing women's clothes and a wig and running around the streets, "but I never actually *did* drag." It was the movie *The Adventures of Priscilla, Queen of the Desert* that spurred him to add makeup to his repertoire for the first time.

Paradoxically, drag both created a way to hide and attracted attention. Milla says, "I found a place where I could be, I could hide, I could mask myself behind wacky makeup, crazy hair colors, the wildest outfits, and feel strong, feel good. Overpowering." About the first time Milla dressed in drag in Key West, she says, "people gave me love, I got all the attention, all the things I never got from a man." Kylie says much the same thing: "I wanted attention. I wanted love, really." Inga also talks about dressing in drag to get attention. "When I was younger, I always had a need to get all the attention, so I was dressing in freaky clothes during the daytime, hats, capes, but never in drag." But then she realized that performing in drag, "with all this makeup and this fake costume, . . . I got attention this way." Dressing in costume, then, allowed them to play with gender and to reject its supposed authenticity.

Perhaps most important in their stories of becoming drag queens is *sexual attraction to and desire for men*. Inga says directly that she started to do drag because of "coming out being gay." It was striking how many of them answered the question of how they began to dress in drag by talking first about having sex with other males. When we ask Scabby how she started to do drag, she says, "I've always been gay, always been attracted to men." Milla answers, "I always knew what I liked, which was I knew I liked boys." Gugi says "I've always known I was gay. I always knew I was attracted to men."

Despite the different stories, certain common themes emerge in the making of a drag queen. Effeminacy and gay sexuality play an important role. (Of course, not all effeminate gay boys grow up to be drag queens, but what is significant is that the 801 Girls connect these parts of their histories to their identities as drag queens.) The cultural styles of the 1980s—like the foppish dress of earlier centuries (Rey 1985)—made room for flamboyance that could easily edge into true drag. Dressing in drag allows one to hide, attracts attention, expresses an in-your-face attitude, and makes clear the performative nature of gender. But what does it really mean to be a drag queen?

What It Means to Be a Drag Queen: Personal Identities

What it means to be a drag queen is different for the various girls, although in telling stories about themselves, the 801 Girls point to two kinds of personal identities linked to the performance of drag as a collective identity and strategy for undermining normative gender arrangements. For some, being a drag queen is about expressing a *transgender identity*. Sushi describes herself as "some place in between" a woman and a man. "I've always been a drag queen," she says another time.

In fact, Sushi's sense of being in between male and female led her to think about becoming a woman for awhile. She lived as a woman for about a year and a half, as did Milla. When she was younger, "I thought, 'Oh my god, I look like such a woman, maybe I am a woman' and it sort of confused me." But "I know I'm a drag queen, I finally realized that." Now, she says: "That's who I am, . . . there aren't that many people like me." Yet Kylie says Sushi "has a struggle . . . whether she should be a woman or a man."

That struggle came to the fore in the spring of 2001, when Sushi saw a television show about transgendered people in America. Over dinner, she tells us about this transformative experience: "For some reason, by the end of it I was crying my eyes out. . . . And I finally realized, oh my God, I'm not a drag queen. I'm a closeted transsexual—transgendered person. And I've been harping and hooting and tooting my horn for years now about being a drag queen—an openly, out, drag queen. And here I finally realize, I'm not a drag queen. I'm a closeted transgendered person." We ask about the difference. "A drag queen is someone like Kylie who never has ever thought about cutting her dick off. Ever. I think about it once a day, sometimes more." She says she really wants to do it but never will, partly because "it's a religious thing, . . . I was born this way," and partly because "I've been a drag queen for so long, and my whole persona—I don't want to try to change my whole personality again into Susie." We remind Sushi about telling us about her discovery that she was a drag queen, not a woman-wannabee. "But now I'm realizing that it's not that I realized I was a drag queen, I learned how to become a drag queen," Sushi explains.

Gugi, too, has a sense of herself as transgendered in some ways. She talks about the femininity in herself and says, "What I've always wanted was to be a woman." Making the link to sexual identity, she adds, " I don't know if it is because I wanted to be a woman or because I was attracted to men that I preferred to be a woman. . . . Out of drag, I feel like I'm acting. In drag, I feel like myself." The other girls tell us that they worried about Gugi when she went through a phase of never getting out of drag, going out in public all the time as a woman. "That means you've lost your identity," they say, making a distinction between being a drag queen and being on the move toward becoming a transsexual. Gugi herself seems to admit this. "It's just that certain things, I got too extreme with. . . . I started going to the straight side of town. In drag." And in fact Gugi has not ruled out becoming a woman. She says she does not want to be a tittie queen but, "Yeah, to be honest, I would love" getting breasts. She likes the idea of not having to wear as much makeup. For two months she did take hormones that she got from his best friend, a transgendered person. But she stopped because "It wasn't the right time. I did it for the wrong reasons. I did it to get away from my dad's death and the breakup with my ex bastard husband."

Milla says, "I love being a guy," but as an adolescent, going through problems at home and getting involved in drugs, being sent to what she calls "kiddie jail" and drug treatment, "I decided that I wanted to be a woman." Not just because she liked women's clothes, but because "I didn't like *me*." She got hormones from a counselor she was seeing by threatening to get them from drag queens on the street. She would go out dressed as a woman and "just have the *men fall over*, all over me, and with no clue, no clue." She loved it, "it was so away from everything." For awhile she thought that she really had to be a woman and was seriously considering sex-reassignment surgery. But then "I started to love myself. I pulled away from that whole effeminate side . . . and I became a man." Now, she says, "I'm so pleased with my penis and my body."

Others never thought of themselves as between genders or as women. Margo says, "I don't want to be a woman. I don't understand why anyone would want to do it." As a young gay teenager in New York in the 1950s, he read about Christine Jorgensen's famous transformation from a man to a woman. It scared him. "I did not want to be a woman, and here it is in the paper that this may be what I have to do." Yet even Margo, who reluctantly dressed in drag for the first time as part of her job at a guest house, nevertheless relates being a drag queen to earlier gender experimentations and transgressions: "And the funny thing is when I got dressed and I came out, it was, it became very natural. . . . And I had never done that since when you're five years old and you put on your mother's high heels and walk around the house. "It's fun!" David writes in *Celebrate!*: "One becomes the center of attention and flaunts the feminine side of the psyche" (Felstein 1997).

Being a drag queen also means embracing a *theatrical identity*, and many of them have background in theater. Scabola has been involved in theater since elementary school and always loved it. "I loved creating personas," she says. Although for Milla being a drag queen is more profound, she also identifies as a performer. She, too, was in theater groups from a young age. What she loves is being able to use her feelings, to evoke the pain and anger and love that audience members have felt in their own lives.

Like Milla, Gugi experiences drag as both expressing her transgendered nature and as theatrical. Growing up as a child in Chicago, she performed in church and school plays. She says, "It just comes to me. . . . I want to be loved by everyone. . . . It's just part of my destiny."

R.V. had been in professional summer stock theater as a boy. Two days after he graduated from high school, he took off to Disney World, unwilling to stop smoking marijuana and live by the rules of his family home. Although she is clearly close to and proud of his mother, she describes her home life as dysfunctional and sees the stage as a way that she could create his own little world. She worked for Disney for fourteen years. There she met drag queens who took her to the Parliament House in Orlando, where she started doing drag. She defines herself as an entertainer: "I'm an actor in a dress." But she also identifies as a drag queen.

Inga has been in the theater since she was ten, and she, too, loves performing. For her it was a natural transition from "Romeo and Juliet" and "The Inferno" to Marilyn Monroe and Madonna impersonations. In contrast to some of the other drag queens, she says, "I never had a need to dress as a girl or wanted to have a sex change." Drag, she says, is an act, not a lifestyle. "I would not trade it, even if some nights it's hard, doing the show, being paid to do it, but I would not trade it for anything. It's fun. It's a game."

With their theatrical experience, the drag queens engage in street theater—both in the cabaret and literally on the streets—in a way that brings their work into alignment with their identity politics. At one Saturday night show, Kylie asks a German tourist if he is straight, and the man replies that he is normal. "Normal!" cries Kylie. "I'm normal. You're weird." They take delight in arousing straight men by teasing and fondling them. Before the show, they pass out flyers on the streets, engaging in banter with the people who walk by. "Are you in the show?," a wide-eyed young tourist asks Margo. "Would I be dressed like this if I weren't?" retorts David in his deep smoker's voice. During Bikers' Week, when the town is overrun with Harleys, the drag queens troop down to the straight bars to "sniff the seats"—a ritual they invented—and, as Sushi puts it, "hassle the straight men." If some of this behavior sounds masculine, they view it more as "acting like hookers," deploying the kind of sexual aggressiveness of female prostitutes.

This theatrical identity involves, just as in traditional theater, taking on a new persona. "Sushi

is different than Gary," says Sushi. Even Margo, who became a drag queen late in life, describes David as "an entirely different person" from Margo, although "now they are coming together more and more." Timothy, too, is shy and describes himself as introverted. Given his stage presence, we thought he would talk our ears off when we interviewed him, but then we realized that that was R.V. and this was Timothy. "That's a whole different person up there. Different personality," he says.

Roger also takes on a different style. "As Inga I can do things I could never do as Roger, I would never do." Kevin says, "Kylie is me" but admits that "Kylie is more expressive, . . . when I'm dressed as Kylie I know that I can get away with so much more." Dean describes keeping Dean and Milla separate because he understood that not being able to live apart from your image— he mentions Boy George here—leads to drugs and breakdown. "That's why there's Dean and Milla. For a while there wasn't."

Audience members are curious about why the drag queens do what they do and come up with explanations that mirror those that the girls themselves offer. A gay male couple from New York who have become friendly with the girls say, "They're people just like anybody else and that just happens to be their profession." A straight man, touching on the theatrical identity and comparing them to women who become strippers or porn stars, wonders if they wanted to break into show business and could not do it any other way. A lesbian from New York disagrees, saying, "I think it's a choice. . . . There are so many things on earth that they could be doing that for a man to go as far as to dress up as a woman, there's a leap." Her lover agrees with her: "I think that is something very important to them." A gay male physician from Boston loves drag because "it seems to me a pure expression of self. . . . They get to project exactly what they want to be." "I think there's an acceptance that they get when they're on stage that they don't necessarily get when they're off stage," says a woman photographer. A gay male lawyer who lives in Key West emphasizes the different motivations: "For some of the performers it's an employment of last resort. For some of the performers it's their pattern. For some of them it's a temporary thing between other things. For some of them it's who they are."

Clearly, being a drag queen has different meanings in the 801 Girls' lives, but transgender and theatrical identities emerge clearly from their collective stories. The effeminacy, attraction to masquerade, and same-sex desire that they experienced as boys and young men converge in their drag queen subjectivities. Through their self-presentations and performances, they enact a collective identity that calls attention to the artificiality of gender and sexual binaries. In that sense, they are indeed gender revolutionaries.

Conclusion

Watching the transformation that takes place in the dressing room and listening to the girls' accounts of their gender and sexuality as boys, it is easy to see in concrete terms how unstable the categories of "masculine" and "feminine" and "heterosexual" and "homosexual" really are. The rigidity of the categories in mainstream culture is reflected in the confusion of boys like Sushi, who thought that her sartorial desires meant that she wanted to be a woman. The role of effeminacy and same-sex sexual desires in the girls' stories about becoming drag queens suggests how bound up the identity of drag queen is with deviation from conventional gender expectations and heteronormativity. "Drag queen" emerges as an in-between or third-gender category in a society that insists that there are only two. One gay male audience member captured this when he said that he did not think of them as either men or women, but as "their own thing. I feel like a drag queen is completely different."

In that sense, drag queens are like others who fall between or bridge or challenge the division between masculine and feminine. As other scholars have suggested in considering the butch-fem bar culture of the 1950s or the "fe-

male masculinity" of women who look like men on a permanent or temporary basis, such "in-betweens" are not about aping the other side of the divide (Kennedy and Davis 1993; Halberstam 1998). Rather, these are people who create their own authentic genders, suggesting that, rather than eliminating the notion of gender categories, we need to expand the possibilities beyond two or three to a whole range of possible identities, including drag queen.

The case of the 801 Girls supports those who view drag as ultimately transgressive and a challenge to the gender and sexual order. But by exploring the personal and collective identities of the drag queens at the 801, we go further to show the ways that their gender presentations, performances, and sexual desires play a role in resisting and transforming the gender and sexual systems. Whether "chicks with dicks" or "men in dresses," drag queens create their own transgender and theatrical identities that force their audiences to think in a complex way about what it means to be a woman or what it means to be a man.

Note

1. The drag queens generally use drag names and female pronouns in reference to each other, although they sometimes shift to male names and pronouns. There is no correlation to whether they are in or out of drag. In this article, we primarily use their drag names and female pronouns, except when talking about them in their pre-drag past.

References

Baumeister, R. and L. Newman. (1994). How Stories Make Sense of Personal Experiences: Motives That Shape Autobiographical Narratives. *Personality and Social Psychology Bulletin* 20, 676–90.

Brubach, H. and M. O'Brien. (1999). *Girlfriend: Men, Women, and Drag*. New York: Random House.

Burawoy, M. (1991). Reconstructing Social Theories. In M. Burawoy (Ed.), *Ethnography Unbound: Power and Resistance in the Modern Metropolis* (pp. 8–27). Berkeley: University of California Press.

Butler, J. (1990). *Gender Trouble: Feminism and the Sub-version of Identity.* New York: Routledge.

Butler, J. (1993). *Bodies That Matter: On the Discursive Limits of "Sex."* New York: Routledge.

Connell, R.W. (1987). *Gender and Power: Society, the Person, and Sexual Politics.* Cambridge, Mass.: Polity in association with Blackwell.

Dolan, J. (1985). Gender Impersonation Onstage: Destroying or Maintaining the Mirror of Gender Roles? *Women and Performance: A Journal of Feminist Theory* 2, 5–1.

Felstein, D. (1997). Face to Face with History—Part Four, *Celebrate!* October 24, 9.

Ferree, M., J. Lorber, and B. Hess. (1999). *Revisioning Gender.* Thousand Oaks, Calif.: Sage Publications.

Fleisher, J. (1996). *The Drag Queens of New York: An Illustrated Field Guide.* New York: Riverhead Books.

Foster , J. (1999). An Invitation to Dialogue: Clarifying the Position of Feminist Gender Theory in Relation to Sexual Difference Theory. *Gender & Society* 13, 431–56.

Gagné, P. and R. Tewksbury. (1996). No "Man's" Land: Transgenderism and the Stigma of the Feminine Man. *Advances in Gender Research* 1, 115–55.

Gagnon, J. and W. Simon. (1973). *Sexual Conduct: The Social Sources of Human Sexuality.* Chicago: Aldine Publishers.

Garber, M. (1992). *Vested Interests: Cross-Dressing and Cultural Anxiety.* New York: Routledge.

Goffman, E. (1979). *Gender Advertisements.* Cambridge, Mass.: Harvard University Press.

Greenberg, D. (1988). *The Construction of Homosexuality.* Chicago: University of Chicago Press.

Halberstam, J. (1998). *Female Masculinity.* Durham, N.C.: Duke University Press.

Howard, J. and J. Hollander. (1997). *Gendered Situations, Gendered Selves: A Gender Lens on Social Psychology.* Thousand Oaks, Calif.: Sage.

Kennedy, E. and M. Davis. (1993). *Boots of Leather, Slippers of Gold: The History of a Lesbian Community.* New York: Routledge.

Kessler, S. and W. McKenna. (1978). *Gender: An Ethnomethodological Approach.* New York: Wiley.

Kulick, D. (1998). *Travesti: Sex, Gender and Culture among Brazilian Transgendered Prostitutes.* Chicago: University of Chicago Press.

Lorber, J. (1994). *Paradoxes of Gender.* New Haven, Conn.: Yale University Press.

Lorber, J. (1999). Crossing Borders and Erasing Boundaries: Paradoxes of Identity Politics. *Sociological Focus* 32, 355–70.

Meyerowitz, J. (2002). *How Sex Changed: A History of Transsexuality in the U.S.* Cambridge, Mass.: Harvard University Press.

Muñoz, J. (1999). *Disidentifications: Queers of Color and the Performance of Politics.* Minneapolis: University of Minnesota Press, 1999.

Murray, S. (2000). *Homosexualities.* Chicago: University of Chicago Press.

Nardi, P. and B. Schneider. (1998). *Social Perspectives in Lesbian and Gay Studies.* New York: Routledge.

Newton, E. (1972). *Mother Camp: Female Impersonators in America.* Chicago: University of Chicago Press.

Plummer, K. (Ed.). (1981). *The Making of the Modern Homosexual.* London: Hutchinson.

Rey, M. (1985). Parisian Homosexuals Create a Lifestyle, 1700–1750: The Police Archives. *Eighteenth-Century Life* 9, n.s. 3, 179–91.

Rupp, L. and V. Taylor. (2003). *Drag Queens at the 801 Cabaret.* Chicago: University of Chicago Press.

Schacht, S. (1998). The Multiple Genders of the Court: Issues of Identity and Performance in a Drag Setting. In S. Schacht and D. Ewing (Eds.), *Feminism and Men: Reconstructing Gender Relations* (pp. 202–24). New York: New York University Press.

Schacht, S. (2000). Gay Masculinities in a Drag Community: Female Impersonators and the Social Construction of "Other." In P. Nardi (Ed.), *Gay Masculinities* (pp. 247–68). Newbury Park, Calif.: Sage.

Schacht, S. 2002a. Four Renditions of Doing Female Drag: Feminine Appearing Conceptual Variations of a Masculine Theme. *Gendered Sexualities* 6, 157–80.

Schacht, S. 2002b. Turnabout: Gay Drag Queens and the Masculine Embodiment of the Feminine. In N. Tuana et al. (Eds.), *Revealing Male Bodies* (pp. 155–70). Bloomington: Indiana University Press.

Schwartz, P. and V. Rutter. (1998). *The Gender of Sexuality.* Thousand Oaks, Calif.: Pine Forge Press.

Stryker, S. (1987). Identity Theory: Developments and Extensions. In K. Yardley and T. Honess (Eds.), *Self and Identity: Psychological Perspectives* (pp. 89–103). New York: John Wiley.

Taylor, V. and N. Whittier. (1992). Collective Identity in Social Movement Communities: Lesbian Feminist Mobilization. In A. Morris and C. Mueller (Eds.), *Frontiers in Social Movement Theory* (pp. 104–30). New Haven, Conn.: Yale University Press.

Tewksbury, R. (1993). Men Performing as Women: Explorations in the World of Female Impersonators. *Sociological Spectrum* 13, 465–86.

Tewksbury, R. (1994). Gender Construction and the Female Impersonator: The Process of Transforming "He" to "She." *Deviant Behavior: An Interdisciplinary Journal* 15, 27–43.

West, C. and S. Fenstermaker. (1995). Doing Difference. *Gender & Society* 9, 8–37.

West, C. and D. Zimmerman. (1987). Doing Gender. *Gender & Society* 1, 125–151.

Meika Loe

Fixing Broken Masculinity: Viagra as a Technology for the Production of Gender and Sexuality

This essay centers on the turn of the century heterosexual male body as a new site for medicalization, technological enhancement, and cultural and personal crisis. Using ethnographic data, I explore the ways in which masculinity and heterosexuality are constructed and problematized in light of the Viagra phenomenon. I expose the ways in which consumers and practitioners actively make sense of Viagra in terms of "trouble" and "repair." And I argue that Viagra is both a cultural and material tool used in the production and achievement of gender and sexuality. For the first time in American history, biotechnology is being used to "fix" or enhance heterosexual male confidence and power and thus avert masculinity "in crisis."

In this article I draw from fifty-one interviews (twenty-five male consumers and twenty-six medical professionals) conducted between 1999–2001. All names have been changed to insure confidentiality. The male consumers I spoke with are a self-selected group who responded to my requests for interviews through internet postings, newspaper advertisements, practitioner referrals, senior citizens organizations, personal contacts, and prostate cancer support group meetings. They represent a diverse sample in terms of ethnicity, sexual orientation, and age (seventeen to eighty-six years old). The majority are middle class. Semi-structured conversational consumer interviews

From *Sexuality & Culture* 5(3) Summer 2001.

were primarily conducted over the phone or the internet (for anonymity and confidentiality reasons) with the in-person interview as the exception. In addition, I interviewed twenty-six medical professionals from Boston, Massachusetts, and Beverly Hills, California, two medically sophisticated urban areas with extremely different medical scenes. The majority of these interviews were in-person, semi-structured conversations, with phone conversations as the exception. All interviews were transcribed, and then coded and analyzed using qualitative data analysis software.

Turn of the Century Troubled Masculinity

Problematic Package

In the age of Viagra, most practitioners and consumers agree that loss of erectile function appears to be synonymous with loss of manhood. Early on, some urologists learned that they couldn't treat the penis in isolation from the man. To treat the penis on its own, one prominent psychiatrist commented, was not to see masculinity as a whole package.

> Certainly [the discovery of a chemical injection that could produce an erection] started a new era in understanding sexual response. This really excited urologists who thought they could isolate the erection from the man. Now they have learned they can't detach the man from his penis. [Baker, psychiatrist]

It quickly became clear to many practitioners that masculinity was intimately tied to erectile functioning. A growing field of scholarship on male sexual bodies suggests that sexuality is a proving ground for masculinity (Bordo 1999; Connell 1995; Fasteau 1975; Kimmel 1996; Potts 2000). Thus, for males, gender and sexuality may be difficult to separate out. Masculinity requires sexuality and vice versa.

This conversation between a doctor, his patient, and myself exposes the close relationship between masculinity and erectile function.

> **Doctor:** You see, sexual dysfunction in males is peculiar. I'm sure if someone is a paraplegic and can't walk, he would feel psychologically deprived. But beyond the great obvious lack—people who don't see or hear as well, they don't feel like they have lost their manhood, you see. I must tell you, and I'm not a psychiatrist, but I think it is far more prevalent in males than it would be in females. The fact that if women don't have sexual gratification, or don't have it [sex?], it isn't that they don't miss it, but they don't have the psychological burden that males seem to have. Maybe it's a throwback to the time when the caveman went and dragged a woman out on his shoulder. [Bending, internist]
>
> **Me:** So sexuality is integral to male identity?
>
> **Patient:** Absolutely! [My wife and I] talked about it for a long time—well a couple of weeks before the [prostate] operation itself. We talked about its possible we may not be able to have sex because the apparatuses they had out didn't necessarily work. So you could go for the rest of your life without having sex. And [the doctor] is so right. You feel part of your manhood is gone. [Gray, consumer]

Above, a practitioner and his patient agree that the "trouble" associated with erectile dysfunction is a psychological burden and loss of manhood. Most of my interview subjects were in agreement on this point; that if the penis is in trouble, so is the man.

> You probably wouldn't understand it—it's a big part of manhood. Ever since you're a little boy growing up that's a part of your masculinity. And whether its right or wrong, and however you deal with it—that's, well, I'm dealing with it and I seem to be okay. If a man gets an erection, or the boys in the shower compare each other, that's your masculinity. A lot of men don't like to admit it. [Phil, consumer]

In this way sexuality, or "erectile health," is compulsory for men; integral to achieving manhood. "Every man must pump up for phallocracy" (Potts 2000, 98).

While many men may not discuss their masculinity problems openly with a doctor, the doctor–patient dialogue above and Viagra's recent blockbuster success are representative of a new global concern for the "broken," or impotent male. If gender is "accomplished" in daily life (West and Fenstermaker 1995), then the accomplishment of masculinity is situated, to some extent, in erectile achievement. Fixing the male machine and ensuring erectile functioning, for the patients quoted above and countless others, is to ensure masculinity. Viagra is a technology, or a tool, used to fix the broken machine.

The Poorly Functioning Male Machine

Donna Haraway argues that the postmodern subject is a cyborg, a hybrid creature composed of both organism and machine who populates a world ambiguously natural and crafted (1991, 149). Medical language about the body reflects the overlap between humans and machines as consumers and practitioners describe bodies using mechanical terminology such as "functioning" and "maintenance." The metaphor of the body as a smoothly functioning machine is central to Viagra constructions. In her research into 20th century understandings of health and the body, Emily Martin (1994) found that the human body is commonly compared to a disciplined machine. Like a machine, the body is made up of parts that can break down. Illness, then, refers to a broken body part. To fix this part ensures the functioning of the machine. Drawing on interviews with consumers and practitioners, I argue in this section that the popularity of Viagra has exposed and created a masculinity crisis of sorts. In this section, consumers and practitioners employ industrial and technological metaphors to make sense of body and gender trouble, or masculinity in crisis.

In this section, customers and practitioners make sense of "trouble" by attempting to locate problems in the male body or machine. Such industrial metaphors are regularly used by Dr. Irwin Goldstein, a media-friendly urologist and Pfizer consultant, known for describing erectile functioning as "all hydraulics" and suggesting that dysfunction requires "rebuilding the male machine." Following this metaphor, common treatment protocols for "erectile dysfunction" center on treating the penis (broken part) separately from the body (machine). Physicians are encouraged (by Pfizer representatives) to center their doctor/patient dialogue around the patient's erectile "performance"—asking the patient to rate their erections in terms of penetrability, hardness, maintenance, and satisfaction levels. This construction of the penis as dysfunctional and fixable is exemplified in the following quotes.

> What I do is say [to patients complaining of erectile dysfunction], "Tell me about the erections. When you were 20 years old lets say they were a 10, rock hard. Where would they be now on a scale from 1–10?" So I give them some objectible evidence that they can give me. They'll say, oh, now it's a 2. A lot of guys say its now a 7 or 8. I say "Can you still perform with a 7 or 8?" They say, "Yeah, but its not as good as it was." [Curt, urologist]

The medical professionals I spoke with were clear that if a patient experiences "deficiency" or complete lack of erectile function, Viagra might be of help. But "dysfunction" may not be as black and white. As Pfizer Inc. and its promotional information suggests, "erectile dysfunction" lies on a continuum from complete inability to achieve erection, to consistent ability to achieve an erection. Many patients who are currently looking for treatment for erectile dysfunction inhabit the gray area (in terms of performance rankings from 1 to

10), and appear to be concerned with restoring their "machine" to a "normal," or near-perfect level of functioning. Optimal performance, or the ability to penetrate one's partner and sustain an erection, is desired, as reflected in the above quotes.

Trouble with Normal

While rigidity is the goal, part of optimal penile performance is to appear malleable. In a twentieth century postmodern world, flexibility is a trait cherished and cultivated in all fields, including health (Martin 1994). Thus, the healthiest bodies are disciplined machines which also exhibit current cultural ideals such as reliability, fitness, and elasticity (Martin 1994). Viagra is constructed as a tool used to achieve the ideal flexible body—a body that is always "on call."

In some cases, Viagra is used by consumers who feel that normal penile functioning is not good enough. While these consumers claim they do not "need" Viagra, they are more satisfied with their performance when they do use it. In the quotes below, Bill and Stan imply that the pre-Viagra penis is slow, unpredictable, and uncertain, and thus, problematic.

> I noticed that if I get titillated, [after using Viagra] then the penis springs to attention. Not atypically. But more facile. It's easier. It's more convincing. It's not like maybe I'll get hard and maybe I won't. It's like "Okay, here I am!" [Stanford, consumer]

For these consumers, the Viagra-body may be preferable to the natural body, because it is consistent and predictable. The "on-call" Viagra penis will consistently respond when it is needed, whereas the "natural" body is constructed as too unpredictable.

> Erections are a lot more temperamental than people are willing to admit. But we have this image of masculinity and expectations of male sexuality as being virile and always ready to go and being the conqueror. And I think that this pill allows people to finally live out that myth (laughs). [Stu, consumer]

As Stu points out, Viagra exposes the flawed "natural" body and enables a man to achieve mythic masculinity. In this way, the Viagra story is one that slips between artificial and natural, and even beyond to super-natural levels. For many, the promise of Viagra is the fact that it can deliver "optimal" results, pushing the consumer beyond his own conceptions of "normal" functioning. In this way, practitioners and customers construct Viagra as a miracle cure because it not only "fixes" the problem, but makes things "better." Below, Viagra is constructed as an enhancement drug.

> With Viagra we say it's for a medical condition, not for just anyone. However I know a fellow who was fine who took a Viagra to get himself extra-normal. [Bastine, psychiatrist]

Practitioners and consumers collaborate in constructing Viagra as a magic bullet that can "extend" the realm of "normal," and push people to the next level: extra-normality, or superhumanness. By pushing the boundaries of erectile function, performance, and sexuality, Viagra sets new standards and constructs countless male bodies in need of repair. Consumers and practitioners use technological metaphors to construct the ways in which Viagra can be used to repair the broken male machine.

Repairing the Broken Male

There is no doubt that at the turn of the century, males may be feeling emasculated, powerless, and lifeless for any number of reasons. For those who are feeling this way, Viagra comes to the rescue, with the potential to avert or repair personal and/or cultural troubles. Acknowledging that culture, the media, or relationships can be a source of trouble is not part of the medical model and appears too complicated to fix. However, when the problem is located solely in the body (as in medical discourse), individualized, and treated as a physiological dysfunction, it can be easier to repair. Even clinical psychologists, who acknowledge that the trouble can be psychological, social,

or relational, may join medical practitioners in seeing Viagra as a tool for regaining body function and repairing confidence, and masculinity.

In the face of troubled masculinity, Viagra is commonly constructed by consumers and practitioners as a pill for masculinity-repair or instruction, to be used either in extreme erectile dysfunction cases where manhood appears to be "lost," to more common "mild E.D." situations where manhood needs a "jump-start" or an extra boost. In this way, Viagra itself is a technology for the production of gender and sexuality. Viagra can be understood as a tool for the repair and/or production of hegemonic masculinity and sexuality. Some consumers take Viagra hoping not only to restore or supplement "natural" physiological function, but also "normal" masculinity and heterosexuality. Others choose not to use Viagra, claiming that Viagra is more "trouble" than solution by producing an artificial and "uncontrollable" body. This idea of trouble will be developed further in a later section.

Techno-Fix and the Viagra "Tool"

With the embrace of Viagra as a biotechnological "wonder," Viagra is invested with myriad technological metaphors. As we have seen, Viagra can be understood as a tool for fixing the broken male machine. The term "jump-start" is used by many practitioners and consumers to understand Viagra's effect on the body, and to symbolize an energetic positive step forward, with biotechnology backing-up and assuring performance. Viagra can jump-start the body and the mind to produce a self-assured masculinity.

> Even the ones with psychological problems, they still try the Viagra to help convince them that everything works okay. I'll give it to them. You need this to *jump-start* your system. See how it works. If it gives you the confidence that you can get an erection, it can work. Then you can taper off of it. [Curt, urologist]

Viagra is employed by practitioners as a tool, similar to jumper cables, to "jump-start" the male machine—to get the patient performing again. In the first quote above, the urologist renders the whole body affected by erectile dysfunction as lifeless, like a dead battery. The urologist and consumers quoted after him use the same metaphor (although they don't know one another) and advocate a rapid return to normal erections, normal performance, and thus, normal masculinity. Below, a consumer uses the same terminology as practitioners to reveal how Viagra works in the body.

> Viagra is a miracle product for men with performance problems. And partners love it too. I've found that it really *jump-starts* things, physiologically. I've talked to many people who say this. But where I'm at right now, with my diet and tantra work, Viagra just doesn't suit me anymore. But I think for some people it might be great to take once in a while to jump-start things. [Bradley, consumer]

Technology-based metaphors pervade practitioner and consumer explanations of Viagra's relationship to the male body. Many medical professionals choose to use machine or automobile-related metaphors to construct the type of treatment now available with Viagra. Here, Viagra does optional repair work (on the male machine) and erections are seen as enhancements or "attachments" to the basic body.

> Viagra has a snap-on component to it. People want it now. It is a metaphor for our culture. [Redding, psychotherapist]

Consumers use similar industrial metaphors to describe how penises are repaired, transformed, and enhanced after using Viagra.

> [My friend] Jack, on the other hand, claimed victory that night and said the little blue confidence pill helped him achieve "pink steel," which impressed his occasional girlfriend, at least that night. [Lue, consumer]

Viagra's promise is one of corporeal technological enhancement—in the form of a snap-on, an accessory, and a ready-made erection. By making such comparisons (car, steel, weapon), consumers attribute masculine characteristics such as power, resilience, hardness, and strength to the Viagra penis, essentially constructing Viagra as a tool for producing masculinity, and enforcing social meanings. In this way, myth and tool mutually constitute each other (Haraway 1991, 164).

Repair = Trouble

Not all consumers buy into the techno-fix model. Some consumers commented that although Viagra may promise bodily repair it can actually cause more trouble than its worth. In this section, Viagra constructs problems, not solutions. Below, Viagra is constructed as techno-trouble, constructing the male body as increasingly out of control.

> I don't ever want to try [Viagra] again. The thing about it is, the side-effects could be very dangerous for someone a little older than I am. Because you do end up with palpitation. Your body is just not your body. So if [your functioning is] not normal, I think its better to just let it go at that. Or make pills that are much much weaker. But I wouldn't recommend it for anybody. [Joel, consumer]

As we saw earlier, some men see Viagra as a tool to create the ideal flexible body. For other consumers, Viagra may produce a body that is overly rigid and inflexible. At this point, the Viagra-effect becomes "unnatural" and uncontrollable, and consequently undesirable.

> Well, I also didn't like it because it was unnatural. Like you were hard and you stayed hard. And I also didn't like the fact that it guaranteed things would be sexual until you weren't hard. [Dusty, consumer]

Rather than lose control of their bodies or experience trouble through repair, these consumers construct alternatives to the pharmaceutical fix model, accepting their bodies as they are or just "leaving it alone." Despite overwhelming evidence that Viagra is associated with the production of normal and/or mythic masculinity, these men work hard at reconstructing masculinity as separate from "erectile health." They insist that masculinity can be achieved without the help of Viagra, or consideration of erectile potential.

I've talked to a lot of different men about this. Some cannot live without sex. They feel their sex makes them the man that they are. And I'm not sure how important that is to me. I'm a man anyways. It's about self-esteem. What do you think about yourself to begin with? [Ollie, consumer]

For many, Viagra fits perfectly in a society that is known for pushing the limits of normal. Consumers may be critical of American culture and Viagra's role in perpetuating the endless pursuit of the quick-fix. Consumers warn of a hedonistic, money-driven, artificial world, where there is a pill for everything. Viagra exists in this world as a crutch or band-aid solution to larger social problems.

I think there is a gross overuse of drugs for "happiness and well-being." Feeling depressed, get a script for a mood enhancer . . . feeling tired, get a pill for energy . . . want to have better sex, get some blue magic. What about the age-proven solution of removing or reducing the problems or stress factors affecting your life and then seeing if pharmacological agents are still needed? [Miles, consumer]

Here, consumers construct society as pharmacologically-infused, producing individuals who are dependent upon pills for health and happiness. Consumers are critical of capitalist and biotechnological attempts at constructing needs, desires, and easy markets for products.

I just see that society is just driving us crazy, making us jump through hoops and do things we really don't need to do. So—a drug for everything. Even if you don't want to do it, you are driven if you pay attention to what's going on. I'm not that kind of person. I just don't believe in it. [Ollie, consumer]

In many ways, consumers are critical of Viagra's potential to enforce social and gendered meanings and realities. Savvy consumers refuse to "buy into" mythic masculinity, and see through problematic discourses of medical progress and widespread public health crises. In this way consumers resist and reframe masculinity, biotechnology,

and medicalization in ways that make sense to them. Rather than construct their bodies and masculinities as troubled, with Viagra as a techno-fix or magical solution, these consumers construct Viagra as problematic, contributing to larger social troubles.

Masculinity, Technology, and Resistance

As my interview data reveals, Viagra can and is being used by consumers and practitioners to enforce and perpetuate such ideal and corporeal masculinities. In this way consumers collaborate with medical professionals and pharmaceutical companies in an attempt to understand and fix "broken" bodies. Perhaps of more interest, my data also reveals consumers and practitioners struggling with the necessity of the Viagra-enhanced body, and what that represents. As they negotiate their relationship to this product, mainstream ideas about sexuality, masculinity, and health are both reinforced and redefined in important ways. For example, some insist that "doing" masculinity does not require sexual performance. Others are critical of a society that increasingly promotes and depends upon biotechnology for achieving health and happiness. This paper reveals men constructing their own ideas about manhood, medicalization, and biotechnology, and creating "various and competing masculinities" in Viagra's midst (Messner 1997).

References

Basalmo, Anne. (1996). *Technologies of the Gendered Body: Reading Cyborg Women*. Duke University Press.

Bordo, Susan. (1999). *The Male Body: A New Look At Men in Public and Private*. New York: Farrar, Straus, and Giroux.

Bullough, Vern. (1987). Technology for the prevention of "les maladies produites par la masturbation." *Technology and Culture, 28*(4): 828–32.

Connell, R. W. (1995). *Masculinities*. Berkeley: University of California Press.

Conrad, Peter & Joseph Schneider. (1980). *Deviance and Medicalization: From Badness to Sickness.* London: Mosby.

Davis, Angela. (1981). *Women, Race & Class.* New York: Vintage.

DeLauretis, Teresa. (1987). *Technologies of Gender.* Indiana: Indiana University Press.

D'Emilio, John & Estelle Freedman. [1988] 1997. *Intimate Matters: A History of Sexuality in America.* Chicago: University of Chicago Press.

Ehrenreich, Barbara & Dierdre English. (1973). *Complaints and Disorders. The Sexual Politics of Sickness.* New York: The Feminist Press.

———. (1979). *For Her Own Good: 150 Years of the Expert's Advice to Women.* New York: Anchor.

Faludi, Susan. (1999). *Stiffed: The Betrayal of the American Man.* New York: Morrow and Co.

Fasteau, Marc Feigen. (1975). *The Male Machine.* New York: Dell.

Foucault, Michel. (1973). *The Birth of the Clinic, an Archaeology of Medical Perception.* New York: Vintage.

———. (1977). *Discipline and Punish: The Birth of the Prison.* New York: Pantheon Books.

———. (1978). *The History of Sexuality, an Introduction.* New York: Random House.

Franklin, Sarah & Helena Ragone. (1998). Introduction. In *Reproducing Reproduction: Kinship, Power, and Technological Innovation.* Eds. Sarah Franklin and Helena Ragone. Philadelphia: University of Pennsylvania Press.

Groneman, Carol. (1994). Nymphomania: The historical construction of female sexuality. *Signs: Journal of Women in Culture and Society, 19*:2.

Hausman, Bernice. (1995). *Changing Sex: Transsexuailsm, Technology, and the Idea of Gender.* London: Duke University Press.

Haraway, Donna Jeanne. (1991). *Simians, Cyborgs, and Women: The Reinvention of Nature.* New York: Routledge.

———. (1999). The virtual speculum in the new world order. In *Revisioning Women, Health, and Healing: Feminist, Cultural, and Technoscience Perspectives,* Eds. Adele E. Clarke and Virginia L. Olesen. New York: Routledge.

Irvine, Janice. (1990). *Disorders of Desire: Sex and Gender in Modern American Sexology.* Temple University Press.

Jacobson, Nora. (2000). *Cleavage: Technology, Controversy and the Ironies of the Man-Made Breast.* New Jersey: Rutgers University Press.

Kimmel, Michael. (1996). *Manhood in America: A Cultural History.* New York: Free Press.

———. & Michael Messner. [1989] 1995. *Men's Lives.* Boston: Allyn and Bacon.

Maines, Rachel. (1999). *The Technology of Orgasm: "Hysteria," the Vibrator, and Women's Sexual Satisfaction.* Johns Hopkins.

Messner, Michael. (1997). *The Politics of Masculinities: Men in Movements.* Thousand Oaks: Sage Publications.

Martin, Emily. (1994). *Flexible Bodies.* Boston: Beacon Press.

Mumford, Kevin. (1992). Lost manhood found: Male sexual impotence and Victorian culture in the United States. *Journal of the History of Sexuality, 3*(1).

Potts, Annie. (2000). The essence of the hard on. *Men and Masculinities, 3*(1): 85–103.

Raymond, Janice. (1994). *The Transsexual Empire: The Making of the She-Male.* New York: Athene.

Reissman, Catherine Kohler. (1983). Women and medicalization: A new perspective. *Social Policy, 14*(1).

Sawicki, Jana. (1991). *Disciplinary Foucault: Feminism, Power, and the Body.* New York: Routledge.

Terry, Jennifer. (1995). The seductive power of science in the making of deviant subjectivity. In *Posthuman Bodies,* eds. Judith Halberstam and Ira Livingston, Bloomington: Indiana University Press.

Tiefer, Leonore. (1998). Doing the Viagra tango. *Radical Philosophy, 92.*

———. (1994). The medicalization of impotence: Normalizing phallocentrism. *Gender & Society, 8*(3).

Watkins, Elizabeth. (1998). *On the Pill: A Social History of Oral Contraceptions, 1950–1970.* Baltimore: Johns Hopkins University Press.

West, Candace & Sarah Fenstermaker. (1995). Doing difference. *Gender & Society, 9*(1): 8–38.

PART EIGHT

Men in Families

Are men still taking seriously their responsibilities as family breadwinners? Are today's men sharing more of the family housework and childcare than those in previous generations? The answers to these questions are complex, and often depend on which men we are talking about and what we mean when we say "family."

Many male workers long ago won a "family wage" and, with it, made an unwritten pact to share that wage with a wife and children. But today, as Barbara Ehrenreich argues in her influential book *The Hearts of Men*, increasing numbers of men are revolting against this traditional responsibility to share their wages, thus contributing to the rapidly growing impoverishment of women and children. Ehrenreich may be correct, at least with respect to the specific category of men who were labeled "yuppies" in the 1980s. But if we are looking at the growing impoverishment of women and children among poor, working-class, and minority families, the causes have more to do with dramatic shifts in the structure of the economy—including skyrocketing unemployment among young black males—than they do with male irresponsibility. Increasing numbers of men have no wage to share with a family.

But how about the new dual-career family? Is this a model of egalitarianism, or do women still do what sociologist Arlie Hochschild calls "the second shift"—the housework and childcare that comes after they get home from work. In this section, Francine Deutsch examines dual-career families and observes how men get out of sharing housework and childcare. Deutsch makes clear that equality will come only when we have dual careers and dual-career families. Anne Shelton and Daphne John examine the different patterns among men of different ethnic groups.

Also in flux are notions of fatherhood and how this role may be changing. Are men becoming more nurturing and caring fathers, developing skills, like the men in Hollywood films such as *Three Men and a Baby*, or simply loving their children more than life itself, as in *Ransom, Jingle All the Way*, and so many others? The articles in this section cause us to expand the debate about fatherhood, recognizing the variety of fatherhoods that are evidenced by different groups of men, such as gay men (Judith Stacey) or Chicano men (Gloria González-López). Scott Coltrane summarizes the research on the effects of inolved fatherhood.

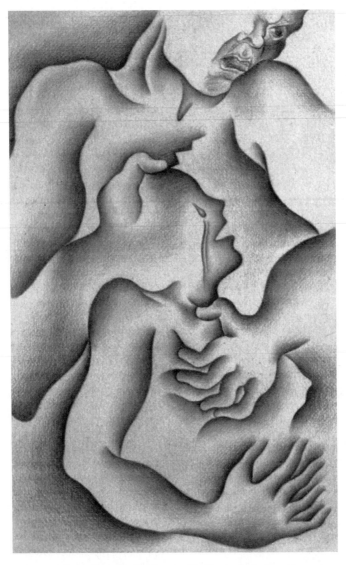

Trying to Kill the Womanly Feelings in His Heart, study from *Powerplay,* Copyright Judy Chicago 1986, prismacolor on hand-made paper, 15″ × 10″. Collection of Jeffrey Bergen, ACA Galleries, New York, NY. Photo: © Donald Woodman.

Francine M. Deutsch

Strategies Men Use to Resist

Women's ambivalence alone certainly doesn't account for the unequal division of labor at home. The unequal men are hardly fighting to do an equal share of the work. In part, they feel entitled to their wives' domestic services, entitled to pursue unfettered careers, and entitled to relax after their day at the job. Yet they don't feel as entitled as their fathers did. They recognize that their wives are out doing paid labor as well. The men in my study virtually never justified their lack of involvement in household work by invoking some inherent right or privilege they held as men. Although even recent statistics show that women do much more of the household labor, the raw spoken claim of male privilege seems to have become taboo. Men do resist, but their strategies are largely indirect. They include: passive resistance, strategic incompetence, strategic use of praise, the adherence of inferior standards, and denial.

Passive Resistance

"Just say nothing!" seems to be the motto of some men who resist their wives' efforts to involve them in household work. The most obvious form of passive resistance is simply to ignore the request. When I asked one father how he responded to his wife's entreaties, he answered, "In one ear, and out the other."

Obliviousness can be another form of passive resistance. Ethan sits with his coffee oblivious to his children's requests for juice. Another mother reports a similar scene at her house:

From *Halving it All* by Francine Deutsch, Cambridge, MA: Harvard University Press, 1999.

He plants himself on the couch. As soon as he's home from work sometimes . . . If there's something going on with kids, the kids could be screaming and yelling. He's totally oblivious to it. I'm listening to it (while preparing dinner) and I have to come out here and say something to them.

Sometimes men give in and perform a particular household duty, but their grouchiness while doing so becomes another form of passive resistance:

He'll help do dishes once in a while . . . He might put up a stink, but he'll end up doing it. I think I . . . try to sleaze out of it (responsibility when at home) as much as I can . . . I try to dicker or make an excuse or something as my first response, but I usually end up, perhaps somewhat nastily, taking care of them (household chores).

Passive resistance is effective because it requires so much energy to overcome. Women, already tired from their double day, may give up the struggle if the cost of getting help looks higher than the benefits of that help. Having to ask a husband to pour the juice when a child asks may feel like more effort than it's worth. As one mother put it: "I have to direct him and it's easier for me to just do it." The sulking, unpleasant compliance of a husband who clearly resents doing a chore will probably cloud whatever satisfaction his wife feels in getting help. Small wonder that the next time she may very well shrink from trying to obtain his help.

Incompetence

Ruining the laundry, leaving grease on the dishes, ignoring children when one is supposed to be watching them, and forgetting to pick them up from activities are all examples of the strategy of incompetence. Incompetence has its rewards. It allows men to justify the gender-based distribution of domestic labor.

> Getting the kids dressed—these buttons are so tiny I can't do these tiny buttons . . . Poor kids, they're always getting dressed backwards.

> Dinnertime. Mom is the cook. When the kids hear that Daddy's going to be making dinner, they'd rather eat out. I'm not talented. I'm just not very good in the kitchen.

> I just don't possess the tools to deal with girls' clothing, whereas she can.

Women may think twice about trying to get their husbands to take more responsibility at home when the way they carry out those responsibilities creates more problems than it solves: "From time to time he's taken on laundry, but that always ends up really a disaster, something being stained or shrunk, so I don't want him to do laundry."

Ruined laundry or mismatched children's outfits may be annoying, but incompetent care for children can be downright frightening. One mother recounted an incident in which her husband forgot her specific instructions to pick up his eight-year-old son before the older one so that the younger child wouldn't be waiting alone. The eight-year-old did end up waiting on a corner for his father, not alone only because another mother discovered his predicament and waited with him. Not surprisingly, she concludes, "Sometimes I don't trust (my husband) . . . He just doesn't pay attention."

Likewise, another mother explained why she worries when her husband watches their two-year-old:

> The other day he was outside with her and he was sitting there reading the newspaper. I never do that, never sit there and read a newspaper, not because I have to see everything that she does. It was more of a safety thing . . . I would like to feel more confident that when he's alone

with her he is watching out for her safety-wise. I sometimes think he's not as conscious of safety.

One might argue that men's "incompetence" in household chores is not a strategy, but simply reflects their lack of skill because of the way they were raised. Boys aren't taught how to take care of children and how to do laundry. According to this argument, even if their incompetence functions to relieve them of domestic responsibility, it doesn't mean that the incompetence is by design. There are two flaws in this argument.

First, although women may be socialized to feel the responsibility for childcare, many have not learned any of the necessary skills before they actually become parents. The difference between them and their husbands is that they know they have no choice. They have to learn how to button those tiny buttons, how to feed solid food, and how to soothe a crying infant. Although these women may have begun parenthood as incompetently as their husbands, the expectations that they and others hold for them as mothers mean that they simply learn what is necessary to learn.

Second, the skills in question can readily be learned. If one took the descriptions of men's incompetence at face value, one would wonder how these men held down jobs. Can it really be the case that a machinist or a man who holds a Ph.D. is incapable of running a washing machine? Women and men often say that women are the managers at home because the women are more organized, but how then do these "disorganized" men manage at work? If a man "forgot" important responsibilities at work the way the father just described "forgot" to pick up his eight-year-old son, he might soon be out of a job.

At heart the issue is not competence, but motivation. If someone wants to learn how to cook, do laundry, take care of children, and manage the household chores she or he can certainly do so. The equally sharing (and alternating-shift) fathers make eminently clear that competence in household skills is not the exclusive domain of women. Some women are not fooled by their husband's cries of incompetence. Listen to this mother's take on what happens when she asks for some help:

> He plays, you know, "How do you do this kind of thing?" and asks me fifteen questions so it would almost be easier for me to do it myself than to sit there and answer all his questions. That makes me angry because I feel like he's just playing stupid because he doesn't want to do it.

The strategy of incompetence often works. Like passive resistance, it is a way of making the cost of the struggle over the work at home too high. This mother sums it up succinctly: "If they act incompetent, then we have to act competent . . . I have this fear that if I didn't do it, then it wouldn't get done or it would be done incompetently." It is a fear that has basis in fact.

Praise

The flip side of men's self-portrayals of incompetence is their praise of their wives' skill in domestic labor. Although praise may be a sincere expression of appreciation, a benefit to its recipient, praise at home may also have the insidious effect of keeping the work within women's domain. The underlying message from men to their wives may sometimes be: "You're so good at it, you should do it." Sometimes the message is hardly subtle: "It would be a struggle for me to do the laundry. I don't think I do it as well as Roz. I think she is better with sort of the *peasant* stuff of life." And the father who said the kids wanted to eat out when they heard Dad was the cook told me: "I only eat to survive, but Dale is just wonderful. She makes these fabulous dinners." In a few couples men used the praise they heaped on their wives to justify why childcare was divided traditionally in their households:

> I definitely wasn't as good as Roz. Roz's just good. She's good if they get a splinter. She's just good at all that stuff.
>
> She's wonderful (as a mother) . . . Some women, like I say, are geared to be business-

women; Florence is geared to be a mother. She loves it. She's good at it. I feel real lucky to have her as a partner because it takes a lot of the burden off me.

Praise can be insidious precisely because women do derive satisfaction from a job well done at home and from receiving recognition for it. Ironically, praise may undermine women's struggle for more help because they don't want to lose the self-esteem they derive from husbands' admiring accolades.

Different Standards

Another strategy men use to resist work at home is to maintain different and lower standards. Their spoken or unspoken claim is that they don't care as much as their wives if the house is clean, if a nutritious dinner is served, or if children have after-school activities.

There are three ways that couples might respond to this difference. First, men could raise their standards to meet their wives'. This rarely happens among the unequal couples. Second, women could lower their standards, which occasionally does occur among this group. Most commonly, however, the difference in standards becomes a driving force behind an unequal division. The person who cares more takes the responsibility and does the work.

Women usually care more about keeping the house neat and clean because they, and not their husbands, are judged to be lacking if the house is a mess: "He wouldn't care if it wasn't dusted once every six months. I care because it's a reflection on me. Now that's another problem. Why should it be a reflection on me? He lives here too. But if anybody comes in here and the house is dirty, they're going to think that I'm a slob." Nonetheless, women are lowering their standards for household care, as sales of paper plates have increased and sales of floor wax have declined.

The problem of what children need is a more troubling one. When the welfare of children is involved, women often feel they can't compromise their standards. Denise gave up a camping trip because she thought one parent should be home with her kids. Other mothers changed their jobs so they could meet the school bus when their husbands wouldn't do it or take their children to the after-school activities that they cared about more than their husbands did.

Denial

Just as a magician tricks us by directing our gaze elsewhere while he makes his move, some fathers deny there is a problem by focusing attention elsewhere while their wives do the work at home. Denial takes a variety of forms. Men exaggerate their own contributions by comparing themselves to previous generations, attribute greater contributions of their wives to their wives' personalities or preferences, and obscure who's doing what by invoking rules and patterns that sound fair and equal.

Men often recall their own fathers' roles at home in order to understand their superior contributions. Ironically, some men who do far less than their wives even see themselves as progressive role models. One father in a dual-earner family said he did 35 percent of the childcare; his wife said 25 percent. Nevertheless, he sees himself as a model of equality. His exaggerated view of his contributions seems to stem from his implicit comparison to himself and his father. When I asked why mothers usually did more at home, he said, "Because of the roles of our parents." (His analysis, of course, ignores that his wife leads a very different life from that of his mother, who was never employed outside the home.) He went on to describe his own contributions in glowing terms:

> We've joked and talked about many of the things that I try and do as far as helping and participating . . . I'm hoping that as our girls are selecting mates later in life, they remember how much I helped out and how caring and listening I was . . . One of the advantages for kids that I'm involved with parenting (is) that they will expect their spouses will be involved. I'm a strong advocate of equal rights of women.

No doubt he is a loving and caring father, but he is far from contributing an equal share at home. He does help out, but his enthusiasm for the benefits of their modern division of labor must be considered in light of the inequality between him and his wife and her response to their division: "Sometimes I get overwhelmed and tired, real tired." By focusing on what he is doing that his father didn't, this man seems to miss what his wife is doing that he is not.

Men sometimes obscure an unequal division of labor by talking about and perhaps thinking about themselves and their wives as interchangeable. When I asked men to describe a typical day, indicating who did what, they sometimes used the word "we." "We get the kids ready for school." "We unloaded the dishwasher." Invariably, on further investigation, "we" meant that their wives were doing it.

Men also suggested by a false interchangeability between themselves and their wives by invoking a rule for dividing household labor that ostensibly applied equally to each, but actually worked in their favor. For example, parents commonly reported that whoever was available did the task at hand. Although that might sound like an equitable procedure, it is not if the father arranges to be unavailable. Consider this family. The father describes the division of responsibility at night: "As far as helping with the homework it's fairly equal . . . We both tend to try to help out—whoever's free that night . . . It's not you're going to do the help in math or I'm going to help in math. It's who's free." That sounds equitable, but listen to his wife's description of what happens in the evening:

> That's been a bone of contention lately. Sawyer goes out a lot . . . He still runs a lot at night so that leaves me to deal with the homework . . . She (one of their children) needs a lot of help with math, so that any homework issues I've been dealing with, and getting the youngest ready for bed.

He goes out, so guess who is available?

Finally, fathers sometimes engage in denial when they acknowledge an inequity in the distribution of labor but attribute it to personality characteristics or personal preferences of their wives. Men exaggerated their wives' enjoyment of the family work. For example, this 75–25 father told me: "Cooking relaxes her. She likes to do it and she likes to keep busy for the most part." But when I talked to his wife, she *complained* that he didn't make dinner when he got home from work early.

By imagining their wives' desire and need to do the domestic labor, these men avoid acknowledging the inequity within the couple. This denial allows them to resist not only the work, but also the guilt they might feel if they viewed the situation accurately.

Clearly, men in the unequal families resist the work at home. But the unequal men are not villains. In fact, most are helpers, not slackers. They do relinquish some male privileges, even while they resist giving up others. However, they also ignore the need for their help, feign incompetence, manipulate their wives with praise, discourage them with very low household and parental standards, and avoid work by denying that there is any conflict at all. All of these strategies work to relieve men of household work without their having to admit directly that they simply don't feel responsible for it. Despite the time their wives spend earning a paycheck, the unequal men often feel entitled to avoid picking up the slack at home. The myth implicitly promulgated by these men is that their wives do the work at home not simply because they are women, but because they notice it, they're better at it, and they enjoy it more.

Although these work-resisting strategies are used mostly by the unequal husbands, the equally sharing husbands are not perfect either. Some resist giving up at least a few traditional male privileges. Housework, in particular, seemed an area of contention. For example, in one of the most explicitly feminist equally sharing couples I interviewed, the father's "incompetence" in doing laundry sounded remarkably familiar. Even in the most equal of households, there may be vestiges of the old ways. Still, even if there are some pockets of resistance, for the most part the equally sharing fathers honor their wives' claims to equality.

Strong Women and Reasonable Men

Strong women and reasonable men resolve the conflict over domestic work by inventing equality. Equally sharing mothers are an assertive crew. They communicate in a clear and direct manner, and use whatever clout they have to elicit their husbands' cooperation. Their husbands acknowledge the strength of these women in establishing equality at home:

> Sally is very strong. There's no question about that. I think it's partly that Sally . . . makes it that we both share. She feels very strongly about that.

> I think the most important reason is that Bernice absolutely, completely insists on it.

However, part of the reason these women appear strong is their success, and although women's strength may be necessary in the fight for equality, it is not sufficient. The strength and assertiveness of the equally sharing mothers is matched by the sense of fairness evident in the behavior of the equally sharing fathers. Equally sharing men have relinquished male privileges to which at least some had initially felt entitled.

In fact, the equally sharing women may argue for principles of equality because they sense they have a shot at success with their husbands. The unequally sharing mothers, realizing the futility of trying for equality in their families, settle for trying to get their husbands to do a bit more. The equally sharing mothers may not have to resort to meltdowns because their husbands have already responded. The rage of the unequal women may express more than the frustration of trying to do the impossible. It may be the rage of impotence at their failure to get more help.

Compare the experience of the equally sharing mothers who won the battles for equality to that of Madeline, a legal services attorney with two children, who began parenthood with strong views about equal sharing. She and her husband agreed that when their first child was born each of them would take parental leave, and subsequently each of them would cut back on paid work to care for their new baby to avoid using too much daycare. Her husband, Aaron, was thrilled with his equally sharing role in the early years of parenting: "I was very excited about it. I had a paternity leave and . . . did sole care . . . and then worked a three- or four-day week for another year . . . There was a lot of time when I was just with my son and I considered that a privilege." Equal sharing was initially achieved in this family with little conflict. But perhaps signs of the dénouement were evident in the meaning Aaron ascribed to his sharing. The language he uses as he enthusiastically describes his role as a new parent is telling. It is the language of personal choice: "It was just great. It completely felt like my own choice and not something that I should do or that I had to do."

It is difficult to imagine a mother speaking these words. No matter how thrilled she is at spending time with a new infant, there is no denying that caring for a new baby is something she "should do." Aaron expresses the thrill of parenting at the same time that he asserts his entitlement not to do it. He immerses himself in parenthood the first time around because he wants to, not because he feels ultimately that it is his responsibility to do so. Thus, after their second child was born, when his career was getting off the ground and he had less passion and energy for parenting, he felt entitled to refuse to do it. He refused to take parental leave or cut back to part-time work. His wife told me:

> If you had come a year after William was born, then you would have found us struggling more about whose responsibility was what. I was feeling very much like Aaron was reneging on the commitment that we made about being with William . . . I had made my commitment and he wasn't keeping his part of the bargain.

Madeline was every bit as assertive as the equally sharing mothers. Yet, although she fought for her belief in equal responsibility for childcare clearly and directly, today she compromises her career while her husband takes a helper role at home. Aaron's analysis of what happens in "society" aptly describes what happened in his own family:

"I think probably men feel they have the option to invest or not invest, whereas I think women feel they're the bottom line and they can't count on anyone else to do that."

Madeline may not appear as strong as other equally sharing mothers simply because she failed. Her husband did not honor her claims of equality. Aaron differed from the equally sharing men because those men accepted the justice of their wives' claims, even if they hadn't internalized as strong a feeling of responsibility for family life as their wives had. One extraordinarily honest equally sharing father acknowledged that although he "irrationally" wished his wife would create a more traditional family life, "rationally" he recognized that it wouldn't be fair: "I'm hardly a raging feminist, but I do have enough sense to see that that's a completely unfair distribution of labor."

Thus a sense of fairness motivates some of the equally sharing men to accept their wives' well-argued claims. Moreover, that sense of fairness drives some of the men to share even without a struggle. Let's not forget Paul, the father of five, who jumped in to help without prompting from his wife. His sense of fairness and love for his wife dictated that it wouldn't be right to shirk while she worked.

The sense of entitlement that men and women bring to marriage affects the content and conduct of their conflicts, but it also changes and develops over time. Feelings of entitlement lead women to fight for principles, make clear and rational demands, and back them up with power-assertive strategies. But the feelings of entitlement expressed by the equally sharing mothers can also be a product, rather than a precursor, of their success. When their husbands accept principles of equality, respond to their demands, or indicate that their relationships are more important than male privilege, they promote a feeling of entitlement in their wives.

For example, consider Paul's wife, Mary, the equally sharing mother of five who didn't demand equality or even fight for it. When I asked her whether she or Paul had more leisure time, she reflected for a few seconds (indicating there wasn't much difference between them) and then replied, "I don't know, maybe he has a little bit more," adding in a light-hearted tone, "I'll have to do something about that." Once achieved, equality feels like a right.

Conversely, when the unequal husbands resist, they undermine their wives' sense of entitlement to their help. Listen to this mother's story:

> There's some things that aren't worth fighting over. I always know when (my husband) has been babysitting for a couple of hours because the living room looks like a demolition derby has come through. And the bathroom looks the same way . . . the dirty diapers are in there and all the dirty clothes are all over the bathroom floor . . . So I just have learned that it's not worth wasting all kinds of extra energy. I just kind of do it, not necessarily that I like it. *He helps much more than a lot of fathers help.*

The futility of some struggles leads women to give up and to read just their expectations. Instead of comparing their husbands' contributions to their own, they shift to comparing their husbands' contributions to those of other men. It is precisely that focus on within-gender comparison that maintains different senses of entitlement between men and women. If a husband does more than his peers, his wife may then conclude she is get-

ting a good deal. But although she may be getting a good deal relative to other women, it's not so good when you compare it to what her husband is getting. The shift in comparisons, however, allows women to live with resistant husbands and not feel exploited.

Men's senses of entitlement are also, in part, products of the struggle with their wives. When you look at the equally sharing men now, they all seem eminently reasonable. For some, the reasonable stance was born out of serious strife with their wives. Interestingly, sometimes these men don't mention the conflicts that led up to their equally sharing role. For example, the husband who had expected his wife to "cook, clean, . . . and box his collars" made no mention of the strikes his wife used to get him to change. His transformation occurred so thoroughly that now his explanation for equal sharing refers only to his own sense of responsibility to do right by his children.

Discovering themselves acting like egalitarians, equally sharing fathers often pat themselves on the back for their enlightened stance. Meanwhile, their wives tout their own assertiveness and strength. Although they look like they have always been strong women and reasonable men, it is important not to forget that female strength and male reason are qualities that are sustained, lost, or developed in the creation of family life.

Anne Shelton
Daphne John

Ethnicity, Race, and Difference: A Comparison of White, Black, and Hispanic Men's Household Labor Time

Most of the recent research on household labor concerns the impact of women's labor force participation on the allocation of tasks or responsibilities. Researchers routinely recognize that women's household labor time is associated with their employment status, as well as with a variety of other sociodemographic characteristics, including age and education. A great deal has been written about the ways in which time commitments and sex role attitudes affect the division of household labor (Coverman 1985; Huber and Spitze 1983; Perrucci, Potter, and Rhoads 1978; Pleck 1985; Ross 1987). Men are by definition included in the analyses that focus on the division of household labor, but these studies typically ignore the relationship between men's work and family roles.

Some researchers have examined the relationship between men's work and family roles (Coverman 1985; Pleck 1977, 1985), but the relative scarcity of these studies means that although some questions about men's household roles have been examined, a number of issues remain unexamined. In particular, there has been little research on the impact of men's paid labor time on their household labor time and there has been only limited research on racial and ethnic variations in men's household labor time.

In this analysis we begin to examine some of the neglected issues in the study of men's household labor time by focusing on how married men's

From *Men, Work, and Family,* Jane Hood (ed.), pp. 131–150. Sage Publications, 1993. Reprinted with permission.

paid labor time affects their family roles as defined by their household labor time and specific household tasks. Although there is less variation in men's paid labor time than in women's, there is some variation, and just as paid labor time affects women's household labor time, it may also affect men's. Moreover, the amount of time men have available to them may affect the specific household tasks they perform, with men with more time performing more nondiscretionary tasks than men who have less time available to them.

Recently, increased awareness of the need to examine links between gender and race have led many to argue that race and gender cannot, in fact, be discussed separately (Collins 1990; Reid and Comas-Diaz 1990; Zinn 1991). Moreover, "gender studies" should not be limited only to women. Therefore, we assess the impact of selected sociodemographic characteristics on men's household labor time with a special emphasis on race and ethnicity.

Literature Review

The changes in women's labor force participation have resulted in a large number of dual-earner couples. Kimmel (1987) notes that this shift has created not only new role demands for women, but also new demands for men. Just as women have expanded their roles in the paid labor force, men also have expanded their roles in the family. The transition in men's and women's roles may, however, vary by race and ethnicity because of the historically different patterns of black, white, and Hispanic women's labor force participation (Beckett and Smith 1981; McAdoo 1990).

Although researchers routinely examine the impact of women's paid labor time on the household division of labor, the impact of men's paid labor time on the household division of labor is generally ignored. The lack of attention to the impact of men's paid work time on their household labor time may reflect the fact that there is less variability in men's paid labor time than in women's. Those studies that have examined the impact of men's paid work time on their household labor time have yielded conflicting results (Barnett and Baruch 1987; Coverman and Sheley 1986; Pleck 1985; Thompson and Walker 1989). Some find that men's time spent in paid labor is negatively associated with their household labor time (Rexroat and Shehan 1987; Atkinson and Huston 1984), whereas others find no association (Kingston and Nock 1985). Because this research rarely focuses on racial/ethnic variation, we have little information about the ways that paid labor and household labor demands may be related differently for white, black, and Hispanic men.

Research on black and Hispanic households indicates that the images of the egalitarian black household and the gender-stratified Hispanic household may be inaccurate depictions of reality derived from superficial examinations. In the case of black households, egalitarianism is commonly attributed to black women's high rates of labor force participation (McAdoo 1990). If, however, black women's labor force participation reflects economic pressures rather than egalitarian sex role attitudes (Broman 1988, 1991), women's employment may be unrelated to the division of labor.

Research on the division of labor in black households does not consistently indicate how black and white households differ. Some research on the division of household labor finds that black families have a more egalitarian division of labor than white families (Beckett 1976; Beckett and Smith 1981; Broman 1988, 1991). Other studies by J. A. Ericksen, Yancey, and E. P. Ericksen (1979) and Farkas (1976) also suggest that black men do more household labor than their white counterparts (see also Miller and Garrison 1982). However, Broman (1991, 1988) argues that although some egalitarian patterns do exist in black households, there is not gender equity. For example, in married couple households the proportions of men who state they do most of the household chores is much smaller than the proportion of women responding that they do all the household chores. Although unemployed men respond that they do more of the household chores more frequently than employed men, they do not make this claim nearly as often as women, regardless of women's employment status. Broman (1988) also notes that women are likely to report being primarily responsible for traditionally female tasks.

Other researchers argue that the image of the egalitarian black family is inaccurate (Cronkite 1977; Staples 1978; Wilson, Tolson, Hinton, and Kiernan 1990). For example, Wilson et al. (1990) point out that black women are likely to be responsible for child care and household labor. Cronkite (1977) says that black men prefer more internal differentiation in the household than do white men. That is, she argues that they prefer a more traditional division of household labor, with women responsible for housework and child care. Others claim that black families are similar to white families in egalitarianism and that the differences that do exist often are based on social class rather than on race per se (McAdoo 1990; Staples 1978). Staples (1978) also claims that class differences are consistent across race. McAdoo (1990) argues, in much the same vein, that black and white fathers are similarly nurturant to their children and that black and white middle- and upper-income fathers have similar parenting styles. In contrast to the view that black men are less traditional than white men, Ransford and Miller (1983) find that middle-class black men have more traditional sex role attitudes than white middle-class men.

The literature regarding the division of household labor within Hispanic households is more limited, and much of what is available deals only with Chicanos, excluding other Hispanics. The research on Hispanic households yields conflicting results. Golding (1990) finds that Mexican American men do less household labor than Anglo men, whereas Mexican American women do more household labor than Anglo women. Differences between Hispanic and Anglo men's housework and child care time, like the differences between black and white men, may be due to other differences between them (Golding 1990; McAdoo 1990; Staples 1978). Golding (1990) finds that education is correlated with ethnicity and household labor time such that after removing the effects of education, the impact of ethnicity on the division of labor in the household is not significant. Thus, although she finds a more traditional division of labor within Mexican American households than in Anglo households, this division of labor reflects educational differences rather than solely ethnicity effects. Similarly, Ybarra (1982) finds that although acculturation does not significantly affect who performs the household labor, wives' employment does. She finds that the division of labor in dual-worker households is more equal than in male provider households.

In other research, Mirande (1979) discusses the patterns of shared responsibility for domestic work in Mexican American households. Although men's participation in household labor may give the appearance of egalitarianism, it does not necessarily indicate equality. For example, men may participate but spend less time than women. Vega and colleagues (1986) argue that Mexican American families are similar to Anglo families but that in terms of their adaptability to change in family roles they appear to be more flexible than Anglo families. Thus the male provider role may be less firmly entrenched in Mexican American than in Anglo households, resulting in a less rigid division of household labor. Similarly, Zinn (1980) asserts that Mexican American women's changing work roles may change their role identification.

There also is research indicating that decision making is not shared in Hispanic households (Williams 1990). Williams (1990) finds that Mex-

ican American men continue to have more authority than wives, but that the patterns of decision making are not as traditional as in the past.

Some research suggests that the differences among white, black, and Hispanic men's family roles may reflect differences in the way that they internalize the provider role. Wilkie (1991) argues that black men's ability to fulfill the provider role may be associated with their rates of marriage (see also Tucker and Taylor 1989). Similarly, Stack (1974) found that when black men are unable to provide financially for their family, they also are less likely to participate in the household (e.g., housework and child care) (Cazenave 1979; Wilkie 1991). Although the findings of Wilkie (1991) and Tucker and Taylor (1989) do not directly indicate a relationship between the provider role and men's participation in the household, we can speculate that this association may exist. Thus, to the extent that there are differences among black, white, and Hispanic men's internalization of the provider role, we might also expect to find that the relationship between work and family roles varies by race/ethnicity.

We focus on the definition of egalitarianism based on the division of labor within the household. Hood (1983) notes that there are a number of ways in which an egalitarian marriage is defined. For our purposes, egalitarianism is defined in terms of household labor time. Some studies discuss decision making and role sharing, which are logically associated with the division of household labor, but which are not unproblematically related to it (Blumstein and Schwartz 1983).

A problem with much of the research on men's household labor time is the failure to incorporate wives' characteristics into the analyses. Just as men's paid labor time may act as a constraint on their household labor time, wives' paid labor time may create a demand for them to spend more time on household labor. The use of couples as the units of analysis in this chapter helps us understand the interaction between spouses' characteristics.

We further examine white, black, and Hispanic men's household labor time to determine the nature of the association between men's paid labor time and household labor time. In addition, we examine racial/ethnic differences in men's household labor time and assess the extent to which any observed differences may reflect differences in paid labor time, education, or other sociodemographic characteristics. We also incorporate wives' paid labor time and attitudes about family roles into our analysis to determine the ways in which husbands' and wives' characteristics interact to affect men's household labor time.

Data and Methods

The data for this study are from the 1987 National Survey of Families and Households (NSFH) (Sweet, Bumpass, and Call 1988), a national probability sample of 9,643 persons with an oversampling of 3,374 minority respondents, single parents, cohabiting persons, recently married persons, and respondents with stepchildren. One adult per household was selected randomly to be the primary respondent and his or her spouse/partner (if applicable) was also given a questionnaire designed for secondary respondents. Portions of the main interview with the primary respondent were self-administered, as was the entire spouse/partner questionnaire. In this analysis, we include only married respondents with a completed spouse questionnaire.

In the analyses to follow we begin by describing black, white, and Hispanic men's and women's household labor time. In addition to comparing household labor time across racial/ethnic groups, we also compare this time by work status.

In the second stage of the analysis, we examine the relationship between ethnicity and men's household labor time after controlling for a variety of other factors, including age, education, sex role attitudes, and both husbands' and wives' paid work. We use multiple regression analysis to determine if there are race/ethnic differences in household labor time or in the impact of paid labor time on household labor time that are independent of sociodemographic differences between white, black, and Hispanic men.[1]

In addition to determining whether or not a race/ethnicity effect on household labor time exists once other characteristics have been taken into account, we look at the relationship between husbands' and wives' paid labor and household labor time. We expect to find that men who spend more time in paid work will spend less time on household labor once other characteristics have been held constant. Moreover, to the extent that wives' market work time may act as a demand on men, we expect to find that the more time wives spend in paid labor the more time husbands will spend on household labor, once other variables have been held constant.

Our analyses include separate estimates of white, black, and Hispanic men's and women's household labor time. Hispanics include Mexican Americans as well as other Hispanic respondents. Paid labor time is measured in hours usually spent per week at work for both respondents and spouses. Education and age are measured in years.

Respondents' and spouses' sex role attitudes are measured by their responses to two attitude items. Each item was scored from 1 to 5. Respondents were asked if they agreed with the following statements:

1. If a husband and a wife both work full-time, they should share household tasks equally.
2. Preschool children are likely to suffer if their mother is employed.

Responses to the two items were summed and divided by two so that the range of the summated measure is 1 to 5. A high score indicates more liberal sex role attitudes and a low score indicates more traditional sex role attitudes.

Presence of children was included as an independent variable in some of the analyses. A score of 0 indicates that the respondent has no children under the age of 18 in the household, whereas a score of 1 indicates that there are children under the age of 18 in the household.

Findings

Findings in Table 40.1 reveal that black and Hispanic men spend significantly more time on household labor than do white men. Women's household labor time also varies by race/ethnicity, but in a different pattern. Hispanic women spend significantly more time on household labor than white women. They also spend more time on household labor than black women, but a t-test of the difference is not significant. Nevertheless, the gap is of substantive interest because the lack of statistical significance is largely a function of inflated standard deviations due to the small number of black and Hispanic respondents. As the results in Table 40.1 indicate, the divergent patterns of variation in household labor time by race and gender combine in such a way that men's proportionate share of household labor also varies by ethnicity.

Black men spend an average of 25 hours per week on household labor compared to 19.6 hours for white men and 23.2 hours for Hispanic men. The absolute size of the gap between black and Hispanic men's household labor time is small, with both groups of men spending significantly more time on household labor than white men. Nevertheless, black men spend more time on household labor than Hispanic men, although the gap is not statistically significant. This pattern both partially confirms and contradicts earlier research. Black men's relatively high household labor time

is consistent with the view that black households may have a more equal division of labor than other households. The data in Table 40.1 do not, however, allow us to determine the source of black men's household labor time investments. It is possible, for example, that on average, black men spend less time in paid labor and therefore more time on household labor. The pattern also could reflect a number of other possible differences in the sociodemographic characteristics of black and white men that we examine in a later section.

Hispanic men's relatively high time investment in household labor is consistent with previous research finding that Hispanic men participate at least as much as Anglo men in household labor, and contradicts those who argue that Hispanic men participate in household labor less than Anglo men. Of course, much of the research on Hispanic men's family roles examines decision making or the distribution of power, rather than household labor time. Most of the research on household labor assumes that it is onerous duty and that only someone without the power to avoid it (or without any decisionmaking authority) will do it (Ferree 1987). Thus, researchers whose focus is on decision making often assume that egalitarian patterns of decision making are associated with an egalitarian division of household labor.

■ **TABLE 40.1**
Household Labor Time by Gender and Race/Ethnicity

	White	**Black**	**Hispanic**	**T-Test Blk/Wht**	**T-Test Hsp/Wht**	**T-Test Blk/Hsp**
Men	19.6	25.0	23.2	2.3**	2.2*	.6
	(19.3)	(28.7)	(19.2)			
Women	37.3	38.0	41.8	.3	1.9*	1.2
	(21.6)	(26.3)	(24.5)			
Men's % of Household Labor Time	34%	40%	36%			

Notes: *p ≤ .05; **p ≤ .01. Standard deviation in parentheses.

Women's household labor time also varies by race/ethnicity, with Hispanic women spending significantly more time on household labor than either black or white women. Hispanic women spend an average of 41.8 hours per week on household labor compared to 37.3 hours for white women and 38 hours per week for black women. Thus, Hispanic men and women spend significantly more time on household labor than white men and women, whereas black women's household labor time is not significantly different from white women's household labor time. Women's and men's different investments in household labor time affect men's proportionate share of household labor time. The data on black men and women indicate that black men do 40 percent of the household labor (done by men and women only) whereas Hispanic and Anglo men do 36 percent and 34 percent of the household labor, respectively. Thus, Table 40.1 confirms earlier research reporting that black households have a more equal division of household labor than white households and also confirms research indicating that Anglo and Hispanic households may have few differences in division of labor. In addition, the findings for Hispanic households suggest that there may be even more changes in the traditional patterns of Hispanic households

than Williams's (1990) research on decision-making indicates.

We begin to examine the source of some of the gap in Table 40.2, where we present white, black, and Hispanic men's household labor time by employment status using multiple classification analysis. We do this in order to determine if black men's relatively high levels of household labor time reflect their lower paid labor time.

With respect to employment status, there are some interesting patterns. For both white and Hispanic men, those who are employed spend less time on household labor than those who are not employed, although the pattern is statistically significant only for white men. For blacks, however, the pattern is quite different. Black men who are not employed spend less time on household labor than black men who are employed, although the difference is not statistically significant. These findings indicate that the relationship between paid labor time and household labor time varies by race/ethnicity and that differences in black, white, and Hispanic men's household labor time are not simply a function of differences in their employment status.

The relationship between black men's employment status and their household labor time may indicate that black men who are not

■ **TABLE 40.2**
Men's Household Labor Time by Race/Ethnicity and Employment Status

	White	Black	Hispanic
Employment Status			
Not employed	23.5	19.5	23.0
Employed PT (1-39 hrs.)	19.1	26.6	22.7
Employed FT	18.2	27.0	22.3
Eta	.12***	.13	.03
N	2798	183	164

Notes: We use 39 hours as our break between part-time and full-time in order to ensure an adequate *n* for the part-time category. Eta is a measure of association.

*** p ≤ .001.

employed are different from nonemployed white and Hispanic men. To the extent that black men are not employed involuntarily, the results in Table 40.2 may reflect the age structure of those who are not employed. It also may indicate the presence of a distinct group of black men characterized by both low time investments in paid labor and low investments in household labor. The argument that the apparent egalitarianism of the black family may be a function of black men's reduced hours in paid labor is not supported by these findings. If anything, these findings indicate that, among blacks, the division of household labor is likely to be more equal in households where the man is employed than in households where he is not. Although this is in some sense counterintuitive, it may indicate that the "breadwinner" role is internalized in such a way that even black men who are not employed may opt out of the family per se, rather than compensating for their reduced paid work with more household labor (Komarovsky 1940; Stack 1974). Among the men in this sample, the expression of their "opting out" may be to avoid household labor. (See Cazenave 1984; Hood 1986, for more discussion of the importance of subjective perceptions of work and family roles.)

Up to this point we have examined men's household labor time without taking into consideration a variety of sociodemographic characteristics, sex role attitudes, or wives' work status. Thus, some of the observed race/ethnic differences may reflect other differences among white, black, and Hispanic households. In Table 40.3 we examine the impact of race/ethnicity on men's household labor time by estimating the direct effect of race/ethnicity on household labor time as well as by estimating the ways that paid labor time may affect white, black, and Hispanic men's household labor time differently, after taking other factors into account. Thus, in Table 40.3 we can determine if the previously observed association between race/ethnicity and household labor time or the race/ethnic differences in the impact of paid labor time on household labor

time are artifacts of other differences among white, black, and Hispanic men.

The results in Table 40.3 show that after controlling for respondents' education, age, children, men's sex role attitudes, wives' sex role attitudes and paid labor time, race/ethnicity is not significantly associated with men's household labor time. Thus, the differences among white, black, and Hispanic men's household labor time that we observed earlier appear to reflect other differences among them. For example, they may reflect differences in social class or education as McAdoo (1990) and Golding (1990) have argued. They may also, however, reflect differences in the presence of children or in wives' paid labor time.

Although we find no direct effects of race/ethnicity on men's household labor time in our multivariate analysis, the differential effect of paid labor time on men's household labor time remains.[2] For white and Hispanic men, each additional hour spent in paid labor is associated with their spending slightly more than six fewer minutes per day on household labor. For black men, however, each additional hour in paid labor is associated with them spending more time on household labor, even after controlling for sociodemographic and household characteristics. Thus, the pattern we observed in the bivariate analyses is repeated in the multivariate analyses. The more time black men spend in paid labor the more time they spend on household labor, whereas the association between paid labor time and household labor time is negative for Anglo and Hispanic men.

There are a variety of possible explanations for the different association between paid labor time and household labor time for black men than for white or Hispanic men. Black men may define the breadwinner role more narrowly than white or Hispanic men, such that when they are not employed and unable to contribute to their family's financial well-being they may retreat from the family in other ways (Stack 1974). The race/ethnic variation in the association between

■ **TABLE 40.3**

Regression of Men's Household Labor Time on Paid Labor Time, Race/Ethnicity, Presence of Children, Education, Age, Sex Role Attitudes, Wives' Paid Labor Time, and Wives' Sex Role Attitudes

	beta	standard error
Paid labor	$-.10^{***}$	.02
Black	-3.4	2.4
Hispanic	$-.67$	3.2
Black/paid	$.27^{***}$	.07
Hispanic/paid	$.08$	.08
Children	3.7^{***}	.81
Education	$-.15$	.12
Age	$.02$	.03
Men's sex role attitudes	1.5^{***}	.52
Wives' paid labor time	$.07^{***}$	.02
Wives' sex role attitudes	$.76$	.51
Constant	13.4	3.4
R^2	.033	
N	2782	

Notes: $^{***}p \leq .001$.

men's paid labor time and household labor time may reflect differences in housing patterns. If households with nonemployed black men are more likely to live in apartments, and those with employed black men are more likely to live in single-family houses, the pattern we see may reflect the amount of household labor that must be done. The different association for white and Hispanic men may be the result of different housing patterns. That is, households with nonemployed white or Hispanic men may not be as concentrated in apartments as is the case with black households. Thus there may be variation in the amount of household labor that must be done associated with men's employment status.

The pattern of the effects of some of the control variables is also interesting. For example, men with children spend more time on household labor than men without children, and men with more egalitarian sex role attitudes spend more time on household labor than men with more traditional attitudes. Wives' sex role attitudes are not associated with men's household labor time, but the more time wives spend in paid labor, the more time husbands spend on household labor. Interestingly, after controlling for other variables, men's age is not significantly associated with their household labor time.

In Table 40.4 we further examine the relationship between men's employment status and their household labor time by examining white, black, and Hispanic men's time spent on specific household tasks, after controlling for sociodemographic and household characteristics. Among those men employed full-time, black men spend more time than white and Hispanic men cleaning house, shopping, and repairing automobiles. Cleaning house and shopping are typically

■ **T A B L E 4 0 . 4**

Men's Time Spent on Specific Household Tasks by Employment Status and Race/Ethnicity

	Not Employed	Employed Part-Time	Employed Full-Time
Preparing Meals			
White	3.3	2.9	2.3
Black	4.2	4.9	3.3
Hispanic	5.8	3.2	2.2
Beta	.09[+]	.09	.02
Washing Dishes			
White	2.7	2.2	1.9
Black	1.6	4.5	2.7
Hispanic	4.0	4.1	2.1
Beta	.06[*]	.22[**]	.05
Cleaning House			
White	2.3	1.8	1.7
Black	2.3	3.2	3.0
Hispanic	4.3	3.9	2.2
Beta	.08[+]	.20[**]	.11[***]
Outdoor Tasks			
White	7.5	5.0	5.6
Black	5.8	4.8	5.4
Hispanic	5.2	3.7	3.9
Beta	.06	.06	.06[*]
Shopping			
White	2.9	2.4	2.3
Black	2.7	2.6	4.0
Hispanic	2.5	3.5	3.1
Beta	.02	.08	.14[***]
Laundry			
White	.7	.8	1.2
Black	.9	1.5	.6
Hispanic	1.3	.4	.6
Beta	.06	.11	.08[***]
Paying Bills			
White	1.6	1.4	1.5
Black	2.5	2.2	2.4
Hispanic	2.1	4.1	2.5
Beta	.07	.26[***]	.09[***]

■ **TABLE 40.4**
Continued

	Not Employed	Employed Part-Time	Employed Full-Time
Auto Maintenance			
White	1.4	1.6	2.0
Black	1.4	2.5	3.4
Hispanic	2.1	3.2	2.9
Beta	.04	.21***	.08***
Driving			
White	1.2	1.3	1.5
Black	1.1	1.7	2.7
Hispanic	1.9	1.4	1.5
Beta	.04	.04	.08

Notes: Controlling for respondents' sex role attitudes, education, age, spouses' paid work time, spouses' sex role attitudes, and number of children. Beta is a partial measure of association. $^+p \le .10$; $^*p \le .05$; $^{**}p \le .01$; $^{***}p \le .001$.

"female-typed" tasks indicating that employed black men's household labor time represents less gender stratification rather than simply more time spent on tasks typically done by men. Nevertheless, there are some "female-typed" tasks on which white men spend more time. White men employed full-time spend more time on laundry than black or Hispanic men. Not all of the differences in housework time result from variation in time spent on "female-typed" tasks. White and black men employed full-time spend more time than Hispanic men on outdoor tasks, and black and Hispanic men employed full-time spend more time paying bills than white men.

Among those who are employed part-time or not at all, Hispanic men are most likely to spend more time on specific household tasks than either white or black men, although in a number of cases black and Hispanic men's household task time is similar. Hispanic men employed part-time spend the most time cleaning house, but black men also spend more time cleaning house than white men. Similarly, black men spend significantly more time washing dishes than other men, although Hispanic men spend almost as much

time as black men. Among those who are not employed, Hispanic men spend more time than black or white men preparing meals, washing dishes, and cleaning house; thus more time among "female-typed" tasks than other men.

The patterns observed in Table 40.4 indicate that there is more variation by race/ethnicity among men who are employed full-time than among those who are employed part-time or not at all. Although we should use care when comparing across employment statuses in Table 40.4 (because there may be sociodemographic differences among the groups), we can see that black men's greater household labor time, with respect to white and Hispanic men, appears to be among those who are employed full-time, whereas there are fewer and less definite patterns among those employed fewer hours or not at all.

With respect to specific household tasks, Table 40.4 shows that black men who are employed full-time spend more time on a variety of household tasks, rather than on only a few or male-typed tasks. The pattern of greater involvement in traditionally female tasks among black men employed full-time indicates that among black households there are more egalitarian patterns of family work when the husband is employed than when he is not.

Conclusion

Our findings point to several important patterns. Just as women's paid labor time is associated with their household labor time, we find that men's paid labor time is associated with their household labor time. Thus, although there is less variation in men's paid labor time than in women's, there is enough that it warrants some research attention. Interestingly, the pattern of association between paid labor time and household labor time varies by race/ethnicity. Employed black men do more household labor than those who are not employed, whereas employed white and Hispanic men do less household labor than those who are not employed. These different patterns illustrate the dangers of analyses that fail to examine not only the direct effect of race/ethnicity on household labor time but also the way that race/ethnicity may affect the relationship among other variables. The relationship between men's work and family roles is not such that we can talk about a relationship: the relationship varies by race/ethnicity. This difference in the relationship between work and family suggests that we need to conduct more research on the nature of work and family trade-offs and how they vary by race and ethnicity.

Our analyses also indicate some differences in the family roles (as measured by household labor time) of white, black, and Hispanic men. Our findings from bivariate analyses show that Hispanic and black men spend more time on household labor than white men. Even with Hispanic women's relatively high levels of household labor time, Hispanic men's proportionate share of household labor time is higher than white men's. Black men's relatively high proportionate share of household labor time confirms earlier research indicating that black households may be more egalitarian than white households. Unlike some speculation, however, we find that this pattern is not the result of differences in black men's paid labor time, but that employed black men are the ones who are spending more time on household labor. This somewhat surprising finding indicates the need to examine the relationship between black men's work and family roles in more detail. Given previous findings about black men's attachment to family and work roles (Cazenave 1979), black men's attachments to the provider role as well as their perceptions of family obligations may be the most fruitful place to begin future studies. In addition, the different patterns observed indicate the complex nature of the work—family linkage for men more generally. Further analyses might also focus on the characteristics of nonemployed black men as compared to nonemployed white and Hispanic men to determine what may account for the different patterns of work and family role trade-offs.

Finally, we find that higher household labor time among black men employed full-time reflects their greater time investments in traditionally female tasks, rather than differences in time investments in "male-typed" tasks. In addition, the pattern of Hispanic men's time spent on specific household tasks indicates that they often spend more time on female-typed tasks than Anglo men. Thus, even though Anglo and Hispanic men's total household labor time is not significantly different once sociodemographic characteristics have been taken into account, Hispanic men may spend more time on typically "female-typed" tasks like meal preparation, washing dishes, and cleaning house than do Anglo men (see also Mirandé 1985; Zinn 1980). In addition, our findings indicate that there may be more changes in the Hispanic household than some who have found changing patterns suggest (Mirandé 1985; Williams 1990).

In future research we must give more attention to racial/ethnic variation in men's family patterns as well as to the different trade-offs that men may make between work and family. We simply cannot assume that the trade-offs are the same for men as for women, just as we have often argued that we cannot assume that women's labor force experiences can be modeled in the same way that we model men's. At the same time, our findings argue for the systematic inclusion of ethnicity and race in studies of the work–family trade-off for both men and women. We need to examine differences among black, white, and Hispanic men's perceptions of their family responsibilities if we are to understand how they balance work and family responsibilities.

Notes

We appreciate the very helpful comments of Jane Hood, Norma Williams, Maxine Baca Zinn, and Marta Tienda.

1. The lack of statistical significance is a result of the relatively small number of black and Hispanic respondents in the survey.

2. To determine the differential effects of paid labor time for white, black, and Hispanic respondents we included interaction terms for race/ethnicity and paid labor time in our analysis. The nonsignificant effect for the interaction term between Hispanic and paid labor time indicates that the impact of paid labor time on Hispanic men's household labor time is not significantly different from the impact of paid labor time on white men's household labor time. The significant interaction term for black men indicates that there is a significant difference in the impact of paid labor time on black and white men's household labor time. By adding the coefficient for paid labor time to the coefficient for the black/paid labor time interaction term, we can see that even after controlling for sociodemographic and household characteristics, paid labor time is positively associated with black men's household labor time. Thus, the more time black men spend in paid labor the more time they spend in household labor, whereas the association between paid labor time and household labor time is negative for Anglo and Hispanic men.

References

Atkinson, J., and Huston, T. L. 1984. "Sex Role Orientation and Division of Labor Early in Marriage." *Journal of Personality and Social Psychology* 46, no. 2: 330–345.

Barnett, R. C., and Baruch, G. K. 1987. "Determinants of Fathers' Participation in Family Work." *Journal of Marriage and the Family* 49: 29–40.

Beckett, J. O. 1976. "Working Wives: A Racial Comparison." *Social Work,* November, 463–471.

Beckett, J. O., and Smith, A. D. 1981. "Work and Family Roles: Egalitarian Marriage in Black and White Families." *Social Service Review* 55, no. 2: 314–326.

Blumstein, P., and Schwartz, P. 1983. *American Couples.* New York: Pocket Books.

Broman, C. 1988. "Household Work and Family Life Satisfaction of Blacks." *Journal of Marriage and the Family* 50: 743–748.

———. 1991. "Gender, Work-Family Roles, and Psychological Well-Being of Blacks." *Journal of Marriage and the Family* 53: 509–520.

Cazenave, N. 1979. "Middle-Income Black Fathers: An Analysis of the Provider Role." *Family Coordinator* 28: 583–593.

———. 1984. "Race, Socioeconomic Status, and Age: The Social Context of Masculinity." *Sex Roles* 11, no. 7–8: 639–656.

Collins, P. H. 1990. *Black Feminist Thought: Knowledge, Consciousness and the Politics of Empowerment.* Cambridge, Mass.: Unwin Hyman.

Coverman, S. 1985. "Explaining Husbands' Participation in Domestic Labor." *Sociological Quarterly* 26, no. 1: 81–98.

Coverman, S., and Sheley, J. F. 1986. "Change in Men's Housework and Child-Care Time, 1965–1975." *Journal of Marriage and the Family* 48: 413–422.

Cronkite, R. C. 1977. "The Determinants of Spouses' Normative Preferences for Family Roles." *Journal of Marriage and the Family* 39: 575–585.

Ericksen, J. A., Yancey, W. L., and Ericksen, E. P. 1979. "The Division of Family Roles." *Journal of Marriage and the Family* 41: 301–313.

Farkas, G. 1976. "Education, Wage Rates, and the Division of Labor Between Husband and Wife." *Journal of Marriage and the Family* 38: 473–483.

Ferree, M. M. 1987. "Family and Job for Working-Class Women: Gender and Class Systems Seen from Below." In N. Gerstel and H. E. Gross, eds., *Families and Work,* 289–301. Philadelphia: Temple University Press.

Golding, J. M. 1990. "Division of Household Labor, Strain and Depressive Symptoms

Among Mexican Americans and Non-Hispanic Whites." *Psychology of Women Quarterly* 14: 103–117.

Hood, J. C. 1983. *Becoming a Two-Job Family.* New York: Praeger.

———. 1986. "The Provider Role: Its Meaning and Measurement." *Journal of Marriage and the Family* 48: 349–359.

Huber, J., and G. Spitze. 1983. *Sex Stratification: Children, Housework and Jobs.* New York: Academic Press.

Kimmel, M. S. 1987. "Rethinking 'Masculinity': New Directions in Research." In M. S. Kimmel, ed., *Changing Men: New Directions of Research on Men and Masculinity,* 9–24. Newbury Park, Calif.: Sage.

Kingston, P. W., and Nock, S. L. 1985. "Consequences of the Family Work Day." *Journal of Marriage and the Family* 47, no. 3: 619–630.

Komarovsky, M. 1940. *The Unemployed Man and His Family.* New York: Dryden.

McAdoo, H. P. 1990. "A Portrait of African American Families in the United States." In S. E. Rix, ed., *The American Woman 1990–1991: A Status Report,* 71–93. New York: Norton.

Miller, J., and Garrison, H. H. 1982. "Sex Roles: The Division of Labor at Home and in the Workplace." *Annual Review of Sociology* 8: 237–262.

Mirandé, A. 1979. "A Reinterpretation of Male Dominance in the Chicano Family." *Family Coordinator* 28, no. 4: 473–480.

———. 1985. *The Chicano Experience: An Alternative Perspective.* Notre Dame, Ind.: University of Notre Dame Press.

Perrucci, C. C., Potter, H. R., and Rhoads, D. L. 1978. "Determinants of Male Family-Role Performance." *Psychology of Women Quarterly* 3, no. 1: 53–66.

Pleck, J. H. 1977. "The Work-Family Role System." *Social Problems* 24: 417–427.

———. 1985. *Working Wives/Working Husbands.* Beverly Hills: Sage.

Ransford, E., and Miller, J. 1983. "Race, Sex, and Feminist Outlooks." *American Sociological Review* 48: 46–59.

Reid, P. T., and Comas-Diaz, L. 1990. "Gender and Ethnicity: Perspectives on Dual Status." *Sex Roles* 22, no. 7–8: 397–408.

Rexroat, C., and Shehan, C. 1987. "The Family Life Cycle and Spouses' Time in Housework." *Journal of Marriage and the Family* 49, no. 4: 737–750.

Ross, C. E. 1987. "The Division of Labor at Home." *Social Forces* 65, no. 3: 816–834.

Stack, C. B. 1974. *All Our Kin.* New York: Harper Colophon.

Staples, R. 1978. "Masculinity and Race: The Dual Dilemma of Black Men." *Journal of Social Issues* 34, no. 1: 169–183.

Sweet, J., Bumpass, L., and Call, V. 1988. *The Design and Content of the National Survey of Families and Households.* Working Paper NSFH-1. Madison: University of Wisconsin–Madison, Center for Demography and Ecology.

Thompson, L., and Walker, A. J. 1989. "Gender in Families: Women and Men in Marriage, Work and Parenthood." *Journal of Marriage and the Family* 51: 845–871.

Tucker, M. B., and Taylor, R. J. 1989. "Demographic Correlates of Relationship Status Among Black Americans." *Journal of Marriage and the Family* 51: 655–665.

Vega, W. A., Patterson, T., Sallis, J., Nader, P., Atkins, C., and Abramson, I. 1986. "Cohesion and Adaptability in Mexican American and Anglo Families." *Journal of Marriage and the Family* 48: 857–867.

Wilkie, J. R. 1991. "The Decline in Men's Labor Force Participation and Income and the Changing Structure of Family Economic Support." *Journal of Marriage and the Family* 53, no. 1: 111–122.

Williams, N. 1990. *The Mexican American Family: Tradition and Change.* Dix Hills, N.Y.: General Hall.

Wilson, M. N., Tolson, T. F. J., Hinton, I. D., and Kiernan, M. 1990. "Flexibility and Sharing of Childcare Duties in Black Families." *Sex Roles* 22, no. 7–8: 409–425.

Ybarra, L. 1982. "When Wives Work: The Impact on the Chicano Family." *Journal of Marriage and the Family* 44: 169–178.

Zinn, M. B. 1980. "Gender and Ethnic Identity Among Chicanos." *Frontiers* 2: 8–24.

———. 1991. "Family, Feminism, and Race in America." In J. Lorber and S. A. Farrell, eds., *The Social Construction of Gender,* 110–134. Newbury Park, Calif.: Sage.

Judith Stacey

Cruising to Familyland: Gay Hypergamy and Rainbow Kinship

Promiscuity was rampant because in an all-male-subculture there was no one to say 'no'— no moderating role like that a woman plays in the heterosexual milieu. (Shilts, 1987)

Because men are naturally promiscuous, two men will stick together as naturally as the two north poles of a magnet. (Davis and Phillips, 1999)

There is room for both monogamous gay couples and sex pigs in the same big tent of gay community. (Rofes, 1998: 221)

Does masculine sexuality threaten bourgeois family and social order? Scholars, critics and activists who hold incommensurate ideological and theoretical views about gender, family and sexuality, nonetheless seem to share the belief that it does. To religious and social conservatives, gay male sexual culture signifies masculine libido incarnate, the dangerous antithesis of family and community. "In the Christian right imagination," as Arlene Stein points out, "homosexuals represent undisciplined male sexuality, freed of the 'civilizing' influence of women" (Stein, 2001: 107). "Untrammeled homosexuality can take over and destroy a social system," warns Paul Cameron, a leading anti-gay ideologue in the US. Indeed, Cameron unwittingly hints that sexual jealousy, marital frustration and not-so-latent homoerotic desire propel his hostility to homosexuality when he concedes that:

Marital sex tends toward the boring end. Generally, it doesn't deliver the kind of sheer sexual pleasure that homosexual sex does. The evidence is that men do a better job on men, and women on women, if all you are looking for is orgasm. (Quoted in Dreyfuss, 1999)

Quite a few mainstream gay male leaders, like the late journalist and AIDS victim Randy Shilts, agree that gay male sexual culture, which legitimates pursuit of recreational sex with an unlimited number of partners as an end in itself, represents the dangerous excesses of *masculine* sexuality. In *And the Band Played On,* Shilts charged unfettered masculine sexuality with escalating the epidemic spread of AIDS. In his view, gay baths, bars and cruising grounds serve masculine, rather than specifically homoerotic male desires: "Some heterosexual males confided that they were enthralled with the idea of the immediate, available, even anonymous sex a bathhouse offered, if they could only find women who would agree. Gay men, of course, agreed quite frequently" (Shilts, 1987: 89). Similarly, pessimistic assessments of undomesticated masculinity that undergird the views of reactionary antifeminists, like George Gilder (1986), echo in the discourse of mainstream gay men. For example, "the conservative case for gay marriage" that neoconservative gay journalist Andrew Sullivan puts forth maintains that:

> . . . the discipline of domesticity, of shared duties and lives, of the inevitable give-and-take of cohabitation and love with anyone, even of the same sex, tends to benefit men more than the option of constant, free-wheeling, etiolating bachelorhood. (Sullivan, 1997: 151)

From *Current Sociology,* March 2004, Vol. 52(2): 181–197 Sage Publications (London, Thousand Oaks, CA, and New Delhi).

421

Right-wing opponents of same-sex marriage endorse the diagnosis that masculine eros is antisocial, but reject the remedy Sullivan proposes as insufficient and naive. Thus, the scornful second extract at the start of this article by Britain's moralistic *Daily Mail* columnist Melanie Phillips concludes: "It is not marriage which domesticates men—it is women" (Davis and Phillips, 1999: 17).

Writing from an antithetical ideological perspective, the late gay sociologist Martin Levine likewise interpreted gay male cruising culture as an arena of hypermasculinity, where men operate free of the restraints that negotiating with women imposes on heterosexual men:

> . . . without the "constraining" effects of feminine erotic standards, gay men were able to focus more overtly and obviously on the sexual activities in finding sexual partners. . . . Cruising, in this sense, is a most masculine of pastimes. Gay men were simply more honest—and certainly more obvious—about it. (Levine, 1998: 79–80)

Likewise, queer theorists, such as Michael Warner (1999), who also hold political and sexual values quite hostile to those of Andrew Sullivan as well as to the right-wing authors quoted above, nonetheless share Sullivan's view (or, in Warner's case, fear) that the contemporary gay rush to the altar and the nursery will erode the liberatory, transgressive character of queer sexual culture. Gays who have succumbed to what comedian Kate Clinton terms "mad vow disease," Warner charges, fail to recognize that "marriage has become the central legitimating institution by which the state penetrates the sexuality of its subjects; it is the 'zone of privacy' outside which sex is unprotected" (Warner, 1999: 128). Critics on all sides take gay male sexual culture to be a potent source of oppositional values and cultural resistance.

In short, sexual radicals and conservatives converge in viewing gay male sexual norms and practices as a realm of unadulterated masculine desire that is subversive to bourgeois domesticity and committed family ties. "If you isolate sexuality as something solely for one's own personal amusement," Paul Cameron warns, "and all you want is the most satisfying orgasm you can get—and that is what homosexuality seems to be—then homosexuality seems too powerful to resist" (quoted in Dreyfuss, 1999).

Yet, *is* orgasm, or even carnal pleasure, all that gay men are looking for when they cruise? And, more to the point, is that all they find? In this article, I draw from ethnographic research I conducted on gay male intimacy and kinship in Los Angeles to challenge these widely shared assumptions. Gay male cruising culture, I suggest, yields social and familial consequences far more complex and contradictory than most critics (or even a few fans) seem to imagine. The gay cruising arena of unencumbered, recreational sex certainly does disrupt conventional family norms and practices. At the same time, however, it also generates bonds of kinship and domesticity. Gay male sexual cruising serves, I suggest, as an underappreciated cultural resource for the creative construction of those "families of choice" (Weston, 1991; Weeks et al., 2001) and "invincible communities" (Nardi, 1999) that scholars have identified as the distinctive character of non-heterosexual family and kinship formations. In particular, the unfettered pursuit of masculine sexuality facilitates opportunities for individual social mobility and for forging rainbow kinship ties that have not yet attracted much attention from scholars or activists.

Gay "El Lay"

Los Angeles is home to the second largest, and likely the most socially diverse, yet comparatively understudied population of gay men on the planet. Arguably no city better symbolizes sexual excess, consumer culture and the antithesis of family values, and perhaps no population more so than the gay male denizens who crowd the bars, beats and boutiques of West Hollywood. To many observers, numerous gay men among them, "Weho" culture particularly signifies gay male decadence in situ, the epitome of the sexual culture that both Andrew Sullivan and Paul Cameron denounce.

Cursory contact with gay culture in Los Angeles readily reinforces stereotypes about gay men's narcissistic preoccupation with erotic allure. Advertisements for corporeal beautification and modification flood the pages, airwaves and websites of the local gay male press: familiar and exotic cosmetic surgery and body sculpture procedures, including penile, buttock and pec implants; liposuction; laser resurfacing; hair removal or extensions; cosmetic dentistry; personal trainers and gym rat regimens; tattooing and tattoo removal; body piercing; hair coloring, growing and styling; tinted contact lenses; manicures, pedicures and body waxing; as well as color, style and fashion consultants and the commodified universe of couture, cosmetics and personal grooming implements that they service.

Nonetheless, conducting local field research on gay men's intimate affiliations from 1999 to 2003, I encountered tinker toys as often as tinsel. Los Angeles might well be the cosmetic surgery capital of "planet out," but much less predictably, the celluloid metropolis is also at the vanguard of gay fatherhood. Organized groups of "Gay Fathers" and of "Gay Parents" formed in the city as early as the mid-1970s and contributed to the genesis of Family Pride, Incorporated, currently among the leading national grassroots organizations of its kind anywhere (Miller, 2001: 226–9). Los Angeles also gave birth to Growing Generations, the world's first and only gay-owned, assisted reproduction agency founded to serve an international gay clientele.[1] Several of its first clients were among nine families who in 1998 organized the PopLuckClub (PLC), a pioneering local support group for gay fathers and their children.[2] The thriving PLC sponsors monthly gatherings, organizes special events and provides information, referrals, support and community to a membership that now includes nearly 200 families of varying shapes, sizes, colors and forms. A PLC subgroup of at-home dads and their children meet weekly for a play-date and lunch in a West Hollywood playground; single gay dads and "prospective SGDs" seeking "to meet others who understand how parenting affects our lives" hold monthly mixers that feature "friendly folks, scintillating snacks, and brilliant banter—about the best brand of diapers!" (PLC listserv, 2003); and additional PLC focus groups, for prospective gay dads or adoptive dads, for example, as well as satellite chapters in neighboring counties continually emerge.

Between June 1999 and June 2003, I conducted field research in the greater Los Angeles area that included lengthy multisession, family life history interviews with 50 self-identified gay men born between 1958 and 1973 and with members of their designated kin, as well as within their community groups, religious institutions and organizations, like the PLC. My primary subjects came of age and came out after the Stonewall era of gay liberation and after the AIDS crisis was widely recognized. Popular discourses about safe sex, the gayby boom, gay marriage, domestic partnerships and "families we choose" informed their sense of familial prospects. This is the first cohort of gay men young enough to be able to contemplate parenthood outside heterosexuality and mature enough to be in a position to choose or reject it. The men and their families include diverse racial, ethnic, geographic, religious and social class backgrounds.[3] They also practice varied relational and residential options. My research sample included 16 gay men who were single at the time of my study; 31 who were coupled, some in open relationships, others monogamous, most of whom cohabited, but several who did not; and a committed, sexually exclusive, trio. It included men who reside or parent alone, with friends, lovers, former lovers, biological, legal and adopted kin, and children of every "conceivable" origin.[4] More than a few of these men cruised their way to several genres of gay hypergamy and to unconventional forms of rainbow kinship.

Cruising to Kinship: Case Studies

In anthropological terminology, hypergamy designates a marriage system in which women, but not men, may "marry up" the social status ladder. In the classic situation, lower rank kin groups trade on the youth, beauty and fertility of their daughters in efforts to marry them (and thereby the fortunes of their natal families) to older, wealthier, often less attractive men from higher ranking families. Modern western residues of this preindustrial patriarchal pattern persist, of course, as the fact that there is a dictionary entry for "trophy wife" (but none for "trophy husband") underscores: "An attractive, young wife married to a usually older, affluent man" (*The American Heritage® Dictionary of the English Language,* 2000). The more pejorative and even more sexist definition for "gold-digger" ("a woman who seeks money and expensive gifts from men") reveals that heterosexual women still can barter youth, beauty and erotic appeal (and sometimes even fertility) for intimate affiliations with older men with greater economic, cultural and social resources (*The American Heritage® Dictionary of the English Language,* 2000).

Two Rainbow Families

And so can some gay men. Cruising culture, combined with the greater fluidity of gay male gender conventions, allows gay men to engage more frequently than is common in intimate encounters that cross conventional social borders. While the majority of these may be fleeting and anonymous, the sheer volume of gay erotic exchanges outside the customary bounds of public scrutiny and social segregation provides opportunities to form more enduring socially heterogeneous attachments. Brief sketches of two cases from my field research illustrate how gay men can cruise their way to creative, multicultural permutations of hypergamous kinship.

Ozzie and Harry—A Gay Pygmalion Fable[5]

Ozzie, Harry and their two young children, a picture-perfect, affluent, adoring nuclear family who own an elegant, spacious Spanish home, represent an utterly improbable, gay fairy-tale romance of love, marriage and the baby-carriage. A

transracial, transnational, cross-class, interfaith couple who have been together eight years, Ozzie and Harry claim to have fallen in love at first sight on a Roman street in 1995. Harry, then 31 years old and a prosperous, white, Jewish, New England ivy-league educated, successful literary agent, was vacationing in Europe when he spotted and cruised 24-year-old Ozzie on a crowded street. Talented but undereducated, a Catholic Afro-Brazilian raised in an improverished single-mother family, Ozzie had migrated to Italy several years earlier as a guest worker.

Although the lovers met by cruising, they both claim to have fallen in love instantly. Ozzie says he told Harry that he loved him that very first night: "I just knew. I just told him what I felt." They report sharing all of their "hopes and dreams" from the moment they met, and preeminent among these was the desire to have children: "When we first met we talked about everything," Harry recalled:

> . . . and all of our dreams, and one of them was to have a family and what it meant to be gay, you know, if we were together, and what we would be giving up potentially, what the sacrifices might be; and so that was one of the things that was going to be a potential sacrifice was not being able to have children.

"Me too," Ozzie interjected. "I always knew I wanted to have children." "But we talked about how we didn't think it was possible to have them together," Harry continued. "We both talked about how it was a dream that we both had, and that it was kind of something that we thought we might have to forsake together."

The new lovers plunged headlong into a deeply romantic, intense, committed, monogamous love affair that seems only to have deepened after nearly a decade of bourgeois domesticity. After a year of transatlantic (and translinguistic) courtship, Harry sponsored his beloved's immigration to the US, financed Ozzie's education in computer technology and vocal music, and assisted his rapid acquisition of fluency in English and bourgeois cultural habitus, all domains in which Ozzie proved gifted. After the couple celebrated their union with an interfaith commitment ceremony in 1998, they had dinner with a gay couple who had recently become fathers through surrogacy. "It was all kind of Kismet," Harry recalled. "They told us about their two sons, and we kind of admitted that it was something we fantasized about." Inspired by this example, Ozzie and Harry contacted Growing Generations and decided immediately to engage a "traditional" surrogate[6] in order to realize the dream of fatherhood that they had feared they would have to sacrifice on the altar of gay love. The agency successfully matched them with a white woman who has since borne them two babies—first a white daughter conceived with Harry's sperm, and three years later, a biracial, genetic half-sister, conceived with Ozzie's.

No gay union in my study encapsulates a more dramatic example of successful hypergamy, or one that transcends a wider array of social structural inequalities and cultural differences than the bond between Ozzie and Harry. Formally, the younger, buff and beautiful Ozzie occupies a disadvantaged position across a staggering number of social divisions and cultural resources—including income, wealth, education, occupation, race, nation, language, citizenship, not to mention access to the ongoing support of his natal world of kin, long-term friendship, community and culture. Moreover, because the co-parents share a strong prejudice against hired childcare, Ozzie has become a full-time, at-home parent and economically dependent on Harry, to boot. "We don't use babysitters at all," Harry boasted, as he burped their first infant daughter during my initial visit. "We don't want any nannies, babysitters, nothing," he emphasized, espousing a childrearing credo few contemporary mothers in the West could contemplate affording, even they were to desire it:

> Nothing, NOTHING. We don't believe in it. No baby nurse, nothing. Just us; and one of us always will be with her. If you wait this long to

do this. We're mature adults. I mean I'm 38. I have no dreams left, other than being a good dad and a good mate for my Ozzie.

"The same with me," Ozzie volunteered, draping both arms around his spouse with adoration. Initially, Harry had stayed home several months blissfully caring for their first newborn while Ozzie was employed. However, because Harry commands far greater earning power, he decided that it was in his family's interest that he resume the breadwinner role. He has supported Ozzie as full-time, at-home parent ever since.

Nonetheless, despite forms of structural inequity glaring enough to make Betty Friedan's (1963) critique of the feminine mystique seem tepid, this is no transvestite version of the male-dominant, female-dependent, breadwinner–homemaker patriarchal bargain of the 1950s' modern family. Defying all sociological odds, Ozzie seems to enjoy substantive and emotional parity with Harry both as partner and parent. In deference to Ozzie's jealous, possessive wishes, Harry relinquished friendships with his former lovers. Harry regards his breadwinner role to be a sacrificial burden rather than a creative outlet or source of status and power: "I hate work," Harry maintains. "It's a necessary evil." He conducts as much of his professional work from home as he can in order to participate as fully as possible in the hands-on burdens and blessings of early parenting—diapering, feeding, dressing, toilet-training, bathing, along with playing, reading, cuddling, educating, cajoling, consoling, disciplining and chauffeuring. Indeed, not only does Harry dread the unavoidable business trips that periodically separate him from his children and spouse, he seems genuinely to envy Ozzie's uninterrupted quotidian contact with the children. "I don't need to make my mark," Harry claims. "There's nothing else I need to accomplish. So that's the most important job [being a parent and mate] I have which is why it's a real conflict." What's more, Harry has voluntarily relinquished the weighty patriarchal power of the purse by taking legal measures to fully share all property, as well as child custody of both daughters, with Ozzie. Few heterosexual marriages—whether hypergamous or homogamous—share resources, responsibilities, or romance so fully or harmoniously as these two seem to do.

Mother Randolph and his Foundling Boys

Dino, an 18-year-old, fresh "wetback," Salvadoran immigrant, was waiting at a bus stop in 1984 when a 45-year-old Anglo entertainment lawyer with a taste for young Latino men cruised by and picked him up. Discovering that his gregarious, sexy, young trick was homeless and unemployed, the lawyer brought Dino home to live and keep house for him for several weeks. There the eager youth began to acquire the mores and mentors, along with the mistakes, from which he has since built his life as an undocumented immigrant among chosen kin in gay L.A.

Among the mentors, Randolph eventually proved to be the most significant. Now in his midsixties, Randolph is a cultivated, but bawdy, financially secure and generous, former interior designer recently disabled by post-polio syndrome. Much earlier, Randolph had met his life partner of 17 years while cruising in a "stand-up sex club." Ten years into the committed, but sexually open, relationship that ensued, Randolph's lover shocked him by choosing to undergo male-to-female sex reassignment surgery. Randolph was traumatized, and the couple's relationship foundered. After a year-long separation and his lover's successful transition from male to female, however, Randolph recognized that his love for the person transcended his strong homoerotic sexual preference, and so the couple reunited. Paradoxically, this gender and sexual upheaval compelled Randolph to perform a semblance of the life of heterosexual masculinity that he had renounced as inauthentic, at considerable risk, but to his great relief, a full decade before the Stonewall rebellion.

Several years after her surgical transformation, however, Randolph's lover was diagnosed with AIDS, a cruel legacy of her prior life as a sexually active gay man. By then too, Randolph's post-polio syndrome symptoms had begun to emerge, and he lacked the physical ability to take care of his lover, or of himself. Blessed with ample financial, social and spiritual resources, Randolph gradually assembled a rainbow household staff of five gay men, who have come to regard him and each other as family.

Chance encounters through sexual cruising generated many of these relationships, as it had the union between Randolph and his lover. A former employee of Randolph's met Dino at a gay bar in 1993 and introduced him to his benefactor. By then Dino had been diagnosed as HIV-positive and was drinking heavily. Randolph has a long history and penchant for rescuing gay "lost boys," and so he hired Dino to serve as his household's primary live-in cook and manager. Now sober, grateful and devoted, Dino remains asymptomatic thanks to the health care that Randolph purchases for him. Dino resides at Randolph's Mondays through Fridays and spends weekends with his lover of five years, a 50-something, Anglo dental hygienist who cruised him at a Gay Pride parade. Dino's lover pays him weekly overnight conjugal visits in Randolph's household and also participates in the holiday feasts that Dino prepares for Randolph's expansive, extended, hired and chosen family.

Randolph employs three additional men who work staggered shifts as physical attendant, practical nurse and chauffeur, and a fourth as part-time gardener and general handyman. The day nurses are Mikey, a 23-year-old, white former street hustler and drug abuser, and Ricardo, the newest of Mikey's three roommates in another multicultural and intergenerational gay male household. The devoutly Catholic Ricardo, who is also 20-something, is a recent illegal Mexican immigrant still struggling with religious guilt over his homosexual desires. Randolph's night nurse, Bernard, is a married, closeted, bisexual African-American man in his fifties with whom Randolph used to enjoy casual sex. Finally, Randolph employs his friend Lawrence as his gardener, a white gay man now in his late forties and also HIV-positive, with whom Randolph has been close ever since they hooked up in a San Diego tea room more than three decades ago.

Randolph refers to Dino and his day nurses parentally as his "boys." "Well, I'm their father and their mother," he explains. Since Randolph's lover died in 1999, "these boys are certainly the most important family that I have these days. They mean more to me, and *for* me than anyone else." From his wheelchair-throne, "Mother Randolph," as he parodically identifies himself, presides with love, wit, wisdom and, it must be acknowledged, financial control, as well as responsibility, over a multicultural, mutually dependent, elastically extended, chosen family somewhat reminiscent of the black drag houses immortalized in the documentary *Paris Is Burning* (1990, directed by Jennie Livingston). Few of these intimate attachments remain erotic. However, a serendipitous series of hypergamous sexual encounters initiated most of the creative kin ties in this expansive rainbow "family of man."

The Gay Family Cruise

Most advocates and opponents of gay, recreational sexual cruising culture, whether straight or gay, believe it threatens mainstream "family values." To be sure, gay male cruising directly challenges norms of heteronormativity, monogamy and premarital chastity. Indeed, unless the pure pursuit of sexual pleasure is culturally sanctioned, in the face of "marital boredom," as Paul Cameron warns, "it seems too powerful to resist" and is often threatening to secure and stable intimate attachments. In fact, for reasons like these, a sizable constituency of gay men find sexual transgression to be as disturbing and threatening as does mainstream heterosexual culture. Although Ozzie and Harry met by cruising, they, along with many men "in the family," practice sexual exclusivity and strongly disapprove of polyamory and recreational sex. These more sexually conservative family values appear to be particularly prevalent among gay men who are fathers, among the religiously observant, and the generation of gay

men who came of age in the period immediately following discovery of the AIDS virus.

However, as my field research illustrates, the gay male arena of sexual sport also spawns less obvious, more productive effects on intimacy and kinship. Sexual cruising, as we have seen, initiates lasting familial ties more than is commonly recognized. Anonymous erotic encounters occasionally yield fairly conventional forms of love and "marriage." "Sexual encounters are often pursued as a route to more long-term, committed, emotional relationships," as Weeks et al. (2001: 144) observe. "Particularly for some men who are not in a couple relationship, casual sexual relationships can offer the potential for meeting the 'right' person." Or, as a gay friend of mine puts it more humorously, "Sex can be a great icebreaker." Randolph, as we have seen, cruised his deceased mate, Dino met his current lover, and even the implausibly idyllic, romantic, monogamous union and nuclear family formed by Harry and Ozzie commenced on a sexual cruise. Many other interviewees also reported histories of long-term relationships initiated through anonymous sexual encounters.[7]

Within what Giddens (1992) has termed the modern western "transformation of intimacy," the search for everlasting "confluent love" occupies a status akin to a religious quest. Just as Puritans who subscribed to the Protestant ethic took material success to signify their spiritual salvation, so do many believers in the "pure relationship" seek its earthly signs in the appearance of instantaneous erotic "chemistry." Syndicated gay sex advice columnist-provocateur Dan Savage endorses this comparatively mainstream family cruise route with uncharacteristic sentimentality:

> Desire brought my boyfriend and me together. And it's simple desire that brings most couples, gay or straight, together. Responsibly acted on, this desire is a good thing in and of itself, and it can often lead to other good things. Like strong, healthy families. (Savage, 2003)

Momentary sexual adventures also yield more innovative genres of "healthy" family life.

Anonymous gay sexual encounters do not ordinarily lead to conjugal coupling, but not infrequently they commence enduring friendships that evolve into kin-like ties, whether or not sexual interest continues. Through such side-effects of casual sex, Randolph met his close friend and gardener; Dino acquired, at first temporary, and later his long-term lodging, employment and familial support; and Mikey repeatedly found refuge from Hollywood's mean streets. Thus, even when a gay man ostensibly *is* "only looking for the most satisfying orgasm" he can get, sexual cruising allows him to find a whole lot more. "Some people like the sport of chasing somebody and seeing if they can get them," Mother Randolph acknowledged. "For some people the game is worth more than the candle. My interest is specifically in the candle." When I asked Randolph, however, whether an orgasm constituted the candle, he quickly identified more enduring embers:

> Yes, and also the love-making, if it was that sort of situation. If I had a guy home in bed, I was big on foreplay and all of that. In fact, often I didn't want my partner to go home after fucking. I often liked them to stay over. And a lot of my sexual partners became eventual friends. Mr. Baldwin [the gardener] over there at the sink being one of them.

A venerable gay history of cruising to kinship and community long antedated the contemporary popularity of gay family discourse. Even in the first two decades of the 20th century, as George Chauncey's (1994) prize-winning historical study, *Gay New York,* copiously documents, gay men frequented bars and bathhouses seeking not only quick sexual encounters, but also because they "formed more elaborate social relationships with the men they met there, and came to depend on them in a variety of ways." Chauncey draws on the extensive diaries of Charles Tomlinson Griffes, a successful early 20th-century composer who:

> . . . was drawn into the gay world by the baths not just because he had sex there, but because he met men there who helped him find apart-

ments and otherwise make his way through the city, who appreciated his music, who gave him new insights into his character, and who became his good friends. (Chauncey, 1994: 224)

Thus, socially heterogeneous intimate affiliations (whether long-term or more ephemeral) are among the underappreciated byproducts of gay cruising grounds. Thanks in part to this arena of sexual sport, interracial intimacy occurs far more frequently in the gay world, and particularly among gay men, than in heterosexual society. US census data indicate this contrast, even though, because they only tabulate co-residential couples who elected to self-identify as same-sex partners, they vastly understate the degree of both gay and interracial intimacy in the US. In 1990, the first time the US census form allowed co-residing, same-sex partners to declare their couple status, 14.6 percent of those who did so were interracial pairs, compared with only 5.1 percent of married heterosexual couples. In the 2000 Census, 15.3 percent of declared same-sex male couples and 12.6 percent of lesbians compared with 7.4 percent of married and 15 percent of unmarried heterosexual pairs bridged racial differences.[8] The percentage of interracial pairs in my nonrepresentative sample was substantially higher, a product, most likely, of my decision to stratify in order to encompass broad racial and social diversity. Of 31 men in my sample who identified themselves as coupled at the time of the interviews, 14 were paired with someone of a different race.[9]

One of the provocative byproducts of sexual cruising culture is the greater access to social mobility that it offers gay men from subordinate social classes, races and cultural milieux than their straight siblings and peers enjoy.[10] In the unvarnished prose of William J. Mann (1997), an established gay writer in the US, "the dick dock in Provincetown is a great equalizer. I've watched my share of condo owners suck off their share of houseboys." While it is likely that only a small percentage of those "houseboys" garner more than a quickly lit "candle" from these encounters, these nonetheless represent a social mobility opportunity very few of their non-gay peers enjoy. Marveling over his personal meteoric rise from working-class origins in a small factory town, Mann reflects:

> *"How the hell did you ever wind up here, kid?"* I've asked myself time and again . . . how did I end up sharing a house in the tony west end of Provincetown every summer for the entire summer, year after year? It's simple: I'm gay. Had I not been gay—had I been my brother, for example—I would never have discovered the access that led me to a different place. (Mann, 1997: 221)

Both Mann and his brother attended the same state university near their hometown. "But only *I* ventured into a world my parents had never known. Had I not been a gay kid," Mann recognizes, "I would never have been invited into that world." A visiting gay lecturer, for example, took the youthful Mann to dinner and later introduced him to prominent writers, and to a gay world: "I met people, I read books, I listened to speeches" (Mann, 1997: 221).

Ozzie, Dino, Mikey and Ricardo are among 10 of the 50 gay men in my study who have traversed even greater social, geographic, economic and cultural distances, all beneficiaries of what I am choosing to call gay hypergamy. But for its gender composition, the Cinderella fairy-tale character of Ozzie's marriage to Harry, represents hypergamy in nearly the classic anthropological sense of marrying up through an exchange of beauty and youth for cultural status and material resources. In no way do I mean to imply that Ozzie or Harry intentionally deployed strategic, let alone manipulative, bartering tactics in this exchange. By the same token, I do not believe that most contemporary, hypergamous, heterosexual marriages involve the cynical exploitation or motives connoted by terms like "gold-digger" or "trophy wife." Rather, I aim to highlight some unrecognized gender and social effects of the asymmetrical exchanges of sex appeal for status that represent the contemporary cultural residue of patriarchal hypergamy.

Expanding the concept somewhat, gay hypergamy can be used to designate even relatively brief and informal intimate affiliations between exotic, erotic youth and older men with greater material resources and cultural capital. Cruising on the "dick dock" in Provincetown, in the baths of old New York, at a bus stop in Los Angeles, and at beats, cottages, tea rooms and ports of call around the world (see, for example, Altman, 2001; Dowsett, 1996) allows for more democratic social mixing and matching and greater opportunities for upward mobility than heterosexual society generally offers. Whether or not the "candle" ignites a satisfying orgasm, it can melt social barriers—as icebreakers are meant to do—and thereby expand the bonds of kinship, as in the rainbow family ties between Mother Randolph and his adopted, and hired, "boys." In this respect, the world of sexual sport resembles athletic sport, which also provides some ghetto male youth opportunities for social mobility and cross-racial bonds, but because sexual sport is simultaneously more intimate and unregulated, it is also far more socially transgressive.[11]

It turns out that gay male "promiscuity" is not as inherently antithetical to healthy, committed, or even to comparatively conventional, family values, as its critics and some of its champions imagine. However, gay men who breach sexual norms often find themselves challenging social divides as well, cruising their way into hypergamous intimate attachments and a social rainbow of kinship bonds. The culture of unbridled masculine sexuality represents no utopian arena of egalitarian, liberated "sexual citizenship." Hypergamous, erotic exchanges among gay men that cross racial, generational and social class boundaries can yield the same sort of exploitative, abusive, humiliating and destructive effects on the more vulnerable party that women too often suffer in asymmetrical heterosexual exchanges. Gender does effect a crucial difference, however, in the social geometry of heterosexual and gay hypergamy. The exclusively masculine arena of gay hypergamy allows for greater reciprocity of sexual and cultural exchanges over the life-cycle than women can typically attain. The heterosexual double standard of beauty and aging inflicts severe

erotic and romantic constraints on even very prosperous, high status, aging "gold-diggers" or "trophy" widows. Although aging gay men also suffer
notable declines in their erotic options, they operate on a gender-free playing field. Unlike heterosexual women, formerly subordinate beneficiaries
of gay hypergamy, like Ozzie and Dino, can come
to enact the opposite side of the exchange over the
life course. Gay men who cruise to higher status
can anticipate ultimately enjoying the power to exchange whatever cultural and material capital they
attained through gay hypergamy for intimacy with
less socially privileged, younger, attractive men.

Gay men aboard the family cruise ship are
reconfiguring eros, domesticity, parenthood and
kinship in ways that simultaneously reinforce
and challenge conventional gender and family
practices and values.[12] Although by no means a
utopian arena of race and class harmony, gay
cruising does facilitate more democratic forms of
intimate social (as well as sexual) intercourse
across more social boundaries (including race,
age, class, religion, nation, education, ideology
and even sexual orientation) than occur almost
anywhere else. Enduring bonds of chosen family
and kinship are among the significant consequences of these transgressive assignations.
Whether or not Melanie Phillips is correct in her
view that men are "naturally promiscuous," she
is clearly wrong that masculine erotic impulses
preclude two men from forming enduring attachments. Whether for "monogamous gay couples"
like Ozzie and Harry, or for unapologetic "sex
pigs" like Mother Randolph and his foundlings,
it turns out that sexual cruising can be a creative
mode of family travel.

Notes

1. See www.growinggenerations.com

2. See www.popluckclub.org

3. My primary sample of 50 men included 10 Latinos, seven blacks, four Asians and 29 of white Anglo
or Jewish origins. Nine men were also immigrants,
both documented and undocumented, five of these
from Latin America, two from the Caribbean and two
from Europe. Religious upbringings and affiliations
ranged from fundamentalist, Catholic, Jewish and
Protestant, to Buddhist and atheist. Social class locations in the US are, of course, vastly more difficult to
conceptualize or assign. The men's natal family backgrounds ranged from destitute to almost aristocratic,
with the majority, unsurprisingly, from self-identified
"middle-class" origins. Current income and occupational statuses encompassed the unemployed and indebted as well as extremely wealthy and successful
members of the local professional, creative, managerial and community elite.

4. In order to study the broad array of paternal strategies and configurations, I intentionally oversampled
gay fathers. Thus, 26 of the 50 men have some sort of
paternal relationship to children, whether biological,
social and/or legal, and whether or not their children
reside with them.

5. I employ pseudonyms and have altered identifying
details to protect privacy of informants.

6. In the terminology of assisted reproduction clinics
in the US, a "traditional" surrogate is also the biological mother of a child conceived via alternative insemination with sperm, generally supplied by a contracting
father. A "gestational" surrogate, in contrast, does not
contribute genetic material to the child she bears under
contract, but is hired to gestate an ovum supplied by
an egg donor, fertilized in vitro and transplanted to
her uterus.

7. Because I cannot reliably tally the aggregate number of couple relationships which all 50 interviewees
have collectively experienced over their lifespans, I
cannot provide meaningful data on the proportion of
these that were initiated through sexual cruising. However, 10 of the 31 men who were in committed couple relationships when interviewed reported that they
had met their mates in this way.

8. An analysis of these census data by the Williams
Project at the UCLA School of Law examined 23
cities where most same-sex couples are concentrated.
Project director William Rubenstein reports that 7
percent of married couples and 14.1 percent of unmarried heterosexual couples are interracial compared
with 18.4 percent of same-sex couples in these urban
areas. The project defines "interracial" as the mix of
two racial groups and/or a Hispanic partner and

non-Hispanic partner. For more information, contact William Rubenstein, The Williams Project, UCLA School of Law.

9. Of these 14 interracial intimacies, eight were in black/white couples, four were Latino/white and two were an Asian/white couple. Additional men in the sample reported prior cross-racial unions.

10. Studies have found substantial differences in occupational ladders and career paths between heterosexual and non-heterosexual individuals. Nimmons (2002: 51) cites the as yet unpublished study by Dr. John Blandford at the University of Chicago, who analyzed a large sample from standard US census figures to find that gay men in same-sex partnered households were "greatly over-represented" compared with heterosexual counterparts in "Professional and Specialty" occupations, particularly in teaching, nursing and the arts. Gay men, however, were scarcely represented at all in traditionally masculine working-class jobs, such as heavy equipment operators, miners, explosive workers, brick layers, etc. Rothblum and Factor's (2001) study of lesbians and their straight sisters found that sisters who grew up in the same age cohort, of the same race/ethnicity and with parents of the same education, occupation and income displayed quite dissimilar outcomes on demographic variables. Lesbians were significantly more educated, more likely to live in urban areas and more geographically mobile than their heterosexual sisters.

11. See, for example, Messner (1992: 90): "several white and black men told me that through sport they had their first real contact with people from different racial groups, and for a few of them, good friendships began . . . competitive activities such as sport mediate men's relationships with each other in ways that allow them to develop a powerful bond while at the same time preventing the development of intimacy."

12. These contradictory practices have historical antecedents. Chauncey (1994: 290) describes the "idiom of kinship" popular in the early 20th century among gay men who used camp culture "to undermine the 'natural' categories of the family and to reconstitute themselves as members of fictive kinship systems." Men involved in relationships that enacted a gendered division of labor often defined themselves as "husbands" and "wives," thereby inverting and undermining the meaning of "natural" categories, while repeated use simultaneously confirmed their significance.

Bibliography

Adam, Barry (2003) "The 'Defense of Marriage Act' and American Exceptionalism;" *Journal of the History of Sexuality* 12(2): 259–76.

Altman, Dennis (2001) *Global Sex*. Chicago, IL: University of Chicago Press.

Asher, Jon ben (2003) "Pope Declares Gay Families Inauthentic," *Integrity-L Digest* 28 January (#2003–29) from PlanetOut News Front; at: www.365Gay.com

Barbeau v. British Columbia (Attorney General) (2003) BCCA 251, Court of Appeal for British Columbia.

Bawer, Bruce (1993) *A Place at the Table: The Gay Individual in American Society*. New York: Simon and Schuster.

Browning, Frank (1994) *The Culture of Desire: Paradox and Perversity in Gay Lives Today*. New York: Vintage Books.

Budgeon, Shelley and Roseneil, Sasha (2002) "Cultures of Intimacy and Care Beyond 'The Family': Friendship and Sexual/Love Relationships in the Twenty-First Century," paper presented at the International Sociological Association, Brisbane, July.

Butler, Judith (1990) *Gender Trouble: Feminism and the Subversion of Identity*. New York: Routledge.

Chauncey, George (1994) *Gay New York: Gender, Urban Culture, and the Making of the Gay Male World 1890–1940*. New York: Basic Books.

Davis, Evan and Phillips, Melanie (1999) "Debate: Gay Marriage," *Prospect Magazine* 40 (April): 16–20.

Dowsett, Gary W. (1996) *Practicing Desire: Homosexual Sex in the Era of AIDS*. Stanford, CA: Stanford University Press.

Dreyfuss, Robert (1999) "The Holy War on Gays," *Village Voice* 18 March: 38–41.

Fagan, Craig (2002) "Buenos Aires Legalizes Same-Sex Unions"; at: www.salon.com/mwt/wire/2002/12/13/brazil_marriage/index.html

Friedan, Betty (1963) *The Feminine Mystique*. New York: Norton.

Giddens, Anthony (1992) *The Transformation of Intimacy: Sexuality, Love and Eroticism in Modern Societies*. Cambridge: Polity Press.

Gilder, George (1986) *Men and Marriage*. Gretna: Pelican.

Heath, Melanie and Stacey, Judith (2002) "Transatlantic Family Travail," *American Journal of Sociology* 108(3): 658–68.

Integrity Press Release (2003) "Integrity Uganda Begins Same-Sex Blessings," 12 April; at: www.integrityusa.org/UgandaJournal/index.htm

Levine, Martin (1998) *Gay Macho: The Life and Death of the Homosexual Clone*. New York: New York University Press.

Lewin, Ellen (1998) *Recognizing Ourselves: Ceremonies of Lesbian and Gay Commitment*. New York: Columbia University Press.

Mann, William J. (1997) "A Boy's Own Class," in Susan Raffo (ed.) *Queerly Classed*, pp. 217–26. Boston, MA: South End Press.

Messner, Michael A. (1992) *Power at Play: Sports and the Problem of Masculinity*. Boston, MA: Beacon Press.

Miller, John C. (2001) "'My Daddy Loves Your Daddy': A Gay Father Encounters a Social Movement," in Mary Bernstein and Renate Reimann (eds) *Queer Families, Queer Politics: Challenging Culture and the State*, pp. 221–30. New York: Columbia University Press.

Nardi, Peter (1999) *Gay Men's Friendships: Invincible Communities*. Chicago, IL: University of Chicago Press.

Nimmons, David (2002) *The Soul Beneath the Skin: The Unseen Hearts and Habits of Gay Men*. New York: St. Martin's Press.

"Oppose the Federal Marriage Amendment" (2003) at: www.petitiononline.com/0712t001/petition.html (accessed 30 May 2003).

PLC listserv (2003) "The Lusty Month of May Mixer," 5 May.

Rauch, Jonathan (1994) "A Pro-Gay, Pro-Family Policy," *Wall Street Journal* 29 November: A22.

Rofes, Eric (1998) *Dry Bones Breathe: Gay Men Creating Post-AIDS Identities and Cultures*. New York: Harrington Park Press.

Rothblum, Esther D. and Factor, Rhonda (2001) "Lesbians and Their Sisters as a Control Group: Demographic and Mental Health Factors," *Psychological Science* 12: 63–9.

Savage, Dan (2003) "G.O.P. Hypocrisy," *New York Times* 25 April: A31.

Shilts, Randy (1987) *And the Band Played On*. New York: St Martin's Press.

Stein, Arlene (2001) *The Stranger Next Door: The Story of a Small Community's Battle over Sex, Faith, and Civil Rights*. Boston, MA: Beacon Press.

Stuever, Hank (2001) "Is Gay Mainstream?," *Washington Post* 27 April: C1.

Sullivan, Andrew (1997) "The Conservative Case," in Andrew Sullivan (ed.) *Same-Sex Marriage: Pro and Con*, pp. 146–54. New York: Vintage Books.

The American Heritage® Dictionary of the English Language (2000) 4th edn. Boston, MA: Houghton Mifflin.

United States Congress (1996) *The Defense of Marriage Act: Committee on the Judiciary, United States Senate*. Washington, DC: US Government Printing Office.

Warner, Michael (1999) *The Trouble with Normal: Sex, Politics, and the Ethics of Queer Life*. New York: Free Press.

Weeks, Jeffrey, Heaphy, Brian and Donovan, Catherine (2001) *Same Sex Intimacies: Families of Choice and Other Life Experiments*. London: Routledge.

Weston, Kath (1991) *Families We Choose: Lesbians, Gays, Kinship*. New York: Columbia University Press.

Wetzstein, Cheryl (2003) "Bill to Define Marriage Tried Again in House as 2 States Mull Cases," *Washington Times;* at: www.washingtontimes.com/national/20030525-155459-1812r.htm

Gloria González-López

Fathering Latina Sexualities: Mexican Men and the Virginity of Their Daughters

A dominant perspective in the literature on Mexican families and fatherhood has projected an inaccurate characterization of men and masculinity. Mexican fathers are frequently portrayed as rigid and authoritative macho men controlling their families (e.g., Barkley & Salazar-Mosher, 1995; Lewis, 1961; Madsen, 1964; Peñalosa, 1968). For instance, being jealous and possessive of "their women" has been identified as a cultural trait of Mexican men in some publications. On one hand, ethnographic research with fathers from the United States (Secunda, 1992), Europe (Sharpe, 1994), and South America (Olavarría, 2001) has similarly reported some men's feelings of possessiveness and difficulty in acknowledging their children—daughters in particular—as sexualized individuals. On the other hand, family and adolescence studies have challenged monolithic and static ideas of fathers of Mexican origin living in both Mexico and the United States (Bronstein, 1984; Cromwell & Ruiz, 1979; Falicov, 1982; Mirandé, 1991).

Mexican men and fathers also have been excluded from the traditionally woman-centered models of reproductive health-related research in Mexico (Figueroa Perea, 1999) and the United States. Sexuality and reproductive health research with populations of Mexican origin began to examine youth sexuality after the mid-1980s. And in the last decade, the parent-child relationship has

From *Journal of Marriage and Family* 66 (December 2004): 1118–1130. Copyrighted by the National Council on Family Relations. Reprinted by permission.

received special attention with regard to sex education, information, and knowledge (Baird, 1993), the first sexual experience (Upchurch, Aneshensel, Mudgal, & Sucoff McNeely, 2001), the absence of sexual activity (Liebowitz, Calderón Castellano, & Cuellar, 1999), and pregnancy out of wedlock (Erickson, 1994). However, these studies focus more frequently on the maternal figure (e.g., Villarruel, 1998), including large-scale quantitative research on Latino adolescents' sexual behavior (e.g., Hovell et al., 1994).

Immigration research with families of Mexican origin also has ignored fatherhood, focusing instead on how and why migration and settlement may restructure gender relations (Hondagneu-Sotelo, 1994), motherhood (Hondagneu-Sotelo & Avila, 1997), young couples' redefinitions of marital quality and sexuality across borders and between generations (Hirsch, 2003), and the sex lives of both homosexual (Cantú, 1999) and heterosexual Mexican immigrants (González-López, 2000, 2003). Culturally defined traits such as familismo, personalismo, machismo, marianismo, the madonna/whore dichotomy, and Catholic religion have long been the dominant theoretical categories that researchers have used in the extensive scholarship on Latino family values and beliefs, and Latina/o sexuality and gender studies across disciplines.

Using ethnographic data from in-depth interviews with 20 Mexican immigrant fathers, this article proposes a bridge between fatherhood, gender and sexuality, and immigration studies in order to examine Mexican fathers' views of sexuality as they educate their daughters with regard to virginity in the United States. Inspired by qualitative Latino family research conducted by Hondagneu-Sotelo (1994) and Hondagneu-Sotelo and Avila (1997), I propose an alternative paradigm in which migration experiences, fatherhood, sexuality, and gender relations are mutually interdependent and interconnected processes. My central thesis is that Mexican immigrant men express greater concern about their daughters' socioeconomic futures and life opportunities than a rigidly ideological concern for maintenance of their daughters' premarital virginity. This is explained by two central factors: regional patriarchies and immigration experiences.

Regional Patriarchies

I suggest that Mexican fathers decide whether to advocate for the premarital virginity of their daughters based on the gender inequalities they were exposed to as young men educated in specific socioeconomic contexts before they migrated. I introduce the concept of *regional patriarchies* to examine these dynamics—that is, the distinctive types of patriarchies that women and men construct in diverse geographical regions of Mexican society. I introduce this concept and identify two of its modalities: *urban patriarchies* and *rural patriarchies.* Urban and rural refer to specific socioeconomic contexts and do not attempt to essentialize or polarize them in oppositional categories. Each of these patriarchies promotes multiple forms and various levels of gender inequality, which shape the ways that Mexican families construct their values and beliefs with regard to sexuality and sexual morality. The concept of regional patriarchies is based on Belinda Bozzoli's (1983) examinations of South African regions, and R. W. Connell's (1987, 1995) analyses of gender and multiple masculinities as social constructions. Gender relations and diverse representations of masculinity are not the same across historical, social, and cultural contexts. They are fluid and reproduced in social interaction, through social

practice, and in particular, in social and geographical situations (Connell, 1987).

In Mexico, regional patriarchies possess the following characteristics: (a) they are fluid and contestable, depending on socioeconomic and political contexts in which women and men live (i.e., the fewer opportunities women and men have to obtain equal education and paid employment, the greater the gender inequalities [Amuchástegui, 2001] and the more emphasized the regional patriarchies); (b) women as well as men actively participate in the social reproduction of different expressions of multiple masculinities in contemporary urban (Gutmann, 1996) and preindustrialized colonial societies (see Stern, 1995); and (c) these dynamics have their historical roots, in part, in the formation of the Mexican state, which has been constructed through and within local hegemonies promoting and reproducing regionally specific constructions of social and political power and control since the early 1930s (Rubin, 1996), and through the regional expressions of bourgeoisie and proletariat shaped by international capital and free-market economies in contemporary society (Besserer, 1999).

Thus, men who are exposed to disguised or de-emphasized expressions of gender inequalities (i.e., urban patriarchies) are more likely to develop more liberal attitudes toward premarital sex for their daughters. This process is prompted by men's exposure to urban settings, which offers women and men multiple possibilities for education, paid employment, well-informed sex education and training, and women's rights organizations (Amuchástegui, 2001; Figueroa Perea, 1997). In contrast, men raised in small provincial locations, or *pueblos,* are exposed to deeply ingrained gender inequalities (i.e., rural patriarchies), and thus, they are less likely to embrace progressive values with regard to the virginity of their daughters. Lack of education and paid employment opportunities characterizes the lives of women living in rural and semi-industrialized contexts (Canak & Swanson, 1998), which has reinforced the lack of equality between women and men, and between fathers and their daughters.

Immigration Experiences

I argue that Mexican working-class fathers' migration and settlement journeys shape their views of their daughters' sex lives. The men I interviewed perceive the cities they migrate to and the immigrant barrios where they settle as sexually dangerous for their daughters. Fear is at the core of the sex education that these fathers offer their daughters: fear of pregnancy out of wedlock and its negative consequences (e.g., fear of a daughter not attending and completing college); fear of sexual violence; fear of sexually transmitted diseases; fear of being in an abusive relationship; and fear of crime, gangs, drugs, and violence. While promoting an ethic of sexual moderation and personal care, these fathers protect daughters who are vulnerable to these high-risk living conditions in the neighborhood. Safeguarding a daughter from these dangers becomes a priority after migration. For these fathers, virginity becomes secondary.

Fear, the universal emotion shared by these men, reveals the existence of a socially constructed and individually experienced *culture of sexual fear* in the Mexican immigrant communities where these fathers live. This culture of sexual fear is fluid and dynamic, and it is shaped by premigration ideologies and patriarchal processes, and by postmigration socioeconomic segregation. Both shape these fathers' views of women and sexuality as they figure out how to protect their daughters within alternatively more restrictive or more permissive sexual discourses.

The notion of a culture of sexual fear is inspired by Barry Glassner's conceptualization. Glassner (1999) examines the hidden dynamics responsible for the social fears permeating the daily lives of North American mainstream society (i.e., fear of crime, drugs, diseases, and other dangers). He reveals how these fears are used, manipulated, and reproduced by the political establishment and other social institutions, generating high costs in money, energy, and time paid by frightened White middle-class North Americans. Mexican immigrants may not escape these fears.

In addition, they also must fear police brutality, racism, and anti-immigrant sentiments.

Sexual fears are confirmed by current Latino demographics on sexual health-related issues and concerns. The 2000 Census indicated that 35.3 million residents in the United States were of Latino origin, 35% of whom were under the age of 18 (Guzmán, 2001). Teenagers represent the most vulnerable age group in the nation to be infected with sexually transmitted diseases (STDs; Centers for Disease Control, 2000). Also in 2000, Latinas had the highest fertility rates among all ethnic groups, and gave birth to 30% of the children born out of wedlock (Bachu & O'Connell, 2001). Residents of Mexican origin represent 58.5% of the Latino population (Guzmán, 2001). Within this group, immigrants represent most of the 4.1 million laborers and seasonal farmworkers living in the United States (Organista, Organista, Garcia de Alba, Castillo Moran, & Ureta Carrillo, 1997). These immigrants tend to settle in California, the state ranked second in AIDS cases (Centers for Disease Control, 1998). California is the destination of immigrants from Jalisco, the state that sends the highest number of immigrant workers to the United States, and the state with the highest incidence of AIDS cases related to migration (Salgado de Snyder, Díaz-Pérez, & Maldonado, 1996).

Method

The present study is part of a larger qualitative research project that examines the individual sex life histories of 60 adult Mexican immigrants living in Los Angeles (40 women and 20 men). I conducted in-depth tape-recorded open-ended individual interviews in Spanish, lasting an average of 3 hours.

Sample

The focus here is on data obtained from interviews with the 20 men, who are from a wide range of educational, socioeconomic, and marital status backgrounds. Men eligible for participation were between the ages of 25 and 45, who migrated from either Jalisco or Mexico City at the age of 20 or older, and who had lived in the Los Angeles area for at least 5 years. I asked interviewees to identify their sexual orientation during the formal interview; all identified themselves as heterosexual.

Socioeconomic differences between Jalisco and Mexico City offer contrasting social scenarios influencing men's views of female sexuality in distinctive ways. Mexico City is the capital and the largest city of the nation. The urban sophistication of Mexico City has been associated with increased employment and educational opportunities for women, which in turn may promote more egalitarian views between women and men with regard to sexuality (Amuchástegui, 2001; Figueroa Perea, 1997). Jalisco encompasses the city of Guadalajara (the second largest city in Mexico and the state capital), but also includes pre- and semi-industrialized rural areas or *pueblos* (towns) and *ranchos* (ranches). Jalisco is also the birthplace of *tequila, mariachi* music, and a *charro* culture, all dominant folklore images frequently associated with the creation of national masculinist identities. Based on my clinical experience with Mexican immigrant women and men, 5 years of permanent residence in the United States offers a minimum period of time to establish a relatively stable personal life.

I identified and interviewed the male informants in the 2000–2001 academic year. To identify my sample, I visited and contacted professionals in four community-based agencies and three elementary schools. In addition, I attended meetings at the consulate of Mexico in Los Angeles and established contact with representatives of hometown associations, community organizations, and employment centers for day laborers. Many of these leaders invited me to attend meetings at their centers and organizations after I described my larger research project with the women, and my desire to expand the project by interviewing men. A snowball sampling technique helped me recruit my final sample of 20 men. They were neither related to nor acquainted

with the women I interviewed in the larger study. I personally conducted all of the interviews mainly at the agencies, schools, employment centers, or their homes. I use pseudonyms here to protect participants' confidentiality.

On average, study participants were 38 years old. Half of the sample (10) was born and raised in the state of Jalisco; the other half (10) was born and raised in Mexico City. All participants have lived permanently in the United States for between 5 and 20 years. On average, men from Jalisco had lived longer in the United States (13.5 years) than the Mexico City group (10.1 years). Most (18) identified themselves as Catholic.

More than half (12) were married, 2 were cohabiting, 3 were never married, 2 were separated, and 1 was divorced. With the exception of never-married men, all had children (M = 2 children); 15 had daughters and 13 had sons, all of whom were being raised in the United States. Only 2 men had children living in Mexico.

The lowest level of formal education for men from both locations was second grade of *secundaria,* equivalent to eighth grade; the highest level was a Master's degree. The average level of education was 12 years, relatively high for Mexico (Canak & Swanson, 1998). Men from Mexico City were more likely to have attended college than their Jalisco counterparts, but no man from Mexico City completed a college education.

Participants held a wide variety of occupations, including construction and maintenance work, truck driving, equipment operation, supervision, and technician work. A minority were employed as administrative assistants, small business owners, or schoolteachers. Study informants reported an average annual income that fluctuated between $12,000 and $24,000.

As part of a larger interview, the men were asked, "Would you like your daughter(s) to have sex before they get married? Why?" This article offers in-depth examinations of the narratives they offered in response. I also studied each informant's interview transcript to identify and examine men's significant reactions and recurrent themes linked to virginity and premarital sex within the context of the father–daughter relationship.

Analysis

This study followed the model for analyzing qualitative data recommended by sociologist Kathy Charmaz (1983). After first collecting the data, I typed verbatim transcripts of my interviews. Second, I conducted *selective* or *focused coding* by sorting out and identifying categories of analysis. Third, I analyzed and worked on informants' interpretations of these categories by creating *memos*—that is, "written elaborations of ideas about the data and the coded categories" (Charmaz, p. 120). I also reviewed fieldwork notes (my personal observations and informants' comments and reactions) that I had written during and immediately after each interview to identify relevant themes. As I typed the interview, I studied these notes while listening carefully to examine the informant's reactions and actual words as he talked about specific themes (e.g., views of sex education of girls in Los Angeles, perceptions of family life after migration, and opinions of young women and sex in contemporary society). I created separate computer files for each theme in order to classify information offered by each informant. I assigned a specific code or category of analysis for each theme. By creating theme files as a technique of data classification and coding, I was able to accomplish a crucial methodological goal: to pay close attention and explore specific research areas in more depth in subsequent interviews (Charmaz). For example, as I discovered that a father's views of his daughter's virginity were associated with his socioeconomic and urban versus rural backgrounds, I created additional questions while investigating men's views of their daughters' sex lives.

Finally, I established analytical interpretations and regional comparisons (i.e., Jalisco vs. Mexico City) with regard to the recurrent themes based on empirical research and theory on Mexican families, fatherhood, gender and sexuality, and migration.

Results

Regional Patriarchies

In the Name of My Daughter   Virginity in a daughter's life is not a priority for any of the fathers born and raised in Mexico City. About half of the men from Jalisco (rural and urban) offered similar views. Some of these rural men migrated to urban areas to attend college. Although they do not expect premarital sexual abstinence in a young woman's life, men from Mexico City and Jalisco demand sexual moderation from their daughters. These fathers described their concerns for a new generation of young women being raised in urban settings. They perceived their social surroundings as sexually dangerous for various reasons: high rates of pregnancy out of wedlock, sexually transmitted diseases and HIV/AIDS, casual sex and promiscuity, and sexual harassment and violence against women.

As these men expressed an interest in helping their daughters postpone premarital sex, sexual protection and care became crucial. For these fathers, delaying sex becomes strategic in their single daughters' lives. It protects their daughters from becoming pregnant while promoting the intellectual and emotional maturity necessary to improve their opportunities to attend and to graduate from college. Although the overwhelming majority of these fathers identified this goal as "the dream" they have for their daughters, men raised in urban areas more frequently articulated these views. With regard to their daughters engaging in premarital sex, first Jacobo (35, from Guadalajara, administrative assistant, married, father of a 15-year-old daughter) expressed,

> I would try to see it objectively. I had sexual relations before I became married. I would talk with her about it but openly and without intending to punish her, or anything like that. Nor would I get into any details with her. Simply to clarify and to motivate her to take care of herself, so she can take care of herself in all respects. But, above all, that she would not stop attending school. That is my main concern. I do not

want her, for any reason, to stop attending college. She is doing so well, and I want her to continue doing the same. That's about it.

Ernesto (43, from Guadalajara, technician, married, father of a 10-year-old girl) similarly commented,

> I am worried about her having a child, that she would not be able to take care of herself and leave the family home. I would not like it. I would love her to have a formal life, that is, that she goes to school, and that she is studying. Because for me . . . my preoccupation is that she makes it all the way to a university and graduates from college. That is my preoccupation and I will always fight for it.

In Mexico, "taking care of herself" or *cuidarse*, has more than one meaning. For women of reproductive age, "taking care" also indicates successfully using a contraceptive method in a healthy and safe manner to prevent pregnancy. Jacobo, Ernesto, and many of the men in this study used this expression while addressing pregnancy before marriage and its negative consequences as risks of being sexually active. Consequences included not completing high school or attending college, becoming poor, being abandoned, and encountering social stigma and sexism as a single mother. Thus, some fathers promote sexual abstinence as the best strategy a daughter can use to take care of herself and increase her chances of obtaining a college degree. Two fathers from Mexico City exemplify this dynamic. Alejandro (37, small business owner, married, father of a 6-year-old girl) elaborated,

> I would like her, before she has sexual relations, to focus on establishing a goal with regard to her studies. I want her to study. In other words, when the day comes that she becomes someone who is self-confident in this country, or in Mexico, wherever, then she may look for a partner. And then she may have sexual relations. Before or after getting married, in other words, it does not affect me. It would affect me, let's say, that she is going to school, she has sex, and then she gets pregnant. That would affect

me, right? because that would completely cut her off as a person, and at the academic level.

And Alfredo (36, construction worker, cohabiting, father of a 13-year-old girl) similarly described,

> I tell my daughter, "The day you are going to have sexual relations, do it. Not now, of course, when you get older. No problem, but use your brain, because you have a brain. If you do not want to get married, no problem, but think about it very well. Complete your education. Figure out how you are going to survive, and then do it when you know how to survive and have a job."

Fathers such as Jacobo, Ernesto, Alejandro, and Alfredo want to prevent what one father regretted that he was unable to accomplish. Emiliano (43, born and raised in Mexico City, technician, married, father of two young adult women and a 9-year-old girl), talked with sadness about the out-of-wedlock pregnancy of one of his daughters. He stated,

> She got married because of the same, she became pregnant and then she left. We [my wife and I] told her to stay here with us so she could continue studying. And at some point, I talked with her about having an abortion, because I told her "Consider it, eh . . . I will give you my support in whatever you want, whatever decision you make."

As he continued, I asked him how he felt that she had sexual relations before marriage. He replied,

> It was not the fact that she was having sexual relations. In fact, I always talked to her, because I used to drive my daughters to school, and when we saw a young girl in our way to school, a young girl who was pregnant, I used to tell her, "My daughter, if you, young girls, want to do it and you have such a great need, how come you don't use a contraceptive method? What's the deal about making your life complicated." That was for me, the worst thing that ever happened to me, that she was not able to take care of herself."

He emphasized,

I used to tell her, "You have to study, you have to educate yourself." So that was the worst thing that ever happened to me. I told her, "You destroyed your life, you could have become someone in your life, but not anymore." I felt sad.

As illustrated, maintaining their daughters' virginity was not of the utmost importance for these five urban fathers. A similar pattern was evident in other men born and raised in or exposed to urban settings. This finding supports previous research with men from Mexico City who expressed more progressive views of female sexuality after experiencing higher education and college life. These men challenged some of the traditional values that they had learned within family, peer groups, and neighborhood contexts (Amuchástegui, 2001; Módena & Mendoza, 2001).

Men from urban contexts reported that they were not concerned about the moral, religious, and family values traditionally associated with virginity, such as a social perception of virginity as a virtue in women. Other sex research with Mexican populations has similarly found no association between religion and the actual sexual values and practices of Catholic women and men (Amaro, 1988; Carrillo, 2002; González-López, 2000).

Beyond the Hymen   Urban fathers sometimes commented on a daughter's sex life beyond the topic of virginity. They believed in a daughter's sexual autonomy and her right to actively seek and experience desire and pleasure, prior to and after marriage. Diego and Alfonso, from Mexico City, elaborated. Diego (36, school teacher, separated, father of an 11-year-old girl) exclaimed,

Aha! I would tell my daughter to talk with her partner a lot about sex, that she should tell him what she wants, what she would like to do, how she would like to do it, about her fantasies and that she should have a lot of communication with him.

Alfonso (33, construction foreman, married, father of two daughters, 7 and 13 years old) similarly elaborated,

When I get to talk with them about it, I will simply tell them that their moment should feel pleasurable to them, that they should feel comfortable with themselves, and that nothing should force them to do it, and that nobody has the right to make sex conditional and that depending on how they feel about it, they should proceed.

Thus, these fathers illustrate how and why regional patriarchies shape the way in which they perceive female sexuality. They embrace distinct social norms of sexual morality for their daughters based on the gender inequalities they experienced before migrating. Urban fathers were not concerned about the virginity of their daughters. It appears that sexually permissive expressions of urban patriarchies, masculinities, and gender equality, along with exposure to the complexities of survival in a competitive and industrialized society, are responsible for this dynamic. Fathers born and raised in rural patriarchies are exposed, in contrast, to more restrictive social norms with regard to women and sexuality.

Between Tradition and Modernity   Fathers from rural Jalisco were more likely to expect their daughters to refrain from premarital sexual activity. For these men, virginity assures the continuation of an ideal of family tradition and social symbolism, which also contributes to a conflict-free relationship with extended family members. These fathers had abstained from premarital sexual activity with their wives. Two fathers born and raised in small towns exemplify these dynamics. Fidel (37, technician, married, father of three daughters) used the expression, "I am the favorite son-in-law of my wife's parents" to explain that his mother- and father-in-law had always had deep respect for him because of the decision he and his wife made to refrain from premarital sex. Fidel hopes that his daughters will practice sexual abstinence and similarly benefit from this pre-scription. He exclaimed, "I don't want to know who, tell me who would not wish for his daughter to possess integrity while wearing white on her wedding day? Do you think that would not be my wish?" However, he explained why this may not happen:

> I know it is difficult because my girls are going to get older and they will feel attraction toward men. And this is almost, this is a thing that none of us, neither me as a father nor her siblings can stop from happening.

Fidel was not the only man who reported that he may lose control over a coming-of-age daughter because of her "natural" heterosexual desire. This pattern was reported by all fathers in this study. These fathers' view of heterosexual sexual attraction and love as something "normal" and expected in a daughter's personal life resonates with multidisciplinary scholarship examining heterosexuality as a socially constructed norm imposed upon women (and men) (Katz, 1995; Rich, 1980).

Felipe (44, truck driver, married, father of one young adult and two adolescent daughters) reported,

> We [my wife and I] have taught [our daughters] that they have to respect and that they have to demand respect from others, and that you should not have sex . . . just like my wife and I did, that they should not have sexual relations until the day they get married. And that is what we learned and we try to transmit the same.

He emphasized why, beyond the family context, specific social institutions also shape a young woman's sexuality, "However, we are aware that these days, schools and television already show it, so they see all that more frequently."

Fidel and Felipe reported they were struggling emotionally but were willing to accept their daughters' sexual agency and desire. Both used the expression "*fracasar*" to explain that young women "morally fail" when they experience sex or become pregnant before marriage. In spite of the

emotional discomfort they might experience, fathers reported that they would be supportive and loving if that was the unfortunate fate of any of their daughters. Both stated that they would explore the possibility of their daughters getting married as a way to cope with an out-of-wedlock pregnancy, but never in a coercive manner. All informants were critical of coercive marriage—that is, the decision to force a daughter to marry as a way "to repair" the moral damage done by out-of-wedlock pregnancy. Many recalled stories of coercive marriages within their own immediate and extended families, and they expressed interest in helping their daughters become well-informed with regard to reproductive health and contraceptive use before becoming sexually active.

My previous work with the 40 mothers in the larger study showed that women follow a similar yet gendered pattern; mothers also decide whether to advocate for premarital virginity for their daughters based on the regional patriarchies that they were exposed to as young women (González-López, 2003). For these mothers, motherhood becomes a developmental stage that they use to revisit and organize their beliefs and practices with regard to premarital sex learned before migrating. Mothering a daughter serves as an opportunity to resolve unfinished issues—such as the issue of protection from gender inequality that they experienced before migrating—that shape daughters' sex education. Rural women whose husbands reproached them for not being virgins at marriage advocate provirginity values before marriage to protect their daughters from similar experiences. Others, especially mothers from urban areas, advocate more egalitarian values for a new generation of women. Most want their daughters to climb the education ladder, develop a professional career, and obtain a well-paid job. As these mothers replace marriage goals with career goals for their daughters, their ideas about appropriate sexual behavior also change. Virginity depreciates as a form of social capital, or *capital femenino,* a concept that I introduce in the larger study with these mothers (González-López,

2003). To some extent, virginity is replaced by new forms of capital emerging in the United States: education and employment opportunities.

Many of these fathers (including men from urban areas) expressed a preference for not knowing whether their daughters become sexually active before marriage because of their admitted feelings of discomfort and jealousy as men, or what some identified as *el celo de hombre*. This subjective experience is not exclusive to Mexican men. Some fathers from the United States, Europe, and South America experience similar feelings with regard to the sex lives of their daughters (Secunda, 1992; Sharpe, 1994; Olavarría, 2001).

Immigration Experiences

Fathers in this study reported that they experienced a transformation of their views of female sexuality after migrating to and settling in the United States. All fathers perceived their Los Angeles immigrant barrios as sexually dangerous for their daughters. They were concerned about the high rates of adolescent pregnancy and single motherhood, violence against women, sexually transmitted diseases (including HIV/AIDS), and a daughter's romantic involvement with men who were drug dealers and addicts, gang members, unemployed, and high school dropouts—all perceived as undesirable. For these fathers, protecting a daughter from these risks became a priority after migration; they perceived U.S. cities as dangerous. For them, then, virginity becomes secondary.

Urban fathers, especially those educated in poor and marginalized areas in Mexico City and Guadalajara, reported both their urban *colonias* and barrios in Mexico and their immigrant communities in Los Angeles to be equally dangerous for young women. However, they were more concerned about the safety of their daughters after migration. In contrast, rural fathers more frequently reflected on the remarkable difference between their small towns and their immigrant neighborhoods. Mainly for those promoting premarital abstinence, socioeconomic segregation

became an important social force in shaping their views of female sexuality after migration. For example, Fidel expressed his reaction to my inquiry about any of his three daughters potentially engaging in premarital sex:

> It is not so much that they are going to lose their virginity . . . it would hurt me that any *cabrón* [asshole] would be the one with whom they would lose it! In other words, it is not that they are going to lose their virginity, because I know that they will lose it some day. But it will make me sad to see that they would lose it with just any *cabrón*. Imagine, how am I going to feel if my daughter gives it to a fucking marijuana user? *un pinche vato* [a damn homeboy] that you see all the time, lazy, selling drugs on the streets? . . . It would hurt me, because as a father, I want the best for my daughters.

I probed to learn more about his concerns. He responded,

> I am so afraid, yes, because I don't know, because of all the things that you find out there, things that happen, that happen these days. All these girls who get pregnant or those who are raped and then abandoned. To put it simply, the other day I was talking with a relative of mine, and I learned that a girl in my family who is 14 or 13, and she is already pregnant! Can you imagine? I am a father and when I listened to those stories, it gives me the chills!

Fidel illustrates the fear that many informants reported as they talked about their views of female sexuality in Los Angeles. Fear was the central emotion involved in the social construction of fathers' views of a daughter's sexuality. Regardless of their place of origin, many fathers reported feeling more apprehensive about the sex education of their children—their daughters in particular—after they migrated as compared with before. They expressed their concern about the kidnapping and sexual abuse of children, gang and violence activity, and exposure to drugs. A few had thought about sending their daughters to live with family in Mexico.

Thus, for these fathers, maintaining virginity is secondary to fear of a daughter becoming pregnant out of wedlock and its potential negative consequences, such as not completing an education; fear of a daughter becoming a single mother and being abandoned, poor, or exposed to stigma; fear of a daughter becoming infected with a sexually transmitted disease, including HIV/AIDS; and fear of a daughter being involved with an undesirable partner who might be a high school dropout, gang member, or drug addict or dealer.

Men experienced these emotions of distress and apprehension individually and reproduced them collectively. Deciphering how to educate their daughters with regard to sex takes time, energy, and emotion work within the culture of sexual fear that permeates these men's segregated immigrant barrios. These fathers' views of female sexuality are also shaped by the sexual panic emerging from the postmigration socioeconomic contexts surrounding the dating experiences and the loving relationships of their daughters.

Regardless of their origins, all fathers talked about the fear that their daughters might become involved in abusive relationships or with objectionable partners living in their L.A. barrios. From a small town, Felipe described the emotional difficulties he experienced as he talked about the loving relationship of one of his daughters with a young Latino boyfriend who was sent to prison. From Mexico City, Sebastián (40, married, father of 8- and 15-year-old daughters) shared his fear:

> Look, I have talked with my oldest daughter about it, and I have been telling her all the time, "*¡Aguas!* [Watch out!]" I tell her, "You have *un tesorito,* a little treasure." I tell her, "And I would like you to give it to the person that you love. The first time should be a wonderful experience, something that you long for, something that you desire. Besides that, what better than doing it with the person you love? Because what happens many times is that men just come, they use you, and then they leave."

For men like Sebastián, a daughter's first sexual experience becomes an initiation loaded with special emotional meaning; virginity is a symbol exchanged for an emotionally safe first sexual experience. A man must "deserve" to be the first sexual partner of a virgin daughter. For fathers like them, teaching a daughter to perceive virginity as something of special value may help her in more than one way. She may use it as an expression of love and emotional intimacy; virginity also can be exchanged for formality and respect in a relationship. She may also use it to protect herself from a potentially abusive man.

Sebastián's fathering practices are shaped by the gender inequalities he learned with regard to sexuality and social interactions before migrating. For instance, many men used the expression "*El hombre llega hasta donde la mujer quiere* [The man goes as far as the woman wants it]" to explain how they are teaching their daughters to demand respect from men. A popular saying in Mexican society, both rural and urban men used it either to assert that women had enough power to stand up for their rights, demand respect, and challenge a man's sexual advances, or to argue that women were responsible for becoming pregnant out of wedlock and for provoking the inappropriate sexual behavior of men. Alfredo, for example, talked about his relationship with his 13-year-old daughter: "I make her strong, she has a very strong character because I have made her that way." As a way to protect his daughter, he explained that he is teaching her—more than his son—to be able to demand respect. He clarified, "With regard to sexuality . . . it might be that I am harder with her, by telling her, 'You are a woman and as a woman, you have to take care of yourself because some men may treat you like a whore.' " Alfredo's paradoxical parenting style (caring and protecting with "a tough hand") seems to be a response to his fear, and it may not coincide with the gentle treatment that some Mexican fathers may use to educate their daughters relative to their sons (Bronstein, 1984). It resonates, however, with the childrearing practices of some Mexican fathers (Buriel, 1993) and Mexican American families in Texas (Williams, 1990), promoting double standards and stricter norms for girls as compared with boys.

Alfredo's narrative also illustrates an ethic of *respeto a la mujer,* a social norm promoting respect for women in Mexican society (Módena & Mendoza, 2001). This also conveys a social message: A woman needs to learn (and practice) morally appropriate sexual behavior as a way to protect herself from sexual harassment and other expressions of sexual violence. For Alfredo and the vast majority of these fathers, a daughter experiences her personal and sex life while being exposed to potential harm in a society perceived as sexually dangerous for young women. As illustrated by the same men (urban, in many cases), however, a daughter is entitled to explore avenues leading to pleasure, emancipation, and education—all of them, it is hoped, leading to social justice and change.

Discussion

Immigrant men enter the United States with gendered ideologies and practices with regard to women and sexuality, virginity in particular. Men reconstruct these norms via fatherhood as they unpack their "sexuality luggage"—the regional patriarchies and masculinities alternatively promoting or challenging gender inequalities in the locations in which they were educated. The concept of regional patriarchies not only contests the idea that patriarchy is uniform or monolithic but it also explains how and why regionally defined masculinities and local socioeconomic forces may influence Mexican immigrant men's ideas about the sex education of their daughters. After heading north, these multiple expressions of masculinity intertwine with the paradoxical challenges that immigrants face within contexts of socioeconomic segregation. The United States—what once was a promised land for these men—becomes a sexual threat as they reflect on the sex education of their daughters. A culture of sexual fear permeating the everyday lives of immigrants who settle in inner-city and marginalized barrios begins to shape their views of a daughter's virginity and premarital sex. Virginity becomes secondary for these working-class men, who instead promote an

ethic of protection and care that may safeguard a daughter from pregnancy out of wedlock, sexually transmitted diseases, sexual violence, casual sex and promiscuity, and sexual dangers associated with drugs, alcohol use, and gang violence, among other risks. In the process, fathers expect their daughters to practice sexual moderation and to delay premarital sex. For them, this is a strategy that their young daughters may use to attend and complete college, and thus improve their living conditions and socioeconomic future as they survive in an increasingly competitive society.

Fathers raising both girls and boys expressed more concern and spent more time talking about their daughters when the topic of sex education of children was first introduced in interviews. Fathers identified child sexual abuse, gang activity, violence, and drug use as risks threatening the safety of a young son, who at times was identified as someone "who sooner or later will learn about sex and to take care of himself, anyway." Emesto (father of a girl and a boy) best articulated what many fathers expressed:

> You have to put much more emphasis on women, because the woman is more, she has the hardest job, the most difficult one with regard to sexuality, to have a child, and tolerate all that. That is why I say, poor women.

To what extent are regional patriarchies and immigration each responsible for the findings in this study? A mutually reinforcing and fluid interaction among these forces seems to be responsible for these fathers' perceptions of a daughter's sex life. In addition, fatherhood is a subjective and personal gender process (Chodorow, 1995). Men experienced and contested some of the gender inequalities that their own fathers, brothers, uncles, and male cousins have reproduced within a family context. Some men expressed anger or pain while describing incidents of sexual abuse, rape, and domestic violence that their own mothers and sisters had endured; some were critical of the ways in which their sisters had been raised by their own fathers. Thus, fatherhood may become a family emotional process (Nichols & Schwartz, 1991) through which men may begin to resolve and disrupt family patterns that promote gender inequality as they educate a new generation of Mexican American women with regard to sexuality.

The testimonies of the men I interviewed challenge stereotypical images of Mexican fathers as macho, dominant, and authoritative. They build on men and masculinities scholarship that is gradually disrupting the reproduction of these static images and archetypes of Mexican men and masculinity in both Mexico (Gutmann, 1996) and the United States (Baca Zinn, 2001; Coltrane, 1996; Mirandé, 1991). In addition, even though some of these fathers said that they lack the knowledge, self-confidence, or comfort to talk with their daughters about sex, others shared their actual conversations with their daughters about sex-related themes. This finding challenges the increasingly popular concept of "sexual silence." A notion frequently identified in HIV/AIDS studies with Latino populations, it argues that Latino families are silent with regard to sexuality (Carrillo, 2002; Díaz, 1998).

Finally, research in the social, behavioral, and reproductive health sciences continues to interpret Latino families' beliefs and practices through culturally defined theoretical concepts such as machismo, marianismo, hembrismo, familismo, personalismo, and the madonna/whore dichotomy, among others, including a so-called "Latino culture." Besides the need to recognize not one but many "Latino cultures," an overemphasis on these categories of analysis may promote inaccurate images of Latinas and Latinos who live in the United States. Without compromising the importance of cultural forces, we need to explore alternative and comprehensive theoretical frameworks aimed at examining how and why socioeconomic structures shape parenting styles and fatherhood experiences, gender relations, and the sex education of a new generation of Latina and Latino children.

Implications and Future Research

Professionals working with Latino families and sexuality issues have been frequently reminded of the cultural sensitivity and competency required to effectively work with these families. Many times, however, this emphasis is placed on Spanish-speaking fluency and cultural familiarity—understood by many as Latino beliefs, customs, and traditions. Thus, such sensitivity and competency skills have the potential to be enhanced and expanded if we become social critics who also uncover and explore the structural forces influencing the sex lives of the members of these communities. As indicated in this study, some of these social factors shaping sexuality, fatherhood, and migration experiences include socioeconomic segregation, unemployment, poverty, racial discrimination, legal status, anti-immigrant laws, lack of access to education, language limitations, and other forces emerging from inequality and social injustice.

A comprehensive and critical examination of Latino men and their fatherhood experiences requires exploration within the context of their relationships with partners. Central topics include Latino fathers' and their partners' views and redefinitions of the sex education of their daughters and sons within contexts of social marginality, and these couples' perceptions and renegotiations of sexual health as part of the immigration experience. Research on the sex lives of young Latino men with regard to sexual initiation and early erotic experiences also has been neglected. Future research cannot offer comprehensive and accurate reflections of Latino communities if it excludes the sexual experiences of men of all ages. Finally, the most marginalized of all Latino family arrangements calls for equally sensitive examinations: same-sex parents of Latino origin and the sex education of their children.

Limitations and Strengths

Results from this qualitative study are not generalizable to the experiences of other self-identified heterosexual Mexican immigrant fathers. Additionally, I do not offer concrete linear analyses of men's views before and after migration. I conceptualize sexuality as a malleable process in constant flux. I look at how and why pre- and postmigration social and economic complexities intertwine with and shape these men's views of their daughters' sexuality in Los Angeles. This project provides an examination of how and why fatherhood, masculinity, and sexuality are nuanced processes formulated and transformed by, through, and within social practice. It offers an alternative perspective to study the sexualities of young Mexican American girls as fluid and dynamic processes linking gender and migration, and socioeconomic forces of discrimination and inequality. These men's narratives of fatherhood should help to "demythologize" Mexican fathers and their families (Vega, 1990). They invite us to place the latter at the center of our research with Latino populations, and put to rest misinterpretations and stereotypes of the families in the fastest growing minority group in the nation.

Author's Note: The author expresses her gratitude to Robert W. Connell, María Patricia Fernández-Kelly, and Barrie Thorne for their intellectual guidance in the early stages of the larger project with these men, and to Patricia A. Emerson, Matthew C. Gutmann, Pierrette Hondagneu-Sotelo, and Kelly Raley for their recommendations and comments in the preparation of this article. Carol Ann Chavez kindly collaborated in various tasks in the completion of this manuscript. The author gratefully acknowledges a faculty award from the Ford Foundation through the Sexuality, Inequality and Health: Practitioner Training Initiative at San Francisco State University (Gilbert Herdt, project director).

References

Amaro, H. (1988). Women in the Mexican-American community: Religion, culture, and reproductive attitudes and experiences. *Journal of Community Psychology, 16,* 6–20.

Amuchástegui, A. (2001). *Virginidad e Iniciación Sexual en México* [Virginity and sexual initiation in Mexico]. Mexico City: EDAMEX and Population Council.

Baca Zinn, M. (2001). Chicano men and masculinity. In Michael S. Kimmel & Michael A. Messner (Eds.), *Men's lives* (5th ed., pp. 24–32). Boston: Allyn & Bacon.

Bachu, A., & O'Connell, M. (2001). *Fertility of American women: June 2000* (Current Population Reports). Washington, DC: U.S. Census Bureau.

Baird, T. L. (1993). Mexican adolescent sexuality: Attitudes, knowledge, and sources of information. *Hispanic Journal of Behavioral Sciences, 15,* 402–417.

Barkley, B. H., & Salazar-Mosher, E. (1995). Sexuality and Hispanic culture: Counseling with children and their parents. *Journal of Sex Education and Therapy, 21,* 255–267.

Besserer, F. (1999). *Moisés Cruz: Historia de un transmigrante* [Moisés Cruz: Story of an immigrant]. Mexico City: Universidad Autónoma Metropolitana, Iztapalapa.

Bozzoli, B. (1983). Marxism, feminism and South African studies. *Journal of Southern African Studies, 9,* 139–171.

Bronstein, P. (1984). Differences in mothers' and fathers' behaviors toward children: A cross-cultural comparison. *Developmental Psychology, 20,* 995–1003.

Buriel, R. (1993). Childrearing orientations in Mexican American families: The influence of generation and sociocultural factors. *Journal of Marriage and the Family, 55,* 987–1000.

Canak, W., & Swanson, L. (1998). *Modern Mexico.* Boston: McGraw-Hill.

Cantú, L. (1999). Border crossings: Mexican men and the sexuality of migration (Doctoral dissertation, University of California–Irvine). *Dissertation Abstracts International, 60*—08A, 163.

Carrillo, H. (2002). *The night is young: Sexuality in Mexico in the time of AIDS.* Chicago: University of Chicago Press.

Centers for Disease Control and Prevention. (1998). National Center for Health Statistics. Table 56: Acquired immunodeficiency syndrome (AIDS) cases, according to geographic division and state: United States, selected years 1985–98. Retrieved October 23, 2001, from http://www.cdc.gov/nchs/fastats/aids-hiv.htm.

Centers for Disease Control and Prevention. (2000). *Tracking the hidden epidemics: Trends in STDs in the United States, 2000.* Atlanta, GA: Author.

Charmaz, K. (1983). The grounded theory method: An explication and interpretation. In R. M. Emerson (Ed.), *Contemporary field research* (pp. 109–126). Prospect Heights, IL: Waveland Press.

Chodorow, N. (1995). Gender as a personal and cultural construction. *Signs, 20,* 516–544.

Coltrane, S. (1996). *Family man: Fatherhood, housework, and gender equity.* New York: Oxford University Press.

Connell, R. W. (1987). *Gender and power: Society, the person, and sexual politics.* Stanford, CA: Stanford University Press.

Connell, R. W. (1995). *Masculinities.* Berkeley: University of California Press.

Cromwell, R. E., & Ruiz, R. A. (1979). The myth of macho dominance in decision making within Mexican and Chicano families. *Hispanic Journal of Behavioral Sciences, 1,* 355–373.

Díaz, R. M. (1998). *Latino gay men and HIV: Culture, sexuality, and risk behavior.* New York: Routledge.

Erickson, P. I. (1994). Lessons from a repeat pregnancy prevention program for Hispanic teenage mothers in East Los Angeles. *Family Planning Perspectives, 26,* 174–178.

Falicov, C. J. (1982). Mexican families. In M. McGoldrick, J. K. Pearce, & J. Giordano (Eds.), *Ethnicity & family therapy* (pp. 134–163). New York: Guilford.

Figueroa Perea, J. G. (1997). Algunas reflexiones sobre el enfoque de género y la representación de la sexualidad [Some reflections on gender and the representation of sexuality]. *Estudios Demográficos y Urbanos, 12,* 201–244.

Figueroa Perea, J. G. (1999). Fecundidad, anticoncepción y derechos reproductivos [Fertility, contraception, and reproductive rights]. In B. García (Ed.), *Mujer, Género y Población en México* (pp. 61–101). Mexico City: El Colegio de México y Sociedad Mexicana de Demografía.

Glassner, B. (1999). *The culture of fear: Why Americans are afraid of the wrong things.* New York: Basic Books.

González-López, G. (2000). Beyond the bed sheets, beyond the borders: Mexican immigrant women and their sex lives (Doctoral dissertation, University of Southern California). *Dissertation Abstracts International,* A 62/06, 2241.

González-López, G. (2003). De madres a hijas: Gendered lessons on virginity across generations of Mexican immigrant women. In Pierrette Hondagneu-Sotelo (Ed.), *Gender and U.S. migration: Contemporary trends* (pp. 217–240). Berkeley: University of California Press.

Gutmann, M. C. (1996). *The meanings of macho: Being a man in Mexico City.* Berkeley: University of California Press.

Guzmán, B. (2001). *The Hispanic population.* Washington, DC: U.S. Census Bureau.

Hirach, J. S. (2003). *A courtship after marriage: Sexuality and love in Mexican transnational families.* Berkeley: University of California Press.

Hondagneu-Sotelo, P. (1994). *Gendered transitions: Mexican experiences of immigration.* Berkeley: University of California Press.

Hondagneu-Sotelo, P., & Avila, E. (1997). "I'm here, but I'm there": The meanings of Latina transnational motherhood. *Gender & Society, 11,* 548–571.

Hovell, M., Sipan, C., Blumberg, E., Atkins, C., Hofstetter, C. R., & Kreitner, S. (1994). Family influences on Latino and Anglo adolescents' sexual behavior. *Journal of Marriage and the Family, 56,* 973–986.

Katz, J. N. (1995). *The invention of heterosexuality.* New York: Dutton.

Lewis, O. (1961). *The children of Sánchez.* New York: Random House.

Liebowitz, S. W., Calderón Castellano, D., & Cuellar, I. (1999). Factors that predict sexual behaviors among young Mexican American adolescents: An exploratory study. *Hispanic Journal of Behavioral Sciences, 21,* 470–479.

Madsen, W. (1964). *Mexican-Americans of South Texas.* New York: Holt, Rinehart & Winston.

Mirandé, A. (1991). Ethnicity and fatherhood. In F. W. Bozett & S. M. H. Hanson (Eds.), *Fatherhood and families in cultural context* (pp. 53–82). New York: Springer.

Módena, M. E., & Mendoza, Z. (2001). *Géneros y generaciones: Etnografía de las relaciones entre hombres y mujeres de la ciudad de México* [Gender and generations: Ethnography of relationships between women and men in Mexico City]. Mexico City: EDAMEX and Population Council.

Nichols, M. P., & Schwartz, R. C. (1991). *Family therapy: Concepts and methods* (2nd ed.) Boston: Allyn & Bacon.

Olavarría, J. A. (2001). *¿Hombres a la deriva? Poder, trabajo y sexo* [Men with no direction? Power, work and sex]. Santiago, Chile: FLACSO-Chile.

Organista, K. C., Organista, P. B., Garcia de Alba, J. E., Castillo Moran, M. A., & Ureta Carrillo, L. E. (1997). Survey of condom-related beliefs, behaviors, and perceived social norms in Mexican migrant laborers. *Journal of Community Health, 22,* 185–198.

Peñalosa, F. (1968). Mexican family roles. *Journal of Marriage and the Family, 30,* 680–689.

Rich, A. (1980). Compulsory heterosexuality and lesbian existence. *Signs: Journal of Women in Culture and Society, 5,* 631–660.

Rubin, J. W. (1996). Decentering the regime: Culture and regional politics in Mexico. *Latin American Research Review, 31,* 85–126.

Salgado de Snyder, V. N., Díaz-Pérez, M. J., & Maldonado, M. (1996). AIDS: Risk behaviors among rural Mexican women married to migrant workers in the United States. *AIDS Education and Prevention, 8,* 134–142.

Secunda, V. (1992). *Women and their fathers: The sexual and romantic impact of the first man in your life.* New York: Delta.

Sharpe, S. (1994). *Fathers and daughters.* London: Routledge.

Stern, S. J. (1995). *The secret history of gender: Women, men, and power in late colonial Mexico.* Chapel Hill: University of North Carolina Press.

Upchurch, D. M., Aneshensel, C. S., Mudgal, J., & Sucoff McNeely, C. (2001). Sociocultural contexts of time to first sex among Hispanic adolescents. *Journal of Marriage and Family, 63,* 1158–1169.

Vega, W. A. (1990). Hispanic families in the 1980s: A decade of research. *Journal of Marriage and the Family, 52,* 1015–1024.

Villarruel, A. M. (1998). Cultural influences on the sexual attitudes, beliefs, and norms of young Latina adolescents. *Journal of the Society of Pediatric Nurses, 3,* 69–79.

Williams, N. (1990) *The Mexican American family: Tradition and change.* Dix Hills, NY: General Hall.

Scott Coltrane

Fathering: Paradoxes, Contradictions, and Dilemmas

The beginning of the 21st century offers a paradox for American fathers: Media images, political rhetoric, and psychological studies affirm the importance of fathers to children at the same time that men are becoming less likely to live with their offspring. Although the average married father spends more time interacting with his children than in past decades, marriage rates have fallen, and half of all marriages are predicted to end in divorce. Additionally, the proportion of births to unmarried mothers has increased dramatically for all race and ethnic groups, and single-mother households have become commonplace. These contradictory tendencies—more father-child interaction in two-parent families but fewer two-parent families in the population—have encouraged new research on fathers and spawned debates about how essential fathers are to families and normal child development (Blankenhorn, 1995; Silverstein & Auerbach, 1999).

Scholars attribute the current paradox in fathering to various economic and social trends. Whereas most men in the 20th century were sole breadwinners, contemporary fathers' wages can rarely support a middle-class standard of living for an entire family. The weakening of the good-provider model, coupled with trends in fertility, marriage, divorce, and custody, has resulted in the average man spending fewer years living with

From *Handbook of Contemporary Families: Considering the Past, Contemplating the Future,* Marilyn Coleman and Lawrence Ganong (Eds.), pp. 224–243. 2004. Thousand Oaks, CA: Sage.

children (Eggebeen, 2002). Simultaneously, however, men rank marriage and children among their most precious goals, single-father households have increased, and fathers in two-parent households are spending more time with co-resident children than at any time since data on fathers were collected (Pleck & Masciadrelli, 2003). Although married fathers report that they value their families over their jobs, they spend significantly more time in paid work and less time in family work than married mothers, with most men continuing to serve as helpers to their wives, especially for housework and child maintenance activities (Coltrane, 2000). Personal, political, religious, and popular discourses about fathers reveal similar ambivalence about men's family involvements, with ideals ranging from stern patriarchs to nurturing daddies, and public portrayals frequently at odds with the actual behavior of average American fathers (LaRossa, 1997). We can understand these contradictions by recognizing that fatherhood has gained symbolic importance just as men's family participation has become more voluntary, tenuous, and conflicted (Griswold, 1993; Kimmel, 1996).

In this chapter, I summarize how fathering practices have varied across cultures and through history; highlight how different social, economic, and political contexts have produced different types of father involvement; review how social scientists have measured father involvement; and examine findings about causes and consequences of father involvement. I end with a short analysis of debates over family policy and offer tentative predictions about the future of fathering in America.

Cross-Cultural Variation

Fatherhood defines a biological and social relationship between a male parent and his offspring. *To father* means to impregnate a woman and beget a child, thus describing a kinship connection that facilitates the intergenerational transfer of wealth and authority (at least in patrilineal descent systems such as ours). Fatherhood also reflects ideals about the rights, duties, and activities of men in families and in society and generalizes to other social and symbolic relationships, as when Christians refer to "God the Father," Catholics call priests "Father," and Americans label George Washington "the Father" of the country. Fatherhood thus reflects a normative set of social practices and expectations that are institutionalized within religion, politics, law, and culture. Social theories have employed the concept of *social fatherhood* to explain how the institution of fatherhood links a particular child to a particular man (whether father or uncle) in order to secure a place for that child in the social structure (Coltrane & Collins, 2001).

Fathering (in contrast to *fatherhood*) refers more directly to what men do with and for children. Although folk beliefs suggest that fathering entails behaviors fixed by reproductive biology, humans must learn how to parent. In every culture and historical period, men's parenting has been shaped by social and economic forces. Although women have been the primary caretakers of young children in all cultures, fathers' participation in child rearing has varied from virtually no direct involvement to active participation in all aspects of children's routine care. Except for breastfeeding and the earliest care of infants, there are no cross-cultural universals in the tasks that mothers and fathers perform (Johnson, 1988). In some societies, the social worlds of fathers and mothers were so separate that they rarely had contact and seldom performed the same tasks; in other societies, men participated in tasks like infant care and women participated in tasks like hunting (Coltrane, 1988; Sanday, 1981).

Drawing on worldwide cross-cultural comparisons, scholars have identified two general patterns of fathers' family involvement, one intimate and the other aloof. In the intimate pattern, men eat and sleep with their wives and children, talk with them during evening meals, attend births, and participate actively in infant care. In the aloof pattern, men often eat and sleep apart from women, spend their leisure time in the company of other men, stay away during births, and seldom help with child care (Whiting & Whiting, 1975). Societies with involved fathers are more likely than societies with aloof fathers to be peaceful, to afford women a role in community decision making, to have intimate husband–wife relationships, to feature more gender equality in the society, and to include nurturing deities of both sexes in their religions. Aloof-father societies are more likely to have religious systems with stern male gods, social institutions that exclude women from community decision making, marriage systems in which husbands demand deference from wives, and public rituals that focus on men's competitive displays of masculinity (Coltrane, 1988, 1996; Sanday, 1981).

Research on fathering among indigenous peoples such as the African Aka suggests why involved fathering and gender egalitarianism are associated (Hewlett, 1991). Anthropologists such as Hewlett have drawn on Chodorow's (1974) work to suggest that when fathers are active in infant care, boys develop an intimate knowledge of masculinity, which makes them less likely to devalue the feminine, whereas when fathers are rarely around, boys lack a clear sense of masculinity and construct their identities in opposition to things feminine by devaluing and criticizing women (Hewlett, 2000). In reviews of data on father involvement over the past 120,000 years, Hewlett concluded that fathers contribute to their children in many ways, with the relative importance of different contributions varying dramatically; that different ecologies and modes of production have a substantial impact on the contributions of fathers to their children; and that fathers' roles today are relatively unique in human history (Hewlett, 1991, 2000).

Historical Variation

Historical studies have focused on practices in Europe and North America, chronicling and emphasizing men's public lives: work, political exploits, literary accomplishments, scientific discoveries, and heroic battles. This emphasis shows how various economic, political, and legal practices have structured privileges and obligations within and beyond families. For example, the historical concept of family in the West is derived from the Latin *famulus,* meaning servant, and the Roman *familia,* meaning the man's domestic property. Linking institutional arrangements with linguistic forms tells us something important about men's relationships to families. Recent historical studies have focused more directly on men's ideal and actual behaviors in families, thereby documenting complexity and diversity in past fathering practices (e.g., Griswold, 1993; Kimmel, 1996; LaRossa, 1997; Mintz, 1998; Pleck & Pleck, 1997).

Before these studies, many scholars erroneously assumed that changes in fatherhood were linear and progressive (Coltrane & Parke, 1998). For example, early family history emphasized that peasant families were extended and governed by stern patriarchs, whereas market societies produced nuclear families, companionate marriages, and involved fathers. In fact, historical patterns of fathering have responded to a complex array of social and economic forces, varying considerably across regions, time periods, and ethnic or cultural groups. Although it is useful to identify how men's work and production have shaped their public and private statuses, actual family relations have been diverse, and fatherhood ideals have followed different trajectories in different regions of the same country (Griswold, 1993; Mintz, 1998; Pleck & Pleck, 1997).

The economy of the 17th and 18th centuries in Europe and America was based on agriculture and productive family households. For families that owned farms or small artisan shops, their place of work was also their home. Slaves, indentured servants, and others were expected to work on family estates in return for food, a place to live, and sometimes other rewards. In this pattern of household or family-based production, men, women, and children worked together. Regional variations could be large, and fathers and mothers often did different types of work, but many tasks required for subsistence and family survival were interchangeable, and both mothers and fathers took responsibility for child care and training (Coltrane & Galt, 2000).

Because most men's work as farmers, artisans, and tradesmen occurred in the family household, fathers were a visible presence in their children's lives. Child rearing was a more collective enterprise than it is today, with family behaviors and attitudes ruled primarily by duty and obligation. Men introduced sons to farming or craft work within the household economy, oversaw the work of others, and were responsible for maintaining harmonious household relations. The preindustrial home was a system of control as well as a center of production, and both functions reinforced the father's authority (Griswold, 1993). Though mothers provided most direct care for infants and young children, men tended to be active in the training and tutoring of children. Because they were moral teachers and family heads, fathers were thought to have greater responsibility for and influence on children than mothers and were also generally held responsible for how the children acted outside the home (Pleck & Pleck, 1997).

Because the sentimental individualism of the modern era had not yet blossomed, emotional involvement with children in the Western world during the 17th and early 18th centuries was more limited than today. Prevailing images of children also were different from modern ideas about their innocence and purity. Religious teachings stressed the corrupt nature and evil dispositions of children, and fathers were admonished to demand strict obedience and use swift physical punishment to cleanse children of their sinful ways. Puritan fathers justified their extensive involvement in children's lives because women were seen as unfit to be disciplinarians, moral guides, or intellectual teachers. Griswold (1997) pointed out, however, that stern unaffectionate fathering, though not confined to Puritans, was not representative of all of the population. In fact, most American fathers attempted to shape and guide their children's characters, not break them or beat the devil out of them. As more privileged 18th-century fathers gained enough affluence to have some leisure time, many were affectionate with their children and delighted in playing with them (Griswold, 1997).

As market economies replaced home-based production in the 19th and 20th centuries, the middle-class father's position as household head and master and moral instructor of his children was slowly transformed. Men increasingly sought employment outside the home, and their direct contact with family members declined. As the wage labor economy developed, men's occupational achievement outside the household took on stronger moral overtones. Men came to be seen as fulfilling their family and civic duty, not by teaching and interacting with their children as before, but by supporting the family financially. The middle-class home, previously the site of production, consumption, and virtually everything else in life, became a nurturing, child-centered haven set apart from the impersonal world of work, politics, and other public pursuits. The separate-spheres ideal became a defining feature of the late 19th and early 20th centuries (Bernard, 1981; Coltrane & Galt, 2000; Kimmel, 1996).

The ideal that paid work was only for men and that only women were suited to care for family members remained an unattainable myth rather than an everyday reality for most families. Many working-class fathers were not able to earn the family wage assumed by the separate-spheres ideal, and a majority of African American, Latino, Asian American, and other immigrant men could

not fulfill the good-provider role that the cultural ideal implied. Women in these families either had to work for wages, participate in production at home, or find other ways to make ends meet. Although the emerging romantic ideal held that women should be sensitive and pure keepers of the home on a full-time basis, the reality was that women in less advantaged households had no choice but to simultaneously be workers and mothers. In fact, many working-class and ethnic minority women had to leave their homes and children to take care of other people's children and houses (Dill, 1988). Even during the heyday of separate spheres in the early 20th century, minority women, young single women, widows, and married women whose husbands could not support them worked for wages.

As noted above, attempts to understand the history of fatherhood have often painted a simple before-and-after picture: *Before* the Industrial Revolution, families were rural and extended, and patriarchal fathers were stern moralists; *after* the Industrial Revolution, families were urban and nuclear, and wage-earning fathers became companionate husbands, distant breadwinners, and occasional playmates to their children. This before-and-after picture captures something important about general shifts in work and family life, but its simple assumption of unidirectional linear change and its binary conceptualization contrasting men's patriarchal roles in the past with egalitarian roles in the present is misleading (Coontz, 1992). Stage models of family history have ignored the substantial regional and race/ ethnic differences that encouraged different family patterns (Pleck & Pleck, 1997). For example, as most of the United States was undergoing industrialization, large pockets remained relatively untouched by it. The experience of white planters in the antebellum South was both like and unlike that of men in the commercial and industrial North (Griswold, 1993). Another major drawback of early historical studies is the tendency to overgeneralize for the entire society on the basis of the experience of the white middle class. Even during the heyday of separate spheres at the turn of the

20th century, minority and immigrant men were unlikely to be able to support a family. Race and class differences also intersect with regional differences: Not only did southern fathering practices differ from northern ones, but slave fathers and freedmen in the South had much different experiences than either group of white men (Griswold, 1993; McDaniel, 1994).

The Emergence of Modern Fathering

Throughout the 20th century, calls for greater paternal involvement coexisted with the physical presence, but relative emotional and functional absence, of fathers (LaRossa, 1997). Nevertheless, some fathers have always reported high levels of involvement with their children. By the 1930s, even though mothers bore most of the responsibility for care of homes and families, three out of four American fathers said they regularly read magazine articles about child care, and nearly as many men as women were members of the PTA (Kimmel, 1996). Increases in women's labor force participation during the 1940s briefly challenged the ideal of separate family and work roles, but in the postwar era, high rates of marriage and low rates of employment reinforced the ideology of separate spheres for men and women. The ideal father at mid-century was seen as a good provider who "set a good table, provided a decent home, paid the mortgage, bought the shoes, and kept his children warmly clothed" (Bernard, 1981, pp. 3–4). As they had during the earlier Victorian era, middle-class women were expected to be consumed and fulfilled by wifely and motherly duties. With Ozzie and Harriet–style families as the 1950s model, women married earlier and had more children than any group of American women before them. Rapid expansion of the U.S. economy fueled a phenomenal growth of suburbs, and the consumer culture from that era idolized domestic life on radio and television. Isolated in suburban houses, many mothers now had almost sole responsibility for raising children, aided by occasional reference to expert guides from pediatricians and child psychologists (Hays, 1996).

Fathers of the 1950s were also told to get involved with child care—but not *too* involved (Kimmel, 1996). The separate spheres of white middle-class men and women were thus maintained, though experts deemed them permeable enough for men to participate regularly as a helper to the mother (Coltrane & Galt, 2000; Hays, 1996).

During the mid–20th century, separate-spheres ideology and the popularity of Freud's ideas about mother-infant bonding led to widespread acceptance of concepts like *maternal deprivation,* and few researchers asked who besides mothers took care of children, although some researchers began to focus on *father absence* during the baby boom era (roughly 1946–64). Empirical studies and social theories valued the symbolic significance of fathers' breadwinning, discipline, and masculine role modeling, even though few studies controlled for social class or measured what fathers actually did with children. Studies including fathers found that they were more likely than mothers to engage in rough and tumble play and to give more attention to sons than daughters (Parke, 1996; Pleck, 1997). In general, research showed that child care was an ongoing and taken-for-granted task for mothers but a novel and fun distraction for fathers (Thompson & Walker, 1989).

Compared to the wholesome but distant good-provider fathers pictured on television programs like *Ozzie and Harriet* and *Father Knows Best* in the 1950s, a new father ideal gained prominence in the 1980s (Griswold, 1993). According to Furstenberg (1988), "[T]elevision, magazines, and movies herald the coming of the modern father— the nurturant, caring, and emotionally attuned parent. . . . Today's father is at least as adept at changing diapers as changing tires" (p. 193). No longer limited to being protectors and providers, fathers were pictured on television and in magazines as intimately involved in family life. Fatherhood proponents focused on the potential of the new ideals and practices (Biller, 1976), but researchers in the 1980s reported that many fathers resisted assuming responsibility for daily housework or child care (Thompson & Walker, 1989).

Some researchers claimed that popular images far exceeded men's actual behaviors (LaRossa, 1988), and others suggested that men, on the whole, were less committed to families than they had been in the past (Ehrenreich, 1984). In the 1990s, researchers also began to examine how the modern ideal of the new father carried hidden messages about class and race, with some suggesting that the image of the sensitive and involved father was a new class/ethnic icon because it set middle-class fathers apart from working-class and ethnic minority fathers, who presented a more masculine image (Messner, 1993). Others suggested that the sensitive or androgynous parenting styles of new fathers might lead to gender identity confusion in sons (Blankenhorn, 1995).

Measuring Father Involvement

Before the 1980s, the rare researchers who included fathers focused on simple distinctions between father-present and father-absent families, finding that children from families with co-resident fathers generally fared better, on average, than those without co-resident fathers. Although the structural aspects of fatherhood (marriage, paternity, co-residence) sometimes correlate with various child and family outcomes, most researchers now agree that what fathers do with and for children is more important than co-residence or legal relationship to the mother and recommend that dichotomous measures (e.g., father presence/absence) be replaced by more nuanced ones.

The most influential refinement in fathering measurement was offered by Lamb, Pleck, Charnov, and Levine (1987), who suggested three components: (a) interaction, the father's direct contact with his child through caregiving and shared activities; (b) availability (or accessibility), a related concept concerning the father's potential availability for interaction, by virtue of being accessible to the child (whether or not direct interaction is occurring); and (c) responsibility, the role the father takes in ascertaining that the child is taken care of and in arranging for resources to

be available for the child. Within each of these categories, two further distinctions should be made. First, it is critical to distinguish the amount from the quality of involvement: Both are important to child development and parental well-being (Parke, 1996). Second, absolute as well as relative (in relation to partner) indices of involvement are independent and may affect children and adults in different ways (Pleck, 1997).

A recent tabulation of father involvement assessment in 15 large social science family data sets showed that all but one measured father "presence/absence," with most also measuring some aspects of fathers' "availability," "teaching," "monitoring," or "affection." About half measured the fathers' "communication" or "emotional support," only a few measured "thought processes" (e.g., worrying, dreaming) or "planning" (e.g., birthdays, vacations, friend visits), and none measured "sharing interests" (e.g., providing for instruction, reading together) or "child maintenance" (e.g., cleaning or cooking for the child) (Federal Interagency Forum, 1998, pp. 144, 400; Palkovitz, 1997, pp. 209–210). Structural availability is thus the most common fathering indicator, with various routine parent-child interactions and support activities sometimes assessed, and with fathers' planning and responsibility rarely measured. In addition, many studies collect fathering data from just one reporter, even though self-reports of fathers' involvement tend to be higher than mothers' reports of fathers' involvement, especially for nonresident fathers (Coley & Morris, 2002; Smock & Manning, 1997).

Levels and Predictors of Fathers' Involvement

Research on fathering in two-parent households shows a noticeable and statistically significant increase in men's parenting involvement, both in absolute terms and in relation to mothers. Simultaneously, however, average levels of fathers' interaction with, availability to, and responsibility for children lag well behind those of mothers (Marsiglio, Amato, Day, & Lamb, 2000; Parke,

1996; Pleck & Masciadrelli, 2003). Measurement strategies vary, with time-use diaries generally producing the most accurate estimates of fathers' interaction and availability. On average, in the 1960s to early-1980s, fathers interacted with their children about a third as much as mothers and were available about half as much as mothers (Lamb et al., 1987). During the mid-1980s to early-1990s, the average co-resident father interacted about two fifths as much as mothers and was available to his children almost two thirds as much (Pleck, 1997). In the late 1990s, he was available to his children about three fourths as much as mothers, interacting on weekdays about two thirds as often, but over four fifths as much on weekends (Pleck & Masciadrelli, 2003; Yueng, Sandberg, Davis-Kean, & Hofferth, 2001). In an estimated 20% of two-parent families, men are now about as involved as mothers interacting with and being available to their children. At the same time, in most families, fathers share much less of the responsibility for the planning, scheduling, emotional management, housework, and other maintenance activities associated with raising children (Deutsch, 1999; Hochschild, 1989).

Researchers have begun to isolate the effects of income, race/ethnicity, education, family structure, marriage, employment, work schedules, and other factors on father involvement, though results are often incomplete or contradictory. For example, the relation between socioeconomic status and father involvement is complex. Income is often found to be positively correlated with father involvement among various ethnic groups (Fagan, 1998; Parke, 1996). Relative income contributions by wives are also associated with higher proportionate levels of father involvement in housework and child care (Coltrane, 2000; Yeung et al., 2001), though some studies still find that financially dependent husbands do less domestic work than others (Brines, 1994). Wealthier men do little routine family work, but the amount their wives do varies dramatically, with higher-earning wives more likely to purchase domestic services (e.g., child care, house cleaning, laundry) (Cohen, 1998; Oropesa, 1993).

Although most contemporary studies of fathering have been based on white, middle-class, two-parent families, we are beginning to get a more complete picture about similarities and differences across family types. When financial stability is hard to achieve, fathers only minimally involved with their children may nevertheless see themselves as "good fathers" because they work hard to provide financially. Because of inequities in the labor market, men of color are disproportionately likely to face difficulties being adequate providers (Bowman & Sanders, 1998; Hamer & Marchioro, 2002). Comparisons between white, African American, and Latino fathers suggest similar levels of involvement with infants and similar styles of engagement with young children (e.g., proportionately more play and less caretaking than mothers; Coltrane, Parke, & Adams, 2001; Toth & Xu, 1999). Contrary to cultural stereotypes, some research also shows that Latino fathers are more likely than their European American counterparts to spend time in shared activities with children, to perform housework and personal care, and to engage in monitoring and supervising children's activities (Coltrane et al., 2001; Toth & Xu, 1999; Yeung et al., 2001). Results for African American fathers in two-parent households are mixed, with most reporting levels of father-child interaction comparable to other race/ethnic groups, and several studies finding that black men do more housework than white men, net of other predictors (Ahmeduzzaman & Roopnarine, 1992; Broman, 1991; Hossain & Roopnarine, 1993; John & Shelton, 1997), and that nonresident black fathers contribute more to children than nonresident white fathers (Wilson, Tolson, Hinton, & Kiernan, 1990). Studies of African American and Latino fathers reveal a wide range of behaviors across families, depending on employment, income, education, gender and religious ideology, family structure, marital status, age of children, immigration status, neighborhood context, cultural traditions, and presence of extended or fictive kin, and a similar pattern of association between social contextual variables and levels and styles of paternal participation

(Auerbach, Silverstein, & Zizi, 1997; Cabrera, Tamis-LeMonda, Bradley, Hofferth, & Lamb, 2000; Hossain & Roopnarine, 1993; Hunter & Davis, 1994; Padgett, 1997; Pleck & Steuve, 2001; Silverstein, 2002).

Fathers tend to spend more time with young children than they do with older children and adolescents, probably because younger children require more attention and care, even though many men feel more comfortable interacting with older children. Most research finds that a father's availability (as determined by work hours) is a strong predictor of his involvement in child care. When mothers of preschool children are employed, a father's time availability predicts whether he will serve as a primary caregiver (Brayfield, 1995; Casper & O'Connell, 1998). Fathers and mothers with nonoverlapping work shifts are the most likely to share child care (Presser, 1995). When mothers of school-aged children are employed more hours, their husbands tend to do a greater portion of the child care and housework, and fathers tend to be more involved to the extent that they view their wives' career prospects more positively (Pleck, 1997). For instance, Brewster (2000) found that fathers in the late 1980s and 1990s were likely to use nonworking discretionary hours for child care, whereas in the late 1970s and early 1980s they tended to use those hours for other activities.

As demonstrated in comprehensive reviews (Pleck, 1997; Pleck & Masciadrelli, 2003), father involvement is multiply determined, with no single factor responsible for the different types of involvement. In addition, studies often report contradictory effects of factors like income, education, age, family size, and birth timing. One of the most consistent findings is that men are more involved with sons than with daughters (Harris, Furstenberg, & Marmer, 1998; Harris & Morgan, 1991; Marsiglio, 1991; McBride, Schoppe, & Rane, 2002), especially with older children (Pleck, 1997). However, some recent studies have found no differences in father involvement by sex of child (Fagan, 1998; Hofferth, 2003), leading Pleck and Masciadrelli (2003) to suggest that fa-

thers' preference for sons may be weakening. Some researchers also find that if fathers get involved during pregnancy or early infancy they tend to sustain that involvement later in children's lives (Coltrane, 1996; Parke, 1996).

Lamb, Pleck, and colleagues suggested that for fathers to become actively involved, they required four facilitating factors: (a) motivation, (b) skills and self-confidence, (c) social approval, and (d) institutional support (Lamb et al., 1987; see also Pleck, 1997). Many studies find that fathers are more involved and show more warmth if they believe in gender equality (Cabrera et al., 2000; Hofferth, 1998), though others find no significant association (Marsiglio, 1991; Pleck, 1997). Others find that fathers get more involved when they have a strong fatherhood identity or actively embrace the father role (Beitel & Parke, 1998; Hawkins, Christiansen, Sargent, & Hill, 1993; Pasley, Ihinger-Tallman, & Buehler, 1993; Rane & McBride, 2000; Snarey, 1993). In general, fathers feel more competent as parents when they are more involved with their children, though it is difficult to say whether this competence is a precursor or a result of active fathering (Beitel & Parke, 1998; McHale & Huston, 1984). Evidence suggesting that competence leads to involvement comes from interventions designed to develop fathers' parenting skills (e.g., Cowan & Cowan, 2000; McBride, 1990). In terms of social support, fathers tend to be more involved when the children's mothers facilitate it, when the mothers had positive relationships with their own fathers when they were children (Allen & Hawkins, 1999; Cowan & Cowan, 2000; McBride & Mills, 1993; Parke, 1996), and when kin and other community members support father involvement (Pleck, 1997). Finally, institutional supports can include factors such as fewer work hours and more flexible work schedules (Pleck, 1993).

Another approach to identifying predictors of father involvement is based on a process model of parenting (Belsky, 1984; McBride et al., 2002). This framework suggests that fathering is shaped by three categories of influence: (a) characteristics of the father (e.g., personality, attitudes toward child rearing), (b) characteristics of the child (e.g., temperament, age, gender), and (c) contextual sources of stress and support (e.g., marital relationships, social support networks, occupational experiences). Many of these facilitating influences overlap with factors in the Lamb and Pleck model, but this approach also includes consideration of things like child temperament and parental stress. Emergent findings suggest that child temperament or other characteristics may have a larger influence on father–child involvement than mother–child involvement, probably because fathering is seen as more discretionary than mothering (Cabrera et al., 2000; McBride et al., 2002).

The nature of the marital relationship is also associated with paternal involvement, though causality is sometimes difficult to assess. Some find that greater marital satisfaction leads to greater father involvement (Parke, 1996), and others suggest that higher levels of men's relative contributions to child care lead to women's greater marital satisfaction (Brennan, Barnett, & Gareis, 2001; Ozer, Barnett, Brennan, & Sperling, 1998). In addition, satisfaction with men's levels of family involvement appears to be strongly related to mothers' and fathers' gender ideals and expectations. We cannot simply assume that more father involvement is better for all families. As the emerging gatekeeping literature (e.g., Allen & Hawkins, 1999; Beitel & Parke, 1998) attests, too much involvement by fathers can be interpreted as interference rather than helpfulness. In general, if family members want a father to be more involved, his participation has positive effects on family functioning. If family members feel that fathers should not change diapers or do laundry, then such practices can cause stress (Coltrane, 1996).

The Potential Influence of Fathers

As scholars pay more attention to fathers, they are beginning to understand what influence their involvement might have on child development. Most researchers find that father-child relationships are influential for children's future life chances (Federal Interagency Forum, 1998; Parke, 1996; Pleck & Masciadrelli, 2003). The focus of this research tends to be on the positive aspects of fathers' involvement, though it should be noted that because men are more likely than women to abuse children or to use inappropriate parenting techniques, increased male involvement can lead to increased risk and negative outcomes for children, particularly if the father figure does not have a long-term relationship with the mother (Finkelhor, Hotaling, Lewis, & Smith, 1990; Margolin, 1992; National Research Council, 1993; Radhakrishna, Bou-Saada, Hunter, Catellier, & Kotch, 2001).

Many researchers continue to focus on fathers' economic contributions to children and report that fathers' resources improve children's life chances. Longitudinal research shows that children from one-parent households (usually mother headed) are at greater risk for negative adult outcomes (e.g., lower educational and occupational achievement, earlier childbirth, school dropout, health problems, behavioral difficulties) than those from two-parent families (Marsiglio et al., 2000; McLanahan & Sandefur, 1994). Although comparisons between children of divorced parents and those from first-marriage families show more problems in the former group, differences between the two are generally small across various outcome measures and do not necessarily isolate the influence of divorce or of father involvement (Crockett, Eggebeen, & Hawkins, 1993; Furstenberg & Harris, 1993; Seltzer, 1994). For children with nonresident fathers, the amount of fathers' earnings (especially the amount that is actually transferred to children) is a significant predictor of children's well-being, including school grades and behavior problems (Amato & Gilbreth, 1999; McLanahan, Seltzer, Hanson, & Thomson, 1994; Marsiglio et al., 2000). Because the great majority of children from single-parent homes turn out to be happy, healthy, and productive adults, debates continue about how such large-group comparisons should be made and how we should interpret their results in terms of fathers' economic or social contributions (Amato, 2000; Coltrane & Adams, 2003).

Earlier reviews suggested that the level of father involvement has a smaller direct effect on infant attachment than the quality or style of father interaction, though time spent parenting is also related to competence (Lamb et al., 1987; Marsiglio et al., 2000). Preschool children with fathers who perform 40% or more of the within-family child care show more cognitive competence, more internal locus of control, more empathy, and less gender stereotyping than preschool children with less involved fathers (Lamb et al., 1987; Pleck, 1997). Adolescents with involved fathers are more likely to have positive developmental outcomes such as self-control, self-esteem, life skills, and social competence, provided that the father is not authoritarian or overly controlling (Mosley & Thomson, 1995; Pleck & Masciadrelli, 2003). Studies examining differences between the presence of biological fathers versus other father figures suggest that it is the quality of the father–child relationship rather than biological relationship that enhances the cognitive and emotional development of children (Dubowitz et al., 2001; Hofferth & Anderson, 2003; Silverstein & Auerbach, 1999). Reports of greater father involvement when children were growing up have also been associated with positive aspects of adult children's educational attainment, relationship quality, and career success (Amato & Booth, 1997; Harris et al., 1998; Nock, 1998; Snarey, 1993). Because of methodological inadequacies in previous studies such as not controlling for maternal involvement, most scholars recommend more carefully controlled studies using random samples and multi-rater longitudinal designs, as well as advocating caution in interpreting associations between fathering and positive child outcomes (Amato & Rivera, 1999; Parke, 1996; Pleck & Masciadrelli, 2003). It will take some time to isolate the specific influence of fathers as against the influence of mothers and other social-contextual factors such

as income, education, schools, neighborhoods, communities, kin networks, and cultural ideals.

We do know that when fathers share child care and housework with their wives, employed mothers escape total responsibility for family work, evaluate the division of labor as more fair, are less depressed, and enjoy higher levels of marital satisfaction (Brennan et al., 2001; Coltrane 2000; Deutsch, 1999). When men care for young children on a regular basis, they emphasize verbal interaction, notice and use more subtle cues, and treat sons and daughters similarly, rather than focusing on play, giving orders, and sex-typing children (Coltrane, 1996, 1998; Parke, 1996). These styles of father involvement have been found to encourage less gender stereotyping among young adults and to encourage independence in daughters and emotional sensitivity in sons. Most researchers agree that these are worthy goals that could contribute to reducing sexism, promoting gender equity, and curbing violence against women (but see Blankenhorn, 1995).

Demographic Contexts for Father Involvement

As Furstenberg (1988) first noted, conflicting images of fathers are common in popular culture, with nurturing, involved "good dads" contrasted with "bad dads" who do not marry the mother of their children or who move out and fail to pay child support. Recent research suggests that both types of fathers are on the rise and that the demographic contexts for fatherhood have changed significantly over the past few decades. In many industrialized countries, at the same time that some fathers are taking a more active role in their children's lives, growing numbers of men rarely see their children and do not support them financially. In the United States, for example, single-parent households are increasing, with only about half of U.S. children eligible for child support from nonresident parents via court order, and only about half of those receive the full amount (Scoon-Rogers, 1999). Both trends in fatherhood—toward more direct involvement and toward less contact and financial support—are responses to the same underlying social developments, including women's rising labor force participation and the increasingly optional nature of marriage.

Marriage rates have fallen in the past few decades, with people waiting longer to get married and increasingly living together without marrying. Women are having fewer children than they did just a few decades ago, waiting longer to have them, and not necessarily marrying before they give birth (Eggebeen, 2002; Seltzer, 2000). One of three births in the United States is to an unmarried woman, a rate that is three times higher than it was in the 1960s, with rates for African American women highest, followed by Latinas, and then non-Hispanic whites (National Center for Health Statistics, 2000). It is often assumed that nonmarital births produce fatherless children, but recent studies show that most of the increase in nonmarital childbearing from the 1980s to the 1990s is accounted for by the increase in the number of cohabiting women getting pregnant and carrying the baby to term without getting married. Historically, if an unmarried woman became pregnant, she would marry to legitimate the birth. Today, only a minority of women do so.

In addition, an increasingly large number of American fathers live apart from their children because of separation or divorce. Because most divorcing men do not seek (or are not awarded) child custody following divorce, the number of divorced men who are uninvolved fathers has risen (Eggebeen, 2002; Furstenberg & Cherlin, 1991), although recent research shows that the actual involvement of fathers with children after divorce varies enormously, sometimes without regard to official postdivorce court orders (Braver, 1998; Hetherington & Stanley-Hagan, 1999; McLanahan & Sandefur, 1994; Seltzer, 1998). The number of men with joint physical (residential) custody has grown, though joint legal (decision-making) custody is still a more common postdivorce parenting arrangement (Maccoby & Mnookin, 1992; Seltzer, 1998). And although single-father households have increased in recent

years, single-mother households continue to outpace them five to one. Demographers suggest that because of all these trends, younger cohorts will be less likely to experience sustained involved fathering than the generations that immediately preceded them (Eggebeen, 2002).

Marriage and the traditional assumption of fatherhood have become more fragile, in part because an increasing number of men face financial difficulties. Although men continue to earn about 30% higher wages than women, their real wages (adjusted for inflation) have declined since the early 1970s, whereas women's have increased (Bernstein & Mishel, 1997). As the U.S. economy has shifted from heavy reliance on domestic manufacturing to global interdependence within an information and service economy, working-class men's prospects of earning a family wage have declined. At the same time, women's labor force participation has risen steadily, with future growth in the economy predicted in the areas where women are traditionally concentrated (e.g., service, information, health care, part-time work). The historical significance of this shift cannot be overestimated. For most of the 19th and 20th centuries, American women's life chances were determined by their marriage decisions. Unable to own property, vote, or be legally independent in most states, daughters were dependent on fathers and wives were dependent on their husbands for economic survival. Such dependencies shaped family relations and produced fatherhood ideals and practices predicated on male family headship. As women and mothers have gained independence by entering the labor force in record numbers, it is not surprising that older ideals about marriage to a man legitimating childbearing have been challenged.

Gender and the Politics of Fatherhood

In the 1990s, popular books and articles revived a research and policy focus that had been popular in the 1960s: father absence. For example, Popenoe (1996) suggested that drug and alcohol abuse, juvenile delinquency, teenage pregnancy, violent crime, and child poverty were the result of father-lessness and that American society was in decline because it had abandoned traditional marriage and child-rearing patterns. Such claims about father absence often rely on evolutionary psychology and sociobiology and define fathers as categorically different from mothers (Blankenhorn, 1995; Popenoe, 1996). Even some proponents of nurturing fathers warn men against trying to act too much like mothers (Pruett, 1993). Following this reasoning, some argue for gender-differentiated parenting measurement strategies: "[T]he roles of father and mother are different and complementary rather than interchangeable and thus the standards for evaluating the role performance of fathers and mothers should be different" (Day & Mackey, 1989, p. 402). Some label the use of measures developed on mothers to study fathers and the practice of comparing fathers' and mothers' parenting as the *deficit model* (Doherty, 1991) or the *role inadequacy perspective* (Hawkins & Dollahite, 1997).

Because parenting is a learned behavior for both men and women, most social scientists focus on the societal conditions that create gender differences in parenting or find proximate social causes of paternal investment that outweigh assumed biological causes (e.g., Hofferth & Anderson, 2003). Nevertheless, questioning taken-for-granted cultural ideals about families can cause controversy. When Silverstein and Auerbach (1999) challenged assertions about essential differences between fathers and mothers in an *American Psychologist* article entitled "Deconstructing the Essential Father," they received widespread public and academic criticism. Their scholarly article (based on a review of research findings) was ridiculed as "silliness" and "junk science" by Wade Horn (1999; formerly of the National Fatherhood Initiative and now Assistant Secretary in the U.S. Department of Health and Human Services), and the U.S. House of Representatives debated whether to pass a resolution condemning the article (Silverstein, 2002). Clearly, debates about fathers, marriage, and

family values carry symbolic meanings that transcend scientific findings. The contentious political and scholarly debates about fathers that emerged in the 1990s appear to be framed by an older political dichotomy: Conservatives tend to focus on biological parenting differences and stress the importance of male headship and breadwinning, respect for authority, and moral leadership (Blankenhorn, 1995; Popenoe, 1996), whereas liberals tend to focus on similarities between mothers and fathers and stress the importance of employment, social services, and possibilities for more equal marital relations (Coontz, 1992; Silverstein & Auerbach, 1999; Stacey, 1996).

A full analysis of contemporary family values debates is beyond the scope of this chapter, but elsewhere I analyze marriage and fatherhood movements using data and theories about political opportunities, resource mobilization, and the moral framing of social issues (Coltrane, 2001; Coltrane & Adams, 2003; see also Gavanas, 2002). In general, cultural tensions in the larger society are mirrored in policy proposals and academic debates about the appropriate roles of fathers and the importance of marriage. One cannot adjudicate among various scholarly approaches to fathering without acknowledging gendered interests and understanding the political economy of expert knowledge production. Recent policies and programs promoting marriage and fatherhood using faith-based organizations are designed to advance a particular vision of fatherhood. Whether they will benefit the majority of American mothers and children is a question that cannot be resolved without more sophisticated research with controls for mothers' parenting and various other economic and social-contextual issues (Marsiglio et al., 2000; Marsiglio & Pleck, in press).

Prospects for the Future

The forces that are driving changes in fathers' involvement in families are likely to continue. In two-parent households (both married and cohabiting), men share more family work if their female partners are employed more hours, earn more money, and have more education. All three of these trends in women's attainment are likely to continue for the foreseeable future. Similarly, fathers share more family work when they are employed fewer hours and their wives earn a greater portion of the family income. Labor market and economic trends for these variables are also expected to continue for several decades. Couples also share more when they believe that family work should be shared and that men and women should have equal rights. According to national opinion polls, although the country has become slightly more conservative about marriage and divorce than it was in the 1970s and 1980s, the belief in gender equality continues to gain acceptance among both men and women. In addition, American women are waiting longer, on average, to marry and give birth, and they are having fewer children—additional factors sometimes associated with more sharing of housework and child care. Thus, I predict that increasing economic parity and more equal gender relations will allow women to buy out of some domestic obligations and/or recruit their partners to do more. Middle- and upper-class wives and mothers will rely on working-class and immigrant women to provide domestic services (nannies, housekeepers, child care workers, fast food employees, etc.), thereby reducing their own hours of family labor but simultaneously perpetuating race, class, and gender hierarchies in the labor market and in the society. Some fathers in dual-earner households will increase their contributions to family work, whereas others will perform a greater proportion of housework and child care by virtue of their wives' doing less. Other men will remain marginal to family life because they do not stay connected to the mothers of their children, do not hold jobs allowing them to support their children, or do not seek custody or make regular child support payments. These two ideal types—of involved and marginalized fathers—are likely to continue to coexist in the popular culture and in actual practice.

The context in which American couples negotiate fathering has definitely changed. The future is likely to bring more demands on fathers to be active parents if they want to stay involved with the mothers of their children. For fathers to assume more responsibility for active parenting, it may be necessary to change cultural assumptions that men are entitled to domestic services and that women are inherently predisposed to provide them. Further changes in fathering are likely to be driven by women's increasing independence and earning power. Ironically, women's enhanced economic position also makes them able to form families and raise children without the father's being present. In the future, men will be even less able to rely on their superior earning power and the institution of fatherhood to maintain their connection to families and children. Increasingly, they will need to adopt different fathering styles to meet specific family circumstances and to commit to doing things men have not been accustomed to doing. Some men will be able to maintain their economic and emotional commitments to their children, whereas others will not. Some men will participate in all aspects of child rearing, whereas others will hardly see their children. Unless living wages and adequate social supports are developed for all fathers (as well as for mothers and children), we can expect that the paradoxes, contradictions, and dilemmas associated with fathering described in this chapter will continue for the foreseeable future.

Author's Note: This chapter incorporates some material from a November 21, 2002, National Council on Family Relations (NCFR) Annual Conference Special Session "Future Prospects for Increasing Father Involvement in Child Rearing and Household Activities," reprinted as "The Paradox of Fatherhood: Predicting the Future of Men's Family Involvement" in *Vision 2003* (Minneapolis, MN: NCFR/Allen Press). I thank Marilyn Coleman, Lawrence Ganong, Joseph Pleck, Carl Auerbach, and two anonymous reviewers for valuable feedback on an earlier draft of this chapter.

References

Ahmeduzzaman, M., & Roopnarine, J. L. (1992). Sociodemographic factors, functioning style, social support, and fathers' involvement with preschoolers in African American intact families. *Journal of Marriage and the Family, 54,* 699–707.

Allen, S. M., & Hawkins, A. J. (1999). Maternal gate-keeping. *Journal of Marriage and the Family, 61,* 199–212.

Amato, P. (2000). Diversity within single-parent families. In D. H. Demo, K. R. Allen, & M. A. Fine (Eds.), *Handbook of family diversity* (pp. 149–172). New York: Oxford University Press.

Amato, P., & Booth, A. (1997). *A generation at risk: Growing up in an era of family upheaval.* Cambridge, MA: Harvard University Press.

Amato, P., & Gilbreth, J. (1999). Nonresident fathers and children's well-being: A meta-analysis. *Journal of Marriage and the Family, 61,* 557–573.

Amato, P., & Rivera, F. (1999). Paternal involvement and children's behavior problems. *Journal of Marriage and the Family, 61,* 375–384.

Auerbach, C., Silverstein, L., & Zizi, M. (1997). The evolving structure of fatherhood. *Journal of African American Men, 2,* 59–85.

Beitel, A. H., & Parke, R. D. (1998). Paternal involvement in infancy: The role of maternal and paternal attitudes. *Journal of Family Psychology, 12,* 268–288.

Belsky, J. (1984). The determinants of parenting. *Child Development, 55,* 83–96.

Bernard, J. (1981). The good provider role: Its rise and fall. *American Psychologist, 36,* 1–12.

Bernstein, J., & Mishel, L. (1997). Has wage inequality stopped growing? *Monthly Labor Review, 120,* 3–17.

Biller, H. B. (1976). The father and personality development. In M. E. Lamb (Ed.), *The role of the father in child development.* New York: John Wiley.

Blankenhorn, D. (1995). *Fatherless America.* New York: Basic Books.

Bowman, P. J., & Sanders, R. (1998). Unmarried African American fathers. *Journal of Comparative Family Studies, 29,* 39–56.

Braver, S. L. (1998). *Divorced dads.* New York: Jeremy Tarcher/Putnam.

Brayfield, A. (1995). Juggling jobs and kids. *Journal of Marriage and the Family, 57,* 321–332.

Brennan, R. T., Barnett, R. C., & Gareis, K. C. (2001). When she earns more than he does: A longitudinal study of dual-earner couples. *Journal of Marriage and Family, 63,* 168–182.

Brewster, K. L. (2000, March). *Contextualizing change in fathers' participation in child care.* Paper pre-sented at "Work and Family" Conference, San Francisco.

Brines, J. (1994). Economic dependency, gender, and the division of labor at home. *American Journal of Sociology, 100,* 652–688.

Broman, L. L. (1991). Gender, work, family roles, and psychological well-being of blacks. *Journal of Marriage and the Family, 53,* 509–520.

Cabrera, N., Tamis-LeMonda, C., Bradley, R., Hofferth, S., & Lamb, M. (2000). Fatherhood in the 21st century. *Child Development, 71,* 127–136.

Casper, L. M., & O'Connell, M. (1998). Work, income, the economy, and married fathers as child-care providers. *Demography, 35,* 243–250.

Chodorow, N. (1974). Family structure and feminine personality. In M. Z. Rosaldo & L. Lamphere (Eds.), *Woman, culture and society* (pp. 43–66). Palo Alto, CA: Stanford University Press.

Cohen, P. N. (1998). Replacing housework in the service economy: Gender, class, and race-ethnicity in service spending. *Gender and Society, 12,* 219–231.

Coley, R. L., & Morris, J. E. (2002). Comparing father and mother reports of father involvement among low-income minority families. *Journal of Marriage and the Family, 64,* 982–997.

Coltrane, S. (1988). Father-child relationships and the status of women. *American Journal of Sociology, 93,* 1060–1095.

Coltrane, S. (1996). *Family man.* New York: Oxford University Press.

Coltrane, S. (1998). *Gender and families.* Newbury Park, CA: Pine Forge/Alta Mira.

Coltrane, S. (2000). Research on household labor. *Journal of Marriage and the Family, 62,* 1209–1233.

Coltrane, S. (2001). Marketing the marriage "solution." *Sociological Perspectives, 44,* 387–422.

Coltrane, S., & Adams, M. (2003). The social construction of the divorce "problem": Morality, child victims, and the politics of gender. *Family Relations, 52,* 21–30.

Coltrane, S., & Collins, R. (2001). *Sociology of marriage and the family* (5th ed.). Belmont, CA: Wadsworth/Thomson Learning.

Coltrane, S., & Galt, J. (2000). The history of men's caring. In M. H. Meyer (Ed.), *Care work: Gender, labor, and welfare states* (pp. 15–36). New York: Routledge.

Coltrane, S., & Parke, R. D. (1998). *Reinventing fatherhood: Toward an historical understanding of continuity and change in men's family lives* (WP 98–12A). Philadelphia: National Center on Fathers and Families.

Coltrane, S., Parke, R. D., & Adams, M. (2001, April). *Shared parenting in Mexican-American and European-American families.* Paper presented at the biennial meeting of the Society for Research in Child Development, Minneapolis, MN.

Coontz, S. (1992). *The way we never were.* New York: Basic Books.

Cowan, C. P., & Cowan, P. A. (2000). *When partners become parents.* Mahwah, NJ: Lawrence Erlbaum.

Crockett, L. J., Eggebeen, D. J., & Hawkins, A. J. (1993). Fathers' presence and young children's behavioral and cognitive adjustment. *Journal of Family Issues, 14,* 355–377.

Day, R. D., & Mackey, W. C. (1989). An alternate standard for evaluating American fathers. *Journal of Family Issues, 10,* 401–408.

Deutsch, F. (1999). *Halving it all.* Cambridge, MA: Harvard University Press.

Dill, B. T. (1988). Our mother's grief: Racial ethnic women and the maintenance of families. *Journal of Family History, 13,* 415–431.

Doherty, W. J. (1991). Beyond reactivity and the deficit model of manhood. *Journal of Marital and Family Therapy, 17,* 29–32.

Dubowitz, H., Black, M. M., Cox, C. E., Kerr, M. A., Litrownik, A. J., Radhakrishna, A., English, D. J., Schneider, M. W., & Runyan, D. K. (2001). Father involvement and children's functioning at age 6 years: A multisite study. *Child Maltreatment, 6,* 300–309.

Eggebeen, D. (2002). The changing course of fatherhood. *Journal of Family Issues, 23,* 486–506.

Ehrenreich, B. (1984). *The hearts of men.* Garden City, NY: Anchor Press/Doubleday.

Fagan, J. A. (1998). Correlates of low-income African American and Puerto Rican fathers' involvement with their children. *Journal of Black Psychology, 3,* 351–367.

Federal Interagency Forum on Child and Family Statistics. (1998). Report of the Working Group on Conceptualizing Male Parenting (Marsiglio, Day, Evans, Lamb, Braver, & Peters). In *Nurturing fatherhood* (pp. 101–174). Washington, DC: Government Printing Office.

Finkelhor, D., Hotaling, G., Lewis, I., & Smith, C. (1990). Sexual abuse in a national survey of adult men and women. *Child Abuse and Neglect, 14,* 19–28.

Furstenberg, F. F. (1988). Good dads—bad dads. In A. Cherlin (Ed.), *The changing American family and public policy* (pp. 193–218). Washington, DC: Urban Institute Press.

Furstenberg, F. F., & Cherlin, A. (1991). *Divided families.* Cambridge, MA: Harvard University Press.

Furstenberg, F. F., & Harris, K. (1993). When and why fathers matter. In R. Lerman & T. Ooms (Eds.), *Young unwed fathers* (pp. 150–176). Philadelphia: Temple University Press.

Gavanas, A. (2002). The fatherhood responsibility movement. In B. Hobson (Ed.), *Making men into fathers* (pp. 213–242). New York: Cambridge University Press.

Griswold, R. L. (1993). *Fatherhood in America: A history.* New York: Basic Books.

Griswold, R. L. (1997). Generative fathering: A historical perspective. In A. J. Hawkins & D. Dollahite (Eds.), *Generative fathering* (pp. 71–86). Thousand Oaks, CA: Sage.

Hamer, J., & Marchioro, K. (2002). Becoming custodial dads: Exploring parenting among low-income and working-class African American fathers. *Journal of Marriage and the Family, 64,* 116–129.

Harris, K. H., Furstenberg, F. F., & Marmer, J. K. (1998). Paternal involvement with adolescents in intact families. *Demography, 35,* 201–216.

Harris, K. H., & Morgan, S. P. (1991). Fathers, sons and daughters: Differential paternal involvement in parenting. *Journal of Marriage and the Family, 53,* 531–544.

Hawkins, A. J., Christiansen, S. L., Sargent, K. P., & Hill, E. J. (1993). Rethinking fathers' involvement in child care. *Journal of Family Issues, 14,* 531–549.

Hawkins, A. J., & Dollahite, D. C. (1997). Beyond the role-inadequacy perspective of fathering. In A. J. Hawkins & D. C. Dollahite (Eds.), *Generative fathering: Beyond deficit perspectives* (pp. 3–16). Thousand Oaks, CA: Sage.

Hays, S. (1996). *The cultural contradictions of motherhood.* New Haven, CT: Yale University Press.

Hetherington, E. M., & Stanley-Hagan, M. M. (1999). Stepfamilies. In M. E. Lamb (Ed.), *Parenting and child development in "nontraditional" families* (pp. 137–159). Mahwah, NJ: Lawrence Erlbaum.

Hewlett, B. S. (1991). *The nature and context of Aka pygmy paternal infant care.* Ann Arbor: University of Michigan Press.

Hewlett, B. S. (2000). Culture, history, and sex: Anthropological contributions to conceptualizing father involvement. *Marriage and Family Review, 29,* 59–73.

Hochschild, A. R. (1989). *The second shift.* New York: Viking.

Hofferth, S. L. (1998). *Healthy environments, healthy children: Children in families.* Ann Arbor: Institute for Social Research, University of Michigan.

Hofferth, S. L. (2003). Race/ethnic differences in father involvement in two-parent families: Culture, context, or economy? *Journal of Family Issues, 24,* 185–216.

Hofferth, S. L., & Anderson, K. G. (2003). Are all dads equal? Biology versus marriage as a basis for paternal investment. *Journal of Marriage and the Family, 65,* 213–232.

Horn, W. (1999). Lunacy 101: Questioning the need for fathers. Retrieved April 29, 2003, from the Smart Marriages Web site: http://listarchives.his.com/smartmarriages/smartmarriages.9907/msg00011.html.

Hossain, Z., & Roopnarine, J. L. (1993). Division of household labor and child care in dual-earner African-American families with infants. *Sex Roles, 29,* 571–583.

Hunter, A. G., & Davis, J. E. (1994). Hidden voices of black men: The meaning, structure, and complexity of manhood. *Journal of Black Studies, 25,* 20–40.

John, D., & Shelton, B. A. (1997). The production of gender among black and white women and men: The case of household labor. *Sex Roles, 36,* 171–193.

Johnson, M. (1988). *Strong mothers, weak wives.* Berkeley: University of California Press.

Kimmel, M. (1996). *Manhood in America: A cultural history.* New York: Free Press.

Lamb, M. E., Pleck, J., Charnov, E., & Levine, J. (1987). A biosocial perspective on parental behavior and involvement. In J. B. Lancaster, J. Altman, & A. Rossi (Eds), *Parenting across the lifespan* (pp. 11–42). New York: Academic Press.

LaRossa, R. (1988). Fatherhood and social change. *Family Relations, 37,* 451–457.

LaRossa, R. (1997). *The modernization of fatherhood: A social and political history.* Chicago: University of Chicago Press.

Maccoby, E., & Mnookin, R. (1992). *Dividing the child.* Cambridge, MA: Harvard University Press.

Margolin, L. (1992). Child abuse by mother's boyfriends. *Child Abuse and Neglect, 16,* 541–551.

Marsiglio, W. (1991). Paternal engagement activities with minor children. *Journal of Marriage and the Family, 53,* 973–986.

Marsiglio, W., Amato, P., Day, R. D., & Lamb, M. E. (2000). Scholarship on fatherhood in the 1990s and beyond. *Journal of Marriage and the Family, 62,* 1173–1191.

Marsiglio, W., & Pleck, J. H. (in press). Fatherhood and masculinities. In R.W. Connell, J. Hearn, & M. Kimmel (Eds.), *The handbook of studies on men and masculinities.* Thousand Oaks, CA: Sage.

McBride, B. A. (1990). The effects of a parent education/play group program on father involvement on child rearing. *Family Relations, 39,* 250–256.

McBride, B. A., & Mills, G. (1993). A comparison of mother and father involvement with their preschool age children. *Early Childhood Research Quarterly, 8,* 457–477.

McBride, B. A., Schoppe, S., & Rane, T. (2002). Child characteristics, parenting stress, and parental involvement: Fathers versus mothers. *Journal of Marriage and the Family, 64,* 998–1011.

McDaniel, A. (1994). Historical racial differences in living arrangements of children. *Journal of Family History, 19,* 57–77.

McHale, S. M., & Huston, T. L. (1984). Men and women as parents: Sex role orientations, employment, and parental roles with infants. *Child Development, 55,* 1349–1361.

McLanahan, S., & Sandefur, G. (1994). *Growing up with a single parent: What hurts, what helps.* Cambridge, MA: Harvard University Press.

McLanahan, S., Seltzer, J., Hanson, T., & Thomson, E. (1994). Child support enforcement and child well-being. In I. Garfinkel, S. S. McLanahan, & P. K. Robins (Eds.), *Child support and child well-being* (pp. 285–316). Washington, DC: Urban Institute.

Messner, M. (1993). "Changing men" and feminist politics in the U.S. *Theory and Society, 22,* 723–737.

Mintz, S. (1998). From patriarchy to androgyny and other myths. In A. Booth & A. C. Crouter (Eds.), *Men in families* (pp. 3–30). Mahweh, NJ: Lawrence Erlbaum.

Mosley, J., & Thomson, E. (1994). Fathering behavior and child outcomes. In W. Marsiglio (Ed.), *Fatherhood* (pp. 148–165). Thousand Oaks, CA: Sage.

National Center for Health Statistics. (2000, January). Nonmarital birth rates, 1940–1999. Retrieved on April 29, 2003, from the Centers for Disease Control and Prevention Web site: www.cdc.gov/nchs/data/nvsr/nvsr48.

National Research Council. (1993). *Understanding child abuse and neglect.* Washington, DC: National Academy Press.

Nock, S. (1998). *Marriage in men's lives.* New York: Oxford University Press.

Oropesa, R. S. (1993). Using the service economy to relieve the double burden: Female labor force participation and service purchases. *Journal of Family Issues, 14,* 438–473.

Ozer, E. M., Barnett, R. C., Brennan, R. T., & Sperling, J. (1998). Does childcare involvement increase or decrease distress among dual-earner couples? *Women's Health: Research on Gender, Behavior, and Policy, 4,* 285–311.

Padgett, D. L. (1997). The contribution of support networks to household labor in African American families. *Journal of Family Issues, 18,* 227–250.

Palkovitz, R. (1997). Reconstructing "involvement." In A. Hawkins & D. Dollahite (Eds.), *Generative fathering* (pp. 200–216). Thousand Oaks, CA: Sage.

Parke, R. D. (1996). *Fatherhood.* Cambridge, MA: Harvard University Press.

Pasley, K., Ihinger-Tallman, M, & Buehler, C. (1993). Developing a middle-range theory of father involvement postdivorce. *Journal of Family Issues, 14,* 550–576.

Pleck, E. H., & Pleck, J. H. (1997). Fatherhood ideals in the United States: Historical dimensions. In M. E. Lamb (Ed.), *The role of the father in child development* (3rd ed., pp. 33–48). New York: John Wiley.

Pleck, J. H. (1993). Are "family-supportive" employer policies relevant to men? In J. C. Hood (Ed.), *Men, work, and family* (pp. 217–237). Newbury Park, CA: Sage.

Pleck, J. H. (1997). Paternal involvement: Levels, sources, and consequences. In M. E. Lamb (Ed.), *The role of the father in child development* (3rd ed., pp. 66–103). New York: John Wiley.

Pleck, J. H., & Masciadrelli, B. P. (2003). Paternal involvement: Levels, sources, and consequences. In M. E. Lamb (Ed.), *The role of the father in child development* (4th ed.). New York: John Wiley

Pleck, J. H., & Steuve, J. L. (2001). Time and paternal involvement. In K. Daly (Ed.), *Minding the time in family experience* (pp. 205–226). Oxford, UK: Elsevier.

Popenoe, D. (1996). *Life without father: Compelling new evidence that fatherhood and marriage are indispensable for the good of children and society.* New York: Free Press.

Presser, H. B. (1995). Job, family, and gender. *Demography, 32,* 577–598.

Pruett, K. D. (1993). The paternal presence. *Families in Society, 74,* 46–50.

Radhakrishna, A., Bou-Saada, I. E., Hunter, W. M., Catellier, D. J., & Kotch, J. B. (2001). Are father surrogates a risk factor for child maltreatment? *Child Maltreatment, 6,* 281–289.

Rane, T. R., & McBride, B. A. (2000). Identity theory as a guide to understanding father's involvement with their children. *Journal of Family Issues, 21,* 347–366.

Sanday, P. R. (1981). *Female power and male dominance.* New York: Cambridge University Press.

Scoon-Rogers, L. (1999). Child support for custodial mothers and fathers. *Current Population Reports,* P60-196. Washington, DC: U.S. Bureau of the Census.

Seltzer, J. A. (1994). Consequences of marital dissolution for children. *Annual Review of Sociology, 20,* 235–266.

Seltzer, J. A. (1998). Father by law: Effects of joint legal custody on nonresident fathers' involvement with children. *Demography, 35,* 135–146.

Seltzer, J. A. (2000). Families formed outside of marriage. *Journal of Marriage and the Family, 62,* 1247–1268.

Silverstein, L. B. (2002). Fathers and families. In J. McHale & W. Grolnick (Eds.), *Retrospect and prospect in the psychological study of fathers* (pp. 35–64). Mahwah, NJ: Lawrence Erlbaum.

Silverstein, L. B., & Auerbach, C. F. (1999). Deconstructing the essential father. *American Psychologist, 54,* 397–407.

Smock, P., & Manning, W. (1997). Nonresident parents' characteristics and child support. *Journal of Marriage and the Family, 59,* 798–808.

Snarey, J. (1993). *How fathers care for the next generation.* Cambridge, MA: Harvard University Press.

Stacey, J. (1996). *In the name of the family.* Boston: Beacon.

Thompson, L., & Walker, A. J. (1989). Gender in families: Women and men in marriage, work, and parenthood. *Journal of Marriage and the Family, 51,* 845–871.

Toth, J. F., & Xu, X. (1999). Ethnic and cultural diversity in fathers' involvement: A racial/ethnic comparison of African American, Hispanic, and white fathers. *Youth and Society, 31,* 76–99.

Whiting, J., & Whiting, B. (1975). Aloofness and intimacy of husbands and wives. *Ethos, 3,* 183–207.

Wilson, M. N., Tolson, T. F. J., Hinton, I. D., & Kiernan, M. (1990). Flexibility and sharing of childcare duties in black families. *Sex Roles, 22,* 409–425.

Yueng, W. J., Sandberg, J. F., Davis-Kean, P. E., & Hofferth, S. L. (2001). Children's time with fathers in intact families. *Journal of Marriage and Family, 63,* 136–154.

PART NINE

Masculinities in the Media

Men are daily bombarded with images of masculinity—in magazines, television, movies, music, even the Internet. We see what men are supposed to look like, act like, be like. And social scientists are only now beginning to understand the enormous influence that the media have in shaping our ideas about what it means to be a man.

For one thing, it is clear that the media can create artificial standards against which boys as well as girls measure themselves. Just as idealized human female models can only approximate the exaggeratedly large breasts and exaggeratedly small waistline of Barbie, virtually no men can approach the physiques of the cartoon version of Tarzan or even G.I. Joe. The original G.I. Joe had the equiva-

lent of 12.2-inch biceps when he was introduced in 1964. Ten years later, his biceps measured the equivalent of 15.2 inches. By 1994, he had 16.4-inch biceps, and today his biceps measure a simulated 26.8 inches—nearly 7 inches larger than Mark McGwire's 20-inch muscles. "Many modern figures display the physiques of advanced bodybuilders and some display levels of muscularity far exceeding the outer limits of actual human attainment," notes Dr. Harrison Pope, a Harvard psychiatrist.

Media masculinities create standards against which men measure themselves. No wonder we often feel like we fail the test of physical manhood. At the same time, the media encourage us to evaluate and judge the manhood of others by those same standards. As the articles in this section suggest, we are constantly "seeing" masculinity, in the movies, in commercials (Mike Messner and Jeffrey Montez de Oca), in pornography (Beth Eck), and especially in sports (Shari Lee Dworkin and Faye Linda Wachs and David Nylund). Any effort to understand—let alone transform—masculinity must take account of the ways in which we see ourselves reflected through the lenses that record our fantasy lives.

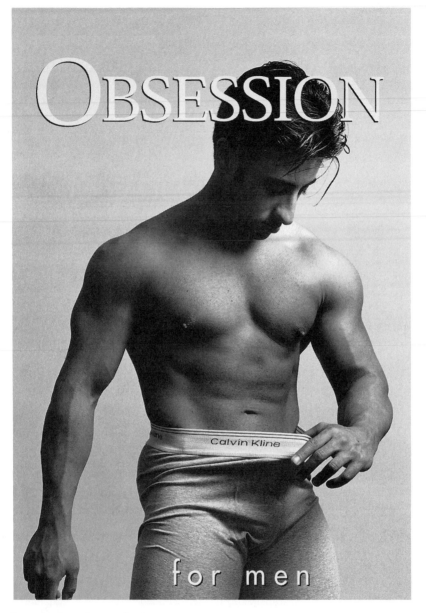

Image courtesy of www.adbusters.org.

Shari Lee Dworkin
Faye Linda Wachs

The Morality/Manhood Paradox:
Masculinity, Sport, and the Media

In a world where women do not say no, the man is never forced to settle down and make serious choices. His sex drive—the most powerful compulsion in his life is never used to make him part of civilization as the supporter of a family. If a woman does not force him to make a long-term commitment—to marry—in general, he doesn't. It is maternity that requires commitment. His sex drive only demands conquest, driving him from body to body in an unsettling hunt for variety and excitement in which much of the thrill is in the chase itself. (Gilder, 1986, p. 47)

Journalists articulated the "body panic" surrounding HIV/AIDS and sport in ways that framed heterosexual women as the virulent agents and heterosexual men as the "innocent" victims. These accounts are readily acceptable because they simultaneously produce and reproduce a gender regime that privileges heterosexual male "promiscuity" and devalues, pathologizes, or criminalizes other forms of sexuality. (McKay, 1993, p. 77)

On November 7, 1991, Earvin "Magic" Johnson announced that he had tested positive for the HIV virus. The public registered immediate shock and dismay that arguably one of the greatest and most beloved players in NBA history contracted the highly stigmatized virus. After Johnson, a self-identified heterosexual, made his announcement, once-quiet HIV/AIDS information hot lines were suddenly jam-packed with millions of concerned inquiries as to who gets HIV and how. Johnson became a national spokesman for safe sex and began to urge abstinence, citing his unsafe "accommodation" of thousands of women. More than four years later, on February 22, 1996, pro-

From *Masculinities, Gender Relations, and Sport*, Jim McKay, Michael A. Messner, and Don Sabo, eds. Sage Publications. © 2000 by Sage Publications, Inc. Reprinted by permission.

fessional diver Greg Louganis announced that he had AIDS and that he had been HIV-positive during the 1988 Seoul Olympics. Mainstream news coverage focused on the now infamous "blood in the pool" incident after Louganis struck his head on a springboard and still went on to win an Olympic gold. Although no shock or dismay was expressed vis-à-vis Louganis, concern was expressed that Louganis, who identifies as gay, had not informed others of his HIV status—and what effect his virus may have had on the doctors who stitched his bleeding head and on others in the pool. During the same month, on February 11, 1996, white working-class professional boxer Tommy Morrison let the public hear his own HIV story. Morrison expressed shock, regretfully blamed his "fast lane lifestyle," and is described by friends as the "world's biggest bimbo magnet." This chapter examines paradoxes that juxtapose the public perception of athletes as role models against media accounts rife with "moral" turpitude. These paradoxes are particularly timely in the wake of recent attention paid to AIDS in sport. Our exploration of the widespread print media coverage of these prominent sports figures reveals cultural and historical assumptions about masculinity, sexuality, and HIV/AIDS.

In U.S. mainstream culture, athletes and sports have specific cultural meanings. Athletes in mediated sports are role models, heroes, and are often featured as successful individuals. Our analysis of dominant print media coverage of these athletes' HIV announcements highlights two important and interrelated issues surrounding bodies, morality, sexuality, and masculinity (the Appendix contains citations to all articles examined in this study). First, a contradiction between dominant norms of morality and masculinity becomes apparent. Second, the complexity of current and historical dynamics of race/class/gender/sexuality are explicated.

Hegemonic Masculinity, Sport, and Bodies

Hegemonic masculinity provides cultural icons or mythic images of masculinity that privilege the most powerful half of multiple dichotomous social locations. Hegemonic masculinity, the most dominant form of masculinity (white, middle-class, heterosexual) in a given historical period, is defined in relation to femininity and subordinated masculinities (Connell, 1987). As Foucault (1979) demonstrated, individuals live at the intersection of multiple hierarchicalized dualities, some of which are privileged, others of which are stigmatized. An individual's social location is determined by his or her positioning within multiple and fragmented hierarchies and dualities. For example, African Americans historically have been framed by the media as being "closer to nature" (Collins, 1990). Within sport, African American male athletes are assumed to be "natural" athletes, whereas white men are praised for their intelligence and hard work (Edwards, 1973). Although

at times both privileged and subordinated male bodies may be said to enjoy male privilege and are seen as physically superior to female athletes, marginalized masculinities are indubitably stigmatized through comparisons with white middle-class norms (Majors, 1990). The body, then, and its discursive interpretations, are sites at which the material effects of power can be explored (Foucault, 1979). It is a tangible enactment and representation of these intersections.

In Western thought, the athletic male body has been a mark of power and moral superiority for those who bear it (Synnott, 1993; Dutton, 1995). Those who have these characteristics, along with other such as the "correct" race and class status, are assumed to be inherently "morally" superior. Which bodies are marked as superior is not static, but is contested. At the turn of the 20th century, the definition of morality was being debated within and between many social institutions, especially religious, medical, legislative, psychiatric, and social welfare agencies. The definition of morality was influenced by religious norms of good versus evil, prohibitions on nonprocreative sex (Katz, 1995b), and the Protestant work ethic that stressed hard work, individualism, and self-abnegation (Turner, 1984). This definition privileged the white, heterosexual middle class as "moral" against assumptions made about subordinated "others."

When urbanization and industrialization created changes in economic opportunities at the turn of the 20th century, many of these changes presented challenges to ideologies of gender and the position defined as hegemonic masculinity. The creation of white-collar occupations, an expanding middle class, and greater acceptance of women in the workforce facilitated a crisis in the definition of masculinity. Women's increasing presence in the public sphere, coupled with changes in men's work, fed fears of social feminization. The rise of competitive team sports in the United States is said to be a backlash, a means for white middle-class men to reaffirm symbolically their physical and moral superiority over women and socially subordinated men (Messner, 1988; Crosset, 1990; Kimmel, 1990). The sports that were popularized in the United States did not promote any type of masculinity and femininity but rather reflected specifically middle-class ideals of masculinity and femininity (Gorn & Goldstein, 1993). Individuals who participated in hegemonic sports were deemed heroes by virtue of their participation. Their bodies became signifiers of power and masculinity. With this power came the assumption of not only physical but also moral superiority.

In recent decades, most of the American public have increasingly experienced sport through the mass media (Wenner, 1989; Sage, 1990). This is not surprising, as sport and the mass media have enjoyed a mutually beneficial or "symbiotic" relationship over the last century (Jhally, 1989; McChesney, 1989). Mediated sports function largely to naturalize values and points of view that are generally consistent with cultural hegemony and come to appear as "common sense" (Jhally, 1989). Ideologies about gender, race, class, and sexuality are reproduced explicitly in media texts, in the assumptions that underlie the text, and in which sports and athletes are valued as culturally significant (Duncan & Hasbrook, 1988; Duncan, Messner, & Jensen, 1994; Kane, 1988, 1996; Messner, Duncan, & Wachs, 1996). For example, numerous works demonstrate how women and femininity are constructed as inferior through mediated sports and how men and masculinity are implicitly defined and constructed as superior (Theberge, 1987; Duncan & Hasbrook, 1988; Kane & Snyder, 1989; Whitson, 1990; Nelson, 1994; Kane, 1995; Messner et al., 1996). Furthermore, other works demonstrate how mediated sports reinforce stigmatizations of marginalized masculinities (Pronger, 1990; Messner & Solomon, 1993; Cole & Denny, 1994; Lule, 1995; Cole & Andrews, 1996; Wachs & Dworkin, 1997; Dworkin & Wachs, 1998). Although some works have examined HIV in sport (King, 1993; McKay, 1993; Cole & Denny, 1994), the cultural paradox that simultaneously represents male athletes as "moral" leaders and protects male privileges that are inconsistent with dominant norms of morality has not yet been problematized.

Given that sport is one of the most powerful socializing institutions for masculinity (Messner, 1992b) that privileges male heterosexual bodies, it provides an interesting forum for exploring norms of sexual behavior. Some scholars have argued that hegemonic male sexuality contributes to sexually aggressive locker room talk (Curry, 1991; Kane & Disch, 1993), violence against women (Kane & Disch, 1993; Messner & Sabo, 1994; Nelson, 1994; Crosset, Benedict, & McDonald, 1995), violence against other men (Messner, 1988; Young, 1993), and [. . .] difficulty in having lasting intimate relationships with women (Connell, 1990; Messner, 1992b; Klein, 1993). To be a man in our culture (and in sport in particular) is to have an assumed naturally aggressive sexual virility that brings with it access to multiple women's bodies. The case of athletes with HIV/AIDS presents a compelling arena in which to explore the discourse on masculinity and sexuality, and specifically "promiscuity" or "virility." Without the stigma that comes with HIV/AIDS, sexually active (heterosexual) men, by definition, are adhering to masculinity successfully. Given that HIV/AIDS is associated with the gay community (Weeks, 1985; Connell, 1987; Sontag, 1989; Watney, 1989; Patton, 1990) and carries a heavy "moral" stigma, we ask: How does the dominant print media frame male athletes and their concomitant normative sexual privilege when they acquire the highly socially stigmatized virus HIV? How will the public discourse—in our example, print media coverage—frame these announcements in the mass cultural discourse given its dual tendency to support hegemonic masculinity and stigmatize and blame infected (and often othered) bodies as immoral? How does mainstream media coverage reconcile hero status, dominant norms of masculinity, and morality in the body of the HIV-positive athlete? For which men?

Methodology

We used textual analysis to explore how cultural discourses that define gendered norms of sexuality shape and constrain men's and women's behaviors. Foucault (1979) observed that power operates both constitutively and repressively. Power operates to constitute dominant discourses, whereby some assumptions shape the acceptable public discourse and appear as common sense; this leaves many potentialities outside the realm of the fathomable. This constitution of power then creates a basis for power to operate repressively, whereby it seems "natural" to accept certain behaviors as "normal" and "moral" while policing "deviant" and "immoral" behaviors (Foucault, 1979). We explored dominant print media framings as one of power's material effects. Our interest was to deconstruct dominant assumptions about male and female sexual agency that survey and police "public" bodies and acts. We also explore the tensions and contradictions within these assumptions.

To explore these assumptions, we performed a textual analysis on all available articles from the *Los Angeles Times, The New York Times,* and *The Washington Post* that followed the HIV-positive announcements of professional basketball player Earvin "Magic" Johnson, Olympic diver Greg Louganis, and professional boxer Tommy Morrison. Articles were coded for content, tone, and implications and were cross-coded for validity. Out of the initial read of the articles emerged two areas for analysis. First, articles were analyzed as to how the status of the HIV-positive athlete was framed: Was he framed as a hero or as a "carrier"? The selective usage of the word hero in titles and/or bodies of articles demonstrates the morality/manhood paradox and reveals how the social location of individuals predetermines their access to hero status. Second, articles were coded for how men's and women's sexual agency is framed. This theme demonstrates how mainstream media coverage maintains this paradox by reinforcing cultural discourses that protect norms of hegemonic masculinity and male (hetero) sexual privilege while blaming and stigmatizing women and subordinated men.

Due to the enormous number of articles on Magic Johnson, many of which focused exclusively on his career, we limited our collection to all articles for three months following his announcement and 10% of the articles that appeared thereafter. Three mainstream newspapers were chosen from three major cities in the United States to represent the dominant or mainstream print media's treatment of gender norms, sexuality, and HIV/AIDS. Indeed, other newspapers, such as *USA Today,* may have large circulations, and the gay and alternative press might offer different framings of these events. However, the selected newspapers garner prestige and respect as mainstream media sources and, as such, are valuable sites in which to analyze dominant discourses on these subjects.

One striking feature of the HIV-positive announcements of Johnson, Louganis, and Morrison is the vast difference in the number of articles written. There are more than 100 articles about Magic Johnson, 12 articles about Greg Louganis, and 8 articles about Tommy Morrison. Perhaps the difference in sheer number of articles highlights not only Magic Johnson's celebrity status within the basketball community but also the fact that basketball is part of the triad of sports that reinforces hegemonic masculinity and is one of the most watched sports in our culture. By contrast, the fewer number of articles about Louganis and Morrison may reflect their lesser popularity as individuals or the status of the sports in which they participate. Furthermore, one cannot ignore the effect of the symbiotic relation between sports and the mass media (Jhally, 1989; Sage, 1990). Sport is promoted by the mass media as a means for targeting the hard-to-reach male middle-class market aged 18 to 45 years. Hence, sports that are considered middle-class and "masculine appropriate" (Kane, 1988) garner the bulk of media coverage (Messner, 1988; Jhally, 1989).

Boxing is a blood sport that has been widely contested as violent and immoral. Participation in such a sport has been largely linked to working-class men, who have been disproportionately represented in the sport since its inception (Gorn & Goldstein, 1993). Although boxing is widely accepted, popularized, and aired in mainstream sports media, it still retains stigma through its historical association with the working class. Thus, although Morrison participates in a sport with heavy doses of physical contact that aids the status of boxing in terms of hegemonic masculinity, its popularity suffers because it is not a team sport with signifiers linked to the dominant class. Although it is true that Morrison is hardly the equivalent of Johnson in terms of the success of his career, it is interesting to note that he received almost as much coverage as did Louganis despite his being a mediocre professional compared to Louganis, who dominated his sport for most of his career.

The relative lack of coverage of Louganis likely reflects that diving, which involves no direct physical confrontation, is not linked to the construction of hegemonic masculinity. In general, team sports are considered male-appropriate, whereas sports that emphasize grace are associated with femininity (Kane, 1988). Male team sports often involve overcoming opponents' defenses and asserting mastery and control of the field of play. The "female-appropriate" sports, like gymnastics and figure skating, involve one receiving an individual score that (in theory) is in no way dependent on the other participants' actions. Men who participate in sports that are not "masculine-appropriate" do not acquire the status of hegemonic masculinity; indeed, their participation may even mark them as less than masculine. Greg Louganis participates in an individual, graceful sport. His athletic body does not have the same status as an exemplar of hegemonic masculinity. Furthermore, as a gay man, he is linked to a number of negative body stigmatizations, especially the (assumed to be) diseased body. Thus, all of these factors contributed to keeping the mainstream media from more in-depth coverage of his announcement.

The "Hero" and the "Whore": Privileging and Protecting Hegemonic Masculinity

In mainstream Western culture, AIDS is associated with the gay community (Weeks, 1985; Con-

nell, 1987; Sontag, 1989; Watney, 1989; Eisenstein, 1994) and other marginalized subpopulations and is therefore highly stigmatized. Despite the widespread invisibility and marginalization of gay men with AIDS, Magic Johnson, a self-identified heterosexual man, was not stigmatized when he publicly announced he had contracted the HIV virus. He was framed by the mainstream American print media unequivocally as a hero and was lauded for courageously battling a socially stigmatized illness (Wachs & Dworkin, 1997). Although coverage of Johnson's announcement may destabilize popular assumptions around AIDS and sexual identity through its statements that "straights can get it too," racist ideologies of black male sexuality most likely linger in the public imagination. As is demonstrated by the print media coverage, ideologies reveal a way in which power relations operate to reproduce the stigmatization of subordinated men and women while protecting the privileges of dominant social categories.

More than 100 articles covered Magic Johnson's announcement. Although the primary framing and content of 27 was that Magic Johnson is a hero, numerous other articles also framed him as a hero through reference to his exemplary career and described his profound influence in professional basketball. Articles titled "Magic Johnson's Legacy" (Berkow, *The New York Times,* 11/8/91) and "A Career of Impact, a Player of Heart" (Brown, *The New York Times,* 11/8/91) ran the day after his announcement. Off the court, Johnson was framed as a hero to at-risk subpopulations, sports fans, activists, the medical community, and the public at large. One article featured Los Angeles Mayor Bradley's comparison of this news to the assassination of former President Kennedy (Thomas, *The New York Times,* 11/9/91). Other articles stated that Magic Johnson "became a hero to a new set of fans—the community of activists and medical professionals" (Harris, *Los Angeles Times,* 11/8/91) and "I think he's obviously a hero to many Americans . . . so I think he would have a tremendous impact" (Cimons, *Los Angeles Times,* 11/11/91).

Johnson's hero status was even openly conferred by President George Bush: "President Bush on Friday described Los Angeles Lakers basketball star Earvin (Magic) Johnson as 'a hero to me' and 'to everyone (who) loves sports'" (Gerstenzang & Cimons, *The Los Angeles Times,* 11/9/91). This status conferral was also reflected in the titles of several articles in which the words hero and icon became synonymous with Johnson: "Los Angeles Stunned as Hero Begins Future With HIV" (Mathews, *The Washington Post,* 11/9/91), "An Icon Falls and His Public Suffers the Pain" (Murphy & Griego, *Los Angeles Times,* 11/8/91). Furthermore, Johnson was framed as a hero for gracefully and honestly dealing with a socially stigmatized illness. For example, he was described as handling his announcement as a "gentleman" (Gerstenzang & Cimons, *Los Angeles Times,* 11/9/91) "with grace and candor," and as a "challenge to fans to put aside shock and dismay" (Kindred, *Los Angeles Times,* 11/8/91). Despite the long negative history of HIV/AIDS, when Magic was found to have contracted the disease, the press reported, "You don't have to avoid Magic Johnson. He is not contaminated. He is not a leper. He is still Magic Johnson" (Downey, *Los Angeles Times,* 11/8/91). These articles demonstrate the media's willingness to remove the stigma of HIV/AIDS when it was contracted by a self-identified heterosexual sports star.

Other articles framed Johnson as a hero for his role as an educator about HIV/AIDS to the heterosexual community and the role he would play as a national spokesman for AIDS. For example, the *Los Angeles Times* and *The Washington Post* published articles titled "Announcement Hailed as a Way to Teach Public" (Harris, *Los Angeles Times,* 11/8/91) and "Hero's Shocker Leaves Teens Grasping for Answers" (Shen, *The Washington Post,* 11/9/91). Johnson was credited with bringing AIDS to the general public's attention and for putting AIDS on the national agenda, for example, "An Epidemic the Public Might Finally Confront: Johnson Could Help End Stigma of AIDS" (Gladwell, *The Washington Post,* 11/10/91), "Legend's Latest Challenge: Sports

Hero's Message May Resonate" (Gladwell & Muscatine, *The Washington Post,* 11/8/91), and "They say he can help shatter myths about HIV, AIDS" (Harris, *Los Angeles Times,* 11/8/91).

However, given the fact that the social discourse that has surrounded AIDS has been one of individual blame, it is interesting to note that Magic Johnson was not vilified for the risk at which he put himself, nor the risk at which he put the numerous people with whom he was physically intimate. The way in which the blame for AIDS transmission was framed shows how the discourse on sexuality serves to exonerate heterosexual men, blame women, and marginalize gay men. Magic Johnson's "promiscuity" was not problematized as his responsibility or his "risk" but rather was blamed on aggressive female groupies. As McKay (1993) argued, the media coverage of Johnson privileged and protected virile male heterosexuality in sport, while making consistent references to "wanton" women who wait for the athletes. What is implied is that any "normal man" would have done the same thing (e.g., "boys will be boys"). Magic Johnson's "promiscuity" is not only blamed on women, but he is painted as a kind man who is quoted as "accommodating" as many women as possible. In one article, Magic Johnson was quoted as saying, "There were just some bachelors that almost every woman in Los Angeles wanted to be with: Eddie Murphy, Arsenio Hall and Magic Johnson. I confess that after I arrived in L.A. in 1979 I did my best to accommodate as many women as I could" (Editor, "Sorry but Magic Isn't a Hero," *New York Times,* 11/14/91). A second article agreed: "The groupies, the 'Annies.' They are the ancient entitlements of the locker room, the customary fringe benefits of muscles" (Callahan, *The Washington Post,* 11/10/91). It is assumed that sports stars, as icons of masculinity, have a right to abundant sexual access to women's bodies.

Four years later, when white, working-class, heterosexual, professional boxer Tommy Morrison announced his HIV-positive status, he was not similarly valorized. Rather than elevating Morrison to hero status for overcoming the stigma of the illness, mainstream print media coverage treated him as a tragic figure, who, through his own "ignorance" about HIV transmission, destroyed a promising career. However, heterosexual masculine privilege was protected, through a reassignment of blame to women's sexual aggressiveness. As in the coverage of Johnson, women were framed as pursuers in the Morrison coverage, and Morrison is framed as a man who is unable to resist temptation. For example, one article pointed to the women who wait "outside the door fighting over who was going to get Tommy that night" (Romano, *The Washington Post,* 2/16/96) as the problem, not Morrison's pursuit of these women or his failure to practice safe sex. Although Morrison was blamed on an individual level for making "irrational, immature decisions," in his fast-lane lifestyle, he clearly was not framed as the pursuer, threat, or sexual agent, but rather as the "world's biggest bimbo magnet." Although the articles held Morrison accountable for his ignorance of HIV/AIDS, he was not held responsible for the risk at which he may have put others. One article highlighted how Morrison's inner circle summed up the situation: "It wasn't uncommon for me to go to his hotel room and find three or four women outside the door fighting over who was going to get Tommy that night. We had groupies all the way up to career women" (Romano, *The Washington Post,* 2/16/96). As in their treatment of Johnson, the media confirmed Morrison's heterosexuality and affirmed his sexual desirability to women through his acquiescence to temptation—what any "normal" man also would have done.

"Normal" under Western ideals of masculinity can include sexual conquest with multiple desirable women. Because sports define and reproduce ideologies of masculinity, it is hardly surprising that athletes are expected to demonstrate their masculinity off as well as on the field. Even when media framings call men into question for their actions, agency and responsibility are displaced onto the bodies of women, while masculine privilege is protected. As noted, women are framed as aggressive groupies who are responsible for tempting men, whereas men are framed as doing what "any normal" man would have done. Reminiscent of 19th century ideologies of gender and sexuality, these ideologies featured cultural narratives that claimed that men's sexual appetites were naturally more powerful and aggressive than women's. Given this claim, it is women who were (and are still) held responsible for controlling men's sexuality (Gilder, 1973). Repopularized during the Reagan and Bush era by leading conservative thinkers such as George Gilder (1986), these ideologies are maintained, reinforced, and celebrated under the rubric of "family values." This conceptual framework refers to women as the "moral guardians of civilization" through the expectation that they will not elicit, provoke, or satisfy male desire outside of heterosexual monogamous marriage. Hence, when mainstream media coverage presents Magic Johnson and other athletes as having "accommodated" as many "bimbos" as they could, the implication is that these men were merely yielding to aggressive females who are depicted as "out of control." Thus, through the framing of female groupies as responsible for tempting male sports stars into "promiscuity," the norm of aggressive male (hetero)sexual conquest common under masculinity remains unproblematized. Furthermore, the idea that women are responsible for control of men's morality means that male athletes are still presumed to be inherently moral. As we show, when individual athletes' morality is called into question, media frames do not link the "moral" transgressions to the norms of hegemonic masculinity but to each man's subordinate status.

Blaming Marginalized Masculinities

The mainstream print media coverage of Greg Louganis reveals a compelling contrast to the coverage of Johnson and Morrison. Although "shock" and "surprise" were abundantly referenced with regard to Johnson's and Morrison's announcements, there were no references to shock or surprise in the print media when Greg

Louganis made his HIV-positive announcement. Unlike the articles on Morrison and Johnson, which featured phrases like "he got it from heterosexual sex," there were no inquiries as to how Louganis could have contracted the virus. The assumed linkage between homosexuality and AIDS was so profound that none of the 11 articles on Louganis even posed the question as to how he contracted HIV/AIDS. We argue that the profound questioning as to how self-identified heterosexual men contracted the virus, coupled with the lack of inquiry into how Louganis could have contracted the disease, works to reinforce the idea that HIV/AIDS is a "natural" and expected part of the gay life course (Weeks, 1985; Watney, 1989; Wachs & Dworkin, 1997; Dworkin & Wachs, 1998). This works to perpetuate the historic assumption that gay bodies are inherently diseased and immoral.

The athletes also were framed differently vis-à-vis the risk of transmission they present to others. Although the "blame" or responsibility for the pollution of the bodies of Magic Johnson and Tommy Morrison was placed on the aggressive women who pursued successful male sports stars, there is no corollary absolution of blame or fault for Greg Louganis. There was no discussion surrounding male groupies who may have pursued Louganis. Furthermore, Magic Johnson and Tommy Morrison's threat to women was nearly always discussed in relation to their wife and fiancée, respectively; they generally were not presented as a threat to their numerous other sex partners. In contrast, the print media did not even begin to ponder the men Greg Louganis may have infected in sex, nor did they ever mention his long-term partner. Several stories, however, expressed concern for the presumably heterosexual divers and doctor who came into contact with Louganis and his blood during the 1988 Olympics. All articles that covered Louganis's announcement discussed this incident and the potential risk of transmission. In this way, gay men and "promiscuous" women are viewed as the virulent agents or problematic vehicle for transmission (Treichler,

1988) while hegemonic masculinity, and the norm of virile male (hetero)sexuality is protected and reaffirmed.

Although data show how heterosexual masculinity is protected at the expense of women and gay men, print media coverage simultaneously subtly reinvigorates the link between blame and working-class and minority status. Johnson was presented as being an African American man with "special" importance as an educator and role model for minority communities. Although he was lauded more generally for raising public awareness on heterosexual AIDS and its prevention, numerous articles focused specifically on this special importance. For example, one article highlighted that the National Minority AIDS Council wanted Johnson to lobby for much-needed increases in financing for health care and prevention (Gross, *The New York Times,* 11/13/91), whereas Johnson himself "has indicated that his personal efforts will focus on AIDS education in the black community" (Harris, *Los Angeles Times,* 11/13/91). Articles claimed, "He speaks best for African Americans" (Gross, *The New York Times,* 11/13/91) and focused explicitly on how "the message" would be loudest for those "who need to hear it most," as quoted in an article titled "Magic's Loud Message for Young Black Men" (Specter, *The New York Times,* 11/8/91, p. B12). Although funding and education are of paramount importance in often-overlooked minority communities whose AIDS rates are disproportionately high, the suggestion that African Americans "need to hear it most" can all too easily become a historical "reminder" that links minorities to stereotypes of excess and a lack of control (Adam, 1978; Collins, 1990). Similarly, articles cited Morrison's poor rural upbringing and broken home and concurrently noted his "irresponsible, irrational, immature decisions," how he "lacked the discipline to say no" (Romano, *The Washington Post,* 2/16/96), and his "ignorance" (Vecsey, *The New York Times,* 2/16/96).

We find it ironic that in the furor over cases involving sexual assaults and athletes, particularly athletes in hegemonic sports, the norm of male sexual conquest in sport goes largely unquestioned (Curry, 1991; Nelson, 1994; Crossett et al., 1995). However, when an athlete acquires a highly stigmatized, potentially deadly virus such as HIV/AIDS, which historically is associated with the gay community, "mistakes" and "ignorance" regarding male (hetero)sexuality are abundantly recognized by the media. Print media coverage of both Morrison and Johnson simultaneously displaced blame onto the bodies of women and framed the two men as having made bad "choices" or "mistakes." For instance, articles on Morrison noted his "ignorance" around proper HIV and AIDS transmission information, quoted him as saying that he thought he had a "better chance of winning the lottery than contracting this disease," and featured how he "lacked the discipline to say no" (Romano, *The Washington Post*, 2/16/96). An article on Johnson featured a young man who was cited in a *Los Angeles Times* article as saying, "It is good [Magic Johnson] is not ashamed he made a mistake" (Almond & Ford, 11/18/91, *Los Angeles Times*). What, however, is the mistake, precisely—is it "promiscuity"? Or is it "getting caught" conforming to the norm of male sexual conquest only when men have acquired HIV? Instead of highlighting how hegemonic masculinity in sport fuels the discourse on male sexual conquest as part of its cultural norm, popular discourse embraces the idea that it is the individual athlete's bad decision making or ignorance that is to blame.

We also argue that the transgression does not just stand on its own as a bad "individual" decision, but becomes available as a negative signifier of subordinate social categories, that is, in the same way that male privilege is protected while women are blamed, we argue that white middle-class heterosexuality is protected, whereas working-class, black, and gay male sexualities are blamed. The social location of white middle-class heterosexuals is left out of the picture, and working-class, black, and gay male sporting bodies are featured in the spotlight as "guilty."

Because the dominant position remains unscrutinized by the mainstream media press, it becomes the "normal" or moral category against which the "other" categories are negatively compared. Indeed, this is the case because working-class and minority men are the ones held up in the sports limelight due to a limited structure of opportunity that disproportionately funnels subordinated men into a sports career (Edwards, 1973; Messner, 1992b). By featuring Morrison's working-class background and "ignorance," along with Johnson's "mistakes" and his role in speaking to African Americans who "need to hear it most," the print media reinforces "others'" bad individual decision making. Those in the dominant race, class, and sexuality position remain the invisible good against which the "bad" sexually excessive and/or out of control "other" is juxtaposed.

Myths in Sport: Productive Bodies, Moral Men?

We have noted the historical significance of how the muscled male body has been associated with moral superiority (Dutton, 1995). Male athletes who display this body and are successful at culturally valued sports receive widespread public attention and are elevated to the status of hero. As "heroes" with cultural fame and popularity, these athletes enjoy numerous social and economic privileges, one of which is the assumption of morality. Yet, simultaneously, one of the social privileges that (heterosexual) men in hegemonic sports are said to enjoy is access to the bodies of numerous women. We are left with a paradox between "moral" standards of heterosexual monogamy and how to attain high status under dominant norms of masculinity. For "fallen heroes" in sport, print media coverage rarely if ever acknowledges norms in sport or in U.S. culture at large that equate masculinity with sexual prowess. Sexual access to women is a cultural privilege associated with being a man, yet, in turn, the powerful then use this privilege to stigmatize subordinated masculinities and women while dominant men remain invisible to the watchful media eye.

Our analysis of print media coverage of the HIV announcements of Magic Johnson, Tommy Morrison, and Greg Louganis is consistent with those who argue that our culture gradually will add to the list of "others" who have been tagged as "deserving AIDS," to distinguish them from "innocent" victims (Eisenstein, 1994). The lack of inquiry into how Louganis acquired HIV, coupled with concern for the threat of transmission only to the heterosexual public, reinforces a tendency to blame gay sexuality for HIV transmission. It is also notable that lesbians are often left out of the discourse on HIV/AIDS, and sexuality in general, because popular culture tends to render lesbians and the kinds of sex they have invisible (Butler, 1993; Kane & Lenskyj, 1998). For Morrison and Johnson, media frames that emphasize "better decision making" for individual "promiscuous" black and working-class bodies reinvigorate negative stigmatizations as to which bodies are inherently "bad" or immoral. Heterosexual male privilege is protected, and "immorality" is linked to "other" categories. Johnson and Morrison are simultaneously featured for behaving "as any normal" man would, while also highlighting their "ignorant" individual decisions and "mistakes" amid discussions of their class and race, respectively. Thus, it is masculinity that is privileged as "normal," whereas it is the social categories of otherness upon which the responsibility for "deviance" is subtly foisted. Thus, dominant coverage works to displace blame onto the bodies of gay, working-class, and black male, and what becomes implied is that through the proper education and assimilation (to heterosexual middle-class values), "the problem" will be solved. This is consistent with Cole and Denny's (1994) argument that such rhetoric "obscures the responsibility of multinational capitalism and the Reagan–Bush administration for the erosion of social welfare programs and the neglect of AIDS" (p. 123). Furthermore, we argue that the articles reinvigorate a white, heterosexual, middle-class

moral gaze on gay, black, and working-class manhood.

Afterword: "God Saved Me": Family Values, Masculinity, and Sexual Conquest

Rather than revealing the paradox between the dominant norms of morality and masculinity, the position of sports stars with AIDS demonstrates how the social location of individuals defines their moral status, not their behavior. Although gay male bodies with HIV are featured often in the media as decaying, diseased, and unproductive (Crimp, 1990), recently, Magic Johnson's body was featured as healing, healthy, and productive. Johnson even announced that the virus in his blood has dropped to "undetectable levels," proof that "God" has "saved him" (Editor, *The New York Times,* 4/5/97). Whereas earlier articles featured Johnson as a spokesman for safe sex, later articles featured his pro-God, promonogamy, profamily rhetoric. Whereas gay men are not framed as having the option of "being saved" from HIV, Johnson, a self-identified newly monogamous heterosexual, is lauded for battling the virus to a level at which it is undetectable. Instead of seeing Johnson as having access to the finest medical care in the world due to his class status, his body is held up as morally deserving of beating the stigmatized illness. Once Johnson renounces his "fast-lane lifestyle" in favor of marriage, family, and monogamy, he is saved. The power of this rhetoric also underlies the critiques of Morrison as irresponsible and assumes that a fast-lane lifestyle is the culprit. The discourse on risk assumes that particular lifestyles and family statuses are safe, and others are dangerous. By conflating lifestyle with risk, erroneous information about HIV transmission is perpetuated (Dworkin & Wachs, 1998). Furthermore, these assumptions reproduce ideologies that privilege particular family forms and relationships and stigmatize others. By contrast, Louganis and other gay men, even if monogamous or family-oriented, are rarely if ever featured for courageously battling HIV or for educating the public; rather, media accounts seem to imply that they "deserve" their fate (Wachs & Dworkin, 1997). For instance, whereas Johnson has become an acclaimed national spokesman and educator for people with HIV/AIDS, a U.S. senator attempted to ban Greg Louganis from speaking on a college campus, citing his talk as "immoral" (Associated Press, *Los Angeles Times,* 1/26/97). Because mainstream print media have identified (assumed to be) immoral acts that require blame, and they have reassigned this blame to "others," coverage of HIV/AIDS announcements reveals the paradox between manhood in hegemonic sports and dominant notions of morality. This is accomplished without ever problematizing hegemonic masculinity in sport or long-held mythic ideals associated with gender, family, and sexuality.

Appendix

Print Media Coverage of HIV Announcements by Prominent Athletes

Magic Johnson

11/8/91 Aldridge, David. Lakers Star Put Imprint on Finals, Records, Money. *The Washington Post,* p. C1.

11/8/91 Araton, Harvey. Riley Leads the Prayers. *The New York Times,* p. B11.

11/8/91 Berkow, Ira. Magic Johnson's Legacy. *The New York Times,* p. B11.

11/8/91 Bonk, Thomas. Even Hearing News Was Not Believing It. The *Los Angeles Times,* p. C1.

11/8/91 Brown, Clifton. A Career of Impact, A Player With Heart. *The New York Times,* p. B11.

11/8/91 Cannon, Lou. Basketball Star Magic Johnson Retires With AIDS Virus. *The Washington Post,* p. A1.

11/8/91 Castaneda, Ruben, & Rene Sanchez. Johnson's AIDS Virus Revelation Moves Teenagers, Fans. *The Washington Post,* p. D1.

11/8/91 Downey, Mike. Earvin Leaves NBA, But His Smile Remains. The *Los Angeles Times,* p. C1.

11/8/91 Gladwell, Malcolm, & Alison Muscatine. Legend's Latest Challenge. *The Washington Post,* p. A1.

11/8/91 Harris, Scott. Announcement Hailed as a Way to Teach Public. The *Los Angeles Times,* p. A32.

11/8/91 Heisler, Mark. Magic Johnson's Career Ended by HIV-Positive Test. The *Los Angeles Times,* p. A1.

11/8/91 Kindred, Dave. Magic's Gift for Inspiring Us Tests Reality. The *Los Angeles Times,* p. B7.

11/8/91 Murphy, Dean E., & Tina Griego. An Icon Falls and His Public Suffers the Pain. The *Los Angeles Times,* p. A1.

11/8/91 Specter, Michael. Magic's Loud Message for Young Black Men. *The New York Times,* p. B12.

11/8/91 Springer, Steve. Through the Years, He Stayed the Same. The *Los Angeles Times,* p. C1.

11/8/91 Stevenson, Richard W. Basketball Star Retires on Advice of His Doctors. *The New York Times,* p. A1.

11/8/91 Thomas, Robert McG., Jr. News Reverberates Through Basketball and Well Beyond It. *The New York Times,* p. B13.

11/9/91 Bonk, Thomas, & Janny Scott. "Don't Feel Sorry for Me," Magic Says. The *Los Angeles Times,* p. A1.

11/9/91 Cannon, Lou, & Anthony Cotton. Johnson's HIV Caused by Sex: "Heterosexual Transmission" Cited; Wife Is Pregnant. *The Washington Post,* p. A1.

11/9/91 Editor. A Magical Cure for Lethargy. The *Los Angeles Times,* p. B5.

11/9/91 Lacey, Marc, & Hugo Martin. Student's Cry a Bit, Learn Life Lessons. The *Los Angeles Times,* p. A26.

11/9/91 Gerstenzang, James, & Marlene Cimons. Bush Calls Johnson a Hero, Defends Administration's Policy on AIDS. The *Los Angeles Times,* p. A26.

11/9/91 Horovitz, Bruce. Sponsors May Use Magic in Ads to Encourage Safe Sex. The *Los Angeles Times,* p. D1.

11/9/91 Mathews, Jay. Los Angeles Stunned As Hero Begins Future With HIV. *The Washington Post,* p. A12.

11/9/91 McMillen, Tom. Magic, Now and Forever. *The New York Times,* p. 23.

11/9/91 Shen, Fern. Hero's Shocker Leaves Teens Grasping for Answers. *The Washington Post,* p. A1.

11/9/91 Specter, Michael. When AIDS Taps Hero, His "Children" Feel Pain. *The New York Times,* p. A1.

11/9/91 Stevenson, Richard W. Johnson's Frankness Continues. *The New York Times,* p. 33.

11/9/91 Thomas, Robert McG., Jr. A Day Later, It Remains a Shock Felt Around the World. *The New York Times,* p. A33.

11/10/91 Aldridge, David. For Moments Like These. *The Washington Post,* p. D4.

11/10/91 Callahan, Tom. What It Boils Down to Is Playing With Fire. *The Washington Post,* p. D2.

11/10/91 Gladwell, Malcolm. An Epidemic the Public Might Finally Confront. *The Washington Post,* p. A1.

11/10/91 Jones, Robert A. A Shock That Shifted the World. The *Los Angeles Times,* p. A3.

11/10/91 Lipsyte, Robert. A Jarring Reveille for Sports. *The New York Times,* p. S1.

11/10/91 McNeil, Donald. On the Court or Off, Still Magic. *The New York Times,* p. E9.

11/10/91 Muscatine, Alison. Magic's Revelations Transcends Sports. *The Washington Post,* p. D1.

11/11/91 Chase, Marilyn. Johnson Disclosure Underscores Facts of AIDS in Heterosexual Population. *The Wall Street Journal,* p. B1.

11/11/91 Cimons, Marlene. White House May Name Johnson to AIDS Panel. The *Los Angeles Times,* p. A1.

11/11/91 Horovitz, Bruce. Advertisers Try to Handle This Magic Moment Carefully. The *Los Angeles Times,* p. D1.

11/13/91 Gross, Jane. For Anyone but Johnson, a Daunting Pile of Requests for Help. *The New York Times,* p. A14.

11/13/91 Harris, Scott. Johnson Brings New Stature to AIDS Funding. The *Los Angeles Times,* p. A1.

11/14/91 Editor. Converse's AIDS Efforts Features Magic Johnson. *The New York Times,* p. D10.

11/14/91 Editor. Sorry but Magic Isn't a Hero. *The New York Times,* p. B19.

11/18/91 Almond, Elliot, & Andrea Ford. Wild Ovation Greets Magic at Lakers Game. The *Los Angeles Times,* p. A1.

11/31/91 Editor. Keep Magic in the Mainstream. *The New York Times,* p. B7.

1/1/92 Araton, Harvey. Advertisers Shying From Magic's Touch. *The New York Times,* p. 44.

1/14/92 French, Mary Ann. Magic, Rewriting the Rules of Romance. *The Washington Post,* p. B1.

4/5/97 Editor. Johnson's HIV Level Drops (AIDS Virus in Earvin "Magic" Johnson Is Significantly Reduced). *The New York Times,* p. 36.

Greg Louganis

2/23/95 Longman, Jere. Doctor at Games Supports Louganis. *The New York Times,* p. B15.

2/23/95 Sandomir, Richard. Louganis, Olympic Champion, Says He Has AIDS. *The New York Times,* p. B11.

2/23/95 Weyler, John. Olympic Diver Louganis Reveals That He Has AIDS. The *Los Angeles Times,* p. A1.

2/24/95 Boxall, Bettina, & Frank Williams. Louganis Disclosure Greeted With Sadness. The *Los Angeles Times,* p. B1.

2/24/95 Editor. Louganis: Breaks His Silence, Another World-Famous Athlete Disclosed He Has AIDS. The *Los Angeles Times,* p. B6.

2/24/95 Longman, Jere. Olympians Won't Have to Take H.I.V. Test. *The New York Times,* p. B7.

2/24/95 Vecsey, George. Tolerance, Not Blame, For Louganis. *The New York Times,* p. B7.

2/26/95 Longman, Jere. Olympian Blood: Debate About HIV Tests Sparked by Diver With AIDS. *The New York Times,* p. 2.

2/28/95 Quintanilla, Michael. The Truth Shall Set You Free. The *Los Angeles Times,* p. E11.

3/5/95 Alfano, Peter. The Louganis Disclosure: AIDS in the Age of Hype. *The New York Times Magazine,* p. E1.

5/5/95 Ammon, Richard. Gay Athletes. The *Los Angeles Times,* p. M5.

1/26/97 Associated Press. Senator Seeks to Ban Louganis. The *Los Angeles Times.*

Tommy Morrison

2/12/96 Eskenazi, Gerald. Morrison Suspension: An HIV Concern. *The New York Times,* p. B6.

2/13/96 Eskenazi, Gerald. Morrison Confirms Positive HIV Test. *The New York Times,* p. B13.

2/13/96 Springer, Steve. Magic Johnson Plans to Call Boxer. The *Los Angeles Times,* p. A9.

2/13/96 Springer, Steve, & Earl Gustkey. Boxer's HIV Test Heats Up Debate Over Risk to Others. The *Los Angeles Times,* p. A1.

2/14/96 HIV Test for Morrison Ref. *The New York Times,* p. B11.

2/16/96 Eskenazi, Gerald. Remorseful Morrison Has Words of Caution. *The New York Times,* p. B7.

2/16/96 Romano, Lois. Heavyweight Deals With Serious Blow. *The Washington Post,* p. A1.

2/16/96 Vecsey, George. Morrison Didn't Pay Enough Attention. *The New York Times,* p. B20.

9/20/96 Kawakami, Tim. HIV-Positive Morrison Says He'll Fight Again. The *Los Angeles Times,* p. C9.

References

Adam, B. (1978). *The survival of domination: Inferiorization and everyday life.* New York: Elsevier North-Holland.

Butler, J. (1993). *Bodies that matter: On the discursive limits of "sex."* Boston: Routledge & Kegan Paul.

Cole, C. L., & Andrews, D. L. (1996). Look, it's NBA Showtime! A Research Annual. *Cultural Studies,* (1), 141–181.

Cole, C. L., & Denny, H., III. (1994). Visualizing deviance in post-Reagan America: Magic Johnson, AIDS and the promiscuous world of professional sport. *Critical Sociology, 20*(3), 123–147.

Collins, P. H. (1990). *Black feminist thought: Knowledge, consciousness, and the politics of empowerment.* New York: HarperCollins.

Connell, R. W. (1987). *Gender and power: Society, the person, and sexual politics.* Stanford, CA: Stanford University Press.

Connell, R. W. (1990). An iron man: The body and some contradictions of hegemonic masculinity. In M. Messner & D. Sabo (Eds.), *Sport, men, and the gender order: Critical feminist perspectives* (pp. 83–96). Champaign, IL: Human Kinetics.

Crimp, D. (1990). *AIDS demographics.* Seattle, WA: Bay.

Crosset, T. (1990). Masculinity, sexuality, and the development of early modern sport. In M. Messner & D. Sabo (Eds.), *Sport, men and the gender order: Critical feminist perspectives* (pp. 45–54). Champaign, IL: Human Kinetics.

Crosset, T., Benedict, J., & McDonald, M. A. (1995). Male student athletes reported for sexual assault: Survey of campus police departments and judicial affairs offices. *Journal of Sport and Social Issues, 19,* 126–140.

Curry, T. J. (1991). Fraternal bonding in the locker room: A profeminist analysis of talk about competition and women. *Sociology of Sport Journal, 8,* 119–135.

Duncan, M. C., & Hasbrook, C. A. (1988). Denial of power in televised women's sports. *Sociology of Sport Journal, 5,* 1–21.

Duncan, M. C., Messner, M. A., & Jensen, K. (1994). *Gender stereotyping in televised sports: A follow-up to the 1989 study.* Los Angeles: Amateur Athletic Foundation.

Dutton, K. (1995). *The perfectible body: The Western ideal of male physical development.* New York: Continuum.

Dworkin, S. L., & Wachs, F. L. (1998). "Disciplining the body": HIV positive male athletes, media surveillance, and the policing of sexuality. *Sociology of Sport Journal, 15,* 1–20.

Edwards, H. (1983). *Sociology of sport.* Belmont, CA: Dorsey.

Eisenstein, Z. (1994). *The color of gender: Reimaging democracy.* Berkeley: University of California Press.

Foucault, M. (1979). *Discipline and punish: The birth of the prison.* New York: Vintage.

Gilder, G. (1973). *Sexual suicide.* New York: Quadrangle.

Gilder, G. (1986). *Men and marriage.* Gretna: Pelican.

Gorn, E. J., & Goldstein, W. (1993). *A brief history of American sports.* New York: Hill & Wang.

Jhally, S. (1989). Cultural studies and the sports/media complex. In L. A. Wenner (Ed.), *Media, sports, and society* (pp. 41–57). Newbury Park, CA: Sage.

Kane, M. J. (1988). Media coverage of the female athlete before, during, and after Title IX: *Sports Illustrated* revisited. *Journal of Sport Management, 2,* 87–99.

Kane, M. J. (1995). Resistance/transformation of the oppositional binary: Exposing sport as a continuum. *Journal of Sport and Social Issues, 19,* 191–218.

Kane, M. J. (1996). Media coverage of the post Title IX athlete: A feminist analysis of sport, gender, and power. *Duke Journal of Gender Law and Policy, 3,* 95–127.

Kane, M. J., & Disch, L. J. (1993). Sexual violence and the reproduction of male power in the locker room: The "Lisa Olsen incident." *Sociology of Sport Journal, 10,* 331–352.

Kane, M. J., & Lenskyj, H. (1998). Media treatment of female athletes: Issues of gender and sexualities. In L. Wenner (Ed.), *MediaSport: Cultural sensibilities and sport in the media age* (pp. 186–201). Boston: Routledge & Kegan Paul.

Kane, M. J., & Snyder, E. (1989). Sport typing: The social "containment" of women in sport. *Arena Review, 13,* 77–96.

Katz, J. (1995). *The invention of heterosexuality.* New York: Dutton.

Kimmel, M. (1990). Baseball and the reconstitution of American masculinity, 1880–1920. In M. Messner & D. Sabo (Eds.), *Sport, men and the gender order: Critical feminist perspectives* (pp. 55–66). Champaign, IL: Human Kinetics.

King, S. (1993). The politics of the body and the body politic: Magic Johnson and the ideology of AIDS. *Sociology of Sport Journal, 10,* 270–285.

Klein, A. (1993). *Little big men: Bodybuilding subculture and gender construction.* Albany: State University of New York Press.

Lule, J. (1995). The rape of Mike Tyson: Race, the press and symbolic stereotypes. *Critical Studies in Mass Communication, 12,* 176–195.

Majors, R. (1990). Cool pose: Black masculinity in sports. In M. Messner & D. Sabo (Eds.), *Sport, men and the gender order: Critical feminist perspectives* (pp. 109–114). Champaign, IL: Human Kinetics.

McChesney, R. W. (1989). Media made sport: A history of sports coverage in the United States. In L. A. Wenner (Ed.), *Media, sports, and society* (pp. 49–69). Newbury Park, CA: Sage.

McKay, J. (1993). "Marked men" and "wanton women": The politics of naming sexual "deviance" in sport. *Journal of Men's Studies, 2*(1), 69–87.

Messner, M. A. (1988). Sport and male domination: The female athlete as contested ideological terrain. *Sociology of Sport Journal, 5,* 197–211.

Messner, M. (1992a). Like family: Power, intimacy, and sexuality in male athletes' friendships. In P. Nardi (Ed.), *Men's friendships.* Newbury Park, CA: Sage.

Messner, M. A. (1992b). *Power at play: Sports and the problem of masculinity.* Boston: Beacon.

Messner, M. A., Duncan, M. C., & Wachs, F. L. (1996). The gender of audience-building: Televised coverage of women's and men's NCAA basketball. *Sociological Inquiry, 66,* 422–439.

Messner, M. A., & Sabo, D. (Eds.). (1994). *Sex, violence and power in sports: Rethinking masculinity.* Freedom, CA: Crossing.

Messner, M. A., & Solomon, W. S. (1993). Outside the frame: Newspaper coverage of the Sugar Ray Leonard wife abuse story. *Sociology of Sport Journal, 10,* 119–134.

Nelson, M. B. (1994). *The stronger women get, the more men love football: Sexism and the American culture of sports.* Orlando, FL: Harcourt Brace.

Patton, C. (1990). *Inventing AIDS.* Boston: Routledge & Kegan Paul.

Pronger, B. (1990). *The arena of masculinity: Sport, homosexuality, and the meaning of sex.* New York: St. Martin's Press.

Sage, G. (1990). *Power and ideology in American sport: A critical perspective.* Champaign, IL: Human Kinetics.

Sontag, S. (1989). *AIDS and its metaphors.* New York: Farrar, Straus & Giroux.

Synnott, A. (1993). *The body social: Symbolism, self and society.* Boston: Routledge & Kegan Paul.

Theberge, N. (1987). Sport and women's empowerment. *Women's Studies International Forum, 10,* 387–393.

Treichler, P. (1988). AIDS, gender and biomedical discourse: Current contests for meaning. In E. Fee & D. Fox (Eds.), *AIDS: the burden of history* (pp. 190–266). Berkeley: University of California Press.

Turner, B. (1984). *The body and society: Explorations in social theory.* Oxford, UK: Basil Blackwell.

Wachs, F. L., & Dworkin, S. L. (1997). There's no such thing as a gay hero: Magic = hero, Louganis = carrier: Sexual identity and media framing of HIV positive athletes. *Journal of Sport and Social Issues, 21,* 335–355.

Watney, S. (1989). *Policing desire: Pornography, AIDS, and the media.* Minneapolis: University of Minnesota Press.

Weeks, J. (1985). *Sexuality and its discontents: Meanings, myths, and modern sexualities.* Boston: Routledge & Kegan Paul.

Wenner, L. A. (1989). Media, sports, and society: The research agenda. In L. A. Wenner (Ed.), *Media, sports, and society* (pp. 13–48). Newbury Park, CA: Sage.

Whitson, D. (1990). Sport in the social construction of masculinity. In M. Messner & D. Sabo (Eds.), *Sport, men and the gender order: Critical feminist perspectives* (pp. 19–29). Champaign, IL: Human Kinetics.

Young, K. (1993). Violence, risk, and liability in male sports culture. *Sociology of Sport Journal, 10,* 373–396.

Michael A. Messner
Jeffrey Montez de Oca

The Male Consumer as Loser: Beer and Liquor Ads in Mega Sports Media Events

The historical development of modern men's sport has been closely intertwined with the consumption of alcohol and with the financial promotion and sponsorship provided by beer and liquor producers and distributors, as well as pubs and bars (Collins and Vamplew 2002). The beer and liquor industry plays a key economic role in commercialized college and professional sports (Zimbalist 1999; Sperber 2000). Liquor industry advertisements heavily influence the images of masculinity promoted in sports broadcasts and magazines (Wenner 1991). Alcohol consumption is also often a key aspect of the more dangerous and violent dynamics at the heart of male sport cultures (Curry 2000; Sabo, Gray, and Moore 2000). By itself, alcohol does not "cause" men's violence against women or against other men; however, it is commonly one of a cluster of factors that facilitate violence (Koss and Gaines 1993; Leichliter et al. 1998). In short, beer and liquor are central players in "a high holy trinity of alcohol, sports, and hegemonic masculinity" (Wenner 1998).

Gender, Men's Sports, and Alcohol Ads

Although marketing beer and liquor to men is not new, the imagery that advertisers employ to pitch their product is not static either. Our analysis of past Super Bowls and *Sports Illustrated* beer and liquor ads suggests shifting patterns in the gender themes encoded in the ads.

Adapted from *Signs: Journal of Women in Culture and Society* 2005, vol. 30, no. 3 © 2005 by The University of Chicago. All rights reserved.

Ads from the late 1950s through the late 1960s commonly depicted young or middle-aged white heterosexual couples happily sharing a cold beer in their suburban backyards, in their homes, or in an outdoor space like a park.

In these ads, the beer is commonly displayed in a clear glass, its clean, fresh appearance perhaps intended to counter the reputation of beer as a working-class male drink. Beer in these ads symbolically unites the prosperous and happy postwar middle-class couple. By the mid-1970s, women as wives and partners largely disappeared from beer ads. Instead of showing heterosexual couples drinking in their homes or backyards, these ads began primarily to depict images of men drinking with other men in public spaces. Three studies of beer commercials of the 1970s and 1980s found that most ads pitched beer to men as a pleasurable reward for a hard day's work. These ads told men that "For all you do, this Bud's for you." Women were rarely depicted in these ads, except as occasional background props in male-dominated bars (Postman et al. 1987; Wenner 1991; Strate 1992).

The 1950s and 1960s beer ads that depicted happy married suburban couples were part of a moment in gender relations tied to postwar culture and Fordist relations of production. White, middle-class, heterosexual masculinity was defined as synonymous with the male breadwinner, in symmetrical relation to a conception of femininity grounded in the image of the suburban housewife. In the 1970s and early 1980s, the focus on men's laboring bodies, tethered to their public leisure with other men, expressed an almost atavistic view of hegemonic masculinity at a time when women were moving into public life in huge numbers and blue-collar men's jobs were being eliminated by the tens of thousands.

Both the postwar and the postindustrial ads provide a gendered pedagogy for living a masculine lifestyle in a shifting context characterized by uncertainty. In contrast to the depiction of happy white families comfortably living lives of suburban bliss, the postwar era was characterized by anxieties over the possibility of a postwar depression, nuclear annihilation, suburban social dislocation, and disorder from racial and class movements for social justice (Lipsitz 1981; May 1988; Spigel 1992). Similarly, the 1970s and 1980s beer ads came in the wake of the defeat of the United States in the Vietnam War, the 1972 gas crisis, and the turbulence in gender relations brought on by the women's and gay/lesbian liberation movements.

The 2002 and 2003 ads that we examine here primarily construct a white male "loser" whose life is apparently separate from paid labor. He hangs out with his male buddies, is self-mocking and ironic about his loser status, and is always at the ready to engage in voyeurism with sexy fantasy women but holds committed relationships and emotional honesty with real women in disdain. To the extent that these themes find resonance with young men of today, it is likely because they speak to basic insecurities that are grounded in a combination of historic shifts: deindustrialization, the declining real value of wages and the male breadwinner role, significant cultural shifts brought about by more than three decades of struggle by feminists and sexual minorities, and challenges to white male supremacy by people of color and by immigrants. This cluster of social changes has destabilized hegemonic masculinity and defines the context of gender relations in which today's young men have grown toward adulthood.

Two Mega Sports Media Events

This article examines the gender and sexual imagery encoded in two mega sports media events:

the 2002 and 2003 Super Bowls and the 2002 and 2003 *Sports Illustrated* swimsuit issues.

Mega sports media events are mediated cultural rituals (Dayan and Katz 1988) that differ from everyday sports media events in several key ways: sports media actively build audience anticipation and excitement throughout the year for these single events; the Super Bowl and the swimsuit issue are each preceded by major pre-event promotion and hype—from the television network that will broadcast the Super Bowl to *Sports Illustrated* and myriad other print and electronic media; the Super Bowl and the swimsuit issue are used as marketing tools for selling the more general products of National Football League (NFL) games and *Sports Illustrated* magazine subscriptions; the Super Bowl and the swimsuit issue each generate significant spin-off products (e.g., videos, books, "making of" TV shows, calendars, frequently visited Web pages); the Super Bowl and the swimsuit issue generate significantly larger audiences than does a weekly NFL game or a weekly edition of *Sports Illustrated;* and advertisements are usually created specifically for these mega sports media events and cost more to run than do ads in a weekly NFL game or a weekly edition of *Sports Illustrated.*

Super Bowl Ads

Since its relatively modest start in 1967, the NFL Super Bowl has mushroomed into one of the most expensive and most watched annual media events in the United States, with a growing world audience (Martin and Reeves 2001), the vast majority of whom are boys and men. Increasingly over the past decade, Super Bowl commercials have been specially created for the event. Newspapers, magazines, television news shows, and Web sites now routinely run pre–Super Bowl stories that focus specifically on the ads, and several media outlets run post–Super Bowl polls to determine which ads were the most and least favorite. Postgame lists of "winners" and "losers" focus as much on the corporate sponsors and their ads as on the two teams that—incidentally?—played a football game between the commercials.

Fifty-five commercials ran during the 2003 Super Bowl (not counting pregame and postgame shows), at an average cost of $2.1 million for each thirty-second ad. Fifteen of these commercials were beer or malt liquor ads. Twelve of these ads were run by Anheuser-Busch, whose ownership of this Super Bowl was underlined at least twenty times throughout the broadcast, when, after commercial breaks, the camera lingered on the stadium scoreboard, atop which was a huge Budweiser sign. This represented a slight increase in beer advertising since the 2002 Super Bowl, which featured thirteen beer or malt liquor commercials (eleven of them by Anheuser-Busch), at an average cost of $1.9 million per thirty-second ad. In addition to the approximately $31.5 million that the beer companies paid for the 2003 Super Bowl ad slots, they paid millions more creating and testing those commercials with focus groups. There were 137.7 million viewers watching all or part of the 2003 Super Bowl on ABC, and by far the largest demographic group watching was men, aged twenty-five to fifty-five.

Sports Illustrated Swimsuit Issue Ads

Sports Illustrated began in 1964 to publish an annual February issue that featured five or six pages of women modeling swimsuits, embedded in an otherwise normal sixty-four-page magazine (Davis 1997). This modest format continued until the late 1970s, when the portion of the magazine featuring swimsuit models began gradually to grow. In the 1980s, the swimsuit issue morphed into a special issue in which normal sports coverage gradually disappeared. During this decade, the issue's average length had grown to 173 pages, 20 percent of which were focused on swimsuit models. By the 1990s the swimsuit issue averaged 207 pages in length, 31 percent of which featured swimsuit models. The magazine has continued to grow in recent years. The 2003 issue was 218

pages in length, 59 percent of which featured swimsuit models. The dramatic growth in the size of the swimsuit issue in the 1990s, as well as the dropping of pretense that the swimsuit issue had anything to do with normal "sports journalism," were facilitated by advertising that began cleverly to echo and spoof the often highly sexualized swimsuit imagery in the magazine. By 2000, it was more the rule than the exception when an ad in some way utilized the swimsuit theme. The gender and sexual themes of the swimsuit issue became increasingly seamless, as ads and *Sports Illustrated* text symbiotically echoed and played off of each other. The 2002 swimsuit issue included seven pages of beer ads and seven pages of liquor ads, which cost approximately $230,000 per full page to run. The 2003 swimsuit issue ran the equivalent of sixteen pages of beer ads and thirteen pages of liquor ads. The ad space for the 2003 swimsuit issue sold for $266,000 per full-page color ad.

The millions of dollars that beer and liquor companies spent to develop and buy space for these ads were aimed at the central group that reads the magazine: young and middle-aged males. *Sports Illustrated* estimates the audience size of its weekly magazine at 21.3 million readers, roughly 76 percent of whom are males. Nearly half of the male audience is in the coveted eighteen- to thirty-four-year-old demographic group, and three quarters of the male *Sports Illustrated* audience is between the ages of eighteen and forty-nine. A much larger number of single-copy sales gives the swimsuit issue a much larger audience, conservatively estimated at more than 30 million readers.[1]

The Super Bowl and the *Sports Illustrated* swimsuit issue are arguably the biggest single electronic and print sports metlia events annually in the United States. Due to their centrality, size, and target audiences, we suggest that mega sports media events such as the Super Bowl and the swimsuit issue offer a magnified view of the dominant gender and sexual imagery emanating from the center of the sports-media-commercial complex.

Losers and Buddies, Hotties and Bitches

In the 2002 and 2003 beer and liquor ads that we examined, men's work worlds seem mostly to have disappeared. These ads are less about drinking and leisure as a reward for hard work and more about leisure as a lifestyle in and of itself. Men do not work in these ads; they recreate. And women are definitely back in the picture, but not as wives who are partners in building the good domestic life. It is these relations among men as well as relations between men and women that form the four dominant gender themes in the ads we examined. We will introduce these four themes by describing a 2003 Super Bowl commercial for Bud Lite beer.

Two young, somewhat nerdy-looking white guys are at a yoga class, sitting in the back of a room full of sexy young women. The two men have attached prosthetic legs to their bodies so that they can fake the yoga moves. With their bottles of Bud Lite close by, these voyeurs watch in delight as the female yoga teacher instructs the class to "relax and release that negative energy . . . inhale, arch, *thrust* your pelvis to the sky and exhale, *release* into the stretch*.*" As the instructor uses her hands to push down on a woman's upright spread-eagled legs and says "focus, focus, focus," the camera (serving as prosthesis for male spectators at home) cuts back and forth between close-ups of the women's breasts and bottoms, while the two guys gleefully enjoy their beer and their sexual voyeurism. In the final scene the two guys are standing outside the front door of the yoga class, beer bottles in hand, and someone throws their fake legs out the door at them. As they duck to avoid being hit by the legs, one of them comments, "*She's* not very relaxed."

We begin with this ad because it contains, in various degrees, the four dominant gender themes that we found in the mega sports media events ads:

1. Losers: Men are often portrayed as chumps, losers. Masculinity—especially for the lone

man—is precarious. Individual men are always on the cusp of being publicly humiliated, either by their own stupidity, by other men, or, worse, by a beautiful woman.

2. Buddies: The precariousness of individual men's masculine status is offset by the safety of the male group. The solidity and primacy—and emotional safety—of male friendships are the emotional center of many of these ads.

3. Hotties: When women appear in these ads, it is usually as highly sexualized fantasy objects. These beautiful women serve as potential prizes for men's victories and proper consumption choices. They sometimes serve to validate men's masculinity, but their validating power also holds the potential to humiliate male losers.

4. Bitches: Wives, girlfriends, or other women to whom men are emotionally committed are mostly absent from these ads. However, when they do appear, it is primarily as emotional or sexual blackmailers who threaten to undermine individual men's freedom to enjoy the erotic pleasure at the center of the male group.

To a great extent, these four gender themes are intertwined in the Super Bowl "Yoga Voyeurs" ad. First, the two guys are clearly not good-looking, high-status, muscular icons of masculinity. More likely they are intended to represent the "everyman" with whom many boys and men can identify. Their masquerade as sensitive men allows them to transgress the female space of the yoga class, but they cannot pull the masquerade off and are eventually "outed" as losers and rejected by the sexy women. But even if they realize that they are losers, they do not have to care because they are so happy and secure in their bond with each other. Their friendship bond is cemented in frat-boy-style hijinks that allow them to share close-up voyeurism of sexy women who, we can safely assume, are way out of these men's league. In the end, the women reject the guys as pathetic losers. But the guys do not seem too upset. They have each other and, of course, they have their beers.

Rarely did a single ad in our study contain all four of these themes. But taken together, the ads show enough consistency that we can think of these themes as intertwined threads that together make up the ideological fabric at the center of mega sports media events. Next, we will illustrate how these themes are played out in the 2002 and 2003 ads, before discussing some of the strains and tensions in the ads.

Real Friends, Scary Women

Five twenty-something white guys are sitting around a kitchen table playing poker. They are laughing, seemingly having the time of their lives, drinking Jim Beam whiskey. The caption for this ad reflects the lighthearted, youthful mood of the group: "Good Bourbon, ice cubes, and whichever glasses are clean." This ad, which appeared in the 2002 *Sports Illustrated* swimsuit issue, is one in a series of Jim Beam ads that have run for the past few years in *Sports Illustrated* and in other magazines aimed at young men.[2] Running under the umbrella slogan of "Real Friends, Real Bourbon," these Jim Beam ads hail a white, college-age (or young college-educated) crowd of men with the appeal of playful male bonding through alcohol consumption in bars or pool halls. The main theme is the safety and primacy of the male group, but the accompanying written text sometimes suggests the presence of women. In one ad, four young white guys partying up a storm together and posing with arms intertwined are accompanied by the caption, "Unlike your girlfriend, they never ask where this relationship is going." These ads imply that women demand levels of emotional commitment and expression undesirable to men, while life with the boys (and the booze) is exciting, emotionally comfortable, and safe. The comfort that these ads suggest is that bonding and intimacy have clear (though mostly unspoken) boundaries that limit emotional expression in the male group. When drinking with the guys, a man

can feel close to his friends, perhaps even drape an arm over a friend's shoulder, embrace him, or tell him that he loves him. But the context of alcohol consumption provides an escape hatch that contains and rationalizes the eruption of physical intimacy.

Although emotional closeness with and commitment to real women apparently are to be avoided, these ads also do suggest a role for women. The one ad in the Jim Beam series that includes an image of a woman depicts only a body part (*Sports Illustrated* ran this one in its 2000 swimsuit issue in 3-D). Four guys drinking together in a bar are foregrounded by a set of high-heeled legs that appear to be an exotic dancer's. The guys drink, laugh, and seem thoroughly amused with each other. "Our lives would make a great sitcom," the caption reads, and continues, "of course, it would have to run on cable." That the guys largely ignore the dancer affirms the strength and primacy of their bond with one another—they do not need her or any other women, the ad seems to say. On the other hand—and just as in the "Yoga Voyeurs" commercial—the female dancer's sexualizing of the chronotopic space affirms that the bond between the men is safely within the bounds of heterosexuality.

Although these ads advocate keeping one's emotional distance from women, a commitment to heterosexuality always carries the potential for developing actual relationships with women. The few ads that depict real women portray them consistently as signs of danger to individual men and to the male group. The ads imply that what men really want is sex (or at least titillation), a cold beer, and some laughs with the guys. Girlfriends and wives are undesirable because they push men to talk about feelings and demonstrate commitment to a relationship. In "Good Listener," a 2003 Super Bowl ad for Budweiser, a young white guy is sitting in a sports bar with his girlfriend while she complains about her best friend's "totally self-centered and insensitive boyfriend." As he appears to listen to this obviously boring "girl talk," the camera pulls to a tight close-up on her face. She is reasonably attractive, but the viewer is not supposed to mistake her for one of the model-perfect fantasy women in other beer ads. The close-up reveals that her teeth are a bit crooked, her hair a bit stringy, and her face contorts as she says of her girlfriend that "she has these *emotional* needs he can't meet." Repelled, the guy spaces out and begins to peer over her shoulder at the television. The camera takes the guy's point of view and focuses on the football game while the speaking woman is in the fuzzy margins of his view. The girlfriend's monologue gets transposed by a football announcer describing an exciting run. She stops talking, and just in time his gaze shifts back to her eyes. She lovingly says, "You're such a great listener." With an "aw-shucks" smile, he says "thanks," and the "Budweiser TRUE" logo appears on the screen. These ads suggest that a sincere face and a bottle of beer allow a guy to escape the emotional needs of his partner while retaining regular access to sex. But the apparent dangers of love, long-term commitment, and marriage remain. The most overtly misogynist ad in the 2003 Super Bowl broadcast was "Sarah's Mom." While talking on the phone to a friend, a young, somewhat nerdy-looking white guy prepares to meet his girlfriend's mother for the first time. His friend offers him this stern advice: "Well, get a good look at her. 'Cause in twenty years, that's what Sarah's gonna look like." The nerd expresses surprised concern, just as there is a knock on the door. Viewed through the door's peephole, the face of Sarah's mother appears as young and beautiful as Sarah's, but it turns out that Sarah's mother has grotesquely large hips, thighs, and buttocks. The commercial ends with the screen filled mostly with the hugeness of the mother's bottom, her leather pants audibly stretching as she bends to pet the dog, and Sarah shoveling chips and dip into her mouth, as she says of her mother, "Isn't she incredible?" The guy replies, with obvious skepticism, "yeah."

The message to boys and men is disturbing. If you are nerdy enough to be thinking about getting married, then you should listen to your male friends' warnings about what to watch out for and what is important. If you have got to have a wife,

make sure that she is, and always will be, conventionally thin and beautiful.

In beer ads, the male group defines men's need for women as sexual, not emotional, and in so doing it constructs women as either whores or bitches and then suggests ways for men to negotiate the tension between these two narrow and stereotypical categories of women. This, we think, is a key point of tension that beer and liquor companies are attempting to exploit to their advantage. They do so by creating a curious shift away from the familiar "madonna-whore" dichotomy of which Western feminists have been so critical, where wives/mothers/girlfriends are put on a pedestal and the women one has sex with are put in the gutter. The alcohol industry would apparently prefer that young men not think of women as madonnas. After all, wives and girlfriends to whom men are committed, whom they respect and love, often do place limits on men's time spent out with the boys, as well as limits on men's consumption of alcohol. The industry seems to know this: as long as men remain distrustful of women, seeing them either as bitches who are trying to ensnare them and take away their freedom or as whores with whom they can party and have sex with no emotional commitment attached, then men remain more open to the marketing strategies of the industry.

Winners and Losers

In the 2002 and 2003 Super Bowls, Budweiser's "How Ya Doin'?" ads featured the trope of a country bumpkin, or hick, in the big city to highlight the rejection of men who transgress the symbolic boundaries of the male peer group. These ads also illustrate the communication and emotional processes that police these boundaries. Men may ask each other "how's it goin'," but they do not want to hear how it's *really* goin'. It is these unspoken limits that make the group bond feel like an emotionally safe place: male buddies at the bar will not ask each other how the relationship is going or push each other to get in touch with their feminine sides. But men who transgress these boundaries, who do not understand the unwritten emotional rules of the male group, are suspect, are branded as losers, and are banished from the inner circle of the group.

Revenge of the Regular Guys

If losers are used in some of these ads to clarify the bounds of masculine normality, this is not to say that hypermasculine men are set up as the norm. To the contrary, overly masculine men, muscle men, and men with big cars who flash their money around are often portrayed as the real losers, against whom regular guys can sometimes turn the tables and win the beautiful women. In the ads we examined, however, this "regular guy wins beautiful fantasy woman" outcome was very rare. Instead, when the regular guy does manage to get the beautiful fantasy woman's attention, it is usually not in the way that he imagined or dreamed. A loser may want to win the attention of—and have sex with—beautiful women. But ultimately, these women are unavailable to a loser; worse, they will publicly humiliate him if he tries to win their attention. But losers can always manage to have another beer.

If white-guy losers risk punishment or humiliation from beautiful women in these ads, the level of punishment faced by black men can be even more severe. Although nearly all of the television commercials and print ads that we examined depict white people, a very small number do focus centrally on African Americans.[3] In "Pick-Up Lines," a Bud Lite ad that ran during the 2002 Super Bowl, two black males are sitting at a bar next to an attractive black female. Paul, the man in the middle, is obviously a loser; he's wearing a garish shirt, and his hair looks like an Afro gone terribly wrong. He sounds a bit whiny as he confides in his male friend, "I'm just not good with the ladies like you, Cedric." Cedric, playing Cyrano de Bergerac, whispers opening pickup lines to him. The loser turns to the woman and passes on the lines. But just then, the bartender brings another bottle of beer to Cedric, who asks the bartender, "So, how much?" Paul, thinking

that this is his next pickup line, says to the woman, "So, how much?" Her smile turns to an angry frown, and she delivers a vicious kick to Paul's face, knocking him to the floor. After we see the Budweiser logo and hear the voice-over telling us that Bud Lite's great taste "will never let you down," we see a stunned Paul rising to his knees and trying to pull himself up to his bar stool, but the woman knocks him down again with a powerful backhand fist to the face.

This Bud Lite "Pick-Up Lines" ad—one of the very few ads that depict relations between black men and black women—was the only ad in which we saw a man being physically beaten by a woman. Here, the African American woman as object turns to subject, inflicting direct physical punishment on the African American man. The existence of these very few "black ads" brings into relief something that might otherwise remain hidden: most of these ads construct a youthful white masculinity that is playfully self-mocking, always a bit tenuous, but ultimately lovable. The screwups that white-guy losers make are forgivable, and we nearly always see these men, in the end, with at least a cold beer in hand. By contrast, the intersection of race, gender, and class creates cultural and institutional contexts of suspicion and punishment for African American boys and men (Ferguson 2000). In the beer ads this translates into the message that a black man's transgressions are apparently deserving of a kick to the face.

Erotic Intertextuality

One of the dominant strategies in beer and liquor ads is to create an (often humorous) erotic tension among members of a "threesome": the male reader/viewer, a woman depicted as a sexy fantasy object, and a bottle of cold beer. This tension is accomplished through intertextual referencing between the advertising text and the sport text. For instance, on returning to live coverage of the Super Bowl from a commercial break, the camera regularly lingered on the stadium scoreboard, above which was a huge Budweiser sign.

One such occasion during the 2003 Super Bowl was particularly striking. Coors had just run its only commercial (an episode from its successful "Twins" series) during this mega sports media event that seemed otherwise practically owned by Anheuser-Busch. Immediately on return from the commercial break to live action, the handheld field-level camera focused one by one on dancing cheerleaders (once coming so close that it appears that the camera bumped into one of the women's breasts), all the while keeping the Budweiser sign in focus in the background. It was almost as though the producers of the Super Bowl were intent on not allowing the Coors "twins" to upstage Anheuser-Busch's ownership of the event.

Omnipresent advertising images in recent years have continued to obliterate the already blurry distinction between advertising texts and other media texts (Goldman and Papson 1996). This is surely true in the world of sport: players' uniforms, stadium walls, the corner of one's television screen, and even moments within telecasts are regularly branded with the Nike swoosh or some other corporate sign. When ads appropriate or make explicit reference to other media (e.g., other ads, celebrities, movies, television shows, or popular music), they engage in what Robert Goldman and Stephen Papson call "cultural cannibalism" (1998, 10). Audiences are then invited to make the connections between the advertised product and the cultural meanings implied by the cannibalized sign; in so doing, the audience becomes "the final author, whose participation is essential" (O'Donohoe 1997, 259). As with all textual analyses that do not include an audience study, we must be cautious in inferring how differently situated audiences might variously take up, and draw meanings from, these ads. However, we suspect that experiences of "authorship" in the process of decoding and drawing intertextual connections are a major part of the pleasure of viewing mass media texts.

The 2002 and 2003 *Sports Illustrated* swimsuit issues offer vivid examples of texts that invite the reader to draw intertextual connections between erotically charged ads and other non-ad texts.

Whereas in the past the *Sports Illustrated* swimsuit issue ran ads that were clearly distinct from the swimsuit text, it has recently become more common for the visual themes in the ads and the swimsuit text to be playfully intertwined, symbiotically referencing each other. A 2003 Heineken ad shows a close-up of two twenty-four-ounce "keg cans" of Heineken beer, side by side. The text above the two cans reads, "They're big. And yeah, they're real." As if the reference to swimsuit models' breast size (and questions about whether some of the models have breast implants) were perhaps too subtle, *Sports Illustrated* juxtaposed the ad with a photo of a swimsuit model, wearing a suit that liberally exposed her breasts.

For the advertisers and for *Sports Illustrated,* the payoff for this kind of intertextual coordination is probably large: for the reader, the text of the swimsuit issue becomes increasingly seamless, as ads and swimsuit text melt into each other, playfully, humorously, and erotically referencing each other. As with the Super Bowl ads, the *Sports Illustrated* swimsuit issue ads become something that viewers learn not to ignore or skip over; instead, the ads become another part of the pleasure of consuming and imagining.

In 2003, Miller Brewing Company and *Sports Illustrated* further developed the symbiotic marketing strategy that they had introduced in 2002. The 2003 swimsuit issue featured a huge Miller Lite ad that included the equivalent of fourteen full pages of ad text. Twelve of these pages were a large, pull-out poster, one side of which was a single photo of "Sophia," a young model wearing a bikini with the Miller Lite logo on the right breast cup. On the opposite side of the poster were four one-page photos and one two-page photo of Sophia posing in various bikinis, with Miller Lite bottles and/or logos visible in each picture. As it did in the 2002 ad, Miller invites viewers to enter a contest to win a trip to the next *Sports Illustrated* swimsuit issue photo shoot. The site of the photo shoot fuses the text-based space of the magazine with the real space of the working models in exotic, erotic landscapes of desire that highlight the sexuality of late capitalist colonialism (Davis 1997). The accompanying text invites the reader to "visit http://www.cnnsi.com" to "check out a 360 degree view of the *Sports Illustrated* swimsuit photo shoot." And the text accompanying most of the photos of Sophia and bottles of Miller Lite teasingly encourages the reader to exercise his consumer power: "So if you had to make a choice, which one would it be?"

This expansive ad evidences a multilevel symbiosis between *Sports Illustrated* and Miller Brewing Company. The playful tease to "choose your favorite" (model, swimsuit, and/or beer) invites the reader to enter another medium—the *Sports Illustrated* swimsuit Web site, which includes access to a *Sports Illustrated* swimsuit photo shoot video sponsored by Miller. The result is a multifaceted media text that stands out as something other than mere advertisement and other than business-as-usual *Sports Illustrated* text. It has an erotic and commercial charge to it that simultaneously teases the reader as a sexual voyeur and hails him as an empowered consumer who can freely choose his own beer and whichever sexy woman he decides is his "favorite."

"Life Is Harsh": Male Losers and Alcoholic Accommodation

In recent years, the tendency in the *Sports Illustrated* swimsuit issue to position male readers as empowered individuals who can "win" or freely choose the sexy fantasy object of their dreams has begun to shift in other directions. To put it simply, many male readers of the swimsuit issue may find the text erotically charged, but most know that these are two-dimensional images of sexy women who in real life are unavailable to them. In recent years, some swimsuit issue ads have delivered this message directly. In 1997, a two-page ad for Tequila Sauza depicted six women in short red skirts, posing flirtatiously, some of them lifting their blouses provocatively to reveal bare midriffs, or opening their blouses to reveal parts of their breasts. In small letters, across the six women's waists, stretching all the way across the two pages, the text reads, "We can say with 99.9%

accuracy that there is no possible way whatsoever in this lifetime that you will ever get a date with one of these women." Then, to the side of the ad is written "LIFE IS HARSH. Your tequila shouldn't be." A similar message appears in other ads. For instance, in the 1999 swimsuit issue, a full-page photo of a Heineken bottle included the written text "The only heiny in this magazine you could actually get your hands on."

These ads play directly to the male reader as loser and invite him to accommodate to his loser status, to recognize that these sexy fantasy women, though "real," are unavailable to him, and to settle for what he can have: a good bottle of Tequila Sauza or a cold (rather than a hot) "Heiny." The Bud Lite Super Bowl commercials strike a similar chord. Many Bud Lite ads either titillate the viewer with sexy fantasy women, point to the ways that relationships with real women are to be avoided, or do both simultaneously. The break that appears near the end of each Bud Lite ad contrasts sharply with the often negative depiction of men's relations with real women in the ad's story line. The viewer sees a close-up of a bottle of Bud Lite. The bottle's cap explodes off, and beer ejaculates out, as a male voice-over proclaims what a man truly can rely on in life: "For the great taste that won't fill you up, and never lets you down . . . make it a Bud Lite."

Revenge of the Losers

The accommodation theme in these ads may succeed, momentarily, in encouraging a man to shift his feelings of being a sexual loser toward manly feelings of empowerment through the consumption of brand-name beers and liquor. If the women in the ads are responsible for heightening tensions that result in some men's sense of themselves as losers, one possible outcome beyond simply drinking a large amount of alcohol (or one that accompanies the consumption of alcohol) is to express anger toward women and even to take revenge against them. This is precisely a direction that some of the recent ads have taken.

A full-page ad in the 2002 swimsuit issue showed a large photo of a bottle of Maker's Mark Whiskey. The bottle's reflection on the shiny table on which it sits is distorted in a way that suggests an hourglass-shaped female torso. The text next to the bottle reads, "'Your bourbon has a great body and fine character. I WISH the same could be said for my girlfriend.' D. T., Birmingham, AL." This one-page ad is juxtaposed with a full-page photo of a *Sports Illustrated* model, provocatively using her thumb to begin to pull down the right side of her bikini bottom.

Together, the ad text and *Sports Illustrated* text angrily express the bitch-whore dichotomy that we discussed above. D. T.'s girlfriend is not pictured, but the description of her clearly indicates that not only does she lack a beautiful body; worse, she's a bitch. While D. T.'s girlfriend symbolizes the real woman whom each guy tolerates, and to whom he avoids committing, the juxtaposed *Sports Illustrated* model is the beautiful and sexy fantasy woman. She is unavailable to the male reader in real life; her presence as fantasy image highlights that the reader, like D. T., is stuck, apparently, with his bitchy girlfriend. But at least he can enjoy a moment of pseudo-empowerment by consuming a Maker's Mark whiskey and by insulting his girlfriend's body and character. Together, the Maker's Mark ad and the juxtaposed *Sports Illustrated* model provide a context for the reader to feel hostility toward the real women in his life.

This kind of symbolic male revenge toward women is expressed in a different way in a four-page Captain Morgan rum ad that appeared in the 2003 *Sports Illustrated* swimsuit issue. On the first page, we see only the hands of the cartoon character "Captain Morgan" holding a fire hose spraying water into the air over what appears to be a tropical beach. When one turns the page, a three-page foldout ad reveals that "the Captain" is spraying what appears to be a *Sports Illustrated* swimsuit issue photo shoot. Six young women in tiny bikinis are laughing, perhaps screaming, and running for cover (five of them are huddled under an umbrella with a grinning male character who

looks suspiciously like Captain Morgan). The spray from the fire hose causes the women's bathing suits to melt right off their bodies. The readers do not know if the swimsuits are painted on or are made of meltable candy or if perhaps Captain Morgan's ejaculate is just that powerfully corrosive. One way or the other, the image suggests that Captain Morgan is doing a service to the millions of boys and men who read this magazine. Written across a fleeing woman's thigh, below her melting bikini bottom, the text reads "Can you say birthday suit issue?"

Two men—apparently photographers—stand to the right of the photo, arms raised to the heavens (with their clothing fully intact). The men in the picture seem ecstatic with religious fervor. The male reader is perhaps invited to identify with these regular guys: like them, he is always good enough to look at these beautiful women in their swimsuits but never good enough to get them to take it off for him. But here, "the Captain" was clever enough to strip the women naked so that he and all of his male buddies could enjoy a vengeful moment of voyeurism. The relational gender and sexual dynamics of this ad—presented here without overt anger and with cartoonish humor—allegorize the common dynamics of group sexual assaults (Beneke 1982). These sexy women have teased men enough, the ad suggests. First they arouse men, and then they inevitably make them feel like losers. They deserve to be stripped naked against their will. As in many male rape fantasies, the ad suggests that women ultimately find that they like it. And all of this action is facilitated by a bottle of rum, the Captain's magical essence.

Tension, Stabilization, and Masculine Consumption

We argued in our introduction that contemporary social changes have destabilized hegemonic masculinity. Examining beer and liquor ads in mega sports media events gives us a window into the ways that commercial forces have seized on these destabilizing tendencies, constructing fantasy narratives that aim to appeal to a very large group—

eighteen- to thirty-four-year-old men. They do so by appealing to a broad zeitgeist among young (especially white, heterosexual) men that is grounded in widespread tensions in the contemporary gender order.[4] The sexual and gender themes of the beer and liquor ads that we examine in this article do not stand alone; rather they reflect, and in turn contribute to, broader trends in popular culture and marketing to young white males. Television shows like *The Man Show,* new soft-core porn magazines like *Maxim* and *FHM,* and radio talk shows like the syndicated *Tom Leykus Show* share similar themes and are targeted to similar audiences of young males. Indeed, radio talk show hosts like Leykus didactically instruct young men to avoid "girlie" things, to eschew emotional commitment, and to think of women primarily as sexual partners (Messner 2002, 107–8). These magazines and television and radio shows construct young male lifestyles saturated with sexy images of nearly naked, surgically enhanced women; unabashed and unapologetic sexual voyeurism shared by groups of laughing men; and explicit talk of sexual exploits with "hotties" or "juggies." A range of consumer products that includes—often centrally, as in *The Man Show*—consumption of beer as part of the young male lifestyle stitches together this erotic bonding among men. Meanwhile, real women are either absent from these media or they are disparaged as gold diggers (yes, this term has been resuscitated) who use sex to get men to spend money on them and trick them into marriage. The domesticated man is viewed as a wimpy victim who has subordinated his own pleasures (and surrendered his paychecks) to a woman. Within this framework, a young man should have sex with as many women as he can while avoiding (or at least delaying) emotional commitments to any one woman. Freedom from emotional commitment grants 100 percent control over disposable income for monadic consumption and care of self. And that is ultimately what these shows are about: constructing a young male consumer characterized by personal and emotional freedom who

can attain a hip lifestyle by purchasing an ever-expanding range of automobile-related products, snack foods, clothes, toiletries, and, of course, beer and liquor.

At first glance, these new media aimed at young men seem to resuscitate a 1950s "*Playboy* philosophy" of men's consumption, sexuality, and gender relations (Ehrenreich 1983). Indeed, these new media strongly reiterate the dichotomous bitch-whore view of women that was such a linchpin of Hugh Hefner's "philosophy." But today's tropes of masculinity do not simply reiterate the past; rather, they give a postfeminist twist to the *Playboy* philosophy. A half-century ago, Hefner's pitch to men to recapture the indoors by creating (purchasing) one's own erotic "bachelor pad" in which to have sex with women (and then send them home) read as a straightforwardly masculine project. By contrast, today's sexual and gender pitch to young men is delivered with an ironic, self-mocking wink that operates, we think, on two levels. First, it appears to acknowledge that most young men are neither the heroes of the indoors (as Hefner would have it) nor of the outdoors (as the 1970s and 1980s beer ads suggested). Instead, the ads seem to recognize that young white men's unstable status leaves them always on the verge of being revealed as losers. The ads plant seeds of insecurity on this fertile landscape, with the goal of creating a white guy who is a consistent and enthusiastic consumer of alcoholic beverages. The irony works on a second level as well: the throwback sexual and gender imagery—especially the bitch-whore dichotomization of women—is clearly a defensively misogynistic backlash against feminism and women's increasing autonomy and social power. The wink and self-mocking irony allow men to have it both ways: they can engage in humorous misogynist banter and claim simultaneously that it is all in play. They do not take themselves seriously, so anyone who takes their misogyny as anything but boys having good fun just has no sense of humor. The humorous irony works, then, to deflect charges of sexism away from white males, allowing them to define themselves as victims, as members of an endangered species. We suspect, too, that this is a key part of the process that constructs the whiteness in current reconstructions of hegemonic masculinity. As we have suggested, humorous "boys-will-be-boys" misogyny is unlikely to be taken ironically and lightly when delivered by men of color.

Caught between the excesses of a hyper-masculinity that is often discredited and caricatured in popular culture and the increasing empowerment of women, people of color, and homosexuals, while simultaneously being undercut by the postindustrial economy, the "Average Joe" is positioned as the ironic, vulnerable but lovable hero of beer and liquor ads. It is striking that the loser is not, or is rarely, your "José Mediano," especially if we understand the construction as a way to unite diverse eighteen- to thirty-four-year-old men. This is to say that the loser motif constructs the universal subject as implicitly white, and as a reaction against challenges to hegemonic masculinity it represents an ongoing possessive investment in whiteness (Lipsitz 1998).

Our analysis suggests that the fact that male viewers today are being hailed as losers and are being asked to identify with—even revel in—their loser status has its limits. The beer and liquor industry dangles images of sexy women in front of men's noses. Indeed, the ads imply that men will go out of their way to put themselves in position to be voyeurs, be it with a TV remote control, at a yoga class, in a bar, or on the *Sports Illustrated/ Miller Beer* swimsuit photo shoot Web site. But ultimately, men know (and are increasingly being told in the advertisements themselves) that these sexy women are not available to them. Worse, if men get too close to these women, these women will most likely humiliate them. By contrast, real women—women who are not model-beautiful fantasy objects—are likely to attempt to ensnare men into a commitment, push them to have or express feelings that make them uncomfortable, and limit their freedom to have fun watching sports or playing cards or pool with their friends.

So, in the end, men have only the safe haven of their male friends and the bottle.

This individual sense of victimization may feed young men's insecurities while giving them convenient scapegoats on which to project anger at their victim status. The cultural construction of white males as losers, then, is tethered to men's anger at and desire for revenge against women. Indeed, we have observed that revenge-against-women themes are evident in some of the most recent beer and liquor ads. And it is here that our analysis comes full circle. For, as we suggested in the introduction, the cultural imagery in ads aimed at young men does not simply come from images "out there." Instead, this imagery is linked to the ways that real people live their lives. It is the task of future research—including audience research—to investigate and flesh out the specific links between young men's consumption of commercial images, their consumption of beer and liquor, their attitudes toward and relationships with women, and their tendencies to drink and engage in violence against women.

Notes

1. In addition to *Sports Illustrated's* 3,137,523 average weekly subscribers, the company's rate card claims 1,467,228 single-copy sales of the swimsuit issue. According to the same multiplier of 6.55 readers per magazine that *Sports Illustrated* uses for estimating the total size of its weekly audience, the swimsuit issue audience is over 30 million. More than likely, the multiplier for the swimsuit issue is higher than that of the weekly magazine, so the swimsuit issue audience is probably much larger than 30 million.

2. Most of the Jim Beam "Real Friends" ads discussed here did not appear in the two *Sports Illustrated* swimsuit issues on which we focus. However, it enhances our understanding of the gender themes in the Jim Beam ads to examine the thematic consistencies in the broader series of Jim Beam "Real Friends" ads.

3. Of the twenty-six beer and malt liquor ads in the two Super Bowls, twenty-four depicted people. Among the twenty-four ads that depicted people, eighteen depicted white people only, three depicted groups that

appear to be of mixed race, and three focused on African American main characters. Thirteen of the twenty-four beer and liquor ads in the two *Sports Illustrated* swimsuit issues depicted people: twelve depicted white people only, and one depicted what appears to be the silhouette of an African American couple. No apparent Latino/as or Asian Americans appeared in any of the magazine or television ads.

4. These same beer companies target different ads to other groups of men. Suzanne Danuta Walters (2001) analyzes Budweiser ads, e.g., that are aimed overtly at gay men.

References

Beneke, Timothy. 1982. *Men on Rape.* New York: St. Martin's.

Collins, Tony, and Wray Vamplew. 2002. *Mud, Sweat, and Beers: A Cultural History of Sport and Alcohol.* New York: Berg.

Curry, Timothy. 2000. "Booze and Bar Fights: A Journey to the Dark side of College Athletics." In *Masculinities, Gender Relations, and Sport,* ed. Jim McKay, Donald F. Sabo, and Michael A. Messner, 162–75. Thousand Oaks, CA: Sage.

Davis, Laurel L. 1997. *The Swimsuit Issue and Sport: Hegemonic Masculinity in* Sports Illustrated. Albany, NY: SUNY Press.

Dayan, Daniel, and Elihu Katz. 1988. "Articulating Consensus: The Ritual and Rhetoric of Media Events." In *Durkheimian Sociology: Cultural Studies,* ed. Jeffrey C. Alexander, 161–86. Cambridge: Cambridge University Press.

Ehrenreich, Barbara. 1983. *The Hearts of Men: American Dreams and the Flight from Commitment.* New York: Anchor Doubleday.

Ferguson, Ann Arnett. 2000. *Bad Boys: Public Schools in the Making of Black Masculinity.* Ann Arbor: University of Michigan Press.

Goldman, Robert, and Stephen Papson. 1996. *Sign Wars: The Cluttered Landscape of Advertising.* New York: Guilford.

———. 1998. *Nike Culture: The Sign of the Swoosh.* Thousand Oaks, CA: Sage.

Koss, Mary, and John A. Gaines. 1993. "The Prediction of Sexual Aggression by Alcohol Use, Athletic Participation, and Fraternity Affiliation." *Journal of Interpersonal Violence* 8(1):94–108.

Leichliter, Jami S., Philip W. Meilman, Cheryl A. Presley, and Jeffrey R. Cashin. 1998. "Alcohol Use and Related Consequences among Students with Varying Levels of Involvement in College Athletics." *Journal of American College Health* 46(6):257–62.

Lipsitz, George. 1981. *Class and Culture in Cold War America: "A Rainbow at Midnight."* New York: Praeger.

———. 1998. *The Possessive Investment in Whiteness: How White People Profit from Identity Politics.* Philadelphia: Temple University Press.

Martin, Christopher R., and Jimmie L. Reeves. 2001. "The Whole World Isn't Watching (but We Thought They Were): The Super Bowl and U.S. Solipsism." *Culture, Sport, and Society* 4(2):213–54.

May, Elaine Tyler. 1988. *Homeward Bound: American Families in the Cold War Era.* New York: Basic Books.

Messner, Michael A. 2002. *Taking the Field: Women, Men, and Sports.* Minneapolis: University of Minnesota Press.

O'Donohoe, Stephanie. 1997. "Leaky Boundaries: Intertextuality and Young Adult Experiences of Advertising." In *Buy This Book: Studies in Advertising and Consumption,* ed. Mica Nava, Andrew Blake, Ian McRury, and Barry Richards, 257–75. London: Routledge.

Postman, Neil, Christine Nystrom, Lance Strate, and Charlie Weingartner. 1987. *Myths, Men, and Beer: An Analysis of Beer Commercials on Broadcast Television, 1987.* Washington, DC: AAA Foundation for Traffic Safety.

Sabo, Don, Phil Gray, and Linda Moore. 2000. "Domestic Violence and Televised Athletic Events: 'It's a man thing.'" In *Masculinities, Gender Relations, and Sport,* ed. Jim McKay, Don Sabo, and Michael A. Messner, 127–46. Thousand Oaks, CA: Sage.

Sperber, Murray. 2000. *Beer and Circus: How Big-Time College Sports Is Crippling Undergraduate Education.* New York: Henry Holt.

Spigel, Lynn. 1992. *Make Room for TV: Television and the Family Ideal in Postwar America.* Chicago: University of Chicago Press.

Strate, Lance. 1992. "Beer Commercials: A Manual on Masculinity." In *Men, Masculinity, and the Media,* ed. Steve Craig, 78–92. Newbury Park, CA: Sage.

Walters, Suzanna Danuta. 2001. *All the Rage: The Story of Gay Visibility in America.* Chicago: University of Chicago Press.

Wenner, Lawrence A. 1991. "One Part Alcohol, One Part Sport, One Part Dirt, Stir Gently: Beer Commercials and Television Sports." In *Television Criticism: Approaches and Applications,* ed. Leah R. Vende Berg and Lawrence A. Wenner, 388–407. New York: Longman.

———. 1998. "In Search of the Sports Bar: Masculinity, Alcohol, Sports, and the Mediation of Public Space." In *Sport and Postmodern Times,* ed. Genevieve Rail, 303–32. Albany, NY: SUNY Press.

Zimbalist, Andrew. 1999. *Unpaid Professionals: Commercialism and Conflict in Big-Time College Sports.* Princeton, NJ: Princeton University Press.

David Nylund

When in Rome: Heterosexism, Homophobia, and Sports Talk Radio

I am negotiating the traffic in my car on a typical harried Monday morning. As an avid sports fan, I turn on my local sports radio station. A commercial plugging the local radio station is airing: "Your hair's getting thinner, your paunch is getting bigger. But you still think the young babes want you! That's because you listen to Sports 1140 AM—it's not just sports talk, it's culture." Next comes the loud, rhythmic guitar riffs from the Guns N' Roses song, "Welcome to the Jungle." As Axl Rose begins to sing the lyrics to the heavy metal song, an announcer bellows, "Live from Los Angeles. You're listening to the Jim Rome Show." Next, the distinct, brash voice of Jim Rome, the nation's most popular sports talk radio host, addresses his audience of 2 million sports fans:[1] "Welcome back to the Jungle. I am Van Smack. We have open phone lines. But clones, if you call, have a take and do not suck or you will get run."[2] Over the next 3 hours, the well-known host interviews famous sports figures, articulates his notoriously controversial opinions on various topics using urban slang, and takes phone calls from his loyal listeners/sports fans who speak in Rome-invented terms such as *Jungle Dweller, bang,* and *Bugeater.*[3] I listen to the program with mixed feelings. As a sports fan and long-time listener of sports talk radio, I find myself engrossed and amused; I want to know what each "in-group" term means. As a critical feminist scholar, I am uneasy with his confrontational and insulting style, not to mention the aggressive and

From *Journal of Sport & Social Issues,* Volume 28, No. 2, May 2004, pp. 136–168.

uncritical content of his speech. I wonder, "What will Rome say next?"[4]

The Jim Rome Show reflects a growing cultural trend in the United States—sports talk radio. According to sportswriter Ashley Jude Collie (2001), Jim Rome is the "hippest, most controversial, and brutally honest voice" (p. 53) in mediated sports. In addition to his nationally syndicated radio program that airs on more than 200 stations, the 40-year-old hosts ESPN's *Rome is Burning,* a weekly 1-hr television sports talk show (and his second show on ESPN). Rome began his radio career broadcasting University of California, Santa Barbara (UCSB), basketball games. After graduating from UCSB in 1986 and serving seven nonpaying radio internships, Rome earned a local weekend job at XTRA in San Diego, a powerful 77,000-watt station. The "clever fashioning of a streetwise persona" (Mariscal, 1999), his raspy voice, staccato delivery, and fiercely independent opinions separated him from the talk radio crowd, and he soon moved into hosting a primetime radio show. Eventually, his popularity earned him a television spot on ESPN2, *Talk2,* a cable show that Rome hosted in the early 90s. The Noble Sports Network syndicated Rome's radio show in 1995, and Premiere Radio Networks acquired the rights to the show 1 year later. Rome also hosted Fox Sports Net's *The Last Word,* a sports talk television program that ran from 1997 to 2002.

However, despite the variety of venues in which he plays, it is the radio show's format that contributes to Rome's controversiality and popularity. Loyal callers, whom he calls "clones," phone in with their opinion (referred to as a "take") on what's happening in the world of sports. Rome listens intently and either "runs" the caller with a buzzer (meaning he disconnects the call) or he allows them to finish their take and says, "rack'em" (meaning he saves the call as an entry into the huge call-of-the-day contest). As opposed to other talk radio programs where there is some dialogical interaction between the caller and hosts, Rome and his callers do not engage in a back-and-forth interchange. The caller's comments are highly performative, full of insider language, and monological. Rome silently listens to the call and only comments when the caller is finished with his or her monologue or Rome disconnects the call. Rarely, if ever, does a caller disagree with Rome.[5] "Huge" calls are those that Rome considers good "smack" speech—his term for sports talk that is gloatful, uninhibited, and unbridled. According to Rome, only the strong survive in this 3-hr dose of smack and irreverence. Rome's in-group language and his unique interaction (or lack thereof) make his radio show distinctive. His "survival of the fittest" format is responsible for the show's reputation as sports version of hate-speech radio (Hodgson, 1999).

The Jim Rome Show epitomizes the growing trend of talk radio. Presented as a medium in which citizens/callers can freely "air their point of view," talk radio has become a very popular forum for large numbers of people to engage in debate about politics, religion, and sports. The media culture, with talk radio as a prominent discourse, plays a very powerful role in the constitution of everyday life, shaping our political values, gender ideologies, and supplying the material out of which people fashion their identities (Kellner, 1995). Hence, it is crucial for scholars to furnish critical commentary on talk radio; specifically, we should critique those radio texts that work to reinforce inequality.

Talk radio formats, particularly political talk radio, exploded in the 1980s as a result of deregulation, corporatization of radio, and niche marketing (Cook, 2001).[6] Deregulation, which loosened mass-media ownership and content re-

strictions, renewed interest in radio as a capitalist investment and galvanized the eventual emergence of its two 1990s prominent showcase formats: hate radio talk shows and all-sports programming (Cook, 2001). By the late 1990s, there were more than 4,000 talk shows on 1,200 stations (Goldberg, 1998).[7] Sports talk radio formats have, according to cultural studies scholar Jorge Mariscal (1999), "spread like an unchecked virus" (p. 111). Currently, there are more than 250 all-sports stations in the United States (Ghosh, 1999).

As a result of deregulation and global capitalism, new media conglomerates emerged as the only qualified buyers of radio programming.[8] Infinity Broadcasting, the largest U.S. company devoted exclusively to owning and operating radio stations, owns WFAN[9] and Sacramento's local all-sports station, 1140 AM. Its competing company, Premiere Radio Network, owns the popular nationally syndicated programs hosted by Howard Stern, Rush Limbaugh, Dr. Laura, and Jim Rome. Schiller (1989) refers to this homogenizing, modulated trend as "corporate speech" (p. 40) that encourages censorship and contains public expression within corporate, capitalist ideologies that reinforce dominant social institutions.

With the corporatization of radio came niche marketing that caters to targeted demographic groups. Talk radio is aimed at a very desirable demographic: White middle-class men between the ages of 24 and 55 years. Research shows that talk-radio listeners are overwhelmingly men who tend to vote Republican (Armstrong & Rubin, 1989; Hutchby, 1996; Page & Tannenbaum, 1996). The most popular program, the *Rush Limbaugh Show,* has 20 million daily listeners who laugh along with the host as he rants and vents, opening a channel for the performance of the angry White male. Roedieger (1996) remarked, in a fascinating read of Limbaugh's cultural significance in the United States, that "banality can carry much more social power than genius where White consciousness is concerned" (p. 42). Douglas (2002) argued that although most of the research on talk radio is on the threat it poses to democracy, what is obvious, but far less discussed, is talk radio's central role in restoring masculine hegemony:

> Talk radio is as much—maybe even more—about gender politics at the end of the century than it is about party politics. There were different masculinities enacted on the radio, from Howard Stern to Rush Limbaugh, but they were all about challenging and overthrowing, if possible, the most revolutionary of social movements, feminism. The men's movement of the 1980s found its outlet—and that was talk radio. (Douglas, 2002, p. 485)

Similarly, sports talk radio, according to Goldberg (1998), enacts its White hegemony via hypermasculine posing, forceful opinions, and loudmouth shouting. Sports talk radio "pontificates, moralizes, politicizes, commercializes, and commodifies—as it entertains" (p. 213). Although Rome's masculine style is different from Limbaugh's and Stern's, all three controversial hosts have built reputations through their rambunctious, masculinist, and combative styles (Farred, 2000). With White male masculinity being challenged and decentered by feminism, affirmative action, gay and lesbian movements, and other groups' quest for social equality, sports talk shows, similar to talk radio in general, have become an attractive venue for embattled White men seeking recreational repose and a nostalgic return to a prefeminist ideal (Farred, 2000).

This article offers a critical analysis of the most prominent sports talk-radio program, *The Jim Rome Show*. My study does not critique and dissect *The Jim Rome Show* in isolation from other media texts or discourses about sports; rather, I aim to provide a historicized and contextualized study based in cultural studies methodology. I show how *The Jim Rome Show* is situated within a broader set of social, gender, racial, political, economic, and cultural forces. In particular, I examine the ways in which the show reinforces and (less obviously) calls into question heterosexism as well as what gender scholars call *hegemonic masculinity*. As a prelude to this analysis, I discuss

sports talk radio and its link to traditional masculinity, homophobia, and heterosexism.

Sports Talk Radio and Hegemonic Masculinity

Many cultural critics and feminists are interested in examining the media industry's participation in the construction and maintenance of oppressive gender and sexual ideologies. One such dominant ideology is hegemonic masculinity. Media critics and scholars of gender have described at least five distinctive features of hegemonic masculinity in U.S. culture: (a) physical force, (b) occupational achievement, (c) patriarchy, (d) frontiermanship, and (e) heterosexuality (Brod, 1987; Kimmel, 1994). Connell (1990) defined hegemonic masculinity as "the culturally idealized form of masculine character" (p. 83) that emphasizes "the connecting of masculinity to toughness and competitiveness," as well as "the subordination of women" and "marginalization of gay men" (p. 94). Connell also suggested that hegemonic masculinity is not a static phenomenon but is an always contested, historically situated, social practice.

Historically, sports have played a fundamental role in the construction and maintenance of traditional masculinity in the United States (Messner, 1992). Communications scholar Trujillo (1996) stated, "No other institution in American culture has influenced our sense of masculinity more than sport" (p. 183). The mass media have benefited from institutionalized sports and have served to reaffirm certain features of hegemonic masculinity. As Trujillo (1994) wrote:

> Media coverage of sports reinforces traditional masculinity in at least three ways. It privileges the masculine over the feminine or homosexual image by linking it to a sense of positive cultural values. It depicts the masculine image as "natural" or conventional, while showing alternative images as unconventional or deviant. And it personalizes traditional masculinity by elevating its representatives to places of hero-

ism and denigrating strong females or homosexuals. (p. 97)

Mediated sports texts function largely to reproduce the idea that hegemonic masculinity and heterosexuality are natural and universal rather than socially constructed (Jhally, 1989). Because these dominant texts have detrimental effects on women, gays, lesbians, and some men, Trujillo argued that mediated sport should be analyzed and critiqued.

Many scholars have taken up Trujillo's call, and in the past decade we have seen an explosion of research on sports and mass media (Wenner, 2000). Most of these studies examine televised sports and its link to violent masculinity, sexism, and homophobia (Messner, Dunbar, & Hunt, 2000). However, scholars have also turned their attention to the impact and meaning of "sports talk."[10] Farred (2000) described sports talk as an "overwhelmingly masculinist (but not exclusively male), combative, passionate, and apparently open ended discourse" (p. 101). Farred described sports radio talk shows as "orchestrated and mediated by rambunctious hosts" providing a "robust, opinionated, and sometimes humorous forum for talking about sport" (p. 116). Likewise, Sabo and Jansen (2000) posited that sports talk serves as an important primer for gender socialization in current times. They wrote:

> Sports talk, which today usually means talk about mediated sports, is one of [the] only remaining discursive spaces where men of all social classes and ethnic groups directly discuss such values as discipline, skill, courage, competition, loyalty, fairness, teamwork, hierarchy, and achievement. Sports and sports fandom are also sites of male bonding. (p. 205)

Sports radio does appear to have a communal function and is a particularly interesting site to study how men perform relationships and community. Haag (1996) found something inherently democratizing about sports talk radio, for she thinks it promotes civic discourse and "teaches us how to make community of and for a lot of people who lead isolated, often lonely lives in America" (p. 460). Haag also suggested that sports talk radio serves a different function than political talk radio, despite serving a similar largely White middle-class audience, because the values that it emphasizes focus on community, loyalty, and decency. The appeal of sports talk radio, according to Haag, lies in the idiosyncrasies of its hosts and the regionalism of the issues covered, in direct opposition to the increased national corporate control of radio. Farred (2000), in speaking to the communal function of sports, suggested that sports talk on the radio can "temporarily break down barriers of race, ethnicity, and class." As he put it, "White suburbanites, inner-city Latino and African-American men can all support the New York Knicks or the Los Angeles Dodgers" (p. 103).

Why is sports talk radio so popular at this particular time in history? Examining the historical and social context of masculinity suggests some interesting answers. With post-Fordist industrialization came economic changes that challenged the ideology of hegemonic masculinity. Women's increased presence in the public sphere, along with the changes in men's work and increased visibility of sexual diversity, provoked a "crisis in masculinity" (Dworkin & Wachs, 2000).[11] This crisis made many men fearful of becoming "feminized." Consequently, organized sports, with its emphasis on strength and physicality, functions as a popular homosocial institution to counter men's fear of feminization in the new economy and to help men cope with changes in the gender and economic order (Messner, 1992; Pronger, 1990).

Thus, as Douglas argued about talk radio in general, the emergence of sports talk radio can be understood as another attempt to retain certain aspects of traditional male identity. Its popularity with men coincides with other current media trends, including men's magazines such as *Maxim* and *FHM,* or Comedy Central Cable Network's hypermasculine TV show, *The Man Show.* It can be argued that these forms represent a nostalgic (and perhaps an ironic) attempt to return to a prefeminist masculine ideal. In particular, White, middle-class, heterosexual men may feel threatened and uncertain with changes encouraged by feminism and gay rights. Sports talk radio may represent an attempt to symbolically reassert their superiority over women and homosexuals (Horrocks & Campling, 1994). In this vein, Goldberg (1998) suggested that sports talk radio, far from being a democratizing force (here disagreeing with Haag), reinscribes dominant discourses and is a leading forum for reproducing male domination. He contended that "Sports talk radio facilitates this masculine self-elevation, the ideological reproduction of hegemony—risk and cost free but for the price of the toll call" (p. 218).[12]

As a casual listener to *The Jim Rome Show* over the past 3 years, I have noticed themes of misogyny, violence, and heterosexual dominance appear to recur with considerable frequency. Rome's persona embodies an aggressive masculinity with unassailable expertise and authority. This aggressive persona climaxed in 1994 on the set of Rome's ESPN show *Talk 2* while interviewing NFL quarterback Jim Everett. During the interview, Everett knocked Rome off his chair after Rome taunted Everett by calling him "Chris" (i.e., female tennis star, Chris Evert), a veiled reference to the quarterback's reputed lack of toughness. Rome's reference to Everett as "Chris" on the show was not the first time he had done so. In fact, Rome has used this term on Everett throughout the 1993 NFL season on his local radio show on XTRA 690 AM. This hypermasculine event increased Rome's fame and reputation among some of his audience as a host who "tells it like it is" even if it means insulting someone. However, many in the media criticized Rome's lack of professionalism and predicted the end of his career (Sports Illustrated Editors, 1994). Although Rome left ESPN2 soon after the Everett incident, his radio career slowly continued to grow to the prominence it now holds. Rome's reputation as intolerant and abusive continues to this day because his rapid-fire, masculinist-laden opinion on sports provoked OutSports.com—a Web site that caters to gay and lesbian sports fans—to refer to him as "the commentator who makes a name for himself by saying stupid things with an obnoxious style, that for some reason, attracts many straight sports fans" (Buzinski, 2000, p. 5).[13]

As a cultural studies scholar and committed sports fan, I am compelled to study *The Jim Rome Show* to examine the sexism and homophobia present in the show. When in Rome do the clones do as the Romans do? This question led me to conduct a textual analysis that identifies those features that appear to reinforce or promote homophobia and sexism. I also researched audiences in various sports bars in the United States to achieve a better understanding of what *The Jim Rome Show* means to listeners. I was particularly curious whether certain audience members resist the dominant, hegemonic, textual themes.

Method

It is important to note that my research is influenced by my pleasure in listening to the show as a sports fan. Because I write as a scholar and as a fan, my study reflects these two levels of knowledge, which are not necessarily in conflict but are also not necessarily in perfect alliance. Being a fan allows me certain insights into sports talk radio that an academic who is not a fan might not have, particularly when his or her analysis of texts is isolated from actual audiences. I thus avoid Jenkins's (1992) critique of academic textual analysis that is distant from audiences and consequently "unable to link ideological criticism with an acknowledgment of the pleasures we find within popular texts"(p.7).

To help work against the limitations of critiquing texts in isolation from context, I hung out in sports bars and interviewed listeners of *The Jim Rome Show* to better understand the complex relationship between audiences and texts. These interviews were conducted in sports bars in Sacramento, Tampa, Las Vegas, and Fresno (see the appendix for interview script). I conducted interviews with 18 people who described themselves as fans of *The Jim Rome Show*. The average age of participants was 32 years. Ten were White, three were African American, three were Latino, and two were Asian American. Sixteen of the participants were men, and two were women, all identified as heterosexual.[14] Given that my research was limited to a small number of participants and because the audience members I interviewed may not be representative of *The Jim Rome Show*'s North American audience, the results are not necessarily generalizable. Yet my hope is that my findings will promote future research on the ways that listeners decode sports talk radio texts.

As I reviewed each interview transcript, I made notes about its content, analyzing the responses to each question. I was particularly interested in looking for common themes, key phrases, ways of talking, and patterns of responses that occurred in my conversations with the participants. Instead of a positivist model of research, my audience research is provisional, partial, and situated in a particular social and historical location. As Ang (1996) stated, "Critical audience studies should not pretend to tell the 'truth' about 'the audience.' Its ambitions should be more modest" (p. 45).

Sports Bars

I chose to research sports bars because many of the patrons who frequent these spaces are avid listeners of *The Jim Rome Show*.[15] In addition, because it is a primary site for male bonding, the sports bar is an extension of the social practices and discourses evident in sports talk radio (Wenner, 1998). Nevertheless, conducting research as a sports fan in the highly masculinized space of a sports bar produced some interesting ethical dilemmas; specifically, the issue of power relations. I attempted to be self-reflexive of my privileged subject position (White, male, heterosexual, sports fan) as to not inadvertently reproduce male hegemony. This privilege was evident when I was discussing my research with a male friend who identifies as gay. As he said to me, "I could never do that research; a sports bar is a dangerous place for a gay man. I would feel very unsafe there." Taking his comments into account helps me to continually reflect on my privileged status

as researcher and straight, middle-class, White male fan. I also need to ask critical questions that invite my male participants to examine and interrogate masculinity.

Being a sports fan who has frequented many sports bars has advantages and disadvantages. The main risk is overidentifying with my research participants and not having enough critical distance. The main advantage of being a sports fan is that it helps to facilitate nuanced understandings and forms of access impossible from other subject positions. Conducting this study as a fan inspired me to a high degree of accountability— I have included verbatim materials, edited and selected from my taped interviews, as a way of privileging their voice (all the names of my research participants have been changed to preserve anonymity).

The sports bar is a fascinating site to conduct fieldwork. In his assessment of the cultural space of modern and postmodern sports bars, Wenner (1998) argued that alcohol, sports, and hegemonic masculinity operate as a "holy trinity." He distinguished the modern sports bar, a traditionally gendered place, from the postmodern sports bar, a place where gender relations are rearranged into a commodified hybrid. The modern sports bar, according to Wenner, is a place to talk to your male peers, have a drink, and watch and discuss sports—places I remember hanging out with my father and grandfather after Detroit Tigers' games. In contrast, the postmodern sports bar is "designed as an experience as opposed to a real place" (Wenner, 1998, p. 323). He wrote,

> The postmodern sports bar does not seek to stimulate the "authenticity" of a local place. Designed for out-of-towners to catch the game and for the realization that fewer and fewer people live in the places they were from, the postmodern sports bar offers "memorabilia in the generic." A wide net is cast so that there is some identity hook for everyone, no [matter] what their favorite team, level of fanship, or geographic past. (p. 325)

The bars I frequented were of the postmodern type that Wenner described. Distinct from the smell (I remember the local taverns in Detroit as smelling like men's locker rooms) and look of local sports bars (worn furniture, photos of local sports heroes, and virtually all men—no women—sitting at bar stools), the bars I conducted my research in were airy, bright, lively, loud, and smelled good. The bar areas looked very similar in each city—a large rectangular perimeter that resembled a large table with four corners and a "wet area" in the middle serviced by bartenders. In contrast to the local sports bar, the sexual geography of the postmodern bars I frequented was more egalitarian. Men and women worked as bartenders and waiters. During the time I spent observing, the majority of people sitting at the bar were men, but women also sat there without noticeable harassment. The space was a metaphor for postmodern culture in general—a constant tension between democratization and commodification. In this space, I found that male hegemony was still present as in the older bar context but in a more understated way. As Wenner (1998) wrote, "In the postmodern sports bar, male hegemony does not go away, it is merely transformed by its reframing" (p. 327).

In each bar I visited, I sat at the large bar area and began socializing with patrons, discussing sports and current events. After some small talk, I asked them if they listened to *The Jim Rome Show.* Virtually all the men I approached stated that they listened to the show. I then informed them of my research project and asked them to do an audiotaped interview about their experience of the show. All agreed enthusiastically after I assured them of confidentiality. The interviews, generally lasting 20 min, were enjoyable and surprisingly substantive and informative. Although the common initial explanation for listening to *The Jim Rome Show* was "it's entertaining," the conversations also focused on issues of homosexuality, masculinity, and other social topics. Often, people shared very personal stories and thanked me for an "enlightening" or "thought-provoking" experience. The interviews confirmed the notion that sports talk can provide an oppor-

tunity for men to discuss and even raise their awareness of gender and sexual issues that they might not otherwise have.

In addition to interviewing people at sports bars, I taped *The Jim Rome Show* from April 30 through September 7, 2001—roughly 390 hr of programming (130 shows). I listened to each taped show and classified the content of the program into two general categories: (a) discussion of sports that centers on statistics and player/team performance and (b) discussion of larger social and political issues including racism, sexism, and homophobia. In my estimation, roughly 80% of the content of *The Jim Rome Show* was devoted to the former whereas social issues were the main topic 20% of the time. I also grouped the sociopolitical content into two general categories: hegemonic and counterhegemonic and found that roughly 70% of the discussion on such issues was hegemonic in nature.[16] In addition to grouping the show's content into these categories, I transcribed portions of the program when sexuality was discussed to conduct a close "reading" of the text. During the period in which I transcribed and analyzed *The Jim Rome Show,* four instances stand out as particularly important moments, what journalists often call "pegs"—critical events that generate a flurry of coverage (Grindstaff, 1994). In this case, the pegs generated discussion of homosexuality, prompting further commentary on other sports media programs. In the pages that follow, I analyze four topics that were widely discussed on *The Jim Rome Show* and other sports media programs as well as among the fans I interviewed. My analysis is connected to the larger media and cultural context. The period in which I taped the show was/is representative of a post-Clinton/Lewinsky, post-Bush inauguration, and pre–September 11, 2001, period of U.S. history. I intend to show links between the topics discussed on *The Jim Rome Show* and larger mediated discourse in general. By examining these pegs and placing them in their historical context, I hope to provide a forum in which to think through some of the ways that capitalism, hegemonic masculinity, sexuality, race, class, and consumption operates in contemporary U.S. culture.

Hegemonic Themes

As stated earlier, my analysis of the text confirms that much of the discourse on the show contains themes of misogyny, violence, and heterosexual dominance including themes that reinforced sexism and lesbian baiting. The following examples highlight these instances. The first is from an infamous program date July 23. On this date, Rome was commenting on the breaking story that several professional male athletes (Patrick Ewing, Terrell Davis, and Dekembe Motumbo) had testified in an Atlanta court that they regularly attended a strip club (The Gold Club) and engaged in sex acts with the some of the club's dancers.[17] This tabloidlike story was a great opportunity for Rome to engage in his sardonic "smack" talk. Here are Rome's acerbic comments on Patrick Ewing's admission that he received "free oral sex" at the Gold Club:

> Want some free oral sex Patrick [Ewing]? Nah, I'm good. Maybe next time! Come on! He said he'd been there 10 times. He said he had free oral sex 2 times. And by the way, who's going to say 'no' to free oral sex? I mean, clones, would you like some free oral sex? Who's going to say no to that [laughing]? Most athletes go to a club or restaurant and get comped some free drinks, chicken wings. . . . not Patrick, he gets comped free oral sex.
>
> [later in his monologue] Meanwhile, a former stripper testified. And it's a good thing. We finally have some good testimony. She testified that she performed sex acts or witnessed other dancers perform sex acts on celebrities including Terrell Davis and Dekembe Motumbo. So in response to the proverbial question, "who wants to sex Motumbo?" The answer obviously is whichever skank's turn it is at the Gold Club.

In this section of the transcript, Rome employs a very common, taken-for-granted

discourse—"the heterosexual male sexual drive discourse" (Hare-Mustin, 1994). This dominant ideology is predicated on the notion that women are objects (Rome misogynistically refers to the dancers as "skanks") who arouse men's heterosexual urges, which are assumed to be "natural and compelling" (Hare-Mustin, 1994, p. 24). Accordingly, men cannot control their primitive sexual yearnings, and women are blamed for inflaming them. This assumption, reproduced by Rome's rhetorical question, "who is going to turn down 'free' oral sex," reinforces women's subjugation as they become defined as existing solely for men's pleasure.

Rome's language takes on homophobic tones later in the same program. In this excerpt, Rome ridicules a former dancer's testimony:

> Finally we are getting somewhere. I thought Ewing's testifying of getting 'hummers' was going to be the best that the trial had to offer. Thankfully, it's not. In fact, not even close! After Patrick was done humiliating himself, one of the hookers got on the stand. That's when it really got good. A former dancer at the club starting naming names! This is just the beginning. This 'tramp' also testified that she went back to the hotel room of a former wrestling executive, to perform sex acts, not on him, but on his wife! Now, we are getting somewhere. Sex with athletes; lesbian sex acts with the wives of executives. That's what I was hoping for from the beginning! And this tramp also added that she and another dancer performed a lesbian sex show for Ewing and some friends before he was given free oral sex by other dancers. And perhaps the most amazing thing, this tramp that ratted everybody out, is now working at a day care center in Georgia. Wonderful. Who wouldn't want to leave their kids with a woman who used to be a hooker? There's no one I would trust my kids with more than a woman who used to perform lesbian sex shows for NBA centers and sex with wrestling executive's wives. What a perfect person to have around children! Man, I can't wait to see what happens today in the trial. I wonder who else's life will be ruined today?

Many of the callers on the September 9 program also reproduced male hegemony during their takes. Here is the call of the day:

Dan: [Contemptuously] I feel sorry for those skanks. I mean Ewing, Motumbo![18] Hopefully, the dancers got time and a half! I guess America has finally found a job worse than Assistant Crack Whore. About the only thing good to come out of this sordid mess is that Motumbo finally found a bar where his pickup line works.

Rome: [Laughing] Good job Dan!

Rome and his production staff chose this take as the call of the day, and in doing so, they support offensive, masculinist humor.[19] Dan's behavior reflects a common social practice for many men—the desire to earn the homosocial approval of other, more powerful men such as Jim Rome. Rome has power over the discourse and decides that Dan's wit gives him the right to enter the homosocial space of male privilege. Yes, Dan attempts to hold the players accountable for their behavior. However, the underlying tone of Dan's comments—"crack whore" and "skanks"—are racialized and sexist.

Rome's comments on athletes receiving oral sex at a strip club references the Clinton/Lewinsky affair and the increasing media focus on sex scandals in the lives of public figures. Although the "tabloidization" of the media has many negative consequences, Lumby (2001) posited that it is not completely destructive. In fact, the increased media attention on private sexuality is because of, in part, the "feminist project of politicizing the private sphere and its attendant issues, such as sexual harassment, domestic violence, and child care" (p. 234). "Bad" tabloid style press may actually stem from some "good" political motives that have focused on issues that were once seen as merely personal. Yet the media focus on Clinton and Rome's focus on athletes at the Gold Club elides a feminist analysis of structures of power (Clinton with an intern or famous athletes with female sex workers). Hence, the entertainment value of sex scandals undermines the feminist goal of politicizing the private and reinforces "patriarchal sexuality morality: a proscription of sexual behavior outside the bounds of heterosexual monogamous marriage and the violation of that proscription by power and privileged males" (Jakobsen, 2001, p. 307).

Entertainment and Male Hegemony

How do fans themselves make sense of and respond to Rome's problematic masculinist commentary? Not surprising, many of the fans I spoke to found it humorous; "It's entertaining" was the most common response. In fact, 2 days after Rome's acerbic comments about the incidents at the Gold Club, the topic came up with George (all the names of my research participants have been changed to preserve anonymity), a 27-year-old White male, in a sports bar in Sacramento. While inquiring about what he finds appealing about Rome, he replied,

I listen every day. He tells like it is. He lets it rip. He doesn't hold back. I like that! And he's entertaining! He pokes fun at people like the other day when Rome went off about the Ewing [Gold Club incident]. It's funny! It reminds me of locker room humor. Yes, I get a kick out of his smack talk. It's pure entertainment. Like when he trashes NASCAR and the WNBA.

His friend, John (a 26-year-old White male), echoed similar sentiments:

Yeah, Rome is hilarious. I thought it was hilarious when he called Jim Everett, "Chris." That's what sticks in my head when someone says something about Rome. He's kind of like the Rush Limbaugh or Howard Stern of sports talk radio. Like he thinks he's God. But I don't mind it because he's entertaining. And it's a way for him to get the ratings and the market share. I admire that because I am a stockbroker. You need to market yourself to stand out. You need to be aggressive and controversial to be successful in today's society. The show makes men cocky—like the clones. I listen to it for the entertainment. And he does know his sports.

Such comments are fairly representative of the participants that I interviewed. Many men valorize Rome's "transnational business masculinity," a term coined by Connell (2000) to describe egocentrism, conditional loyalties, and a commitment to capital accumulation. In addition, as stated above, many participants found the program pleasurable because Rome is knowledgeable, authoritative, and comedic. Implied here is the notion that listening to Rome is a natural as well as an innocent pleasure. One person, when asked about the so-called harmlessness of the program, said, "If you don't like it, turn the radio dial. No one is forcing you to listen. Its just entertainment!" This is a common response to critiques of the negative effects of media culture and audience pleasure. Yet amusement is neither innate nor harmless. Pleasure is learned and closely connected to power and knowledge (Foucault, 1980b). As media scholar Dougas Kellner (1995) observed,

> We learn what to enjoy and what we should avoid. We learn when to laugh and when to cheer. A system of power and privilege thus conditions our pleasures so that we seek certain socially sanctioned pleasures and avoid others. Some people learn to laugh at racist jokes and others learn to feel pleasure at the brutal use of violence. (p. 39)

The media industry, therefore, often mobilizes pleasure around conservative ideologies that have oppressive effects on women, homosexuals, and people of color. The ideologies of hegemonic masculinity, assembled in the form of pleasure and humor, are what many of my participants found most enjoyable about *The Jim Rome Show,* including Rome's aggressive, masculinist, "expert" speech that ridicules others. Thus, many of the pleasurable aspects of the program may encourage certain male listeners to identify with the features of traditional masculinity.

Calling The Rome Show: Homosociality and Approval

I was also interested in what listeners of the program thought of callers' comments and if they

had ever called the program themselves. Many enjoyed listening to callers such as Dan and found their commentary to constitute comical moments of the show. I was particularly interested in what calling in to the show might mean for men who subscribe to traditional masculinity. One of the main aspects of traditional masculine homosociality involves men's striving and competing for prestige and approval within their peer groups (Wenner, 1998). This striving provides the basis for an affiliation. Many people I interviewed stated that the ultimate compliment would be for Jim Rome to approve of their take if they called. To have your call "racked" by the leading sports media personality would be a revered honor. What's more, from within the terms of hegemonic masculinity, having one's call rejected may signify a "failure" of masculinity. The following dialogue occurred between me and Fred (a 44-year-old Black male):

David: Have your called the program before?

Fred: No, I never have called. I thought about calling but I would hate to get run [Rome disconnecting the call]. Man, that would hurt! I sometimes think, "Man, I could give a good take . . . but if I call and 'suck' . . . you know . . . get run, start stuttering . . . man that would be embarrassing.

David: What would be embarrassing about getting run?

Fred: It's embarrassing 'cause it's Jim Rome. He's the man [laughing]! He's the pimp in the box![20] Man, if you get racked and are the caller of the day, you're the man!

As stated earlier in this article, some scholars believe that sports and the media expanded to create a homosocial institution that functions to assuage men's fear of feminization in current postmodern culture. Some of my interviews appear to confirm this view. When asked why *The Jim Rome Show* and other sports talk radio programs are so popular among heterosexual men, about one half of the men told me that they feel anxious and uncertain because of the changes in men's work and women's increasing presence in the public sphere. Moreover, several participants believed that sports talk provides a safe haven for men to bond and reaffirm their essential masculinity. Here's what a 27-year-old White male said in a bar in Tampa:

> It's [*The Jim Rome Show*] a male bonding thing, a locker room for guys in the radio: You can't do it at work, everything's PC [politically correct] now! So the Rome Show is a last refuge for men to bond and be men. It's just in your car, Rome, and it's the audience that you can't see. I listen in the car and can let that maleness come out. I know its offensive sometimes to gays and women . . . you know . . . when men bond . . . but men need that! Romey's show gives me the opportunity to talk to other guy friends about something we share in common. And my dad listens to Romey also. So my dad and I bond also.

This comment is telling about the mixed effects of sports talk. On one hand, sports talk radio allows men to express a "covert intimacy"[21] (Messner, 1992) and shared meaning about a common subject matter. This bonding can bring forth genuine moments of closeness and should not necessarily be pathologized or seen as completely negative. However, much of the bonding is, as the interviewee stated, "offensive sometimes to gays and women." Many of the men I interviewed were speaking in a group context in the presence of other male peers. The gender displays (sexist and homophobic jokes, for example) by the men I interviewed in the homosocial space of a sports bar were interesting to observe as they confirmed Messner's (2002) point that men in groups define and solidify their boundaries through aggressive misogynistic and homophobic speech and actions. Underneath this bonding experience are homoerotic feelings that must be warded off and neutralized through joking, yelling, cursing, and demonizing anybody who does not conform to normative masculinity. Pronger (1990) argued the arena of sports is paradoxical: on one hand, sports is a primary for the

expression of heterosexual masculinity, and on the other hand, there is a powerful homoerotic undercurrent subliminally present in sports. Sports radio operates similarly as an extension of this paradoxically homosocial and homoerotic space. Shields (1999), in his analysis of sports radio, stated, "It would be impossible to overstate the degree to which sports talk radio is shadowed by the homosexual panic implicit in the fact that it consists almost entirely of a bunch of out-of-shape White men sitting around talking about Black men's buff bodies" (p. 50).

Lesbian Baiting

Sabo and Jansen (2000) suggested that radio talk shows are regular forums for men to lament and demonize lesbians or "dykes" in sport. A vivid example of lesbian baiting occurred on Jim Rome's September 7 show. Rome began the program with comments about a story in *Sports Illustrated* that claimed that ex-coach of the Detroit WNBA team, Nancy Lieberman, was rumored to have had an affair with one of her players. Consider Rome's bombastic and derisive comments about this rumor:

> Not surprisingly, Liebermen is divorced from her husband right now. I can't imagine why! I would think that your wife having a lesbian affair with one of your players would make your marriage that much stronger! Lieberman continues to deny the accusation. "I did nothing wrong. I was never in a relationship with her [the guard]. I mentored her to the best of my ability. If the media can write that Hilary Clinton's gay, write that Oprah Winfrey's gay, write that Rosie O'Donnell is gay, I guess that is the hand I am dealt with. Again, I did nothing wrong" end of quote. Wow! Look Nancy, stop the lies [Yelling]! . . . She has inferior ability. You are kicking it with her by the pool. You don't think your players are going to resent that? And leave Hilary, "Obese" Winfrey, and Rosie "O'Fat" out of this. I imagine they loved you tracking their name through this by pointing the finger at them as lesbians by the media.

This is another instance of Rome's loyalty to hegemonic masculinity. One way to interpret the above passage is that Rome is simply criticizing the unethical behavior of a coach supposedly having an affair with a player. Closer scrutiny, however, reveals that he is also marginalizing the presence of lesbians in sports.[22] Lesbians present a unique threat to the maintenance of male hegemony in sport as do women generally. The visibility of lesbians in sport contests the idea that sports are naturally a "manly" pursuit by rupturing cultural associations between masculinity and heterosexual potency. As Crosset (1995) posited, "The media industry has a stake in maintaining the image of sport as a resource for doing masculinity. It sells" (p. 126). For this reason, Rome's ridiculing of lesbians preserves male hegemony in sport.[23]

While talking to a heterosexual couple (both listened to the program and described themselves as committed sports fans), I asked the husband, Sam, what he made of Rome's sexist humor. Sam said that he thought it was ironic and should not be taken literally:

> **Sam:** I mean Rome's joking about lesbians and women is tongue in cheek. Neither he nor the clones mean it literally. I mean it's not like you are going to start gay bashing or treating your wife or daughter poorly! It's just playful satire!
>
> **Dave:** But why find that type of humor funny—humor at the expense of lesbians and women—even if it is tongue-in-cheek humor?
>
> **Sam:** I don't know, maybe men are feeling mixed . . . unsure about being all gender sensitive and politically correct.

Sam is suggesting that the humorous content of *The Jim Rome Show* provides men a space to playfully mediate the changing and tenuous nature of hegemonic masculinity; he describes Rome's misogyny as "ironic" not as sexist. However, as Jackson, Stevenson, and Brooks (2002) stated about satire and men's magazines (*Maxim* and *Loaded,* for example), "Irony allows you to have your cake and eat it. It allows you to express an unpalatable truth in a disguised form, while

claiming it is not what you mean" (p. 103). Hence, irony, while making visible the ambivalence men feel toward traditional masculinity, ultimately works to mask oppressive, patriarchal aspects of this masculinity in the form of humor. More interesting, Sam's wife Susan, a self-proclaimed feminist, fervently disagreed with her husband's views about the so-called innocence of the humor on the show:

> Okay, Jim Rome may know his sports. But he's a macho asshole like Rush or Stern. Sarcastic humor is not innocent [looking at Sam]! But I mostly hate the program because of the men I know that are fans of the show. I know some men at work who love the show, and call themselves, "clones." These guys have never grown up! It's like they are still in a fraternity! The Jim Rome Fraternity of men who never grow up! And they are all very sexist and make homophobic jokes all the time. I think Rome is dangerous and wrong.

Counterhegemonic Themes

As the above analysis illuminates, *The Jim Rome Show* reinforces male hegemony. However, a close reading of the show reveals some contradiction and fissures to hegemony. The following transcripts of the program exemplify times when the text and its voices (Jim Rome, audience members) partially subvert hegemonic masculinity and homophobia. The first example is from the show dated April 30 when the topic of bigotry was raised by Rome. Here, Rome, in his belligerent vocal style, is taking issue with the homophobic comments made by Chicago Cubs pitcher, Julian Tavares, about San Francisco Giants fans:

> Julian Tavarez, a pitcher for the Cubs said this about San Francisco Giants fans—his words not mine—"they are a bunch of a-holes and faggots." . . . You know, it would be nice to go a week without some racist or bigot comment . . . but no, Julian. Nice job Julian. . . . And here's a thought, Julian Rocker [reference to John Rocker, a pitcher who became famous for making racist and homophobic comments during an interview in *Sports Illustrated*], just

because San Francisco has a significant gay population, I would be willing to bet that not everybody at a Giants game is a homosexual. Maybe. Can't document that. Just a thought . . . I feel pretty secure in saying that? How do you come up with this garbage? I mean how do you get to the point where the proper response to heckling fans is to drop racist, anti-Semitic, or homophobic bombs on people? And even if you had those bigoted views, you would have the sense to keep it yourselves. They might realize that not everybody hates everybody else. I think there is only one solution to this problem of overcrowding in the racist frat house. We are going to have to have honorary members.

In this instance, the host clearly positions himself as antiracist and antihomophobic. This stance is noteworthy and a possible contradiction to dominant sports talk discourse. Rome uses his masculine authority to stand against the intolerance often engendered by homophobia.

Rome's comments on the subject appear to be progressive and reasonable.[24] On closer examination, however, Rome's location of the problem of homophobia in a few bigoted, intolerant individuals leaves unchallenged the larger societal structures that perpetuate heterosexism. The stance taken up by the host is rooted within liberal discourse, which reduces analysis to an individual, private endeavor (Kane & Lenskyj, 2000; Kitzinger, 1987) and forecloses any serious discussion of homophobia as structural and political issues related to power, gender, and sexuality. When Rome denounces a few athletes as "bigots," it prevents a wider analysis of the link between the institution of organized sports and its heterosexual, masculinist, and homophobic agenda. Addressing the thorny questions of sexuality, politics, power, and privilege would be a risky and bold move for *The Jim Rome Show,* as it would offer a more radical challenge to the institution of heterosexual privilege and sports.

The next seemingly subversive segment relates to an editorial letter in the May 2001 issue of *Out* magazine. In that issue, editor in chief, Lemon, stated that his boyfriend was a Major League baseball player. Lemon did not give names but hinted that the player was from an East Coast franchise. Rome and other mainstream media programs reacted quickly to the editorial. A media firestorm resulted in a rumor mill: Players, fans, owners, and sports talk radio hosts swapped guesses and anxieties over the athlete's identity.

On May 18, Rome's monologue pondered the questions, What would happen if that person's identity became public? What would it mean for baseball, gays, and lesbians in sports in general, and for the man himself? Given that Lemon's boyfriend would be the first athlete in one of the "big four" major league team sports (baseball, football, basketball, and hockey) to come out "during" his career, what effect would this have on the institution of sport? Rome decided to pose this question to one of his interview participants that day, well-respected baseball veteran Eric Davis.

> **Rome:** What would happen if a teammate of yours, or any baseball player, would come out of the closet and say, "I am gay"? What would the reaction be like? How badly would that go?
>
> **Eric:** I think it would go real bad. I think people would jump to form an opinion because everybody has an opinion about gays already. But I think it would be a very difficult situation because with us showering with each other . . . being around each other as men. Now, you're in the shower with a guy who's gay . . . looking at you . . . maybe making a pass. That's an uncomfortable situation. In society, they have never really accepted it. They want to come out. And if that's the cause fine but in sports, it would definitely raise some eyebrows. . . . I don't think it should be thrown at 25 guys saying, "yeah I am gay."
>
> [Rome changes the subject . . . no follow-up]

Rome asks a pointed question to Davis whose predictable homophobic response warrants more follow-up questions. Yet Rome shifts the subject to something less problematic, letting Davis off the hook. After Rome ends the interview, he addresses Davis's comments in another monologue:

> That's [Eric Davis] a 17-year respected major league ballplayer. And I think that's a representative comment of a lot of these guys. . . . He is very highly regarded guy. This is why I asked him the question. And he answered it very honestly. He would be concerned about having a gay teammate. . . . For instance, when he's showering. Personally, I don't agree with the take. It's my personal opinion. However, I posed the question to see what the reaction would be. And this is what I have been saying since this story broke. This is why it would not be a good thing. This is why the editor of that magazine clearly was wrong and has never been in a locker-room or clubhouse. That's why it hasn't happened. Eric Davis' reaction is what you would expect. Not everybody would feel that way, but a large majority would. It would make it nearly impossible for a gay player to come out.

Here, Rome is aware of the difficulties that would occur for an openly gay ballplayer. However, he shares his opinion in the safety of his "expert" monologue, not in the presence of Eric Davis. He does not risk compromising his masculinity or his relationship with Davis by endorsing this unusually progressive stance in the presence of a famous ballplayer such as Davis. However, when a listener calls immediately after the Davis interview, Rome responds differently:

> **Joe:** I never imagined my first take would be on gays but I had to call. Being gay, it matters to no one but gays themselves. Why don't you guys, girls or gays . . . whatever you guys are. Just do us a favor, do yourselves a favor and keep it to yourselves. I mean . . . [Rome runs the caller with the buzzer and disconnects the call]
>
> **Rome:** I think that's a very convenient response—"It's an issue only because you make it an issue." I don't agree with that frankly. It's an issue because they are often persecuted against, harassed, assaulted, or killed in some cases. That's why it is an issue.

They are fired from jobs, ostracized. It's not only an issue because they are making it an issue. What you are saying is keep your mouth shut, keep it in the closet; you are not accepting them for whom they are and what they are. It's not an issue because they are making it an issue. It's an issue because of people saying things like, "keep your mouth shut. . . . We don't want you around. . . . We don't want to know you people exist." That's why it's an issue because of that treatment.

Again, Rome takes a strong stance against homophobia and demonstrates a fairly nuanced appreciation of the injustices of homophobia and heterosexism. This position is worth mentioning, particularly in the context of a program referred to as "The Jungle" with an audience of mostly men steeped in traditional masculinity and for whom heterosexuality is the unquestioned norm. Rome's antihomophobic stance represents a fissure in hegemonic masculinity. It can potentially foster a new awareness in Rome's listeners and invite new voices into this important conversation about masculinity and sexuality, potentially spurring a rethinking of masculinity and sports. Cutting off the first-time caller because of his homophobic comment could be viewed as a productive accountable maneuver, which is notable because straight men do not have a rich history of holding other straight men responsible for homophobic slurs.[25]

The historic May 18 radio show generated further substantive discussion on the issue of sports and heterosexual dominance in various media sites. This included a two-part show on Jim Rome's Fox TV show, *The Last Word,* titled "The Gay Athlete." The show's guests included two out athletes: Diana Nyad and Billy Bean. The show's discussion was very rich with the host asking fairly nuanced and enlightened questions. Since this show, Rome has interviewed other athletes who have come out since they left professional sports including football players, Esera Tuaolo and David Kopay. In these interviews, Rome asked perceptive questions about the prevalence of homophobia in male sports and applauds their courage in coming out. ESPN also addressed the same topic and conducted a poll that showed that a substantial number of sports fans would have no problem with a gay athlete ("Outside the Lines," 2001). What's more, the *Advocate* magazine published an article by cultural critic Toby Miller (2001) where he argued that the media firestorm generated by Brendan Lemon's article could potentially create a moment "for unions and owners of the big four to issue a joint statement in support, to show that queers are a legitimate part of the big leagues" (p. 3).

Another significant moment occurred on the May 18 show when Rome read the "huge e-mail of the day," usually reserved for the nastiest comments. Rome chose an e-mail from "Mike from San Gabriel," who wrote the following:

> Jim, Eric Davis is perhaps the quintessential baseball player/human being who has overcome tremendous odds in battling and overcoming cancer and physical challenges. He's faced and battled a disease that strikes fear into the heart, and understands that life must be taken a day at a time.
>
> Yet, despite this brush with death and the clarity in some areas that it brings, Eric's reaction to your question regarding baseball players' reactions to knowing that a teammate is gay spoke volumes, and none of it particularly heartening. Eric's fear (speaking for the average baseball player, that is) that a gay player may be checking him out in the shower is representative of the stereotypes foisted upon homosexuals in our society, and in baseball in particular. I find it a little sad and ironic that an African-American player would espouse a viewpoint—fear, ignorance and intolerance—that for much of baseball's history had kept some of the best players in history—African-Americans—out of the Major Leagues.
>
> Perhaps, though, baseball may play a progressive role in our society once again. Like it did in helping to erase the "color" barrier in the 1950s, so too it may be able to play a part in fostering tolerance and acceptance in society today. I think it's going to take someone the

stature of a Jackie Robinson from the gay community to help allay the fears of baseball players, and in turn our society, before progress can be made. Until then, gay baseball players will be relegated to a shadowy world of fear and intolerance once reserved for African-Americans and other minorities.
>
> Mike

Mike's comments caught the attention of the editor of Outsports.com, Mike Buzinski, who commented that Mike's e-mail of the day was "well-written" and "gay-positive." In the Web site article titled "Give the Media Good Marks: Coverage of Closeted Gay Baseball Player was Positive and Non-Judgmental," Buzinski (2001) went on to write:

> Lesbian basketball fans and gay Major League Baseball players have been all the rage in the sports media the past two weeks. This alone is unprecedented. The mainstream media barely acknowledges the existence of gay athletes or fans. Having the issue raised in, among others, *The New York Times, The Los Angeles Times,* Internet discussion boards and sports talk radio is all to the good. Even better is that, overall, the coverage was balanced, informative and non-homophobic. (p. 1)

Later in the same article he refers to Jim Rome:

> The tenor of talk radio (at least when I was listening) was not as Neanderthal as one might have expected. Jim Rome, the guy who called Jim Everett "Chris" a few years ago, has been very enlightened on the gay issue, saying it's nobody's business, while at the same time acknowledging the difficulties an "out" athlete might face. (p. 2)
>
> Rome's stance against homophobia is groundbreaking and historic in sports talk radio.

Ultimately, however, the perspective articulated by "Mike" and supported by Rome once again confines the meaning of homophobia in sports to the intolerant or ignorant behavior of individuals and locates the responsibility for changing that behavior in gay players and/or Black athletes, who, after all, should "understand" about discrimination. Mike's letter and Rome's comments also innocently presume that African Americans have achieved equality in sports and in the larger society. This presumption, common in sports talk radio discourse, is informed by what Goldberg (1998) referred to as a "feel-good colorblindness of sports talk hosts" (p. 221).[26] Queer scholars have discussed how sexuality is often produced through the process of racialization (Gopinath, 1997; Munoz, 1999). By ignoring the intersection of race and sexuality, Rome saves sports from a more biting and transgressive critique, one that would expose the deep, institutional sexism and racism in sports. Instead, Rome refocuses the audience on the simple metaphors of sports—bad guy bigots and heroic gay athletes—rather than the larger discursive environment of sports and media that keep White, heterosexual masculinity at its center, thereby systematically excluding and oppressing all "others," including women, racial minorities, and gays.

Hence, there are contradictions in, and limitations to, Rome's "progressive" stance on sexuality. His comments espouse a liberal discourse that views homophobia as fearful behavior enacted by intolerant individuals.[27] Take, for example, Rome's careless dismissal of the caller who wants gays to stay in the closet. Although the caller's comments certainly reflect a homophobic viewpoint, Rome locates the blame in the caller as an individual, as if the caller is one of just a few, unenlightened bigots. A closer look at Rome's own discursive practices on the show, including homophobic references, jokes, and name calling, all point to the same homosocial fears that motivate the caller's concern. Perhaps the caller's comments are better understood as a reasonable (but repugnant) apprehension of gays and lesbians based on the widely shared perception that out gays and lesbians challenge heteronormativity and patriarchy. As Card (1995) pointed out, hatred and hostility toward homosexuals is not a pathological disorder of a few individuals. Rather, homophobia is a pervasive affliction that is not isolated in its effects.

Also embedded in this discourse is the assumption that the right, best way for gays and lesbians to live is out. Almost all parties in this dialogue refer to coming out, including Mike, Rome, Eric Davis, and the editor of *Out* magazine. As Gopinath (1997) observed, the "coming out narrative" assumes that people who have same-sex desire need to reveal their sexuality and become visible and also presupposes a universal gay subject. Coming out is viewed by Rome as a contested privilege, a "right," and the natural and logical next step in achieving "health" and an "authentic life." This identitarian narrative is supported by many people and institutions, including the mental health industry, straight allies, and in particular, by the dominant discourses of the urban gay community.

The Jim Rome Show suggests that coming out signifies freedom and egalitarianism. Although this stance can provide a very powerful option for persons who identify as gay or lesbian, coming out can also be another standard for sexual expression that people may feel obligated to meet. In addition, privileging the coming-out narrative can unwittingly work in the service of heteronormativity. Coming out requires that a person claim an identity as gay or lesbian. Foucault (1980a) suggested that claming a fixed identity as homosexual may be personally liberating but unintentionally relocates heterosexuality in the privileged center. Because straights are not required to come out and claim a heterosexual identity, heterosexuality is assumed to be natural and normal. Although Rome and his callers discuss homosexuality, heterosexuality is never interrogated or discussed hence remaining an unmarked and naturalized category.

It is important to note that Rome's interviewing of out athletes such as Billy Bean and David Kopay is a unique outcome in the world of heteronormative sports. To allow visibility of the gay athletes cannot be taken lightly in terms of its potential ramifications. Yet it is equally important to ask which athletes are allowed to become visible? What is their social location? How is their sexuality represented? Virtually all the gay athletes who have been on *The Jim Rome Show* are White males (an exception is Esera Tuaolo who is Samoan) who define homosexuality as an essentialist identity. Foucault (1980b) contended that although visibility opens up some new political possibilities, it is also "a trap" because it creates new forms of surveillance, discipline, and limits. Sure, Bean and Kopay are given space to discuss their experience as a gay athlete, however it must be contained within a very limited, private discourse. Scholar Duggan (2001) claimed that much of the recent visibility of gays and lesbians are framed within a post-Stonewall, identitarian, private discourse. She referred to this discourse as homonormativity—"a politics that does not contest dominant heteronormative assumptions and institutions, but upholds and sustains them, while promising the possibility of a demobilized gay constituency and a privatized, depoliticized gay culture anchored in domesticity and consumption" (p. 179). According to Duggan, homonormativity is privatizing much as heteronormativity is, and each lends support to the other. As much as Rome's recognition of gays in the sporting world is noteworthy, it is very much contained with a homonormative frame that reproduces the sex and gender binary. Hence, Rome's show although it may be influenced by traditional gay and lesbian identity politics; it is not a queer space. Athletes, including women who perform a more transgressive, non-normative sexuality, are invisible in sports radio.

Don't Ask Don't Tell

Sexuality and sports was again the subject of discussion of Rome's show on August 29. On the program that day, Rome was interviewing heavyweight boxers Lennox Lewis and Hasim Rahman about their upcoming title fight. During the interview, a war of words broke out because Rahman questioned Lewis's heterosexuality. Lewis became quite perturbed stating, "I am not gay! I'm 100% a woman's man." This verbal conflict continued later that day on an ESPN interview program. During the ESPN taping, a physical scuffle broke out between the two boxers as they

pushed each other and rolled around on the ground. The following day, Rome discussed the incident, and the subsequent brawl on ESPN on his program focusing mainly on the question of whether the incident was staged to hype the fight. Rome argued that the harsh feelings between Rahman and Lewis were "genuine," that the incident was not staged. Yet in focusing on the theatrics or authenticity of the scuffle, Rome failed to address the inappropriateness of Rahman's homophobic slur.

The host did make an attempt, however, to address some of his callers' heterosexist/homophobic comments in the wake of the incident. On the August 30 radio show, many clones called pronouncing that Lewis' strong reaction to Rahman's assertion proves that Lewis is gay. Hence, homophobic gossip questioning Lewis' sexuality became the spotlight of the talk. In this next excerpt, Rome criticizes Rahman's allegations and the callers' fixations with Lewis' sexual orientation:

> Personally, I don't care. It's nobody's business what that guy [Lewis] does outside of the ring. It's nobody's business but Lennox's. I don't care. But apparently, he does. He says he is not. I don't care whether he is or isn't. I tell you what—HE'S NOT GOING TO STAND FOR ANYBODY SAYING HE IS. He made that pretty clear. I don't think Rahman should have said what he said. He should not have said quote, "That was gay of you to go to court to get me to fight." But, I tried to point out to Lennox that he's not calling you a homosexual, he's saying "it was gay to go to court." Lennox didn't want to hear it. He didn't make the distinction. And yes, it is a little peculiar that he got that hot that quickly, but I don't really care.

Here again, Rome takes up a "tolerant" position by asserting that sexual orientation should not matter and gossip about Lewis's sexuality is improper. Yet, by stating that sexual orientation makes no difference to him, Rome is once again invoking a liberal, privatized argument that contradicts his previous intolerance of the same "don't ask, don't tell position" held by a caller. In addition, his comments mirror the "don't ask, don't tell policy" on gays in the military. Queer theory scholar McWhorter (1999) critiqued this personalized approach to homophobia:

> When tolerant people insist that that my homosexuality doesn't matter to them, they say in effect that my homosexuality is not a social or cultural phenomenon at all but rather some sort of brute quality inherent in me and totally disconnected from them; they say in effect that my homosexuality is a kind of object that is obviously there but has nothing to do with me as a person. Thus, this "tolerance" in the final analysis amounts basically to the same stance as that taken by reductivistic homophobes. (p. 3)

In summary, Rome's position of tolerance is praiseworthy. Yet his stance is less than revolutionary if one takes critiques such as McWhorter's into account. Rome's discourse replicates essentialism—the idea that sexuality can be reduced to some biological essence—an ideology that replicates heternormativity by failing to examine sexuality in a historical, social, and political context.

Many of the people I interviewed in sports bars appreciated that Rome and his show addressed larger, social issues. The overwhelming majority of interviewees respected and agreed with Rome's opinion or takes on the issues of gender and sexuality. For many, the show was the main forum for them to discuss and reflect on wider, political matters. The following is a conversation I had with Nick, a 26-year-old Latino male in Fresno that reflects the dominant discourse of don't ask, don't tell:

Nick: Romey is like a sports sociologist with humor. He's entertaining. He's really into the gay issue. He's an advocate for gay rights. I respect him for it but because he speaks his mind.

David: Why do you respect him for that?

Nick: Personally, I don't care what gays do. But it's not cool that gays have to stay in the closet. But I don't think gays in team sports won't work because so many athletes are macho and homophobic.

Nick's comments are fairly representative of the conversations I had with fellow fans. All 18 people I interviewed respected and agreed with Rome's tolerant position on the issue of homosexuality and sport—a position, although progressive in the context of sports talk radio, is limited because it ignores larger structures that promote heterosexism. Although all made it clear that they were heterosexual, my interviewees indicate that some men who listen to sports talk radio are somewhat open minded on the issue of homosexuality and sports.

I don't know if this attitude is representative of the larger Rome audience. It may not be, because *The Jim Rome Show* Web site (www.jimrome.com) contained 16 pages in which self-described clones passionately opposed Rome's antihomophobic takes. Here's an example of the deep-seated homophobia expressed on the Web site message board. It reveals how those who subscribe to dominant masculinity feel threatened by Rome's position:

> My 13-year-old was working with me at my business today, and we were listening to Rome when he takes off in his "gay defender" mode. My son looks at me and says, "Dad, what's wrong with this guy? He thinks homosexuality is normal?" Well, clue-in Romey—it IS wrong: morally, and in every other way. Why you pander to this group is beyond comprehension.

There were other responses on the fan message board that questioned Rome's genuineness stating that his progressive stance on homophobia was primarily motivated as a marketing strategy to stir up controversy and recruit new listeners. Some on the message board found Rome's stance to be hypocritical as Rome himself has made homophobic references in the past. One of the men I interviewed also stated that Rome's position on homosexuality was hypocritical:

> A contradiction! He's totally a hypocrite. Here is a so-called gay advocate on one breath and in the next breath, he refers to the LPGA as the

"dyke" tours. And remember, he's the guy who got famous for calling Jim Everett, "Chrissie." Plus, he panders to athletes and celebrities such as Jay Mohr. I was listening to Romey in May when Mohr called Mike Hampton [a baseball pitcher] a "gay Curious George." Rome laughed at this and lauded Mohr's brilliant humor. He's not progressive. If he were progressive, he would confront homophobes. He's just another macho dude who's using social issues and controversy to gain market share, profits, and more radio affiliates.

Female Listeners

Because many of Rome's comments were sexist, I was also interested in finding out how women listeners experience the show. In addition to Susan, I interviewed Joan, a 31-year-old White woman hanging out in a bar in Las Vegas. Diverging from Susan's opinion, Joan believed Rome to be progressive on gender and sexual issues, In fact, she was the only person I interviewed who actually called the program. Here's part of our dialogue at a bar in Las Vegas:

> **Joan:** I actually called. My voice was heard. He was cool. He didn't bag me. I didn't speak the clone language. I am me! I called to state that violence should stay in hockey—hockey is not hockey without violence—I feel very strong about that.
> **David:** What was cool about Rome?
> **Joan:** He's cool to women. He's not sexist or homophobic. He respected my call. I know sexist guys. I have lived with them. My ex-husband was one. He was very violent and mean. I lived in a bad environment. I left him and moved to Vegas. I no longer will be around men who are offensive or demeaning to women.
> **David:** And you don't experience that from Rome, him saying sexist comments?
> **Joan:** No, I don't feel that from him. I don't see him as demeaning to women. If he were a sexist, I wouldn't listen to his show.

Joan's comments could be seen as firmly grounded in postfeminist discourse that replicates hegemonic masculinity.[28] Her comments advocate continued violence in hockey, and she does not experience Rome as sexist despite Rome's repeated misogynistic references on the show. Joan presents herself as "one of the guys" and replicates a patriarchal view of the show and its contents. Her response is further indication the listeners of *The Jim Rome Show,* dependent on their social location, read the text in multiple ways.

Conclusion

At this historical moment when hegemonic masculinity has been partially destabilized by global economic changes and by gay liberation and feminist movements, the sports media industry seemingly provides a stable and specific view of masculinity grounded in heterosexuality, aggression, individuality, and the objectification of women. *The Jim Rome Show,* with its aggressive, male-talking host and masculinist themes, is located within this hypermasculine space.

However, my analysis indicates that *The Jim Rome Show* is not a simple, completely obnoxious site of monolithic masculine discourse. Rather, the show represents a complex, paradoxical, ambivalent, and polyvalent text. *The Jim Rome Show* fosters a mix of masculine styles, identities, and discourses, ranging from highly misogynistic to liberal humanist. My article notes some of the discontinuous and contradictory moments that disrupt hegemonic masculinity and heterosexual dominance; it considers Jim Rome's antihomophobic stance to be somewhat progressive given the context and hypermasculine discursive space of sports talk radio.

In my effort to recognize the complexity and contradictory elements of the text, I suggest that the antihomophobic tenor of the radio program, although laudable, is informed by a liberal-humanist approach that elides substantive interrogation and political discussion of the structures of heterosexual domination. Moreover, Rome's examination of homophobia focuses entirely on sexuality and sexual identity; issues of race fall by the wayside, making his analysis monothematic. Whiteness and hetero-normativity stay at the privileged center.

It is also important to note that *The Jim Rome Show* is a highly popular, commercialized radio program owned by a giant corporation (Premiere Radio Network) that privileges profits, niche marketing, and audience ratings over challenging oppressive practices and institutions. Consequently, Rome's show tends toward a more conservative "reproductive agency" (identification with corporate consumerism that stabilizes oppressive social institutions) than a more radical or transgressive "resistant agency" (Dworkin & Messner, 1999).

My audience analysis suggests that *The Jim Rome Show* may, in the end, stabilize the institution of heteronormativity. I showed how the textual content greatly influences the ways audience members understand the show's messages. The participants interviewed generally held conservative opinions about gender and sexuality that conform to the hegemonic masculine ideal. However, most of my interview participants did support Jim Rome's antihomophobic posture. Thus, further research should explore whether the text helps to transform the beliefs of men who have not yet acquired a sincere commitment to antihomophobia.

In addition, future research needs to investigate how gays and lesbians may experience this discursive space. *The Jim Rome Show* has been specifically created for heterosexuals to publicly discuss sports. Even if Rome is sometimes antihomophobic, how does this space feel for a gay or lesbian person? Even if Rome defends gays (and usually not lesbians), is his show a "safe haven" for queers? Does *The Jim Rome Show* simply re-create hierarchical power relations or is it a democratic site that opens up the potential for achieving real social justice? These questions are critical for future feminist inquiries into radio sports talk programs. Moreover, how has the discourse of the Rome show and other sports radio

programs changed since September 11, 2001? Has the discourse become more nationalistic?

It is also crucial to consider the role of pleasure in listening to sports talk radio while steering clear of the problems associated with uncritical, moralistic, and/or celebratory accounts of popular culture. I myself enjoy listening to the program even though I am aware of the sexist, homophobic themes. Pleasure is a double-edged sword: It provides opportunities for relaxation, bonding, but also makes the sexist and homophobic content seem more innocent and easier to dismiss or laugh off. Hence pleasure cannot be valorized per se but needs to be critically examined to determine whether the pleasure of a given moment in the text of the program is progressive, emancipatory, or destructive.

Regardless, it is important for critical media scholars and activists to leverage and build on those moments in the text that disrupt hegemonic masculinity and heterosexism. McKay, Messner, and Sabo (2000) suggested that there is a tendency for critical media studies and sports sociology to overemphasize negative outcomes for men in sports. They argued that this overemphasis on negative outcomes leads to a simplistic view of the incongruities in talk and commentary about sports.

Following this thesis, I think it is important for critical scholars and activists to be vigilant in noticing and promoting the possibilities for disruption and resistance within dominant media sport structures. The antihomophobic tenor of *The Jim Rome Show* is an opportunity to address heterosexual dominance in sports. Yes, Rome's radio program reveals the limits of liberal discourse, however, his progressive stance may be a starting point to influence men who are deeply embedded in hegemonic masculinity. Remember, Rome was not built in a day! Rome likely has more influence with many men who are recruited by the specifications of dominant masculinity than academic scholars and political activists. In other words, a radio community of men discussing sports may not be just simply reproducing hegemony—there is more complexity in this discursive space, including opportunities for men to engage in relationship building and to reinvent masculinity. Perhaps Haag's (1996) suggestion that sports talk discourse may serve as a blueprint for civic discourse has some merit here.

Although Rome's radio program is deeply embedded within corporate consumerism and tends more toward a more reproductive than resistant agency, it remains a potential channel for challenging hegemonic masculinity and homophobia. The contradictions, fissures, and ambivalences within the discursive space of *The Jim Rome Show* should not be trivialized. It is through those contradictory spaces that Rome's show may have potential for generating new conversations about masculinity and sexuality. Although *The Jim Rome Show* is situated within commercial culture, it does offer heterosexual men a rare public space for dialogue on homophobia and contemporary masculinity. Furthermore, I would assert that this discursive space is occupied in a multiplicity of ways, not all of which are immediately colonized by consumer capitalism. Hence, my study neither uncritically celebrates the show nor views the show in purely negative terms as a backlash against feminism and gay rights. Rather *The Jim Rome Show* offers a potential site to change gender relationships and identities, while concurrently reinscribing particular forms of traditional masculinity.

Appendix

In general, I asked the interviewed audience members the following questions:

1. How often do you listen to *The Jim Rome Show*?
2. What do you like most about the show?
3. What do you like least about the show?
4. What do you think the show means to most men who listen regularly to the program?
5. Why is the show popular with many men?
6. What is your view on Rome's position on various social issues?
7. Have you ever called the program?
8. What do you think of most of the takes of the callers?
9. What is your age? Race or ethnic group? Sex? Sexual orientation? Occupation if any? Sport participation?
10. What other television and radio programs do you consume?

Acknowledgments

Funding for this project was provided by a research grant from the Gay Lesbian Alliance Against Defamation (GLAAD), Center for Study of Media and Society. Permission granted by GLAAD to reprint/publish this article. Special thanks to Van Cagle, Kent Ono, Laura Grindstaff, Susan Kaiser, Gayatri Gopinath, Judith Newton, and Debora Nylund for their helpful suggestions as this article developed. I am also grateful to Van Cagle and GLAAD for their support of this project.

Notes

1. According to Arbitron ratings, *The Jim Rome Show* is ranked eighth in radio talk audience share. The most popular radio talk hosts, according to the ratings, are Rush Limbaugh and Dr. Laura. All three shows, Jim Rome, Rush Limbaugh, and Dr. Laura, are owned by Premiere Radio Network, a company worth U.S. $330 million dollars. These statistics are from Premiere Radio's Web site: www.premiereradio.com.

2. "Run" refers to the host hanging up on the caller.

3. Jim Rome's Web site (www.jimrome.com) has a 24-page glossary (known as "city jungle gloss") that lists his terms and the definitions. For instance," Jungle Dweller" refers to a frequent telephone contributor to Rome's show. "Bang" means to answer phone calls. "Bugeater" refers to a Nebraskan who is a fan of the Nebraska Cornhuskers' college football team.

4. The comment "What will Rome say next?" has been applied several times to listeners of the *Howard Stern Show,* for those who enjoy and despise it. This is (even) mentioned in the Howard Stern autobiographical movie, *Private Parts.*

5. Rome's relationship with his caller, similar to most talk-show power relations between caller and host, is quite asymmetrical. Hutchby (1996) in his study of the discourse in talk radio stated that although the host has an array of discursive and institutional strategies available to him or her to keep the upper hand, occasionally callers have some resources available to resist the host's powerful strategies. Hence, Hutchby argued that power is not a monolithic feature of talk radio. Hutchby's argument does not appear to work with *The Jim Rome Show* as callers hardly ever confront Rome's authority. Rather, Rome's callers want his approval.

6. Deregulation was championed by then FCC chairman Mark Fowler who sold it as a form of media populism and civic participation. However, this public marketing campaign masked increased economic consolidation and increased barriers to entry into this market for all but very powerful media conglomerates such as Infinity Broadcasting and Premiere Radio. Commenting about the success of conservative White male talk radio due to deregulation of the 1980s, Douglas (2002) claimed that Reaganism was successful by "selling the increased concentration of wealth as a move back toward democracy" (p. 491).

7. In 1960, there were just two radio stations in the United States that were dedicated to talk radio formats (Goldberg, 1998).

8. The other significant deregulatory move in the 1980s was the abandonment of the Fairness Doctrine, which the FCC announced it would no longer enforce. The doctrine required stations to offer access to air alternative opinions when controversial issues were discussed. The goal of the doctrine was to promote a balance of views. Opponents of the doctrine, including Fowler and Reagan, felt it inhibited freedom of speech. Stations, they argued, avoided giving airtime to opinionated individuals because of the requirement to broadcast competing points of view. Unrestricted by the Fairness Doctrine's mandate for balance, Limbaugh and a legion of ultraconservative imitators took off the gloves and revived the financial state of AM radio.

9. The largest sports station in the United States based in New York. WFAN is also the largest ad-billing radio station in the United States.

10. These popular hosts are known for being rude and abrupt to their callers. If the host disagrees with the callers' opinion, they are likely to be disconnected by being buzzed, flushed down the toilet, or run over by a bus.

11. The idea that contemporary masculinity is in crisis is an arguable point. Beynon (2002) suggested that it is misleading to assume that the current alleged crisis is new and unique to current times; that there are many historical periods when masculinity appeared to be in crisis. In fact, he argued that crisis is constitutive of masculinity itself.

12. Mariscal also disagreed with Haag's stating the national syndicated programs such as *The Jim Rome Show* undermines the regionalism of sports radio.

13. In a recent interview in *Sports Illustrated,* Rome stated he regrets the Everett interview and has matured into a well-reasoned interviewer. In the article, Rome stated that he was "wiser" because of being married and having a child (Deitsch, 2003).

14. I invited several women to be interviewed about *The Jim Rome Show.* However, only two stated that they listened to the show.

15. The local Sacramento sports talk affiliate runs a commercial that says, "Belly up to the bar and pour yourself a cold one! You are listening to your sports bar on the radio."

16. It is important to note that my coding scheme was based on my interpretation of what constitutes hegemony and counterhegemony; it is not an objective measure.

17. The court in Atlanta was prosecuting the owner of the Gold Club for mob connections and other illegalities. This event received a great deal of media attention.

18. Ewing and Motumbo are Black men. The caller of the day, Dan, is implying that they are unattractive men. Dan's disdainful "smack talk" could be understood to reproduce racist representations of Black athletes.

19. As a sidebar, Cook (2001) challenged the common notion that radio talk shows are a natural two-way dialogue between the caller and host that allow the caller to "freely air their point of view" (p. 62). The production process reveals that it is a complex, mediated process that constrains the dialogue through a range of in-studio control techniques. These hidden maneuvers include off-air talk decisions on what gets included on the program, what gets omitted,

and time control cues. Cook argued that examining the complex relational politics in radio talk is important to examine to contest its negative power and influence.

20. The term *pimp in the box* refers to Rome's "pimping" of NHL hockey in Los Angeles during 1992–1993 when the Los Angeles Kings made it to the Stanley Cup Finals. Rome's show was the first in Los Angeles to actively talk about hockey on sports talk stations and book hockey players as guests. This made national news as Wayne Gretzky was to appear on the show following every playoff game the Kings played that season to the point where Gretzky thanked Rome during a televised interview after the Kings won Game 7 of the Western Conference Finals to advance to the Finals. After thanking Kings management and players he said, "To my friend Jim Rome, we've got the karma going."

21. Messner (1992) defined "covert intimacy" as doing things together rather than mutual talk about inner lives.

22. Rome has consistently "bashed" the LPGA and the WNBA, sports with lesbian visibility.

23. Rome has a history of marginalizing lesbian athletes including Martina Navratilova, referring to her as "Martin" because of embodying qualities that are usually associated with maleness, such as strength, authority, and independence. In her book, *Female Masculinity,* Halberstam (1998) made a compelling argument for a more flexible taxonomy of masculinity, including not only biological men, who have historically held the power in society, but also women who perform a traditionally masculine persona. Halberstam argued "a major step toward gender parity, and one that has been grossly overlooked, is the cultivation of female masculinity" (p.3). Utilizing Halberstam's framework, Heywood and Dworkin (2003) suggested that athletes who perform female masculinity, such as Navratilova, create fissures in the heterosexual male preserve of sport.

24. When I refer to Rome in this section, I am referring not to Rome, the individual person. Rather, I am referring to Rome's discourse.

25. However, it is important to note that Rome asserts his authority over a person with less power—a first-time caller. Rome doesn't take this strong a stance with Eric Davis, a high-status person who likely has more influence within the sports world. This textual example reveals the power relations of talk radio;

hosts and famous athletes have more authority than callers.

26. Goldberg (1998) and Mariscal (1999) suggested that sports talk radio is more racialized than any other radio format.

27. Mariscal (1999), in his analysis of *The Jim Rome Show,* noted Rome's contradictory stance on race. At times, Rome is very progressive and antiracist, and other times Mariscal noted that Rome engaged in derogatory stereotypes toward Latinos. Mariscal stated that Rome's inconsistent stance on "racially charged topics reveal[s] the basic slippage in liberal discourse," (p. 116) a situation where citizens engage in post-civil rights speech that "slides easily from tepid antiracism to the reproduction of deeply ingrained racist clichés" (p. 116).

28. Postfeminism refers to the idea that women have already achieved full equality with men (Humm, 1995).

References

Ang, I. (1996). *Living room wars: Rethinking media audiences for a postmodern world.* New York: Routledge.

Armstrong, C. B., & Rubin, A. M. (1989). Talk radio as interpersonal communication. *Journal of Communication. 39*(2), 84–93.

Beynon, J. (2002). *Masculinities and culture.* Philadelphia: Open University Press.

Brod, H. (Ed.). (1987). *The making of masculinities.* Boston: Unwin Hyman.

Buzinski, J. (2000, July 13). *Week in review.* Available at www.outsports.com/

Buzinski, J. (2001, May 20). *Give the media good marks: Coverage of closeted gay baseball player was positive and non-judgmental.* Available at www.outsports.com/

Card, C. (1995). *Lesbian choices.* New York: Columbia University Press.

Collie, A. J. (2001, August 8). Rome rants. *American Way,* pp. 50–54, 56–57.

Connell, R. W. (1990). An iron man: The body and some contradictions of hegemonic masculinity. In M. A. Messner & D. F. Sabo (Eds.), *Sport, men, and the gender order* (pp. 83–95). Champaign, IL: Human Kinetics.

Connell, R. W. (2000). *The men and the boys.* Berkeley: University of California Press.

Cook, J. (2001). Dangerously radioactive: The plural vocalities of radio talk. In C. Lee & C. Poynton (Eds.), *Culture and text: Discourse and methodology in social research and cultural studies* (pp. 59–80). New York: Rowman & Littlefield.

Crosset, T. W. (1995). *Outsiders in the clubhouse: The world of women's professional golf.* Albany: State University of New York Press.

Deitsch, R. (2003, May 12). Under review: Rome returning. *Sports Illustrated, 98,* 28.

Douglas, S. J. (2002). Letting the boys be boys: Talk radio, male hysteria, and political discourse in the 1980s. In M. Hilmes & J. Loviglio (Eds.), *Radio reader: Essays in the cultural history of radio* (pp. 485–504). New York: Routledge.

Duggan, L. (2001). The new homonormativity: The sexual politics of neoliberalism. In R. Castronovo & D. D. Nelson (Eds.), *Materalizing democracy: Toward a revitalized cultural politics* (pp. 175–194). Durham, NC: Duke University Press.

Dworkin, S. L., Messner, M.A. (1999). Just do what? Sports, bodies, gender. In J. Lorber, M. M. Ferree, & B. Hess (Eds.), *Revisioning gender* (pp. 341–364). Thousand Oaks, CA: Sage.

Dworkin, S. L. & Wachs, F. L. (2000). The morality/manhood paradox: Masculinity, sports, and the media. In M. A. McKay, M. A. Messner, & D. F. Sabo (Eds.), *Masculinities, gender relations, and sport* (pp. 47–66). Thousand Oaks, CA: Sage.

Farred, G. (2000). Cool as the other side of the pillow: How ESPN's Sportscenter has changed television sports talk. *Journal of Sport & Social Issues, 24*(2), 96–117.

Foucault, M. (1980a). *The history of sexuality: An introduction.* New York: Vintage.

Foucault, M. (1980b). *Power/knowledge: Selected interviews and other writings, 1972–1977.* (Colin Gordon, Ed. & Trans.). New York: Pantheon.

Ghosh, C. (1999, February 22). A guy thing: Radio sports talk shows. *Forbes,* p. 55.

Goldberg, D. T. (1998). Call and response: Sports, talk radio, and the death of democracy. *Journal of Sport & Social Issues, 22*(2), 212–223.

Gopinath, G. (1997). Nostalgia, desire, and diaspora: South Asian sexualities in motion. *Positions, 5*(2), 467–489.

Grindstaff, L. (1994). Abortion and the popular press: Mapping media discourse from *Roe* to *Webster.* In T. G. Jelen & M. A. Chandler (Eds.), *Abortion politics in the United States and Canada: Studies in public opinion* (pp. 58–88). Westport, CT: Praeger.

Haag, P. (1996). The 50,000 watt sports bar: Talk radio and the ethic of the fan. *South Atlantic Quarterly, 95*(2), 453–470.

Halberstam, J. (1998). *Female masculinity.* Durham, NC: Duke University Press.

Hare-Mustin, R. T. (1994). Discourses in the mirrored room: A postmodern analysis of therapy. *Family Process, 33,* 19–35.

Heywood, L., & Dworkin, S. L. (2003). *Built to win: The female athlete as cultural icon.* Minneapolis: University of Minnesota Press.

Hodgson, E. (1999, August 18). King of smack. *Fastbreak—The Magazine of the Phoenix Suns,* pp. 1–5.

Horrocks, R., & Campling, J. (1994). *Masculinity in crisis: Myths, fantasies and realities.* New York: Routledge.

Humm, M. (1995). *The dictionary of feminist theory* (2nd ed.). New York: Prentice Hall.

Hutchby, I. (1996). *Confrontation talk: Arguments, asymmetries, and power on talk radio.* Mahwah, NJ: Lawrence Erlbaum.

Jackson, P., Stevenson, N., & Brooks, K. (2002). *Making sense of men's magazines.* London: Polity.

Jakobsen, J. R. (2001). He has wronged America and women: Clinton's sexual conservatism. In L. Berlant & L. Duggan (Eds.), *Our Monica, ourselves: The Clinton affair and the national interest* (pp. 291–314). New York: New York University Press.

Jenkins, H. (1992). *Textual poachers: Television fans and participatory culture.* New York: Routledge.

Jhally, S. (1989). Cultural studies and the sports/media complex. In L. W. Wenner (Ed.), *Media, sports, and society* (pp. 70–93). Newbury Park, CA: Sage.

Kane, M. J., & Lenskyj, H. J. (2000). Media treatment of female athletes: Issues of gender and sexualities. In L. W. Wenner (Ed.), *Mediasport* (pp. 186–201). New York: Routledge.

Kellner, D. (1995). *Media culture: Cultural studies, identity, and politics between the modern and postmodern.* New York: Routledge.

Kimmel, M. (1994). Masculinity as homophobia. In H. Brod & M. Kaufman (Eds.), *Theorizing masculinities* (pp. 119–141). Thousand Oaks, CA: Sage.

Kitzinger, C. (1987). *The social construction of lesbianism.* Newbury Park, CA: Sage.

Lumby, C. (2001). The President's penis: Entertaining sex and power. In L. Berlant & L. Duggan (Eds.), *Our Monica, ourselves: The Clinton affair and the national interest* (pp. 225–236). New York: New York University Press.

Mariscal, J. (1999). Chicanos and Latinos in the jungle of sports talk radio. *Journal of Sport & Social Issues, 23*(1), 111–117.

McKay, M. A., Messner, M. A., & Sabo, D. F. (Eds.). (2000). *Masculinities, gender relations, and sport.* Thousand Oaks, CA: Sage.

McWhorter, L. (1999). *Bodies and pleasures: Foucault and the politics of sexual normalization.* Bloomington: Indiana University Press.

Messner, M. A. (1992). *Power at play: Sports and the problem of masculinity.* Boston: Beacon.

Messner, M. A. (2002). *Taking the field: Women, men, and sports.* Minneapolis: University of Minnesota Press.

Messner, M. A., Dunbar, M., & Hunt, D. (2000). The televised sports manhood formula. *Journal of Sport & Social Issues, 24*(4), 380–394.

Miller, T. (2001, June). Out at the ballgame. *Advocate,* pp. 1–3.

Munoz, J. E. (1999). *Disidentifications: Queers of color and the performance of politics.* Minneapolis: University of Minnesota Press.

Outside the lines: Homophobia and sports. (2001, May 31). ESPN.com. Available at http://espn.go.com/otl

Page, B. I., & Tannenbaum, J. (1996). Populistic deliberation and talk radio. *Journal of Communication, 46*(2), 33–53.

Pronger, B. (1990). *The arena of masculinity: Sports, homosexuality, and the meaning of sex.* New York: St. Martin's.

Roedieger, D. (1996). White looks: Hairy apes, true stories, and Limbaugh's laughs. *Minnesota Review, 47,* 41–52

Sabo, D. F., & Jansen, S. C. (2000). Prometheus unbound: Constructions of masculinity in the sports media. In L. W. Wenner (Ed.), *Mediasport* (pp. 202–217). New York: Routledge.

Schiller, H. (1989). *Culture, Inc.* New York: Oxford University Press.

Shields, D. (1999). *Black planet: Facing race during an NBA season.* New York: Crown.

Sports Illustrated Editors. (1994, April). The fall of Rome. *Sports Illustrated, 80,* 14.

Trujillo, N. (1994). *The meaning of Nolan Ryan.* College Station, TX: Texas A & M University Press.

Trujillo, N. (1996). Hegemonic masculinity on the mound: Media representations of Nolan Ryan and the American sports culture. In S. K. Foss (Ed.), *Rhetorical criticism: Exploration and practices* (pp. 181–203). Prospect Heights, IL: Waveland Press.

Wenner, L. W. (1998). The sports bar: Masculinity, alcohol, sports, and the mediation of public space. In G. Rail & J. Harvey (Eds.), *Sports and postmodern times: Gender, sexuality, the body, and sport* (pp. 301–322). Albany: State University of New York Press.

Wenner, L. W. (Ed.). (2000). *Mediasport.* New York: Routledge.

Beth A. Eck

Men Are Much Harder: Gendered Viewing of Nude Images

Recent scholarship in the sociology of culture has paid a lot of attention to issues of audience interpretation or the construction of meaning (Griswold 1987; Liebes and Katz 1990; Shivley 1992). The issue of cultural use has similarly garnered attention (Beisel 1992; Corse 1997; Griswold 1987; Long 1986; Radway 1984, especially chap. 4). The two literatures obviously intertwine since what people use culture for influences their interpretations of it. Little of this research, however, has seriously considered systematic differences in how men and women both interpret and use cultural works. I investigate both how men and women interpret nude images through highly patterned, gendered lenses and, simultaneously, how the process of interpretation allows men and women to construct their sexual identities.

Through focused interviews with 45 people, I demonstrate that heterosexual men and women respond to and discuss opposite- and same-sex nude images publicly (i.e., in the presence of an unknown researcher) in distinctive ways. Both men and women have access to shared, readily available cultural scripts for interpreting and responding to female nude images (it is part of the "cultural toolkit") (see Swidler 1986), although there are gendered differences in those interpretations and responses. Neither men nor women, however, are culturally adept at the interpretation and use of nude male images; they have particular difficulty commenting on the male in the

From *Gender & Society,* Vol. 17, no. 5, October 2003, pp. 691–710. Copyright © 2003. Reprinted by permission of Sage Publications, Inc.

soft porn pose. Thus, some images of male nudes require more "work" by individual viewers because cultural scripts are less readily available. The process of viewing nudes provides a clear opportunity to observe the sexual and gender identity work men and women perform when confronted with this cultural object.

The research presented here is an extension of an earlier study that investigated the significance of the frame in one's reception of nude images (Eck 2001). That project asserted that there are three frames that help one understand nude images—art, pornography, and information (e.g., medical texts). In addition, the commodified frame of advertising provides an increasingly important fourth frame. In that earlier work, I argued that frames come to adhere to images. The content of an image is important, but the meaning of the content is importantly aided by the context. For example, one female nude (Titian's *Venus of Urbino*) is recognized as art because of the conceptual frame that surrounds her: the old-looking paint that conveys her body and position, her body shape that suggests a model from a past time, and her pose that harkens back to a particular period of art. These cues frame her and instruct respondents on how to understand her: She is to be revered, admired, kept in the sacred realm of art, where the bodies are not presented for sexual pleasure. Thus, the context and content of nude images exist in a dialectical relationship.

My earlier work, then, was concerned with how people apply a variety of frames to nude images. I now ask, what other resources, in particular gender, do people draw on when making sense of these images? What do men and women do differently when they look at images of nude men and women? How do these different ways of seeing simultaneously allow for the mobilization and elaboration of identity work?

Literature Review

The historical prevalence of female nude images cannot be denied (Berger 1977; Bordo 1993; Callaghan 1994; Clark 1985; Nead 1992; Pollock 1988). The availability of these nudes has affected how men and women receive them. Both understand that the female nude is there to be looked at, an active process by the assumed male viewer (De Lauretis 1987; Gamman and Marshment 1989; Metz 1982; Modleski 1982; Mulvey 1975), and that she invites the gaze, the passive position of being viewed (Berger 1977).

Looking at the nude is an interactive process, one that calls on individuals to "do gender" (West and Zimmerman 1987)—to "reflect or express" who they are. For men, gazing at images of nude females helps to remind them of their masculinity (Dines 1992; Kimmel 1990). For women, gazing at these same images offers them lessons on how "women" look. However, the viewing experience for women is more complicated than it is for men. As Betterton (1987, 3) suggested, "Women have an ambiguous relationship to the nude visual image. This is because they are represented so frequently within images yet their role as makers and viewers of images is rarely acknowledged."

Understanding the viewer/viewed experience as outlined above has come under criticism from Bordo (1999). She noted that "passive" does not describe what is going on when one is the object of the gaze. "Inviting, receiving, responding . . . are active behaviors" (p. 190). Furthermore, attention to appearance involves a lot of hard work and is about more than "sexual allure"; it also indicates one is disciplined and has "the right stuff" (p. 221).

While female nude images are prevalent in society (though their positioning as active or pas-

sive may be disputed), the opposite is true of male nudes. These images are less common and less available for objectification (Coward 1985; Davis 1991; Saunders 1989). However, Bordo noted the recent increase in images of nude and scantily clad men, particularly in fashion advertising. She argued this increase is not a response to heterosexual female pleas for more naked men but a product of the gay male aesthetic—gay photographers "eroticizing the male body, male sensuousness, and male potency"—as well as the buying power of gay men (Bordo 1999, 183). While Betterton (1987, 11) asserted that when women are given the opportunity to view nude males that "power and control are not so easily reversible" as who "has the power to look is embedded in cultural forms," Bordo suggested the same uneasiness for men. "For many men," Bordo (1999, 172) stated, "both gay and straight, to be so passively dependent on the gaze of another person for one's sense of self-worth is incompatible with being a real man." A similar assertion has also been made by Coward (1985) and Davis (1991), who argued this is because men have controlled who looks at whom.

In fact, looking at nude men can call into question men's own heterosexuality. For example, Pronger's (1990) examination of heterosexual and homosexual men in sport suggests that all men, gay or straight, look at one another in locker rooms. However, the men he interviewed said that they were taught early on that one should not get caught looking lest he be thought a "fag." If he looks too long or likes looking, it raises serious questions about his sexual identity and, hence, his masculinity. Similarly, Kimmel (1994, 133) stated, "The fear—sometimes conscious, sometimes not—that others might perceive [men] as homosexual propels [them] to enact all manner of exaggerated masculine behaviors and attitudes to make sure that no one could possibly get the wrong idea about [them]."

For women, looking at men is complicated as well. Disch and Kane (1996) noted there can be ramifications associated with "peeking excessively" at naked men. To look critically at men goes against the feminine role and disrupts the power relationship. Everyone seems more comfortable when a woman gives up her authoritative position and assumes a docile one.[1]

Bordo (1999, 177) noted that women "are not used to seeing naked men frankly portrayed as 'objects' of a sexual gaze." Women are just learning to be voyeurs. Although women may be more accustomed to seeing male bodies, they are not as accustomed to having those bodies "offered" to them.

In short, the literature suggests that men and women have a certain facility with viewing images of nude women but lack the same vocabulary and comfort level looking at men. What happens, then, when men and women confront the male nude image in a public setting?

Research Design

This study involved in-depth, face-to-face interviews with 45 people collected through snowball sampling. Given the potentially "delicate" nature of the research, I found it useful to be introduced to potential interviewees by acquaintances or previous interviewees. This method also allowed for purposive selection of respondents to ensure appropriate distribution across gender, age, and education. My sample included 23 men and 22 women (see Table 47.1). Most of the respondents were non-Hispanic white, with 2 African Americans, 1 Mexican American, and 1 Korean American in the sample. The respondents ranged in age from 18 to 65 and were roughly divided between those younger than 35 and those older. The interviews took place in various locations including New Hampshire, Ohio, Pennsylvania, California, Virginia, and the District of Columbia where a snowball sample was started in each.[2] Half of my respondents held a high school diploma as their highest degree, and half held at least a bachelor's degree, with a significant minority holding advanced degrees at the time of the interview. I interviewed the majority of my respondents individually but also interviewed 5 couples to explore the effect of gendered interaction on the interpretive work I was asking interviewees to do. The interviews averaged 1.5 hours.

I presented the respondents with 23 images of the nude drawn from four contexts—medical texts (information frame), "adult entertainment" magazines (pornographic frame), mainstream magazines (commodified frame), and art books (art frame) (see the appendix for a list of images). I arranged the images in sets of two to four, grouped by similarity of pose and subject matter.[3] The selection of the images was both purposive and exploratory. That is, I wanted to ensure some similarity of pose as the initial project was focused on the importance of contextual cues, and I wanted to be sure the images came from a variety of sources; however, I was not concerned with including particular periods of art or specific magazine titles. I selected images with attention to poses, positions, and mediums. For example, I selected an "artistic" image of a pregnant woman to juxtapose against the commercially stylized photograph of Demi Moore nude and pregnant on the cover of *Vanity Fair* magazine. Each image was color xeroxed to a similar size, pasted onto a neutral background, and laminated. During the interviews, I passed each set of images to the interviewees so that the respondents controlled the length of time they viewed each image.

The larger study, within which this research is located, was focused on complicating the simplistic public discussions that revolve around publicly funded art. Those discussions frequently focused on the "types" of people in the debate, classifying those who defend Robert Mapplethorpe's work as "art," for example, as "pedophiles" and those who do not as "Christians" (Eck 1995). Missing from those discussions was the important role context plays in the interpretation process. Hence, the focus of the interview asked respondents to identify and discuss the origin of each image and its social meaning. In most cases, viewers knew the correct origin (e.g., images from *National Geographic* and *Penthouse* were

■ **TABLE 47.1**
Respondent Characteristics

Characteristic	Women (*n* = 22)	Men (*n* = 23)
Mean age	37 years	38 years
Education		
High school	12	11
B.A.	4	3
M.A./M.S.	3	5
Ph.D.	3	0
M.D.	0	2
J.D.	0	2
Religion/spirituality		
Religious	10	8
Spiritual	7	6
Both	2	2
Neither	3	7
Political affiliation		
Conservative	4	8
Moderate	8	9
Liberal	7	3
Libertarian	0	2
Socialist	1	0
None	2	1

easily identified as were images from "art books"). Other times, respondents guessed (e.g., the Calvin Klein ad was thought by some to be a photograph taken during the depression). The following gender analysis exists within that interview framework (see Eck [2001] for an examination of context on the interpretation process). The initial questions and discussion of context were followed by (1) a discussion of art and pornography (e.g., How does one define each of these concepts?), (2) the respondent's cultural consumption habits (e.g., Does one read a newspaper? How much does one watch television?), and (3) questions about the respondent's religious and political orientation as well as his or her positions on a variety of social issues (e.g., homosexual parenting, condom avail-

ability in public schools). The original design was set up to see if "types" of people and their interpretations of nudes could be so easily classified. I did not ask respondents about their sexual orientations. Only two men, a couple, volunteered to me that they were homosexual. This couple had been together for five years, and both of the men were physicians. Their reactions to the body are complicated by the confluence of these two factors, and so in this article I only focus on assumed heterosexual responses.[4] An examination of homosexual responses is certainly warranted by another study.[5]

There are some limitations to this study. Because of the small sample size, I hesitate to make generalizations about how men and women view nudes, and I cannot make any claims about non-white respondents as a group. The sample is mostly white and heterosexual, and so the important work of intersecting gender with nonwhite racial and ethnic cultures (and the corresponding standards of beauty and ways of looking) is not done here. Within this study, the responses of nonwhite respondents did not vary from those of the white respondents. It should also be noted that most of the subjects in the images were white, with the exception of a Robert Mapplethorpe photograph (*Thomas*) and the two images from *National Geographic* (for some discussion about race within the images, see Eck [2001]). Furthermore, a retrospective view from this inductive analysis suggests that there are surely more pointed questions that could be asked. However, this exploratory work does begin to shed light on how heterosexual men and women understand and, hence, interact with images of nudity, particularly male nudity.

I first turn to a discussion of how heterosexual men and women view female nudes. Because of the existing research on the viewing of female nudes, my summary is relatively brief. The bulk of my discussion focuses on the less studied topic of both genders viewing male nudes.

Looking at Women

The first set of images that respondents in this study see contains four bodies, all photographed. Cindy Crawford poses on the cover of *Rolling Stone,* arms crossed over her bare breasts. The image is cropped at midthigh, and a piece of fabric covers her pubic area. Calvin Klein model Kate Moss faces the camera in an ad, cropped at the waist, one bare breast exposed. There is also a black-and-white photograph of former body-builder Lisa Lyon taken by Robert Mapplethorpe. She is coming out of the water fully nude. Finally, the set includes a heavy-set woman photographed by Hariette Hartigan. She is seated, her nude body three-quarters exposed to us. The second set of female images that respondents view includes reclining nudes—Titian's *Venus of Urbino,* a Pent-

house nude, and a black-and-white photograph of Demi Moore from *Vanity Fair* magazine.

Men, as previous researchers have demonstrated, view the female body with a sense of ownership (Berger 1977). They interpret female nudes as objects of pleasure or derision and by so doing reproduce and sustain heterosexual masculinity on a daily basis. Men's status as "men" is reaffirmed every time they encounter and pass judgment on the female form. Consider the following comments from men about Cindy Crawford, Lisa Lyon, and Kate Moss. "I think she's beautiful physically. Personally I think she is attractive." "I like that. That's what we dream about." From an older man, "She's a good-lookin' girl." One man repeatedly told me that Cindy Crawford is a "professionally sexy, good-looking woman." Conversely, men's responses to the Hartigan nude dismiss her as a potential candidate for desire, quickly labeling the images as "art"—an antiseptic term that removes the body from potential erotic pleasure (Nead 1992). When men look at these images, they reveal no sense of embarrassment or self-consciousness in rendering an opinion on these models. They assume a culturally conferred right to evaluate the female nude—as do the female respondents.

The Cindy Crawford and Lisa Lyon images elicit these comments from women: "I wish I had a body like that," or "She's an attractive woman. I'd love to look like that." Many women echoed this response from 26-year-old Sophie:

> If I'm waiting in a doctor's office I'll open up a *Glamour* or a *Mirabella* or something but I really don't buy them. I think it's more, just the portrayal of these thin models and I just get depressed. . . . I'm very hard on myself, wanting to be that way.

Like the men, the women I interviewed look at the female nude with an evaluative eye. Unlike the men, their eyes were simultaneously on their own appearances. Women viewers use female nudes to reflect on their own bodies and whether these bodies are acceptable to themselves and others. Because the definition of the "ideal" female body is partly imposed from the outside (e.g., the media, other women, and men), evaluating, judging, and even obsessing about the body are part of being female. In viewing the image of the heavier woman, women, like men, first define her as art. About one-half of them then use pejorative terms such as *repulsive, unattractive,* or *ugly* to describe her. Finally, and importantly, they often identify with her. For example,

> Oh this is what I'm going to look like in 10 years. (Rachel, 56, newspaper editor)

> Well, this is unfortunate because I am disgusted by it because she is fat, but I'm also, it's right after Christmas and I need to lose about 10 pounds so it's a sensitive issue. (Roxanne, 29, legal assistant)

> I don't necessarily find her body that attractive. She is overweight. Her stomach looks like mine (*laughing*). (Lori, 31, lobbyist)

> I don't think this is done in good taste. . . . Americans [*sic*] now it's showin'us that thin is the way. And thin is healthy and I've lost 60 some pounds myself lately because I'm getting into my 40s and it's all in how you carry yourself and what you feel about yourself. (Paula, 38, short-order cook)

For women, female nudes are objects to be studied, viewed, judged, and, above all, used as a comparison for the self—"her stomach looks like mine," and "I need to lose 10 pounds myself." Women both view the image and respond as if the image represents a part of themselves being viewed. Becky, a 42-year-old librarian, is a little heavier than the other women in my sample. She identifies fully with the Hartigan nude, but her negative reaction is not toward the image itself but toward how society evaluates that image. "I always say I was born in the wrong century. I need to go back to a time when men appreciated women like this." She indicates that it is men who would not appreciate a body like this, a body like hers. Women judge other women based on what they have learned makes the female form pleasing to men. Furthermore, women's expertise

on female forms raises no alarms or challenges to female heterosexuality. Only one respondent made it a point to tell me she was not a lesbian. Tammy noted,

> I think that women are beautiful creatures. And, maybe I think that just because I am a woman, I am not really sure. I don't have sexual tendencies toward my same sex so I don't want that point to come across, but I think women are beautiful. I really think God knew what he was doing when he made us.

Both men and women in this study easily find a language with which to discuss the naked female image. For men, this everyday practice of viewing allows them to enact their heterosexuality and their power; for women in my sample, this practice is more complicated, suggesting a sensitivity toward and even passive acceptance of external definitions of female beauty and desirability. Both genders, however, talk freely about female nudes in a way that they cannot do when confronted with the male nude.[6]

Looking at Men

Viewing male nudes in classical Western art allows for a separation, a physical distancing between the viewer and the viewed. Thus, when asked to comment on a fifth-century B.C. sculpture of a sleeping satyr, respondents have little to say past "it's art." It does not seem imposing, threatening, or particularly relevant. Viewing contemporary male nudes, however, is another matter.

My respondents look at two sets of the male nude. The first set includes three images of frontal poses including a fifth-century B.C. sleeping satyr sculpture, a twentieth-century painting by Lucian Freud, and an image from *Playgirl.* All of these men are sitting/reclining with legs apart and one hand behind their heads. The second set includes a side-view photograph by Mapplethorpe of a man leaning on a podium (*Thomas*), a photograph titled *The Boxer* in which the shading all but conceals the genitals, and a photograph of Sylvester Stallone posed as Rodin's *Thinker* from the cover of

Vanity Fair. The images are handed to the respondents stacked in this order.

Although the respondents in my sample have the opportunity to comment on six images of men, the image that receives the most reaction is the *Playgirl* nude. This is unlike viewing images of women in which comparable time is given to each. They comment on the other images primarily as they relate to this soft porn pose. For men, this is apparent as they are viewing the images. For example, Jamie, 31, looks through the first set of images and comments,

> My initial reaction is of course less positive because I am less interested in looking at nude males than nude females. This looks like it came right out of *Playgirl* or I don't know what they call the equivalent women's magazine.

All of the images are not as pleasing to look at as the images of women are, but the *Playgirl* image is the one that he will use to talk about the others; it is the one he is drawn to first. Similarly, Gary, 32, notes on being handed the first set of images, "Hmm. Men are much harder. This one is definitely out of a porno." This practice of commenting on the *Playgirl* image first occurred for one-half (12) of the men in my sample, the half who laid out all the images first rather than discuss them in order. Interestingly, this ordering of responses happened with only six women. Most of the female respondents were like Rachel who laid out the images and said, "This is the high end [sculpture], this is in the middle [painting], and this is totally exploitative [*Playgirl*]." Women's use of the *Playgirl* image to talk about the others came out later in the interview, when images were discussed more generally and respondents were asked about their level of comfort looking at images. Men also used this time as an opportunity to return to the image.

The male response to the *Playgirl* image is more uniform than the female response. A couple in their late 20s offers an illustrative case. They sit at the dining room table of their Cleveland apartment mulling over the first set of male images presented to them. In the following interview excerpt, they are discussing the first set of male nudes.

Brian: I have no feeling about any of these pieces.

Holly: What do you mean?

Brian: I have no response. I have no response at all. Big deal. I don't know what to say. So what?

Holly: You know I think he's a good-looking guy [*Playgirl*] but I would rather just see him like that (*she covers up the bottom half of the photo with her hand*). That kind of turns me off a little bit.

Brian: I don't care for any of them. I have no feelings on it. . . . I can't comment much on the male body because I have a male body.

Holly: Why? I commented on the female.

Brian: Yeah. But it's different for a guy. It's different.

Holly: No it's not.

Brian: Guy looks at another guy and goes "so what." I bet you look at another girl and go "so what."

Holly: I actually don't. I pick her apart like crazy.

Brian: Really? It's different between guys. Big deal. That's a guy. So what.

Holly: Alright. If you say so.

Three key points are illuminated by this exchange. First, Holly mistakenly assumes that when Brian views men he will mimic her response to women and "pick [them] apart like crazy." She is surprised when she finds that he does not and that he has no other way to discuss them. Second, Holly covers up the lower half of the image from *Playgirl* because she is uncomfortable with exposed male genitalia (at least in front of a stranger). She says that it "turns her off." Third, Brian mentions several times that he is a "guy" and as such has "no response." Both Brian and Holly are reciting bits of the social script. For Holly, her female identity involves her ability to judge, evaluate, and compare herself to female images. It also involves a certain caution about looking at naked men. Brian must be careful too. Whereas Holly seems repulsed and maybe embarrassed, Brian suggests there is something troubling about one man looking at a nude image of a man. These three themes reverberate through the responses in this study. I now turn to a broader discussion of men viewing male nudes.

"I Like Women"

Heterosexual men respond to male nudes in two ways—with overt rejection and with stated disinterest. Both responses construct a hypermasculinity, with more than one-half of the men in this sample implicitly distancing themselves from homosexuality. They also indicate that because they "don't go looking" for images of men, viewing them is just not something they are used to doing. Their responses suggest that when men look at both women and men they affirm their heterosexual masculinity—in the first case by gazing and evaluating and in the second by not gazing and evaluating. Looking at male nudes involves more elaborate responses than those responses directed toward female nudes. Only two men in my sample noted that they had the same level of comfort looking at nude men as they do nude women. Gary, a 32-year-old floral arranger, had told me that "men are much harder" when looking at the *Playgirl* nude, but when I asked him if he had a different level of comfort looking at same-sex versus opposite-sex images he said, "It doesn't matter. Really." Sid, a 58-year-old stockbroker, noted, "I mean that doesn't particularly bother me. I don't see very much of the same sex." What these men note is not a preference for male images but a stated indifference to them. Most men, however, were like Jorge, who stated, "Definitely I like to look at women." When asked if this meant he was uncomfortable looking at men, he said, "No. I just like women."

Interestingly, men do not identify with naked male images the way women identify with naked female images. For example, the sample of male images contains well-defined bodies as well as one overweight individual. Only one male remarked,

with reference to the heavy male, "That'll be me in 50 years."[7] And only two men in my study identified with the well-built men. For example, Arthur, a 38-year-old professional manager who defined himself as a "stick-up-the-ass-preppie-type," noted, "This is a stud. I would love to look like him." But it is Arthur's subsequent discussion of male nudes that speaks to viewing as a means of affirming his masculine heterosexuality. Being interviewed along with his wife Cassie, a college professor, gives him some freedom to admire the male body without fear of being seen as a homosexual. But he can further assert his machismo through his language.

Arthur's response below is to an image from *Playgirl,* and it provides a useful illustration of his efforts to maintain a "manly front" (Kimmel 1994).

> You have to be careful with nudity. So looking at Demi Moore for sort of 10 seconds is okay, but looking at this guy's balls for more than 5 seconds might be a bit much. I mean, you look at that and someone's going to say, "What color are his eyes?" Fuck if I know. But "How many testicles does he have?" Two. "Is he circumcised?" Yeah. (Arthur)

Here, Arthur is trying to distance himself from the sexually seductive male in the photograph. He cannot help but notice "this guy's balls," but he has to be "careful" about doing so. He is not overt in his identification with the model the way most women were in their discussions of female nudes. He does not talk of fear or hope for himself when encountering this image. Rather, Arthur, along with the other men in my sample, speaks awkwardly about the image and in doing so reflects his discomfort and perhaps disassociation with man as object. More important, the chance to state the way he receives this image provides a site where his own heterosexual masculinity can be demonstrated. This masculinity precludes looking "for more than 5 seconds."

Similarly, let's return to Holly and Brian and listen to Brian: I ask them if they have a different level of comfort looking at same-sex versus opposite-sex images. Holly, like most (16) of the women in my sample, would rather view women and so would Brian, like all but two male respondents (again these exceptions did not prefer looking at men but simply did not have one preference over another). Now remember that Brian stated that he could not really comment on men because he is a man. He told me later in the interview, "Yeah, I'd rather look at the opposite sex. I would rather look at a picture of a girl than a guy." I reminded him that when he looked at the pictures of men he set them aside and announced he had no reaction to those. I asked him what he meant by that. Holly interjected, "Are you afraid that if you look at it too long we'll think you're gay?" Brian laughed in response to this, "I just don't care for this. He's a man. I have what he has and as far as the pornographic issue, it does nothing for me. Big deal. Big deal. I'd rather see this" he said, stabbing the image of Lisa Lyon with his finger.

This exchange highlights how heterosexual men respond to images of male nudes. Brian begins by noting, "He's a man. I have what he has." This is a quick acknowledgment that he sees some of himself in the image. Unlike women's compulsive self-reflexivity in viewing female nudes, however, with attendant comments about themselves and how they compare, Brian brushes quickly past a similar opportunity for comparison. He moves on to stress that it does "nothing" for him. The male as the object of the picture is meant to sexually titillate. Men are not used to viewing other men in this position and refuse the opportunity for doing so.

In fact, more than half of the men I talked with stated they were virtually unable to comment on the male form. Two stated their heterosexual orientation explicitly, as if that explained their inability to comment. Others made implicit reference to their sexual preference by noting how they were raised or that they "like women" as a way of justifying their lack of response to the male nudes. One man noted,

> Well, that one don't turn me on. . . . And if I had to exercise my imagination and say where did it come from for somebody who painted

something like this I would say that maybe it is someone who is part of the gay community.

This comment explicitly connects the nude male positioned for display as only accessible through the homosexual gaze. This is stated even more emphatically by Arthur:

> OK, I am a product of society and guys who take too much interest in guy's anatomy are voyeurs at best and gay at worst and in a lot of the world which I have to occupy, for better or worse, gayness is not a highly regarded lifestyle. And I do find, yeah, I do have a different level of comfort. I would not say that I recoil at men's naked bodies but to sit here and gaze at it for too long would make someone suspect my character.

That men reactively construct their heterosexuality through a disavowal of interest in male nudes can be further illustrated. Jack is 60 years old. Retired from the Navy, he now works as a benefits counselor for the service. I ask him if he has a different level of comfort looking at same-sex images versus opposite-sex images. He says,

> I think so. I'm more comfortable looking at a woman's picture. But I think that's part of your makeup. My belief is that human beings come in every possible degree of totally heterosexual all the way down to homosexual and all the way back up the other side again. Some people are asexual. So I think, I don't find myself uncomfortable but I would think that if I found that the male pictures were more attractive then I would have to wonder about my own sexuality which I don't normally do.

Other men also allude to not having to wonder about their sexuality when they note that nude males are "less appealing" than women, that they "don't do anything for them," and that naked men make them "less comfortable."

Hank's comments illustrate this point. Hank is a native Virginian. He is retired from the food service industry. He told me that we have always seen naked women because "it's reality. It's the way it is." He told me that he "actually stumbled into a bar in New Orleans about 30 years ago with a buddy" of his, and indeed there were paintings of naked men there. I asked him if he stayed.

> No. I didn't care for it because I figured it was either a queer bar or a transvestite bar and that's what it turned out to be and I was with a good friend from high school and he said something like "let's get the hell out of here and go see some women," and I said, "Yeah. I don't think we want to stay here too long."

Hank makes it quite clear that real men should not want to be in bars where naked male images are displayed. Those places could never be associated with a heterosexual environment, one with "real men."

Older men are not the only ones to speak uneasily about the male nude. Matt, 32, admits that I really threw him when I introduced the pictures of men: "It was like wow! Am I going to see old people next?" For Matt, images of naked males and naked "old people" occupy the same space in the margins—unusual and inappropriate objects for viewing.

The male voice is concerned, perhaps even alarmed, that his viewing of the male will be misconstrued. Male viewers fear that looking at or thinking about male nudes may say something inaccurate about the kind of men they are. Jamie, 31, states this even more explicitly than Jack, Matt, or Hank. Jamie and I sat at his kitchen table in New Hampshire to discuss the images:

> I don't want to look at any contemporary pictures of a nude male. . . . I'm just a bit uncomfortable looking at a man who is trying to be looked at kind of sexually and so I find it mildly uncomfortable staring at it for too long. (Jamie)

With that, Jamie's mouth gave way to a slight smile, and he covered up the image from *Playgirl* with a female image.

If looking at men forces these men to actively, and even defensively, construct their heterosexuality in elaborated ways, what does it ask of women?

The Tables Turned

Unlike the fairly uniform responses men gave to the sexually available male nude, women's responses are more complicated. I find that women respond in three ways—a few welcome the advance, some are attracted but with feelings of guilt, and some reject the seductive image altogether.

Three women in my sample said that looking at images of naked men is or could be stimulating.

> Am I blushing? Yes. Um, is it done in bad taste because the genitals are showing? He has a nice body. I would definitely say pornography. . . . He has a fantastic body (*laughs*) and the genitals are not bad either (*laughs*). . . . Yeah, he's attractive; I guess you can say your pulse is elevated. (Paula, 38)

> As far as when you get into *Playgirl, Playboy* and all of that, sure I can look at the pictures and get physically turned on, stimulated anyway, and I can read the nasty articles and realize that it's garbage, but the trick is working. I've read this a lot, totally nasty, scummy articles and I've felt bad. I've felt perverted because I was being stimulated but then I really tried to just let it go because I don't see it as a bad thing. (Zoe, 26)

> I'm more uncomfortable looking at the male image because I am a woman and I know my body and it's uncomfortable in that yes, I find an attraction or I'm excited to see the male part so maybe it makes me uncomfortable. (Sophie, 28)

While Zoe and Sophie can be stimulated by images of nude males, they still must work out their feelings of shame. The three women are anomalous, however, as most of the women I interviewed were not accustomed to looking at images of men in terms of arousal and found the idea "absurd." For example:

> Well, it's like Chippendale dancers and these women, I said, gosh, I don't. That doesn't do anything for me. I don't see how anyone can get excited about that. I don't know. I guess maybe I'm weird. (Diane, 46)

I just think it's absurd. . . . I just can't imagine this would arouse any woman. I think they would look at it and laugh. . . . I had this friend in college who used to get it [*Playgirl*] and I think a lot of times women will get it for the shock value. I don't know. I've never heard of anybody getting it because they really enjoy it, although maybe they do and they are embarrassed to say. I don't know. But I had a friend who had a few of them in college and I had never seen them in my life and almost died and then one day someone brought one in here [workplace], I can't remember which one, and it was just really ridiculous (*laughs*). . . . We were all laughing. I mean, it's ironic because I assume they sell quite a few magazines. I can't imagine why. There's no appeal whatsoever. So, I would imagine people buy it as a joke. (Roxanne, 29)

Debbie said the same about *Playgirl* when she noted that her brother bought a subscription for her when she was in college, as a joke, and all the girls would run down the hall to her room to see the forbidden. She continues,

I see the purpose of *Playgirl* being the same as *Penthouse,* but maybe women aren't as desperate as men. I think *Penthouse* subscribers are really lonely old men or teenage boys who really haven't figured out how to get girls yet. Maybe very lonely and ugly (*laughs*) 20- and 30-year-olds and maybe that's not true but I see sort of *Penthouse* is desperate. *Playgirl* is sort of harmless but not really serious in any way. I don't think *Playgirl* has the subscription rate and there is only one of them and that sort of tells you something right there. There's only one magazine that exploits men for women and yet there are all these [magazines that exploit women for men], there are a lot of them. (Debbie, 34)

While *Playgirl* might be adult entertainment for women, these two women suspect that few women take it seriously—or even know what to do with it. This comes across in the responses from other women. Women, like men in my sample, lack the tools to speak about these images of men, particularly the *Playgirl* male. They speak of the offensiveness of male genitalia and the com-

parative comfort they feel looking at nude female images. The women in my sample also acknowledge that if they saw images of men more often then they might come to view them as easily as they view female images. As Debbie puts it,

I think I'm just more used to looking at nude women than nude men because that's what we're barraged with. I think we're sort of indifferent, well, maybe not indifferent but it's much more acceptable to go out and see a nude woman than a nude man just because everywhere we turn there are images of nude women. We're taken to museums and we're told, "Well, it's OK that she is naked because she's art."

As a woman it is OK to look at nude women because "everywhere we turn" there they are. In fact, many are even taken by the hand to museums and instructed on the appropriateness of looking at naked women. Debbie notes how extensive this education is by bringing up *National Geographic.*

As long as they were dark brown it was okay to see naked women. *National Geographic* is a very standard middle-class magazine. We had it; all of our friends had it in their homes. There were never naked men. So we grew up with that idea, that it's OK to look at naked women and not naked men.[8]

By omitting or de-emphasizing images of nude men, high culture and popular culture inform women—and men—of who is the appropriate object. Peggy, 51, an administrative assistant in a university town in Ohio, makes the same statement: "I'm more comfortable probably looking at women rather than men. I think that I'm shy. And just a cultural thing. It's OK to look at women but it's not OK to look at men." In this context, it is not "OK," and perhaps not desirable, for women to assume the role of actor/aggressor/maker in this relationship.[9]

Men and women are both uncomfortable viewing male nudes, but their discomfort is different. Diane, a 44-year-old legal secretary from Cleveland, states,

Well, as much as I hate to admit this, I don't much like any of these. That's my personal feeling. Of course, I feel that the male body is not real attractive to look at (*laughing*). That's really sexist, but other than muscle form it does nothing for me.

Diane notes the male form "does nothing for her." She does not mean this in the same way the men mean it when they look at women. Not one man said that the female body is "not attractive." Heterosexual men in my sample evaluate all kinds of women in terms of sexual arousal—whether a particular woman does anything for them. Diane's statement is a blanket one—"I don't much like any of these." Any of these. The male body, male genitalia in particular, is offensive to her. As Becky notes, "I don't know. I'm just not into men's genitalia. . . . It's just not something I enjoy looking at. . . . It's like, excuse me, I would rather you didn't point at me." For men and for the women who feel ashamed or embarrassed, then, looking at the male nudes raises fears about identity and sexuality. But the fears are different. Men fear too long a gaze will suggest a homoerotic interest and thus a homosexual identity. For women, the fear is that the active subject who captures the nude male in her gaze is not a properly heterosexual, "feminine" subject.

From the responses above, it appears that the men and women in my sample demonstrate the inadequacy of the scripts available to them. Men, over and over again, reject the seductive advance. While some women welcome the advance, most feel a combination of shame, guilt, or repulsion in interacting with the image—or, at least, in doing so publicly. It is worth nothing that this response spans age categories. Younger women in the sample are not any more adept at viewing these images. Furthermore, it appears that these women have been socialized to find the naked male body unattractive, perhaps by men themselves as Coward (1985) suggested. At the same time, they acknowledge that if they saw the male body more often they would be more comfortable in their role as the viewer here.

Conclusion

There is a dialectical experience in viewing nudes. Gender informs how one looks, and how one looks informs gender, particularly as it is linked to sexual identity. Individuals use nudes to comment on the acceptability of a sexual advance. When women view the seductive pose of the female nude, they do not believe she is "coming on to" them. They know she is there to arouse men. Thus, they do not have to work at rejecting an unwanted advance. It is not for them. They look at her and respond to her with longing ("I wish I looked like that") and fear ("I can't look like that"). The casual way that men respond to female nudes suggests that the assumptions of male heterosexual judgments prevail without much question. Women may resent these images, they may uneasily identify with them, but they are also accustomed to the mundane practice of viewing them and accepting them. The way men assume the active subject in this relationship and all that it entails barely warrant comment. The man reaffirms his masculinity by conferring judgment as well as his heterosexuality by showing that he is, as one respondent said, "headed in the right direction."

Nude male images are more difficult. Because viewing male nudes, particularly in seductive poses, is still unusual, the respondents stumble through their responses (with laughter, embarrassment, and even disinterest). Their very hesitancies and embarrassment indicate the incomplete and fragmented cultural scripts on which they are relying. Because these men are used to being the subject in the viewer-viewed relationship, they reactively construct a hypermasculine heterosexuality when the viewed object is male. The male viewer must distance himself from the male object, speak about his own sexuality to reassert his privilege, and stress that "men don't interest me." Even though they know that *Playgirl* is an "adult entertainment magazine for women," these men cannot dismiss the seductive pose of the male nude the way women can in the reverse case.

Women, in my sample, are unaccustomed to taking on the role of subject in the viewing experience. However, whether they are repulsed, indifferent, or intrigued, women are active viewers. These women are working to evaluate and assess images as well as actively producing their own responses. The produced response is of a "feminine" sexuality—hesitant, shy, disinterested.

If certain frames come to adhere to images making the content and context one, then it appears from examining gendered responses to the *Playgirl* nude that this is one subject that does not fit the frame. The pornographic frame (context) is presumed to encompass the female body (con-

tent). With the *Playgirl* image, the pose is right, the look is clear, but the genitalia are all wrong. Female respondents in this study suggest that they might be aroused by the male in the soft porn pose if they were more familiar with it. Only then would this image fit the frame for them. However, it is not clear from this research that men are on their way to blending the two. What is desirable is constructed in and reflective of the dynamics of power (MacKinnon 1987). Examining how men and women view nude images guides our attention to how desire is structured, how sexuality and identity are linked, and how object-subject relations are still gendered.

Appendix

List of Images

Set 1: Female frontal

1. Cindy Crawford [C], cover of *Rolling Stone,* 23 December 1993 to 6 January 1994
2. Kate Moss [C], Calvin Klein ad, inside cover of *Elle Magazine,* August 1994
3. *Lisa Lyon* [A], 1990 (Kardon, Janet, ed. 1994. *Robert Mapplethorpe: The perfect moment.* Philadelphia: Institute of Contemporary Art, University of Pennsylvania Press)
4. Photograph by Harriette Hartigan [A], 1993 (Haldeman Martz, Sandra, ed. 1994. *I am becoming the woman I've wanted.* Watsonville, CA: Papier-Mache Press)

Set 2: Female reclining

5. *The Venus of Urbino* [A], Titian, 1536 (Bohm-Duchen, M. 1992. *The nude.* London: Scala Publications)
6. Female reclining [P] in *Penthouse,* September 1994
7. Demi Moore [C], black and white, inside *Vanity Fair,* 1992

Set 3: Male reclining

8. "Sleeping Satyr" [A], plate 157a (Sismondo Ridgway, Brunilde. 1990. *Hellenistic sculpture I: The styles of ca. 331–200 b.c.* Madison: University of Wisconsin Press)
9. Male reclining [P], *Playgirl,* September 1994
10. Male reclining [A] (Lampert, Catherine. 1993. *Lucian Freud: Recent work.* London: Whitechapel Art Gallery)

Set 4: Male focus on musculature

11. Sylvester Stallone [C], cover of *Vanity Fair,* November 1993
12. *The Boxer* [A], by James A. Fox (Weiermair, Peter. 1988. *The hidden image: Photographs of the male nude in the nineteenth and twentieth centuries.* Cambridge, MA: MIT Press)

13. *Thomas* [A], by Robert Mapplethorpe (Weiermair, Peter. 1988. *The hidden image: Photographs of the male nude in the nineteenth and twentieth centuries.* Cambridge, MA: MIT Press)

Set 5: Anatomy

14. Anatomy diagram of woman [I] (Boston Women's Health Book Collective. 1984. *The new our bodies/ourselves.* London: Touchstone)

15. Anatomy diagram of man [I] (Anson, Barry J. 1992. *Morris' human anatomy.* 12th ed. New York: McGraw-Hill)

Set 6: Nursing females

16. Woman breastfeeding [I], photograph (Launois, John. 1972. "Stone age caveman of Mindanao," *National Geographic* 142 (2): 244)

17. Woman breastfeeding [C], cover of *Life* magazine, December 1993

Set 7: Pregnant females

18. "Pregnant Nude" [A], by Imogene Cunningham, 1959 (Ewing, William A. 1994. *The body.* San Francisco: Chronicle)

19. Demi Moore [C], cover of *Vanity Fair,* August 1991

Set 8: Children

20. Boys playing soccer [I], photograph (Conger, Dean. 1971. "Java: Eden in transition," *National Geographic* 139 (1): 34)

21. "Jessie McBride" [A], by Robert Mapplethorpe (Kardon, Janet, ed. 1994. *Robert Mapplethorpe: The perfect moment.* Philadelphia: Institute of Contemporary Art, University of Pennsylvania Press)

22. "Virginia at 4" [A] (Mann, Sally. 1992. *Immediate family.* Carson, CA: Treville)

23. "Virginia at 3" [A] (Mann, Sally. 1992. *Immediate family.* Carson, CA: Treville)

Note: [A] = art frame; [P] = pornographic frame; [I] = informational frame; [C] = commodified frame, as designated by the author in selecting the images.

Author's Note: An earlier version of this article was presented at the 1997 International Visual Sociology Association meetings in Boston. For their comments on an earlier draft of this article, the author wishes to thank Jill Fuller, Sharon Hays, James Davison Hunter, Karin Peterson, Bess Rothenberg, and Saundra Westervelt. For their assistance on later versions of this article, the author wishes to thank Sarah Corse, Shari Dworkin, Fletcher Linder, and the anonymous reviewers at *Gender & Society.*

Notes

1. In Disch and Kane's (1996) analysis of an incident involving female sports reporter Lisa Olson, the authors noted how many female sports reporters play by the rules of the locker-room game. They are expected to look at the naked men parading about them but not for long. If, like Olson, they do, they may be called "dick-watching bitches."

2. A lack of resources limited my research sites to places I traveled to visit friends and/or attend conferences.

3. The respondents viewed the sets of images in the following order: female frontal, female reclining, male reclining, male with a focus on musculature, pregnant female, nursing female, anatomy diagrams, and images of children.

4. For example, in viewing the *Playgirl* nude, Thad noted, "I've seen three *Playgirl*s in my life and all the

men have long hair like Fabio. And it also it looks like [looking at genitals], does he shave? Probably shaves." Kevin responded, "Or at least plucks." Thad goes on to say, "Interesting that his left testicle hangs lower than his right and it's usually the other way around. I remember that from anatomy." Kevin replies, "I don't think you're right." Thad looks at the genitals again and agrees, "Oh, you're right. His is correct." While the first part of this exchange may reflect a gay male aesthetic, the rest of the exchange reflects their experience as physicians. This type of responding happened on at least four other occasions during the interview.

5. In doing this project, I had to take into account my own status characteristics as a researcher. I am a female, and at the time of the research I was in my early 30s and unmarried; hence, I wore no marital badges. I was conscious of both my physical appearance and my body language during the interviews and kept the environment as formal as possible. Doing the interviews in cold weather environments allowed me to wear turtlenecks, slacks, and blazers to all interviews. Only one respondent, a male, openly appeared to flirt with me. In a conversation about the female images, he said, "Men like to fantasize. I could have a fantasy about you."

6. I do not discuss responses to the female reclining nudes in this article. An examination of the responses to the *Penthouse* nude can be found in Eck (2001). In short, men and women discuss the *Penthouse* nude with more ease than they do the *Playgirl* nude discussed within this article. Most of the discussions about the image revolve around issues of context. Also, unlike the *Playgirl* image, the *Penthouse* nude does not garner significantly more attention from the respondents than other female nudes they are shown.

7. The overweight male is painted. It is possible men and women would have commented more on this image if it had been a photograph. However, women did comment more than men on this painting and stated that the man in the picture "looks sad." The comments by both men and women were rarely about size but about his circumstances: "Why are his sheets on the floor?" "He looks poor." "Is he in a mental hospital?" This line of commentary and lack of focus on his size suggest that "fatness" is gendered.

8. See Lutz and Collins (1993) for an examination of the dark female nude in *National Geographic*.

9. Segal (1994) noted that many women even admit that they change themselves into men when engaging in sexual fantasy. Sometimes they read homoerotic literature or construct homosexual stories that allow women to identify with both characters—the person who desires and the person being desired.

References

Beisel, Nicola. 1992. Constructing a shifting moral boundary: Literature and obscenity in nineteenth century America. In *Cultivating differences: Symbolic boundaries and the making of inequality,* edited by Michele Lamont and Marcel Fournier. Chicago: University of Chicago Press.

Berger, John. 1977. *Ways of seeing.* London: Penguin.

Betterton, Rosemary. 1987. *Looking on: Images of femininity in the visual arts and media.* London: Pandora.

Bordo, Susan. 1993. *Unbearable weight: Feminism, western culture and the body.* Berkeley: University of California Press.

———. 1999. *The male body: A new look at men in public and in private.* New York: Farrar, Straus and Giroux.

Callaghan, Karen A. 1994. *Ideals of feminine beauty: Philosophical, social and cultural dimensions.* Westport, CT: Greenwood.

Clark, T. J. 1985. *The painting of modern life: Paris in the art of Manet and his followers.* London: Thames and Hudson.

Corse, Sarah M. 1997. *Nationalism and literature: The politics of culture in Canada and the United States.* London: Cambridge University Press.

Coward, Rosalind. 1985. *Female desires: How they are sought, bought, and packaged.* New York: Grove Weidenfeld.

Davis, Melody D. 1991. *The male nude in contemporary photography.* Philadelphia: Temple University.

De Lauretis, Teresa. 1987. *Technologies of gender.* Bloomington: Indiana University Press.

Dines, Gail. 1992. Pornography and the media: Cultural representations of violence against women. *Family Violence & Sexual Assault Bulletin* 8 (3): 17–20.

Disch, Lisa, and Mary Jo Kane. 1996. When the looker is really a bitch: Lisa Olson, sport and the heterosexual matrix. *Signs: Journal of Women in Culture and Society* 21 (winter): 278–308.

Eck, Beth. 1995. Cultural conflict and art: Funding the National Endowment for the Arts. *Virginia Review of Sociology* 2:89–113.

———. 2001. Nudity and framing: Classifying art, pornography, information, and ambiguity. *Sociological Forum* 16 (4): 603–32.

Gamman, Lorraine, and Marcia Marshment. 1989. *The female gaze: Women as viewers of popular culture.* London: Women's Press.

Griswold, Wendy. 1987. The fabrication of meaning: Literary interpretation in the United States, Great Britain and West Indies. *American Journal of Sociology* 5 (March): 1077–117.

Kimmel, Michael. 1990. *Men confront pornography.* New York: Crown.

———. 1994. Masculinity as homophobia: Fear, shame, and silence in the construction of gender identity. In *Theorizing masculinities,* edited by Harry Brod and Michael Kaufman. Thousand Oaks, CA: Sage.

Liebes, Tamar, and Elihu Katz. 1990. *The export of meaning: Cross cultural readings of Dallas.* New York: Oxford University Press.

Long, Elizabeth. 1986. Women, reading and cultural authority: Some implications of the audience perspective in cultural studies. *American Quarterly* 38:591–612.

Lutz, Catherine A., and Jane L. Collins. 1993. *Reading National Geographic.* Chicago: University of Chicago Press.

MacKinnon, Catharine. 1987. *Feminism unmodified: Discourses on life and law.* Cambridge, MA: Harvard University Press.

Metz, Christian. 1982. *The imaginary signifier: Psychoanalysis and the cinema.* Bloomington: Indiana University Press.

Modleski, Tania. 1982. *Loving with a vengeance: Mass-produced fantasies for women.* Hamden, CT: Archon.

Mulvey, Laura. 1975. Visual pleasure and the narrative cinema. *Screen* 16 (3): 6–18.

Nead, Lynda. 1992. *The female nude: Art, obscenity, and sexuality.* New York: Routledge.

Pollock, Griselda. 1988. *Vision and difference: Femininity, feminism, and histories of art.* New York: Routledge.

Pronger, Brian. 1990. *The arena of masculinity: Sports, homosexuality and the meaning of sex.* New York: St. Martin's.

Radway, Janice. 1984. *Reading the romance: Women, patriarchy and popular literature.* Chapel Hill: University of North Carolina Press.

Saunders, Gill. 1989. *The nude: A new perspective.* Cambridge, UK: Harper and Row.

Segal, Lynne. 1994. *Straight sex: Rethinking the politics of pleasure.* Berkeley: University of California Press.

Shivley, Joellen. 1992. Perceptions of western films among American Indians and Anglos. *American Sociological Review* 57 (December): 725–34.

Swidler, Ann. 1986. Culture in action: Symbols and strategies. *American Sociological Review* 51 (3): 273–86.

West, Candace, and Don H. Zimmerman. 1987. Doing gender. *Gender & Society* 1 (2): 125–51.

PART TEN

Violence and Masculinities

Nightly, we watch news reports of suicide bombings in the Middle East, terrorist attacks on the United States, racist hate crimes, gay-bashing murders, or Colombian drug lords and their legions of gun-toting thugs. Do these reports ever mention that virtually every single one of these terrorists, suicide bombers, or racist gang members is male?

This fact is so obvious that it barely needs to be mentioned. Virtually all the violence in the world today is committed by men. Imagine, for a moment, if all that violence were perpetrated entirely by women. Would that not be *the* story?

Take a look at the numbers: Men constitute 99 percent of all persons arrested for rape, 88 percent of those arrested for murder, 92 percent of those arrested for robbery, 87 percent for aggravated assault, 85 percent of other assaults, 83 percent of all family violence, and 82 percent of disorderly conduct. Nearly 90 percent of all murder victims are killed by men.

From early childhood to old age, violence is the most obdurate, intractable behavioral gender difference. The National Academy of Sciences puts the case starkly: "The most consistent pattern with respect to gender is the extent to which male criminal participation in serious crimes at any age greatly exceeds that of females, regardless of source of data, crime type, level of involvement, or measure of participation." "Men are always and everywhere more likely than women to commit criminal acts," write criminologists Michael Gottfredson and Travis Hirschi.[1]

What can we, as a culture, do to understand, let alone prevent the casual equation of masculinity and violence? The articles in this section approach that equation in a variety of arenas. James Gilligan describes how perceived humiliations are the pretext that legitimates the use of violence, and Jack Katz's ethnography of "badass" masculinity applies that model to street crime. Nick Pappas, Patrick McKenry, and Beth Catlett look at violence in sports, especially ice hockey. (Ice hockey is especially interesting because the rules of the game are so gendered: For men, aggression and fighting are prescribed, but female ice hockey strictly prohibits them.)

Violence isn't only interpersonal; it is also institutional. Carol Cohn's chilling ethnography of war intellectuals shows how rational men making rational plans can come up with some of the most irrationally terrifying proposals.

[1]National Academy of Sciences, cited in Michael Gottfredson and Travis Hirschi. *A General Theory of Crime* (Stanford: Stanford University Press, 1990), p. 145. See also Steven Barkan, "Why Do Men Commit Almost All Homicides and Assault?" in *Criminology: A Sociological Understanding* (Englewood: Prentice Hall, 1997); Lee Bowker, ed., *Masculinities and Violence* (Thousand Oaks, CA: Sage Publications, 1998).

Image courtesy of THINK AGAIN 2006, www.agitart.org

James Gilligan

Culture, Gender, and Violence: "We Are Not Women"

Even those biological factors that do correlate with increased rates of murder, such as age and sex, are not primary determinants or independent causes of violent behavior. They do not spontaneously, in and of themselves, create violent impulses; they act only to increase the predisposition to engage in violence, when the individual is exposed to the social and psychological stimuli that do stimulate violent impulses. In the absence of those stimuli, these biological factors acting alone do not seem to stimulate or cause violence spontaneously or independently.

That is good news; for while we cannot alter or eliminate the biological realities of age and sex, which are made by God, we can bring about fundamental changes in the social and cultural conditions that expose people to increased rates and intensities of shame and humiliation, since culture and society are made by us. In this chapter I will analyze some of the cultural patterns, values, and practices that stimulate violence, and how they might be altered to prevent violence.

When these conditions are altered the exposure of human populations to shame is dramatically reduced—and so is violence. Those economically developed democracies all over the world that have evolved into "welfare states" since the end of the Second World War, including all of Western Europe, Japan, Canada, Australia, and New Zealand, offer universal and free health care, generous public housing, unemploy-

ment and family leave policies, and so on. Every one of those countries has a more equitable (and hence less shame-inducing) socioeconomic system than the United States does. There is a much greater sharing of the collective wealth of the society as measured, for example, by the smaller gap between the income and wealth of the most and least affluent segments of their populations. Our rate of violent crime (murder, rape) is from two to twenty times as high as it is in any of the other economically developed democracies. This is precisely what the theory presented in this book would predict.

Other cultures have also altered their social conditions so as to protect their members from exposure to overwhelming degrees of shame and humiliation, and have experienced the dramatic diminution in rates of violence that the theory espoused in this book would lead us to expect. They demonstrate the degree to which rates of violence are determined by social, cultural, and economic conditions. One example would be those societies that practice what has been called "primitive Christian communism," and are truly classless societies whose economic systems are based on communal sharing—Anabaptist sects such as the Hutterites, Mennonites, and Amish. One remarkable feature of these societies is that the incidence of violence in them is virtually zero. The Hutterites, for example, do not appear to have had a single confirmed case of murder, rape, aggravated assault, or armed robbery since they arrived in America more than a hundred years ago. They also practice a strict and absolute pacifism, which is why they had to emigrate to America from Europe in the last century—to escape becoming victims of genocide at the hands of governments there which were persecuting them. While that aspect of their experience is one reason why I do not propose them as a model for our own society to emulate in any concrete, literal way, they do demonstrate that violence does not have to be universal; and that altering social, cultural, and economic conditions can dramatically reduce, and for all practical purposes eliminate, human violence from the face of the earth.

One apparent exception to the generalizations I am making here is Japan, which has often been cited as a "shame culture." If frequent exposure and intense sensitivity to shame (in the absence of a correspondingly powerful exposure to guilt) stimulates violence toward others, then why does Japan have a relatively low homicide and high suicide rate—the same pattern that characterizes those societies that have sometimes been called "guilt cultures," namely, the European and other economically developed "welfare state" democracies? There are two answers to that question, one that refers to the period before World War II, and the other, the time since then.

During both periods, Japan has been described by those who know it best as an intensely homogeneous and conformist society, with strong pressures against individual deviations from group norms and behaviors. That social pattern had, and still has, a powerful influence on the patterns of Japanese violence. Until the end of the Second World War, Japan was an extremely violent society—indeed, one of the most violent in the history of the world; they have been described, both by themselves and by their neighbors, as "a nation of warriors" since they first emerged as an independent nation two to three thousand years ago. However, that violence was directed almost entirely toward non-Japanese. Some cultures, such as Japan's, have been more successful than others in channeling the homicidal behavior of their members toward members of other cultures, so that it is labeled warfare or genocide, rather than toward members of their own culture, which is called murder. Thus, the Japanese engaged in

a degree of violence toward their Asian neighbors from 1930 to 1945 that was just as genocidal as what the Germans perpetrated in Europe. When compared to the number of suicides that Japanese citizens committed during the first half of this century, the number of homicides that they committed (in the form of warfare) during that same period was astronomical—exactly as the theory proposed in this book would predict.

However, since 1945 the social and economic conditions in Japan have changed remarkably. Japan today has the lowest degree of economic inequity among its citizens in the world (as judged by the World Bank's measures of relative income and wealth). So it is not surprising that Japan also has a remarkably low frequency both of violent crime and of structural violence. For if socioeconomic inequities expose those at the bottom of the ladder to intense feelings of inferiority; if relative equality protects people from those feelings; and if inferiority feelings stimulate violent impulses, then it is not surprising that Japan's current socioeconomic structure would be marked by a low level of violence toward others, as indeed it is—even if the Japanese are unusually sensitive to feelings and experiences of shame, and even if (as some observers have claimed) they are not especially sensitive to or likely to experience guilt feelings. For their socioeconomic system, even if it does revolve primarily around sensitivity to shame rather than guilt, actively protects most individuals from being exposed to overwhelming degrees of shame, and also provides them with nonviolent (e.g., economic) means by which to prevent or undo any "loss of face" that is experienced.

If the main causes of violence are these social and psychological variables (shame versus honor), an apparent anomaly lies in the fact that men are and always have been more violent than women, throughout history and throughout the world. If shame stimulates violence; if being treated as inferior stimulates shame; and if women have been treated throughout history as inferior to men, then why are women less violent than men? (And they are indeed vastly less likely than men are to commit homicide, suicide, warfare, and assault, in every culture and every period of history.)

The Making of "Manhood" and the Violence of Men

To understand this apparent anomaly, we must examine the cultural construction of masculinity and femininity, and the contrasting conditions under which the two sexes, once they have been cast into patriarchally defined "gender roles," are exposed to feelings of private shame or public dishonor. To understand physical violence we must understand male violence, since most violence is committed by males, and on other males. And we can only understand male violence if we understand the sex roles, or gender roles, into which males are socialized by the gender codes of their particular cultures. Moreover, we can only understand male gender roles if we understand how those are reciprocally related to the contrasting but complementary sex or gender roles into which females are socialized in that same culture, so that the male and female roles require and reinforce each other.

Gender codes reinforce the socialization of girls and women, socializing them to acquiesce in, support, defend, and cling to the traditional set of social roles, and to enforce conformity on other females as well. Restrictions on their freedom to engage in sexual as well as aggressive behavior is the price women pay for their relative freedom from the risk of lethal and life-threatening violence to which men and boys are much more frequently exposed (a dubious bribe, at best, and one which shortchanges women, as more and more women realize).

The outpouring of scholarship across disciplines on the asymmetrical social roles assigned to males and females by the various cultures and civilizations of the world, including our own, has included works in history, economics, literary theory, philosophy, sociology, anthropology, psychology, science, law, religious studies, ethnic studies, and women's studies. One thing all this

work has made clear to me (and to many others) is that listening to women (for the first time), and opening up a dialogue between men and women, rather than merely continuing what has throughout most of the history of civilization been primarily a male monologue, is a necessary prerequisite for learning how to transform our civilization into a culture that is compatible with life. And to do that requires that men and women both learn to interact in ways that have simply not been permitted by the gender codes of the past.

My work has focused on the ways in which male gender codes reinforce the socialization of boys and men, teaching them to acquiesce in (and support, defend, and cling to) their own set of social roles, and a code of honor that defines and obligates these roles. Boys and men are exposed thereby to substantially greater frequencies of physical injury, pain, mutilation, disability, and premature death. This code of honor requires men to inflict these same violent injuries on others of both sexes, but most frequently and severely on themselves and other males, whether or not they want to be violent toward anyone of either sex.

Among the most interesting findings reported by social scientists is the fact that men and women stand in a markedly different relationship to the whole system of allotting honor in "cultures of honor." For example, one observation that has been made recurrently is that men are the only possible sources, or active generators (agents), of honor. The only active effect that women can have on honor, in those cultures in which this is a central value, is to destroy it. But women do have that power: They can destroy the honor of the males in their household. The culturally defined symbol system through which women in patriarchies bring honor or dishonor to men is the world of sex—that is, female sexual behavior. In this value system, which is both absurd from any rational standpoint and highly dangerous to the continued survival of our species given its effect of stimulating male violence, men delegate to women the power to bring dishonor on men. That is, men put their honor in the hands of "their" women. The most emotionally powerful means by which women can dishonor men (in this male construction) is by engaging in nonmarital sex, i.e., by being too sexually active or aggressive ("unchaste" or "unfaithful") before, during, or even after marriage.

These themes are prominent in one well-known "culture of honor," for example, the American South. Bertram Wyatt-Brown illustrated this by quoting from a letter Lucius Quintus Cincinnatus Lamar wrote to Mary Chesnut in 1861, in which he compares the men of the South to Homer's heroes, who "fought like brave men, long and well," and then went on to say "We are men, not women." The real tragedy for Lamar, as Wyatt-Brown saw, was that "for him, as for many, the Civil War was reduced to a simple test of manhood."

And women can adopt those same views of manhood, as Mary Chesnut recounts in her diary: "'Are you like Aunt Mary? Would you be happier if all the men in the family were killed?' To our amazement, quiet Miss C. took up the cudgels—nobly: 'Yes, if their life disgraced them. There are worse things than death.'" These attitudes are exactly the same as those of the men I have known in maximum-security prisons.

That the same relative differences between the two gender roles can be found in many civilizations throughout history and throughout the world emphasizes the importance of understanding that it is men who are expected to be violent, and who are honored for doing so and dishonored for being unwilling to be violent. A woman's worthiness to be honored or shamed is judged by how well she fills her roles in sexually related activities, especially the roles of actual or potential wife and mother. Men are honored for activity (ultimately, violent activity); and they are dishonored for passivity (or pacifism), which renders them vulnerable to the charge of being a non-man ("a wimp, a punk, and a pussy," to quote the phrase that was so central to the identity of the murderer I analyzed in Chapter Three). Women are honored for inactivity or passivity, for not engaging in forbidden activities. They are shamed or dishonored if they are active where they should not be—sexually or in realms that are forbidden (professional ambition, aggressiveness, competitiveness and success; or violent activity, such as warfare or other forms of murder). Lady Macbeth, for example, realized that to commit murder she would have to be "unsex'd," i.e., freed from the restraints on violence that were imposed on her by virtue of her belonging to the female sex; and even then, she was unable to commit murder herself, but had to shame her husband into committing murder for her, so that she could only participate in violent behavior vicariously (just as she could only gain honor vicariously, through the honor she would obtain through being his queen when he became king).

Further evidence that men are violence objects and women, sex objects, can be found by examining the kinds of crimes that are committed against each sex. Men constitute, on the average, 75 percent or more of the victims of lethal physical violence in the United States—homicide, suicide, so-called unintentional injuries (from working in hazardous occupations, engaging in violent athletic contests, and participating in other high-risk activities), deaths in military combat, and so on. And throughout the world, men die from all these same forms of violence from two to five times as often as women do, as the World Health Organization documents each year. Women, on the other hand, according to the best available evidence, seem to be the victims of sex crimes (such as rape and incest) more often than men are. Both men and women seem to feel that men are more acceptable as objects of physical violence than women are, for both sexes kill men several times more often than they kill women. Even in experimental studies conducted by psychologists, both men and women exhibit greater readiness and willingness to inflict pain on men than on women, under otherwise identical conditions. Studies of child abuse in those countries in which reasonably accurate statistics are available find that boys are more often victims of lethal or life-threatening violent child abuse (being treated as violence objects), whereas girls are more often victims of sexual abuse (being treated as sex objects)—with few exceptions. Virtually every nation that has had a military draft has decided either that only men should be drafted, or that only men should be sent into combat. Again, none of this should surprise us, given the competition between men for status, valor, bravery, heroism—and honor—in patriarchal societies.

We cannot think about preventing violence without a radical change in the gender roles to which men and women are subjected. The male gender role generates violence by exposing men to shame if they are not violent, and rewarding them with honor when they are. The female gender role also stimulates male violence at the same time that it inhibits female violence. It does this by restricting women to the role of highly unfree sex objects, and honoring them to the degree that they submit to those roles or shaming them when they rebel. This encourages men to treat women as sex objects, and encourages women to conform to that sex role; but it also encourages women (and men) to treat men as violence objects. It also encourages a man to become violent if the woman to whom he is related or married "dishonors" him by acting in ways that transgress her prescribed sexual role.

Since culture is itself constructed, by all of us, if we want to take steps to diminish the amount of violence in our society, both physical and sexual, we can take those steps. To speak of eliminating the sexual asymmetry that casts men and women into opposing sex roles is to speak of liberating both men and women from arbitrary and destructive stereotypes, and to begin treating both women and men as individuals, responding to their individual goals and abilities, rather than to the group (male or female) to which they belong.

There is a deep and tragic paradox about civilization. On the one hand, it has been, up to now, the most life-enhancing innovation the human species has created. The sciences have made it possible for more people to live, and to live longer lives, and to live better lives, freer of pain and illness, cold and hunger, than was ever possible before civilization was invented; and the many forms of art that could not and did not exist except under conditions of civilization are among the main things that make life worth living. But the paradox is that civilization has also increased both the level of human violence, and the scale of the human potential for violence, far beyond anything that any precivilized human culture had done. In the past, the primary threat to human survival was nature, now it is culture. Human suffering before civilization was mainly pathos; since the creation of civilization, it has become, increasingly, tragedy. In fact, it would not be going too far to say that violence is the tragic flaw of civilization. The task confronting us now is to see whether we can end the tragic (violent) element of civilization while maintaining its life-enhancing aspects.

Why has civilization resulted in the most enormous augmentation of human violence since the human species first evolved from its primate forebears? I believe that that question can only be answered by taking into account the psychology of shame. Shame not only motivates destructive behavior, it also motivates constructive behavior. It is the emotion that motivates the ambition and the need for achievement that in turn motivates the invention of civilization.

But—and this is the crux of the matter—this same emotion, shame, that motivates the ambition, activity, and need for achievement that is necessary for the creation of civilization also motivates violence. And when the enormous increase in technological power that civilization brings with it is joined to the enormous increase in violent impulses that shame brings with it, the stage is set for exactly the drama that the history (that is, the civilization) of the world shows us—namely, human social life as an almost uninterrupted, and almost uninterruptedly escalating, series of mass slaughters, "total" and increasingly genocidal wars, and an unprecedented threat to the very continuation not only of civilization itself (which brought this situation about, it cannot be emphasized too strongly) but much more importantly, of the human species for the sake of whose survival civilization was invented in the first place.

Through my clinical work with violent men and my analysis of the psychodynamics of shame and guilt, I have come to view the relationship between civilization and violence in a way that is the diametrical opposite of Freud's. Freud saw violence as an inevitable, spontaneously occurring, natural, innate, instinctual impulse, and civilization and morality as attempts at "taming," neutralizing, inhibiting, or controlling that violent impulse. I see violence, in contrast, as defensive, caused, interpretable, and therefore preventable; and I see civilization, as it has existed up to now (because of class, caste and age stratification, and sexual asymmetry), as among the most potent causes of violence.

One of the puzzles of this century is the phenomenon of Nazism: how could one of the most civilized nations on earth have been capable of such uncivilized, barbaric behavior? (One could ask the same question about Japan's record in World War II.) But from the perspective being elaborated here, genocide is not a regression or an aberration from civilization, or a repudiation of it. It is the inner destiny of civilization, its core tendency—its tragic flaw. Genocide has characterized the behavior of most of the great world civilizations, from ancient Mesopotamia to Rome, to medieval Europe, to the African slave trade and the conquest of the Americas, to the Holocaust and atomic weapons.

How to deal with violence, then? The moral value system (which I will call "shame-ethics") that underlies the code of honor of those patriarchal cultures and subcultures in which behavioral norms are enforced primarily by the sanctions of shame versus honor, such as the Mafia, urban street gangs, and much of the rest of American culture, rationalizes, legitimates, encourages, and even commands violence: it does not prohibit or inhibit it.

The kind of morality that I am calling guilt-ethics (that says "Thou shalt not kill") is an attempt at a kind of therapy, an attempt to cure the human propensity to engage in violence, which is stimulated by shame-ethics. And that was a noble attempt, which one can only wish had been successful. Why has it not worked? I think that the analysis of violence presented in this book can enable us to see the answer to that question. The reason that guilt-ethics has not solved and cannot solve the problem of violence is because it does not dismantle the motivational structure that causes violence in the first place (namely, shame, and the shame-ethics that it motivates). Guilt, and guilt-ethics, merely changes the direction of the violence that shame has generated, it does not prevent the violence in the first place. It primarily redirects, onto the self, the violent impulses that shame generates toward other people. But it does not prevent violence, or even inhibit it. Suicide is no solution to the problem of homicide; both forms of violence are equally lethal. Masochism is no solution to the problem of sadism; both forms of pathology are equally destructive and painful.

Neither shame nor guilt, then, can solve the problem of violence; shame causes hate, which becomes violence (usually toward other people), and guilt merely redirects it (usually onto the self). But to say simply that we need more love, and less shame and guilt, is vacuous. What we really need is to be able to specify the conditions that can enable love to grow without being inhibited by either shame or guilt. And it is clear that shame and guilt do inhibit love. Shame inhibits people from loving others, because shame consists of a deficiency of self-love, and thus it motivates people to withdraw love from others and ration it for the self. Guilt, on the other hand, inhibits self-love, or pride, which the Christian guilt-ethic calls the deadliest of the seven deadly sins. Guilt motivates people to hate themselves, not love themselves, because the feeling of guilt is the feeling that one is guilty and therefore deserves punishment (pain, hate), not reward (pleasure, love).

If we approach violence as a problem in public health and preventive medicine then we need to ask: What are the conditions that stimulate shame and guilt on a socially and epidemiologically significant scale? The conditions that are most important are relative poverty, race and age discrimination, and sexual asymmetry. If we wish to prevent violence, then, our agenda is political and economic reform.

The social policies that would be most effective in preventing violence are those that would reduce the amount of shame. To reduce the amount of shame, we need to reduce the intensity of the passive, dependent regressive wishes that stimulate shame. And to reduce the intensity of those wishes, we must gratify those wishes; by taking better care of each other, especially the neediest among us—particularly beginning in childhood, when the needs for love and care are most intense and peremptory. To quote again the phrase that Dostoevsky put in the mouth of Father Zossima, we then would recognize that "all are responsible for all."

We have a horror of dependency in this country—particularly dependency on the part of men. No wonder we have so much violence—especially male violence. For the horror of dependency is what causes violence. The emotion that causes the horror of dependency is shame. Men, much more than women, are taught that to want love or care from others is to be passive, dependent, unaggressive and unambitious or, in short, unmanly; and that they will be subjected to shaming, ridicule, and disrespect if they appear unmanly in the eyes of others. Women, by contrast, have traditionally been taught that they will be honored if, and only if, they accept a role that restricts them to the relatively passive aim of arranging to be loved by men and to depend on men for their social and economic status, foregoing or severely limiting or disguising activity, ambition, independence, and initiative of their own. This set of injunctions decreases women's vulnerability to behaving violently, but it also inhibits women from participating actively or directly in the building of civilization, in part by reducing them to the role of men's sex objects.

We Americans, as a society, appear to be horrified by the thought that a man could be dependent on anyone (other than himself), and that a woman could be dependent on anyone (other than "her man," that is, her father or husband). The extent of our horror of dependency can be seen in our horror of what is somewhat misleadingly called "welfare dependency"—whether it is the "dependency" on society of an unemployed or disabled man, of an unmarried mother, or of a child without a father. This conceals, or rather reveals, that we as a nation do less for our own citizens than does any other democracy on earth; less health care, child care, housing, support to families, and so on. So that we end up shaming and blaming those whose needs are exposed. Therefore it is not surprising that we also have more violence than does any other democracy on earth, as well as more imprisonment—since we shame some people for having needs that all people have.

For needs that are repressed do not get met, nor do they just disappear. The return of repressed needs, in unconscious, disguised form, is what the various symptoms of psychopathology consist of. One form in which repressed needs for care return is chronic institutionalization—that is, long-term imprisonment or mental hospitalization—which allows us as a society to punish massively, while we gratify grudgingly, those needs of which we are so intolerant.

In fact, the violence of our society reveals our shame at being less "independent" than we "declared" ourselves to be two centuries ago. In contemporary America, to want love, to depend on others, to be less than completely self-sufficient, is to be shamed by all the institutions of our society, from welfare offices to mental hospitals to prisons. One can pretend that one is in an institution only because one is so tough and dangerous and scary, so active and aggressive, and so independent of the community's standards, that the courts insisted on locking one up against one's own wishes. But nevertheless, it is true that for many men in our society it is only in prison that one is given three meals a day, a warm bed to sleep in at night, a roof over one's head, and people who care enough about one to make sure that one is there every night.

Those are among the reasons why the most effective way to increase the amount of violence and crime is to do exactly what we have been doing increasingly over the past decades, namely, to permit—or rather, to force—more and more of our children and adults to be poor, neglected, hungry, homeless, uneducated, and sick. What is particularly effective in increasing the amount of violence in the world is to widen the gap between the rich and the poor. We have not restricted that strategy to this country, but are practicing it on a worldwide scale, among the increasingly impoverished nations of the third world; and we can well expect it to culminate in increasing levels of violence, all over the world.

Relative poverty—poverty for some groups coexisting with wealth for others—is much more effective in stimulating shame, and hence violence, than is a level of poverty that is higher in absolute terms but is universally shared. Shame exists in the eye of the beholder—though it is more likely to exist there if the beheld is perceived as richer and more powerful than oneself. In that archaic, prescientific language called morality, this gap is called injustice; but most people throughout the world still think in moral terms, and the perception that one is a victim of injustice is what causes shame, which in turn causes violence.

From the standpoint of public health, then, the social psychology of shame, discrimination, and violence becomes central to any preventive psychiatry. The causes and consequences of the feelings of shame as well as their psychodynamic parameters have become more urgently compelling as a focus of investigation, given the potential ultimacy of violence in a nuclear age, as well as the continuing high rate of violence in American society. In my analysis of the psychological consequences of the feelings of shame, I have set out to show how such seemingly trivial events as personal experiences of chagrin or embarrassment can explode into epidemics of violence, just as the physical consequences of organisms as insignificant as microbes can have the gravest implications for public health. As Rudolph Virchow, who helped to lay the foundations of preventive medicine and public health more than a century ago, put it, "Medicine is a social science, and politics is simply medicine on a larger scale."

If cleaning up sewer systems could prevent more deaths than all the physicians in the world, then perhaps reforming the social, economic, and legal institutions that systematically humiliate people can do more to prevent violence than all the preaching and punishing in the world. The task before us now is to integrate the psychodynamic understanding of shame and guilt with the broader social and economic factors that intensify those feelings to murderous and suicidal extremes on a mass scale.

Jack Katz

Ways of the Badass

In many youthful circles, to be "bad," to be a "badass," or otherwise overtly to embrace symbols of deviance is regarded as a good thing. How does one go about being a badass? How can that become a compelling project?

One can develop a systematic understanding of the ways of the badass by distinguishing among three levels or degrees of intimating aggression. Someone who is "real bad" must be tough, not easily influenced, highly impressionable, or anxious about the opinions that others hold of him; in a phrase, he must not be morally malleable. He must take on an existential posture that in effect states, "You see me, but I am not here for you; I see you, and maybe you are here for me."

The second stage in becoming a badass is to construct alien aspects of the self. This construction may be achieved barbarically, by developing ways of living that appear hostile to any form of civilization, or by inventing a version of civilization that is not only foreign but incomprehensible to native sensibilities. If being *tough* is essentially a negative activity of convincing others that one is not subject to their influence, being *alien* is a more positive projection of the world in which one truly fits. The existential posture of the alien states in effect, "Not only am I not here for you, I come from a place that is inherently intractable by your world." The foreigner may often be charming; the alien is unnerving. Managing the difference between appearing to be interestingly foreign and disturbingly alien is a subtle business; much of the work of the adolescent badass plays on the fineness of the distinction.

Either alone or in combination with a posture of toughness, the perfection of an alien way is not sufficient to achieve the awesomely deviant presence of the badass. Toughs who set off sparks that call for attention but never explode risk being regarded as "punks." And many who elaborate alien ways achieve nothing more than the recognition of being "really weird." In addition to being tough and developing an alien style, the would-be badass must add a measure of meanness.[1]

To be "bad" is to be mean in a precise sense of the term. Badasses manifest the transcendent superiority of their being, specifically by insisting on the dominance of their will, that "I mean it," when the "it" itself is, in a way obvious to all, immaterial. They engage in violence not necessarily sadistically or "for its own sake" but to back up their meaning without the limiting influence of utilitarian considerations or a concern for self-preservation. At this level, the badass announces, in effect, "Not only do you not know where I'm at or where I'm coming from, but, at any moment, I may transcend the distance between us and destroy you. I'll jump you on the street, I'll 'come up side' your head, I'll 'fuck you up good'—I'll rush destructively to the center of your world, whenever I will! Where I'm coming from, you don't *want* to know!"

To make vivid sense of all the detailed ways of the badass, one must consider the essential project as transcending the modern moral injunction to adjust the public self sensitively to situationally contingent expectations. The frequent use of phallic metaphors is especially effective for making this process bristle with sensational moves. At the end of the chapter, I will clarify the distinctive relevance of masculine sexual symbols and suggest why being a badass is so disproportionately seductive to males. I will relate class and ethnic status to differences in adolescent cultures of deviance. Knowledge of the ways of the badass contributes to the explanation of the self-consciously criminal careers of hardened stickup men.

Being Tough

The ways of being tough may be summarized along two lines. First, a tough appearance may be accomplished by using symbols and practical devices that suggest an impenetrable self. Here we can place the attractions, to those who would effect a tough appearance, of leather clothing and metal adornments. Here, too, we can understand the connection of a publicly recognizable "toughness" with signs that unusual physical risks have been suffered and transcended; scars are an example. High boots frequently enhance a tough look, in some styles suggesting cowboys or motorcyclists, in other styles implying that the wearer has passed or expects to pass through some sort of disagreeable muck.[2]

Prominent among the devices of toughness are dark sunglasses. As the street name suggests, "shades," unlike sunglasses in general, pull down a one-way curtain in face-to-face interaction, accomplishing nicely the specific interactional strategy that is toughness. On the folk assumption that the eyes are windows to the soul, in face-to-face interaction we regularly read the eye movements of others for signs of the focus of their consciousness, to grasp their subjective location, and to track what is "here" to them. Simultaneously, we manage the direction of our gaze to shape the perception by others of what is "here" to us. Thus, we usually avert our gaze from passersby after an implicitly understood interval, so that our apparent continued attentions do not suggest an improperly intimate interest; conversely, if we want to suggest that the other is intimately "here" for us, we do not avert our gaze. Shades permit the wearer to detect what is "here" to passersby, while the wearer's focus of conscious

ness remains inaccessible to them. When this interactional reading does not hold, for example, when we know the wearer is blind, darkly tinted glasses will not work as a device for intimating toughness.

Because toughness manifests that one is not morally or emotionally accessible, one recognizable style of being tough is to maintain silence, sometimes referred to as a "stony" silence, in the face of extensive questions, pleadings, comic antics, and other efforts to evoke signs of sympathy. As an audible analog to the eyes' "shades," when "tough" guys have to say something to get things from others, they may mumble or speak in a voice muffled by gum, a tightly closed mouth, or a downcast face.

The symbols and devices of impenetrability are a simple ready-made way of being tough; many of them can literally be bought off the rack. What is culturally more complex and individually more challenging is the requirement to offset the moral malleability inevitably suggested when one enters communicative interaction. I may easily appear tough to you when I am not attempting to shape your understanding to any effect other than that I am tough. But if I want to do any other sort of business with you, my apparent rigidity will, sooner or later, become a problem. If I want to communicate substantive desires, I must attend to whether you have correctly interpreted my messages; if not, I am constrained to alter my expression to get the point across—all of which risks suggesting that, to shape your experience of me, I am willing to shape and reshape myself and, hence, that I am not so tough.[3]

It is common for young people to take on the first layer of toughness without being accomplished in the second. What appears to be a hard-and-fast toughness often dissolves in the first moments of substantive interaction. Thus, in the privacy of a bedroom, one may drape the body in leather and chains, practice a hard look in the mirror, apply apparently permanent but really erasable tattoos of skulls and crossbones, and so forth. When one enters a store to buy cigarettes, however, it may feel impossible not to wait one's turn with the clerk politely, and even to finish the transaction with a muttered "thanks."

The openings and closings of face-to-face interactions in public are routine occasions for indicating that one has the moral competence to be in society. With "How are you?" we often formally open and move into an interaction. The response, "And how are you?" without a pause is accepted and thus the interaction proceeds smoothly without either party explicitly responding to the question.[4]

The primary project of the questioner is usually to indicate that he is the sort of person who cares. Even though his failure to await a response might logically be taken to indicate just the opposite, the move makes sense to the participants because it indicates that the speaker is open to moral concerns. He has used convention to indicate that he is open to change based on the state of the other's being. Here is a little ceremony performed to ritualize the beginning of interaction, a ceremony in which each indicates to the other that he is capable of mediating his existence with others through social forms.

Compare a common ritual opening of interaction among adolescents who are attempting to be tough. When boys in American junior high schools pass each other in the halls while changing classes, they sometimes exchange punches aimed at each others' shoulders. They may then continue past each other or, even more oddly, they may abruptly abandon the dramatization of hostilities and pause for a short interchange of affable comments that make no reference to the opening blows. Literally, the thrust of the message is the thrust of the message. Familiarity with this ritual breeds a competition to be first in detecting the other's presence and to land the first punch. In a little ceremony performed to mark the initial moments of interaction, each attempts to indicate to the other that he exists for the other in the first instance physically, independent of civility and social form.

Note that not only is the implicit statement the inverse of that made by the customary civil ritual, so is its irony. The tactful adult shows that

he is the sort of person who cares by inquiring about the other's sensibilities and then proceeding without pausing for a response. But the playfully combative adolescent shows that he is present most fundamentally in his socially unrestrained physical being, by more or less artfully employing a well-established social form.

One of the most elemental ways of being tough is to mark the beginning and the ending of an interaction gutturally, with a sound that emanates from deep in the body and whose form indicates that the sound maker ("speaker" would not be quite accurate here) exists outside of civil conventions. Members of street gangs in Italian sections of Brooklyn in the 1950s would often signal their entrance into a streets corner assemblage of their fellows with an "eh" (or "ay") that would trigger a cycle of responsive "ehs."[5] This utterance is guttural, both in significance and sensual practice; the physical exertion indicates to the others that he is present for them from his stomach—not from his mind or from any socialized sensibility.

Endings of interactions are again typical occasions for expressing a competently socialized moral character. The strength of the moral demands made during an interaction is revealed by the amount of culture and proficiency of skill required to end an interaction without retrospectively undermining its moral framework. Such verbal and written civil endings as "Take Care," "Yours Truly," and "Have a Nice Day" reaffirm the person's competent social sensibility. Despite a near-universal awareness of the banality of these forms, they remain difficult to avoid.

Such ritual endings are executed because people who have been interacting anticipate that a new threat will emerge at the end of the interaction. This threat is not to the future of their relationship (these conventions are used as much, perhaps more, among strangers who may well never see each other again as among friends), but to the reinterpretation of what has just transpired. Often formally prospective *(Have* a nice day: I *remain* sincerely yours, *take* care, best *wishes),* these devices are implicitly and more fundamentally retrospective. In effect, farewells assert that even though my care for you is so limited that I can now move on to other cares—even though by ending this interaction I may suggest that I have not been authentically here for you—I really have been deeply, sensitively involved with you all the while. The misleadingly prospective direction of the form is essential to suppress awareness of the implicit retrospective doubt, the existential doubt that either participant was (and perhaps ever can be) really "here" for the other. As phenomenal worlds begin objectively to separate, civil interactors rush to reaffirm that those worlds really were isomorphic and that each person really was morally sensitive to the other. I anticipate your sense that if I can break off abruptly from you, you may reflect, "He never really gave a shit about what I felt in the first place!"

To produce toughness is, in part, a matter of failing to perform these prophylactic rituals on the moral health of everyday life, but it is also a matter of inventing substitutes. Consider as a striking example of a guttural exiting ceremony, the *cholo's* "Shaa-haa!" In East Los Angeles, adolescent *vatos, cholos,* or "homeboys" frequently mill about in a casual mood that shows no particularly malevolent spirit until the assemblage is brought to a close when one of the participants utters a forceful or cool statement of bravado to which he appends a "Shaa" or "Shaa-haa," which the others join in.

The following instance was part of a homeboy's recollection of his first day in the tenth grade at Garfield High School in East Los Angeles. He was "holding up the wall" with fellow homeboys from his *barrio*—a traditional practice in which groups congregate at traditional spots, lean against the wall, and look out at groups clustered in other spots. The school bell rang to call students to class. The homeboys continued to mill about, aware that, with time, their passivity would take on an increasingly deviant significance as a tacit rebellion against the school's attempt to control their interaction. A vice principal came over to urge the group to go to class, and one homeboy responded,

"'Say, professor, don't you have something better to do? If you don't take my advice, go sit on the toilet and flush yourself down. Shaa-haa!'"[6]

Like "eh," "Shaa-haa" (which can be short or long and more syncopated or less, depending on the occasion) comes from deep in the body, from the very bottom of the throat, if not from the guts. It involves letting out a burst of air audibly, over a jutting jaw, with mouth open but without shaping lips to form letters, all to accomplish a broad, deep, serpentine hiss that is often succeeded by a machine-gun burst of belly laughing. Having publicly defined the interaction that preceded the termination as one in which all the boys were present in a gutturally direct, socially uninhibited way, the aggregation can disband and the participants can head toward class.[7] With this utterance, a group of young men can harmoniously articulate a common moral posture of being tough without fear that the medium will contradict the message.

In addition to opening and closing interactions, those who would be tough must routinely counter the moral vulnerabilities suggested in the very nature of human existence. For human beings eating, for example, is a figurative, as well as a literal, opening of the self. For tough guys, eating (and defecating, ejaculating, extracting mucus from the nose and throat, and so on) must be carefully cultivated to offset the breach of self inherent in the process. Sweating, however, should require no special ceremony for toughs: perspiring occurs simply in a transpiring; no act of opening the body is necessary to make visible these drops from inside.

In adolescent cultures, toughness is commonly displayed as a subtle negativity, barely glossed onto an otherwise morally sensitive interaction. Consider two everyday ironies from black street life, hand-slapping rituals and the use of "shit" to begin a turn at speaking in conversation. Handshaking is a conventional form for displaying a civil sensibility when face-to-face interactions begin or end. It expresses a gentle man's spirit by physically enacting a moral malleability and a moral vulnerability: I open my hand, my self, to feel the force of your presence, and vice versa; we are united by social form, such that each may be influenced by the other's will.

Young men in black ghettos have constructed from this convention a means of displaying a paradoxical form of social contract. With the hand slap, the moral malleability suggested by the handshake becomes a cooperative hitting—I hit you and I let you hit me. The moral vulnerability suggested by the offer and acceptance of physical contact is simultaneously countered by its opposite. The hitting or slapping, an action that in other contexts might be humiliating punishment, usually passes as an unremarkable gloss of toughness.

This dialectical principle is elaborated within ongoing group interactions as speakers and listeners seek and confer agreement. The more a listener agrees with a speaker, the harder he hits him, and conversely. As R. Lincoln Keiser noted:

> In general, when a hand-slapping episode occurs during social interaction it emphasizes agreement between the two parties. If an individual has said something someone thinks particularly noteworthy, he will put out his hand to be slapped. By slapping it, the alter in the relationship signals agreement. Varying the intensity of the slap response indicates varying degrees of agreement. A Vice Lord may say, "Five Lords can whup fifty Cobras!" and then put out his hand, palm up. Another club member responds by slapping the palm hard, thus indicating strong agreement. The first Vice Lord might then say, "I can whup ten Cobras myself!" and again put out his hand. This time, however, the second individual may respond with a much lighter slap.[8]

The more the listener indicates that he has been moved by the speaker, the more emphatically he simultaneously acknowledges and counters his malleability through enacting aggression.

"Shit," pronounced melodically over long vowel sounds ("Sheee-it"), has had an extraordinary run of popularity in black street life. It is a way for a speaker to begin a turn in conversation or to mark publicly the movement of his consciousness from one theme to another within a monologue. Compare, as the inverse in form and function, the British use of "Right" to begin a turn in conversation, for example, the Bobby's "Right, what's going on here?" the Mexican's use of "Bueno, es que" to begin a response to a question; and the use of "okay" by white middle-class adolescents in the U.S. to begin a turn and repeatedly to reorient a narrative account in a conversation. Although with "shee-it" the speaker pulls himself out of a communal moral order even as he audibly begins to enter it, "Right," "Bueno," and "Okay" invoke a transcendent moral order to tie people together into a conversation at moments when the coordination of their sensibilities has become problematic. With "Right," the Bobby invokes a framework of moral approbation to begin the assertion of his authority. With "Bueno, es que," the Mexican begins to respond to a question by formally overcoming the dim, horrific possibility that the asking has inexorably alienated the speakers. With "okay, okay, okay," the young suburban American asserts his moral commitment to sustain order in conversation just as he anticipates that, because of problems in the evolving structuring of a narrative, it may soon fall into doubt.[9]

"Sheee-it" is elegantly negative, both in content and in form of delivery. When pronounced in a descending melody, the phrasing gives the word, even apart from its content, a cynical, negating tone. In content, shit is about as purely negative an image as any that could be thrown into a conversation. The existential fact that we are, each of us, literally (if also narrowly), walking, talking containers of excrement is remarkable for its typical absence from overt public attention. When used to start a speaker's turn in conversation, "shee-it" brilliantly executes a simultaneous expression of two dialectically related themes: (1) the fact that I speak to you coherently displays my ability to shape myself to fit into your understanding and (2) the fact that I begin by tying your impression of me to shit suggests that the social form I take on is but a thin veneer over a nature that is obdurately beyond social domination. The following example, which illustrates the point both in form and content, came from an interview with a member of a black street gang in San Francisco:

> I feel my high school education is the most important thing in my life right now. That's how I feel.
> [Interviewer:] How long have you felt this way? Shit. Maybe a year.[10]

These subculturally varied devices for producing a veneer of toughness are all counterveiling commentaries on the image of personal moral openness that is persistently implied in social interaction. To sustain interaction while remaining tough, one can repeatedly negate the continuously resurrected implication that one is sensitive to others by throwing shit onto the scene, with guttural outbursts, by physically hitting at the image of moral sensibility, and so forth. Attacks on the conventions and cliches of civil demeanor constitute one of the stock ways of being tough. An account of street gang violence in Glasgow, Scotland, provides a final illustration. According to one retelling by members of the "Young Team" of an attack on a solitary victim, the victim, a boy aged 14, rolled himself into a ball for self-protection and was then stabbed seventeen times in the back. Just before the attackers ran off, Big Sheila, a barmaid who was sympathetic to the Young Team, created a memorable closing line by dropping a handkerchief on the boy and offering: "That'll help ye tae mop yir brow."[11]

Being Alien

Being tough is essentially a process of negation, achieved either with a visual block, a symbolic sartorial shield, an audible muffle, or a maneuver that inverts the suggestions of a morally open self that are inevitably born in such everyday activities as eating, meeting friends, and conversing. Of course, being tough is not sufficient to construct a deviant identity; we admire poker players, respect businessmen, and honor political leaders who appear to be "tough." In all cases, the quality being celebrated is a negative moral capacity—an ability not to give away, not to give up, and not to give in.

By developing ways of being alien, adolescents can move positively beyond the negativity of a tough posture without abandoning it and without embracing respectable conventions. In congruence with the statement made from the stance of toughness, "I am not here for you," adolescents have fashioned an ever-expanding set of subcultures in which they can style great swaths of their everyday lives with indications that they come from some morally alien place.

Street Styles

Across subcultures would-be badasses exploit the hermeneutic possibilities in walking. Young blacks who would strike up the admirable image of the "bad nigger" work on orchestrating their pace to a ghetto "bop." John Allen, a black from Washington, D.C., who became a "professional" stickup man, recalled that when he was first committed to a juvenile detention facility,

> I learned a lot of things. . . . it was a place where you fought almost every day because everybody trying to be tougher than the next person. As a kid you pay so much attention to how a dude's supposed to be a bad nigger, he really having his way around the joint with the counselors and with everybody. . . . So you wanna be like him, you wanna act like him and talk like him. I think down there I must of changed my voice about hundred times 'cause I had a high-pitched voice and was bothered being small. And I changed my walk from supercool to ultracool.[12]

In East Los Angeles, the night before his first day in high school, a barrio homeboy anxiously anticipated humiliating challenges. He debated whether to take a gun to school and practiced his "barrio stroll": "a slow, rhythmic walk with ample flamboyant arm movement, chesty posture, and head up towards the heavens."[13]

Each of these styles transforms walking from a utilitarian convention into a deviant esthetic statement made routinely in the practice of getting from here to there. Each suggests that the walker takes some special pleasure in the existential necessity of putting one foot in front of the other to get ahead. Each suggests that the walker will not take a simple "straight" path through the social structure. He will take up more attention and more space in his social mobility than is called for by civil routines, perhaps, with those flamboyantly swayed arms and his side-to-side gait or slightly jumping bop causing problems for pedestrians who are attempting to pass unnoticed in the other direction.

Most notably, each style of walking suggests not only that the walker is not here for the others around and "walks to a beat of a different drummer," but he is from a morally deviant place. The *ghetto* bop and the *barrio* stroll identify the walker as a native of a place that is outside and antagonistically related to the morally respectable center of society. Similarly, the streetcorner male's habit of repeatedly making manual contact with his genitals and hoisting up his pants is a prominent way of pointing to the walker's animal life, a life carried on somewhere beyond the perception of respectable society. The currently popular "sag" look makes the same point by inverting these symbols. Pants are held by tight belts below the buttocks, where they permit the display of a "bad" ass covered by florid boxer shorts, which are often worn over a second, unseen pair of underpants.[14]

From Japan to Scotland to East Los Angeles, tattoos are appreciated as devices for embracing a deviant identity. Tattoos may be used minimally to suggest toughness by drawing attention to the skin as a barrier between the tattooed person and others. They also conjure up toughness by suggesting that the person has suffered and survived pain. Tattoos are not necessarily ominous, but often their content conveys an additionally "bad," alien theme by suggesting a totemic relationship with evil. In one circle of street fighting young men in Glasgow in the early 1970s, "Mick . . . sported on his forearm a red dagger entering the top of a skull and reappearing through its mouth. It was considered to be the finest tattoo in the neighbourhood."[15] Los Angeles cholos are partial to

black widow spiders and death skulls. Hell's Angels sport swastikas, German crosses, and skulls-and-crossbones.

These symbols suggest that the wearer presumes himself fundamentally rooted in a world of deviance and so is unresponsive to conventional moral appeals. What is more interesting is that the same effect is often achieved with tattoos that are traditional, respectable symbols of moral content—of "Mom," "love," and American Eagles; in the Japanese criminal subculture of *yakuza,* the whole body may be tattooed with chrysanthemums.[16] Beyond suggesting toughness and almost regardless of content, tattoos emphasize personal intransigence and are symbols of permanent loyalty to a particular subgroup's interpretation of the Good. They seem to say, "Wherever I am, whatever is going on, without my even trying, this will be fundamental to who I am." Even when the moral commitment is to "Mom" or to the American flag, the tattoo will often have threatening, deviant overtones. (Contrast the morally innocuous wearing of pins bearing club or patriotic images: unlike tattoos and like college ties and tie-clips, these can be taken off.)

Like walking, the would-be badass may also fashion talking into a deviant esthetic. John Allen, the professional "bad nigger" whose recollections of his street education in a juvenile detention facility were quoted earlier, noted: "There was a big thing there about talking. You had to express yourself, and you saying, 'Damn, jive, Listen man' and going through all the motions and changes."[17] In Glasgow, young street fighting men use a slang, reminiscent of Cockney forms, that hides its meaning through a multistep process of alteration from conventional expression. Thus, "It's jist yir Donald" means "It's just your luck": "Donald" calls up "duck," and "duck" rhymes with "luck." "Ya tea-leaf ye!" means "You thief!," which, if pronounced with their accent, would sound something like, tea-eef. "Ah fancy yir tin flute" means "I like your suit."[18]

The ethnographer who recorded these phrases grew up in Glasgow but was initially frustrated in attempting to understand the young toughs' everyday conversations. As Allen indicates with regard to the United States, "jive" talk is not a natural talent of ghetto blacks.[19] Within the local context of ghettoes, these argots are resources for taking the posture of an alien presence, a being who moves cooly above the mundane realities of others. As with being tough, being alien is not necessarily a posture taken toward conventional society. It is a way of being that may be taken up at any moment. As Allen's quote made clear, being ultra cool is most essential in the company of other tough young men. Being alien is a way of stating, "I am not here for you," when anyone—friend, family, or foe—may be the "you."

The ways of being alien begin to define an alternative deviant culture. As such, they call for the study of their distinctive esthetic unities. Here, I can only indicate a few lines of analysis that might be elaborated by investigations devoted solely to ethnographic documentation.

The Cholo

A coherent deviant esthetic unites various manifestations of the low-income youth culture of the barrio known as *la vida loca* and identified with the cholo, vato loco, or Mexican-American homeboy. Language, body posture, clothing fashions, car styles, and graffiti exhibit a distinctive, structurally similar, "bad" perspective. As individuals, young people in the barrio take on and shed this esthetic from situation to situation and to different degrees, but they continuously take for granted that affiliation with it will signify, to their peers and to adults alike, the transcendence of a line of respectability and the assumption of a high-risk posture of moral defiance.

In its essential thrust, the cholo esthetic assumes an inferior or outsider status and asserts an aggressive dominance. In body posture, this dialectic is achieved by dropping below or falling back and simultaneously looking down on others. Thus, when Mexican-American young men wish to take up a cholo or "bad" posture for a photograph, they often squat, placing their buttocks just off the ground, sometimes on their heels, while

they throw their heads slightly back to a position from which they can glare down at the camera. This posture is not easily sustained; its accomplishment is at once an athletic test and an esthetic demonstration of "bad" toughness.[20]

This position might be characterized as an aristocratic squat. Reminiscent of a resource known to peasants throughout the world, the cholo's squat creates a place for him to sit when there are no chairs. But by throwing his head sharply back, the cholo takes on a paradoxically aristocratic air. Once in the lowered and reared-back position, a sense of superiority is attached to him, as it is to one who is born to privilege: naturally and necessarily, like a law of nature.

Faced by a squatting cholo, an observer sees himself observed by a down-the-nose glance, like the stereotype of a peasant under the regard of an aristocrat. For his part, the cholo accomplishes something magical: he simultaneously embraces and transcends an inferior status. Before your very eyes and dressed in an undershirt that has no sleeves to put anything up, the cholo drops down to the ground, becoming lower to you in physical position but putting you down morally. Miraculously, the cholo manages literally to look down on you from beneath you.

The dialectical structure and aggressive symbolic force of this body posture is also carried out in the classic *pachuco* stance and in the contemporary "barrio stroll." Unlike the cholo's aristocratic squat, the pachuco style is both historically dated and well-known outside Mexican-American barrios, in part because of the popularity of the play and then movie, *Zoot Suit*. Although the pachuco's Zoot Suit or "drapes" were fashions of the 1930s and 1940s, contemporary cholos proudly, and sometimes self-consciously, continue elements of the pachuco style, wearing overly large, multiply pleated, sharply pressed khaki pants and pointed, brightly shined black shoes. And if the narrator of *Zoot Suit* took an exaggerated back-leaning stance, the contemporary cholo is similarly inclined.[21]

When being photographed, a group of cholos will often divide up into some who squat, lean forward, throw their heads back, and cast their eyes down to meet the camera and some who stand, maintaining the wide angle between their side-pointed feet that the squatters also adopt, throwing the trunk slightly back, throwing their heads back even more, and casting their eyes down to meet the camera. This standing position is put into motion in the barrio stroll. In forward movement, the foot position adopted by squatting and stationary cholos is maintained, but now it becomes far more noticeable, causing a duck-like waddle. To balance out the waddle and the backward slant of the trunk, the barrio stroller bends his elbows sharply, drawing the hands up parallel to the ground.

In the stationary position and in the stroll, the "being low" of the squat is replaced by a "being outside." While the squatting cholo is in a remarkably low social position, the backward-inclined, standing and strolling cholo is remarkably beyond reach. The magical effect is that while being emphatically beyond conventional reach, the cholo appears to be unusually aggressive and assertive as he strides into your world.

The low position of the cholo's aristocratic squat is repeated in the automobile esthetic of the low rider. By altering stock shocks and springs, cholos make cars ride literally low. If the rear is lowered more than the front, the driver will naturally incline backwards. Even without mechanical alterations, they may achieve the same effect by driving with their arms fully extended, their trunk and head inclined back, and their eyes cast down at the world above.

The overall effect is less an approximation of the advertised modern man in an up-to-date car than a fantasy image of a prince in a horse-drawn chariot, sometimes racing with other chariots and sometimes promenading slowly through public boulevards. The cars themselves are restored and dressed up at a substantial expense. The challenge is to demonstrate a transcendent esthetic power by raising the dead and discarded to a vividly displayed superiority. The low-rider is a distinctively American construction of alien being; foreign cars are not used, but the style is pointedly differ-

ent from anything Detroit has ever tried to get Americans to buy.

The form of graffiti that is popular among Mexican-American youths in Los Angeles also has an emphatically alien esthetic and a backward leaning slant. In New York City, graffiti, produced by blacks, Puerto Ricans, and others, is often colorful and graphic, sometimes extensively narrative, and cartoon figures are often mixed in with individual and gang names, threats, and ideological slogans. New York graffiti writers consider one of their highest achievements to be the creation of an integrated set of images running over up to ten subway cars. In East Los Angeles, graffiti is primarily monotonic calligraphy; as one writer put it, everything is in the line:

> Graffiti is all the same line, the same feeling, even though different people use it for a different purpose. . . . Anyway, I dig that line, I dug that line. That's how I got involved. It's my thing—that line.[22]

Experienced graffiti "writers" in New York denigrate "tags" (writing only a name or nickname) as amateurish and unsophisticated. But in Los Angeles, graffiti is called *plaqueasos*—from *placa,* which in various contexts means a car license plate, a policeman's badge, or a plaque announcing one's business to the world. The plaqueasos of Los Angeles are elaborated in line and adornment far beyond the "tags" derided by New York writers.

Mexican-American plaqueaso writers appear to be working from traditions that are so ancient and foreign as to make the content of their graffiti routinely indecipherable to outsiders, often even to residents of their own barrios. The emphasis in the content is on individual and gang names, phrases of bravado and threats, nightmarish (black widow spiders, laughing skulls) and deviant (the number 13 for the letter "M" for marijuana) iconography, and a protective curse (*Con Savos* or *Con Safos,* often written simply as C/S) that is reminiscent of those inscribed on Egyptian tombs. Individual letters in words, designed in a style that is unfamiliar to any written tradition known in the barrio, are often mixed with symbols (for instance, stars between letters), as in a hieroglyphics.

In a sensitive study of East Los Angeles graffiti, Jerry and Sally Romotsky argued that major styles of plaqueasos are based on Old English, Gothic, Dürer-like calligraphy.[23] Perhaps the style that is most difficult for outsiders to decipher is what plaqueaso writers call the "point" style. Romotsky and Romotsky showed that the point style is achieved essentially by tracing the outlines of blocky, Old English-style letters. In effect, plaqueaso writers achieve a strange, alien appearance by working out of Anglo-Saxon cultural traditions in a disguised way. They achieve a distinctive presence by the ingeniously simple device of negation, that is, leaving out the substance of letters.

A superior posture for plaqueaso is achieved by using the same dialectical technique that is used in body posture. When drawn in three dimensions, the letters sometimes march to one side or huddle together like colorful cartoon characters engaged in a light, comic spirit. But in their "bad" forms—when they announce the names of gangs or make ominous declarations, three-dimensional letters often rear back and come down heavily on the observer as they declare their author's existence.[24]

The same esthetic runs through clothing and language. Cholos favor armless undershirts, as if to embrace a sign of the working-class status that has been abjured by conventional fashion. Unlike garments that are manufactured to be worn as "tops," these tops are also bottoms: traditionally worn beneath shirts, their display is a negation that emphasizes what is not worn. And by studiously maintaining their undershirts in brilliant white, cholos proclaim their transcendence of dirty work. Plaid shirts, referred to in the barrios as "Pendletons," are part of the everyday uniform of many school-age cholos. Worn over a bright white undershirt, the Pendleton recalls the cotton plaid shirts common among impoverished Mexican immigrants as well as the expensive wool shirts associated with the Oregon manufacturer.

As a practical matter, the style is alien to the reality of the cholos, whose first days of classes in the fall often have temperatures topping 100 degrees. With colorful bandanas wrapped around their foreheads, cholos look like they come from rural Indian areas rather than urban barrio neighborhoods.

Homeboys in East Los Angeles speak and write graffiti with elements from Calo, a unique amalgam of Spanish and English that continues a "pachuco" argot whose roots are in pre–World War II, Mexican-American gang life.[25] On the one hand, cholos often ridicule recently arrived Mexicans who are incompetent in English.[26] On the other hand, their version of Spanish is incomprehensible to native Mexicans as well as to many of their U.S.-born parents. Pachuco or Calo is not a foreign language; it is ubiquitously alien.

In sum, the cholo-pachuco style is a deviant posture of aggressive intrusiveness made from a position that is proudly outside the reaches of the various societies it addresses. Through the stationary and the walking body and in clothing, cars, everyday language, and stylized writing, the pachuco-cholo-homeboy-vato loco conjures up a deviance rooted in a world that is self-consciously and intrinsically alien. The special claim of this esthetic is not just that its bearers are tough, but that they are from a spiritually rich, morally coherent place that Anglo authorities, native Mexicans, parents, or conventionally styled peers may only grasp minimally and at a distance as existing somewhere over "there."

The Punk

Consider next the novel way in which the punk culture locates its bearers in an alien moral system. An observer of the original British working class–based punk culture offered this summary:

> The punks turned towards the world a dead white face which was there and yet not "there." These "murdered victims"—emptied and inert—also had an alibi, an elsewhere, literally "made up" out of vaseline and cosmetics, hair dye and mascara. But paradoxically, in the case of the punks, this "elsewhere" was a nowhere—

a twilight zone—a zone constituted out of negativity.[27]

The alien character of punk culture has been achieved in several ways. One is to embrace as appearance enhancing the devices that, according to strong moral injunctions and contemporary fashion, ought to be kept hidden. Thus, safety pins and sanitary napkins are worn as adornments on shirts and skirts, lavatory chains are draped like a necklace on the chest, and makeup is applied in degrees and places that ensure that its application will be seen. And hair is not only dressed in unconventional ways but is dyed blue, green, intense red, yellows, and combinations of these colors that are not found naturally on any humans. The suggestion is of an alien culture whose standards are the opposite of conventional esthetic standards. The thrust of punk culture is not only foreign or "weird" but consistently antipathetic.

The alien theme in punk culture has not been limited to dress and appearance. Dancing "was turned into a dumbshow of blank robotics." The pogo—a dance style of jumping up and down, hands clenched to the sides, as if to head an imaginary ball, the jumps repeated without variation in time to the strict mechanical rhythms of the music—"was a caricature—a reductio ad absurdum of all the solo dance styles associated with rock music." Bands took names like the Unwanted, the Rejects, the Sex Pistols, the Clash, and the Worst and wrote songs with titles like "I Wanna Be Sick on You" and "If You Don't Want to Fuck Me, Fuck Off." There was a "wilful desecration and the voluntary assumption of outcast status which characterized the whole punk movement."[28] A memorable example was a sort of pet hairdo constructed by carrying live rats perched on the head.[29]

Another alien theme, one that was given a particular reading in punk culture but that has had broad appeal to many "bad" youth cultures, might be called, being inured to violence. Clothes display holes and rips that suggest not wear but war; hair is shaped into daggers; makeup may suggest bruises, scars, and black eyes. In this theme,

the suggestion of an alien origin for the punk is that he or she has just come to the instant social situation, to what is going on here, from a place that is, to all in civil society, somewhere inhospitably "there."

Despite radical differences in the substance of their symbols, the punk and cholo cultures dramatize a tough invulnerability and the status of a visitor in the conventional world. For the individual adolescent, the adoption of the cholo or punk style has often meant a weighty decision of moral citizenship. On the one hand, the bearer sets himself off as a member of an alien culture in the eyes of school and police authorities, parents, and conforming peers. On the other hand, the alien style enables even the loner to induct himself, through what sociologists call collective behavior, into a deviant community.

Punk culture was manifested during its classic stage in the mid-to-late 1970s by an informal social organization underlying a strong esthetic coherence. The punk style inevitably became commercialized, softened, and sold to "normal" adolescents and to middle-aged adults through beauty salons, high-priced boutiques, and massmarketed music. But for several years, tens of thousands of adolescents were working out a personal style and helping to produce the emerging collective esthetic. By acquiring pieces of used clothing, costume jewelry, and miscellaneous "junk"; altering items already in their closets; and applying makeup and assembling outfits with a care for detail; adolescents, male and female, were literally fitting themselves into a controversial collective movement. That the culture as a whole achieved a persistent coherence even while the details of the punk "look" constantly changed could be taken by individual members as proof both of the autodidactical, idiosyncratic creativity of individual punks and of the existence of a common spiritual bond running through the age group, cutting across formal divisions of school classes, neighborhoods, sex, and ethnicity.

Many adolescents live alien subcultures with far more everyday meaning than simply that of a bizarre dressing ritual. Beyond exploring the reactions of conventional others, adolescents who are dressed in an alien style are recurrently challenged to behave in a distinctively cholo or punk (or "bad nigger," or Hell's Angel) style in routine interactions. How, for example, does one order food at a restaurant in punk style? How does one answer a teacher's question like a cholo?

If the alien adolescent is in exile from a society that does not and never has existed, we still must appreciate the transcendent loyalties that are being evoked. Alien adolescent subcultures are collective movements on the way toward class consciousness, but they rarely reach explicit self-awareness or survive efforts to organize them formally. The cholos' aristocratic squat and other elements of arch style suggest their inchoate collective efforts to weave themes from their unique historical reality: the Mexican peasant origins and U.S. agricultural exploitation of earlier generations combined with a revolutionary tradition in which battles between peasants and aristocrats were joined by bandit leaders. Just as the black ghetto pimp, dressed in a white suit and a planter's hat, defiantly embodies the stereotype of slave owners he has never known, so the cholo, looking down on his environment by taking up a stance beneath and outside, unwittingly but defiantly gives expression to his people's historical subjugation.

The punk movement in the United States emerged in the mid-1970s, coincident with the recession, rapid inflation, and the passage into political quiescence of the "sixties" generation. It emerged after the withdrawal from Vietnam, after the culmination of Watergate, and as the oil crisis was beginning to push up prices throughout the economy. Meanwhile the sixties generation, which originally gained collective self-consciousness, in part by taking over radio station formats and displacing the pop stars of the fifties, was now in its thirties, moving into higher income brackets, but still holding onto its cultural representation of youth. In rock music, the arena in which adolescents uniquely attempt to detect and define the waxing and waning of generations, scores of bands struggled for mass recognition in a youth market that was tena-

ciously dominated by stars and styles nearing middle age. Styled like a militant vanguard, the punk band represented, in the market of collective symbols, the distinctive historical struggle of the emerging generation. The punk movement was bitterly antihippie; rumors of attacks on sixties youth types were constant. And the punk music and performance style was not simply raucous but a move back to an historical era before the sixties. It was an effort to get back to the fertile, earliest, crudest days of rock and roll in the fifties, as if to begin the youth culture again but in a way in which the currently young could take their place.

To regard these as more than speculations is to miss the open-ended, protean quality of the subculture. What the movement is about in terms of collective material interest and historical position is necessarily unclear as long as it retains the openness to individual esthetic creativity that makes it a compellingly exciting process to its members. But not to speculate on underlying, implicitly sensed themes of collective class interest is to miss an essential element in the excitement of being in these movements. The alien subcultures of adolescence are vehicles for cooperative speculation, means of exploring, through the reactions of others to clothing and new speech forms, which devices "work" and which do not; which fit the alien soul and which are incomprehensible in it; and which compromise the alien order by evincing a subtle sympathy to mainstream conventions. To the extent that young people who do not know each other can create, through indirect interactions and informality, a rich coherence among such minor details as the shape of a line in graffiti, the colors painted on hair, a rag worn around the head, a stirring accent, or a memorable phrase uttered before a class, they can sense the reality of an alien spiritual home—a place as yet concretely present in no definable geography, but surely "there."

The Animal and the Cool

Cutting across the various alien adolescent subcultures is a dualism between the animalistic and the cool. One way to indicate that you are not just tough but essentially outside contemporary civilization is to manifest an animal incapacity for moral responsiveness. Hell's Angels embraced this folk anthropology with their studied affinity for dirt. Inverting the practice of teenagers who shrink "designer" jeans through multiple washings before wearing them skin tight in public, Hell's Angels would train new denim jackets through multiple baths in dirt and grease before wearing them on the road. To shock outsiders, they turned rituals of civil society into occasions for displaying their animal natures, as when one 250-pound Hell's Angel would greet another in a bar by taking a running jump into his arms and planting a wet kiss on his lips.[30] To be animal is to suggest chaotic possibilities—that, through you, at any moment, forces of nature may explode the immediate social situation.

Being cool is a way of being alien by suggesting that one is not metaphysically "here" in the situation that apparently obtains for others, but is really in tune with sensually transcendent forces in another, conventionally inaccessible dimension. To be cool is to view the immediate social situation as ontologically inferior, nontranscendent, and too mundane to compel one's complete attentions. A common way of being cool is to realize or affect a moderate drug mood: the "cool cat" of black street life has its origins in the culture of the heroin world.[31] In Los Angeles barrios, an analogous, drug-related phenomenon is *tapaoism,* an air of being so into a deviant world *(la vida loca)* that one cannot "give a shit" about any situational restraints. In contexts of extreme poverty, a cool version of a "bad" look may be achieved by a self-consciously exaggerated display of luxury in the form of flashy styles worn casually. In their ghettoes, the pachuco who is "draped" in overflowing fabric and the black cat who is "dripping" in jewelry imply sources of wealth that must exist at a distance from conventional morality, in some underground realm, perhaps that of the pimp or the drug dealer.[32]

The two emphases of alien style have spawned different descriptions of fighting. On the

animal side, in Puerto Rican street gangs in New York in the 1970s, to be beaten up was to be "dogged up." In many black ghettoes, group attacks on isolated individuals are described as "rat packing" or "wolf packing." In East Los Angeles, attempting to intimidate others with a fierce expression is known as doing a "maddog" look.

On the cool side, to Chicago's Vice Lords of the early 1960s, a fight was a "humbug," and some of the West Side branches became known as the "Conservative" Vice Lords. With "conservative" as with "humbug," they were assuming a pose of calm reserve toward what others find extremely upsetting. It also is cool to refer to risky deviant activities with a diminutive. John Allen, the "professional" stickup man, liked to talk about a period in his life in Washington, D.C., that was nicely organized—a time when he could do "my little sex thing," "my little drug thing," and "a little stickup."[33]

As used in black street culture, "shit," "jive," and "stone" have been used to express both the animal and the cool sides of an alien posture. To talk "jive" is to talk in a cool, poetically effective way, but it may also be to talk nonsense and to bullshit, as in the pejorative "don't give me that jive talk!" or "you jive motherfucker!" "Jive" and "shit" also refer to a gun. In this sense they suggest an overwhelming force that puts the individual beyond the restraints of civilized morality. To be "stoned" is, in one aspect, to be drugged beyond competence for morally responsive interaction. Stone is also a cool object; metaphysically, it emphasizes a hard, unmovable reality, as in the praiseworthy, "He's a stone motherfucker," or in The Black P. Stone Rangers, a famous gang name in Southside Chicago in the 1960s. The gang's name was supercool, since it exploited a double entendre ("stone" played off the name of a local street, Blackstone). Actually, the phrase was ultracool, in that it fortuitously created a triple or quadruple entendre; the club's name was celebrated by poetically inserting a "P" within the street name, which audibly set "stone" apart from "black" just long enough to register racial as well as metaphysical connotations.

Finally, a lack of expressiveness is used widely to construct alien adolescent subcultures in both animal and cool forms. "Animals" in fraternity houses and on sports teams represent a frequently admired way of being "bad" by showing themselves, in loud and wild forms, as being governed by inarticulate, uncivilized forces. On the cool side is the use of silence to affect the style of the professional killer or the Mafia chief. When asked by a sociologist, "What would you like to be when you grow up?" it is cool to answer, "an assassin."[34]

More elaborately, it is dramatically "bad" style to exercise power publicly through silent codes. Turtle, "the Chicano 'Fonz,'" first verbally dressed down homeboys from another barrio in a dangerous face-to-face confrontation and next gave a hand signal and walked away; then twenty or so of *his* homeboys "spontaneously" attacked in unison.[35] This move is "supercool" or extraordinarily "bad" owing to its doubly silent structure. It is a silent message that mobilizes a more profoundly silent dialectic. That is, the most minimal imaginable physical move causes a major physical attack, a momentary shift in posture produces a permanent change in being, a silent signal creates screaming pain, and a cool move turns on the heat and burns the victim.

No attack need follow such a silent message, however. A gesture by one, apparently undifferentiated, man that turns all the others in a place into his servants—for instance, in a bar, at the snap of a finger, an aisle is cleared and a central table is left vacant—also shows a bad "cool." Watching the silent signal and its results, both the participants and bystanders suddenly appreciate a powerful, alien presence. The indications are not only that a structure of authority clearly exists in the group, but that it is implicitly illicit: no formal indicia demarcate those who act as waiters, chauffeurs, and couriers from those who are served as customers, car owners, and chiefs. Exercised with an aura of mystery, "bad" because it cannot show its sources publicly, this power always exists at a distance from the situation that obtains here and now. For those under its spell, its sources are always in some unreachable location vaguely apprehended as over "there."

Being Mean

The person who would be tough must cultivate in others the perception that they cannot reach his sensibilities. Adolescents who would achieve a foreign and hostile presence in interaction must go further and participate in a collective project to produce an alien esthetic. But the shaping of a tough image and the practice of an alien sensibility are insufficient to ensure that one will be "bad." Those who would be bad are always pursued by powerful spiritual enemies who soften tough postures and upset the carefully balanced cultures of alienation, making them appear silly, puerile, and banal and thus undermining their potential for intimidation. To survive unwanted imitators, you must show that unlike the kids, you're not kidding; unlike the gays, you're not playing; unlike the fashionable middle class, you understand fully and embrace the evil of your style. You must show that you mean it.

By being mean, I refer to a distinctive sensuality worked into the experience of interaction. To complete the project of becoming a badass, it is necessary to impress on others the apprehension that, however carefully they may maintain a respectful comportment, you might suddenly thrust the forces of chaos into their world. If he is serious about being tough and alien, the would-be badass can inundate the routine social settings of his everyday life with this "awe-full," ominous character. But how can he show that he means it so clearly that he is never confused with childish, playful, or otherwise inauthentic imitators?

The key distinction is not between physical action and its symbolic representation. If the badass is to make everyday social situations routinely ominous, he cannot, as a practical matter, depend simply on violently harming others.[36] As has frequently been found in studies of street "gangs," those with the "baddest" reputations are not necessarily the best nor even the most frequent fighters. And in the qualitative materials which follow, the actual infliction of physical harm seems always imminent but is not.

Whether through physical attack or via dramatization at a distance, the badass conveys the specific message that he means it. If we ask, what is the "it" that he means? we miss the point. To construct and maintain an awesome, ominous presence, the badass must not allow others to grasp the goals or substantive meaning of his action. He must seem prepared to use violence, not only in a utilitarian, instrumental fashion but as a means to ensure the predominance of his meaning, as he alone understands it, whatever "it" may be.

To make clear that "he means it," the badass celebrates a commitment to violence beyond any reason comprehensible to others. For example, at a dance hall in Glasgow, Tim, a dominant personality in the Young Team, turned to Dave and pointed to a bystander," 'Ah don't fancy the look o' his puss. Go over an' stab him fur me.' Dave had duly carried out the request."[37] From London's East End, an ex-skinhead recalled, "We only 'it people for reasons, didn't we? . . . like if they looked at us."[38]

In conflicts between street gangs, there is little room for a reasoned exchange of grievances; "discussion" and "debate" risk suggesting a deferential bow to rational order that would undermine the project of the badass. Manny Torres, a member of the "Young Stars" in Spanish Harlem in the late 1950s, recalled that in his work as "warlord," debate was not a means of avoiding conflict but a signal that a fight was inevitable:

> My job was to go around to the other gangs, meet with their chiefs, and decide whose territory was whose. And if we had any debate about it, it was my job to settle on when and where we would fight it out and what weapons we would use.[39]

Physically, badasses are always vulnerable; in U.S. ghettoes, someone can always "get to" them, since guns are widely available. But if they communicate that they will persevere without limitation until they dominate, then they force others to confront the same choice: are they willing to risk bodily injury, and even if they escape injury, are they willing to risk arrest? Is a momentary sensation of dominance worth it? The badass's logic of domination is to mean nothing more or less than meanness. He succeeds by *inducing others* to reason, to reflect on the extraneous meaning of violence, to weigh the value of experiencing dominance against the fear of physical destruction and legal punishment, when *he* will not make the calculation. Now and again, he must go at least a little bit mad.

Ethnographic details demonstrate the would-be badass's awareness of the necessity to dramatize his transcendence of rationality. Badasses are not irrational or antirational, and they certainly are not stupid. They understand precisely the nature of rationality and they position themselves carefully to manifest that their spirit, their meaning, is not limited by their need to make intelligible to others or even to themselves the purposive coherence or utilitarian sensibility of their action. Within this framework, we can understand the following comments by black Philadelphia street toughs to sociologist Barry Krisberg not as evidence of intellectual incompetence or moral insensitivity, but as the opposite. A group leader named William told Krisberg that he "wouldn't argue with someone—just stab them."[40] There was no need to argue or explain because: " 'whatever comes to my mind, I know it got to be right because I'm thinking of it.' "[41] Another leader, Deacon, characterized his everyday posture with:

> Doesn't have to be anything, it could be just the principle of a conversation. If I thought it was justifiable, like, they was trying to, like fuck over me, I would shoot them, whatever way that came into my mind at that moment.[42]

Where badasses congregate, showdowns are likely. In showdowns, we can sometimes see the eminently rational use of seemingly irrational violence to manifest a transcendence of rationality. In the following incident, drawn from R. Lincoln Keiser's ethnography of Chicago's Vice Lords, there is no suggestion of sadism or even of much anger; rather, there is a mutual recognition of the meanness required to be a badass. The background is a fight between two cliques within the Vice Lords, the Rat Pack and the Magnificent Seven. The speaker, a member of the Rat Pack, began a fistfight with Fresh-up Freddie of the Magnificent Seven:

> He couldn't touch me, so I said, "I quit," and I dropped my guard. That mother fucker, he hit me in the nose, hit me in the mouth, and my mouth started bleeding. Now Cool Fool had my jive [gun]. I said, "Fool, gimme my jive!" and Fool, he gave me my gun. I said to Fresh-up, "I ought to shoot you!" Now Fresh-up got the intention of snatching the gun. He done snatched three or four guns out of different fellows hands, and he started walking at me. He said, "Shoot me if you want to. I don't believe you going to shoot me." I knew what he's going to do when he got close, he going to grab the gun. I didn't want to kill him so I shot him in the arm. I had to shoot him. You see, if I hadn't done it, he would of took my gun away from me.[43]

Fresh-up was attempting to be the baddest, first by manifestly not limiting himself by principles of honor or conventional morality (he struck out at the speaker after the latter had "quit") and second, in moving to snatch the gun away, by demonstrating the other's moral weakness—the other's fear not of him but of the consequences of using the gun he possessed. The speaker shot, not necessarily out of fear that Fresh-up would take the gun and shoot him, but so Fresh-up would not transform the speaker's pretense of meanness into an evident bluff.

Being mean, then, is a pristinely rational social logic for manifesting that one has transcended rationality. Having grasped its paradoxical rationality, we can now more readily understand various ways in which badasses breathe awesomely mean airs into everyday life. To the would-be badass, being mean is not an abstract commitment but an exciting world of distinctive phenomena. Becoming a badass becomes seductive when one senses in interactional detail the transcendent sig-

nificance of manifesting meanness. I will trace three segments of esthetically and sensually compelling ways of being mean under the categories: "Soulful Chaos," "Paraphernalia of Purposiveness," and "Mind Fucking."

Soulful Chaos

The ominous presence of the badass is achieved in one respect by his ways of intimating chaos. The person who is most fearsomely beyond social control is the one who does not appear to be quite in control of himself because his soul is rooted in what, to us, is chaos.

The following is a poem written by an ex-skinhead.

> Everywhere they are waiting, In silence.
> In boredom. Staring into space.
> Reflecting on nothing, or on violence. . . .
> Then suddenly it happens. A motor-cycle
> Explodes outside, a cup smashes.
> They are on their feet, identified
> At last as living creatures,
> The universal silence is shattered,
> The law is overthrown, chaos
> Has come again. . . . [44]

In this poem, chaos is represented as the force that moves one from boredom to liveliness, awakening one's senses, providing essential energy, making the world a seductive place again. The suggestion is that chaos is at the very source of one's spiritual being.

If badasses are not often poets, they are most fundamentally creators of a special culture. Consider the explanation offered by Big L, a member of a Puerto Rican gang in Brooklyn in the 1970s, of why the Bikers have the reputation of being the baddest:

> Rape old ladies. Rape young girls. Kick people out of their homes. Steal. Vandalize the whole neighborhood. Burn cars and all this. And they're bad. That's why they consider them bad. They're bad.[45]

Beyond the specific acts cited, the Bikers have, for Big L, a transcendent, ringing reality as bad, real bad, the baddest: his description quickly becomes a recitation in which the intonation of evil goes on and on, resonating in choruses of awe.

Rape and mayhem may sometimes be useful to construct a bad reputation, but as a routine matter, the badass will exploit a more cultured, symbolically economic means of sustaining an awful presence. He may dramatize a sadistic pleasure in violence to suggest that chaos is natural to him and, therefore, that it is always his potential. Skinheads described cutting someone with a razor as "striping," as if there was an esthetic appeal, a matter of artistic achievement, in the process of destruction. In Glasgow, another place where knives have been a favorite instrument of group violence, "team" fighters distinguish between being "slashed" and being "ripped" (the latter involving a special turning of the knife) and they further distinguish a method of kicking aimed at opening the wound.[46] When gangs have successfully established terrifying reputations, they are often accorded myths of bestial sadism. Ellison reported that in the 1950s in Brooklyn, members of the most feared gang, the Puerto Rican Flyers, were said to drink blood.[47]

By celebrating hedonism as the underlying motivation for their violence, badasses avoid the interpretation that their violence is contingent on the prospect of extrinsic rewards and, therefore, ultimately controllable by others. A Vice Lord explained to Keiser the essential attraction of "wolf packing":

> Wolf packing—like for instance me and some other fellows go out and knock you down 'cause we feel like it. That's what it is. I might take your money, but I really want to kick some ass anyway, so I decide to knock the first thing in my way down.[48]

Across various sociocultural settings, badasses sometimes seem to attack victims because they "need" a beating. A graffiti writer from the South Bronx recalled a time when a few Black Spades arrived at their clubhouse with guns, turned lights on, and discovered that some of those present were not of their group: "first they took and beat up a couple of guys because, though they weren't in a gang, they just needed a good ass-kicking at the time."[49] There is an ambiguity in this statement as to who "needed" the beating, the attackers or the victims. In some contexts, badasses posture virtually as altruistic servants of their victims' "need" for a beating. At other times, the "need to kick ass" is more clearly their own. In either case the suggestion is of soulful chaos: of a nature governed by overwhelming, destructive forces that demand release through the instrumentality of the badass or of irresistibly seductive weaknesses in victims that compel the badass to attack, like a priestly servant who is duty bound to preserve a certain harmony of evil in the world.

Being mean is achieved with a special economy by attacks directed at especially vulnerable victims and especially respectable places. Accompanying a Glasgow gang, Patrick described a rush into a public library. They began setting fire to newspapers in the Reading Room, knocked a magnifying glass out of the hand of an elderly man, and en route to the street, a male attendant in a green uniform was punched and kicked out of the way. "Some, behind me," he noted, "could hardly run for laughing."[50]

Ex-skinheads recalled an excursion to London's Hyde Park: "When we got to the Park we just went wild." Disturbing "Pakis," for example, by putting fingers in the way of a man taking pictures of his wife and children, was a focal activity. At the local park, they would throw stones at ducks; go to the cafe, order food, and not pay; and hide behind bushes waiting for a boat to come by, say to the child in it, "give me a lift, mate," and then collectively jump in, promptly sinking the boat.[51] Their targets were "nice" in a conventional moral sense. The attacks had no utilitarian purpose; many were treated exclusively as "fun." With these elements of context, meanness may be manifest with remarkably little physical effort.

In fights, meanness may be demonstrated by exceeding moral limitations and utilitarian justification. From the white ethnic gang scene of 1950s Brooklyn, Ellison recited the primer for gang kids. . . . When he's down, kick for the head and groin. . . . gang warfare is typified by a callous disregard for Marquis of Queensbury rules, or for that matter, rules of simple decency. When they fight, they are amoral . . . totally without mercy . . . almost inhuman. A cat that's down is a cat who can't bother you, man! Stomp him! Stomp him good! Put that lit cigarette in the bastard's eye! Wear Army barracks boots—kick him in the throat, in the face, kick him where he lives. Smash him from behind with a brick, cave in his effin' skull! Flat edge of the hand in the Adam's Apple! Use a lead pipe across the bridge of his nose—smash the nose and send bone splinters into the brain![52]

Paraphernalia of Purposiveness

All manner of weapons contribute to the badass's project of being mean. From a Philadelphia black gang leader, Krisberg recorded this spontaneous expression of affection:

> I love shotguns. . . . And if anybody ever bother me, that's what they better look out for. Cause I'm going to bring it. . . . Cause I know I ain't going to miss you.[53]

In adolescent "bad" society, weapons and their incidents are matters for sacred ritual. In the South Bronx in the early 1970s, the Savage Nomads were ordered by their leader to clean their guns meticulously twice, sometimes three times, in weekly, group sessions.[54] In Chicago, Ruth Horowitz observed Mexican-American gang members' fascination with the special instruments of violence.

> One afternoon I was sitting on a bench talking with the Lions. Suddenly all conversation stopped and attention was focused on Spoof and Fidel, two Senior Nobles in their mid-twenties. Spoof flipped his keys to the nearest Lion and told him to get his lounge chair from the trunk of the car. His orders were carried out silently. Spoof settled comfortably in his chair. He proudly produced three bullets: one had a cutoff head, one had a flattened head, and the third was unmodified. He carefully described just how each of the bullets reacted inside the

body. Everyone listened quietly and a few asked technical questions. No one was allowed to hold the bullets. . . . Then we were treated to a show and history of their scars while the Lions nodded their approval and were properly awed. Even after the two departed, the Lions discussed nothing else for the rest of the evening.[55]

As Ellison observed in Italian gangs in 1950s Brooklyn, "the weapons of the gang kid have a charm all their own." In this setting, the charmed objects resembled a medieval knight's battery of arms: garrison belts with razor-sharp buckles to be wrapped around fists, raw potatoes studded with double-edged razor blades, zip guns, barracks boots with razor blades stuck between toe and sole, and Molotov cocktails.[56] One fellow drew special attention for possessing a flare-shooting Navy Very pistol. As Robert DeNiro effectively captured in the movie *Taxi Driver* (after he asks the mirror, "Are you looking at me?"), would-be badasses may spend hours practicing the rapid production of a knife or a gun with a special flourish.[57] Among Chicago's Vice Lords, a three-foot sword was, for a time, a popular weapon for robbing passengers on the El. A gang member named Cupid recalled the time "my mother came up and busted me with six shotguns!" including a buffalo gun, and Cupid will

> never forget this. It was . . . crazy ass King Solomon, [in a fight with the Comanches] he had one of these little Hookvilles. It's a knife, a linoleum knife. Got a hook on the end. . . . [which he used when he caught "Ghengis Khan" and] Cut the stud's whole guts out![58]

Among the fighting teams in Glasgow, a member named Baggy kept a "sword" in his scooter and would often recount how, in a battle with the Milton Tongs at a bowling center, he had rushed to his scooter, taken up his sword, cut one boy, and watched the rest scatter. When stopped by bouncers at a dance hall, members of the Young Team were required to give up a concealed hatchet and bayonet, but one got by with a hidden, open razor. In a fight outside a dance hall, Tim charged into battle, brandishing his open razor, but only after grabbing a wine bottle that he broke on the wall, cutting his hand badly. Later, Tim embroidered his account of the fight, adding an air rifle. "The open razor and the broken wine bottle he had carried were apparently not sufficient to create the image he hankered after."[59] In the United States today, we might find the objects of awesome charm to be Uzi machine guns and Ninja stars.

Fascinated, charmed, seduced—the badass is completely taken by the paraphernalia of his purposiveness. Note that although some of these objects might fit presumptions about the power of phallic imagery, others (stars, garrison belts, and linoleum knives) surely do not. Note also that the fascination persists apart from any envisioned practical context of the use of these objects. Just to have these things, to hold them, inspect them, and observe them swiftly introduced into the focus of the moment is exciting. These objects suggest that others will have to take seriously the intentions of the badass who controls them, whatever those intentions may be—that he will mean it, whatever he may make of "it."

We might attribute the significance of these things to the power they represent, but "power" is an impoverished metaphor for this world of experience. "Being mean" picks up the evil undertones set off by the display of these objects. Many of these weapons are notable not just for their power but for their brutish, sadistic character; others, fitted for covert possession, are notably illicit in design. In contrast to "power," "being mean" captures the project at stake: to assume a tough, alien posture beyond all danger of mockery and metaphysical doubt that ensures that one will be taken seriously. These things excite by attesting to a purpose that transcends the material utility of power.

Mind Fucking

In various languages, badasses have a special affinity for the culture of "fuck you!" Chas, an East Los Angeles graffiti writer, recounted his transformation from "Chingaso."

A friend gave me that nickname. Started calling me that about three years ago. . . . Now it's funny. I don't like "Chingaso" any more because it's too "bad," it's too heavy. "Chingaso" means the one who's a fucker. Not a stud, just one who fucks people up. I don't like that. I feel like I'm not saying the right thing out there. I like it, but I think I'm telling the right people the wrong thing. So I write "Chas" now.[60]

In Glasgow, both the police and the street toughs they attempt to control are deeply involved in the same culture. In the following account, Patrick, Tim, and Dave from the Young Team were at Saracen Cross, on their way to a dance hall:

Tim was prevented from moving forward by the approach of two policemen, one of whom shouted across at him: "So fuckin' Malloy is oot again? Is yir fuckin' brothers still in fuckin' prison?" Tim's answers also made liberal use of Glasgow's favourite adjective. The second policeman turned to Dave and me, and, noticing the marks on Dave's face he began: "So ye goat fuckin' scratched, trying' tae get yir fuckin' hole."[61]

The confrontation ended when one of the policeman said, "Weil, get aff this fuckin' Cross, or Ah'll fuckin' book ye."

Used gramatically in myriad ways and conveyed through posture and conduct perhaps more generally than in explicit verbal form, the distinctive thrust of the "fuck" culture is captured nicely in the English form, "fuck you!" Although it may seem obvious, it is worth a moment's pause to articulate just what makes this phrase so effectively "bad." To wish sex on another is not necessarily negative, but this is clearly not an alternative form for "Have a nice lay." Nor is the use of "fuck" for denoting sex necessarily negative; the phrase is universally "bad" while crude sex is not.[62]

At the essence of "fuck you!" is the silent but emphatic presence of the "I." "Fuck you!" implies the existence of the speaker as the key actor (compared to "get fucked!" and the appropriately feminine form, "fuck off!"). It is the assertion of an anonymous insertion—a claim to penetrate the other in his most vulnerable, sensitive center, in his moral and spiritual essence, without revealing oneself to the other. "Fuck you!" thus achieves its force through projecting an asymmetry of the most extreme sort between the fucker and the fucked; I will force myself to the center of your existence, while you will not grasp even the most superficial indication of my subjectivity.

In its essence, then, "fuck you!" is a way of being mean as a transcendent existential project. "Fuck you!" equals "I'll thrust my meaning into your world, and you won't know why, what for, what I mean; I'll hide the 'I' from you as I do it." Of course, in context "fuck you!" may connote anything from a dare to a muted message uttered on retreat. But with the existential significance of "fuck you!" in mind, we may more readily grasp, as devices for mind fucking, several widespread, practical strategies of would-be badasses that are otherwise deeply enigmatic.

The Bump

Consider the "accidental" bump, used either to begin a fight or to force a humiliating show of deference. Manny Torres recalled from his adolescent years in Spanish Harlem,

> walking around with your chest out, bumping into people and hoping they'll give you a bad time so you can pounce on them and beat 'em into the goddamn concrete.[63]

In the literature on adolescent street violence, there are innumerable analogous examples of fights beginning from what in one light appears to be accidental and minor physical contact. Sometimes the badass is the one arranging the accident, sometimes he is the one who is accidentally bumped. Thus, when some laborers accidentally nudged Pat at a Glasgow bar, he challenged them to a fight, immediately moving his hand into his jacket as if he had a weapon. Wee Midgie hit the laborers on their heads with a lemonade bottle, Pat and others kicked them in the face, and Tim cracked a bottle over their heads. The fighting

team suddenly exited when someone shouted, "Run like fuck."[64]

To understand specifically what is happening in these scenes, it is insufficient to interpret the attackers as "looking for a fight." The enigmatic aspect is the dramatization of a "bump"—an accidental physical clash—as the necessary condition or catalyst of the violence. Pat and his friends seemed so intent on attacking these laborers that one wonders why they waited for the chance, unintentional nudge.

Nor will it do to project onto the attackers a felt necessity to neutralize moral prohibitions against unwarranted attacks, that is, that the attack would make no compelling sense to them until and unless they had the "excuse" of a bump. The same young men can be seen at other moments proudly attacking without the moral necessity of any excuse or justification, as when the party attacked is treated simply as one who "needs his ass kicked."[65] Attackers often arrange bumps that are publicly, self-consciously transparent. Why do they bother to feign accidents?

Because their focus is not on physical destruction or moral self-justification, but on the transcendent appeal of being mean. The feigned accident is not a moral necessity for attack; it is, however, a delightful resource for constructing from the attack the stature of the attacker as a badass. Manny and Pat did not "have to have an excuse" to attack. Nor were they compulsive sadists "getting off" on physical destruction. They were seduced by the bump. They rejoiced in the special reverberations that could be given the interaction by making the attack the product of a transparently "accidental" bump.

At its first, most superficial, level of appeal, the bump clarifies and enhances the meaning of a subsequent physical attack as the work of a badass. After a bump, an attack inevitably reflects the spatial metaphor, the existential dilemma of "here" and "there" with which all the ways of the badass are concerned.

The badass does not invent the revolutionary moral potential in the bump; he simply seizes on it. When you and I, two polite members of civil society, bump into each other, there is at once a literal and figurative invocation of the toughness of each of us. Wishing to avoid giving offense, with bated breath we race each other to the stage of apology. Through my apology, I drop any possible pretense of toughness, showing you that I am morally responsive to your well-being. In apologizing, I enact a shameful recognition that the bump occurred because, as far as I could tell, our phenomenal worlds had been independent; I had practiced an apparent indifference to your existence.

In the bump, what had been "here" to you, bounded off from me, penetrates my phenomenal isolation and becomes "here" to me, and vice versa. As quickly as polite members of civil society scurry to avoid the moral tensions that they sense have suddenly become potential, so can the badass flood the situation with awful possibilities. By treating the accidental bump as an obdurate, unforgettable fact of history, the badass opens up a glorious array of nasty courses of action.

No matter who was at "fault" for the bump, once the "bump" has occurred the badass can exploit a precious ambiguity to charge the situation with the tensions of a moral crisis. Any fool can see and only a coward would deny that the bump takes each into the other's phenomenal world. In the bump, you become "here" for me and I become "here" for you. The bump provides the grounds for each to wonder, Was it accidental? Or were you "fucking" with me, thrusting yourself into my world for purposes I could not possibly grasp?

At this stage, the least the would-be badass can do is obtain public testimony to his badass status. If the other tries to ignore the bump, the badass can easily make this attempt an obvious pretense for repeating the bump. He may stop at any point in this process, taking as his sole booty from the situation the victim's evidently artificial posture that "nothing unusual is happening."

More enigmatically, immediately after he has produced an intentional bump or received an obviously accidental bump, the badass may launch an attack without waiting for an apology, whether sincere or pretended. This, an even tougher, "badder" move, plays off the metaphor of mind fucking.

Once we have accidentally bumped for all to see, everyone knows that you must wonder whether I will let it go as an accident or charge you with an intentional attack. Everyone knows that you are wondering about my purpose and spirit and that merely by wondering, you are taking me into your world of moral judgment and putting me at risk of negative judgment. In other words, the bump suddenly raises the momentous possibility that "you are fucking with me." I can now, without more provocation, strike out physically to "fuck you up" as a transcendent response to your publicly visible "fucking with me."

Before examining elaborations on this interaction, we should take special note of the profound explosion of meaning that has already occurred. Through the most inarticulate, most minor physical contact between two individuals, without any apparent plan, intention, or reason, without any forewarning any man could detect, a small moral world has suddenly burst into full-blown existence. Once the bump has occurred, for whatever original cause or antecedent reason, everything has forever changed; the bump cannot be removed from moral history. A chain reaction can then sensibly follow in a spirit of coherent determinism. The badass, as it were, struts out as the Great Creator, capable of arranging the most transcendent cosmological experience from the chance encounters of everyday life; with a little bump, he has occasioned a moral Big Bang.

But this is only the first theme of significance that may be drawn by the badass from the "accidental" bump. That the accidental quality of the bump should be put in quotes is not only obvious to the would-be badass; he may arrange the bump so that it is obvious to all that the fictive accidental character of the bump is obvious to him, to the victim, to all. And with this move into universal moral transparency, the would-be badass moves the drama to the level of what might be called on the streets, "royal mind fucking."

"Whachulookinat?"

In perhaps all subcultures of the badass, there is a homegrown version of a mind-fucking strategy that is deeply rooted in the danger of eye contact. It is recognizable with the opening phrase, "Whachulookinat?"

A badass may at any moment treat another's glancing perception of him as an attempt to bring him symbolically into the other's world, for the other's private purposes, perhaps to "fuck with" him. This may be treated as a visual bump. As with the physical bump, the badass may allow the victim to cower his way out of danger by enacting a transparently artificial display of deference, for example, through offering profuse excuses and literally bowing out of the situation.

Of more interest are those situations in which the badass wishes further to exploit the potential to construct a transcendent theme of evil. Victims of "Whachulookinat?" frequently answer "Nothing;" with this response, they open up what sometimes seems to be an irresistible opportunity to fill the air with awesomely threatening meaning. "You callin me nothin?" is the well-known reply.

Just as he thought he had regained a measure of self-protective control over the situation through an effusive display of deference, the victim realizes that he has damned himself, for he has been caught in a lie. *He* is now the immoral party. Everyone knows that he had glanced at the badass. "Nothing" was intended as a ritual of deference, but the badass will not go along with the fiction. The badass suddenly adopts the posture of the only honest man in the transaction: he's being lied to, as all can see. But, he now has the right to ask, why? What malevolence moves the victim to lie and answer, "Nothing?" Has he been fucking with the image of the badass in the privacy of his mind? What is he covering up?

From this point, the badass can readily build tension by playing for a while with the victim, tossing him from one to the other horn of his dilemma. Now the badass treats the victim's "Nothing" as a lie, a fiction designed to cover up a shameful or hostile perspective. Next, the badass insists on a literal interpretation, that the victim's response should be taken as a claim that the existential value of the badass is really "nothing." Then, the badass mocks his own metaphysical stance; everyone knows that the badass knows that the "Nothing" was artificial and, therefore, that the badass's indignation is artificial. All know, as they have known all along, who is the victim and who is the badass—who is attempting to avoid any association with evil and who is embracing it.

In short, all recognize that by feigning victimization, the badass is really mind fucking the victim. The universal transparency of the badass's moral posturing makes it "royal mind-fucking"—a high art that may be practiced through a variety of analogous strategems. Thus, analogous to the simple mind fucking of attacking after a bump is the strategy described by Yablonsky of a New York boy who

> will approach a stranger with the taunt, "What did you say about my mother?" An assault is then delivered upon the victim before he can respond to the question.[66]

And analogous to the royal mind fucking constructed from the visual bumping of "Whachulookinat?" is the Vice Lords's practice of wolf packing. With several mates present, a Vice Lord begins an interaction with a stranger passing by with the formal request, but informal demand, "Hey, man, gimme a dime!" As Keiser noted, "If a dime were given, then a demand for more money would be made until finally the individual would have to refuse."[67]

Physical dominance is not the key concern, since it often seems a foregone conclusion. And, what is even more interesting is that, as some of the Glasgow incidents showed, it sometimes seems not to matter to the badasses that they might lose the battle. From the standpoint of physical power and outcome, these mind-fucking maneuvers are gratuitous. After all, one could physically destroy victims without entering into any interaction with them, for example, by shooting them without warning from a distance and without emerging from camouflage. The ambush of a stranger might maximize one's physical success, but it would not necessarily construct an identity as a badass.

Mind fucking, however, shows the badass in control of the meaning of the situation. Bumps are accidents or intentional provocations, depending on what the badass has in mind. The badass controls the moral ontology of the moment. On the one hand, he may allow life its little bumps, its give and take, recognizing that, owing to imperfections in the nature of social life for which no one is responsible, men must have at least small spaces free from responsibility. On the other hand, he may make life inexorably purposive, affording a man no rest from the moral implications of his conduct. The badass rules the moment as the master of its metaphysics. Moral pretenses become real and unreal as if by magic, at the snap of his finger. At his discretion, words mean just what they say on the surface or are revealed to mask shamefully hidden intentions. "Nothing" will mean nothing at all or everything fateful, as he chooses. Apart from physical dominance, mind fucking allows the badass to demonstrate the transcendent character of his meaning.

Foreground and Background: The Sex of the Badass

I have attempted to demonstrate that the details of the distinctive adolescent culture of the badass can be grasped as a series of tactics for struggling with what the adolescent experiences as a spatially framed dilemma—a challenge to relate the "here" of his personal world to the phenomenal worlds of others who he experiences as existing at a distance, somewhere over "there." Thus, being tough positions the self as not "here" for others. Being alien goes further, indicating that the self is not only not here for others but is native to some morally alien world, inevitably beyond the intimate grasp of others who are present here. And

being mean produces its awful air by intimating that where the self is coming from is a place that represents chaos to outsiders and threatens constantly to rush destructively to the center of their world, attacking their most intimate sensibilities.

The ultimate source of the seductive fascination with being a badass is that of transcending rationality. What "rationality" means to the adolescent, as a challenge that stimulates his seduction to a world of deviance, is not primarily legal authority, institutional discipline, or social expectations of an ordered and integrated competence to reason. These phenomena may, at times, become the foils for badasses of all types, but more routinely, the provocative issue is a matter of demonstrating rationality as the modern moral competence to adjust the self to situationally specific expectations.

To understand the seductive quality of this project and why the data have been overwhelmingly though not exclusively from males, we might consider what, after all, makes the phallus so powerful a symbol for the badass. Phallic imagery is obviously prominent in the ways of the badass, from the "hardness" of the tough posture, to the "hot rodder" style, to the "cool" quality conferred on speech by random thrusts of "fuck," to the drama of "mind fucking." But the motivating, emotionally compelling concerns of the badass cannot simply be reduced to a sexual metaphor; the distinctive presence of the badass is not particularly erotic. Posed like a phallus, the badass threatens to dominate all experience, stimulating a focus of consciousness so intense as to obliterate experientially or to transcend any awareness of boundaries between the situation "here" and any other situation, "there." And in this appreciation, the phallus has the further, socially transcendent power to obliterate any awareness of boundaries between the ontologically independent, phenomenal situations of different people. The fascination here is with the paradoxical, distinctively masculine potential of the phallus: by threatening to penetrate others, the badass, this monstrous member of society, can absorb the whole world into himself.

Notes

1. The differences between the three stages are not on a scale of symbolism versus real action. A physical fight can be nothing more than a show of toughness, while a stare-down can accomplish a consummate act of meanness.

2. As Werthman noted, "Not all black leather jackets communicate the same quality of 'toughness.' . . . One almost has to be committed to a fashion in order to read the nuances of self-image that can be expressed within it." See Carl Werthman, "Delinquency and Authority" (master's thesis, University of California at Berkeley, 1964), p. 118.

3. If these terms seem abstract for the realities of street life, consider the following dialogue between two Puerto Rican women who were members of a Brooklyn street gang and became uncomfortable with the tough image they embraced in their early adolescent years.

> [WEEZA:] We ain't really tough. We don't consider ourselves tough—not me.

> [BOOBY:] Because we try to communicate with people. But when they don't want to communicate with us, then that's their problem, not ours.

Anne Campbell, *The Girls in the Gang* (Oxford: Basil Blackwell, 1984), p. 155.

4. For a treatment of such interactions, see Erving Goffman, *Relations in Public* (New York: Harper & Row, 1971), pp. 75–77, 81. For an analysis of "How are you?" as a "greeting substitute," see Harvey Sacks, Everyone Has to Lie," in *Sociocultural Dimensions of Language Use.* ed. Mary Sanches and Ben Blount (New York: Academic Press, 1975), pp. 57–79.

5. See Harlan Ellison, *Memos from Purgatory* (New York: Berkley, 1983).

6. Gus Frias, *Barrio Warriors: Homeboys of Peace* (n.p.: Diaz Publications, 1982), p. 21.

7. As ethnographic observers have emphasized, toughness, as opposed to socially sensitive, deferential civility, is hardly a constant feature of Mexican-American adolescent society. In the street gangs of Chicago, Horowitz noted, "Most [of these] young men have conventional social skills;" they take a woman's arm when crossing the street and walk on the curb side, skillfully order dinner in a restaurant, and shake hands and make polite conversation when introduced to a stranger. See Ruth Horowitz, *Honor*

and the American Dream (New Brunswick, N.J.: Rutgers University Press, 1983), pp. 86–87. The point is that toughness is a contingent social production.

8. R. Lincoln Keiser, *The Vice Lords* (New York: Holt, Rinehart & Winston, 1979), pp. 43–44.

9. On the last point, comments by my colleague, Emanuel Schegloff, were helpful.

10. Werthman, "Delinquency and Authority," p. 88.

11. James Patrick, *A Glasgow Gang Observed* (London: Eyre Methuen, 1973), p. 69.

12. John Allen, *Assault with a Deadly Weapon,* ed. Dianne Hall Kelly and Philip Heymann (New York: McGraw-Hill, 1978), pp. 19, 22–23.

13. Frias, *Barrio Warriors,* p. 19.

14. My thanks here to Paul Price, a sociology graduate student and a staff member in a Los Angeles home for delinquent boys.

15. Patrick, *Glasgow Gang Observed,* p. 83.

16. Florence Rome, *The Tattooed Men* (New York: Delacorte Press, 1975).

17. Allen, *Assault with a Deadly Weapon,* p. 23.

18. Patrick, *Glasgow Gang Observed,* pp. 32, 33.

19. Allen, *Assault with a Deadly Weapon.*

20. See, for example, the photographs of the Maravillos of the 1940s and 1980s, in Frias, *Barrio Warriors,* p. 16.

21. Descriptions of dress and walk are available in Frias, *Barrio Warriors;* Alfredo Guerra Gonzalez, "Mexicano/Chicano Gangs in Los Angeles: A Sociohistorical Case Study" (Ph.D. diss., School of Social Welfare, University of California at Berkeley, 1981); Carlos Manuel Haro, "An Ethnographic Study of Truant and Low Achieving Chicano Barrio Youth in the High School Setting" (Ph.D. diss., School of Education, University of California at Los Angeles, 1976); and Hilary McGuire, *Hopie and the Los Homes Gang* (Canfield, Ohio: Alba House, 1979).

22. Gusmano Cesaretti, *Street Writers: A Guided Tour of Chicano Graffiti* (Los Angeles: Acrobat Books, 1975), p. 8.

23. Jerry Romotsky and Sally R. Romotsky, *Los Angeles Barrio Calligraphy* (Los Angeles: Dawson's Book Shop, 1976), pp. 23–24, 29, 32–33.

24. See, for example, the laughing skull in Cesaretti, *Street Writers,* and in Romotsky and Romotsky, *Los Angeles Barrio Calligraphy.* pp. 58–59.

25. George Carpenter Barker, *Pachuco* (Tucson: University of Arizona Social Science Bulletin, no. 18, 1958).

26. Frias, *Barrio Warriors,* p. 23; and Haro, "Truant and Low Achieving Chicano Barrio Youth," p. 363.

27. Dick Hebdige, *Subculture: The Meaning of Style* (London: Methuen, 1979), p. 65.

28. Ibid., p. 110.

29. Sandy Craig and Chris Schwarz, *Down and Out: Orwell's Paris and London Revisited* (London: Penguin Books, 1984), p. 107.

30. Hunter Thompson, *Hell's Angels* (New York: Ballantine Books, 1967), p. 253.

31. Harold Finestone, "Cats, Kicks, and Color," in *The Other Side,* ed. Howard S. Becker (New York: Free Press, 1964), pp. 281–97.

32. By the 1970s in New York ghettos, being "cool" had been around for decades and had apparently lost some of its force. It was replaced by "too cool" as a superlative in the adolescent lexicon. See Campbell, *Girls in the Gang.* p. 183. Now "chill out" is popular.

33. Allen, *Assault with a Deadly Weapon,* pp. 199–200.

34. Admiration for the "killer" is reported in David Dawley, *A Nation of Lords: The Autobiography of the Vice Lords* (Garden City, N.Y.: Doubleday Anchor Press, 1973), p. 32.

35. Frias, *Barrio Warriors,* p. 45.

36. Being a badass is not a status obtained in a fatefully violent moment and guaranteed for life. Like other charismatic figures, the badass is subject to the double challenge: (1) that he must always be open to challenge—there is no time off for the badass, no vacation from this occupation, which is indeed a vocation; and (2) that he must never fail any challenge. Cf. Max Weber, *Economy and Society* (New York: Bedminster Press, 1968), 3: 1112–13.

37. Patrick, *Glasgow Gang Observed,* p. 49.

38. Pat Doyle et al., *The Paint House: Words from an East End Gang* (Harmondsworth, England: Penguin Books, 1972), p. 31.

39. Richard P. Rettig, Manual J. Torres, and Gerald R. Garrett, *Manny: A Criminal Addict's Story* (Boston: Houghton Mifflin, 1977), p. 19.

40. Barry Alan Krisberg, *The Gang and the Community* (San Francisco: R & E Research Associates, 1975), p. 15.

41. Ibid.

42. Ibid., p. 24.

43. Keiser, *Vice Lords,* p. 18.

44. Doyle et al., *Paint House,* p. 23.

45. Campbell, *Girls in the Gang,* p. 164.

46. Patrick, *Glasgow Gang Observed,* p. 43.

47. Ellison, *Memos from Purgatory,* p. 86.

48. Keiser, *Vice Lords,* p. 35.

49. Craig Castleman, *Getting Up: Subway Graffiti in New York* (Cambridge, Mass.: MIT Press, 1982), p. 93.

50. Patrick, *Glasgow Gang Observed,* p. 77.

51. Doyle et al., *Paint House,* pp. 28, 30.

52. Ellison, *Memos from Purgatory,* pp. 58, 61. Note that the evidence is of a "primer," not of a pattern of violence.

53. Krisberg, *Gang and Community,* p. 14.

54. William Gale, *The Compound* (New York: Rawson Associates, 1977).

55. Horowitz, *Honor and the American Dream,* p. 92.

56. Ellison, *Memos from Purgatory,* pp. 48, 60, 61.

57. Cf. Ellison's account of his practice before a mirror with a twelve-inch Italian stiletto in ibid.

58. Keiser, *Vice Lords,* p. 62.

59. Patrick, *Glasgow Gang Observed,* pp. 54, 56.

60. Cesaretti, *Street Writers,* p. 57.

61. Patrick, *Glasgow Gang Observed,* pp. 52–53.

62. No doubt in some erotic uses, the "bad" quality of "fuck you" is deemed delicious. As many a wag has noted, "fuck" is an especially versatile condiment in courses of conversations. An anonymous list, provided to me by an engineer who found it circulating in a local metal-coating plant, includes "positive" uses, as in "Mary is fucking beautiful"; inquisitive uses, as in "What the fuck?"; and ad hoc, sometimes ambiguous enhancements of emphasis, as in "It's fucking five-thirty." "Fuck" draws attentions beyond civility, and it is therefore widely attractive as a means by which a speaker suggests he has more passion or a more idiosyncratic feeling about a matter than convention will allow him to express. Our concern here is to grasp the specifically hostile and threatening forms, the "bad" power that the phrase can achieve.

63. Rettig, Torres, and Garrett, *Manny,* p. 18.

64. Patrick, *Glasgow Gang Observed,* p. 54.

65. See also ibid., p. 32. At a dance hall, Pat pushed his way onto the floor and bumped into three big guys who said, "Who the fuck are you pushin'?" Pat responded with "Ah'm pushin' you, thug face," whereupon fists began to fly, this time to Pat's great disadvantage.

66. Lewis Yablonsky, *The Violent Gang* (Baltimore: Penguin Books, 1966), pp. 202–3.

67. Keiser, *Vice Lords,* pp. 44, 45. See also Robert Lejeune, "The Management of a Mugging." *Urban Life* 6 (July 1977): 123–48.

Nick T. Pappas

Patrick C. McKenry

Beth Skilken Catlett

Athlete Aggression on the Rink and off the Ice: Athlete Violence and Aggression in Hockey and Interpersonal Relationships

Athletes recently have appeared on television and in news headlines because of their involvement in instances of aggression and violence. Although much of the documented violence takes place in the context of sports competition, not all athlete aggression is restricted to sports opponents. Indeed, the past decade has witnessed documentation of athlete aggression directed toward other males outside the sports arena, as well as aggression directed toward women in both intimate and nonintimate situations. What remains unclear, however, is whether athletic participation—in particular, the violent strategies learned in sport—contributes to the likelihood that athletes will be violent in interpersonal relationships (Coakley 1998; Crosset 1999).

Public concern about the links between sports participation and interpersonal violence has spawned work over the past decade that documents athlete violence, especially in the area of sexual aggression. Specifically, several studies have indicated that college athletes are overrepresented among those who are involved in aggressive and violent sexual behavior on college campuses. In a study of male undergraduates at a large southeastern university, Boeringer (1996) found that 60 percent of athletes reported at least

one instance of using verbal coercion to obtain sexual favors, 28 percent reported using alcohol and drugs to obtain sexual favors, and 15 percent reported using physical force. Moreover, Boeringer found that athletes reported higher percentages than nonathletes in all such categories of aggressive behavior. In a similar vein, Frintner and Rubinson (1993) found that although the population of male athletes at a large midwestern university was less than 2 percent of the male student population, 21 percent of the reported sexual assaults, 18 percent of the attempted sexual assaults, and 14 percent of the cases of sexual abuse were committed by members of sports teams or sports clubs on campus. Berkowitz (1992) similarly reported that in one review of alleged gang rapes by college students since 1980, twenty-two out of twenty-four documented cases were perpetuated by either members of fraternities or intercollegiate athletic teams. And Crosset, Benedict, and McDonald (1995) reviewed police records at twenty colleges and universities as well as the records of offices of judicial affairs and found that male athletes were overrepresented in reports of sexual assault; while athletes accounted for 3 percent of the male student population, they perpetrated 35 percent of the physical battering reports on the college campuses.

Young (1993) argues that the links between sport and interpersonal violence parallel the

Men and Masculinities, Vol. 6 No. 3, January 2004 291–312. © 2004 Sage Publications.

problems of violence elsewhere in society. In fact, this notion is consistent with research that indicates that violence in one social domain is highly correlated with violence in other domains (Fagan and Browne 1994; National Research Council 1996). Yet it should be noted that while much is known regarding athlete-athlete violence as a part of the sport, there is little empirical validation of athlete violence outside the sports arena (Benedict and Klein 1997; Coakley 1998; Young 2000). Moreover, while initial explorations have theorized a link between athletic participation and interpersonal violence, many studies have found only a weak association between sports violence and outside the sport violence (e.g., Koss and Gaines 1993) and some have found no association at all (Carson, Halteman, and Stacy 1997; Schwartz and Nogrady 1996).

The mixed results of early empirical research highlight the need to clarify the connections between athletic participation and violence. Indeed, researchers such as Boeringer (1996) and Crosset (1999, 2000) note the pressing need to explore the dynamics surrounding athlete violence beyond the sports context, including inquiries into how team members, coaches, and fans promote and defend violent behavior, variations in the experiences of athletes in different sports contexts, and the role of intervening variables that may be more predictive of male violence than athletic participation per se (Crosset 1999; Crowell and Burgess 1996). One intervening variable, alcohol consumption, is worth particular note. As Crosset (1999) argues, missing from current discussions of athletes and violence is any discussion of drinking. This omission is conspicuous in light of the strong association between drinking and sport. Furthermore, alcohol has been strongly implicated in much of the research on violence against women; although alcohol consumption is not necessarily considered a cause of such violence, many scholars theorize that it has a complex role in men's violence.

The need for such exploration is perhaps nowhere more pertinent than in the sport of hockey. In recent years, several incidents in pro-

fessional hockey have resulted in an intensified concern regarding aggression and violence associated with the sport. For instance, Toronto Maple Leafs' Nick Kyupreos sustained a severe concussion that led to his early retirement from hockey. In another incident, Vancouver's Donald Brashear was struck on the head by Boston's Marty McSorley; he missed 20 games because of the injury. Furthermore, several publicized incidents of athlete violence outside the sports context have caused substantial concern, in particular, about the links between male athletic participation and violence against women. One case, for example, involves AHL Wilkes-Barre rookie, Billy Tibbetts, who lost four seasons of hockey due to a jail sentence for raping a 15-year-old girl at a party.

Thus, the purpose of this study is to explore, through in-depth interviews with five former college/professional hockey players, the nature of aggression and violence in their sport and its relationship to violent interpersonal behaviors both inside and outside the sport. Violence is defined as male-to-male physical sport-related violence, male-to male physical out-of-sport interpersonal violence; and male-to-female physical, sexual, and emotional aggression and abuse.

Socialization for Violence

While an instinctive drive and a drive stimulated by frustration may partially explain sports aggression, Terry and Jackson (1985) contend that a powerful socialization process is the primary determinant of sport and sport-related violence. Hargreaves (1986) notes that sports offers an ideal means for males to develop and exhibit traditional masculine qualities including power, strength, and violence while rejecting traditionally ascribed feminine values. Terry and Jackson see sports aggression as behavior learned in a culture that reinforces and models violence. In sport, reinforcement for acts of violence emanate from a variety of sources, which may be grouped under three categories: (1) the immediate reference group of the athlete, especially coaches, teammates, and family; (2) the structure of the sport and the implementation of rules by governing bodies and referees; and (3) the attitude of the fans, media, courts of law, and society in general.

Reference Groups

Cultural ideals of sport and of masculinity combine to create a context within which violence in athletics is not only tolerated but encouraged (Messner 1995). Coaches and parents contribute to the legitimacy of sports violence as they argue that sport aggression prepares boys for success as a man in an adult world (Fine 1987). Messner and Sabo (1990) contend that male tolerance of risk and injury in sports is not a socially passive process but rather is one through which violence, injury, and disablement become reframed as masculinizing by society at all levels. Demonstration of these behaviors is thus linked to gender legitimacy.

In a review of biographies of athletes who come to understand the rewards of aggression and violence, Crosset (1999) suggests that these individuals learn from coaches and peers to be violent. Studies of hockey players, in particular, provide prototypic examples of such socializing influences. For instance, Smith (1979b) found that displays of toughness, courage, and willingness to fight are important means of establishing a positive identity among both peers and coaches in hockey. Moreover, Weinstein, Smith, and Wiesenthal (1995) found that players' aggression, demonstrated especially through fistfighting, often produced greater teammate and coach perceptions of player competence than playing or skating skills. In general, players who backed away from fights were often labeled as "chicken" and were viewed as exhibiting signs of personal failure and weak character. These authors suggest that players will often participate in hockey fights and violence to avoid demeaning labels, which are not easily removed.

Key concepts from West and Zimmerman's (1987) classic work on "doing gender" provide an apt interpretive framework for understanding the impact of hockey culture on athletes' displays

of violence and aggression. Under this view, violent behavior can be seen as a way of constructing oneself as masculine and demonstrating one's place in the masculinity hierarchy (Connell 1995). Violence and aggression may be displayed as a way to meet the gender expectations of the peer group as well as the hegemonic notions of masculinity more broadly (Coakley 1989; Levinson 1989).

Furthermore, Crosset (1999) argues that training for sport in the context of an already patriarchal society may also be training men to be violent toward women. For example, coaches employ images of antifemininity and castration to chastise players. The descriptive works of Curry (1991, 1998, 2000) found team dynamics that openly express support for violence against women and demonstrate how resistance to these norms is discouraged. Indeed, teammates in many contact sports clearly reinforce and model sexist behaviors, focusing on sex, aggression, and negative attitudes toward women (Curry 1991).

Structure of the Sport and Implementation of the Rules

Many athletes are presented with a conflict inherent to competitive sports—that is, they are presented with the apparent dilemma of having to win at all costs and yet, at the same time, to adhere to moral and ethical sport behavior. Young (1993) reflected this conflict when he compared professional sports to a hazardous and violent workplace with its own unique form of industrial disease. Male athletes are expected to be tough and to live up to cultural expectations of manliness, which often encourage the use of violence and performance-enhancing drugs such as steroids. Indeed, Messner (1990) contends that violent behaviors are occupational imperatives in contact sports with practical consequences if not performed. Athletes constantly are encouraged to ignore their own pain and at the same time are encouraged to inflict pain on others or they risk being belittled by their coaches and peers.

Smith (1979a) specifically describes the hockey subculture in terms of an occupational culture based on a theme of violence. By age 15, boys are identified by coaches for their ability to mete out and withstand illegal physical coercion—attributes desired by professional hockey teams. The structure of the system compels conformity to prevailing professional standards that include the necessity of employing violence. Weinstein, Smith, and Weisenthal (1995) found even among youth and preprofessional junior hockey teams that there was a strong imperative toward violence. These authors state that fighting and intimidation are essential elements in the tradition and culture of hockey.

From an early age, hockey players undergo a specialized socialization process in the production of a tough fighting unit; players are taught that competence is linked to aggressive play, including penalties (Vaz 1979, 1980; Weinstein, Smith, and Wiesenthal 1995). Toughness and willingness to fight are attributes that impress coaches and management (Smith 1983). Players understand the possibility of violence on the ice, and they know that fighting is advocated as a proactive means for not being easily intimidated and guarding against further aggression. Players also are required to create trouble for opponents and to employ tactics that create anxiety in adversaries (Faulkner 1974; Weinstein, Smith, and Wiesenthal 1995).

Attitudes of the Community and Society in General

In general, there appears to be widespread support, both institutional and community, for violence associated with sport, both within and outside the sports context. Institutional support for alleged perpetrators of violence outside the sport often blames the victims and fails to hold athletes responsible for their actions. The inability of institutions to hold athletes accountable also extends to the court system (Crosset 1999). In spite of higher rates of violence within sport communities, conviction rates present a striking difference that favors the accused athlete (Benedict and Klein 1997). Benedict and Klein examined arrest and conviction rates for collegiate and professional athletes accused of felony sexual assaults against women and compared these with national crime data to determine differential patterns of treatment in the criminal justice system. In sum, these authors found that of 217 athletes who were initially reported to police for a felonious sex crime, only 24 percent were successfully prosecuted. The comparison national sample was 54 percent of arrests leading to conviction. In addition, Benedict (1997) found in their 150 case studies of reported violence that athletes were convicted in only 28 cases, mainly through plea-bargaining agreements. Only 10 cases went to trial, and 6 of these resulted in guilty verdicts.

Curry (2000), among others, has focused on the sports bar as a safe haven in the community arena for aggression outside the sport. Curry found that aggression and assault are encouraged by bars' privileging of male athletes—allowing them to drink for free, taking their sides during fights, and giving them an arena in which to operate. Curry describes the striving for status among peers in the bars through drinking, fighting, and public display of sexual activity. Indeed, Curry (1998) contends that these bars were permissive to the point of allowing the male athletes to take advantage of situations where they could prey on the physical inequalities of others.

Fans also play an important role in the reinforcement of violence, in particular within hockey culture. For example, in a national opinion poll, 39 percent of Canadians reported that they like to see fighting at hockey games (Macleans-Goldfarb 1970, cited in Smith 1979a). In a similar vein, Smith (1979b) found that 61 percent of the players he surveyed perceived spectators at these games as approving of fighting.

Based on this overview of the literature and the socialization into a culture of violence theoretical perspective, the following research questions were developed and addressed: (1) In what ways does participation in hockey promote a culture of aggression and violence? and (2) To what extent does hockey aggression and violence affect off-ice behavior, and what factors seem influential?

Method

Participants in this study were five former hockey players whose ages ranged between twenty-five and thirty years old with a mean age of twenty-six years. Four of the five athletes consisted of former players that the researcher formerly coached at the collegiate level. Each of the athletes had competed at either the collegiate level, the professional minor league level, or both. Four of the athletes played collegiate hockey, two of the athletes played professionally in the minor leagues, and one player played both college and professional hockey. Three of the five players were Canadian and played Canadian junior hockey before playing collegiate or professional hockey. It is important to note that the style of Canadian junior hockey is fundamentally different from collegiate hockey in that it allows and encourages fighting to a much greater extent than American collegiate hockey. The two American players had competed at either the high school and/or prep school level before playing collegiate hockey.

The first author has a history of extensive involvement in the culture of ice hockey, with a keen understanding of the perspectives of the players, as well as the phenomenon of violence inside and outside the sports arena. This experience has occurred through participation in American and Canadian junior hockey, over five years of professional playing experience in both the minor leagues and in Europe, and coaching at numerous levels, including three years at the men's collegiate level. It is through being deeply involved in the culture of ice hockey as both a player and a coach over the span of twenty years that the first author has a unique, insider knowledge of ice hockey and its associated violence.

In fact, the first author's unique position as a participant observer within the culture of hockey allowed him ready access for recruitment of players to participate in this study. Four of the five informants were players that the first author coached

in college, and the fifth was a referral from one of the four former players. Each of these athletes has at least ten years of professional competition and is thought to be fully immersed into the culture of ice hockey. In addition, the researcher has a long personal and professional relationship with the four players he coached.

The primary source of data for this study was in-depth interviews. The interviews can be considered as semistructured because they were guided by a set of predetermined questions with a number of branching questions that were used to facilitate more detail and more focused attention to the study's domains of interest. Probing questions were also used in a spontaneous manner to prompt elaboration and specificity. The questions were derived from previous inquiries into sport violence as well as previous focused discussions with participants in ice hockey regarding the use of violence. Five major questions were asked during the interviews: (1) Describe your overall experience as a player in organized hockey; (2) How do you think contact sports such as hockey promote violence/aggression within the sport itself; (3) Describe any situations of violence/aggression perpetrated by athletes that you have either seen, heard of, or participated in that occurred outside of sports competition; (4) What are some of the ways that you think participation in hockey encourages off-ice aggression; and (5) What are some ways to prevent athlete violence and aggression off-ice. The participants determined the settings for the interviews, which, in four of the five cases were their homes; this helped to ensure privacy and confidentiality.

It is important to note that these participants were asked to (1) discuss their own personal involvement in hockey, both on and off the ice and (2) to comment on their observations of others in the sport and their overall view of violence and aggression associated with the culture of hockey. Because the principal investigator had a strong personal connection to and history with the respondents, and because he wanted to ensure honest and open exploration of sensitive topics such as violence, sexual aggression, and alcohol and drug use, he did not insist that participants specify whether their narrative responses pertained to their own personal experiences or experiences observed of other athletes. Thus, these participants are best considered key informants who inform this in-depth exploration of the culture of violence and aggression among hockey players.

The data analysis began with a verbatim transcription of the audio-recorded interviews. Once this was completed, a qualitative content analysis was conducted by two independent coders. Specifically, coders first identified and subsequently organized themes that emerged from the transcribed text. The interview responses were examined for salient topics covered, patterns, regularities, and differences within and across the cases. Then, initially coded categories were generated from the topics and patterns, and these coding schemes were developed, continuously modified, and redefined through the data collection process and afterwards (Miles and Huberman 1994). Finally, the topics and patterns were placed into conceptually focused analytical themes related to the study's theoretical foundation (Berg 1998; Bogdan and Biklen 1992).

Results

All of the participants' narratives contained detailed accounts of both their own and other athletes' involvement in violence and aggression within the context of sports competition, as well as outside of the competitive arena. These narratives described varied experiences with and observations of aggression perpetrated against teammates, opponents, bystanders, and women. Moreover, each of the participants provided their own subjective insights about the interconnections between hockey and aggression/violence. In this analysis, we first discuss, in an introductory fashion, the participants' accounts of the extent of violence in ice hockey. Next, we review the ways in which hockey socialization and athletes' notions of masculinity combine to create a culture of aggression and violence. We then turn to an examination of two central factors—consumption

of alcohol and the objectification of women—that contribute to exporting violence outside the athletic arena.

Frequency of Violence

All of the research participants were easily able to identify a number of situations in which they had either participated in violence or they had observed such violence among their friends and teammates. Moreover, these narratives illustrate the way in which such violence and aggression is considered routine in this population. For example, one athlete described his social life in this way:

> It seemed like every time we would go out . . . at someone's house or a bar . . . at least once a weekend, there would probably be a fight . . . if you took a random sample of 20 guys that didn't play sports and went out on a Friday or Saturday, I don't think you would find the frequency in them getting into fights compared to the 20 guys that I hung out with that I played hockey with.

The narrative accounts of two other participants reflected parallel sentiments with respect to the conventions of aggression and violence in this community:

> More things I've seen has been guys hitting other guys—in a bar—get a couple of drinks in some of these guys, and they want to fight everyone as if they're invincible—the worst I've seen is that guys will get a bunch of teeth knocked out or their face beat in—black eyes and brown eyes and all of that . . .

> I mean, I had quite a lot of brawls in the summer—one time, a guy had sold drugs to my younger sister and I confronted the guy, and he brought back a bunch of his friends, and I went after the whole gang of them and . . . I beat them up quite badly . . . they beat me over the head with a fishing bat and they cut me open, but I'd also cut a bunch of them open pretty bad too—and I went to the hospital and they had come after me at the hospital. I was out of town very shortly after that, so that was good.

These players' perspectives align well with extant research that asserts that conformity to a violent sport ethic is common and that this conformity can lead male athletes to see aggression as a natural part of their sport and a natural part of who they are as athletes and men (Young 1993). The question that remains, however, is, Are people who choose to play heavy contact sports more likely than others to see aggression as an appropriate way to deal with life stressors? An answer to this question is embedded within the research participants' reflections on the potential causes of aggressive behavior among hockey players. In particular, several respondents speculated that men with aggressive tendencies may be attracted to the sport of hockey:

> It's the old what-came-first-the-chicken-or-the-egg syndrome—were these guys violent before they played hockey or did they become violent because they played hockey . . . I think that guys I played with . . . had some antisocial behavior and had it before they ever got into hockey, and then you mix the two and you can get yourself into a lot of trouble. . . . I played junior C in Canada, and guys were getting out of jail on weekends to play hockey—you know, get in trouble with the law and all sorts of crazy stuff before they were really ever really involved with the game, and I think the game for them was almost a chance to vent their anger or whatever it was they were dealing with in a way that wouldn't get them thrown [back] into jail . . .

> I played against guys that do a lot of fighting in hockey that were just plain whacked—you know, that would sit there across from you before the game, hyperventilating and stuff, some of them I knew that were actually crazy—but . . . with one guy in particular, I knew that he had a chemical imbalance and he just happens to also be a really good hockey player that snaps . . .

> I think, from my experiences, with some of these guys who are getting into trouble on the ice have a lot more going on off the ice than you think. The rink becomes the hunting grounds for a lot of these guys, and I don't know all their stories in and out, but troubled guys getting in trouble on the ice as well whether it's

family, school, or what. . . . I think it's a place for violence to come out—because it's allowed.

These narratives are somewhat inconsistent with a sports socialization perspective. That is, these informants' speculations that men with pre-existing aggressive tendencies actualize such proclivities within the acceptable context of hockey play is somewhat contrary to an explanation that emphasizes the socialization of the athlete in which violence learning takes place within sport culture. However, the multifaceted interpretations offered by the informants in this study are compatible with Coakley's (1989) assertion that the origins of this phenomenon are heterogeneous, and that there is no single cause of violence in sport.

Hockey Socialization and the Culture of Masculinity

The socialization of hockey differs from socialization for other contact sports because fighting plays a central role in hockey competition. Indeed, according to Gruneau and Whitson (1993), high rates of violence in hockey are to be expected because physical contact affords opportunities for hockey sticks to be defined and used as weapons, and norms within the community celebrate toughness and a willingness to fight, seek retribution, and intimidate opponents. According to the participants in this study, this context promotes a unique set of dynamics that is unlike most other contact sports. Players enhance their value to their team by demonstrating toughness through display of fighting skills; indeed, the ability to fight effectively becomes a coveted trait, operating even as a means to indirectly win games through intimidation of the opposition and targeting of key opposing players. Fighting is seen to be far more important than skating skills to player success (Weinstein, Smith, and Wiesenthal 1995). These concepts can be seen in the following observations of three study participants:

> Hockey definitely promotes violence. . . . I mean, they have a penalty for fighting . . . and

just the reasoning behind that is that they say hey, we don't want fighting in the game, but if they didn't want fighting in the game, they wouldn't have a penalty for it—they would just basically kick the person out of the sport . . . and just the nature of the sport . . . how you win a game—you're physically dominant over another person—being bigger, stronger, faster than the person . . . it's just inherent in the nature of the sport . . . that promotes violence . . .

Hockey players or others in a contact sport could be prone to instigate a fight . . . hockey players instigating fights is part of the game . . . instigating a fight can work to your advantage . . . you can get them [opposition] off their game . . . you know . . . make them push themselves, push their manhood . . . I'm not sure if it [hockey] makes you more prone to violence, but it almost does . . .

Actually, it [fighting] was the thing that was paying my meal ticket so to speak, you know—and you get good at it and you have to do it—or you weren't going to play or they would find somebody else that would do it. I mean, if I was going to make it to the NHL, I was going to have to fight my way there, and it wasn't going to be through some other role on the team, and you have your role on the team.

The narrative data in this study also reflect the pressure that hockey players feel from coaches who are perceived to promote aggression in their players. These athletes' accounts are replete with references to coaches' win-at-all-cost mentality, as well as descriptions of the ethically questionable methods that a number of their former coaches used against their players to motivate them toward aggressive behavior. For example, one player described the way in which a coach used aggression himself as a sort of modeling strategy:

There's pressure from all around. The coaches will use name calling or in some situations use physical—not to hurt, but wrestle you around a bit—if they don't think you are doing your job and being aggressive and taking guys out of the play, that kind of thing. I've been in situations where coaches have used their hand or

their stick in certain ways to get you fired up—hand in the back of the head, stick in the balls, you know.

Other coaches may not have engaged in aggressive behavior themselves, but players certainly believed that their coaches had a role in encouraging aggression, perhaps by active promotion or simply tacit acceptance of violent and aggressive behavior. The following narratives serve as prototypic examples:

Your teammates may expect you to watch their back . . . but, generally, it's the coach that will tell you to start with the violence . . . to agitate—sometimes those are elements that the team is lacking . . . it really is . . . coaches like guys . . . who take a hit . . . most coaches I've played with have not had a problem with sending someone out . . . a heavy person [enforcer] out . . . if they believe that a rival would possibly injure one of his good players . . . it makes sense . . . you've got to keep your scorers to win the game . . .

I've been involved in situations before where people are asked to go and fight [by the coach]. Someone is being dirty on the ice—takes a cheap shot at a smaller guy and basically they [coach] will . . . say, hey, I want you to go fight that guy just because they don't want them to take liberties and try to intimidate . . . so that's a definite influence, and, of course, you are rewarded by the coaches . . .

I smacked a guy in the dressing room one time and the coach asked me why I did it at the next practice. I said he shot his mouth off in front of the whole team and I told him to shut it or I was going to smack him—if I back down in front of the whole team and let him shoot his mouth off, how do you expect these guys to rely on me the next game out there—he [coach] said that's fine.

These quotes are consistent with Crosset's (1999) findings that athletes fully understand that their knowledge of the rewards for being mean are linked to coaching behaviors.

Fan pressures and influences also promote aggression and violence because the reinforcement through cheering and positive comments is extremely appealing to the athletes. Although winning was usually viewed as being most important, the use of aggression and violence could at times be considered an extremely significant secondary aspect in terms of what hockey fans wanted to see. The pressure players felt as a result of spectator comments is described through the following accounts:

> The first thing that comes into my head is the cheering every time somebody gets hit into the boards and a fight breaks out everyone stands up and cheers—that kind of thing, and when they see blood. A lot of fans came to see that and they got bored if there wasn't some kind of violence going on. In my personal conversations with them and how they react to the game, it was enough for me to see that they wanted to see that violence thing, and it does promote it—I mean, when the crowd is behind you and cheer when you knock people into the boards—I'm not going to lie, it gets you fired up and wants to make you do more banging of guys into the boards, and lots of times, if it takes that to get the team fired up, then that's what you're going to do. It always helps to get the fans behind you—they definitely have a role in promoting violence in the sport.

> Like even at universities or . . . back in the days of juniors . . . basically, if you go out in a fight and beat someone up . . . after the game . . . you'd get recognition for that—fans would come up to you and say, that's a great fight you were in, you really beat the crap out of that guy . . . and, basically, you're getting rewarded for . . . fighting with someone, and people remember that . . . if you're constantly getting rewarded for something you do . . . you're going to do that again and again.

Such findings are consistent with Smith's (1979b) findings that 61 percent of the players perceived spectators at hockey games approved of fighting.

The reinforcement of violent behaviors can be usefully framed with the observations offered by Vaz (1980). He found that violence is virtually non-existent among young boys just starting to play hockey. But as they are influenced by older

players and professionals within the hockey community, rough play is encouraged and "under certain conditions, failure to fight is variously sanctioned by coaches and players" (145). This hockey subculture plays itself out against a larger backdrop of conventions of masculinity in contemporary society. For instance, several players discussed the ways in which hockey players are likely to equate manliness with a willingness to engage in violent behavior. Three narratives, in particular, illustrate this inclination:

> I think of people that you know and hang out with . . . expect you to be strong, kind of macho, and stick up or you know stick up for yourself . . . someone would never walk up to you and say, hey that was a great move you made walking away from fighting that guy, I mean I probably never heard that in my life but I definitely heard a person being put down because he backed away from a physical confrontation both on the ice and off the ice . . . you were generally perceived as weak if you didn't go fight . . . it would lower their opinion of you whereas if you went out and fought . . . you were generally seen . . . in higher standards . . . you're a team guy, you're a guy that would stick up for the other players . . . you were tough . . . you're a lot of things that people respected back then . . .

> I think it's more trying to prove yourself . . . trying to prove your physical dominance . . . to yourself, your coach, your teammates, the fans that you know . . . hey, I might of lost the last fight, but hey, I'm strong enough to win this fight against this guy . . . and trying to make yourself look better in front of . . . especially your teammates . . . your teammates tend to remember a lot of things that I think most of the fans that come will forget . . .

> If someone were to try to fight you on the ice and you backed away . . . it would be more perceived as he's weak, he's backed away from a physical confrontation and generally most people don't want to be seen like that . . . so I think there was a lot of pressure to stick up for yourself and I think the same goes over into your social behavior often . . . you're kind of expected to stick up for yourself and people

think you should and kind of have the perception that if you are not, you're not as manly.

As this last narrative reflects, embedded within many of these players' narratives is the implicit recognition that the tendency to draw parallels between manliness and violence extends beyond the competitive arena into broader social relations (cf. Coakley 1989). For example, one player described the similarities between problem solving in hockey competition and problem solving in social relationships in this way:

> You might have something like guys having problems in school and with their girlfriend or . . . away from home and pressure from not being around his family . . . maybe at an older level, like in juniors, maybe leaving home for the first time, a combination of all those things contributing to maybe a little bit more of a downer attitude—not feeling good about themselves—and maybe having to beat someone up to feel better about themselves—you get a lot of that with athletes.

As this thematic analysis indicates, hockey socialization and players' ideals of masculinity combine to create a culture of aggression and violence within the sport. Specifically, the socializing influences on which the research participants focused their attention included hockey competition per se, teammates, coaches, and fans. Cultural imagery surrounding masculinity—in particular, ideals of physical dominance, strength, and toughness—joins with these primary hockey influences to create a culture within which violence and aggression are not only tolerated but even encouraged. Moreover, the narrative data in this study demonstrate that the conventions of aggression and violence that typify sports competition apply as well in the nonsports environment. In fact, one player's narrative powerfully illustrates his belief that this link is indeed inevitable:

> They make demands on athletes to be tough because they want to see it, it [aggression] automatically carries over when you see some guy who's huge and charged with beating his wife.

It's like, what—so they think this is some sort of surprise, because if you're paying a guy three million dollars a year to knock somebody's block off, do you expect them to turn it off? No way, and you're praising him to be this animal, you know, you want him to be a destructive force on the field but then you want him to be some sort of pussy cat off the field?

In addition to discussing this inherent connection between violence within and outside of sports competition, the athletes discussed two factors that promoted the exportation of violence outside the athletic context: (1) consumption of alcohol and (2) objectification of women.

Alcohol Consumption

Previous research—for example, Gallmeier (1988)—has found that alcohol use is nearly universal among professional hockey players. Its use is apparently related to the extreme pressures of the game, as well as to the desire to suppress or deaden feelings. Likewise, all of the participants in this study discussed the common role of alcohol in the lives of hockey players. Moreover, these athletes associated violence with consumption of alcohol and other substances. For some, alcohol consumption was mentioned merely as a contextual feature in their descriptions of violent episodes. Some of the participants, however, perceived alcohol as a causal agent, explaining that it facilitated the transition of violence from the competitive venue into everyday social interaction. One player explained it in this way:

> It is the major factor of talk and off-ice violence—alcohol and testosterone and after-sport smack talking—you know, I was doing this and I did that and I played great, and when they start drinking, they think that they can do anything . . . it's the major factor in off-ice violence. Alcohol is the thing that leads to fights—in my experience in college, there wasn't one sober, off-ice violence [incident] that I ever witnessed or heard of or anything—never.

Other players may not have identified alcohol as "the major factor" but they certainly described, with great clarity, the role alcohol and drugs often play in creating a context within which athletes can act out their machismo. Two narratives illustrate this phenomenon:

> Alcohol after a game adds a strange element—I think it makes a person more conducive to violence off the ice—definitely—just because beer and muscles . . . you feel a little bit more invincible once you have a six-pack in you . . . that much more macho . . . alcohol is good for socializing, helps you relax, but it can also get people on edge . . . especially more high-strung people . . .

> I think it just adds fuel to the fire—if you've already got a kid who's aggressive by nature and you throw a catalyst in there [alcohol], it just makes everything worse—especially with hockey as there's a lot of drinking that goes on with it—you mix that with guys who are maybe lonely or depressed and you got trouble off the ice—if things are going on on the ice that they may not be happy with and then you're drinking and doing drugs, it makes everything worse—so it's just adding fuel to the fire.

In essence, all these players describe some way that alcohol and drugs act to promote aggression and violence. Indeed, these findings are consistent with previous work in this area. For instance, although alcohol has not been identified as the cause of abuse, it has been associated with violence and is thought to play a complex role in its occurrence; it may impair reasoning and communication, be part of premeditated strategy (Crowell & Burgess 1996), and/or be used to excuse violent behavior (Benedict 1997). Furthermore, the complex relationship between alcohol, violence, and constructions of masculinity that is implicated in the narrative data in this study is mirrored by Messerschmidt (1993), who theorizes that alcohol cannot be separated from demonstrating masculinity as it is often used to decrease communication and increase men's capacity to be violent.

Although the athletes in this study talked about the connection between alcohol and violence rather generally, there is research to indicate that excessive alcohol use within male peer groups contributes to sexual violence against women (Koss and Dinero 1988). In addition, Koss and Gaines (1993) linked alcohol consumption, athletic participation, and violence against women; they found that while athletic participation per se was associated with sexual aggression, alcohol consumption was even more highly correlated with sexual aggression. Thus, this analysis now turns to an examination of the role of hockey players' sexual relationships with women.

Objectification of Women

Commentaries, theoretical analyses, and empirical studies have begun to focus on whether participation in certain sports is related to misogyny, high rates of physical and sexual assault, and the occurrence of rape and gang rape (Coakley 1998). For instance, Sanday (1990) argues that when men become emotionally bound together in all-male groups that emphasize physical dominance, they often express their sense of togetherness by demeaning women. The narrative data in this study provide support for these assertions. For example, two participants talk extensively about the way in which their peers objectify women:

> I think that date rape is prevalent among the jock culture. There are things that are not violent but they just seem kind of wrong that guys do in terms of how they relate to women—off ice. They treat women like objects—sexual objects. They talk about them as if they aren't there, as if they [the athletes] were in the locker room talking . . . and don't care what they say at all because they think they're still going to have sex or whatever. Things like that machismo group mentality, that locker room mentality, comes out in off-ice behavior . . . treating women really bad . . . like one-nighters or short-term girlfriends or someone they didn't care very much, just as objects or sex partners.

> Locker room talk [is] definitely machismo without doubt, and that carries over when the team is all out . . . you're talking to a girl and all the team's around and they say, what are

you going to do to her—and all that stuff. That kind of talk breeds, does breed that kind of certain behavior in the group when men have the group thing going with a not-caring attitude towards women—that kind of carries over when a guy's with a girl—he doesn't care what happens to the girl as long as he is getting what he wants—or getting what the group wants—like, sometimes, I've heard where two guys will have sex with one woman, group sex, or, if she's drunk or passed out or whatever—sometimes, the girl's into it—and that's a rarity—and then you hear about that stuff in the locker room—I mean, it happens, and sometimes they're willing and sometimes they're not—I'm not sure . . . if they're kind a coaxed, you know, 'cause there are more than one male in the room—stuff like that.

From the first author's knowledge of athlete behavior, these players are describing situations that are very common to the male sport culture, and they reflect only a small extent of the actual sexual behaviors that occur. It has been this researcher's experience that objectification of women occurs as a natural outgrowth and continuation of traditional male socialization that begins in early childhood. Such socialization encourages boys and men to see women as inferior and as sexual objects who are supposed to meet the needs of men. The culture of hockey reinforces this objectification because of the focus on traditional male behaviors conducive to sports success and the large amount of time men spend exclusively with other males. These conversations occur frequently as part of the bonding experience.

Moreover, according to the athlete informants in this study, such demeaning attitudes and talk often carry over into actual violent behaviors. One player's account provides an apt illustration:

A guy back in juniors I played with when he was 16—a tough kid off the farm—cucumber farm—he got his girlfriend pregnant—knocked her up—she was about 15—and while I never saw it—he was actually taken away right out of the rink one night because she went to the cops

and told them he had been beating her when she was even pregnant with the kid—so that was probably one of the worst stories I had heard because there was a baby involved.

Two other players also commented on their knowledge of violence against women. Although these athletes do not concede to engaging in violence against women themselves, they discuss it as if it is a somewhat routine occurrence within male hockey cultures:

Yeah, I remember certain things that had happened. . . . My friends would get abusive with their girlfriends and stuff like that. I definitely know people that have gotten like that—not necessarily hit, but they'd be abusive and kind of push them and things like that, and we'd always stop them.

I'd heard stories of guys roughing up a girl a bit. Most of it was guys talking about other guys they knew that were in situations like that.

Summary and Conclusions

The findings of this study indicate that interpersonal aggression is common in the lives of these hockey players, both on and off the ice. For these hockey professionals, aggressive behaviors were seen as manifestations of existent tendencies as well as products of sport socialization. Future studies should examine personality characteristics and psychological symptoms of particularly aggressive athletes to determine the role of individual factors as opposed to the culture of sport in producing violent behaviors. Increasingly, studies of interpersonal violence are employing biopsychosocial perspectives, noting the relevance of all three domains in predicting violence (e.g., McKenry, Julian, and Gavazzi 1995).

The participants in this study readily explored the ways in which hockey socialization created a context within which violence and aggression are not only tolerated but also encouraged. Much was said about the culture of hockey itself as an instigating mechanism of male violence. Clearly, hockey was viewed as a violent sport and a sports culture that encouraged violent behaviors on the ice; the players, management, and indeed the fans expected and desired it. It was not mindless violence but functional despite some prohibition. Consistent with Weinstein, Smith, and Wiesenthal's (1995) survey of youth and preprofessional junior hockey players, violent behaviors were seen as only mildly penalized and generally viewed as essential for team and individual player success. For example, referees do not intervene in professional hockey fights as long as only two players are involved, and teammates and coaches judge players' competence more on their willingness to engage in violence (especially fist fighting) than playing and skating skills. Messner (1995) notes that men are raised to view the world as competitive and hierarchal, taught to get the job done regardless of the consequences to others—what Balkan (1966) termed "unmitigated agency." Thus, when tasks become more important than people, violence is sometimes a problem-solving mechanism, for example, intentionally hurting an opposing player. Aggression and violence were important components to competitive success, and they were not limited to the ice rink; a united front perpetuating violent behaviors carried over to social situations. In addition, coaches often were negligent, if not somewhat encouraging, of players remaining tough and aggressive off the ice.

A culture of masculinity can be seen to characterize the teams the players described. The athletes tended to share a set of ideological beliefs related to traditional forms of masculine expression, for example, preoccupation with achievement and maintaining status through fighting or risk taking, acquiring an identity of toughness (Weisfeld et al. 1987). Research has found that hockey players with the strongest levels of endorsement of traditional masculine ideologies are more likely to fight than are other players (Weinstein, Smith, and Wiesenthal 1995). Kilmartin (2000) contends that violent behaviors by athletes are motivated by one athlete's perception that another is trying to hurt him. This too was represented in the players' comments regarding the need to be on guard, the necessity to protect oneself from the violence inherent in the game, and the dominance perspective wherein the athlete is constantly battling against teammates and opposition who are motivated toward domination. The culture of masculinity was also seen in the pack mentality that emerged among the players and carried over to off-ice activities. The strong bonds that emerged reinforced aggressive behaviors but also resulted in strong bonds of allegiance and loyalty.

In his examination of sport and violence, Young (2000) asserts that while knowledge of player violence within sport is substantial, little is actually known about other forms of sport-related violence. This in-depth exploration of hockey culture begins to fill this knowledge gap; its unique contribution is a more nuanced understanding of athletes' expressions of aggression and violence outside the sports context. As noted previously, the players in this study viewed aggression in broader social relationships as a logical extension of on-ice violent behavior. This relationship between participation in violence in sport and in other social contexts is consistent with the well-established relationship between and among various types of violent displays consistently found in the literature (Fagan and Browne 1994; Levinson 1989). Moreover, when asked specifically to provide explanations for off-ice violence based on their experiences, many mentioned the role of alcohol specifically, but also in combination with other factors. The players typically drew a causal relationship between alcohol use and violent behaviors. Alcohol was used to a great extent to self-medicate as a means of handling the stresses associated with the game. Gustafson (1986) contends that alcohol is a societally sanctioned aggressive solution for men to use when frustrated. Also, hockey seems to be a culture that is defined, in part, by the use of alcohol in leisure. Others have noted that drinking is a cultural symbol of masculinity (Lemle and Mishkind 1989). The complex role that alcohol plays in aggression should be explored in greater depth, especially as it interacts with social situations, psychological factors, and other drugs.

The informants in this study also identified athletes' tendency to objectify women as a factor that contributes to the exportation of violence off the ice. Interestingly, the men defined sexual abuse of women broadly to include verbal aggression and general disrespectful behaviors, that is, treatment of women as sexual objects. Some connected sexual aggression or violence to what they termed a locker-room-talk mentality wherein certain male sexual bravado in the peer culture was carried off the ice to their relationships with women. The respondents tended to differentiate between general physical violence and sexual aggression or violence, seeing the latter as less serious and more understandable than general physical violence. In general, the athletes seemed to speak of a culture that had a lesser regard for women.

In general, the findings of this study have illuminated men's subjective experiences as participants in the sport of hockey. As such, they have brought personal insights to bear on our understanding of aggression and violence in sports. Because this was a small-scale intensive study, the voices of a variety of other participants who could have provided more insights into couple violence were excluded, for example, actual male aggressors of women and women victims. The researchers rely on the perspectives of respondents who had a particularly close relationship with the first author; perhaps a larger number of informants who were not acquainted with the researcher would have yielded additional information. Many questions remain to be addressed. Because violent behaviors first emerge in high school and continue into college play, these would be useful arenas for generating a fuller understanding of the development of violent behaviors in this sport. Other sports have also been associated with violence outside the sport itself, for example, football and basketball; a question emerges as to whether the development of violence is similar for other sports. In addition, as more women enter contact sports, it would be interesting to see if they create a similar sport culture and become more aggressive both in and outside the sport. Factors that have been implicated in domestic violence research in general, for example, masculine identity, family-of-origin issues, male peer group influences, and stress need to be explored in future work on this topic.

References

Balkan, D. 1966. *The duality of human existence.* Chicago: Rand McNally.

Benedict, J. R. 1997. *Public heroes, private felons.* Boston: Northeastern University Press.

Benedict, J., and A. Klein. 1997. Arrest and conviction rates for athletes accused of sexual assault. *Sociology of Sport Journal* 14:86–94.

Berg, B. L. 1998. *Qualitative research methods in the social sciences.* Needham Heights, MA: Allyn & Bacon.

Berkowitz, A. 1992. College men as perpetrators of acquaintance rape and sexual assault: A review of recent literature. *Journal of American College Health* 40:157–65.

Boeringer, S. 1996. Influences of fraternity membership, athletics, and male living arrangements on sexual aggression. *Violence Against Women* 2:135–47.

Bogdan, R. C., and S. K. Biklen. 1992. *Qualitative research for education: An introduction to theory and methods.* 2d ed. Boston: Allyn & Bacon.

Carson, S. K., W. A. Halteman, and G. Stacy. 1997. Athletes and rape: is there a connection? *Perceptual and Motor Skills* 85:1379–83.

Coakley, J. J. 1998. *Sport in society: issues and controversies.* Boston: Irwin McGraw-Hill.

Connell, R. W. 1995. *Masculinities.* Los Angeles: University of California Press.

Crosset, T. W. 1999. Male athletes' violence against women: A critical assessment of the athletic affiliation, violence against women debate. *Quest* 51:244–57.

———. 2000. Athletic affiliation and violence against women: toward a structural prevention project. In *Masculinities, gender relations, and sport,* edited by J. McKay, M. A. Messner, and D. Sabo, 147–61. Thousand Oaks, CA: Sage.

Crosset, T. W., J. R. Benedict, and M. M. McDonald. 1995. Male student-athletes reported for sexual assault: A survey of campus. *Journal of Sport and Social Issues* 19:126–40.

Crowell, N., and A. Burgess, eds. 1996. *Understanding violence against women.* Washington, DC: National Academy Press.

Curry, T. J. 1991. Fraternal bonding in the locker room: A profeminist analysis of talk about competition and women. *Sociology of Sport Journal* 8:119–35.

———. 1998. Beyond the locker room: Campus bars and college athletes. *Sociology of Sport Journal* 15:205–15.

———. 2000. Booze and bar fights: A journey to the dark side of college athletics. In *Masculinities, gender relations, and sport,* edited by J. McKay, M. A. Messner, and D. Sabo, 162–75. Thousand Oaks, CA: Sage.

Fagan, J., and A. Browne. 1994. Violence between spouses and intimates: Physical aggression between women and men in intimate relationships. In *Understanding and preventing violence: social influences,* edited by A. J. Reiss, Jr., and J. A. Roth, 115–292. Washington, DC: National Academy Press.

Faulkner, R. 1974. Making violence by doing work, selves, situations and the world of professional hockey. *Sociology of Work and Occupations* 1:288–312.

Fine, G. A. 1987. *With the boys: Little league baseball and preadolescent culture.* Chicago: University of Chicago Press.

Frintner, M. P., and L. Rubinson. 1993. Acquaintance rape: The influence of alcohol, fraternity, and sports team membership. *Journal of Sex Education and Therapy* 19:272–84.

Gallmeier, C. P. 1988. Juicing, burning, and tooting: Observing drug use among professional hockey players. *Arena Review* 12:1–12.

Gruneau, R., and D. Whitson. 1993. *Hockey night in Canada: Sport, identities, and cultural politics.* Toronto, Canada: Garamond.

Gustafson, R. 1986. Threat as a determinant of alcohol-related aggression. *Psychological Reports* 58:287–97.

Hargreaves, J. 1986. Where's the virtue? Where's the grace? A discussion of the social production of gender relations in and through sport. *Theory, Culture, and Society* 3:109–21.

Kilmartin, C. T. 2000. *The masculine self.* Boston: McGraw-Hill.

Koss, M. P., and T. E. Dinero. 1988. Predictors of sexual aggression among a national sample of male college students. *Annals of the New York Academy of Sciences* 528:133–46.

Koss, M. P., and J. A. Gaines. 1993. The prediction of sexual aggression by alcohol use, athletic par-

ticipation, and fraternity affiliation. *Journal of Interpersonal Violence* 8:94–108.

Lemle, R., and M. E. Mishkind. 1989. Alcohol and masculinity. *Journal of Substance Abuse Treatment* 6:213–22.

Levinson, D. 1989. *Family violence in cross-cultural perspective.* Newbury Park, CA: Sage.

McKenry, P. C., T. W. Julien, and N. Gavazzi. 1995. Toward a biopsychosocial model of domestic violence. *Journal of Marriage and the Family* 57:307–20.

Messerschmidt, J. W. 1993. *Masculinities and crime: Critique and reconceptualization of theory.* Lanham, MD: Rowman & Littlefield.

Messner, M. 1990. When bodies are weapons: Masculine violence in sport. *International Review for the Sociology of Sport* 25:203–21.

———. 1995. Boyhood, organized sports, and the construction of masculinity. In *Men's lives,* edited by M. A. Kimmel and M. S. Messner, 102–14. Boston: Allyn & Bacon.

Messner, M., and D. Sabo. 1990. *Sports, men, and the gender order: Critical feminist perspectives.* Champaign, IL: Human Kinetics.

Miller, M. B., and A. M. Haberman. 1994. *Qualitative data analyses: A new sourcebook of methods.* Newbury Park, CA: Sage.

National Research Council. 1996. *Understanding violence against women.* Washington, DC: National Academy Press.

Sanday, P. 1990. *Fraternity gang rapes: Sex, brotherhood, and privilege on campus.* New York: New York University Press.

Schwartz, M., and C. Nogrady. 1996. Frat membership, rape myths, and sexual aggression on a college campus. *Violence Against Women* 2:158–62.

Smith, M. D. 1979a. Hockey violence: A new test of the violent subculture hypothesis. *Social Problems* 27:235–47.

———. 1979b. Towards an explanation of hockey violence: A reference other approach. *Canadian Journal of Sociology* 4:105–24.

———. 1983. *Violence and sport.* Toronto, Canada: Butterworths.

Terry, P. C., and J. J. Jackson. 1985. The determinants and control of violence in sport. *Quest* 37:27–37.

Vaz, E. W. 1979. Institutionalized rule violation and control in organized minor league hockey. *Canadian Journal of Sports Sciences* 4:83–90.

———. 1980. The culture of young hockey players: Some initial observations. In *Jock: Sports and male identity,* edited by D. F. Sabo and R. Runfola, 142–57. Englewood Cliffs, NJ: Prentice Hall.

Weinstein, M. D., D. S. Smith, and D. L. Wiesenthal. 1995. Masculinity and hockey violence. *Sex Roles* 33:831–47.

Weisfeld, G. E., D. M. Muczenski, C. C. Weisfeld, and D. R. Omark. 1987. Stability of boys' social success among peers over an eleven-year period. In *Interpersonal relations: family, peers, and friends,* edited by J. A. Meacham, 58–80. Basel, UK: Karger.

West, C., and D. H. Zimmerman. 1987. Doing gender. *Gender & Society* 1:125–51.

Young, K. 1993. Violence, risk, and liability in male sports culture. *Sociology of Sport Journal* 10:373–96.

———. 2000. Sport and violence. In *Handbook of sports studies,* edited by J. Coakley and E. Dunning, 23–59. London: Sage.

Carol Cohn

Wars, Wimps, and Women: Talking Gender and Thinking War

I start with a true story, told to me by a white male physicist:

> Several colleagues and I were working on modeling counterforce attacks, trying to get realistic estimates of the number of immediate fatalities that would result from different deployments. At one point, we remodeled a particular attack, using slightly different assumptions, and found that instead of there being thirty-six million immediate fatalities, there would only be thirty million. And everybody was sitting around nodding, saying, "Oh yeah, that's great, only thirty million," when all of a sudden, I heard what we were saying. And I blurted out, "Wait, I've just heard how we're talking—Only thirty million! Only thirty million human beings killed instantly?" Silence fell upon the room. Nobody said a word. They didn't even look at me. It was awful. I felt like a woman.

The physicist added that henceforth he was careful to never blurt out anything like that again.

During the early years of the Reagan presidency, in the era of the Evil Empire, the cold war, and loose talk in Washington about the possibility of fighting and "prevailing" in a nuclear war, I went off to do participant observation in a community of North American nuclear defense intellectuals and security affairs analysts—a community virtually entirely composed of white men. They work in universities, think tanks, and as advisers to gov-

ernment. They theorize about nuclear deterrence and arms control, and nuclear and conventional war fighting, about how to best translate military might into political power; in short, they create the discourse that underwrites American national security policy. The exact relation of their theories to American political and military practice is a complex and thorny one; the argument can be made, for example, that their ideas do not so much shape policy decisions as legitimate them after the fact. But one thing that is clear is that the body of language and thinking they have generated filters out to the military, politicians, and the public, and increasingly shapes how we talk and think about war. This was amply evident during the Gulf War: Gulf War "news," as generated by the military briefers, reported by newscasters, and analyzed by the television networks' resident security experts, was marked by its use of the professional language of defense analysis, nearly to the exclusion of other ways of speaking.

My goal has been to understand something about how defense intellectuals think, and why they think that way. Despite the parsimonious appeal of ascribing the nuclear arms race to "missile envy," I felt certain that masculinity was not a sufficient explanation of why men think about war in the ways that they do. Indeed, I found many ways to understand what these men were doing that had little or nothing to do with gender. But ultimately, the physicist's story and others like it made confronting the role of gender unavoidable. Thus, in this paper I will explore gender discourse, and its role in shaping nuclear and national security discourse.

Reprinted by permission of the author.

I want to stress, this is not a paper about men and women, and what they are or are not like. I will not be claiming that men are aggressive and women peace loving. I will not even address the question of how men's and women's relations to war may differ, nor of the different propensities they may have to committing acts of violence. Neither will I pay more than passing attention to the question which so often crops up in discussions of war and gender, that is, would it be a more peaceful world if our national leaders were women? These questions are valid and important, and recent feminist discussion of them has been complex, interesting, and contentious. But my focus is elsewhere. I wish to direct attention away from gendered individuals and toward gendered discourses. My question is about the way that civilian defense analysts think about war, and the ways in which that thinking is shaped not by their maleness (or, in extremely rare instances, female-ness), but by the ways in which gender discourse intertwines with and permeates that thinking.

Let me be more specific about my terms. I use the term *gender* to refer to the constellation of meanings that a given culture assigns to biological sex differences. But more than that, I use gender to refer to a symbolic system, a central organizing discourse of culture, one that not only shapes how we experience and understand ourselves as men and women, but that also interweaves with other discourses and shapes *them*—and therefore shapes other aspects of our world—such as how nuclear weapons are thought about and deployed.

So when I talk about "gender discourse," I am talking not only about words or language but about a system of meanings, of ways of thinking, images and words that first shape how we experience, understand, and represent ourselves as men and women, but that also do more than that; they shape many other aspects of our lives and culture. In this symbolic system, human characteristics are dichotomized, divided into pairs of polar opposites that are supposedly mutually exclusive: mind is opposed to body; culture to nature; thought to feeling; logic to intuition; objectivity to subjectivity; aggression to passivity; confrontation to ac-

commodation; abstraction to particularity; public to private; political to personal, ad nauseam. In each case, the first term of the "opposites" is associated with male, the second with female. And in each case, our society values the first over the second.

I break it into steps like this—analytically separating the *existence* of these groupings of binary oppositions, from the association of each group with a gender, from the valuing of one over the other, the so-called male over the so-called female, for two reasons: first, to try to make visible the fact that this system of dichotomies is encoding many meanings that may be quite unrelated to male and female bodies. Yet once that first step is made—the association of each side of those lists with a gender—gender now becomes tied to many other kinds of cultural representations. If a human activity, such as engineering, fits some of the characteristics, it becomes gendered.

My second reason for breaking it into those steps is to try to help make it clear that the meanings can flow in different directions; that is, in gender discourse, men and women are supposed to exemplify the characteristics on the lists. It also works in reverse, however; to evidence any of these characteristics—to be abstract, logical or dispassionate, for example—is not simply to be those things, but also to be manly. And to be manly is not simply to be manly, but also to be in the more highly valued position in the discourse. In other words, to exhibit a trait on that list is not neutral—it is not simply displaying some basic human characteristic. It also positions you in a discourse of gender. It associates you with a particular gender, and also with a higher or lower valuation.

In stressing that this is a *symbolic* system, I want first to emphasize that while real women and men do not really fit these gender "ideals," the existence of this system of meaning affects all of us, nonetheless. Whether we want to or not, we see ourselves and others against its templates, we interpret our own and others' actions against it. A man who cries easily cannot avoid in some way confronting that he is likely to be seen as less than fully manly. A woman who is very aggressive and incisive may enjoy that quality in herself, but the fact of her aggressiveness does not exist by itself; she cannot avoid having her own and others' perceptions of that quality of hers, the meaning it has for people, being in some way mediated by the discourse of gender. Or, a different kind of example: Why does it mean one thing when George Bush gets teary-eyed in public, and something entirely different when Patricia Shroeder does? The same act is viewed through the lens of gender and is seen to mean two very different things.

Second, as gender discourse assigns gender to human characteristics, we can think of the discourse as something we are positioned *by*. If I say, for example, that a corporation should stop dumping toxic waste because it is damaging the creations of mother earth (i.e., articulating a valuing and sentimental vision of nature), I am speaking in a manner associated with women, and our cultural discourse of gender positions me as female. As such I am then associated with the whole constellation of traits—irrational, emotional, subjective, and so forth—and I am in the devalued position. If, on the other hand, I say the corporation should stop dumping toxic wastes because I have calculated that it is causing $8.215 billion of damage to eight nonrenewable resources, which should be seen as equivalent to lowering the GDP by 0.15 percent per annum (i.e., using a rational, calculative mode of thought), the discourse positions me as masculine—rational, objective, logical, and so forth—the dominant, valued position.

But if we are positioned *by* discourses, we can also take different positions *within* them. Although I am female, and this would "naturally" fall into the devalued term, I can choose to "speak like a man"—to be hard-nosed, realistic, unsentimental, dispassionate. Jeanne Kirkpatrick is a formidable example. While we can choose a position in a discourse, however, it means something different for a woman to "speak like a man" than for a man to do so. It is heard differently.

One other note about my use of the term *gender discourse:* I am using it in the general sense to refer to the phenomenon of symbolically organizing the world in these gender-associated opposites. I do not mean to suggest that there is a single discourse defining a single set of gender ideals. In fact, there are many specific discourses of gender, which vary by race, class, ethnicity, locale, sexuality, nationality, and other factors. The masculinity idealized in the gender discourse of new Haitian immigrants is in some ways different from that of sixth-generation white Anglo-Saxon Protestant business executives, and both differ somewhat from that of white-male defense intellectuals and security analysts. One version of masculinity is mobilized and enforced in the armed forces in order to enable men to fight wars, while a somewhat different version of masculinity is drawn upon and expressed by abstract theoreticians of war.

Let us now return to the physicist who felt like a woman: what happened when he "blurted out" his sudden awareness of the "only thirty million" dead people? First, he was transgressing a code of professional conduct. In the civilian defense intellectuals' world, when you are in professional settings you do not discuss the bloody reality behind the calculations. It is not required that you be completely unaware of them in your outside life, or that you have no feelings about them, but it is required that you do not bring them to the foreground in the context of professional activities. There is a general awareness that you *could not* do your work if you did; in addition, most defense intellectuals believe that emotion and description of human reality distort the process required to think well about nuclear weapons and warfare.

So the physicist violated a behavioral norm, in and of itself a difficult thing to do because it threatens your relationships to and your standing with your colleagues.

But even worse than that, he demonstrated some of the characteristics on the "female" side of the dichotomies—in his "blurting" he was impulsive, uncontrolled, emotional, concrete, and attentive to human bodies, at the very least. Thus, he marked himself not only as unprofessional but as feminine, and this, in turn, was doubly threatening. It was not only a threat to his own sense of self as masculine, his gender identity, it also identified him with a devalued status—of a woman—or put him in the devalued or subordinate position in the discourse.

Thus, both his statement, "I felt like a woman," and his subsequent silence in that and other settings are completely understandable. To have the strength of character and courage to transgress the strictures of both professional and gender codes *and* to associate yourself with a lower status is very difficult.

This story is not simply about one individual, his feelings and actions; it is about the role of gender discourse. The impact of gender discourse in that room (and countless others like it) is that some things get left out. Certain ideas, concerns, interests, information, feelings, and meanings are marked in national security discourse as feminine, and are devalued. They are therefore, first, very difficult to *speak,* as exemplified by the physicist who felt like a woman. And second, they are very difficult to *hear,* to take in and work with seriously, even if they *are* said. For the others in the room, the way in which the physicist's comments were marked as female and devalued served to delegitimate them. It is almost as though they had become an accidental excrescence in the middle of the room. Embarrassed politeness demanded that they be ignored.

I must stress that this is not simply the product of the idiosyncratic personal composition of that particular room. In other professional settings, I have experienced the feeling that something terribly important is being left out and must be spoken; and yet, it has felt almost physically impossible to utter the words, almost as though they could not be pushed out into the smooth, cool, opaque air of the room.

What is it that cannot be spoken? First, any words that express an emotional awareness of the desperate human reality behind the sanitized abstractions of death and destruction—as in the physicist's sudden vision of thirty million rotting corpses. Similarly, weapons' effects may be spoken of only in the most clinical and abstract terms, leaving no room to imagine a seven-year-old boy with his flesh melting away from his bones or a toddler with her skin hanging down in strips. Voicing concern about the number of casualties in the enemy's armed forces, imagining the suffering of the killed and wounded young men, is out of bounds. (Within the military itself, it is permissible, even desirable, to attempt to minimize immediate civilian casualties if it is possible to do so without compromising military objectives, but as we learned in the Persian Gulf War, this is only an extremely limited enterprise; the planning and precision of military targeting does not admit to consideration of the cost in human lives of such actions as destroying power systems, or water and sewer systems, or highways and food distribution systems.) Psychological effects—on the soldiers fighting the war or on the citizens injured, or fearing for their own safety, or living through tremendous deprivation, or helplessly watching their babies die from diarrhea due to the lack of clean water—all of these are not to be talked about.

But it is not only particular subjects that are out of bounds. It is also tone of voice that counts. A speaking style that is identified as cool, dispassionate, and distanced is required. One that vibrates with the intensity of emotion almost always disqualifies the speaker, who is heard to sound like "a hysterical housewife."

What gets left out, then, is the emotional, the concrete, the particular, the human bodies and their vulnerability, human lives and their subjectivity—all of which are marked as feminine in the binary dichotomies of gender discourse. In other words, gender discourse informs and shapes nuclear and national security discourse, and in so doing creates silences and absences. It keeps things out of the room, unsaid, and keeps them ignored if they manage to get in. As such, it degrades our ability to think *well* and *fully* about nuclear weapons and national security, and shapes and limits the possible outcomes of our deliberations.

What becomes clear, then, is that defense intellectuals' standards of what constitutes "good thinking" about weapons and security have not simply evolved out of trial and error; it is not that the history of nuclear discourse has been filled with exploration of other ideas, concerns, interests, information, questions, feelings, meanings and stances which were then found to create distorted or poor thought. It is that these options have been *preempted* by gender discourse, and by the feelings evoked by living up to or transgressing gender codes.

To borrow a term from defense intellectuals, you might say that gender discourse becomes a "preemptive deterrent" to certain kinds of thought.

Let me give you another example of what I mean—another story, this one my own experience:

One Saturday morning I, two other women, and about fifty-five men gathered to play a war game designed by the RAND Corporation. Our "controllers" (the people running the game) first divided us up into three sets of teams; there would be three simultaneous games being played, each pitting a Red Team against a Blue Team (I leave the reader to figure out which color represents which country). All three women were put onto the same team, a Red Team.

The teams were then placed in different rooms so that we had no way of communicating with each other, except through our military actions (or lack of them) or by sending demands and responses to those demands via the controllers. There was no way to negotiate or to take actions other than military ones. (This was supposed to simulate reality.) The controllers then presented us with maps and pages covered with numbers representing each side's forces. We were also given a "scenario," a situation of escalating tensions and military conflicts, starting in the Middle East and spreading to Central Europe. We were to decide what to do, the controllers would go back and forth between the two teams to relate the other team's actions, and periodically the controllers themselves would add something that would ratchet up the conflict—an announcement of an "intercepted intelligence report" from the

other side, the authenticity of which we had no way of judging.

Our Red Team was heavily into strategizing, attacking ground forces, and generally playing war. We also, at one point, decided that we were going to pull our troops out of Afghanistan, reasoning it was bad for us to have them there and that the Afghanis had the right to self-determination. At another point we removed some troops from Eastern Europe. I must add that later on my team was accused of being wildly "unrealistic," that this group of experts found the idea that the Soviet Union might voluntarily choose to pull troops out of Afghanistan and Eastern Europe so utterly absurd. (It was about six months before Gorbachev actually did the same thing.)

Gradually our game escalated to nuclear war. The Blue Team used tactical nuclear weapons against our troops, but our Red Team decided, initially at least, against nuclear retaliation. When the game ended (at the end of the allotted time) our Red Team had "lost the war" (meaning that we had political control over less territory than we had started with, although our homeland had remained completely unviolated and our civilian population safe).

In the debriefing afterwards, all six teams returned to one room and reported on their games. Since we had had absolutely no way to know why the other team had taken any of its actions, we now had the opportunity to find out what they had been thinking. A member of the team that had played against us said, "Well, when he took his troops out of Afghanistan, I knew he was weak and I could push him around. And then, when we nuked him and he didn't nuke us back, I knew he was just such a wimp, I could take him for everything he's got and I nuked him again. He just wimped out."

There are many different possible comments to make at this point. I will restrict myself to a couple. First, when the man from the Blue Team called me a wimp (which is what it felt like for each of us on the Red Team—a personal accusation), I felt silenced. My reality, the careful reasoning that had gone into my strategic and tactical choices, the intelligence, the politics, the morality—all of it just disappeared, completely invalidated. I could not explain the reasons for my actions, could not protest, "Wait, you idiot, I didn't do it because I was weak, I did it because it made sense to do it that way, given my understandings of strategy and tactics, history and politics, my goals and my values." The protestation would be met with knowing sneers. In this discourse, the coding of an act as wimpish is hegemonic. Its emotional heat and resonance is like a bath of sulfuric acid: it erases everything else.

"Acting like a wimp" is an *interpretation* of a person's acts (or, in national security discourse, a country's acts, an important distinction I will return to later). As with any other interpretation, it is a selection of one among many possible different ways to understand something—once the selection is made, the other possibilities recede into invisibility. In national security discourse, "acting like a wimp," being insufficiently masculine, is one of the most readily available interpretive codes. (You do not need to do participant observation in a community of defense intellectuals to know this—just look at the "geopolitical analyses" in the media and on Capitol Hill of the way in which George Bush's military intervention in Panama and the Persian Gulf War finally allowed him to beat the "wimp factor.") You learn that someone is being a wimp if he perceives an international crisis as very dangerous and urges caution; if he thinks it might not be important to have just as many weapons that are just as big as the other guy's; if he suggests that an attack should not necessarily be answered by an even more destructive counterattack; or, until recently, if he suggested that making unilateral arms reductions might be useful for our own security. All of these are "wimping out."

The prevalence of this particular interpretive code is another example of how gender discourse affects the quality of thinking within the national security community, first, because, as in the case of the physicist who "felt like a woman," it is internalized to become a self-censor; there are things professionals simply will not *say* in groups,

options they simply will not argue nor write about, because they know that to do so is to brand themselves as wimps. Thus, a whole range of inputs is left out, a whole series of options is foreclosed from their deliberations.

Equally, if not more damagingly, is the way in which this interpretive coding not only limits what is *said,* but even limits what is *thought.* "He's a wimp" is a phrase that *stops* thought. When we were playing the game, once my opponent on the Blue Team "recognized the fact that I was a wimp," that is, once he interpreted my team's actions through the lens of this common interpretive code in national security discourse, he *stopped thinking;* he stopped looking for ways to understand what we were doing. He did not ask, "Why on earth would the Red Team do that? What does it tell me about them, about their motives and purposes and goals and capabilities? What does it tell me about their possible understandings of *my* actions, or of the situation they're in?" or any other of the many questions that might have enabled him to revise his own conception of the situation or perhaps achieve his goals at a far lower level of violence and destruction. Here, again, gender discourse acts as a preemptive deterrent to thought.

"Wimp" is, of course, not the only gendered pejorative used in the national security community; "pussy" is another popular epithet, conjoining the imagery of harmless domesticated (read demasculinized) pets with contemptuous reference to women's genitals. In an informal setting, an analyst worrying about the other side's casualties, for example, might be asked, "What kind of pussy are you, anyway?" It need not happen more than once or twice before everyone gets the message; they quickly learn not to raise the issue in their discussions. Attention to and care for the living, suffering, and dying of human beings (in this case, soldiers and their families and friends) is again banished from the discourse through the expedient means of gender-bashing.

Other words are also used to impugn someone's masculinity and, in the process, to delegitimate his position and avoid thinking seriously about it. "Those Krauts are a bunch of limp-dicked wimps" was the way one U.S. defense intellectual dismissed the West German politicians who were concerned about popular opposition to Euromissile deployments. I have heard our NATO allies referred to as "the Euro-fags" when they disagreed with American policy on such issues as the Contra War or the bombing of Libya. Labeling them "fags" is an effective strategy; it immediately dismisses and trivializes their opposition to U.S. policy by coding it as due to inadequate masculinity. In other words, the American analyst need not seriously confront the Europeans' arguments, since the Europeans' doubts about U.S. policy obviously stem not from their reasoning but from the "fact" that they "just don't have the stones for war." Here, again, gender discourse deters thought.

"Fag" imagery is not, of course, confined to the professional community of security analysts; it also appears in popular "political" discourse. The Gulf War was replete with examples. American derision of Saddam Hussein included bumper stickers that read "Saddam, Bend Over." American soldiers reported that the "U.S.A." stenciled on their uniforms stood for "Up Saddam's Ass." A widely reprinted cartoon, surely one of the most multiply offensive that came out of the war, depicted Saddam bowing down in the Islamic posture of prayer, with a huge U.S. missile, approximately five times the size of the prostrate figure, about to penetrate his upraised bottom. Over and over, defeat for the Iraqis was portrayed as humiliating anal penetration by the more powerful and manly United States.

Within the defense community discourse, manliness is equated not only with the ability to win a war (or to "prevail," as some like to say when talking about nuclear war); it is also equated with the willingness (which they would call courage) to threaten and use force. During the Carter administration, for example, a well-known academic security affairs specialist was quoted as saying that "under Jimmy Carter the United States is spreading its legs for the Soviet Union." Once this image is evoked, how does ra-

tional discourse about the value of U.S. policy proceed?

In 1989 and 1990, as Gorbachev presided over the withdrawal of Soviet forces from Eastern Europe, I heard some defense analysts sneeringly say things like, "They're a bunch of pussies for pulling out of Eastern Europe." This is extraordinary. Here they were, men who for years railed against Soviet domination of Eastern Europe. You would assume that if they were politically and ideologically consistent, if they were rational, they would be applauding the Soviet actions. Yet in their informal conversations, it was not their rational analyses that dominated their response, but the fact that for them, the decision for war, the willingness to use force, is cast as a question of masculinity—not prudence, thoughtfulness, efficacy, "rational" cost-benefit calculation, or morality, but masculinity.

In the face of this equation, genuine political discourse disappears. One more example: After Iraq invaded Kuwait and President Bush hastily sent U.S. forces to Saudi Arabia, there was a period in which the Bush administration struggled to find a convincing political justification for U.S. military involvement and the security affairs community debated the political merit of U.S. intervention. Then Bush set the deadline, January 16, high noon at the OK Corral, and as the day approached conversations changed. More of these centered on the question compellingly articulated by one defense intellectual as "Does George Bush have the stones for war?" This, too, is utterly extraordinary. This was a time when crucial political questions abounded: Can the sanctions work if given more time? Just what vital interests does the United States actually have at stake? What would be the goals of military intervention? Could they be accomplished by other means? Is the difference between what sanctions might accomplish and what military violence might accomplish worth the greater cost in human suffering, human lives, even dollars? What will the long-term effects on the people of the region be? On the ecology? Given the apparent successes of Gorbachev's last-minute diplomacy and Hussein's series of nearly daily small concessions, can and should Bush put off the deadline? Does he have the strength to let another leader play a major role in solving the problem? Does he have the political flexibility to not fight, or is he hellbent on war at all costs? And so on, ad infinitum. All of these disappear in the sulfuric acid test of the size of Mr. Bush's private parts.

I want to return to the RAND war simulation story to make one other observation. First, it requires a true confession: *I was stung by being called a wimp.* Yes, I thought the remark was deeply inane, and it infuriated me. But even so, I was also stung. Let me hasten to add, this was not because my identity is very wrapped up with not being wimpish—it actually is not a term that normally figures very heavily in my self-image one way or the other. But it was impossible to be in that room, hear his comment and the snickering laughter with which it was met, and not to feel stung, and humiliated.

Why? There I was, a woman and a feminist, not only contemptuous of the mentality that measures human beings by their degree of so-called wimpishness, but also someone for whom the term *wimp* does not have a deeply resonant personal meaning. How could it have affected me so much?

The answer lies in the role of the context within which I was experiencing myself—the discursive framework. For in that room I was not "simply me," but I was a participant in a discourse, a shared set of words, concepts, symbols that constituted not only the linguistic possibilities available to us but also constituted *me* in that situation. This is not entirely true, of course. How I experienced myself was at least partly shaped by other experiences and other discursive frameworks—certainly those of feminist politics and antimilitarist politics; in fact, I would say my reactions were predominantly shaped by those frameworks. But that is quite different from saying "I am a feminist, and that individual, psychological self simply moves encapsulated through the world being itself"—and therefore assuming that I am unaffected. No matter who else I was at

that moment, I was unavoidably a participant in a discourse in which being a wimp has a meaning, and a deeply pejorative one at that. By calling me a wimp, my accuser on the Blue Team *positioned* me in that discourse, and I could not but feel the sting.

In other words, I am suggesting that national security discourse can be seen as having different positions within it—ones that are starkly gender coded; indeed, the enormous strength of their evocative power comes from gender. Thus, when you participate in conversation in that community, you do not simply choose what to say and how to say it; you advertently or inadvertently choose a position in the discourse. As a woman, I can choose the "masculine" (thoughtful, rational, logical) position. If I do, I am seen as legitimate, but I limit what I can say. Or, I can say things that place me in the "feminine" position—in which case no one will listen to me.

Finally, I would like to briefly explore a phenomenon I call the "unitary masculine actor problem" in national security discourse. During the Persian Gulf War, many feminists probably noticed that both the military briefers and George Bush himself frequently used the singular masculine pronoun "he" when referring to Iraq and Iraq's army. Someone not listening carefully could simply assume that "he" referred to Saddam Hussein. Sometimes it did; much of the time it simply reflected the defense community's characteristic habit of calling opponents "he" or "the other guy." A battalion commander, for example, was quoted as saying "Saddam knows where we are and we know where he is. We will move a lot now to keep him off guard."[1] In these sentences, "he" and "him" appear to refer to Saddam Hussein. But, of course, the American forces had *no idea* where Saddam Hussein himself was; the singular masculine pronouns are actually being used to refer to the Iraqi military.

This linguistic move, frequently heard in discussions within the security affairs and defense communities, turns a complex state and set of forces into a singular male opponent. In fact, discussions that purport to be serious explorations of the strategy and tactics of war can have a tone which sounds more like the story of a sporting match, a fistfight, or a personal vendetta.

> I would want to suck him out into the desert as far as I could, and then pound him to death.[2]
>
> Once we had taken out his eyes, we did what could be best described as the "Hail Mary play" in football.[3]
>
> [I]f the adversary decides to embark on a very high roll, because he's frightened that something even worse is in the works, does grabbing him by the scruff of the neck and slapping him up the side of the head, does that make him behave better or is it plausible that it makes him behave even worse?[4]

Most defense intellectuals would claim that using "he" is just a convenient shorthand, without significant import or effects. I believe, however, that the effects of this usage are many and the implications far-reaching. Here I will sketch just a few, starting first with the usage throughout defense discourse generally, and then coming back to the Gulf War in particular.

The use of "he" distorts the analyst's understanding of the opposing state and the conflict in which they are engaged. When the analyst refers to the opposing state as "he" or "the other guy," the image evoked is that of a person, a unitary actor; yet states are not people. Nor are they unitary and unified. They comprise complex, multifaceted governmental and military apparatuses, each with opposing forces within it, each, in turn, with its own internal institutional dynamics, its own varied needs in relation to domestic politics, and so on. In other words, if the state is referred to and pictured as a unitary actor, what becomes unavailable to the analyst and policy-maker is a series of much more complex truths that might enable him to imagine many more policy options, many more ways to interact with that state.

If one kind of distortion of the state results from the image of the state as a person, a unitary actor, another can be seen to stem from the image of the state as a specifically *male* actor. Although states are almost uniformly run by men, states are not men; they are complex social institutions, and they act and react as such. Yet, when "he" and "the other guy" are used to refer to states, the words do not simply function as shorthand codes; instead, they have their own entailments, including assumptions about how men act, which just might be different from how states act, but which invisibly become assumed to be isomorphic with how states act.

It also entails emotional responses on the part of the speaker. The reference to the opposing state as "he" evokes male competitive identity issues, as in, "I'm not going to let him push me around," or, "I'm not going to let him get the best of me." While these responses may or may not be adaptive for a barroom brawl, it is probably safe to say that they are less functional when trying to determine the best way for one state to respond to another state. Defense analysts and foreign policy experts can usually agree upon the supreme desirability of dispassionate, logical analysis and its ensuing rationally calculated action. Yet the emotions evoked by the portrayal of global conflict in the personalized terms of male competition must, at the very least, exert a strong pull in exactly the opposite direction.

A third problem is that even while the use of "he" acts to personalize the conflict, it simultaneously abstracts both the opponent and the war itself. That is, the use of "he" functions in very much the same way that discussions about "Red" and "Blue" do. It facilitates treating war within a kind of game-playing model, A against B, Red against Blue, he against me. For even while "he" is evocative of male identity issues, it is also just an abstract piece to be moved around on a game board, or, more appropriately, a computer screen.

That tension between personalization and abstraction was striking in Gulf War discourse. In the Gulf War, not only was "he" frequently used to refer to the Iraqi military, but so was "Saddam," as in "Saddam really took a pounding today," or "Our goal remains the same: to liberate Kuwait by forcing Saddam Hussein out."[5] The personalization is obvious: in this locution, the U.S. armed forces are not destroying a nation, killing people; instead, they (or George) are giving Saddam a good pounding, or bodily removing him from where he does not belong. Our emotional response is to get fired up about a bully getting his comeuppance.

Yet this personalization, this conflation of Iraq and Iraqi forces with Saddam himself, also abstracts: it functions to substitute in the mind's eye the abstraction of an implacably, impeccably evil enemy for the particular human beings, the men, women, and children being pounded, burned, torn, and eviscerated. A cartoon image of Saddam being ejected from Kuwait preempts the image of the blackened, charred, decomposing bodies of nineteen-year-old boys tossed in ditches by the side of the road, and the other concrete images of the acts of violence that constitute "forcing Hussein [*sic*] out of Kuwait."[6] Paradoxical as it may seem, in personalizing the Iraqi army as Saddam, the individual human beings in Iraq were abstracted out of existence.

In summary, I have been exploring the way in which defense intellectuals talk to each other—the comments they make to each other, the particular usages that appear in their informal conversations or their lectures. In addition, I have occasionally left the professional community to draw upon public talk about the Gulf War. My analysis does *not* lead me to conclude that "national security thinking is masculine"—that is a separate, and different, discussion. Instead, I have tried to show that national security discourse is gendered, and that it matters. Gender discourse is interwoven through national security discourse. It sets fixed boundaries, and in so doing it skews what is discussed and how it is thought about. It shapes expectations of other nations' actions, and in so doing it affects both our interpretations of international events and conceptions of how the United States should respond.

In a world where professionals pride themselves on their ability to engage in cool, rational, objective calculation while others around them are letting their thinking be sullied by emotion, the unacknowledged interweaving of gender discourse in security discourse allows men to not acknowledge that their pristine rational thought is in fact riddled with emotional response. In an "objective" "universal" discourse that valorizes the "masculine" and deauthorizes the "feminine," it is only the "feminine" emotions that are noticed and labeled as emotions, and thus in need of banning from the analytic process. "Masculine" emotions—such as feelings of aggression, competition, macho pride and swagger, or the sense of identity resting on carefully defended borders—are not so easily noticed and identified as emotions, and are instead invisibly folded into "self-evident," so-called realist paradigms and analyses. It is both the interweaving of gender discourse in national security thinking *and* the blindness to its presence and impact that have deleterious effects. Finally, the impact is to distort, degrade, and deter roundly rational, fully complex thought within the community of defense intellectuals and national security elites and, by extension, to cripple democratic deliberation about crucial matters of war and peace.

Notes

1. Chris Hedges, "War Is Vivid in the Gun Sights of the Sniper," *New York Times,* February 3, 1991, A1.

2. General Norman Schwarzkopf, National Public Radio broadcast, February 8, 1991.

3. General Norman Schwarzkopf, CENTCOM News Briefing, Riyadh, Saudi Arabia, February 27, 1991, p. 2.

4. Transcript of a strategic studies specialist's lecture on NATO and the Warsaw Pact (summer institute on Regional Conflict and Global Security: The Nuclear Dimension, Madison, Wisconsin, June 29, 1987).

5. Defense Secretary Dick Cheney, "Excerpts from Briefing at Pentagon by Cheney and Powell," *New York Times,* January 24, 1991, A 11.

6. Scarry explains that when an army is described as a single "embodied combatant," injury, (as in Saddam's "pounding") may be referred to but is "no longer recognizable or interpretable." It is not only

that Americans might be happy to imagine Saddam being pounded; we also on some level know that it is not really happening, and thus need not feel the pain of the wounded. We "respond to the injury . . . as an imaginary wound to an imaginary body, despite the fact that that imaginary body is itself made up of thousands of real human bodies" (Elaine Scarry, *Body in Pain: The Making and Unmaking of the World* [New York: Oxford, 1984], p. 72).

PART ELEVEN

ELEVEN

Men, Movements, and the Future

Q: Why did you decide to record again?

A: Because *this* housewife would like to have a career for a bit! On October 9, I'll be 40, and Sean will be 5 and I can afford to say, "Daddy does something else as well." He's not accustomed to it—in five years I hardly picked up a guitar. Last Christmas our neighbors showed him "Yellow Submarine" and he came running in, saying, "Daddy, you were singing . . . Were you a Beatle?" I said, "Well—yes, right."

—John Lennon, interview for *Newsweek*, 1980

Are men changing? If so, in what directions? Can men change even more? In what ways should men be different? We posed many of these questions at the beginning of our exploration of men's lives, and we return to them here, in the book's last section, to examine the directions men have taken to enlarge their roles, to expand the meaning of masculinity, to change the rules.

The articles in this section address the possibility and the direction of change for men: How shall we, as a society, understand masculinity in the modern world? Richard Goldstein examines the use of masculinity rhetoric in the post 9/11 era, while R. W. Connell pulls back and provides a more global overview of similar issues. Feminist writer bell hooks argues that feminists, especially African-American feminists, need to see men as potential allies. And the Statement of the United Nations Commission on the Status of Women outlines the importance of involving men in the global struggles for gender equality.

Richard Goldstein

Neo–Macho Man: Pop Culture and Post-9/11 Politics

Say what you will about oil and hegemony, but the pending invasion of Iraq is more than just a geopolitical act. It's also the manifestation of a cultural attitude. To understand how this war is being packaged and sold, you have to look at the fantasies Americans consume as they graze through the vast terrain of TV, radio, movies and the Internet. In this charged environment, pop culture and politics swirl around each other like strands of DNA. The product of this interplay is the current crisis.

From Colin Powell dissing the French as cowards to Donald Rumsfeld raising his fists at the podium, the Bush Administration bristles with an almost cartoonish macho. It's a little like watching pro wrestling in a global arena. Why is this smackdown style acceptable to many Americans now? Bill Clinton has an explanation. "When people feel uncertain," he said after the Democratic Party's recent electoral rout, "they'd rather have somebody who's strong and wrong than somebody who's weak and right."

This truism seems to resonate with human nature, but other crises have produced a very different response. Faced with the Great Depression, not to mention Pearl Harbor, Americans chose a President who seemed strong and right. It's a measure of how the nation has changed that when we were attacked this time we closed ranks behind a leader whose program leaves many with a sinking feeling. Polls show a similar ambivalence about the war, yet it hasn't led to a revolt against the Ad-

From *The Nation*, March 24, 2003. Reprinted by permission.

ministration. Why are people willing to suspend their disbelief in Bush? Why are we drawn to the strong man who is wrong?

The answer lies not in our stars but in our superstars. To understand how America has changed since 9/11, it's necessary to examine the attitudes that dominated movies and music before 9/11. The mindset of manly belligerence was already in place when the planes struck. In the horror that followed, we struggled for a way to respond—and we found it in the icon of neo–macho man.

Not so long ago, you couldn't say "macho man" without thinking of the Village People. Hypermasculinity was so thoroughly discredited that it seemed fit for camp. Now it's back, in earnest. But this revival was no bolt from the blue. The neo-macho hero has a history.

He sprang from the reaction to feminism that began in the 1980s and advanced in the '90s, even as the empowerment of women became a tenet of Democratic politics. As women rose, so did male anxiety, and in this edgy climate a new archetype appeared in pop culture: the sexual avenger. His rage often focused on personal betrayal, but implicit in his tirades was a sense of the world turned upside down.

By 1990 the revolt against feminism was a hip commodity. Shock-jocks like Howard Stern and Don Imus dominated drive-time radio, misogynistic comics like Sam Kinison and Andrew Dice Clay were late-night TV sensations, rock marauders spat variations on Axl Rose's final solution for bitchy women: "Burn the witch." Meanwhile, at the multiplex the sexually cornered male, embodied by Michael Douglas in a series of films from *Fatal Attraction* (1987) to *Disclosure* (1994), was the new Dirty Harry.

At first, these performers combined racial and sexual resentment for a double thrill. Imus and his sidekicks did cottonfield imitations of black celebrities, Axl railed against "immigrants and faggots [who] come into our country and . . . spread some fucking disease," the Diceman vowed vengeance on immigrants. But racism was an impediment to crossover success. Misogyny, however, was not. In the Clinton era, the backlash reached a fever pitch—and Hillary was hardly its only target. Pop culture invited men of all races and ages to bond over bitch-bashing, and as the 1990s progressed every market niche had its version of the sexual avenger.

The most commercial hip-hop fronted for this backlash. Veering from its radical roots in the black community, gangsta rap became a spectacle of male conquest. Its paragon was the player (pimp) ruling over abject hos and raining violence on resistant bitches. Because these top dawgs trafficked in sadism, they were sexy in a way that angry white males of the 1980s could never be. And because they were for the most part black, their rage could be cast as progressive. Many liberals who would never buy into Rush Limbaugh's "feminazi" rants were drawn to neo-macho rappers who carried the imprimatur of the street. Postmodernists saw this music as an exercise in role-playing or an outlet for fantasies that would never be carried out in life, certainly not in politics. Armed with denial, even a pro-feminist man could enjoy the spectacle—and critics called it art.

The most unexpected boost to backlash culture came from young women who gravitated to its forbidden games. It was hot to play the ho and cool to call yourself a bitch. You could always tell yourself that this was just an erotic pose. But the return of fetishized femininity was about more than sex. Men were not the only ones made anxious by the new female agency. Many women feared the loss of desirability that their power might bring—and teenagers were especially prone to these uncertainties. The new model offered a way out for boys and girls alike.

Without the backlash, other, more progressive tendencies in hip-hop might have prevailed. But the flight from feminism had created a huge market for bitch-bashing anthems. By meeting this demand in a powerful musical form, gangsta rappers tapped into the choice demographic of suburban teens. Sexual violence was only part of the thug package, but it turned millions of white kids on, resonating with the broader culture of misogyny. The male avenger was emerging as the insignia of rebellion for a new generation.

Still, there were alternatives to the backlash in the 1990s. Daytime TV was as wild as talk-radio, but with a far less patriarchal slant on sex and society (to suit its largely female audience). Celebrities like RuPaul offered a potent dissent from the polarities of gender. Female comics and rappers could be as wicked as their male counterparts, and Madonna was a bigger draw than any neo–macho man. Eminem was still a guilty pleasure. Today Madonna gives interviews extolling the virtues of matrimony, and Forbes.com proclaims that Eminem "may be the most popular man in America." What has changed?

The short answer is 9/11. In its wake, the once-mocked figure of the dominant male has become a real-life hero. Saluting the new spirit of patriarchal vitality, *People* included Rumsfeld in its most recent list of the sexiest men alive. In his feckless swagger we see the timeless union of militarism and macho. Then there's Rudy Giuliani, who emerged from 9/11 as "America's mayor." His authoritarian streak has been repackaged as the mark of leadership. Like any alpha male, Rudy can confer macho on other Republicans, as he did for George Pataki in a campaign ad proclaiming New York's pallid governor "a real man."

That phrase can now be uttered without a trace of irony. It informs the banter of Jay Leno, who reacted to the rescue of trapped miners last summer by remarking, "It's great to see real men back in the news. I'm so sick of weasels." It even colors the prose of style writers in the *New York Times,* as in this observation from a female reporter shortly after the dust of 9/11 cleared: "A certain kind of woman [is] tired of the dawdlers, melancholics and other variants of genius who would not know what to do with a baseball mitt or a drill press." Eminem put it more succinctly when he called his sensitive rival Moby "a little girl." Such rhetoric no longer reads like an expression of ideology. The real man seems vital—and necessary in a crisis.

We haven't always been so attuned to the need for our leaders to be macho. It wasn't the measure of FDR's strength. But Roosevelt arose from a culture that regarded protecting the weak as an important manly virtue. The pop heroes of his day were loner lawmen, reluctant warriors or world-weary survivors with a secret decent streak. There were bad boys, to be sure. The denizens of Depression-era crime films were as violent and vital in their narcissism as today's gangsta rappers. But something crucial has changed. The bad boy's primary target is no longer the system but strong women and weak men. Power is the ability to turn both into "my bitches," in the parlance of prison and pop. It may be wrong to rule others, but it's strong, and these days dominance is its own reward.

Not that the good guys have disappeared. The firefighters who gave their lives in the Twin Towers are heroes of 9/11, as they should be. But this benign image allows us to forget that the dark side of macho has also been unleashed. Male grievance has found a geopolitical target in Saddam. Sexual revenge has been sublimated into military payback. Underlying this process is a sense of the world as a jungle where friendship is transient, danger is everywhere and one can never have enough power. This is the classic rationale for macho. Feminism teaches us that it's a pretext for preserving the order. Liberalism tells us it's paranoid. But what once seemed like paranoia is regarded as reason, and what was piggy now feels natural.

No one plies the neo-macho trade like Eminem. Talent notwithstanding, what made this blue-eyed rapper a star was his baroque misogyny (as in: "My little sister's birthday, she'll remember

me/For a gift I had ten of my boys take her virginity"). Eminem is the hottest recording artist in America, a singular honor for a man who never wrote a love song to a woman. Instead, he struck gold (or rather, platinum) by ruminating about raping his mother and slaughtering every bitch in sight. At first, these attitudes were impossible for critics to ignore. Those who praised Eminem felt compelled to issue a caveat about his hate. There was a line in liberal culture he couldn't cross. But that changed with his first starring role in a film. *8 Mile* is a fictionalized biopic set in streets so mean that even the sun stays out of sight. It opened in November 2002 to rave reviews, and it's raked in more than $100 million since. A little cleaning up is all it took to transform this monster from the id into a populist hero, a Rocky for our time.

Gone are Eminem's attacks on women and gays (as in: "Hate fags? The answer's yes"). In *8 Mile* he never busts a rhyme against a bitch, not even his mom; he adores his little sister and sticks up for a homo. The film firemanizes Eminem by placing him in the tradition of working-class heroes and blunting his sexism with stirring images of racial harmony. This is balm to liberals—and it's allowed mainstream critics (nearly all of whom are men) to overlook the meaning of Eminem's rise.

A similar sublimation occurred when Elvis Presley became a mainstream icon. His first feature film, *Love Me Tender,* was a historical romance that didn't call for pelvic action. As his public broadened, he didn't need to grind in order to be understood. Of course, Elvis embodied a different morality than Eminem does. His appeal was Dionysian rather than sadistic; his lewdness didn't preclude the possibility of love. These values fueled not just Elvis's ascendance but also a sexual revolution that would change society. A radical new vision, which began as the stuff of pop, evolved into a generational norm. The Eminem experience is producing something similar—with very different consequences.

It's no coincidence that *8 Mile* ruled the box office right after Bush's GOP romped at the polls. These two young patriarchs seem utterly opposite, but they have fundamental things in common. Both are social conservatives who stand for a male-dominated order. Both owe their appeal to anxiety over sexual and social change. Both offer the spectacle of an aggrieved man reacting with righteous rage. These qualities, which once seemed dangerous, now read as reassuring. The macho stance that once looked stylized is now a mark of authenticity.

Sexual terror is rarely dealt with as a factor in politics. The intimate nature of this anxiety prevents it from being addressed, and as a result, it operates in powerful, unapparent ways. That's certainly how sex played out in the 2000 campaign, when Al Gore was tarred with the priss brush while Bush butched his way to the White House.

It's easy for Republicans to seem manly, for the same reason pundits call the GOP the Daddy Party. Their tough-love style represents patriarchal values of strength and order. If the Democrats are (often disparagingly) called the Mommy Party, it's because their attitude expresses feminist values of empathy and equity. Democratic men are not less masculine than Republicans, but they tend to be less macho in their manner, reflecting an etiquette that allows both sexes to project power. This is also why Democratic women tend to be less courtly and decorated than the daughters of the GOP. When voters see these qualities in a candidate, they are reminded of the underlying sexual politics. If Democratic men seem weak and Democratic women all too strong, it has much less to do with character than with the angst that the party of feminism generates.

Clinton brought a trickster's charms to the table, but Gore was running against that type, and he never figured out how to combine probity with vitality. A marathon kiss from Tipper didn't do the trick, since she was another one of those bitches—a kinder, blonder Hillary—while Laura Bush left no doubt about her proper place, three steps behind her husband. Then came Naomi Wolfe, whose effort to counsel Gore on color schemes was met with the same scorn that greeted

Jimmy Carter when he got attacked by a rabbit. Dubya didn't have to count on a gal to tell him how to dress—he was his own Man! Even his flubs at identifying world leaders made him seem like a dude. After all, no one ever lost macho points for being stupid.

Gore won the popular vote, but as heir to an Administration that had produced peace and prosperity he should have triumphed. It wasn't just his stiffness that hurt him; it was the backlash. By then it was so embedded in mass consciousness that Bush's good-old-boy affect seemed natural while Gore's New Age style seemed politically correct. Too many moderates were lulled by Dubya's charming macho. The culture had clouded their ability to read its ideological content. Bush didn't look right wing; he just looked right.

Now that patriarchy is associated with survival, how can the party of feminism prevail? It's easier to see the problem than the solution, but a good start would be for Democrats to reject the idea that they are weak. This image is a figment of the backlash, meant to demean those who support the empowerment of women. It can't be dispelled by butching up, since the real issue—sexual equity—will remain. The only option for the Mommy Party is to embrace its identity. That means stripping Republican macho of its mystique. This is a moment for speaking truth to power.

The Democrats should hammer the point that virtually every issue—not just abortion—is a women's issue. Take Bush's plan to privatize large swaths of the federal government. Any attempt to cut wages will have an undue effect on women, since so many of them work in the public sector. Then there's the signal Bush sends when he defunds women's bureaus in federal agencies and closes the White House Office for Women's Initiatives and Outreach. There's a pattern here, but it's hard to see because gender is the great unmentionable in public life, and women are especially invisible as citizens in a time of crisis.

It's even harder to address the culture that animates these policies. No progressive wants to be a censor, a puritan or, worse still, a fogy. But attention must be paid, because cultural values are central to social reality. A norm can only be undone if people understand the damage it does, and macho is a stunting force even when it looks fresh and young. Under its thumb, a generation is growing up with attitudes that will warp their lives, not to mention the course of American politics.

Fortunately, this is not another lost liberal cause. The public's doubts about Bush persist, as his seesawing popularity attests. There's a lingering uncertainty about the war, and not just among doves. These misgivings reflect a deep ambivalence about the macho code. Yet this primal issue is rarely broached. What will it take for the best and brightest Democrats to address the relationship between male dominance and the current crisis? Don't count on courage. Politicians usually arrive when the coast is cleared by culture. It remains for artists to challenge the backlash and for critics to criticize it.

It's time to create a new vocabulary of dissent, one that makes a clear connection between war fever and thug power. There's no more urgent task. The dawgs of war are about to be unleashed. Thousands will die, billions will be spent and most of us will have to do with less. These are the wages of following a leader who is strong but wrong. He's the man; we're his bitches.

R. W. Connell

Change among the Gatekeepers: Men, Masculinities, and Gender Equality in the Global Arena

Equality between women and men has been a doctrine well recognized in international law since the adoption of the 1948 *Universal Declaration of Human Rights* (United Nations 1958), and as a principle it enjoys popular support in many countries. The idea of gender equal rights has provided the formal basis for the international discussion of the position of women since the 1975–85 UN Decade for Women, which has been a key element in the story of global feminism (Bulbeck 1988). The idea that men might have a specific role in relation to this principle has emerged only recently.

The issue of gender equality was placed on the policy agenda by women. The reason is obvious: it is women who are disadvantaged by the main patterns of gender inequality and who therefore have the claim for redress. Men are, however, necessarily involved in gender-equality reform. Gender inequalities are embedded in a multidimensional structure of relationships between women and men, which, as the modern sociology of gender shows, operates at every level of human experience, from economic arrangements, culture, and the state to interpersonal relationships and individual emotions (Holter 1997; Walby 1997; Connell 2002). Moving toward a gender-equal society involves profound institutional change as well as change in everyday life and per-

sonal conduct. To move far in this direction requires widespread social support, including significant support from men and boys.

Further, the very gender inequalities in economic assets, political power, and cultural authority, as well as the means of coercion, that gender reforms intend to change, currently mean that men (often specific groups of men) control most of the resources required to implement women's claims for justice. Men and boys are thus in significant ways gatekeepers for gender equality. Whether they are willing to open the gates for major reforms is an important strategic question.

In this article, I will trace the emergence of a worldwide discussion of men and gender-equality reform and will try to assess the prospects of reform strategies involving men. To make such an assessment, it is necessary to set recent policy discussions in the wider context of the cultural problematization of men and boys, the politics of "men's movements," the divided interests of men and boys in gender relations, and the growing research evidence about the changing and conflict-ridden social construction of masculinities.

In an article of this scope, it is not possible to address particular national agendas in detail. I will refer to a number of texts where these stories can be found. Because my primary concern is with the global character of the debate, I will give particular attention to policy discussions in UN forums. These discussions culminated in the 2004 meeting of the UN Commission on the Status of Women, which produced the first world-level policy document on the role of men and boys in re-

From *Signs: Journal of Women in Culture and Society* 2005, vol. 30, no. 3. © 2005 by The University of Chicago. All rights reserved.

lation to gender equality (UN Commission on the Status of Women 2004).

Men and Masculinities in the World Gender Order

In the last fifteen years, in the "developed" countries of the global metropole, there has been a great deal of popular concern with issues about men and boys. Readers in the United States may recall a volume by the poet Robert Bly, *Iron John: A Book about Men* (1990), which became a huge best seller in the early 1990s, setting off a wave of imitations. This book became popular because it offered, in prophetic language, simple solutions to problems that were increasingly troubling the culture. A therapeutic movement was then developing in the United States, mainly though not exclusively among middle-class men, addressing problems in relationships, sexuality, and identity (Kupers 1993; Schwalbe 1996).

More specific issues about men and boys have also attracted public attention in the developed countries. Men's responses to feminism, and to gender-equality measures taken by government, have long been the subject of debate in Germany and Scandinavia (Metz-Göckel and Müller 1985; Holter 2003). In anglophone countries there has been much discussion of "the new fatherhood" and of supposed changes in men's involvement in families (McMahon 1999). There has been public agonizing about boys' "failure" in school, and in Australia there are many proposals for special programs for boys (Kenway 1997; Lingard 2003). Men's violence toward women has been the subject of practical interventions and extensive debate (Hearn 1998). There has also been increasing debate about men's health and illness from a gender perspective (Hurrelmann and Kolip 2002).

Accompanying these debates has been a remarkable growth of research about men's gender identities and practices, masculinities and the social processes by which they are constructed, cultural and media images of men, and related matters. Academic journals have been founded for specialized research on men and masculinities,

there have been many research conferences, and there is a rapidly growing international literature. We now have a far more sophisticated and detailed scientific understanding of issues about men, masculinities, and gender than ever before (Connell 2003a).

This set of concerns, though first articulated in the developed countries, can now be found worldwide (Connell 2000; Pease and Pringle 2001). Debates on violence, patriarchy, and ways of changing men's conduct have occurred in countries as diverse as Germany, Canada, and South Africa (Hagemann-White 1992; Kaufman 1993; Morrell 2001a). Issues about masculine sexuality and fatherhood have been debated and researched in Brazil, Mexico, and many other countries (Arilha, Unbehaum Ridenti, and Medrado 1998; Lerner 1998). A men's center with a reform agenda has been established in Japan, where conferences have been held and media debates about traditional patterns of masculinity and family life continue (Menzu Senta 1997; Roberson and Suzuki 2003). A "traveling seminar" discussing issues about men, masculinities, and gender equality has recently been touring in India (Roy 2003). Debates about boys' education, men's identities, and gender change are active from New Zealand to Denmark (Law, Campbell, and Dolan 1999; Reinicke 2002). Debates about men's sexuality, and changing sexual identities, are also international (Altman 2001).

The research effort is also worldwide. Documentation of the diverse social constructions of masculinity has been undertaken in countries as far apart as Peru (Fuller 2001), Japan (Taga 2001), and Turkey (Sinclair-Webb 2000). The first large-scale comparative study of men and gender relations has recently been completed in ten European countries (Hearn et al. 2002). The first global synthesis, in the form of a world handbook of research on men and masculinities, has now appeared (Kimmel, Hearn, and Connell 2005).

The rapid internationalization of these debates reflects the fact—increasingly recognized in feminist thought (Bulbeck 1998; Marchand and Runyan 2000)—that gender relations themselves have an international dimension. Each of the substructures of gender relations can be shown to have a global dimension, growing out of the history of imperialism and seen in the contemporary process of globalization (Connell 2002). Change in gender relations occurs on a world scale, though not always in the same direction or at the same pace.

The complexity of the patterns follows from the fact that gender change occurs in several different modes. Most dramatic is the direct colonization of the gender order of regions beyond the metropole. There has also been a more gradual recomposition of gender orders, both those of the colonizing society and the colonized, in the process of colonial interaction. The hybrid gender identities and sexualities now much discussed in the context of postcolonial societies are neither unusual nor new. They are a feature of the whole history of imperialism and are visible in many contemporary studies (e.g., Valdés and Olavarría 1998).

Imperialism and globalization change the conditions of existence for gender orders. For instance, the linking of previously separate production systems changes the flow of goods and services in the gendered division of labor, as seen in the impact of industrially produced foods and textiles on household economies. Colonialism itself often confronted local patriarchies with colonizing patriarchies, producing a turbulent and sometimes very violent aftermath, as in southern Africa (Morrell 1998). Pressure from contemporary Western commercial culture has destabilized gender arrangements, and models of masculinity, in Japan (Ito 1992), the Arab world (Ghoussoub 2000), and elsewhere.

Finally, the emergence of new arenas of social relationship on a world scale creates new patterns of gender relations. Transnational corporations, international communications systems, global mass media, and international state structures (from the United Nations to the European Union) are such arenas. These institutions have their own gender regimes and may form the basis for new configurations of masculinity, as has re-

cently been argued for transnational business (Connell 2000) and the international relations system (Hooper 2001). Local gender orders now interact not only with the gender orders of other local societies but also with the gender order of the global arena.

The dynamics of the world gender order affect men as profoundly as they do women, though this fact has been less discussed. The best contemporary research on men and masculinity, such as Matthew C. Gutmann's (2002) ethnographic work in Mexico, shows in fine detail how the lives of particular groups of men are shaped by globally acting economic and political dynamics.

Different groups of men are positioned very differently in such processes. There is no single formula that accounts for men and globalization. There is, indeed, a growing polarization among men on a world scale. Studies of the "super-rich" (Haseler 2000) show a privileged minority reaching astonishing heights of wealth and power while much larger numbers face poverty, cultural dislocation, disruption of family relationships, and forced renegotiation of the meanings of masculinity.

Masculinities, as socially constructed configurations of gender practice, are also created through a historical process with a global dimension. The old-style ethnographic research that located gender patterns purely in a local context is inadequate to the reality. Historical research, such as Robert Morrell's (2001b) study of the masculinities of the colonizers in South Africa and T. Dunbar Moodie's (1994) study of the colonized, shows how a gendered culture is created and transformed in relation to the international economy and the political system of empire. There is every reason to think this principle holds for contemporary masculinities.

Shifting Ground: Men and Boys in Gender-Equality Debates

Because of the way they came onto the agenda of public debate, gender issues have been widely regarded as women's business and of little concern to men and boys. In almost all policy discussions, to adopt a gender perspective substantially means to address women's concerns.

In both national and international policy documents concerned with gender equality, women are the subjects of the policy discourse. The agencies or meetings that formulate, implement, or monitor gender policies usually have names referring to women, such as Department for Women, Women's Equity Bureau, Prefectural Women's Centre, or Commission on the Status of Women. Such bodies have a clear mandate to act for women. They do not have an equally clear mandate to act with respect to men. The major policy documents concerned with gender equality, such as the UN *Convention on the Elimination of All Forms of Discrimination against Women* (United Nations [1979] 1989), often do not name men as a group and rarely discuss men in concrete terms.

However, men are present as background throughout these documents. In every statement about women's disadvantages, there is an implied comparison with men as the advantaged group. In the discussions of violence against women, men are implied, and sometimes named, as the perpetrators. In discussions of gender and HIV/AIDS, men are commonly construed as being "the problem," the agents of infection. In discussions of women's exclusion from power and decision making, men are implicitly present as the power holders.

When men are present only as a background category in a policy discourse about women, it is difficult to raise issues about men's and boys' interests, problems, or differences. This could be done only by falling into a backlash posture and affirming "men's rights" or by moving outside a gender framework altogether.

The structure of gender-equality policy, therefore, created an opportunity for antifeminist politics. Opponents of feminism have now found issues about boys and men to be fertile ground. This is most clearly seen in the United States, where authors such as Warren Farrell (1993) and Christina Hoff Sommers (2000), purporting to speak on behalf of men and boys, bitterly accuse

feminism of injustice. Men and boys, they argue, are the truly disadvantaged group and need supportive programs in education and health, in situations of family breakup, and so forth. These ideas have not stimulated a social movement, with the exception of a small-scale (though active and sometimes violent) "father's rights" movement in relation to divorce. The arguments have, however, strongly appealed to the neoconservative mass media, which have given them international circulation. They now form part of the broad neoconservative repertoire of opposition to "political correctness" and to social justice measures.

Some policy makers have attempted to straddle this divide by restructuring gender-equality policy in the form of parallel policies for women and men. For instance, some recent health policy initiatives in Australia have added a "men's health" document to a "women's health" document (Schofield 2004). Similarly, in some school systems a "boys' education" strategy has been added to a "girls' education" strategy (Lingard 2003).

This approach acknowledges the wider scope of gender issues. But it also risks weakening the equality rationale of the original policy. It forgets the relational character of gender and therefore tends to redefine women and men, or girls and boys, simply as different market segments for some service. Ironically, the result may be to promote more gender segregation, not less. This has certainly happened in education, where some privileged boys' schools have jumped on the "gender equality" bandwagon and now market themselves as experts in catering to the special needs of boys.

On the other hand, bringing men's problems into an existing framework of policies for women may weaken the authority that women have so far gathered in that policy area. In the field of gender and development, for instance, some specialists argue that "bringing men in"—given the larger context in which men still control most of the wealth and institutional authority—may undermine, not help, the drive for gender equality (White 2000).

The role of men and boys in relation to gender equality emerged as an issue in international discussions during the 1990s. This development crystallized at the Fourth World Conference on Women, held in Beijing in 1995. Paragraph 25 of the *Beijing Declaration* committed participating governments to "encourage men to participate fully in all actions towards equality" (United Nations 2001). The detailed "Platform for Action" that accompanied the declaration prominently restated the principle of shared power and responsibility between men and women and argued that women's concerns could be addressed only "in partnership with men" toward gender equality (2001, pars. 1, 3). The "Platform for Action" went on to specify areas where action involving men and boys was needed and was possible: in education, socialization of children, child care and housework, sexual health, gender-based violence, and the balancing of work and family responsibilities (2001, pars. 40, 72, 83b, 107c, 108e, 120, 179).

Participating member states followed a similar approach in the twenty-third special session of the UN General Assembly in the year 2000, which was intended to review the situation five years after the Beijing conference. The "Political Declaration" of this session made an even stronger statement on men's responsibility: "[Member states of the United Nations] emphasise that men must involve themselves and take joint responsibility with women for the promotion of gender equality" (United Nations 2001, par. 6). It still remained the case, in this and the accompanying "Outcome Document," that men were present on the margins of a policy discourse concerned with women.

The role of men and boys has also been addressed in other recent international meetings. These include the 1995 World Summit on Social Development, its review session in 2000, and the special session of the General Assembly on HIV/AIDS in 2001. In 1997 the UN Educational, Scientific, and Cultural Organization (UNESCO) convened an expert group meeting about "Male Roles and Masculinities in the Perspective of a Culture of Peace," which met in Oslo and produced studies on the links among personal violence, war, and the construction of masculinities (Breines, Connell, and Eide 2000).

International meetings outside the UN system have addressed similar issues. In 1997 the Nordic Council of Ministers adopted the *Nordic Action Plan for Men and Gender Equality.* In the same year the Council of Europe conducted a seminar on equality as a common issue for men and women and made the role of men in promoting equality a theme at a ministerial conference. In 1998 the Latin American Federation of Social Science (FLACSO) began a series of conferences about masculinities, boys, and men across Latin America and the Caribbean. The first conference in this series had the specific theme of gender equity (Valdés and Olavarría 1998). The European Commission has recently funded a research network on men and masculinities.

Divided Interests: Support and Resistance

There is something surprising about the worldwide problematizing of men and masculinities, because in many ways the position of men has not greatly changed. For instance, men remain a very large majority of corporate executives, top professionals, and holders of public office. Worldwide, men hold nine out of ten cabinet-level posts in national governments, nearly as many of the parliamentary seats, and most top positions in international agencies. Men, collectively, receive approximately twice the income that women receive and also receive the benefits of a great deal of unpaid household labor, not to mention emotional support, from women (Gierycz 1999; Godenzi 2000; Inter-Parliamentary Union 2003).

The UN Development Program (2003) now regularly incorporates a selection of such statistics into its annual report on world human development, combining them into a "gender-related development index" and a "gender empowerment measure." This produces a dramatic outcome, a league table of countries ranked in terms of gender equality, which shows most countries in the world to be far from gender-equal. It is clear that, globally, men have a lot to lose from pursuing gender equality because men, collectively, continue to receive a patriarchal dividend.

But this way of picturing inequality may conceal as much as it reveals. There are multiple dimensions in gender relations, and the patterns of inequality in these dimensions may be qualitatively different. If we look separately at each of the substructures of gender, we find a pattern of advantages for men but also a linked pattern of disadvantages or toxicity (Connell 2003c).

For instance, in relation to the gender division of labor, men collectively receive the bulk of income in the money economy and occupy most of the managerial positions. But men also provide the workforce for the most dangerous occupations, suffer most industrial injuries, pay most of the taxation, and are under heavier social pressure to remain employed. In the domain of power men collectively control the institutions of coercion and the means of violence (e.g., weapons). But men are also the main targets of military violence and criminal assault, and many more men than women are imprisoned or executed. Men's authority receives more social recognition (e.g., in religion), but men and boys are underrepresented in important learning experiences (e.g., in humanistic studies) and important dimensions of human relations (e.g., with young children).

One could draw up a balance sheet of the costs and benefits to men from the current gender order. But this balance sheet would not be like a corporate accounting exercise where there is a bottom line, subtracting costs from income. The disadvantages listed above are, broadly speaking, the conditions of the advantages. For instance, men cannot hold state power without some men becoming the agents of violence. Men cannot be the beneficiaries of women's domestic labor and "emotion work" without many of them losing intimate connections, for instance, with young children.

Equally important, the men who receive most of the benefits and the men who pay most of the costs are not the same individuals. As the old say-

ing puts it, generals die in bed. On a global scale, the men who benefit from corporate wealth, physical security, and expensive health care are a very different group from the men who provide the workforce of developing countries. Class, race, national, regional, and generational differences cross-cut the category "men," spreading the gains and costs of gender relations very unevenly among men. There are many situations where groups of men may see their interest as more closely aligned with the women in their communities than with other men. It is not surprising that men respond very diversely to gender-equality politics.

There is, in fact, a considerable history of support for gender equality among men. There is certainly a tradition of advocacy by male intellectuals. In Europe, well before modern gender-equality documents were written, the British philosopher John Stuart Mill published "The Subjection of Women" (1912), which established the presumption of equal rights; and the Norwegian dramatist Henrik Ibsen, in plays like *A Doll's House* ([1923] 1995), made gender oppression an important cultural theme. In the following generation, the pioneering Austrian psychoanalyst Alfred Adler established a powerful psychological argument for gender equality (Connell 1995). A similar tradition of men's advocacy exists in the United States (Kimmel and Mosmiller 1992).

Many of the historic gains by women's advocates have been won in alliance with men who held organizational or political authority at the time. For instance, the introduction of equal employment opportunity measures in New South Wales, Australia, occurred with the strong support of the premier and the head of a reform inquiry into the public sector, both men (Eisenstein 1991). Sometimes men's support for gender equality takes the form of campaigning and organizing among men. The most prominent example is the U.S. National Organization of Men against Sexism (NOMAS), which has existed for more than twenty years (Cohen 1991). Men's groups concerned with reforming masculinity, publications advocating change, and campaigns among men against violence toward women are found widely, for instance, in the United Kingdom, Mexico, and South Africa (Seidler 1991; Zingoni 1998; Peacock 2003).

Men have also been active in creating educational programs for boys and young men intended to support gender reform. Similar strategies have been developed for adult men, sometimes in a religious and sometimes in a health or therapeutic context. There is a strong tradition of such work in Germany, with programs that combine the search for self-knowledge with the learning of antisexist behavior (Brandes and Bullinger 1996). Work of the same kind has developed in Brazil, the United States, and other countries (Denborough 1996; Lyra and Medrado 2001).

These initiatives are widespread, but they are also mostly small-scale. What of the wider state of opinion? European survey research has shown no consensus among men either for or against gender equality. Sometimes a third/third/third pattern appears, with about one-third of men supporting change toward equality, about one-third opposing it, and one-third undecided or intermediate (Holter 1997, 131–34). Nevertheless, examinations of the survey evidence from the United States, Germany, and Japan have shown a long-term trend of growing support for change, that is, a movement away from traditional gender roles, especially among members of the younger generation (Thornton 1989; Zulehner and Volz 1998; Mohwald 2002).

There is, however, also significant evidence of men's and boys' resistance to change in gender relations. The survey research reveals substantial levels of doubt and opposition, especially among older men. Research on workplaces and on corporate management has documented many cases where men maintain an organizational culture that is heavily masculinized and unwelcoming to women. In some cases there is active opposition to gender-equality measures or quiet undermining of them (Cockburn 1991; Collinson and Hearn 1996). Research on schools has also found cases where boys assert control of informal social life and direct hostility against girls and against boys perceived as being different. The status quo can

be defended even in the details of classroom life, for instance, when a particular group of boys used misogynist language to resist study of a poem that questioned Australian gender stereotypes (Kenworthy 1994; Holland et al. 1998).

Some men accept change in principle but in practice still act in ways that sustain men's dominance of the public sphere and assign domestic labor and child care to women. In strongly gender segregated societies, it may be difficult for men to recognize alternatives or to understand women's experiences (Kandiyoti 1994; Fuller 2001; Meuser 2003). Another type of opposition to reform, more common among men in business and government, rejects gender-equality measures because it rejects all government action in support of equality, in favor of the unfettered action of the market.

The reasons for men's resistance include the patriarchal dividend discussed above and threats to identity that occur with change. If social definitions of masculinity include being the breadwinner and being "strong," then men may be offended by women's professional progress because it makes men seem less worthy of respect. Resistance may also reflect ideological defense of male supremacy. Research on domestic violence suggests that male batterers often hold very conservative views of women's role in the family (Ptacek 1988). In many parts of the world, there exist ideologies that justify men's supremacy on grounds of religion, biology, cultural tradition, or organizational mission (e.g., in the military). It is a mistake to regard these ideas as simply outmoded. They may be actively modernized and renewed.

Grounds for Optimism: Capacities for Equality and Reasons for Change

The public debates about men and boys have often been inconclusive. But they have gone a long way, together with the research, to shatter one widespread belief that has hindered gender reform. This obstacle is the belief that men *cannot* change their ways, that "boys will be boys," that rape, war, sexism, domestic violence, aggression, and self-centeredness are natural to men.

We now have many documented examples of the diversity of masculinities and of men's and boys' capacity for equality. For instance, life-history research in Chile has shown that there is no unitary Chilean masculinity, despite the cultural homogeneity of the country. While a hegemonic model is widely diffused across social strata, there are many men who depart from it, and there is significant discontent with traditional roles (Valdés and Olavarría 1998). Though groups of boys in schools often have a dominant or hegemonic pattern of masculinity, there are usually also other patterns present, some of which involve more equal and respectful relations with girls.

Research in Britain, for instance, shows how boys encounter and explore alternative models of masculinity as they grow up (Mac an Ghaill 1994; O'Donnell and Sharpe 2000).

Psychological and educational research shows personal flexibility in the face of gender stereotypes. Men and boys can vary, or strategically use, conventional definitions of masculinity. It is even possible to teach boys (and girls) how to do this in school, as experiments in Australian classrooms have shown (Davies 1993; Wetherell and Edley 1999).

Changes have occurred in men's practices within certain families, where there has been a conscious shift toward more equal sharing of housework and child care. The sociologist Barbara J. Risman (1998), who has documented such cases in one region of the United States, calls them "fair families." It is clear from her research that the change has required a challenge to traditional models of masculinity. In the Shanghai region of China, there is an established local tradition of relative gender equality, and men are demonstrably willing to be involved in domestic work. Research by Da Wei Wei (Da 2004) shows this tradition persisting among Shanghai men even after migration to another country.

Perhaps the most extensive social action involving men in gender change has occurred in Scandinavia. This includes provisions for paternity leave that have had high rates of take-up, among the most dramatic of all demonstrations of men's willingness to change gender practices. Øystein Holter sums up the research and practical experience: "The Nordic 'experiment' has shown that a *majority* of men can change their practice when circumstances are favorable. . . . When reforms or support policies are well-designed and targeted towards an on-going cultural process of change, men's active support for gender-equal status increases" (1997, 126). Many groups of men, it is clear, have a capacity for equality and for gender change. But what reasons for change are men likely to see?

Early statements often assumed that men had the same interest as women in escaping from restrictive sex roles (e.g., Palme 1972). Later experience has not confirmed this view. Yet men and boys often do have substantial reasons to support change, which can readily be listed.

First, men are not isolated individuals. Men and boys live in social relationships, many with women and girls: wives, partners, mothers, aunts, daughters, nieces, friends, classmates, workmates, professional colleagues, neighbors, and so on. The quality of every man's life depends to a large extent on the quality of those relationships. We may therefore speak of men's relational interests in gender equality.

For instance, very large numbers of men are fathers, and about half of their children are girls. Some men are sole parents and are then deeply involved in caregiving—an important demonstration of men's capacity for care (Risman 1986). Even in intact partnerships with women, many men have close relationships with their children, and psychological research shows the importance of these relationships (Kindler 2002). In several parts of the world, young men are exploring more engaged patterns of fatherhood (Olavarría 2001). To make sure that daughters grow up in a world that offers young women security, freedom, and opportunities to fulfil their talents is a powerful reason for many men to support gender equality.

Second, men may wish to avoid the toxic effects that the gender order has for them. James

Harrison long ago issued a "Warning: The Male Sex Role May Be Dangerous to Your Health" (1978). Since then health research has documented specific problems for men and boys. Among them are premature death from accident, homicide, and suicide; occupational injury; higher levels of drug abuse, especially of alcohol and tobacco; and in some countries at least, a relative unwillingness by men to seek medical help when it is needed. Attempts to assert a tough and dominant masculinity sustain some of these patterns (Sabo and Gordon 1995; Hurrelmann and Kolip 2002).

Social and economic pressures on men to compete in the workplace, to increase their hours of paid work, and sometimes to take second jobs are among the most powerful constraints on gender reform. Desire for a better balance between work and life is widespread among employed men. On the other hand, where unemployment is high the lack of a paid job can be a damaging pressure on men who have grown up with the expectation of being breadwinners. This is, for instance, an important gender issue in postapartheid South Africa. Opening alternative economic paths and moving toward what German discussions have called "multioptional masculinities" may do much to improve men's well-being (*Widersprüche* 1998; Morrell 2001a).

Third, men may support gender change because they see its relevance to the well-being of the community they live in. In situations of mass poverty and underemployment, for instance in cities in developing countries, flexibility in the gender division of labor may be crucial to a household that requires women's earnings as well as men's. Reducing the rigidity of masculinities may also yield benefits in security. Civil and international violence is strongly associated with dominating patterns of masculinity and with marked gender inequality in the state. Movement away from these patterns makes it easier for men to adopt historically "feminine" styles of nonviolent negotiation and conflict resolution (Zalewski and Parpart 1998; Breines, Connell, and Eide 2000;

Cockburn 2003). This may also reduce the toxic effects of policing and incarceration (Sabo, Kupers, and London 2001).

Finally, men may support gender reform because gender equality follows from their political or ethical principles. These may be religious, socialist, or broad democratic beliefs. Mill argued a case based on classical liberal principles a century and a half ago, and the idea of equal human rights still has purchase among large groups of men.

Grounds for Pessimism: The Shape of Masculinity Politics

The diversity among men and masculinities is reflected in a diversity of men's movements in the developed countries. A study of the United States found multiple movements, with different agendas for the remaking of masculinity. They operated on the varying terrains of gender equality, men's rights, and ethnic or religious identities (Messner 1997). There is no unified political position for men and no authoritative representation of men's interests.

Men's movements specifically concerned with gender equality exist in a number of countries. A well-known example is the White Ribbon Campaign, dedicated to mobilizing public opinion and educating men and boys for the prevention of men's violence against women. Originating in Canada, in response to the massacre of women in Montreal in 1989, the White Ribbon Campaign achieved very high visibility in that country, with support from political and community leaders and considerable outreach in schools and mass media. More recently, it has spread to other countries. Groups concerned with violence prevention have appeared in other countries, such as Men against Sexual Assault in Australia and Men Overcoming Violence (MOVE) in the United States. These have not achieved the visibility of the White Ribbon Campaign but have built up a valuable body of knowledge about the successes and difficulties of organizing among men (Lichterman 1989; Pease 1997; Kaufman 1999).

The most extensive experience of any group of men organizing around issues of gender and sexual politics is that of homosexual men, in anti-discrimination campaigns, the gay liberation movement, and community responses to the HIV/AIDS pandemic. Gay men have pioneered in areas such as community care for the sick, community education for responsible sexual practices, representation in the public sector, and overcoming social exclusion, which are important for all groups of men concerned with gender equality (Kippax et al. 1993; Altman 1994).

Explicit backlash movements also exist but have not generally had a great deal of influence. Men mobilizing as men to oppose women tend to be seen as cranks or fanatics. They constantly exaggerate women's power. And by defining men's interests in opposition to women's, they get into cultural difficulties, since they have to violate a main tenet of modern patriarchal ideology—the idea that "opposites attract" and that men's and women's needs, interests, and choices are complementary.

Much more important for the defense of gender inequality are movements in which men's interests are a side effect—nationalist, ethnic, religious, and economic movements. Of these, the most influential on a world scale is contemporary neoliberalism—the political and cultural promotion of free-market principles and individualism and the rejection of state control.

Neoliberalism is in principle gender neutral. The "individual" has no gender, and the market delivers an advantage to the smartest entrepreneur, not to men or women as such. But neoliberalism does not pursue social justice in relation to gender. In Eastern Europe, the restoration of capitalism and the arrival of neoliberal politics have been followed by a sharp deterioration in the position of women. In rich Western countries, neoliberalism from the 1980s on has attacked the welfare state, on which far more women than men depend; supported deregulation of labor

markets, resulting in increased casualization of women workers; shrunk public sector employment, the sector of the economy where women predominate; lowered rates of personal taxation, the main basis of tax transfers to women; and squeezed public education, the key pathway to labor market advancement for women. However, the same period saw an expansion of the human-rights agenda, which is, on the whole, an asset for gender equality.

The contemporary version of neoliberalism, known as neoconservatism in the United States, also has some gender complexities. George W. Bush was the first U.S. president to place a woman in the very heart of the state security apparatus, as national security adviser to the president. And some of the regime's actions, such as the attack on the Taliban regime in Afghanistan, were defended as a means of emancipating women.

Yet neoconservatism and state power in the United States and its satellites such as Australia remain overwhelmingly the province of men—indeed, men of a particular character: power oriented and ruthless, restrained by little more than calculations of likely opposition. There has been a sharp remasculinization of political rhetoric and a turn to the use of force as a primary instrument in policy. The human-rights discourse is muted and sometimes completely abandoned (as in the U.S. prison camp for Muslim captives at Guantanamo Bay and the Australian prison camps for refugees in the central desert and Pacific islands).

Neoliberalism can function as a form of masculinity politics largely because of the powerful role of the state in the gender order. The state constitutes gender relations in multiple ways, and all of its gender policies affect men. Many mainstream policies (e.g., in economic and security affairs) are substantially about men without acknowledging this fact (Nagel 1998; O'Connor, Orloff, and Shaver 1999; Connell 2003b).

This points to a realm of institutional politics where men's and women's interests are very much at stake, without the publicity created by social movements. Public-sector agencies (Jensen 1998;

Mackay and Bilton 2000; Schofield, forthcoming), private-sector corporations (Marchand and Runyan 2000; Hearn and Parkin 2001), and unions (Corman et al. 1993; Franzway 2001) are all sites of masculinized power and struggles for gender equality. In each of these sites, some men can be found with a commitment to gender equality, but in each case that is an embattled position. For gender-equality outcomes, it is important to have support from men in the top organizational levels, but this is not often reliably forthcoming.

One reason for the difficulty in expanding men's opposition to sexism is the role of highly conservative men as cultural authorities and managers. Major religious organizations, in Christianity, Islam, and Buddhism, are controlled by men who sometimes completely exclude women, and these organizations have often been used to oppose the emancipation of women. Transnational media organizations such as Rupert Murdoch's conglomerate are equally active in promoting conservative gender ideology.

A specific address to men is found in the growing institutional, media, and business complex of commercial sports. With its overwhelming focus on male athletes; its celebration of force, domination, and competitive success; its valorization of male commentators and executives; and its marginalization and frequent ridicule of women, the sports/business complex has become an increasingly important site for representing and defining gender. This is not traditional patriarchy. It is something new, welding exemplary bodies to entrepreneurial culture. Michael Messner (2002), one of the leading analysts of contemporary sports, formulates the effect well by saying that commercial sports define the renewed centrality of men and of a particular version of masculinity.

On a world scale, explicit backlash movements are of limited importance, but very large numbers of men are nevertheless engaged in preserving gender inequality. Patriarchy is defended diffusely. There is support for change from equally large numbers of men, but it is an uphill battle to articulate that support. That is the political context with which new gender-equality initiatives have to deal.

Ways Forward: Toward a Global Framework

Inviting men to end men's privileges, and to remake masculinities to sustain gender equality, strikes many people as a strange or utopian project. Yet this project is already under way. Many men around the world are engaged in gender reforms, for the good reasons discussed above.

The diversity of masculinities complicates the process but is also an important asset. As this diversity becomes better known, men and boys can more easily see a range of possibilities for their own lives, and both men and women are less likely to think of gender inequality as unchangeable. It also becomes possible to identify specific groups of men who might engage in alliances for change.

The international policy documents discussed above rely on the concept of an alliance between men and women for achieving equality. Since the growth of an autonomous women's movement, the main impetus for reform has been located in women's groups. Some groups within the women's movement, especially those concerned with men's violence, are reluctant to work with men or are deeply skeptical of men's willingness to change. Other feminists argue that alliances between women and men are possible, even crucial. In some social movements, for instance, environmentalism, there is a strong ideology of gender equality and a favorable environment for men to support gender change (Connell 1995; Segal 1997).

In local and central government, practical alliances between women and men have been important in achieving equal-opportunity measures and other gender-equality reforms. Even in the field of men's violence against women, there has been cooperation between women's groups and men's groups, for instance, in prevention work. This cooperation can be an inspiration to grassroots workers and a powerful demonstration of women and men's common interest in a peaceful and equal society (Pease 1997; Schofield, forthcoming). The concept of alliance is itself important, in preserving autonomy for women's groups, in preempting a tendency for any one group to speak for others, and in defining a political role for men that has some dignity and might attract widespread support.

Given the spectrum of masculinity politics, we cannot expect worldwide consensus for gender equality. What is possible is that support for gender equality might become hegemonic among men. In that case it would be groups supporting equality that provide the agenda for public discussion about men's lives and patterns of masculinity.

There is already a broad cultural shift toward a historical consciousness about gender, an awareness that gender customs came into existence at specific moments in time and can always be transformed by social action (Connell 1995). What is needed now is a widespread sense of agency among men, a sense that this transformation is something they can actually share in as a practical proposition. This is precisely what was presupposed in the "joint responsibility" of men invoked by the General Assembly declaration of the year 2000.[1]

From this point of view, the recent meeting of the UN Commission on the Status of Women (CSW) is profoundly interesting. The CSW is one of the oldest of UN agencies, dating from the 1940s. Effectively a standing committee of the General Assembly, it meets annually, and its current practice is to consider two main themes at each meeting. For the 2004 meeting, one of the defined themes was "the role of men and boys in achieving gender equality." The section of the UN secretariat that supports the CSW, the Division for the Advancement of Women, undertook background work. The division held, in June–July 2003, a worldwide online seminar on the role of men and boys, and in October 2003 it convened an international expert group meeting in Brasilia on the topic.

At the CSW meetings, several processes occur and (it is to be hoped) interact. There is a presentation of the division's background work, and delegations of the forty-five current member countries, UN agencies, and many of the nongovernmental organizations (NGOs) attending make initial statements. There is a busy schedule of side events, mainly organized by NGOs but some conducted by delegations or UN agencies, ranging from strategy debates to practical workshops. And there is a diplomatic process in which the official delegations negotiate over a draft document in the light of discussions in the CSW and their governments' stances on gender issues.

This is a politicized process, inevitably, and it can break down. In 2003 the CSW discussion on the issue of violence against women reached deadlock. In 2004 it was clear that some participating NGOs were not happy with the focus on men and boys, some holding to a discourse representing men exclusively as perpetrators of violence. Over the two weeks of negotiations, however, the delegations did reach consensus on a statement of "Agreed Conclusions."

Balancing a reaffirmation of commitment to women's equality with a recognition of men's and boys' potential for action, this document makes specific recommendations across a spectrum of policy fields, including education, parenthood, media, the labor market, sexuality, violence, and conflict prevention. These proposals have no force in international law—the document is essentially a set of recommendations to governments and other organizations. Nevertheless, it is the first international agreement of its kind, treating men systematically as agents in gender-equality processes, and it creates a standard for future gender-equality discussions. Most important, the CSW's "Agreed Conclusions" change the logic of the representation of men in gender policy. So far as the international discourse of gender-equality policy is concerned, this document begins the substantive presentation of gender equality as a positive project for men.

Here the UN process connects with the social and cultural possibilities that have emerged from the last three decades of gender politics among men. Gender equality is an undertaking for men that can be creative and joyful. It is a project that realizes high principles of social justice, produces better lives for the women whom men care about, and will produce better lives for the majority of men in the long run. This can and should be a project that generates energy, that finds expression in everyday life and the arts as well as in formal policies, and that can illuminate all aspects of men's lives.

Note

1. Twenty-third special session, UN General Assembly, "Political Declaration," par. 6.

References

Altman, Dennis. 1994. *Power and Community: Organizational and Cultural Responses to AIDS.* London: Taylor & Francis.

———. 2001. *Global Sex.* Chicago: University of Chicago Press.

Arilha, Margareth, Sandra G. Unbehaum Ridenti, and Benedito Medrado, eds. 1998. *Homens e Masculinidades: Outras Palavras.* Sao Paulo: ECOS/Editora 34.

Bly, Robert. 1990. *Iron John: A Book about Men.* Reading, MA: Addison-Wesley.

Brandes, Holger, and Hermann Bullinger, eds. 1996. *Handbuch Männerarbeit.* Weinheim, Germany: Psychologie Verlags Union.

Breines, Ingeborg, Robert Connell, and Ingrid Eide, eds. 2000. *Male Roles, Masculinities and Violence: A Culture of Peace Perspective.* Paris: UNESCO.

Bulbeck, Chilla. 1988. *One World Women's Movement.* London: Pluto.

———. 1998. *Re-orienting Western Feminisms: Women's Diversity in a Postcolonial World.* Cambridge: Cambridge University Press.

Cockburn, Cynthia. 1991. *In the Way of Women: Men's Resistance to Sex Equality in Organizations.* Ithaca, NY: ILR Press.

———. 2003. *The Line: Women, Partition and the Gender Order in Cyprus.* London: Zed.

Cohen, Jon. 1991. "NOMAS: Challenging Male Supremacy." *Changing Men* (Winter/Spring): 45–46.

Collinson, David L., and Jeff Hearn, eds. 1996. *Men as Managers, Managers as Men: Critical Perspectives on Men, Masculinities and Managements.* London: Sage.

Connell, R. W. 1995. *Masculinities.* Berkeley: University of California Press.

———. 2000. *The Men and the Boys.* Sydney: Allen & Unwin Australia.

———. 2002. *Gender.* Cambridge: Polity.

———. 2003a. "Masculinities, Change and Conflict in Global Society: Thinking about the Future of Men's Studies." *Journal of Men's Studies* 11(3):249–66.

———. 2003b. "Men, Gender and the State." In *Among Men: Moulding Masculinities,* ed. Søren Ervø and Thomas Johansson, 15–28. Aldershot: Ashgate.

———. 2003c. "Scrambling in the Ruins of Patriarchy: Neo-liberalism and Men's Divided Interests in Gender Change." In *Gender—From Costs to Benefits,* ed. Ursula Pasero, 58–69. Wiesbaden: Westdeutscher.

Corman, June, Meg Luxton, D. W. Livingstone, and Wally Seccombe. 1993. *Recasting Steel Labour: The Stelco Story.* Halifax: Fernwood.

Da Wei Wei. 2004. "A Regional Tradition of Gender Equity: Shanghai Men in Sydney." *Journal of Men's Studies* 12(2):133–49.

Davies, Bronwyn. 1993. *Shards of Glass: Children Reading and Writing beyond Gender Identities.* Sydney: Allen & Unwin Australia.

Denborough, David. 1996. "Step by Step: Developing Respectful and Effective Ways of Working with Young Men to Reduce Violence." In *Men's Ways of Being,* ed. Chris McLean, Maggie Carey, and Cheryl White, 91–115. Boulder, CO: Westview.

Eisenstein, Hester. 1991. *Gender Shock: Practising Feminism on Two Continents.* Sydney: Allen & Unwin Australia.

Farrell, Warren. 1993. *The Myth of Male Power: Why Men Are the Disposable Sex.* New York: Simon & Schuster.

Franzway, Suzanne. 2001. *Sexual Politics and Greedy Institutions.* Sydney: Pluto.

Fuller, Norma. 2001. "The Social Constitution of Gender Identity among Peruvian Men." *Men and Masculinities* 3(3):316–31.

Ghoussoub, Mai. 2000. "Chewing Gum, Insatiable Women and Foreign Enemies: Male Fears and the Arab Media." In *Imagined Masculinities: Male Identity and Culture in the Middle East,* ed. Mai Ghoussoub and Emma Sinclair-Webb, 227–35. London: Saqi.

Gierycz, Dorota. 1999. "Women in Decision-Making: Can We Change the Status Quo?" In *Towards a Women's Agenda for a Culture of Peace,* ed. Ingeborg Breines, Dorota Gierycz, and Betty A. Reardon, 19–30. Paris: UNESCO.

Godenzi, Alberto. 2000. "Determinants of Culture: Men and Economic Power." In Breines, Connell, and Eide 2000, 35–51. Paris: UNESCO.

Gutmann, Matthew C. 2002. *The Romance of Democracy: Compliant Defiance in Contemporary Mexico.* Berkeley: University of California Press.

Hagemann-White, Carol. 1992. *Strategien gegen Gewalt im Geschlechterverhältnis: Bestandsanalyse und Perspektiven.* Pfaffenweiler, Ger.: Centaurus.

Harrison, James. 1978. "Warning: The Male Sex Role May Be Dangerous to Your Health." *Journal of Social Issues* 34(1):65–86.

Haseler, Stephen. 2000. *The Super-Rich: The Unjust New World of Global Capitalism.* London: Macmillan.

Hearn, Jeff. 1998. *The Violences of Men: How Men Talk about and How Agencies Respond to Men's Violence to Women.* Thousand Oaks, CA: Sage.

Hearn, Jeff, and Wendy Parkin. 2001. *Gender, Sexuality, and Violence in Organizations: The Unspoken Forces of Organization Violations.* Thousand Oaks, CA: Sage.

Hearn, Jeff, Keith Pringle, Ursula Müller, Elzbeieta Oleksy, Emmi Lattu, Janna Chernova, Harry Ferguson, et al. 2002. "Critical Studies on Men in Ten European Countries: (1) The State of Academic Research." *Men and Masculinities* 4(4):380–408.

Holland, Janet, Caroline Ramazanoğlu, Sue Sharpe, and Rachel Thomson. 1998. *The Male in the Head: Young People, Heterosexuality and Power.* London: Tufnell.

Holter, Øystein Gullvåg. 1997. *Gender, Patriarchy and Capitalism: A Social Forms Analysis.* Oslo: Work Research Institute.

———. 2003. *Can Men Do It? Men and Gender Equality—The Nordic Experience.* Copenhagen: Nordic Council of Ministers.

Hooper, Charlotte. 2001. *Manly States: Masculinities, International Relations, and Gender Politics.* New York: Columbia University Press.

Hurrelmann, Klaus, and Petra Kolip, eds. 2002. *Geschlecht, Gesundheit und Krankheit: Männer und Frauen im Vergleich.* Bern: Hans Huber.

Ibsen, Henrik. (1923) 1995. *A Doll's House.* Cambridge: Cambridge University Press.

Inter-Parliamentary Union. 2003. "Women in National Parliaments: Situation at 30 December 2003." Available online at http://www.ipu.org/wmn-e/world.htm.

Ito, Kimio. 1992. "Cultural Change and Gender Identity Trends in the 1970s and 1980s." *International Journal of Japanese Sociology* 1(1):79–98.

Jensen, Hanne Naxø. 1998. "Gender as the Dynamo: When Public Organizations Have to Change." In *Is There a Nordic Feminism? Nordic Feminist Thought on Culture and Society,* ed. Drude von der Fehr, Bente Rosenberg, and Anna G. Jóasdóttir, 160–75. London: UCL Press.

Kandiyoti, Deniz. 1994. "The Paradoxes of Masculinity: Some Thoughts on Segregated Societies." In *Dislocating Masculinity: Comparative Ethnographies,* ed. Andrea Cornwall and Nancy Lindisfarne, 197–213. London: Routledge.

Kaufman, Michael. 1993. *Cracking the Armour: Power, Pain and the Lives of Men.* Toronto: Viking.

———, ed. 1999. "Men and Violence." Special issue, *International Association for Studies of Men Newsletter* 6, no. 2.

Kenway, Jane, ed. 1997. *Will Boys Be Boys? Boys' Education in the Context of Gender Reform.* Canberra: Australian Curriculum Studies Association.

Kenworthy, Colin. 1994. " 'We want to resist your resistant readings': Masculinity and Discourse in the English Classroom." *Interpretations* 27(2):74–95.

Kimmel, Michael S., Jeff Hearn, and R. W. Connell, eds. 2005. *Handbook of Studies on Men and Masculinities.* Thousand Oaks, CA: Sage.

Kimmel, Michael S., and Thomas E. Mosmiller. 1992. *Against the Tide: Profeminist Men in the United States, 1776–1990: A Documentary History.* Boston: Beacon.

Kindler, Heinz. 2002. *Väter und Kinder.* Weinheim, Germany: Juventa.

Kippax, Susan, R. W. Connell, G. W. Dowsett, and June Crawford. 1993. *Sustaining Safe Sex: Gay Communities Respond to AIDS.* London: Falmer.

Kupers, Terry. 1993. *Revisioning Men's Lives: Gender, Intimacy, and Power.* New York: Guilford.

Law, Robin, Hugh Campbell, and John Dolan, eds. 1999. *Masculinities in Aotearoa/New Zealand.* Palmerston North, NZ: Dunmore.

Lerner, Susana, ed. 1998. *Varones, sexualidad y reproducción: Diversas perspectivas teórico-metodológicas y hallazgos de investigación.* El Colegio de México, México.

Lichterman, Paul. 1989. "Making a Politics of Masculinity." *Comparative Social Research* 11:185–208.

Lingard, Bob. 2003. "Where to in Gender Policy in Education after Recuperative Masculinity Politics?" *International Journal of Inclusive Education* 7(1):33–56.

Lyra, Jorge, and Benedito Medrado. 2001. "Constructing an Adolescent Father in Brazil." Paper presented at the Third International Fatherhood Conference, Atlanta, May 28–30.

Mac an Ghaill, Mairtin. 1994. *The Making of Men: Masculinities, Sexualities and Schooling.* Buckingham: Open University Press.

Mackay, Fiona, and Kate Bilton. 2000. *Learning from Experience: Lessons in Mainstreaming Equal Opportunities.* Edinburgh: Governance of Scotland Forum.

Marchand, Marianne H., and Anne Sisson Runyan, eds. 2000. *Gender and Global Restructuring: Sightings, Sites and Resistances.* London: Routledge.

McMahon, Anthony. 1999. *Taking Care of Men: Sexual Politics in the Public Mind.* Cambridge: Cambridge University Press.

Menzu Senta (Men's Center Japan). 1997. *Otokotachi no watashisagashi* (How are men seeking their new selves?). Kyoto: Kamogawa.

Messner, Michael A. 1997. *The Politics of Masculinities: Men in Movements.* Thousand Oaks, CA: Sage.

———. 2002. *Taking the Field: Women, Men and Sports.* Minneapolis: University of Minnesota Press.

Metz-Göckel, Sigrid, and Ursula Müller. 1985. *Der Mann: Die Brigitte-Studie.* Hamburg: Beltz.

Meuser, Michael, 2003. "Modernized Masculinities? Continuities, Challenges, and Changes in Men's Lives." In *Among Men: Moulding Masculinities,* vol. 1, ed. Søren Ervø and Thomas Johansson, 127–48. Aldershot: Ashgate.

Mill, John Stuart. 1912. "The Subjection of Women." In his *On Liberty; Representative Government; The Subjugation of Women: Three Essays,* 427–548. London: Oxford University Press.

Mohwald, Ulrich. 2002. *Changing Attitudes towards Gender Equality in Japan and Germany.* Munich: Iudicium.

Moodie, T. Dunbar. 1994. *Going for Gold: Men, Mines and Migration.* Johannesburg: Witwatersrand University Press.

Morrell, Robert. 1998. "Of Boys and Men: Masculinity and Gender in Southern African Studies." *Journal of Southern African Studies* 24(4):605–30.

———, ed. 2001a. *Changing Men in Southern Africa.* Pietermaritzburg, S.A.: University of Natal Press.

———. 2001b. *From Boys to Gentlemen: Settler Masculinity in Colonial Natal, 1880–1920.* Pretoria: University of South Africa Press.

Nagel, Joane. 1998. "Masculinity and Nationalism: Gender and Sexuality in the Making of Nations." *Ethnic and Racial Studies* 21(2):242–69.

Nordic Council of Ministers. 1997. *Nordic Action Plan for Men and Gender Equality, 1997–2000.* Copenhagen: Nordic Council of Ministers.

O'Connor, Julia S., Ann Shola Orloff, and Sheila Shaver. 1999. *States, Markets, Families: Gender, Liberalism and Social Policy in Australia, Canada, Great Britain, and the United States.* Cambridge: Cambridge University Press.

O'Donnell, Mike, and Sue Sharpe. 2000. *Uncertain Masculinities: Youth, Ethnicity and Class in Contemporary Britain.* London: Routledge.

Olavarría, José. 2001. *Y todos querían ser (buenos) padres: Varones de Santiago de Chile en conflicto.* Santiago: FLACSO-Chile.

Palme, Olof. 1972. "The Emancipation of Man." *Journal of Social Issues* 28(2):237–46.

Peacock, Dean. 2003. "Building on a Legacy of Social Justice Activism: Enlisting Men as Gender Justice Activists in South Africa." *Men and Masculinities* 5(3):325–28.

Pease, Bob. 1997. *Men and Sexual Politics: Towards a Profeminist Practice.* Adelaide: Dulwich Centre.

Pease, Bob, and Keith Pringle, eds. 2001. *A Man's World? Changing Men's Practices in a Globalized World.* London: Zed.

Ptacek, James. 1988. "Why Do Men Batter Their Wives?" In *Feminist Perspectives on Wife Abuse,* ed. Kersti Yllö and Michele Bograd, 133–57. Newbury Park, CA: Sage.

Reinicke, Kenneth. 2002. *Den Helc Mand: Manderollen i forandring.* Aarhus, Denmark: Schønberg.

Risman, Barbara J. 1986. "Can Men 'Mother'? Life as a Single Father." *Family Relations* 35(1):95–102.

———. 1998. *Gender Vertigo: American Families in Transition.* New Haven, CT: Yale University Press.

Roberson, James E., and Nobue Suzuki, eds. 2003. *Men and Masculinities in Contemporary Japan: Dislocating the Salaryman Doxa.* London: Routledge.

Roy, Rahul. 2003. "Exploring Masculinities—A Travelling Seminar." Unpublished manuscript.

Sabo, Donald, and David Frederick Gordon, eds. 1995. *Men's Health and Illness: Gender, Power, and the Body.* Thousand Oaks, CA: Sage.

Sabo, Donald, Terry A. Kupers, and Willie London, eds. 2001. *Prison Masculinities.* Philadelphia: Temple University Press.

Schofield, Toni. 2004. *Boutique Health? Gender and Equity in Health Policy.* Sydney: Australian Health Policy Institute.

———. Forthcoming. "Gender Regimes in Public Policy Making." Unpublished manuscript, Faculty of Health Sciences, University of Sydney.

Schwalbe, Michael. 1996. *Unlocking the Iron Cage: The Men's Movement, Gender Politics, and American Culture.* New York: Oxford University Press.

Segal, Lynne. 1997. *Slow Motion: Changing Masculinities, Changing Men.* 2nd ed. London: Virago.

Seidler, Victor J., ed. 1991. *The Achilles Heel Reader: Men, Sexual Politics and Socialism.* London: Routledge.

Sinclair-Webb, Emma. 2000. " 'Our bülent is now a commando': Military Service and Manhood in Turkey." In *Imagined Masculinities: Male Identity and Culture in the Modern Middle East,* ed. Mai Ghoussoub and Emma Sinclair-Webb, 65–92. London: Saqi.

Sommers, Christina Hoff. 2000. *The War against Boys: How Misguided Feminism Is Harming Our Young Men.* New York: Simon & Schuster.

Taga, Futoshi. 2001. *Dansei no Jendâ Keisei: "Otoko-Rashisa" no Yuragi no Naka de* (The gender formation of men: Uncertain masculinity). Tokyo: Tôyôkan Shuppan-sha.

Thornton, Arland. 1989. "Changing Attitudes toward Family Issues in the United States." *Journal of Marriage and the Family* 51(4):873–93.

United Nations. 1958. *Universal Declaration of Human Rights.* New York: Department of Public Information, United Nations.

———. (1979) 1989. *Convention on the Elimination of All Forms of Discrimination against Women.* New York: Department of Public Information, United Nations.

———. 2001. *Beijing Declaration and Platform for Action, with the Beijing +5 Political Declaration and Outcome Document.* New York: Department of Public Information, United Nations.

United Nations Commission on the Status of Women. 2004. *The Role of Men and Boys in Achieving Gender Equality: Agreed Conclusions.* Available online at http://www.un.org/womenwatch/daw/csw/csw48/ac-men-auv.pdf.

United Nations Development Program (UNDP). 2003. *Human Development Report 2003.* New York: UNDP and Oxford University Press.

Valdés, Teresa, and José Olavarría. 1998. "Ser hombre en Santiago de Chile: A pesar de todo, un mismo modelo." In their *Masculinidades y equidad de género en América Latina,* 12–36. Santiago: FLACSO/UNFPA.

Walby, Sylvia. 1997. *Gender Transformations.* London: Routledge.

Wetherell, Margaret, and Nigel Edley. 1999. "Negotiating Hegemonic Masculinity: Imaginary Positions and Psycho-Discursive Practices." *Feminism and Psychology* 9(3):335–56.

White, Sara C. 2000. "Did the Earth Move? The Hazards of Bringing Men and Masculinities into Gender and Development." *IDS Bulletin* 31(2):33–41.

Widersprüche. 1998. "Multioptionale Männlichkeiten?" Special issue, no. 67.

Zalewski, Marysia, and Jane Parpart, eds. 1998. *The "Man" Question in International Relations.* Boulder, CO: Westview.

Zingoni, Eduardo Liendro. 1998. "Masculinidades y violencia desde un programa de acción en México." In *Masculinidades y equidad de género en América Latina,* ed. Teresa Valdés and José Olavarría, 130–36. Santiago: FLACSO/UNFPA.

Zulehner, Paul M., and Rainer Volz. 1998. *Männer im Aufbruch: Wie Deutschlands Männer sich Selbst und wie Frauen Sie Sehen.* Ostfildern, Ger.: Schwabenverlag.

bell hooks

Men: Comrades in Struggle

Feminism defined as a movement to end sexist oppression enables women and men, girls and boys, to participate equally in revolutionary struggle. So far, contemporary feminist movement has been primarily generated by the efforts of women—men have rarely participated. This lack of participation is not solely a consequence of anti-feminism. By making women's liberation synonymous with women gaining social equality with men, liberal feminists effectively created a situation in which they, not men, designated feminist movement "women's work." Even as they were attacking sex role divisions of labor, the institutionalized sexism which assigns unpaid, devalued, "dirty" work to women, they were assigning to women yet another sex role task: making feminist revolution. Women's liberationists called upon all women to join feminist movement but they did not continually stress that men should assume responsibility for actively struggling to end sexist oppression. Men, they argued, were all-powerful, misogynist oppressors—the enemy. Women were the oppressed—the victims. Such rhetoric reinforced sexist ideology by positing in an inverted form the notion of a basic conflict between the sexes, the implication being that the empowerment of women would necessarily be at the expense of men.

As with other issues, the insistence on a "woman only" feminist movement and a virulent anti-male stance reflected the race and class background of participants. Bourgeois white women,

especially radical feminists, were envious and angry at privileged white men for denying them an equal share in class privilege. In part, feminism provided them with a public forum for the expression of their anger as well as a political platform they could use to call attention to issues of social equality, demand change, and promote specific reforms. They were not eager to call attention to the fact that men do not share a common social status; that patriarchy does not negate the existence of class and race privilege or exploitation; that all men do not benefit equally from sexism. They did not want to acknowledge that bourgeois white women, though often victimized by sexism, have more power and privilege, are less likely to be exploited or oppressed, than poor, uneducated, nonwhite males. At the time, many white women's liberationists did not care about the fate of oppressed groups of men. In keeping with the exercise of race and/or class privilege, they deemed the life experiences of these men unworthy of their attention, dismissed them, and simultaneously deflected attention away from their support of continued exploitation and oppression. Assertions like "all men are the enemy," "all men hate women" lumped all groups of men in one category, thereby suggesting that they share equally in all forms of male privilege. One of the first written statements which endeavored to make an anti-male stance a central feminist position was the "Redstockings Manifesto." Clause III of the manifesto reads:

> We identify the agents of our oppression as men. Male supremacy is the oldest, most basic form of domination. All other forms of exploitation and oppression (racism, capitalism, imperialism, etc.) are extensions of male

supremacy: men dominate women, a few men dominate the rest. All power situations throughout history have been male-dominated and male-oriented. Men have controlled all political, economic, and cultural institutions and backed up this control with physical force. They have used their power to keep women in an inferior position. All men receive economic, sexual, and psychological benefits from male supremacy. All men have oppressed women. (1970, p. 109)

Anti-male sentiments alienated many poor and working class women, particularly non-white women, from feminist movement. Their life experiences had shown them that they have more in common with men of their race and/or class group than bourgeois white women. They know the sufferings and hardships women face in their communities; they also know the sufferings and hardships men face and they have compassion for them. They have had the experience of struggling with them for a better life. This has been especially true for black women. Throughout our history in the United States, black women have shared equal responsibility in all struggles to resist racist oppression. Despite sexism, black women have continually contributed equally to anti-racist struggle, and frequently, before contemporary black liberation effort, black men recognized this contribution. There is a special tie binding people together who struggle collectively for liberation. Black women and men have been united by such ties. They have known the experience of political solidarity. It is the experience of shared resistance struggle that led black women to reject the anti-male stance of some feminist activists. This does not mean that black women were not willing to acknowledge the reality of black male sexism. It does mean that many of us do not believe we will combat sexism or woman-hating by attacking black men or responding to them in kind.

Bourgeois white women cannot conceptualize the bonds that develop between women and men in liberation struggle and have not had as many positive experiences working with men politically. Patriarchal white male rule has usually devalued female political input. Despite the preva-

lence of sexism in black communities, the role black women play in social institutions, whether primary or secondary, is recognized by everyone as significant and valuable. In an interview with Claudia Tate (1983), black woman writer Maya Angelou explains her sense of the different role black and white women play in their communities:

> Black women and white women are in strange positions in our separate communities. In the social gatherings of black people, black women have always been predominant. That is to say, in the church it's always Sister Hudson, Sister Thomas, and Sister Wetheringay who keep the church alive. In lay gatherings it's always Lottie who cooks, and Mary who's going to Bonita's where there is a good party going on. Also, black women are the nurturers of children in our community. White women are in a different position in their social institutions. White men, who are in effect their fathers, husbands, brothers, their sons, nephews, and uncles say to white women or imply in any case: "I don't really need you to run my institutions. I need you in certain places and in those places you must be kept—in the bedroom, in the kitchen, in the nursery, and on the pedestal." Black women have never been told this. . . .

Without the material input of black women, as participants and leaders, many male-dominated institutions in black communities would cease to exist; this is not the case in all-white communities.

Many black women refused participation in feminist movement because they felt an anti-male stance was not a sound basis for action. They were convinced that virulent expressions of these sentiments intensify sexism by adding to the antagonism which already exists between women and men. For years black women (and some black men) had been struggling to overcome the tensions and antagonisms between black females and males that is generated by internalized racism (i.e., when the white patriarchy suggests one group has caused the oppression of the other). Black women were saying to black men, "we are not one another's enemy," "we must resist the socialization that teaches us to hate ourselves and one another." This affirmation of bonding between black women and men was part of anti-racist struggle. It could have been a part of feminist struggle had white women's liberationists stressed the need for women and men to resist the sexist socialization that teaches us to hate and fear one another. They chose instead to emphasize hate, especially male woman-hating, suggesting that it could not be changed. Therefore no viable political solidarity could exist between women and men. Women of color, from various ethnic backgrounds, as well as women who were active in the gay movement, not only experienced the development of solidarity between women and men in resistance struggle, but recognized its value. They were not willing to devalue this bonding by allying themselves with anti-male bourgeois white women. Encouraging political bonding between women and men to radically resist sexist oppression would have called attention to the transformative potential of feminism. The anti-male stance was a reactionary perspective that made feminism appear to be a movement that would enable white women to usurp white male power, replacing white male supremacist rule with white female supremacist rule.

Within feminist organizations, the issue of female separatism was initially separated from the anti-male stance; it was only as the movement progressed that the two perspectives merged. Many all-female sex-segregated groups were formed because women recognized that separatist organizing could hasten female consciousness-raising, lay the groundwork for the development of solidarity between women, and generally advance the movement. It was believed that mixed groups would get bogged down by male power trips. Separatist groups were seen as a necessary strategy, not as a way to attack men. Ultimately, the purpose of such groups was integration with equality. The positive implications of separatist organizing were diminished when radical feminists, like Ti Grace Atkinson, proposed sexual separatism as an ultimate goal of feminist movement. Reactionary separatism is rooted in the conviction that male supremacy is an absolute aspect of our culture, that women have only two alternatives: accepting it or withdrawing from it to create subcultures. This position eliminates any need for revolutionary struggle and it is in no way a threat to the status quo. In the essay "Separate to Integrate," Barbara Leon (1975) stresses that male supremacists would rather feminist movement remain "separate and unequal." She gives the example of orchestra conductor Antonia Brico's efforts to shift from an all-women orchestra to a mixed orchestra, only to find she could not get support for the latter:

> Antonia Brico's efforts were acceptable as long as she confined herself to proving that women were qualified musicians. She had no trouble finding 100 women who could play in an orchestra or getting financial backing for them to do so. But finding the backing for men and women to play together in a truly integrated orchestra proved to be impossible. Fighting for integration proved to be more a threat to male supremacy and, therefore, harder to achieve.
>
> The women's movement is at the same point now. We can take the easier way of accepting segregation, but that would mean losing the very goals for which the movement was formed. Reactionary separatism has been a way of halting the push of feminism. . . .

During the course of contemporary feminist movement, reactionary separatism has led many women to abandon feminist struggle, yet it remains an accepted pattern for feminist organizing, e.g. autonomous women's groups within the peace movement. As a policy, it has helped to marginalize feminist struggle, to make it seem more a personal solution to individual problems, especially problems with men, than a political movement which aims to transform society as a whole. To return to an emphasis on feminism as revolutionary struggle, women can no longer allow feminism to be another arena for the continued expression of antagonism between the sexes. The time has come for women active in feminist movement to develop new strategies for including men in the struggle against sexism.

All men support and perpetuate sexism and sexist oppression in one form or another. It is crucial that feminist activists not get bogged down in intensifying our awareness of this fact to the extent that we do not stress the more unemphasized point which is that men can lead life affirming, meaningful lives without exploiting and oppressing women. Like women, men have been socialized to passively accept sexist ideology. While they need not blame themselves for accepting sexism, they must assume responsibility for eliminating it. It angers women activists who push separatism as a goal of feminist movement to hear emphasis placed on men being victimized by sexism; they cling to the "all men are the enemy" version of reality. Men are not exploited or oppressed by sexism, but there are ways in which they suffer as a result of it. This suffering should not be ignored. While it in no way diminishes the seriousness of male abuse and oppression of women, or negates male responsibility for exploitative actions, the pain men experience can serve as a catalyst calling attention to the need for change. Recognition of the painful consequences of sexism in their lives led some men to establish consciousness-raising groups to examine this. Paul Hornacek (1977) explains the purpose of these gatherings in his essay "Anti-Sexist Consciousness-Raising Groups for Men":

> Men have reported a variety of different reasons for deciding to seek a C-R group, all of which have an underlying link to the feminist movement. Most are experiencing emotional pain as a result of their male sex role and are dissatisfied with it. Some have had confrontations with radical feminists in public or private encounters and have been repeatedly criticized for being sexist. Some come as a result of their commitment to social change and their recognition that sexism and patriarchy are elements of an intolerable social system that needs to be altered . . .

Men in the consciousness-raising groups Hornacek describes acknowledge that they benefit from patriarchy and yet are also hurt by it. Men's groups, like women's support groups, run the risk of overemphasizing personal change at the expense of political analysis and struggle.

Separatist ideology encourages women to ignore the negative impact of sexism on male personhood. It stresses polarization between the sexes. According to Joy Justice, separatists believe that there are "two basic perspectives" on the issue of naming the victims of sexism: "There is the perspective that men oppress women. And there is the perspective that people are people, and we are all hurt by rigid sex roles." Many separatists feel that the latter perspective is a sign of co-optation, representing women's refusal to confront the fact that men are the enemy—they insist on the primacy of the first perspective. Both perspectives accurately describe our predicament. Men *do* oppress women. People *are* hurt by rigid sex role patterns. These two realities co-exist. Male oppression of women cannot be excused by the recognition that there are ways men are hurt by rigid sex roles. Feminist activists should acknowledge that hurt—it exists. It does not erase or lessen male responsibility for supporting and perpetuating their power under patriarchy to exploit and oppress women in a manner far more grievous than the psychological stress or emotional pain caused by male conformity to rigid sex role patterns.

Women active in feminist movement have not wanted to focus in any way on male pain so as not to deflect attention away from the focus on male privilege. Separatist feminist rhetoric suggested that all men shared equally in male privilege, that all men reap positive benefits from sexism. Yet the poor or working class man has been socialized via sexist ideology to believe that there are privileges and powers he should possess solely because he is male often finds that few if any of these benefits are automatically bestowed him in life. More than any other male group in the United States, he is constantly concerned about the contradiction between the notion of masculinity he was taught and his inability to live up to that notion. He is usually "hurt," emotionally scarred because he does not have the privilege or power society has taught him "real men" should possess. Alienated, frustrated, pissed off, he may attack, abuse, and oppress an individual woman or women, but he is not reaping positive benefits from his support and perpetuation of sexist ideology. When he beats or rapes women, he is not exercising privilege or reaping positive rewards; he may feel satisfied in exercising the only form of domination allowed him. The ruling class male power structure that promotes his sexist abuse of women reaps the real material benefits and privileges from his actions. As long as he is attacking women and not sexism or capitalism, he helps to maintain a system that allows him few, if any, benefits or privileges. He is an oppressor. He is an enemy to women. He is also an enemy to himself. He is also oppressed. His abuse of women is not justifiable. Even though he has been socialized to act as he does, there are existing social movements that would enable him to struggle for self-recovery and liberation. By ignoring these movements, he chooses to remain both oppressor and oppressed. If feminist movement ignores his predicament, dismisses his hurt, or writes him off as just another male enemy, then we are passively condoning his actions.

The process by which men act as oppressors and are oppressed is particularly visible in black communities, where men are working class and poor. In her essay "Notes for Yet Another Paper on Black Feminism, or Will The Real Enemy Please Stand Up?" (1979) black feminist activist Barbara Smith suggests that black women are unwilling to confront the problem of sexist oppression in black communities:

> By naming sexist oppression as a problem it would appear that we would have to identify as threatening a group we have heretofore assumed to be our allies—Black men. This seems to be one of the major stumbling blocks to beginning to analyze the sexual relationships/sexual politics of our lives. The phrase "men are not the enemy" dismisses feminism and the reality of patriarchy in one breath and also overlooks some major realities. If we cannot

entertain the idea that some men are the enemy, especially white men and in a different sense Black men, too, then we will never be able to figure out all the reasons why, for example, we are beaten up every day, why we are sterilized against our wills, why we are being raped by our neighbors, why we are pregnant at age twelve, and why we are at home on welfare with more children than we can support or care for. Acknowledging the sexism of Black men does not mean that we become "manhaters" or necessarily eliminate them from our lives. What it does mean is that we must struggle for a different basis of interaction with them.

Women in black communities have been reluctant to publicly discuss sexist oppression, but they have always known it exists. We too have been socialized to accept sexist ideology and many black women feel that black male abuse of women is a reflection of frustrated masculinity—such thoughts lead them to see that abuse is understandable, even justified. The vast majority of black women think that just publicly stating that these men are the enemy or identifying them as oppressors would do little to change the situation; they fear it could simply lead to greater victimization. Naming oppressive realities, in and of itself, has not brought about the kinds of changes for oppressed groups that it can for more privileged groups, who command a different quality of attention. The public naming of sexism has generally not resulted in the institutionalized violence that characterized, for example, the response to black civil rights struggles. (Private naming, however, is often met with violent oppression.) Black women have not joined the feminist movement not because they cannot face the reality of sexist oppression; they face it daily. They do not join feminist movement because they do not see in feminist theory and practice, especially those writings made available to masses of people, potential solutions.

So far, feminist rhetoric identifying men as the enemy has had few positive implications. Had feminist activists called attention to the relationship between ruling class men and the vast majority of men, who are socialized to perpetuate and maintain sexism and sexist oppression even as they reap no life-affirming benefits, these men might have been motivated to examine the impact of sexism in their lives. Often feminist activists talk about male abuse of women as if it is an exercise of privilege rather than an expression of moral bankruptcy, insanity, and dehumanization. For example, in Barbara Smith's essay, she identifies white males as "the primary oppressor group in American society" and discusses the nature of their domination of others. At the end of the passage in which this statement is made she comments: "It is not just rich and powerful capitalists who inhibit and destroy life. Rapists, murderers, lynchers, and ordinary bigots do too and exercise very real and violent power because of this white male privilege." Implicit in this statement is the assumption that the act of committing violent crimes against women is either a gesture or an affirmation of privilege. Sexist ideology brainwashes men to believe that their violent abuse of women is beneficial when it is not. Yet feminist activists affirm this logic when we should be constantly naming these acts as expressions of perverted power relations, general lack of control over one's actions, emotional powerlessness, extreme irrationality, and in many cases, outright insanity. Passive male absorption of sexist ideology enables them to interpret this disturbed behavior positively. As long as men are brainwashed to equate violent abuse of women with privilege, they will have no understanding of the damage done to themselves, or the damage they do to others, and no motivation to change.

Individuals committed to feminist revolution must address ways that men can unlearn sexism. Women were never encouraged in contemporary feminist movement to point out to men their responsibility. Some feminist rhetoric "put down" women who related to men at all. Most women's liberationists were saying "women have nurtured, helped, and supported others for too long—now we must fend for ourselves." Having helped and supported men for centuries by acting in complicity with sexism, women were suddenly encour-

aged to withdraw their support when it came to the issue of "liberation." The insistence on a concentrated focus on individualism, on the primacy of self, deemed "liberatory" by women's liberationists, was not a visionary, radical concept of freedom. It did provide individual solutions for women, however. It was the same idea of independence perpetuated by the imperial patriarchal state which equates independence with narcissism and lack of concern with triumph over others. In this way, women active in feminist movement were simply inverting the dominant ideology of the culture—they were not attacking it. They were not presenting practical alternatives to the status quo. In fact, even the statement "men are the enemy" was basically an inversion of the male supremacist doctrine that "women are the enemy"— the old Adam and Eve version of reality.

In retrospect, it is evident that the emphasis on "man as enemy" deflected attention away from focus on improving relationships between women and men, ways for men and women to work together to unlearn sexism. Bourgeois women active in feminist movement exploited the notion of a natural polarization between the sexes to draw attention to equal rights effort. They had an enormous investment in depicting the male as enemy and the female as victim. They were the group of women who could dismiss their ties with men once they had an equal share in class privilege. They were ultimately more concerned with obtaining an equal share in class privilege than with the struggle to eliminate sexism and sexist oppression. Their insistence on separating from men heightened the sense that they, as women without men, needed equality of opportunity. Most women do not have the freedom to separate from men because of economic inter-dependence. The separatist notion that women could resist sexism by withdrawing from contact with men reflected a bourgeois class perspective. In Cathy McCandless's essay "Some Thoughts About Racism, Classism, and Separatism," she makes the point that separatism is in many ways a false issue because "in this capitalist economy, none of us are truly separate" (1979). However, she adds:

Socially, it's another matter entirely. The richer you are, the less you generally have to acknowledge those you depend upon. Money can buy you a great deal of distance. Given enough of it, it is even possible never to lay eyes upon a man. It's a wonderful luxury, having control over who you lay eyes on, but let's face it: most women's daily survival still involves face-to-face contact with men whether they like it or not. It seems to me that for this reason alone, criticizing women who associate with men not only tends to be counterproductive, it borders on blaming the victim. Particularly if the women taking it upon themselves to set the standards are white and upper or middle class (as has often been the case in my experience) and those to whom they apply these rules are not.

Devaluing the real necessities of life that compel many women to remain in contact with men, as well as not respecting the desire of women to keep contact with men, created an unnecessary conflict of interest for those women who might have been very interested in feminism but felt they could not live up to the politically correct standards.

Feminist writings did not say enough about ways women could directly engage in feminist struggle in subtle, day-to-day contacts with men, although they have addressed crises. Feminism is politically relevant to the masses of women who daily interact with men both publicly and privately, if it addresses ways that interaction, which usually has negative components because sexism is so all-pervasive, can be changed. Women who have daily contact with men need useful strategies that will enable them to integrate feminist movement into their daily life. By inadequately addressing or failing to address the difficult issues, contemporary feminist movement located itself on the periphery of society rather than at the center. Many women and men think feminism is happening, or happened, "out there." Television tells them the "liberated" woman is an exception, that she is primarily a careerist. Commercials like the one that shows a white career women shifting from work attire to flimsy clothing exposing flesh, singing all the while "I can bring home the bacon,

fry it up in the pan, and never let you forget you're a man" reaffirm that her careerism will not prevent her from assuming the stereotyped sex object role assigned women in male supremacist society.

Often men who claim to support women's liberation do so because they believe they will benefit by no longer having to assume specific, rigid sex roles they find negative or restrictive. The role they are most willing and eager to change is that of economic provider. Commercials like the one described above assure men that women can be breadwinners or even "the" breadwinner, but still allow men to dominate them. Carol Hanisch's essay "Men's Liberation" (1975) explores the attempt by these men to exploit women's issues to their own advantage, particularly those issues related to work:

> Another major issue is the attempt by men to drop out of the work force and put their women to work supporting them. Men don't like their jobs, don't like the rat race, and don't like having a boss. That's what all the whining about being a "success symbol" or "success object" is really all about. Well, women don't like those things either, especially since they get paid 40% less than men for working, generally have more boring jobs, and rarely are even allowed to be "successful." But for women working is usually the only way to achieve some equality and power in the family, in their relationship with men, some independence. A man can quit work and pretty much still remain the master of the household, gaining for himself a lot of free time since the work he does doesn't come close to what his wife or lover does. In most cases, she's still doing more than her share of the housework in addition to wife work and her job. Instead of fighting to make his job better, to end the rat race, and to get rid of bosses, he sends his woman to work—not much different from the old practice of buying a substitute for the draft, or even pimping. And all in the name of breaking down "role stereotypes" or some such nonsense.

Such a "men's liberation movement" could only be formed in reaction to women's liberation in an attempt to make feminist movement serve the opportunistic interests of individual men. These men identified themselves as victims of sexism, working to liberate men. They identified rigid sex roles as the primary source of their victimization and though they wanted to change the notion of masculinity, they were not particularly concerned with their sexist exploitation and oppression of women. Narcissism and general self-pity characterized men's liberation groups. Kanisch concludes her essay with the statement:

> Women don't want to pretend to be weak and passive. And we don't want phony, weak, passive acting men any more than we want phony supermen full of bravado and little else. What women want is for men to be honest. Women want men to be bold—boldly honest, aggressive in their human pursuits. Boldly passionate, sexual and sensual. And women want this for themselves. It's time men became boldly radical. Daring to go to the root of their own exploitation and seeing that it is not women or "sex roles" or "society" causing their unhappiness, but capitalists and capitalism. It's time men dare to name and fight these, their real exploiters.

Men who have dared to be honest about sexism and sexist oppression, who have chosen to assume responsibility for opposing and resisting it, often find themselves isolated. Their politics are disdained by antifeminist men and women, and are often ignored by women active in feminist movement. Writing about his efforts to publicly support feminism in a local newspaper in Santa Cruz, Morris Conerly explains:

> Talking with a group of men, the subject of Women's Liberation inevitably comes up. A few laughs, snickers, angry mutterings, and denunciations follow. There is a group consensus that men are in an embattled position and must close ranks against the assaults of misguided females. Without fail, someone will solicit me for my view, which is that I am 100% for Women's Liberation. That throws them for a loop and they start staring at me as if my eyebrows were crawling with lice.

> They're thinking, "What kind of man is he?" I am a black man who understands that women are not my enemy. If I were a white man with a position of power; one could understand the reason for defending the status quo. Even then, the defense of a morally bankrupt doctrine that exploits and oppresses others would be inexcusable.

Conerly stresses that it was not easy for him to publicly support feminist movement, that it took time:

> . . . Why did it take me some time? Because I was scared of the negative reaction I knew would come my way by supporting Women's Liberation. In my mind I could hear it from the brothers and sisters. "What kind of man are you?" "Who's wearing the pants?" "Why are you in that white shit?" And on and on. Sure enough, the attacks came as I had foreseen but by that time my belief was firm enough to withstand public scorn.

> With growth there is pain . . . and that truism certainly applied in my case.

Men who actively struggle against sexism have a place in feminist movement. They are our comrades. Feminists have recognized and supported the work of men who take responsibility for sexist oppression—men's work with batterers, for example. Those women's liberationists who see no value in this participation must re-think and re-examine the process by which revolutionary struggle is advanced. Individual men tend to become involved in feminist movement because of the pain generated in relationships with women. Usually a woman friend or companion has called attention to their support of male supremacy. Jon Snodgrass introduces the book he edited, *For Men Against Sexism: A Book of Readings* (1977), by telling readers:

> While there were aspects of women's liberation which appealed to men, on the whole my reaction was typical of men. I was threatened by the movement and responded with anger and ridicule. I believed that men and women were oppressed by capital, but not that women were oppressed by men. I argued that "men are

oppressed too" and that it's workers who need liberation! I was unable to recognize a hierarchy of inequality between men and women (in the working class) not to attribute it to male domination. My blindness to patriarchy, I now think, was a function of my male privilege. As a member of the male gender case, I either ignored or suppressed women's liberation.

My full introduction to the women's movement came through a personal relationship. . . . As our relationship developed, I began to receive repeated criticism for being sexist. At first I responded, as part of the male backlash, with anger and denial. In time, however, I began to recognize the validity of the accusation, and eventually even to acknowledge the sexism in my denial of the accusations.

Snodgrass participated in the men's consciousness-raising groups and edited the book of readings in 1977. Towards the end of the 1970s, interest in male anti-sexist groups declined. Even though more men than ever before support the idea of social equality for women, like women they do not see this support as synonymous with efforts to end sexist oppression, with feminist movement that would radically transform society. Men who advocate feminism as a movement to end sexist oppression must become more vocal and public in their opposition to sexism and sexist oppression. Until men share equal responsibility for struggling to end sexism, the feminist movement will reflect the very sexist contradictions we wish to eradicate.

Separatist ideology encourages us to believe that women alone can make feminist revolution—we cannot. Since men are the primary agents maintaining and supporting sexism and sexist oppression, they can only be successfully eradicated if men are compelled to assume responsibility for transforming their consciousness and the consciousness of society as a whole. After hundreds of years of anti-racist struggle, more than ever before non-white people are currently calling atten-

tion to the primary role white people must play in anti-racist struggle. The same is true of the struggle to eradicate sexism—men have a primary role to play. This does not mean that they are better equipped to lead feminist movement; it does mean that they should share equally in resistance struggle. In particular, men have a tremendous contribution to make to feminist struggle in the area of exposing, confronting, opposing, and transforming the sexism of their male peers. When men show a willingness to assume equal responsibility in feminist struggle, performing whatever tasks are necessary, women should affirm their revolutionary work by acknowledging them as comrades in struggle.

References

Angelou, Maya. 1983. "Interview." In *Black Women Writers at Work*, edited by Claudia Tate. New York: Continuum Publishing.

Hanisch, Carol. 1975. "Men's Liberation," In *Feminist Revolution* (pp. 60–63). New Paltz, NY: Redstockings.

Hornacek, Paul. 1977. "Anti-Sexist Consciousness-Raising Groups for Men." In *A Book of Readings for Men Against Sexism*, edited by Jon Snodgrass. Albion: Times Change Press.

Leon, Barbara. 1975. "Separate to Integrate." In *Feminist Revolution* (pp. 139–144). New Paltz, NY: Redstockings.

McCandless, Cathy. 1979. "Some Thoughts About Racism, Classism, and Separatism." In *Top Ranking*, edited by Joan Gibbs and Sara Bennett (pp. 105–115). New York: February Third Press.

"Redstockings Manifesto." 1970. In *Voices from Women's Liberation*, edited by Leslie B. Tanner (p. 109). New York: Signet, NAL.

Smith, Barbara. 1979. "Notes for Yet Another Paper on Black Feminism, or Will the Real Enemy Please Stand Up?" *Conditions: Five* 2 (2): 123–127.

Snodgrass, Jon (ed.). 1977. *For Men Against Sexism: A Book of Readings*. Albion, CA: Times Change Press.

Commission on the Status of Women
Forty-eighth session, March 1–12, 2004

The Role of Men and Boys in Achieving Gender Equality

Agreed conclusions March 12, 2004, as adopted

1. The Commission on the Status of Women recalls and reiterates that the Beijing Declaration and Platform for Action[1] encouraged men to participate fully in all actions towards gender equality and urged the establishment of the principle of shared power and responsibility between women and men at home, in the community, in the workplace and in the wider national and international communities. The Commission also recalls and reiterates the outcome document adopted at the twenty-third special session of the General Assembly entitled "Gender equality, development and peace in the twenty-first century"[2] which emphasized that men must take joint responsibility with women for the promotion of gender equality.

2. The Commission recognizes that men and boys, while some themselves face discriminatory barriers and practices, can and do make contributions to gender equality in their many capacities, including as individuals, members of families, social groups and communities, and in all spheres of society.

3. The Commission recognizes that gender inequalities still exist and are reflected in imbalances of power between women and men in all spheres of society. The Commission further recognizes that everyone benefits from gender equality and that the negative impacts of gender inequality are borne by society as a whole and emphasizes, therefore, that men and boys, through taking responsibility themselves and working jointly in partnership with women and girls, are essential to achieving the goals of gender equality, development and peace. The Commission recognizes the capacity of men and boys in bringing about change in attitudes, relationships and access to resources and decision making which are critical for the promotion of gender equality and the full enjoyment of all human rights by women.

4. The Commission acknowledges and encourages men and boys to continue to take positive initiatives to eliminate gender stereotypes and promote gender equality, including combating violence against women, through networks, peer programmes, information campaigns, and training programmes. The Commission acknowledges the critical role of gender-sensitive education and training in achieving gender equality.

5. The Commission also recognizes that the participation of men and boys in achieving gender equality must be consistent with the empowerment of women and girls and acknowledges that efforts must be made to address the undervaluation of many types of work, abilities and roles associated with women. In this regard, it is important that resources for gender equality initiatives for men and boys do not compromise equal opportunities and resources for women and girls.

6. The Commission urges Governments and, as appropriate, the relevant funds and programmes, organizations and specialized agencies of the United Nations system, the international financial institutions, civil society, including the private sector and nongovernmental organizations, and other stakeholders, to take the following actions:

a) Encourage and support the capacity of men and boys in fostering gender equality, including acting in partnership with women and girls as agents for change and in providing positive leadership, in particular where men are still key decision makers responsible for policies, programmes and legislation, as well as holders of economic and organizational power and public resources;

b) Promote understanding of the importance of fathers, mothers, legal guardians and other caregivers, to the well being of children and the promotion of gender equality and of the need to develop policies, programmes and school curricula that encourage and maximize their positive involvement in achieving gender equality and positive results for children, families and communities;

c) Create and improve training and education programmes to enhance awareness and knowledge among men and women on their roles as parents, legal guardians and caregivers and the importance of sharing family responsibilities, and include fathers as well as mothers in programmes that teach infant child care development;

d) Develop and include in education programmes for parents, legal guardians and other caregivers information on ways and means to increase the capacity of men to raise children in a manner oriented towards gender equality;

e) Encourage men and boys to work with women and girls in the design of policies and programmes for men and boys aimed at gender equality and foster the involvement of men and boys in gender mainstreaming efforts in order to ensure improved design of all policies and programmes;

f) Encourage the design and implementation of programmes at all levels to accelerate a socio-cultural change towards gender equality, especially through the upbringing and educational process, in terms of changing harmful traditional perceptions and attitudes of male and female roles in order to achieve the full and equal participation of women and men in the society;

g) Develop and implement programmes for pre-schools, schools, community centers, youth organizations, sport clubs and centres, and other groups dealing with children and youth, including training for teachers, social workers and other professionals who deal with children to foster positive attitudes and behaviours on gender equality;

h) Promote critical reviews of school curricula, textbooks and other information education and communication materials at all levels in order to recommend ways to strengthen the promotion of gender equality that involves the engagement of boys as well as girls;

i) Develop and implement strategies to educate boys and girls and men and women about tolerance, mutual respect for all individuals and the promotion of all human rights;

j) Develop and utilize a variety of methods in public information campaigns on the role of men and boys in promoting gender equality, including through approaches specifically targeting boys and young men;

k) Engage media, advertising and other related professionals, through the development of training and other programmes, on the importance of promoting gender equality, non-stereotypical portrayal of women and girls and men and boys and on the harms caused by portraying women and girls in a demeaning or exploitative manner, as well as on the enhanced participation of women and girls in the media;

l) Take effective measures, to the extent consistent with freedom of expression, to combat the growing sexualization and use of pornography in media content, in terms of the rapid development of ICT, encourage men in the media to refrain from presenting women as inferior beings and exploiting them as sexual objects and commodities, combat ICT- and media-based violence against women including criminal misuse of ICT for sexual harassment, sexual exploitation and trafficking in women and girls, and support the development and use of ICT as a resource for the empowerment of women and girls, including those affected by violence, abuse and other forms of sexual exploitation;

m) Adopt and implement legislation and/ or policies to close the gap between women's and men's pay and promote reconciliation of occupational and family responsibilities, including through reduction of occupational segregation, introduction or expansion of parental leave, flexible working arrangements, such as voluntary part-time work, teleworking, and other home-based work;

n) Encourage men, through training and education, to fully participate in the care and support of others, including older persons, persons with disabilities and sick persons, in particular children and other dependants;

o) Encourage active involvement of men and boys through education projects and peer-based programmes in eliminating gender stereotypes as well as gender inequality in particular in relation to sexually transmitted infections, including HIV/AIDS, as well as their full participation in prevention, advocacy, care, treatment, support and impact evaluation programmes;

p) Ensure men's access to and utilization of reproductive and sexual health services and programmes, including HIV/AIDS-related programmes and services, and encourage men to participate with women in programmes designed to prevent and treat all forms of HIV/AIDS transmission and other sexually transmitted infections;

q) Design and implement programmes to encourage and enable men to adopt safe and responsible sexual and reproductive behaviour, and to use effectively methods to prevent unwanted pregnancies and sexually transmitted infections, including HIV/AIDS;

r) Encourage and support men and boys to take an active part in the prevention and elimination of all forms of violence, and especially gender-based violence, including in the context of HIV/AIDS, and increase awareness of men's and boys' responsibility in ending the cycle of violence, inter alia, through the promotion of attitudinal and behavioural change, integrated education and training which prioritize the safety of women and children, prosecution and rehabilitation of perpetrators, and support for survivors, and recognizing that men and boys also experience violence;

s) Encourage an increased understanding among men how violence, including trafficking for the purposes of commercialized sexual exploitation, forced marriages and forced labour, harms women, men and children and undermines gender equality, and consider measures aimed at eliminating the demand for trafficked women and children;

t) Encourage and support both women and men in leadership positions, including political leaders, traditional leaders, business leaders, community and religious leaders, musicians, artists and athletes to provide positive role models on gender equality;

u) Encourage men in leadership positions to ensure equal access for women to education, property rights and inheritance rights and to promote equal access to information technology and business and economic opportunities, including in international trade, in order to provide women with the tools that enable them to take part fully and equally in economic and political decision-making processes at all levels;

v) Identify and fully utilize all contexts in which a large number of men can be reached, particularly in male-dominated institutions, industries and associations, to sensitize men on their roles and responsibilities in the promotion of gender equality and the full enjoyment of all human rights by women, including in relation to HIV/AIDS and violence against women;

w) Develop and use statistics to support and/or carry out research, inter alia, on the cultural, social and economic conditions, which influence the attitudes and behaviours of men and boys towards women and girls, their awareness of gender inequalities and their involvement in promoting gender equality;

x) Carry out research on men's and boys' views of gender equality and their perceptions of their roles through which further programmes and policies can be developed and identify and widely disseminate good practices. Assess the impact of efforts undertaken to engage men and boys in achieving gender equality;

y) Promote and encourage the representation of men in institutional mechanisms for the advancement of women;

z) Encourage men and boys to support women's equal participation in conflict prevention, management and conflict resolution and in post-conflict peace-building;

7. The Commission urges all entities within the UN system to take into account the recommendations contained in these agreed conclusions and to disseminate these agreed conclusions widely.

Notes

1. Report of the Fourth World Conference on Women, Beijing 4-15 September 1995 (United Nations publications, Sales No. E.96.IV.13).

2. A/RES/S-23/3, annex.

CONTRIBUTORS

JUDI ADDELSTON, Ph.D., received her doctorate at the City University of New York Graduate School and University Center in 1996. She is currently a professor of psychology at Valencia Community College in Orlando, Florida. In addition, she has a private practice in marriage and family therapy and mental health counseling.

ERIC ANDERSON is a Lecturer in the Department of Education at the University of Bath. He is author of numerous articles on sport, gender and sexuality. His most recent book is *In the Game: Gay Athletes and the Cult of Masculinity* (State University of New York Press, 2005).

TIM BENEKE is a freelance writer and editor living in the San Francisco Bay Area. He is the author of *Men on Rape* and *Proving Manhood*.

A. AYRES BOSWELL is a supervisor at a foster care agency in New York City. She works with abused and neglected children, trying to achieve permanency in the children's lives by reunification with their birth parents or by locating adoptive resources.

ROCCO L. (CHIP) CAPRARO, Senior Associate Dean and Assistant Professor of History, is the founding coordinator of the men's studies program and founding director of the rape prevention education program for men at Hobart and William Smith Colleges, Geneva, New York. He received his B.A. from Colgate University and his Ph.D. from Washington University, and is a consultant and public speaker in the areas of gender and diversity, with an emphasis on masculinity, and is currently writing a brief history of rock and roll from a men's studies perspective.

BETH SKILKEN CATLETT is a visiting professor of Women's Studies at DePaul University. She received her doctorate from the Ohio State University, where her studies focused on feminist approaches to studying families. She has been particularly interested in applying a feminist paradigm to understanding male aggression.

JUDY CHICAGO is an artist, author, feminist, and educator. One of the pioneers of Feminist Art, her installation, "The Dinner Party" (1974–1979), was a monumental media project, a symbolic history of women in Western Civilization. Subsequent projects have included "The Birth Project," "The Holocaust Project," and "Powerplay." She lives in New Mexico.

CAROL COHN is the Director of the Boston Consortium on Gender, Security, and Human Rights, and a Senior Research Scholar at the Fletcher School of Law and Diplomacy, Tufts University. Her research and writing have focused on gender and international security, ranging from work on discourse of civilian defense intellectuals, gender integration issues in the US military, and, most extensively, weapons of mass destruction, including: "Sex and Death in the Rational World of Defense Intellectuals," *Signs: Journal of Women in Culture and Society*, vol. 12, no. 4 (Summer 1987), and, most recently, with Sara Ruddick, "A Feminist Ethical Perspective on Weapons of Mass Destruction," (in *Ethics and Weapons of Mass Destruction: Religious and Secular Perspectives*, eds. Sohail H. Hashmi and Steven P. Lee, Cambridge University Press, 2004). Her most recent research, supported by the Ford Foundation, examines gender mainstreaming in international peace and security institutions; a central focus is the passage of UN Security Council Resolution 1325 on women, peace and security, and the ongoing efforts to ensure its implementation. She also does consulting on gender and organizational change.

SCOTT COLTRANE is Professor of Sociology and Associate Dean of the College of Humanities, Arts and Social Sciences at the University of California, Riverside. His research focuses on families, gender, and social inequality.

RAEWYN CONNELL is University Professor at the University of Sydney, and author, co-author or editor of nineteen books, including *Ruling Class*

Ruling Culture, Making the Difference, Gender and Power, Schools and Social Justice, Masculinities, The Men and the Boys, and *Gender*. A contributor to research journals in sociology, education, political science, gender studies, and related fields, her current research concerns social theory, changing masculinities, neo-liberalism, globalization and intellectuals.

ANGELA COWAN is a postgraduate student in the Department of Sociology at the University of Newcastle. Her thesis topic is an investigation of the discursive world of young children. She is a trained primary school schoolteacher and has worked as an observer on a number of psychiatric research projects.

JULIA O'CONNELL DAVIDSON is Professor of Sociology at the University of Nottingham in the United Kingdom with a focus on gender, race, class and global inequalities, and contract, employment relations, selfhood, and human rights. She has conducted studies of entrepreneurial prostitution, sex tourism, and children's involvement in the global sex trade.

FRANCINE M. DEUTSCH is Professor of Psychology at Mount Holyoke College, and the author of *Halving It All: How Equality Shared Parenting Works* (1999, Harvard University Press), a study of the division of domestic labor among dual-earner couples. Her articles on gender and the family have been published in *Journal of Personality* and *Social Psychology, Psychology of Women Quarterly, Sex Roles, Journal of Family Issues,* and *Current Directions in Psychology*. Her most recent research examines the gendered life plans of Chinese college seniors in the People's Republic of China, and plans for egalitarian marriage among graduating college seniors in the United States.

SHARI LEE DWORKIN is a Post-Doctoral Research Fellow at the HIV Center for Clinical and Behavioral Studies (New York State Psychiatric Institute and Columbia University, Mailman School of Public Health) where she carries out gender, sexuality, and HIV research. Her journal articles have appeared in *Sociological Perspectives, The Sociology of Sport Journal,* and *The Journal of Sport and Social Is-*

sues. She was guest coeditor (with Michael A. Messner) of a special issue of *Sociological Perspectives* on gender and sport (Winter, 2002) and currently serves on the editorial board of *Gender and Society*. She is coauthor of *Built to Win: The Female Athlete as Cultural Icon* (April, 2003, University of Minnesota Press).

BETH A. ECK is an Associate Professor of Sociology at James Madision University. Her other work about viewing nudes can be found in *Sociological Forum* (2001). Professor Eck's current work is a qualitative investigation into the lives of single men in mid-life.

YEN LE ESPIRITU is Professor of Ethnic Studies at the University of California, San Diego. She is the author of *Asian American Panethnicity: Bridging Institutions and Identities, Filipino American Lives,* and *Asian American Women and Men: Labor, Laws, and Love*. She is also serving as the President of the Association of Asian American Studies.

DANIEL FARR is a doctoral student in sociology at SUNY Albany.

JULES FEIFFER is a syndicated cartoonist and was a regular contributor to *The Village Voice*.

ANN FERGUSON is Assistant Professor of Women's Studies and African American Studies at Smith College. She received her Ph.D. in Sociology from University of California at Berkeley.

MICHELLE FINE, Distinguished Professor of Social Psychology at the Graduate Center, CUNY, has taught there since 1990. Her work concerns questions of social injustice in schools, prisons, and communities. She draws from feminist psychology, critical race, and Marxist thought. She looks at the spaces of possibility in which youth struggle for what could be and against what is; the relation of scholarship and activism; and questions of theory, ethics, and method in participatory research.

THOMAS J. GERSCHICK is Associate Professor of Sociology at Illinois State University. His research focuses on identity, and marginalized and alternative masculinities.

JAMES GILLIGAN has been on the faculty of the Department of Psychiatry at the Harvard Medical School since 1966, for whom he directed mental health services for the Massachusetts prison system for many years; and is Director of the Center for the Study of Violence, Immediate Past President of the International Association for Forensic Psychotherapy, author of *Violence: Reflections on a National Epidemic* and *Preventing Violence*, and a member of the Academic Advisory Council of the National Campaign Against Youth Violence.

RICHARD GOLDSTEIN, an executive editor of the *Village Voice,* is at work on a book about Eminem and the culture of cruelty.

GLORIA GONZALEZ-LOPEZ is Assistant Professor in the department of Sociology at the University of Texas-Austin. She is author of *Erotic Journeys: Mexican Immigrants and their Sex Lives* (Berkeley: University of California Press, 2005).

JULIA MARUSZA HALL received her Ph.D. from the University at Buffalo, State University of New York. Hall is the author of articles that have appeared in *Anthropology, Education Quarterly,* and *The Urban Review,* among others. She currently teaches Social Foundations of Education at D'Youville College in Buffalo, New York.

SHAUN R. HARPER is an Assistant Professor and Research Associate in the Center for the Study of Higher Education at The Pennsylvania State University.

KEVIN D. HENSON is Associate Professor of Sociology at Loyola University Chicago. He is the author of *Just a Temp* (1996) and co-editor of *Unusual Occupations* (2000). His research focuses on gender and nonstandard employment. He has written about the role of clerical temporary employment in recreating racial and gender inequalities, and is currently working on a project on traveling nurses.

BELL HOOKS is a writer and lecturer who speaks on issues of race, class, and gender. She teaches at CUNY Graduate Center. Her books include *Ain't I a Woman, Feminist Theory,* and *Talking Back.* Her column, "Sisters of the Yam," appears monthly in *Z* magazine.

DAPHNE JOHN is associate professor and chair of the department of sociology at Oberlin College. Her teaching and research focuses on issues related to work and family, and gender stratification.

ELLEN JORDAN is Senior Lecturer in the Department of Sociology at the University of Newcastle. She was for many years a teacher in primary schools. Her major research interests are women's work in nineteenth-century Britain and gender construction in early childhood.

JACK KATZ is Professor of Sociology at UCLA and the author of *Seductions of Crime.*

MICHAEL S. KIMMEL is Professor of Sociology at SUNY at Stony Brook. His books include *Changing Men* (1987), *Men Confront Pornography* (1990), *Men in the United States* (1992), *Manhood in America* (1996), *The Politics of Manhood* (1996) and *The Gendered Society* (2000). He is the editor of *masculinities,* a scholarly journal, and national spokesperson for the National Organization for Men Against Sexism (NOMAS).

PAUL KIVEL is a trainer, activist, writer, and a violence prevention educator. He is the author of several books including *Men's Work, Uprooting Racism,* and *Boys Will Be Men.* He is also co-author of several widely used curricula including Making the Peace, Young Men's Work, and Young Women's Lives. His newest book is *You Call This a Democracy? Who Benefits, Who Pays, and Who Really Decides.* He can be reached at *pkivel @mindspring.com,* or at *www.paulkivel.com.*

BARBARA KRUGER is an artist in New York City.

TERRY A. KUPERS practices psychiatry in Oakland, California, and is Institute Professor at The Wright Institute in Berkeley. He consults with several public mental health agencies, and has testified in many class action lawsuits about the psychological consequences of harsh prison conditions, the quality of mental health services "Inside," and the issue of prison rape in men's and women's prisons. He is active in the National Organization for Men Against Sexism, California Prison Focus, Critical Resistance, and Stop Prisoner Rape (website: www.spr.org). His books include *Revisioning Men's*

Lives: Gender, Intimacy and Power (Guilford, 1992) and *Prison Madness: The Mental Health Crisis Behind Bars and What We Must Do About It* (Wiley/Jossey-Bass, 1999). He is also co-editor of *Prison Masculinities* (Temple University Press, 2001).

MEIKA LOE is Assistant Professor of Sociology and Women's Studies at Colgate University in New York. She is the author of *The Rise of Viagra: How the Little Blue Pill Changed Sex in America*, NYU Press, 2004.

PETER LYMAN is University Dean of Libraries at the University of California, Berkeley.

PATRICK MCKENRY is a professor of Human Development and Family Science at the Ohio State University. He received his doctorate from the University of Tennessee in Child and Family Studies. His research has focused on family conflict, including domestic violence. He has published over 100 journal articles and book chapters.

JAMES MESSERSCHMIDT is Professor of Sociology in the Criminology Department at the University of Southern Maine. His research interests focus on the interrelation of gender, race, class, and crime. In addition to numerous articles and book chapters, he is the author of *The Trial of Leonard Peltier* (South End Press, 1983), *Capitalism, Patriarchy, and Crime: Toward a Socialist Feminist Criminology* (Rowman & Littlefield, 1986), *Masculinities and Crime: Critique and Reconceptualization of Theory* (Rowman & Littlefield, 1993), *Crime as Structured Action: Gender, Race, Class, and Crime in the Making* (Sage, 1997), *Criminology* (3rd edition), with Piers Beirne (Westview, 1999), and *Nine Lives: Adolescent Masculinities, the Body, and Violence* (2000, Westview Press).

MICHAEL A. MESSNER is Professor of Sociology and Gender Studies at the University of Southern California. He is co-editor of *Through the Prism of Difference: Readings on Sex and Gender* (1997). His books include *Power at Play: Sports and the Problem of Masculinity* (1992), and *Politics of Masculinities: Men in Movements* (1997).

ADAM STEPHEN MILLER was a master's degree student in journalism at University of Michigan

and an organizer of an Internet disability support group. He died in 1997.

JEFFREY MONTEZ DE OCA is a doctoral candidate in sociology at the University of Southern California. He teaches classical and contemporary theory as well as media analysis. His dissertation examines postwar physical education and American football's relation to cold war masculinities.

PETER M. NARDI is Professor of Sociology at Pitzer College. He has published articles on AIDS, anti-gay crimes and violence, magic and magicians, and alcoholism and families. His books include *Men's Friendships* (1993) and *Growing Up Before Stonewall* (1994), with David Sanders and Judd Marmor. He has served as co-president of the Los Angeles chapter of the Gay and Lesbian Alliance Against Defamation.

DAVID NYLUND is a doctoral student in cultural studies at the University of California, Davis, and an assistant professor of social work at California State University, Sacramento. He is the author of *Treating Huckleberry Finn: A New Narrative Approach with Kids Diagnosed ADHD/ADD* (Jossey-Bass, 2000).

NICK T. PAPPAS is a graduate of the Ohio State University in Human Development and Family Science. He is a former professional hockey player and coach and former adjunct professor at Indiana University of Pennsylvania. Dr. Pappas is presently the founder of Personal & Athletic Solutions, working as a motivational speaker and personal life coach (www.drnickpappas.com).

C. J. PASCOE is completing a dissertation entitled, "'Dude, You're a Fag': Masculinity in High School," about the social construction of masculinity in adolescence among both boys and girls.

JENNIFER PIERCE is Associate Professor of American Studies at the University of Minnesota. She is author of *Gender Trials: Emotional Lives in Contemporary Law Firms* (California 1995).

KEVIN POWELL is an activist, poet, journalist, essayist, editor, cultural curator, hiphop historian, songwriter, music producer, public speaker, political consultant and fundraiser, and businessman. A product of extreme poverty, welfare, fatherlessness, and a single mother-led household, he is a native of Jersey City, New Jersey and was educated at New Jersey's Rutgers University. Kevin Powell is a longtime resident of Brooklyn, New York, and it is from his base in New York City that Powell has published six books, including his current title, *Who's Gonna Take The Weight? Manhood, Race, and Power in America.*

BETH A. QUINN is an Associate Professor in the Department of Sociology at Montana State University-Bozeman. She received her Ph.D. in Criminology, Law, and Society from the University of California-Irvine. Drawing primarily on feminist and masculinity theories and neo-institutional organizational theory, her research focuses on legal complaint-making and discrimination law. This research has been published in journals such as *Law and Social Inquiry* and *Gender & Society.* She is currently exploring how human resources understand and deal with sexual harassment law.

M. ROCHLIN is the creator of "The Heterosexual Questionnaire."

JACKIE KRASAS ROGERS'S research interests include gender and racial inequality in work and employment. She explores issues of inequality and employment in her book entitled, *Temps: The Many Faces of the Changing Workplace.* The book documents and analyzes the experiences both of temporary clerical workers and temporary lawyers. Presently, Professor Rogers is working as part of an interdisciplinary research team funded by the National Science Foundation to investigate the underrepresentation of women in the information technology field. Her work has appeared in *Gender & Society* and *Work & Occupations.*

LILLIAN B. RUBIN is a Research Associate at the Institute for the Study of Social Change at University of California, Berkeley, and a psychotherapist in private practice. Her books include *Intimate Strangers, Just Friends, Erotic Wars, Worlds of Pain,* and, most recently, *Families on the Fault Line* and *The Transcendant Child.*

LEILA J. RUPP is Professor and Chair of Women's Studies at the University of California, Santa Barbara. She is coauthor with Verta Taylor of *Drag Queens at the 801 Cabaret* (2003) and *Survival in the Doldrums: The American Women's Rights Movement, 1945 to the 1960s* (1987) and author of *A Desired Past: A Short History of Same-Sex Sexuality in America* (1999), *Worlds of Women: The Making of an International Women's Movement* (1997), and *Mobilizing Women for War: German and American Propaganda, 1939-1945* (1978). She joined Verta Taylor and Nancy Whittier as co-editor of the seventh edition of *Feminist Frontiers.*

DON SABO is a Professor of Social Sciences at D'Youville College in Buffalo, New York. He has co-authored *Humanism in Sociology, Jock: Sports & Male Identity,* and *Sport, Men and the Gender Order: Critical Feminist Perspectives.* His most recent books include, *Sex, Violence and Power in Sports: Rethinking Masculinity,* and *Men's Health & Illness: Gender, Power & the Body.* He has conducted many national surveys on gender issues in sport, is a trustee of the Women's Sports Foundation, and co-authored the 1997 Presidents' Council on Physical Fitness and Sports report "Physical Activity & Sport in the Lives of Girls."

RITCH C. SAVIN-WILLIAMS is Professor of Human Development at Cornell University. He is co-editor, with Kenneth M. Cohen, of *The Lives of Lesbians, Gays, and Bisexuals* (Harcourt Brace 1996).

STEVEN SCHACHT was professor of sociology at SUNY Plattsburgh. His ethnographic research included work on masculine identity construction and performance among rugby players, transgendered individuals, and college students. He died in 2003.

KIRBY D. SCHROEDER is a University of Chicago doctoral student in sociology.

JASON SCHULTZ is an attorney with the Electronic Frontier Foundation, a non-profit specializing in protecting civil liberties online, and an adjunct professor at University of California, Berkeley. Prior to law school, Jason attended Duke University where he received degrees in Public Policy

Studies and Women's Studies and co-founded Men Acting for Change, a pro-feminist men's activist group. He currently lives in San Francisco and maintains a personal blog at lawgeek.net.

ANNE SHELTON is professor in the department of sociology and anthropology at the University of Texas at Arlington. She is author of *Women, Men and Time: Gender Differences in Paid Work, Housework and Leisure*, Westport, CT: Greenwood, 1992.

JOAN Z. SPADE is Associate Professor of Sociology at Lehigh University. Her previous publications have focused on the interstices of work and family, including the effects of men's and women's parental values. She is currently examining the effects of grouping students in middle schools.

JUDITH STACEY is Professor of Sociology and Professor of Gender and Sexuality at New York University. She is author of many articles and books on gender, sexualities and families, including *In the Name of the Family: Rethinking Family Values in a Postmodern Age* (Boston: Beacon Press, 1996).

GLORIA STEINEM is a founding editor of *Ms.*, and the author of *Outrageous Acts and Everyday Rebellions* and *Revolution from Within*.

JACQUELINE SANCHEZ TAYLOR is a researcher on adult sex tourism and child sexual exploitation in Latin America, India, South Africa, and the Caribbean. Her Ph.D. focuses on sexual economic exchanges between female tourists and local men in Jamaica and the Dominican Republic. She is currently a sociology lecturer at the University of Leeds.

VERTA TAYLOR is Professor and Chair of Sociology at the University of California, Santa Barbara. She is coauthor with Leila J. Rupp of *Drag Queens at the 801 Cabaret* (University of Chicago Press) and *Survival in the Doldrums: The American Women's Rights Movement, 1945 to the 1960s* (Oxford University Press); author of *Rock-a-by Baby: Feminism, Self-Help and Postpartum Depression* (Routledge); and co-editor of seven editions of

Feminist Frontiers. Her articles on the women's movement, the gay and lesbian movement, and social movement theory have appeared in journals such as *The American Sociological Review, Signs, Social Problems, Mobilization, Gender & Society, Qualitative Sociology, Journal of Women's History*, and *Journal of Homosexuality*.

FAYE LINDA WACHS is an Assistant Professor of Sociology in the Behavioral Sciences Department at Cal Poly Pomona. Current research projects include a content and textual analysis of men's and women's health and fitness magazines, and interviews with women who participate in sports historically considered "male appropriate." Past projects have examined gender relations in the field of coed softball, and media coverage of HIV+ athletes.

KAREN WALKER has completed her doctorate in the Department of Sociology at the University of Pennsylvania. She is Vice President of Research at Public/Private Ventures in Philadelphia.

LOIS WEIS is the author or co-author of numerous books and articles pertaining to social class, race, gender and schooling in the United States. Her most recent books include *Silenced Voices and Extraordinary Conversations: Re-Imagining Schools* (Teachers College Press, 2003, with Michelle Fine); *The Unknown City: The Lives of Poor and Working Class Young Adults* (Beacon Press, 1998, with Michelle Fine); *Speed Bumps: A Student Friendly Guide to Qualitative Research* (Teachers College Press, 2000, with Michelle Fine); and *Beyond Black and White: New Faces and Voices in US Schools* (State University of New York Press, 1997, with Maxine Seller). She sits on numerous editorial boards and is the editor of the *Power, Social Identity, and Education* book series with SUNY Press.

CHRISTINE L. WILLIAMS is Professor of Sociology at the University of Texas at Austin. She is author of *Gender Differences at Work* (1989), *Still a Man's World* (1997), and editor of *Doing "Women's Work": Men in Nontraditional Occupations* (1993).